Praise for

Henry James: The Young Master

"Like a movie of James's life, as it unfolds moment to moment . . . lends the book a powerful immediacy." —*The New York Times*

"Splendidly written . . . Novick has aimed to bring James back to life and he has succeeded brilliantly. The biography itself reads like a novel. . . . It is no small ambition to write a biography of James that is in any way commensurate with that master, and Sheldon Novick has done it." —*The Washington Post Book World*

"Beautifully written, with a grace that enables him to weave his subject's words in and out of his own." —*The New Republic*

"Masterful in bringing James and his world to life." —*San Francisco Examiner-Chronicle*

"A finely nuanced recounting of James's life from childhood to the cusp of his major works . . . an uncluttered narrative of an emerging artist, backed with scrupulous documentation." —*The New York Times Book Review*

"Sheldon Novick's *The Young Master* is much the best biography of Henry James that I've encountered. We seem to walk and think with Henry James in these pages. Something infinitely valuable in James's sense of self is caught here with grace and clarity." —HAROLD BLOOM

"It rescues America's greatest novelist from the dread clutches of psy- chobiographers, and proves that there is no substitute for lucid, schol- arly narrative. A book suffused, like James's own novels, with mellow nostalgia for temps perdu." —EDMUND MORRIS

ALSO BY SHELDON M. NOVICK

Henry James: The Mature Master

Honorable Justice: The Life of Oliver Wendell Holmes

The Collected Works of Justice Holmes
(edited by Sheldon M. Novick)

HENRY
JAMES

HENRY JAMES

The Young Master

SHELDON M. NOVICK

RANDOM HOUSE TRADE PAPERBACKS
NEW YORK

2007 Random House Trade Paperback Edition

Published in the United States by Random House Trade Paperbacks,
an imprint of The Random House Publishing Group,
a division of Random House, Inc., New York.

RANDOM HOUSE TRADE PAPERBACKS and colophon
are trademarks of Random House, Inc.

Grateful acknowledgment is made to the following for permission to reprint previously published material:

Brown University Press: Excerpt from *Henry James and John Hay: The Record of a Friendship*, edited by George Monteiro (Providence, R.I.: Brown University Press, 1965). Copyright © 1965 by Brown University. Reprinted by permission.

Harvard University Press: Excerpts from *The Letters of Henry James*, Vol. 1, edited by Leon Edel (Cambridge, Mass.: Harvard University Press, 1974.) Copyright © 1974 by Leon Edel (editorial). Copyright © 1974 by Alexander R. James (James copyright material). Reprinted by permission of the publisher.

Oxford University Press: Excerpts from *The Complete Notebooks of Henry James*, edited by Leon Edel and Lyall Powers. Copyright © 1987. Reprinted by permission of Oxford University Press.

University Press of Virginia: Excerpt from letter which appears on pages 13–14 from *The Correspondence of William James*, Vol. 1, edited by Ignas Skrupskelis and Elizabeth Berkeley (Charlottesville, Va.: University Press of Virginia, 1992). Reprinted by permission.

Library of Congress Cataloging-in-Publication Data

Novick, Sheldon M.
Henry James : the young master / Sheldon M. Novick.
p.   cm.
Includes bibliographical references and index.
ISBN 978-0-8129-7883-4
1. James, Henry, 1843–1916—Childhood and youth.   2. Authors,
American—19th century—Biography.   I. Title.
PS2123.N58   1996
813'.4—dc20
95-53088

www.atrandom.com

Printed in the United States of America

2 4 6 8 9 7 5 3 1

Book design by Caroline Cunningham

For Carolyn

What he wanted himself was . . . the very tick of the old stopped clocks. He wanted the hour of the day at which this and that had happened and the temperature and the weather and the sound, and yet more the stillness, from the street, and the exact look-out, with the corresponding look-in, through the window and the slant on the walls of the light of afternoons that had been. He wanted the unimaginable accidents, the little notes of truth for which the common lens of history, however the scowling muse might bury her nose, was not sufficiently fine. He wanted evidence of a sort for which there had never been documents enough, or for which documents mainly, however multiplied, would never be enough.

—HENRY JAMES
The Sense of the Past

PREFACE

No one sees a life as a whole except the person who lives it. The story, when there is one, lives in memory alone. The biographer therefore must make a choice—to penetrate that private reality and write a book that gives some sense of the life as it was lived; or to write some other sort of book, a commentary from the outside.

To gain a true sense of a life as it was lived is not always possible. The data may have been lost, the world in which the life was lived may have vanished beyond recall. But when the critical details of ordinary life can be reconstructed, there is a sensibility, almost a separate sense, that one may use to understand the subjective existence of another person. We use this sensibility to understand almost without speech people we care for, and so writing a life is a little like falling in love. One need not like or even admire the subject of a life, but one must be able to use this particular sensibility.

In the case of Henry James, the materials for such a life are ample, thanks in large part to the work of devoted scholars. It is true that he did his best to conceal his private affairs from the public; he hated newspaper photographs. But like many private persons, James left clues to his inner life, hoping to be understood. In his last years he prepared a revised edition of his novels and stories, with prefaces explaining their genesis; he wrote memoirs of his father and brother, and a scattering of autobiographical essays and stories; all of this taken together amounts to a huge self-portrait of Henry James as an artist. He felt it was his duty to the young, to his inheritors, to record his own development, and in this great work of his old age he embedded the best of his fiction in the matrix of his own story, revising his fiction into a single tale, the story of its own telling. He could not resist including in these last works recollections even of his first sexual encounters. But to read the books of his old age in this way one needs a fund of sympathy, and must immerse oneself in the language and customs of James's private world. The style of his last work requires patience and attention, moroever, and many of his memories are shrouded in private references and multilingual puns. He built up portraits of people and events by a pointillist technique, so that a great deal of description must be absorbed together, without direct statements of fact.

When the necessary trouble has been taken, however, the autobiographical works provide a unique self-portrait of an acutely self-aware artist, doing his painstaking best to explain himself, the processes of his art, and the manner in which his work evolved itself from his life. In preparation for writing the book that follows, I have traced the private references, and have compressed his vast impressionist self-portrait into a thinner and more conventional sketch. James's published and unpublished writings were my primary materials, but I have tried also to re-create the context that gave them meaning. I have taken a standpoint a little outside and above James's, but as far as possible I have used James's own sensibility as a lamp to illumine the subject matter, in the way that he himself used the sensibility of a fictional character to light the scenes of his novels.

The historical Henry James is, of course, a large, stubborn, and unwieldy tool. Trying to use him as a camera or a paintbrush is like the royal game of croquet in *Through the Looking Glass*, in which flamingos were used as mallets. He wrote some of the greatest stories and novels in the English language, and originated a whole new school of critical theory. He served as the gatekeeper to Europe for two generations of Americans, was mentor to numberless writers and painters and scientists, and labored artfully to help build an English-speaking alliance in Europe. But above all, he was a master of personal relation, of love and friendship. He devoted all his artistry, experience, and force to shaping the sensibility of his readers—you and me, dear reader. With a powerful but most benevolent intention, he rests his dove-like hand upon your shoulder; he grasps you by the nape of the neck; and soon you are gazing through his eyes, recalling his memories as if they were your own.

In short, to *use* James's point of view to illumine his life and his world requires a sort of jujitsu: rather than simply bowing under his hand, I have been wrestling with the master, and cannot be sure that I have always remained in command of this extraordinarily powerful material. Here at any rate is the ground of my own position.

I have taken it for granted that Henry James underwent the ordinary experiences of life: that he separated himself from his enveloping family, that he fell in love with the wrong people, that his first sexual encounters were intense but not entirely happy. He formed friendships, stable loving relations, worried about money, had problems with his health, grew old. He wrote about these experiences, both in his fiction and in his memoirs, but we do not always know the details. The meaning that these experiences, or more precisely the memories of these experiences, had for James and that he saw they had for others were the raw materials of his fiction. I have tried to show both the memories themselves and the ways in which James used them. To show, in short, how his criticism and fiction grew out of the materials of his experience. For memories are as much historic facts as the events that give rise to them, and it is in memory alone, and not in the meaningless facts, that one finds a narrative with unity and meaning, with moral significance.

The lack of any such biography until now can be attributed partly to James's having loved young men. Few who knew this were willing to talk openly about it, and for others it has been difficult to accept that despite the privacy in which he shrouded his intimate relations, he shared the common experiences of life. I have not made any special discoveries about James's sexuality; James's sexual orientation, as we now say, has been an open secret for a hundred years. Although he disliked publicity in such matters, and lived a conventional life, he was reasonably open with his family and friends. His first biographer, Leon Edel, was most certainly aware of this side of his life, but evidently did not care to be explicit in the vast five-volume biography that he published in the 1950s and 1960s and that dominated scholarly discussions for a generation. Instead of James's life, Edel wrote of the unconscious, impersonal machinery of the Oedipal conflict.

In recent works, biographers have been somewhat more open, but they still feel obliged to deny that James shared the common experiences of humanity, the experiences of realized passion, of love and family. Edel and those who have followed him have hewn closely to what now seems a rather old-fashioned, Freudian view of "homosexuality" as a kind of failure. The "passive male" in the Freudian account was wounded and frightened by a powerful mother and a weak, absent father. This mythic figure retreated from the terrors of heterosexual rivalry into a world of delicate imagination.

I have tried as much as possible to look at the data with a fresh eye, without any preconceptions except the ordinary ones of day-to-day life. Seen in this way, James evidently had both loves and friendships. In the absence of contrary evidence, it has seemed most reasonable to assume that when he seemed to be having a love affair, he was; that when he seemed to be expressing an idea, he was consciously doing so. When James described some experience with apparent firsthand knowledge, when he evoked with stunning sensuality the experience of being kissed by a man or the memory of a successful seduction, his raw materials—as he always insisted—most likely were his own memories. Why should we suppose that he accomplished so many miracles of imagination? Why imagine, as the Scholastic philosophers of the sixteenth century did, that in order to preserve the perfection of the heavenly spheres, the valleys of the moon were filled with invisible glass? James wrote about the possibility of joy: the fusion of love and passion, of experience and ideal, of theory and practice. His single, endlessly repeated message was "Live!"—for it was only in the practice of life itself that this fusion could be accomplished. I believe that he knew what he was talking about. Of course, one needs a certain degree of *imagination* to relate the details of James's writings to the historical facts of his most intimate experiences. It is particularly difficult to reconstruct the emotional truths of early childhood. But as one of James's heroes, Ernest Renan, said of a much more serious subject, "I have learned that history is not a simple game of abstractions. . . . In such an effort as this, to restore life to the great souls of the past, an element of divination and conjecture must be permitted."

In its broad outlines, however, the story of James's own life, as it existed in memory, is clear and definite enough; and that is the story I have compressed into the comparatively small space of a biography.

The society James knew was a performance—a play in which the performers wore masks and costumes. The masks and the costumes were what transformed life into art, into civilization. For him, the most interesting play of all was being enacted on the stage of Europe, where America and a united Germany had just entered from left and right. Powerful personalities, the self-made aristocrats of a free society, artfully dressed in their appropriate costumes, performed the dance of history on that stage. The audience was expected to imagine the actual bodies beneath the costumes and the secret acts of love and violence that occurred offstage. The performance was a dance of the powerful, who loved, abused, and sometimes freed their beloved victims, and of the victims themselves, who, all too rarely, succeeded in achieving freedom and power.

In the effort to bring James's story into the present, I have been immensely aided by copious and often marvelous new scholarship. James's unpublished letters—of the roughly twelve-thousand letters that have survived, only about two thousand have been published—

have been located and are slowly being cataloged. There is the equally magnificent treasure of modern theoretical studies in Great Britain, France, and the United States, which in some ways have returned to James's sensibilities and even to his ideas. I have tried to acknowledge my manifold debts to those who are doing this work, and who have helped me in many more direct ways, in a separate note at the end of this volume. I have been touched and flattered by the support and friendship extended by these young scholars over the years in which this book was in preparation; they have been openhanded in sharing their work with me, and while the work that follows is my own, and all its defects are upon my own head, I hope that they will see at least a dim image of their historical Henry James and the all but vanished world in which he lived and which they have done so much to restore.

The time for a new biography is right. The wonderful scholarly work going on now is a reflection of our time. The ninety years since James's death were a period of only briefly interrupted war and revolution. We have now, however, if only temporarily, returned to peaceful life. In the course of my research I visited his own peaceful, prewar world—the country-house gardens and parlors where he was given tea, the study in which he wrote at Lamb House. I looked through his reading glasses, and handled the seal he used for formal letters—smooth, beautifully carved and balanced amber—and his silver-headed malacca cane, which had a curious dent on the handle. I walked up the front steps of No. 19, Washington Square, and looked back over the still-barren parade ground; and up the worn, canted marble staircase of the Palazzo Barbaro. I followed the Roman pavement out of Florence and up among the olive groves on Bellosguardo to Elizabeth Boott's villa.

These houses and villas are accessible, although they are older and more worn than in his day, and evidently are not to be with us much longer. Chickens were pecking on the lawn at Hardwicke, where I, like Isabel Archer and James himself, was given tea. The Palazzo Barbaro is splitting and sinking, very slowly, into the Grand Canal. But, for a while longer, James and his world can still be visited. One can still imagine the flame of Daisy Miller's courage alight in the Colosseum, and feel the impact of Isabel Archer, a new moral force unleashed in Europe, as she makes her way on straight steel rails to Rome.

In Henry James's Europe and America, in short, someone of my generation feels like an immigrant returning home after a long war. Nothing is just as it was in his day. After so many years of war, one had forgotten or ceased to believe that the rooms James moved in had ever existed. There is a touching passage in Virginia Woolf's essay "A Room of One's Own," in which she hesitantly returned to James's central theme, the terrible need for practical means with which to create a personal identity, a private place of one's own: a room in which to love and work. She puzzled over the cataclysm that separated her from James's world, where such things had seemed possible:

> Before the war at a luncheon party like this people would have said precisely the same things but they would have sounded different, because in those days they were accompanied by a sort of humming noise, not articulate, but musical, exciting, which changed the value of the words. Could one set that humming noise to words? Perhaps with the help of the poets one could. A book lay beside me and, opening it, I turned casually enough to Tennyson. And here I found Tennyson was singing:
>
> > *There has fallen a splendid tear*
> > > *From the passion-flower at the gate.*
> > *She is coming, my dove, my dear;*
> > > *She is coming, my life, my fate;*
> > *The red rose cries, "She is near, she is near";*
> > *And the white rose weeps, "She is late";*
> > > *The larkspur listens, "I hear, I hear";*
> > *And the lily whispers, "I wait."*
>
> Was that what men hummed at luncheon parties before the war? And the women?

It was the music of a time in which one took for granted the possibility of happiness. James, too, had felt it a bitterly hard thing to find a room of his own, and he had particular sympathy for the hardships faced by women. In his books, the heir, the inheritor of all the ages, is almost always a young woman.

James knew both Tennyson and Virginia Woolf, and he lived to see the destruction of Tennyson's world and the birth of Virginia Woolf's century. He was fond of her, and hoped that she, and even you and I, dear reader, with all our wealth and liberty, would inherit the honor, virtue, and beauty, the possibility of joy, that was the great treasure of the Old World; that we would receive this treasure stripped of at least some of the evils and injustices committed in its accumulation.

But please allow me, after this brief preface, to direct your attention to Henry James, with whom I would like you to become better acquainted. He is sitting comfortably at a sidewalk table on a broad crowded boulevard. Perhaps he is in Paris. He has just come from the theater, and there is his usual pink grenadine glacée, with two straws, on the white tablecloth beside him. He is wearing a black coat and a colorful tie; he sits calmly, watching the passersby with grave eyes. He has a fine head, with a broad, strongly modeled forehead, and striking gray eyes. There is something grand, even Napoleonic, in his posture and in his repose. He is clean-shaven and his mouth is soft and expressive; despite his dignity, he seems to invite confidences. A young man stops to talk, and then sits down with him. A couple in evening dress stop. Soon there is a circle of young people around him, and they remain until long after midnight, talking.

CONTENTS

BOOK III
Solitude and Power

APPENDIX:

Henry James's First Published Work:

BOOK I

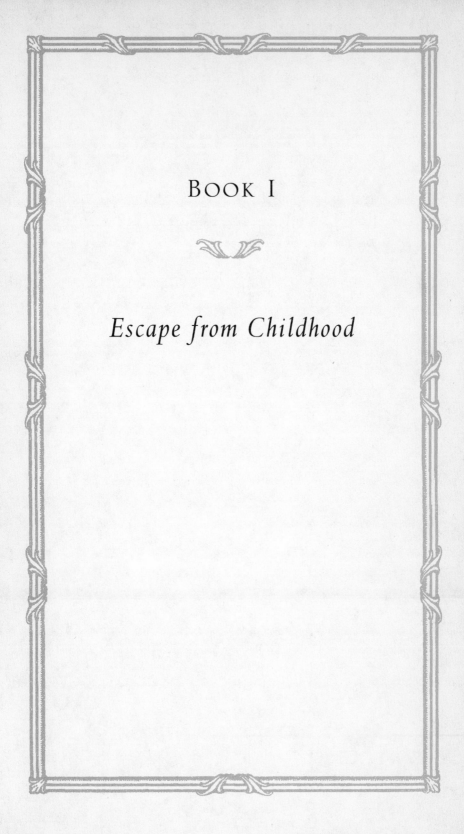

Escape from Childhood

1

EARLIEST MEMORIES:
ALONG THE HUDSON

He had long lived in the country, in an old brick house on the south coast of England, where atmospheric conditions sometimes produced a quivering mirage of his beloved France, just over the horizon. But now that he had grown old and ill, the dark and solitary country winters were too oppressive to be borne, and he had taken a flat in London, or rather in Chelsea, which was like a little riverside village loosely attached to the metropolis, and where the light, movement, and companionship helped him to ward off the depression that always threatened to descend upon him in winter. His flat was in a spanking new and bright red-brick building, with an elevator! He had been ill, and the elevator was a wonderful innovation. He who had thought nothing of twenty-mile walks had even allowed little Noakes to push him along the Embankment in a Bath chair, enjoying the sense of space and of passersby, a delicious mixture of privacy and publicity.

The flat's windows looked southward over the treetops on the Embankment to the river that flowed past with massive opacity.

In that spring of 1913, when he was seventy years old, it was almost ten years since he had published a new novel; he met a woman who was surprised to find that he was still alive. He had been engaged for the past two years, since shortly after the death of his older brother, William, in writing about their shared childhood. As the last survivor of the family, he felt it was his duty to record his memories of his celebrated brother and their once celebrated but now all but forgotten father.

The new flat was a wonderful place to work in. He had turned a sunny, south-facing front room that in years past would have been his bedroom into a large and comfortable office. His Remington typewriter was solidly placed on a desk, and before it sat erectly Theodora Bosanquet, whom he called his "literary secretary," with her slender fingers on the keys. James had spent an hour or two that morning refreshing his memory with old letters, composing his thoughts; now he was dictating the text of the memoir, and Miss Bosanquet was transcribing his dictation directly on the typewriter.

How complex is even the simplest relation between friends. Between Henry James and Miss Bosanquet, for instance: Like every genuine friendship it had its open, physical expression. She sat quite still, except that her fingers played on the keys of the typewriter. He stood at the window, looking out over the river, or paced the room, gesturing with his head, eyes, and hands, dictating; or he would collapse on the mantel with a groan, audibly searching for the word that they both awaited. Miss Bosanquet has described him for us, as he appeared to her in the early months of their friendship:

> He was much more massive than I had expected, much broader and stouter and stronger. I remembered that someone had told me he used to be taken for a sea-captain when he wore a beard, but it was clear that now, with the beard shaved away, he would hardly have passed for, say, an admiral, in spite of the keen grey eyes set in a face burned to a colorable sea-faring brown by the Italian sun. No successful naval officer could have afforded to keep that sensitive mobile mouth. . . . he might perhaps have been an eminent cardinal in mufti, or even a Roman senator amusing himself by playing the part of a Sussex squire. The observer could at least have guessed that any part he chose to assume would be finely conceived and generously played, for

his features were all cast in the classical mold of greatness. He might very well have been a merciful Caesar or a benevolent Napoleon. . . .[1]

He dictated slowly, unreeling the sentences that formed themselves in his mind, his deliberate speech occasionally interrupted by the shadow of a stutter that sometimes obstructed the flow of words; but for the most part he spoke smoothly, in a beautiful voice, without the slightest hesitation. Punctuation was carefully stated, every new proper noun spelled out.

With occasional pauses, the clatter of the Remington machine answered him in a rhythm that he and the young woman had established, and that would be audible in the style of the finished work. They were performing a little dignified and highly accomplished dance to a shared music; and just as an actor or a painter's model intimately collaborates in the performance of a work of art, and sometimes confers upon it its inner quality, so Miss Bosanquet joined Henry James in the production of his last and greatest works. Their vast and intricate score for light and sound passed through her strong, boyish fingers, and what we read and see and hear now is this shared performance. James inscribed a copy of a novel to his typist, "from your collaborator"—a truth as well as a delicate compliment.

Those last works were experiments in the re-creation of memory itself. Just as the brushstrokes of the Impressionist painters were meant to fuse in the eye, combining to reproduce the sensation of light, Henry James's phrases and sentences magically coalesced in the listener's ear into an image of a person, of a situation; the memory itself was re-created and performed on the blank screen of the listener's imagination, a kind of hologram.

At the age of twenty-seven, Miss Bosanquet had eagerly sought the position with Mr. James, and at thirty she was now his practiced accompanist; his work was more intimately familiar to her than perhaps to any other person except James himself. Yet she herself was always something of a mystery to him.

His first stenotypist, twenty years earlier, had been William MacAlpine, a wiry young Scot with whom he had formed a household. James was still living in London then, and MacAlpine was a sort of spouse. They traveled and paid calls together, and MacAlpine was in a sense a protégé. But when James moved to the country, in 1898, MacAlpine remained in London, and James arranged with the improbably named Miss Petherbridge's Secretarial Bureau for a female stenotypist to be sent to him. A female secretary was an innovation, like an elevator or a telephone, and James was a little clumsy getting used to it. The first, Miss Mary Weld, was a cheerful and plain little creature, skillful and uncomprehending. She added the bright rhythm of her typing to the master's dictations, and every Christmas he gave her a bonus and a little decorated box, the sort of gift one gave a servant. He arranged for her to learn bookbinding, which seemed to him a suitable profession for a young woman of the middle class. She stayed six years, and then married and left him.

Miss Bosanquet was an altogether different person. Dark-haired, intelligent, handsome, well educated, and despite her youth a confirmed spinster, as James was a bachelor; she shared her apartment with a companion, but she entered into the inner life of James's work. It is curious to think of James striding about the Chelsea flat evoking for her powerfully sensuous images, and at the last, when he was close to death, dictating *The Ivory Tower*, an intricately constructed phallus around which he set his characters dancing to Miss Bosanquet's music.

Intimate as their intellectual relation was, however, James was growing old and his magnificent receptivity had begun to fail him. He gave Miss Bosanquet, as he had Miss Weld, a little decorated glue box each Christmas. He did not quite understand her position and her pride in it; to him it would have been a cage to be escaped. At first it did not occur to him that he needn't spell out the hard words for her. It would have been better if he had set aside his generosity and his duty toward her—toward us—more often, or entirely, and simply explored and enjoyed their collaboration.

But at the moment we have looked in on them, it is the early summer of 1913, and there is a peculiar richness in their work together. As the memoirs of his childhood with his father and older brother unfolded, the grandmothers, mother, sister, sisters-in-law, little brothers, and cousins who occupied the space of his early life began to enter and to fill the little sun-washed flat in Chelsea, like cherubs filling the heavens of an old Italian painting with their plump limbs. These were ghosts, they were nearly all dead, now; James had been left in all but intolerable solitude.

He is dictating, now: he has taken hold of himself and caught up his typist and his readers in the gigantic effort not only to see his life and work as a whole but to lift her up, to lift us all up, by the strings of our curiosity to the frightening heights to which he himself has climbed.

.   .   .

His earliest memory was this: held in his nurse's strong hands and plunged gasping into the cold sea. At New Brighton, it would have been, at the Pavilion hotel, fronted with painted white columns.[2] In that summer of 1846, his mother was in Albany, waiting for Bobby to be born; Wilky was just a year old, and Alice, of course, had not yet been born. Where was William? He couldn't recall. He himself, three-year-old Harry, was with his nurse at the Pavilion. He remembered the bright sun, the nurse's hands, the cold water of the bay.

In that first remembered New Brighton summer, there was another image: his father, whose name he bore. His father's spectacles with their iron frames and distorting glass, his big round face with its uneven fringe of dark beard; his father stumping awkwardly and vigorously on his cork leg, taking little Harry with him on a social call.

The village of New Brighton was where the steamboat had landed in that vanished time. The great white-and-yellow temple of the Pavilion faced the blue water, and far behind the Pavilion white painted houses climbed the green slopes of adjoining hills, and looked back over a bay flickering with reflected sunlight and spotted with islets, steamers, and sails, toward the clustering brick houses at the foot of Manhattan island, among which rose the slender black spire of Trinity Church.

Tables were spread on a sloping lawn; a family with all their children were having an outdoor meal. Harry remembered being lifted onto a dog's back—an immense black dog, perhaps a Newfoundland—and sitting as if astride a horse, to be exhibited. He wore proper leather shoes and socks, despite the heat, but the other children's legs and feet were remarkably bare; and the profusion of bowls of fruit and heaped platters on the tablecloths, and of smooth, white bare legs and white bare feet, were his first memories of wealth and liberty.[3] Many years later, an outdoor meal on a long, sloping lawn would be his image of Eden.[4]

They had come to New Brighton by steamboat, from Albany, for a part of the summer. Father's widowed mother lived in a large house in Albany, and they lived with her in the wintertime while Father waited to come into his inheritance. Grandfather, who died before Harry was born, was a Presbyterian Ulsterman who had become wealthy, and had left shops and mills to be divided among a dozen children. Grandmother, who now presided over the family and the estate, was descended from English landowners in Ireland. Her forebears, and some cousins on Father's side, had tried to make a nation of Ireland, and had fled to America when their Irish revolution failed.

Robert Emmet, the martyred English leader of their revolt, had been a distant cousin; Grandmother's numerous relations and these Emmet cousins had gathered in Albany, a wealthy and rebellious Anglo-Irish and American crowd with a long pedigree, just the sort of forebears an independent young man of aristocratic tastes might wish to have.[5]

In this grandmother's house in Albany, on North Pearl Street, with its immense—as it seemed to Harry—walled garden that sloped down to the stable, peaches were carried in from the garden in bushel baskets. Catherine James's tall house seemed to be a generous sort of orphanage or inn, filled with children.

There were dozens of aunts and uncles and cousins nearby or with standing invitations to come and stay; and the Jameses accordingly lived in a cloud of cousins that were always in the house, filling the space with their plump little bodies. There were motherless cousins and orphaned cousins: Harry yearned to be one of these, romantically unparented and free.

The vanished grandfather who had once presided in this house, William James, seemed to have left few traces of himself. There was only a mysterious "office" behind an unused entrance. To Harry it was his grandmother's house, and he had a persistent fantasy that he would be an orphan and would join his English cousins under their grandmother's wing. He lived to realize it, in a way; in many of his stories an American orphan would come to England.

After that New Brighton summer, he and his father had gone up to Albany to rejoin his mother and the other children. Harry, the nurse, and his father took the side-wheel steamer up the Hudson, a memorable night of huge strange paddling and pattering and shrieking and creaking.[6] They docked in the early dawn and waited for a long hour on the quay while their baggage was unloaded from the boat and reloaded into a wagon. Then they rode rattling on the cobbles up the sweep of Broadway, up the wide causeway of State Street, straight up the hill from the harbor. Above them on the crest of the hill Harry could see the cupola of the little state capitol, like the seat of some great family, and the spires of a church. Before they reached the crest, the wagon turned to the right where the old elm grew into the wide way. North Pearl Street was lined with little high-peaked Dutch red and yellow brick houses. At his grandmother's house, breakfast waited.

He would make this the childhood home of the heroine of *The Portrait of a Lady*, and would confer upon her his own memories of the house.[7]

The new baby, Robertson—Bobby—was the fourth in five years. William was the eldest, and no longer had a nurse: William spent his mornings across the way in Miss Bayou's school, in an old house that they called the Dutch House, a peculiar gabled house of yellow brick, surrounded by a rickety wooden paling. Harry absolutely refused to be evicted from the nursery or taken to school there when it began in September. Nurse dragged him crying and kicking across the street, through the little swinging gate and up to the front door—with the fanlight that sixty-five years later he still could picture vividly—but no farther. Nurse surrendered on the doorstep, and they went home. That fall he remained with Nurse in his grandmother's house, undisturbed, hearing through the open window with inextricably mingled pleasure at his freedom and regret at his exclusion the sounds of children reciting the multiplication tables. He delighted in choosing books from the big empty library that lay behind the sealed and unused door, and he would carry them into the deserted office, where he would lie on his stomach and read as well as he could, and study the mysterious engravings.[8]

In the old brick house on the shoulder of the hill, Grandmother was the center around which all the others warmed themselves: the cousins, uncles, and aunts. She stood quite erect, and even when she smiled, her beautiful gray eyes were sad. Harry remembered that in the evenings, sitting quietly after the day's excitements, she would read a novel by the light of a single tall candle that stood straight between the page and her eyes.[9] The glare of the flame seemed not to disturb her, and her gaze was steady. She did not seem to Harry to be a widow; she was simply there, his own chosen ancestor.[10]

Very near Grandmother's house was Aunt Catherine's, his father's dearest sister's. She lived alone with her five children, her husband, Captain Robert Emmet Temple, having gone to fight in the war with Mexico. The captain was named for their distant martyred cousin, Robert Emmet, to whom he was now doubly if remotely related. The two Temple boys, Catherine's sons, Bob and Willy, were a little older than Harry. The Temple girls, Kitty, Mary, and Ellen, were just the ages of the James boys. A fourth daughter, Henrietta, would be born later.[11]

Grandmother's house was the home shared by these ten Temple and James children, and by another dozen neighboring cousins, among whom the image of red-haired little Gus Barker, an immense year older than Harry, shone most brightly. The cousins did not have enough entirely distinct names, all the Catherines and Williams and Roberts seemed to share and merge and blur in memory.

In the spring, Harry's father and mother detached themselves and their children and drifted down the Hudson River to New York City, to live with Harry's other grandmother, Elizabeth Robertson, on Washington Square. She, too, was a widow; she, too, had married a wealthy Presbyterian Ulsterman. His name was Walsh, and like the Albany grandfather, he had died long ago; Grandmother's own family, the Scottish Robertsons, somehow had filled the space he once occupied in the house on Washington Square.

Looking back on the two households, James was conscious of their different religious and national characters, and that his own father did not seem to fit entirely into either. The Albany grandmother and cousinhood were liberal, republican Anglo-Irish and Anglo-American gentry, who had owned estates in Ireland and America and who had imagined heading republics of their own. The Washington Square household was Presbyterian, conservative, Scottish and Scots-Irish. They, too, were wealthy; but whereas the Albany family were landowners, the Washington Square family were in the linen trade with Ireland. Father himself belonged to neither.

Washington Square remained in memory one of the two homes of Harry's early childhood. He was to set the novel *Washington Square* in his grandmother's house and would confer on another heroine, Catherine Sloper, his memories of it.[12] The house, No. 19,[13] was a big, mild red-brick structure with a walled garden that ran down to a little carriage house. The garden was narrower and smaller than the one on North Pearl Street. Everything here was compact, urban, new; red-brick houses were joined to Grandmother's on both sides. Hers had a broad front, however; wide steps led up to a welcoming over-sized door. From the top step one looked across the parade ground, a blank expanse of grass littered with leaves. It was a little rural wilderness bounded by white-painted pickets and a fringe of ailanthus trees. Soldiers, the 7th Regiment of Volunteers, sometimes drilled on the parade ground in their long-tailed blue coats and their high hats, while men who wore loops of gold braid on their shoulders stood by and observed. On the pavement in front of this grandmother's house Harry had taken his first walks outdoors, following his nurse with uneven steps. The odd smell of the ailanthus trees came back to him in memory.[14]

The high-ceilinged front parlor on Washington Square had a Dutch tile fireplace, and a cut-glass chandelier. Great-grandfather Alexander Robertson, for whom little Bobby was named, frowned down from his portrait over the mantel. Harry remembered being given tea, a generous tea, in the front parlor. The comfortable furniture was covered in chintz. A narrow mirror hung between the long front windows.[15]

Harry's mother and her sister, Catherine, and a nearby cousin on the Robertson side, Helen Wyckoff, had grown up together like sisters in the house on Washington Square. Catherine—Aunt Kate—and their cousin Helen made up Harry's sense of near relations in New York.[16]

Mother, Aunt Kate, and Cousin Helen together had gone to the same Murray Street Presbyterian church of which Grandfather Robertson had been a founder, and where an uncle, the William James for whom Harry's big brother was named, had preached for a time, in the heart of the old Calvinist New York. Looking back, Harry imagined them in a portrait by a grave Dutch master, in their lace caps and dark colors.

It must have been the following year, while they were still in Albany, that Father had received his inheritance. The Albany grandfather's vast estate, from which Father had for many years received an allowance, was at last being distributed. He could now buy a house of his own, and it was to be in New York.[17] Harry's long, fair curls were shorn—he remembered his tearful protest—and the James family, Father and Mother, William, Harry, Wilky, and Bob, with nurse Fanny, their servants and baggage, boarded the steamer and traveled the familiar river route to Manhattan. Mother and Father were full of optimism.

Mother, although she no longer went to the Murray Street church, still spoke the earnest biblical language of her upbringing. "Do not weary in well-doing," she exhorted her brothers—confident that they would not. She had grown up in a simpler world, as it seemed to Harry, a world of clear bright colors, of moral certainties. Father, who had also grown up in the Calvinist church, spoke the same language, and they shared as well an optimistic faith. They studied the vision of socialist Charles Fourier of an earthly heaven.

> My dear [husband] and I have lately been receiving a whole flood of light and joy . . . by an insight into the glorious plans and prospects which Fourier opens upon the world. . . . Those forms will be prepared into which the divine love and mercy will flow without measure, and the earth become a paradise indeed.[18]

Harry's mother was a devoted wife and mother, nursing her babies, managing husband and servants on the moderate income derived from Father's inheritance. When the young family moved to New York, she was pregnant with her fifth child in seven years, proud of her health and her strength and the health of her children. She was careful to see that the young family lived where the air and the water were healthful. The religion she taught her children was compounded of confident optimism and moral clarity. Doubt and anger seemed impious to her. She shone with vigor and pride and affection, and unembarrassed passion.

When Harry thought of her in later years, he remembered her as he often saw her, sitting and working while his father read aloud from his latest book. His father seemed always to have been reading pages he had just written that would show he had, this time, at last done it.[19] Mother would look down at her embroidery, listening, entirely attentive, entirely available, and reassuring.

Among her chores was the writing of letters to uncles and aunts and cousins, and above all to the grandmother in Albany, the grandmother who smiled a little sadly and sighed, thus preserving the web of relations in their widely extended family:

Dear Ma

Henry has I believe acknowledged receipt of the basket of poultry and thanked you for your kind remembrance of us at the New Year. He has wanted to go up and see you and would have done so had he not been, and still is, entirely engrossed with his book. . . . When it is out I wish you would read it for I am sure you will like it better than any thing he has ever written. It is addressed to the church and meets so rationally and satisfactorily so many of the difficulties, that every one in the church . . . must some time have felt in many of its teachings, that I am sure you will read it with interest. It fills too with new meaning and beauty, so many of the old Scriptures. . . .

Yours affect[ly]
Mary[20]

Harry remembered often being present when his father read aloud these latest pages of his latest book, and memories of that reading aloud had a particular significance for him. Mother's downcast eyes and attentiveness, all supportive of the father as they were, still communicated somehow to Harry as well a certain protective tolerance.

Father read with intensity, impatient with the stutter[21] that occasionally interrupted him, concentrating on his ideas.

There was a singleness of purpose in Father that Harry found disturbing. Harry would have preferred that the family had gone to church and had an ordinary religion, or that they had had no religion at all, rather than having only Father's fierce vision. But Mother with her downcast eyes gave Harry assurance of his own safety and liberty.[22]

They had rented part of a house at No. 11, Fifth Avenue, a few paces from the house on Washington Square, in the fall of 1847.[23] They moved in with their small children and their immense optimism like a young vicar and his wife into a new parish. The father planned to write and give public lectures, and the mother was to share the work, make a home, and raise the children.

The father had been trained for the Presbyterian ministry, and he had a sense of mission; but he had found that he did not believe in the outward forms of Christian religion. He wanted only its inner truths. As a young man he had tried to decipher the Old Testament, to find the Cabalistic message encoded there. In these studies he had come upon the voluminous works of Emanuel Swedenborg,[24] the Swedish theologian of the previous century, whose books in their faded and loosened red bindings Harry remembered were a fixture of Father's library. Swedenborg was a scientist whose thirst for understanding was limitless. He had extended science into the realm of the spirit, and in a series of extraordinary visions had described the architecture of the universe. He had seen that the material world of the ordinary senses was only a segment of a larger, spiritual reality. Inert and senseless matter was like a line that transected an angle, or an angle that cut a shape from a larger sphere. The world of spirit was not in some distant, future life, after death or in heaven; it was present like a higher dimension of the ordinary world, giving it life and movement. Heaven and hell were all about them. It was this world in which Harry was reared.

In his father's family, Harry recalled, the spiritual world lost all the ominousness it had for others. Harry was accustomed to hearing the passage by death to the spiritual world as freely alluded to as the prospect of dinner or the call of the postman.[25] Death was an enlargement, a liberation.

Modern, nineteenth-century science was confirming these visions of Swedenborg's. The great Joseph Henry, who taught at the Albany

Academy and had tutored Harry's father when he was a boy, had explored the mystery of magnetism, the force that seemed to act through the higher spiritual dimension without any material medium.[26] Then Father had also met Michael Faraday, discoverer of electrical induction and inventor of the dynamo, who was much admired by the Swedenborgians.

A subtle ether pervaded the whole of the material world, Faraday had discovered, through which the mysterious forces of gravity and magnetism acted. The human mind and the passionate affections alike were expressions of this ether that suffused the world. By subtle movements, or even by a direct act of will, one could control the mind of another: mesmerize. Demonstrations of the new science were startling, magical. The newly discovered forces could be used to heal disease, to move objects, to communicate with the spirits of the dead. A larger sphere extended outward, invisibly, from every point of the material world.[27]

Human history, like the movements of the planets, was governed by the natural laws of the spiritual realm, and Charles Fourier was the Newton of the new passional forces. Just as gravity bound the planets in their orbits, passions bound men and women and children into families and societies. Sexual attractions, the binding force between parents and children, the intense cohesion of a religious community, these were the Strong Forces of society, overcoming repulsion and rivalry.

Harry's father was one of the founders of the new Fourierist movement in America, to which he devoted a large part of his inheritance. He believed that the laws of motion of human society had been uncovered, that history henceforth would be a science, and that the future was to be consciously molded. Human institutions would be scientifically designed, harmonious; all the affectional passions would be allowed to follow their natural courses. Society would become a single phalanx, a unity drawn from multiplicity.

Father corresponded with the founders of a utopian community at Brook Farm, near Boston, who were converting to French socialism and becoming a phalanx. The Phalanx of North America was being organized outside New York City; in Illinois and Ohio and Indiana other new phalanxes appeared. Prominent men had joined the phalanxes; the Whig party began to include prominent socialists in its ranks; Horace Greeley, publisher of the New York daily *Tribune*, with Father's support made his newspaper an organ of the phalangists.[28] Grandfather William James's millions had been secretly won in sharp dealing, trading on the basis of inside knowledge; he had foreclosed mortgages and otherwise acquired property along the route of the projected Erie Canal. Father's thousands, derived from those victories, were now to be openly devoted to the socialist cause.

Despite his stutter, Father began to give public lectures. His first venture, in Albany, was a talk before the YMCA on "What Constitutes the State," in which he explained the principles of Christian socialism. Humanity was hastening to the prophesied millennium, to the New Jerusalem. What a spectacle the past half century of progress represented! The sciences had proclaimed their true mission to be the melioration of our common life.

> Our steamboats, our railroads, our magnetic telegraphs, which laugh
> to scorn the limitations of time and space . . . [are] gigantic throb-
> bings whereby our dumb nature herself confesses the descent of
> that divine and universal spirit, which even now yearns to embrace
> all earth's offspring in the bonds of a mutual knowledge and a mu-
> tual love.[29]

At the new phalanx of Brook Farm, the journal *The Harbinger* commented favorably on the speech and on Father's philanthropy.[30] He was giving a part of his income to the experiment at Brook Farm and *The Harbinger*,[31] and when Brook Farm failed and the newspaper moved to New York, he invested the immense sum of ten thousand dollars, a significant portion of his capital, in Horace Greeley's *Tribune*,[32] which provided a home for *The Harbinger*—an office upstairs in the *Tribune* building on Spruce Street—and Greeley became its publisher. Father visited the office daily, and wrote for *The Harbinger* violent reviews and scathing notices. In vigorous Swedenborgian language he reported on trade unions and socialist colonies. He was no churchman; he berated the Swedenborgians themselves for having founded a church, a "pretentious little Papacy," instead of a social movement.[33]

Father contributed twenty-seven articles to *The Harbinger* in the first year of his ministry in New York City. At the same time, with immense energy, he translated and published at his own expense Fourier's *Love in the Phalanstery*, an exposition of the arrangements of the phalanx with regard to sexual attraction: Every sexual appetite, being God-given, was to be satisfied. For men who wished to be promiscuous, there would be women who wished to make themselves accessible. For the naturally virtuous, apartments were likewise to be available, to house families and celibate workers. As in Swedenborg's heaven, every type of moral character was to be given a suitable apartment and complementary neighbors, in the great harmony of the spiritual laws.[34]

This religion of his, which Father considered the latest and highest evolution of Protestantism, was the enemy of all churches. No pious forms were observed, and the Sabbath was not kept, in the James house. The rule of duty was denied, and conventional morality was declared the enemy of the spiritual. Every impulse was held to be natural, and true morality was sweetly spontaneous. Yet Father himself, the only minister of his church, was troubled, restless, violent.

New York lay all about them. The city was noisy, and in winter the air was thick with woodsmoke and coal smoke, and filled with the racket of horseshoes and wooden wheels rattling over paving blocks, of cries, shouts, arguments, songs, all of which blended into a distant dull daytime roar. In early winter mornings, the chimney-sweep boys would call out, "Sweep O, sweep O," and in the dusky afternoons the bakers' boys, each with a basket of fresh tea rusk, would cry in their high voices, "Tea ruk, ruk, ruk, tea ruk." The junkmen's carts were festooned with jangling cowbells, and the junkmen called, "Rags! rags! rags!—and old rags! Old Clo', old clo', and old clo'! Scissors to grind!" When the warm weather came, women with bandanna-swathed heads carried steaming pails and cried, "Baked pears!" or "Hot corn, hot corn, here's your lily-white hot corn; hot corn, all hot, just come out of the boiling pot!"[35] It was noisy and lively, but there were few machine noises. The sounds of violent life were all around them, but indoors, in their own private realm, all the loud cries of life would become faint and disappear.

That winter, Father brought Harry to see a new house on Fourteenth Street. So far north as that, there were still spaces between the houses and the rubble of construction in empty lots. Father showed him a modest, narrow house, on the south side of the street close to Sixth Avenue, one of a block of joined houses in which a few gaps still remained. The house was just twenty feet wide, but perfectly new. It had gaslights, and the new piped Croton water; there was a toilet instead of a privy. Men on ladders wearing folded paper caps were still putting up the plaster moldings and hanging patterned yellow wallpaper adorned with dragons and sphinxes.[36]

In the spring of 1848, when Harry was turning five, they moved into this new house. Bob was less than a year old, and Mother was near her time with Alice. Aunt Kate came up from Washington Square to help. She was cheerful and kind and practical and energetic, if a little severe. Her stiff black dresses were adorned with bugles and buckles that protruded uncomfortably when one embraced her. When Alice was born in August, Mother was a good deal absorbed in the new baby. Harry, stout blond Wilky, and dark little Bobby shared the nursery, and were cared for by the governess. William, the eldest, went to school during the day and slept in his own room at night, so that Harry saw him only in glimpses and at meals. Father, too, was away a great deal, making his daily journey down Broadway to Spruce Street and the *Tribune* office, a journey that he made by horsecar, the public tramcar drawn by a single weary little horse or mule that ran on buried rails. Father had lost a leg in a childhood accident, and his cork leg made walking laborious. On principle, and to avoid the expense of keeping a carriage, he rode the democratic, even socialist, horsecars.

He had taken advertisements in the *Tribune* to announce a new journal of Fourierism, *The New Times*, to be published and edited by himself. He had burst the confines of *The Harbinger* and needed his own newspaper in which he could add his own discoveries to the doctrines of the new science, simultaneously to educate and to inspire the public.[37]

In February 1848, however, just before the planned move to their new house on Fourteenth Street, their spiritual world had turned upside down. Harry recalled that two of the Albany uncles, Father's elder brothers Augustus and James, had come to their door on Fifth Avenue, to announce the momentous news of revolution in France. The king of France had fled to England; socialism was proclaimed.

Through the spring, as they moved into their new house, Father spent more and more time at the *Tribune* office; bulletins from abroad displaced all other interests. There were disturbances in Ireland, Europe was in upheaval, revolution broke out in Germany, in Italy. Venice had become a republic once more; the pope had fled from Rome. Refugees from war and disorder poured into New York.

By June the revolution that had begun in France had started to falter, however. *The Harbinger* blamed Lamartine's government for having raised expectations but having done nothing to bring socialism into being. An insurrection in Paris was followed by repression of the socialists. On July 29 the newspaper reported glumly,

> The progress of the Revolution in France is suspended in favor of
> the conservative interest. The tendency to reaction is now dominant;

the panic produced by the insurrection is still widely felt; the mass of the people are distrustful; social ideas are winked out of sight. . . .

In America, the violent failure of the revolution dampened hopes. No matter how often Father explained that socialism had not in truth been tried and was still awaiting its opportunity, the European failure cast doubt on the authenticity of Fourier's revelation. American phalanxes, too, were failing, as across Europe, one by one, the new republics disappeared under a tide of reaction.

A few months later *The Harbinger* itself was no more. Father's plans for a newspaper of his own were abandoned. He turned again, and more furiously, to his own ideas. Cork-legged, limping, spectacled, stuttering, he resumed his public lectures; wrote letters for the *Tribune*; began work on a new book that would explain the true principles of Christian socialism once and for all.

The Jameses lived modestly, for people of means, having invested so much of their capital in the unremunerative cause of the phalanx. Their house, while comfortable, was much smaller than Grandmother's, and they kept only two female servants to begin with,[38] and no manservant. The cook did not live in. Because of his cork leg, Father could not walk very far, but they did not keep a carriage, and they had no carriage house or stable.[39] The house was rather remote, but Father rode the horsecars that traveled up and down each of the major avenues. In winter there was no heat in the cars; men spat in the straw that was spread on the floors for insulation. The fare was six cents. Father often had stories to tell of conversations on the horsecars. He described them as a sort of moving phalanx of democracy.

Mother was proud of having brought five children through the dangers of infancy, the cholera and the diarrhea that swept away so many in the late summers. She had a theory, one of her many theories on the subject of the children's health, that diarrhea showed weakness of constitution. Her own children were not troubled in that way; if anything, they tended to be costive, which she thought was a sign of strength. Their appetites were good, and mealtimes were cheerful and even enthusiastic.[40] When Father was at home he ate greedily. He himself said that he fed like the devil, and was ashamed to be seen at his orgies by a gentleman.[41]

Dinner was eaten at midday; the evening meal was "tea." The eldest boy, William, often grew excited and there was a great deal of shouting, hilarity, and rivalry for Father's attention at the tea table. Harry did not feel the same excitement, but he ate quite as much as the others. There was always talk at the table, Father stuttering, genial, and eloquent despite the stutter, telling his stories, and William, teasing and laughing. They spoke a family language, compounded of Calvinism, spiritualism, and slang. In the back parlor and the upstairs nursery, the windows were hung in winter with heavy red moreen. Later in the day, beside the nursery fire, Harry delighted in the stories that Nurse would tell him, and in the fairy tales she read from the fat *Boy's Own Book*. It seemed to him, remembering, that a blue river of truth curled through the tales.[42]

From these fables an impression of an ancient world, not found in America, began to form, its emblems an old woodcutter and a ruined castle. This was the world of legend and fable, of mysterious truths.

Father also read to the children; he read chapters alternately from the New Testament and the Old;[43] the Bible was another world of truthful fables. And he told stories about his trips and travels. Father had been in Europe in 1837, and again with his wife and two infant sons in 1844; his stories were filled with railroads and hotels and great people. The best and most often repeated were his stories of his trips to England, in which Father moved familiarly among the great people, and to Ireland to see his relations, who were made to seem impoverished and ignorant. Yet Europe somehow was the land of fables, the place where their truths could be found.

Sometimes, Harry went with his mother in the morning as basket on arm she walked briskly down Sixth Avenue to the Washington Market. Seckel pears, Isabella grapes, peaches, figs, and pineapples were heaped as high as his young head in front of the grocer's shops at every corner. Most delectable were the peaches: bushels of peaches, peaches white and peaches yellow, peaches cut up and eaten with cream at every meal, peaches brandied and eaten with ice cream, the greatest treat of all.[44] From the foot of Sixth Avenue they made their way through the narrow crooked streets of the oldest part of the city to the farmers' market on the Hudson River. The market extended into the river on piers, a great covered square of wooden stalls filled with produce from the farms of Manhattan and New Jersey and Brooklyn.[45]

Near their own house, hogs ran in the streets off Sixth Avenue, scavenging garbage. Brick and brownstone houses were spreading outward from Fifth Avenue, but had not yet reached past Sixth. The streets farther west were still lined by low wooden houses, brightly painted, and these soon gave way to coal yards and livery stables. In Harry's memory, it seemed that the shabbier, poorer houses were always painted red, giving a sort of red tone to the neighborhoods beyond the broad avenues.[46] The symbol and embodiment of this shabby other world was the policeman, a figure never seen on Washington Square—a man in ordinary clothes but wearing a brass star on his breast and a varnished leather fireman's hat who loitered in the parks and walked in the streets at night, calling the hours.

Each of the neighborhoods beyond the boundaries of their own world had its volunteer fire brigade, to which the working men and boys swore allegiance. The boys wore the emblems of the brigades on their coats, and were careful not to wander into foreign neighborhoods among rival brigades. Fires in the wooden houses were marked by fights among the rival gangs.

Harry began school in the fall of 1848, the year that they moved to Fourteenth Street, and each morning he and Nurse walked down Sixth Avenue to Waverly Place, and crossed the street to No. 102, the next house but one to Washington Square. The school was kept by the Misses Taylor in a little two-story house with a low stoop and freshly painted ironwork, within sight of Grandmother's house.[47]

The school was popular with the more progressive clergy of the city, and was highly democratic: at one time, both a grocer's daughter and a Jewish girl were pupils. On entering the school for the first time, students were greeted by Miss Taylor, the eldest of the four sisters, in the downstairs front parlor. The older children, who could read, were sent upstairs to be taught in two rooms on the second floor. Harry, who was five years old and had learned very early to read, went upstairs to the room at the back, where the coats were kept, with the boys. Girls were in the front room, which had three windows looking out over the street. Folding doors between the two rooms were left open for the first exercises of the morning, when the children read aloud or recited a passage of Scripture, usually a psalm. These were responsive readings, for language in this intimate little world was always a performance. The girls asked, "Who is the King of Glory?" and the boys responded, "The Lord of Hosts, He is the King of Glory." Together they sang hymns and sentimental songs: "I Dreamt that I Dwelt in Marble Halls," and "Sweet Alice, Ben Bolt." Then the doors between the rooms were closed, and the children had spelling or wrote from dictation, or copied a set text into their books.

Compositions were sometimes required of the girls, and once a week the folding doors were thrown open and the girls read their best compositions. The boys, on such occasions, recited "pieces" they had memorized: poems like "Lochinvar," and "Lochiel, Lochiel, beware of the day," or a passage from Shakespeare; sometimes two boys would take different parts.

They learned by rote. The older children learned arithmetic, and weights and measures, by memorizing tables that they recited in chorus to singsong tunes that made a strange accompaniment to the smaller children's exercises:

> 20 pence are one and eight pence
> 30 pence are two and six pence
> 40 pence are three and four pence
> 50 pence are four and two pence
> 60 pence are five shillings

Alone among the children, Harry, like his father, stuttered, which must have made the recitations trying. In his first year of school there was a great deal of examination and consultation about this, but the verdict was that his stutter was incurable, and Harry went on as he had before. The stutter made him cautious in speech. Unlike his impatient father and the ebullient William, Harry prepared his sentences carefully beforehand, mentally navigating their difficulties. The stutter was least troublesome when he was reading aloud or reciting passages thoroughly memorized beforehand; slowly, over the years, he learned to speak without more than occasional hesitations.[48]

The children brought their lunches to school, and brought coins to buy doughnuts, pies, and gingerbread at Walduck's bakery on Eighth Street, for dessert. In fine weather they played tag or "ball" in the backyard, where an apricot tree held forbidden fruit. At recess the boys were turned into Washington Square, to play in the parade ground. Looking back, dictating to Miss Bosanquet, James said it seemed always to have been autumn, the ground muffled in twigs and ailanthus leaves. The small boys kicked up the leaves—the circus smell, the semisweet rankness of the ailanthus, was all in the air—as they galloped about, whacking their steeds. After school, Harry would have tea at Grandmother's, and then walk up Fifth Avenue to Fourteenth Street, past the two big churches, lingering in the dusk at the corners where theater bills were posted.

On holidays he played in Union Square, at the northern boundary of his world. This was a little oval park in a square at the top of Broadway, with a fountain in its center, ringed by an elegant painted ironwork fence; it was far more grand than the half-rural parade ground in Washington Square. The elegant little park in Union Square was presided over by a policeman—not one of the ordinary men who wore a badge and a varnished leather hat, but a strange, dilapidated functionary who somehow belonged to the solemn, four-story brick houses that stood about the square. He carried a little cane and wore, with a very copious and very dirty white shirtfront, a gentleman's long-tailed coat and tall hat.[49]

Harry's world lay between Sixth Avenue and Broadway, from Union Square in the north to Washington Square in the south. Whenever later he was to find a city apartment for himself, in any city of Europe or America, he would reproduce the essential features of this sheltered little world: the stolid block of brick housefronts on a side street, with a broad avenue and a park at one end and a little private square on the other. Its nested spheres of privacy would be the setting of his novels. Beyond the boundaries of this realm lay a wilderness of roving gangs, pigs, soldiers, and policemen. But within its borders Harry moved familiarly among family houses, schools, and parks, in an atmosphere of cousins, aunts, and grandmothers. And at the end of the day, or at odd moments, he returned to a purely private realm of his own, a place he had begun to make for himself at the heart of this world, a nest of secrecy, hidden from the adults and children who filled the space between park and avenue with their complex relations.

His old nurse, Fanny, who had cared for him in Albany, and whose strong hands had lifted him into the water at New Brighton, vanished. Nurses and tutors thereafter seemed to appear and disappear abruptly; schools began and ended inexplicably, and he was alone a great deal. The Misses Taylor's school was followed in rapid succession by Miss Rogers', Miss Sedgwick's, and Lavinia T. Wright's schools; this last was far uptown, on Twenty-first Street; and then abruptly he was tutored at home by small, brown, snappy Mlle. Delavigne and then still more suddenly by a large Russian lady in a short cape, whose French was strangely accented. At each change, Father expressed optimistic enthusiasm for the new arrangement. The changes were always, he said, for the children's sake. Miss Rogers was not so churchly as the Misses Taylor; Miss Sedgwick had excellent manners; Mlle. Delavigne spoke French very well.[50] Each excitement gave way to new hopes. Yet the changes were frightening and disruptive, and constantly tore away the only stable relation in Harry's life, other than his mother's often distracted affection.

Cheerful, commanding Father was busy with his affairs, and these

interventions in the nursery, and the consequent appearances and disappearances of the young women, were fitful and impatient. There
was something unstated, mysterious, about the constant turmoil over
the young female servants. Harry was left to deal with it as he might.
Affectionate, distant Mother was busy caring for Father and the in-
fants. There were unstated tensions between the adults, muffled arguments. Father, laughing, conspired with the children. William was
at school. Sometimes Harry was left with one of the smaller boys, and
sometimes he was sent to school with William; sometimes Father or
Mother alone, but not both, took him along on an errand or a visit. At
times, as in memory he was puzzled to recall, he found himself with
his mother, inexplicably, at a grown-ups' dance. The only principle in
all this turmoil, it seemed, was that he should forget his nurse and not
attach himself to anyone else, that he should patiently await his father's infrequent attention. He remembered that Father, dangerous
and affectionate, Father above all, ruled these movements.[51]

Early in his childhood, then, self-protectively he began to live in
the private place that he had built himself. In his memoirs, dictated to
Miss Bosanquet, when he talked about his father and brother, he recalled the sense of separation that began at this time. This separation
from family would be a constant theme of his fiction. It was necessary
for the formation of a self, a powerful identity. It always began with a
secret, with concealment.

Dictating more than sixty years later, James still kept his secret,
whatever it was. One saw only the results: the carefully defended,
oddly secure little individuality of the growing boy. He gazed outward
from the photographs of the time—and from his own memories—
gentle and affectionate but quite distinct, his own person.

The father, on the other hand, was like a feudal monarch, whimsical and arbitrary, his little domain in constant turmoil as he flung the
family and servants about. There was something disturbing about his
violent expressions, the preoccupation of his writings with the sexual
relation, his insistence on the benevolence of his passions, his demand
for spontaneity, his need for responsiveness without attachment, his
constant restless flight and return, the abrupt departures of young female servants.[52]

In the later years, when Harry returned to his childhood memories, tyrannical fathers were frequently the villains of his tales. Their
villainy lay in their abuse of power. Miss Bosanquet, listening to these
last dictations, described them this way:

When he walked out of the refuge of his study into the world, he saw a place of torment, where creatures of prey perpetually thrust their claws into the quivering flesh of the doomed, defenseless children of light. . . . He realized how constantly the tenderness of growing life is at the mercy of personal tyranny and he hated the tyranny of persons over each other.[53]

But victims need not remain defenseless. Sometimes they achieve power of their own. It begins with their finding a firm place to stand, a fulcrum for their will. Those who had achieved this sort of indirect power had a certain quality of aristocratic repose. James would say that they had learned patience.

In *What Maisie Knew*, written when he was returning to his memories of his own childhood, the heroine was six years old at the beginning of the story. A nurse had inadvertently revealed something that frightened the child, and that was kept secret. It was a hint, a clue that her parents were using the child for their own purposes, using her in their quarrels.

This discovery, that the infinitely powerful monarchs of the household were capable of such abuse, would have been abrupt and horribly frightening, as Maisie's discovery was. Harry James traced the beginning of his sense of his own separate self to a discovery that had this emotional quality.

As James described such an awakening in a child to the awareness of evil, the first step toward freedom, "it seemed to color the air in the nursery. The stiff dolls on the dusky shelves began to move their arms and legs; old forms and phrases began to have a sense that frightened one. The young child had puzzled out her secret from imperfect signs, and the discovery had given her a new feeling, a feeling of danger; at which rose a remedy, the idea of an inner self; of concealment."[54]

2

TEMPORARY QUARTERS
IN UNION SQUARE

The family was at New Brighton again, after a long absence, and Father brought Harry into the city to have their daguerreotype taken by Mr. Mathew Brady at his establishment on Broadway. At eleven years of age, Harry was still a child, but he was a favorite in the family; they were all very fond of him, and called him "angel." He looked at his father with intelligent, innocent gray eyes. His hair had darkened to brown. Father still cultivated separate alliances with the children, and Harry, who loved his father, intensely enjoyed their excursions together. But he had long ago learned to hold himself in reserve, to keep his feelings enclosed in the muffled room of his inner privacy.

Father and he were on the side-wheel ferry in the midst of the harbor, in the beauty of light and air, the great scale of space, and far away to the west they could see the majestic gates of the Hudson. Harry would recall the sensation of that early-morning summer ferry ride, "the stretched awnings, the scoured decks, the smell of new ropes and polished brasses, the sight of other steamers clear in the blue air. Ahead of them, and all around, was the vehemence of the great city":

> The aspect the power wears then is indescribable; it is the power of the most extravagant of cities, rejoicing, as with the voice of the morning, in its might, its fortune, its unsurpassable conditions, and imparting to every object an element, to the motion and expression of every floating, hurrying, panting thing, to the throb of ferries and tugs, to the plash of waves and the play of winds and the glint of lights and the shrill of whistles and the quality and authority of breeze-borne cries . . . its sovereign sense of power.[1]

It was his own intimately known city. Harry's family had lived on West Fourteenth Street, at No. 58, for six years, until the smaller boys and Alice were ready for school. After that, Father's impatient restlessness could no longer be restrained. But those six years were the years of Harry's childhood.

In those New York years, after the revolutions of 1848 and the repressions that followed, Father was principally occupied in writing books and articles for the newspapers, and in giving public lectures in behalf of the seemingly lost cause, lectures for which he had great hopes. Father would read his talks to Mother beforehand, and then in evening dress, when the children were going upstairs to bed, he would stump impatiently down the front steps to the waiting carriage; sometimes he would rush back to the door for his forgotten speech, tuck the papers into the tail pocket of his coat, and go off again. Harry remembered watching these flurried departures from the upstairs parlor window.

Generally, Father's lectures were given in one of the halls on lower Broadway, or near the park, the old town common, that surrounded the city hall. There were placards and poems on the low iron fence around the park. The audience for Father's lectures was a mixture of working men and women; typographers from the *Tribune*, union men in short jackets and caps; immigrants; women who kept schools; and men of the world, as Harry thought of them, who wore long coats and high hats, and called at the house. Some of the gentlemen and ladies were ill dressed, as if on principle; and the hall, rented by the Fourierists or by Father himself, would be hot and rank. Although Father assiduously advertised, the audiences were small. He would read from his carefully composed sheets, copies of which, set up in type, had been carefully delivered to newspaper offices.

> Henry James has been reading some lectures in New York, lately, on art, property, the Church, &c., of which last the *Tribune* of this week gives some notice. James is one of the ablest men now speaking— bold, clear, comprehensive, deep, the champion of Socialism for this country, and armed with a certain club-logic which makes his thought more formidable than any other man's in the country.[2]

But, despite notices in the dependent and faithful *Tribune*, there was not much perceptible effect. Reflecting on Father's lack of success, the absence of public enthusiasm, of newspaper notices, the perfect absence of any Movement,[3] Harry, looking back, thought perhaps the failure had something to do with the simple ugliness of the whole business, Father's refusal to make himself, to make his ideas, in any way attractive. With his cork leg and his iron spectacles and his ragged fringe of beard, in the stuffy gaslit halls, Father genially, fiercely grasped his audience by the collar and declared to them: You shall understand.

In Boston, where the graceful Emerson's lectures had made such a success, the reception for Father's lectures was even less enthusiastic than in New York. He stood before the same small audiences that Emerson had captured, and found them only polite. Bronson Alcott, veteran of Brook Farm and connoisseur of movements, was unimpressed. The phalanx was passé.

> Henry James advertises his lectures in the city papers. . . . His themes . . . are a little unpopular just now, and his bearing too consequential and knowing, as of a man with Kingdom-come in his brain, to make friends. . . . It were safer for all grades and complexions to keep out of his way on pain of being gobbled down. Perhaps this our New England is not quite the place for one of his Thracian mettle. Metropolitan New York were fitter, or the Wild West.[4]

The great men and women, however much Father desired their aid, were obstacles in the path of his movement; and Father's failure to conquer them was part of his whole failure. Elizabeth Peabody, the great mentor of abolition and reform, especially infuriated Father. He raged at her calm, positive, conventional charities, her mild saintly tolerance. When the phalangists had captured Brook Farm, she wished them well, albeit with misgivings, but declined to join them. Even Emerson, who should by all rights have been a leader of the phalanx, obstinately refused to agree with Father's ideas or even to disagree with them.[5]

When Father was back from his expeditions into the wilderness of railroads, the harsh gaslight that seemed to flatten all surfaces and erase all distinctions, he would revile the great men. He complained, in his edgily humorous way, about Carlyle, Emerson, and Thoreau sizzling like sausages in a pan, putting a nice brown on one another. In his speeches there was the violence of anger and jealousy, mingled with his passionate love for the people on the horsecars. The great men of Boston and New York stimulated him to "show off," but the men on the horsecars never did that; they shrank into themselves to make room for one another. "They talk so heartily of household expenses and weather and raising chickens that it is sweet to be near them."[6]

> I continually witness so much mutual forbearance [in the horse-cars] . . . so much spotless acquiescence . . . such a heavenly self-shrinkage in order that "the neighbor," handsome or unhandsome, wholesome or unwholesome, may sit or stand at ease; that I not seldom find myself inwardly exclaiming with the patriarch: *"How dreadful is this place! It is none other than the house of God, and the Gate of Heaven!"*[7]

The restlessness, the dread, was not merely a rhetorical device. Father was unable to be at ease even in his own carefully decorated, civilized house, in the cultivated rooms that his wife kept for him. This incapacity was somehow appealing; even Father's refusal to be loved was parodoxically attractive.[8] Self-denial and death were familiar and queerly cheerful topics of household discussion. "We have all been educated by Father to feel that death was the only reality," little Bob recited.[9]

The children intensely interested him—at least the older boys did. Father aspired to be intimate with William in particular, to be his best friend, and he was always at work, as he said, in the children's behalf.[10] His letters were filled with reflections on William and Harry: "the dear chickens, it seems to me, come under my wing every night with an increasing sense of benediction."[11] Harry by now was practiced in preserving his sense of himself, of keeping clear of the enveloping paternal wing. But in any case it was William, the eldest, who was more frequently in the paternal grasp, where he struggled excitedly. William was fretful, impatient, loudly protesting of discomforts; at the tea table in the evenings, William was likely to argue with Father. He squabbled with and teased the smaller children, but did not escape from his beaming father's embrace.

On Sunday mornings Father worked in his library and the children were allowed to go to Barnum's "Lecture Room" or, if they chose, to wander at will in the churches of the neighborhood. There were the great Episcopal and Presbyterian churches on Fifth Avenue, and the more modest Dutch Reformed churches just beyond Broadway to the east and Sixth Avenue to the west. Lutheran, Baptist, Methodist, and Congregational churches were all nearby. Just to the north on Fifteenth Street there was an immense Catholic church and seminary building, recently built in the fashionable Gothic Revival style. Harry was aware that his New York family, the descendants of Alexander Robertson, were Presbyterian, but he was equally aware that his own father belonged to no denomination.

"What church do you go to?" would come the friendly question as Harry was welcomed into a church that he had never entered before. But he had no religion, no pew, of his own. At last, Harry brought his uneasy question to his parents. What should he answer, when he was asked about his church?

"We are Christians," Father answered, amusedly, "and there is no communion, even that of the Catholics, even that of the Jews, even that of the Swedenborgians, from which we need be excluded."

To Harry, this was colder than any criticism.[12] Nurse, teachers, friends had all been taken away as soon as he had formed any attachment to them, and now it was plain that he would not share in the warm candle-lighted communion of any church. He was not to have any church of his own, nor any communion but that of his father's ideas. The purpose of this was to prevent his forming the stubborn selfhood that was the source of all evil; or so his father said. Father's doctrine was this: Redemption lay in the extinction of the individual, the separate, the private. The sinfulness of individual life was to be extinguished in the spirit of humanity, which was simply the divine spirit.

> And my true property in mankind is not my mere natural father and
> mother and brother and sister, and the great tiresome dispensation of
> uncles and aunts and cousins and nieces thereunto appended, but the

whole vast sweep of God's harmonies in the realms of human passion, intellect, and action.[13]

The essence of the matter, Father concluded, was that I live only in my race; not in my self or my family; and consequently I must will myself to surrender myself to my fellows, and lose myself in the Lord; that is, in Society.[14]

> Mr. James's uniqueness as a thinker lies precisely in this identification
> of the spiritual and social. . . . He would have understood the religion
> of Sovietism, with its almost mystical devotion to the State. . . .[15]

But Harry, in silent defiance, had learned to cultivate his secret independence.

Father's brother Uncle Augustus would often come down from his estate, Linwood, on the Hudson, traveling on the new railroad; often he and Uncle James and Uncle John came together—Harry seemed to remember them as a threesome, all in identical, jauntily forward-tilted top hats. Father would go to see them at the New York Hotel, and they would come to Fourteenth Street. This band of uncles seemed to be a miniature of the Reformed Society of Man: a happy band of lads. Brothers-in-law were inducted into this band: Captain Robert Emmet Temple, sister Catherine's husband, and *his* brother-in-law, Edmund Tweedy. Father was very warmly fond of these men; when Tweedy married Captain Robert's sister and went to Italy, Father began to write longing letters to them, and said he would come abroad to join them if Edmund would only promise to remain long enough in Europe.[16]

Father, indeed, did not like to be alone and would often take Harry with him as he went here and there in the city, so that Harry became a sort of honorary, junior member or mascot of the band—with his own thoughts and feelings carefully tucked out of sight. Harry warmly remembered these trips at his father's side, the sense both of danger and of the now settled security of his private self. Father inveighed against the self, against all barriers and self-protections, but he seemed to enjoy affectionate, bright Harry's secure independence.

Harry remembered that on the day of the ferry ride across the harbor, his father and he had ridden the horsecar up Broadway from the ferry landing. He remembered the bare-armed men at the *Tribune*, hurrying amid the racket of the machinery, and the clever, easy, jocular gentlemen in their shirtsleeves in the August heat, chatting with Father in the midst of the agitation.[17] He remembered a visit with Father to a little shop on Fourth Street near Broadway, near the uncles' hotel. Mrs. Cannon's shop was mysteriously reached by a stairway going down from the street, and it was furnished more like a parlor than a shop. Father and the uncles bought handkerchiefs, umbrellas, and eau de cologne there, and were waited upon in a faintly risqué household. Mrs. Cannon, like Mother, had the knack of listening attentively while busy with her needlework. Father gossiped with her about the uncles as to where they were or when they might be expected and, above all, *how* they were. There was something unstated about the uncles' condition that Father and Mrs. Cannon understood—the condition of Mr. John in particular was often a subject of concerned discussion—that Harry did not quite follow.[18] Mrs. Cannon created a social space in which Father's little band could warmly extend their relations.

Not long after the Fourteenth Street era began, Harry's Scottish grandmother had died, and the house on Washington Square had been sold. Grandmother's death at a great age occasioned no sadness on her behalf. Aunt Kate was freed at last from the duty to care for her. Free to choose her own course in life, she was courted and wed by a Captain Marshall.

Father had been amused at this middle-aged romance, but it was short-lived, and Aunt Kate, who would not discuss what had happened, came to live with Harry's family on Fourteenth Street for a time. The house had had to be enlarged to accommodate her and the baby, Alice. In a crowded house, with few servants, Mother was often busy; always a refuge for Harry in time of need, she nevertheless had little time for the ordinary, momentary cares of a small child. His solitude deepened.

There were occasional family excursions into the country, in a rented carriage, and one of Harry's most vivid, pictorial memories of the first years on Fourteenth Street was this: Their carriage passed a lady on horseback—seated sidesaddle, wearing a curious flat riding cap, she had stopped to address with some vivacity certain men at work by the road. Just as the image passed Mother exclaimed, "Why, it's Fanny Kemble!" Harry did not recall having seen a woman on horseback before, and there was something striking in the image; he gathered the confused impression that riding on horseback was somehow connected with her fame, as if she performed in a circus.[19]

Helen Wyckoff, she who had grown up like a third sister with Mother and Aunt Kate on Washington Square, had married a man named Perkins; Harry had never learned his first name, for she always called him "Mr. Perkins." Cousin Helen and her husband had no children of their own. With them lived Helen's retarded brother, Henry, and her orphaned nephew, Albert, who were both her wards; they all shared a house across Sixth Avenue from the Jameses. This was the "other house" of his New York years, where he was perfectly at home. In Cousin Helen's house some of Harry's favorite books were to be found, and there he read the illustrated volumes of Dickens. (Father had only a moderate opinion of Dickens's merits, and there was no illustrated edition on display at home, as there was at the Wyckoffs'.) But the important part of Cousin Helen's house was the attic, a vast dusty expanse, where Harry, Albert, and other children dressed up in costumes from the dusty trunks and acted dramas. This was part of an important ritual of his boyhood; all of their attics were secret theaters. Another was the neighboring Van Winkleses'.

Dear Eddy

As I heard you were going to try to turn the club into a theater, and as I was asked whether I wanted to belong here is my answer. I would like very much to belong.

Yours truly
H. James[20]

William sometimes played with the younger children; he would be excited, make jokes and boss the business, inventing the play, directing the actors and performing the principal role himself. Harry remembered that on these occasions he himself would spend most of his time waiting, bare-legged, for his costume and his lines.

Theaters were an important feature of the adult world, as well, as were all sorts of spectacles and performance, great dances and assemblies. Father, of course, could not dance; but the family was often at assemblies and balls in the evenings, where Mother danced, and Harry was occasionally a spectator. There were "German" dances on the polished deck of Jim Pendleton's yacht, and assemblies at the Emmets' on Washington Place. To the childish eye, the dances were much like the attic theatricals at Cousin Helen's. Beautiful young Kitty Emmet presided over the assemblies.[21] The furniture would be taken away and an immense white cloth spread over the floor, converting it into a ballroom, and there Harry would meet his girl cousins, who waltzed in tightly laced waists and immense crinolines, at sovereign ease on their bright stage—more at ease, it seemed to him looking back, than any growing young girls that he would ever find again.

Little red-headed Gus Barker ran onstage and off again repeatedly. He was one of the motherless Albany cousins, and his appearances were always vivid and memorable to Harry. Gus was sent to a variety of schools, in the experimental spirit of the family. For a time he was at the Institut Charlier, in New York, to learn French and good manners, and then he would occasionally appear at Fourteenth Street on holidays.

The memory of Gus that was most brightly illumined for Harry was connected with a trip by steamer up the Hudson, with a group of Albany cousins, to the modern prison at Sing Sing. Gus was at a military school in the village near the prison, and he appeared in uniform, a most beautifully made athletic little person of twelve, in the highest degree appealing and engaging, to show them about the school and the great prison. It seemed that state prisons were on the whole delightful places, vast, bright, and breezy. The children brushed against gentlemanly prisoners who were guilty of gentlemanly crimes. One prisoner, in his white uniform, lounged at the foot of a stair, and stared back at them; his hands were white and fair, and were adorned with a gold signet ring. Harry envied this bold-eyed celebrity as much as he envied the masterful Gussy.[22]

Gus, the athletic, manly, beautiful Gussy in his military costume, Harry regarded with a kind of possessive envy, the feeling he had for such boys: Gus was so *other*, and yet Harry yearned to taste what his life was like. Harry was conscious that he entirely lacked the passion of jealousy. He had no wish to compete, he never dreamed of competing, with Gussy; he yearned toward Gus like a little boy with his nose pressed against the hard glass of a confectioner's window.[23] Gus belonged to the world of the uncles, to the band of lads. Harry remembered visits to Uncle Gus, at Linwood, with its immense views across the Hudson River, with its gardens and draperies, which to Harry were only a pretext for a reunion with Gussy, for their games and conversations.

In that summer of 1854, the summer of the Brady photograph, after their dutiful visit to the gently sighing Albany grandmother,

Harry's family had returned to the Pavilion, in New Brighton. They took their meals in the collective dining room as if in a phalanstery. Harry reveled in hotel existence, and felt some of the romance of the fortunate orphans, so superior to the merely homebound existence of ordinary children. Here there was no crushing intrusive pressure; he could carry his private world about with him and observe the spectacle of Father's utopia, the play of forces in the impersonal air. Across the columned front of the hotel there was a vast veranda, overlooking the wide farthest reaches of New York harbor, and this seemed to Harry to be the literal stage on which the summer's dramas were enacted.

Immediately about the hotel there was only the poverty of a rural village—dust and glare and mosquitoes and pigs and shanties and rum-shops. The family took no walks in this wilderness, rarely even drove; their summer was the hotel, and above all the remarkable veranda of Harry's memory, a raft of rescue from the wilderness so immediately near.[24]

The veranda was interestingly peopled. There were the De Coppets, for instance. She, an American, had married a French-speaking Swiss, and Harry was awed by their tale of a family celebration, in the Canton de Vaud, in which Mr. De Coppet had worn armor and ridden on horseback. The De Coppets were theoretically American, and lived in America, but they had just returned from Geneva, where their eldest son, Louis, had been at school. They had brought Louis home with them, presumably so that he would acquire some firsthand knowledge of his native land. He spoke an English that while fluent was still not precisely native American. He was that remarkable being, the first that Harry had encountered: a cosmopolite. Louis was Harry's age and intensely fascinating. He did not play games, but he did not seem to feel this as a lack. He was slender and dark, confident, easy, and sporting in his own way, and to Harry he seemed sublime. He had an odd, delicate, precise way of saying local place names— O-*ee*-oh for Ohio, and Ee-oh-wah for Iowa—that seemed both foreign and correct. Through the whole long summer, Harry and Louis confabulated on the veranda and in the shady rooms of the hotel. Louis had decided in his clear way that Harry would be a writer, and would have a talent for writing romances; and that he, Louis, would arrange to have them published. For long hours they discussed the exciting question of the getting published; how this was to be managed, through what friends and acquaintances and blandishments. The question of publishing seemingly had to be decided first, and as these delicious conversations prolonged themselves no romance was ever indeed written.

Louis, with his manner, his confidence, his courage, seemed to open vistas for Harry; he seemed to prefigure the manners, the tone, of a European young man, splitting Harry's loyalty. Until then, the American had been his only ideal—the American as personified by manly little Gus Barker. But Louis's toy hammer drove in the very point of a golden nail, and Harry was thenceforth always to be divided.[25]

There had been at least one new school for him to attend each winter. As the boys grew older, the wild succession of dame schools and female instructors had given way to a series of masculine schools. Harry found himself among a new set of strange boys each year. One season, the winter of 1851–52 it must have been, at the Institution Vergnès, on lower Broadway, a black and ill-heated room, the other pupils were the sons of Cuban and Mexican émigrés, and there was a great deal of shouting. The next year, the Institution gave way to the school of Richard Puling Jenks, two rooms that were up a flight of stairs from Broadway. In the front room there was a stove that somehow scorched without warming. Mr. Coe, the drawing master, and Mr. Dolmidge, the writing master, hovered about this stove in the early mornings, drawing out their delays. Mr. Jenks was the principal teacher, and he wielded a ferule with which he whacked the boys.

Father's relentless churning of family arrangements kept Harry from forming friendships or attachments, and each of the schools Father chose was more foreign and repellent than the last. Looking back on it from old age, Harry James saw it all dispassionately, even humorously, but it was a sad business at the time. Of all the schools and teachers of those years, Harry remembered only Mr. Coe and Mr. Dolmidge with anything like affection; they had been the only ones whose teaching he wished to have. Mr. Coe, the drawing master, was a fat man who wore a great gathered cloak with a velvet collar. He had many little white cards on which he had drawn, with incongruous delicacy, little scenes for the boys to copy, and he handed these out to the boys, his great cloak billowing, like an immense bird dropping tiny eggs. Mr. Dolmidge was quite different. He taught penmanship, and as if by some law of illustration, was painfully thin and tall. He wore a swallowtail coat and black satin stock, and he taught the boys to write in great calligraphic flourishes, exhibiting great scrolls in the form of surging seas and beaked eagles for them to copy. But after a single winter Harry was removed from Jenks's school and whisked into another, maintained by Messrs. Forrest and Quackenbush, just across the avenue from their home, on the northwest corner of Sixth Avenue and Fourteenth Street.

At the new school, for the first time, Harry was among boys from families like his own, but they were not boys with whom he had played. Mr. Forrest, who wore a black swallowtail coat and a white neckcloth, sat on a little rostrum and listened to recitations, and whacked the boys freely. Mr. Quackenbush, who taught Latin, did not beat the boys himself; he sent them to Mr. Forrest for that.

The school was sociable and gay, in its fashion, but its atmosphere was nevertheless thin. Harry sat in the large, brightly crowded, smelly and smoky front room in the mornings, and listened to the roll being called—Colgate, Havermeyer, Hoe, Phelps, Stokes—the English and Scottish and Dutch names. He was no longer among the very small-est boys, although the eldest were still crushingly bigger. The big boys seemed at home in arithmetic, and had great sheets of figures, ledgers drawn in columns, and other arcane appliances, that to Harry were blankly incomprehensible.

At recess the boys played in a barren courtyard on Fourteenth Street; in the passageway a black woman would set up a little portable stove and sell the boys hot, soft, brown waffles drenched in syrup. The boys would crowd into the doorway and jostle each other and thrust forward their copper pennies, and eat seemingly hundreds of hot, sticky waffles.

In the courtyard itself, the bigger, stronger boys displayed knowl-edge and attainments that Harry admired respectfully, and a little yearningly, but, as with Gussy, without jealousy. A tall boy, Simpson, whom Harry particularly admired, did magic tricks with a pocket-knife, a handkerchief, and a key. Harry asked to be shown how to do the tricks—a request that Simpson, from the height of his greater years, treated with scorn. Harry asked again, and another boy said, "Oh, oh, oh, I should think you'd be too proud—!"

He neither was too proud nor imagined that one might be; but it flashed on him that with his self-contained reserve, he had failed or missed sharing a high privilege; and that cool little voice gave him a pang that never entirely subsided.[26] As from that first day when he had refused to be taken to school in Albany, the pleasure of being at liberty was mixed with regret at being excluded; almost from the mo-ment he began to construct his secure, private little self, he felt the pain of loneliness.

After school he would wander idly in the streets. One of the few ameliorations of solitude in that dreary, lonely winter were evenings at the theater with his parents. The theater was an approved form of education, Fourier having pointed out the importance of affecting all the senses simultaneously. Father thought a sensuous education more important than the rote learning the boys received in school, and Mother liked the children to share the theater as innocent amusement. And so at a very young age, Harry had often found himself with Father and Mother, in a stall at a theater, waiting impatiently for the curtain to rise.

The first play he remembered seeing was Shakespeare's *A Comedy of Errors*,[27] at William Burton's small theater on Chambers Street, just off Broadway near the city hall. Harry remembered the sacred thrill, then experienced for the first time, of waiting for the green curtain to rise. They often went as a family to other productions of Shakespeare, romantic comedies, and performances of such family fare as *Uncle Tom's Cabin*. But Harry was free on holidays to attend less edifying performances, and he went regularly to Barnum's lecture room and to the circus; he saw the French acrobats, the Ravels, and Signor Léon Javelli, who danced on the tightrope, leaped and bounded and wavered and recovered closely face-to-face with his young audience—he bounded highest of all, this brave Signor Javelli.

Harry remembered the stage performances of Dickens's works far more intensely than the books themselves. Dickens had shaped the imagination of his generation, and Harry would always class people mentally as Murdstones or Little Dorrits or Oliver Twists. But once he had seen a character acted on the stage, it was the living person that he remembered, not the books themselves. The immense authority of the stage, the mightiest of engines, its mechanism like a dynamo constantly being improved, stamped his memories.[28] He was already curious to know how the effects were achieved. The actors and actresses wore costumes, and Harry found himself examining their manner and their dress, very much as he scrutinized the persons in the ballrooms and on the verandas of his social world. The actress Mrs. Holman to his relentless eye had a receding chin. Mr. Nagle, Harry recalled, had rather a blue chin and a noticeable brogue. Mrs. Russell, performing in *Love in a Maze*, had a bony chest for such a low-cut gown.

Ah, how tenderly and yearningly enthusiastic he could be, though. For Miss Mary Taylor, in *The Debutante's Father*, a charming, panting dark-haired creature in a flowing white dress, a gold tiara, and a golden scarf, throwing herself upon the neck of the broken-down old gentleman in a blue coat with brass buttons![29] And for Julia Bennett, whose speech was English, not American, and who made her first appearance in a becoming white bonnet, as a brilliant adventuress; for Fanny Wallack, flushed and vociferous in a riding habit, and Laura Keene; for Madame Céleste's wonderful, majestic, and voluptuous stride, in a short skirt and leggings, swinging a riding crop.[30]

But in that remembered summer of 1854, the last summer of his childhood, the summer of his friendship with Louis De Coppet, the family was staying at the Pavilion hotel in New Brighton when eleven-year-old Harry rode the ferry to Manhattan with his father to have their portrait taken. Harry was perfectly conscious of stepping onstage in his own small way, and, head clasped in the photographer's steel brace, he looked at Mr. Brady, to one side of the camera, with his self-possessed, receptive gaze; his hand rested as if forgotten on his father's shoulder, where Brady had put it; his lips were almost parted, in a characteristic expression, as if he were about to speak. Father, his eyeglasses set aside, looked intently into some vision of his own, his jaws firmly clenched.[31]

That summer a drama had begun to play itself out in Albany. Father's dear sister, Catherine, and her husband, Robert Emmet Temple—Colonel Robert now—were both ill and bitterly unhappy. Catherine had been ordered away from the contagion of her husband's tuberculosis, against her own wishes. The children were with Grandmother on North Pearl Street, and she had fled to Uncle Gus's ample house, Linwood, leaving Robert dying. Father had come up to see her. He had once again boarded the ferry, taking Harry with him. They again crossed the bright, sunlit harbor in the early morning. By evening they were in spacious Linwood, and for the first time Harry was in the presence of actual tragedy, feeling that an audience was superfluous and wondering why he was there.

Father was somewhere in the interior of the house, trying to persuade Catherine not to return to Albany, and Harry waited in the warm, lamplit parlor with Uncle Augustus and his family. Cousin Marie, who was just Harry's age, sat beside him, and Uncle Gus said that it was time for her to go to bed. Marie, as Harry knew, was "spoiled"; she protested, and Uncle Gus said something short-tempered, whereupon Marie fled across the room to her mother's arms. But her mother only said, "Come now, my dear; don't make a scene—I *insist* on your not making a scene!"

Harry had never heard this expression before. To Harry, the "scene," *la scène,* was the theater, was action on a stage. He had been witness to a great many scenes, of tragedy and romance and comedy; he was seeing one now. The great thing revealed to him by Aunt Elizabeth's remark, the immense illumination, was that one made them; one could make "scenes" or not, as one chose.[32]

3

FATHER'S ASSAULT ON PARIS

Only weeks after the scene at Linwood, Catherine and Robert Temple had both died, their six children were orphans, and the Jameses' own lives were thrown into turmoil. Father's restlessness became acute, and he began a long period of impulsive travel, of dashes across the ocean and back, trailing his young family behind him.

Anticipation of this prolonged restlessness was in the air from the time of the Temples' deaths. Harry was sent rather late to Forrest and Quackenbush's school in the fall, and it was plain this would be temporary; everything in their lives had become impermanent. Father said schools in Europe were better, and the boys would learn languages there. They would go abroad without definite arrangements; Father would look out for suitable schools, not only for his own children but for the two orphan Temple boys. The little girls would go to school in Albany.

Father and Mother had talked for some time of going to Italy, where the Edmund Tweedys, Catherine Temple's surviving sister and her husband, had settled; Aunt Kate, who adored Florence, was for this. But the Tweedys returned to the United States, in part because of straitened circumstances, and in part under the weight of their own multiple tragedies. They had lost their own children to disease, and now they came home to Albany to care for the orphaned Temple girls.

Father and Mother turned to the possibility of Geneva. The city of Calvin, undisturbed by the revolutions of 1848, was considered a proper place to learn French and German, and the Swiss had made a positive industry of progressive education for the children of the well-to-do. Furthermore, Mother's cousin Charlotte King had settled in Geneva with her children. In the autumn of 1854, accordingly, Father began to talk of going there. Harry was glad to hear the talk and to sense the impending upheaval. He was not very happy as he was.

He was for the most part alone. He read a great deal, books ordered from a shop on Broadway, whose proprietor was English and whose shop, which smelled of fresh paper and leather, seemed an embassy of England. The books and magazines that Harry read were English—Dickens, *Punch*, which seemed to bring London with it, and *The Charm*, a yellow-covered magazine for children that Father had ordered from the bookshop.[1] The language of his reading was the English of England, the language of another country.

When he was not reading or wandering the streets, he drew. That winter he had formed the ambition to be a painter, and in his quiet moments he practiced drawing and painting with watercolors. He and William had been taught the elements of drawing, and through diligence he had kept pace with his older brother. William, it was true, aside from being older, had more facility, but Harry worked hard, and was determined to paint, and felt that he was keeping up.

When Harry was twelve he was taken to see a great show of European painting. A Crystal Palace had been built uptown, a replica of the high-technology, glass-and-steel pavilion in London's Hyde Park. The Crystal Palace was a sort of world's fair, in the wilderness near the reservoir on Forty-second Street, and the horsecar line had been extended up Sixth Avenue to carry visitors there. There was a vast display, a sort of jungle, of art in the greenhouse of the Crystal Palace; it was an outpost of continental Europe. Books were English, but art was European.

Harry, dressed in a clumsy and unbecoming overcoat with troublesome stiff embroidered buttonholes, visited the Crystal Palace with

Albany cousins, and was cold and hungry. The paintings, in room after room, asked questions and addressed feelings he had not yet examined. The strong forces of sexual passion and religious feeling were visible, tangible. He remembered Kiss's formidable *Mounted Amazon* in marble, a great muscled superheroine attacked by a leopard. Thorvaldsen's enormous *Christ and the Twelve Apostles*, a shining marble company ranged within a semicircle of dark maroon walls, was beautiful indeed; Harry rose to it in wonder.[2]

But Harry's initiation into art as something accessible, as something he himself might undertake, occurred more modestly in the Broadway picture galleries. He went alone, or with visiting cousins—most memorably with Gus Barker—to see the shows. German and French paintings, scandalously nude figures, great brilliantly colored canvases, were on sale. The colors, as Harry recalled them, lustrous in the fresh American light, were more vivid than any he would ever see later. No single impression was as intense as the exhibition of Mr. Leutze's vast canvas *Washington Crossing the Delaware*. The James family went to see it one evening, as if going to a play. They went after supper, past Harry's usual bedtime, not renting their own carriage but traveling in the Fourteenth Street stage to Stuyvesant Hall, where the picture was displayed under whitely flaring gaslight. The vividness, the importance of details in the picture had the effect of a revelation. The marvel of the wintry light, the sharpness of the ice blocks, the sickness of the sick soldier, the strands of rope and a soldier's boots—all stood out with an uncanny effect; and above all, the tension, the vividness of Washington's posture, of the whole drama of his standing *up* in the boat, in such difficulties, made Harry begin to think of how such dramatic works were composed.[3]

And so Harry undertook to draw, to paint, dramatically. He bought some quarto sheets at a shop on Sixth Avenue. These were ruled, and had the peculiar virtue that they were folded into little books, the fourth page of each of which was blank. In the seclusion of his room, Harry filled these little books. In each, on the first three pages he would write a miniature drama. Time passed in these stories, words were spoken, events occurred. They were scenes. He wrote quickly, impatiently, combining in himself author, actor, and stage manager, in haste to reach the fourth page. There he drew a picture of the scene as it would be performed on a stage. He did not draw easily, but he was determined to draw well, if only by the intensity of his grip on the pencil. The pictures were scenes not of ordinary life but of artful performance, and he carefully rendered the details of the stage as well as the actors, drawing the boards of the stage floor in proper perspective, lines converging toward the vanishing point of infinite space.[4]

These childish efforts were a prelude to Europe, where Harry knew that art was to be found. On June 27, 1855, the Jameses sailed for Liverpool, en route to Geneva, and Harry's childhood came to an end. They sailed in a flurry of last-minute preparations, Father in an agony at severing himself from family and friends. Before leaving New York he arranged to send back letters and reports on political and social conditions in Europe for publication in the grateful *Tribune*.[5] At the last possible moment he wrote to arrange for a letter of credit to a London bank, Baring Brothers, through their American correspondent, Samuel G. Ward, a distant connection of his. Mother's eldest brother, Robertson, would manage their financial affairs in their absence, and make regular deposits to an account at Ward's to cover drafts against the letter of credit.[6] In this manner they would have access to their income while abroad; and Father characteristically set the terms of the letter of credit in excess of his income, so that he would be able to draw on his capital as well, or receive gifts and loans from his family as in the past. To Ward, Father also promised to send along with his accounts reports of his evangelical work among the corruptions of Europe: "I keenly desire to make you sharer of my views. . . ."[7] The house on Fourteenth Street was rented on a long-term lease. They were off into the world, without a perch to which they could return: Father, Mother, Aunt Kate, two female servants, and five children whose ages ranged from five to thirteen years, bound for Paris and Geneva, to bring Father's ministry to Europe. They traveled modestly, by the standards of their class and their day; they did not have a manservant, for instance. They relied on friends and relations for information about housing and schools; they planned to settle among familiar faces.

It was a bad crossing, in a frail steamer with twin side-wheels and twin black smokestacks rising between them, which was very much like and hardly bigger than the overnight boats that had carried Harry between Albany and New York. They met storms and unseasonably cold weather, and all became ill in various degrees. Harry was sick and remained in the cabin, among familiar creakings and groanings and splashings. Aunt Kate remained well enough to nurse Mother and the children, but only Father and little Bobby were able to take meals at the captain's table.[8]

Harry did not much remember their landfall off Queenstown or their Sunday embarkation at Liverpool, where they spent the night.

His illness seemed to persist, and by the time the family had reached London, where they meant to stop only long enough to change trains, he was shaking with chills and fever. A doctor was consulted and the diagnosis was intermittent fever—malaria—which the elders characteristically decided had an invisible source; they thought the illness had been contracted the summer before in the wilderness of New Brighton and had lain dormant, only to break the surface now. Mother was particularly fond of this sort of moral diagnosis, of tracing illnesses back to chills, carelessness, lapses barely noticed at the time that would have historic consequences later on.[9]

The family halted for a day at the railroad hotel, at the London and Northwestern Station, where they waited for one of the periodic breaks in Harry's fever. He lay at ease on the great fusty curtained hotel bed, a four-poster with a canopy that seemed medieval, a big bed in a smallish room crowded with other furniture. It was Harry's first remembered experience of Europe, which was then to him only the land of fairy tales and of Louis De Coppet's mysterious sophistication. Experienced now at firsthand, the air seemed thicker and the light richer than in New York, dense with history and the memory of coal smoke. When the doctor and the family left Harry alone for part of the afternoon, he tasted the thick and heavy suggestions of a London room, the very smell of which was ancient and strange. The open window let in a hum of a thousand possibilities on the July air, and he trembled with pleasurable anticipation.[10]

The family continued on their journey into Europe, and Harry's next distinct memory was of Paris, which after long delays and journeyings would prove to have been Father's destination all along. They had taken rooms for the night, in a hotel on the Rue de la Paix, two flights up. Harry remembered leaning on the narrow balcony's wrought-iron railing above the broad Parisian boulevard. Just opposite their windows was a dressmaker's with lighted uncurtained windows. He remembered feeling as if he were at the theater, precisely the theater he had imagined Paris to be, where the vast social realm with its rich history and complexities was as much open to him as the attics and drawing rooms of New York had been. Serious young women sat at their work, just behind the windows, while other figures flitted past. Harry stared and imagined and seemed almost to remember having experienced just this scene, this air, this spirit. He felt that he was a Parisian.[11]

The railroad as yet went only as far as Lyons. Debarking there, the family entered a much older world of travel, the world of the horse-drawn traveling carriage with a postilion on the box. The Jameses, now accompanied by a black-bearded courier, Jean Natali, to assist them in their travels, loaded themselves and their baggage into two carriages and lumbered on to Switzerland. Harry, intermittently feverish, lay on a little makeshift bed in one and gazed out the window as the carriage climbed higher each hour into the Jura Mountains. They paused in a village on a short, narrow cobbled street that opened on an entrancing vista. In the distance, on higher ground, was a crumbling ruined castle, and in the middle distance a peasant woman stooped to labor in a field. This picture, framed by the cottages of the village, was Europe, the world of legend, of reading and anticipation, like a scientific hypothesis that was now richly confirmed.[12]

The carriage ride to Geneva brought him past the doorstep of the De Coppets' home in the Canton de Vaud, and the town of Coppet itself, on Lake Geneva, with its memories of Madame de Staël. In Geneva the Jameses rented an apartment on the lake, with a fine view of Mont Blanc, beside the apartment of the Henry A. Stones of New York City. The Stones, who were in Geneva to be near their children's school, played host to the arriving Jameses. On the first morning, Father with characteristic energy went promptly to interview schoolmasters whose names Stone had given him, and after a single round of visits chose for his boys the Pensionat Roediger, a new school in a comfortable country house just outside the city. It was not a school that many Americans attended, the pupils being principally French and German; the instruction was almost entirely carried out in those languages. But Roediger was a vigorous, compelling, manly man, whom Father liked immensely and to whom he impulsively entrusted his children, with a perverse disregard for their ordinary needs.

William, Wilky, and Bob, accordingly, were packed off to the Roediger school,[13] and a governess, a young Vaudoise woman, was hired to give little Alice lessons. Father took his remaining, much reduced, family to a suburban villa, the Campagne Gerebsow,[14] away from the lake but in a very pretty spot on the Rhône. A few days after their arrival, Father wrote home to Grandmother that the schools were good and would do for the Temple boys as well as his own—although on second thought perhaps the Roediger school was not for the Temple boys after all. He sent off a letter to be printed in the *Tribune* praising Geneva: John Calvin had been a progressive mayor for the city, Father said; Geneva was Calvin's successful experiment in scientific good government and education. Father entertained the readers of the *Tribune* with personal details of his hosts, the Stones, who were thus named and publicly thanked. He described the view from his bedroom window, mentioned the rent he was paying at the Campagne Gerebsow, ten dollars a week, and the tuition for the boys at the Roediger school, "little short of $350 per annum, including washing and the necessaries." He systematically, on principle, sacrificed their privacy.[15]

Harry was unaware at the time of this invasion. He spent his days at the villa, sometimes in bed, in the big high-ceilinged room with deeply recessed windows that to his delight he had to himself. He spent his time reading. The deep window embrasures were a constant reminder of the massive and ancient stone walls that surrounded him, so different from the thin wooden or brick shells of even the grandest houses at home. The vast dim spaces around him seemed to harbor depth upon depth; the room had a spirit that he could not penetrate but that was somehow expressed in the early twilight, in the great homely green wooden shutters, the occasional small sound of a voice or a footfall in the garden beneath his window. When it grew too dark to read in his room, and when the fever was in remission, he would go down to the salon to join Mother and Aunt Kate. They would chat idly until the waiter entered and with a graceful, tactful bow would announce, *"Mesdames et messieurs, le diner est servi."*[16]

Invalid Harry was a little emperor, and communicated with his realms through messengers and ambassadors, of whom the principal, essential ambassador was his younger brother, Garth Wilkinson—Wilky. Harry profited from handsome, happy Wilky's genius for friendship: when Wilky came to visit in the late afternoons after school he came with stories and reports. Wilky met everyone, befriended everyone, and his omnivorous explorations fed Harry's intense imagination. Wilky had tales to tell of the masters and pupils at the Roediger school, where Harry was to join him when his health allowed, and of their hostess, the glamorous Countess Gerebsow. For the first time Harry saw the world through someone else's eyes, experiencing it vicariously through imagination. For the rest of his life he would supplement his own experiences in this way, and would write about his ambassadors in the very act of using them.

When Harry at length recovered, he was not enrolled at the Roediger. Father by then wished to return to Paris. Geneva had quickly revealed its secrets to him, and there was little company that he cared for, but he did not want to live in Paris alone. After a few weeks of growing impatience, Father began to complain of the expense of the Pensionat Roediger, soon to be increased by Henry's tuition. He confided his dilemma to his Swedenborgian friend Garth Wilkinson, who responded with an invitation to join the Wilkinsons in London;[17] the two families were close, and young Wilky had been named for him, as the Wilkinsons' daughter Mary had been named for Mrs. James. Within days, with characteristic abruptness, the James boys were taken out of school. Father wrote to Grandmother again, this time to say that Swiss schools were overrated, and that he was taking his family to London, and would look about there for something better.[18] Three months after their arrival in Europe, they sped through Paris again. The Vaudoise governess, Mlle. Cusin, went with them, and they landed briefly in London, but only long enough to hire a tutor for the older boys.

Although the superiority of English schools was the ostensible reason for their abrupt removal from Geneva, the boys were not sent to school in England. Neither Father nor Mother approved of the corporal punishment that was part of the famous English boarding-school regime. And then, too, the schools were expensive, and wanted tuition paid a full year in advance,[19] which would have committed Father to a course of action. As ever, he refused to be committed. A tutor accordingly was engaged for the James children, a tutor who could be dismissed as easily as he had been hired: Mr. Robert Thomson, a tall, thin, awkward, very young and dark-haired Scot, who had come to London from Edinburgh and was saving money to open his own school. Thomson was a mild and friendly man of whom Harry quickly grew fond, and who seemed fond of him.

While the question of schools and tutors was being resolved the family lingered for a month in London, at No. 3, Berkeley Square, a London in which it was always a rainy evening. Then they rented a house in suburban St. John's Wood, near the Wilkinsons. Mlle. Cusin lived with them, and Mr. Thomson rented a little flat nearby, over a shop, where William and Harry sometimes were given a stale cake as a special treat. Wilky, Bob, and Alice were given lessons by Mlle. Cusin. It was strange to have come so far for the children's education, only to hire a tutor and governess who could have been found at home.

Harry enjoyed the new arrangements, however, unaware of their temporary character. Mr. Thomson was a very pleasant and intelligent man; he did not whip the boys, and in the morning lessons his harshest command was "Come now, be getting on!" Harry fondly recalled the tutor's fresh complexion, his very round clear eyes, his tendency to trip over his long legs or feet while thoughtfully circling around the boys, his constant black dress coat and gray trousers.

Separated from Wilky, Harry was now thrown together with his older brother, William, for the first time. Lessons were given in the morning, and on most afternoons Harry and William were left to their own devices. For lack of anything better to do they simply walked about together with no particular object, looking into shopwindows and being stared at by passersby. William was growing up tall and thin, and had dark hair and a turned-up Irish nose. He was restless and bored by idle strolls in the company of his little brother. But little, round-faced Harry enjoyed his big brother's company on these long walks, which were so much like the walks he had been obliged to take alone in New York.

London was glimpsed only during these long rambles with William: Harry remembered best the gaslit Strand, then still literally on the river's bank, a glistening street filled with carriages of every kind and lined by shops and theaters. He was struck by the variety in costume and manner and accent in London: postmen in red frock coats and beaver hats; milkwomen in little shawls and immense boots, milk pails swaying from wooden yokes on their shoulders; the swell men in their distinctive dress and their tall hats; ladies riding in all sorts of carriages, large and small; footmen in livery, carrying staves, hooked behind the larger coaches; the horseback riders in Hyde Park, ladies riding sidesaddle in their voluminous skirts, each followed by a mounted, uniformed groom; the picture glimpsed from a cab window, and never forgotten, of a shabbily dressed woman reeling backward as a man felled her to the ground with a blow in the face.[20]

In the evening, sometimes the whole family with Mr. Thomson and Mlle. Cusin would clamber into two carriages rented for the occasion and journey into the West End, where the vividness of costume and language in the audience, illumined by the undimmed gaslights, was reflected on the stage, and one set of players seemed to be entertaining another.

On an outing of another kind he again saw Fanny Kemble, the horseback rider he had once glimpsed in New York; this time she was reading Shakespeare. The Jameses had gone to a small community hall, the Assembly Rooms, in St. John's Wood, where Mrs. Kemble read not excerpts or favorite speeches but entire plays. In middle age, divorced from her husband and long since retired from the stage, she had undertaken this singular new career. Father, who had admired her of old, brought the family to hear her reading of *King Lear.*

She was a small plump woman dressed in black velvet and point lace who stepped out on a bare stage adorned only with table and chair, reading table and lamp. She bowed with stately gravity right and left, and seated herself on the chair, spread out her flowing skirts and opened her little book—and the audience was utterly hers. Her voice was remarkably beautiful, Harry thought, deep and sometimes hoarse, and it adapted itself to every character with masculine power. Her voice rose to a splendid volume, a sort of human thunder-roll, for the old king in the storm: "Howl, howl, howl!"[21]

A few days later they all returned to the Assembly Rooms to hear a reading of *A Midsummer Night's Dream*, for which Mrs. Kemble was dressed in lavender,[22] again with point lace but with a good deal of décolletage, and the wonderful fairy tale seemed to fill the room with perfect lightness and grace.

But the London experiment proved to be as short-lived as the Genevan. The Wilkinsons, to whom they had once felt so close, somehow were not sympathetic, and Father, as if having now exhausted all possible objections, took his family to Paris. Neither Mr. Thomson nor Mlle. Cusin accompanied them, however. The Swiss governess had become engaged to be married, and would stay on in London. Mr. Thomson's reasons for failing to accompany them were not made so clear.

"Do you like my father and mother very much?" Harry asked him, familiarly.

"Dear me, yes, they're charming people."

Harry received this in silence, and then unexpectedly, but affectionately, remarked, "You're a jolly old humbug!" For some reason, the words made Thomson change color, whereupon Harry turned red himself, and the pupil and master exchanged a longish glance. The memory of the separation from this loved tutor sank into the depths of his private world, and joined his secret awareness of the earlier discharged nurses, governesses, and tutors. He was to portray such a scene repeatedly in his later stories.[23]

Just after his thirteenth birthday, in the spring of 1856, Harry found himself in a house on the Avenue of the Champs-Élysées. It was by far the grandest house the Jameses had had to themselves. They rented the house from its American owner for the summer months, while they looked for a permanent lodging. There was a walled courtyard in front, paved with cobblestones, and a walled garden behind, so that the house itself stood as if in a little rural village of its own. One came in through a wrought-iron door in the wall, across the paved courtyard and up a narrow stair. Harry, dozing in the warm afternoons at a window over the courtyard, would hear the jangle of the old bell, followed by the clatter of the concierge's wooden sabots on the uneven flags, sounds that were ever afterward to call up the savor of old Paris for him. The house harbored queer graces and inconveniences: the glassy polished floors, the perilous staircase, the immense repeated mirrors and redundant ormolu vases, the red brocade panels outlined in gold on the white walls, the uncomfortable gilt-framed chairs and sofas, upholstered in stiff red damask.

The Avenue of the Champs-Élysées, not yet widened into immensity, was a grand tree-shaded boulevard, and carried one's eye from the Palace of the Tuileries to the Arch of Triumph. Pleasant, grand old houses stood behind their walls, the great houses interspersed with cabarets and cafés of a homely, almost rural kind. The immediate neighborhood was a little enclave of American and Anglo-Irish gentry: the Jameses' own cousins, and some people named Stewart and Parnell, to whom perhaps they were distantly related.

The old Palace of the Tuileries, Catherine de Médicis's great country house as it once had been, rambled across the foot of the avenue and down to the bank of the Seine. The setting sun, striking down the Champs-Élysées, illumined the complex façade of the Tuileries with its sloping roofs and central dome. It was now the empress Eugénie's palace, the home of the beautiful young Spanish girl who had married Napoleon III and with him now commanded an empire.

Mr. Thomson was replaced by M. Larembert, a formal and reserved young man. M. Larembert was not greatly interested in the small American boys who were put in his care for a few hours in the warm summer mornings in the schoolroom above the courtyard, but he was intelligent and correct. A new governess for the smaller children had also been engaged: Mlle. Danse, of slender, supple figure and smiling, protuberant green eyes. In the mornings, seven-year-old Alice was under her care, but in the afternoons she took all the boys as well, except William, on walks and excursions. Mlle. Danse was ambitious in her own way, and most certainly as bored with the Americans as was M. Larembert, but she was better able to be genuinely attentive to her small charges than he. On sunny afternoons they walked along the Champs-Élysées to the "Avenue of the Empress,"[24] and watched the procession of carriages with their display of fashion. Mlle. Danse was remarkably free in her commentary on these sights and on her own hopes and plans.

The most thrilling exhibition on the avenue was the baby Prince Impérial, borne forth for his airing in the Bois in a splendid open coach that gave a glimpse of appointed, costumed nursing breasts and laps, beside which the imperial guard, all light blue and silver and intensely erect, rattled with pistols raised and cocked.[25]

On clear afternoons they went on picnics in the Bois itself, the great anciently cultivated, wooded park that to Harry seemed so much older than the wilderness he had seen in his own country. Wilderness had no history, and so had no duration. It was as evanescent as America itself. But the carefully tended, slowly evolving park seemed ancient indeed.

They had their house only for the summer, and soon accordingly were obliged to move again. Finding suitable quarters for the winter was difficult. Parisian families were small, children were sent to the country to nurse, and Parisian apartments were correspondingly small and excruciatingly dear. When they at last found an apartment with six bedrooms, on the nearby Rue d'Angoulême, near an old convent that had been turned into a girls' school, the rent was more than they could continue to pay for any long period of time, and this prompted Father to talk of cutting expenses.[26] But all the same he took the apartment on a year's lease. They were at last fairly settled in a fashionable quarter of Paris, and were once again in a cloud of uncles, aunts, and cousins. Father's brother Howard had just arrived, and stepbrother Robert had been in Paris for some time. There were former New York neighbors, the Masons; Lydia Mason and her daughters were company for Mother. Twenty years later, one of the daughters, Alice, would be company for Harry on his first sojourn alone in Paris. Cousin Charlotte King, too, had settled in this quarter of Paris while her son—fresh-faced, lightly bearded Vernon—who had been at school in Geneva, attended the Sorbonne, and her daughter was being "finished" by French tutors. Cousin Caroline Sturgis, Mrs. Tappan, was nearby; and Father was especially fond of young Fanny MacDaniel, who lived with the Sturgises.

Despite the wealth of company, Mother was not happy. Paris really was very dear. There was the exorbitant rent, twenty-two hundred dollars for the year, nearly half their ordinary income, and the servants seemed to cheat her and to steal. A single peach cost from five to twelve sous, and was likely to be sour—which summoned up ironical memories of bushel baskets carried in from Grandmother's garden.[27]

The apartment on the Rue d'Angoulême opened another view of Paris for Harry, however: the view from the balcony of their parlor just one flight up and overlooking the narrow street. At the corner across the way was the baker who supplied the softly crusty crescent rolls they had with warm milk flavored with coffee every morning;

then came a small crémerie, white picked out with blue, which by some secret process produced from its tiny interior lunches for cab-drivers in uniform and workingmen in white or blue smocks; next, the little niche where the oyster lady dispensed her wares; the narrow cage of the wood merchant; and so on down to the next corner. The street was a perpetual parlor and household center into which servants in their caps and little householders stepped at every opportunity to display their neat ankles and to talk.

Harry's long walks with William in the afternoons after their lessons were briefly renewed. They often took one walk in particular, southward across the Avenue of the Champs-Élysées to the nearest little bridge across the Seine. On the far side, the Left Bank, among the bookstalls on the quays they sometimes lingered to rummage through the dusty boxes displayed on the parapets.[28] The quarter to the south was gently hilly, and they mounted by the long perspective of the Rue de Seine, past old houses with low windows, that seemed to conduct the boys into an ancient realm. At the crest of the long walk they turned into the wide Rue de Tournon, where grass grew among the cobbles, that made a little antechamber to the Luxembourg Palace and its gardens.[29] The Luxembourg Palace housed the Senate of the Empire, and some of its grand rooms served as the state museum of contemporary painting.

Here Harry and William saw the new realistic art; William admired Delacroix above all. Harry for his part especially remembered a painting by Thomas Couture, *The Falconer*,[30] a splendid fair youth in black velvet and satin who, while he mounted a marble staircase, showed off a falcon on his forefinger with a grace that showed him off as well.[31]

The Palace of the Louvre, however, the great storehouse of European art, overwhelmed and bewildered him. He was allowed to go there alone; and it was as if the paintings and sculpture had gathered in a vast deafening chorus and filled the halls with a complicated sound, diffused and reverberant. The rooms of the palace themselves made an impression, their arched ceilings and moldings in golden riot and relief, opening into windows from which one could regally view Paris. In these rooms the people—in pairs, in groups, and alone like himself—were like the artworks on display. There were the poor, the Louvre splendidly ironical for them, who came in for the sake of the warmth. There were families of tourists, and couples making private rendezvous. Europe passed before him, and America as it looked to Europe: society, manners, types, characters, possibilities, prodigies, and mysteries of fifty sorts. Harry imagined himself as he looked to them; imagined himself an orphan; wondered what people thought he was, a boy alone, fancied they looked at him askance.[32]

In the galleries of the Louvre and especially in the wondrous corridor of the Galerie d'Apollon, where, on the domed ceiling, Apollo wrestled with a thick serpent, Harry was conscious of the monarchy of which this was the center. The red-and-gold room was adorned with portraits in which kings and artists were given equal rank; great windows looked out on the Seine from deep embrasures. Harry inhaled the sense of *glory*. The empire seemed present there, palpable to a sense that he could only call imagination. The empire was so new and so queer and perhaps even wrong, but there at least on that spot it was amply radiant and elegant. The sign of the empire, the mystic "N," greeted him from the cornices.[33] It stood for glory, which meant many things to the small boy—not only beauty and art and supreme design, but history and fame and power, the material world raised to its richest and noblest expression. Harry had a half-frightened premonition that a glorious scene of his own would be played in this very corridor of the Galerie d'Apollon; a premonition that would be realized a lifetime later.[34]

Just after Harry's fourteenth birthday, when the family seemed to have settled into Paris for a long stay, M. Larembert was abruptly dismissed—rather bitterly, as he had wished to remain—and the two older boys were enrolled as day pupils at the Institution Fezandié, a Fourierist enterprise. The socialist movement that had briefly flourished in 1848 had almost vanished under the reaction and repression that had followed. But Father had learned of the Institution Fezandié, which was in all but name a Fourierist phalanx. Housed in a big square mansion in the Rue Balzac, with a courtyard before and a walled garden behind, it was a little community of men and women ranging from early youth to advanced age, with all the multiplicity of Paris. The school was a source of income for the phalanx; the pupils were principally English-speaking young men who wished to learn French. Lessons were given in a schoolroom by the magnificent M. Bonnefons, who dictated to the boys and young men in French and listened to their recitations from the classics.

He was an elderly, retired actor, who perhaps did not get enough to eat, and who interrupted the recitations with wondrous anecdotes of other times and reminiscences of performances at the Théâtre-Français. He moved among them in a cloud of legend, wigged and wrinkled, this impassioned M. Bonnefons. When one of the American children encountered the sacred word *liberté* in a recitation and failed to give the *r* its due, M. Bonnefons mimicked and derided, splendidly sounding about thirty *r*'s.[35]

In Paris in the spring of 1857, Harry became friendly with New York cousins, Gertrude Pendleton's four daughters, who with a Parisian companion, Honorine,[36] had taken to early-morning rambles, in which Harry now joined. They strolled in the deserted streets near the Palais-Royal, studying the playbills of the theaters and discussing the actresses whose names appeared there: the incomparable Rachel, then aging and consumptive; the younger rivals, Rose Chéri, Mélanie, Delaporte, Victoria, Mlle. Fargeuil, and a seventeen-year-old ingenue of the season whom Harry was to befriend decades later, Mlle. Pierson.

In the portico of the Théâtre-Français, looking at the bills, Harry felt a certain envy of his cousins, these women who commanded the evening hours as well as the dawns, who attended the plays and wept at *La Dame aux Camélias* and yet were fresh and beautiful in the early morning. He would have given a great deal to be allowed to attend those evening performances.

The greatest events of these morning excursions under the guidance of Honorine were the slow wanderings in the Avenue of the Palais-Royal as the shutters of the shops were taken down, seemingly for the children's benefit. In the little windows of the jewelry shops that congregated there, diamonds and pearls and rubies and sapphires were displayed in necklaces, bracelets, and rings. To Harry, it seemed appropriate for a young man of the world to express an intelligent preference for this piece of jewelry or that, but he was alarmed and fascinated by his companions' lust for gems and felt that as a boy he showed less feeling than the girls. Honorine said that she would do anything, everything, for the richest ruby; and the Pendleton girls passionately approved. If the cousins understood as little as Harry himself what this "anything and everything" might amount to, yet he still felt the warmth of the passion.[37]

Father, settled at last in Paris, now made frequent trips to London to see his new book through the press.[38] The Americans on whom the Jameses depended for company were leaving Paris for the summer, however, and an unnerving economic depression was widening in the United States. The Jameses began to feel a little uncomfortable being alone in Paris, and Parisian rents came to seem insupportable. In the summer of 1857, accordingly, the boys were taken out of the Institution Fezandié; the wonderful apartment on the Rue d'Angoulême was sublet for the balance of the lease, and the Jameses, bag and baggage, fled to Boulogne-sur-Mer, leaving behind Mlle. Danse and the greater part of their expenses.

Boulogne, a fishing port on the Pas-de-Calais, had recently been linked by rail with Paris, and the English coast was just visible on the horizon. Steam ferries left twice each day for Folkestone, where there were hourly trains to London. Father was in constant motion between Paris and London, on the railroads and steamships, while his family waited at the seaside.[39]

The older boys—William, Harry, and Wilky—were clapped into the highly democratic municipal school of Boulogne, grandly named the Collège Impérial,[40] where the tuition was only ten francs per month.[41] Harry's memories of this school were two: the first was of a black-eyed boy, the son of English parents. The boy was standing in the sun-washed wide playground of the school. The other memory was of Benoît-Constant Coquelin, the son of the pastrycook whose shop was nearby, who would become an actor—and his good friend— in later years; otherwise he remembered only the stale air of the schoolroom, the odor of unwashed clothes worn day after day.[42]

The stone school building sat well above the port to which Catherine de Médicis had fled from Paris centuries before, and where elderly, mid-Victorian English ladies now came because it was cheap to live in the gray, weather-beaten houses. Harry walked in the tree-shaded grounds of the castle in the old part of the city, and down the steep Grand Rue to the harbor and the shining beaches, where un-selfconscious young women of Picardy tucked up their skirts and waded bare-legged after crabs and shrimp.

The Jameses' apartment was a vast space above some little shops on the Neuve Chaussée, in the unfashionable, new part of town beside the harbor. The rent at 150 francs per month, about thirty dollars, was an eighth the price of their apartment in the Faubourg Saint-Honoré.[43] It looked out over a busy street, and was filled with the clear seaside summer light. Harry felt the air and the light and even the stale odors of the place as an intensified experience, and was prepared to be happy. There were ample sensations to feed upon.

They had no American friends in Boulogne, however, and consequently had very little society of any sort. Harry did a great deal of reading in his sunny bedroom and in the family parlor. Seeing that he was reaching out for more adult fare, Mother gave him a copy of Edmond About's *Tolla*, a novel that had been popular in Paris the year before. The exquisite heroine, Tolla, had lived and died in Rome, the very heart and center of the Old World. The novel was to become for Harry a kind of legend of Europe, with the truth of a fable, and would add its note of enchantment to Rome when he came to live there; he would rework its plot in his own novels and plays.

Rome was populated by fairy-tale figures. The innocent and beautiful heroine loved a handsome prince: tall, broad-shouldered, with flashing dark eyes and crisp black hair that clustered around a throat whiter than any woman's. The cosmopolitan Mme. Fratieff, a widow who traveled from the Russian court to German spas, to Paris and now to Rome, was the great progenitor of villainous mothers in many of the novels Harry would write, such as the powerful Mme. Merle in *The Portrait of a Lady*. Mme. Fratieff hoped to maneuver her own daughter into Tolla's place, into a rich marriage with the prince. There was a worldly, scheming cardinal, and the prince was made to marry yet another rival. The virtuous Tolla was sacrificed to her rivals' intrigues. She was imprisoned in a convent, where she wasted away and beautifully died—triumphing in this way, the only way left to her.[44]

Tolla was set in a world of tyrannies, of arranged marriages and ancient enmities, and in the end it was the figures disposed in this colorful background that affected Harry most strongly. The aristocratic Roman families were miniature totalitarian states; and Rome itself was under the absolute dominion of the pope. Politics were obscure and underground, newspapers were censored and insignificant; life was lived and history was made in private. Much of the drama was played in the salon of the marchioness Trasemini, who had entered into an arranged marriage as if into a convent; she had been sold into marriage with an evil, abusive man. Yet her house was the most agreeable and she was the most charming woman in Rome; she lived for others—for the children especially; on her Thursday evenings the young people danced to the pianoforte in the tapestried salon, with its lofty frescoed ceiling; the colors of the tapestries had been softened and muted by time. The ebony furniture, with its almost imperceptible cracks; the old rock crystal lusters of the chandeliers; the Vienna piano, whose sounds were dampened by the hangings—all wore the stamp of a stately and rather mournful hospitality. A few dowagers indolently watched their daughters' amusements, while the papas played whist in the boudoir of the marchioness. In the garden outside the tall windows a dozen or so smokers walked about in the gathering darkness, lighted only by their cigars.

Soon after reading this book, on a bright summer afternoon, Harry suffered a strong headache and a fever. Mother promptly put him to bed, where he remained for a time that he could not gauge. That same afternoon, or the next, he woke to find himself alone and in distress. He was conscious of the soft, late afternoon, the mild animation of the Boulogne street through the half-open windows. He had a strange sense that something was happening to him, that something of grave importance had begun. The day was ending, and night was coming on. Awed and half frightened, he tumbled weakly out of bed and wavered toward the bell just across the room. He felt a strong sick whirl of everything about him and fell unconscious. It was typhus, a life-threatening disease—a louse-borne infection acquired, perhaps, at the municipal school. His survival was in question for a time, and the illness extended into the autumn and merged with a series of disasters.

In July, while Father was in London seeing to his book, news came that Grandmother had suffered a stroke that had left her partly paralyzed. Father reacted to this news with disbelief. Such illnesses had moral causes, and it did not seem possible for such a blameless life as his mother's to be afflicted with paralysis. Father was sure the stroke was not serious.[45]

The economic depression in America was deepening, just as a feverish speculation in railroad securities was rising to its peak. On August 7 the failure of a Midwestern stockbroker to honor his obligations pricked the speculative bubble, setting off a cascade of demands by creditors for repayment, demands that could not be met. Brokerages and banks failed or stopped making payments in gold; bankruptcies multiplied and fed on one another. French and British investors withdrew their capital and nascent, protected American industries simply collapsed. Payments of dividends on bonds and rents from the Jameses' properties in Syracuse, Albany, and New York City all but ceased; Uncle Robertson was unable to make deposits with Samuel Ward, and as the panic spread, the family's drafts on Baring Brothers in London stood in danger of being dishonored. Father wrote urgently to Grandmother, despite her illness, and to his brothers in Albany, to deposit as much cash as they could in his account with Ward.[46]

Despite the deepening crisis, in September 1857, and heedless of the cost to others, Father, having seen his book through the press in London, determined to return with his family to Paris. Harry was convalescent, strong enough to travel, and the family boarded the railroad for Paris and took a new and very expensive apartment on the Rue Montaigne, in the Faubourg Saint-Honoré, not far from their last perch.

By December, however, the economic depression in America having continued and worsened, simple lack of cash drove them back to Boulogne. For the first time, uncertainty as to the future struck Father, and he wrote to his elder brother William that as soon as he had the means they would return to America.[47] Nonetheless, the family lingered in France through the winter and spring, with Father making regular visits to Paris and the family making the best of it in Boulogne. They had neither friends nor relatives near them. The boys, except Harry, whom Mother considered still too delicate after his illness, were again sent to the municipal school. Marie Boningue again gave lessons to Alice in the mornings, and a tutor, M. Ansiot, came to their apartment and taught Harry a little about the French classics from a few worn books of his own.

M. Ansiot was immensely fat, and puffed and blew like a pallid porpoise, a creature that had emerged from another, older time. His unwashed person was dosed with scent, and as soon as the tutor left the room at the end of their hour Harry rushed to open the window. He afterward imagined that M. Ansiot's odor was the very smell of the old regime. There was a sinister note in Harry's remembrance of M. Ansiot, whom he disliked at the time but who planted the seed of Harry's later acquaintance with the art and the tone of the Old World—a sinister tone that was washed over with a weak mixture of that earlier summer's premonition of death.[48]

He was fifteen years old, often on his own, silently living through his pubescence. In Boulogne he achieved manhood: he knew that he was not afraid of death or of the wickedness that rose like a pale fish from the depths of the past. His inner privacy had grown immensely richer, and he looked about him with new eyes.

When he was better, Harry liked to walk in the old castle grounds, bounded by a stone parapet that overlooked the sea, as well as in the working-class streets near the harbor. When Father was at home, Harry sometimes joined him on walks, as he had done long ago in New York; and one afternoon they walked near the beach, Father talking as usual, his eyes following a young fisherwoman as with fine stride and shining limbs she waded from the sea with her basketful of glistening black shrimps.[49]

4

THE FAMILY RETREATS TO NEW ENGLAND

Harry's once-blond curls were now dark brown, thick, and un-ruly. His complexion was rich and full-blooded, his forehead broad and strongly modeled, the veins faintly visible at his temples. His wide, gray, heavy-lidded eyes spoke of intelligence. He listened with lips almost parted, as if on the brink of speech. The family's wanderings in Europe might not have been the education to rec-ommend, but it had produced an air of refinement in Harry; he had come a little to resemble his childhood friend Louis De Coppet.[1] The striking quality, anomalous in such a young boy, was the sense one had of his reserve. Although he was talkative in his careful way, there was a deep reserve like a little gentleman's that set him apart in a family in which the father and the other boys were given to spon-taneous, boisterous expressions of feeling and riotous laughter.

The family had returned to America in the summer of 1858, and after a brief visit to his grandmother in Albany, who had not recovered from her stroke, they settled in Newport, on an island on the New England coast midway between New York and Boston. It was a little seaport town that, like Boulogne, was a temporary refuge, conveniently near, from the heat and expense of cities. There was an excellent little harbor, with a picturesque jumble of great rocks and a long jetty where the steamer tied up. Just above it was a small, pleasant parade-ground square, with a Georgian city hall—formerly the market—and a great wooden "athenaeum" building, which held a good library and a fifty-foot reading room, the legacy of its frugal Quaker founders.

Those Quakers of an earlier age, in their little island republic, had become rich in the rum trade, but Newport's brief time of glory was all but forgotten, and it remained now a small seafaring town, with its weather-beaten gray square Georgian houses, fronting closely on the streets, and a few half-timbered houses dating from the seventeenth century climbing the steep bluff behind the harbor. It had an air that was becoming familiar to Harry, of inexpensive seaside resorts for the despoiled and disillusioned, the mildly desperate who lived upon reminiscence.[2]

A handful of Southern families, plantation aristocracy from South Carolina and Virginia, had established summer houses in Newport's years of prosperity; after the collapse of the French colonies in the West Indies, a few expropriated French plantation owners had joined them. The island town, with its Spanish-Jewish cemetery, its old French and Catholic families, its remnant of Tory and Quaker gentry, was quite disconnected from the American hinterland. The Newporters did not send their sons to nearby Brown University, but sent them to Europe, or to New York, or to Harvard. Admiral Perry's widow had settled in Newport; white-haired George Bancroft, with his old-fashioned muttonchop whiskers, who had been ambassador to the Court of St. James's and was writing a magisterial history of the United States, lived on Bellevue Avenue, where he grew roses behind a sheltering wall and walked with his cane on the bluff overlooking the sea. Harry had been sorry to leave Paris, but Newport was a little European missionary outpost or colony in the wilderness of America.[3]

In summer, steamships now brought crowds of Bostonians; it was the fashion in the younger set to rent a farmhouse on the island for the weeks of hot weather. Father's friend Samuel Ward and his recently married sister Julia Ward Howe took farmhouses, as did the Longfellows and Mrs. Longfellow's dapper, handsome bachelor brother, Tom Appleton. A newly fashionable painter, William Hunt,[4] had just returned from Paris and opened a studio in Newport, where he painted portraits of the summer visitors. Newport too was the refuge to which Edmund and Mary Tweedy had come with the Temple orphans, whom they had adopted. It was a frugal retreat. There were American children of the Jameses' ages; there were horseback riding and boating, and a school for the younger boys.

The school[5] was conducted by young William C. Leverett, recently married, recently a father, who also served as curate in the white-spired Trinity Church. Leverett's name amused Harry: a leveret is a young hare.[6] The school was a great deal like Forrest's, as to both its pupils and its curriculum, and prepared the boys for careers in trade. Harry's family alone seemed not to be in a business of some sort, or to expect to be in one. Harry patiently sat through recitations in Latin and declamations of set speeches, and prepared his own exercises carefully. He struggled through the detested mathematics.

Father had abandoned Paris only with great reluctance, trailing letters of farewell behind him.[7] But in Newport the Jameses' life was more placid than it had been for some time. A local governess was found for Alice, and a cook was retained. (Harry, spoiled by Paris, twitted Mother with the poor quality of American cooking.) William was too old for the children's school—at seventeen he was already past the usual age for a university—but Father forbade the children to attend college. Perhaps this prohibition was partly the result of Father's own unhappiness at college, but he justified it on philosophic grounds. He thought William should attend not a liberal arts college but the new Lawrence Scientific School, and accordingly he began looking for an inexpensive house in Cambridge. In the meantime William simply idled at home. He had indeed begun to take an interest in science, and experimented with chemicals and electrical batteries. But perhaps in muffled rebellion, the experiments were often practical jokes. Members of the family learned to examine their chairs before sitting down.[8]

William fought ever more violently, if jokingly, with Father at the tea table; Father would stammer out his ideas with zeal and strong language, goading William into dispute. To a visitor Father said in amused explanation, "You see, dear Ellen, I have to stimulate William's intellect."[9] When Father was away, William turned about and teased the women of the family. He composed mock-heroic and mock-chivalric poems, addressed to Aunt Kate and little Alice, and he became so excited that the other children joked about his having to be committed to an asylum.[10]

Harry remained aloof from William's struggle with Father and from his teasing, and withdrew into the citadel of his privacy. As when he had been ill, he remained alone a good deal, reading and drawing, and writing poems and dramas that he illustrated himself. Visits with the four orphaned Temple sisters at the Tweedys'—their brothers had been sent away to school—and trips to New York to see his cousins there broke the solitude. Father bought a horse for the children, and Harry, like the others, learned to ride, but for the most part he walked on the island. Behind the low cliffs that faced the sea there were wide, flat, empty pastures divided by tumble-down stone walls and spotted with ponds. Here and there a stream cut a low valley into the flat terrain, a valley that would lead one to a rocky cove and a sudden view of Narragansett Bay or the uninterrupted Atlantic.

Happy, rosy-cheeked Wilky was Harry's principal companion, when he had one; Wilky and a lovely, sweet-tempered boy, Sarge Perry, grandson of the admiral and great-nephew of the commodore who had opened Japan to the West.[11] Sarge Perry was Wilky's age, and Wilky had drawn him into the circle. Sarge now often tagged after Harry on his reflective rambles, and Harry called him "chéri," and "petit Peri."[12] On one long ramble to the Lily Pond, Harry loyally explained to his new young friend Fourier's great scientific plan for reforming the world.[13]

But the great event of this period in their lives was William Hunt's arrival. Hunt was a Boston painter who had taken a two-story commercial building in the old harbor district, on Church Street, for a studio. Upstairs was his own work space, where he painted portraits of young Boston matrons and rural landscapes with peasant figures in them, in the new French fashion. The downstairs served him as classroom and gallery. Hunt had just begun to take students, and had only two: a Newport woman, Theodora Watson, and a New Yorker, John La Farge.

Hunt was a swarthy, sunburned man, wiry and strong, with a spreading black beard turning prematurely gray, a hawk's profile, and intense black eyes. In his velvet jacket he was Harry's image of a painter, or a sculptor, personified. Everyone said that Hunt looked like an Oriental sheik; Harry thought him like Don Quixote. He would come down downstairs and look at his two pupils' work, comment tactfully, and discourse widely and charmingly on art. When he had a sitter, he would invite the students up for refreshments, and they would entertain her with their conversation. On the walls were the famous *Sower* and other remarkable pictures by Jean-François Millet, painted not in the studio but out of doors and painted in rough patches of color.

Harry took to visiting the classroom, to see the pictures and hear the talk; he entered through the back door, on the cobbled courtyard, rather than the door on the street, and so came directly into the room where Miss Watson and La Farge were working.[14]

La Farge, at twenty-three, was only a little younger than Hunt, and he too had just returned from Paris. He was remarkably tall and thin, and in winter he dressed all in elegant black, in summer in fastidious white. When out of doors, he wore the wide-brimmed black hat and carried the furled black umbrella that were the badges of the Parisian art student. He was intensely fastidious, as exacting about his handkerchief as about his brushes and colors or the Japanese paper on which he drew. But this care in small things was not cold or repellent. If he seemed a little foppish, he was also the kindest of men, and looked or listened with his head thrust forward, and all his attention in his large, nearsighted, dark eyes. He wore eyeglasses when reading or painting,[15] and while these were unattractive, they further emphasized his intelligent, feeling eyes.

When Harry and La Farge became better acquainted, they went riding together over the empty pastures, Harry on the hack that Father had bought for the children, and La Farge, a striking figure in black, on a beautiful Arabian chestnut with arched neck and flying mane.

La Farge was not studying painting only to be a painter; he was studying to *understand;* he was a man of letters in the Parisian mold, and his talk was as much of Sainte-Beuve and the Goncourt brothers and the *Revue des Deux Mondes* as it was of Millet and Barbizon. La Farge in short was wonderful. William was as smitten with him as Harry was, and they both found reasons to visit Hunt's studio, to walk with La Farge and listen to his talk.

On August 18, 1859, a little more than a year after they had returned to America, Harry's grandmother died; she was buried in the Rural Cemetery at Albany. The household furniture and silver went to four maiden nieces, the Gourlay sisters, who were given a modest annuity and a two-story house in Albany.[16] Her substantial estate, which had been held in trust all these years, was promptly distributed to her surviving children and grandchildren.

Like Aunt Catherine's, Grandmother's death upset their world and sent them traveling. Within days, as if fleeing the death, Father, who now again had the means to travel and was no longer tied to his mother's deathbed, wrote to Paris of his plans to return. On October 8 the Jameses sailed from New York on the new side-wheel steamer *Commodore Vanderbilt*, bound for Le Havre. La Farge, little Perry, walks with Wilky on the bluffs—everything that for a year Harry had grown to love now vanished like smoke.

This wrenching departure was more agonized and desperate than any before, and would be their last voyage as a family. Little Perry came sadly to see them off at the Newport harbor. The stated purpose of the journey was to arrange a scientific education for William. It was Father's heart's desire to return to Paris, and a scientific education for William was a colorable motive. Yet they did not go to Paris after all. Presumably at Mother's insistence, Father's aim was deflected, and the Jameses again went to Geneva. Their means having been restored and the Panic of 1857 having vanished into memory, they stayed very comfortably at the Hôtel de l'Écu, on the lake. In the four years since their first visit, the railroad had been extended and now ran directly from Paris to Geneva, so that Father was able to leave his family in Geneva and to visit Paris quite easily.

Unhappily, Harry was sent alone to a preparatory school for the Polytechnic, a school where future engineers and civil servants were trained, and where he was taught mathematics and physics from six in the morning until five in the evening. This unfortunate choice was the result of Father's belief in scientific education, and of a feeling that he and Mother shared, that Harry spent too much time reading novels. The scheme to provide a scientific education for William had simply been extended to Harry, all absentmindedly.

Wilky and Bob went to a boarding school in the country, so that Harry did not have even their company. Round-faced little Alice, at eleven still with her governess, was hardly yet a companion, and William was attending the scientific courses at the University of Geneva.[17] So Harry attended the Polytechnic preparatory school alone. Looking back, he could hardly believe his own perfect acquiescence in this business. Father and Mother together had explained the need for him to get away from novel reading and to learn science, and he had cheerfully agreed.

The preparatory school, presided over by a M. Rochette, was in a narrow stone house at the top of the Cité, on a queer crooked narrow street directly behind the cathedral. There were classes in mechanics, algebra, and geometry, and it was perfectly horrible. After only a few weeks, Harry lodged a protest and the experiment was abandoned, under the thin rationale that he was still too delicate to attend school. For the first time he felt the miserable sense of failure.

Tutors were now engaged to teach him German and French literature at home, and there were no further forays into algebra. Harry's German tutor, a noisy little professor whose name he did not later remember, had given him an introduction to the great art form of Germany, idealist philosophy, and Harry read Goethe's and Schiller's verse as well as the formal verse plays of Gotthold Lessing. For the rest, he wandered about the narrow streets of Geneva and attended a few lectures with William. He went once to see an anatomy class, where the corpse of a muscular gendarme was being dissected, an experience that fully satisfied his curiosity as to this kind of science. All this Geneva time was blighted by the shadow of the preparatory school, and the only nourishing impressions he received he got vicariously, through William, who became his ambassador, as Wilky had been before. But Harry fed more on the energy and warmth of William's feeling, on his enthusiasm and his stories, than on the abstract subjects of his study.

Of the whole Geneva experiment in education he remembered only one moment as remarkable. It was the smallest, almost invisible germ of the novel *The Tragic Muse*, that he would write thirty years later. One morning when they were reading Racine's *Phèdre*, Harry, entranced, listened to his French tutor M. Toeppfer's tales of the actress Rachel. Her genius had revived the classical French theater, had given it life and interest. She had infused the Alexandrines of Racine with the strongest force. When Toeppfer had seen her perform, in her first entrance as Phèdre, borne down in her languorous passion for her stepson by the weight of her royal robes—"These useless ornaments, these veils oppress me!"[18]—the long lapse of time before she spoke and while she sank upon a seat filled itself extraordinarily with her visible woe.[19] The space seemed to fill itself with palpable feeling, and on the stage that Harry had not yet seen, behind the little Jewish girl who played the queen of Thebes, he saw Poseidon lift his immense shoulders.

When summer came, Harry began to take long hikes in the countryside, and he learned to swim. His health was restored, and he felt thoroughly vigorous again.

Father had in the end removed himself entirely to Paris; Mother, Aunt Kate, and Alice had followed him there. Little Bob had gone off on a tour of Italy with his classmates, and the older boys—Harry, William, and Wilky—were now packed off to Bonn to pursue their scientific studies. For Harry, even if he had no interest in science, Germany was at least a new country, an adventure of impressions, exciting in itself, and to make it more pleasant he and Wilky boarded together. They were placed with a professor from the Gymnasium; William boarded with a university professor nearby.

Harry still accepted all this passively and was prepared to be happy. But scientific studies of history and philosophy were cold and lifeless. He had not yet seen a way of using the scientific to make sense of his impressions; life and books seemed utterly distinct. There was nothing in the middle-class home where he boarded to interest him, beyond the library. He did begin to read Goethe's prose, scientific and historical works, which he found more difficult than the poetry he had sampled in Geneva. In the gaps of studies he began to read Goethe's novel *Wilhelm Meister's Lehrjahre*, the simple narrative slowly becoming clear to him. The tale was plain and realistic, the persons were ordinary, the setting was the moral landscape in which he had been raised. This was simple realism, a scientific investigation of the ideal.[20]

It was William who at last rebelled; he wanted to return to Newport. The reason he gave was that he wished to study painting in Hunt's studio, with La Farge. This surprising determination was communicated to Father, in Paris, by letter. And Father, confronted with open opposition, gave up for a time his insistence on science.[21]

The boys returned to Paris, to join their parents briefly there, in a little apartment overlooking the Louvre, where Harry renewed his sense of the magnificence of the new French empire, of the Louvre's mystic "N" and its mysterious promise of glory. But the family remained in Paris only long enough for Harry to come to a settled conviction of how odd it was, how very much a mistake, to be leaving Paris at this moment to study art in Newport. People stared or laughed when Harry, with innocent truthfulness, explained the reason for their leaving.[22]

But nineteen-year-old William was fleeing to Newport, and Father, with the family trailing behind, pursued him. A little more than a year from the day they left, the Jameses were in a house at 13 Kay Street, across the street from where they had been the year before. They were next door to the Tweedys and the adopted Temple girls, and within easy visiting distance of little Perry.

The abrupt termination of Harry's European education left him without a clear path to pursue. He, too, was now past the age at which university studies should begin, but college was forbidden by Father. And so, albeit with an uncertain sense of vocation, Harry joined William as a student in Hunt's studio, with La Farge and Miss Watson. In the downstairs classroom that they had once idly visited, the brothers set up their easels side by side. The older pupils, La Farge and Miss Watson, were at one end of the room, Harry and William at the other.[23]

For Harry, La Farge himself was the principal attraction of the studio. At that time, this slender, elegant man was painting cut flowers—a most idiosyncratic choice of subject. He would ask the serving girl to choose flowers at random; or he would simply paint whatever was on the corner of his table. This method sometimes obliged him to work furiously into the night, to capture with all the precision of academic technique the moment in which these particular flowers briefly lived.

La Farge wanted to learn to paint landscapes in this way, to record the whole vivid complexity of the light at a place, at a particular moment, with all the care of the academy.[24] Hunt discouraged him, saying that this would be immensely difficult, and that few would know or care what he had done when he succeeded. Only one painter in a hundred was trained to see the discriminations of light that he wanted to capture. But La Farge answered that this only confirmed his purpose.

> Each little or big blade of grass in front of me, and there are millions, has its shape and its composition. The colors are exquisite. . . . As I lift my eyes from the wonderful green (never painted yet by man) I see a pale blue sky with pale cumulus clouds, white, with violet shadows, and on the other side the blue is deep, and in an hour, shall be deeper still.[25]

La Farge had grown up on Washington Square; he had traveled to Paris for the first time almost at the same moment that the Jameses had first gone to Geneva. The very same *Falconer* of Thomas Couture that Harry had admired in the gallery of the Luxembourg Palace had excited La Farge's ambition to paint. He was mastering the highly evolved technology of academic painting: the careful preparation of canvases, the scientific rules of color and composition, the techniques of invisible brushwork and perfect finish—painting that was possible only in the timeless, anonymous, unvarying light of a studio. But he wished to go beyond the formal, lifeless classicism that was taught in Parisian studios. As the young French painters were doing, he learned to adapt academic techniques to a freer, more realistic style and subject matter. He was seeking to capture the unique particularity of experience. Like a marauding sea captain, he looted the French Academy, learning from Couture and Millet, and the Venetian treasure houses, learning from Titian to apply his colors in layers of translucent, tinted glaze. He worked at self imposed tasks, applying classical technique to his own purposes..[26]

La Farge, perhaps even more than Hunt, was Harry's teacher and mentor, and his principal lesson was the example of his own manner of work. To La Farge, the practice of art was a religious observance. There was no detail of ordinary life that he did not submit to the discipline of art.

> His person was always absolutely neat, and scrupulously adapted to whatever he was undertaking to do. He had his own kind of pen, his own kind of paper, his own distinctive way of doing everything; every gesture of his body seemed to relate to the ultimate ends of his life and work.[27]

In his painting, this meant rendering a subject with supersubtle taste, with infinite pains; when La Farge was painting he put back the clocks and ignored every timetable but his own. He wished to render the subject—a wreath of flowers, a landscape—as he *saw* it, with the precise details that gave it reality and life. This devotion to original vision, to the child's eye, made his painting an act of worship. Harry, entranced, devoted himself to exercises like those La Farge had invented for himself, to train himself in seeing. He drew a stone, on a white sheet of paper, and a single flower.[28]

Harry was studying with John Ruskin as much as with Hunt or La Farge. He had absorbed with astonishment the early volumes of Ruskin's *Modern Painters* and the just-published, pirated American edition of *Elements of Drawing*. Ruskin taught him: "The greatest thing a human soul ever does in this world is to *see* something, and tell what it *saw* in a plain way. . . . To see clearly is poetry, prophecy, and religion, all in one."[29]

Every shadow was filled with reflected light, every color trembled in relation to surrounding colors. A composition was not merely an assemblage of facts, however truly observed, it was a fabric of relations, of balances and dependencies and reflections and contradictions, making a unity, a *tone*.[30] Drawing could be taught, but composition was a matter of inborn genius. One was not free to invent; one had to see the unity.

In the downstairs classroom that they shared, often La Farge would set up a still life; at times Hunt would give them a model, whom they painted in oils or watercolor. Harry, whose work was less advanced, betook himself to another room during these life studies, and practiced drawing from plaster casts. In the cool, constant, indirect light of the studio, with admirable examples of Hunt's work on the walls, Harry for the first time felt he was an artist. Occasionally, Hunt would wander in and discourse charmingly, saying little about Harry's work but encouraging him by his presence.

Alone with the plaster casts of classical antiquity, Harry felt he had *genius,* the ability to render not just a fact but a vision, to see with the eye of imagination. La Farge told him, "You have a painter's eye"—but gave him a volume of Prosper Mérimée's poetry, and urged him to read Browning.

Harry's illusion ended with his first life class. He came upstairs to Hunt's studio and found William and La Farge already at work with charcoal and sketch paper, and Gus Barker perched, nude, on a pedestal, "the gayest as well as the neatest of models," as he recalled many years later, dictating to Miss Bosanquet. His beloved cousin, on a visit to Newport, was their model. Nude, he had a beauty that inspired sacred awe, and the sight brought down Harry's illusions with a crash. There was something here of which Ruskin's exercises and Harry's niggling with plaster casts took no account. "I put my pencil in my pocket for that day," he said. But he asked for and kept William's drawing.[31]

Another morning, soon after, dark-haired Kitty Temple, at sixteen the oldest of the orphaned sisters and generally considered the pretty one, sat in the middle of the room working at her needlepoint while Hunt, La Farge, William, and Miss Watson drew and painted her portrait.[32] Harry felt even farther from them now. He could not transmit the intensity of his impressions to the canvas. There was an element missing in his work.

Little by little he abandoned the studio. La Farge continued to befriend him, but when they went out, as the weather grew warmer, Harry became his model rather than his sketching companion. Harry sat for him out of doors, as La Farge continued his pursuit of the light. Painting did not inhibit his talk, and these were happy moments for Harry, who listened to the flow of thoughtful reflection, the long sentences adorned with dependent clauses and parentheses designed to capture every opalescent nuance of light and thought. La Farge would lean forward, peering intently; or stand in a characteristic posture—hands thrust in coat pockets, head jerked back, mouth twisted, the muscles of his face taut with comic amazement—good-humoredly astounded at what he was hearing or seeing.[33]

Harry visited La Farge's house in Paradise Valley, and they would talk in the library, La Farge gesturing with long, slender hands in his papal manner, first and second fingers together, or with the eyeglass that hung from a black ribbon about his neck. It gradually came to Harry that La Farge talked to him of literature, and not of painting. One afternoon, La Farge showed Harry a beautiful set of Balzac, with the famous illustrations of Tony Johannot, that he had inherited from his father. In the opening pages of *Eugénie Grandet*, under La Farge's instruction, a landscape opened for Harry. It was a rural landscape, like the ones the new painters were doing: a village, Saumur, in wine-growing, farming country. The history of the countryside was in the three-hundred-year-old wooden houses of the village, with their massive projecting blackened beam-ends, and in the stone mansions of the nobility, now ruined and deserted. The medieval world and the Revolution were still fresh memories. Poverty had left them no privacy, no culture; the peasants and artisans who had so recently become tradesmen lived out of doors, like animals. Grandet, a cooper who battened on the ruins of the aristocracy, was like a gnarled vine, a growth of the place. He loved gold, the glowing, imperishable metal that had erupted into the rural landscape. A girl grew up in this half-medieval, newly bourgeois world: Grandet's daughter. She came of age, and learned that a woman in love must never reveal her feelings, that love and civilization rest on secrets.

Harry could almost see the Grandets' musty little sitting room, the gray painted wainscoting, the faded curtains, the rickety card tables, the framed samplers on the walls. Mme. Grandet's foot warmer evoked the unheated room, and the table was set for a meager dinner. Into this dim atmosphere came Charles Grandet, his Parisian trousers, his watch chain, his cravat, the curl of his hair, all vividly imagined, and gleaming like lucent gold in the gray room.[34]

Sexual energy was palpable. Old Grandet's money power and Eugénie's innocent sexual passion met on the stage that Balzac had set.

The scene was rendered in natural light, as it were, rendered with the coolly detached passion of the painter, and in the perfect dramatic form of classic theater.

In the spring of 1861 the war began, however, and Harry's studies came to an end.

5

HENRY BECOMES AN AMERICAN

When Abraham Lincoln, a gaunt lawyer from Springfield, Illinois, took the oath of office as president of the United States, he swore to defend the Constitution and to see that escaped slaves were returned to their owners. Abolitionists of the North were offended and the South was not conciliated. Seeing that Lincoln meant to rule, the leaders of the plantation societies began to withdraw their states from the Union, and to prepare a new empire of their own.

In the spring of 1861, accordingly, the United States was dissolving. New England, contemptuous of a constitution that recognized slavery, openly defied the fugitive slave laws and the president. Chief Justice Lemuel Shaw of Massachusetts dissolved a warrant issued in Washington for the arrest of conspirators in John Brown's raid on the slaveholding South. In New York City, Horace Greeley's *Tribune*, equally disdainful of the conciliatory Unionists and the slaveholding

South, was leading a movement for secession of the city. Mayor Fernando Wood—whom Harry's father and Horace Greeley had both supported—introduced a resolution of secession in the city council. Their Christian socialist movement had been absorbed into abolitionism: destruction of the slave power was to be the first step in establishing a new order of society. "What a world, what a world!" Father wrote to Emerson. "But once we get rid of Slavery the new heavens and new earth will swim into reality."[1]

In April, skirmishing began between the rival nascent empires of North and South. Lincoln ordered that an effort be made to resupply Fort Sumter, commanding Charleston harbor. South Carolina now claimed the fort as its own, and forcibly took it. Treating this as an act of war, on April 15, 1861, Harry's eighteenth birthday, Lincoln asked the loyal states to call up their militias.

The Jameses were still at 13 Kay Street, but the old Newport life was disintegrating. Southerners were leaving and would not return. Bostonians were going home, and the talk was all of the war to come. Bill Hunt's studio began to break up. Hunt was spending more time in Boston. La Farge wanted a commission in the Union army, but his eyesight was too poor. Sarge Perry wanted to enlist, but was too young. The James cousins were obtaining commissions; Will Temple, eldest of the orphaned children of Catherine and Robert, obtained a commission and was leaving school to join the army. In deference to his late father's rank, Will in one stroke was made a captain in the regular army.[2]

Father gave a public address on the Fourth of July. Secession of the slave states and dissolution of the federal constitution did not trouble him. Father had been among the supporters of John Brown's raid, which he had hoped would spark a violent slave rebellion in the South. But Lincoln's growing war did not yet aim to abolish slavery. Lincoln's cautious legalism, his reaffirmation of the constitutional protection for slave property, earned only Father's resentment. He blamed England and New England for tolerating the slave power that was the modern source of all evil simply for the sake of supplying their cotton mills. The disease of slavery had corrupted the Union itself, even the presidency:

> We find shameless God-forsaken men, holding high place in government, become so rabid with its virus as to mistake its slimy prurient ooze for the ruddy tide of life, and commend its foul and fetid miasm as the fragrant breath of assured health.[3]

Father would have been glad to go to war to free the slaves, to take the first step toward the New Jerusalem. But for Lincoln's war to salvage the Union he had not one word of interest or sympathy. When William and Harry wanted to enlist, Father stopped them, saying to a friend, "No existing government, nor indeed any now possible government, is worth an honest human life and a clean one like theirs, especially if that government is like ours in danger of bringing back slavery again under one banner: than which consummation I would rather see chaos itself come again."[4]

Harry was not afraid of going to war, and wanted to join in the excitement of the time, but he bowed to his father's wishes. It would have been difficult to obtain a commission without Father's support, even if Harry had felt able to disagree openly on fundamental moral questions; and it was hard to breach family ties, to resist the lifelong habit and duty of obedience.

Father had again forbidden Harry to attend college, and so he was left without practical alternatives. He simply drew into himself, into the security of himself, for a while longer, and lived imaginatively in the reports of distant ambassadors. For his external life he was obliged to remain on the edge of American life, in the little island community of Newport.

The family circle, too, was dissolving. With Bill Hunt's studio breaking up, William was without a clear path to pursue, and without a mentor. After less than a year as a painter, therefore, he abandoned art entirely, and to Father's intense pleasure he agreed to enroll in the Lawrence Scientific School at Harvard. In August, he moved to Cambridge. Wilky was gone as well. Too young for the army, Wilky and his little brother, Bob, were enrolled in the progressive, coeducational Sanborn School, in Concord, Massachusetts. The redoubtable Elizabeth Peabody, who had traveled alone to the slaveholding South to plead with the governor of Virginia to spare John Brown's life, had founded this school. Frank Sanborn, the headmaster, had fled to Canada to avoid the investigations into John Brown's raid. Brown's orphaned daughters were enrolled there, and Emerson and Hawthorne sent their children. But the war had begun, and it was humiliating to be schoolboys. Wilky and Bob were restless and bored. Wilky remained at school, but Bob—thin, dark, intense, and in many ways Wilky's opposite—soon returned home, and began spending much of his time aimlessly sailing a little boat that Father bought for him.

Frustratingly immobilized by Father's prohibitions, Harry was alone much of the time. Father's high moral principle was difficult to dispute, but it left no space for ordinary life, it denied his children the possibility of choice. Forbidden any practical alternative, Harry remained in solitude. He walked a great deal. Young Perry sometimes came with him on these long rambles. With Perry he was kind but aloof and withdrawn.[5] Sometimes Alice walked with him. At twelve years old she was attending a school for girls, and had a little circle of friends of her own age. She was growing talkative, even somewhat excitable. She kept Harry company on their long walks, and seemed to enjoy his silent presence.

Harry still sometimes sat for La Farge, who wanted to paint portraits out of doors. On one memorable occasion in the summer of 1861, La Farge invited Harry to drive early in the morning to the Glen, about six miles from the town of Newport, where both of them would set up easels. *We* paint! Harry thought. They rode in an open buggy, with plank seats, and at an inn at the Glen they had a rustic breakfast under the trees, a breakfast overflowing with coffee and griddle cakes. Afterward they worked, Harry at a respectful distance from La Farge, and Harry remembered the sound of the leaves and the sense that the eye of La Farge's friendship might illumine his work.[6]

Painting, aside from the chance for La Farge's friendly illumination, was no longer a serious endeavor, however. Harry spent his time reading, horseback riding, paying calls. An Albany cousin, young Kitty James, stayed with them for a few weeks; she was in love with her psychiatrist, Dr. William H. Prince, which was interesting.

The great excitements in Newport were occasional fires, to which the volunteer firemen, followed by all the boys of the neighborhood, turned out. Harry enlisted in these ad hoc brigades, this children's army, and, on one warm evening that he remembered, found himself in an awkward position in the angle of a fence, furiously working a pump handle, which left his back sore.[7]

He took the steamer to New York occasionally to visit family and friends. He stayed with Robertson cousins, the Rodgerses, at their new house far uptown on Murray Hill, and escorted their daughters Katie and Nellie to concerts and lectures and sociables, and on splendid ten-mile walks from Central Park to the Battery.[8] With Bob Temple, home for the summer from school in Scotland, he went to services in odd little churches: to hear the preaching of Mrs. Cora V. L. Hatch, in an underground lecture room on Astor Place, and to the "congregation of the new dispensation," on Broadway.

In October he spent a weekend in Cambridge with William. William's sleeping room was cheerless, in a depressing household, but at the boardinghouse where William took his meals, Miss Upham's, the table talk was lively and pleasant. William was rather tensely engaged in laboratory studies of chemistry at the Lawrence School, and as usual experimented when at home. He had begun to take psychoactive drugs, and with a sort of disinterested curiosity recorded their effects upon himself. Having bowed at last to Father's wishes, William seemed nervous, agitated, and frequently tired, and he was far behind in his chemistry assignments. Harry's visit seemed to cheer him.

Father, too, was ill, suffering from back trouble and from inexplicable fainting spells. But he was happy with William's new career and visited Boston and Cambridge often. At home, although it was his own moral strictures that immobilized Harry, he chided his son for aimlessness, and said that if Harry would only fall in love, that would be the making of him.[9]

There was a cupboard under a stair in the house on Kay Street, where Father kept back numbers of the *Revue des Deux Mondes*, and these opened a window in Harry's captivity. The salmon-covered volumes, after lying for a time on a table in the parlor, were added to the heaps in the under-stairs closet. Harry remembered this magical place, discovered in the family's first Newport time, when he was still sickly and the shelf with its mountain of reviews seemed high and out of reach. Now it was at eye level. The *Revue des Deux Mondes* reopened Europe to his mind's eye, to the imagination that was now his only sense for perceiving the social landscape. The great figures in that world were writers, critics, actresses; above all, they were men of letters like Sainte-Beuve, the Goncourts, Mérimée, and Renan, a sort of person who did not exist in the United States.

The *Revue* was the newspaper of his spiritual home, but Harry's Baedeker of spiritual Europe was *The Human Comedy* of Honoré de Balzac. Balzac, who had been a lawyer, who had been a man of the world, had donned the white robe of devotion to his art. "I invent nothing," he had proclaimed, and sat down to paint the portrait of France in his time. Through *The Human Comedy* one saw with a scientist's eye, with a painter's eye, the sweep of France through the first half of the nineteenth century—the first Napoleon, the restored Bourbon monarchy, the July revolution of 1830 and the reign of the citizen king Louis-Philippe, the yearning for monarchy and glory, the intimations of 1848 of a future republic. One saw interiors as well as landscapes, the inner history: old family estates, rooted in place and nature, disintegrating and dissolving under the corrosive attack of the marketplace. One saw the corruption and death of glory, and the triumph of money and prostitution. One saw and felt the sensual power of gold, its soft luminosity, its beauty. Democracy was rising; palpable was the new force of public opinion, the magnetic force of the mob. In the bare, anonymous public spaces of the marketplace, freshly made princes of the media were great powers: the newspaper men, opera singers, and actresses.

Alone in his room, Harry wandered in Balzac's landscape. He observed the pure strong force of which marital love and the most dissolute and abandoned sexual passion were only different aspects. The force of love was an imponderable fluid, like electricity or magnetism. Its force was vast, oceanic; it burst from the powerful gaze of heroes and villains.

Most fascinating of the men and women of Balzac's Paris was the squat, powerful, perversely attractive Vautrin: lover of boys, seducer, archcriminal, master of disguise, whose very body could be altered like a costume. " 'The parts we play in the world are mere appearances; the reality is the idea!' "[10] Vautrin conquered by wielding sexual and money power; his soldiers were journalists and whores. He was a Napoleon of the democratic era, an artist of the actual, invading every border, his powerful legs bestriding a new empire. "All great men are monsters," Vautrin said, smiling. The laws of human society were no more than the rules of a game, reflections of a time and place. Ethics had become self-conscious, ironical. Masquerading as a Jesuit, Vautrin expounded the rules of the game of glory:

> There are two kinds of history: official history, all lies, the history which is taught in schools. . . . Then there's secret history, which explained how things really happened. . . . Have you studied the means whereby the Medicis, once simple merchants, came to be Grand Dukes of Tuscany? . . . Look upon men, and women particularly, as mere tools. . . . Let there be behind all your fine qualities a force which is *semper virens* . . . and nothing in the world will stand against you.[11]

Harry attempted, tentatively, to write. He began with exercises. As Ruskin had once set him to drawing a round stone, so La Farge now set him to making translations. He began with Prosper Mérimée. The Parisian's stories were small, perfectly constructed narratives written in an impeccable, classical style with barely a word of description. Sober, unemotional, they yet struck Harry sharply and deeply. How was this done? The subjects were as bare as the style. The stories were set in curious, primitive societies. The characters were Basques, Gypsies, Corsicans, Africans. Each tale was like an experiment or an anatomical demonstration: it seemed to exhibit some primitive feature of human character and national type, with all the obscuring overlay of civilization stripped away. The stories were so simple that the trick must have lain in the selection of details.

He translated three of Mérimée's stories. The first two, "Mateo Falcone" and "Tamango," were each sufficiently sensational to launch a succès de scandale. He recopied his work, rolled it neatly, and sent it to an illustrated weekly newspaper.

But it was the third story that remained in Harry's memory, that in his imagination developed a life of its own: "La Vénus d'Ille." An ancient bronze Venus had been unearthed in a little Basque village. It was an embodiment of disconcerting female lust. In metaphoric, ghostly fashion it destroyed the little vanities and pretensions of men. Harry, who had gazed with fascination at the female passions displayed before jewelry-shop windows, carefully rendered the story into English and sent it to a journal in New York.[12] The first two tales came back, still neatly rolled, from the illustrated weekly, but "La Vénus d'Ille" vanished, never to be published, its receipt never to be acknowledged.[13]

Undiscouraged, he translated a play, Alfred de Musset's *Lorenzaccio*. This was a considerable labor. Harry patiently deconstructed and rebuilt the five-act tragedy, in which the multiform Lorenzino de' Medici, wearing one costume after another, worked secretly through seduction and murder. It was a work of history à la Vautrin: secret history. Harry confided this work to dear Perry alone; it was itself a secret to be kept from his family.[14]

Early in 1862, Father put his family into motion once again. He had found a house in Newport that he thought was a bargain.[15] It was on Spring Street, just a short stroll from the MacKayes and the Tweedys. Mother was pleased to have a house of their own, and spent much of her time that spring and summer in fixing it up; they moved into the house in June.

Harry's back had begun to trouble him severely;[16] he was beginning to feel obscurely that the pain was a permanent condition. Perhaps, he thought, the weakness could be traced to the incident of the previous year, when he had strained his back while working the handle of the fire brigade's pump. After a long interval without trouble, he now found that standing and even sitting was painful; he spent a considerable part of each day lying on his back on a hard sofa. At first he had preserved the secret of his hurt, in a now habitually protective reflex. But soon he was obliged to explain to his family his long hours of inactivity. Harry told his parents and Aunt Kate of his trouble.[17]

The revelation provoked sympathy, support, and reassurance. But once it was known to his father, Harry was chagrined to learn, his injury quickly became generally known among friends and relations as well. What was worse, his father took the injury as a form of malingering.[18]

As the character of the war had changed, Harry's father had grown impatient at having all his sons at home. The campaign of the summer of 1862 had revealed the gathering change; the struggle had slowly become not a war to preserve the Union but to extirpate a civilization founded on slavery. The president issued a call that summer for three hundred thousand volunteers. In Boston a committee of notables was established to manage Massachusetts' contribution, and recruiting tents were set up on Boston Common.[19] Parades were held, and Bill Hunt's recruiting posters were everywhere. On September 17, in the bloodiest battle of the war, federal troops at Antietam Creek broke a Confederate advance into the north. Military victory seemed possible, and the president warned that he would free the slaves of the seceding states if the rebellion was not ended.

Having sons at home under the new conditions was to some extent a reflection upon Father himself. William, of course, would remain: William had shouldered his duty to Father and begun his scientific studies. But Harry was of age and not occupied in any way. With characteristic suddenness, Father was impatient to see him enlist. In the summer of 1862, he said that he gravely disapproved of inactivity. Accordingly, and as Harry truly did wish to enlist if he could, Father took him to see a surgeon in Boston, the head of his profession in that city, to see what could be done about the back injury. Medicine was a primitive business in those days, but the doctor was a clever man,[20] and perhaps he saw that Harry was bookish and lacked violence. He examined Harry and with bottomless assurance declared the affliction to be nothing at all. The doctor made light of Harry's injury, and failed utterly to prescribe care or even caution. Harry was sent home to carry on as well as he could, and the injury to his back again became a part of his private existence.[21]

Harry did not rebel against the doctor's judgment as yet, although he knew perfectly well how seriously wrong it was. He could not enlist in the army, but he had been deprived of any open reason for his failure. He tried to live normally, as ordered by the physician, but this was not possible. It was again necessary to explain the long hours he was obliged to spend on his back, and Harry struck on a device that seemed to him beautiful. He decided to enroll in the Harvard Law School, for which he could say he was preparing. The cynicism of lying down, book in hand, was decked with a certain fine plausibility.[22] He was allowed to return to his solitude, his secret protected by a lie.

William remained in Cambridge for the summer, Wilky and Bob had both abandoned the Sanborn school, little Alice was still at home, and so the house was full and there was sympathetic company to lighten Harry's solitude. The other children came often to Harry's room, and he sometimes had to close his door against their noise so that he could work. He was not preparing for law school, as advertised, but was reading every word that Nathaniel Hawthorne had written and published. Harry was reading Hawthorne's works with great pleasure and also as a sort of amends for his inability to enlist in the American cause. Hawthorne was the chronicler of America, as Balzac was of France. A curious chronicler, to be sure, a student of the deeper psychology, more concerned with the realm in which mesmeric forces worked beneath the visible surface, than with the externals of American life.

But the great thing was that Hawthorne existed. Harry had begun to conceive an ambition, still inarticulate, to be a man of letters. He knew of no American men of letters who were of European stature. But here at last was Hawthorne, writing with a great moral and historic sweep. Hawthorne seemed to know how important it was to show that this could be done.

Hawthorne's America was the old New England of the China trade, of seaport villages like Salem and Newport that had been blighted by greed and war, that had long been settling into decay and a consciousness of ancient wrongs. Harry saw in these stories his father's Concord and Brook Farm, and glimpses of Father himself, his radicalism benignantly allegorized. These tales were romances, not novels like Balzac's; they were not so much observed as imagined, and their truths were general and moral. In Hawthorne, one found, however, if not real people and places, the perfectly portrayed *spirit* of New England, the consciousness of personal guilt and original sin, of penalties to be paid, of the darkness and wickedness of life. His work was an investigation of moral psychology, and the results of the investigation were presented in allegory and romance. He did not dive deeply, however, as Balzac had. In Hawthorne's world there was evil, but it was distant and fanciful. Here was portrayed a psychology that began with a consciousness of evil, puzzled out from imperfect signs. Harry was entranced.[23]

In August, Harry took a steamboat to an army hospital on the far side of his island, doing his duty as a noncombatant. The landing was at Portsmouth Grove, where the hospital had been erected in a field,[24] its broad canvas tents pitched over the bare earth. Harry visited the wounded and sick in the hospital tents, his pockets filled with coins and small bills.

The wounded young men sat or lay, stoical, melancholy. Sitting with a soldier, perched on the edge of his cot, Harry found that he could easily draw out the man's tale. Harry listened attentively. He only half understood the heavily accented army slang, but he heard each soldier's complaint, his particular hardship, with deep sympathy. In a few minutes he felt he had struck up a friendship, gave the man his address, asked him to write, and sealed the new comradeship with an offer of money, which was always accepted. This singular experience was repeated and repeated, through the afternoon. One after another, the sad young men yielded up their melancholy reserve to his sympathy, and accepted the newly printed greenbacks that he offered.

In the slanting sunlight in the hot afternoon, among the rough tracks and worn paths between the tents, the stolid young men lay in rows on their cots, as if for his examination. Harry strained to understand, to *sympathize*, and it seemed to him that with affection and sympathy he had reached across a barrier, he had imaginatively entered into a kinship with these men.

He later thought that Walt Whitman's tender, elegiac emotion was like his own. When, years afterward, he read Whitman's book he thought that Whitman, too, had felt something of the unity, the American quality, of this multitude of young men. There was a freshness, a strangeness of unfamiliarity in this Americanism, which for the first time Harry recognized as his own.[25]

How young they were! So many were less than twenty, were even younger than himself, only fifteen or sixteen or seventeen. It was surprising how many more were sick than wounded, perhaps twice as many, sick with fevers of various kinds, with bowel disorders, with pneumonia and venereal disease. Even the wounded suffered more from infection than from the injuries themselves, and underwent successive amputations as gangrenous infections spread. The principal medicines were whiskey and morphine. The men were stoical about their pain. Whitman recorded his experience, much like Harry's:

> In my visits to the hospitals I found it was in the simple matter of personal presence, and emanating ordinary cheer and magnetism, that I succeeded and help'd more than by medical nursing, or delicacies, or gifts of money, or anything else. . . . My habit, when practicable, was to prepare for starting out on one of those daily or nightly tours of from a couple to four or five hours, by fortifying myself with previous rest, the bath, clean clothes, a good meal, and as cheerful an appearance as possible. . . .[26]

> I spent a long time with Oscar F. Wilber, company G, 154th New York, low with chronic diarrhoea, and a bad wound also. He asked me to read him a chapter in the New Testament. I complied, and ask'd him what I should read. He said, "Make your own choice." I open'd at the close of one of the first books of evangelists, and read the chapters describing the latter hours of Christ, and the scenes at the crucifixion. The poor, wasted young man ask'd me to read the following chapter also, how Christ rose again. I read very slowly, for Oscar was feeble. It pleased him very much, yet the tears were in his eyes. He ask'd me if I enjoy'd religion. I said, "Perhaps not, my dear, in the way you mean, yet may-be, it is the same thing." He said, "It is my chief reliance." He talk'd of death, and said he did not fear it. I said, "Why Oscar, don't you think you will get well?" He said, "I may, but it is not probable." He spoke calmly of his condition. The wound was very bad, it discharg'd much. Then the diarrhoea prostrated him, and I felt that he was even then the same as dying.[27]

On the steamboat that evening, paddling slowly back to Newport with familiar creakings and shriekings, Harry sat in a deck chair, leaning against a bulkhead, to ease his painful back as best he could. The afternoon had strained it badly. He felt as if he, too, had been wounded, and that his poor hurt sealed his kinship with the soldiers. He was enveloped by emotion born of his tender sympathy with the wounded men and the intensity of his effort to *imagine* what he had been kept from experiencing directly: a single emotion that infused his whole consciousness with a new sense of his own shared identity that was never afterward to leave him.[28]

Wilky had turned seventeen that summer, and on September 12, as the armies were gathering at Antietam, Father took him up to Boston to enlist. Father had entirely lost his reluctance to see the boys serve. The war was plainly going to mark a social revolution, as Father had hoped. A new national state was being formed, into which all localisms and personalities would be submerged, and in which slavery and its corruption of public life accordingly would be ended. The plantation society of the South would not be brought back under the rule of law, but would be destroyed. And although he had failed with Harry, Father dedicated Wilky to the struggle as he would have sacrificed himself if he had been able.[29] Little Bob, not quite sixteen, impatiently waited at home for his chance.

Wilky's departure was a painful loss for Harry, but Wilky wrote home faithfully and his letters opened a channel for Harry's sympathy. As in the Geneva days, when Harry was first bedridden, Wilky was an extension of himself, an ambassador. In imagination, Harry felt himself enlisted in the war.[30]

In the same month as Antietam, pursuing the fiction of his law career, Harry went up to Cambridge and found a room. More cautious than William, he inquired and learned that the best lodgings were the few rooms given to students in the Divinity Hall, and he managed to get one of these. He arranged to take his meals with William, however, at Miss Upham's on Kirkland Street.

Harry, faithful to his tale, did attend the lectures that were given in the mornings at the law school. These were given in a modest, new building designed in the Greek Revival style, its portico ornamented by four wooden pillars, on a corner of the College Yard just off the street. Harry listened faithfully to the dry and technical lectures of Judge Parker, Dr. Parsons, and Governor Washburn, who together made up the entire law faculty, successful and unimaginative lawyers all; but the subject seemed to him as alien as mathematics.

Harvard itself, however, was like a great golden apple that had dropped into his lap, and that his father at last had allowed him to have. He had an ample circle of friends and free access to the wonderful library.

The older buildings in the College Yard were simple, handsome, unornamented brick, Puritan in their severity, overhung by slender elms. Harry was struck by the way the university buildings were open to the public life of the town, with only a nominal wooden fence around the College Yard, like the rustic fence around Washington Square, humbly open to passersby.[31] He was to go where he liked and do what he liked, Father having inexplicably dropped his opposition to college as well as to the army.[32] But Harry clung to his law school plan. At nineteen he was rather old to begin college, where the freshmen were only fifteen, and eighteen-year-olds were leaving for the army. But the law school was attended by students even older than he, and Harry felt that by training for the law, he would be preparing for an active life.

What mattered most for the moment, in any event, was that he was in Cambridge. His family's house in Newport had been an outpost of Europe on the shore of America, but now he had entered into the country itself, or so it seemed.[33] The wide street on which Divinity Hall opened was overhung with sycamores. The Norton woods were nearby, and the town of Cambridge was a rural village, disturbed only by the sound of voices and an occasional carriage. It was Hawthorne's New England. By November the trees had massed themselves in scarlet and orange. After his morning lectures, Harry mounted the wooden stair of Divinity Hall, knocked at a friendly door and upon its being opened sank into the familiar window bench. It was a college hall in the forest. The windows were opened to Indian summer, and Harry inhaled at once the golden November and the thick suggestion of a young man's room, where thought struggled to be formed.[34] It was a great square, low-browed room with deep window benches; prints from Johann Overbeck and Ary Scheffer were on the walls, and books were arranged with great refinement of classification in alcoves beside the high mantel. In the evenings he occasionally shared a bowl of hot punch and an evening of conversation beside the fire with two or three of the divinity students.[35]

One morning, soon after arriving in Cambridge, Harry saw Gus Barker across the little square fronting the Yard. Gus was attending the college, but he had obtained a commission in a new cavalry regiment that was being formed. Harry did not stop him, and he was sorry afterward that he had not done so, for he did not see Gus again. Just fifty years later he paused in his dictation and remembered what grace and agility poor slaughtered Gus had shown in every movement; remembered his bright-colored wagging head and the large gaiety of his young smile.[36]

That autumn, Harry went down to Readville, just south of Boston, to see Wilky in camp with the 44th Volunteer Infantry Regiment. It was a bright breezy day; the laughing, sunburned young men of Boston welcomed Harry, and he was astonished to find Wilky among them in a blue uniform. His little brother was suddenly his superior in the realm of doing.[37]

In the huge procession of months that followed, Harry had to content himself with knowing the war in indirect and muffled fashion, from Wilky's letters and the newspaper reports; which did not keep it from being an indescribably intensified time, intensified by the very effort to imagine, to sympathize.[38] Wilky's regiment, after the briefest training, went to North Carolina, and Wilky, like the other new recruits, wrote letters that were confident and excited. He viewed the war as a chance for honorable glory, and expected to distinguish himself. This temper carried him through his first weeks in North Carolina, marching inland from the coast twenty or thirty miles in a day, the enemy retreating before them, the men wishing for a battle if only for a chance to throw down their knapsacks. Like all new soldiers, they constantly imagined enemy snipers. Lying facedown on a riverbank, beside his comrade Cabot Russell, Wilky fired away at the treetops.

On December 14, 1862, the 44th was in its first fight, near Kinston. They charged across an open field under fire, yelling, their blood up, and the enemy retreated. Wilky, who was now a sergeant, reported that the charge across the field was the greatest moment of his existence: "I don't think Sergeant G.W. has ever known greater glee in all his born days."[39]

The 44th marched again, and then halted and fought. The fighting continued for several days, and rumors spread that the Southerners were bringing up reinforcements. Now it was the 44th's turn to retreat, and a routine of forced marches on meager rations began. It was a chilly and wet winter in North Carolina, and there were wounded and sick among them now. Wilky was brevetted lieutenant, as casualties opened gaps among the officers. The regiment returned to winter quarters on the coast and waited, while camp fevers and dysentery did far greater damage than the enemy had done.

Like the waiting wives and lovers, Harry anxiously read newspapers and waited for letters.[40] Will Temple, Gus Barker, and Wilky were all safe. Cousin Charlotte King's son Vernon had been killed fighting for the Confederacy. Some regiments were returning after three or nine months' enlistments, and were greeted on Boston Common by waiting mothers, wives, and sisters; new regiments departed, marching before the statehouse steps and down Beacon Street, under the young elms, pausing to be reviewed on the Common.

At Harvard the war hung on the horizon, but life went on in its usual currents. A new president of the college arrived early in 1863; a new chemistry laboratory and natural science museum were flourishing. The school had an adolescent air. French and German were tentatively offered as electives, with no credit given, but in the classrooms the students still recited their lessons in Latin and classical history like boys at school.

In the spring term, Harry moved from Divinity Hall to a set of rooms in a wonderful old house on Winthrop Square, where a huge desk stood before a wide window that provided a handsome view of the Brighton Hills. Here he reveled in complete independence. He could all the more easily conceal the writing that he had begun to do and the long hours he was obliged to spend on a hard sofa. He kept a pile of lawbooks on a table, but these remained undisturbed. In his hours on the sofa he read not law but the collections of Sainte-Beuve's critical essays,[41] a wonderful procession of Monday-morning newspaper columns: hard-minded, absolute judgments, insistently factual, analytic. Sainte-Beuve had sneered at Balzac's coarseness, and was utterly hostile to the novelist's copious intuitions. He had demanded the seen, not the imagined, framed in the perfections of classical form and style. "It is the glory and eternal honor of the domain of thought, of art, that charlatanism never penetrates it. That is why this noble part of man is inviolable."[42]

Harry read voraciously, omnivorously. The college library was open to him, and modest as it was it contained a wealth of European treasures unheard of at home. The marvelous *Thousand and One Nights*[43] opened a world for him: a world in which polymorphous sensuality was as much taken for granted as in a Fourierist utopia. The stories told of the overwhelming concupiscence of women, their shrewdness and wisdom; the nobility and foolishness of men. There were tales of tale-telling, of cleverness and trickery and violence. One especially captured his imagination: "The Story of Prince Camaralzaman and Princess Badoura." The prince was the most beautiful man in the world, so beautiful that the princess fell in love with him after only glimpsing his sleeping face. They were as alike as twins, and exchanged clothes. When they were magically separated, the princess ruled in his place, and married as a man, but in the end the prince returned and restored order. He married both the princess and her queen, and ruled over all.[44]

The blue river of truth wound through *The Thousand and One Nights* as through Hawthorne, and the fairy tales of his childhood. The prince and princess enacted a story that could not be told directly, realistically, but could only be conveyed as a fable. Beautiful as the moon, the prince and princess would appear by name or in various guises in many of Harry's novels and stories.

At the law school, summoned back from the world of myth, Harry on one occasion was obliged to present an argument in moot court. He was prevented by back pain from preparing his case, and so he stood unprepared before the judge in the classroom in the fashion (he said later) of Rousseau standing before an audience with a fiddle and a bow, and attempting to rub them together desperately enough to make some semblance of music. When he looked at the faces of the older students, he quavered into a silence that was like the merciful fall of the curtain on an actor who has forgotten his lines.[45]

Harry was on good terms with the other law students, however, and with them he went into Boston in the evenings, riding the foul-smelling, crowded horsecars of which his father was so fond. They ate and drank at Parker's, and went to the poor theaters that Boston had to show, still masquerading as "lyceums" and "athenaeums." Harry wandered the snowy streets and tried to assimilate this new aspect of America, to fit it with the New York and the Albany and the Newport that he knew.

On many dusky afternoons, he escaped from the law school with irresponsible zeal into the small room in which Mr. James R. Lowell lectured on literature. Among the small somnolent Harvard faculty of a dozen men, there was no professor of English. The boys studied literature by reciting Latin verses and chapters from Gibbon. Lowell was the sole professor of modern languages, and instead of listening to the boys recite, he lectured, as in a European university. Harry remembered the glow of the lamp on Lowell's desk in the small, still room; the lamp illuminated his fine head and graceful hands. He lectured on English literature and the Old French romances of chivalry that had so influenced the English. He spoke of style; nowhere else had Harry heard such talk. It made a romance of the lecture hour, a picture of the scene.[46]

In the first week of January 1863 he wrote his own first work of criticism. He had seen a play at the Howard Athenaeum, *Fanchon the Cricket*, about the awakening of a young girl, and was struck with admiration for Miss Maggie Mitchell, who had performed the title role.[47] With Sainte-Beuve beside him in his room in Winthrop Square, Harry wrote a review of Maggie Mitchell's performance. He tried to speak in the authoritative tone of the French critic. Miss Mitchell did not perform stylized gestures and intonations representing various emotions; she plainly felt and performed the emotions themselves. He admired the performance, without entirely endorsing the method, and sent his review to a Boston newspaper, *The Daily Traveller.* It was his first venture into letters. He waited nervously; but the wait was brief. To his delight the review appeared in the evening edition of the newspaper.[48]

His article was published anonymously, as all such reviews were, but he sent the notice to Miss Mitchell with a brief letter identifying himself. Shortly there came back to him from the actress a little pamphlet, the "acting edition" of the play, inscribed by her to him. He was a little amused by the gesture. The inscription was sufficiently romantic to make him think he had been mistaken for the love-smitten adolescent hero of *Pendennis.* But Harry, without illusions or at least without confusions, had addressed himself to Miss Mitchell's artistic genius alone. He was not only an American now, he felt he was becoming an American man of letters.[49]

Early in the new year, President Lincoln issued his long-threatened proclamation, freeing the slaves in the states that were in rebellion. This was justified only as a war measure; the slaves were still treated as property, and in effect were confiscated as war matériel. Wilky, writing home, using army slang called them "contraband." The president had not disturbed the Constitution, but no one could doubt the import of his action. As if to underline the open change from civil war to revolution, the president directed Governor John Andrew of Massachusetts to organize a regiment of black troops.

Andrew moved quickly to establish the new regiment. African-Americans came from all over the North, and those chosen were a remarkable band. It was not thought possible to choose officers from among them, however; Andrew asked instead for the sons of the Boston aristocracy to lead the new regiment, which became the 54th Massachusetts Volunteer Infantry Regiment.

Regular officers and some of the volunteers who had been in combat since the beginning of the war declined the invitation. The new regiment was not a military measure, it was a moral and political gesture. It was a kamikaze regiment: the 54th would be sacrificed. It was officered by young and untried men, courageous and chivalrous.

Wilky was one of those who volunteered for this honor. His name and that of a comrade, Cabot Russell, were submitted by his colonel, Frank Lee, and in March of 1863 he was back in camp in Readville, where Harry once more went to see him. Wilky, so recently a boy, was to be the new regiment's adjutant. Eighteen-year-old Russell, who, like Wilky, had served only in a single battle, was in command of a company. The easy informality of the earlier time was gone, and the nature of the new task was evident. Harry felt the air of the camp was vaguely sinister, and sad.[50]

In the spring, Wilky's regiment had completed its training. The young officers had learned some of their task, and the enlisted men had learned to drill and to shoot. In May they prepared to leave camp. Young Bob, who was sixteen, could no longer be restrained and he, too, went up to Boston and enlisted, lying about his age. Father did not interfere. On May 21, Bob went to the camp at Readville for training; two days later, on May 23, Wilky's new regiment left the camp, paraded down Beacon Street and boarded steamers for the South. Harry, immobilized by back trouble at home, was bitterly unable to join the crowd cheering Wilky's regiment on its way. His Cambridge experiment was over, and he had returned to Newport.[51] William, too, was in Newport for the summer, suffering from vague nervous ailments and a new eye trouble,[52] as was Alice, helplessly waiting with the others.

It was an intensely trying summer of waiting. Bob's new regiment was put to quelling a draft riot in Boston, and then he, too, was accepted for a black regiment, the 55th Volunteer Infantry. On June 3, Wilky's regiment, the 54th, reached South Carolina. After an excursion into Florida, they were chosen with careful symbolism to lead the assault on Fort Wagner, the fortified earthworks guarding the ruins of Fort Sumter, where the war had begun.

In that summer of waiting Harry learned that both Will Temple and Gus Barker had been killed.

On the first of July 1863 (a hot day in Newport, Harry remembered), the great battle of Gettysburg began. The Confederates had outflanked Union forces and were sweeping through Pennsylvania; if not halted they would threaten Washington from the north, and sympathetic England might at last intervene in their behalf. The Jameses sat in the garden of their house, not quite able to move or to remain still, neither to go in nor to stay out, and actually *listened* together, in their safety and stillness, as if to the boom of faraway guns.[53]

On July 10, when they had already learned of the gigantic cost of the victory at Gettysburg, Wilky's regiment approached the entrance to Charleston harbor. It was the beginning of the violent end of the war. Wilky sent a letter home:

We are to have the honour of charging the first rebel batteries on Morris Island, and to push on as far as we can get. It will no doubt be a fearful fight; all we ask for the 54th is a good fair fight, no matter how many we lose. . . . The men behaved admirably so far, and you can't commence to imagine how pleasing it is to us to reap such success. They are cut out for soldiers every way. Every negro ought to be armed, it is a crying shame the gov't doesn't take the thing in hand more earnestly and devote itself to it. It is already beginning to break its faith with the negro. They promised him the same pay as the white soldier, and they only give him $10 a month—$3 of that for clothing making only $7 in cash instead of the white man's $13. But the negro will bear it, they are patient and used to being roughed. By the time you receive this Charleston I hope will be ours.[54]

On the morning of July 16, just before dawn, a squadron of Confederate cavalry attacked the left flank of Wilky's regiment, but the men held their ground under the sharp, brutal assault. By the morning of July 18 they had resumed their advance.

We are sailing down the Edisto River, on our way to the front. I have only time to say that we came out of the fight on the 16th with 47 killed and wounded. The regiment behaved nobly; and I would give my right arm to keep up the good name it has won. Some of the bravest little episodes were performed by the men. Sergeant Wilson, for example, of Capt. Rapell's company, killed three men out of the four who assailed him, and was himself cut down by the fourth man, whom he also wounded severely with his bayonet. We are now on our way to Morris Island, the new attack on Fort Wagner commencing tomorrow at dawn. I hope and pray to God that the regiment will do as nobly there as it did at James Island.[55]

The 54th was placed at the head of the assault column with inadequate support, and marched straight up a narrow spit of land in a futile and gallant attack on the strongly defended earthworks.

News came to Newport only slowly. The attack of the first day had been a disastrous failure. The 54th had behaved with immense courage. Casualties were great. There were no names. There was a rumor that President Jefferson Davis had ordered to be hanged any white officers of the 54th who were captured. The newspapers reported that Wilky's good friend Cabot Russell and another captain had been captured. Colonel Robert Gould Shaw, leading the assault, had been killed early in the battle, and it was reported that a Confederate officer had said, "He is buried with his niggers."

Wilky had been gravely wounded. At first there was no definite news. About a week after the battle a telegram came from Cabot's father, William C. Russell, who had gone to the battlefield to search for news of his son. He had not succeeded in finding Cabot, but he had found Wilky; and after more days of futile search for his own son, he brought Wilky home to Newport.

They arrived at night. Wilky was on a stretcher, and at first there was a question whether he was not dead. He was pitifully haggard and seemed pitifully young. He had been wounded in the side and the leg, and the wounds were deeply infected. He lay on his stretcher in the entry hall of the new house in Spring Street, too weak after his journey even to be carried upstairs into a bedroom. At first, only his mother and the doctor were permitted to remain with him, and Harry was sent away. Harry took a covering from the heap that had been hurriedly tossed down in the hall: it was an old army blanket. He took it outdoors with him, and sat on the steps with his head on the blanket. An earthy smell lingered in it, and an odor of tobacco. Instantly his senses were transported to the battlefields, and he seemed to see men lying in their blankets, under this same night sky, puffing their kindly pipes.[56]

Wilky's recovery was very slow. Even after a few days when he was strong enough to be carried to his room and could talk a bit, he seemed closer to death than to life. Finally he was able to tell the story of the disastrous assault. He seemed not to mind having been so nearly sacrificed in an attack that was, in strictly military terms, senseless.[57]

The 55th Regiment was sent to reinforce the 54th, and so in August Bob, too, joined the attack on Fort Wagner, which had settled into a siege. The two black regiments with their young white officers labored at building gun emplacements, and cringed under enemy artillery fire. Their camp lacked drinkable water, and they suffered bowel disorders and vermin. At last, on September 7, a final attack on the fort was ordered. The black regiments were again given the place of honor leading the assault. The enemy retreated, however, and they entered the fort without opposition.

6

ARRIVING AT MANHOOD
IN THE WAR YEARS

Newport had grown more quiet. The old town was like a walled
garden, and the war went on outside the walls. As he restlessly
waited in the fall of 1863, Harry continued to train himself for the
craft of letters. He had translated Musset's play and Mérimée's short
stories; he had written a little newspaper criticism. Now he undertook
his own first original fiction, a short story, "A Tragedy of Error." It
opened theatrically, as if on a stage setting where the company was engaged in a dance of gestures:

> He stood before the carriage a moment before getting in. She gave
> him her parasol to hold, and then lifted her veil, showing a very pretty
> face. This couple seemed to be full of interest for the passersby, most
> of whom stared hard and exchanged significant glances. Such persons
> as were looking on at the moment saw the lady turn very pale. . . .

Her companion saw it too and instantly stepping into place beside her, took up the reins, and drove rapidly down the main street of the town, past the harbor, to an open road skirting the sea.[1]

The heroine, an adventuress, sat beside her lover in the open carriage, in a French seaside town that resembled Boulogne-sur-Mer. The deftly rendered opening scene once past, however, the characters spoke only the words Harry put in their mouths; he could not seem to get them to speak their own words. The story of adultery and murder was told in minimalist fashion, with little description, as in a tale by Mérimée, but the tone and point of view wobbled wildly, and there was still an element missing from his work, as there had been from his drawings. It failed to come to life. Still, Harry sent it to a New York magazine, *Continental Monthly*, where it was published anonymously in February 1864.[2] He rashly showed the published story to his family. William teased him, and his father was amused but disapproved of both the moral tone of the story and the direction Harry's interests were taking; he nevertheless proudly told everyone at Newport about Harry's success.[3] But Newport was not Paris: there was a certain amount of adverse comment, and the orphaned Temple sisters were forbidden to read the story.[4]

For some time afterward, Harry kept his writing hidden, but he persevered, and he thought of his gathering little collection of anonymous pieces as a "secret garden."[5]

Wilky, although not entirely recovered and still limping from his wound, returned to his regiment in the fall. Soon he was with Sherman's army in its march across Georgia. Wilky was not yet sufficiently healed to stand the rigors of service in the field, however, and after a few weeks he was obliged to return to Newport for another attempt at recovery.

They were a pair of invalids, as Harry's back continued to keep him immobile for much of the time. Despite the pain and the difficulty of sitting for any long period, however, Harry continued to write. His repeated efforts to break into the New York periodicals, with translations from the French and original stories that imitated Balzac and Mérimée, had made little impression. He had caused a mild scandal in Newport without a corresponding succès de scandale in Manhattan. Harry turned instead to the didactic, aging Boston journals.

His assault on Boston began with a very different and more ambitious effort, a short novel—"a novelette," Perry said, when Harry confided the project to him. It was the tale of a young soldier in the Civil

War and a pretty but trivial young woman, his fiancée, whom he had left behind. The soldier's mother was the powerful figure in the tale; she embodied the moral force of New England. She disapproved of her son's engagement and tried to break it up, but he returned home gravely wounded and died, so that the mother's tyranny ended only in ashes. This sad tale was not the story of the soldiers or their battles, but of the matrons and businessmen in whose behalf the war was fought, and of the young women who waited at home. The stories of the battles had been told in the newspapers, Harry said: "My own taste has always been for the unwritten history, and my present business is with the reverse of the picture."[6]

The Perrys and other summer people had gone back to their city houses, and Newport was quiet. On March 25 Harry wrote to Sarge Perry in Philadelphia that despite back troubles he was struggling to complete his novel, and would submit it to the leading Boston journal, *The Atlantic Monthly:*

> [I]t is almost finished and will go in a day or two. I have given it my best pains: bothered over it too much. On the whole, it is a failure, I think, tho' nobody will know this, perhaps, but myself. . . . I shall take the liberty of asking the Atlantic people to send their letter of rejct. or accept. to you. I cannot again stand the pressure of avowed authorship (for the present.) and their answer could not come here unobserved. Do not speak to Willie of this. I will not begin again the old song about being lonely; although just now I am quite so; Wilkie is gone to New York. As for John La Farge, he comes to Newport so seldom that his company goes for little.[7]

At the same time, he was working on a piece of criticism for the *North American Review,* the oldest and most prestigious of Boston journals. This essay was a careful appreciation of Sir Walter Scott, whom Balzac had admired and whom Harry now called the founder of the modern novel: a strong and kindly elder brother to the modern writers.

> "Waverly" was the first novel which was self-forgetful. It proposed simply to amuse the reader, as an old English ballad amused him. It undertook to prove nothing but facts. It was the novel irresponsible.[8]

Harry delicately sketched a general view of the modern craft of fiction. There were "romances," of which he quietly said to himself that

Hawthorne was the American master. Romances were openly inventions, in which events departed from probability, but in which a certain kind of moral truth could be beautifully displayed. They had the truth, if they succeeded, of fairy tales or the *Arabian Nights*. But *novels*, properly speaking, were quite different. They were histories, and of these Scott was the master.

> Fiction? These are the triumphs of fact. In the richness of his invention and memory, in the infinitude of his knowledge, in his improvidence for the future, in the skill with which he answers, or rather parries, sudden questions, in his low-voiced pathos and his resounding merriment, he is identical with the ideal fireside chronicler. And thoroughly to enjoy him, we must become as credulous as children at twilight.[9]

The novel was like a story told by a father or elder brother at the fireside—not a romance but a memory, artfully recovered and performed.

A few weeks later he was in Boston, swept there by one of his father's abrupt scene changes. He never knew precisely why the James family gave up their house in Newport so soon after buying, renovating, and decorating it with such great effort and expense. But William had begun to take courses at the Medical College in Boston while Father had begun to think of Europe again. In February 1864, bringing Harry with him for company, Father had gone up to Boston to look at houses. He said then that he was ready to cut his ties to Newport, and wanted a furnished house for a year or two until their departure for a new assault on Paris.[10] The Newport house was sold, and they were loose from their moorings again.[11]

In May the Jameses took a rented house in Boston, on Beacon Hill. They had gathered William up into the family again, and were once more poised on the brink of uncertainty.

Harry was glad of the change. Being in Boston seemed to make more real the possibility of a career as man of letters. Boston was alive with industry and war. Soldiers in uniform and wounded men, evident veterans, were in the streets. Their ragged beards and dashing wide-brimmed hats gave a new, wild look to the city. Old wooden houses were being torn down—the John Hancock house had been razed—and rows of prosperous brick fronts went up in their place. New red-brick houses with lines of chimneys on their level roofs stood side by side on narrow streets on the slopes of Beacon Hill. The peak and shoulders of the hill had been cut off and carted away to fill marshes and make way for the houses of the newly wealthy railroad and mill owners, securities traders, and bankers. On the flattened top of the hill rose the blank rock walls of an immense granite reservoir, a marvel of modern technology, that supplied water under pressure to the new houses. At the foot of the eastern slope, running down toward the harbor, a new commercial city was going up, of multistory brick office buildings and new granite warehouses to serve the booming railroads and steamship lines. From Beacon Hill to the east, over the roofs, one could see a forest of masts rising from the harbor.

The Jameses' house was a narrow, high, red-brick house, neither old nor new, at No. 13 Ashburton Place, a little street on Beacon Hill that ran eastward and down toward the harbor. The children's bedrooms were on the third floor; Harry and William shared a room[12] at the front of the house, whose tall windows could be covered by green wooden shutters. It was a sunny room, and in the hot weather Harry would work alone with the window open and the slatted shutters closed. Although small for such a large family, the house was conveniently located for both William and Father. It was only a short walk from the Medical College, and for Father the house was only a few paces from the library at the Athenaeum, or from the horsecar line on Beacon Street that led to the new railroad depots and the harbor. Nearly everyone Father wanted to see was on Beacon Hill or in the business district, easily reached on foot or within range of horsecar, railroad, and steamer. Father's new publisher, James T. Fields, was on Charles Street, and one could walk quite easily over the top of Beacon Hill and down the sharp slope to the Fieldses' house. Also on Charles Street, looking out over the Back Bay, was the house of Dr. Oliver Wendell Holmes, dean of the medical school where William was taking courses.

Sixteen-year-old Alice, struggling alone through her puberty, was blissfully freed from the isolation of Newport and was allowed to go to school, where she made friends. She soon met and grew to love Fanny Morse, a cousin of the Holmeses. Her health improved. For Harry, too, and in much the same way, Boston was a release from a long isolation, and he was now surrounded by life and society. He was twenty-one years old and his own master. He let his beard grow: he was grateful for the new fashion for beards, for he thought his face too round. By October he had a neatly trimmed, curly dark beard that nicely lengthened and squared off the lower half of his face.[13] He began to see people outside the narrow circle of family and Newport friends.

The center of their social life was now on Charles Street, where the Holmeses and the Fieldses lived. Looking back at that time, Harry combined the two addresses into a memory of "a certain door of importances, in fact of immensities," in Charles Street.[14]

On the western fringe of Beacon Hill, on the "water side" of Charles Street, the shore of the still-unfilled Back Bay, was the Holmeses' house, a tall, narrow red-brick in a solid new row. Both the dining room at the back of the ground floor and the family parlor one flight up looked out over the bay. There were marshes along the Boston shore, and for an urban view it was strangely rural. In the evenings the sun struck across the water.[15]

Dr. Holmes was an energetic little man: he managed the Harvard medical school's business affairs, presided over the dissection of cadavers in the gross anatomy class, and gave entertaining lectures on physiology at one o'clock every weekday during term. Before the war he had achieved celebrity and made a success of the then new *Atlantic Monthly* magazine with his serial, *The Autocrat of the Breakfast-Table.* The doctor was tiny, barely more than five feet tall, round-faced and talkative. Sometimes in the evening he took out the violin he was teaching himself to play, and sawed away at a popular song to accompany his rather plain, round-faced daughter, Amelia, who sang and played the piano. At larger parties the little doctor might be lifted on to a table to recite a comic verse he had composed for the occasion.

His eldest son, named for him, was called Wendell, and was tall and long-jawed like his mother, but intensely, cheerfully talkative like his father. His brown hair was still cropped short in military fashion, and he had a becoming, blond guardsman's mustache that he had grown while in the service, and that moderated his long upper lip. He had returned that summer from three years' service in the volunteer infantry, brevetted lieutenant colonel, veteran of Ball's Bluff, the Peninsula campaign, Antietam, the Wilderness. Exhausted by constant service, by a diet of morning whiskey rations and hot coffee, by wounds, by chronic bowel disorders, by the dysentery that had nearly killed him, Wendell Holmes had come back at the end of his three-year enlistment "soaked with death." He had been struck three times by bullets or shell fragments, but he had never been seriously disabled, which toward the end was for him almost a cause of regret. His regiment had been destroyed, leaving him without a commission, and he was too anxious and weary to seek another for the time being. There was something touching about his very fierceness, his intelligence, his humor; it was to be on Wendell's account that the door on Charles Street took on importances and immensities.

Like Wilky and many other furloughed officers, Wendell Holmes was anxious when he was away from the fighting. He followed the war news very closely, and thought that it would be his duty to return to service in the spring if the war continued. He kept a scrapbook of news clippings, following the deaths and injuries of his remaining comrades who were scattered among other regiments, and wrote striking memorial poems for the newspapers as one by one they died. He had gone to the army directly from school, and so at the age of twenty-four he had had almost no experience of ordinary social intercourse, had had little contact with women outside his own family; his idleness was filled by dissipated amusements with fellow veterans. A few months after they met and became friends, Harry described him this way:

> For three years he had been stretched without intermission on the rack of duty . . . constantly exposed to hard service . . . until his health broke down. With an abundance of a certain kind of equanimity and self-control . . . he was yet in his secret soul a singularly nervous, over-scrupulous being. . . . The sense of lost time was, moreover, his perpetual bugbear—the feeling that precious hours were now fleeting uncounted. . . . This feeling he strove to propitiate as much as possible by assiduous reading and study, in the loathsome leisure of winter-quarters. . . . He was . . . a very accomplished scholar, as scholars go, but a great dunce in certain social matters.[16]

Wendell Holmes's ambition, held in abeyance while the war went on, was, like Harry's, to be a man of letters; he had written poetry, had read widely in philosophy, and had begun to set down his own ideas in a series of pocket notebooks. And then, Holmes was like La Farge in some ways: over six feet tall, and exquisitely thin; rather pale, with a long thin neck, about which his father teased him. He had a magnificent head, fine gray eyes, and long, graceful hands. His skyrocketing intelligence let off flashes of poetry. He had taught himself wood-block engraving, and had done a historical study of Dürer that was well regarded and had won a prize. He called the great Emerson

"Uncle Waldo," and he had published a prize-winning essay in which he said that Plato's venerated philosophy had been disproved by modern science. "When you strike at a king, you must kill him," Emerson said dryly, upon reading this essay; and Holmes took characteristic pleasure in telling this story.[17]

Holmes's steady stream of talk, always cheerful, sometimes incongruously so, had earned him the nickname "Chain-pump" among his fellow officers—it was a continuous rattle of carefully rehearsed anecdotes and of philosophical speculations that flattered his audience, a performance that only barely concealed his war-weariness.

Harry at first held himself back a little. Wendell Holmes and William James were just of an age, and the two men drank a great deal. After dinner at the Holmeses', Wendell, Harry, and William would go upstairs to talk and drink. Wendell was addicted to cigars, and the smoke would fill his little bedroom.

Harry drank very little whiskey, only enough to be companionable on these occasions, and he did not yet smoke. He often lay flat on the floor or on a sofa to ease his back, listening. Wendell and William would argue late into the morning hours in the upstairs bedrooms at Ashburton Place and Charles Street, Harry listening more than he spoke, intensely enjoying himself. His private and personal emotions were entertained in a chamber of his heart so remote from the portals of speech that no sound of revelry found its way into the world.[18]

One May morning, just after they came to Boston, while Harry sat half dressed on the side of his bed, green shutters closed across the open windows, he heard the news that Hawthorne had died. This violence struck into his private realm, and out of sadness for his own loss and out of loyalty to Hawthorne, he wept.[19]

That summer his first literary criticism, an essay on Sir Walter Scott, was accepted by the *North American Review*.[20] Admission to the *Review* was a necessary first step for a prospective man of letters, and Harry was immensely gratified to receive a prompt reply from the editor, Charles Eliot Norton, accepting his article, enclosing a check for twelve dollars and inviting Harry to call. This was not his first published work, and it was not a major effort; but it was his first payment, and it seemed to be a guarantee that he had only to work hard and write well and he would be published and paid. The question of how one would live—a question that was so tormenting William—seemed to have been solved for Harry almost before it was stated. He would be an American man of letters. He went out and cashed the check, taking the faintly dubious wartime greenbacks in exchange, and in his room he spread the bills on his writing table and stared at them in the rich afternoon light.[21]

A few days later, he walked to Norton's house in Cambridge. When he asked directions in Boston, he was told simply to walk across the bridge and continue straight on until he reached Shady Hill. There, in the long library of the house, Norton, a slender blond young man with a drooping mustache, sweetly praised him and invited him to write again for the review. The *North American Review* had been moribund, and Norton who had just become its active editor in the past year—he nominally shared the work with Professor Lowell, whose lectures Harry had attended—was energetically reviving the journal with enthusiastic religious and political articles. The journal was now the organ of the new morality, the new crusading spirit that the Union troops were carrying south. Norton had good reason to seize eagerly on Harry's work, which fell perfectly within his program. As a result, on this occasion for the first time Harry's work had been intelligently praised, and for the whole half hour the filtered sunshine touched serene bookshelves and pictures with what seemed a golden light of promise, an assurance of things to come; the moment was something like a consecration.[22]

Harry's modest essay on Scott appeared in the very next number of the review—anonymously—and he promptly set to work, struggling a little as he tried to frame his thoughts, on a new series of reviews of recent popular novels sent to him by Norton. His method was to think over the premises of the novel that had been given him, the situation in which the characters found themselves. He would imagine what he himself might have made of the situation, morally speaking, as a person or as an author, and then he compared his imaginary novel with the much poorer one that he had been given to review.

Anne Crane, for instance, had written a successful book, *Emily Chester,* one of the first widely popular novels by an American author. It was about a woman, married to an ugly man, who nursed a helpless passion for a handsome one. The author made her heroine purely a creature of physical attractions; the book was a modern study of the body, and in the end the heroine wasted and died, a victim of her passion.[23]

It had been a scandalous book because of its frank treatment of the sexual instinct. But Harry found nothing wrong in that, in itself. The problem was that there was no more than instinct—the author had erased the spiritual dimension of her characters. Her heroine gave herself up to an attraction to a handsome man whom she did not love. But she exercised no choice, she felt no affection; the author represented her as helpless. The book, in short, was fashionably materialist, which Harry thought was just a meager sort of sentiment: "We are not particularly fond of any kind of sentimentality; but Heaven defend us from the sentimentality which soars above all our old superstitions, and allies itself with anything so rational as a theory." Against the flimsy cleverness of scientific materialism, Harry wanted to contrast the strength of genuine feeling. It did not seem to Harry, alone in his room, that Emily Chester had truly loved; she was a light woman, and her arbitrary passion was not serious. There was no *serious* condition short of love.[24]

The next step on the path to his career brought him to that other Charles Street address of immense importance, the Fieldses' house at No. 37, another new red-brick house with a Georgian façade. It was his father who introduced him to the Fieldses, although, to be sure, without any intention of advancing anything so material as a career.

The Fieldses' reception room was dotted with chairs and settees upholstered in dark blue velvet, and the room was filled with plants. Every patch of wall was hung with paintings. It seemed very modern and European. Beyond the double doors, one caught a glimpse of the dining room. Passing upstairs, one entered a single long, book-filled parlor, crowded with guests, that stretched from front to back of the house, the green carpet matched by green drapes framing tall windows at either end of the house. The parlor was already a famous room, as Harry knew, in which the Fieldses maintained a sort of Parisian *salon*. Fields was the active partner in Ticknor & Fields, proprietors of the Old Corner Bookshop in Boston, publishers of Emerson, Hawthorne, Longfellow, Whittier, and Dr. Holmes. They had published Harry's father's books, and those of Bronson Alcott and Samuel Ward, and now they were publishing Louisa May Alcott, Harriet Beecher Stowe, and Julia Ward Howe. The Ticknor & Fields imprint appeared on the title page of every book of importance written by an American, as it seemed to Harry.[25] Fields, forty-five years old when Harry met him, was a powerfully built and handsome man, not tall but broad and strong, with ample glossy black hair combed back from a high forehead and a rich full beard flowing in waves over his chest. He was gentle and kind, unremittingly fatherly to his young wife, and to the young writers whose work he encouraged.

Although Fields seemed to Harry to be almost a mythological

figure, one of the Brahmins, he had only recently become a partner in the publishing house,[26] and only in the last year had he become editor of *The Atlantic Monthly*. He was a sort of peaceful Napoleon of the publishing world, having come to Boston at the age of fourteen from a Maine village, with neither money nor education. Beginning as a clerk in the Old Corner Bookshop, he had charmed the clientele and the elderly owner, had become a partner in the firm, and quickly became its principal partner, the sole editor of its books and of *The Atlantic*. Fields had drawn authors to his firm by establishing personal relations with them; he invited them to dinner, charmed them, and made common cause with them. He arranged favorable reviews of their books, puffed them mercilessly in the newspapers and in his own magazines. *The Atlantic* had become a kind of advance display for the books of Ticknor & Fields. He was in the process of buying the *North American Review*, which would give him control of the most authoritative reviewing medium; he was beginning a weekly illustrated magazine to compete with *Harper's;* he was launching an annual review and a children's magazine. He had become the gatekeeper of American literature.[27]

Harry, although conscious of all this and the newness of it, the wartime exuberance and inflation of it, still felt that Fields was invested with a stately past, perhaps because of the aura of those imposing title pages bearing his name at the bottom. A secret pleasure of the meeting for Harry was that he had submitted his short novel to Fields (he had called it "A Story of a Year") anonymously, and the manuscript was presumably upstairs in Fields's study, when Harry called at Charles Street with his father in July.

He met there Annie Adams Fields, who became his earliest mentor and lifelong friend. She had married Fields in 1857, when she was not yet twenty years old. The publishers had built the house on Charles Street for her, as if to house their latest acquisition. She was small and slender, a singularly graceful young wife, her lovely hair parted in the center and modestly covering her forehead with two dark wings. She was wealthy, she was of the Boston aristocracy, she was everything an ambitious man could ask in a wife. Her voice was beautiful and warm.

Fields was just twice her age when they married. He was not merely conventional, he was convention itself. He and Annie walked on fine Sunday mornings to a Unitarian church in Roxbury. He opposed slavery, without quite being an abolitionist; he supported the Union, without quite being a Republican. He was a collector of beautiful things, and the drawing room on Charles Street was filled with photographs and paintings, books and manuscripts, mementos on display in glass cases. Annie confided in later years that entering marriage was like being engulfed in an icy tide. But she had made her choice, and while they were childless, they appeared to be happy—he bearded and paternal, she devoted and daughterly.

Annie had a talent for languages, and when they traveled made friends for the publishing house in Paris, Rome, and London. Perhaps her greatest charm was her sense of humor, her easily provoked laughter, which seemed to fill with her abundant affection. She was herself an accomplished poet and essayist, and a circle of women writers and poets of her generation gathered in her drawing room, and under her tutelage entered the pages of *The Atlantic:* Elizabeth Prescott, Gail Hamilton, Helen Hunt, Louisa May Alcott, Celia Thaxter, writers who, like Longfellow and Whittier of the older generation, wrote consistently at a certain pitch, and made the magazine popular among the women who had become the majority of its readers. European and American authors, painters, singers, and actors came to Annie Fields's house and became her friends. This wide circle of people helped the Fieldses, helped one another, and each was helped in turn.

In short, she was, as Harry saw, a lady, a remarkable woman of just under thirty years in whom American principle and European culture were united. She represented an ideal that would animate his early novels; she was the marchioness Trasemini, who lived for others, who was the most charming woman in America.

Harry first came to dinner at the Fieldses' on an evening when among the other guests was Senator Charles Sumner, who talked of affairs in Washington.[28] The company was pessimistic about the civil government, and had more faith in the military. General Sherman was spoken of as a potential president. Harry's father was quiet; he was an admirer of Lincoln, as Harry himself was. In the course of the evening Harry managed to impress himself upon Mrs. Fields, who courteously attended to him.[29] He soon began to receive invitations in his own right to Mrs. Fields's late-morning Continental breakfasts, where he sometimes met Wendell Holmes, and where they lingered in the dining room, with its view of the Fieldses' long shady garden and the bay, so nearly identical with the view from the Holmeses' dining-room windows. The conversation was often fine, although maintained within limits. It was mainly gossip, the gossip of famous people. Harry's father contributed his funny, belittling stories of great men. The talk was often of Europe, of British writers and French politicians.

The new sciences were represented at the Charles Street table solely by devout men. Fields had declined to publish Darwin's *Origin of Species* five years earlier; the book had been serialized in New York but not in Boston. Dr. Holmes, who went as far as any of them, said broad-mindedly that Darwin's doctrine was only a hypothesis, which never could be proved or disproved, but Louis Agassiz was quite against it.

Agassiz, a Swiss-born Parisian, broad-faced, smiling, a student of Cuvier, had brought French natural science to America. He had founded the natural history museum in Cambridge, and was a professor of biology at Harvard. He had compiled the definitive classification of the fossil fishes, and at the invitation of the emperor of Brazil was planning to lead an expedition of naturalists up the Amazon River. His work in geology had established the remarkable fact that glaciers had once swept over North America and Europe. The fossil record was a history of cataclysms—gigantic eruptions, all-enveloping floods, and the grinding of glaciers. Fossils of extinct species, whole families of genera and species, seemed to appear abruptly among the earth's strata, persist for geologic ages and then vanish in a new upheaval. This history of cataclysms seemed to contradict Darwin's theory of evolution by natural selection, which apparently required vast untroubled ages during which the gradual process of evolution would proceed. Darwin's meager ideas seemed wholly inadequate to explain the creation and extinction of whole classes of species or the sudden appearance of the human race. Darwin's theory seemed not even wrong, only trivial and inadequate.

One evening, someone fell to discoursing on imagination. "Let us stop here," Agassiz said, "we each define imagination differently. Imagination to me is the perfect conception of truth which some minds attain, of what cannot be proved through the senses. For instance, the planet Jupiter is so many miles from us, it has a certain determined size, and certain peculiarities. The mind that can comprehend and use this knowledge clearly as if the senses had touched the planet, that mind has imagination."[30] This "imagination" was the investigative tool of the idealist sciences, the faculty that Immanuel Kant had described that produced knowledge or understanding; and it was in this sense that Harry used the word in later years.

In August, when Boston emptied, instead of joining his family at the seashore Harry went to Northampton, Massachusetts, a town that lay in the Connecticut River valley in the mountainous western part of the state, a resort that had just come within reach of Boston rail-

roads and Boston fashion. He went there to drink the water and recover his health. It was his first experience of living alone.

He had taken a room in a solitary inn that stood on a dirt road behind a flower garden and a wooden gate. His little oblong upstairs
room had patterned yellow paper on the walls and a tattered grass
mat on the floor, in deference to the heat of summer, and was filled
with reflected sunlight in the afternoons. In the early evenings tea was
served on a veranda framed by climbing roses, and there Harry met his
fellow sufferers: Mrs. Haviland, a middle-aged lady, was accompanied
by her husband; Miss Wheeler was alone; Duncan Pell, from Newport,
was with his brother.[31]

Harry spent much of his time on his back in his room, reading.
He would hear the serving girl, Jennie, in the hallway telling Miss
Wheeler, who was in the little room over the kitchen, that there was
hot water for a bath. Through the open window he could hear the
handyman, Fred, slowly lugging a load of firewood to the kitchen, frequently setting it down to rest. From the front hall the driver Ben's
voice would come up the stairs, announcing a trip into town.

He occasionally accepted Ben's invitation, climbed into the wagon
and rode down the dusty, unpaved road to Northampton. The village
lay about a wide, unpaved street overhung by immense elms. There
were a few grand old white-painted wooden houses from which
mossy brick paths ran down to the road between clipped hedges. Here
and there one saw a climbing rose or wisteria, but as in Newport there
were few flowers, little color or scent. It was bare, frugal, decaying.

He remained at the inn, drinking the water copiously at meals, re-
laxing, resting, and reading, until the heat and illnesses of summer had
passed over Boston. Harry's principal company was Mr. Haviland,
who would regularly tap at his door and with hat and stick in hand
would enter and propose a walk.

Most often they would walk at a steady, leisurely pace eastward
toward the river, through woods and between fields, to a grassy hill
studded with mossy rocks and red cedars. Just beneath them, in a
great shining curve, flowed the generous Connecticut. They sat on the
grass, tossed stones into the river, and talked like old friends. Haviland talked of his daughter and Harry talked of his ambitions. They
watched the shadows on Mount Holyoke, listened to the gurgle of the
river, and sniffed the balsam of the pines. On the far side of the river
the meadows had just been cut for hay. It seemed to him beautiful,
and a strange feeling of prospective regret took possession of him.[32]

In November, when he returned to Boston, the attractions of

Charles Street were somewhat reduced. Wendell Holmes had begun to attend lectures at the Harvard Law School, taking a room in Cambridge as Harry had done. Harry frequently went out to see him and listen to his coruscating talk, and sometimes, after dinner, Wendell would come to Boston to see Harry in Ashburton Place.

A piece of good news was waiting for him in Boston. Fields had written (via Sarge Perry) in October to say that he liked "A Story of a Year," despite some difficulties. The story was too long, for one thing; and Harry set about revising it. In the completed tale the absent, doomed soldier took on some of Holmes's qualities.

It was a satisfactory story and would be published, but Harry was conscious of how far, even as a beginning, it fell short of his ambition to write the inner history of his time. The ambition itself was inflamed, however, at this moment, by the appearance of a new book by Ernest Renan, *The Life of Jesus*, which had been published first in Paris in French, and then very rapidly in English translation in America. It was already a European and American best-seller.

Anthropologists and historians had sent a tremor through the world of faith by questioning the literal truth of the Gospels. German scholars had claimed to show the inconsistencies, the historical roots, and the varying authorship of the biblical texts. Renan, whose idealist, scientific writings William had so much admired in the Newport years, was a linguist and philologist, and he had added significantly to these recent studies of the Bible. He had traveled in the Holy Land and had studied in detail the environment that had shaped Jesus' development. Now Renan composed all of these investigations into a single, realistic tale, a novel. In an elegant, precise style he told the story of Jesus' life as a man.[33]

> In such an effort as this, to restore life to the great souls of the past, an element of divination and conjecture must be permitted. A great life is an organic whole, which cannot be portrayed merely by assembling little facts. It requires a profound sensibility to embrace them all, fusing them into perfect unity.[34]

The sensibility that Renan used to reconstruct the past was identical with Agassiz's scientific "imagination." It was a kind of sense organ for the detection of meaning; it was the very opposite of fancy, of the playful invention of dreams and fairy tales. Renan was a scientist whose powerful intellect was an active, creative force, but what he sought to achieve was literal, historical truth. In imagination he visited the moons of Jupiter and the landscape of Galilee almost two thousand years in the past. Scientific understanding was by no means passive; the most intense effort and courage were required to penetrate the veil of time and distance to "fuse" scattered traces into a story, into historical or scientific truth.[35]

Renan's retelling of Jesus' life as a work of imaginative history, as a realistic novel, had a profound effect upon Harry. The book itself, as a historical event—it seemed almost a new Bible in which the lesson of Jesus' life was retold—inflamed a young man's ambition. A man of letters like Renan, by writing a book, could alter the consciousness of Europe and America, and change history. And embedded within this example was the still greater inspiration of Jesus' own life. Renan taught that Jesus was not a deity, he was only the first person in the history of the world to say that true religion was this: the approach of one with a pure heart to God the father. Stripped of the supernatural and retold as if it were one of Balzac's tales, his was the story of a poet who went from the sweet fields of Galilee to Jerusalem, the metropolis, and changed all the human history that would follow.[36]

In November 1864 Wilky once more returned to service with his regiment and spent weeks under fire. He still limped from the old injury, but he managed to keep up. "The 54th are all well. They are an awful looking set of men. Armed to the teeth with spirit & pluck they prowl along the road in their ragged uniforms, and verily frighten southern birds. . . . They have a fiendish swing about them entirely foreign to the contraband."[37] His letters again gave Harry eyes in the dark:

> Sherman leaves to-night from Beaufort with Logan's Corps to cross Beaufort Ferry and come up on our right flank and push on to Poco-taligo bridge. We are waiting anxiously for the sound of his musketry announcing him. We all propose to Hdqrs to take our stores out and ride up to the bank of the river and watch the fight on the other side. We are praying to be relieved here—our men are dying for want of clothing; and when we see Morris Island again we shall utterly rejoice.[38]

Harry felt Wilky's feelings, seemed to see Wilky's sights. Never in his life would he wait to hear the sound of musketry, but how he waited with Wilky for that sound announcing General Sherman! And how Sherman's whole army moved before him, as a vast epic vision![39] The intensity of his affection for Wilky inflamed his imagination.

By February the old wound that still kept Wilky limping had made it impossible for him to remain with his regiment, and he obtained a post as aide to General Gillmore, so that at least he was more often on horseback than on foot. Wilky was with General Gillmore when the army returned to Fort Sumter. The commander who four years earlier had been forced to surrender the fort, General Robert Anderson, raised the American flag there once more. In the gathering spring, the air seemed to become lighter, the prospect of Wilky's and Bob's return to be more certain.

Yet for the moment, Harry's solitude deepened. William, always at best a distant companion, early in 1865 departed on an adventure of his own: he joined Agassiz's expedition to Brazil, which was for him a sort of moral equivalent of war.[40] Tom Ward, his dear friend and fellow student, the son of his father's friend Samuel Ward, had volunteered to join Agassiz's expedition up the Amazon River to collect specimens for a new natural history museum in Cambridge. William abruptly decided to leave the medical school for a year to join his friend. Father happily acceded to the considerable expense of this plan—volunteers were expected to pay their own way—as it pointed toward pure science and philosophy. Quite abruptly, William set off in a carriage for Boston harbor and took a steamer to New York and thence to Brazil; Harry was left quite alone in their third-floor bedroom.

In March, Lincoln was inaugurated for his second term. All the old Whig sentiment was now with him. Doubting Boston had come to admire the manner in which he had relentlessly prosecuted the war. Sherman was the great man, perhaps, who they all hoped would lead the nation after the war, but for now, Lincoln's ravaged eyes gazed from every window.

The war effort was most nobly if oddly personified by Fanny Kemble, who was reading the plays of Shakespeare at benefits for the aid of the soldiers. A fierce abolitionist, she was now giving readings in Boston, although long retired from the stage, to benefit the Union cause. Harry went to hear her read *Henry V;* in later years, after they had become friends, he heard her declare that it was the play she loved best to read. It was gallant and martial. Her splendid voice and her face, lighted like that of a war goddess, seemed to fill the performance with the hurrying of armies and the sound of battle. He would always recall the ring of her voice in the culminating "God for Harry, England, and Saint George!"[41]

The spring arrived, a late New England spring of faint green and glimmering white flowers, of moist indirect light, of stalks that had been bleached by winter darkness and uncovered by the melting snow. Harry's novel about a returned soldier, now reduced in length and rewritten, appeared in *The Atlantic.*

The detested war was ending. General Robert E. Lee surrendered his troops to General Ulysses S. Grant; the federal army, survivors of the black regiments leading, Wilky and Bob among them, marched unopposed into Richmond, the capital of the ruined Confederacy.

In that epochal spring, in a rooming house in Cambridge and in his own shuttered bedroom in Ashburton Place, Harry performed his first acts of love. Years later, while on a visit to America, he recorded the memory in his journal:

> How can I speak of Cambridge at all. . . . The point for me (for fatal, for impossible, expansion) is that I knew there, *had* there, in the ghostly old C. that I sit and write of here by the strange Pacific on the other side of the continent, *l'initiation première* (the divine, the unique), there and in Ashburton Place. . . . Ah, the "epoch-making" weeks of the spring of 1865![42]

It was his first initiation, the premier, his "prime," as he was to say discreetly, so many years later, in his cosmopolitan Parisian English. In a secret act, in a private place, his long passivity had ended. He was to describe such a moment, or rather the intensely vivid memory of it, renewed each time that he returned to his bedroom afterward, in a novel:

> What had come to pass within his walls lingered there as an obsession importunate to all his senses; it lived again, as a cluster of pleasant memories, at every hour and in every object; it made everything but itself irrelevant and tasteless. It remained, in a word, a conscious, watchful presence, active on its own side, for ever to be reckoned with . . . the fact of the idea as directly applied, as converted from a luminous conception to historic truth. . . .

> It played for him—certainly in this prime afterglow—the part of a treasure kept at home in safety and sanctity, something he was sure

of finding in its place when, with each return, he worked his heavy old key in the lock. The door had but to open for him to be with it again and for it to be all there; so intensely there that, as we say, no other act was possible to him than the renewed act, almost the hallucination, of intimacy.[43]

He was a writer, and nearly overwhelming as this experience had been, he used it. Looking back at this time, it seemed to Harry that a memory of such intense and seemingly independent life was the product of imagination warmed by passion, a creative imagination that fused all the tales of romance he had read with his own direct experience. This memory showed him what was meant by love: the fables of Tolla, *The Arabian Nights*, and of chivalry, were illuminated for him; he now believed in all the fanciful exaggerations of love.

The element that had been missing from his work was the strong force that binds people together, that confers on the imagination the power to give meaning to experience. This inexhaustible force was now at his disposal. From that time forward, he understood his life as an active expression that required to be composed, like a painting, to have meaning. In his work, the writing of fiction took on new importance; he loved his fictional creations with some of the same affection he felt for his lover. And a dimension of realism entered his criticism.[44] When in later years, he dictated his memoir of this time to Miss Bosanquet, he spoke of himself as a man of "imagination," which was to say, understanding.[45]

In the spring of 1865, then, he had come to momentous understandings.[46] He had received his first payments in cash—the slightly greasy dollars received from the *North American Review* and *The Atlantic Monthly*; he had his first encounters with death; and in the spring of 1865, the spring of his prime, there was this climactic "momentous relation," in Cambridge and Ashburton Place. In later years when he recalled this epochal moment, he could not resist leaving clues to the identity of the other figure in the scene. He seemed to be a veteran, an officer. Harry hinted that he was Wendell Holmes.

The encounters with Henry James, in his Cambridge rooming house and James's Ashburton Place bedroom, evidently were not of great importance to Holmes. He was drinking very heavily, in bouts, at this time. In later years, writing to James himself and to mutual friends, Holmes referred to the "difference in the sphere of our dominant interest,"[47] by which he meant their different interests in such experiences. But to James their encounter was a self-revelation.[48]

Linked with this experience in memory and imagination was the knowledge of death. In that spring of 1865, an actor, John Wilkes Booth, during the performance of a play in a Washington theater, leaped from the stage into the boxes and fired a revolver at the president, killing him. An idea was realized in historic fact then as well. The news came to Boston in fragments during the early hours of April 15, Harry's twenty-second birthday. A shriek seemed to go out from their house on Ashburton Street. Driven out of doors into the numb streets, Harry peered into shopwindows for newspapers, for news of any kind. That morning was the hour of the streets, when the huge general gasp filled them like a great earth shudder and people's eyes met people's eyes without the vulgarity of speech.[49]

7

HENRY DIRECTS A SCENE

The barrier between the compartments of his formerly divided privacy had broken, and the vivid light of imagination shone on his ordinary experience.[1] Henry had been set free from a cage, and could wander, gaping, in the great social spaces of Boston, where scenes were being enacted around him that he now understood in a way that had been lacking.[2] He had a sense of confidence in his work. Ideas, visions, came bubbling up. One afternoon, in a horsecar, he saw with the eye of imagination the hero of a novel, an officer who had served in the Civil War, whose peaceful good nature would now conquer Europe.[3]

He was intensely fond of the characters in his few short stories, and sensitive to their difficulties. The bantering, teasing tone of his earliest efforts, the defensive teasing of the family tea table, was gone. He entered most sympathetically into the lives of the slim, handsome young men and women, so innocent and vulnerable to abuse by parents, lovers, spouses. His love for Holmes and his affection for the characters in his stories, some of whom now resembled his younger brothers and Holmes himself, warmed each other.[4] This was his inner life, kept quite hidden from those around him. As to both his work and his inner life, it was a pleasure never to so much as speak of the loved object; the rites of art and love, when they were performed, were performed with a perfect freedom of mind, because they were done in private.[5]

The vast federal army was demobilizing. When James wandered down the east slope of Beacon Hill into the new commercial center, the streets were filled with hurrying people, and there seemed almost an odor of military service in the air. Many of the men were still in uniform; in front of shops and on street corners there were heaps of cast-off and faded blue coats, of army blankets, of buckles and sword belts, offered at a discount.

Wilky and Bob came home, sunburned from their last campaign in Virginia, and in other ways much altered. Wilky, although more inward than before, was genial as always, but Bob was restless and prone to bursts of anger. He had gone into the army at seventeen, and was still so young that he had had no chance to form his manners or find a place for himself in life; yet somehow he had grown old, and there was an edge of bitterness to him.

A great many schemes were being organized for the returning veterans: business ventures, railroad enterprises in the newly conquered realm to the south and to the west. State Street was the moral center of a new empire, and the men were eager to exploit their new domain. Both Wilky and Bob began to talk of businesses that they might enter.

The returning soldiers and officers, in the early weeks of the summer, filled the streets and houses of Boston. They had brought home with them an accumulation of experiences that made Henry feel as if the little world of Boston had been lifted and pushed forward into a new cosmopolitanism.[6] What James began most to feel with the return of the veterans and the huge vitalization of Boston that followed was the promise of peace. They had won the war, these young men fighting in behalf of Boston and New York and Philadelphia; now they felt a deep revulsion against violence. They were all taking a deep breath and beginning to allow themselves to appreciate the magnitude of the victory that had been won and of the immense extent of the peace that had now descended. In the Charles Street drawing rooms and in their own, the Jameses met almost daily the rulers of the new empire of reason.[7]

In May a New Yorker, Edwin L. Godkin, came up to Boston for a visit and called upon the Holmeses, the Fieldses, and the Jameses, in rapid succession, to discuss a new journal, *The Nation*.[8] He was Anglo-Irish, and had fought for Irish independence; defeated, he had settled in New York and had espoused the Union cause. He might have been a cousin of the Jameses. His new journal was to be a voice of the new empire, and would issue from its true capital. The new journal would speak for the victors in the war; it was to be financed by Norton, Fields, and other former Whigs, now leading Republicans of a moderate bent, and would be reinforced by a network of books and magazines. Ticknor & Fields, which already owned the monthly *Atlantic* and had purchased the quarterly *North American Review*, now had just begun weekly and annual magazines, as well as a weekly for children, all to be published from Boston. James Fields had turned his attention to the new metropolis as well, and had opened an office in New York for his book-publishing business. He and his colleagues at *The Atlantic* and the *Review* were among the principal investors in *The Nation*; it would be their organ in New York.

Godkin, a short, mustachioed, balding man just entering middle age, came to see James at home.[9] He called indeed on both father and son, as he had just called on the Holmeses, father and son. To Henry's delight, Godkin invited him to *contribute*—magical word: to review books regularly for the new weekly. The editorial program of these linked publications was to uplift the moral and intellectual tone of the new nation; to establish American letters on a solid basis; to assimilate immigrants and educate voters. Henry joined with a good will. His part of the effort would be to help found an American school of criticism equal to the French. He continued to write occasional lurid short stories for *The Galaxy*, but the greater part of his renewed energy was devoted to the work of writing reviews worthy of the capital city of the Western world.

One summer afternoon, Fields gave him the proofs of Matthew Arnold's new book of essays to read and review, and James settled on his back on a sofa at Ashburton Place and read them with intense delight. Ticknor & Fields had purchased the right to publish Arnold's essays from advance sheets of the English edition, and it was these smeared sheets, marked for the American compositor, that Henry held almost reverently.[10]

He had been given the proofs because he was expected to write about the book for Fields's *North American Review*; yet it was part of

Fields's genius that there was nothing strained or false in this. Henry James resonated like a bell to the tones of Matthew Arnold's essays.

Criticism had no concern with party politics or local religious disputes, Arnold began; the function of the critic was to get at the best thought that was current—to see things in themselves, as they were, to be disinterested. Criticism was to be "a free play of the mind on all subjects which it touched. . . . Its business is simply to know the best that is known and thought in the world, and, by in turn making this known, to create a current of true and fresh ideas."[11]

This was the credo for Henry James. He had long admired the French criticism that had inspired Arnold. Here was a call for a truly European mode of thought. While "Mr. Arnold is too wise to attempt to write French English," yet he managed, as James was struggling to do, to put French thought and expression into English forms.[12]

Sarge Perry wrote an affectionate letter from Philadelphia, praising "The Story of a Year," the tale that he had seen through all its stages of gestation, that had now appeared in *The Atlantic*, and chatting along with James about religion and philosophy as if they were walking together, and asked his opinion, of all things, of the Book of Job. James answered warmly:

> A myriad thanks, dear Boy, for your heaven-inspired letter. Of course it is more delightful than I can say to have your good opinion of the romance; which I value infinitely more than a chorus of promiscuous praise. But what I am especially grateful for is the fact that you should have written to me at the dictate of a mood of feeling so kindly and expansive. "Keep a doin' of it." I have had nothing in a very long time please me so much as yr. expression—so full and so spontaneous—of confidence and sympathy.—Yr. letter touches on great questions.— The Book of Job! I know it but little. W. Holmes has often spoken of its charm to me.—I appreciate yr. sense of mystery.—I delight in seeing you *ferment*. One day a rich wine will come of it.[13]

As the summer came on, Boston slowly grew deserted; and while his father and mother remained in town, James, having emerged from his long inertia, resolved on a program of visits to the country. He went first to Newport, going as to a summer resort, in his new character as a published author and critic, a man of letters.

He stayed first with the Tweedys, on Mt. Vernon Street, whose house had been almost a second home to him in the Newport years. The Temple girls were at home, and so the house was a center of life and warmth. Kitty and Ellen were being seriously courted by Emmet cousins from Pelham, New York. At the center of the scene was Mary Temple, called "young Mary," or "Minny," to distinguish her from *Aunt* Mary Tweedy, her guardian. Young Mary was two years younger than James, just twenty years old, and the two had a friendship distinct from the general family relation that reached back to those distant times when they had played together in his grandmother's house in Albany. She was a young woman now, of marriageable age, beautiful, rebellious, intelligent, and charming.

As a girl she had cut off all her red hair, impatiently cutting it short like a boy's; now she wore it quite long but carelessly, loosely. In memory, Harry saw her glide swiftly, toss her head characteristically, and laugh with her whole mouth.[14] He admired and tenderly envied the way in which this slender girl became the center of everything that took place around her, simply by giving the open attention of her wide gray eyes and dark brows to the truth of each person beside her. She was utterly indifferent to appearances and hierarchies. She seemed to take a deep pleasure in seeing the play of life in others, the acting out of their force or weakness—at no matter what cost to herself.[15]

James stayed at Mt. Vernon Street through the early part of the summer, walking along the cliffs as he had before, but now most often going down the hill to the Point, the little district just above the harbor, where he imagined he could see old Quaker faces still peeping through the little panes of the old houses. The young writers and painters who came down from Boston took rooms there that looked out over the placid bay toward the Rhode Island shore. An ancient, ruined stone tower whose history was unknown, but which some thought had been built by Norsemen a thousand years before, stood in a little park in the Point.

The friends of his family were in the bigger, newer houses on Bellevue Avenue—to Newporters simply "the Avenue"—on the crest of the hill above the town, from which one had views to the east, over the open Atlantic. The Point was filled with little wooden houses crowded companionably together, overhung by ivy and flowering shrubs; there were no stables and no one kept a horse or a carriage. On the Avenue, however, the big brick houses were widely spaced, surrounded by wide formal gardens and backed by carriage houses and stables.

All of James's worlds, the Point and the Avenue, Boston and New

York, seemed to meet in a sort of outdoor drawing room, Lawton's Valley. This was a garden-salon created by the Howes, who presided benignly over Newport society. Samuel Gridley Howe was a physician then in his sixties, a remarkably romantic figure, whose long blond hair, flowing mustache, and beard were just beginning to turn white. Like Lord Byron, he had served, forty-five years before, in the guerrilla army that fought for Greek independence. He had then fought with the Poles for their independence, and had been imprisoned in Berlin. He had become a physician and had achieved worldwide renown by teaching sign language to a blind, deaf, and dumb child. Charles Dickens had written an account of this achievement, and Dr. Howe had become a transatlantic celebrity.

His wife, Julia Ward Howe, was hardly less well known. Her elegant poem, "The Battle Hymn of the Republic," published in *The Atlantic* early in the war, had been taken up by the troops and had become the anthem of the victory. Of a wealthy New York family, she was the sister of family banker and friend Samuel G. Ward and was related by cousinship and marriage to the Astors and the old Dutch ruling class of New York. Twenty years younger than her husband, handsome, red-haired, strong-featured, she had been one of the leaders of the abolition movement. With her friends Maria Chapman—proudly known as Captain Chapman—and Lydia Child, she had provided a guard for the threatened abolitionist lecturer Francis Parkman, and had stared down a mob that had intended to hang him. She had carefully educated herself in German philosophy and European letters, and had become a public lecturer herself, a propagandist for abolition. She had labored to understand the philosophy of Hegel, who was highly regarded by the Transcendentalists, but she now admired above all the sermons of the charismatic Unitarian minister Theodore Parker and the philosophical writings of Immanuel Kant.

The works of Kant were Mrs. Howe's great guide in practical morality, a subject upon which she had begun to lecture. As to the wisdom of Kant she said, "If we have found our master, if we are satisfied with him, what need have we of starting again, to make the same journey with a new guide. Once we have got there, it seems better to abide."[16] The great principle that she drew from Kant concerned the use of power. One was forbidden to use other people as if they were solely a means, forbidden to use them solely for one's own profit.

She seemed to feel that she had reached commanding heights, and James admired her complacency. Of the gatherings at Lawton's Valley, Mrs. Howe herself said that "society rarely attained anywhere a higher level." In later years, when he wanted to describe Boston, James described the circle around Julia Ward Howe and Annie Fields, and when he wanted to personify the New England spirit, he freely used Mrs. Howe's handsome remembered figure.[17] She would be the American monarch of *The Ambassadors*, affectionately and humorously portrayed in all her justified complacency.

Lawton's Valley was a summer place the Howes had purchased very cheaply just before the war. The property was a long carriage drive northward from Newport, and it held a small, tumbledown farmhouse with just enough room for them and their three children. In order to entertain, consequently, they went outdoors. At the distance of a short walk, about an eighth of a mile from the farmhouse, a nameless stream ran for a little way through a deep, wooded gorge. At the upper end of the gorge was a waterfall, and above it the picturesque ruin of an old stone mill. The gorge had been marshy and overgrown with brambles, but Julia Ward had pulled up the brambles and slowly filled the marsh with sod; she had deepened the stream and restrained it between stone-lined banks. She had had old stumps pulled out and replaced them with carefully chosen specimen trees. Soon the gorge had become a spacious room, where tables could be laid on the shaded lawns, beside the tamed stream.

To Lawton's Valley she brought the new English fashion for afternoon tea, perfectly suited to outdoor entertaining on summer afternoons. At her teas there would be serious talk as well as games and childish comic songs, as at a family's Sunday outing. James entered easily into the spirit:

> *I'll come distinguished Julia,*
> *With the greatest satisfaction!*
> *'T would be indeed peculiar*
> *To resist such an attraction!*[18]

Arriving at one of Julia Ward Howe's teas, James was always amused to see the grand carriages of the Avenue parked beside the shabby, hired rigs that came overloaded from the Point. One might expect to meet the leaders of the party of progress—Senator Sumner, James and Annie Fields, Dr. and Mrs. Holmes, all great friends of the Howes—as well as Democrats like George Bancroft, a man who clung to the old conservative spirit, who wore old-fashioned muttonchop whiskers and whose extremely courtly manner hinted a little of sarcasm.

At the hospitable tables spread beside the stream in this carefully cultivated outdoor salon, Julia Ward Howe poured tea. She had a compelling voice and a warm manner, and if Annie Fields was the more charming, Julia Ward had greater presence, and was undisputed queen of Lawton's Valley.

At these tea tables, James regularly met Dr. Holmes, Mr. Godkin, up from New York, and Charles Norton, solidifying useful friendships. His companion often was Sarge Perry. But Wendell Holmes, despite invitations, remained in Boston, reading law.

When Henry went down to Newport in the summer of 1865, the war already seemed to have receded far into the past. A new reign of peace had begun, and there was a cosmopolitan air to the gathering, as if one were among the aristocrats of Europe. The late President Lincoln, once so despised, was now much admired, in part because of the contrast with his successor, Andrew Johnson, who was reported to have traveled to Philadelphia by rail with one servant and two demijohns of whiskey, from which he personally helped everyone on the train and copiously imbibed himself.

Father's anecdotes about meeting Thomas Carlyle, and about Carlyle's insolent rudeness about America, were very happily received, and he was encouraged to work them up into a public lecture. There were many stories about Walter Savage Landor, who had recently died. Fields remembered meeting the poet in Paris and in Rome. He spoke of George Washington as the greatest hero in the noble galaxy: "He had a large hand," he said, "which is an excellent sign. Assassins have small hands. Napoleon, the most wholesale of assassins, had a very small hand. . . ."

In May, an unauthorized play made from Dr. Holmes's fine novel *Elsie Venner* had appeared in Boston. The doctor had gone to see it, and said, "It was a great shock to me, that performance, a great shock. It was the novel vulgarized, and I should not like to see it again."[19] In the doctor's tale a woman bitten by a snake had given birth to a poisoned, viperish daughter. The book was a long meditation on moral responsibility, on the heritage of evil, and James thought it the best of the doctor's work, a classic.[20] But the play had made it into merely a sensational case.

Elizabeth Peabody, whose conventional morals and charities Father had long derided, was a friend of the Howes, but she rarely attended Lawton's Valley teas or other social gatherings. She was, however, a frequent topic of conversation. Longfellow liked to tell the story of their first meeting. As soon as introductions were complete and they were both seated, she had leaned forward confidentially and said, "Mr. Longfellow, I have long wanted to meet you—can you tell me of a good Chinese grammar?" Twenty years later, James would people his novel *The Bostonians* with this Lawton's Valley circle.

After his long visit with the Tweedys, Henry went to stay for a few days with La Farge, who was now living on a farm near Newport, overlooking the sea. John was painting the landscapes that he had been working toward for years. Henry sat for him outdoors, as in the old days.[21] They sometimes spoke again of Browning, whose poems evoked the ideas, the pictures, that occupied them, and who opened to Henry an understanding of what the heterosexual relation could be. Two summers before, when La Farge had guided Henry's reading of Balzac, he had persuaded him also to read Browning's *Men and Women*, which they now read again.

La Farge read aloud gracefully. James was struck by "A Light Woman," a tale of a nobleman who rescues a young friend from an adventuress by taking her for himself.

> *'Tis an awkward thing to play with souls*
>
> . . . .
>
> *One likes to show the truth for truth;*
> *That the woman was light is very true:*
> *But suppose she says,—Never mind that youth—*
> *What wrong have I done to you?*[22]

It seemed a challenge, a problem in morality like doing a difficult sum, that James would later try his own skill upon.[23]

Wendell Holmes did not come to Newport. James wanted to see him, but there was the question of what relation with Wendell he really might expect. They exchanged letters; Holmes wrote to say that he had liked Harry's essay on Scott's novels, which had just appeared. Wendell wrote a little hesitantly that he would have more to say about it when they met. He was working hard.

In July, Henry made a decision. The Temple girls were going up to North Conway, New Hampshire, for the balance of the summer to stay with a great-aunt, Ellen Gourlay, one of the Albany great-aunts. Henry could not stay at La Farge's indefinitely, and the girls had invited him to join them.

Henry accepted, and he evidently decided to use the occasion as a means of putting his friendship with Holmes on an easier footing. Holmes had refused all invitations to join him in Newport. Henry now invited Holmes to join him in New Hampshire—to meet Mary

Temple. He was making the best of the patent limitations on his own relationship with Holmes.

It was easily done. Minny wrote that she would try to find a room for them both in North Conway, a little village that stood at the foot of a mountain, not far from the head of a lovely lake. Holmes, offered the lure of a houseful of young women, was agreeable, and writing from La Farge's little house, James completed his arrangements.

July 14th

Dear Holmes:

Your kind letter just recd., together with one from our young friend of the Wh. Mts. I had been waiting for it to write to you. It is I regret to say only half satisfactory. After superhuman efforts she had ferreted out a single room, the only one in the place, high or low—far or near. This the wretch who owned it refused to furnish with 2 beds; but she took it and when we get up there we can pull his own out from under him. . . . I shall be in town towards the end of the mo. and shall let you know when, and await your order for marching. Meanwhile I am living a delicious life, far away from men women & newspapers, with a sky & sea of cobalt (to talk what is for the moment, shop) before the window at wh. I write. . . . Glad your term is up, and that you like my article. I shall certainly ask for "more"; don't be afraid. . . . As I say, I will write again. I pant for the 1st of August. I hope you will have a jolly interval. I will keep Minny Temple on the lookout for a larger room. We shall shift well enough. Farewell. Excuse unseemly haste.

Ever dear H. most truly yrs.

July 24th

Dear Holmes—

. . . Of course one room is better than two, etc. If you don't mind it, I don't, as the young lady said when the puppy dog licked her face. . . .[24]

James went up to Boston on July 28, and visited at home. On July 31 there was a great ball for the Beacon Hill families to celebrate the end of the war. It was held at the Boston Theater, where a false floor was laid over the seats, on a level with the stage, for dancing. Wendell took sharp-tongued Clover Hooper to the ball, and nearly everyone of their mutual acquaintance was there. But Henry pleaded his back, and did not attend.[25]

Early in August, Henry James and Wendell Holmes traveled to New Hampshire together by railroad for an extended visit.[26] From the railroad station in Conway a coach took them over a wide white dusty road along the rim of a rocky ledge; beyond the ledge and below them, the Saco River wound through the broad flat farmland of its valley, snow-peaked Mount Washington overhanging all. The coach ride heightened their sense of anticipation. The little shingle and clapboard village of North Conway lay at the foot of Mount Washington. After settling into their rented room, the two young men went to call on the Tweedys.

The country house was presided over by Miss Gourlay, one of the four unmarried sisters who had inherited the Albany house and its obligations. To James's young eye she resembled a portrait of George Washington, with white hair and false teeth. The house was filled with young women and their friends, as full of life as the Albany house had been, and at its center was straight, slim young Mary. James would often later recall her first meeting with Holmes. He was struck as he always was by her odd beauty.[27]

Wendell Holmes, too, was tall and slim, and, like Mary, had a remarkably handsome head and beautiful gray eyes. They were like the prince and princess in the tale, who fell in love with each other's beauty. He had an oddly vulnerable quality and spoke lightly of his wartime experiences, telling of the courage of others. But he had fought and offered his own life, even if it had not been taken.[28]

The young people—the Temple sisters, Henry, and Wendell—spent long hours on the grass under the pines; Henry remembered Mary as the center of the picture. He described the scene in his memoir, dictating to Miss Bosanquet. And he described the feelings of a man looking at just such a scene, in a story:

> I couldn't have said what I felt about her except that she was undefended; . . . protection was wholly absent from her life and she was wholly indifferent to its absence. . . . She held her little court, in the crowd, upon the grass. . . . She presently moved her eyes . . . and I felt them brush me again like the wings of a dove.[29]

The seductive Holmes courted and charmed her, and Mary fell in love. In his memoir James mildly recalled this difficult moment, which he had purposely brought about. The choice he had made was a complex one, but it evidently seemed right to him, joyously so; there was a golden light cast upon this scene in each of his evocations of it.

What was the inwardness of the experience? Surely it was the experience of freedom that came from the realization of his own nature, and of conscious choice, that he so often described. In his first novel he described a young woman in the moment of choice finding her own moral center. She felt strangely, almost absurdly, light of spirit. Her anxieties had vanished. The sky was blazing blue overhead, and she hailed the joyous brightness of the day with a kind of answering joy. She seemed to be in the secret of the universe.[30] Many years later, another young heroine of another novel, similarly accepted her fate as the Dove.

James himself, with a certain awareness of the subtle absurdity of the situation, had become an actor instead of a victim; dressed incongruously in dignified motley, he had taken his first spring onto the tightrope.

8

FORMING AN IMAGE

OF GREATNESS

James kept a photograph of Mary Temple taken at this time: Her strongly modeled face, framed by luxuriant, unruly red hair, was in alert repose, open and sad. He said later that the picture made one wish for her smile of attention and welcome, as one had delighted in pleasing her.

James brought Holmes with him to North Conway, where the Temple sisters were staying;[1] on a second visit, Holmes brought another veteran of the recent war, John Gray,[2] who was a dark, heavily bearded man two or three years older than the rest. Gray was quiet and composed; his brief remarks revealed a critical intelligence and conservative religious views. He did not join easily in the light general conversation under the trees when Holmes was rattling on. But in the evening after dinner he would tell his thoughts to one or another of the four Temple women. He was a lawyer, already busy with his share of the task of building a peaceful rule of law in the new empire. Young Mary Temple later would tease him about these early visits; she told Gray that he had been such a *middle-aged* man,

> smoking and gravely discussing Trollope's novels with Elly or Kitty, good, perhaps, but not interesting . . . to whom I never felt disposed to speak, & in whose society I used to get sleepy at eight o'clock, & wonder how the other girls could stay awake until eleven.[3]

Mary Temple held them together in a way that James alone could not have done: Holmes, "the companion of his own pilgrimage"; Gray, whom he thought handsome and wise, and for whom he cherished a tenderness that Mary came to share; and young Tom Perry, who was in his third year of college and had grown too old to be called "Sargey" or "Petit Peri" any longer. They revolved like planets around the four Temple girls, with Mary Temple the sun at the center of all their orbits. They were serious young people, and talked about the new poetry, and the truth of revelation, and gossiped, and made a little friendly salon of themselves. They talked about Matthew Arnold, and Robert Browning's *Dramatis Personae*, just published in Boston by Ticknor & Fields.

Gray grew fond of the eldest Temple sister, Kitty; Mary was in love with Holmes; and Henry, who had set the circle in motion, felt himself full of tender yearnings and promptings and envy. Their relations were intensely intimate, infused with a feeling that was equally sexual and spiritual.

Miss Gourlay's chaperonage was nominal and they were quite free to do as they liked, but their dealings with one another were highly, intensely moral. "Our circle," Henry fondly called it

> a little world of easy and happy interchange, of unrestricted and yet all so instinctively sane and secure association and conversation, with all its liberties and delicacies, all its mirth and its earnestness protected and directed so much more from within than from without. . . .[4]

They were to become, all of them, the heroes and heroines of his tales. The air of freedom, the American liberty they took, protected them; they were not innocent, exactly, but their liberty to do wrong, to abuse their relations with one another, was inextricably part of the air of doing right.[5] This spontaneous moral sense would be the distinctive American trait in the stories and novels that would culminate with *The Portrait of a Lady.*

At the end of August, Henry returned to Ashburton Place, where his mother, growing stout and middle-aged, busy with the charities of the postwar world, presided with her firm cheerful brightness. She beamed upon Henry's growing health and independence.

His father, too, although increasingly ill, was very busy. The war having been won, the great public enterprise now was the reconstruction of the economy of the slave states. He believed trustingly that victory in the war had made possible the creation of a good society, of a genuine fellowship, and in the old Fourierist fashion he invested his money in a cotton plantation in Florida that was to be worked by freedmen. A group of young veterans, like a new civilian army, were gathered from Boston and Concord, and he invested ten thousand dollars, a significant part of his remaining capital, in the project. Aunt Kate invested some of the capital on which she depended for her own support, and they sent Wilky and Bob to manage the plantation. Bob was bitter; he had wished to study architecture, but both his father and mother urged him on to this new battle.

Father smiled a great deal, although it was the fashion for men to be solemn, and he neglected his appearance and his health. He allowed his beard to grow into unbecoming chin whiskers; his little round eyeglasses made his nose look still more snub and Irish, made his eyes seem small and intense. He limped badly and he stammered, and he groaned under the burden of recurrent inexplicable illnesses: back trouble, eruptions of boils. Yet he was intensely, dangerously charming, and there was something bleak and bottomless behind his eyes, something like a yearning for the embrace of white emptiness. Henry renewed his childhood intimacy with this old man and they resumed their custom of visits paid together in companionable silence. His own feelings were not less dangerous than his father's, and part of the pleasure in his new freedom was his conscious self-control, his trust in his own moral instinct.

With his father, and increasingly often alone, he paid visits to the Holmeses' and Fieldses' houses on Charles Street. Wendell Holmes was back at law school in Cambridge, attending lectures in the mornings and lingering in Cambridge for afternoon and evening meetings of a club the young men had organized, a moot court in which they practiced their arguments. Henry did not see him often.

Annie Fields's famous salon, however, became familiar to him. In the long, narrow second-floor drawing room, with its green carpet and curtains, the high windows looked out over a long garden and the Back Bay. The salon was an enclosed world, its air of intimacy spoiled only a little by the too-wide sliding doors that stood open to the stairway and hall. It was decorated in the new supercharged fashion of imperial Paris: every possible surface was filled. Palm trees stood in corners, ferns lifted their fronds from pots, and English ivy cascaded down étagères in the drawing room, beside doors and windows and between the high bookcases; a gardener came in daily to attend them. Annie Fields disliked the artificial quality of cut flowers in winter, and welcomed the new fashion for houseplants and complex interior decorations that allowed her to fill her rooms with life and spirit. As in the old James house in Albany, cherubs seemed to fill the empty spaces with their plump limbs. Annie's drawing room was richly composed; it had *tone*, the composition of light and shadow that was a reminiscence of Europe; it was in that sense like a museum, with busts, framed photographs and paintings, books, and green growing things covering every blank surface. A piano brought from abroad made a little plant-shrouded alcove out of one corner of the room, near the windows. On the walls were French landscapes, a charcoal sketch by Bill Hunt, and portraits of Dickens and Alexander Pope. Books rose on shelves to the ceiling, rare old volumes and new treasures, inscribed copies of novels by Thackeray, Dickens, and George Sand with individually handmade leather bindings. In glass cases set about the room were other inscribed books and mementos of French and English authors. At teatime, the guests watched the sun set over the golden stretch of water beyond the garden. In the evening there would be music, or someone would read from a work in progress.

Fields would sometimes join them, benignly paternal, his flowing rabbinical beard now going white, and Annie would regard him with her calm daughterly affection. More often she presided alone, young and masterly, and the guests included women poets of whom she was passionately fond. There was always something to eat or drink at the right moment, and her light touches brought the conversation to life.

Henry also called at Bill Hunt's studio, which was now in the new Mercantile Building on Summer Street. After the war's end, Hunt had resumed painting portraits, and James could chat with the sitter and other guests while Hunt worked or admire the pictures on the walls. There were always some examples of La Farge's work among the French paintings that Hunt regularly brought home from Paris for sale.

At other times, James would stop at the Doll and Richards Gallery on Tremont Street, opposite the Fitchburg railroad station, where contemporary French paintings were also offered for sale, and from this incongruous dirty Boston setting he would step into the cool green countryside outside Paris and in imagination join a group of young painters on an outing. There, within the oblong frame of a Lambinet landscape, bathed in green light, were the poplars, the willows, the rushes, the Seine, the sunny silver sky, the shady wooded horizon.[6]

He always hoped to meet La Farge in this virtual French landscape, but in that first winter of the peace La Farge alarmingly vanished. He had grown ill, was bedridden in Newport, paralyzed by lead poisoning. La Farge had been mixing his own colors and experimenting with stained glass, and had breathed an atmosphere of poisonous fumes, but after the first alarm it appeared that he would recover. He was terribly pale and impatient to resume his dangerous explorations.[7]

At Ashburton Place, the front bedroom on the third floor was now Henry's own room, the place where he worked. William's letters came to him from Brazil. The letters were filled with scientific observations and reports of the tropical diseases that were eroding William's health; filled too with troubled affection, resentment, and longing. "I feel more sympathy with Bob and Wilky than ever," William wrote, and "Father is the wisest man I know" in a letter that ended, characteristically, "Kiss Alice to death."[8]

In the Ashburton Street bedroom, Henry read books and magazines that, like William's letters, were messages from emissaries abroad. Alfred de Musset:

> In the streets they ask me why I wander staring at the long-legged birds, the street girls, smoking my cigar in the sun; how I am passing the years of my youth. . . .

> Your mouth burns, Julie; then let us find some madness in which we may lose both soul and body. . . . As it is through you I die, Déjanire, open your gown that I may mount my pyre.[9]

In the solitude of his Ashburton Street bedroom, James wrote steadily, turning the light of imagination on his richest memories. There in his bedroom he felt the pleasure of freedom. No experience, no feeling, was closed to him. He thought that no one could ever have made a seriously artistic attempt without becoming conscious of this immense increase—a kind of revelation—of freedom.[10]

He was learning to write, as he had once learned to draw, by careful observation, with the whole world of possibility now open to his gaze. He thought out loud about this in essays that he wrote almost every week for *The Nation*, and for each quarterly number of the *North American Review*. Every book that he reviewed was a testing ground for his thought.[11]

He reflected that one could do nothing as an artist without mastering the first steps to success in practical affairs. He would have to reach a wide audience if he meant to make a difference in the world, and literature, besides being an art, was also the business of selling books. It was a business he now set himself to learn.

The successful English writer Mary Braddon taught him his first lessons. She was not an admirable figure, but she had succeeded in the marketplace. Indeed, she seemed to have set out with a grim determination to succeed in the business, like one of Balzac's young men, without too many scruples over the means; while the result was not admirable, still it was worthwhile to study how she had succeeded.

She began with an assessment of her market. Miss Braddon wrote for a particular audience that she always kept in mind. "The great public . . . is made up of a vast number of little publics, very much as our Union is made up of States, and it is necessary to consider which of these publics is Miss Braddon's," he ruminated. She wrote her books for the vast audience of middle-class women who bought books, but who read "neither George Eliot, George Sand, Thackeray, nor Hawthorne."[12] Her readers wished simply to be given an interesting sensation, and she tried to meet this demand.

James thought about his own audience: the readers of *The Atlantic* and *The Nation*. They too were women, by and large, but they were quite different from Miss Braddon's. They did read Eliot, Sand, Thackeray, and Hawthorne, and their expectations were more complex. He invited them to join him in understanding Miss Braddon's success.

The next step in the formula, after knowing one's reader, was to gain her interest. Miss Braddon's purpose was to make a hit. It was a difficult task, but audacity could accomplish it. Miss Braddon had the necessary audacity and resorted to extreme measures. She had created the sensation novel.[13] Her object was simply to play on the feelings of her readers for her own profit, and for this James had only contempt.

One did not use people solely as a means to one's own profit. But if her aims were despicable, the *methods* she used, the techniques of popular fiction, were worth study.

Miss Braddon's medium was terror, created by the intrusion of crime and the supernatural into the ordinary world of domestic relations. How was this made believable? Her audience—and his— had grown accustomed to newspapers and photographs; the thin imaginings of the old romances no longer carried conviction. In the modern age,

> to be satisfactory to the general public, art has to specify every indi-
> vidual fact of nature; when, in order to believe what we are desired to
> believe of such a person, we need to see him photographed at each
> successive stage of his proceedings. . . .[14]

Braddon proceeded to "get up her photograph" by assembling details that conveyed a realistic impression: brand names, the use of weapons, slang culled from newspaper reports.

> It is the peculiar character of these details that constitute her chief
> force. They betray an intimate acquaintance with [the] disorderly
> half of society. . . . Miss Braddon "has been there." . . . She knows
> much that ladies are not accustomed to know, but that they are ap-
> parently very glad to learn. The names of drinks, the technicalities
> of the faro-table, the lingo of the turf, the talk natural to a crowd of
> fast men at supper, when there are no ladies present but Miss
> Braddon. . . .[15]

Braddon's were skillful books of the modern day; her characters were placed in real settings encrusted with detail, but they lacked a moral dimension. The trick of the photograph compelled a reader to partic- ipate in the sensations of the tale of terror. But it could be a shabby sort of trick.

An artist must seduce her reader, but without some moral purpose Miss Braddon's arts were on a par with the allures of the long-legged street girls. The author's power over the reader, like the power of the beloved, should not be misused. With the arrogance and self-absorption of youth, James lumped the novels of Trollope and Flaubert with the sensational romances of Mrs. Braddon and her lesser sisters. These books were instructive, he said, but they lacked the essentials of truth.

The photograph, with all its detail, lacked what only a painting or a performance could convey, the portrayal of character.

> Mr. Trollope accomplishes his purpose of being true to common life. But in reading his pages, we are constantly induced to ask ourselves whether he is equally true to nature; that is, whether in the midst of the multitude of real things, of uncompromisingly real circumstances, the persons put before us are equally real. . . . The persons should reflect life upon the details, and not borrow it from them. To do so is only to borrow the contagion of death.[16]

The business of the artist was not to accumulate accurate details alone, the dead machinery of materialism, but to enact the truth. To engage the intellect and the moral imagination of the reader, the author must provide more than tales of mere wickedness, lies, and adulteries; she must portray the struggle of good and evil. *Moral* realism was created not by newspapers and photographs but by the great philosophical writers, by Goethe and Renan.

The trick to master for a young man like himself was evidently to harness the technology of the photograph and the crime report, but to use it for creating interest in a tale of imagination. James, imitating Miss Braddon, would assiduously read crime reports and proceedings of criminal trials in search of details that lent an air of truth. His plots like hers would often be sensational tales drawn from the newspapers. The trick for the modern writer of fiction was to use these materials honestly: to create interest, without losing the moral dimension of his story.

James was staking out a position, and he sneered at older writers. The course of literature was at a branching point, and James was taking the turning that Hawthorne had marked but had not been able to follow.[17] It was the path that, in Great Britain, George Eliot, Meredith, and Hardy would follow, and that in France was the great highway of Balzac, Hugo, Sand, Musset, and Mérimée. In the end, James would follow it farthest of all, to the distant vanishing point at which all paths converge. But now, at the age of twenty-two, he was staking out his position and building upon it a personal philosophy. At its center was the love inspired by the victims of injustice, of life itself.

Maurice de Guérin, to take a concrete instance, had been such a victim. He had been a graceful French writer of minor verse in the last generation. His poetry, although filled with an exquisite sensitiveness, was one long record of moral impotence. He had a sister, Eugénie, who loved him despite—or even because of—his helplessness. She seemed to have the same affection for him that Henry felt for every man who was deficient in will.[18] With a profound humility that expressed itself in a perfect style, she filled her diary with daily letters to Maurice. In unconscious emulation of her God, she bent her head in love for her weak brother.[19]

This humility, this subordination of strength to weakness, was one of the lessons of Europe. Paradoxically, it required a powerful will to submit oneself in this way. The old pagan teaching of the Stoics was that a man's happiness lay in his own hands, in the godlike principle of his own nature from which he derived courage, modesty, and religion. This Stoic principle, the great teaching of the old order, was a doctrine for a world without liberty.

In the modern Christian world the ideal was freedom—freedom to choose, to abolish injustice, to succor the beloved victims of life. The old order had not entirely passed away, however, and there still was slavery and oppression enough. One was not always free to put down the mask of self-control: "for we still suffer and as long as we suffer we must act a part."[20]

He scattered these reflections through a series of inconsequential book reviews. They were only notes for a personal philosophy that would be the background of all his art.

When he remembered this time as he prepared for his dictation to Miss Bosanquet, he recalled his growing fascination with the idea of America, where the new order of liberty had been established, and the contrast between the American and the European ideals. The two ideals had appeared to him most vividly embodied in the characters of men. There were Europeanized young men whom one met in New York: finished fops dressed in the perfection of Savile Row in its prime, wearing a monocle and a contemptuous air of boredom—the embodiment of world-weariness. To young Henry they seemed to represent a peculiarly European type unknown to America, and to hint of more appetites and yearnings than America was consciously aware of. In memory he set down beside the European type, by way of contrast, the American man who had "such a flush of life and presence."[21]

These young men translated ideals into embodied art. A gentleman of the old order simply submitted himself to a style that had been long in the making; the American, while fully capable of submitting himself to necessity, was also wholly original, freely self-created, and that for James counted double.[22]

And so Henry James formed his ideas upon the men and women he loved. Europe was a perfect style; the American was an image of freedom. Freedom meant choosing, when necessary, self-sacrifice, as the American soldiers had done, but it was freedom all the same.

Henry now marked his departure, not quite a rebellion, from his father. Father taught selflessness; *his* ideal was derived from his yearning to merge himself into the divine spirit of humanity. Henry James's hero and heroine of the modern age, however, were powerful personalities, who subordinated themselves not to superior power, as in the old order, nor to Humanity, as in Father's teaching, but only to their own idea, to their own genius.[23]

He wrote two stories that winter that might have been portraits of a single American heroine taken from different angles. She greatly resembled Mary Temple; she might have been Holmes's sister—tall, slim, gray-eyed, intelligent, and charming. She was conscious but heedless of being observed; one might have spoken of her stage presence. She had a long, graceful throat and a musical laugh, and her dress was delicately feminine, worn with a style that James could not yet easily describe.

From her manner and expression one could see that James had imagined her older, less innocent than Holmes or Mary Temple. She was a lady, a gentlewoman by instinct and breeding, and a shade more cosmopolitan than her surroundings seemed to warrant. Her experience of life, the unstated common experience of women, of love and loss, had left her as gentle as the officers who had returned from the war. She spoke reflectively, in complete sentences and paragraphs not unlike James's own. She was the woman Mary Temple might become when she had acquired James's knowledge of life, his self-awareness and self-control. His heroine had gained moral certainty without losing her brave openness, her spontaneity, her charity, her genius, her imagination.

He saw her in a rural New England village, too generalized to be exactly Northampton; it was simply rural America. At times she was poor and trapped there; in the first story, she was wealthy. She was visiting her scientist brother. Briefly she was left alone in the house while her brother attended a scientific congress.[24] James placed her there, under the strong clear American light as if on a laboratory bench or on a stage.

She was courted by a sweet, solemn Unitarian minister, rather like Gray. But another young man interested her more, if only because he suited her mood. Answering the requirements of the hour, this visitor was of a sex as different as possible from her own. He was vigorously masculine, talkative, energetic, conventionally blunt, yet blushing at his own cleverness in a large, manly way. A good-looking fellow, open and vulnerable, with

> head so well-shaped as to be handsome, a pair of inquisitive, respon-
> sive eyes, and a large, manly mouth. . . . he stood leaning against the
> window-shutter, outside the curtain, with folded arms. The morning
> light covered his face, and mingled with that of his radiant laugh,
> showed . . . that his was a nature very much alive.[25]

Hardly more than a boy, this fellow had wandered into the heroine's scene; he sensed an extraordinary possibility concerning her; but he lacked audacity, or confidence, or imagination. His work absorbed him, he was about to begin a journey to Europe. He was businesslike, and did not want to miss the steamer for New York. As he stood for a moment with the heroine in her doorway, saying good-bye, he sensed that he was at a branching of the way: yet he was unable to rise to her courage, to step into the unknown. Thinking only that he was being reasonable, and without a heart's choice, he chose. In an instant the opportunity was past; he had failed to grasp the moment.[26]

In the second tale, "A Landscape Painter," a wealthy young gentleman from New York, handsome, complacent, self-regarding, came onstage. The heroine in her New England village liked him well enough, perhaps not as well as she had liked the first young man; but in this story she was poor and a stoic. A woman without means must marry. Her task was to wear the prescribed costume and the smiling mask, and to marry well, but without dishonesty and on the basis of genuine affection.

The task of attracting the wealthy gentleman, it seemed, was an artist's problem, very much like the difficulty a writer faced who was obliged to stimulate interest in his readers. The author's selfish motive could not be allowed to dominate; the reader had to make the advances, had to take a genuine interest. How to generate this interest without seeming to do so, and without dishonesty, was the problem of all affectionate relations, as it was of every art. Artifices and lies were required. One was obliged to respect oneself and yet also to live. And so the heroine was artful, and yet truthful. She had an original style of her own.

The gentleman was an amateur painter, and pretended to be poor to test her. But she read him as if he were a text, and learned the secret of his wealth. She was cleverer than he, and made a greater mystery of herself and her feelings. She knew the difference between artifice and falsity, and she did not pretend to love him, but straining to read her secret, he fell in love with her, helplessly. She, after all, was the artist and actor; he only the audience, the reader, the victim.[27]

The two brief stories appeared that winter, and they seemed to James to vindicate his growing sense that he was a man of letters. He was writing very well, in a style that he had begun to make his own. He described scenes not from the perspective of omniscience, but through his heroine's eye; his own memories were illumined by imagination, and rendered with La Farge's precision of detail. "A sex as different as possible from her own. . . . The morning light covered his face and mingled with the radiance of his laugh. . . ." He was learning to say what could not ordinarily be said.

A book of verse was published that year that interested him greatly and was making a stir in Boston. Walt Whitman's *Drum Taps* was a product of the war, of his visits to army hospitals and his love for the wounded and dying youths he had nursed there. Through the soldiers, Whitman had imagined himself into the spirit of America, as James had.

> *From Paumanock starting, I fly like a bird,*
> *Around and around to soar, to sing the idea of all. . . .*
> *To sing first (to the tap of the war-drum, if need be)*
> *The idea of all—of the western world, one and*
> *inseparable. . . .*

These verses had been much admired by James's father and by Emerson. But James dismissed them almost with anger, for Whitman was on a course that diverged widely from his own. James addressed the poet directly; his review was like a letter. Whitman, you have audacity and will enough; but you lack patience, intellect, education; your book is filled with impatient self-regard. It is monstrous; an offense against art.

> You came to woo my sister, the human soul. . . . But for a lover you talk entirely too much about yourself. In one place you threaten to absorb Canada. In another you call upon the city of New York to incarnate you, as you have incarnated it. In another you inform us that

neither youth pertains to you nor "delicatesse," that you are awkward
in the parlor, that you do not dance, and that you have neither bearing, beauty, knowledge, nor fortune. In another place, by an allusion
to your "little songs," you seem to identify yourself with the third person of the Trinity. . . . We find art, measure, grace sneered at on every
page. . . . [28]

This was not good enough. One needed more than courage, one
needed to acquire the virtues of the Old World as well, a powerful
will subordinated to necessity: a style. "You must forget yourself in
your ideas. . . . You must be *possessed*, and you must strive to possess
your possession."[29]

So he lectured Whitman, as he would always lecture his readers. A
great writer had no theory, only an idea: an idea that would be embodied in his own life and work.[30]

He felt that he himself was, would be, a great writer. The idea that
he had formed, and to which he willingly submitted himself, was the
idea of America. It presented itself in an image: an American heroine,
straight and tall, auburn-haired, gray-eyed. She was freely frank and
courageous, a woman of intellect, charm, and moral force. James's
beloved Holmes and Mary Temple and his image of his reader fused
in this character, an American heroine who combined the graces of
Europe with the freedom and sure moral instinct of New England.
She loved the weak and will-less victims of life with an undivided innocent passion. Her coming of age, her self-awareness and freedom,
was that of history itself. James's greatest telling of her story would be
The Portrait of a Lady.

To be a great artist one would have to enact this idea, to be great
oneself. The artist must combine the heart of Eugénie de Guérin, the
powerful will of Balzac and Hugo, the courage and self-control of
Epictetus, the scientific intelligence of Renan, the moral certainty of
Julia Ward Howe. One must be the Goethe and the Shakespeare of a
new age, mad with the ambition of youth.

9

FLEEING TOWARD THE LIGHT

Father's dream of Europe had been postponed, and so necessarily had Henry's as well. The Florida venture strained the family's resources—even by the most optimistic calculation the investment in the cotton plantation could not hope to begin paying dividends for years—and the virulent inflation of the war years continued. The Jameses' income had effectively been cut in half. With the return of the troops, housing grew scarce and even Boston now seemed very expensive. Father and Mother began to look about for something cheaper.

William returned in February from the Brazilian expedition, sun-browned and mustachioed but in weakened health. He said that he wanted to return to the medical school and complete his degree as his friend Tom Ward was doing. He talked of their practicing medicine together. Medicine would be a midpoint compromise between Mother's concern for practicality and Father's insistence on science, the pure life of the mind.[1] Accordingly, William took a furnished room in Boston conveniently near the Massachusetts General Hospital and medical school. The family was poised to depart for a cooler and healthier atmosphere, but William planned to remain in the hot city through most of the summer. He worked long hours, stooping over the dissecting table, and began to complain of his back.[2]

When their lease at Ashburton Place expired in May 1866, however, the Jameses gave up their house and in the old way went to rented summer lodgings without having any fixed place to which to return. They went to Swampscott, a seashore resort north of Boston, while they looked for a smaller, year-round house that would be within their shrunken means.

Just as they were moving to Swampscott, Wendell Holmes, like the young man in James's story, went to New York and boarded a steamer for a four-month visit to Europe. Even forty years later, Henry recalled the intensity with which he had imagined Wendell on his travels:

> I can't help . . . just touching with my pen-point (here, here, only here) to the recollection of that . . . day when I went up to Boston from Swampscott and called in Charles St. for news of [Wendell Holmes], then on his first flushed and charming visit to England. . . .[3]

The doctor and Mrs. Holmes were not in. Henry was received by Wendell's plump sister, Amelia, in the cool drawing room. The rugs had been taken up, there were bamboo mats on the floor and bamboo shades over the windows. They talked of the heat, and Amelia said with amusement that Mary Temple had already called for news of Wendell.[4] He had had a great success in London from the very first, Amelia said, and had been invited to pay a visit to the Duke of Argyll's castle in Scotland in August, after the London season ended. Henry asked Amelia to send his love.[5] Wendell was in Europe; and Henry

> *vibrated* so with the wonder and romance and curiosity and dim weak tender (oh, tender!) envy of it, that my walk up the hill, afterwards, up Mount Vernon St. and probably to the Athenaeum was all coloured and gilded, and humming with it, and the emotion, exquisite of its kind, so remained with me that I always think of that occasion, that hour, as a sovereign contribution to the germ of that inward

romantic principle which was [to] determine so much later on (ten years!) my own vision-haunted migration.[6]

On that brief visit to Boston, he went also to Massachusetts General Hospital, where William bent over his dissections. He recalled of this visit only the sense of the busy and genial hospital community of which William had become part, all housed in "a great porticoed and gardened setting."[7] William had been drawn into this busy, masculine community, and was beginning to talk of obtaining an appointment at the hospital.[8]

Boston otherwise seemed deserted. Bill Hunt had taken his family for an extended visit to Italy and France. Those of Henry's acquaintances who had not joined the migration abroad had scattered to the mountains and seaside resorts, fleeing from the cholera that swept through the poorer quarters of the crowded city in the hot months and threatened even the well-to-do.

Tom Perry, too, had gone abroad. He had graduated from Harvard College that summer, and after making a grand tour of Europe he was to complete his studies at the University of Berlin.

Germany was the center of scientific thought in Europe, and Berlin was the capital of a new German empire. That summer of 1866, the King of Prussia, who was uniting the kingdoms and baronies of northern Germany into a federal state, had shown himself to be a master of the new technology of warfare in a lightning seven-weeks' war on the Austrian Empire, a war of telegraphed orders, troop movements by railroad, and artillery bombardments at long range. He was now a rival of the French emperor, and to American eyes increasingly more attractive. Where the French emperor was Catholic and absolute, and had restored the pope to power in Italy, the emerging German state was Protestant, a constitutional monarchy with a federal system like the American. German philosophy, science, and law were provoking great excitement in Boston and Cambridge, and the new German state seemed to the Lawton's Valley circle to be a sister empire, a new force of reason. The first transatlantic telegraph cable was successfully completed that summer, and the first message transmitted to America was the news of Germany's victory over Austria: "Peace in Europe."

James, who yearned to follow his friends to Europe, and Alice were each other's sole companion in Swampscott. They walked and talked as in the Newport days. Alice had studied German, and during the war had joined one of the sewing circles formed in Boston to supply the troops; after the war the circles had continued doing charitable work, a part of which was teaching young Irish and German immigrant girls to sew. She now missed all this activity, and above all the close friendships she had formed with intelligent, independent young women—especially Fanny Morse and Ellen Hooper, for both of whom Alice had a great affection.[9]

Alice worked very hard to keep her feelings in check and dress herself in neutral tints.[10] But that summer she had her first outbreaks of hysteria, of uncontrollable excitement and rage, followed by hysterical weakness. She was immobilized by weakness thereafter, until the family moved to Cambridge, and she would sit quietly with a book in her hand, apparently reading.[11]

Henry spent much of the summer on his bed, yielding to his bad back, and reading novels by a woman who wrote under the name of George Eliot. He read the novels with great excitement: Eliot seemed to him the first English novelist of genius who had both a clear intellect, an analytical mind worthy of the French, and a powerful moral imagination. But her stories were artificial; she had no great idea, nor any hero or heroine to embody one. Eliot drew only portraits of average humanity, of mild people whose doings in the aggregate made up the sum of national history. The action of her plots illustrated the author's points instead of growing out of the personality of the actors, and accordingly seemed arbitrary and unreal.[12] But her novels were an event; James's review of Eliot's novel of politics, *Felix Holt: The Radical*, appeared in *The Nation* in August and his long essay-review of her work appeared in *The Atlantic* in October.[13] Eliot had demonstrated that intellect and vivid realism could be combined in a novel, and he was conscious of having needed this proof to enable him to turn from criticism to fiction again.[14]

He imagined himself writing Eliot's novels, imagined how he would have done them, pondering the technical questions of craft. Eliot engaged the reader's intellect, but this was not enough. One had to engage the reader's imagination. Surely, the technology of writing that the Miss Braddons of the world had developed could find some application in serious fiction? The trick needed for all fiction was to make the reader see the point: to *want* to see the point, to find out the author's hidden treasures. Eliot clumsily told the reader everything, and James thought that on the contrary, like the young woman in *A Landscape Painter*, she should somehow have given the reader hints to *deduce* what the future would hold for her characters: "the reader would be doing but his share of the task; the grand point is to get him to [do] it. I hold that there is a way. It is perhaps a secret; but until it is found out, I think that the art of story-telling cannot be said to have approached perfection."[15]

James began, for the first time in two years, an extended work of fiction of his own: "Poor Richard."[16] It was set once again in the New England countryside, but this was no longer a bare stage. As in Eliot's novel, the country houses, farms, gardens, and ancient towns were the soil from which the characters grew. It was Hawthorne's New England. At its center was a new character. She was by no means a heroine: she was neither slender nor beautiful; she was dark, she was plump, and she would have been called plain if it had not been for her charming smile. She was not romantically poor, she had adequate means; but neither was she romantically wealthy. She was a woman of the middle class, rather like Henry himself, only a little older; like him she dressed well, in somber colors. In both moral and practical questions she chose wisely, exercising good taste, courage, and a fine moral instinct. Her name, Gertrude, was not that of a romantic heroine. In a romance she might have been the heroine's aunt.

James plunged into the heart of this character. He told the reader in his own voice that Gertrude sometimes felt weak, although she always appeared strong; that she had been bruised and had learned caution; that her feelings were kept in a place so distant from the surface that no sounds of revelry ever escaped.

The story was set in the last year of the Civil War. Gertrude had been courted by three men: the first was a wounded captain who had come home to recover his health. He anxiously followed the war news and feared that he would have to return if the war continued.[17] His history and circumstances were like Holmes's, but his taciturn, dignified manner was Gray's. Gertrude and the captain loved each other, but she was wealthy and he was poor. Each was too proud and too cautious to make a confession of love to the other; and so this strong woman watched a great happiness sink below the horizon and disappear.

The villain was also an officer, one who had served himself well during the war, and who now wanted Gertrude's money and social position. He was clever but used his talents for evil purposes; he was evil in the only way that James recognized evil: he abused his power. He tried to use Gertrude for his own profit.

And there was a young man, Richard. He was adolescence itself: passionate, innocent, impatient, and violent, lacking in will and self-control. Helpless to control his passions, he drank too much, went into rages, and woke after his dissipations into an agony of awareness. He was not unlike William, or Bob, or Tom Perry: a young American who had not yet acquired confidence or patience, an embodiment of the nation's character before the war. He was a young man of whom the author was very fond.

Poor Richard was in love with Gertrude and suffered agonies of jealousy. And Gertrude, like an affectionate aunt, like James himself, helped him to gain patience and self-control. The ending was sadly sweet. Poor Richard had become a man, and the future lay before him. The villain was exposed and dismissed; the captain silently returned to the war and was killed. Gertrude, now alone, set sail for Europe.

Despite his strictures on George Eliot, James told the story as if he saw it with the eye of God, and left nothing for the reader to imagine. He sent "Poor Richard" to Fields, who liked it and paid him the magnificent sum of two hundred dollars. But as the story was long, Fields said that he would hold it in reserve until it could be serialized in two or three successive numbers of *The Atlantic*.[18]

In October 1866 the much diminished James family moved to a house at 20 Quincy Street in Cambridge. A carriage loaded with Jameses rolled across the bridge from Boston westward through the port and the growing factory district into the countryside. Cambridge lay in a low, marshy plain through which the little Charles River meandered. Still farther to the west, the land rose gently to the rounded slope of Mount Auburn, skirted by the Charles, and the hilly farms to the north and west.

Their new home in Cambridge was a square frame house on a little rise of ground, overhung by trees. The interior of the house was shaded by climbing wisteria and overhanging trees; after the noise and crowds of Boston it seemed like a country retreat, a cloister. There was only the jingle of the horsecars and an occasional burst of laughter from a group of students, to break the quiet. James had a pleasant room upstairs overlooking the street, a room with a big soft bed and good chairs.[19] From his window he could see across Quincy Street the red-painted wooden house of the president of the university, Thomas Hill, who had been inaugurated in the war year 1862, during James's brief tenure as a law student.

Harvard was still rather bare. Plain brick buildings stood in a rectangular yard, overhung by slender elms, their uncurtained windows disapproving of privacy or adornment; there was still only a low wooden fence around the yard, and the gates were open to every

passerby. On the far side of the yard the town square was shaded
by the great elm that grew at its center. Cambridge was still a rural
village, but the wooden houses scattered around the square were
giving way to blocks of brick buildings. Immigrants were beginning
to move into little houses on muddy lanes in the district north of
the square, and every few minutes a jingling horsecar left the square
for Boston.

The horsecar ride to Charles Street took forty minutes, in a long
wooden omnibus pulled along a buried track by two weary little mis-
matched horses. Working men and women filled the cars going into
Cambridgeport and Boston in the morning, and in the evening it was
filled by college men going into town for a night of drinking at the
Parker's House bar, for a dancing party on Beacon Hill, or to the
whores on Shawmut Avenue. The men going to Shawmut were a
distinct group, proud of their exploits and even of the diseases that
ravaged them.[20]

The rural village was visibly giving way to suburb. But carriages
were still rare, and there was little traffic on the unpaved roads. A few
minutes' walk took one among farms and orchards.[21]

William helped the family move from Boston, and drifted with the
others to Cambridge, giving up his furnished room without explanation. The project of completing his medical degree and securing an
appointment at the hospital had been vaguely deferred. He was as excitable as ever, but his spirit was depressed and he seemed resigned to
ill health and a kind of dependency.[22] Alice, too, was ill; her immo-
bilizing hysteria had not greatly improved, and in the fall after they
were settled in Cambridge Aunt Kate accompanied her to New York
for treatment.[23] A physician, Charles F. Taylor, had had great success
in treating hysteria with a course of vigorous exercise and the lifting
of weights; Alice was to be in residence in his little sanitarium for a
long course of such treatments.[24]

Other than William, who was ill, there was little company for
Henry in Cambridge that winter. Wendell Holmes, it was true, had
come back from his European triumph and he visited in Quincy
Street regularly to spend evenings with Henry and William.[25] Holmes
was greatly enriched in knowledge and self-confidence, and spoke
easily of the London season; his manner was becoming ever more
blunt and masculine. He and Henry continued to exchange visits,[26]
but a visit was no longer a question of strolling over the brow of the
hill, and both had their work. Holmes had gone into an office in
Boston and begun his law career, having set aside his ambition to be a

poet and a man of letters, at least temporarily, while Henry, persisting in his own program, was equally busy. He sat painfully at the desk in the Quincy Street parlor writing reviews. *The Nation* continued to ask for regular contributions. To his annoyance, there was never enough time for the weekly to send him proofs of his articles, which always appeared with errors that pained him. But *The Atlantic* and *The Nation* wanted all his output, and paid him well enough, and when *The Galaxy* wrote to ask for his next story, he answered a little sharply that he had nothing for them just now and didn't expect to write any fiction for a while.[27]

To vary his solitude, and to replenish his store of materials, he began a systematic program of paying calls. He made it a rule to see someone outside the family, no matter who it was, every day.[28] This quickly became a habitual exercise: paying calls and laying plans for the calls of the future became a part of his daily routine,[29] habits that remained with him to the end of his life. Eventually he would create for himself a web of hundreds of friendships, assiduously maintained, in Europe and America, that would serve him like a network of observation posts, an array of satellites that gave him a constantly changing map of the Western world.[30]

The institution of being "at home" was a great help to James's program of paying calls. The hostesses of Cambridge and Boston in those postwar years, following Annie Fields's example, had begun to adopt the fashions of Europe. Some were "at home" to visitors on regular days; a few were at home on every weekday afternoon until seven, when it was the hour to dress for dinner. James could put these houses on his calendar. Boston and Cambridge hostesses, like their European sisters, aside from being excellent company themselves, mediated friendships among the men; each made a nucleus around which the men could gather; and James who had no club, no place of business, relied on the new salons in which to make friends among his peers.

James called regularly on the Nortons at Shady Hill, for instance, the estate just outside Cambridge where the widowed matriarch of the family, Catherine Eliot Norton, presided. It was a low, white-columned house like an Italian villa, on fifty acres that had come to her from her father's family, the Eliots, and where three of her six children continued to live. She was an heir to the great interlinked merchant families of Nortons and Eliots that had taken Harvard College as their special responsibility. She kept a carriage, unique in

Cambridge, with her late husband's and her initials on the doors like a crest.

When her son Charles married, he brought his bride, Susan Sedgwick, home to Shady Hill; it was in the library there that Henry James in the summer of 1864 had received from Norton like a sword-tap on the shoulder the promise of a career in letters. Norton remained a cool and somewhat distant figure, however, and Susan was preoccupied with their five small children. But Grace Norton, the younger of two sisters who had remained at Shady Hill, was an intelligent and charming woman who made James especially welcome.

Another sociable scene to which James had access was Longfellow's magnificent old house on Brattle Street, appropriated from its Tory owners in the Revolution and still known as the "Craigie house" for the clever Whig doctor who had claimed it as the spoils of war. The house looked down from its formal garden across the Cambridge marshes to the river. Longfellow, whose fame was long a fact of his existence, his flowing beard and tousled locks almost as familiar to the general public as the portrait of General Washington, in his old age had immersed himself in a great undertaking, a translation of Dante's *Divine Comedy* into English verse. A little circle of gentlemen met with him on Wednesday evenings to talk over the latest cantos of the translation. They were a genteel band of Pre-Raphaelites, a masculine company, whose center was the college.

After Longfellow himself, the leading figure in the group was James Lowell, whose lamplit lectures Henry had attended in his own solitary stay at Harvard two years before. Lowell lived at Elmwood, in the rural outskirts of Cambridge, an easy walk or drive from the college that was the center of his world. He was a handsome man who wore the full square beard of the day. His blond hair was parted in the center, combed back from his broad forehead, and worn a little longer than was fashionable. He was a teacher, poet, and scholar, and while his poems had grown very popular during the war he seemed resigned to doing no great work of his own, and to nourish instead the careers of his pupils.

Henry enjoyed visits to Elmwood, which seemed to embody the New England spirit. The great square wooden house, painted dove-gray and shaded by the high slender trees that gave it its name, seemed somehow ancient, although in truth it was only a little older than its inhabitants. The rooms were white and bare, doors and uncurtained windows were left open in good weather, and the house was sunlit and clean as a dairy. Lowell's books and steel engravings set a tone of high intellectual pleasure, and Lowell himself for all his inner sadness was addicted to jokes and childlike puns, to every sort of study and play with language. He would become a good, lifelong friend, and would appear as a character in two of James's novels.[31]

James and Lowell soon found that they shared an interest, an avuncular fondness for William D. Howells, an attractive blond young man whose drooping dark mustache screened a wide sensitive mouth, always a little parted. Howells had come to Cambridge just the summer before, and he was already a frequent visitor at Elmwood. There was a hint of belligerence, not unattractive, in Howells's heavy eyes and lax square jaw. He looked as if he had been spoiled by attentions. He was twenty-nine—six years older than James—had lived abroad, had been American consul in Venice, and had just published a book of travel sketches, but for all this he seemed the younger of the two. James and he soon became friends, and on their long walks together Howells usually listened as the other spoke. He would always be a sort of pale alter ego, his life the mild, stay-at-home one that James would reject, and the choice between their two courses would be the theme of some of James's greatest works.[32]

Howells had just begun work at *The Atlantic Monthly*, reading manuscripts and making recommendations to the editor, Fields; he also read proofs, checked facts, answered inquiries, and wrote book reviews. Soon after his arrival, Fields had handed him the manuscript of Henry James's "Poor Richard," and told him that they wanted everything that James would give them. And so one of Howells's first duties had been to write to James to inform him that "Poor Richard" had been accepted. Howells wrote with the real warmth of his own admiration for the story, and expressed the wish that James would submit more of his work.[33]

Perhaps they first met at Lowell's; James did not clearly recall their first meetings in the fall of 1866, but they soon settled into a habit of long walks through Cambridge on Sunday afternoons. This became a fixed part of James's calendar. The two young men in their tall hats and long coats, swinging their walking sticks idly, followed Concord Street up its gradual rise to the Fresh Pond, where there were ice-skaters that winter; or still farther into the unpeopled countryside, among the soundless fields, the stony pastures, the clear-faced ponds, the rugged little orchards,[34] and then still farther up into the Arlington hills, from which they could look back at the distant blue plain of Boston and the sea beyond. On their return, on a sunny winter day, they might stop to stroll through the sandy paths or rest on the benches of the Botanic Garden that the college kept on Linnaeus Street. Sometimes James took Howells to his viewpoint in Mt. Auburn Cemetery, on the bluff over the Charles, where new graves lay beside winding tree-shaded paths.

They began by talking literature, and soon progressed to talking of themselves. They had already made different choices, and their paths had begun to diverge. Howells, too, was the son of a Swedenborgian socialist, but he had remained within his father's orbit and become a newspaper reporter and a halfhearted abolitionist. He had been given the chance to write Lincoln's campaign biography and, as a reward for the biography, had been given three years in Venice as American consul and so had escaped the war. Returning from Venice, he had lived briefly in New York, but he soon put himself under Fields's tutelage and allowed himself to be brought to Cambridge.

Now Howells had settled down in a house on Sacramento Street in Cambridge, with a wife, Elinor Mead, a thin and pale woman of exactly his own age. The two were well matched. Howells was a composed listener, and Elinor Mead was nervously, energetically talkative. They had obscure fears; they clung to each other, and adored their pretty blond three-year-old daughter. (She was very like himself, Howells said.) They had used every penny of their savings to furnish their little house in Cambridge.[35]

On his first visit to the house on Sacramento Street, James found it on a quiet, unpaved street, "a little, high-perched wooden house."[36] Twin pine trees framed the gate, and a prettily blooming vine hung over the door. Behind the house, there was a profusion of pear trees and grape vines, blackberries, currants, and rhubarb, and indoors it was snugly if simply furnished. James had been invited to Sunday dinner, and this was a great occasion for the modest household. The little girl, Winifred, was dressed in her best blue gingham dress with white edging at the neck. Elinor wore a dress decorated with rosettes, and had wound a purple ribbon into her braided blond hair. Dinner was poached salmon, a sirloin roast, and a salad served with wooden spoon and fork. At the end the African cook, Mrs. Little, served a bread pudding with sauce. James warmly admired the little girl, Winifred, which endeared him to Elinor, and the dinner was a success.[37] Soon he began to dine twice a month at Sacramento Street, and then nearly every Sunday, after his walk with Howells.

On those Sunday walks, James spoke of his ambition to write criticism that would outdo the French, and to use the new technology of realism in fiction. He opened his heart and his ambitions, and How-ells listened ever so patiently and genially and suggestively, and this active listening won him to James irresistibly.[38]

The little circle of calls that Henry had begun to make did not sat-isfy him. Despite the difficulty of sitting up at his writing desk, each night before retiring he wrote letters, maintaining relations with his family and friends in America and abroad, in Florida, New York, New-port, Boston, Paris, and Berlin.

Tom Perry proved to be a good and dutiful correspondent, and so they kept up a long-distance conversation that required persistent ef-fort. Perry was dividing his time between Berlin and Paris, and to Henry he was now "Mon cher vieux Thomas":

> I'm very glad to think of you as being as much as possible in Paris—city of my dreams! I feel as if it would count to my advantage in our future talks (& perhaps walks.) When a man has seen Paris somewhat attentively, he has seen (I suppose) the biggest achievement of civi-lization in a certain direction & he will always carry with him a cer-tain little *reflet* of its splendour. . . .
>
> When I say that I should like to do as Ste. Beuve has done, I don't mean I should like to imitate him, or reproduce him in English: but only that I should like to acquire something of his intelligence & his patience and vigour. One feels—I feel at least, that he is a man of the past, of a dead generation; and that we young Americans are (with-out cant) men of the future . . . we can deal freely with forms of civilization not our own, can pick and choose and assimilate. . . . We must of course have something of our own—something distinctive and homogeneous—& I take it that we shall find it in our moral con-sciousness, our unprecedented spiritual lightness and vigour.[39]

Mary Temple remained the center of the circle that James had put into motion around her. But she no longer seemed to be in love with the increasingly worldly Holmes; instead her gentle gaze rested most often upon the scholarly, doctorial John Gray.[40]

Early in the spring, Henry was writing fiction again. He began with a short story for *The Atlantic*. It was another telling of the tale he had written the previous winter. His heroine was again visiting a New England village. Her hair was lighter, and her eyes were a darker blue, but it was she, slender and upright. The village had become a seaside resort like Swampscott. She was poor, and a widow, more deeply plunged into destitution than she had been the year before. A wealthy young man had again come up from town, and again he and she were at swords' points.

Strolling with a shotgun, he accidentally killed the heroine's little boy. It was a perfectly imagined hunting accident, shockingly unexpected, yet characteristic of the idle young man.

After this terrible accident, in the very moments afterward, the young man began to fall in love with the heroine. Strange to say, she did not immediately rebuff him. She was profoundly gentle. Her child after all was not to be pitied; the least harm one can do a human being is to kill him, James reflected. The reader saw that she was desperately poor, and that neither she nor the child had had much of a prospect of life. And so as time passed she set aside her own grief and self-pity, and did not reject the man's overtures. She kept herself intact, and she did not hate him; that was not in her character.

A friend was present when, with a few seemingly irrelevant words, she implicitly accepted an offer of marriage from the rich young man, whose name was George Bingham:

> I am at a loss to express the condensed force of these rapid words,— the amount of passion, of reflection, of experience, which they seemed to embody. They were the simple utterance of a solemn and intelligent choice; and, as such, the whole phalanx of the Best Society assembled in judgment could not have done less than salute them. What honest George Bingham said, what I said, is of little account. The proper conclusion of my story lies in the highly dramatic fact that out of the depths of her bereavement—out of her loneliness and her pity—this richly gifted woman had emerged, responsive to the passion of him who had wronged her all but as deeply as he loved her.[41]

It was a story for the women that he knew and admired, and who were his readers: who knew the reality of the death of children, the narrow limits of choice. It was their story, intensified; not so much told as performed.

Henry James was showing his skill at using the techniques of sensational fiction to tell his stories, to create suspense and interest, the lesson he had learned from Miss Braddon. But he had also begun carefully to use a new method of narration. The whole story was told by a friend, who saw it only in fitful glimpses, briefly illuminated scenes.

The story told itself through the way the characters stood as he observed them, and the action progressed as much through gestures as through their words. It was a performance, a dance on a tightrope, and the reader watched and strained to interpret, to understand: to do her share of the work. The central image was a tableau of gestures: a marriage ceremony, in which the slender American heroine enacted the solemn and joyous ritual of choice.

James felt he was learning to write, and that perhaps he had found the secret of interesting his reader: the new technique that would perfect the art of storytelling. As if stamping the mark that an artisan puts on his first piece of work as a master, he spoke in his own voice at the end:

> The reader will decide, I think, that this catastrophe offers as little occasion for smiles as for tears. My narrative is a piece of genuine prose.[42]

The story appeared in March, and Howells, who continued to admire, yet said that people were puzzled by James's stories and didn't like them, that James would have to make an audience for his work.

In April, William revealed a secret: he too had a bad back. He had developed the pain and weakness that afflicted Father and Henry, and it had kept him from continuing work at the hospital or taking his degree. He had nursed the disability in secret, and as it did not get better, he had consulted a physician at the hospital, Charles Brown-Séquard, who now recommended a course of ice treatments and a trip to Europe for a more thorough cure.

The two brothers shared their secrets for the first time. Henry too had had a downturn in health; his own back trouble had become more severe and was compounded by another difficulty that he had not shared with his family. The sedentary habits that his back imposed, and the costive diet that his mother prescribed for her children, had resulted in a persistent and painful constipation that mingled with the other pain in his lower back into a single, miserable malady, which he now confessed to William.

In this sharing of secret illnesses, Henry's affection for his older brother found for the first time an easy mode of expression. He was able to be solicitous of William's health, yet tactfully respectful of William as physician and older brother. And so they shared secrets upon which they founded a friendship.

William was applying ice to his back, which he recommended to

Henry, and he had determined to go abroad and take the cure at a German spa. Perhaps he would continue his scientific education in Germany as well, if the baths should help him. Father and Mother were now told, and their support gained; and within a week Father had arranged a letter of credit for William and a berth on the *Great Eastern*, the most modern of the new side-wheel steamers, which was to sail from New York on April 16. William set off for New York with the abruptness characteristic of all the family's movements. Henry was alone again, but with another cable link of affection to Europe.

> Dear Willie—We have not heard from you yet, altho' we daily expect a letter; but I nevertheless venture to presume upon your being alive and well—well enough at least to care to get a line from home. I am more anxious than I can say to hear how you endured your journey & in what condition you found yourself at the end of it.—I hope your letter when it comes will be very explicit on this point. We had the satisfaction of learning thro' the Cable of the safe arrival of the Great Eastern—which was a great blessing; but the message didn't mention whether you had been sick or not.—But your back, *that* is what I want to hear about. . . .The Spring arrives with little steps; the grass is green but the air is almost as cold as March.[43]

If the air still held the chill of winter, the sunlight was intense and the wide bare streets grew leafy. It was time to choose a fabric and be fitted for summer's light suits. To mark their new friendship, he chose the fabric that William had worn the year before. And as Henry was considered within the family to have infallible taste, Mother reported this as a great compliment to his brother.[44]

Henry was not entirely solitary, as he often had Alice's company. Shortly after William's departure, she had returned from New York, apparently fully recovered. They paid calls together and went into town to the theater and to lectures. Even more than Henry, Alice felt a stranger in Cambridge. She had found no congenial women friends except Susan Norton's relations: the Sedgwick sisters and Annie Ashburner, whom she described happily as "the most astonishing and delightful old maid."[45] Her Cambridge world consisted of these women, her sewing circle, and the polite charitable societies. She traveled diligently into Boston to hear lectures at Elizabeth Peabody's house on women's rights and the education of children; it was rather an arid life, brightened only by her Boston friendships with Fanny Morse and

Ellen Hooper. And then, while on a visit to Fanny Morse in Boston, Alice suffered a new attack of nerves, of hysteria that left her helpless, seemingly immobilized by inarticulate rage. Mother was obliged to go into town and bring her home in a carriage. A continuing helpless weakness of back and legs kept Alice bedridden much of the summer. When she could sit up, she again spent her hours reading in the study, silently keeping Father company.

In that difficult summer of 1867, Henry too was all but continuously bedridden, and he went out little. The ice treatments that William recommended seemed to help for a few days, but the back pain then returned redoubled, and Henry began to think that the best thing for him was simply rest. Bed rest and a heavy diet added to his malaise, which in turn made it more difficult for him to go out. Deprived of exercise and company, he felt himself losing the energy to resist his deepening depression. His horizon narrowed to his pleasant room, his big soft bed and good chairs. He spent the increasingly hot days in shirtsleeves in his room, reading.[46]

William wrote regularly from Europe, dwelling affectionately and with a curious verve on their mutual disability.

> I have been this morning to consult Dr. Duchenne (of Boulogne) who is the French authority for everything concerning the muscles. He says that he has seen many cases like ours. He counsels as Brown-Séquard does a counter-irritant, not ice which he says is dangerous, but cutaneous faradization. I am going to buy an apparatus for 180 francs. . . .[47]

As well as "faradization," electrical stimulation of the muscles, Duchenne recommended a corset, and in addition to these treatments William also planned to take the water cure at a spa near Dresden. He took an interest in each of these conflicting schemes as if it were a problem in chemistry, or as if his illness were that of a particularly interesting patient.

William was not a very satisfactory ambassador to Europe. The few days that he had been in Paris he spent resting from his journey, and Henry was disappointed to have so little news. William had little to say except that he had gone every night to the theater, which he adored: the actors' grace and the perfection of every movement and glance were astonishing, and yet the actors remained perfectly natural.[48]

Other messengers brought Henry more interesting reports. Tom

Perry was on a tour of Italy, writing ravishing accounts of the pictures, and was out of reach of replies for the time being. Howells was bringing out another book of travel sketches of Italy that summer. On his back on a sofa, Henry read Hippolyte Taine's intensely interesting journal of a trip through Italy.[49] This was criticism of an order that one did not find in English. It gave him a sense of accompanying William, Tom Perry, and Bill Howells on their travels. Everything around him seemed to pcint toward Europe, toward Italy, and the certainty that his education required him to go there. But it was not possible, and that summer he sank into depression as if into a comforting lap.

His mother grew concerned about his low spirits,[50] but her prescription continued to be bed rest and the heavy, costive diet to which Henry passively continued to submit, although he sank more deeply into depression. He did not leave Cambridge that summer, did not sleep one night away from home.[51] He ceased writing his weekly reviews for *The Nation*.[52]

A rival, John R. Dennett, had written a sour and condescending review of "Poor Richard" in the weekly.[53] The story was appearing serially in *The Atlantic*, having been held over from the previous summer because of its length. Dennett in his review simply sneered. The heroine Gertrude's affection for vulnerable, impatient young Richard he treated with contempt. How could a woman feel affection for Richard, who was so plainly inferior to the fine officer?—the officer whose correct manner and shrewd calculations Henry had meant to make the embodiment of evil. James's careful, realistic descriptions of the relations among the characters were derided as "delicate" and "over-refined."[54]

There were a few bright spots in the gloom. Howells came to the house to visit with all of the Jameses, talked Swedenborg and socialism with Father and Alice, talked shop with Henry, and shared his dismay at Dennett's stupid review.[55] Dear La Farge came up from Newport for a few days and stayed with them; he had been in New York working on a mural, and had brought some sketches with him to show. He had turned more positively to the Church and was working in murals and stained glass, on commissions. The stained glass especially entranced him, and he was mastering the difficult materials that were poisoning him, working directly in the medium of light itself. His subjects now were classical or biblical, portrayed in careful and realistic detail; he remained Henry's mentor in moral realism. He, too, was ill, recovering from another episode of lead poisoning. He went to Boston nearly every day and returned exhausted, so that to Mother's relief he did not take Henry on the long talking walks that were so hard on Henry's back.

By July the regime of rest and solitude at last seemed to be having some positive effect. Henry thought that he was steadily getting better, and he began work on a new story. He wrote a dutiful, warm review of Howells's *Italian Journeys* for Norton's *North American Review*. He started to pay calls again, and early in August he spent a Sunday afternoon reading aloud to Bill and Elinor Howells his new ghost story, a potboiler for the New York magazines, "The Romance of Certain Old Clothes."[56]

He was able to take walks again, and the exercise helped his spirits, but what he craved was stimulating company, intimate friendship. Holmes was fishing for Atlantic salmon in the rocky streams of Maine. Boston was deserted, and Cambridge had very little to offer him. Even in the fall, when friends began to return from mountains and seashore, Henry found himself still solitary. Alice was bedridden and could no longer accompany him on jaunts into Boston. Bill Howells's mother died that fall, and he had gone to Ohio for a long stay with his father. Henry was twenty-four years old, and his intimate life was locked in solitude and secrecy.[57]

Even the Fieldses had failed him as a social resource. After years of being courted, Charles Dickens had come to them in America. He had come to Boston to begin a lecture tour that Fields had arranged, to promote the books that Fields would publish.[58] Annie and James devoted themselves body and soul to Dickens and the success of his lecture tour. Their salon was suspended until further notice.

The Florida plantation had had a disastrous harvest. The first year the price of cotton had been low; and now there was very little cotton at all. Insects had rotted the bolls. Bob came home in October, looking thin and angry, drinking too much and racked by a persistent cough. After miserably searching in Boston for work, he took a clerk's position in a railroad office at Burlington, Vermont. Within a month of his arrival in Cambridge, he too was gone.

Wilky returned just as Bob was leaving. The plantation was foundering, but Wilky had not yet given it up. He thought he might do better with Bob gone. But he had come down with malaria, and after a fearful time he had come home to recover, just as he had, exhausted and wounded, from the battlefield of the war. Wilky was nearly overwhelmed with attentions from his Boston friends, and the house was made cheerful for a time by baskets of fruit and flowers and a steady stream of guests.[59]

Despite the boys' brief appearances at home, Cambridge was a prison for Henry. The social fabric was so thin that the departure of a few friends left it rent and bare. Only writing would earn his release into a larger world, and that autumn, although his health was not much improved, he systematically began writing reviews for the *North American Review*, and stories for *The Atlantic* and *The Galaxy*, again. It was hard work and required a steady expenditure of energy.

To F. P. Church, editor of *The Galaxy*:

> I sent you a fortnight ago a letter & an M.S. in different packages. As I have received no answer as yet, I am afraid one or the other has mis- carried—if not both. Or perhaps your answer has gone astray. If the M.S. has reached you—a story with my name inscribed—I beg you will let me know at your earliest convenience.[60]

The neglectful Church thereupon sent the check that was due, and James thanked him, but firmly declined to make requested changes.[61]

James's essays and tales again appeared in New York and Boston, but not in *The Nation*, where Dennett had sneered at "Poor Richard." Godkin asked Henry to resume writing reviews for *The Nation*, but he did not answer for a time.

In that dreary Cambridge winter he wrote another Civil War story. The leading character closely resembled Holmes as he had been in that epochal spring of 1865; James barely altered the details of his history and appearance. The officer, whom he called Mason, had returned from three years' service a brevetted colonel. He had been wounded and ill. He was anxious when he was away from the fight- ing, and followed the war news closely. "For three years he had been stretched without intermission on the rack of duty . . . a very ac- complished scholar, as scholars go, but a great dunce in certain social matters."

The officer was cared for by an aunt, "Mrs. Mason," who was very like Gertrude in the earlier story, very like James himself. She nursed the exhausted officer back to health. By her tenderness and affec- tion, she revived the officer's spirits; she reminded him of the ex- quisite side of life.

> The two accordingly established a friendship—a friendship that promised as well for the happiness of each as any that ever undertook to meddle with that province. If I were telling my story from Mrs. Mason's point of view, I might make a very good thing of the state-

ment that this lady had regularly determined to be very fond of my
hero; but I am compelled to let it stand in this simple shape.[62]

She brought the soldier to her own house. Generously sacrificing her
own feelings, Mrs. Mason introduced the colonel to her beautiful orphaned niece, a young heroine with whom all the young men were in
love. The officer's cure was all but completed by his falling in love
with her. But she did not fall in love with him, as she was meant to do,
for his sake; she fell in love instead with the doctor, who was learned
and modest, and rather like John Gray. The officer thereupon sank
into a sudden decline and died. "A most extraordinary case," the doctor said, quite oblivious of having killed his friend.

There was an element of black humor in the tale; Henry's spirits
evidently were recovering, for he had found an efficacious treatment
for his compounded illnesses. Imitating the course of treatment Alice
had received, he exercised with weights, and arranged for a young
Irishman to come in every day to massage his back. His health and his
appetite improved most markedly.[63]

His stories and reviews appeared steadily in other journals, and finally *The Nation* made its peace with him. Dennett wrote a review of
the new Civil War story, "A Most Extraordinary Case," and called him
one of the best American writers of short stories; James thereupon resumed writing his regular reviews for the weekly.

With a revived appetite for work, he seized upon a cartload of
hapless books that served him merely as the premise for a manifesto.
Most of the books were perfectly terrible. Historical novels and romances were selling well just then. The popular writers in their long,
simpering procession—Anne Manning,[64] James Froude,[65] Mrs. R. H.
Davis,[66] Anne Crane,[67] William Alger,[68] and Sarah Tytler[69]—all in
their different ways committed the same sin. They spread a haze of
correct sentiment over their subject, obscuring its details and difficulties. Sentiment was the enemy of historic truth.

The popular writers of historical novels made intimate judgments
of moral worth. They took their heroine's side or took up the cause of
some distinguished historical figure. What struck Henry, however, was
the vast difficulty of deciding questions of goodness. Moral qualities
showed themselves in the choices that people made privately, in
complex circumstances and with unforeseeable results. It was almost
impossible to pronounce a person positively good or bad without
knowing his secret, perhaps unknowable, history—without, that is,

detaching him from relations and surroundings in a way that was fatal to the truth of history.[70]

Even Howells, Henry said very carefully and nicely, was a sentimental writer who sacrificed historical fact to style.[71] The romance novelists were guilty of the same fallacy, and it came all the more easily to them because storytellers were unused to limiting their imagination or being restrained by fact. But that self-imposed restraint was what criticism, history, and the realistic novel all required.

True historians, like Francis Parkman, told their tale without blinking. When the Church sent Jesuits to Canada to convert the Indians, the missionaries were sacrificed in a hopeless cause; no effort had been made to establish thriving colonies. The missionaries found not noble but brutal savages, engaged in warfare, torture, and cannibalism. There was no simple, sentimental moral to be learned from the true history, but a truthful recounting of the disaster was one of the interesting chapters in the history of Mind.[72]

Let men of imagination go for their facts and research to the men of science and judgment, and let them consult the canons of historical truth.[73] Writers of imagination must master science and subject themselves to the discipline of fact. Only then would they create history, criticism, and a new realistic art; only then would they be worthy successors to the writers of the older generation, to John Ruskin,[74] to Balzac, Sainte-Beuve,[75] Renan, and Sand.[76]

Henry issued his manifesto. At the same time, he answered his own call. He reached out to review a pious biography of Father Lacordaire of the Dominican order, translated into English and published in Dublin the year before.[77] This was not the sort of reading that *The Nation*'s audience ordinarily troubled themselves with; only a few months before, Henry had told them that "we are all Protestants now."

And indeed, Henry did not give more than a few dismissive words to the book itself, the pious labor of a Dominican priest. Instead, he drew his own portrait of the famous Lacordaire. Like Renan, like Balzac imagining the villain Vautrin, Henry sketched a portrait of the inner life of a man who had shaped history.

Lacordaire had possessed the authority that accompanies great intensity of will, as well as the irresistible charm that belongs to passionate tenderness of feeling. He had both these gifts and that ambiguous virtue of the Old World, spiritual submission. He submitted himself to his order, but Henry thought it was hard to say how much he did this simply from a taste for discipline, and how much from spiritual necessity. It was impossible and unnecessary to know. They order these things much better in the Catholic Church than we do in the world, he mused. Lacordaire practiced the most painful and degrading mortifications—causing himself to be lashed to a column and scourged, having his brothers spit in his face, kissing and washing their feet. There was a certain audacity, even impudence, in his fervor.

> A certain young man of wealth, satiated with pleasure, and longing for spiritual light and repose, had presented himself to the reverend father in quest of those treasures. Lacordaire had prescribed a retreat and meditation in a religious house, and ultimately the assumption of the Dominican habit; but the young man's friends had interfered and by their importunities had prevented him from acting on this advice. . . . The reverend father received him with great severity and rebuked him for his weakness and cowardice. Then, suddenly inflamed by a sacred ardor, he commanded him to fall on his knees and lay bare his shoulders. The young man felt that it was not in him to disobey. Lacordaire seized a discipline of leathern thongs and inflicted a sound scourging. With the first blow the happy victim felt an ecstatic sense of relief. He had received his baptism.[78]

To perform such acts as this, one certainly needed that sacred audacity which is a result of grace, but one also needed a little of that grosser sort of assurance which is merely a gift of nature.

Father Lacordaire, submissive to his Church, yet exerted his ascendancy over his brothers. He founded monasteries, revived the Dominican order in France, founded schools. He became well known even in England, and his followers liked to repeat his prophecy that the stronghold of Protestant faith would fall to the old religion as a result of his work. He was a shaper of history, but whether in his inner life he was a good man, Henry declined to say. That was a quite different question.

Retreat into monastic life and purely masculine company might be a weakness, rather than an exhibition of strength. Wrestling with his own solitude, Henry ended by saying that the cloister was a temptation to passivity, a kind of death. One's duty was to enter into the world of women and men, the shackles and embarrassments of one who honestly attempts to *live*. That was the precondition of art, of courageous accomplishment.[79]

He began to pay calls again. He went down to Newport in February and visited old friends, although the place was chilly and horrible.[80] A new theater had opened in Boston, and he took the horsecar into town occasionally, alone, to see a play. But there was little intimate company. Howells was still away, and the Cambridge circle was not much larger than before. There were the Nortons, and Mrs. Norton's brother, Arthur Sedgwick, and the Lowells, Feltons, and Dixwells. The Longfellows were preparing for a long trip to Europe.

Charles Norton surprised Henry one evening by saying that he too was going abroad that summer, with his family, for an extended stay. Charles was ill, and he thought travel and a rest would be good for his health. His mother, wife, sisters, and sisters-in-law looked forward to a long stay in Europe. They would live together in the south of France and visit Italy. This would be a heavy loss to both Henry and Alice. The four young Norton and Sedgwick women made up a large part of the meager social resources that Cambridge offered.

There was the editorship of the *North American Review*. Would Henry be willing to take it over?

This required some thought. Presumably the offer had come with Fields's endorsement. Perhaps Fields was eager for the change; the *Review* had been struggling to keep itself above water. But an editor had duties that were often menial, as Henry knew from his conversations with Howells, and was always self-effacing. It was work that was the antithesis of art. It was the labor of an employee. He delicately turned the offer down.[81] Instead, he turned to writing more of the smooth, distanced, skillful stories for which he was now being paid very well,[82] and dreamed of Europe.

William was having a difficult time abroad. He was taking the cure at Teplitz, in Bohemia, bathing in cold running water. At first this had produced good results, and he wrote optimistically about his health. A new doctor had prescribed vesicants, irritating plasters applied to his back, which William thought had done him good and which he recommended to Henry (he said nothing more about electricity):

> Apply one every night on alternate sides of the spine over the diseased muscles. In the morning, prick the bubbles, and cover with a slip of rag with cerate, fastened down by cross straps of sticking plaster. Try a dozen in this way at first. Then wait two weeks and try ½ dozen more. . . .[83]

William was the only one of the James sons who had no work to do, and who was not contributing to his own support. He had exhausted the letter of credit that his father had given him, and was obliged to ask for another. In an effort to earn something, he wrote reviews of books that he came upon in Germany, and sent them to Henry, asking his help in getting them published.

> After sweating fearfully for three days, erasing, tearing my hair, copying, recopying, etc., etc., I have just succeeded in finishing the enclosed. . . .[84]

> With a mighty sweat and labor I forged the accompanying, wh. I beg you will take care of & smooth if possible the style.[85]

Each of William's submissions came with these cries of agony, but Henry, who was happy enough to make their shared illness a bond, drew the line here. This was business. He answered briskly that William would learn to write well in time; he could not understand his brother's strange intensity of feeling about the work of writing. William apologized generously:

> The "strange intensity of my feeling" on the subject of article writing, of wh. you speak is to be explained by the novelty of the exercise, & by the enormous difficulty I experience in turning out my clotted thought in logical & grammatical procession. I find more freedom however in each successive attempt, and hope before long to write straight ahead as you do. What an activity by the bye you are displaying in the *Nation*! I like your last articles very much indeed.[86]

Henry carefully revised William's reviews, and sent them on to *The Nation*, turning the fees over to his father. He revised one book review extensively, removing William's remarks on the French character, and William protested half humorously that the heart of his article had been cut out. It was all terribly difficult for William, as Henry knew, and he tried to be cheerful and empathetic. Henry's own work was appearing in all the journals that William read, and American tourists in Teplitz, not knowing of their relation, innocently praised Henry to him. In February, Henry wrote confidingly that he had been offered the *North American Review* and had turned it down.

William replied on March 4, in despair that his cure had failed completely. He was worse than before. He thought perhaps he had overdone the baths. He did not know what to do, except to linger on in Germany and try the cure again more carefully. Abruptly he began to criticize Henry's stories, and now that he had begun it was as if he could not stop—he went on for pages, bitterly. Henry's stories showed a "certain neatness & airy grace" but they dealt with sexual subjects that William found unsympathetic. Besides, they lacked sentiment. There was something cold in them, a want of heartiness and *unction*. The material of the stories was *thin*, "so that they give a certain impression of the author clinging to his gentlemanliness tho' all else be lost." William adopted Dennett's manly, condescending tone, and repeated Dennett's complaint: Henry's stories were delicate, overrefined:

> If I were you, I'd select some problem, literary or philosophical, to study on. There's no comfort to the mind like having some special task, and then you cd. write stories by the way for pleasure & profit.[87]

This sad letter arrived on March 26, and cost Henry a great deal of deep regret and pain. But he immediately wrote a long reply. He ignored William's criticisms, and responded in warm and brotherly fashion to William's despair. He sent his sympathy at the failure of William's cure and with it of all his immediate hopes.[88] A few weeks later William wrote again, apologetically. He praised Henry's latest story, "A Most Extraordinary Case," which he thought must be drawn from life, but he failed to recognize Holmes or Henry himself in the tale, or to quite see what it was about.[89]

Summer was approaching. Another summer in the damp Cambridge heat, with only his invalid family for company, was out of the question. Henry wanted the cool mountain air, and while his limited means allowed him few choices, he at last settled on a remote inn in Jefferson, New Hampshire, thirty miles north of North Conway. Like Balzac, he said, he would put on the white robes of a monk for the summer and concentrate himself upon his work. But absolute solitude evidently was not required, for he invited Wendell Holmes to visit him. Holmes's acceptance was a little vague; he was busy, and would write when he was free.[90]

Henry brought books and writing paper with him to New Hampshire, and alone for the moment, under the trees in a parklike evergreen woods, he surrendered himself to imagination. "To sit in the open shade, inhaling the heated air, and while you read . . . to glance up from your page at the clouds and trees, is to do as pleasant a thing as the heart of man can desire."[91]

He had brought with him George Eliot's and George Sand's most recent books to review. Henry thought of both women as having accomplished what they were likely to do. The Englishwoman, Eliot, had a more mature and masculine intellect than any novelist of the day. But Sand, although she lacked scientific philosophy, was the greater novelist; she was indeed the greatest novelist writing in English or French. Her style and her spirit were superior not only to the meager naturalism of Thackeray and Dickens, but to the intellectualized tales of George Eliot. Her mind seemed not to have isolated and contracted itself in the regions of perception, but had expanded with longing and desire.[92]

There was a new French novel from Octave Feuillet; and a biography of Mme. Swetchine, that touched him in a still more personal way. The two French works had been translated into English, but after looking at the English versions Henry turned to the French originals.

The translation of Feuillet was just badly done: pretentious, vulgar, and incorrect.[93] Perhaps the novel was untranslatable. Feuillet's book was a perfectly successful novel in French, but in English the story itself seemed somewhat bizarre. The protagonist, M. Camors, was a cynical villain. In his youth, he had fallen in love with a young widow who had an infant daughter. She was prevented by her family from marrying him, and in compensation the widow offered to bring up her little girl to be his wife. He assented coldly and vaguely. The little girl submitted when the time came; this in itself was odd, a reminder of the tyrannical authority of the French mother. But the girl was not a victim; she conquered Camors with her beauty and her scorn. He fell in love with her, and knowing that there was nothing he could do to alter her contempt for him, he committed suicide.

This all struck Henry as unreal, unnatural, and morbid, from the American point of view. Still, it was ingenious. He put it in the back of his mind.[94]

The biography of Mme. Swetchine was also translated very poorly, and made one ask troubling questions. Her life, even more than the language in which it was recorded, was inaccessible to the American temperament. But it was not the moral principle that was lost in translation, it was the touch and feel and odor of the Old World. National character, like conventional distinctions of dress between men and women, was a costume that one might put on or take off. But the person who knew only one language, like the ordinary American or

Frenchman, hardly knew even that one well. Mme. Swetchine was a cosmopolite; and there was something especially intriguing to Henry in a woman from the provinces who had come to the capital of Europe and triumphed there.

Mme. Swetchine had lived in St. Petersburg, and Russia, like America, was a province on the distant borders of Europe. She had gone to Paris after the July revolution of 1830, and for twenty years thereafter, until the second Napoleon had transfigured the landscape once more, she had maintained a salon. She had been a major figure in the history of France, and it was through her salon that her influence was chiefly exerted. The phenomenon was strange to American eyes (or so Henry assumed, condescendingly): she had held no position in government, and had made no claims to literary distinction. It was only that a small circle of people exercised power in France and shaped its history, and she was in the center of that circle.[95] Here was a bit of the true history of Europe, the secret history whose inner life Balzac had portrayed. But some firsthand experience of the world in which she lived, the air of reality, somehow had to be conveyed if the reader was to understand the moral qualities that were embodied in her life.[96]

The inn at Jefferson was a good place to work, and when he had written reviews of these books for *The Nation* and *North American Review* he continued to develop his thoughts in a series of stories that were half literary theory and half sensational fiction. One, "Gabrielle de Bergerac," was a historical novelette, for which Fields on receiving it later that summer paid him the astonishing sum of eight hundred dollars. It was set in the last days of the old regime in France: a story of a young boy and his tutor, fleshed out with realistic details drawn from his own memory.

The second story was a romance in which an ancient curse, transmitted in the blood of an old family, hinted at the reality of venereal disease.[97] There was a curious, wise old priest in this story, a highly self-controlled man, his passions deeply hidden, who greatly resembled James himself, and who was at work on a great history of the Catholic Church in America, a history that was respectful but perfectly factual. This work would never be published, he knew, because it lacked heartiness and *unction*.

Finally, at the end of the summer James wrote a realistic story, quite different from the others. In it, two young men, Osborne and Grahame, had a loving friendship. Osborne was big, hearty, and handsome in a manly way. Grahame was slim, intelligent, and perceptive.

The friendship between the two men was intense: it was the first and deepest tie—the brotherly bond. But then Grahame became obsessed with a woman, and Osborne lost him. The heroine was bewitching. Intelligent and charming, she was an American Swetchine. She was not a beauty, but her intelligence, moral clarity, and charm made her irresistible. Her frank gaze drew both Grahame and Osborne to her. The big man was overwhelmed by a confused passion of love, anger, jealousy, and suspicion. He imagined the woman was a devil, but his fear and hatred of this gentle woman were only the distorted face of his own jealousy and loss.[98] The effeminate Grahame conveniently died, and for Osborne the author devised a happy ending in a complacent marriage. With the help of the American heroine, he left the easy path of brotherly relations, and entered the world of women and men.

July 29

Dear Wendell,

. . . I have now been here quite long enough to learn the long and short of the place & have at least proved that it is habitable. At the present moment, I am sorry to say, it is very little more. . . . I inhabit a great racketing roadside tavern, where I feel sadly remote & unfriended. . . . Come as soon as you can, & write me, if your letter will precede you. I have lots of questions, but I keep them. Farewell. . . .

P.S. Let me fairly get it off my conscience that it's mortally slow & stupid here. *Dixi;* now if you're bored, don't say I lied.[99]

Wendell declined. He had begun to write digests of court reports for a new law journal. This was a first step toward writing scientifically about the law; their old shared ambition of being men of letters had revived. But as this scholarly work was undertaken in addition to his labors in a Boston law office, he was stretched to the limit and could not take any time away from his work. He, too, was ill with the familiar intestinal disorder that they called "the common enemy."

Dear Wendell,

I'm sorry you're worked so hard—sorry you can't come up—sorry you've been ill—& sorry that while you were at it, you didn't write me the least little bit longer letter. Of course, with so many sorrows,

I can't expect to write a very long one myself. Damn the digests! My Wendell, you're a truly noble soul & I pray the Lord that something fine will come of it all. . . . The brevity of your note broke my heart. But, seriously, of course, you've far other deeds [to perform] than to scribble gossip to such as me & I grant you a delicious pardon. I note within the book & volume of my soul in indelible letters, your approbation of my article. I wish you were here to sniff & twig the view. The breeze is cool & moist, the clouds low & heavy, the mountains dark and sullen. But if you can't, you can't. . . .[100]

His work for the summer was done, and there was a certain letdown of feeling as a result. He had evidently reconciled himself to the necessary limitations of the friendship with Holmes, but still it was difficult to be alone, and in August, as the early northern autumn drew on and the light waned, he became depressed. This second episode was a warning that depression was a state that would recur with varying severity throughout his life. The colors drained from his world, and he was tempted to sink into the languorous dusk.

He returned to Cambridge in September, his present work done and nothing else immediately at hand. He found that Alice was still housebound, a semi-invalid, troubled in back, legs, and nerves. Word had come back from England that Charles Norton had grown more seriously ill on his voyage, and that the family would linger in England until he was better, before going on to France. Lowell, too, was thinking of going abroad. The landscape would be increasingly barren.

A new family had arrived in the Jameses' circle, it was true: Francis and Elizabeth Boott, widower father and daughter, home from a long sojourn in Italy, had descended like exotic birds into the plain fields of Newport and Cambridge. Although they had returned in 1865, after the war, it was now that the Jameses made their acquaintance. Elizabeth was twenty-two, three years younger than Henry, and they had returned to reacquaint themselves with American men and women, and perhaps for her to marry.

But Henry did not cultivate an intimacy with the Bootts. He sank into his depression: stopped writing, stopped paying calls, stopped even reading.[101]

He again tried the "lifting" therapy that had helped Alice, exercising with the weights for two months. He found that his muscles were strengthened and his back was eased, and his spirits recovered considerably.[102] But he was now persuaded that he could not live in

Cambridge. He, too, would try the curative powers of travel. William suggested a tour of England, and his father recommended the water cure at an English resort, Great Malvern, from which he himself had benefited at Henry's age. Henry agreed to go to Malvern. He thought he might then go on to Paris, if the baths lightened his spirits and eased his back sufficiently. And once on the Continent, Italy was not far off. He yearned for light, for congenial company, for materials with which to work.

BOOK II

The Difficulty of Uniting

Work and Love,

Justice and Beauty

10

RESTORING HIS SPIRITS
IN ENGLAND

Steamers bound for England departed from the foot of Manhattan, and the path to Europe accordingly led Henry back to New York in February 1869. Aunt Kate went back with him; she and Cousin Helen Perkins were planning a journey to Italy of their own, and Aunt Kate would spend the winter with the Perkinses on Fourteenth Street until it was time for them to go. Henry visited for a few days with them, and the ladies helped him shop and pack. The visit also gave him time to call on Mary Temple, who was visiting her newly married sister, Kitty, in Pelham, a rural town just north of the city.

Pelham was only a brief ride by carriage or rail from Manhattan, where the winter round of assemblies, balls, and dances was in full spate, and Mary Temple moved through them surrounded by a cloud of male Emmet, Temple, and James cousins. She wrote faithfully to John Gray.

Dear Mr. Gray—I will write you as nice a letter as I know how, but I would much rather have a nice talk with you. . . . I feel as if I were in Heaven to-day and all because the day is fine and I have been driving all morning in a little sleigh in the fresh air and sunshine, until in spite of myself I found I had stopped asking for the time being the usual inward question of why I was born. . . . Then we are so near the town that we often go in for the day & do a little shopping, lunch with some of our numerous friends, and come out again, with a double relish for the country. We all went in, on a spree, the other night and stayed at the Everett House; from which, as a starting point, we poured in a strong force, upon Mrs. Gracie King's ball—a very grand affair, given for a very pretty Miss King, at Delmonico's.[1]

She adored music and she loved to dance. She had a singular grace in movement, Henry remembered, original and unconventional as it was careless and natural. But to his eye, she never looked better than when she was at the piano, in which she delighted, at which she had ardently worked, and where, slim and straight, her head and shoulders constantly, sympathetically swaying, she played with an admirable touch and a long surrender.[2]

This free movement and surrender was one mood; the other, more frequent, was her ceaseless, restless intellectual doubt. She was troubled at her lack of perfect faith, and she struggled to arrive at an intellectual resolution of her fears. Her long conversations with William James and John Gray were questioning and introspective. She believed that in some way her life should be an emulation of Jesus', but she was unable to find the manner in which this could be true.

Henry visited her in Pelham, where they had their first talk in many months. He remembered her coming into the parlor, ever so erectly slight, so pale and fair. She had been ill, but her thinness and pallor were becoming, and she had lost none of her charm. She glided as swiftly and gracefully to him as ever, tossed her head characteristically, and laughed as unreservedly, her wide mouth parted, showing her white teeth.[3]

She was not quite recovered from her illness. He asked how well she slept, if coughing still kept her up at night. "Sleep," she said. "Oh, I don't sleep, *I've given it up!*" She said it with her old laugh, and Henry was reassured, although later the memory of this moment would take on an ominous tone.[4]

The house was quiet and spacious, empty in the early afternoon, and they talked comfortably for an hour. She called him "Harry" in the old way. He would go to England, first, he said, and try to recover his health. Then he would go on to the Continent, certainly to Paris and perhaps, if he could manage it, to Italy. It was to be an indefinite stay; he hoped to return with his health restored.

Mary was pleased for him, and thought that a trip to Europe was just what he needed. She immensely admired George Eliot, as he knew. Perhaps in London he would meet the great novelist; if he did, he was to give her Mary's love. She envied Henry, and wished she were going with him. It was wholly detestable that he was going without her. A trip to Europe was just what she needed, and she hoped to go abroad next summer for her own health, to spend the winter in Italy. Perhaps she would be able to travel with friends. She and Henry would meet in Rome next winter. There, that was agreed; she smiled. He left her standing at the door, her face open and affectionate; the memory he carried away was of her solitary struggle, in the wide American desert.[5]

The *China* sailed the next day for Liverpool. It was more than nine years since Henry had last crossed the ocean, in another of these old steamers, but the nighttime creakings and shriekings were familiarly unchanged. It went swiftly, scudding before a steady winter wind.

He had no definite plans. He had turned over to his father the substantial earnings of his fruitful summer and fall, more than two thousand dollars, including the miraculous eight hundred dollars that Fields had paid for his historical novelette, *Gabrielle de Bergerac*, and he had received in exchange, most generously, a letter of credit for five thousand dollars in gold, one thousand British pounds sterling. This would be ample for the costs of travel and of taking the waters at Malvern. Other than Dr. Raynor's sanatorium at Malvern, he did not know where he would live, or what he would do. He was keyed up to an intensity of anticipation greater than he had ever experienced.

The *China* landed in Liverpool on a gusty, cloudy, overwhelmingly English morning at the end of February.[6] Black steamers knocked about in the yellow Mersey, under a sky so low that they seemed to touch it with their funnels, and in the thickest, windiest light. Most of the passengers hurried to join a stream of dark-coated people setting off for the railroad station and the train to London. Others were being met at the wharf. Some of his shipboard American companions invited Henry to come with them for a look around Liverpool or to meet later at a hotel. But he stole away from everyone and gave his day and evening to taking his first draft of Europe on his own. He had no appointments to keep, and so he wandered in the soot-blackened streets like a man who finds more money than usual in his pocket and chinks it idly and pleasantly before addressing himself to the business of spending. He had such a consciousness of personal freedom as he hadn't known for years; a deep taste of change and liberty, of having nobody and nothing to consider.[7]

He had his trunk taken to the Adelphi Hotel, and after his first walk through the blustery streets he had a late breakfast alone in the hotel coffee room, Radley's. He had buttered muffins and tea, perhaps also a boiled egg and a dab of marmalade. Trying to recall the moment, as Miss Bosanquet's fingers rested on the keys, he only distinctly remembered the muffins. The waiter had poured steaming hot water from the kettle into a slop bowl, and had set the covered plate of buttered muffins on the bowl. He continued dictating:

> I was again and again in the aftertime to win back the homeliest notes of the impression, the damp and darksome light washed in from the steep, black, bricky street, the crackle of the British "sea-coal" fire, much more confident of its function, I thought, than the fires I had left, the rustle of the thick, stiff, loudly unfolded and refolded "Times," the incomparable truth to type of the waiter, truth to history, to literature, to poetry, to Dickens, to Thackeray . . . an arrangement of things hanging together with a romantic rightness that had the force of a revelation.[8]

He sat in the window seat eating his breakfast, looking out into the street. He pictured himself walking into the future, down the middle of an endless waiting display that was divided between the familiar and the strange.

He remembered England from his visits as a child; and then too he had so intensely imagined the world of Thackeray and Dickens. The buttered muffins and the scrawny waiter led to everything else; it was one fabric of language, dress, religion. He felt as if he were a stranger abruptly introduced into a circle of people, preoccupied and animated with their own concerns, and yet he had a miraculous awareness of the matters they conversed about, so as to need no word of explanation before joining in.[9]

The next day, having slept late and lingered in Liverpool for his midday meal, he went by rail to London. He had telegraphed ahead for a room at Morley's Hotel, on Trafalgar Square. On his arrival he identified himself to the clerk and went into the coffee room while the clerk investigated the available rooms. He remembered the shining mahogany wainscots and the cheerful coal fire. He lounged beside the fire and read a newspaper; at last he was summoned to inspect a large, dim chamber filled by a great four-poster. He took the room, and after he had dined in the coffee room, he went upstairs to bed. The towering, flickering shadows cast by his bedroom candle made the room unutterably romantic.

In the morning, Trafalgar Square was filled with a steady stream of noisy traffic. Morley's stood beside the spare old church of Saint Martin's-in-the-Fields. To his left as he came out into the square was the wide mouth of a broad avenue, the Strand, that swept past the new railroad station and came to an end at Charing Cross. There was a little shop in Charing Cross, where he hastened to buy a pair of gloves, conscious of a sense of deflowering this first delight. Still farther to the south lay a murky realm of crooked streets stretching down to the Thames.[10]

London straddled the Thames. The opaque river meandered through its broad plain from the west, and then ran swiftly through the old city. The gaslit Strand lay on the north bank, a well-remembered street of shops and theaters, flowing with life. Pedestrians crowded the streets, and an extraordinary variety of carriages, hackney cabs, and horse-drawn lorries crowded the road. As he went eastward along the Strand from Trafalgar Square he plunged back in time. The Strand became Fleet Street, the streets opening from it grew narrower and more crooked; wandering into them he found himself in the little courts and mews of Dickens's London: the Inns of Court, where miniature staircases ran up from tiny courtyards and dark twisting overhung streets ran down to the Thames.

To the west, however, lay the new imperial London of the Horse Guards and Buckingham Palace, immense and fashionable; and still farther west, the comfortable enclave of Mayfair, with its dignified little squares of grand houses. Beyond that again lay Hyde Park and Kensington Garden. Fashionable London had slowly migrated westward over the years, into cleaner air and water, more spacious parks and gardens.

He sent a message to the Nortons, who were in a Kensington flat. The previous summer they had lingered in the country, but Charles's health seemed to have been restored sufficiently for them to plan a winter in London before going on to the Continent. An invitation to dine came promptly back, and Henry took a hansom cab westward down Piccadilly to half-suburban Kensington. The light two-wheeled hansom was a wonderful way to travel; the passenger had an unobstructed view; the driver was behind him on a high little perch, like a Venetian gondolier.

The Nortons' warm, brightly gaslit flat in Queen's Gate Terrace, just south of Kensington Gardens, was a cheerful refuge from the dark, cold streets. The elder Mrs. Norton had let Shady Grove on a long-term lease to cousins, and had moved her entire household to England—her daughters Grace and Jane, her son Charles, his wife, Susan, their four children; Susan's sister, Sara Sedgwick, joined them as well, making her first visit to England and English cousins, the Darwins. The Eliot-Norton-Sedgwick extended family made up a charming little Anglo-American society by themselves. Charles Norton, whose supposed illness had been the premise for the whole household's moving to England, did seem pale; perhaps his pallor was exaggerated by his very high forehead and drooping blond American mustache. He was as always rather distant and condescending; Henry and he had little rapport; but the women made a charming circle of talk. On that first evening there was another guest, Albert Rutson, a kind, slim, well-dressed gentle young man of an old Cumberland family, just old enough himself to have distinctly taken up the character of confirmed bachelor.[11]

The next morning, Henry began his search for rooms that he could take by the month. He meant to see London before making his way to the water cure at Malvern. The search was dispiriting. London was immense, dark, and noisy. It was far bigger than any city in which he had been, far denser; the very air was thick with age and dirt. London was a northern city; even in the rare intervals of pale sun, the light had a thin watery cast, the sky a brownish tint; soot fell in visible flakes from the smoky chimneys. When there was not a thin persistent drizzle, the dark air soon filled with yellowish acid fog.[12] Landladies were coarse, and the rooms he saw were dark and dreary, impossible to imagine taking.

It was Albert Rutson who solved the problem of rooms. Rutson himself had a second-floor flat in Mayfair, in a little house that was kept by a pensioned family retainer, Mr. Lazarus Fox. At Rutson's suggestion, Henry presented himself to Mr. Fox. The ground-floor rooms were vacant, and Henry took them on the spot.

The flat was on Half Moon Street, whose evocative name summoned up vague associations with Lord Byron, who had lived there forty or fifty years earlier. The narrow street ran for only a few hundred feet from Piccadilly, opposite the Green Park, up to a little square, and was solidly lined with the sooty brick façades of the last century. It was not entirely unlike the older streets near Washington Square. The ground floor was rather dark, and the rooms were decorated with heavy furniture and framed, glazed, colored pictures cut from the *Illustrated London News* and waxed flowers. The uproar of Piccadilly hummed away at the end of the street, and the rattle of a hansom passed in the street close by. A sudden horror of the whole place came over him, like a tiger-pounce of homesickness. London was hideous, vicious, cruel, and overwhelming, as indifferent as nature herself to the single life.[13]

> My own dearest Mother, I have been debating with myself for the past half hour as to whether my being horribly homesick this evening is a reason for scribbling these few lines. . . . What is the good of having a mother—and such a mother—unless to blurt out to her your passing follies and miseries? At all events, sitting here in this dreary London, between my fire and my candles, I must begin a letter, or else I shall begin to howl and drive the poor landlord to send out for a policeman. Yes, I confess it without stint or shame, I am homesick—abjectly, fatally homesick. Tomorrow, doubtless, I shall be better—the crisis will have passed, but meanwhile until bedtime, let me be my own dear mother's son.[14]

Morning indeed restored his spirits. The landlord, Lazarus Fox, was a type of the old family retainer, and Henry gratefully found himself cared for with great intelligence and tact. He was aware that despite Aunt Kate's, Cousin Helen's, and his own best efforts, everything he owned from his trunk to his boots was indelibly provincial and American. Mr. Fox took him in hand, however, and he gradually supplied himself with clothes, boots, hairbrushes, hair wash, brilliantine. He trimmed his curly beard and brushed brilliantine into it. He consulted Mr. Fox as to where he might go for dinner.

"Well, there is the Bath Hotel, sir, a very short walk away, where I should think you would be very comfortable indeed. Mr. So-and-So dines at his club, sir—but there is also the Albany in Piccadilly, to which I believe many gentlemen go."[15]

Henry made a single venture into the coffee room of the Bath

Hotel, which was on Piccadilly above the Green Park, not far from the new quarters of the Royal Academy. He dined that evening in solitary state at a heavy mahogany table, with neither company nor atmosphere, and did not return. He fell back on the Albany, a little eating house a few steps farther up Piccadilly. The eating house had taken its name from the grand block of apartments across the road, formerly the town residence of the Duke of York and Albany. But the eating house itself was not in the least grand. It was small, to begin with, and was divided into a half-dozen booths like horse stalls. The shoulder-high mahogany partitions were each furnished with a narrow, un-cushioned ledge; two randomly assorted pairs of male diners faced each other across the narrow oak table between. Above the darkened mahogany wainscoting, the sooty dark-yellow walls were decorated with a dozen sallow prints—the Derby favorite of 1807, the Bank of England, Her Majesty the Queen. The air was filled with smoke and noise and bodies; Henry bathed in English company and atmosphere.

His dreams of lamb and spinach and a charlotte russe quickly evaporated, and he sat down to a mutton chop and a rice pudding at a crowded table.[16] The Albany was cheap and vulgar, and noisy with talk; scraps of conversation overheard in the racket seemed to cast light on the larger scene. The very coarseness of the place and of the men was eloquent. It was part of a scheme, and it implied an aristocracy above as well as an abyss below; the image seemed to him rounded and complete, as definite as a Dutch picture hung on a museum wall. The vast inequalities of English life were wrong, but their highlights and black shadows were intensely more *interesting* than his monotonously prosperous, democratic America.[17]

Rutson soon invited him to breakfast to meet some friends, and James accepted with trepidation, but he was encouraged that Mr. Fox approved of his hat, coat, cravat, and gloves. Rutson's flat, two flights up, was much less gloomy than his own; Henry seemed to ascend into brightness. Pale sunlight filtered through tall windows into a Georgian sitting room, cool and classical, that seemed quite private and re-moved from the domestic arrangements in the rest of the flat. The food was simple and very good. Henry was obliged to talk, and he did so carefully and slowly, choosing his words beforehand as he always did, navigating past his stutter, so that often the rapid conversation simply flowed on past him.

Nevertheless, he was invited to a series of these late-morning breakfasts to meet a series of important men, alone or in pairs. Ten or fifteen years older than Henry, these men had quiet good manners, were well dressed and graceful. They wore neatly trimmed whiskers like his own, and they sat down promptly to their midday breakfast—often a grilled sole and a dash of marmalade—but they made a leisurely meal. There were no offices or shops to run off to. Hunting was over for the winter, and the young men had come into town for the session of Parliament that had just begun. Rutson himself was parliamentary private secretary to the newly appointed home secretary, Henry Bruce; other guests were often fellow members of the House of Commons, with positions in Gladstone's newly formed ministries, parliamentary undersecretaries of the Home Office or the Foreign Office. Parliament did not begin its sittings until late in the afternoon, and their midday breakfasts were leisurely affairs.

They spoke of the United States, where the newly elected president, General Grant, was waiting to assume office. These young Liberals were curious about their new ally. Grant would reveal himself with his first cabinet appointments. There was speculation as to whether he would make Charles Francis Adams his foreign minister—Adams had been an effective ambassador to the Court of St. James's, and would find it easy to deal with a reform-minded Liberal government. The Englishmen were prepared to admire a victorious general like Grant in his new role.

Henry had nothing to say about any of this, and was surprised and alarmed to find himself an object of curiosity, when he had hoped simply to observe and to listen. Although he had met Mr. Adams and his younger son, Henry, in Boston, he knew nothing about the other candidates for cabinet posts or their prospects. He felt he appeared foolishly ignorant of his own country's affairs. At home, political affairs in Washington—barring the president's impeachment or a war—were not really topics for polite conversation. But here one bumped into politics constantly.[18]

He received a steady stream of invitations to tea or dinner with the Norton clan at Queen's Gate Terrace, or to excursions with Grace or Susan Norton or with Sara Sedgwick. They introduced him to intellectual and artistic men of the upper middle class not unlike their Cambridge cousins. Rutson's circle were parliamentary Liberals, and the Nortons' circle were academic and intellectual Liberals: editors and contributors to the *Edinburgh Review,* on which Norton had modeled the *North American Review,* and experts on sanitary reform and poor relief. Prominent among them was Leslie Stephen, who had visited America repeatedly and knew the Lowells, the Nortons, and the Holmeses very well. Stephen seemed to live in a cloud of mutual friends and relations, an extension of the one James had left behind in Boston.

There were differences, however. The London circle was far more materialist and practical, for instance: Charles Darwin, a cousin of the Sedgwicks, was taken far more seriously than in Boston, and here Agassiz was unknown.

One Sunday morning, Leslie Stephen took James to see the zoo-logical gardens in Regent's Park, which were for Stephen a great scientific enterprise, a vast device for probing the secrets of life through studies of anatomy, physiology, and behavior. They went by underground railroad, and for Henry, who was not interested in natural history, the principal sensation of the visit to the zoo was the steam-driven train itself, roaring through its great loop under London, that carried them in minutes the whole breadth of the city from South Kensington to the edge of Regent's Park.

After breakfasting the following Monday morning at the Nortons', where he had been invited to meet a socialist scholar and an expert on sanitation,[19] Henry descended into the underground again and traveled from Kensington eastward into the City. The trip cost only sixpence—a hansom cab would have cost several shillings. In the City, he called at Baring Brothers for his mail, and was greatly pleased and cheered to find a letter from his mother.[20]

By and large, despite the novelty and economy of the underground railroad, however, he traveled by hansom cab so that he could see London all about him; he went off on his own as much and as often as he could. While Stephen was a good fellow and hospitable to a fault, he had remarkably little to say. James found the whole Norton circle charming, and he approved of their moral reforms, but he himself had as little to contribute on the questions of evolution and political economy as he had had on Grant's cabinet. He had met no literary people at all, and to his great disappointment, both the National Gallery and the Royal Academy were closed for the whole of his visit while preparations were made to move the Academy's collection to its new quarters on Piccadilly, and so he was unable even to look at paintings.

The Nortons took him one evening to hear John Ruskin lecture at University College; another day they brought him out to Ruskin's country house at Denmark Hill, which appeared to James as if it might have been the setting of a Jane Austen novel. But Ruskin was engaged when they called, and James did not meet the great man. At least he did get to see some paintings—Ruskin's remarkable collection

of Turners and an ineffably handsome portrait by Titian.[21] The following week, they made another effort and succeeded in dining with
Ruskin. He had a simple manner, but to Henry he seemed to have
been frightened by life. Dinner was charming and easy, however,
owing to two very young nieces, one Scottish and one Irish, who lived
with him.[22]

By prearrangement, one Wednesday afternoon after their midday
meal, James met Charles and Susan Norton and Sara Sedgwick at the
door of William Morris's house in Bloomsbury. Henry had known of
Morris principally as a poet, but here he was an artificer, the creator
of a Gothic world:

> To begin with, he is a manufacturer of stained glass windows, tiles,
> ecclesiastical and medieval tapestry, altar-cloths, and in fine every-
> thing quaint, archaic, Pre-Raphaelite—and I may add, exquisite. Of
> course his business is small and may be carried on in his house: the
> things he makes are so handsome, rich and expensive (besides being
> articles of the last luxury) that his *fabrique* can't be on a large scale.[23]

Morris's wife and daughters, it appeared, aided him in the weaving of
the tapestries, and Henry sent Alice a description of these women for
her amusement.

> Oh, ma chère, such a wife! . . .—she haunts me still. A figure cut out
> of a missal—. . . Imagine a tall lean woman in a long dress of some
> dead purple stuff, guiltless of hoops (or of anything else, I should say,)
> with a mass of crisp black hair heaped into great wavy projections on
> each of her temples, a thin pale face, a pair of strange sad, deep, dark
> Swinburnian eyes, with great thick black oblique brows, joined in
> the middle and tucking themselves away under her hair . . . a long
> neck, without any collar, and in lieu thereof some dozen strings of
> outlandish beads.[24]

They stayed to dinner, and afterward Morris read one of his unpublished poems. Having a toothache, his wife lay on a sofa, with a handkerchief to her face. There was something quaint and remote from
actual life, it seemed to Henry, in the whole scene: Morris reading in
his flowing antique diction a legend of prodigies and terrors; around
them all the picturesque bric-a-brac of the apartment; and in the corner a dark silent medieval woman with her medieval toothache. Just

under his own careful good manners Henry's sense of fun was beginning to bubble.[25]

That Friday morning, after breakfast with Rutson to meet the Honorable George Brodrick ("son of Lord Middleton, you know"), James returned to his flat for a rest, and began a determinedly cheerful letter to William. The experiment of England had been a great success, so far as its principal purpose went. His depression had lifted: "I go thro' everything that comes up, feeling the better & better for it; I feel every day less fatigue." To prove his stamina he went to the British Museum to look at the Elgin marbles for two hours, and then dined with the Stephens in South Kensington.[26] In the evening he completed his letter to William and posted it to catch Saturday's steamer for Boston.

He was seeing and learning a great deal, but as yet he did not know what to do with his harvest. London was not at all like Paris or New York; it had no similarity to the capital cities that he knew. There was little public life. London lived within doors, and was thoroughly and complacently English. "We may like it or not, but it's positive," Henry made an American visitor to London say in a story soon afterward. "No more dense and stubborn fact ever settled down on an expectant tourist. It brings my heart into my throat."[27] It seemed to have its complacent back turned to strangers.[28]

Alone he visited all the places that tourists were expected to go. He went to Westminster Abbey and Saint Paul's and the Tower of London. He took a penny steamer down the black Thames to Greenwich, but as the weather was bad he did not go up to the observatory. On another afternoon he went up the Thames to Hampton Court, a royal castle of the Tudor era, where, in the seemingly eternal, chilly, and somber afternoon, he strolled alone through empty corridors, through audience chamber, chapel, and great hall hung with trophies of hunting and warfare.

He had taken his flat only for the month of March, and he resolved that in April he would go as planned to Malvern for the summer, as his father had recommended. Although his back and his spirits were better, his digestion had not improved, and had even worsened under the onslaught of the immense heavy breakfasts, teas, dinners, and suppers that he was eating, washed down with copious quantities of English beer (for which he was acquiring a decided taste). He hoped that Malvern might help him in that respect.

He paid a last call on the Nortons, and Charles recommended that when the weather grew warmer he should go up to Scotland. To his mother Henry wrote on the eve of departure, "During the last week I have been knocking about in a quiet way and have deeply enjoyed my little adventures. The last few days in particular have been extremely pleasant."[29] But it was time to put himself into motion once more. London, dark, huge, and prodigious, loomed and spread, too mighty a Goliath as yet, even for this fast-growing David.

> I could somehow only fear him as much as I admired him and that his proportions reached away beyond all expectation. He was always the great figure of London. . . . I had crept about his ankles, I had glanced adventurously up at his knees, and wasn't the moral for the most part the mere question of whether I should ever be big enough to so much as guess where he stopped?[30]

And so he took a return ticket for Malvern, his last impressions of London gathering about him. Chief among the little adventures of which he had spoken to his mother were the accidental encounters on his solitary walks—unexpected vistas of a little street or an old court-yard—that called to him with the passion of an only chance. If the commonest street vista was a heart-shaking image,

> so the great sought-out compositions, the Hampton Courts and the Windsors, the Richmonds, the Dulwiches, even the very Hampstead Heaths and Putney Commons, to say nothing of the Towers, the Temples, the Cathedrals and the strange penetrabilities of the City, ranged themselves like figures in a sum, an amount immeasurably huge, that one would draw on if not quite as long as one lived, yet as soon as ever one should seriously get to work.[31]

That spring he wrote "A Light Man," which was in a way addressed to Robert Browning, whom he had not yet succeeded in meeting.[32] It was not quite the serious work of his own that he meant to do—it was only another technical exercise. It was a variation on Browning's "A Light Woman." In that long-ago Newport summer, James had puzzled over the poem's moral conundrum. An Italian count, like an eagle, had snatched up the "light woman" who had seduced his friend. By doing this, the aristocrat had revealed the light woman's falsity, but at the same time he had exploited her and destroyed his own friendship with her intended victim. Henry put this trio into fancy dress. The light woman was daringly disguised as a seductive old man, Mr.

Sloane, who lured young men into his clutches by promising to make each his heir. A handsome young American was about to become the latest victim of the old man. This innocent had an aristocratic, eagle-like friend, who had just returned from Europe. Henry now felt fully equal to portraying this jaded character, a materialist and a villain, who used his artistry and skill to seduce the old man for him- self—perhaps to show Sloane's falsity but also, incidentally, to profit himself.

With a new impudence, James told the story from the point of view of the villain, who conquered the old man's affections and then literally brought him to his knees by threatening to leave him.

> I have lost no time. This evening, late, . . . I repaired to Mr. Sloane, who had not yet gone to bed, and informed him that I should be obliged to leave him at once, and pick up a subsistence somehow in New York. He felt the blow; it brought him straight down on his mar- row-bones. . . . The remainder of this extraordinary scene I have no power to describe: how the *bonhomme*, touched, inflamed, inspired by the thought of my destitution, and at the same time annoyed, per- plexed, bewildered, at having to commit himself to doing anything for me, worked himself into a nervous frenzy which deprived him of a clear sense of the value of his words and his actions; how I, prompted by the irresistible spirit of my desire to leap astride of his weakness and ride it hard to the goal of my dreams, cunningly con- trived to keep his spirit at the fever-point, so that strength and reason and resistance should burn themselves out. I shall probably never again have such a sensation as I enjoyed to-night—actually feel a heated human heart throbbing and turning and struggling in my grasp; know its pants, its spasms, its convulsions, and its final sense- less acquiescence.[33]

This audacious description of sexual conquest was the central inci- dent in the tale. The count in Browning's poem was shown to be evil—to use another human being as a means, rather than as an end in himself, was evil—and in Henry's tale the villain ended badly. The vil- lain gained nothing; and the handsome young American went on with his virtuous life.

·   ·   ·

On the first of April a railroad took Henry west, beyond the water-shed of the Thames, into the Severn valley. At the far side of the Severn rose the Malvern hills that looked out over the wide midland plain of England. A stiff climb from his inn brought him up to the crest of a ridge. The Severn and the Avon wound away into the distance. At his feet whole counties were displayed: the dark, rich farms of Worcestershire, divided into little fields by green hedges, and the whitely blossoming apple groves of Hereford.

> At widely opposite points of the large expanse two great cathedral towers rose sharply, taking the light, from the settled shadow of their encircling towns,—the light, the ineffable English light! . . . The whole vast sweep of our surrounding prospect lay answering in a myriad of fleeting shades the cloudy process of the tremendous sky. . . .[34]

The sanatorium that his father had recommended, Dr. Raynor's establishment, lay on steep ground, so that it was difficult to walk very much, however, and the weather was bad. Henry spent a good deal of time indoors with the other inhabitants of the sanatorium, who were mostly male, mild and pleasant and inexpressibly British. A retired officer who had returned from India with a yellowish complexion and alcoholic liver told long improbable stories at the common table. The guests read the *Telegraph* and the *Standard*, and played billiards and whist.[35]

The cold baths that were the chief feature of Raynor's treatment simply made James tired, and did nothing to help his digestion. He began to think the baths might even be hurting his back, and he wrote to William asking if there was not some other cure for his constipation. Was the "injection-douche" that William had tried in Divonne worth going to France for?

> A line on this point dispatched immediately would greatly oblige me. I am rather at a loss to say where it would find me. My ambition is to stay here a month—to May 1st. I shall stay as long as I don't find the systems detrimental to my back.[36]

He spent some time writing letters, refreshing his network of friend-ship. Wilky was in Florida, and was hoping to entice more immigrants from the North to join him, to do the backbreaking work of cultivating cotton. The former slaves had proved to be difficult employees; they had not fallen into the spirit of the project. Bob had given it up and gone west to take a job with a railroad. William's back evidently was worse again, but William and Wendell Holmes seemed to have become truly good friends. William seemed definitely to have softened toward Mary Temple, too, and had become willing to accept her affection. Mary herself, as intellectually restless as ever, had gone to Philadelphia to hear the famous Episcopalian minister Phillips Brooks preach. But his sermons had proved merely comfortable and emotive, and had failed to still her questioning.[37] She was coughing badly again. Wendell refused to answer letters—was he dead? Tom Perry was at home. Bill and Elinor Howells had a second child, a little boy. The new arrivals in the Cambridge circle, the Bootts, were much loved by the Jameses and Temples. Mary Temple and Elizabeth Boott had grown intimate, and Henry was interested in the picture of these two together—Mary, with her clear gray eyes and intense, restless, spontaneous, pure Albany character, and Elizabeth, dark and cosmopolitan, in perfect repose.[38]

The best news was that Alice was better; she was up and about, and had gone to Newport with young John Bancroft, over Father's protests, escaping for a little while from the suffocating atmosphere of home.[39]

After his first week at Malvern, James was already planning his departure. The simple, regular meals, the mild exercise, and the large quantities of plain water had ended his painful constipation, but his depression of spirits threatened to return. His goal was the Continent, but he was obliged to wait until the unhealthy heat of the summer was past. He thought over Norton's suggestion of a trip up to Edinburgh and back along the eastern coast of Great Britain. This seemed too much to undertake; he thought instead of traveling a little in the beautiful midland countryside that was visible from the brow of his hill. He decided to get a closer look at the cathedrals that dotted the perspective, and at Oxford, on his leisurely way down to Dover; then he would wait out the rest of the hot summer in Switzerland until it seemed safe to continue his voyage south into Italy. He unburdened himself in a confidential letter to William, fretting about his health and the expense of travel.[40]

He wrote to the Nortons of his new plan, and the ladies responded promptly with letters of introduction to friends and acquaintances at Oxford, and with these in his pocket, on April 20, after less than three weeks of "cure," he set out in gradual stages eastward, following the Avon River to Stratford, Warwick, and Leamington, admiring Elizabethan inns and abbeys along the way. The land was one teeming garden, and the late April rains had brought out flowers everywhere. The castles and cathedrals failed to inspire, however, and at Stratford-on-Avon, especially, his enthusiasm most embarrassingly hung fire. He had been nourished on Shakespeare's plays from his earliest youth, but he shared the general Bostonian skepticism as to the authorship of the plays—Stratford to him was an empty shrine.[41]

When he came to Oxford, it was a different matter. He had his trunk brought to the Randolph Hotel, and at five in the lengthening afternoon he went out to deliver his letters of introduction.

It was a perfect evening & in the interminable British twilight the beauty of the whole place came forth with magical power. There are no words for these colleges. As I stood . . . within the precincts of the mighty Magdalen, gazed at its serene tower & uncapped my throbbing brow in the mild dimness of its courts, I thought that the heart of me would crack with the fullness of satisfied desire.[42]

He had entered for the first time the walled gardens of aristocratic life. The old stone façades, with their windows open on private courtyards and gardens; the mixture of athletic and scholarly energies, the beauty and intelligence of the place—it was perfect.[43]

After two days in Oxford—dining in hall at Christ Church, and, thanks to the Norton and Sedgwick ladies' letters, being treated in every way as an honored guest—much revived in spirits, James went back to London. His health was quite restored. His back no longer troubled him, and he felt prepared for any adventure. Paris had dropped from his itinerary, as perhaps inconsistent with a trip undertaken for reasons of health. He now planned to go on from London to Geneva and, if his strength and his funds continued to support him, to Italy. Regular travel seemed to be the prescription for all his ills.

He lingered two weeks in London, where the "season" had begun. At Baring Brothers, he was pleased to find that he still had almost nine hundred pounds in his line of credit.[44] There was an accumulation of mail, including an angry letter from William.

Perhaps he had been angered by Henry's having so casually rejected the theory of cold baths, William's own chosen course of action. He lashed out with denunciations of the expense to which

Henry was putting the family, and demanded that he go to Germany, learn German, and submit himself to the baths there, as William had done. William said that he had read aloud at the family breakfast table Henry's confidential letter from Malvern, and he now asserted that both Father and Mother were greatly concerned about the expense Henry was incurring and the poor results in health that he was reaping in consequence.[45]

This last cost Henry a pang, and required a series of conciliatory letters to William, Mother, and Father. To William he wrote mildly: "I can't help feeling as if you had gone back on me a little."[46] He said he was going on to the Continent—not to Germany but to Switzerland and Italy. The experiment of travel had succeeded: he was in excellent health. And he planned to continue on the program he had begun. "Movement, & more movement & still movement—de l'audace et encore de l'audace et toujours de l'audace."

He artfully asked William to be his spokesman to the family. It was a matter both of Henry's putting his health right and of gaining the education he needed to do his work, which he forbore to say too directly that he had been denied. It was a matter of setting him up in his profession. He felt confident that after a year of travel, he would be in good health and prepared for his work.

> I don't forget that you too have a "situation" of your own. I wish I could prescribe for it as well. I wish I heard from you oftener, but don't write a line but when you feel like it. Give my love to father & mother & bid them to be charitable to the egotism of my letter.[47]

But to Alice he burst out more frankly, *"I know what I am about."*[48]

London in the season was quite different from London in winter. Mayfair had come to life, and Piccadilly and Hyde Park were no longer so exclusively masculine. The ring road in Hyde Park was filled with open carriages in which were exhibited the most beautifully dressed women, in pairs or with escorts. The "ten thousand," the aristocratic families and owners of great wealth, had come to London from their country houses, and had begun a systematic round of breakfasts, lunches, dinners, and balls. Henry observed these manifestations with interest, but from a distance. He learned that in Hyde Park one could rent a chair for a penny and watch the parade of carriages on the ring road or the horseback riders on "Rotten Row," the old Route du Roi whose sandy surface put him in mind of a circus ring.[49]

The National Gallery and the Royal Academy in its new quarters in Piccadilly were now both open, and he went almost daily to look at paintings. He disliked the new British pictures at the Royal Academy, but the National Gallery was filled with treasures looted from Italy and France. He spent happy hours there, looking at the pictures and at the people looking at the pictures, just as he had in the Louvre so many years before.

Early in May he met George Eliot. Susan Norton brought him to the novelist's house in North Bank, an unfashionable region above Regent's Park.

Eliot lived with a G. H. Lewes, without being married to him, and was known as Mrs. Lewes. Despite this seeming bohemianism, theirs was a conventional household in a middle-class suburb. James came upon her in a domestic crisis. He and Susan had been admitted into a cool drawing room, and the novelist came to them from another room. Henry was moved to see such a great celebrity quite humanly and familiarly agitated. She introduced herself as Mrs. Lewes, and apologized for her husband's absence. There was a domestic emergency. Mr. Lewes's son had suffered a serious injury to his back some years before; Henry confusedly gathered that while in the West Indies he had been tossed by a bull. The injury still troubled him. He had just had a terrible onset of pain, and Mr. Lewes had gone to the chemist for a remedy of which they knew, but when he returned he would only have to go off again for Mr. Paget, the surgeon.

The author wore a black dress and a lace mantilla, and the visitors sat down in the drawing room with her to keep her company while she waited for Lewes to return. She helped them to help her in this way by making conversation. Henry was struck by the dignity with which she did this, by a certain high grace despite her anxiety.

To his young eyes she was terribly plain. He stored up the impression for Mary Temple, to be told on his return. Eliot was magnificently ugly—deliciously hideous. She had a low forehead, a dull gray eye, a vast pendulous nose, a huge mouth full of uneven teeth, and a long chin.

> Now in this vast ugliness resides a most powerful beauty which, in a very few minutes, steals forth and charms the mind, so that you end as I ended, in falling in love with her. Yes, behold me literally in love with this great horse-faced bluestocking.[50]

She spoke of a short holiday she had taken with Mr. Lewes in the south of France, from which they had just returned. The wind of the south, the mistral, was the scourge of their expedition. It had blown them into Avignon, where they had gone to see J. S. Mill, and then had blown them straight out again. They had had their pleasure further poisoned by the frequency of evil faces: "oh the evil faces!" Henry had never heard a traveler's anecdote told with so little of the superficial or the banal, told with such art and such moral earnestness. As he was himself engaged in compiling his own impressions of travel, he took careful mental note; but he was struck with the absence of color in her story, the overall tone of gray.

The earnestness, the sensitivity to evil faces, was only a part of the same large tenderness that the occasion had caused to overflow. Susan said that perhaps they should go, and Mrs. Lewes insisted that they remain; Henry was impressed by the moral delicacy with which she was doing them the courtesy of allowing them to humor her. Henry then asked if he could help, and they all went into the adjoining room, where the afflicted young man lay stretched on his back on the floor, fair and young and flushed. Henry knelt beside him and asked if there was any way he could ease the pain. They all tried to make normal conversation over the prostrate body while Mr. Lewes still failed to arrive.

Henry was inspired to ask whether *he* couldn't go for the surgeon, Mr. Paget. Mrs. Lewes and her stepson instantly agreed, and leaving Susan behind, Henry ran outside to search for a cab. The long blank avenue disclosed a single lumbering four-wheeler in the distance; Henry commandeered this and set off to Hanover Square. At the great man's door Henry learned that though he was not at home Mr. Paget was expected without delay; assured that the surgeon would receive the message as soon as he arrived, Henry returned to North Bank.

Mr. Lewes soon returned, and the visit was over. Henry took Susan home. But he always carried with him after that episode a distinct sense of relation to George Eliot, and to the great treasure of beauty and humanity, of applied and achieved art that she had collected.[51]

Henry arrived in Geneva by rail, in the middle of May, and stayed at the family's old haunt, the Hôtel de l'Écu. Geneva was still the little city of his school days, but the dark homely-featured mass of the town was now relieved by a rim of white-walled hotels along the fringe of the blue lake. It was still the city of Calvin, however, the capital of the Scottish and Dutch world of his childhood, the Presbyterian mother city.[52] But the cool blue Rhône gushed from the lake, and it seemed to Henry that the river was like the impetus of faith shooting in deep indifference past Calvinist doctrine.[53]

Early summer blossomed. He took long walks into the country-side, and then boarded a steamer to the eastern end of the lake, where Byron's legend had spawned an industry: the Castle of Chillon was crowded with polyglot tour groups led about by their guides. He wandered away from the lake into the countryside, among the little villages, each with a great stone fountain in the village square, where the tinkling cattle drank, where the lettuce and linen were washed, and where hot and dusty, he would drink from the spout, casually in-different to the bare brown arms of the muscular women who leaned over the trough.[54]

Rain fell for a full week and dampened his spirits, but when the weather cleared he began assiduously hiking with a rucksack, with any companions he found. The best company by and large were the young Englishmen, among whom mountain climbing in Switzerland was a new fashion. Toward the end of June, with two Englishmen and a German, he set off at midnight to climb the Roche de Neige so as to see the sunrise at the summit. It was a stiff four-hour hike.

> The sunrise was rather a failure owing to an excess of clouds; but the red ball shot up with the usual splendid suddenness. The summit was extremely cold. . . . We descended in about half the time and reached the hotel by 7 a.m. in time for a bath and breakfast.[55]

He sent a long letter home, telling of his improved health, and saying that he now thought quite definitely of spending the winter in Italy. Despite the expense, he felt this would be justified for both his health and his education.[56]

At the end of a month the Norton clan joined him at the eastern end of Lake Geneva, near Vevey. He spent a pleasant four days there with them. He himself stayed in a picturesque old farmhouse a little farther down the lake, enjoying the Vaudois countryside and the com-pany of the Norton and Sedgwick women as much as ever, but Charles's cold, superior manner had begun to wear on him. Neither Charles nor Susan seemed to be in good health.

Henry resumed his summer walking tour, hoping to gain in strength and spirits until the hot weather was past and he could re-sume his journey into Italy. He left the cultivated rural scenes around the lake and traveled into the mountains. The railroad carried him up the Rhône valley from the lake, the tremendous peaks of the Alps rising six or seven thousand feet above the railbed on either hand, as far as the resort town of Aigle, which he found hot and crowded with English and American tourists. Accordingly he went on a little farther, by post chaise in the remembered old-fashioned style, a little higher into the wilderness of mountains. But the wilderness was even less hospitable than the resort town: "Decidedly this was not a place to stop at: a vast amphitheater, surrounded by bleak towering desolate walls of snow-covered rock—grim, horrible & uninteresting."[57]

He set off yet again, this time on foot, with a porter pulling his trunk in a little car, across the Col de Pillon and down into German-speaking Switzerland. It was a delightful walk, and he reached the village of Gsteig. "Here at the inn I met four lovely Englishmen—the flower of the earth," he wrote to William.

> I am getting, by the way, absolutely to adore the English. At this place, my brother, there came over me a rich & vivid recollection of the little foot-journey we made together years ago, when we had no aches and pains. As I sat in the little German-Swiss dining room, I could almost fancy you at my side & myself ten years younger.[58]

He continued to follow the flow of the streams down from the Alps in easy stages northward to Thun and Bern. From there he went on eastward by rail to the Lake of Lucerne. The mountains about the lake were all shrouded in a hot haze, but they loomed in dim grandeur, outcrowding and over-topping each other.[59] Henry had determined to spend some time in a mountain resort, and before he left Malvern the yellow-faced officer had recommended that he visit the mountains at the far end of this lake, above Gersau. A steep two-and-a-half-hour climb, with a sweating porter carrying his trunk, brought him to a bare, rocky peak, the Scheidegg. Here James took a room in a rough hotel crowded with German hikers, which he made a base for further excursions. The exercise of hiking was addictive, and he felt himself growing stronger and more eager to lengthen his walks every week. A stiff hike and short climb to the west brought him up to the peak of the Rigi, which rose steeply up beside the Lake of Lucerne and had magnificent views. He settled in at the Scheidegg hotel, and sent his regular report to William, Alice, Father, and Mother:

> The obvious drawback is the total absence of shade & the violent glare produced by the "view" & by the clouds being as much below as above you. Nevertheless owing to the great elevation (I believe about 6,000

feet,) the air even at noon-day is light & cool & stirring—it has a sort of flavor.[60]

In walking you quite sweat the rhapsodical out of you & have no eloquence left for talk. Mountain-climbing is an awfully silent process. I nevertheless should be very glad to be able to give you some hint of one or two of my sensations—the great snow-&-ice world I gazed upon from the summit of the Rigi—& the spectacle before me when, on the summit of the Wengen-Alp I sat on the bench outside the inn & surveyed, directly opposite, the towering gleaming pinnacles of the Silberhorn, the Eiger, the Mönch. . . .[61]

He found the regular regime of the hotel healthful and dull, and characteristically German. There was no wandering in to meals at all hours. Breakfast was at eight, dinner at twelve-thirty, tea at five, and supper at seven-thirty.[62] There was little English-speaking company, but he was able to go off on excursions into the more crowded resort areas. His mail caught up with him. There was a lovely letter from Mary Temple:

My darling Harry—(You don't mind if I am a little affectionate, now that you are so far away, do you?) Your most welcome letter came to me some time ago, & was doubly welcome, as it reached me while I was in the very act of having the third hemorrhage of that day, & it quite consoled me, for them. By which you perceive that I still continue in my evil courses, which however don't seem to have killed me, yet. Since then I have had one other slight attack, last week, here, in Newport. . . . I shall miss you, my dear—but I am most happy to know that you are well & enjoying yourself. I wish I were there too. If you were not my cousin I would write to ask you to marry me & take me with you—but as it is, it wouldn't do. . . . If I were, by hook or by crook, to spend next winter, with friends, in Rome, should I see you at all?—. . . There is nothing new to tell you. John Gray & Lizzie Boott were both as nice as ever—the former rather handsomer than ever. Elly & Kitty are at Pelham, well & happy. I shall stay there quietly all summer, & shall think of you. You mustn't be homesick. I hear you find it expensive. How much money would you like me to send you? I have lots. Do write to me, if you have time. Just think how I like to get your letters, & remember that of all the princes &

princesses (so to speak) who now seek your society, none of them love you half so well as I do. I am now going to bid you good-by. . . . God bless you, dear. Don't forget me—or that I am,

> Always your loving cousin
> Mary Temple.[63]

The James family had gone to Pomfret, Connecticut, for the summer, where the Bootts had also gone. Wendell Holmes sent affectionate remembrances to Harry via William, but did not write himself. Alice was continuing to improve steadily in health.

William himself wrote that he had had a serious collapse earlier in the summer, both physical and spiritual. William now suffered both from the mingled back pain and constipation of which Henry had just freed himself and from a depression of spirits. But he was taking the examinations to complete his medical degree, at last. He and Father both thought that Henry should go to Germany and spend the winter studying there.[64] Henry must have sighed.

There was a letter from Howells, who wrote to praise "A Light Man," which had just appeared in *The Galaxy*, and to ask if Henry would not do a travel piece for *The Atlantic*.[65] And there was a letter from his mother in her old-fashioned, beautiful hand that somehow conveyed her inconsequent, regal manner:

My dear beloved child, I have been cut off from writing for several weeks, finding that the rest had got the start of me; and now although Alice wrote but two days ago I can forbear no longer—Your letter last evening opens the deepest fountains in my soul, and my bosom seems as if it must burst with its burden of love and tenderness. If you were only here, and we could talk over this subject of expense, I could, I know, exorcise all these demons of anxiety and conscientiousness that possess you, and leave [you] free as air to enjoy to the full all that surrounds you, and drink in health of body and mind in following out your own safe and innocent attractions. Just here we desire dear Harry to leave you, only exacting from you the promise that you will hence forth throw away prudence and think only of your own comfort and pleasure, for our sakes as well as your own—I am sure you may confide in your prudent old mother to take care of that side of the question—You must have got my letter suggesting you go to Italy for the winter, very soon after writing your last, so you see we are quite of one mind—Italy will be just the place for you; and do not I pray you cramp yourself in any way to hinder your fullest enjoyment of it. You dear reasonable overconscientious soul! Take the fullest liberty and enjoyment your tastes and inclination crave, and we will promise heartily to foot the bill.[66]

11

THE LESSONS OF ITALY

The first great masterwork that he encountered after coming down into Italy from Switzerland was Leonardo's mural *The Last Supper*. Much damaged and darkened, it covered a wall in what had been the refectory of a monastery in Milan and which was now occupied by a regiment of Napoleon III's cavalry. Horses stamped in the cloisters.

He spent a long time gazing at the solemn work in its incongruous surroundings, which were a part of the oddness of the experience. *The Last Supper* had been so badly damaged that at first he was not sure of understanding the picture. But as he gazed, his imagination found delight in filling the vacant spaces, stripping away the smoke and grime, repairing the damage of centuries as far as it was possible to do. Slowly the beautiful central image of Christ clarified, and James perceived its radiation right and left along the sadly broken lines of the

disciples. One by one, out of the depths of their grimy disorder the figures of the Apostles trembled into meaning and life, and the vast serious beauty of the work stood revealed to him.[1]

The viewer had become a creator, and it seemed to James that the
fresco's greatness lay in its very incompleteness, that the fullness of art
lay in the lost, omitted, and suppressed details, brought to life and
meaning by the reader's effort; it became not a representation at all,
but a kind of newly invented memory of the viewer's own, illumined
by imagination.

But Milan otherwise made little impression upon him, and he did
not feel that he was fully in Italy until he reached Venice. There, a few
days after his arrival, Henry rode in a gondola across the placid lagoon
until he was out of sight of land. He planned to spend the day on the
lagoon before returning to his hotel in Venice. It was a fine day, the sun
shed the strong light of the south, and the gondola moved forward
sinuously, undulating gently to the plunges of the long oar at the rear.
Henry lounged on the soft cushioned seat under the canopy and
observed the light. Sea and sky seemed to meet halfway and to blend
their tones into a soft iridescence, a lustrous compound of wave and
cloud and a hundred nameless local reflections. It was a perfect bath
of light, and he couldn't get rid of the feeling that he was cleaving the
upper atmosphere on some hurrying cloud skiff.[2]

The island of Torcello, the object of the day's expedition, proved
to be a low green marshy island, utterly silent. The gondola pulled into
the mouth of the one little stream, near the grassy square of the village. There was a half-ruined church, the ancient cathedral of the
place, and a few houses. Twelve hundred years before, this had been
the mother-city of Venice. Now there was no visible life except the
tremor of the brilliant air and the cries of a half-dozen young children
who followed him clamoring for coins. They were beautiful children,
sunburned, nearly naked.

They scampered and sprawled in the soft, thick grass, grinning like
suddenly translated cherubs and showing their hungry little teeth . . .
one little urchin—framed, if ever a child was, to be the joy of an aristocratic mama—was the most expressively beautiful creature I had
ever looked upon. He had a smile to make Correggio sigh in his grave;
and yet here he was running wild among sea-stunted bushes, on the
lonely margin of a decaying world, in prelude to how blank or dark
a destiny?[3]

Torcello seemed to help explain Venice, a medieval village built on a cluster of islands. Pilings had been sunk into the marshy sands, and palaces erected upon them. The hundred tiny islands had gradually been covered by a vast structure like a rambling country house that had been added to and built upon for centuries. A thousand-year-old republic, Venice lay between the German north, the Italian south and the Turkish east, housed as if in a single vast apartment, a salon for cosmopolitan Europe. Without streets and vehicles, the uproar of wheels or the brutality of horses, and with its little winding ways where people crowded together, the human step circulated in the streets of Venice as if it skirted the angles of furniture.[4] Henry walked everywhere. A narrow street hardly more than a corridor would pass under an arch like a doorway, and, turning, would open suddenly into a little paved square with its café and its church. The Piazza San Marco was like a formal drawing room, and the cathedral that opened off the square, hung inside with treasures looted from Byzantium, was like a private chapel on a vastly enlarged scale.

The little islands on which the city had been built had long ago disappeared beneath this immense Gothic construction and one rarely saw the earth, or a garden. The pavement met the water, and the canals flowed into dark loggias beneath the palaces; the effect was of a floating village, suspended between air and sea. It was lovely to tour the city on a gondola, floating as if in midair.

On close examination, he found that the Venetian effect was achieved with the most remarkable materials—rotting pilings, flaking plaster, broken marble, refuse; the water left its green slime on the walls. Venice was terribly poor. But at a little distance the city was remarkably beautiful, although it was composed from these materials of poverty and decay, and as he drifted along a canal past picturesque figures on a gracefully arched bridge, while looking up at the same angle that one looked up at the stage from the stalls, he felt as if he were in a theater.

He stayed at the Hotel Barbesi, which occupied a crumbling palace on the Grand Canal, just where it began to broaden into a placid green lagoon. In the morning after coffee and a hot bath, in the bathing facilities provided by the establishment—Venice was a city without central plumbing, and bath houses were listed in guidebooks and advertisements—he would set out by gondola, sheltered by a canopy and cooled by the breeze on the water, to visit museums and churches.

In the evenings, mosquitoes rose from the canals. It was too hot to close his window and his lamp attracted insects, so that it was difficult to read or write. Beside the smoky lamp, he answered the letters from home that had come to him with their strange air of having been written to him from the past. A touching note from La Farge, in Newport:

> I did not have the courage to write to you all summer. Whenever I thought of the lovely time I might have been having with you & the rest & quiet of (literally) another world, I put it off until I should feel more satisfied at having stayed here. My physician thought I had better not go. . . . I am little better now than I was and suffer from a continual dullness of mind and body. . . . How much there will be for you in Italy—and for me too I hope. Sargie is here who sends love to you & intends to write when he gets to Cambridge in September.[5]

Mother's letter brought news of the family at Pomfret. The Bootts had come and gone; Wendell Holmes and John Gray had visited. Alice continued better in health, and had enjoyed the visit and their outings. Her twentieth birthday had been marked by a solar eclipse. Kitty Temple had given birth to a boy, to be named William Temple Emmet. Nineteen-year-old Elly Temple had married another Emmet cousin from Pelham, Christopher Temple Emmet, who was forty-seven, even older than Kitty's husband.[6] This struck Henry as terribly sad.[7] Emmet was a good fellow, but old and plain and bald. How sad for Elly to lose the chance for life, for beauty.

When the mosquitoes grew intolerable, he went to dinner at Quadri's on the Piazza San Marco, where he could look out at the darkened square and the lamplit church of Saint Mark. After dinner he would stroll across the square to the scattered tables outside Florian's, where graceful young Italian men in tall hats and soft gray summer trousers drank and laughed and listened to the music. He would eat an ice at Florian's and linger. Early in his visit he met a young American painter, and most evenings they sat together and gossiped, feeling the sea breeze throb languidly between the two pillars of the piazzetta and over the low black domes of the church. At these moments Henry felt that he was as happy as was consistent with the preservation of reason.[8]

He had brought with him Murray's handbook for travelers, Ruskin's *Venetian Index*,[9] and Théophile Gautier's *Italia*. With these tools he attacked Venice as an intellectual problem. It was Ruskin's

Venice that he studied, the ancient Christian republic uncorrupted by the Renaissance. He went nearly every day to the Doge's Palace, landing his gondola on the steps to the piazzetta beside the immense rose-colored palace, the center of the old seafaring empire. The palace seemed to float in the light: heavy upper stories poised on graceful arches below. Henry mounted the Staircase of Giants and wandered among the rooms, studying the vast wall-covering canvases.

Nearly every day he went as well to the Academy, where treasures of painting had been collected, and using Ruskin as a guide, he sought out little churches where remarkable paintings hung in the dusky light, blackened by the smoke of lamps and heaters, decaying in the sea air.

He was disappointed by Titian, whose work he had admired in the Louvre and the National Gallery. At the Church of Santa Maria Gloriosa dei Frari, the artist's own church, Henry saw what many considered to be the greatest picture in the world, Titian's *Assumption of the Virgin*. In the lower part of the painting a number of men were painted nearly life-size, staring upward, astonished at the miracle they were witnessing. These figures stood in a cool bluish light under a cloudy sky. The Madonna was rising into another realm, just over their heads. The space above the clouds, near enough for the unseeing crowd to touch, was heaven, enclosed in a vast sphere of warm light and filled with the plump bodies of winged little boys. This spiritual realm dwarfed and submerged the empty infinities below. The Heavenly Father spread his cloak to shield the Madonna's astonished and unaccustomed gaze from the intensity of the Light that was a palpable presence behind him.

Henry was impressed but unmoved. *The Assumption* seemed to him only a great work of the second class, a masterpiece of technique.[10] It would be many years before he came to a mature appreciation of Titian and would in some degree model his work upon the painter's. At this time he sought principally to understand Tintoretto, whose work Ruskin had praised above all the others. Little was known of the painter himself, but as Henry studied the dozens of works Tintoretto had executed, the man himself began to appear to him, a great shadowed figure of genius and bottomless energy, whose bleak vision seemed like Shakespeare's to penetrate every recess. He had covered the walls of the guild halls and the churches with acres of magnificent paintings, his genius overflowing into shadowy chapels and dark naves. Blackened and corroding as they were, the works slowly became clear to Henry. He lingered before a dimly lighted *Last Supper,* utterly unlike Leonardo's depiction of the same scene.[11] The long table lay at a diagonal in a rectangular room. The disciples were gathered about the table, engaged in their own conversations. Jesus was in the center of the scene, all unnoticed, bending to give the bread and wine, while in the foreground a servant clattered in a basket. The space was filled with the smoky light of an oil lamp, but the halo of light behind Jesus' bent head was the ineffable light of Venice, in which ghostly angels swam.

> It was the whole scene that Tintoret seemed to have beheld in a flash of inspiration intense enough to stamp it ineffaceably on his perception; and it was the whole scene, complete, peculiar, individual, unprecedented, that he committed to canvas with all the vehemence of his talent . . . its long, diagonally-placed table, its dusky spaciousness, its scattered lamp-light and halo-light, its startled, gesticulating figures. . . .[12]

The secret of Tintoretto's genius was this mastery of composition. The scene's dark colors and crowded gesticulating figures all seemed to belong just as they were. The work had a *tone*—a central unity, to which every vagrant detail contributed—that was evidently a product of the imagination, of the organ of perception with which somehow the painter had seen the complete tableau. It was this unity of composition that Henry studied. Tintoretto had solved the problem of realistic art—the problem of giving form and meaning to a scene seemingly ripped from historical reality.

A Crucifixion scene by Tintoretto, in a little church on its own square,[13] gave James the hint of the nature of the solution. Alone among the paintings that he had seen, it had been kept clean and whole; the muted colors were as fresh as when they were painted. It was hung in a good light and he could study it at his leisure. It seemed to have been painted almost carelessly, for the painter's own delight. The foreground was filled with brambles, as if the observer were looking up at the brow of a hill or at a stage. In the background the heads of a row of Roman soldiers looked over from the far side of the stage setting, their spears a thin row against the sky. The three crosses were at the far right, Jesus' powerful sinewy figure illuminated by the pale moist light. The Madonna and Saint John were on the ground at the far left.

At the center of the picture were the executioners, the uppermost executioner reaching down from his ladder for the taunting sign that was to be set over the figure of Christ on his Cross.[14] The executioners, intent upon their task, brought the scene into motion, into time.

The secret of this strange and compelling composition, over which the eye seemed to wander aimlessly before coming upon the Cross, was this. The painter had grasped something with his imagination, an image of the executioners on their ladder, from which all the rest had unfolded.

> When once Tintoretto had conceived the germ of a scene it defined itself to his imagination with an intensity, an amplitude, an individuality of expression, which make one's observation of his pictures seem less an operation of the mind than a kind of supplementary experience of life.[15]

After two weeks he had "done" Venice, and he had another store of impressions. It was time to resume the movement that guarded him from depression. He spent a final day in taking his leave of the city; in the Academy he saw Arthur and Katherine De Kay Bronson, who had summered in Newport in the long-ago times. Mrs. Bronson seemed haggard and pale and did not recognize him.[16]

In Florence he brought his trunk to the Hôtel de l'Europe, walked about a little, and then wrote to Alice:

> Now that I behold her no more I feel sadly as if I had done [Venice] wrong—as if I had been cold and insensible—that my eyes scowled and blinked at her brightness and that with more self-oblivion I might have known her better and loved her more.[17]

His spirits were low, despite the change of scene, and whether because of this or as a result no one could have said, but various disorders deeply afflicted his bowels. Italian water was poisonous, and he drank principally coffee and beer. A local doctor dosed him with pills, and William suggested enemas of hot soapsuds and oil—or galvanic currents applied to the rectum.[18] Henry thanked William for his advice, but cautiously ignored it.

Despite the expense he settled at a hotel, and planned only a short stay in Florence. He could not face the isolation of an apartment, nor the bad food and the dreary boardinghouse company at the cheap pensions. He was terribly disappointed not to find any letters waiting for him. But he set to work.

This meant at first simply walking about in the compact precincts of the old city-state of Florence that lay within its five-sided walls. This little community was built upon ancient Etruscan foundations. The Medici, like the merchants and bankers of New England, their wealth earned in trade with the Orient, had built a new republic on this ground. Henry walked in their streets and admired the perfect taste of the squares in front of the churches, and of Giotto's slender, graceful bell tower covered with geometrical patterns. The great houses stood in solid stuccoed ranks that reminded him of the brownstone façades of Boston.

A church that Brunelleschi had built for the Medici had revived classical forms, and harnessed them to the new science of design. A double row of interior columns led the eye past the altar to a vanishing point in infinite space. Older churches were dark hollows in which the spirit of the little community took refuge, but this new church was open to the light. It was built in infinite space, as seen by a single motionless eye, the timeless geometrical space of the material world, mapped scientifically from a single point and subject to the laws of design and perspective. The cool gray light fell from the windows onto the bare stone, and a silent wind seemed to blow through it.

The Medici had established their central laboratory at the Academy of Design; it was there that science was applied to the task of redesigning the world. Giorgio Vasari in his vast history exclaimed that in Florence this science of design had reached perfection. The environment designed by Michelangelo—the master of architecture, sculpture, and painting, united into one by a single science of design— was more perfect than those of nature itself.

The yellow Arno cast its reflections on the yellow plaster walls, and as in Venice, a close inspection showed only poverty and filth. Florence was the temporary capital of a new, very poor nation that had been painfully assembled in the past decade from the ancient kingdoms and dukedoms of the Italian peninsula. King Victor Emmanuel II was in residence at the Pitti Palace. The Five Hundred, the chamber of deputies, were meeting in the great council chamber of the Old Palace, surrounded by vast murals of past military glory. The city's ancient wall was being pulled down, and the Anglo-Italian Bank had undertaken to finance the construction of whole new quarters reaching outward from the old boundaries, great boulevards, squares, and office buildings to house the new government. Railroads were slowly linking the former duchies of Tuscany and the north into a single nation, and modern hotels were filled with visitors and tourists.

This new Florence was overawed—or at least James was—by the ghostly presence of Dante, Machiavelli, Petrarch, Benvenuto Cellini, Leonardo da Vinci, Raphael, Michelangelo, Botticelli. In the square before the Old Palace stood Michelangelo's immense nude *David*. Something more than an imitation of human form, it was terribly alive, as if with the life of the stone itself.

Time had turned on itself, and this new rebirth of Florence had awakened the older renaissance, when Duke Cosimo de' Medici had brought to the fortress of the Old Palace his bride, the seventeen-year-old Eleanora di Toledo. She had come to this foreign city a beautiful blond, dark-eyed child. In her apartment in the Old Palace she had designed for herself a study of perfect simplicity, and her modest chapel was decorated in passionate colors by Bronzino. After her children were born, she had purchased the great Pitti Palace across the Arno, and the grand duke filled it for her with the treasures of antiquity and the best of modern art. Henry wandered through the Pitti Palace, stunned by rooms filled with Raphaels, Bronzinos, Botticellis; art had been heaped up like booty.

He returned to his hotel and wrote an agonized and depressed letter to William. His health was bad and it continued to depress his spirits. But after a while there were letters from home, and these cheered him.

> My darling Mammy. . . . I've hardly until within a day or two exchanged five minutes' talk with anyone but the servants in the hotels and the custodians in the churches. . . . The "hardly" in the clause above is meant to admit two or three Englishmen with whom I have been thrown for a few hours. One especially, whom I met at Verona, won my affection so rapidly that I was really sad at losing him. But he has vanished, leaving only a delightful impression and not even a name—a man of about thirty-eight, with a sort of quiet perfection of English virtue about him, such as I have rarely found in another.[19]

As he struggled through the palaces and museums with Murray's guidebook and Vasari's *Lives of the Artists* in hand he chatted at long range with his old friends. He especially treasured a new letter from Mary Temple:

> I was much interested in your account of George Eliot. I want to go abroad and I mean to think about it, and try to get there. . . . Mrs. Jones most kindly offers to take me with her to Rome next winter, and by all that's blissful, if I can arrange it pecuniarily, I shall go! I shall write to Mrs. Jones, and ask her what the expense will be, and if it is at all reasonable for me to think of going, I shall make my arrangements for a year at least. Think, my dear, of the pleasure we should have together in Rome. I am crazy at the mere thought. . . . I wrote this letter to you a week ago, and according to my usual habit of forgetfulness have left it until now lying in my desk. . . . I have taken no steps about the European trip, and truth to tell, dear, I have no heart for it. . . . I am really not strong enough to go abroad even with the kindest friends. . . . My dearest Harry what a charming tale is Gabrielle de Bergerac! *Just* as pretty as ever it can be. I am proud of you, my dear, as well as fond—have you any special objections? Good bye. All send love. Write soon and believe me as ever your loving
>
> M. Temple[20]

In the great museum that had been made of the Uffizi, the "offices" of the ancient and vanished republic, there was a round chamber like a drawing room where Medici family portraits and treasures had been collected. There hung Bronzino's portrait of his young patron the grand duchess Eleanora, the bride of Cosimo de' Medici. She sat erect in a ceremonial dress whose magnificent brocade bespoke her rank. One aristocratic hand lay on her lap and the other rested lightly on the shoulder of a little boy, her son Giovanni, whose plump face was bursting with manly life. Her expression was unfathomably sad. It was the face of a lady, exiled and wed to a stranger.

There was a second portrait by Bronzino, of a lady in Eleanora's court, Lucrezia Panciatichi. She sat erect in the same pose as Eleanora, albeit in the more modest plain red satin suitable to her rank. Her expression was one of open arrogance. In color and expression she was like a negative impression of the portrait of the grand duchess. And it was odd: her red hair and pale skin, her strongly marked brows were remarkably like Mary Temple's. If the two Bronzino portraits had somehow been fused they would have shown his lovely, affectionate friend as a grand duchess, with all the knowledge of suffering in her eyes that young Mary had not yet learned. The heroine of *The Portrait of a Lady* and *The Wings of the Dove* was forming herself in his memory.[21]

The weather had turned cold, and a chilly rain settled in as if to stay for the winter. There were no cabs, which made it difficult to avoid the rain, and he felt he had *done* Florence as he had done Switzerland and Venice. He took the overnight train in the evening of October 29, and in the pale morning light of autumn he arrived in Rome.

The ancient city upon its little hills was half overgrown and abandoned. The broken stonework of the Colosseum was shrouded by mist in the morning light. From the broad piazza on the brow of the Pincian Hill, one looked back over the Tiber, swift and dirty as history,[22] toward the Vatican, where the dome of Saint Peter's seemed to float like an ageless planet. He walked for five hours through the city on his first day; the gods and fables, the palaces and princes, the residue of ancient virtues and evils were visible and tangible. The world of sense and imagination fused, and he went reeling and moaning through the streets, wondering in which of these palaces the exquisite Tolla had lived, loved, wasted, and died.[23]

French soldiers in their short blue coats and high-waisted red trousers—they seemed to be all red leg—lounged in every public square. The city lay under French occupation. The pope, its ruler, had been restored to the secular throne of his city-state by the imperial hand of Louis Napoleon. Now the aged Pius IX had summoned a great Vatican Council, which was to convene in December, and the city was crowded with the clerics of a hundred nations, the Church's still-undiminished spiritual empire.[24]

In the papal city, James somewhat to his surprise found a congenial society of American expatriates and leisurely tourists. The Nortons had come to Rome for a brief stay before settling in Florence. Aunt Kate and Cousin Helen, with Helen's ward, poor Henry Wyckoff, in tow, arrived early in December. James had as much of their company as he wished, and through them he met some of the permanent American colony in Rome. Anna Ward, looking old and fat and accompanied by her maid, encountered him in the street and invited him to dinner, and took him to mass at the Church of Saint Cecilia, on the eve of that martyr's day, where the music and singing were quite beautiful.

Henry James and his father. Daguerreotype by Mathew Brady, New York City, probably summer of 1854, when Harry was eleven years old. (By permission of the Houghton Library, Harvard University.)

Henry James, summer of 1858 or 1859, toward the end of the family's travels in Europe. (By permission of the Houghton Library, Harvard University.)

Henry James, 1860 or 1861, Newport. (The portrait by La Farge on the dust jacket was probably painted the following year in Newport.) (By permission of the Houghton Library, Harvard University.)

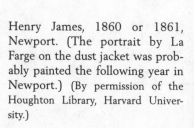

Henry James. Daguerreotype, probably taken in Boston, 1863 or 1864. Damage on the plate gives the appearance of hair *en brosse*. A light mustache and beard are discernible. (By permission of the Houghton Library, Harvard University.)

Catherine Barber James, Henry's Albany grandmother, his chosen ancestor, in old age, probably late 1850s. (By permission of the Houghton Library, Harvard University.)

Catherine Barber James. Oil painting, at the time of her marriage to William James, Sr., in 1803. She was thirty years old. (By permission of the Houghton Library, Harvard University.)

Above and at left: Mary Robertson James, née Walsh, Henry's mother, probably in Boston in the early 1860s. (By permission of the Houghton Library, Harvard University.)

Henry James, Sr. Daguerreotype, probably at the time of his marriage in New York City, July 1840. He was thirty-nine years old. The resemblance of his son at the same age is striking; compare the last portrait of this photo insert. (By permission of the Houghton Library, Harvard University.)

Henry James, Sr., in old age, probably late 1870s in Cambridge, Massachusetts. (By permission of the Houghton Library, Harvard University.)

Robertson James, the youngest brother, in Milwaukee at the time of his marriage, November 1872. (By permission of the Houghton Library, Harvard University.)

Garth Wilkinson James, Henry's next younger brother, in Boston just before enlisting in the Union army, September 1862. (By permission of the Houghton Library, Harvard University.)

Alice James, Henry's sister. Daguerreotype, Newport, about 1862, when Alice was fourteen. (By permission of the Houghton Library, Harvard University.)

William James, Henry's older brother. Daguerreotype, Newport, 1862,
when William was twenty. (By permission of the Houghton Library,
Harvard University.)

Alice James, Cambridge, 1870, at age twenty-two. (By permission of the Houghton
Library, Harvard University.)

William James, 1869, at the time of his visit
to Henry in Italy. (By permission of the
Houghton Library, Harvard University.)

Mary Temple, who as a child was known as Minny, about 1865, when she was twenty and the center of Henry's circle. (By permission of the Houghton Library, Harvard University.)

Edmund Tweedy, Mary Temple's uncle, in the late 1860s. Mary grew up in the Tweedy household after the death of her parents in 1855. (By permission of the Houghton Library, Harvard University.)

Mary Tweedy, Mary Temple's aunt and adoptive mother. Daguerreotype, 1850. (By permission of the Houghton Library, Harvard University.)

Oliver Wendell Holmes, the future Supreme Court justice, known as Wendell, second from right, with his family. From left: Edward, Mary Jackson Holmes, Amelia, and Dr. Oliver Wendell Holmes. About 1860, when Wendell was nineteen. (Courtesy Harvard Law School Art Collection)

Oliver Wendell Holmes, Boston 1865, shortly before he enrolled in the Harvard Law School. Holmes was twenty-four years old. (Courtesy Harvard Law School Art Collection)

Oliver Wendell Holmes, Boston, 1872, when his ambition to be a man of letters had briefly revived. The character Basil Ransome in *The Bostonians* is based on Holmes at this time. (Courtesy Harvard Law School Art Collection)

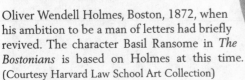

Thomas Sargent Perry, Henry's neighbor and friend in Newport, about 1860. (By permission of the Houghton Library, Harvard University.)

John La Farge. Sketch by William James, Newport, about 1861. William probably scribbled over the sketch in dissatisfaction, but kept it nonetheless. (By permission of the Houghton Library, Harvard University.)

John La Farge, from a damaged glass plate negative, Newport, 1859. This was a study for a self-portrait in oils. (Unidentified photographer, detail from *John La Farge in his Studio*, ca.1859, Yale University Art Gallery. Gift of Frances S. Childs in memory of Henry A. La Farge.)

Elizabeth Boott, always known as Lizzie, probably photographed in Boston at the time of her first visit to the United States, with her father, in 1865 or 1866, at age twenty. (By permission of the Houghton Library, Harvard University.)

Francis Boott, Elizabeth's father, photographed in Florence, c.1880, most likely a study for Duveneck's 1881 portrait of Boott as one of Titian's aristocrats, which is now in the Boston Museum of Fine Arts. (By permission of the Houghton Library, Harvard University.)

Pen-and-ink drawing from Elizabeth Boott's notebook, at about the time of Henry James's visit to Rome 1869–70. (Private collection: photograph Robert Boyajian.)

Elizabeth Boott. Oil on canvas, portrait by her future husband, Frank Duveneck, probably painted in Florence 1880–81. (Private collection: photograph courtesy Owen Gallery, New York City.)

Francis Boott. Watercolor by his daughter, Elizabeth, Florence, July 1882. (Private collection: photograph Robert Boyajian.)

The Holy Family, by Paul Zhukovsky, oil, 1881. The painting portrays the tableau vivant arranged by Zhukovsky at Christmas, 1880, in the Wagners' villa at Posillipo: the Wagners' son, Siegfried, as Jesus; their eldest daughter, Daniela von Bülow, as Mary; and the younger daughters as angels. Zhukovsky painted himself as Joseph; in the original tableau this part was played by his ward, Pepino. (The painting is now at Haus Wahnfried, Bayreuth; photograph courtesy Richard Wagner Museum, Bayreuth)

Pavel Vassilievich Zhukovsky, known as Paul, probably in Paris in 1875, when he and Henry James "swore an eternal friendship." Zhukovsky was thirty-five years old. (By permission of the Houghton Library, Harvard University.)

Paul Zhukovsky, about 1881, the time of his friendship with Richard and Cosima Wagner, when he was forty-one, and sat for his portrait as Gilbert Osmond in *The Portrait of a Lady*. (Courtesy Richard Wagner Museum, Bayreuth.)

The Wagner household, 1881, on their return to Bayreuth, Bavaria, shortly after Henry James's visit. From left: Richard and Cosima Wagner, Heinrich von Stein, Paul Zhukovsky. (Courtesy Richard Wagner Museum, Bayreuth.)

Frank Duveneck, Venice, 1870s. (Courtesy Owen Gallery, New York City.)

Frances Anne Kemble, always known as Fanny, probably in Boston during the Civil War, when she did benefit readings of Shakespeare's *Henry V,* and seemed to embody the martial spirit of the abolitionist cause. (By permission of the Houghton Library, Harvard University.)

Fanny Kemble, at about the time (1877–78) that she and Henry James each settled in London. (Courtesy Robert Hale & Co., London.)

Constance Fenimore Woolson, probably 1870s. Henry James became her mentor in Florence in 1881, as he was beginning work on *The Portrait of a Lady.* (By permission of the Houghton Library, Harvard University.)

Henry James, in the early 1880s, about the time that *The Portrait of a Lady* was published, securing his place as first among American novelists. (By permission of the Houghton Library, Harvard University.)

He called on William and Emelyn Story in their famous apartment in the Palazzo Barberini. The Storys were Bostonians, good friends of the Nortons and Lowells, who had settled in Rome some years before. He was a sculptor, and his friend Nathaniel Hawthorne had put his *Cleopatra* into *The Marble Faun;* as a result Story had become famous. He was well formed to be a celebrity, tall and handsome, his blond hair just beginning to show gray. He wore a thick drooping mustache and a thin pointed beard in a distinctly archaic fashion that gave him the look of a Renaissance princeling. Despite his fifty years, he and Emelyn were always the youngest and the best-looking in a gathering; they were wealthy and talented and famous, and wonderfully charming hosts.

Their palace had been built in the seventeenth century for Pope Urban VIII. It was on the sharp slope of the Quirinal, halfway down the valley formed by the opposite slope of the Pincian Hill. Approached on foot, the yellow marble structure faced one, as so many of the Roman monuments seemed to do, like some great natural fact. The left wing of the palace housed a gallery to which American tourists came in a steady stream with guidebooks in hand to see the pictures and sculptures that Hawthorne had described. In the right wing one mounted a steep circular staircase to the Storys' apartment. Elderly Cardinal Barberini, heir of the papal family, occupied the ground floor and was visible through the wide door, left open in the warm evening, as he played cards with two or three obsequious priests. James recalled the scene—like a magic-lantern picture lighted by candles—he had glimpsed through the open door: the intelligent resigned smile of the others when *Sua Eminenza ha vinto!*[25]

At crowded gatherings in the vast Story apartment that rambled through fifty rooms on the upper stories, the spirit of the old papal Rome presided. The spirit of the place was the master conductor of a great harmonious band in which differences of rank were disallowed, so that every performer came near to being as important—in other words as insignificant—as any other. That certainly was the great charm and the great ease of the place—no one, really, could be a bore. People might elsewhere be stupid, might elsewhere be vulgar or cross or ugly; here, you cared so little whether they were or not that it was virtually as good as not knowing.

James met Matthew Arnold one evening at the Palazzo Barberini, and became conscious then and there of the interesting influence of this spirit of the place. Arnold had been one of the idols of his reading time in Boston, and he had imagined that to meet him face-to-face would have made him fairly stagger with a sense of privilege. What actually happened, however, was that the sense of privilege found itself postponed; when he met Arnold again in London, years later, then it had free play. On this Roman evening, however, it was as if they were *equally* great and happy; before the overwhelming fact of Rome each bore himself with the same good manners.[26]

On another day, Henry paid a delighted visit to William Story's studio in the Via San Nicola da Tolentino, just a short walk up the Pincian Hill. It was not a place of solitary creation: Story was the head of a large enterprise of Roman workmen and assistants and servants. His own part in the work was to sketch an idea, in clay. Italian workmen then would realize the idea in a full-size armature, roughed in with clay. He and they would finish the clay model, and the workmen would then cast the fragile clay figure in more sturdy plaster, and finally—if there was a commission—the workmen would carve it in marble under his direction.

The rooms that he had taken for his studio were filled with plaster casts and marble statues in various stages of completion. In the studio there were expert Italian carvers who specialized in drapery, in fruit, in flesh; the studio and the gardens were loosely filled with workmen and guests. Story himself was the director of an orchestra, superintending this manufactory of artistic creation.

> The poetry of life . . . is in the slight dimness of the high rooms, lighted from above and with a *tone* for all their figures; it is in the space and sunshine of the garden outside, where a vague, easy pressure of business flickers and drops, where odd morsels of marble shine and shade as in their natural light, where happy human adjuncts make labour look like leisure, like luxury, like love, like something independently sweet. A door stands open to a court (there are glimpses, vistas everywhere,) and impressions so multiply that you go to meet them—meet them in the form of workmen of the pleasant race, delightful one would say as partakers of one's thought and diviners of one's intention; propitious with their fine hands and mild handsome faces and hereditary skill. . . .[27]

Casts of the famous *Cleopatra* and other works that had been carved in marble were on display. Although Story loved the nude, his own subjects were heavily draped and costumed. The costumes were necessary for the scenes he portrayed, but whether there was an element of calculation in this it would be difficult to say. Victorian England and America did not care for the nude, and Story's sensuous but draped figures were a great popular success.

In Rome, as in Venice and Florence, Henry felt driven to work. In the morning he would walk to Saint Peter's basilica, which was filled with foreign ecclesiastics, great priestly armies camped in prayer on the marble plains of its pavement, gathered for the Vatican Council. The simple impact of Saint Peter's was immense. The great dome enclosed a universe of color and sound; the greatest sculpture in the world stood in the shadows. It was the beating heart of the Catholic Church, but after a tremendous initial impression Henry put up his guard. It did make him think of Michelangelo's chapel for the Medici in Florence, where Cosimo and Eleanora were buried: a small, dimly lighted room, filled with unutterable grief, pity, and despair. It was a completely realized world.

On most mornings, however, he went through Saint Peter's as if it were only a gigantic anteroom to the Vatican. He pushed aside a leather curtain and passed through a narrow corridor into the papal enclave, where he wandered among antiquities, and peeped from the windows into the gardens of the papal household. In December, despite the crowds of Council attendees, he went to the Sistine Chapel and spent long hours studying the paintings on the ceiling, the work of Michelangelo's young manhood, and the vast and terrible end wall, *The Last Judgment*, the work of his old age. These were compositions in flesh, an essay in the theology of the body. The ceiling and walls were not paintings, exactly, at least not as Tintoretto's *Last Supper* was. A painting meant a single scene, portrayed from a single point of view. Such a painting's greatness lay in the composition of contrasting values, of bright light and deep darkness. A painting had a tone, a moral quality. But the ceiling and walls of this high-roofed chapel were not a painting or a series of paintings. The room was an architectural environment, like the vast space of Saint Peter's, half shrouded with smoke and the grime of centuries, in which one wandered among writhing figures.

Henry walked in the ruins of ancient Rome. He visited the Capitol museum, and often lingered in the square outside, at the head of Michelangelo's remarkable stairway, to admire the equestrian statue of Marcus Aurelius. He walked down among the ruins of the Forum, and then mounted up into the grassy and earth-filled Colosseum, where on a sunny afternoon he lounged, stretched out at length, watching strollers among the little shrines that had been set up beneath the ruined walls.

The greatest pleasure of all was riding outside the walls of the city. He would always remember the first carriage ride that he had taken through the ancient Porta del Popolo and along the old posting road to Florence. The winter light was infused with a kind of mellow purple glow, and bathed in this light he drove for an hour, and halted.

> The country rolled away around me into slopes and dells of long-drawn grace, chequered with purple and blue and blooming brown. The lights and shadows were at play on the Sabine Mountains—an alternation of tones so exquisite as to be conveyed only by some fantastic comparison to sapphire and amber. In the foreground a contadino in his cloak and peaked hat jogged solitary on his ass; and here and there in the distance, among the blue undulations, some white village, some grey tower. . . . It was so bright and yet so sad, so still and yet so charged, to the supersensuous ear, with the murmur of an extinguished life, that you could only say it was intensely and adorably strange. . . .[28]

The custom of the English and Americans in Rome was to ride on horseback on this great level plain, the vast granary and vineyard and market garden of Rome, ringed by distant hills and stretching westward to the sea. He resolved that when he returned to Rome he would take up horseback riding again, and join them.[29]

In the evenings he dined at a restaurant and then settled with an ice or a glass of beer at the Caffè Greco, near the Spanish Steps, where expatriate artists gathered in their wildly varied cloaks and tall hats, whitely lighted by the brass and crystal lamps.

He settled into the life of art; it became a liquid element, in which he could bathe and splash. In such an element one could sit up to one's neck, quite as one sat in a German bath.[30] There was always a meeting, a junket, an excursion—some church feast, some curiosity of color and sound not to be missed, some *rendezvous* of fraternizing artists, costumed, polyglot, theatrical, farcical, delightful; something finished, reported of, in somebody's, a poor fellow's, a clever chap's studio; some actor worth seeing at the Mausoleum of Augustus; some singer, somewhere else, singing for sixpence an old opera never heard but in Italy; some hospitality, for the evening, offered at a painted and storied palace.[31]

At a Roman ball, in this last moment of the golden age, the early evening was quiet and dancing was in suspense; nothing was done until the cardinals had arrived, princes of the secular Church, preceded up the great staircases by the four torches to which they had a right and which were carried before them in a like manner on their urbane departure. Then, when the cardinals had come and gone, beneath the great lusters that clarified the rich old ceilings, the dancing began. A majordomo stood behind the hostess to indicate, when necessary, the identity of the arriving guests, with a hint of the degree of salutation required. There were cases, apparently, in which the degree was high: *"Due reverenze, tre reverenze—reverenza profunda!"* [32]

At another gathering, at the Barberini late in the evening, it seemed as if everyone had been breathing the golden air of the artistic life of Rome. James listened to the rich voices of the women at the piano and found them all charged with the quality of the day. For there had always *been* a day—a day that moreover had been supercharged with the expectation of the evening. Rome spread its soft ancient cloth for a cosmopolitan banquet. [33]

His studies in Rome drew to a close. In the end, they turned on the central figure of the city, Michelangelo. In *Lives of the Artists*, Vasari had proclaimed Michelangelo the greatest artist of antiquity or the modern world, and Henry set himself to assess this judgment. Michelangelo was certainly a living presence in Florence and Rome. He had secured the patronage of popes and kings, had thrown up fortifications, libraries, chapels, churches; had painted and modeled and carved. He seemed to work directly in the strong forces.

Toward the end of December, Henry went one morning to bid farewell to Michelangelo's *Moses*, and he stood agitated by all the forces of his soul. The statue called up for him again the memory of the Medici Chapel, and of the painted figures in the Sistine Chapel. He could not yet express to himself a critical judgment. The figure of Moses was not precisely beautiful; he felt that it narrowly missed being ugly. Other works of art succeeded by achieving an effect; this seemed to be great by its very absence of any limited effect. That evening he tried to set down his thoughts:

This energy—positiveness—courage—call it what you will—is a simple primordial quality in the supremely superior genius. Alone it makes the real man of action in art & disjoins him effectually from the critic. I felt this morning irresistibly how M. Angelo's greatness lay above all in the fact that he *was* this man of action—the greatest almost, considering the temptation he had to be otherwise—considering how his imagination embarrassed & charmed & bewildered him—the greatest perhaps, I say, that the race has produced.[34]

He had been staying on from day to day, reluctant to leave Rome; but it was time to get himself in movement again. As in Florence and Venice, he had found what he had come to find, and his health and spirits had begun to sag again. On the first of the New Year, 1870, therefore, he retraced his steps northward.

12

ENGLAND, AGAIN:
THE ANCHOR CHAIN
IS BROKEN

Returning as he had come, Henry spent the first two weeks of the new year in Florence, where the Nortons had opened doors for him; now that his work in Italy in a sense was done, he relaxed into the graceful tone of the city and was less oppressed by its imperious greatness.[1] The good company, the good taste of the Medici palaces, and the excellent accommodations available at the best hotels made it a very pleasant place to spend a little time. The little English-speaking colony on the crest of Bellosguardo, overlooking the valley of the Arno, was a particularly lovely and graceful spot that seemed to lend its temper to the houses there.

A lifetime later, preparing for his dictation to Miss Bosanquet, the thought of Bellosguardo summoned up a vivid memory of his visit to Miss Isa Blagden, an English friend of the Nortons: he recalled the feel of the sun of Florence in the morning walk out of the ancient city gate and up the long winding hill—the sense of the large, cool villa. Her garden looked out over the valley of the Arno, vast and delicate, as if it were a painted picture.

Miss Blagden was an eager little lady whose gentle, gay black eyes and rich complexion hinted to Henry of the East Indian ancestor of whom he had been told. She had been an intimate friend of Robert Browning and Harriet Hosmer, the sculptor, and she liked to talk of the great romantic figures who had passed through Florence in her lifetime, and of the books she would have liked to read, the news she would have liked to receive, of her wide Italian acquaintance. It seemed wonderful to Henry how much they talked in an hour, and it made him reflect how deeply one might sink into Italy.[2] Their conversation struck a chord with Miss Blagden, too, for she wrote a poem for James before he left.[3]

Another letter from Mary Temple reached him in Florence, answering one he had written on his first unhappy visit to the city:

> My darling Harry, I was at Cambridge last week when your letter came to your father and Willy, from Florence, giving an account of your health and spirits that went to my heart. To think that you should be ill and depressed so far away, just when I was congratulating myself that you, at all events, were well and happy, if nobody else was. Well, my dearest Harry, we all have our troubles in this world. I only hope that yours are counterbalanced by some true happiness, which Heaven sends most of us, through some means or other. I think the best comes through blind hanging on to some conviction, never mind what, that God has put deepest into our souls, and the comforting love of a few chosen friends. . . . Don't you think so?[4]

He wrote a long answer, saying how much better he was, and telling her of his deep satisfaction with Italy. Perhaps he and she would travel in Italy together, soon.

He planned now to journey in a leisurely way along the Mediterranean coast, which he had been told was extraordinarily beautiful, as far as Marseilles, and then to work his way northward by stages to Paris, where he planned to spend a month or more. He would return dutifully to Malvern for the spring, for his health, and then, if his parents were willing to bear the added expense, perhaps he would linger in Switzerland for the summer and return to Italy for a last visit when the weather was cooler. Venice would be so close, he could drop down without any trouble. He found he had an extreme reluctance to part finally with Italy.[5]

After two sunny and happy days at Genoa spent waiting for a carriage to take him along the Corniche, the famous drive along the upper Riviera, into France,[6] he set off in the soft sunlight of an early morning, through the zone of eternal spring.

> The country is a land of universal olive—a foliage as gentle and tender as the feathers on the breast of a dove—of olives and lusty cacti and fierce fantastic date-palms, perfect debauches of light and heat. Two moments stand out beyond the rest in my memory of the last three days—the night I spent at Oneghi—and the two sweet hours I spent at San Remo, yesterday. The first had a peculiar sanctity from the fact that it was my last night on Italian soil . . . it was the moonlight which set its stamp on the event—the biggest brightest moon I ever beheld—a few pale stars looking on and the Mediterranean beneath, a sheet of murmurous silver. At San Remo, as the Italian coast draws to a close it gathers up on its lovely bosom the scattered elements of its beauty. . . . The color of the Mediterranean there is something unutterable—as blue as one has dreamed the skies of heaven. . . . There, too, the last sweet remnant of the beautiful Italian race looks at you with kindly dark eyed wonder as you take your way to the stupid unlovely North.[7]

He had breakfast at San Remo in the bosom of the olive groves, and there was something hideous about getting into his carriage to leave. He would have given much, to feel free to remain there.[8] But he could not afford to remain. It would be more than a decade before he returned.

For the remainder of the drive the road turned inland, climbing and winding among the low mountains. To his right he watched a succession of grand masses of hill scenery, clad in purple and spotted and streaked with broken lights, and on his left, seen intermittently through the openings of shady gorges, the vast blue glitter of the Mediterranean. But for all the grandeur of the scene it lacked the lovely, swarming detail of the Italian Riviera.[9]

At Nice he was truly in France, having left behind both Italy and fine weather. It was winter, and the cold affected him badly; he regretted Italy all the more. The countryside was characterized no longer by the olive groves that grew in their own sweet fashion, but by plowed fields, order, method, decency, and prosperity. The inn at Menton produced a meal of several courses, perfectly served with no apparent effort. But this modest, middle-class virtue made him yearn to return to Italy, where the whole spectrum of sensation filled the public spaces, where fact and legend fused, and even the landscape was both sensuous and intellectual; the sense of smell, of touch, of sight, and of the highest imagination were all engaged there. Having reached after so many centuries the ultimate elaboration of a civilized community, in Italy all was in harmony. As in Rome, where everyone and no one was important, so in the Italian countryside no one asserted dominion. All was pliant, feminine, peaceful. Italy had outlived glory and nationality; it was cosmopolitan and gentle; or so he believed.

He detoured briefly to visit the casino at Monaco, but gambling did not interest him. He had no taste for surrendering himself to impersonal forces. He wandered outside and walked along the beautiful shore as far as Menton, where he had dinner and reminisced about Italy.[10]

> Dearest father—I drew from my bankers in Florence the day before I left your excellent and most welcome letter of Dec. 22d . . . tho' it please you to call it a sermon. For heaven's sake don't fear to write exactly as the spirit moves you. . . . Be very sure that as I live more I care none the less for these wise human reflections of yours. I turn with great satisfaction to any profession of interest in the fate of collective humanity—turn with immense relief from the European world of idlers and starers and self-absorbed pleasure seekers. I am not prepared perhaps to measure the value of your notions with regard to the amelioration of society, but I certainly have not travelled a year in this quarter of the globe without coming to a very deep sense of the absurdly clumsy and transitory organization of the actual social body. The only respectable state of mind, indeed, is to constantly express one's perfect dissatisfaction with it—and your letter was one of the most respectable things I have seen in a long time. . . . I am *tout desolé* to find myself in this ugly pretentious sprawling Nice. I speak on the evidence of half an hour's stroll before dinner. Here Italy quite gives it up and Imperial France reigns supreme—France which I used to love—but somehow love no more.[11]

He continued westward to Marseilles by rail, a seven-hour journey that was unremarkable except for his being thrown in with a young

Englishman very gone with tuberculosis, traveling back to England alone, though he seemed to Henry quite unfit to do so. Henry tried to make him comfortable on the journey, and helped him to his hotel at Marseilles, and on their departure in the morning the young man pledged his "eternal gratitude"; but Henry had profound doubts that he would reach England alive.[12] The young traveler was to be the first in a succession of models for the charming, genteel, consumptive Ralph Touchett, in *The Portrait of a Lady*.

James himself reached Arles at noon of the next day. Winter had settled down on the countryside and a cold wind, the mistral that George Eliot had hated so, blew relentlessly. After a brief exploration he returned to his hotel. It was evident folly to try to see sights in winter. He opened a newspaper—the *Figaro*—and found it filled with descriptions of the horrible Troppmann, the murderer of the Kink family; the very names repelled him. He yearned for the familiar beauty and justice of home.[13]

He wrote dispiritedly to Alice that since it was to the savage accompaniment of the mistral—the hurtling roaring paralyzing mistral—that he visited the ancient city of Arles, he asked to be excused for not finding it the most interesting spot on earth.[14] At Avignon, the weather was worse, if anything, and the massive Palace of the Popes held little interest for him. He decided to push on quickly to Paris. He now planned to stay there not a month but only perhaps two weeks.

The capital was a city very much changed from his boyhood. His memories of the city were compounded from Balzac's novels and his own wanderings about the Palais-Royal, under the lax supervision of tutor and nurse; his was a Paris of narrow, crooked streets and little block-long neighborhoods. But this was a new Napoleonic Paris. Wide sweeps of boulevard had been cut through old half-sinister neighborhoods. Broad gaslit avenues swept outward from the Palace of the Tuileries, where Empress Eugénie dwelled, a modern-day Eleanora, cultivating the society and arts of the new empire. From the well-remembered precinct of the National Theater, beside the Palais-Royal, a broad avenue now swept northward to the new Opéra, making a striking vista. From the Opéra itself, vast new boulevards radiated east and west, lined by high-rise apartment buildings that had quickly filled with newly wealthy French, English, and Americans. The new boulevards were smoothly paved with asphalt, lighted by gas lamps, their globes piled in pyramids on the stanchions, and bordered by new theaters and cafés.

William had recommended a hotel on a little street off the Rue de la Paix,[15] and this proved pleasant and comfortable. Every evening on his return to the hotel Henry found a wood fire laid in the little fireplace, a refuge from the chill winds. But the broad boulevards with their theaters and cafés were all about. The new Paris of vistas and monuments struck Henry as pedantic and excessively symmetrical, and the big apartment buildings were garish. Paris evidently was now the capital of a European empire, of which Rome was only a remote dependency.

Once again he set to work. After his morning brioche and coffee, he walked up to the Louvre and systematically toured its vast collection. In the well-lighted rooms he found paintings that had been looted from Venice, Florence, and Rome. The French had brought order and method to the works of painters that in Italy he had seen only in dimly lighted churches and smoky guildhalls. The pictures were more intelligible but somehow less interesting when so displayed. He visited the Cathedral of Notre Dame, a vast, impossibly graceful, and light structure of stone and glass. After the day's studies he would dine in a restaurant and then retire to his room, to warm himself before the cheerful wood fire and read or write letters. He was grateful for this evening release from the weight of imperial Paris.

The great event of his stay in Paris was the national theater company, the Comédie-Française, housed in its own great palace beside the Palais-Royal. It was a company of actors descended from Molière's troupe. On his second evening in Paris he saw them perform.

In what would become his regular habit, on the evening of the performance he bought an inexpensive ticket for a stall, and took his place on a narrow uncomfortable wooden seat on the orchestra floor. He looked up at the immense proscenium, whose high arch was upheld by the half-nude figures of Apollo and Poseidon. Around and behind him, the rings of boxes rose to the distant ceiling, from whose center depended an immense chandelier. At seven the traditional *toc-toc-toc* sounded and the immense curtain lifted. The inflexible gaslights of the chandelier remained on, and the actors played to the visible wigged and costumed patrons of the boxes, so that in his stall below them, James seemed to be watching a play within a play.[16]

The great stage, the gilt and stained plaster, the red plush of the boxes, all were emblems of the tradition of the national theater. Even the foul, stale air seemed to be part of the mystic effect. The same footlights had shone on the now-vanished and legendary Rachel, she of the placards in the Palais-Royal over which he had lingered with his cousins in those early morning hours, fifteen years before.

The company of actors was self-governed, under a sort of common-law constitution that allowed its traditions to accumulate. He felt the superior influence of these traditions as soon as the curtain went up. He was in a theater that was not like other theaters. It had a peculiar perfection—something consecrated, historical, academic. This impression was delicious, and he watched the performance in a tranquil ecstasy.

Never had he seen anything so smooth and harmonious, so artistic and completed. He had heard all his life of attention to detail, and now, for the first time, he saw something that deserved that phrase. He saw that there were no limits to possible "finish," and that so trivial an act as taking a letter from a servant or placing one's hat on a chair might be made a suggestive and interesting incident. He saw these things and a great many others besides, but he did not analyze them as yet—he gave himself up to sympathetic contemplation. He was in an ideal and exemplary world.

The women were not all beautiful—decidedly not, indeed—but they were graceful, agreeable, sympathetic, ladylike; they had the best manners possible and were perfectly dressed. They had charming musical voices and they spoke with irreproachable purity and sweetness; they walked with the most elegant grace, and when they sat, it was a pleasure to see their attitudes.

As for the men, they were not all handsome either. They looked perfectly what they were intended to look, however, and when it was intended that they look handsome, they succeeded well enough. They were as well mannered and well dressed as their fairer comrades, and their voices were no less agreeable and effective.

The play was a romantic comedy, *The Adventuress*,[17] in which a brother and sister conspired to entrap a rich man, a provincial from Padua, into marriage. The adventuress was played by Mlle. Favart, no longer young and perhaps never very beautiful, but supremely elegant and exquisitely dramatic.[18] Her seduction of the middle-aged, provincial Paduan was perfectly portrayed in gesture and intonation.

Here was the ultimate realism in art: life itself made ideal. Ten years later he would render the play as a novel, *The Europeans*, and twenty-five years later, still in the grip of this vivid experience, he would try but fail to reproduce its critical scene upon the English stage.

Four times in the space of eight days Henry went to the national theater, and the intense week's experience, like his introduction to Italian painting, would shape his work thenceforth. But he was tired, and cold, and after a year of intense work he was weary and lonely. His allotment of time for Paris shrank from a month to two weeks to little more than a week; abruptly at the end of January he was on his way to Malvern, which somehow called with the voice of home.

Dr. Raynor's establishment, if not precisely home, was sufficiently familiar. English was spoken and the food was ordinary and familiar: boiled or roast mutton, or beef chops, with fried eggs and toast added in the morning, boiled potatoes, stewed vegetables, and rice pudding added at dinner.

He came down each day to find the little table in the hall filled with letters for the other residents, and searched through the envelopes for the blue stamp that meant a letter from America.[19] Then he would go for his morning walk, weather permitting.

At first the weather had been miserable and cold, and snowstorms kept him indoors in front of the British coal fire. Between storms, he took long walks in the mornings. The English countryside in February was lovely, only a shade less lovely than the greeneries of late April, when he had last been at Malvern. The fields and hedges had kept their deep green through the winter, and the trees seemed already to be in bud.

Among the twenty or so fellow boarders at Dr. Raynor's establishment was the retired Indian officer Major James, whom Henry had met the year before, he of the jaundiced complexion, who again regaled them over their common dinner table with whoppers about tigers in India and wild feats in Chinese Tartary. There was a young widow, Mrs. Hooper, who spent her days and evenings in an armchair beside the fire in the drawing room, and talked with a sort of cheerful, thick-waisted English charm to anyone who came within range about her daddy and her daddy's claret and her daddy's sayings.

While James pined for Italy, a number of Scots had come to this southern establishment—everything being relative—for the sake of its warm climate. Mr. Bruce Campbell was the swell of the house. He had soft blond whiskers and a dozen different coats, and silly Mrs. Hooper had fallen in love in with him. He was with a friend, Captain Adams, a beautiful specimen of honest, simple, stammering young British naval officer. There was heavy Mr. Fraser, a Scottish laird and a gentleman, who had placid, insipid, ladylike manners; and flaming-haired Mr. Ray, another and greater Scottish laird, with a nice young wife who carried her arms a bit like Mary Temple.[20] There were a number of ladies who dressed in brown dresses with dirty collars, linsey-woolsey trains, and dowdy beads. Their conversation never went beyond formulas and they made him wish for Mary Temple's moral spontaneity.

"Have you ever been in Florence?"

"Oh yes."

"Isn't it a most peculiarly interesting city?"

"Oh yes, I think it so very nice."[21]

And there was a certain poor young fellow, Jameson, who was in a condition of wretched semiblindness. He was an Oxford man, slender, wiry, gray-eyed; he had been a good deal of a traveler when his sight was better. Henry was glad to take up his company—cautiously, not too often. Toward the end of February they took their morning walk together, he and his gentleman, arm in arm, four miles across the hedgy Worcestershire fields to the bank of the narrow, gliding Severn. That evening, Henry wrote to Alice a long letter about his friend and the walk they had taken together. There was nothing remarkable about the walk—only that England seemed to come home to him more closely than ever. England was in the faraway group of stately blue-black trees of Birken Foster, in the mist on a sheep-cropped manorial slope, and in the turfy common that bordered the highway, dotted with cattle; and in a shaggy, mauve-colored donkey, with its mane over its eyes, browsing innocently among the very thickest brambles of the hedge. Three geese cackled and expanded their wings. Henry and his friend had walked along companionably, saying little, and had come upon an old woman—*the* very old woman of Europe in person, in her red cloak and black bonnet frilled all around the face, triple-frilled beside her placid old cheeks. The stalwart rustic young man beside her called her Granny. England was in his white smock, puckered on the chest, his standing collar and scarlet neckerchief, his vast blue-stockinged calves and tremendously high shoes, his big red rural face. In the background, beyond the common, was *the* cottage of ancient England with its steep heavy thatch, its broad low-latticed windows, waist-high door, and curling smoke, its general rich expression of having been lived in and died in and worked and played in since a happy English day when Yankees were babies unborn.

But all this picture is nothing without the darksome light—the mist-softened air—the damp black hedges, the springing turf, and the great band above the horizon—the band of watery light, playing through the stems of distant copses. . . . sometimes as I glance at some ancient bit of greenery by the wayside it will break in upon me as a revelation and I seem to feel England for the 1st time. To *feel England* is a satisfaction which I heartily wish you for some future day.[22]

The morning's walk with Jameson made him think about the possibility of living in England, although, as before, he did not find it welcomed him, or any stranger. It still seemed to sit with its back turned, intent on its own familiar faces.

> To live in England, "respectably," you have somehow to draw more
> heavily on your manhood—your substance and courage than in other
> countries;—how much more, alas! than in that sweet relaxing Italy.
> But I wish my pen had the power to make you feel the land as I felt
> it this morning. . . .[23]

Jameson, he mused, was a gentleman, which was a great deal to the purpose in this pleasant England. To be or not to be respectable was to stand on one side or the other of a very visible line.[24]

After his morning and afternoon walks, Henry sat alone in the cold, running sitz bath that Dr. Raynor had prescribed, but as before he had an uneasy suspicion that they did not aid his bowels and that they made his back worse.

Letters from home at last began to arrive. Bob wrote in an odd formal way to tell Henry that he had moved to Milwaukee in search of business opportunity. Wilky, too, had now abandoned the Florida venture and was moving west. The plantation had been a near-total loss. William wrote to say that the family had decided to buy the Cambridge house in which they had lived for the past five years. Father had evidently given up at last the theory that the family was only temporarily lodged, awaiting a return to Europe. There were letters from Mother and Alice and Aunt Kate. Alice told him that Mary Temple had had another bout of hemorrhages.[25] The Temple sisters had visited the Jameses in Cambridge during the winter, and William and Mary Temple had become close friends, which amused and troubled Mother.[26] There was news of Holmes, Gray, Howells, and the Bootts, and Henry asked for more.

Malvern was not having the favorable effect on his health that he had hoped. The cold baths seemed to make his lower-back pain worse, if anything, and memories of the abundant gardens of home suddenly filled him with yearning:

> I sometimes think I shall never get well until I get a chance for a year at
> a pure vegetable diet—at unlimited tomatoes & beans & pease &
> squash & turnips & carrots & corn—I enjoy merely writing the words.[27]

He turned over plans for the spring and summer—he would travel in England during the spring, perhaps using Malvern as his base, visiting London and Jameson's Oxford. Then, when the weather grew hot, perhaps he would go to Switzerland while he waited for his chance to return to Italy in the fall. But it would be a great deal of expense, for perhaps only modest gains. His spirits were good, and he had filled his trunks; he began to think of returning to America. He felt confident that his health would continue to improve at home, aided by fresh food and the magic of regular travel. He had succeeded, after all, in making capital out of this difficult year, capital on which he would draw for a long time. He was conscious of the change in himself that Europe had made. But there was the circle of friends and family that he had so carefully built around himself in America, and to which he longed to return. Yet even while he revolved these thoughts in his mind, the center of that circle, Mary Temple, had been lost.

March 29, 1870

Dearest mother—I rec'd this morning your letter with father's note, telling me of Minny's death—news more strong and painful than I can find words to express. Your last mention of her condition had been very far from preparing me for this. The event suggests such a host of thoughts that it seems vain to utter them. You can imagine all I feel. Minny seemed such a breathing immortal reality that the mere statement of her death conveys little meaning; really to comprehend it I must wait—we must all wait—till time brings with it a poignant sense of loss & irremediable absence. I have been spending the morning letting the awakened swarm of old recollections & associations flow into my mind—almost *enjoying* the exquisite pain they provoke. Wherever I turn in all the more recent years of my life I find Minny somehow present directly or indirectly—and with all that wonderful ethereal brightness of presence which was so peculiarly her own. And now to sit down to the idea of her *death*! . . . Oh dearest Mother! oh poor struggling suffering *dying* creature! . . . There is absolute balm in the thought of poor Minny & rest—rest & immortal absence! But viewed in a simple human light, by the eager spirit that insists upon its own—her death is full of overflowing sadness. It comes home to me with irresistible power, the sense of how much I knew her and how much I loved her.[28]

It was the first death of someone close to him, and as a writer he took an intense interest in his own reaction. With a sort of tender concern he opened himself to feeling. He spent the day walking, allowing the news to sink into him.

He had not been in love with her, as more or less everyone was supposed to have been, but he had loved her—they had loved each other. Mary and he had shared a great deal from infancy onward; they were close cousins and friendly rivals, and he had long been in the habit of trying to project the lines of her life into the future. But those lines had been cut now, and he was constantly brought up short. What would have become of such intellectual and spiritual yearning, such defenseless generosity? With her open affections she had seemed destined to be victimized by life. What prospect had there been for her to *complete* herself, she who had not yet lived?[29] In his novels he would repeatedly imagine the completion, her passage from victimhood to active life.[30]

That evening, his mind still filled with the thoughts and feelings that the news of her death had provoked, he sat down to write a long clinical letter to William. He had already made her death an element of a composition of contrasting light and shadow. While he had been crawling from weakness and inaction and suffering into strength and health and hope, she had been sinking out of brightness and youth into decline and death. There was a tinge of pleasure in his imaginings, not entirely to be accounted for by the natural relief that is felt by a survivor. Mary had suffered very badly in the final weeks of her disease, and Henry could not help repeatedly imagining her sufferings and her final release.[31] He lingered on at Malvern, taking occasional walks—not too often—with Jameson. They went up to London, and to Oxford, together.

Despite William's urgings and all the conventional wisdom, the cold baths of Malvern were adding to his back pain, which otherwise had been manageable. In April he returned to London for a few days, over William's objections, to consult a specialist who told him that sitting in the baths had been affecting his kidneys adversely. It was time to travel again, to return to America.

13

RETURNING TO THE HUDSON,
AS A VISITOR FROM ABROAD

Elizabeth Boott had befriended Mary Temple and had been with her in the agonized final weeks. Henry wanted every scrap of news about Mary, and they had long conversations about her; this was the beginning of their friendship.

To Henry, child of his parents, death in itself was not to be regretted. The saddest part of the whole tale was that Mary had clung desperately to life, even at the last, when there was nothing more for her to expect but continued suffering. She had never found her courage, it seemed, or her faith; she had clung to consciousness and would have given anything to live—and the image of this was to remain for him the essence of the tragedy, to have died without having found her freedom, without properly having lived.[1]

If Mary had been spontaneous and incomplete, Elizabeth was self-aware and complete to a high finish—markedly *produced*.[2] While

Mary had been a child finding her way alone in the world, Elizabeth had been guarded and cultivated and nurtured by her father, Francis.

Frank Boott—a bit narrow in the shoulder, elegantly dressed, his full beard carefully trimmed—was fifty-seven years old. His father and uncle had been among the founders of the mill town at Lowell— the Boott Mills were famous—and he was a man of moderate but independent means. He had lived in Boston with his young wife, had studied music and begun to compose; his music was one of their great shared pleasures. He wrote songs for his wife to sing: ballads, romantic and very modern songs, settings for poems by Sir Walter Scott or their friend Mrs. Norton.[3] Their first baby did not survive his infancy, and shortly after their daughter, Elizabeth, was born, the mother had died. Boott had then taken his little daughter abroad with him. The sad little family had settled in Florence, and Boott had devoted himself to music and to his daughter's education. As she grew older they became inseparable companions, a deep sympathy uniting them; they had traveled together in Italy and Europe, and now he had brought her home. In the evenings she sang the sweet, sad songs he had written for her mother while he accompanied her on the piano.

There was a marked similarity between them, especially in their large, liquid brown eyes, the brows drawn together a little quizzically. Her features were delicate, and her mouth was wide and expressive, with a lingering memory of a sad smile in the corners. She had smooth brown hair drawn down in two wings across her forehead and a lovely pale complexion, and though she was rather small, she stood and carried herself in a graceful way, both conscious and heedless of being observed. She spoke perfectly colloquial English, French, and Italian. Her conversation touched lightly and intelligently on the art and literature of Europe; she had begun to paint in watercolors.

The Bootts were in Boston, and Henry met them there and in Cambridge, as he took up his old round of calls. The society of Cambridge seemed thinner and more barren than ever. The Norton and Sedgwick sisters were still abroad, and for society he made do with their in-laws, the Gurneys, who had rented Shady Hill, and the Sedgwick family on Kirkland Street. Young Arthur Sedgwick had remained at home, and Henry found him good company. He had taken a law degree, but, like Henry, was preparing himself for a career as a man of letters. Lowell was back from Europe, but somehow Henry did not resume his calls at Elmwood.

The Holmes and Fields houses on Charles Street seemed unchanged. Wendell Holmes was rather busy and distracted. He had opened a law office with his younger brother, Ned, and had undertaken to edit a comprehensive treatise of American law. He had also been appointed an instructor to teach constitutional law to the juniors and seniors at Harvard College; he seemed pale and tense, and was evidently struggling to establish himself.[4] Sedgwick and Holmes had become joint editors of a new journal, the *American Law Review.*

John Gray, by contrast, pursued his even course as before. Like Holmes, he was now teaching at the university, but with less sense of strain. Old Professor Washburn was on leave of absence, and Gray was taking his classes.[5] Howells, too, was a university lecturer, talking on Italian literature in the evenings in classes that were open to the public. He was preoccupied with this work, with proofreading for *The Atlantic,* and with household cares. He hoped for a raise in salary. Tom Perry came up to Boston regularly, but he was courting Lilla Cabot, a fiercely intelligent young woman, a cousin of Wendell Holmes's, and James rarely saw him. The circle that had briefly drawn them together was broken, and each was flying off in his own direction; Henry saw them very little.

At home at Quincy Street, the family circle had been restored, except that the two youngest boys were absent, looking for work in the west. Alice was sarcastic and increasingly imperious, but she was full of life and energy, enmeshed once more in intimate friendships. William was thirty years old, and he had his medical degree, but he remained at home, somehow inert. He talked vaguely of practicing psychiatry with Tom Ward. He had had a difficult winter and had sunk into a deep depression. He discussed his own symptoms, as always, with great interest. Henry felt out of place, restless, impatient. When a letter from Grace Norton arrived, redolent with the air of Florence, he had a spasm of regret.

Here I am—here I have been for the last ten days—the last ten years. It's very hot: the window is open before me: opposite thro' the trees I see the scarlet walls of the President's *palazzo.* . . . Howells is lecturing very pleasantly on Italian literature. I go to the lecture room in Boylston Hall: I sit with my eyes closed, listening to the sweet Italian names & allusions & trying to fancy that the window behind me opens out into Florence. But Florence is within & not without. When I'm hopeful of seeing Florence again not ten years hence—that *is*

Florence:—all that you tell me is delightful. I can fancy what a game Florence & May are playing between them. Poor May just here has rather an irresponsive playmate. . . .

I wish I could tell you how characteristic everything strikes me as being—everything from the vast white distant sky—to the stiff spare individual blades of grass.[6]

The Jameses and the Bootts were often together; Henry found himself in frequent conversation with Elizabeth. She knew Italy intimately, of course, and when he told his stories of his trip she knew the places and the pictures, and she responded warmly and with feeling. It was like retracing the route with a companion. They stood together before Tintoretto's terrible *Crucifixion*, and as Henry described its perfect realism there were tears in her eyes. But she had been moved by the subject; and he, by the painter.

The only great virtue of Cambridge was negative—the isolation and silence it provided in ample measure. It was a place to work, and in his shirtsleeves, in his familiar second-floor bedroom looking out at President Eliot's red house and the gray mass of the new library through the thin trees, he began to write again, for the first time in a year.

He had promised Howells a travel piece for *The Atlantic*, but what came from his pen was a story set in Italy. In his hot bedroom he imagined himself back over the course of his trip, and the lessons of the voyage crystallized as he wrote. He remembered, above all, standing before Leonardo's *Last Supper*—the epitome of the treasures of the past, half destroyed, demanding to be imagined into wholeness.

In the story, an American girl stood before the picture—it was Elizabeth Boott, with her dark hair combed in two wings over her forehead and a sad smile lurking in the corners of her mouth. She and her father were traveling together, intimate and sufficient to themselves. Henry imagined meeting her in Italy, but she was a tourist like himself, not an old inhabitant. He would accompany her to the churches and museums he had visited; they would dine at Quadri's, and walk across the piazza to Florian's to listen to the music. They would visit the old Hebrew cemetery on the island of the Lido, and lounge among the grass-grown headstones. In the tale he was a young man of the north, more like William than himself, a serious scientific young man. The father would die, of course; and he imagined the young man's hot passion for the daughter in all its ambiguous complexity. In his summer bedroom he imagined being aroused by her pain and weakness and loneliness. He loved her, and she rested her head on his breast.[7]

The simple, realistic style in which he wrote matched the beauty of the setting. Hawthorne, Stendhal, and George Sand were gracefully evoked; the great Italian paintings seemed to glimmer with the light of Venice. He called the story "Travelling Companions," and gave it to *The Atlantic.* A few days later Annie Fields lay in the grass at the bottom of her garden on the bank of the Charles River while James Fields read the story to her, and she wept—with pleasure at Henry's success, she said. It was so terribly hard to succeed.[8] But also, perhaps, she wept with sympathy, for her feeling for the young heroine was not unlike James's.

Howells joyfully repeated to him Fields's remark that the editors would like to have as much as Henry James could give them, and in June he unpacked his European bags for them, writing in rapid succession another long story, "The Passionate Pilgrim,"[9] and a long book review.[10] In these he reflected on the aristocratic idea that seemed to dominate English society. Romantic it was, indeed, and he liked to see it celebrated. But complacent and unjust and narrow it was also. In his story, a passionate American pilgrim yearned for the romance of England while a ruined Englishman yearned for the liberty and justice of America. Each dreamed of living in the other's country, but the two visions seemed to be incompatible, and each character died without realizing his ideal in the other's land.

It was his first extended reflection on the seeming incompatibility of justice and art. In Italy, beauty seemed to rest upon centuries of evil; the new Italian republic had seemed to usher in an age of modern ugliness as well as justice. In England and France the old order persisted, with its grace and beauty, and its tyranny. In America there was liberty and justice, but it was the liberty of a wilderness.

This emptied his bag, for the moment.[11] It was time to put himself into motion again. The Bootts planned to spend their summer in Newport; the Jameses would go to the seashore north of Boston. He, too, would have to flee the summer heat, but he did not know where he would go or what he would do, "now that he had got American again."[12] He wrote to Godkin, proposing to write a series of travel pieces about American summer resorts. When July came he was on his way westward, as if he were a foreign traveler once more.

His plan was to travel up the Hudson River, the great artery of his America, and to visit the famous resort at Saratoga Springs, where he might take the waters himself and observe others doing so, and then continue northward, fleeing the hot weather, through Lake George and Lake Champlain, into Vermont. He would end with a return to Newport, which, since the war, had itself become a fashionable resort.

The Hudson River valley above Albany, and western New York State, in his childhood had always been talked of at home as a frontier country; the old Robertson lands in "the west" were vaguely in this trackless desert. He had formed an idea of Saratoga as a resort buried in a sort of elegant wilderness, a region of shady forest drives with a bright, broad-terraced hotel gleaming here and there against a background of mysterious groves and glades—an image compounded of his own childhood memories of summers in New Brighton, and those vague stories of the lands in the "west." But the Saratoga of reality was immensely different.[13]

"The hotel system is unrivalled in any country," the guidebook proclaimed, "being equal to the accommodation of 18,000 visitors . . . while over 3,000 private carriages, together with the cavalcades, join in the parade of fashion on Broadway. . . ."[14] The Grand Union Hotel occupied almost the entire square at Broadway and Congress Streets, and it proclaimed itself the largest hotel in America: a vast, modern, six-story brick edifice. Directly facing it across Broadway was the all but equally vast Congress Hotel, which would claim as its own the famous Congress spring, whose effervescent waters were bottled and sold throughout the United States, and whose medicinal qualities were the foundation of the resort's fame.[15]

Henry was prepared to concede the superior qualities of the water, which indeed agreed with him remarkably well. With a certain bemusement he was also willing to concede that the Grand Union's veranda, which was mounted on cast-iron pillars and ran across the first story of the façade, was the largest in the world. It certainly provided a vast amount of space for sitting outdoors and looking at the crowds of vehicles—light two-wheelers, open-topped four-wheel carriages, big yellow horse-drawn cavalcades—and the pedestrians below. Henry made notes for *The Nation:*

> In the evening, when the "boarders" have all come forth and seated themselves in groups, or have begun to stroll in . . . couples, the big heterogeneous scene affords a great deal of entertainment. . . . The rough brick wall of the house, illumined by a line of flaring gas-lamps,

forms a natural background to the crude, impermanent, discordant tone of the assembly.[16]

He stayed at the Grand Union, which the guidebook said was the "center of fashion." The gaslights on the veranda were strangely cold, and their harsh light flattened and erased the gradations of light that might have given it tone. Tall windows opened at regular intervals from the veranda into an immense parlor—he supposed it was the largest in the world—furnished only with a few dozen scattered rocking chairs; small tables beside them bore pitchers of iced water.

The population of Saratoga Springs was overwhelmingly female, the men having remained in their offices in New York (a fast train now ran in the summers). The couples that strolled in the evening or danced in the ballroom that blazed with hot lights, were often pairs of women.

The men who were present had arrived from the West, and were hopelessly out of range of their offices. They seemed to spend a great deal of time tilted back in chairs, feet up, hat down, a cigar jutting from the corner of the mouth at yet another acute angle. They were dressed in the roughest, most casual clothes, even for the ballroom in the evening. They interested Henry, these western men, whose thin faces spoke of decisive activity.[17] They were utterly disconnected from the women.

> If the men are remarkable, the women are wonderful. . . . Your first impression is . . . of the—what shall I call it?—of the abundance of petticoats. Every woman you meet, young or old, is attired with a certain amount of richness. . . . You behold an interesting, indeed a quite momentous spectacle; the democratization of elegance.[18]

It was a curious and somehow sad spectacle: lovely young women dressed for an appearance before the crowd of tavern loungers. They were not dressed for anyone in particular, they were dressed for publicity. One woman especially struck him. Her dress was tremendously modern, and every evening of the two weeks he remained in Saratoga she appeared in a fresh creation.

> She ought to sit on the terrace of a stately castle, with a great baronial park shutting out the undressed world, and bandy quiet small-talk

with an ambassador or a duke. My imagination is shocked when I behold her seated in gorgeous relief against the dusty clapboards of the hotel, with her beautiful hands folded in her lap, her head drooping slightly beneath the weight of her *chignon*, her lips parted in a vague contemplative gaze at Mr. Helmbold's well-known advertisement on the opposite fence, her husband reading the New York *Herald*.[19]

America had failed them, these women who had neither public work to do like the men nor a private world where history was made. They remained passive, for they had no chance to become active; the young women had been denied an education in life, had been denied their coming-of-age.

Henry's theme returned to him, with a strangely ambiguous addition. He began to think of writing a novel about an American girl who becomes a woman. She would be an orphan, and all alone. A man would take the young woman in his charge. He would not be like the detached, oblivious businessmen at Saratoga; he would be a man with a heart, rather like one of the middle-aged Emmet cousins or Frank Boott: father, tutor, mentor, husband. He would create a private world for the heroine, and there he would educate her to self-awareness and freedom.[20]

The newspapers were filled with intensely interesting reports from Europe that hinted at momentous events that were hidden from view. The ruling families of the European powers had begun to quarrel seriously. A cousin of the king of Prussia, a Hohenzollern prince, had secretly been offered the throne of Spain. The emperor of France had not been consulted; the Prussians seemed to be encircling France with a hostile alliance. The empress, the beautiful Eugénie, conceived the notion that her emperor had been insulted. She was not ill disposed to a war against the Prussians that would leave France the undisputed power in Europe. She insisted on treating the matter as an affair of honor. In July the newspapers that came up from New York were filled with rumors and alarms. The Prussians seemed deliberately to provoke the empress further, and on the fourteenth, France declared war. The next day Wilhelm, king of Prussia, ordered a mobilization of his army and of the armed forces of the North German Confederation. He persuaded the independent kingdoms of South Germany, who would meet the first advance of the French, to join him as well.

It was easy to laugh at the Prussians and their army of clerks and opticians, their patient diligence and their passionate idealism. But the English correspondents began to report that this was a new kind of war. Helmuth von Moltke, years before, had advised the king of Prussia to prepare for an attack by France, and now the shining steel rails that reached across Europe—the rails that had carried so many travelers—were blackened with troops and matériel flowing westward, in response to carefully drafted orders, toward preordained marshaling points. With frightening speed an immense German army gathered.

The emperor Napoleon III went to the front to take personal command of his army, and on August 2, 1870, his advance into the South German states began. This advance was quickly repulsed, and the Prussian-led armies of the German confederation began to move forward into France. The reverses of the French army came in rapid succession; the army that was to invade Germany had been trapped at Metz; Napoleon III, with more than one hundred thousand troops, fell back upon the seventeenth-century fortress at Sedan.

As these extraordinary events were unfolding, Henry ended his stay at Saratoga and returned to the Hudson River valley. He resumed his journey northward by rail, and drove into the thickening hills and along the bases of half-grown mountains to Lake George. Henry found himself in utter wilderness. He could not put a name to anything. He could not describe the mountains in any but the most vague and general terms. The few traces that people had left on the land only emphasized the general wildness:

> Here, on the left shore of the lake, is a saw-mill with a high black chimney, a dozen little white wooden houses, and a little promontory of planks on posts, in the nature of a steamboat-pier. This brave little attempt at civilization looks as transient and accidental as the furniture of a dream.[21]

In the late afternoon he went upon the lake lazily, with a rednecked, brown-eyed young man as his oarsman; it was, of course, delicious.

> In the evening, at the hotel, there was the usual array of placid, sauntering tourists—the usual spectacle of high-heeled young ladies in those charming puffed and paniered overdresses of white muslin which are now so picturesquely worn. . . . The New York papers had just come in, and I had been reading of the great deeds of Prussia and the confusion of France. I was filled with a sense of Prussian greatness. Strolling toward the place where the band was stationed, I beheld

behind every trumpet a sturdy German face and heard in every note an uplifted German voice. My sense of German greatness was hugely magnified. Here, while their strong fellow-citizens were winning battles and making history in Alsace and Lorraine, they were making music in a distant land for a crowd of unmelodious strangers. What a splendid range of prowess and powers! What an omen for the Prussian future! The air seemed a brazen paean of triumph and joy. Their simple Teutonic presence seemed a portent.[22]

After a brief return to Cambridge, in accordance with his plan, he went to Newport. Prosperity had come once again to the old seaport, but without seeming to damage its tone. The Avenue had been extended and now ran along the once-deserted shore where he and Tom Perry had wandered long ago; the occasional carriage that passed along the road did not disturb its solitude much, and the walk along the fringe of the ocean was, if anything, improved. The immense white sky reminded him of the Venetian light, and the little orchards with their ancient twisted trees were like the olive groves of the Italian coast. It was a domesticated landscape, filled with memories and associations. Perhaps, after all, beauty and justice might be reconciled; here, at least, was a civilized democracy.

In the town itself, the little twisted, cobbled main street was filled with beautifully dressed women carrying little baskets on their arms, making their daily purchases. The old village trailed off as of old into the weathered, gray, barnacled houses of the Point.

On the Avenue, and along the low eastern cliffs, some very large new "cottages" had been built; many of them had been designed by Bill Hunt's brother, Richard, in emulation of the classic villas of Italy. The effect, although not subtle, was not unlovely; the long afternoons in these grand houses especially appealed to his fancy; it was here that liberty and beauty combined.[23] In Newport as elsewhere, women ruled the lovely houses and governed the society in them, but if in Europe women were required to do so by indirection and sophisticated arts, here they ruled openly and innocently. When he walked along the Avenue, and doffed his hat to a young woman alone in her open little basket phaeton, she bowed confidently to him, with an open and frank smile, without shyness or coquetry. He heard a woman tell another, with a quiet ecstasy of tone, that she had been having "a most perfect time." This seemed to him the very poetry of pleasure.[24]

Nor was there, as in Saratoga, an absence of men. There was an ample number, but they were not sharp-faced businessmen taking a grudging hour from their offices. Young men of leisure galloped their shining horses or reclined in submission beside young women in open carriages. The relations of the men and women were complex, leisurely, and without visible signs of vice. So he described them for *The Nation*, warming to his subject and the ideal of life that it represented. It was a perfectly American scene, far superior in its complacent virtue, its confident freedom, to the civilization of Europe—and yet it was not Saratoga. It was not precisely *democratic*.[25]

The extraordinary news from abroad, alarming and awful as it was, yet contributed to his sense of American complacency. The German confederation, under the leadership of the king of Prussia, continued to inflict humiliations upon the French. Early in September, correspondents with the Prussian army reported that Napoleon III had been surrounded at Sedan. On the sixth, there came the astounding news that the emperor had surrendered and was taken prisoner with his army of one hundred thousand. By the end of October the French had lost the entire army of five hundred thousand men that the emperor had put into the field. There had been no equivalent defeat in European history.

The empress secretly left the Tuileries and fled with her son to the coast of England, crossing at Boulogne, over the path that so many exiles had trodden over the centuries, and established a tiny court in exile. The empire had fallen, and a new government of the left proclaimed itself in Paris, a Government of National Defense. There was no cessation of the war: Prussian armies marched steadily toward Paris and encircled it. Supplied by rail, they encamped themselves to besiege the quondam capital of Europe. The new French government declared that there could be no peace, and began to raise new armies. It was now to be a war, not between kings for honor, but a People's War to the knife.

The French troops that had occupied Rome were called back to France to assist in the defense of Paris; and the new Italian state of Victor Emmanuel II took Rome for its own capital almost without firing a shot. The pope peacefully withdrew into the Vatican; the secular power of the Church in Europe was no more.

Day by day, the historic order of Europe was being permanently altered. The little German-speaking duchies and dukedoms of central Europe were being absorbed into a single empire; once-provincial Berlin had become a world capital. The powers looked on a little uneasily. Newspapers began to report atrocities committed by German troops. The German chancellor, Bismarck, was reported to have announced that the aim of the war was the permanent destruction of France as a military power. The provinces of Alsace and Lorraine would be taken, and Paris would be invested by German troops. In London, Parliament began to struggle with the unfamiliar question of whether it should intervene on the side of France, its ancient rival.

Henry tried to imagine the cataclysms that were convulsing France. He was fortunate to have returned from Europe when he had. He would visit again, when the war had ended; he was full of admiration for the comparatively peaceful Italians. As he made his way back to Cambridge he was conscious of a constant desire to return to Italy, not for a brief visit but for an indefinite stay of years.[26] His own circumstances did not yet allow him this freedom, but he and Arthur Sedgwick talked of going to Italy together, to share expenses, in a year or two, and the idea of joining the Norton-Sedgwick colony in Florence began to crystallize as a definite plan.

Grace Norton had written a lovely long letter about the family's life in Florence that summer. The Nortons had taken a villa on the hill just outside the city, Bellosguardo, where Henry had paid a visit to Miss Blagden. They had a magnificent view of Florence and the valley of the Arno, with the distant hills beyond. Grace recalled for him the winding, walled road that led down the hill to the gardens of the Pitti Palace; from there one could stroll across the old bridge, pausing midway to look at the yellow Arno casting its light on the dirty yellow plaster walls of the houses that lined its banks. Henry passionately imagined himself with them, observing from the relative peace and tranquillity of Florence the turmoil convulsing France and Germany.

At home on Quincy Street, as in Cambridge generally, the tide of sympathy had begun to shift from the Germans to the new French Government of National Defense, but Henry shuddered at the new People's War they had undertaken, and sat down in imagination with Grace Norton, to tell her his troubled thoughts:

> But it is useless talking or guessing or sermonizing about France. She is a grim object enough. She holds her fate in her own hands—no one can help her or advise her but herself—she who feels her bosom torn and shaken with all the raging elements of the problem. All one can say is *poor poor France!* & yet there is a kind of resignation in our pity: the healthy sentiment of satisfaction that we *must* feel in seeing folly & vanity & iniquity attended by a smothering, stifling, trampling suc-

cession of mortifications, defeats & penances. What Germany has done, in a broad way, has simply been to give France over to herself: that self so weak so vain, so unveracious . . . she receives the great gift & charges into a yawning bloody gulf of disorder—a vainer vanity than ever! The Germans have done more than they dream—haven't they?—and builded better than they knew. They have enforced certain homely truths as never in all history they can have been enforced, & the silent economy of one's moral life draws vigor from their example. Live for the shows & names and glory of things & not for their bitter, nutritious essential forces and values—and you'll have the trampling Germans of the universe let loose upon you.[27]

He had been a man of leisure all summer; it was now time to work. If he were to go to Italy, he would have to save some money for the expenses of travel and establish himself sufficiently as a writer to support himself by his writings from abroad. He thought that these tasks might take two or three years. His travel pieces and reviews were appearing in *The Nation*, and his two stories would appear early in the following year in *The Atlantic Monthly*.

He wrote a story for the New York *Galaxy*, the other steady market for his work. It was an audacious analysis of the sensual forces within the family. A woman had given herself up to passion, selfishly, and a son—Master Eustace—had been born from her adultery. She lived alone with the son, and transferred to him all her undisciplined affection. He grew into a wicked, self-indulgent adolescent, and when his natural father returned, the boy attacked him with violence and loathing.[28]

This was a calculated piece of work; the language of the tale evoked references to Hamlet and Oedipus, on the one hand, and modern scientific anthropology on the other. It seemed somehow cold and contrived, however; perhaps the very skillfulness and attention to detail had obtruded themselves.

My dear Church, many thanks for your cheque; it reached me this morning. May I express the hope that you will be able to print *Master Eustace* in the *larger type*—undivided pages—of the magazine? as it is very little broken up by paragraphs or talk there will be little waste of space in so doing.[29]

But without materially altering his circumstances, he had exhausted the opportunities for short articles and stories for the moment. He would have to do something more substantial: a novel. Fields, like other publishers who had captive magazines, could publish a book in chapters, in serial form; Henry would be paid for his work, month by month, as it appeared; and the magazine version would create interest in the eventual book. If the book succeeded, then there was a chance of additional royalties from its sales.

Yet he was not quite ready to write the full-scale novels that the logic of writing as a profession seemed to require. He would begin with a kind of exercise, a sketch of the novel that he had been turning over in his mind, about a mentor and his ward. It could be serialized in perhaps five numbers of *The Atlantic*. It would be another sensational treatment of the strong forces of sexual attraction, still more audaciously, between father and daughter. It would be a study composed with the clarity and precise form of a French play or a scientific experiment.

The central figure was a slim young girl, with the auburn hair and gray eyes that marked her as the heroine. She was to have two fathers—one bad and one good. The first father was an adventurer, a man of uncontrolled passions. He had lost everything but his twelve-year-old daughter. Wife and friends and money were all gone; in his need he carried his daughter about with him in aimless travels, so that she had no education and no friends but himself. She developed a certain prematurely elderly air and an incongruous familiarity with foreign languages and mores—echoes of James's own childhood.

Father and daughter came to be marooned in a New York hotel. Late one night he came into his daughter's bedroom and knelt at her side; she awakened to find him kissing her, fondling her, and raving over her. Then he bade her good night and passed into the adjoining room. Later she was awakened again: he was calling her.

When she came into his room he was standing in shirtsleeves, with the gas turned low; she heard a report and felt the wind of a bullet as it went past her head. Her father had fired a pistol at her. She fled back into her own room, and she heard a second report. Returning, she found his corpse, the face covered with blood and the pistol still in his hand.

This much was rendered like a newspaper report. One could be utterly frank about the father's violent passions, a mixture of tenderness and cruelty, so long as they were not named. Indeed, one had no name to give these strong forces. They were there, in the gaps and suppressions of the picture, for the reader to imagine.

A second man became, in effect, another father. He adopted the twelve-year-old girl—out of charity, as he said to himself, but he loved her as passionately, as ambiguously, as her true father had. If the heroine somewhat resembled the orphaned Temple girls, this second father was like the older Emmet cousins who had courted them. Balding, shy, formal in manner, gently affectionate, he was as much a doting grandmother as he was a father; he gave the little girl her freedom, and an affection that did not intrude, that was like the background of her life. They lived in a house in the country. He educated her and provided her with friends, and eventually sent her to school. He felt a strong aversion to claiming in his ward that prosaic right of *property* that belongs to the father.[30] But his feelings for her were complex.

As she grew older, her adoptive father admitted to himself that he loved her, and that he wished her to love him in return. He did not wish to impose his will, but to have their relation ripen as a perfect matter of course. He watched patiently, like a botanist searching for the first woodland violets of the year, for the shy field-flower of spontaneous affection. He aimed at nothing more or less than to inspire the child with a passion. When he sent her away to school, it was with the conscious awareness that he was educating her to be his wife—if she should choose him, as he had chosen her.

> Until he had detected in her glance and tone the note of passionate tenderness, his experiment must have failed. It would have succeeded on the day when she should break out into cries and tears and tell him with a clinging embrace that she loved him.[31]

She outgrew her awkward adolescence and became a striking young woman, with unexpected charm and beauty—but with James's own or Elizabeth Boott's deep reserve. And she began to fall in love, but not with her adoptive father. First she loved a cousin, a western go-getter, and then an unctuous and hypocritical cleric. They were each, in their different ways, cold and abusive.

The story drove the girl from the violent manly cousin to the hypocritically moral minister. The two men were types; they were meant to represent the world. She saw that each would use her for his own profit. At last she consulted her own inner being and renounced her passion for them. At this, she experienced an epiphany: The sky was blazing blue overhead; she hailed the joyous brightness of the day with a kind of answering joy. She seemed to be in the secret of the universe.[32] She had acquired genuine understanding, and was now therefore free to choose. She joyfully accepted her own nature, the complex character shaped by her inheritance and her upbringing. She chose to be what she could not help being; she chose to be her adoptive father's wife. Love and duty were one. And he, the mentor, having left her free to choose, could embrace her guiltlessly.

This strange tale in itself was not unlike some of Dickens's sentimental stories; benevolent uncles and grateful nieces were forever providing the happy endings of romantic novels. What made James's novel peculiar and sensational was the intense naturalism of his portrayal. It was a fairy tale decked out with the details of a newspaper story.

It was as audacious in its way as "A Light Man"; it dripped with sexuality, with suggestive metaphors. The very title, "Watch and Ward"— a "ward" was the little key used to wind up a pocket watch—suggested couplings and insertions. The little girl, who was also a ward, fumbled with her mentor's keys with her childish fingers; his sunlike rays penetrated her opening blossom. He embraced her, and the reader felt her thin boyish limbs.

The story was written as if in a constant state of arousal. Perhaps it was, but this was self-conscious technique, all the same. James was a rather cool seducer. "I have tried to make a work of art," he wrote to the Nortons, "and if you are good enough to read it I trust you will detect my intention. A certain form will be its chief merit."[33] But the form and content had not fused into a work of art; it was only a strangely sensational piece of intellectual work, to which the arts of Miss Braddon had been annexed; "cold as an icicle," Henry thought when he reread it. Howells liked the story, however, and recommended it to Fields, who liked it as well, and it appeared in *The Atlantic*. For a few months James had an income, but nothing was said of book publication as yet.

When James came to dictate his reminiscences, he said nothing about this first attempt at a novel, and although in due course he arranged for it to appear as a separate volume, he never referred to it in later life. But clumsy, unsuccessful, and even repellent as the product was, the writing of "Watch and Ward" was a step forward. He was learning to portray a broad landscape and the development of characters over time. He had had a vision of liberty—now he had added a vision of the exercise of power. This tale was the mentor's, more than the ward's.[34]

The elements of the old circle that James and Mary Temple had constructed was scattered, and new relations were forming. Chauncey

Wright, whose blotched, empurpled complexion, and plump mincing walk, as if on tiptoe, testified to his solitude,[35] made the nucleus of one new circle, a sort of salon of young men. Wright called regularly at Quincy Street, where his young friends were often found, and genially argued philosophy with Father and William; if Holmes or Gray was present, the discussion would embrace them all. Wright was a much loved teacher, who quietly presided over the clash of materialism and idealism, with its strange echo of the war going on in France.[36]

Charles Darwin's *Descent of Man* appeared that winter, a book that sought to demonstrate simply that human beings had descended from animals. Wright's manner and his intelligence both recommended the modesty and simplicity that the Darwinian theory suggested. Smiling benevolently on the young men, Wright was teacher and mentor and friend, but he remained alone. Henry divined that this solitude called for great sacrifices on his part, so that in memory Henry loved and befriended and pitied him. Looking back from his Chelsea flat, when he too was an old man fond of younger men, who knew what it was to grow old and be afraid of dying alone, he regretted that he could say no more, do no more, to preserve the memory of Chauncey Wright.[37]

The women of the old circle who had not married had their own gatherings. In the spring of 1871 they began meeting as the Saturday Morning Club for conversation, and each month one of the members delivered a paper. Marian Hooper (whom everyone called Clover) organized a German club to practice the language and discuss the literature—an act that had its political implications.[38] Henry and William James were nominally members, but in practice the German club was principally female. Alice, who had continued to struggle along in her German lessons, attended these meetings, as did her friend Fanny Morse. Alice again went into town for the discussions and lectures at Elizabeth Peabody's unfashionable house in South Boston. There the proponents of women's rights and women's solidarity now gathered. And there, fifteen years later, James would locate his novel on the women's movement, *The Bostonians*. Cambridge and Boston had little to offer these women. Clover wrote tartly to a friend that she had had a pleasant little dinner in Boston, with soup, fish, Sayles and Gray, and then had dined again at the Jameses', "with the variation which Boston affords of raw oysters, then soup Gray & Holmes that was quite different you see if only one thought so."[39] It was not an invigorating environment for an intelligent or ambitious person.

James, too, was growing restless. In the spring of 1871, with *Watch and Ward*, his sketch of a novel, done and the winter quickly melting away, he resumed his round of calls and visits in this little world. The Fieldses were now holding regular receptions on Friday evenings. He went every Sunday afternoon for his walk and dinner with Bill Howells. Howells had been given an increase in salary, and would soon become editor of *The Atlantic Monthly;* he could afford a larger house for his growing family, and a nurse and servant to help Elinor. After dinner, Howells read aloud the latest chapter of a new novel, *Their Wedding Journey*, which was a sort of literary photograph, a novel that consisted in the ordinary events of a trip that Howells and Elinor had taken. Howells made no effort to idealize or generalize, or to see beneath surfaces in any way.[40] Henry admired the gracefulness and humor of the effect. But he was disappointed; instead of presenting a rich realism, the fusion of memory and perception, of imagination and historical fact, Howells was setting down static little pictures, impressions as they fell on the retina; he was reproducing the physical act of perception alone. It seemed hardly worth the considerable effort involved.

> The more I think of it, the more I deprecate the growing tendency— born of the very desperation of the writer—to transfer directly and bodily, without any intellectual transmutation, all the crude accidents of his life as they encursively befall, into the subject matter of literature. Before we are fairly launched here we are being swamped by the dire vulgarity of it.[41]

He thought continually of Europe; the war in France continued to dominate his awareness and his conversation. The king of Prussia had established his headquarters outside besieged Paris, at the royal palace of Versailles. On January 18, 1871, the dukes and princes of the German alliance gathered in the Hall of Mirrors at Versailles and proclaimed Wilhelm their emperor—successor to the conquering Romans, the new Caesar.

By the end of January the People's War had ground to its bloody conclusion; the French republic was as decisively beaten as Napoleon III had been. The German army of eight hundred thousand men, a vast body whose relentless deployment and inexhaustible supply were the single inexorable fact of the war, had entered Paris in triumph. It was a great victory of management and technology, reproducing in Europe the American victory of Northern railroads and manpower over Southern courage and dash, the new order over the old. Boston looked on with intense interest.

An armistice followed defeat; the French elected a new national government. The conservative countryside returned an overwhelmingly royalist assembly. In March, the left-wing political clubs rebelled against this new government and established a Commune in Paris. The elected assembly fled to German protection at Versailles. As the Germans smilingly looked on, the national government attacked its own capital. The Communards of Paris took hostages and, as the siege tightened, executed them. The Communards burned the Palace of the Tuileries, the Palace of Justice, and the Hôtel de Ville. But the Commune inevitably fell, and triumphant national troops began a wholesale execution of the revolutionaries and their supporters. The newly crowned Kaiser quietly encouraged the violence; the war against France had been extended into its very houses. Liberal opinion in England and America favored a compassionate peace, but this was not to be. With the defeat of the Commune the peace terms were disclosed. The French were compelled to pay a crushing indemnity of five billion francs; German troops would occupy France until the indemnity was paid; and the provinces of Alsace and Lorraine would pass to the German empire. France was to be humiliated.

Boston radicals who had supported the Commune had organized themselves to provide relief to the French. Two young women, Katharine Loring and Ellen Hale, began a newspaper called the *Balloon Post* in honor of the airships that provided the only link between Paris and the outside world during the siege. When they asked Henry to contribute something to the *Balloon Post*, he agreed, bowing to its avowed humanitarian purpose, and gave them a light, one-act play modeled on the French design.[42]

But James's sympathy for France was limited. Italy was the center of his thoughts, and his wish to live in Italy had formed itself into a definite plan. He would go in the spring of 1873, two years hence. He would support himself there by writing about Italy for American magazines and newspapers. He and Arthur Sedgwick would share expenses, but it would still take a certain amount of capital to carry him through the transition. He would have to work and save.[43] He wrote to Grace Norton in Florence:

> Every one hereabouts is just now talking about Darwin's *Descent of Man*—many of course with great horror at his fundamental proposi-

tions, but here is poor old France, doing its very best apparently to convince a reluctant world that we have only to be scratched a bit in certain places to reveal a very fair intimation of the missing link? . . . In my secret heart I do nothing but weep for the French; but when I come to talk aloud—even to myself, I find that propriety holds my tears. They have suffered unutterably, but they have sinned unutterably. As for the Germans, you may be very sure I don't care a straw for them!—and how are my dearly beloved Italians all this time?— Would that I could see a few dozen or so. . . .[44]

Summer dawned and broadened. Wilky came home for a visit, to explore opportunities in Boston. The family went to the seashore north of Boston again, fleeing the heat, and the Bootts followed them. But Henry remained at home in Cambridge, bringing his plan into realization. In the mornings he remained in his shirtsleeves in his bedroom, reading, with the summer curtains drawn to keep out the sun. After a light noon meal, his European breakfast, he would walk out of Cambridge, sometimes crossing the bridge into Boston. If he had no errands in town he would walk into the Waltham and Arlington hills; on the return the familiar blue plain of Boston, and the ocean beyond, would lie before him. Despite the appearance of lassitude, he was working. His morning reading was devoted to French fiction, and the afternoon walks to reflection. He was studying the form of the novel.

The best of the recent writing was that of Gustave Droz, who had the genius of treating serious matters lightly. Droz and other writers had begun to restore Henry's optimistic hopes for France. Henry hoped that when the destruction of the war had been repaired and Paris returned to normal life, it would have become a very different nation.

> It was the pretension of the system which perished at Sedan to pervade and invade all things,—to set the tune, to pitch the universal voice, to leave its visible stamp in every corner. On the top of the page, in every clever novel of the last ten years, you seem to read that mysterious N. which greeted you endlessly from the cornices of the Louvre.[45]

But that totalitarian era was over, and he had high hopes for the great established figures—Sand and Renan—and the finest of young writers who had preserved their independence and carried on the liberal tradition. The best of the new work was realistic, an accurate history of the time. It was not simply photographic, as the new American tales were; it was deepened by the tools of thought, of analysis, and so it penetrated to the moral substrate. Droz's novel told a graceful tale of the fierce irruption of modern life into the little mountain parish of a poor curate: it was the fruitless strife between old and new, between the consecrated past and the cold future.[46] He thought that Droz's novel was a truly analytic work, applying the clarity of modern thought without any loss of civilized values. It had the tone of a great painting, and Henry took a good deal of comfort from it.

In the evenings he would sit on the Sedgwicks' veranda or his own, with Arthur, sharing news of their friends in Italy, gossiping about Cambridge and Boston and Harvard. And then Arthur Sedgwick, too, left Cambridge; E. L. Godkin was ill, and Arthur went to New York to help manage *The Nation*. The plan for Italy would have to be redrawn.

Henry had no great project for which the solitude of Cambridge in August might be put to use. His story "Passionate Pilgrim" had appeared in *The Atlantic,* and while it was widely praised, only the cosmopolitan Bootts and Nortons seemed to have had any notion of what it was about. The first of the five serial installments of *Watch and Ward* was appearing, and he foresaw a still more puzzled audience.

To pay for a visit to a cooler climate, he decided to do another set of travel pieces for *The Nation,* and set off to the north again, to Quebec City and Niagara Falls.

Quebec charmed him; it was a French town, transported from an earlier and more Catholic age. It was not Paris, to be sure, but a French provincial town lifted and moved to America with its modest plain gentry still intact and its air of having nothing in particular to do. When he settled into his rented room he found that the casement window, something one never found in America, looked over that essentially European sight, a convent, whose shabby little chapel sat among plane trees in a walled garden beneath his window.[47] After a few days of wandering in the city he wanted to see the surrounding countryside, and took a carriage out to an inn near the falls of Montmorency, one of the great beauties of the place. But the falls did not have any great interest for him. The wild, fierce, suicidal plunge of the living flood was undoubtedly beautiful, but it seemed to make an appeal, to demand admiration. It was essentially trivial and violent.[48]

With some foreboding, therefore, he went on to his next destination, Niagara. The countryside was plain and American, and the village of Niagara Falls was a perfectly terrible agglomeration of shanties and shops. The road to the falls themselves was lined with little taverns, from whose doorways hawkers darted out upon the hapless traveler. But when James stood at the verge of the falls, surrounded by thundering violence, he stared his fill at the most beautiful object in the world.

The meager arrogance of the cataract at Montmorency was forgotten. The Niagara Falls seen from the Canadian side were a graceful semicircle, an immense line drawn between dark stone abutments. It was not in the least monstrous; it was in ideal taste, Michelangelesque.

> The perfect curve melts into the sheet that seems at once to drop from it and sustain it. . . . A green more vividly cool and pure it is impossible to conceive. It is to the vulgar greens of earth what the blue of a summer sky is to artificial dyes, and is, in fact, as sacred, as remote, as impalpable as that. You can fancy it the parent-green, the head-spring of color to all the verdant water-caves and all the clear, subfluvial haunts and bowers of naiads and mermen in all the streams of the earth. The lower half of the watery wall is shrouded in the steam of the boiling gulf—a veil never rent nor lifted. At its heart this eternal cloud seems fixed and still with excess of motion—still and immensely white. . . .[49]

This was the vast masculine Rome of cataracts, the ancient heart of violence, uncaring and beautiful, millennia beyond any appeal for admiration or wonder.

In Cambridge the leaves were turning and dropping, the greens darkening into red and brown; the sky was clouded and pale. Darkness of winter descended on Cambridge and Boston. Henry went out less and read more. In midwinter, he paid a visit to New York, refreshing his acquaintance with Robertson and Wyckoff and Perkins cousins. He wrote a notice of a new museum that had opened on Fifth Avenue— "La Musée de New York," as the *Revue des Deux Mondes* had grandly styled it—the future Metropolitan Museum, which was at the moment housed in a former dancing school at Fifty-third Street and Fifth Avenue. He wrote to Elizabeth Boott, tentatively sketching his plan to visit Italy the following year; perhaps they would rendezvous in Perugia, on the lovely road from Florence to Rome:

But aren't all the old towns on the road from Florence to Rome—
perched on their mountain sides & hosed and belted in their black
walls—the most enchanting visions in the world?—My ideal of perfect earthly happiness is a slow pilgrimage through the whole chain
of them, from Arezzo to Narnio. . . .[50]

Early in March 1872, Wendell Holmes and Fanny Dixwell announced
their engagement; within a few days Henry Adams and Clover
Hooper announced theirs. Almost at the same moment came the
news that Susan Norton had died.

Henry sent a brief letter of condolence to Charles and a longer letter to Grace: he had been meaning to write to her at any time the past
month, and little thought that when he should really do so, it would
be over poor Susan's grave.

My own memory of her will always be a bright presence in the foreground of that year of mine in Europe which seems to me now
weighted with so many things. . . . It's a grand illusion, I imagine, dear
Grace, to suppose I must write you a funereal letter, or that you are
not still on generous terms with life. I was confident of this from the
moment I heard of your troubles—confident in spite of it as regards
all the imaginable trials of your situations. . . . Tell me then how
Charles is bearing himself, & how it is with your mother. Give them
my love—as well as to Theodora and Jane. For yourself, dear Grace,
I devoutly trust you are fairly strong. . . .[51]

Henry could no longer think of joining the Norton and Sedgwick clan
in Florence. The Nortons in any case would now be returning to
Shady Hill. In April, as the dreary winter was breaking up, however, it
was agreed within the James family that Henry should take Alice
abroad. Cambridge was as difficult for her as it had been for him, and
it was her turn for a European tour, for health and education. Aunt
Kate would come with them, to care for Alice as a man could not.
Henry arranged with Godkin to write a series of letters from abroad
for The Nation, and so, after all, despite everything, he would be returning to Europe, perhaps even to Italy.

He left behind him a long story for The Atlantic, "Guest's Confession," which was to appear when Howells had space for it. It was the
last of the studies of American life he wrote before leaving. It was a
study of the relations of men with men. Like all the stories he had

written since his visit to Europe, it was audaciously sexual. It was set in an American spa, an amalgam of Saratoga Springs and Swampscott, peopled with men he had seen on the piazza in Saratoga Springs— sinewy western miners, soft genial stockbrokers, sharp-faced men.

A hard little fellow who traded on the stock exchange came to the resort with a grave illness; he did not realize at first that he had come there to die. He brought with him a big, clumsy, boyish half brother, more youth than man.

The older brother, whose name was Edgar Musgrave, liked to exercise power. He was a rigidly moral man, but he calculated what was due to him, and was certain to get it. Having caught a stockbroker, John Guest, speculating with his money, Musgrave humiliated him; Guest, in his shirtsleeves, half undressed, was forced down onto his knees. "Fold your hands, so. Now beg my pardon."

> It was a revolting sight,—this man of ripe maturity and massive comeliness on his two knees, his pale face bent upon his breast, his body trembling with the effort to keep his shameful balance; and above him Edgar, with his hands behind his back, solemn and ugly as a miniature idol, with his glittering eyes fixed in a sort of rapture on the opposite wall.[52]

Guest was forced to write a confession in abject language, on a sheet of paper that the little man kept. There was to be no escaping his wrath. Musgrave was a vengeful Calvinist godling, the embodiment of predestinated vengeance.

But the godling Musgrave died, and the confession passed to his young brother, David. The younger man was tempted to use the power that the secret gave him, but he was not vengeful; he burned the paper with its secret and its power. He turned away from the dangerous relation with Guest and fell in love instead with Guest's daughter: a slim, boyish, gray-eyed heroine; he married her with Guest's blessing.[53]

It was a story of the conflict of the old and the new, treated lightly, yet with a cosmic dimension. The Old Testament gave way to the New; the violent primary bond of father and son gave way to the gentle, heterosexual union; the old feudal, Calvinist order gave way to the new empire of liberty.

Yet clear, light, and well made as the tale was, there was a chasm between the intensely interesting events and their ideal or intellectual dimension, which remained unbridged. The story was interesting, disturbingly realistic, but it was not understood. The characters and their surroundings were too thin and new to suggest the immense spaces and depths Henry wanted his reader to imagine. The story was like a performance of *Medea* on the veranda of the Grand Union Hotel.

The war in France was over, and the waves of revolution had subsided. Constitutional government was being established everywhere. Rome was the capital of a new Italy. The ancient accumulations of dirt that covered the floor of the Colosseum were being excavated and removed; the grime that had coated the statues and monuments of Rome for centuries was being stripped and sandblasted away. Winter was breaking up, and Henry James turned toward spring. He would not suffer another Cambridge winter of isolation, cold, and darkness. On May 11, 1872, with Alice and Aunt Kate, he embarked from New York on a new Cunard steamer, the *Algeria*, bound for Liverpool. He was returning to Europe; henceforth it would be his home.[54]

14

Henry Opens the Doors
of Europe for Alice

The journey to Europe under Henry's care did restore Alice's health, and established a friendship between them that would deepen over the years. On this first journey together, they and Aunt Kate spent a night in Liverpool at the familiar Adelphi Hotel, and went to Chester the next day, where they paused, and Henry wrote his first travel letter for *The Nation*. It was difficult to keep a fresh eye. But Alice had the same enthusiasm for England that he had, and walking with her around the city wall was a little like conducting his own younger self, giving her permission to enjoy herself, recording her own fresh impressions as much as his own. The odd feeling of being twinned, and of escorting his own younger self, would echo through his later novels.[1]

The three travelers settled into a comfortable small hotel, where they indulged in the expense of a shared sitting room, with a bow window that overlooked a little garden and flooded the room with the cool light of May. They spent a happy two weeks in that hotel, while Aunt Kate recovered from the indispositions of the voyage. Alice herself seemed to flourish and to bloom, and walked about with Henry in the town, exploring shops and making small purchases. They were regularly taken for husband and wife. She had Henry's rich brown hair, his thoughtful expression, and sad dark eyes. She parted her hair in the middle, and braided and coiled it in the German fashion, so that her clear forehead and delicate ears were unfashionably bare, like his. Strolling arm in arm, Henry carried Alice's parasol in his free hand.[2]

They made daylong excursions through the green countryside, to castles, abbeys, and cathedrals. When they resumed their journey, Henry brought his companions by easy stages southward, resting overnight at little midland towns. They settled in Oxford for a few days, which Alice found as wonderful as Henry had two years before. They walked from college to college, wandering among the courtyards and the walled gardens.

Henry took a good deal of pleasure in managing the expedition, and in smoothing the way for Alice and Aunt Kate. He planned each day's excursion with care, so that there was ample opportunity to rest. At five or ten minutes before the breakfast hour, he would knock at their doors. He would order a carriage for the day's expedition, and would see that their shawls and umbrellas were tucked around them. Alice was cheerful and bright, a good-natured monarch, generous and thoughtful, her imperious sarcasms much in abeyance. Henry liked to see her come into her own. Aunt Kate wrote to their mother,

> If you were to see him folding in the most precise manner, the shawls and rugs, which are brought in from our drives, and smoothing them down in some quiet corner, with the parasols and umbrellas, tears would flow from your eyes, and you would say he is my own son indeed. He forgets nothing, and his care and consideration for Alice is unceasing. He is proving himself thoroughly *practical* in all respects. . . .[3]

Each morning, before the expedition of the day, he would write, and sometimes he would stay behind to continue his work while the ladies went on a local excursion. His travel pieces were thoughtful and light, the work of a man having a quiet but thoroughly pleasant time. Excursions to cathedrals and castles gave him an opportunity to reflect on religion and class in England, and to contrast England and America in these respects. He admired the great Anglican cathedrals, which reminded him that the established church in England had all the charm; dissent and democracy and other vulgar variations, like his father's socialism, had nothing but their bald logic—justice and beauty were no more easily reconciled in this realm than in any other.[4]

The threesome moved by easy stages, never traveling overnight but stopping in villages along the rail line southward into Devonshire. Henry was curious to see the seaside, and finding that the railroad had not yet reached so far, he left Alice and Aunt Kate behind and went by coach, in the ancient fashion, to the little village of Ilfracombe, where a steep cliff looked out over the Irish Sea. Even here, almost at land's end, England was crowded; the cliff face was scarred by convenient paths, to which access could be gained for a penny, and there were domesticating little signs and crowds of people, so that for once he yearned for the solitude of American wilderness.[5]

James had planned that they should spend the hottest weeks of the summer in Switzerland, and then drop down briefly into Italy before returning through Germany, to England and home. On their way to Switzerland, hurrying to escape the summer heat, they stopped only briefly in London, where they consulted Leslie Stephen on Swiss resorts, and in Paris, where they shopped for clothes and went to the theater.

At Villeneuve, on Lake Geneva, letters from home reached them. Wilky and Bob had both settled in Milwaukee, and each had announced his engagement: Wilky to a young woman from modest circumstances, Caroline Cary, a silent motherless girl whom he loved with a passion, and who seemed to return his love. Neither she nor he had any means, and his job as a clerk at the railroad did not allow them to marry, so the engagement would be prolonged. Moody Bob was engaged to marry a pretty, ambitious, and perhaps slightly hard young woman, Mary Holton, from one of the leading families of Milwaukee. Their marriage would not be delayed.

The much diminished Cambridge family—Father, Mother, and William—had gone to Mount Desert for the summer. William would remain at home in Cambridge: he had been promised an appointment at Harvard College as an instructor of physiology, and he would begin by teaching a course in psychology, in the science of the mind. Father wrote happily to Henry about this. All the news of recent weeks had pleased him—the youngest boys' engagements, Henry's tutelage of Alice, and her revived health and spirits; but above all, he was happiest at William's having finally adopted a course of action, a place in life:

> It is a delight above all delights, to see one's children turn out—as ours have done—all that the heart covets in children; and my delight is so full that I sometimes fancy my heart will have to burst for its own relief.[6]

The good news concerning William, he added a little later, was not only that he would begin to teach scientific philosophy, but that William had accepted his father's ideas. It was as if William had become the ward in Henry's story, accepting the place for which he had been shaped.

> He came in here the other afternoon [Father wrote to Henry] when I was sitting alone, and after walking the floor in an animated way for a moment, exclaimed "Dear me! What a difference there is between me now and me last spring this time: then so hypochondriacal" (he used that word, though perhaps in substantive form) "and now feeling my mind so cleared up and restored to sanity. It is the difference between death and life." He had a great effusion. I was afraid of interfering with it, or possibly checking it, but I ventured to ask what specially in his opinion had promoted the change. He said several things . . . but especially his having given up the notion that all mental disorder required to have a physical basis. This had become perfectly untrue to him. He saw that the mind did act irrespectively of material coercion, and could be dealt with therefore at first-hand, and this was health to his bones. It was a splendid confession. . . .[7]

Henry imagined the scene vividly: William agitated, in his burst of confidence, his bright earnestness, moving about Father's study; Father himself, eyeglasses askew, almost holding his breath for the charm of this moment, after all their long struggles, and after William's past hesitations and reserves.[8] William had accepted the career for which he had been prepared; he would be a student and teacher of scientific idealism, and Henry shared some of his father's pleasure in the victory, although he himself had taken care to keep free of that sheltering wing.

Elizabeth Boott joined the travelers in Switzerland, to their mutual satisfaction. She wrote first from Aix-les-Bains, where they were staying with a party of Bostonians, that she and her father thought of going to Geneva. Alice thereupon somewhat peremptorily summoned them to join the James party in Villeneuve—"I do wish we could have half an hour's talk, it wd. be worth all the writing in the world. Why can't you come here from Geneva, if only for a night? When you write, that is within a week—address here, but I shall expect to see you rather than a letter. . . . Yr. loving A. James."[9] When Henry went to post this, he enclosed a tactful note of his own:

> You know the place, & it may not suit you to be indulgent twice. Yet we want enormously to see you. . . . We expect to be here a week or ten days, collecting our wits after our recent furious wanderings. If you are likely, as I suppose you are, to come to Geneva, do drop me a word saying when & where & I will run down hence instantly & seek a personal interview.[10]

The Bootts did not go to either Geneva or Villeneuve, however, but met the Jameses later at Grindelwald, a resort frequented by English mountain climbers. Both Alice and Henry enjoyed Elizabeth Boott's company.[11] She had been studying music in Florence, and her voice was much stronger; now it was not only pleasing but moving.[12] She was like a third sibling, and the three young people shared gossip and speculations about the love affairs and marriages of their mutual friends.

But it was hot and humid, and the Jameses went somewhat abruptly to Thusis, well up in the mountains, in search of more bracing air. Alice was determined to see the mountains, but the Bootts struck off in another direction, and the separation, perhaps, or the cold mountain air, upset Alice and affected her health.[13]

The James party arrived in Venice in September, while it was still very hot and the mosquitoes were terrible. But Alice again summoned the Bootts to join them, and this time Elizabeth answered that they would come as quickly as possible. But the mosquitoes and the heat were intolerable, and after only a week the Jameses fled northward from Venice into Austria. They were gone by the time Elizabeth and Francis Boott arrived, and Henry felt rather bad over their unnecessary discomfort.

The travelers continued northward, and Henry began in his letters to prepare his parents for the fact that he would not be returning but would remain in Europe indefinitely. After a short stay in Paris he would travel to Italy. It was the place for him to learn and to work; his health was now strong and he was able to support himself financially.[14]

On September 20 the three arrived in Paris for a week's stay, settling in the little Hôtel Rastadt, near the Rue de la Paix, which Henry had enjoyed on his last visit. It seemed to him that the city should have shown more signs than it did of the convulsion it had been through, but Paris was surprisingly untouched by the war.[15] The Palace of the Tuileries was a blackened ruin, still smelling of smoke, it was true, but the new boulevards were bustling like Broadway. There was a good-sized American colony, in which Edmund and Mary Tweedy, now childless once more, their surviving adopted daughters all having married, had settled; the Jameses dined with them each night. The Nortons and Sedgwicks were encamped in a suburb, Saint-Germain-en-Laye, awaiting the chance to return home; James Lowell and John Holmes were in a little private hotel on the Left Bank; Chauncey Wright and his companion, Samuel Rowse, the painter, were at the Grand Hôtel. Henry met Wright on the Boulevard de l'Opéra, serenely trundling along as if on tiptoe.[16]

Early in October, Henry accompanied Alice and Aunt Kate to Liverpool, and saw them into their staterooms. He said farewell, and returned to Paris alone.

A letter from his father brought with it a respectful notice in the *Tribune* of "Guest's Confession," which he hardly now remembered writing. Howells wrote to say that it had on the whole been received with more favor than anything he had published in *The Atlantic*. Howells, like the *Tribune* reviewer, was respectful but not entirely comprehending. And he was very sorry to be losing James's company: "I've just come in from a long walk up North Avenue, in which I missed you abominably."[17]

From William, too, there was a letter. Perhaps he, like Howells, was unhappy at losing Henry's company; he would be at home with Alice and his parents now, as yet unable to support himself or to think of marrying, while all his younger brothers had left home. Affection, for whatever reason, became anger, and he lashed out at Henry. William complained of the tendency in his brother's travel letters, as in his fiction, toward overrefinement of language and feeling. It was the old slur: effete.

At this special moment Henry could not let criticism of his writing slide past without comment, and he answered at length, and seriously. Henry courteously acknowledged the objection. He could write more simply, more in the blunt factual manner of the newspapers, to a degree. But:

> Beyond a certain point, this would not be desirable. . . . At the point we have reached[18] all writing not really leavened with thought—of some sort or other—is terribly unprofitable, & to try & work one's material closely is the only way to form a manner on which one can keep afloat—without intellectual bankruptcy at least. I have a mortal horror of seeming to write thin—& if I ever feel my pen beginning to scratch, shall consider that my death-knell has rung.[19]

To write in a way that would please William, in short, would be his death. And so he parted with Cambridge, with a great wrenching of feelings. And despite William's bitterness, he luxuriated in his freedom.

He had planned to spend the winter in Paris, writing, and then to settle in Rome, where Elizabeth and Francis Boott were spending their own winter—where the Tweedys had gone as well. But he made decisions day by day, moment to moment.

> My dear Lizzie—Where are you, how are you, & in the name of ancient friendship & all other respectable things, why don't I hear from you? . . . You're now in Rome I know from Mrs. Tweedy & finding it "delightful." Of course you do & I am forgiving enough to be glad. Where do you live, how much do you pay (nay, neglect this ignoble question . . .) whom do you see, where & what do you paint, & how does your father chase the fleeting hours? I want the more to hear from you, that my own departure for Italy is deferred from week to week & some time may now elapse before I get there. I rather dread the dissipations and distractions of Rome, & am trying to dispatch a few literary wares before I leave Paris. . . . Most affectionate greetings to your father & the best wishes, my dear Lizzie for your self— including the wish that you'll immediately write.[20]

He worked very hard during the day, writing and reading books that he might review. He went to the theater in the evenings, and twice a week visited the Lowells in their little private hotel on the Left Bank, the Hôtel Lorraine, just off the Quai Voltaire. On a few Sunday afternoons he and Lowell went for long walks and conversations; afterward he would dine with the Lowells at their *table d'hôte*.[21] On these visits, Henry and James Lowell gradually overcame the mutual indifference that had settled on their relations in Cambridge. They both had the habit of long walks, and on Sunday afternoons they rambled together through the streets from one border of the city to another. Lowell talked a good deal: he was spending the winter reading Old French, in pursuit of the language, the style, and the traditions of chivalry. He seemed far less professorial, less European and more American than he had in Cambridge.[22]

Their walks were taken in the intermittent drizzling rain; it seemed to rain every day. Henry always remembered the solitary walk back to his hotel after a visit with Lowell, in the cold, rainy November evenings, amid the wet flare of the myriad lamps.[23]

He had agreed to send a letter on Paris to *The Nation*, and he decided to make it a review of the national theater, which seemed to him the distillation of French civilization. His impressions of two years before had been confirmed and intensified. He would never forget the pleasure, he wrote, after a busy, dusty, weary day, repairing to the Théâtre-Français to watch a curtain-raiser by Alfred de Musset and a play by Molière.

> The entertainment seemed to my travel-tired brain what a perfumed bath is to one's weary limbs, and I sat in a sort of liquid ecstasy of contemplation and wonder—wonder that the tender flower of poetry and art should bloom again so bravely over the blood-stained pavements and fresh-made graves.[24]

The performance—not the written play, but the performance—was the national art form, and as practiced in Paris, it was perhaps the greatest art. The fusion of sensation and idea was most perfectly accomplished there: "An acted play is a novel intensified."[25] His praise for the actors and their art was lavish, uncharacteristically unstinting. The actors worked directly with the strong forces, and he confided that he never listened to the *toc-toc-toc* as the curtain went up and settled himself in his chair and grasped his opera glass without exclaiming to himself that, after all, the French were prodigiously great! Yet outside the theater there was little to admire at the moment. The French seemed unable to learn what he believed were the lessons of the war and the Commune. In consequence, as it seemed,

Paris would never again be the capital of Europe. And yet, and yet: there was the new republic, there were the young artists in the cafés. He resolved his thought gradually, and when he came to set it down it was the picture of two men.

Théophile Gautier, whose critical essays had accompanied James on his wanderings in Venice, had recently died, and a commemorative book of his reviews had been issued. Gautier had burst upon the world a generation earlier, with a scandalous novel, *Mademoiselle de Maupin*, that proclaimed absolute indifference to subject, to moral dimension. *L'art pour l'art*. It became a slogan: Art for art alone. The only deities that Gautier recognized were Beauty, Wealth, and Happiness; his poetry was gold, marble, and purple.

Thirty years after this spectacular debut he had become a dominant power in Parisian letters. For the newspapers he wrote a weekly review of the theater, regular reviews of books, and every year a review of the Salon, the exhibition of new paintings. He wrote his own exquisite poetry, travel literature, stories and novels, all with an infinitely light touch. His work was perfect in form and style. Indeed, form was everything, was eternal. To Henry his greatest poem, "Art," seemed to have been written in a kind of aesthetic fever: "The gods themselves die. But sovereign lines of verse remain stronger than brass."

Gautier reveled in language; he had absorbed dictionaries, and his French was infinitely rich and precise. But his art was purely an art of the senses; his infinite analysis never penetrated beneath the skin. The poetry and tales were beautiful, but without any idea, without passion, without the metaphysical and moral dimension that made both life and art.

The second figure was a painter. In the Salon of 1866 this new young arrival had shown a single portrait, an anonymous woman in red velvet. It was stunning, enigmatical. The painter, Henri Regnault, was everything that Gautier was not. He was above all passionate, and his work was a fusion of feeling and intellect, of imagination and sense. The painting opened into the dimension of the spiritual; the *Woman in Red Velvet* was the portrait of an intellect that illumined a charming face and body.

The portrait would have made the young man's fortune in any case, but Gautier made him a celebrity. He wrote a glowing review, and used his now considerable powers to put the young painter forward. Yet, reading over the old reviews, Henry was struck by what a fatally shallow conception of his duty as a mentor the older man had.

Gautier, possibly, claimed no such office; but, at any rate, he spoke with authority; and the splendid, unmeasured flattery which he pours out on the young painter gives us something of the discomfort with which we should see an old man plying a young lad with strong wine. Regnault, fortunately, had a strong head; but the attitude, in Gautier, is none the less immoral.[26]

Gautier, who was a monarchist and took refuge in Versailles during the Commune, died quietly at home, outliving his protégé. Regnault was a passionate republican, and died defending Paris.

Gautier's disposition served him to the end, and enabled him to leave a literary heritage perfect of its kind. He could look every day at a group of beggars sunning themselves on the Spanish Steps at Rome, against their golden wall of moldering travertine, and see nothing but the fine brownness of their rags and their flesh-tints—see it and enjoy it for ever, without an hour's disenchantment, without a chance of one of those irresistible revulsions of mood in which the "mellowest" rags are but filth, and filth is poverty, and poverty is a haunting shadow, and picturesque squalor is mockery.[27]

Despite his moral blindness, Gautier had loved young Regnault. The young painter's death in the siege of Paris seemed to epitomize the tragedy that had stricken France.[28]

Dear Lizzie—I have had in hand for some time your most gracious and graceful of last letters, & I have not sooner answered it because my imminent departure from Paris has given me an unusual lot of things to do & I have wanted to make the most of my last Parisian days. We shall have Roman days together which will be better than letters. . . . I am going tonight, for instance, to the Masked Ball, the 1st of the season, at the Opera. . . .[29]

He joked that he was writing to a loved one, just before departing, as if he were on the way to a duel.[30]

15

SETTLING IN ITALY

James was at liberty, and Rome was to be his home for the indefinite future. He was struck by how small and comparatively dark the city seemed, with its little twisted streets, after the gaslit boulevards of Paris. The installation of the capital of secular Italy in Rome and the withdrawal of the pope into the refuge of the Vatican were reflected in numberless small changes. The newspaper stands on the Corso that had formerly sold only the Vatican newspapers, with their authoritative and carefully limited views, now displayed a spate of raw new journals—*Capitale, Libertà, Fanfulla!* There were a great many more shops, and the Corso was crowded as it had never been before with carriages and pedestrians. But he missed the purple-stockinged monsignors, followed on foot by servants, and the glittering scarlet carriages of the cardinals that had swayed with the weight of the footmen clinging behind.[1]

Henry James was twenty-nine and Elizabeth Boott was twenty-six in that winter of 1872–73. She had begun to study painting seriously and had taken a studio in Rome, where her models were principally children whom she found in the streets and paid in *scudi*, pennies. She painted with rapidly increasing ability; her work was graceful and light, and often beautiful, although in Henry's eyes it lacked the quality of genius.

He and she were friends now, after the tacitly shared burdens of their meetings in Switzerland and Italy, and they conversed in a companionable way. They shared a benevolent interest in each other's family and in the moral crises of their friends, whom they estimated with the same humorous, clear-eyed spirit. They agreed on most questions, and when he wrote to her with his gossip she answered in kind. As to John Bancroft, for instance, who had once gallantly accompanied Alice on her visit to Newport and now had accompanied his own sister to Rome, Elizabeth replied:

> Of course I remember the Bancrofts. Miss B. is charming I think, tho' I cannot reach to a great pitch of enthusiasm about her, & Bancroftino is as you say, most excellent in every respect & I am glad you appreciate him. It would not have been necessary for Cavalier No. 1 to tell him that he was No. 2, for I think he was aware of the fact—bore it philosophically. He thought it perfectly right & natural that it should be so, for I am told that both he and his sister entertained certain suspicions. . . .[2]

This was Elizabeth's tone: light and clear, but falling short of joyousness.

Her father was a strong, handsome, virtuous, single-minded man, whose aquiline profile seemed to express an old Calvinist sense of duty. Francis Boott had a tendency to drift back into calling Henry "Mr. James," and was often severe in his judgments, but he had a boyish sense of humor, and he was much easier when Henry got him laughing, which was not difficult to do. He was visibly happy with his daughter, and she seemed content. They had taken an apartment for the Roman winter season, but they planned to return to the United States early in April.

Henry had come to Rome partly because the Bootts and the Tweedys were there. But shortly before Christmas, while he was still en route, Edmund Tweedy had come down with an intestinal ailment and a high fever, which might have been the symptoms of cholera or typhoid, and Aunt Mary had been gravely alarmed. Summoned by her, he had hastened to Rome without lingering in Florence with friends, two young Englishmen, as he had planned to do. But by the time Henry arrived, Tweedy's fever had subsided and the doctor said that the worst had passed.[3] Henry accordingly went on to the Hôtel de Rome, and notified the Bootts of his arrival, and they most cordially invited him to Christmas Eve supper in their apartment, very near to the Tweedys on the Pincian Hill.

Henry had been able to secure an excellent room at the Hôtel de Rome, in front, with a little balcony. It was only two hundred francs per month, about forty dollars, and in the following days, when he trudged about with Frank Boott looking for lodgings, he decided that he could not live much more cheaply in an apartment, even if he could find one, than at a hotel. Rome was crowded in the brief winter season between Christmas and Easter; on April 10 it would begin to empty of foreigners once again, however, and then he might easily find an apartment. It would have been difficult to better his hotel room, in any case. The sun streamed in through the open window, and he sat at a little writing table looking out at the crowds and the carriages on the Corso, marveling at the January warmth.[4]

During Tweedy's convalescence, Henry devoted himself to Aunt Mary, accompanying her on daily errands and dining with her in the evenings. He felt oddly like a temporary spouse; it was an experience of tedium and constraint, of the destruction of time and energy. But on the positive side, there was the luxury of Aunt Mary's carriage. The coachman spoke the Roman dialect, which Henry imagined was pronounced more as the ancient Latin had been, and which he found easier to understand than the Tuscan dialect that was now the national language. The coachman showed them Rome with a proprietary air, as if he thought all the foreigners were barbarians.

When Uncle Edmund was better and the Tweedys seemed to need him less, Henry walked through Rome, as he had before. He again strolled southward down the length of the Corso to the quadrangle in front of the Capitol, and then down into the Forum, where archaeological excavations were in progress, and up once more into the noble Colosseum, as impressive a stage setting as ever, although the weeds and flowers had been uprooted from the ruined walls. He went the rounds of the great sites of antiquity and of the medieval Church. The simple dome of the Pantheon particularly impressed him. It was still a pagan temple, although a veneer of Catholicism had been thinly laid over it; the huge vacant niches still seemed to hold the phantom images of Juno and Diana, Jupiter and Poseidon.

For a few days he had a cold, and he baked himself on the broad piazza of the Pincio in the afternoon sun, sometimes resting his elbows on the parapet and gazing out over Rome, and sometimes facing inward, watching the thick stream of carriages on the boulevard.

> Such a staring, lounging, dandified, amiable crowd! . . . The ladies on the Pincio have to run the gauntlet; but they seem to do it complacently enough. The European woman is brought up to the sense of having a definite part in the way of manners or manner to play in public. To lie back in an open barouche alone, balancing a parasol and seeming to ignore the extremely immediate gaze of two serried ranks of male creatures on each side of her path, save here and there to recognize one of them with an imperceptible nod, is one of her daily duties.[5]

Every night, or almost every night, he made diligent entries in his journal. There was an irritable note in many of these entries. What, after all, was there fresh to say about the Capitol or the step on which Gibbon sat, and on which Henry dutifully sat in his turn, to contemplate the ruin of the Forum and the fall of Rome? He took the stance of being difficult to please; the famous stairway to the Capitol was only an inclined plane, with a step every two or three paces. The Capitol itself and Michelangelo's quadrangle were smaller than he remembered, really almost dwarfish. Only the statue of Marcus Aurelius retained its freshness for him.

Saint Peter's had been restored, inside and out, but for Henry at the moment this only emphasized the sudden collapse of the temporal power of the Church. The martial, imperial splendor of the square before Saint Peter's and the façade of the basilica itself were now merely sites for the tourist, reminders of a vanished age that was receding rapidly into history. The vast marble expanse of the floor of the church, which when Henry had last visited had been filled with the world in-gathering of the Vatican Council, was now crowded with tourists. The pope's rule had ended, and the reign of the first king of Italy had begun.

Henry was very little interested in contemporary Italian Rome, however. Italy was poor, and quite rightly was turning its attention to the future, but his business was with its past. Even in society, in the little cosmopolitan set that had its winter season in Rome, what interested him were the echoes of the past, of Stendhal's and Edmond About's Rome, the city of Tolla.

Somehow or other, he could not seem to begin working on a novel, which was what would pay best and what he had intended to write. He was dependent for some while longer on journalism, which filled his time and kept him from attempting larger projects. He tried to write more quickly, as he would have to do if he was to live on the hundred-dollar fees he received from weekly and monthly magazines, for book reviews and short stories.

It was difficult to keep meeting his expenses, which came infallibly due, with the irregular and uncertain payments provided by publishers for these little articles. His problems were complicated by his choosing to live and work on his own. There was no one to help him with travel arrangements, housekeeping, banking, shopping, all the myriad problems of daily life.

His father was helpful to a degree. He served as Henry's American banker and literary agent. While Henry was still in Paris, his father as of old had arranged a letter of credit, through Uncle Robertson in New York, on which Henry could draw while he was in Rome. Henry in turn had arranged for *The Nation* and *The Atlantic* and the *North American Review* to send his checks to his father. Henry would draw gold coins from a bank in Italy against the letter of credit, and Father would eventually be asked to reimburse the correspondent bank in Boston in an equivalent amount of dollars.

Even more helpfully, Father was his agent in Boston, answering numerous little problems from day to day that could not wait for the monthlong round trip of ordinary letters to Italy. This and the letter of credit were an immense saving of trouble.

But another drain on his energy and finances was the drudgery of constructing a social environment for himself, a new routine of visits and calls and letters. There was the expense of clothes, rented carriages, and gifts, which this in turn entailed. And his old friends and family all demanded answers to their letters, requiring him to spend additional hours at his writing desk that somehow had to be found, although he was already overwhelmed by the volume of writing he was obliged to do. And, finally, there was the distinct task of entering into society, into the privileged world in which his subject matter, the moral history of his time, was to be found. This in itself was a daunting task. In his two months in Paris he had not succeeded at all, had met none of the French and had not entered even into expatriate society; he had observed solely from the outside, to his regret. But he hoped for better success in Rome, where his first visit had held so much promise. His proper work, in itself, was continually set aside while he made these preparations.

The Bootts were very helpful good friends from the start, especially in the social tasks. Francis and Elizabeth introduced him to the drawing rooms and studios of the little society of foreigners, of *forestieri*, or at least its large American branch, who were to some degree already familiar to him: Alice Sumner, for instance, the former Alice Mason, whom he had met so long ago when they were both children in Paris, gazing idly into jeweler's windows in the Palais-Royal, was separated now from her husband, Senator Charles Sumner, and lived in an apartment on the Via della Croce with young Anne Bartlett, a friend of Elizabeth Boott's. At the palazzo of the Bootts' friends, the Clevelands, he met Fanny Kemble, that almost mythic figure of his youth, who was in Rome with her daughter, Sarah Wister. Mrs. Kemble's lavender velvet and Venetian lace, her lavish décolletage and her beautiful hoarse speaking voice, brought back in vivid detail his memory of her readings in London and Boston. But they barely spoke, and Henry observed her principally from a distance.

Her daughter, Sarah Wister, was tall, like her American father, and wore a great helmet of beautiful shining blond hair; she had the strongly marked features and intelligent eyes of the Kembles, however, and their passionate spontaneity; she startled him at moments with her resemblance to Mary Temple.

> She has a fierce energy in a slender frame & has always some social
> iron on the fire. She rides, walks, entertains, has musical rehearsals,
> writes largely (I believe) and is very handsome in the bargain.[6]

Henry, as a leading young writer whose work she admired, was something of an acquisition for a hostess; Sarah Wister monopolized him for the evening, invited him to her own reception the following night, and secured him for a walk the following day in the Colonna Gardens, on the crest of the Pincian Hill.[7] They wandered for almost two hours down paths lined with ilex, orange, and laurel, among mossy sarcophagi, lingering on benches at the base of damp green statues. Mrs. Wister talked uninterruptedly, learnedly, cleverly; Henry was bemused and impressed. He became a regular visitor at her Saturday-evening receptions, and they continued to take occasional walks together.

Sarah Wister introduced him to the Villa Medici, the magnificent home of the French Academy in Rome, and its director, M. Ernest Hébert, who had painted the portraits of Napoleon III and Princess Marie-Clothilde; he had a little studio of his own in the gardens of the villa, to which Mrs. Wister brought James. The painter was more than twenty years his senior, but soon he and James were on friendly terms.[8] He had known Regnault well, which greatly endeared him to the younger man. They talked of Rome, and Hébert urged him to stay past the tourist season into the early summer, when the city would empty of foreigners and tourists, and Rome would be reborn as herself.[9] There were some beautiful things in the villas, for instance, that could not really be seen when they were crowded with foreigners.

Mrs. Sumner, the Alice Mason who was, had taken a box for the winter season at the Apollo, a beautiful great theater where the boxes were large enough to walk about in. Henry joined her and her companion, Miss Bartlett, at the opera often. One evening, a New Yorker he knew, long settled in Rome, joined him in Mrs. Sumner's box and instructed Henry on the names and identities of the various ladies: the princess Margaret and the lesser princesses, the Lavaggi and the Calabrini, visible in their own boxes in the soft undimmed light.[10]

At a dinner party he met Harriet Hosmer, who struck him forcibly. For a woman to have sculpted nude marble figures was one of the enduring sensations of the Roman colony, and, too, there were her rumored romances with both men and women. She seemed to Henry like a little gray-haired boy, adorned with a magnificent diamond necklace, both vivacious and discreet. And he met Harriet St. Leger, of the Anglo-Irish aristocracy, who was in Rome with her niece Lady Castletown, to whom he was very distantly related through the Emmets, a frail, slim and sadly charming young woman, recovering from the death of her first child. Years later he would give friendly assistance to her romance with Wendell Holmes. He called in due course on the Storys, and was welcomed and invited to their receptions, where young Miss Story sang with her sweetly artless tremolo, and Henry wandered through the ramifying, candle-lit rooms. As before, the golden atmosphere of Rome had collected in the rooms; beauty was an almost palpable medium.

He was invited as well to the palace that was the Storys' social rival, the Odescalchi, where Louisa Ward, Samuel and Anna's daughter, entertained in great state with her husband, the painter Luther Terry, and her amiable, loquacious daughter Annie.[11] Louisa Ward's specialty was the musical evening, where Francis Boott's songs were often performed. Henry received a standing invitation to her receptions, so that already he was booked for four or five evenings a week, every week in the season.

In the mornings, regardless of late hours the night before, he went horseback riding in the Campagna, as he had vowed on his last visit to do. On his first such exercise, he chose a horse carefully, and rode out of the livery stable grounds through an ancient gate in the city wall, the Porta del Popolo, across the Tiber and into the great rolling plain of the Campagna.

The landscape itself, after thousands of years of cultivation, still seemed an expression of a perfect taste. The moist air held the golden light and infused it with a wonderful purple glow; the fields and vineyards and olive groves were carefully arranged, and in the distance here and there was a white village or a gray tower; behind all, the blue Sabine Hills again seemed to glow in the afternoon light in tones of sapphire and amber. After a timeless ride James reached the crest of a low hill and looked back to see Rome clustered within its walls, the dome of Saint Peter's floating above all, and yet small in the distance.

He rode for two hours on that first morning, and came back exhilarated. Not only was the Campagna beautiful, not only did it lend a timeless perspective to Rome, but he had ridden well, and held his seat closely when the horse jumped ditches and hedges. It was a purely idle pleasure, so pleasant indeed that it seemed wrong. He was so unused to long stretches of *dissipation* that he felt he was reading a chapter in the story of a hero of romance, rather than living an episode in his own duty-ridden life.[12]

He rode one morning with Elizabeth Boott and her friend Miss Cleveland, and then more often with Elizabeth alone. To the south there was the long perspective of the Aqueduct of Claudius, slumping periodically under the weight of the centuries, stretching off to a vanishing point under the Alban Hills. One morning he and Elizabeth rode well out of the city and turned off the Tor de Quinto Road to a castellated house among the fields, once a Ghibelline fortress, where Claude Lorraine had painted his famous landscapes. They went into the inner court, ringed by the carved marble columns of a shady loggia. A little girl hung shyly in an opened door, a sketch in bright colors against the black interior. Elizabeth spoke fluently with the pale young farmer, who accepted a coin from Henry. Then they galloped away, a long, long gallop over the daisied turf. The elastic bound of Henry's horse was poetry of motion, he took obstacles easily, and the exhilaration of the ride and the pleasure of Elizabeth's companion-ship affected him almost as a spiritual exercise.[13]

On other mornings, he rode with Mrs. Sumner and Miss Bartlett, who made very handsome figures on horseback and were very fond of galloping cross-country. On a few occasions he went riding with Anne Bartlett alone. They shared an interest in Ariosto's poetry, and formed a regular schedule of reading the poems aloud to each other in the afternoons as a means of improving their Italian.

As the season went on, three or four mornings a week he rode with Elizabeth Boott. They talked in easy, intimate fashion, but there were silent restraints, unstated limits on their friendship. One afternoon on the Pincio, they saw Mrs. Kemble ride past in an open carriage, a survival of another age, regally erect, alone as always. Another day, he came into Elizabeth's studio and found her at work alone with her model, a most handsome young contadino with curly hair and fine legs.

The Bootts were to leave Rome early in April, but neither Henry nor Elizabeth seemed to think that there was anything in their friend-ship to detain her, or would move Henry to follow her. Elizabeth said cheerfully she looked forward to another long visit to Boston and Cambridge. Before she left, however, she showed Henry her favorite riding places, especially a delightful region an hour from the Porta Cavaleggieri that she called Arcadia, where three or four grassy dells stretched away in a chain among low hills. The elements of the land-scape were simple enough, but the composition had extraordinary re-finement. A shepherd had thrown himself down under one of the trees in the foreground; perhaps he had been washing his feet in the neighboring stream, for his short breeches were rolled well up on his thighs. Lying thus in the shade, on his elbow, with his naked legs stretched out on the turf and his soft peaked hat crushed on the back of his head, he struck them both as the perfect figure of romance.[14]

On the last morning before the Bootts were to leave, Henry and Elizabeth went for a ride in the cork woods of Monte Mario, her fa-vorite spot of all for solitary rides. It was her own private place. Strewn among the old trees were shrubs and flowers, like a charming wood-land garden. Casting about for a compliment, Henry said that it re-minded him of the pine woods of New Hampshire; Elizabeth smiled and said that the compliment was double-edged. She showed him the Italian flowers and told him their names, and he then saw, in what had been the featureless botany around him, "the idle elegance and grace of Italy alone, the natural stamp of the land." It was Elizabeth's home, which he loved all but as well as his own country.[15]

"I wonder if we shall ever ride through the cork woods again?" he wrote to Elizabeth when she had departed. He said that he wished neither of them would ever ride there again without the other.[16]

Henry missed Elizabeth after she returned to America, but the warmth and sun filled him with contentment and protected him from depression. He feared only that he was too relaxed, too easy, to do his best work or very much work at all. His letters to his family took on a new apologetic note, as he thought of them struggling with illness and solitude in the Cambridge winter. In his letters to William in particular—whose health was bad and who was finding the work of teaching difficult, and who at thirty-two was still living at home with his parents—with deliberate tact he belittled the pleasures of his new life and wrote a little sourly about the hostesses who were pursuing him; he kept up the old tie of shared unhappiness.

On April 10 the winter season in Rome traditionally ended, and the English, French, and German *forestieri* began to make their way northward. Sarah Wister had taken a house in Hyde Park for the London season, where she would continue to live at the high intensity that Henry thought must be so exhausting for Dr. Wister. Alice Sumner had taken a house in Brittany for herself and Anne Bartlett. The Tweedys prepared to follow the northward migration; the Storys remained a little longer, but gave up their "days" and simply left their door open for visitors.

Henry lingered in Rome; after a few days' visit to a picturesque inn at Albano, he took a now vacant apartment on the Corso for a month. It was his birthday—he was thirty years old—and he viewed the anniversary with a certain solemnity. He was no longer young, in a certain sense; the time of preparation was over. But he was conscious that his book reviews and travel letters, while they paid his rent, were delaying the time when he would begin on his serious work, which was all to come.

M. Hébert had recommended that he see the old villas, especially the Villa Ludovisi and the treasures of antiquity there; but King Victor Emmanuel's wife, known familiarly to society as Rosina, was in residence and the villa was closed to the public. At last, however, when summer was drawing on and the nightingales had just begun to sing, the Villa Ludovisi was vacant again, and James knew that he had found a treasure he would draw upon in the future.

April 27th.—A morning with [a young Mr. Ireland] at the Villa Ludovisi, which we agreed that we shouldn't soon forget. . . . There is
nothing so blissfully *right* in Rome, nothing more consummately consecrated to style. The grounds and gardens are immense, and the great
rusty-red city wall stretches away behind them and makes the burden
of the seven hills vast without making *them* seem small. There is everything—dusky avenues trimmed by the clippings of centuries, groves
and dells and glades and glowing pictures and reedy fountains and great
flowering meadows studded with enormous slanting pines. The day
was delicious, the trees all one melody, the whole place a revelation of
what Italy and hereditary pomp can do together. Nothing could be
more in the grand manner than this garden view of the city ramparts,
lifting their fantastic battlements above the trees and flowers. They
were all tapestried with vines and made to serve as sunny fruit-walls—
grim old defence as they once were; now giving nothing but a splendid
buttressed privacy. The sculptures in the little Casino are few, but
there are two great ones—the beautiful sitting Mars and the head of the
great Juno, the latter thrust into a corner behind a shutter.[17]

The colossal mask of the goddess looked with blank eyes from her
dusky corner;[18] and Henry's companion, saturated with impressions,
refused to look at anything else, at anything less perfect, that day.[19]

He took the Corso apartment for a second month, but on June 12,
when his lease again expired, and the summer's heat and illness were
beginning, he tore himself away from Rome and followed the well-
traveled path northward through Perugia, Florence, and the northern
Italian lakes, to Switzerland, pausing for a few days at each place.

After the intense companionship of the winter, however, he was
lonely. In Perugia, he spent a week going to the theater in the evenings
and letting the music of Italian fill his ear. He spent ten days in Florence, where Francis Boott's angelic tailor made up a summer outfit
for him. On the shore of Lake Maggiore, he waited for the coach that
would carry him into Switzerland, and he wrote to Elizabeth and to
his sister, Alice, that he was sorry to be taking leave of Italy; it was a
wrench, like having one of his back teeth pulled. He lingered, waiting
for the Simplon coach. At last he set off, economically riding outside
on the *banquette* with a young Frenchman, the very type of the imperious young Parisian whom he began by adoring and ended by hating.
They rode at night, in the moonlight, away from all Italian things.[20]

Henry planned to settle in the familiar towns near Lake Geneva for three months, and then to return to Italy. For the summer he would have society only vicariously, through letters. He wrote assiduously, greedily, complaining at the lack of letters from friends and family. To Alice he wrote:

> And now here I am *en pension* at Glion amid multitudinous English whom I shall neither adore nor detest. The place is hardly less lonely than I remembered it & I am settling down to it on a sternly rational basis. The Hotel Byron is twinkling there on the green edge of the blue lake & bringing last summer up to yesterday. The pine clad hills are rising to their snows . . . all around me and making me sigh when I think of gentle Tuscany all festooned in flowers and vines. But they are very handsome indeed, I do them full justice.[21]

He cautioned Alice not to take at all seriously the glum letters he had sent to William; he had enjoyed Italy thoroughly. He had thought it better to leave for the summer, yet in the end it was difficult to leave and he still had doubts. "I suppose I have done the more wholesome thing (with another winter in Italy in view) to come to Switzerland. . . . I am very well indeed. . . ."[22]

He wrote to Elizabeth Boott once a month, complaining when he had not heard from her, and nostalgically recalling their rides in the Campagna. His letters crossed those she wrote to him at the same carefully modulated frequency. In June, not knowing whether she had sailed for America or not, he half seriously suggested that she and her father give up their plan of going to Cambridge in the summer—they were mad—and come to spend it in Switzerland with him. She did not receive this letter before sailing from Liverpool in July. But in June he received a letter she had sent from London before leaving, in ignorance of his movements and his thoughts. Her letter had followed him from Florence; he answered promptly, not knowing where his reply would find her.

> Florence was empty, hottish & most pleasant—as pleasant at least as Rome would let it be. As I read last evening by the lakeside your lovely sentences about the wood & future rides & the past ones, I could have flung myself into the lake for desperate melancholy.[23]

Despite these heroics, he missed her a great deal. But it was time for solitude and work. He had begun to think it was time to write a novel.

But first, unfortunately, and for the immediate future, there was the letter of credit to feed, and so he planned a hasty series of travel letters, short stories, and book reviews.

The travel pieces were not difficult to get out. He had only to pillage his journal. But book reviews were a problem, as he did not have easy access to new books. He was less interested in current releases, in any case, than in putting his own thoughts in order. His thoughts had turned to the novel form, and so he settled down to write a review of the work that seemed to him preeminent in that field: Ivan Turgenev's novels. Although Turgenev wrote in Russian, all of his work had appeared by then in French translation,[24] and Henry had read the stories and novels as they appeared in French. Relying on his excellent memory for the volumes that were not readily at hand in Glion or Montreux, he assessed the novels of Turgenev. He wrote quite a long essay with the *North American Review* in mind, and when it was done he was so pleased with it he offered to write a series of such essays for the *Review*.

Turgenev was the first novelist of the day, and to assess Turgenev's work therefore was to assess the state of the novel. Henry proceeded to his analysis like a man studying a mountain that he planned to climb the next morning.

There were odd elements of similarity between the Russian novelist and himself. America and Russia were two vast countries metaphorically on the edges of Europe, and each nation was just stepping onto the stage of European history. For Turgenev as for Henry James, French was a second language. Christian belief and German philosophy provided the intellectual background of their thought. Each was a man of democratic opinions and aristocratic tastes. And each was an expatriate, who had found it impossible to live in his native land. Turgenev had lived for many years in German-speaking Baden. He was a cosmopolite, a European, who yet was loyal to his native villages and to his native language, who lived in Europe but wrote in Russian, for and about Russians. Henry had never seen a picture of Turgenev, but he imagined the older man to be like a Titian portrait: an aristocrat with thin features, a hawk's nose, and graceful hands. It seemed to Henry that Turgenev was the latest in a line of great writers, a follower of Balzac and Sand, who had come from his province to Paris, the capital of Europe, and yet had not been false to his origins.

In what, then, lay his greatness? Henry began with Turgenev's method, with his fundamental qualities as a writer. At first glance he seemed to have a fatal limitation, like Henry's own.

> He belongs to the limited class of very careful writers. . . . His line is narrow observation. He has not the faculty of rapid, passionate, almost reckless improvisation—that of Walter Scott, of Dickens, of George Sand. This is an immense charm in a story-teller; on the whole, to our sense, the greatest. Turgenev lacks it. . . .[25]

Turgenev's method was fundamentally realistic, and if he lacked the charm of a storyteller, he had the charm of a great portrait painter. His books and stories were filled with people who seemed to be real. "We believe as we read," Henry observed. The trick was worked by the accumulation of telling details that evidently were not invented but observed. Henry thought that Turgenev must have the habit of taking notes, of noting down a fragment of talk, a gesture, a feature, and of preserving them for twenty years if need be, until he found just the spot for placing the observed detail.

> His figures . . . have each something special, something peculiar, that none of their neighbors have, and that rescues them from the limbo of the gracefully general. We remember, in one of his stories, a gentleman who makes a momentary appearance as host at a dinner party, and after being described as having such and such a face, clothes, and manners, has our impression of his personality completed by the statement that the soup at his table was filled with little paste figures, representing hearts, triangles, and trumpets. . . .[26]

Mysteriously, such details gave life and meaning to a portrait. Dickens characterized people in this way, by their idiosyncrasies; but he was an improvisator dancing on the tightrope, and his characters were like a lawless revel of the imagination. Turgenev always proceeded by the book, and his descriptions carried a kind of historical weight. Reading, one felt as if the author could show documents and relics; as if he had an old portrait, or a dozen of the character's old letters. Turgenev believed in the intrinsic importance of the subject; his work was the strongest answer to the school of Gautier, to "art for art alone." There were trivial subjects and serious ones, Henry wrote, and the latter were much the best.

There was something cold about this method, it was true, but it was redeemed by Turgenev's love for the characters who kindled his imagination. For he did love his characters, even those who were evil. And of all his characters, none were more interesting and memorable than the women.

> There are no heroines we see more distinctly, there are none we love more ardently. It would be difficult to point, in the blooming fields of fiction, to a group of young girls more radiant with maidenly charm than M. Turgenev's Hélène, his Lisa, his Katia, his Tatania and his Gemma. . . .[27]

Turgenev's heroines were the best example of his method, in which he united detailed observations of material forms and gestures with an acutely imagined moral dimension. His novel *On the Eve* was essentially a portrait of a lady, Hélène, a heroine in the literal sense of the word: "a young girl of a will so calmly ardent and intense that she needs nothing but opportunity to become one of the figures about whom admiring legend clusters."[28]

Henry thought that the painter owed something to his model, and that Russian women must be in some respects remarkable; their purity, their force of will, their religious passion seemed to be observed rather than invented.

> American readers of Turgenev have been struck with certain points of resemblance between American and Russian life. The resemblance is generally superficial, but it does not seem to us altogether fanciful to say that Russian young girls . . . have to our sense a touch of the faintly acrid perfume of the New England temperament—a hint of the Puritan angularity. It is the women and young girls in our author's tales who mainly represent strength of will—the power to resist, to wait, to attain. In the integrity of Lisa, of Hélène, even of the more dimly shadowed Maria Alexandrovna—a sort of finer distillation, it seems, of masculine honor—there is something almost formidable: the strongest men are less positive in their strength.[29]

Turgenev's portraits of women were drawn with tenderness and yet with an indefinable, an almost unprecedented respect. The male characters, by contrast, rarely exhibited the necessary will. The men were often fools or victims, and the basest passions seemed always to prevail over them. Turgenev was plainly very fond of these victims, and portrayed them with great sympathy; yet, after all, they were moral failures. Turgenev's pessimism was embodied in these men.

What story did these characters tell, in whom individual qualities evoked the largest types and generalizations? It was principally one story, the great theme of so much tragedy, the battle between the old and the new. Turgenev was not in sympathy with the revolutionary movement in Russia; the anarchists and nihilists seemed to him adolescent and unintelligent. Yet he was fond of them, of their youthful violence and passion, and he was sadly aware of the bankruptcy of the old slaveholding aristocracy.

The tone of Turgenev's stories therefore was ironical and pessimistic; his sarcasm seemed to Henry his principal fault. There was something self-indulgent, even morbid, in his pessimism. Henry thought that the ultimate novelist would be a person altogether purged of sarcasm. For if there was some wisdom in Turgenev's sadness, there was also some error. A complete realism, a complete fusion of observed historic fact with imaginatively perceived moral truth would be colored not precisely by joy, but by contentment. The true realist was at home in the world.

> Evil is insolent and strong; beauty enchanting but rare; goodness very apt to be weak; folly very apt to be defiant; wickedness to carry the day; imbeciles in great places, people of sense in small, and mankind generally, unhappy. But the world as it stands is no illusion, no phantasm, no evil dream of a night; we wake up to it again for ever and ever; we can neither forget it nor deny it nor dispense with it. We can welcome experience as it comes, and give what it demands, in exchange for something which it is idle to pause to call much or little so long as it contributes to swell the volume of consciousness. In this there is mingled pain and delight, but over the mysterious mixture there hovers a visible rule, that bids us to learn to will and seek to understand.[30]

In this essay, with its statement of a personal religion, Henry set out also his critical method and his own program for a novel. His old manifesto, the call for a fusion of history and romance, of imagination and historical fact, was reaffirmed. Turgenev had shown the way; it was for James to take the next step. Turgenev, for all his genius, was timid and disappointed. It remained for Henry James to take all of

Europe and America for his stage, to show the drama of the meeting of old and new.

The setting would be Rome, the ancient city, as small as a village constrained within its walls. The streets were narrow and crooked; there were few restaurants or hotels, few public gathering places. The city to James was not a world capital like Paris or London, it was an archaeological site. He loved to watch the excavations going on at the Forum; but one did not need to dig into the earth—layers of history were exposed everywhere. Two-thousand-year-old Juno lay behind a shutter in a medieval villa. Mary Tweedy's coach driver was a living survival of classical Rome. And swarming everywhere in the city were the *forestieri*, who embodied the most modern of civilizations, if not indeed the future itself.

Henry imagined the sweep of history as a story of progress, of maturation. There was a clear progression from more simple and primitive types: from the beautiful amoral Greeks, the sensuous and materialist Rome, and the complex art and culture of Florence to the highly evolved nations of the modern world. It was only necessary to give a moral dimension to the scientific studies that had described this evolution. Violence and empire had had their last spasm, and the future promised to be peaceful. The powerful will of the artist of life would supplant the rule of force.

The great drama he saw being enacted in Europe was this testing of the new type against the older races, the drama of the battle of the past against the future. A young girl's coming-of-age was the story of a whole nation's maturation. In the true, secret history of a nation, alternate futures branched continually, and the choices between them were made in private, in walled enclosures; a woman's choice might decide the course of civilization, as Mme. Swetchine had day by day, in her salon, shaped the moral quality of France.[31]

That summer at Glion and Montreux, James for the first time portrayed the encounter of Europe and America. His heroine was an American woman who had come into her proper inheritance. She was still the fine, slim, heroine of his youth, she of the dove-gray eyes. But she had acquired Annie Fields's or Elizabeth Boott's polish and self-possession. She had been raised by a benevolent father, carefully educated, and was equal to the manners and traditions of Europe. Her new husband was dark, beautiful: a prince, a Louis De Coppet of the Old World, embodying the history of an ancient civilization, its perfect taste and manner.

The prince in the story at first seemed to be a fairy-tale figure, the ideal object of innocent passion; marriage to him promised fulfillment, the intensity of delight. But the prince was of the old order, morally blind. He was capable of thoughtless evil: not only wickedness, of which Henry's heroine took small account, but of evil. Her marriage itself was the encounter of the old and the new orders, and the result was by no means to be foreseen.[32]

Dictating to Miss Bosanquet forty years later, James remembered this moment, the beginning of his ten-year study of the encounter of America and Europe. The reasons for almost always choosing a woman as his protagonist were somewhat complex, although the first reason that offered itself would have been sufficient. The typical American man was in business, and Henry knew very little about any business other than his own. He knew least of all about the businesses that had to be considered typical of America: buying and selling, trading and deal making. This was not a realm that he felt capable of investigating as he had investigated the cities of Europe and the resorts of America.[33] James would continue to sketch securities traders, advertising men, and merchants as he observed them from a distance; but he did not feel confident of the inward dimension of these portraits, and after all he did not wish to be. It was difficult to imagine a romance of trade.[34]

If American businessmen were difficult subjects, their wives and mothers were still more so. The older woman, the power of her beauty lost, her life choices made once and for all, did not strike him as the heroine of a novel.[35] The hero of his international tales, therefore, would be the American girl, just coming into her inheritance and her power, with all her freedom intact and her choices ahead of her.

If his first reasons for choosing this heroine had not sufficed, there were others he might have called on. The audience for his work was principally female, as he knew, and the most popular fiction of his day was written by and for women. The popular novel form was defined as a tale of young love. Books and magazines had to be suitable for unmarried women to read; their sensibilities and experiences were the test for admission to the popular magazines and the lending libraries. This ignoble motive would not have been decisive in itself, perhaps, but it joined with and supported his aesthetic and moral principles. And then, too, there were perceptions, observations, and insights that could be presented only from a female perspective, and that a male author could not offer as his own without violating the conventions of popular fiction. Even in the portrayal of the American man, it was difficult to paint him with affection, and from the outside, as an object of interest and desire, except through a young woman's eye.

But perhaps the final reason and the one he would have offered if all others had failed, was that the American woman, like the Russian heroine of Turgenev's tales, seemed to him to be a superior type. There were men of whom one could say the same, but as a type only the American woman could be imagined as the peaceful conqueror of Europe: a character whose love was still fused with primordial religious feeling, a pure expression of innocent passion unmixed with coquetry, capable of great courage. For all his rebellion against his father, he wrote from within the world in which he had been raised. From the dove-gray eyes of his American heroine gazed the Holy Spirit, the spirit of humanity in its latest and best incarnation. It was this character who most counted on the little stage of his stories, the stage on which history was enacted; she was the character that he observed most carefully and whose part he performed with the most heartfelt and spontaneous power.[36]

That summer, from Switzerland, he sent off to Howells a story set among the ruins of Rome: "The Last of the Valerii."[37] His American heroine had married a noble Roman, a throwback to the old aristocratic type. On the grounds of his villa, a clever dwarfish expert from the new Italian regime had unearthed a statue of Juno, the queen of the gods, the goddess herself, more ancient than Rome. She was at her most imposing in the moonlight: "Juno visited by Diana." The Roman husband helplessly worshiped the goddess; but the American heroine was stronger, and conquered his love—conquered the goddess.[38]

Montreux was uncomfortably hot; Henry felt his spirits flagging and his constitution suffering under the regime of long hours at his desk. It was time to put himself in motion again. Instead of remaining in Switzerland until the fall, he decided to venture eastward to Bad Homburg, the German spa whose waters William continued insistently to recommend, although they had done him so little good. Henry did not find that the waters agreed with him, either. But Homburg was cool, and he found a quiet room, a dampish, dusky, unsunned room. It opened from the courtyard of an inn, and was so dark that he could find his way to his candle and inkstand only by leaving the door open. It was cool and quiet; he let the waters alone and continued his profitable labors.[39]

He was not capable of real solitude for very long, but he did find congenial company in Homburg as well. He met an English bachelor, in Homburg for the cure, an Edmund Parkes who was known in America for his published attacks on homeopathy. Dr. Parkes was staying at Henry's inn, and he had a gentlemanly mind that wore well for daily companionship. James and he suffered from the same complaint, for which Parkes found the waters beneficial, and they became close companions.

Here, in the quiet of Homburg, with the comfort of an undemanding friendship, Henry attempted his first major story on his new theme. It was a portrait of the heroine with dove-gray eyes, who now wore her hair as Alice did. She was an American, but she had the innocent manners and graces of a European *jeune fille*, a young woman of good family. Above all, she had a purity of imagination that was her own, and that was profoundly uncorruptible. This she had nourished on fairy tales, as Henry had done, on the fables of nobility, of aristocratic blood, of Prince Charming. She had a school friend, a little French girl of aristocratic descent, who, like De Coppet and La Farge, had seemed to her to be a realization of the fable. She found American men vulgar, and set her heart upon an aristocratic marriage.[40]

In his dimly lit room in Homburg, Henry was visited by this heroine, the gentle Euphemia, the well-spoken:

> She was slight and fair, and, though naturally pale, delicately flushed, apparently with recent excitement. What chiefly struck Longmore in her face was the union of a pair of beautifully gentle, almost languid gray eyes, with a mouth peculiarly expressive and firm. Her forehead was a trifle more expansive than belongs to classic types, and her thick brown hair was dressed out of the fashion. . . . Her throat and bust were slender, but all the more in harmony with certain rapid charming movements of the head, which she had a way of throwing back every now and then, with an air of attention and a sidelong glance from her dove-like eyes.[41]

Henry sat in the twilight coolness, artfully transcribing the confidences with which Euphemia honored him.[42] But if she herself was a realistic character, the tale she told him was the lightest romance. Her husband was a throwback to the old order. He was a Frenchman, a baron of ancient descent. He was in debt, and she was wealthy. Her wealth allowed her to choose; allowed her the liberty to make profound mistakes.

The aristocrat and his wicked family were literary inventions, drawn from the novels of Droz and Feuillet, and the plays of Alfred de Musset, rather than from direct observation; they were types, not individuals. They were meant to represent manners without morals, art for art alone, historic tradition for its own sake. Henry's Americans, "modern bourgeois," viewed them across the mist of history.[43]

True to his type, the baron treated his wife like a new glove that was to be thrust aside when she was no longer fresh. But Euphemia was stronger than he. She refused to accept her husband's adulteries or to compensate herself with adulteries of her own. She remained true to herself and to the choice that she had made, to the fable that had proved so meager when realized. She gazed at her husband with her open expression, her luminous eyes, and slowly she conquered. The baron fell tragically in love with his own wife. Yet she did not conceal her contempt for him. Withering under her gaze, the baron languished and in the end, like Octave Feuillet's protagonist Camors, he killed himself.[44]

This ending was more a literary convention than a realistic climax. But the tale had an air of reality, largely because of the vividness of its heroine, and because it was told by a believable observer, a new character: Longmore, an American intellectual male. Like Turgenev's Russian intellectuals, whom he greatly resembled, he lacked moral force, lacked *will*. Henry was fond of him, and he had the exquisite sensitivity to serve as an acute observer and narrator; he spared the author the burden of omniscience. The air of reality in the tale was largely created by this device: everything was observed through his rather ordinary, if sharp, eyes. The reader was invited to join with Longmore in trying to decode the secrets of Euphemia's marriage.

In September the hot weather broke at last, and the larger part of his summer's work was behind him: the long essay on Turgenev and "Madame de Mauves," the fine new story about Euphemia, were in the mail to American editors. James relaxed and enjoyed the hilly landscape. Homburg had a pleasant, old-world picturesqueness, and the weather was so pleasant, he wrote to Alice, who was with the family in New Brunswick for the summer, that he could

> hardly write or think, for looking out the window at clouds & light & air and wanting to go into the woods & lie on the edge of a clearing & waste existence in the mere rudimentary consciousness of it. . . . of

our soft, grey, windy days with the breezes wandering about—to the
music of the rustling winds—like couples waltzing. . . .[45]

He was very pleased with the work he had done. The Turgenev essay in
particular he thought "splendid,"[46] and he was conscious that his work
had reached a new plane. He thought that he would write a series of
essays on French writers, and he asked William to send to him his copies
of the works of Balzac, Sainte-Beuve, Musset, and Stendhal.[47]

The summer was ending, and he began to think of returning to
Italy. But Parkes's companionship was so pleasant and undemanding
and the Homburg air so cool and invigorating—he seemed to feel it
was charged with health-giving influences—that he lingered. It was
too soon to be going to Rome in any case. He decided to remain
in Homburg until late in September, and then to work his way in
leisurely fashion down through Florence to Rome, which he had
begun to think of as his permanent base.

He caught up on his neglected correspondence. There was a good
deal of news from Cambridge: Alice had continued to bloom since her
visit to Europe with Henry, and was full of life. She issued her commands and sarcasms with great gusto. William was jealous of her trip
to Europe with Henry and of the vigorous health in which she had
returned.[48] She had learned from Henry that travel was a sovereign
cure, and when she could not bear Cambridge any longer, she went to
New York, alone, to visit Aunt Helen. She informed everyone that
henceforth she would travel alone, convention notwithstanding. Indeed, she thought of returning to Europe for a longer stay. But as
Mother wrote in her own letter, this was not to be thought of now, nor
would it ever be possible during Father's lifetime. Father depended
too greatly on Alice for company, and his health was too frail for her
to be so far away. Alice must remain at home, her father's secretary
and companion during his lifetime.[49]

William wrote that he had completed his first year of teaching and
was resting for the summer. It had been very tiring, and he was afraid
that he would not be permitted to teach psychology again; the new
president, Eliot, wanted him to teach a course in anatomy and physiology instead. The pay was only six hundred dollars for the year, and
at first he had decided to turn it down. He would hold out for psychology or nothing. But Eliot was firm, and it was somewhat humiliating for William to recognize that he was still dependent on his
parents and could not turn down even this modest salary. He wrote
somewhat sadly to Henry,

I have changed my mind & for the present give myself to biology. i.e. accept the tuition here for 600 dollars, & this is virtually tantamount to my clinging to those subjects [anatomy and physiology] for the next 10 or 12 years if I linger so long. On the whole this is the wiser, if the tamer decision—the fact is, I'm not a strong enough man to choose the other and nobler lot in life. . . .[50]

Alice & I keep up a rather constant fire of badinage &c of which you furnish the material; she never speaking of you except as "that angel"—and I sarcastically calling you the "angel–hero–martyr." Usually toward bed-time I wander into the parlor where the three [father, mother, and Alice] are sitting and say "I suppose that angel is now in such and such and attitude," drawing on my imagination for something very "oriental," to which Alice generally finds no better reply than a tirade upon the petty jealousies of *men*.[51]

But it appeared that in truth it was Alice of whom he was jealous. On and off during the summer, William had spoken vaguely of going to Rome to be with Henry, "my in many respects twin brother."[52] Although he had agreed to teach biology to Harvard undergraduates, he was constantly on the point of changing his mind. He would tell Eliot to find someone else to teach the onerous course, and would spend the next fall and winter with Henry in Rome. He wanted time to heal.

Here at home there are various modes of killing time, the ride to Boston and back destroys one hour, there are constantly visitors to the house. . . . This is the point I want you to answer: from your experience of killing time in Rome & elsewhere, should you think the experiment would be a safe one for a man in my state to try? Your being there and with me, (if you are willing) would of course help it through amazingly. . . .[53]

Henry answered very delicately, praising the attractions of Rome and making William welcome, without urging him to one course of action or another. In August, however, William said he had finally decided to remain at home. The expense of travel would be too great for the family to bear. Yet he was obsessed by the state of his health.

I alternate between fits lasting from 4 or 5 days to three weeks of the most extreme languor & depression, weakness of body & head & pain

in the back—during wh. however I sleep well—and fits of equally uneven duration of great exhilaration of spirits, restlessness, compara-
tive bodily & mental activity. . . .[54]

There was other news from Cambridge. Tom Perry, whom no one
thought likely to marry, had announced his engagement to that intelligent, forthright little cousin of the Lowells and Holmeses, Lilla
Cabot. Mother wrote in some amusement that Miss Cabot's masculine charms had captivated sweet Tom.[55] There were the distant rum-
blings of another industrial depression in America. A crash in the
securities markets had sent its reverberations rippling through the
economy, as in 1857. The family's investments were not greatly affected, but cash was tight; there was a sharp deflation in currency, and
Henry wrote to ask whether the Albany relations had been hurt.
Fields had been obliged to sell *The Atlantic* to a rival publisher, Henry
Houghton; ill and growing old, he left the book business to his young
partner, James Osgood, and retired. Henry wrote with concern to
Howells, but Howells was not affected by all the upheavals; he would
continue as editor of *The Atlantic*, and indeed was moving into a large
new house, on Concord Avenue in Cambridge, with a frescoed ceiling
and chestnut bookshelves in the library.

Wendell Holmes asked to be remembered to Henry, in one of
William's letters. His wife, Fanny, had recovered from a bout of
rheumatic fever and they were planning to spend their summer in
England; Wendell hoped to see Henry, perhaps in Switzerland and
perhaps in London.

Henry at last went slowly on to Florence, a little sooner than
planned, but it was intolerably hot; and he reversed course briefly to
Siena. In October, however, when it was cooler, he was back in Florence, in a comfortable hotel room, where another round of letters
found him.

Howells had rejected the tale of Euphemia, "Madame de Mauves,"
apparently because it treated adultery with some frankness. It was the
first time in ten years that one of Henry's tales had been turned down.
Father said that he had forwarded it to *The Galaxy*, in New York,
which was less prudish.

The Turgenev essay, too, had been rejected. Tom Perry had returned it with suggestions for extensive revision. Father had fretted
over whether to forward this article to another journal or to make the
revisions himself, as he sometimes did when they were minor; but in
the end he decided to return the piece to Henry, despite the delays

that this would involve. This rejection was particularly disheartening, but Henry patiently set to making the requested alterations so that the article might appear in the *North American Review*.[56] He wrote to his father:

> I am sorry you should have had any worry of mind about sending me back the Turgenev manuscript & am most glad you decided to do so. I shall not fail to do anything I can to amend it. I am not a little disappointed to know it leaves so much to be desired, for I wrote it with great care, zeal, & pleasure & said to myself when it was finished that it was the best thing I had done & would help me to some reputation.[57]

And then yet another letter came from William; he had changed course once more, and was already on his way to Italy:

> My dear H.—the die is cast! The 600 dollars salary fall into the pocket of another! And for a year I am adrift again & free. . . . Of course I can't wait to take passage till I hear from you, it wd. give me too bad a choice of berths. I only write this word to tell you of my decision, to say that I rejoice at the prospect of so soon communing with you. . . .[58]

Henry's thoughts of setting to work on his novel, at long last, were put aside. There was nothing to be done. He wrote a careful letter of instructions for William that would greet him at the Adelphi Hotel in Liverpool. The overland voyage through France was best; William should buy a through ticket to Rome, or at least to Florence, at the office of Alta Italia Railway Co., behind the Grand Hotel. "Don't forget to buy and bring some of Davis's tooth soap, and Harrison's lozenges, from London."[59]

16

THE AMBASSADOR FROM
LAWTON'S VALLEY

William came straight to Florence, without pausing except to change trains. He came with the plan of spending the winter in Rome with Henry and of bringing him back to Cambridge in the spring.[1] William was thin and intense, and seemed awkward, ill at ease with himself. He had a drooping mustache and furiously blue eyes. The trip had invigorated him, but he found Henry rather subdued.

William lost no time in making his argument: Henry should return with him to the United States and get a job with a salary, perhaps as an editor like Perry, Howells, and Sedgwick. Then, at the end of the day, his work would be done; the pressure to earn money would be off and he could indulge himself in literature in his spare time.[2] This was a belittling view of literature, and of Henry's identity as a man of letters, but William was like a stern minister of the Gospel, impatient of frivolity.[3]

Henry tried to avoid this discussion, but when pressed by William he said that he could not live in America, and when pressed further, he gave his reasons—the provincial quality of life, the thinness, the bareness of culture; the lack of a community of like-minded artists; the lack of society. William then accused him of disloyalty.[4]

Florence, on the other hand, with its narrow dark streets and its poverty, repelled William and reinforced his arguments. Everything spoke to him of ancient injustice; he wished Father were there to utter his vast oaths and imprecations upon the inhumanity of Europe. Henry seemed to find it beautiful. William said he was not sufficiently sensitive to the moral squalor, the filth. Henry listened, but showed him the other aspect of Florence, Eleanora's, and gradually William began to enjoy himself.

> For ten days after my arrival I was so disgusted with the swarming and reeking blackness of the streets and the age of everything, that enjoyment took place under protest, as it were. But I've left all that behind me, and can take the picturesque now without any moral afterthought. It is easier in Italy than elsewhere because of the cheerfulness and contented manners of the common people. They don't take life anything like as hard as we do, and suffer privation without being made desperate by it as we are. My old love of art returns, but not in its full force.[5]

Rome was their goal, and after William had been outfitted by the Florentine tailors, on November 28 they went south, traveling in the day by rail, past walled towns on their little hills. They arrived in Rome in the evening, and after dinner at the Hôtel de Rome, Henry took William for his favorite walk down the Corso. It was a cloudless night, lit by a half-moon. The effects were as dramatic as could be wished, and with mingled excitement and resentment, William felt himself acted upon. The next day he reported this experience to his father:

> I had arrived at Rome with no more sentiment or expectation than if I were going to East Boston, and when in ten minutes after having left the modern shop-lit street, I found myself passing the old wreck-strewn Forum, and advancing under a line of trees in what seemed a common country road with a few distant lamps against the sides of houses, and right and left huge looming shapes of tumbled walls and ruins, not a living being, biped or quadruped, to be seen or heard—

and finally when we entered under the mighty Coliseum wall and stood in its mysterious midst, with that cold sinister half-moon and hardly a star in the deep blue sky—it was all so strange, and, I must say, inhuman and horrible, that it felt like a nightmare. Again I would have liked to hear the great curses you would have spoken. Anti-Christian as I generally am, I actually derived a deep comfort from the big black cross that had been planted on that damned blood-soaked soil. I think if Harry had not been with me I should have fled howling from the place.[6]

The two brothers had not lived on intimate terms for some years, and Henry had a highly developed, private existence of which William as yet knew very little. There was a certain degree of friction as they came to know each other's ways. The little bottle of brilliantine for Henry's beard, for instance, was something of a shock to William. When they were settled in Rome, William renewed the attack on this way of life. The attractions of Rome were perceptible, but they were only a temptation. William attacked from high moral ground, with their father's arguments. The accumulations of the past, the deeply stained individuality of persons and places, the secret histories that one sensed everywhere, all these things that Henry loved were the residues of past evil and injustice. The great churches were monuments to wickedness. And there was the expense for the family, when Wilky and Bob were struggling and needed help, of keeping Henry abroad. Henry was a drain on the family's resources at a time when they could ill afford it; he was not earning as much as he was spending, and Father was obliged to make advances of credit for him.[7] These were powerful arguments that William advanced in the name of the whole family, in behalf of Father especially; but Mother, Alice, and Aunt Kate too wished to see Henry marry, and settle finally in America.

On December 7 these arguments of family piety were strongly enforced by a letter from Father.[8] Wilky had married, and he had brought his new bride, Carrie, home for a visit. And the most joyous news was that Bob and Mary had a boy, the first grandchild to be born into the James family. Both brothers were struggling financially, and needed help.

Henry listened to the family's arguments, and made his replies. These were all questions he had considered; but he would keep an open mind. He would like to meet his new sisters-in-law, and he very much wanted to see his nephew, the first baby in their family. If he could not keep his accounts in balance with Father, perhaps it would be better to return. But William, too, was to keep an open mind; they would explore the question together. When William made his preliminary reports to the family, the question was left in suspense.

> The poor fellow is not quite as blooming as I had hoped to find him when I left home, but nevertheless is in materially better condition than he has been at all. He seems to dislike America, yet there is something desolate in his living here as an alien. I advise him strongly to look out for a wife—but he positively refuses to think of such a thing.[9]

Henry made all their arrangements, and rented two rooms in the Hôtel de Rome, which had proved so comfortable and convenient on his own first visit. He went in search of an apartment they could take, for economy's sake, for a longer term. The little apartment on the Corso he had occupied the previous spring was vacant and could be let by the month. But this was only one room, not large enough for both brothers to share. William was happy to remain in the hotel, however, and Henry moved into his old apartment. They had breakfasts together and toured in the afternoons; they separated in the evenings.[10]

There was a flicker of oddity about these separate arrangements, but Henry carried out the transactions in a perfectly commonplace way and William did not think more about them. It was still early in the season, but the Storys and Terrys had already begun to entertain, and Rome was beginning to grow lively. The Samuel Wards had come to Rome to join their daughter Louisa and Samuel's sister Lilly von Hoffman. The Wards extended their hospitality to the James brothers—a little insistently, indeed, for their father had written to Sam Ward and he was keeping an eye on the boys.[11]

The James family in Cambridge—Father, Mother, Wilky, Alice, and Aunt Kate—were like a little audience gathered to watch a play, awaiting the climax of the scene in Rome. A steady stream of letters from the two brothers gave regular and competing reports. William wrote:

> At present Harry is my spouse. . . . I was disappointed at finding him not completely well as I had hoped; but he seems well enough to

work hard, and that seems now to be the only thing he lives for. I don't know whether he can ever be got to return home and take a position of literary drudgery, editorial or other. . . . his temperament is so exclusively artistic that the vacuous, simple atmosphere of America ends by tiring him to death. So I don't know how it will turn out.[12]

Henry wrote to Father, reporting in his turn about William's health, ignoring the question of his own return. He was immensely pleased with the improvement in William's health, and Henry had the pleasure of being the agent, the mentor, of his flourishing.[13] The season had properly begun, and it was Rome the magnificent. He wrote to Alice:

Never has it seemed more delightful. No too importunate friends,—plenty of time to one's self—yet, with Wards, Hoffmanns, Storys &c. enough society, the divinest weather that ever graced the planet, the lovely afternoon walks and drives, & for me, the especial charm of Willy thriving under it all as if he were being secretly plied with the elixir of life.[14]

But the letters from Rome abruptly ceased. In the silence there were confused movements. After only a few days in Rome, William left abruptly and returned to Florence. After some delay, on the first of the year, Henry followed him.

The family continued to write in turns every few days, with growing insistence. A brief reply from William on January 6 said that he had been ill, and that he had abandoned Rome and its malarial air in consequence, but that he was improving greatly in Florence.[15] Then on January 13 Henry wrote a more complete report, addressed to Alice.

To Rome came duly your lovely letter, to me, of Nov 20th, & then mother's as lovely of Dec 8th, also to me; & then Father's of Dec. 18th & 26th & then yours again to Willy of Dec 15th. So we have had a feast [of] tidings & domestic affection. Willy has written a "vivacious" acknowledgment of all this, which I am to enclose herewith. You will already know of our being in Florence, and why; but I am afraid that since Willy wrote you, a week ago, we have left you too long without news; but it has been simply because Willy is now so completely restored to exuberant health that there seemed no reason for sending bulletins.[16]

At Rome, he said, William had been afflicted with the restless and sleepless nights that characterized his excited states, and a doctor had advised leaving the unhealthy air. William had decided to come back to Florence, which he had enjoyed on his first visit. And Henry, who had not been in the best of health himself, had decided to join William there for the balance of the winter.[17] There was another flicker of oddity in these abrupt movements. Whatever their cause, in a separate letter he confessed privately to Alice that he bitterly regretted leaving Rome.

> I wish I could portray also to your sisterly soul the emotions of one who is called upon, suddenly, in midwinter, to substitute Florence the meager, for Rome the magnificent. I was very willing to abide quietly in Florence till the autumn, & attempt no higher flight; but to go to Rome and take root there, and have all the satisfactions come crowding back on me & call one's self a drivelling fool to have pretended to exist without them—& then to brush away the magic vision and wake up and see the dirty ice floating down the prosy Arno . . . this is a trial to test the most angelic philosophy![18]

With equal suddenness, a few days later and without any further explanation, William left Florence, left Italy entirely, and went north to Germany. He visited Dresden briefly, and then returned to the United States. He sailed from Bremen on a German ship, abandoning the berth he had carefully reserved and the luggage he had left in Liverpool awaiting his return. He appeared to believe that Henry would follow him shortly.[19] And Henry wrote to his family and friends that yes, he was planning to return to the United States.

Neither of them gave entirely frank or complete reports of what had happened. But Henry repeatedly portrayed William's brief visit and abrupt departure in his novels.[20] The first account, written just two years later in *The American*, was the most literal; both William and their mutual friends recognized the portrait.[21] In this first account, William was coldly satirized. He was portrayed as a New England minister, Babcock, rather innocent and aesthetic. Mr. Babcock loved pictures and other expressions of beauty, but could not accept the reality of the world that had produced them. He was innocent, and had to have explained to him the nature of the illicit relations that were so large a feature of the life around him. After only a brief visit in Italy, Babcock abruptly departed, afterward sending a letter of explanation to his host. The letter might have been William's, except that the fictional character was the ambassador of his congregation, instead of his family:

> I am afraid my conduct at Venice, a week ago, seemed strange and ungrateful, and I wish to explain my position, which, as I said at the time, I do not think you appreciate. . . . I have a high sense of responsibility. You seem to care only for the pleasure of the hour, and you give yourself up to it with a violence which I confess I am not able to emulate. Art and life seem to me intensely serious things. . . . You put, moreover, a kind of reckless confidence in your pleasure which at times, I confess, has seemed to me—shall I say it?—almost cynical. Your way at any rate is not my way, and it is unwise that we should attempt any longer to pull together. And yet, let me add, that I know there is a great deal to be said for your way; I have felt its attraction, in your society, very strongly. . . .[22]

When this novel was published, their mutual friend Grace Norton recognized the portrait of William, and confessed that something in her soul trembled like a guilty thing when she read his denunciation of expatriate life in Italy.[23] Henry himself, like the fictional host of the story, felt rebuked and depressed for a time after William's departure.[24]

Six years later, after Henry had happily settled in London, he again put into a novel an encounter in Europe between characters very much like himself and his brother William.[25] By this time his tone was no longer angry or sarcastic, and the story had an added dimension. The novel was *Confidence*.

The illicit relations around him again had to be explained to the innocent William character. The Henry character was in love, in this account, and the plot was contrived in a way that made the love improper: on its surface it was a violation of conventional morals. But to the eye of Henry's moral imagination this love showed itself to be perfectly innocent and joyous.[26] "It was the very truth of his being."[27]

The William character did not at first understand the nature of his relationship, but after some delay the Henry character was obliged to explain. The William character thereupon departed abruptly and angrily for America.[28]

Whatever happened in historic fact between the brothers in Rome, William did leave Italy abruptly, without spending the winter as he had planned. He had asserted the claims of duty, and he returned carrying Henry's promise to follow him shortly. Henry had agreed to try the experiment of living in America. But after William departed he temporized a little, and said that he would stay a while longer in Florence, to begin work on a novel.

Florence too had its season; the opera began after Christmas, and there were late parties that broke up at three or four in the morning.[29] But Florence was far less exciting and demanding than Rome, and it was true, after all, that he had not been able to do any serious work in Rome. Now that the harshest cold weather had passed, and the beautiful flower-filled spring was dawning, Florence was very pleasant. He rented a vast sunny apartment on the Piazza Santa Maria Novella, whose sitting room looked out over the empty square, deserted except for the carriage drivers lounging about the fountain in the center. Their lively conversation drifted through the partly open shutters of his sitting room. Henry settled into Florence: he would stay as long as the climate would allow, and would go north again in the summer. He put off his return to America until the fall.

When he was not working, he walked about the city. Via della Scalla opened a vista toward the distant hills that ringed Florence and seemed to hold it in a cup. The old city wall was gone and the broad new streets that stretched outward were paved with blank white stone and lined with ugly buildings. But the view of the hills that had been revealed was charming, and there was a good French restaurant just around the corner.

The center of Florence for him was the Pitti Palace, where Eleanora had assembled her great art collection, and it was there that he often went to look at paintings and to wander in the old private apartments, to stroll through the long gallery across the Arno to the Uffizi galleries, or simply to linger in the palace's gardens, where clipped hedges climbed up to the last remnant of the old fortified city wall. On the gray and misty days of winter the green aisles and the overhanging trees of the Boboli Gardens were sweetly melancholy.

He occasionally walked up to Bellosguardo, for the view, and thought of the Bootts, and of Miss Isa Blagden of the gentle, gay dark eyes. She had died that winter without his seeing her again, and her personal life, her friendships with Browning and Hattie Hosmer, were the subject of lively gossip in Florence.[30] This gossip perhaps helped to confirm his determination to live without outward scandal.

James Lowell was in Florence, at the old Hôtel du Nord, working and keeping to himself. Henry saw him occasionally, mounting to his high-ceilinged rooms overlooking the square of the Holy Trinity. One evening Lowell read aloud something he had been working at that winter. Agassiz had died, and Lowell had written an elegy that seemed to Henry to be the truest and most passionate work he had ever done:

> I cannot think he wished so soon to die
> With all his senses full of eager heat,
> And rosy years that stood expectant by
> To buckle the winged sandals on their feet,
> He that was friends with Earth, and all her sweet
> Took with both hands unsparingly.[31]

But Henry had set aside the spring for writing, and he paid few calls. There were travel pieces to grind out to feed the letter of credit. He completed and sent to Howells a two-part story, "Eugene Pickering," that he had been working at since the fall. It was set in Bad Homburg, and concerned a certain thin, awkward, young man with furiously blue eyes, Eugene Pickering, who had been raised by his father like a cultivated plant. It was a perfectly crafted little tale, full of private reminiscences. And it too fed the letter of credit. What Henry needed now was uninterrupted time to work on his novel, and he struggled to earn enough to give himself time. The letter of credit was about to expire, and he asked his father to have it extended for six months, for 250 pounds to cover his living expenses through the summer, and the expense of his return home in the fall.

Six months would be enough time to begin his novel, which had been maturing in his imagination.[32] "My story is to be on a theme I have had in my head a long time & once attempted to write something about," he told Howells, who had agreed to pay Father for the installments as they were received so that Henry would not fall further into debt.[33]

It was to be a tale of a sculptor and his patron: a renewal of the theme of guardian and ward. The ward this time was to be a man, Roderick Hudson—an American genius, from the great valley of the Hudson River. He was a sculptor of great talent. Young and lacking in means, he was trapped by poverty in a New England village. Only great wealth could free him to practice his art.

His mentor and patron, Rowland Mallet, was somewhat older than he, and possessed the wealth that he lacked. The older man adopted the sculptor as his protégé, and brought him to Rome, showing himself to be an artist as well, with his own genius. The city itself was the third principal character. It had an atmosphere of beauty, seductive and fatal, that was personified in the character of Christina Light. She was Henry's first female villain—or, perhaps, since she was as much victim as villain, his first bad heroine.[34] She was a light woman, an embodiment of the light that streams from the widened crevice, the opened door. She was the prince Camaralzaman, so beautiful that one fell in love with her, glimpsed while sleeping. Evil and corrupting as she was, she, too, was a victim; James drew her portrait with both love and understanding.

He began with these characters and their relations to one another.[35] Christina was the dominant figure: one saw her walking beside her ambitious, cosmopolitan mother and her dwarfish Italian father; one saw her little family in relation to their own histories and circumstances, in the surrounding fact of Rome. The tapestry filled James's room, as he explored its intricacies.[36]

He felt that he was applying the method of Tintoretto. He began with the central group of figures that had presented themselves to his imagination: Rowland, Roderick, and Christina. From the germ of their triangular relationship, the whole story grew. He explored the figures and the attractions and jealousies among them, almost with his eyes—with the delicate sense of imagination, of understanding.

Henry freed himself from the sense of the pressure of time. He felt that he had to nose into the subject like a dog sniffing out a bone.[37] Slowly he found out what the characters would do. The difficulty was in drawing limits and boundaries, of cutting the fabric of relations somewhere to draw a circle around the work. The difficulty, in short, was the problem of form.[38]

He gazed in imagination at his characters, and at their relations, and waited until they had composed themselves into a picture. It was very much as if he had thrown himself down on a gilded, silk-covered chair in the Pitti Palace, or stood before Leonardo's damaged *Last Supper*, slowly growing to know it intimately. Yet the process was not passive; the exercise of imagination was vigorous and creative. Slowly the picture was composed, and filled with the sights and sounds and odors of his own memories.

Rowland Mallet, the mentor, was a New Englander, descended of British and Dutch Calvinist stock, with great breadth of body, round cheeks, pale golden hair, and flowing beard. He spoke and moved with authority. He had been immediately attracted to Roderick. Roderick was an artist of genius; dark, Southern, tainted with the languorous weakness of a slave-owning society. He had spontaneous brilliance and remarkable audacity. He was thin and tall, and had the long face and gray eyes of the American type; his beauty lay principally in his remarkable eyes. He was not so much thin as narrow, lacking in physical substance, and his voice was high-pitched. These effeminate qualities reflected his moral lack: he had no force of will. But this lack was somehow part of his boyish attractiveness.

> He interrupted, he contradicted, he spoke to people he had never seen . . . he lounged and yawned, he talked loud when he should have talked low, and low when he should have talked loud. Many people in consequence thought him insufferably conceited. . . . But to Rowland and to most friendly observers this was quite beside the mark, and the young man's undiluted naturalness was its own justification. He was impulsive, spontaneous, sincere. . . . His appearance enforced these impressions—his handsome face, his radiant unaverted eyes, his childish unmodulated voice.[39]

James set his story in the now vanished papal, imperial Rome, where, lovingly recalled, memory and fable magically fused. The very names in the story evoked the great resonant myths of Greece and Rome, of Christian Scripture, and medieval chivalry. The two men strolled down the Corso together as if walking into the past, down through archaeological layers to the Forum and the Colosseum. They rode on the Campagna; they pushed past the heavy leather curtain of Saint Peter's, and gazed at the magnificent antique sculptures of the Vatican. At the Villa Ludovisi they admired the head of Juno.

It was there that they met Christina Light, escorted by her corrupt, queenly mother—Juno visited by Venus—looking as if the villa were hers. They made her acquaintance, and in due course Roderick Hudson carved her portrait in the character of Venus, in a white dress with her shoulders bare. He said to Rowland that he had never seen such perfect beauty.

> "I had no idea of it," he said, " 'till I began to look at her with an eye to reproducing line for line and curve for curve. Her face is the most exquisite piece of modeling that ever came from creative hands. Not

a line without meaning, not a hair's breadth that is not admirably finished. And then her mouth! It is as if a pair of lips had been shaped
to utter pure truth without doing it dishonor!"[40]

Rowland Mallett watched them, and, meeting his gaze, Christina
smiled a little, only in the depths of her gray-blue eyes, without
moving.[41]

Rowland and Christina dueled over the handsome artist. Each of
them in their own way loved the handsome, selfish, passionate, passive young man, who had no control over his instincts. She drew first
blood: she corrupted Roderick and made him love her, although it was
impossible for them to marry. He ceased to work, abandoned his art,
and sank into the pleasures of Rome.

Then Rowland made a coup: he appealed to Christina's better
nature. And so she released Roderick, for a time. But Christina Light
in her turn was a victim; her mother had shaped her to marry a prince,
and in the end Christina was sold to an ancient and corrupt family,
and was obliged to become in fully realized fact a princess, the
princess Casamassima. In her own anger and despair she ensnared
Roderick once more. The sculptor remained helpless; a victim of his
own instinct, he drifted with the currents around him. He sank into
depression and lassitude. His mentor, Rowland, seeing that the experiment had been a failure, was at last goaded into confronting Roderick with his egotism and passivity. The sculptor—now violently
deprived of the strong and generous affection on which he had relied,
wandered aimlessly like a child into the wilderness of the mountains,
into the last weakness, the escape of death.

Rowland Mallet was left alone among the ruins of his plans. His
love had taken the form of generosity. He had given his friend material liberty, and with it the freedom to choose. But his beloved Roderick had proved to be selfish and weak, and had not survived the
experiment; he had not chosen to live. Rowland grieved for his friend,
but he had no remorse. Like Madame de Mauves, there was a Calvinist toughness in him. He had loved, he had behaved well, even generously. He had been reasonable, perhaps too reasonable, but he had
taken what life offered and had learned its lessons. There was nothing
to regret.

A fourth character in the tale, Mary Garland, was a pale personification of New England. After the failure of the Roman experiment,
Rowland Mallet dutifully returned to America, to her. And again, with

something of Madame de Mauves's implacable will, he laid siege to her affections. But whether this new enterprise was to succeed was left unresolved at the end.[42]

Henry worked at this novel all through the spring. It called on all his resources, and he went slowly and carefully. The two narratives in all of his recent work were mingled: the meeting of America and Europe and a mentor's gift of freedom to his ward. James called upon *The Song of Roland*, the tale of a chieftain whose beloved warrior companion died in battle under his command—a tale he dressed in realistic detail, drawn from the vivid memories of his encounters with William. Fables fused with historic fact: *The Arabian Nights* and *Tolla* with the tale of the empress Eugénie and the Medici popes; old Greek stories and the parables of the Gospel with the private history of the foreigners in Rome. The complex composition unfolded slowly. He worked patiently and lovingly, stitching figures into the tapestry.

While he was at work, his essay on Turgenev at last appeared in the *North American Review*. He sent a cutting of it to the novelist, who was so much in his mind that summer, addressing it in care of Turgenev's Paris publisher because he had no other address. He heard that Turgenev had a villa at Baden-Baden, however, and he determined to go there for the balance of the summer, hoping to meet the Russian.

Elizabeth Boott sent him a wonderful gossipy letter from Cambridge, where she and her father had now settled:

> Your article on a return to Italy after many years made me desperately homesick & I made a vow never to read anything more of the kind. This is strictly private—I never confess to any Italian homesickness here, nor do I generally feel any, so will you please in the future caro Enrico, be kind enough not to write any more such descriptions as they disturb my equanimity sadly.[43]
>
> . . . Cambridge is well & pretty in its best dress for Class Day. I have never seen the foliage nicer or fuller than it is this year. . . . William seems remarkably well and able to work like other people. His friend Henry Bowditch thinks his condition much improved by his European tour. It is delightful to see him so active but I can never fully believe it as I have never known him when he was well. . . . I hope that you still hold to your plan of coming home—I will be pleased to see you again. Come to see me as soon as you can after your return—Till then dear Henry farewell.[44]

At the beginning of July, James took a room in Baden-Baden, at the Hôtel Royal. It was cool, and there was much more society than at Homburg. The Conversation House, where one sat on the terrace in the evening and listened to band music, was an adequate substitute for the Parisian café; it made a place where one could enter into society, or stay away, as one chose. For exercise there were lovely walks in the hills and in the Black Forest, and one could take the waters. It was an excellent place to work, and Henry sat down to his novel without delay. But he did not meet Turgenev, who had sold his villa that same year and returned to Russia, to write. At the end of the summer, James himself went dutifully home to America.

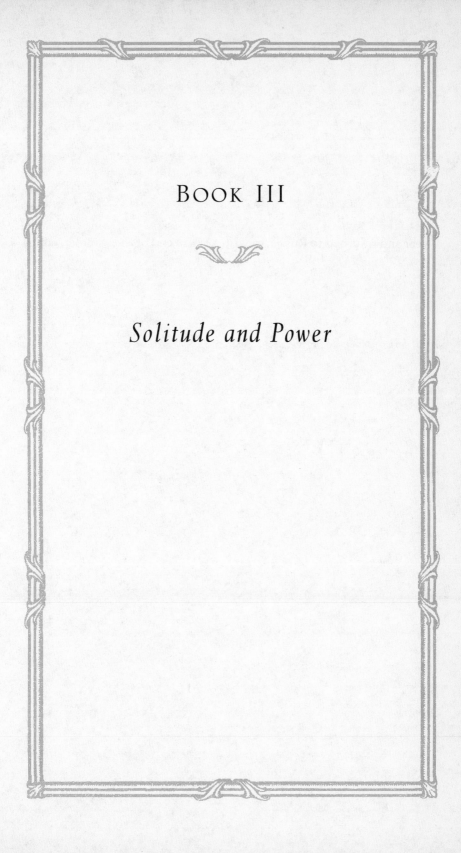

BOOK III

Solitude and Power

17

A Dutiful Experiment:
A Year in Manhattan

Manhattan was home as much as anywhere had been, and New York could claim to be a world capital like London or Paris. The experiment of living in America would be carried out there.

His family was still encamped in the rented house in Cambridge, however, and he spent the month of October there, among his old friends. There was an intense nostalgia in the brightly colored, fallen leaves that one kicked up as one walked. Howells had grown stout; he had a portentous stomach, and a grand new house filled with furniture, and a new baby boy. Tom Perry and Lilla Cabot were happily married; Wendell and Fanny Holmes were in their own little apartment on Beacon Hill, where they entertained most modestly.

Alice and William had both kept up the good health and spirits gained on their visits to Henry in Europe, and each was now settled in Father's house. Father was visibly older and more frail, and Alice was his indispensable secretary and companion. But she was not entirely housebound; she was busy as well with her friends Ellen Hooper, Fanny Morse, and a new friend she had met the previous winter, Katharine Loring, who had been an editor of the short-lived *Balloon Post*, and who was now organizing a correspondence school for the education of women. Alice greatly enjoyed riding expeditions with these friends, and she had acquired a pet, a little dog, which she liked to take with her when riding in a carriage.[1]

William had returned to teaching. He had accepted the course in anatomy and physiology, and had taken charge as well of the college's little natural history museum. It had been the sensible, prudent thing to do; psychology and scientific philosophy would have to wait.

The Bootts had gone on a long expedition into Vermont that summer and were full of cheerful stories; Alice had accompanied them and had enjoyed the trip enormously. Elizabeth, modest and diligent as ever, was making wonderful progress in her work, and in the evenings she sang as always to her father's accompaniment on the piano, singing the songs he had written. She admired Henry's greatly improved Italian, and they exchanged polyglot gossip about Florence and the Roman *forestieri*.

Now that they had both returned to America for an indefinite stay, he could not have avoided being conscious of the question of marriage to Elizabeth, which in so many ways would have been suitable, and which her father seemed tacitly to be urging. Henry evidently answered it for himself now, as he had answered so many times to his family's promptings. He had agreed to make the experiment of living in America, but he was a bachelor; what did he want with a wife?[2]

While he was at home in Cambridge he received a letter from Turgenev, who had written to him in care of the *North American Review*. Turgenev's silence had been disappointing, but now at last there was an encouraging word:

> The letter you wrote to me never reached me. I was in Russia at the time—I know that it was sent to me from Paris, but it did not come to my hands. I received the April no. of "The North American Review" with your article on my writings only in July; and the very day of its arrival I had a violent attack of gout, which has not disappeared even now. . . .
>
> It is rather difficult for an author to judge fairly a critical analysis of his own works—I must confess that I, for instance, find always the

praise too great and the blame too weak. I do not attribute this impression to diffidence or modesty: it is perhaps one of the many disguises which self-love enjoys in. All that I can say—is that your article strikes me as being inspired by a fine sense of what is just and true; there is manliness in it and psychological sagacity and a clear literary taste. I have only to observe that the pessimism you reproach me [with] is perhaps—is certainly—an involuntary one. My "excess of irony," as you call it, does not give me any pleasure—not even the bitter one, of which some people speak.

I have a great sympathy for all that is American—and a great desire to see your country. But I ought to have indulged it earlier in life. . . . Still I do not altogether abandon the idea. It would please me very much indeed to make your acquaintance as well as that of some of your compatriots. In the meantime, believe me, my dear Sir, yours most sincerely,

Ivan Turgenev.

P.S. My permanent address is: Paris, rue de Douai, 50.[3]

This was generous and friendly, if somewhat impersonal. And it contained an implicit invitation. Turgenev had not vanished into the Russian wilderness, after all. Henry could write, or call if he should be in Paris.

Before he left Cambridge, he arranged for publication of two collections of his articles. James Osgood, who had taken over Fields's book business, agreed to bring out a collection of Henry James's travel pieces.[4] It seemed to Henry also that it was time to issue a collection of his short stories, and this he proposed to Henry Houghton, who had taken over publication of *The Atlantic*. They agreed on a volume of tales that had first appeared in that magazine.[5]

When these arrangements were made, Henry returned to New York City, where his trunks had remained, and found an apartment for the winter near Madison Square. The slow northward march of solid brownstone fronts had long since swept past the broad plaza where Broadway mingled somewhat confusedly with Twenty-third Street and Fifth Avenue. The vast white front of the Fifth Avenue Hotel looked down upon the pleasant gardens and the equestrian statue of George Washington in the center of the square. Telegraph poles draped their lines over the broad avenue. On the northwest corner of

Fifth Avenue and Broadway stood the fashionable new uptown branch of Delmonico's Restaurant.

Henry's apartment was at 111 East Twenty-fifth Street, but he shuddered to give this ugly address. Numbers had no identity, no history, no individuality, no meaning. How was one to write a story in New York, where the houses were all of uniform brownstone design, and known only as numbers? How was one to locate the characters, the scene?[6]

It was a cold, sunny autumn. His apartment was pleasant and warm, and his parlor faced on the street. He worked at *Roderick Hudson* in the mornings and walked in the afternoons for exercise, but not, as in Europe, for the picturesque. The brownstone rows reached all the way up to the great Central Park; they had engulfed once rural Murray Hill, where his Rodgers cousins were encamped. The tall rows of houses now faced one another over the Central Park itself.

The park had only recently been completed; the elaborate landscaping, designed by Godkin's friend Frederick Olmsted, was very much admired. New Yorkers liked to say that their city was now a rival of European capitals, but Henry silently demurred. The park seemed to him clumsy and cockneyfied. The asphalt paths, rockwork caverns, and huge iron bridges spanning muddy little lakes were crowded and dirty.[7] The park was only a reminder that private gardens, and privacy generally, were lacking. There was ample public life in streets and hotel lobbies and restaurants, but as in Saratoga Springs he had the sense that everyone was on display for an anonymous audience. It was very big and bustling and full, and there was no sense of privacy or personal relation.

To the east and west, the boundaries of brownstone society were now vividly marked by the elevated railways on Third and Sixth Avenues. The lacy iron trestles shaded these avenues, and roaring steam engines racing overhead dropped black flakes of coal soot and an occasional glowing ember on the streets below as they rattled past with their trains of wooden cars.[8] To the east and west of the elevated railroads lay the shabby, familiar, red-painted rooming houses of the poor.

Godkin, the editor of *The Nation* who had so steadfastly befriended James, lived farther uptown at Forty-eighth Street, in the midst of a modern block of brownstone fronts. The Godkins had lost their eight-year-old daughter, Elizabeth, the previous spring. She had been a treasured child, a friend and companion to Godkin, and he had been distraught by her death. She was the second of their three children to have died, and he seemed stunned by the losses. His wife, too, was gravely ill; she seemed never to have recovered from the shock of Elizabeth's death.

Godkin was oppressed, and his own health was poor. *The Nation*, perhaps in consequence, was noticeably in decline. It had never been profitable, and Godkin drew very little salary. Fields and the other original investors had lost their stake; accepting the philanthropic nature of the enterprise, they had donated their shares to a holding company controlled by Godkin. He was absolute master of the journal now, and it had grown highly personal. But in these years of illness and death he had turned over more and more of the management of the weekly to his two assistants, Arthur Sedgwick, Henry's old friend, and Wendell Garrison. Henry saw Godkin very little; but he dined often with Sedgwick in a little literary, bohemian chophouse near the magazine's office on Beekman Place. Sedgwick wanted to begin a daily edition of *The Nation*, to enter into direct competition with the newspapers. Godkin had given his support to the plan, but Sedgwick had been unable so far to raise the capital that he needed.

As the lonely holidays began to loom, Henry received an invitation from Sarah Wister to spend a long weekend with her family at their country house, north of Philadelphia, and to this he cheerfully acceded. It was in truth Fanny Kemble's house, one of the fruits of her divorce settlement twenty years before. It had become Fanny's residence in the United States, to which she came to see her children and grandchildren for a part of each year. Afflicted with bouts of depression that, like Henry, she treated with ample doses of travel, she moved spasmodically in an immense circle from Pennsylvania to Massachusetts, to London, to Switzerland, to Italy, and then once again to the Pennsylvania country house for Christmas and the New Year. She had left Rome only shortly before Henry had.

The American estate was in reality two farms, facing each other across a road. The smaller house was York Farm, where Fanny was now staying; opposite was the farmhouse at Butler Place, where Sarah Wister and the grandchildren were staying for the holiday season.[9]

The two farmhouses were charming, comfortable, and unpretentious. Snow already lay thick, and paths were icy; Henry took one thumping fall, and stayed behind when Sarah went off on horseback to Germantown, five miles away. He spent his mornings with Mrs. Kemble, across the road. It was to be the beginning of a long friendship, and it began interestingly enough. Mrs. Kemble was sixty-five years old, and on this chill morning she was shrouded in shawls and wore an odd, old-fashioned lace cap. She sat beside a bright fire, in a sunny morning room, and when her visitors entered she was wearing spectacles and had a book opened in her lap. To Henry, at thirty-one years of age, she seemed very old indeed. Over the fireplace hung Sir Thomas Lawrence's magnificent portrait of Fanny's grandmother, Mrs. Roger Kemble, the old lioness, the mother of all the brood, as a young woman; it might have been Fanny Kemble herself, forty years before.

Another visitor that Sunday, a lady, was returning to Mrs. Kemble a volume of Calderón's plays recently translated into English, and she asked Mrs. Kemble to read a favorite passage. This was presumptuous, but the visitor was an old friend. Mrs. Kemble at first demurred, and then allowed herself to be persuaded. She read in her remarkable deep voice. The poetry of the passage was of the noblest, with rising, extreme, and increasing emotion. Abruptly with a cry she flung the book across the room. This startling gesture seemed to Henry both as genuine and as much a performance as the reading itself; all her art was in the incident.[10]

Conversation was the basis of their friendship. Fanny Kemble liked to talk, and as she had just begun writing a memoir of her childhood—on a typewriter, to which she sat up as straight as if at a piano—she was full of reminiscences. As she spoke, delicately re-creating Regency London, she brought into the cheerful morning light her vividly remembered images of Lord Melbourne as prime minister, of Holland House, of her good friend Lady Byron; she seemed to Henry an ambassador from another age.

Henry returned to New York City with a sense of coming home; indeed he felt vastly at ease there.[11] He was surrounded by family and friends, but there was a great deal of work to do. The first installment of *Roderick Hudson* had appeared in *The Atlantic* that month, but he had not yet sent the final chapters to Howells. The final drafting and revisions occupied his mornings.

The hundred dollars he received for each monthly installment of the novel was not enough to live on in New York, which was proving to be expensive indeed. In the afternoons and evenings, therefore, he wrote reviews, principally once again for *The Nation*. John Dennett, his old nemesis and the magazine's principal literary reviewer, had been ill, and he died in December; it was a sad business, he had been little older than James himself, and there was now an immense hole in the weekly's pages to fill. Through the winter, filling the gap, Henry wrote at least one review for each issue, as well as occasional paragraphs for the chatty, gossipy news page.[12]

The books and plays he reviewed were too numerous to be more than mediocre on the average, and there was remarkably little that rose above the average. He had to content himself with nuggets of pleasure embedded in the mass. Madame Ristori, on her farewell tour, was at the Academy of Music, the opera house on Fourteenth Street; while she sang he could imagine himself in Italy.[13] George Rignold, a young English actor, was charming as Henry V, at Booth's Theater.[14] There was even less to praise in the books that streamed into the office. But in an otherwise unremarkable book about London society, he found this:

> I sat alone upon a broken, dirty, iron bench . . . under an old pear tree. [The garden] was a long narrow patch of sod and flowers. The brick walls were rent and decayed, and, except where the peach and vine covered them, were green with moss and black with age. The neighboring gardens I only knew by the tops of the pear- and May-trees. No sound came from them save the rustle of their greenery, which now and then disturbed the heart of the quiet hour. Of the children who played in them, of the maidens who knelt among their flowers, I knew nothing. The same sunshine and yellow haze filled them all, the same Sabbath silence. From out their narrow plots all looked upward to the same blue sky. I used to think that the gardens never ended, but lay side by side the island through, and that the sea washed them round.[15]

"That last is quite exquisite," James wrote for *The Nation*, his own memories touched, "and exactly hits the fancy that the charmed American is apt to have in England concerning any green place in which he may find himself."[16]

But even these reflected pleasures were European. The purely American works were—disheartening. One that particularly struck him was Charles Nordhoff's *The Communist Societies of the United States*.[17] Nordhoff had spent a year touring little utopian communities. The Shakers maintained the largest number and the most successful of these communist enterprises. They were oddly conservative villages, conducted with relentless attention to costs. Many housed successful factories, and the common living arrangements and plain style of life were very economical. Often the communities required celibacy, and this too was economical; there were no children and all the population were able to work without interruption. The enforced celibacy particularly horrified Henry, and he could hardly credit the statements that Nordhoff repeated, praising the celibate state in sometimes ecstatic terms. This seemed perverse to James, even immoral, and he wrote that he was struck "with the existence in human nature of lurking and unsuspected strata, as it were, of asceticism, of the capacity for taking a grim satisfaction in dreariness."[18]

But the Shaker communities, if they seemed to Henry to take economy to perverse extremes and sacrificed all freedom and pleasure, at least might be understood as having improved the circumstances of the unfortunates, the orphans of the poor, who populated the villages. In material terms, communism seemed to be a paying experiment,[19] but it exemplified once more the familiar inability to achieve both justice and beauty.

What horrified him was another aspect of the communities; in this respect by far the worst was the Oneida settlement, led by John H. Noyes, Elinor Howells's uncle. The Oneida community had been much discussed in the James household, as in Swedenborgian circles generally. Noyes had devised a scientific, empirical communism that had overcome the weakness of earlier experiments, phalanxes like Brook Farm. Its purpose was utterly to subordinate the individual to the community, to extirpate any vestige of private existence. The rival powers of family and religion, which had wrecked the earlier experiments, were to be absorbed by the community itself.[20] At Oneida, Noyes himself was the religious leader, the meetings of the community were its only form of worship, and the community itself the only family. There was much that was reminiscent of Henry's father's doctrines in the creed that Oneida adopted. The personal and the private were the source of all sin; selfishness, attachment to the personal, was evil. The sin of keeping secrets was the object of particular attention.[21] But this community was not celibate; they practiced instead a sort of collective marriage, which seemed infinitely worse.

> *We have built us a dome*
> *On our beautiful plantation,*
> *And we have all one home,*
> *And one family relation.*

Henry underscored the last line of this chilling little verse, with its false naïveté. What it meant in practice was that the members of the community, while they lived in pairs, were forbidden to form exclusive attachments. Noyes himself determined the pairings, generally assigning a younger to an older of the opposite sex; when any sign of exclusive attachment appeared, he altered the arrangements. Procreation was permitted only by his order, and children, once weaned, were raised in a common nursery. The state was to have no rivals.

The principal means of maintaining this order was the practice of "criticism," which was Noyes's own invention. The person to suffer criticism sat in silence while the rest of the company, each in turn, told his faults. This ingenious device, Nordhoff reported, was rightly regarded by Noyes and his followers as the cornerstone of their practical community life. "It is in fact their main instrument of government; and it is useful as a means of eliminating uncongenial elements, and also to train those who remain into harmony with the general system and order."[22]

A public-criticism session was described in the book. It was directed at a man that the author called Charles. He sat silently at the center of a circle, while the members of the community took turns in pointing out his faults in very plain language. His principal failings were an attitude of superiority and an excessive attachment. Two women pointedly observed that Charles had been a "respecter of persons"; this sin consisted in showing his liking for a certain woman too plainly. As the accusations multiplied "Charles" grew paler, and the drops stood on his forehead. John Noyes then summed up:

> "Charles, as you know, is in the situation of one who is by and by to become a father. Under these circumstances, he has fallen under the common temptation of selfish love, and a desire to wait upon and cultivate an exclusive intimacy with the woman who was to bear a child through him. This is an insidious temptation, very apt to attack people under such circumstances; but it is nevertheless to be struggled against." Charles, he went on to say, had come to him for advice in this case, and he (Noyes) had at first refused to tell him anything, but had asked him what he thought he ought to do; that after some conversation, Charles had determined, and he agreed with him, that he ought to isolate himself entirely from the woman, and let another man take his place at her side; and this Charles had accordingly done, with a most praiseworthy spirit of self-sacrifice.[23]

After reading this, James wrote only a brief commentary. It suggested more appalled reflections than he could encompass in a book review. The industrial results of the Oneida experiment were no doubt excellent, as Nordhoff's careful reporting showed. But morally and socially, this new invention of the industrial age struck him as hideous. He could not bring himself to describe in detail in his review the public criticism of "Charles," but he recommended that his audience read it.[24]

> In what was apparent here, and still more in what was implied, there seem to us to be fathomless depths of barbarism. The whole scene, and all that it rested on, is an attempt to organize and glorify the detestable tendency toward the complete effacement of privacy in life and thought everywhere so rampant with us nowadays.[25]

In February, Lizzie Boott came to town and they had a fine daylong visit, lunched at Delmonico's, looked at the display of jewelry at Cartier's, drove in the park and talked of Italy. Lizzie may have told him of a young painter of genius who was showing some of his portraits at the Boston Art Club: an Ohioan named Frank Duveneck, who was only in his twenties, and who was studying in Munich. Bill Hunt had arranged the show and was lining up portrait commissions, trying to persuade Duveneck to settle in Boston.[26] Henry would have a look at the pictures and write a review when he next came up to Boston.

On April 11 Mrs. Godkin died, and Godkin himself promptly resigned from *The Nation*. He put his controlling stock interest into trust, and turned over the editorship to Garrison. He fled New York, which he partly blamed for the death of his wife and children, and took his surviving little son, Lawrence, to Cambridge.[27]

It was time for Henry, too, to assess the New York experiment. His principal outlet and professional resource, *The Nation*, was in fragile condition. The journal was having trouble meeting its financial obligations. Circulation was declining, and to cut costs Garrison now began to reduce the number of pages. As a market and source of support, Henry's old mainstay was in parlous circumstances.[28]

He had tried the experiment of living in New York only in part for practical reasons, however; he had done it more from a sense of duty, and thought still that if it was possible he should remain loyal to his family and to the only nationality that he could claim.[29] But it was impossible for him to write fiction in New York, the sandpaper surfaces were blank to his gaze, and the life of trade that was the life of the city meant nothing to him. Both as an artist and in his personal affairs the lack of privacy, of personal relations, would be fatal.

There was also a certain animosity toward him. His English clothes and artistic interests, his quiet manners and his sharp tongue, his lack of sexual violence and his simple lack of enthusiasm for American institutions, provoked a certain hostility in journalists, stock traders, Tammany Democrats and the "muscular Christians" of the Good Government movement. "He bears the same relation to other literary men that a poodle does to other dogs," the leader of the Progressive Republicans in New York, Theodore Roosevelt, said of James.[30]

And then he missed the richness and excitement of Europe. He missed, quite simply, Rome.[31] The only story he wrote during this time in New York was a little allegory. A handsome prince, Benvolio, was torn between his love for poor, little, pale Scholastica, who evidently represented America, and a beautiful, wicked countess, who was Europe. Benvolio himself was like the moon; each of the objects of his affection expressed a side of his character, bright or dark, passive or active. In the story, Benvolio virtuously chose Scholastica, but his poetry became dismally dull.[32]

Both James's new books had been published, and reviews from his colleagues in the press were predictably warm. Howells gushed embarrassingly over the collection of stories, *The Passionate Pilgrim*, without in the process betraying any profound understanding: "We may compare him with the greatest, and find none greater than he," Howells sang. James remarked a little bemusedly that, "if kindness could kill, I would be safely out of the way."[33] A more delicate appreciation came from Louise C. Moulton, who reviewed his collection of travel pieces for the *New York Tribune*.

We have enough books of travel, and too many of them; yet there is room for the "Transatlantic Sketches" of Henry James, jr. . . . If that good old word "sentimental" had not been so misused that it now means "spoony" to the popular apprehension I should call Mr. James a sentimental tourist. I mean that where other people see things in a matter-of-fact way he sees them like a poet. He discerns the sentiment of a scene—the soul of a landscape. A ruin is something more for him than a picturesque pile of stone—a spot where ghosts linger and old voices call. To read his book is to feel more of the atmosphere and the significance of the places he describes than most of us could ever discern on the spot. We are indebted to him for his deeper vision, his deeper insight.[34]

The *Tribune*, the old flagship of Henry James, Senior, had become a leading journal; it was the only newspaper that seemed to achieve commercial success without loss of dignity and taste. The *Tribune*'s publisher now was Whitelaw Reid, Horace Greeley having retired; the head of the newspaper's editorial department was a brilliant young man named John Hay. It was presumably Hay who had assigned James's book to Mrs. Moulton. Hay had been Lincoln's private secretary, had published a book of his own poems, and now, as the leading editorial writer on the leading Republican newspaper, was a power in the land. Yet he had not acquired the coarse manners and tastes of the newspaper business or politics. He was a graceful man, who thought very little of his own poetry and a great deal of others'.

Henry got to know Hay, confirmed that Hay liked his work, and began to sense that here might be a new Godkin, a new *Nation*. But he would have to find some way of tapping this resource from abroad. The New York experiment was a failure, and as the weather grew warm in May, Henry gave up his apartment and went to Cambridge to save money and plan his next move.[35]

He continued to send items to *The Nation;* the very first of these was a paragraph for the news page, about the painter whom Lizzie Boott had admired. Five portraits by Frank Duveneck were being shown at the Boston Art Club. The most important plainly was the full-length portrait of an old man seated, with his hat on, in a sort of Shaker armchair, dressed in plain, ill-made dark clothes. Another striking picture was a half-length of a rather seedy young man in a black slouch hat, with a stump of a cigar in his mouth. The pictures had the kind of strong originality, the powerfully personal expression, that Henry admired.

The discovery of an unsuspected man of genius is always an interesting event. . . . Mr. Duveneck, on the exhibition of these works, was, we believe, invited to come to Boston, where a dozen immediate orders for portraits were assured him. After reflection, he declined the invitation, and decided that before producing on this large scale he needed to fortify his foundations. He is now about to return to Europe. This, doubtless, is the wisest course, and it would be a serious pity that he should adopt any but the wisest. We confess that, as things stand with us at present, almost any young artist of promise is likely to do better out of America than in it.[36]

On a sunny afternoon in July it dawned on Henry that while Rome was too dangerous he might live in Paris.[37] Turgenev and Renan were there; it was in Paris that a man of letters would make his mark, or not. Duty had been served, and he had completed the experiment of living in New York. He had reached a point in his career in which he might expect to support himself in Europe, and when he might begin to measure himself by European standards. The elements of a plan fell quickly into place. He would undertake a new novel immediately. *Roderick Hudson* was still running in *The Atlantic,* and Fields would not be likely to print another long serial of his for another year, but *The Galaxy* was eager to get more of his work and *Scribner's* had already asked for a novel. He would write something quickly, a less substantial work than his first. He offered to F. P. Church of *The Galaxy* his next novel in serial form, beginning that winter, if they would pay $150 for each monthly installment. The novel would run for nine or ten months. He thought that Church seemed interested.

The Nation would be glad to get more book reviews and travel letters from him in Europe, and would use perhaps two a month; that would add another hundred dollars.

But it would be wise to supplement *The Nation* as a market for occasional pieces. His work for the magazine was published anonymously, its future was uncertain, and the future seemed to belong to the daily newspaper. Gossip said that the Paris correspondent of the *Tribune,* Arsène Houssaye, was about to lose his place. Henry approached John Hay, in gingerly fashion, by letter:

> I have a tolerably definite plan of going in the autumn to Europe & fixing myself for a considerable period in Paris. I should like, if I do so, to secure a regular correspondence with a newspaper. . . . When I say "newspaper" I have an eye, of course, upon the *Tribune.* To my ambition, in fact, it would be the *Tribune* or nothing. There is apparently in the American public an essential appetite, & a standing demand, for information about all Parisian things. It is as a general thing rather flimsily and vulgarly supplied, & my notion would be to undertake to supply it in a more intelligent and cultivated fashion—to write in other words from the American (or if it doesn't seem presumptuous to say so, as far as might be from the *cosmopolitan*) point of view a sort of *chronique* of the events and interests of the day. I have thought the thing over in its various bearings, & have satisfied myself

that I could put it through. Indeed I have a dazzling vision of doing very good things. I should have a fair number of strings to my bow, & be able to write on a variety of topics—"social" matters, so-called, manners, habits, people &c, books, pictures, the theater, & those things which come up in talk about rural excursions & dips into the provinces.[38]

Henry had no entrée into the social realm of France, but he thus audaciously offered a weekly letter from Paris in which he would provide, as well as reviews and travel pieces, gossip, "things which come up in talk," reports on the movements of the members of society. It was a proposal out of Balzac.

Hay approved, and passed the proposal on to his publisher. Whitelaw Reid was indeed looking for a replacement for Houssaye. Most writers exhausted their freshness in a few months, and he liked to have a succession of distinguished names appear in his newspaper. He didn't like James, as perhaps James was aware,[39] but he recognized the position James had achieved. He offered to pay a grudging twenty dollars per letter, and the arrangement was to be only temporary.

The rate of pay and the tentative quality of the offer were disappointing, and almost an insult for an established writer; at *The Nation*, Henry was paid fifty dollars for each review, and while it was true that newspapers paid less than magazines, Houssaye had received thirty dollars for his letters to the *Tribune*. But John Hay encouraged James to accept; the low rate of pay would be compensated for in the long run by re-publication of his letters in book form, like Sainte-Beuve's, and by the wider market the *Tribune* would create for his other work. Henry seized on this; it was after all his own young vision. The newspaper had an immensely larger circulation and consequent power than the magazines, and his letters, in the long run, were bound to be both influential and profitable. On August 3, he wrote to Hay:

> First of all let me thank you heartily for the trouble you have taken & for your sympathy & good will. May I ask you to render me a further service. Will you be so kind as to let Mr. Reid know that I accept his offer of $20—gold, & that I expect to be able to write my first letter [from Paris] by October 25th.[40]

There had been a further ominous note in Hay's letter: he himself was leaving the *Tribune* to pursue business opportunities in the West. It would be the skeptical Whitelaw Reid himself to whom James would submit his letters. But James was thirty-two years old, and possessed by his vision.

Preparing himself for his return to Europe, he read the new books from Paris, and wrote a little essay on the current state of French literature, a sort of fusillade fired at long range against the walls of the capital. Recent novels told the story of weak women who were solely creatures of sexual passion; the books lacked a moral dimension.[41] The trouble with the authors of these novels of prostitution—Flaubert, Daudet, and lesser lights—had begun with their master, Balzac. This great novelist who had so much influenced his own youthful ambitions James now held up to the light of moral criticism.

Later in life he would return to his early admiration for the French novelist, but now he was fighting to make a place for himself. James had renounced the pleasures of Rome for duty, and had committed himself to write for the journals of the new American republic. He was a journalist for the higher propaganda, the higher complacency. Firmly renouncing his own temptations, he now denounced what he had once admired and in later years again would love.

He wrote an essay excoriating Balzac, blaming him, perhaps, for the flaws of his own first novel, *Watch and Ward*. The greatness of the man, his simple mass and size, was admitted. Balzac was the founder of the school of realism in fiction, and he was no mere materialist like his shallow successors Gautier and Flaubert. Balzac's unsurpassed merit was a huge, all-encompassing, all-desiring, all-devouring love of reality, not the thin reality of surfaces but the deep truths of imagination united to perception, the fusion of fable and history. The real, for his imagination, had an authority that it had never had for any other writer. His characters were incomparably real and fully realized; if he had a rival—and he did not—it would be Turgenev.

But the secret of the art by which he conveyed this profound realism was the force, the violence, of his own belief. He believed himself to have the creativity of the deity. His female characters surrounded him like the women of a bordello. He was their *gros* licentious father. At his instigation, they were overwhelmed by their passions and were constantly at one another's throats; society was for them a deadly battle for lovers, disguised in a tissue of caresses. Surely, every clever woman in France detested these books.

It was true that realism required one to plumb passions to their depths; no subject was forbidden to the novelist. Balzac had laid his hand upon every kind of passion, had even described passions that were usually deemed unmentionable. But for all his greatness he lacked ideas, lacked moral intelligence. Missing in his work was the philosophy and aristocratic taste that characterized Sand, Turgenev, and Renan. This was not a trivial failing in James's eyes. It made the whole of Balzac's *Human Comedy* a gigantic failure. Balzac's book, James now said, deliberately provocative, read at times like the dreams of an ambitious hairdresser.[42]

Those currently popular authors who had followed Balzac had turned away from what was central and best in the French character, the legacy of the old order, a profound capacity for sacrifice in the service of an ideal.

Some recently published memoirs recalled a great figure in this vanished world: Madame Juliette Récamier, the sovereign of the social world, the friend and protégée of Mme. Swetchine in the Paris of Balzac. At her height, when she was in her forties and fifties, she seemed to bestow an air of tolerance and intelligent affection upon the Paris that she ruled. All her accomplishments had been swept away by the revolution of 1848 and the Napoleonic empire that succeeded it, sadly, but the whole society that was represented in her memoirs—the cultivated liberal France of the period before the empire—made intellectually and morally a very honorable show.[43]

To prove that this France continued to exist there was the surprising popular success of a two-volume life of Joan of Arc. It was an admirable portrait of perhaps the most remarkable woman who had ever lived. It was regrettable that the author, Minister of Public Instruction Henri Wallon, did not attempt a realistic portrait of the Maid, in the manner of Renan. Strenuous efforts were being made in Rome in behalf of her canonization in Rome, and Wallon's perfectly orthodox account was presumably in aid of these efforts. He had removed the Maid of Orléans to the realm of ultramontanist religion. But her story was amply documented in historic fact. Evidence of Joan's career had been found in enormous quantities, and each successive step in it was now almost as vividly illuminated as if, say, she had been a resident of Brooklyn.

The accretion of fact had not dispelled the mysterious quality of her life, which was the most intensely interesting of any but that of Jesus himself. A peasant girl had been accepted by royalty, had become the commander of French armies, and had defeated the English in a series of lightning campaigns that were masterpieces of tactics.[44]

One was obliged to account for this success realistically. The extraordinary thing about Joan from the first hour was the perfect definiteness of her ideas. She had no vagueness, no extravagance, nothing unpractical. She knew exactly what she wished; her undertaking was mapped out before her. Her good sense, her discretion were never at fault. Her sense of detail was extraordinary.[45]

Henry ventured to supply the realism that the biographer had omitted. If the Maid had not been simply a passive vessel through which the saints had spoken, how was one to account for her? Henry's answer was like an examination answer in reply to a question posed by Renan. She had been a woman possessed by the passionate love of place, of patriotism. The presence of the English on French soil had wounded her soul as some cruel physical pressure would have wounded her body, and she would not rest until she had pulled out the sharp weapon. Her visions were simply the response of a mind unaccustomed to dealing with abstractions, a mind that expressed its emotions to itself, as it were, in images, and in the highest images it knew, the painted images of Saint Michael and Saint Margaret in the church windows.[46] The Maid had dressed her own perceptions with the images of legend; her visions were those of an artist, and her brief career was a monument to the possible triumphs of a powerful will.[47]

He himself, Henry James, would go to Paris; if he were not the Maid, at least he would tell her story. Like Turgenev, he would carry on the best traditions of French civilization more ably than the French themselves. A little more than a month after his plan had formed itself in his mind, he was back in New York, boarding a Cunard steamer for England. From London, where he stopped to repair his wardrobe and buy tickets for the last part of the journey to Paris, he wrote to his family in Cambridge: "Dear People all—I take possession of the old world—I inhale it—I appropriate it!"[48]

18

HENRY'S ASSAULT ON PARIS

Paris, in 1875, was still in a sense the capital of Europe. But German tourists now came with an offensive air of visiting a conquered province. Americans were visible on the boulevards, distinguished not so much by their clothes as by their loose-jointed manner and their open, almost childlike faces. American women in pairs and in groups, beautifully dressed, crowded the little shops of the Rue de la Paix and the great new department stores, the Bon Marché, the Louvre, the Compagnie Lyonnaise.

These Americans, who had no racial history and no culture, were a topic of conversation among the French. That winter, a much discussed play by Dumas fils, *The Foreigner*, about a mongrel American adventuress in Paris, was opening at the national theater. The opening of a new play by Dumas was from the Parisian point of view a great event. Judging by the coverage in the *Figaro*, James mused, it would take something like a *coup d'état* by Marshal MacMahon or an invasion of France by Prussia to equal it.[1]

"Madame Bentzon," Marie-Thérèse de Solms, had also written a currently popular novel about an American visitor to Paris. Mme. Bentzon had been to America, and was translating American works of fiction in the *Revue des Deux Mondes;* James was amused and irritated to find that his own story "The Last of the Valerii," presumably translated by Mme. Bentzon, was in the November 15 number of the *Revue* without his knowledge or permission. He registered a mild protest at the piracy. The translation seemed to him execrable. In the following year, two more translations of his stories would appear in the *Revue,* but by his permission.[2]

He used his customary care in selecting a place to live, and after due deliberation found an apartment at 29, Rue de Luxembourg,[3] on the Right Bank. It ran from the Rue de Rivoli, opposite the gardens of the ruined Tuileries palace, to a little *place* that was reminiscent of Union Square. From the little square, a broad boulevard opened toward the Opéra and the Rue de la Paix, with its government ministries, expensive shop fronts, and distinguished little hotels. At the foot of his own street was the Rue Saint-Honoré, crowded with carriages and lined with shops.

But his own street between these centers was quiet and dignified, a little refuge in the heart of the city. It was a respectable neighborhood, and his apartment was up only three flights of stairs; yet it was not too expensive. He had two bedrooms, a parlor, an antechamber, and a kitchen. The principal bedroom was at the front of the house, where the morning sun came in diffusely through the high, narrow windows. This was where he wrote, and through the open casements came the clicking of the small cab horses on the new asphalt, echoing between the high houses.

There were Empire portrait medallions at the center of each white panel of wall. A little fireplace warmed the parlor. The kitchen was fitted out with copper pots and a cupboard filled with glass and china. He had mirrors and clocks and curtains and lamps and picturesque candlesticks. A porter waited upon James; for twenty-five francs, about five dollars, he replenished the woodpile in the kitchen and laid the fires, and brought hot coffee and a brioche in the morning. For another fee, a charming laundress brought clean linen and took away his dirty things to be washed at a barge moored in the Seine, at the Île de la Cité. He dined very well at a restaurant nearby, on the Rue Saint-Honoré, where an excellent dinner composed like a piece of music could be had at a modest price. These amenities were important to a man living alone in rented quarters; they made up the texture of his life.

With his morning coffee and brioche, and again with the midday meal, he read a newspaper: the conservative *Figaro* for the sense it gave him of French life and the news it gave of people and their doings, which he pillaged for the *New York Tribune*, and the *Journal des Débats* for political news. On Sunday evenings after he had unfolded the crisp napkin beside his plate he opened *Le Temps* and read Francisque Sarcey's weekly review of the theater, which he admired for its perfect knowledgeability and craftsmanship.

For exercise he walked in the streets of Paris. From the Rue de Luxembourg he was within a comfortable walk, even in bad weather, of the Louvre, the national theater, the opera and the cafés; he could easily stroll across the Seine to the Faubourg Saint-Germain or the university.

Someone observing James on his walks would have seen a young man with a fresh, somewhat pale, complexion. He had removed his whiskers, in deference to French fashion.[4] He was thinner than he should have been according to the taste of the day, and his hairline was markedly receding, which made him look older. The well-tailored winter suits he had acquired in London became him, and in Paris he bought brightly colored waistcoats and neckties. He had a personal style, conservative with touches of bright color, and he equipped himself with a fashionable hat and cane that carried through the idea of easy elegance. His gait and expression were habitually serious, even grave, and conveyed a certain masculine weight.

The first person he met in Paris was a Cambridge acquaintance, Charles Peirce, one of the little circle of philosophers around Chauncey Wright. Peirce was in Paris on an abstruse scientific task, but one would hardly have suspected that from his appearance. James had known him in Cambridge as a newly married man, living rather modestly and working at the Harvard Observatory. Now he was resplendent in Parisian clothes, living rather grandly and making a study of French restaurants and French wine.

But when they spoke, Peirce seemed terribly lonely and distraught. Peirce called almost as soon as James arrived; he insisted on their dining together that evening. He brought James back to his apartment, and they arranged to meet again soon. His was an odd tale. Peirce was working for the United States Coast and Geodetic Survey, heading the American portion of an international effort to determine more precisely the shape of the earth and the elevation of points on its surface by measuring variations in the force of gravity. This was done by making exquisitely careful determinations of the swing of a pendulum. Peirce had come to Europe months earlier to purchase a German pendulum and to measure its swings at Paris and London observatories, where his own determinations could be compared with those of the more advanced European laboratories.

It had been a difficult year for Peirce. Chauncey Wright, who had been his mentor and friend, had died. Peirce's financial accounts had got in a terrible muddle, and he somehow could not communicate with his headquarters in Washington. In September his wife had left him, and he had remained on in Paris alone. The Académie des Sciences had at first ignored his requests to swing his pendulum at the observatory in Paris, and now that he was finally at work he was being treated as a person of no importance and given no consideration. He knew no one and he was desperately lonely. He had broken out in an odd way in luxurious living, and was spending very freely, occupying himself with a study of wines, and writing a paper on the logic of relations.

James dined with him every second or third evening, and they got on comfortably enough. They did not share intellectual interests, for James had well-settled convictions on metaphysical questions; he did not think it at all mysterious that logic and mathematics, the most abstract of ideas, seemed to have objective reality.[5] But James enjoyed the dinners, and the sense of Peirce's first-class intellect, reflected in his ardent eyes.[6]

For a few weeks Peirce was nearly his only companion, but James had little time for company in any case. As soon as he was settled in his apartment he set immediately to work on a letter for the *Tribune* as well as on the novel he had offered to *The Galaxy*. The arrangement with Church concerning the novel had been a little vague, but James had incurred heavy expenses in London and he now tried to make the details more definite:

> I propose to take for granted, as soon as I can, that you will be ready
> to publish, on receipt of them, the opening chapters of a novel. I have
> got at work upon one sooner than I expected, & particularly desire it
> come out without delay. The title of the thing is "The American."[7]

The balance of what was due him for *Roderick Hudson* and for the books of stories and travel essays would be sent directly to his father, to repay drafts against his letter of credit, but thenceforth payments for monthly installments of the new novel, and for his letters to the *Tribune*, would come to him directly in Paris. He was cutting his last material ties to home.

He would give his new novel a Paris setting, and would use the theme that was popular now on both sides of the Atlantic: the American in Paris. The germ of the story, the central setting from which it would grow, was one that had appeared to him long ago as he descended from a Boston horsecar in the epochal spring of 1865. An old, aristocratic family had cheated a young American. The American would prepare a revenge, he would have them in his power. But in the end he would vanquish them, morally speaking, only by renouncing his revenge. The theme and the characters had blossomed and matured in his mind, and he felt that he could write quickly and smoothly. It would be a relatively short novel; he would evidently have to write such a novel every year, simply to keep himself afloat as a man of letters.

Within days after his arrival he had sent a note to Ivan Turgenev, at the Paris address that Turgenev had given him the year before. The prompt response was joyously received:

> I will be happy indeed to make your acquaintance and shall expect you Monday between 11 and 1 at my house. I hope you will find the time and place convenient and beg you to accept the expression of my best feelings.[8]

Rue de Douai, to which James went at the appointed time, proved to be a little street at the foot of Montmartre. Turgenev was on the top floor, two flights up; the remainder of the house was occupied by his intimate friends the Viardots.

James had imagined the Russian's appearance to be aristocratic in the conventional way: fine-boned and delicate. But Turgenev, who was indeed an aristocrat of old family, proved to be a vast, corpulent man with thick features: big head, big chest, broad stooping shoulders, large hands and feet. At fifty-seven he seemed already aged. His hair, which he had allowed to grow very long, and his full beard were a pure bleached white. His dark eyes were shadowed and sad, and rather too close together for beauty, but his face was strong and handsome. The impression he gave was of an immense gentle, soft sadness, and James felt an immediate fondness and attraction for the older man; he wrote home that he had taken an "unprecedented fancy" to the great novelist.[9]

Turgenev had been in Paris only a few days, and his study was neat and undisturbed. The conversation went easily. He had a fund of polite conversation that was perfectly friendly and gracious, and his manner was unassuming and modest. He lacked the air of contained force, the "consciousness of powers," which marked the men of achievement that James had known, but this distinguished artist was perfectly at home in the world, perfectly gentle and unassuming.

He spoke stiff and bookish English rather than French, out of courtesy to his guest. The Viardots were his greatest friends, he said, and he had established his household with them here in Paris after many years of living abroad. They had lived in Baden, as James knew, until the war, but now they had returned to France, and he with them. Turgenev's great friend Mme. George Sand was rarely in Paris, she lived almost entirely at her country house in Nohant. He would introduce James to Mme. Sand when she came to town. But Gustave Flaubert was in Paris, and Turgenev would introduce James to him. Flaubert was his greatest friend, after Mme. Sand. Indeed, it had been George Sand who introduced them—had made the marriage, as people said. Turgenev himself was unfortunately about to leave for Saint Petersburg for the winter, but he would call on James before he left the city.[10]

It was a polite and friendly conversation, but no single remark remained with James afterward, and while he had the sense that Turgenev liked him, he saw that it would be hard work to establish an intimacy. The novelist's easy flow of polite conversation erected a barrier between them. James had no real access to the Viardots' house, and they were evidently careful gatekeepers; he would have to establish himself with Mme. Viardot if he was to maintain an intimacy with Turgenev.

After a few days, Turgenev did call, briefly. It was a courtesy call, and he stopped only for a moment in James's parlor to talk in his stilted English. A few days later, on a Sunday, he called again, but he had not come to visit; he wanted to introduce James to his good friend Gustave Flaubert. They walked together up the Rue du Faubourg Saint-Honoré, to Flaubert's flat near the lovely Parc Monceau. Flaubert had a sort of literary salon on Sundays, and when they arrived a half-dozen men were present.

Flaubert himself was a striking figure: very tall, stout, and gray-haired, he was handsome, with a serious, sober face, a big mustache, and a mottled red complexion. In his fifties, to James he seemed elderly, but whereas Turgenev was immense and soft, Flaubert was compact and powerful.[11]

The talk was of literary business and literary personalities. Flaubert spoke in a disconcerting tenor bellow, like a guard's trumpet, and altogether put one in mind of a retired military officer. He seemed to James somehow naïve, and was embarrassed at having an American stranger presented to him and bothered over what he could say or do. Turgenev buried himself in an armchair that had evidently been left vacant for him, and when he spoke, it was slowly, in a gentle voice and almost with hesitation. Flaubert listened to him almost reverently, fixing his wide blue eyes with their restless pupils on his friend's face and answering in his loud voice.[12]

James was able to join occasionally in the conversation in his unaccented French, and he was surprised at the fierce partisanship of the group. When he mentioned Cherbuliez, or Gustave Droz, whose works he had admiringly reviewed, someone said, "We think nothing of him; you mustn't talk of him here; for us, he doesn't exist."[13]

Some of those present had famous names—there was Edmond de Goncourt, the man of letters, who appeared to James as the type of the French gentleman, and the young Émile Zola, of whose naturalistic fiction people were just beginning to speak. James was conscious of his dislike for the work of these authors, with the sole exception of Flaubert's *Madame Bovary*. He had repeatedly published his opinion that the vein they were working was very thin to begin with, and had been exhausted. But they were utterly unaware of his writings, and after all he was glad enough to meet them and to be invited to return.

There were a few Americans in Paris whom James knew, principally the cosmopolites he had met in Rome, among whom were Mrs. Sumner, who had been widowed before she could be divorced, and was now known as Mrs. Mason; and Lilly von Hoffman, Sam Ward's sister. In the two weeks after he arrived in Paris, James left his card at their doors. He called also on William H. Huntington, the *Tribune*'s political correspondent in Paris, who proved to be a middle-aged bachelor who had lived in the city for twenty-two years, and with whom James quickly established an easy partnership. Huntington he thought forlorn and womanish, and James was amazed to find that despite his long residence in the city the older man did not speak French.[14] Godkin had given James a letter of introduction to Auguste Laugel, *The Nation*'s correspondent. The greatest treasure of all, however, was a note from Fanny Kemble enclosing a letter of introduction to her dear friend Mme. Mohl, a Frenchwoman, Mme. Récamier's protégée and rival. Mme. Mohl maintained what Kemble said was the last salon in Paris, the last link to the world of Swetchine and Récamier. James left his card at her door.

Until these overtures should be answered he saw no one except Peirce for dinner two or three times a week. He went to the theater regularly, and to the opera once or twice. The imposing new Opéra was very crowded with tourists. It was the newest architectural wonder of Paris; the frescoes in the foyer had just been completed. As the last great work of extravagance of the empire, it was already historic: like the restored Saint Peter's basilica in Rome, it was a monument to a departed regime, to an era of history that had ended forever. "It is nothing but gold—gold upon gold; it has been gilded until it is dark with gold," James scribbled in his notebook. The staircase was light and brilliant, an immense affair of white marble overlaid with agates and alabasters, and swept up to a magnificent foyer, a long golden corridor with high doors that opened into the auditorium. But it could lead to nothing grander than itself. The moldings were heavily gilded, and high up on the faraway ceiling, dimly and imperfectly glimpsed through the dusky glow of gas and gilding, he made out the noble and beautiful new frescoes. "If the world were ever reduced to the dominion of a single gorgeous potentate," James wrote, "the *foyer* would do very well for his throne room."[15]

Americans and other visitors were moving on toward Rome as the weather grew colder and the days grew shorter and darker. The city seemed to grow emptier. Dreading a little the coming of the winter darkness himself, James settled into the routine of work. After morning coffee he sat at a table before the wood fire in the parlor that never quite warmed his feet and worked at his new novel. In the afternoons he walked, and then worked again—reading Taine's *L'Ancien Régime*, or writing a letter for the *Tribune* or a review for *The Nation*.

In each of his different tasks he examined Paris, or rather the relation of an American to Paris. In his novel *The American* the hero was to be a type of the national character, and hence would be a businessman: likable and virtuous but lacking in cultivation. Paris seen through his eyes consisted of the Grand Hotel and the gilded apartments that Americans had taken on the boulevards around the Place d'Étoile. James wished to introduce this American character into the aristocratic quarter, the parlors and salons of the Faubourg Saint-Germain, and observe the results. But as he himself knew nothing at first hand of French society, he studied the works of Taine, his *Notes on Paris* and *The Origins of Contemporary France*. He sent home for his copy of *Country Life in France*.

He drew the French heroine of his novel from these literary sources, and from his reading of the previous summer. She was tall, thin, blond, accomplished, and dignified, no longer a girl. She lived with her family, in a tiny totalitarian state, an ancient mansion between courtyard and garden. The old grandmother of the family ruled it, wielding the power of family affection and religion. The mansion was a microcosm of the old order.[16] It was the sort of society that he had glimpsed in Rome. There was no ambition, no new wealth. Almost every man, almost every woman, was at the very summit of this civilization. "They were all like so many hot-house plants, and which give out their best as you pass them without further trouble to you than to inhale their perfect fragrance."[17]

The American character was named Christopher Newman. James described him with an anthropologist's precision. Newman had a well-formed head, with a shapely, symmetrical balance of the frontal and occipital development. He had all the features of his race: the brown, rather dry hair and gray eyes, the flat jaw and the sinewy neck. Clean-shaven except for an abundant mustache, he might have been Holmes or any of the recently returned Massachusetts officers. And like the returned soldiers that James knew, his hero had a deep dislike for violence.

His past was rather vaguely sketched, but he was a westerner and had done all sorts of things, had manufactured tubs and sold leather, had made and lost fortunes in copper and oil. He had come to feel a revulsion for that kind of combat as well. He had lost interest in further victories on the stock exchange, and had gone to Paris a wealthy man, with the plan of acquiring culture and a wife that he could place proudly on top of the heap of his possessions.[18]

The Frenchwoman that he coveted was equally a type: gentle, sad, proud. The American would conquer her affections, but her family would breach their agreement with the American and prohibit the marriage. This was the wrong that the civilized Europeans would do him, which Henry had imagined ten years before on a Boston horsecar.

To thwart him, the Frenchwoman, like Tolla, would be driven to the living death of a convent. James's distaste for celibacy and physical discomfort almost overcame him when he described her fate; the convent seemed to him the final perversity of the old order.

He tried to describe the conflict between the old and the new with the precision and objectivity, the love of historical fact, that he found in Taine. He took pleasure and pains to show the meeting of the two languages, the communication by gestures. He fleshed out his legend and made it real with his own memories. The type of the French adventuress became Mlle. Danse, the guide of his childhood wanderings in Paris; the detail of her protuberant green eyes brought her to life. He made her a wicked commentary on the empress, and had her provoke a duel between a French gentleman of the old school and a brutal Prussian brewer in which the French gentleman was killed.

Henry could not resist putting William into the story. He dressed William as a young Unitarian minister, Babcock, whose digestion was weak and who lived principally on health foods, Graham bread and hominy. Babcock gave the American hero the lectures that William had given Henry; the detailed, affectionate, and also somewhat malicious portrait was a continuation of their brotherly quarrel, and when the book appeared, William recognized it well enough, as he was meant to do.[19]

Some years later, when Henry James reread this novel, it seemed to him that the French characters and their motives were no more than literary inventions, pure romance. But the American, Christopher Newman, he thought, was fully realized, a man infused with reality by his author's affectionate memory and understanding.[20]

With his work well started, James went to the Palace of Versailles to observe the election that was in progress. He strolled in the gardens of the palace that had become a synonym for the old order. The wartime national assembly was peacefully relinquishing power to a constitutional government. The first stage in this slow process was to be the election of seventy-five life members of the senate. James recorded the moment, and himself observing it, as if in a little snapshot for the readers of the *Tribune*.[21] He went into the red-brick theater in which the Sun King had smiled at the plays of Molière. A crowd of rather ordinary men in business clothes, not especially attractive or intelligent, gathered in little knots under the great gilded angel of the proscenium arch that bore the lilied shield of the Bourbons. The solemn ceremony of voting was being carried on. Seven hundred gentlemen filed slowly before the tribune and dropped their ballots into an urn.[22] A new republic seemed to be bringing itself into being. The dark picture of incompatible races that he had been painting in his novel had a reverse image: the graceful harmony, the marriage, of the old order and the new.

Turgenev did not call, but after a while a note arrived explaining that he was again suffering from gout and could not go out. James received an invitation from Mme. Viardot, but only to attend one of her crowded receptions, where there was very little opportunity for conversation. Turgenev cheerfully confessed to him that Mme. Viardot left him very few unfilled evenings, but he was invited to call again. James resigned himself to a slow process, but assured himself that he would be tenacious and would persist.

He fought the depression and darkness of winter by long walks and relentless work: writing his novel for *The Galaxy*, his letters for the *Tribune*, book reviews for *The Nation*. He sent off the first installment of his novel to Mr. Church, and struggled to keep up with his letters to friends and family, to do his duty to Peirce, and even to amuse himself occasionally. He called regularly on the elderly bachelor Huntington, who showed him a side of Paris he would not otherwise have seen. Early in December it grew bitterly cold, and there were snow squalls. The cheerful wood fire in his parlor was a polite fraud; it did little to warm the apartment, and he went to bed and rose in the damp chill.

About a month after his introduction to Flaubert, James thought it would be time to pay a second call on his own account, and on Sunday afternoon walked up the Rue du Faubourg Saint-Honoré again. He was politely greeted; Turgenev was not present, but they spoke of him.[23] The circle now included Alphonse Daudet, whose novel *Jack*, for which James did not care very much, was selling like loaves of bread, and a handsome twenty-four-year-old, Guy de Maupassant, who had published nothing as yet. Maupassant told a funny and rude story about the English poet Algernon Swinburne, who had been living with a monkey at Étretat. When Swinburne installed a young boatman in the household, the monkey, who had been the favorite until then, became intensely jealous, and somehow committed suicide.

Maupassant told the story with intensity and it was certainly bizarre enough, but for James it showed the peculiar light in which English conduct and manners appeared to these men, their careless sneers at the sodomy they took to be characteristic of the English. From behind the mask of his excellent manners and fluent, colloquial French, he had spied them out—this was how these refined French gentlemen spoke privately: "Here they are at it!"[24]

Silence had descended on his relations with Turgenev. The Russian, having performed the offices of polite hospitality, seemed to have dropped him. In the hope of reviving the acquaintance, James sent Turgenev a newly bound copy of *Roderick Hudson*, which had just gone on sale in the United States. But there was no immediate reply.

Christmas approached. Dusk fell in midafternoon, but the street-lamps and the shopwindows were gaily lighted, and Paris began to make a brilliant picture of itself. The boulevards were bordered by rows of little booths for the sale of everything conceivable, from cotton nightcaps to the oranges that were favorite gifts; one might buy an orange on which a girl's or boy's name had been pricked out in blue letters. The shopwindows on the crowded sidewalks were filled with displays. The confectioners in particular were amazing: the rows of marvelous bonbonnières looked like precious sixteenth-century caskets and reliquaries, chiseled by Florentine artists, in the glass cases of great museums.[25]

James was alone on Christmas Day. He went out walking, up the boulevard, looking into faces and into shopwindows, and then down the Rue de la Paix to the Seine. He had never seen Paris so charming.[26] After lingering for a while on the prow of its little island, he went inside the great cathedral of Notre Dame and listened to vespers, and watched the nave grow dusky.[27]

On New Year's Eve he was alone again. He spent the evening writing letters to old friends who were far away, to Elizabeth Boott, to whom he had not written since his arrival.

> Dear Lizzie—You see, late in the day—or in the year, as I come, I am bent on not letting this familiar old 1875 pass away without answering your letter of several weeks ago. . . . A happy, happy New Year, Cara Lis and an abundant supply of them: such is the ardent wish [of] your unfailing friend. A thousand affectionate compliments to your father!
>
> You will have heard from my people that I am safely housed in this glittering capital, & that I take to it very kindly. Such is the immoral truth: it suits me to a T. It seems, I suppose, from your Cambridge point of view, as if I ought to have a 1000 exciting things to relate & as if my letter should reek & glow with "local color." But alas, it won't; it can't; for I find the Rue de Luxembourg, looking off to the Boulevard as it does, not so very different from Irving St. as you might suppose. I lead a quiet life of it, I see no one to speak of, & I have next to nothing to relate. Paris is of course *per se* extremely agreeable but one grows in this world so shockingly inured to things. . . . I am very

consciously comfortable, of course, & I like the place, & am very fond of it, but it has as yet done no great things for me. I spend quiet days, chiefly in my apartment (which is a most agreeable one & a very happy find) & in the evening I stroll abroad to dine & amuse myself as I most conveniently can. I have no "society," to call such, though I have seen a few people. That is a thing which comes slowly: though if I hang on long enough I hope I shall end by finding it.[28]

He lapsed into Italian and chatted on with his dear Lizzie for another page or two. He had gone to the theater, but not with his old relish; he had seen some mutual friends. Mrs. Mason had gone on to Rome, and really he saw no one at all. "I am writing up to the confines of the old year, & at this solemn hour I invoke upon you all sorts of solemn blessings."[29]

His relative solitude had already begun to lighten, however. After Christmas, Parisians began to visit their boxes at the opera, to call on one another, and to entertain. People began to reply to his cards and letters of introduction. Auguste Laugel, the *Nation* correspondent to whom Godkin had given him an introduction, invited him to a dinner.

Laugel was rather conservative and monarchical in his views, an Orléanist. Conversation revolved around political questions, and Laugel was rather sour in tone over the defeat of the Orléanists by the republicans, who had engineered an alliance for this purpose with the extreme right, in the first round of elections. James felt himself out of sympathy with the general tenor of the talk. He thought the phenomenon of American monarchists rather odd and out of character.

Nevertheless, this first invitation was followed by another. James had evidently expressed his view that Renan was the first man of French letters, for shortly he was asked to dine, to meet Renan and his wife. They were very small and old, and to James's eyes rather plain; Renan indeed struck him as hideous. In the moment of their meeting James felt all his love for the literary face of the old man, the old attraction for the thin and delicate aristocrat of his own youthful imagination, begin to slip into a long descent into cold dislike. He consciously arrested this slide.[30] The white-haired old man was almost dwarfish, and so remarkably corpulent that he had difficulty walking. His head seemed too large for his squat body. The broad, pale forehead seemed distended.

Dinner went off very pleasantly, however. Renan spoke a good deal, and very beautifully. He spoke of persons and told stories of his childhood in Brittany.[31] He who had been the great liberal spirit of the old order was deeply conservative and pessimistic in the new. He thought that Germany and America between them were creating a purely materialist civilization, and he feared that it would be as difficult to strike the note of the ideal in their world as to strike the silver note of Notre Dame's great bell from one cast in lead or tin.[32]

After dinner, James sat beside Renan in a corner and they conversed for half an hour. James spoke of his own admiration for the older man's work, and Renan treated him with great consideration. His gestures were graceful and paternal, like a priest's. James politely asked his view of the elections, and Renan, perhaps because of James's fluent French and European manner, seemed to forget to whom he was speaking.

"Oh, it is done, this time, decidedly it is done," Renan answered in the most mournful tones. "We are Americanizing! Yes, it is done. . . . The republican form is fatally different from those under which France acquired her greatness." Renan spoke with an air of dejection so profound that James refrained from reminding the older man that he was speaking to an American, and that this solemn prophecy perhaps fell something short of perfect courtesy. He felt the need to respond; but he contented himself with saying that some of the forms under which France had grown great would make an ugly figure today.[33]

The last introduction Laugel made for him, playing his greatest social card, was Henri d'Orléans, duc d'Aumal. The duke was a man of charming manners, and James was invited to call on him at a reception. James found himself briefly in the bosom of the Orléans family, whom energetic partisans in the Faubourg were striving to restore to the throne. James was presented to the duke, and to a princess of Saxe-Coburg. The latter was ensconced in an armchair beside the fire. She was old, corpulent, and deaf, and when James was presented to her she plainly knew nothing of him or his work; yet she was so gracious and chatty as to give him a realizing sense of what princesses were trained to.[34] But after these two introductions, in European fashion he was left to his own devices. He observed the gathering of royalty and aristocracy with a critical eye. There were large, majestic men and small, demonstrative men. There were ugly women in yellowed lace and quaint jewels and charming young women with very bare shoulders and backs, who remained nameless and unknown to him.[35]

The season for entertaining had begun, and the little American colony in Paris gathered him up, the success of *Roderick Hudson* having made him once more a lion. As in Rome, he attended a great many receptions and late-evening parties. He no longer had any time for the theater. Many of the faces he saw were familiar; he brought Peirce with him on a few occasions and introduced him to Lilly von Hoffman, who took Peirce up a little. James himself was too busy now for their bachelor dinners.

At a dinner of Bostonians, he met the former Mrs. Edgar, who was now Mme. Bonaparte, married to the grandson of Jérôme, the emperor's brother who had fled to America. She was moving heaven and earth in the Bonapartist cause; if it succeeded she would be a great personage, perhaps a princess.[36] Another New Englander, Lee Childe, a friend of the Nortons, called on James one day in response to a letter from Norton. James was invited to meet Mme. Childe, the former Blanche de Triqueti, who proved to be a distinguished, graceful, and elegant Frenchwoman. She asked James to call, and a day or two later he found her in black velvet by her fire; old decorated counts and generals leaned against her mantelpiece. It was a scene from Balzac. Again, James was not introduced, but he had a brief conversation with Mme. Childe, who was very clever. Perhaps in response to his remarking on the oddity of royalist and imperialist Americans, she spoke pleasantly of a man she had known who was a republican. But she had ceased for some time to see him, he was so violent in his opinions. He had none but republicans at his house, and they were all horrible people.

"No French people," she added in a moment, "are republicans—at least no one that anyone sees." To James this seemed in its way quite sublime.[37]

Working patiently in the mornings at his novel, he filled the imagined drawing rooms of the Faubourg Saint-Germain with anonymous, decorated old gentlemen, former lovers of their hostesses, and with corpulent and charming aristocrats, glimpsed as if from a distance, moving in their warmly lighted private houses, utterly removed from the events of the world.

He came to know the little American colony in Paris, rather languorous and dissipated, whose company he quickly found wearisome. The best of the group was Henrietta Reubell, who kept a salon where one met writers and painters. She was too tall and too thin, but she had lived in Paris all her life and was very elegant; there was something frank, intelligent, and agreeable about her. When her mother gave him a standing invitation to breakfast with them, en famille, it seemed very likely that he might marry Henrietta if he chose.[38] It was not the first such opportunity to present itself, but marriage to wealthy Miss Reubell would be brilliant in so many ways, would solve so many of the problems of life in Europe, and she herself was so agreeable, that he gave it more thought than usual, and even mentioned the possibility to his family. On the whole, however, he thought that he would not marry.[39] He had too strong a sense of his genius, of his calling. But the sense of possibility, of power, was gratifying; in *The Portrait of a Lady* he would describe the sensation, conferring it on a heroine who refused a brilliant marriage out of an inarticulate sense that there was something still better, something more in accord with her genius.

The election campaign for the national assembly which began that winter exemplified the polarization of Parisian life: the extreme polarization of sexes, of parties, of factions. There was an infinite amount of more or less ferocious discussion going on at every moment.

> If one is disposed that way, one may find at every turn the most vivid reminder of the vanity of passionate argument. The intensity of political discussions is sharper in France than it is anywhere else—which is the case, indeed, with every sort of difference of opinion. There are more camps and coteries and "sets" than among Anglo-Saxons, and the gulf which divides each group from every other is more hopelessly and fatally impassable.[40]

This organized combat had its achievements. There was the extraordinary refinement and elaboration of the male and female roles. There were the past military and political glories of commitment to an ideal. The Revolution, Renan had said, was to him like a young woman for whom he had conceived a helpless passion in his youth. French literature abounded in books in which particular tendencies had been pushed to lengths that only a sort of artistic conspiracy among many minds could have reached. But these—James thought of the new naturalist writing—were like blind alleys of thought, where explorers perished. The French seemed incapable of the art of compromise. Ideals were well and necessary, but life, he thought, required a fusion of idea and practice, an art of making choices among actual alternatives.[41]

The most profitable of his ventures into society were his visits to Mme. Mohl. Fanny Kemble's letter of introduction had elicited an invitation from her. This elderly woman seemed to have made a little civilization around herself that carried forward into the modern world the ideals of the Regency and the Restoration. She was near ninety: a little old woman, with her gray hair in disarray and down on her fore-head in wisps, wearing a grotesque cap and a shabby black dress. But then it had always been her style to neglect her appearance and to rely on her extraordinary charm. She was English, the former Mary Clarke, and had married the scholar Jules Mohl, friend and colleague of Renan. She had lived with Mme. Récamier and Chateaubriand, and had been the intimate friend of the queen of Holland. In her old age she and Fanny Kemble and Lady Augusta Stanley, wife of the arch-bishop of Canterbury, made a cosmopolitan circle of friends.

In recent weeks, however, her husband, Jules Mohl, and her dear friend Lady Stanley had both died, and Mme. Mohl was greatly dis-tressed. Despite these great losses and her own great age, she contin-ued to follow her daily routine, and, battered old stoic as she was, to entertain old friends.

Fanny Kemble's letter had ensured him a reception, and Mme. Mohl seemed to take to James, much as Kemble had done. She was very friendly and kind on their first meeting, at any rate, and James un-derstood that he would be able to call as often as he wished. He ex-ercised this privilege, albeit cautiously. It was only at Mme. Mohl's that he met the luminaries of the liberal and republican set, scholars and artists of the older generation.[42]

On the last day of January 1876 there was a letter from Turgenev. An excellent omen: Turgenev, who had been relentlessly polite and had addressed him only in stilted English, now wrote to James in everyday French. He apologized for not having written sooner, but he had mislaid the address! He thanked James most warmly for the gift of his book; he and Mme. Viardot had begun reading it together,[43] and he was happy to tell James of the pleasure it was giving them. One opening scene in particular had been done by the hand of a master. Turgenev himself had been ill and still kept to his bed. But it would be an amiable thing if James were to come to Rue de Douai.[44]

Hurrah! *Roderick Hudson* had done it! He was to be taken seri-ously! Henry sent Turgenev's letter to Alice, as he knew what pleasure she would take in this triumph.[45]

Within the week, but not too precipitately, he went to Rue de Douai, and passed almost the whole of a rainy afternoon with Turgenev, who lay propped on cushions. To James he was a love of a man, immense and gentle. He spoke for the first time about his own writing. He had adopted Balzac's motto—he invented nothing. Every-thing in his stories came from some person he had seen, although often the figure from whom the story began turned out to be a secondary character. He never consciously put anything into his people and things; to his sense all the beauty, the strangeness, the poetry were there, *in* the people and things, the definite ones, the ones he had seen.[46]

Carnival had begun, and a few days later there was another note from Turgenev, enclosing a printed invitation: the Viardots were having a costume ball on the nineteenth of February. Would it amuse James to attend such a ball, where there would be many lovely personations? If James did not want to go to the expense of a costume, there would be a *marmiton*'s white cap and apron in the vestibule for any gentlemen in evening clothes.[47]

He could not afford to have a costume made by a tailor, and he disliked availing himself of the scullion's white cap and apron. In the end he excused himself with the plea of a headache. He did attend the masked ball at the Opéra, but only as a spectator, without wearing fancy dress.

His fellow correspondent Bill Huntington, who by now had become an intimate friend, brought him to the more exotic entertainments, including the infamous artists and models ball at Bullier's, on Montparnasse, where a decent woman could not allow herself to be seen, where men dressed as women, and women were all but naked.[48] The bachelor Huntington, it appeared, was quite an extreme bohemian.[49] James found his aesthetic circle of expatriate English and American young men interesting; he was aware that this was what many young men came to Paris to find, and he recorded its dissipations in his memory, without being greatly tempted by them. During the entertainments of carnival, however, he met a young Italian painter who had taken a house at Versailles. The Italian was a painter of talent and a gentleman; James confided to Elizabeth Boott that he amused himself occasionally with this new friend.[50]

Further invitations from the Viardots arrived; they had regular evenings of entertainments, readings, and musical performances, for which they made printed programs, and James became a recipient of these periodic announcements.[51]

Pauline Viardot was a concert singer of great talent. She had irregular features—very widely spaced, protuberant eyes and a very long upper lip—but she was beautiful nonetheless, and charged with attractive energy. Her husband, utterly conventional in manner and appearance, was a prosperous, dignified dealer in paintings.

Turgenev was openly devoted to Mme. Viardot, but Viardot himself seemed to accept their relationship, whatever it was. The three appeared to live together on cordial terms. Mme. Viardot no longer very often performed on the stage, but her musical evenings were important events in the world of art and letters. They were crowded affairs, and offered little opportunity for talk, and as James cared very little for music, he attended these evenings as a duty. He was also invited to the Viardots' Sunday evening receptions, which were family affairs. Parlor games were played, and James was astonished to see Turgenev capering about on all fours, in a game of charades, draped in Pauline's shawls.

Despite their one cordial meeting, Turgenev seemed as far out of his reach as ever. His health had recovered, and there was no longer any opportunity for intimate visits. James was unable to entertain, and unless Pauline made it possible, as she seemed to have no inclination of doing, he would find no more occasions to see Turgenev at ease.

He had sent the opening chapters of *The American* to *The Galaxy* and had received an acknowledgment, but no confirmation that they would be published or that he would be paid. Bill Howells had written, asking for a new novel, and so he wrote once more to Church, directing him to forward the manuscript to Howells if he did not propose to publish it immediately himself. James set the novel itself aside for a few weeks, and dashed off two short stories set in America, which he sent to *Scribner's*, where they were gratefully received and promptly published and paid for.[52]

The carnival season was hectic, and he was so much in demand that he had exhausted his supply of *carte de visite* photographs. He wrote repeatedly to Alice to send more:

> I *beseech* you to send me a couple of my card-photos in a letter. Imagine me on my knees, with streaming hair, and flaming eyes. I *entreat* you. This is the third request.[53]

Charles Peirce left for Berlin; James had not seen him since the first of the year. He had a sense that Peirce was unhappy at having been dropped, and felt that he, James, could have done more to bring him into society, but James consoled himself that the man had too little social talent, too little art of making himself agreeable. James told himself that he had done what he could.[54]

He was very busy, carrying on as vigorous a social life as in the soft winter in Rome, and yet working as hard at writing as he had ever done in his days of solitude. Society provided him with a rich feast of materials, of life, and he had worked too hard to achieve it, to give it up at its height.

The *Tribune* letter had become a burden to him. Paradoxically, now that he was so busy, he had more trouble finding things to write about, for his time and energies were occupied with people he could not put into a newspaper. Occasionally, a fragment of Renan's or Turgenev's conversation, or an anecdote from Flaubert's Sunday receptions, would find its way into his column. But the personal references were so carefully disguised as to make them useless for newspaper purposes.

He could not retail even harmless gossip about the duc d'Aumale or the princess of Saxe-Coburg, who had received him so graciously, without offending his own sense of propriety. Nor was he in society in a way that would allow him to write of the public movements and entertainments of great people in a knowledgeable and impersonal way. He would have to give up the proposal to write about society. But he did not want to give up the connection with the newspaper entirely, yet. Aside from the lovely payments in gold that arrived periodically from their London office, the status of newspaper correspondent was useful to him; he could not be a man of letters entirely in the void. But he knew that his letters were becoming dull and abstract, and lacked the personal note that was required and that he had promised.[55] He was filling them with reviews of pictures and plays—magazine work.

The winter dragged on into March, and under the weight of steady rains and melting snows, the Seine rose and rose until the working-class suburb of Bercy flooded and its streets resembled the canals of Venice. The black rushing river came up under the arches of the bridges. The weather was growing warmer and there was a promise of spring.

Elizabeth Boott wrote to say that she and her father were returning to Europe so that Lizzie could study painting with Thomas Couture, who had been Hunt's teacher and mentor. The letter plunged James into a mood of tender envy, mingled with impatience, of wealthy dilettantes, artists at leisure. Paris was beginning to seem silky and very charming, spring was about to dawn, and the Bootts would see some very clever painting at the Salon when it opened in May, he told Elizabeth.

"So you are going to Couture?" he asked. "It sounds very pleasant & promising & I wish you all fame & fortune's consequences," he wrote, although fame and fortune were perhaps not the point for Lizzie. "I envy you greatly your vocation[56]—it is better than this dreary abstract scribbling." He would introduce Lizzie to the little

Italian painter (of great talent) with whom he amused himself occasionally, who had a delicious old house and garden at Versailles.[57]

Through the American expatriate hostesses, he had come to know a number of Russian émigrés, including Nicholas Turgenev, the novelist's cousin, and he was invited to call at Turgenev's immense palace on the Rue de Lille, on the western fringe of the Faubourg Saint-Germain, near the river. These rather Bostonian-seeming aristocratic Russians, although not republicans by any means, had devoted themselves to the abolition of serfdom, and they were very like the Abolitionists of Boston; they reminded him of the Norton-Sedgwick clan. At the Nicholas Turgenevs' he met a young man who was to make a great difference to him: a Russian painter, who was introduced, in the Russian fashion, as Pavel Vassilievich Zhukovsky.

They spoke French, in which language the young man became "Paul Joukovsky." He was a perfect cosmopolite, having grown up in Saint Petersburg and Baden, who spoke German, French, and Russian, but not, alas, English. He had lived for many years in Venice, but he had taken an apartment and a studio in Paris for the winter.

He was a man of thirty-five—two years older than James—slender and tall, narrow in the shoulders, with a high forehead and clear, rather sad eyes. There was a reminder of Louis De Coppet in his appearance and in the way he stood aside from his surroundings. He was at the utmost remove from the American whose chronicle James worked at every morning. The fabric and cut of Zhukovksy's clothes were carefully chosen, with a rather luxurious taste, and he wore more jewelry, heavy rings and monogrammed studs than an Anglo-Saxon would. His cheeks were clean-shaven, even the sideburns were shaved smooth, and his hair was combed backward, so that his face was a long smooth oval with high cheekbones. But dark, bushy whiskers stood out rather fiercely from his chin, and made a sharp, almost military contrast with the pale oval of his face and his dark, sad eyes.

The father whose name he bore, Vasily Andreivich Zhukovsky, had been an important Russian poet early in the century, tutor to the then heir apparent, the present czar Alexander II. His son Paul had lived a picturesque life. The father had died when he was small, and Paul had been raised at court by the empress. Free of material cares, he had lived alone for a time in a Venetian palace, attended by servants. He was a very good friend of the Turgenevs. His father had been an intimate friend of Ivan Turgenev's parents, and of the novelist himself in his student days in Saint Petersburg, and they had the easy intimacy of friends who are almost relatives.

Zhukovsky was a painter; he had had two large canvases accepted for the coming Salon, but he was a man of independent means, and in James's eyes an amateur. He was talented but he did not seem to James to be a man of genius; he had great intelligence and a deeply informed taste. There was an air of lassitude about him, the air of someone who has seen and heard only the best. He held himself always in an attitude that seemed a little melancholy and skeptical: the attitude of a young man of talent who stands on the threshold of the future, but without entering.[58]

Henry's interest in Turgenev was the first premise of their friendship, and they talked of the older man at length. Turgenev's absolute goodness and tenderness could not be exaggerated, Zhukovsky said. But neither could his softness, ripeness, his lack of will. He was unable even to choose a pair of trousers for himself. The difficulty in establishing a continuing relation with Turgenev was not a lack of friendliness on his part. After their recent meeting, Turgenev had spoken of James with an appreciation amounting to tenderness, in a way that Zhukovsky had hardly heard him speak of anyone! The difficulty was that Turgenev allowed himself to be utterly dominated by Pauline Viardot, and she was relentlessly protective. She would never create a space for them to meet and become friends. Ah, but that problem could be easily solved. *Zhukovsky* would invite Turgenev, they would entertain him together. They talked over this problem of relations with Turgenev in great detail, making plans to liberate the old man from Pauline Viardot's tyranny.[59]

It was early April, the black floodwaters had receded, and the weather was growing warm. When James sat down to write his letter to the *Tribune*, he found himself writing with joy.

> The spring in Paris, since it has fairly begun, has been enchanting. The sun and the moon have been blazing in emulation, and the difference between the blue sky of day and of night has been as slight as possible. There are no clouds in the sky, but there are little thin green clouds, little puffs of raw, tender verdure, caught and suspended upon the branches of the trees. All the world is in the streets. . . .[60]

Zhukovsky in due course issued the promised invitation, and Turgenev came to dine with them, at a café in the little square opposite the Comic Opera. It was a most pleasant evening. Zhukovsky had invited another Russian friend, the princess Urusova, a thin and dark young woman who smoked cigarettes continuously, of whom Turgenev was fond and who helped to put him at ease. It was brilliantly done; James had never seen the older man so jovial, so talkative.

Turgenev told stories. He spoke in French, rather than in his stilted English. He spoke lightly of himself, and of his friends. The evening went past quickly, and Turgenev excused himself rather early, at nine-thirty, to return to Mme. Viardot, cheerfully acknowledging that he was under her thumb. The three young people remained at the café for a time, and then finished the evening together at the princess's apartment.

Zhukovsky himself had a most enchanting apartment and studio on a top floor flooded with light and filled with antique Italian *objets d'art* and curious drawings by Goethe, which had been given to his father. Zhukovsky's own work, executed with a simple clarity, was talented but lacked intensity. And despite the charm and artistry of his language, his graceful management of his relations to others, he was reserved, withdrawn, even solitary. But these qualities drew James to him all the more.

They saw each other often during the spring, and soon James wrote to Cambridge in a way that might have been considered an announcement. He told William that some Russians he had met were "an oasis of purity & goodness in the midst of this Parisian Babylon," especially a young man who gave him a high opinion of Russian nature. "The young man, Paul Zhukovsky . . . is a very amiable fellow, of about my own age, & we have quite sworn an eternal friendship." He pointedly said that Zhukovsky lived a life of great purity. There was something quite sweet and distingué about him: "He was brought up at court as an orphan by the Empress (wife of Nicolas,) his father having been tutor of the present Emperor; so you see I don't love beneath my station. He is to dine with me tomorrow."[61]

To Alice he wrote with less calculation: "The person I have seen altogether most of late is my dear young friend Zhukovsky, for whom I entertain a tender affection."[62]

James had never spoken in these terms to his family of anyone before, and after these letters William, on behalf of the family, politely asked for a photograph of Zhukovsky.[63]

In May, Turgenev left Paris for Russia on his long-deferred journey. He planned to stay away for the summer to work on his new novel. But James was confident now that he had established a relationship with Turgenev that he would be able to carry forward in the space provided by Zhukovsky when they met again in the fall.

"I am turning into an old and very contented Parisian," he wrote to

Howells, sending along the fourth chapter of *The American*. The first chapter was about to appear in *The Atlantic*, and Houghton at his request had sent a very substantial advance on the balance. Paris was on the whole a very comfortable and profitable place—not Parisian Paris, for he saw very little of the French. It was Paris as a cosmopolitan center that he enjoyed:

> The great merit of the place is that one can arrange one's life here exactly as he pleases—that there are facilities for every kind of habit and taste, & that everything is accepted and understood. Paris itself meanwhile is a sort of painted background which keeps shifting & changing. . . .[64]

Spring was the time of exhibitions in the vast glass-and-steel Palace of Industry, on the riverbank. The great annual horse fair was winding up, and in a few days, on the first of May, the annual Salon would open, the display of thousands of paintings, drawings, and sculptures. A small group of painters, the Impressionists, who had been refused admission to the Salon, had opened their own little rival exhibition. James went to see it and enjoyed the light, pleasant, small canvases that so delicately reproduced the sensation of a momentary appearance. It was another form of the great movement of realism that was transforming all the arts, but Impressionism did not seem to him to be in the first rank. The Impressionists sought only to reproduce appearances without imposed form or arrangement, and hence without meaning. He compared them unfavorably in his mind with the more ambitious realism of Ruskin and La Farge. But it was innocent and pleasurable, all the same.[65]

There was so much to enjoy. He went with Mrs. Strong, of New York, to her box at the Italian Opera to hear performances of Verdi's *Aida* and *Requiem*, conducted by the composer himself with a certain passionate manner and performed by the singers for whom the music had been written. James was not greatly sensitive to music, but he realized that he was witnessing a kind of perfection.[66]

Someone—perhaps Zhukovksy—knowledgeable in the refined pleasures of Paris brought him to see the horse show at the Palace of Industry. It was not the sort of thing in which he would ordinarily have taken an interest. But the last day of the exhibition, before the palace was redone for the Salon, was known as the Carrousel, a display of purely fantastic and picturesque horsemanship.

It was held that year by the cadets of the cavalry school at Saumur, and was in every way a high festival. It was like the mock-medieval jousts and tournaments that had become the fashion in England a generation earlier. The price of admission was made very high to exclude the populace. The president of the Republic and Mme. Mac-Mahon were seated on a dais, like a king and queen, and the knights and cavaliers rode at Saracens' heads with lances in place or hurled their lances at a great mask. The riders were warriors, young knights. It seemed to James all very graceful and gorgeous and effective. Here was the great tradition of French chivalry, realized. A sort of arrested murmur of affection and delight ran constantly through the vast assembly. *"Ah, qu'il est gentil, ce petit Saumurien!"* he heard his neighbor exclaim; and there was a loving cadence in the phrase that made him envy the sentiment that produced it. He knew perfectly well what horrors and evils lay behind the traditions of a warrior class. Yet he envied France the possession of such a brightly dressed institution. It was not exactly that he wished America had a warrior class, but he felt the loss as well as the gain.[67]

The Salon opened on the first of May, and Henry spent hours there, among the sculpture on the ground floor, among potted trees and ferns, and the two thousand canvases on the principal floor upstairs, under acres of glass. There were vast portrayals of military subjects, of the Maid of Orléans, and one striking canvas of vigorous bare-limbed women, fishwives wading with their baskets.

The weather was growing uncomfortably warm; James began to take his meals outdoors, in a garden restaurant in the Champs-Élysées, and to spend the evenings drinking cold beer at a café table. By July, he reflected, he should leave Paris.[68] Zhukovsky, he knew, would be going to Bayreuth, near Munich, where a new theater was being inaugurated, exclusively for the performance of Wagner's operas. James would not follow, but he would need a distraction of his own to spend the weeks of hot weather until they both returned to Paris in September.[69]

On the first of June there was a note from the Bootts, who were in London on their way to Paris.[70] He arranged hotel rooms for them, and a few days later met them at the station. For a week or two they filled his days. He went through the Salon with Lizzie, comparing notes, and before they left, he invited the Bootts to dine, to meet Zhukovsky.

James was fearful that his aristocratic friend would not care for the Bootts, but it went well enough. Zhukovsky found Francis Boott extremely sympathetic, he said afterward; Boott seemed to him like one of Titian's noblemen. And Lizzie, to James's astonishment, revealed a mastery of colloquial French he had never suspected.[71] The evening seemed to have been a success; he knew that the Bootts would write to his family about it.

The next day, the Bootts went on to Villiers-le-Bel, the suburb where Couture had his studio; James remained in Paris, and he and Zhukovsky went together, as a couple, to dine with the Nicholas Turgenevs at their palatial country house on the Seine, a carriage ride of three quarters of an hour. It was a pleasant dinner, *en famille*. The constant topic of conversation was the massacre in Bulgaria of Christian Slavs by the Turkish Empire. Russia must go to war in behalf of her brother Slavs, everyone seemed to think, although England threatened to intervene in behalf of the Turks. The Jew Disraeli had made a great coup by sending the British fleet to protect Constantinople. But the English would not side with the Turks, surely.

Ivan Turgenev had written a patriotic poem in behalf of the rebellion against the Turks, and in the coming days James translated it into English for American publication.[72] The old abolitionist faction in Boston had taken up the cause of Bulgarian independence.

George Sand died at her country house in Nohant; the last words she had put to paper were praise for an essay by Renan; he wrote beautifully of her, in memoriam, and Victor Hugo wrote an address to be delivered at the state funeral.

After Zhukovsky's departure for Munich, James lingered a little later in Paris than he had planned, and then, alone, on July 20, he set off in a little steamer for a cruise down the Seine to Rouen, and continued in stages down the river to its mouth on the coast of Normandy.

Out of old memory and habit he was bound for a seaport, in search of cooler weather and cheaper prices. The Seine led him to Le Havre, where the French transatlantic ships put in, and he paused for a day or two. There he watched a steady stream of arriving and departing Americans; the town had its picturesque quality. He imagined for himself the reactions of the Americans who were getting their first glimpse of Europe.[73] But it was hot and it stank of rotting fish. He got into a little open carriage with all his baggage and set off down the coast to Étretat, a nearby resort that he had seen advertised on placards.[74]

A week after his departure from Paris he was settled in a cottage at Étretat. It was quiet and safe and inexpensive, and after the intensity and struggle of the past year, of the several past years, it was a blessed haven of quiet contemplation. He went for a swim, and then dressed and lay on the shingle beach, throwing little stones into the water, his face shaded by a broad-brimmed white flannel hat, watching the naked children and the all but nude adults swimming and diving from a springboard. They seemed to be one large family party, unembarrassed when they disrobed, seemingly content to spend the whole day bathing and gossiping on the warm pebbles.[75]

The beach lay in a semicircle of enclosing cliffs, which grasped it with two white arms. Above the cliffs lay rolling grassy downs on which one could walk endlessly. James took long walks on the seashore and along the downs; one evening he went so far that he dined in a little nameless fishing village and returned by carriage after midnight. In the evenings he sat on the patio outside the little casino, listening to the music that drifted through the open windows and talking with chance acquaintances.

It was a realization that perhaps had come to him earlier, in Paris in the spring. But in his novel *Confidence*, written four years later when his relations with Zhukovsky were at their best, he described a character very much like himself coming idly to Étretat. The description was this: He felt himself happier than he had been in a long time.[76] The feeling of happiness came upon him somewhat to his surprise, and for a while he savored and examined it without quite understanding why he should be so happy. One evening, he stood on the beach looking at the sea outside the casino. The sea looked huge and black and simple; everything was vague in the unassisted darkness. An immense conviction came over him, abruptly. It was like a word spoken in the darkness: He was in love.[77]

When he described this sensation in the novel, he said that at first the realization of his feelings came over him with positive terror. But as the quiet days passed, as he walked his long walks along the downs and on the beaches, he accustomed himself to his feelings. In the novel it was a forbidden love. But as the days passed, the shadow dropped away, and nothing was left except the beauty of the feeling. He was not thinking of actions or consequences, those were another matter. The feeling was intrinsically the finest one he had ever had, and—as a mere feeling—he had not done with it yet.[78]

James, in Étretat in the summer of 1876, wrote to his former concierge in Paris, saying that he would take the same apartment again for the following winter.[79] He wrote another letter for the *Tribune*. He enclosed with the letter a note to Whitelaw Reid, who had been hinting that it was time for James to give up his column. James said that on the contrary he wanted to write for another year from Paris. He asked for an increase to thirty dollars per letter.[80] And he set to work to finish the final installments of *The American*, which was already appearing in *The Atlantic* to high praise from his friends in Boston.[81]

19

THE ASSAULT IS REPULSED

One morning, breakfasting at the hotel in Étretat where he took his meals, James met a young Englishman, Theodore Child. This young man was a Jew, a handsome fellow, fluent in French, and James thought that he must resemble the angelic hero of George Eliot's new novel, *Daniel Deronda*, which he was just then reading; Deronda in the story was as beautiful as the prince Camaralzaman.[1] The equally beautiful Child gave him an address in London, and invited him to call. But James put the card aside; he was planning to return to Paris for another winter.

He had received only one invitation to a country house: the Château de Varennes, south of Paris, Mme. Childe's family estate. He ended his summer's rest there, and described it for Elizabeth Boott:

> I find myself in the most enchanting quarters—a little moated 15th Century château, which clamors for you to come and paint it—a

château with walls 3 feet thick, turrets & winding staircases & a little green river tied in a circular knot close around its base. From my window I look across the stream, into which I might drop my letter.[2]

Mme. Childe was a graceful hostess; little excursions were arranged for her guest each day. One afternoon she brought James along as she paid calls in the village which was hers. It was an interesting view of a still-feudal way of life. Shortly, the mail, forwarded from Paris, arrived and with it a letter from Whitelaw Reid.

> I am in receipt of your favor of the 25th July requesting an advance of one-half in the payment for your letters.
>   I had been on the point of writing making a suggestion of quite a different nature. It was to the effect that the letters should be made rather more "newsy" in character, and somewhat shorter, and that they should be sent somewhat less frequently. . . .[3]

Reid noted that the newspaper would be crowded with news of the centennial celebrations and the election campaign of 1876, and then he was afraid that James's letters were "sometimes on topics too remote from popular interests to please more than a select few of our readers."[4]

> You must not imagine that any of us have failed to appreciate the admirable work you have done for us. The difficulty has sometimes been not that it was too good, but that it was magazine rather than newspaper work.[5]

This was a dismissal and it stung. James, having ignored Reid's hint that it was time to make way for a fresh voice, and having instead requested a raise in pay, had opened himself to an insult, and here it was. He knew perfectly that his letters were not the gossip that he had promised to the *Tribune*, and that in the event he had found it morally impossible to write.

> I quite appreciate what you say about the character of my letters, and about their not being the right sort of thing for a newspaper. I have been half expecting to hear from you to that effect. I myself had wondered whether you could make room for them. . . . But I am afraid I can't assent to your proposal that I should try and write

otherwise. I know the sort of letters you mean—it is doubtless the sort of thing for the *Tribune* to have. But I can't produce it—I don't know how and I couldn't learn how. . . . If my letters are too "good" I am honestly afraid that they are the poorest I can do, especially for the money![6]

James would explain the failure of his venture into newspaper journalism with variations of this *mot*, but it was a little misleading. The difficulty with his letters was not their literary quality. Both G. W. Smalley and Anthony Trollope wrote perfectly respectable literary letters from London for the *Tribune*. The difficulty was that he was incapable of providing gossip for newspapers without violating his own standards. One hardly knew whether to call it a moral or an aesthetic question. Privacy was the armature on which personality was modeled, the skeleton of the self-created actor, the core of moral certainty on which art and civilized life were built. He could no more intrude on a host's privacy than steal his spoons.

He was not quite ready to face the implication of this belief, which was really a condition of his being, a private religion. He had imagined for himself a success in journalism like Sainte-Beuve's, but though he was in Paris he wrote for the audience at home, and American newspapers had no place for a Sainte-Beuve. What they wanted was gossip: news. It would be twenty years before he fully realized the contradiction, on a London theater stage, where for the first time he looked the mass audience in the face.

It was soon time to return to his apartment on the Rue de Luxembourg, but the *Tribune*'s unexpected dismissal continued to trouble him, and he looked forward to his return to Paris with an unaccountable foreboding.[7] He went up to Paris in the middle of September, shortly before Zhukovsky's expected return, and saw the concierge about his apartment. But despite his letter from Étretat the apartment he had taken the previous winter had been let. This was a great blow. Apartments were scarce and his income had been reduced; it would now be very difficult to find something equally good. Even a small furnished apartment in the desirable part of the city would be very expensive. The concierge said there was an inferior apartment on the top floor, in the rear, and after a brief fruitless search for alternatives, James felt obliged to take it. But it was still very hot and no one had returned to Paris yet, and so he made yet another excursion into the countryside, to Saint-Germain-en-Laye, from which he could easily come into town in the evenings.

He was at work, as always, on *The American*, keeping ahead of the publication of installments in *The Atlantic*, but he was briefly distracted by a miserable, soul-destroying job that had been inflicted upon him by friendship. A young friend of Lizzie's in Rome, a Miss Hall, was in difficult circumstances, and was hoping to make a little money by writing. At Lizzie's suggestion she had sent him a manuscript, a piece of travel writing, which he was tediously transcribing and trying to revise into something that might be published in an American magazine. It was hopeless, however, and after wasted hours he wrote to Lizzie suggesting a hint to Miss Hall to learn to write well, at least to spell and construct sentences correctly, or to find some other way out of her difficulties.[8]

From his suburban perch, James cautiously felt his way back into the Parisian setting. The heat of summer gave way to mists and chill drizzles, and in the early autumn weather he saw Zhukovsky again.

Thirty years later he told a story to Edmund Gosse, a young man of letters who was an intimate friend, one of the few people to whom he ever spoke at all frankly about the Paris year. Gosse made a note of the story, and when he published his own memoirs he described Henry James in the act of telling it:

> He spoke of standing on the pavement of a city, in the dusk, and of gazing upwards across the misty street, watching, watching for the lighting of a lamp in a window on the third story. And the lamp blazed out, and through bursting tears he strained to see what was behind it, the unapproachable face. And for hours he stood there, wet with the rain, brushed by the phantom hurrying figures of the scene, and never from behind the lamp was for one moment visible the face. The mysterious and poignant revelation closed, and one could make no comment, ask no question, being throttled oneself by an overpowering emotion. And for a long time Henry James shuffled beside me in the darkness, shaking the dew off the laurels, and still there was no sound at all in the garden but what our heels made crunching the gravel, nor was the silence broken when suddenly we entered the house and he disappeared for an hour.[9]

One could not be sure that this was a rainy evening in Paris, although it sounded like one, in the fall of 1876. The memory remained unique, a part of James's private existence.

On James's return to Paris, in any case, there was no immediate renewal of what had been the blooming intimacy with Zhukovksy, who now appeared to have a new friend, a French pianist. James attended a musical evening at Zhukovsky's studio, and from nine until two in the morning the pianist performed selections from the *Ring of the Nibelung*, the opera cycle that had been performed at Bayreuth for the first time that summer. The evening was evidently a trial for James. It was not only that he did not really care about music, and for Wagner's music cared least of all. He burst out in a letter the next day, "My friend Zhukovsky is a most *attachant* human creature, but a light-weight and a perfect failure";[10] which disclosed more depth of feeling than the music itself could account for.

He had declined another invitation from Elizabeth Boott to join her in Florence, saying that he was "fixed here" in Paris,[11] but now on October 13 he wrote a brief and hasty note to William, saying, "I am thinking seriously of going to England, but *please say nothing about it until I decide.*"[12]

The situation was another test of his angelic philosophy. Whatever his feelings may have been, he continued to see Zhukovsky at entertainments, and he evidently introduced the young Russian to a young aristocrat, Lady Selina Bidwell, who consented to have her portrait painted by him, and who would recommend him to friends in London. James encouraged the painter to submit his portrait of Selina Bidwell to the British Royal Academy's exhibition that winter; he himself would be Zhukovsky's agent in London, where he hoped that with the lady's patronage, and her portrait on display at the Royal Academy, Zhukovsky would be a success.[13]

Although only days earlier he had written of his plans to remain in Paris for the winter,[14] he was now thinking of departing as soon as possible for London.[15] The American set was returning to Paris, and he could not bear the thought of being among them, of being limited to their company, but "there is nothing else, for me personally, on the horizon. . . ."[16]

With the collapse of the intimacy with Zhukovsky he lost also his opportunities for a close friendship with Turgenev. It seemed likely that now he would see Turgenev no more than he had the winter before.[17] The Russian novelist was still in the country, and he wrote a letter to Zhukovsky offering to come into town to have dinner with him and James. The letter did not reach James, however, and was not answered, and James missed the chance. Zhukovsky would not be the hostess, as it were, who would provide the common ground for their friendship. A black winter loomed ahead, in a dreary apartment, and

James was back at his beginning, without even the modest income and identity of a *Tribune* correspondent. *The American* was all but completed, and there was suddenly no reason for him to remain in Paris.

Italy called to him again. Elizabeth Boott repeated her offer of an apartment in the palace where she and her father were staying for the winter. This would provide warmth, economy, and friendly company; and reading her letter, Rome rose up around him:

> I had a real hallucination; I seemed for a moment to be in that golden Roman air again, to see it trembling around me as I stood in the grass before the Lateran. I can imagine great pleasure, & what an ass—what an abject idiot—I must seem like, to you, that I too should not be there, in the only proper place.[18]

But there was an echo of William's voice—"a letter from William had a great deal to do with it"—and the door to Italy closed once more. He would go to London, the capital of the last great empire—the capital, in a certain sense, of the world. Henrietta Reubell and other American hostesses returning to Paris, just opening their apartments for the season, were half humorously indignant.[19] To leave Paris in December, just as the season was beginning, for the black deserted London winter, was simply eccentric.

James certainly had no thought of returning to New York or Boston. America had been thin and barren. But he had no real ties to England, either. Only in the cosmopolitan set that traveled among the capitals and watering places of Europe—the polyglot Anglo-Saxon hostesses and the charming Russian, English, and Italian men—had he found both the grace of the old order and the tolerance, the inclusiveness of the new. He wanted not so much a new home as simply a base of operations, a fixed point from which to enter the cosmopolitan world.

In London, perhaps, there was an order both aristocratic and liberal: houses and gardens where one might cultivate both progressive convictions and conservative tastes. Why should he not live in London? In November 1876 he gave notice to the concierge that he would not want his apartment for the winter after all, and began to pack his books and clothes. In the middle of December, almost on the eve of the solstice, he crossed the English Channel.

From New York, Whitelaw Reid honored him with a paragraph of the kind that James could never bring himself to write:

Mr. Henry James, jr., whose brilliant letters from Paris in THE TRIBUNE were among the most graceful and finished of last year's contributions to newspaper literature, and whose novel of American Parisian life, now running in *The Atlantic*, promises to be one of the most successful efforts yet made in American fiction, has transferred himself to London, where he seems to be established for the Winter.[20]

20

LONDON

His house was No. 3, Bolton Street, just off Piccadilly, close to his old haunt on Half Moon Street. The flat perfectly suited him, and he was to occupy it for almost ten years. Bolton Street was a little avenue at the eastern verge of Mayfair, opening into the broad busy boulevard of Piccadilly, with its shops, arcades, and galleries. The river was distant and forgotten.

His flat was two flights up, with windows that faced southwest; directly opposite was the monotonous, sooty, gray-brown Jacobean brick wall of Lord Ashburton's house. James's windows captured what little sunlight there was, and they gave an oblique view of the broad boulevard and of the Green Park opposite. An immense cab rank stretched from the head of the Green Park down his side of Piccadilly, and the long row of waiting hansom cabs, with their drivers on perches high up behind, seemed to him unsurpassably modern and majestic.[1] It was the close of the year 1876, and he was thirty-three years old.

The flat was perfectly suitable for a literary bachelor; it was very much like Rutson's upstairs flat at Half Moon Street which he had admired so long ago. The comparatively sunny front room, with a coal grate and a writing desk between the tall front windows, became his drawing room and workplace. In the summer, with the windows open, it would be noisy with the racket of cabs, carriages, and crowds on Piccadilly and the unsleeping roar of London itself. But in the depth of winter it was quiet, a warm and private retreat.

The landlady, Miss Ball, who lived in the house, was stiff and conventional, and while she seemed to harbor as much avidity and calculation as any French shop woman, she utterly lacked French graces and charms. The housemaid, Louisa, a dark-complexioned young woman who spoke in the accents of a duchess, as it seemed to James, had a charming smile, and the rent was cheap and the service was really very good. For two and a half guineas a week, about thirteen dollars, he had the furnished apartment, and every morning a luxurious English breakfast of tea, toast, eggs, and bacon was brought to him before his wonderfully warming coal fire. After breakfast, he sat in comfort at his desk, writing letters. He reflected that in Paris, his feet had never been warm.

It was terribly dark. The brief northern days were shrouded by the poisonous, brownish-yellow London fog that penetrated everywhere. Yet he was in a state of deep delight. He had complete liberty and the prospect of profitable work. He took long walks in the rain; he took possession of London; he felt it to be the right place.[2]

In the bleakness of the London December, he made his first acquaintances. A young man named Benson, who had visited America, came and called on him at someone's suggestion, and took him to dinner at the Oxford and Cambridge Club. James himself looked up young Nadal, the second secretary at the American legation, whose book on London life he had reviewed just before leaving New York; it was Nadal who had so beautifully described England as a collection of walled gardens.

On the day before Christmas, he breakfasted with Theodore Child, the seraphically beautiful Jew whom he had met that past summer, but Child was now on his way to Paris, where he was to be the correspondent of the *Daily Telegraph*. James called on Smalley, the *Tribune*'s European chief and London correspondent, who was most cordial. Smalley invited him to dinner, and introduced him to men of his own Oxford circle, including the historians James Bryce and Albert Dicey.

Christmas Eve and Christmas Day were solitary, weary, and sad. James was almost frightened when his landlady warned him not to expect any clean linen over the long Christmas weekend, for the washerwomen would all be drunk. He momentarily yearned for his flat on the Rue de Luxembourg, where every Saturday evening a young woman, well dressed, with a crisp white muslin cap and a basket on her arm, had returned his bleached and starched and pressed linen, distributing it in his rooms along with a charming conversation.[3]

He wrote a little anxiously to friends in America, to Sarah Wister and Henry Adams, asking for letters of introduction. And yet, for all the darkness and solitude of London, he had a sense of repose, of rightness. He wrote to Lizzie Boott in Rome, who had again invited him to join her in bathing in the warmth and light of Italy.

I have had to content myself with wafting envious sighs toward you— some of which may possibly have reached you, if not (which is probable) converted into the turbid element of the London fog. Your letter of Nov. 22d is before me now, & renews the almost deathly anguish with which I read it when it came. Another like it, I think, rec'd a few days afterward and striking while the iron was hot, would simply have led me straight by the nose to Rome. But instead, behold me in the foggy city. I came hither 2 weeks, or more, since & feel, as I usually do anywhere after the 1st day or two, already like an old inhabitant. The weather is hideous, the heavens being perpetually enstained with a crust of dirty fog-paste, like Thames mud in solution. At 11 a.m. I have to light my candles to read! . . . The dusky seriousness of London doesn't at all displease me [however]: indeed, in spite of fog & isolation & a very dreary Xmas, I rejoice in all things & find that I have the making of a good Londoner.[4]

Lizzie's letter had reached him in Paris just before his departure, and had been full of happy news. Rome was beautiful, and she had formed a romantic friendship with young Anne Bartlett, the boyish, bachelor horsewoman with whom James had once read aloud the poetry of Tasso. Lizzie wrote joyously of riding with Anne Bartlett—in the cork woods!—and that she was painting well. When James wrote in answer he called her wicked for her seductive descriptions of Rome. He promised to come to see her soon, perhaps in the early spring.[5]

This time of quiet, after the rush of his departure from Paris, was not entirely unwelcome. He began to work again, and he centered himself upon his new situation, with practiced skill designing a new costume. Aside from a new high silk hat, dress coat, boots for day wear, and patent-leather shoes for the evenings, there was the question of a beard. In Paris he had been clean-shaven, but beards were very much the fashion in London. By early February, when he began to dine out a good deal, he again had a full beard—closely trimmed on his cheeks, but deep and square on the chin. His high forehead and pale, olive-tinted skin threw into prominence his beautiful eyes, and with his full, glossy brown beard he had the look of a ship's captain of the last century.[6]

In this quiet interval he was able to complete the final two installments of *The American* and send them off to Howells, who complained mightily when he saw them. Howells had very much wanted a happy ending; he had wanted the American to marry the Frenchwoman, Madame de Cintré. That, James patiently explained, could not realistically have happened, and in any case would have defeated the point of the story. But he promised that his next novel for *The Atlantic* would have a happy ending.[7]

With the serial ended and no newspaper column to write, he was obliged to begin a new series of travel pieces and reviews for *The Nation* and *The Galaxy*. He had the expenses of travel and a new English wardrobe, charged to his letter of credit, to make up, and the expenses of daily life to meet. It was a miserable business writing these poorly paid anonymous little magazine pieces. To lighten the burden of critical work, he would have to write another novel for serialization in a magazine every year. He wrote to Church at *The Galaxy* once again, proposing to give them his next novel; he could hardly begin a new one in *The Atlantic* so soon, when his last had been appearing there for almost a year, and still had two numbers to run.[8]

But how and when would he find the leisure for something more substantial? For several weeks he had been revolving in his mind the plan for a new novel, something far more ambitious than *The American*, a far more serious affair than anything he had yet attempted. He had been encouraged by Turgenev,[9] and he had before him the example of George Eliot. Her last novel, *Daniel Deronda*, which he had read at Étretat, was a highly serious, highly intellectual work; yet it had been an immense success commercially. As it had once before, her success encouraged him. She had written on the very theme he had been revolving in his own mind—the awakening of a young girl.[10]

He wrote a review of *Daniel Deronda* in the form of a curious dramatic dialogue between himself and his American audience. He himself appeared, lightly disguised, as a critic, "Constantius," muted and thoughtful after his Parisian reverses.

His readers were two American women. One admired George Eliot uncritically, and the other despised her. "I see; I can understand that," he said mildly to each.

"Oh, you understand too much! This is the twentieth time you have used that formula. . . ."

He was not so partisan and fierce as his audience; he only tried to understand. That was his strength; his weakness was that he had written a novel himself. It was perhaps his weakness speaking, he said, but *Daniel Deronda* was very much to his taste, even though it did not quite succeed. George Eliot, like him, had tried to understand.

Her protagonist in this novel was a beautiful young girl, Gwendolen Harleth. The book was the story of her tragic marriage to an aristocratic villain, Grandcourt. The heroine and the villain were both on the heroic scale. Gwendolen Harleth was absolutely real: an intelligent, sensitive, young woman. Grandcourt too was a reality: cold, abusive, sadistic, the personification of evil. He treated Gwendolen solely as a means to his own gratification. There was the most delicate of hints that he was the type of the British imperialist. Gwendolen was his dominion, and he ruled her mercilessly for the pleasure of exercising power.

The marriage and the experience of evil that it brought was a terrible education in life. The heroine's growing awareness of her difficult condition was the thread of the tale:

> The universe is forcing itself with a slow, inexorable pressure into a narrow, complacent, and yet after all extremely sensitive mind, and making it ache with the pain of the process—that is Gwendolen's story.[11]

She could not escape the marriage, and it was part of her attractiveness that what she regretted most was the loss of her chance for an exalted passion. The very chance of embracing what Eliot liked to call the "larger life," the life of virtuous love, was denied her.[12]

In James's imaginary dialogue, the tough, modern young woman disdained all this idealism. But Eliot's clumsy, noble motives were just what James admired most, he said. Eliot was a teacher, and she put meaning, life itself, into her books. Her idealism was rather awkwardly introduced, it was true, with a parcel of unreal Jewish characters (they made his new friend Child smile); but perhaps the difficulty could have been cured by allowing the burden of the story to be carried by a different sort of heroine, a beautiful woman who did not require a male tutor; perhaps one of Turgenev's Russian heroines—or an American girl.

This brief winter of working solitude ended quickly; with the new year came a series of callers who were to take him into the heart of London, the capital of Europe, and among the makers of history.[13]

How much Fanny Kemble had to do with this cordial reception he would never be quite sure. Her old friend Lord Houghton, who had been at Cambridge with her brother John, and who had admired her in the days of her first appearances on the stage, appeared unbidden at James's door early in January; and then old John Motley, the Europeanized American historian and diplomat, called. James had never met either Houghton or Motley; whatever the cause of these visits, he felt himself the beneficiary of a secret exercise of indirect power. He was being taken up into the quiet society of Mayfair and Belgravia.

Kemble herself arrived in London early in the year, having given up her country house in Pennsylvania once and for all. Her younger daughter, Frances, had married an English clergyman named James Leigh, and they had settled in his rural parish, not far from London. As the elder daughter, Sarah Wister, had formed the habit of spending each spring season in London, Kemble had given up her footing in America entirely, and had purchased the leasehold of a house in Connaught Square, peaceful and elegant, above Hyde Park; she would be with her daughters and grandchildren, at home in London again.[14]

From different worlds and different generations as they were, yet it was remarkable how many points of contact she and James had. Kemble was a cosmopolite: half English, half French, and, as it were, half American. Although she had grown up in the then still-rural Bayswater, among the farms and fields where Paddington Station now stood, her experience of France was like James's: she had gone to school in Boulogne-sur-Mer, and then in Paris, in an odd institution for girls on the Rue d'Angoulême; and as a girl she had wandered in the gardens of the Tuileries and in the gallery of the Luxembourg Palace.

She was sixty-seven years old in the year of James's arrival and her return to London: strong-minded, passionate in her feelings and her opinions. She and James quickly became close friends, even confidants.

> It is . . . a kind of rest & refreshment to see a woman who (extremely annoying as she sometimes is) gives one a sense of having a deep, rich human nature & having cast off all vulgarities. The people of this world seem to me for the most part nothing but *surface*. . . . Mrs Kemble has no organized surface at all; she is like a straight deep cistern without a cover, or even, sometimes, a bucket, into which, as a mode of intercourse, one must tumble with a splash.[15]

She was a wonderful talker, and spun the most complex and gracefully perceptive tales. Little and stout, like the queen, her manner was imperious. She would begin speaking in midstream, with some violent expression:

> I am as stupid as *several* fools—yesterday I said to my daughter, "Henry James is so kind! (that's not the stupidity—I'm coming to it) sending me his photograph, & books, & Reviews to read, & I know not where to write him one word of thanks"—"3 Bolton St. Piccadilly my dear Mother" quoth she—"he has kept his London lodging." "O," said I with much prolongation both of relief & regret at my own imbecility—so now here come thanks & thanks & more thanks. . . . [16]

She had grown up among women, and most of her talk was about the remarkable women she had known. There was her very dear friend of a lifetime, Harriet St. Leger, whom Henry had met in Rome, for instance; her "Aunt Dall," Adelaide de Camp, who had helped raise her, and managed the household and the family's acting company when it went on tour.

One anecdote particularly struck him. It concerned Lady Byron, Kemble's highly esteemed friend. Lady Byron was a heroine to women of Kemble's generation in Great Britain and America, although—perhaps because—she had been a victim of her husband's incestuous infidelities and public abuse. She and Florence Nightingale, at the time of the Crimean War, had made idle, frivolous fine ladies into hospital nurses, Kemble said, and had turned into innumerable channels of newly awakened benevolence and activity "the love of adventure, the desire for excitement, and the desperate need of occupation, of many women who had no other qualifications for the hard and holy labors into which they flung themselves."[17]

A young author, Anna Jameson, had come under Lady Byron's influence at that time. As Fanny told the tale, Anna Jameson was an attractive young woman, with a skin of that dazzling whiteness which generally accompanies reddish hair; her face was capable of a marvelous power of concentrated feeling, such as is seldom seen in any woman's face. She had gone to consult Lady Byron about work that she could do, and Lady Byron had suggested she give public lectures.

> Lady Byron thought a very valuable public service might be rendered by women who so undertook to advocate important truths of which they had made special study. . . .
>
> Lady Byron was a peculiarly reserved and quiet person, with a manner habitually deliberate and measured, a low, subdued voice, and rather diffident hesitation in expressing herself; and she certainly conveyed the impression of natural reticence and caution. But . . . she always struck me as a woman capable of profound and fervid enthusiasm, with a mind of a rather romantic and visionary order. She surprised me extremely one evening as she was accompanying me to one of my public readings, by exclaiming, "Oh, how I envy you! What would I not give to be in your place!". . . "What! to read Shakespeare before some hundreds of people?" "Oh, no," she said, "not to read Shakespeare to them, but to have all that mass of people under your control, subject to your influence, and receiving your impressions." She then went on to say she would give anything to lecture upon subjects which interested her deeply, and that she should like to advocate with every power she possessed. . . .[18]

This picture fixed itself in James's memory: Lady Byron and her red-haired protégée, Anna Jameson, transposed to America, would be the leading characters of his novel *The Bostonians*.[19] It would be only one of a series of stories and novels that would begin with tales told to him by Fanny Kemble.

Even before she was settled in her own house, she set about introducing James to friends of her own—and her parents'—generation. She brought him to old Mrs. Proctor, who was past eighty but still had two days each week to receive her friends, and who appeared in an elegant old lady's toilet and did the honors of afternoon tea herself.[20]

They were an extraordinary circle of friends, among whom Fanny counted Mme. Mohl, as James knew, and Lady Hamilton Gordon, daughter of the remarkable Herschels, a family of astronomers. They were intelligent, beautiful, accomplished, wealthy, and powerful, and they ruled in their private world at the center of the capital. James could not help envying them; their world, although it was based as he knew on the most violent injustices, seemed to have been a realm of grace. He recalled later,

> the fine old felicity of the fortunate and the "great" under the "old" order which would have made it so good to live could one but have been in their shoes. . . . the class, as I seemed to see it, that had had the longest and happiest innings in history—happier and longer, on the whole, than even their congeners of the old French time. . . .[21]

What a passionate, extraordinary people they were! The English race, as he came to study them now, seemed characterized by a curious combination of individualism and convention. There was nothing so purely conventional as English life, and yet how each of them took vigorous advantage of every conventional opportunity for individual expression. Energy, above all, a sometimes violent energy, characterized them.

This circle of Fanny Kemble's friends, the Early Victorians, as he later called them, the rulers of London, were, as it seemed to James, close to the end of their reign. The last of the old order, these elders embodied all its glory and its moral failures.

The remarkable Louisa, marchioness of Waterford, seemed to him a distillation of their virtues. She had been in her youth the most beautiful and characteristic of the Early Victorian maidens, but her beauty was of the subtle kind that was difficult to capture, and escaped a photograph entirely; it was a question of spirit as much as of physiognomy.[22] It was something one could understand only at first hand. She and her sister, Lady Canning, the daughters and heirs of Lord Stuart de Rothesay, spent their early youth in Paris, where their father was the British ambassador. They made a great sensation when they were first presented at court and entered into London society.

Both were tall, imperially formed, and great beauties. Louisa was blond, and her sister was dark. Her portrait had been painted many times, and by the leading painters of her day. These showed a round head set gracefully on a long neck; plump cheeks, a round chin, and a strong, aquiline nose. She wore her long hair in a coil at the back of her head, which emphasized her height, her smooth throat, and her great round eyes. In the portraits her shapely mouth was almost pursed with the faint hint of a smile. She was a woman of interesting qualities, and somehow conveyed strength and dignity, perhaps in the way her head was seated on her long neck; painted in three-quarters profile, with her head slightly inclined and her eyes downcast, she looked like a Renaissance Madonna.

At twenty-one, she had been the most beautiful woman in London. That was 1839, the year of the Eglinton Tournament. Carrying their family armor and escutcheons on the first railroad, the aristocracy had journeyed to the curious festival. It was a revival of the tournaments of the bygone age of Elizabeth, the last age of chivalry.

Henry, third marquess of Waterford, a slim little man who seemed to radiate violence, paid court to the elegant and accomplished Louisa. If she was the most beautiful maiden, he was the most vivid knight, a dark-haired, dark-eyed Irish nobleman who rode recklessly.

> First came music, retainers, men-at-arms [Louisa said, describing the tournament]; then the ladies (Lady Seymour, &c.) led up to the lists on white palfreys beautifully caparisoned; then the knights, each with his body of squires and retainers. When the procession had moved round the lists, the ladies dismounted, and came up into the pavilion in which we were, and then each knight rode to his tent. Lord Waterford dashed full gallop into his, and others more quietly into theirs. Then commenced the tilting, followed by riding at the ring, then a general mêlée, which was most beautiful and real-looking. The banquet took place in an immense temporary room, each knight having his banner held by a page behind him. Then followed a ball in an equally large temporary room. Some of the dresses were absurd, others beautiful. Lord Fitzharris had a magnificent dress of green velvet and fur. . . . The ball and banquet one could easily have dispensed with, being the same as such like in London, but the procession into the lists, the tilting, the mêlée, were such beautiful sights as one can never expect to see again.[23]

She married Lord Waterford, who had worn a red costume with an ermine collar at the tournament, and where he had been in constant attendance upon her. Waterford was a sportsman, whose principal occupations were riding, hunting, and shooting, and she was a young Parisian of intellectual tastes. They were married, and she left London and Paris for the Irish village of Curraghmore. When Lord Waterford was thrown from his horse and died, Lady Waterford then ruled alone, in a realm that reached across Ireland and England. She cultivated the great botanical collections and greenhouses on her estates, and built factories and churches and houses for the villagers and tenants. Her serenity was the temper of one both fortunate and confident of the goodness of the natural order. Like the best of her generation, her expressions of faith were spontaneous and passionate, and her good works were not so much concessions to duty as expressions of intimate interest and concern for her villagers. As the exemplar of her generation she was "accomplished"—she sang beautifully and musically, and painted in watercolors. She studied drawing with Ruskin, and music with Continental masters. She was beautiful, virtuous, and talented, the product of an exquisite system of cultivation that had taken centuries to achieve, and Henry James, for all his sense of the oppressive peonage and tenantry on which all this rested, envied her. They met at a dinner party, given by a friend of Fanny's, and James studied her, tried to imagine himself into her vanished youth and beauty, into "the fine old felicity of the fortunate and 'great' under the old order."[24] Yes, he assured himself, "It may be that the ancient greatness of Britain has been an iniquity, an 'hypocrisy' & an insolence: but to live here is (for me) to feel a kindness for the products of those energetic qualities of the race. . . ."[25] Lady Waterford personified the early Victorian virtues, the beauty and accomplishments of Fanny Kemble's generation; for James she opened a window into the not quite vanished age of the old aristocratic order. He listened to Fanny Kemble's own stories and studied her features for the principle of her vanished beauty.[26]

The other important ambassador from the past was Richard Monckton Milnes, Lord Houghton, who had called unbidden at Henry's door shortly after his arrival in London. He and Fanny's older brother John had been among the first members of the Cambridge Conversazione Society, then and afterward known as the Apostles, a self-selected group of twelve that had included Arthur Hallam and Alfred Tennyson.[27] Thomas Carlyle had described Houghton exuberantly:

> Conceive the man! A most bland-smiling, semi-quizzical, affectionate, high-bred, Italianized little man, who has long olive-blonde hair, a dimple, next to no chin, and flings his arm round your neck when he addresses you in public society![28]

He was white-haired and wrinkled now, but he still had some of his restless, passionate manner; his dark eyes darted about the room as he spoke. He was a good friend of both Fanny Kemble and Mme. Mohl, and it was presumably through Fanny's good offices that he had come, uninvited, to call. Houghton was sixty-eight when he paid his visit[29] in January 1877. He had served in Tory governments but he was not a party man; he liked his independence better than office, and indeed preferred the freedom of indirect power to the rituals and constraints of government. He was a host, a man of the world, the friend of the great, playing a part more often given to women. He said of himself, "The thing I was intended for by nature is a German woman. . . . I think Goethe would have fallen in love with me."[30] At his breakfasts the older generation met young artists, writers, and political aspirants; James found himself invited repeatedly to such gatherings.

The other mysteriously uninvited visitor, John Motley, was of Kemble's and Houghton's generation, and had played gatekeeper to Europe for two generations of American visitors. Without explaining why he had come, he called on James and bestowed on him a treasure whose value James quickly came to appreciate—an honorary three-month membership in the Athenaeum Club. James effusively described it in his letters:

> I am writing this in the beautiful great library of the Athenaeum Club. On the other side of the room sits Herbert Spencer, asleep in a chair (he always is, when I come here) and a little way off is the portly Archbishop of York with his nose in a little book.[31]

> The place is the last word of a high civilization—I wish you could see the great library in which I am writing this. Such bookshelves . . . such lounges and easy chairs![32]

> I find it a little heaven here below. It transfigures the face of material existence for me: & alas! I already find it indispensable![33]

Dinners at the club were much better (and cheaper) than he could easily get in restaurants; and in the two-story library, walled floor to ceiling with a magnificent collection of books, he found all the current newspapers, magazines, and journals he wished to read, and all the current novels issued by Mudie's lending library. He could sit in the library, writing letters on the elegant letterhead of the club, embossed with the profile of the goddess Athena, in the corner where Dickens, Thackeray, Trollope, and Matthew Arnold had written.

The greatest value of the club was social. It was not easy for a visitor to find his way in London; as he had learned on his earlier visits, London sat with its back complacently turned to the stranger. There was no café society, no social life of any importance to which a stranger had free access. But while London was not a hospitable place for a stranger, it was extraordinarily convenient for the households of Mayfair. The postal system, for instance, was like a network of special messengers. One was never more than a short walk from a post office in a grocer's shop or tobacconist's; a note sent in the morning might be answered by midafternoon. This was a great help to social relations. There were cabs and carriages everywhere, and once inside the door, as it were, James could move easily from one drawing room to another. But the greatest social facility for a man was the system of clubs. James found that in a club one might speak to anyone. This was one of the immense satisfactions of the Athenaeum, "the best club in London," at least for literary and intellectual men, as James complacently noted. It was a place where one might make friends, as James did with his remarkable facility.

> Dear Lizzie—. . . . The extreme tranquillity in which I passed the early part of my stay here is being rapidly exchanged for an amount of "merriment" which may become equally extreme if I don't keep a vigilant eye on it: which however I mean to do. . . . I suspect you will take it for granted that I like London much, & you will not be wrong. I find it very interesting & profitable; my personal life is very much less *thin* than on the continent.[34]

Lizzie had written again, urging him to visit her in Rome in the soft spring, but he said that he did not want to break the spell of London so soon. And for the first time he suggested that she come to him, or rather to London: "It strikes me that you had better come here & study with Burne-Jones. I went the other Sunday . . . to B.J.'s studio, & took a great fancy to his work . . . the strongest English painting since Turner."[35] Burne-Jones's work was being exhibited at the new Grosvenor Gallery, along with some impressionists, and the contrast was damning. The impressionists—most especially a young American living in London, James Whistler—were simply not interesting. Whistler had a near-abstract composition called *Nocturne in Black and Gold: the Falling Rocket*. When Ruskin reviewed the show, he said that he "never expected to hear a coxcomb ask two hundred guineas for flinging a pot of paint in the public's face,"[36] and this had prompted a libel suit. James's own reaction was milder. The work seemed to him an object, rather than a representation, and Whistler's paintings were pleasant enough objects to have about. But he thought that paintings should be expressions, not impressions; Whistler's pictures referred to nothing except the act of painting itself.[37] On the whole he hoped that Lizzie would abandon the impressionists and study with Burne-Jones.

The elders of Victorian London had given him freedom of the city, as it were, and with true Victorian practicality, the problems of material existence had been inexpensively and beautifully solved for him. Introduced to London by Kemble's circle, he received a steady stream of invitations to dinners where he found himself seated at the head of the table among the dignitaries, and where he quickly made friends. A stranger was ordinarily left to stand about unintroduced in the brief interval before dinner, and then perhaps paired with a very young woman who took little interest in him. But the circle had opened for James; generally he took in an older woman of the hostess's generation, from whom he would the next day receive an invitation to another such dinner party. ("The old women spoil him," Clover Hooper tartly observed.) And so between club acquaintanceships and dinner invitations, with remarkable speed he found himself taken up and passed from hand to hand.

He had tumbled into a private world of walled gardens and drawing rooms, a polite society presided over by ladies and donnish bachelors, in which history, art, and religion were preserved and handed down. In the world of Mayfair and the country houses of the county families, intimacy was possible; the associated met often, and sounded and selected and measured and inspired one another, and relations and combinations had time to form themselves.[38]

My dearest sister: . . . . This is a rainy London afternoon—a dreadfully dreary sort of thing in London. I usually consecrate Sunday afternoons to visits, it being the only time one has a chance of finding ladies at home; but today I abstain, from an aversion, on the one side, to becoming wet & muddy in my peregrinations, & a thrifty indisposition, on the other, to encounter an accumulation of cab fares. . . . So I will pay an afternoon call on my sister in spite of the fact that she will probably not offer me a cup of 5 o'clock tea in a bit of highly re-

markable old china, on a Japanese table about as high as a foot-
stool. . . . I dined [a few days ago] with a pleasant old gentleman who
seems kindly disposed to me—a Mr. Phillips-Tadreu, who lives round
the corner, in Stratton St., where his dwelling looks into the garden
of Devonshire House. He is an old bachelor of fortune & culture, a
Liberal, charitable, a retired fox-hunter, a valetudinarian, & a friend
of many Americans of 40 years ago. He is very fond of giving small
dinners, talking of old books, &c., & is a very pretty specimen of a certain sort of fresh-colored, blue-eyed, simple-minded yet interested
(two things which go together so much here) old English gentleman.
His dinner consisted of young Liberal M.P.'s &c.—my eternal fate! I
meet none but statistical people. . . . [39]

The talk he heard was often gossip about people who were quickly
becoming known to him, and he delighted in passing it along to Alice,
in brotherly fashion:

Mrs. Norton . . . has just been married, by the way, at 75 years of
age, in a Bath-chair, to a great Scotch laird, Sir Wm. Sterling
Maxwell, the author of "The Cloister Life of Charles I.": a fact that
Mrs. Kemble cited to me the other day as a proof that the English
were the most romantic of all people & the most capable of great passions; Sir Wm. Sterling having been in love with Mrs. N. for the last
40 years & prevented hitherto from marrying her. Lady Morgan, said
Mrs. Duncan Stewart, kept a salon & was a very good maitresse de
maison. "She always drew people out & made them show their best.
To me she always said: 'Come out of your corner there and show your
shoulders!' "[40]

He made friends in this circle, the more democratic, liberal women of
the older generation that he met through Fanny Kemble. He described one of them in a characteristic letter to Lizzie Boott:

I have given a note of introduction to you to a good friend of mine—
Lady Hamilton Gordon, who probably leaves for Rome tomorrow to
be near her daughter who is ill. . . . She is as easy as an old glove,
much, potentially, of a Bohemian, and also much of an artist. She
paints very nicely indeed herself. Make her—or rather let her, for she
will be charmed—come into your studio while you paint, see your

models, &c; and invite her to dinner *en famille*, to meet Miss Bartlett: this last point is essential. She must know Miss B. . . . She is extremely sociable & will delight in your treating her as a sister. She is the daughter of Sir John Herschel (the astronomer &c) & . . . for a good while lady-in-waiting to the Queen; but though a "swell" she hates swellishness & revels in shabbiness. So you needn't to even un-paintify your thumb for her.[41]

He gradually made his way among the Liberal young men, who edited journals and would be helpful to him: Leslie Stephen, whom he had met on earlier visits and who now was editor of *The Cornhill Magazine*; Thomas H. Huxley, the great expositor of evolutionary theory; James Anthony Froude, whose epochal history of England in the fifteenth century was just finished; the young poet and man of letters Andrew Lang. George Howard, who had taken him to see Burne-Jones's paintings, was his mentor and guide in the London art world and for whom he quickly formed a strong affection. Howard would in due course become the ninth earl of Carlisle; at the moment, however, he was an amateur painter with a deep and intense fondness for Italy. He was a good Liberal, immensely wealthy, but theoretically committed to democracy and to the end of his own aristocratic privileges; renamed "Lord Warburton," James described him in *The Portrait of a Lady* as the very type and epitome of the Liberal aristocrat:

> A remarkably well made man . . . a noticeably handsome face, fresh-colored, fair and frank, with firm, straight features, a lively grey eye and the rich adornment of a chestnut beard. This person had a certain fortunate, brilliant exceptional look—the air of a happy temperament fertilized by a high civilization—which would have made almost any observer envy him at a venture.[42]

As indeed James could not help envying him. The circle of young men was less generous than the older generation, and less conscious of him.

> I partook of a very pleasant dinner at the Smalleys'. . . . Present at the dinner were Robert Browning, Mr. & Mrs. Huxley, Mr. & Mrs. Frank Hill, editor & editress of the *Daily News*, & my humble self. The Hills are quite the cleverest folk I have met here . . . though on this occasion [they] were shut up by the chattering and self-complacent Robert B., who I am sorry to say, does not make on me a purely agree-

able impression. His transparent eagerness to hold the [floor] & a sort of shrill interruptingness which distinguishes him have in them a kind of vulgarity. Besides which, strange to say, his talk doesn't strike me as very good. It is altogether gossip & personality & it is not very beautifully worded. But evidently there are 2 Brownings—an esoteric & an exoteric. The former never peeps out in society, & the latter has not a drop of suggestion of *Men & Women.* . . . [43]

The circle who drew him in were in many ways like Americans—idealized, Europeanized Americans, on a grander scale. And James himself, as he joined their circle, took up his share of the work of maintaining and extending the community, and of welcoming new arrivals. Yet he made no intimate personal friendship. "I have framed no 'relation,' " he confided to Grace Norton. His emotional ties were with Paris and Rome.

Zhukovsky was still very much in his thoughts at this time, as he was trying to open doors for the young Russian in London. Zhukovsky's picture had been refused by the Royal Academy, although James thought it better than seven eighths of what they accepted. When the annual exhibition of recent paintings opened at the new Academy building, a few paces up Piccadilly from his flat, James held his own miniature salon for Zhukovsky. In May he wrote home that Zhukovsky's portrait of Lady Selina Bidwell "reposes at this hour on my sofa . . . she has been sending various earls & countesses to look at it all the week, & their presence in my sitting room interferes slightly with literary composition. . . ."[44] But his effort to secure commissions for Zhukovsky to paint portraits in London was unsuccessful. The various earls and countesses ordered no pictures. It was his first venture as a patron, a mentor, in London; later efforts would be more successful.

London was now his permanent base, in any event, at least as long as he remained in Europe.[45] He wrote to Grace Norton: "I feel seriously—I am afraid you would think alarmingly—Londonized, & consider that I have only made a beginning of living here."[46]

He spent much of the hot summer of 1877 in the country, moving from one house party to the next, with brief returns to London. In August he was in the countryside near Stratford-on-Avon, familiar from earlier trips, visiting Fanny Kemble, her daughter Mrs. Leigh, and their neighbors. He wrote from the picturesque countryside to Lizzie Boott:

I wish you could see [the roses] clambering against the wall of this house, just outside my window. I wish, too, you could see, in the distance, straight across the lawn, the beautiful soft mass of Kenilworth Castle. I am staying in this lovely country for a few days, with some very amicable people [the Alexander Carters]—with whom I drove last evening six miles, to a party at an enchanting old rectory where I *danced*—if you please—half the night, with a series of the rosiest shyest sweetest little British maidens![47]

It was the birthday party of the rector's daughter, and James's dance with these maidens became a metaphor for the whole sweet welcome that England had extended to him. When he wrote to Elizabeth in Rome, at the other pole of his emotional world, the dancing maidens often now came back to him, like a long-absent but now warmly remembered friend. "The women dance ill, but they are soft & clinging. Will you take a turn with me to celebrate my arrival?"[48] To his sister, Alice, in his joy he confided a plan that it would take him many years to carry out: "If I were the happy possessor of an English country house I would invite you to come and stay with me. . . ."[49]

Among his visits to the countryside he had included a long return visit to Oxford as well, and that had touched him more closely still. James Bryce had invited him to attend Commemoration Day exercises, and had arranged for him to stay in vacant rooms at Oriel College.

I had had a glimpse of Oxford in former years, but I had never slept in a low-browed room looking out on a grassy quadrangle and opposite a medieval clock-tower. This satisfaction was vouchsafed me on the night of my arrival; I was made free of the room of an absent undergraduate. I sat in his deep armchairs; I burned his candles and read his books, and I hereby thank him as effusively as possible. Before going to bed I took a turn through the streets and renewed in the silent darkness the impression of the charm imparted to them by the quiet college fronts which I had gathered in the former years. The college-fronts were now quieter than ever, the streets were empty, and the old scholastic city was sleeping in the warm starlight.[50]

After the Commemoration Day exercises, at which the undergraduates were conventionally rowdy, there was a lunch party at All Souls. When he came to report the afternoon for a travel piece in *The*

Galaxy, he said that it was the college at which he would find it the highest privilege to reside, the ripest fruit of the old order.

> It is deemed by persons of a reforming turn the best-appointed abuse in a nest of abuses. A commission for the expurgation of the universities has lately been appointed by Parliament to look into it—a commission armed with a gigantic broom, which is to sweep away all the fine old ivied and cobwebbed improprieties. . . . This delightful spot exists for the satisfaction of a small society of Fellows who, having no dreary instruction to administer, no noisy hobbledehoys to govern, no obligations but toward their own culture, no care save for learning as learning and truth as truth, are presumably the happiest and the most charming people in the world.[51]

There was a party in the beautiful gardens of Worcester College—charming lawns and spreading trees, music of Grenadier Guards, iced drinks in striped marquees, mild flirtation of youthful gownsmen and bemuslined maidens—and then a quiet dinner with "the little dons" in common room at Oriel; old portraits on the walls and great windows opened upon the ancient court, where the afternoon light was fading in the stillness, and at dinner,

> superior talk upon current topics, and over all the peculiar air of Oxford—the air of liberty to care for the things of the mind assured and secured by machinery which is in itself a satisfaction to sense.[52]

This was not precisely a portrait, but a fantasy of what college might have been to him, had he not been denied it; an image of loss, like the one Virginia Woolf would paint fifty years later, almost on the same spot: a vision of a room of his own, of freedom from care.

As to the fraternity of actual Oxonians, he sometimes took a more jaundiced view, although this, too, may have been colored by the sense of loss. He grew sarcastic about the characteristic "aesthetic bachelor of a certain age." John A. Symonds, for instance, after a meeting at lunch in London, had invited James down to his modest house in Clifton. Symonds was known for his work celebrating the Greek ideal, and he had been a prominent member of an Oxford circle whose evocations of same-sex love had pressed the limits of what could be said. He was a leading figure in the aesthetic movement, the English followers of Gautier's doctrine of art as a form of pleasure. Now he had published the first volume of a masterwork, *The Renaissance in Italy*, in which he made the great masters of Italian art the originators of aestheticism.[53] He was a figure who represented choices that James had rejected: he had married and fathered a child, despite his all but open celebration of love for young men; he had evidently used his wife as a mask.

James described his visit to Symonds only in a short story, "The Author of *Beltraffio*," in which a young American author calls on a Symonds-like figure at his house in the country; the Symonds figure speaks more openly than he did in his printed works, and regrets his fearful inability to speak the whole truth.[54] In the story, it appears to the American visitor that Symonds's marriage is part of the screen of concealment he has erected around himself; the wife herself is portrayed as wearily knowing, too late, that she has been used in this way.[55]

James had an almost physical repulsion from the immorality that Symonds's marriage represented to him. The man's selfishness was expressed in his perverse appearance and manner. In his letters of this time, James also expressed, not for the first time, a vigorous dislike of effeminacy in men. He wanted men and women to play their parts, to wear their proper costumes, in society. And physical beauty was a matter of great importance to him. Life was an art that depended upon form. But there was an uncharacteristic violence in his expressions that hinted of uneasiness, perhaps a wish to distance himself. When he observed some of the more celebrated Oxonians at the Athenaeum, he seemingly could not contain his revulsion, at least in his letters home:

Lecky the historian, & Green ditto (author of Alice's favorite work— the fat volume which she gave me) have just come & seated themselves in front of me: 2 such grotesque specimens of the rickety, intellectual Oxford cad[56] that I can't forbear mentioning them. Only Du Maurier, in *Punch*, could do them justice; & if Alice could see in the flesh her little wizened, crawling Green, with eyes like ill-made button-holes, she would take to her bed for a month. . . .[57]

The drooping, lackadaisical *Lecky* stands before me at this instant, & if I had only the pen of a Du Maurier I would make you die with laughing at his lolling head, his languid eyes & his willowy limbs.[58]

The Oxford aesthete, the acolyte of selfishness, of art as pleasure, would become the villain of his English tales.[59] And yet Oxford itself continued to represent his ideal of community, seen through his own friends' eyes and colored with his own imagination of what it would have been for him.[60] And so, indeed, he saw all of social England, the world of the walled gardens of his imagination. It was an ideal of community—if only it could have been freed of the injustices that were so much a part of its formation.

Early in March, toward the end of this first winter, he had had a chance to see a representative gathering of London's four millions, the great mass of people whose labor in a certain sense made all this beauty possible. It was the funeral of George Odger, a working-class radical who had campaigned futilely for election to Parliament. Only property owners could vote or hold seats in Parliament. The vast procession of the propertyless that followed Odger's hearse proceeded down the broad expanse of Piccadilly, and James climbed into the high seat of a hansom cab to watch. It was the first and finest sunny day of the dawning spring.

> The hearse was followed by a very few carriages, but the *cortège* of pedestrians stretched away in the sunshine, up and down the classic decorum of Piccadilly, on a scale highly impressive. Here and there the line was broken by a small brass band—one of those bands of itinerant Germans that play for coppers beneath lodging-house windows; but for the rest it was compactly made up of what the newspapers call the dregs of the population. It was the London rabble, the metropolitan mob, men and women, boys and girls, the decent poor and the indecent, who had scrambled into the ranks as they gathered them up on their passage, and were making a sort of solemn "lark" of it. Very solemn it all was—perfectly proper and undemonstrative. They shuffled along in an interminable line, and as I looked at them out of the front of my hansom I seemed to be having a sort of panoramic view of the under side, the wrong side, of the London world . . . of strange, pale, mouldy paupers who blinked and stumbled in the Piccadilly sunshine. I have no space to describe them more minutely, but I found the whole affair vaguely yet portentously suggestive.[61]

The portentous air of the radical, even revolutionary procession was met by none of the signals of alarm that would have greeted it in Paris.

There were no mounted Horse Guards with weapons at the ready; there was no effort to suppress the demonstration.

> It was this that I found impressive as I watched the manifestation of Mr. Odger's underfed partisans—the fact that the mighty mob could march along and do its errand while the excellent quiet policemen . . . stood by simply to see that the channel was kept clear and comfortable.[62]

It was a momentous spring. At the Easter season, the czar declared war on Turkey; the declaration had the quality of a holy war in behalf of the Christian Slavs, whom the Turks had so brutally repressed. From Moscow came money and volunteers to help the insurgents in Bosnia, Herzogovina, Croatia, and Bulgaria. A Greater Serbia and a Christian Bulgaria were to be carved out from the rival empires of Austria and Turkey. These new nations were to be united to Russia by ties of blood and religion, the new ideology of race.

Commerce flowed along the sea-lanes and on the railroads of the empire. It flowed through the great modern steel-and-glass railroad stations, vaulted like cathedrals. In the vast halls of Paddington and Euston stations, James loved to visit the gaslit bookstalls, centers of warmth and light in the smoky caverns. They gave him the idea that literature, too, was a splendid commodity like opium or gold, a dazzling essence. And in the early spring he had the intense pleasure of seeing in the bookstalls a pirated edition—the symbol of popular success—of his *American*, with a colorful illustrated cover.[63] He had known nothing about it, and of course would receive nothing for it. And yet there it was among the glittering spoils of the new Venetian republic.

Even a political post for a moment seemed to beckon. The election of Rutherford B. Hayes as president of the United States had interesting repercussions for James in Great Britain. Hayes was a relation of Elinor Howells, and Bill Howells, editor of the leading Republican literary journal, had supported the victorious candidate. Howells now freely helped his friends to share in the spoils of victory, appointments in the new administration. He lobbied vigorously for Lowell, who was given the post of ambassador to Spain. Then Lowell requested the appointment of Henry James as his secretary. This was more than the president was willing to grant, however; the State Department had its own candidate. After a brief flurry of excitement, and the prospect of a salary and leisure, by the summer of 1877 James knew it was not to be. He was not sorry. He wrote a little impatiently to his family, who were supporting the appointment for him, "There would have been only a moderate salary, and a great deal of annoying work, which I should have both disliked and not known how to do."[64]

In England a Tory government—an energetic, even youthful conservative administration—was in power for the first time in forty years. The prime minister, Benjamin Disraeli, was extending and strengthening the empire. He annexed the Transvaal in April, laying the premise for eventual war with the Boers of South Africa; and he purchased the khedive of Egypt's controlling shares in the Suez Canal. The British Parliament conferred upon the queen, at his request, the new title Empress of India; the great trade routes of the Western world, over which Constantinople and Venice had battled for centuries, were now controlled by the British navy.

James was fascinated and excited by the sense of London's power. Soon, it appeared, England would intervene decisively in the conflict in the Balkans. James could not refrain from viewing the spectacle as a performance, and hoping that England would play its part.

> In the difficult days that are now elapsing a sympathizing stranger finds his meditations singularly quickened. It is the imperial element in English history that he has chiefly cared for, and he finds himself wondering whether the imperial epoch is completely closed. It is a moment when all the nations of Europe seem to be doing something, and he . . . wishes that England *do* something—something striking and powerful, which should be at once characteristic and unexpected. . . . Can't she occupy Egypt? The "Spectator" considers this her moral duty—enquires even whether she has a right *not* to bestow the blessings of her beneficent rule upon the downtrodden Fellaheen. . . . Mr. Gladstone had said that England had much more urgent duties than the occupation of Egypt: she had to attend to the great questions of—What were the great questions? Those of local taxation and the liquor laws! Local taxation and the liquor laws! The phrase, to my ears, just then, sounded squalid. These were not the things I had been thinking of. . . .[65]

Mr. Gladstone perhaps was right, morally speaking, but a spectator could not help hoping for a dramatic extension of the empire at the expense of the despised Turks. He wished the Liberals would show characteristic English energy.[66] The Disraeli government had it, but

Disraeli was allying himself with the sultan of Turkey; there were rumors the Tories would bring England into the war on Turkey's side.

> This I can't believe; though it is all that is talked about. . . .[67] There is
> infinite cynicism and brutality in the Tory government. The sneering
> way in which most people here speak of the subject races of Turkey
> & their sufferings is something too brutally cynical. . . .[68]

He could not bear the Tory sentiment, and was more indignant than he had been concerning public affairs since the conclusion of the Civil War. But public life was a spectacle in which he did not expect to participate directly, except as a writer of books. He was never to play any great role in politics, which, like commerce, he understood only from a distance; nor was he to play a great part in the festivities of the London season, the great carnival of entertainments that accompanied the sitting of Parliament. The season was essentially public, a sort of Protestant carnival, in which the masks were not of velvet or silk but of wonderful deceptive flesh and blood.[69] He did not go to the after-dinner parties that lasted almost until dawn; when he began to receive these invitations, he refused them. Late-night parties were not conducive to work the next morning, and were not profitable in themselves.[70] One read about them in the newspapers; and if one didn't attend the events that were reported in the newspapers, one was held not to be in society at all. But James was not a public man. He was a man of letters, it was true, a theorist and writer of fiction. But his subject was the middle ground, the social space: garden and drawing room, where alliances were created and choices made. And it was in England, above all in London, that this world opened its curtains to him, where he watched, entranced, and where he now joined the actors on the stage.

The American continued its immense popularity; Tauschnitz brought out an edition in English, for sale on the Continent; for this edition Baron Tauschnitz had offered to pay him five hundred marks. There were two pirated German translations, from Stuttgart and Leipzig. The editor of the fashionable new *Century* magazine asked him to write his impressions of England, and Leslie Stephen asked him to do something for *The Cornhill Magazine*.

He had lingered in England during that first summer, at first enticed by the pleasures of the countryside, although he had promised to come to the Bootts in Florence in the fall. He lingered past the time he had intended, and waited in empty and uncomfortable London, feeling that he was losing precious time;[71] he was waiting with increasing impatience for Zhukovsky's return to Paris.

> I think I should hardly have courage to write to you dear Lizzie, this morning, if I had not received your letter from Lucerne last night. . . . I am happy to be able immediately to add that I depart day after tomorrow (on the 9th [of September]) for Paris. I won't tell you when I expect to arrive in Italy, for you must be weary of my procrastinations & (apparently) faithless assurances. I will only say that it will be on the very 1st day that this enchanting event becomes possible. I have (to tell the truth, the whole truth &c.) entered into a promise with my friend Zhukovsky (the Russian whom you will remember) to stay with him—a while before I go southwards. He is ill, unhappy, impoverished & generally uncomfortable by reason of this horrible [war in the Balkans].[72]

21

HENRY JAMES BECOMES
A COSMOPOLITE

Great Britain did not enter the war, but it shared in the spoils. The
Russian armies recovered from their first reverses and advanced
upon Constantinople. Disraeli led the European powers in negotiations that halted this advance, and England was rewarded for
her intervention with concessions from the Turks in North Africa
and the eastern Mediterranean. James fumed at Disraeli, adopting
Zhukovsky's rather personal view of the matter: the old Jew had not
treated the czar with respect.[1]

In America, Grace Norton's beloved sister, Jane, had died, and
Grace was bereaved and alone.

> I want greatly to write to you, & yet I can't attempt to write you a
> letter of what is called "consolation." I can really only tell you that I
> constantly think of you—think of you & think of Jane with an equal

personal tenderness. I have been thinking too that when such a nature as Jane's becomes simply a silent memory to those who have known it, the beautiful form it puts on is almost an unmitigated rebuke to sadness.[2] Unable as I am to believe in the complete extinction of anything that has been sentient as human nature is sentient I feel as if a spirit like Jane's must even enjoy our way of thinking of it—be glad of the way in which what we call regret images what we know of it. Your mind must be full of the shadow of the future, but I suppose you are learning every day that simply living to a certain extent dissipates shadows. The continuous present is always less & less obscure. But there is no pang, dear Grace, in your sense of loss that I can't feel the force of. Give my friendliest love to your mother & to Charles. I won't talk to your sadness, or to theirs, but only to your serenity.[3]

He had his private religion, his core of selfhood, and now after fifteen years of struggle he had a place in the world, if not precisely a home; he had an identity. He was a cosmopolitan man of letters, and in dress, manner, and speech an English bachelor. He had grown stout, which at thirty-four was becoming. His silk top hat, tightly furled umbrella, and boots were gleaming black. A high forehead and rich brown beard were set off by a gleaming white collar and a few glints of color: a gold watch chain, a Parisian necktie. It was not a self-revealing costume, but neither was it false.

I am fast becoming a good enough Englishman to respect inveterately my own habits and do, wherever I may be, only exactly what I want. This is the secret of prosperity here—provided of course one has a certain number of sociable and conformable habits, and civil inclinations, as a starting-point. After that, the more positive your idiosyncrasies the more positive the convenience.[4]

Yet when the question arose, he was patriotically American. In truth, he saw both Europe and America from a certain distance. He confided to Grace Norton that his uprooted childhood had made of him a "cosmopolite," a good deal more of one than the average Briton of culture, and to be a cosmopolite was to be of necessity a good deal alone.[5] He mused upon the question for his audience in America:

It is hard to say exactly what is the profit of comparing one race with another, and weighing in opposed groups the manners and customs

378 Solitude and Power

of neighboring countries; but it is certain that as we move about the world we constantly indulge in this exercise. This is especially the case if we happen to be infected with the baleful spirit of the cosmopolite—that uncomfortable consequence of seeing many lands and feeling at home in none. To be a cosmopolite is not, I think, an ideal; the ideal should be a concentrated patriot. Being a cosmopolite is an accident, but one must make the best of it.[6]

His life, in short, was a series of compromises, of choices between limited alternatives. He was a bachelor, and would not marry,[7] and he lacked the means to make a home, an establishment of his own. He might have married well, of course, and acquired both wealth and an establishment. He felt himself quite capable of marrying and having children. But while he did not object to, and even enjoyed, putting on his conventional costume, his tall hat and furled umbrella, when he went into society, marriage would have been a greater affirmation of the role than he cared to make.

> If I were to marry, I would be guilty in my own eyes of an inconsistency. . . . I am not moved to that way, because I think my opinion of life on the whole good enough. I am attached to it, I am used to it— it doesn't in any way incapacitate or paralyze me (on the contrary), and it doesn't involve any particular injustice to anyone, least of all to myself. Then there are other impressions. An amiable bachelor here & there doesn't strike me as at all amiss, & I think he too may forward the cause of civilization.[8]

Thus he unburdened himself to Grace Norton, herself a confirmed spinster, who answered by sending him an essay on the duty to marry, and its charms. But this was not a topic that he considered open for discussion. He had long ago settled the matter—marriage was not consistent with his sense of his calling. But he did not like to be self-important about this, and with Grace he made light of his sense of having a demon, a genius.

> Your essay on matrimony is charming & ought to be published somewhere—in the *Fortnightly* or the *Cornhill*. My single individuality is quite unworthy of it. Still, I shall not make it public; I shall make it private. That is I shall take it to my heart & assent to everything it contains. But I shall not marry, all the same. I am happy enough as it is,

& am convinced that if I should go further, I should fare worse. I am too good a bachelor to spoil. That sounds conceited—but one may be conceited, in self-defense, about a position with which the rest of the world associates a certain idea of the ridiculous.[9]

His intimate relations were in Paris and Rome, and the round of travels among London, Paris, and the cities of Italy that he had begun was the only home he had ever really known. To a degree, denied the possibility of completion in his own life, he lived for others, and, imaginatively, lived through them. With unremitting energy, through letters and regular visits, he kept up his extended family, his circle of friends and acquaintances, scattered over two continents. He sat down to his writing desk at the front windows on Bolton Street late in the evening, after returning from dinner, and wearily sifted the letters waiting for reply:

Dear Tom—I have before me your last letter & am appalled at the date—nothing less than Dec. 31st. But you will pardon my silence when I tell you that I am fairly crushed by the weight of correspondence imposed upon me by the fact of my expatriation—combined with the fact that so many of my friends live on the continent. This gives me an eternity of letters to write; & often I stagger beneath the burden. Therefore, even now, I must be brief. . . .[10]

He had taken up what would be a growing, lifelong, labor of making introductions—of linking and forging alliances. Day after day, he introduced Britons to America, and Americans to Britain, with patience and skill: Lady Hamilton Gordon to Lizzie Boott; Frederick H. Myers to William James; John Morley to Tom Perry; Thomas Huxley to American men of science, Lady Huxley to American educators. A steady stream of American mothers and daughters, male and female artists and writers, seeking access to London society, passed through his parlor. When Lowell, in the spring of 1880, became minister to Great Britain, James became in many ways his collaborator. A character began to appear regularly in his stories: a skillful gatekeeper of London society, an often weary, middle-aged person.

He maintained his ties with his family and America, however tenuously, and felt a little closer to them in London than he had in Paris. William remained at home, but he was becoming a teacher, and had settled into the task of instructing undergraduates in biology.

Father was growing more frail and was ever more often ill. He had invested in one last utopian enterprise, James R. Osgood's tangled publishing business; a canal scheme had gotten mixed up in it somehow,
and Father was losing a great deal of money, which he could ill afford
to do. The publishing house itself was on the way to bankruptcy. Alice
was more important to her father than ever, but her life had begun to
take her away from him. She was comparatively healthy and busy, a
history professor in the correspondence school that she, Fanny Morse,
and Katharine Loring had founded.

> I wish you could know Katharine Loring [Alice wrote], she is a most
> wonderful being. She has all the mere brute superiority which distin-
> guishes man from woman combined with all the distinctively femi-
> nine virtues. There is nothing she cannot do from hewing wood &
> drawing water to driving run-away horses & educating all the women
> in America.[11]

She and Loring had gradually become intimate friends, after their
meeting six years earlier,[12] a friendship that would continue until the
end of her life. The year before, Alice had borrowed twenty-five hundred dollars from her father and built a cottage near the seashore, at
Manchester, close to Loring's home, where she now spent much of her
time when she could be spared from her own home.[13] She was flourishing, and James took great pleasure in the friendship that was having this beneficent effect,[14] and in telling Alice that travelers came to
London speaking of her beauty and charm.[15] Alice herself began to
think of paying long visits to England, and Henry wrote to welcome
her, and to renew what had now become a shared fantasy: "I hope that
another year or so of prosperity in London will give me a little dwelling
(of some sort) of my own, where I may offer you hospitality."[16]

His year in London had transformed him; when he returned to
Paris in mid-September 1877, James was a man of letters with a place
in the world. He took an apartment on the Right Bank for a month,
and waited a little impatiently for Zhukovsky to arrive. Ivan Turgenev
came into town and breakfasted with him; he visited the Nicholas
Turgenevs at their palatial country estate, where Ivan joined them at
breakfast and was "magnificent." Afterward, James went to see the
curious little *dacha* that Turgenev had built for himself nearby, beside
the Viardots'.[17]

Fanny Kemble was in Paris, and Theodore Child; James saw them,
and dined with "good old" Huntington. Eventually Zhukovsky re-

turned. At least for a few weeks there was a most congenial circle of men in Paris, but it was evidently Zhukovsky who drew and kept James there. He lingered, and was evasive in letters to the Bootts about his plans.[18] The weather was clear and cold, and very pleasant, and when he did write to Elizabeth at last, he continued to put her off. He would come soon to Florence, where she was, or perhaps would join her in Rome after the first of November.[19] Even after the lease on his flat expired, he lingered a few days longer; but when the moment for departure came at last, "for various reasons" he still was little disposed to leave.[20] Yet the visit must come to an end; James certainly did not wish to overstay his welcome. For the moment, he was the unhappy Zhukovsky's benevolent and loving mentor,[21] and made no demands for himself. When the visit was over he left for Italy, to join the Bootts and Anne Bartlett in Florence at the end of October.

Florence suited his mood; it seemed empty, melancholy, bank-rupted by the removal of the capital to Rome. Florence was becoming an old, sleeping, soundless city again. James spent hours in the walled garden of the Bootts' rented villa on the crest of Bellosguardo Hill, sitting in the autumn sunshine and staring stupidly at the never-to-be-enough-appreciated view of the little city of Florence among its mountains.[22] A few days later, he, the Bootts, and Anne Bartlett all traveled together to Rome. For a while, even in Rome, he was sad and out of temper. But the sunny weather was inexpressibly pleasant, and the Bootts made a warm center, almost a home, from which he could venture out to visit the other pleasures of the old city. He was only thirty-four years old, after all, and there was no disapproving presence at his elbow. An initial impatience with lassitude, an irritable wish to get back to London and to work, dissipated;[23] soon the languor of Italy had "potently taken possession" of him, and he was comforted for his solitude.[24]

The Bootts were remarkably happy. It was two years since he had seen them last, and Francis—who had been gravely ill the previous winter—was older and more frail, and still coughed distressingly, but his manner was easier, and he had lost some of his severities. Perhaps the illness had softened him. In the previous winter, thinking he was dying, he had summoned Anne Bartlett to his bedside and committed Lizzie to her keeping; she was more precious to him than ever. And as to her, James observed,

> Lizzie is the same noiseless little active & productive person as ever.
> She is extremely nice, & their life in Rome is a very happy & com-

fortable one. Frank's devotion to his daughter is more intense & absorbing than ever & his unremitting attention to every stroke that she draws or paints, half-touching, half-amusing. . . .[25]

She is happier I imagine than she has ever been, in a sort of antique friendship with the excellent Miss Bartlett.[26]

James made a jocular escutcheon for his two friends—a crossed riding crop and painter's maulstick. When Anne and Lizzie united in denouncing the unhappy ending he had given *The American*, he said he felt rapped about the head with each of these instruments, but that the pleasure and the honor were greater than the pain.[27]

After your approval, *à toute deux*, nothing could give me greater delight than your censures; I indeed am not sure that the thought of moving you to wrath—noble, indignant, magnanimous emotion—has not something even more exquisitely grateful than the idea of your simple tame satisfaction. Generous, admirable, sublime you are, both of you, & I kiss the hem of your garments: that, namely, of Miss Bartlett's riding habit, and your (Miss Boott's) painting blouse. . . . I salute you both to the earth, & adore you completely . . . [Let us] love & admire each other. In that we can't differ.[28]

The air seemed filled with generous, sensual affection, a sort of condensation of the spirit of Rome, to which he entirely surrendered himself for a brief month. But he could not remain through the winter; as always, it was impossible for him to work in Rome.

If I had had no work to do I should certainly have remained in Rome where the prospect of a winter of tender softness & mildness seemed delicious. But it is no place to work & it leads to nothing. My ugly, dusky London will lead to much more.[29]

In mid-December, therefore, he returned to his flat in London.[30] A sort of acrid sleet fell from the sky, and he was obliged to light his candle in the mornings again. "Oh, the foggy Philistinism, the grimy ugliness, of London! After one has been tasting again of the freer intellectual, moral, sensual, life of the Continent, it seems very overwhelming."[31]

He spent the Christmas holiday, always difficult and fraught with risks of depression, with Fanny Kemble at her daughter's house at Stratford-on-Avon. The weather was brilliant, and the picturesque old house, into which the Leighs had only just settled themselves, was charming. It had once been a sort of convalescent hospital, founded in the fourteenth century by the monks of Worcester Abbey, and with its big fires and hangings of holly and mistletoe, it helped him through the holiday.[32] On Christmas Day, there was tea and plum cake for a table full of red-cheeked children belonging to the coachman, the gardener, and the household servants. The little girls bobbed curtsies and the boys tugged salutes at their forelocks in a quaintly old-fashioned manner.[33] James attended services with the family at Shakespeare's church in Stratford, and this part of the visit remained prominent in his memory. To Fanny Kemble, the church was as much a shrine to Shakespeare as to the Deity, but to James's eyes the conjunction only emphasized the ludicrous aspects of an established church. He was not a believer, and he was skeptical as to the true authorship of the plays attributed to the actor named William Shakespeare. He therefore observed the forms of worship with more than a faint sense of the ridiculous, which compounded his sense of playacting the role of an Englishman and a believer. He fashioned the memory of these visits to Stratford into a funny story, a meditation on fancy dress and necessary lies.[34]

On his return to London, the long silence of Mr. Church at *The Galaxy* was explained—the magazine had failed, and its remaining subscription list had been purchased by *The Atlantic*. But *The Atlantic* would hardly consider a long, serious novel from him now. He made haste to offer to Howells a brief serial for *The Atlantic:* a story with the happy ending Howells had demanded—marriages, galore![35] The big novel was set aside for the time being, once again.

He renewed his output of anonymous travel articles and reviews for *The Nation;* but he hoped that by summer, with a serial running in *The Atlantic* and royalties from his various books, he would be able to give these up, at long last, and devote himself solely to serious writing. Then, he thought, when he was freed from the pressure of monthly bills, his real career would begin.[36] He settled at his writing desk, facing the broad, blank wall of Lord Ashburton's house, with a good will. The wall was like a curtain, that soon would lift.[37]

> Dear Lizzie—. . . I don't think my enjoyment of Italy was ever more exquisite than during the last few days in Rome or that my memory of it has ever been more distractedly tender than since I left. . . . And

you, wretched maid, are still revelling, rolling, rollicking, in the Paradise I have abjured! I hate you for it, if I could hate anything in Italy. . . . But I came here with impatience, & since I would have London I have got it with a vengeance. It is positively *slimy* with fog & as dark as Maria's eyes—but by no means as beautiful. . . . I see you there at your little studio window—I see you before the mountain-views in the campagna—you sit gracefully swaying in your saddle & glancing indifferently at the pretty purple mountains—I see you everywhere & everywhere I may[,] even while I bless you. My blessing, & the rest, is for Miss Bartlett, too . . . My love to yr. father.[38]

How late do you remain in Rome & do you go straight to Florence? I envy you the sweet labor of feathering your nest at Bellosguardo, & if I were an angel, would pluck the softest plumes from my own wings, to upholster your own peculiar corner.[39]

The brief novel he wrote in the quiet weeks of the new year, *The Europeans*, was a perfect little work of art. He was greatly aided by strict limits—Howells insisted the serial could not take more than one hundred pages. The story was set in America—which was to say, Cambridge, Massachusetts—and peopled with his Cambridge acquaintances, but it was playfully infused with the air of Rome. He imagined a sort of golden age of innocence, just before the vast upheavals of 1848. He took Longfellow's house, and clapped Lowell into it; and turned Howells into a plump, handsome blond parson. James, himself, peeped out from the gray eyes of his heroine, Gertrude, with disconcerting intelligence.

For this light tale he borrowed the plot of Émile Augier's *Adventuress*, the performance of which had made such a deep impression on him eight years earlier in Paris,[40] and which he had just been studying in a new edition.[41] In his loose translation, a cosmopolitan baroness, an adventuress, came with her brother to Cambridge and tried to entrap a wealthy, provincial American cousin into marriage. James was greatly pleased with the combination of the light French form, and his American subject matter.[42] Like a little play, his novel was a series of scenes. In each there was a fixed set of characters who remained in one place, as if on a stage, and the action was advanced by dialogue. This theatrical staging gave crisp shape to a novel for which ordinarily there was no particular form. At the end, the wicked baroness[43] retired in confusion to Europe; her handsome and charming brother,

Felix, married the American girl, Gertrude. There was an interesting little scene in which Gertrude looked up from her reading—*The Arabian Nights*—to see Felix, handsome as Prince Camaralzaman, standing before her.[44]

The serial was a great success when it ran in *The Atlantic* in the summer and fall of 1878, and was quickly issued in book form both by Osgood, in Cambridge, and Macmillan, in London.

In May a letter from William announced his engagement to Alice Gibbens. Henry was pleased, and not surprised; it appeared the engagement had long been delayed because of William's poor health, but in the end William and Alice had decided to disregard his invalidism and simply to marry. Father and Mother were very pleased, and praised Miss Gibbens in the warmest terms. It seemed she was a sort of paragon. Further letters from home revealed that their own Alice had been ill since March, however, of the distresses that afflicted her periodically; Mother hoped that they would clear up soon under a regime of diet, exercise, and constant care. Mother was heavily burdened with the care of Father, of William, whose eyes and back rendered him a near invalid, and with preparations for the wedding. The burden of nursing Alice therefore fell upon Alice's friends Fanny Morse and Katharine Loring.[45]

Henry wrote a sympathetic letter to Alice. She had suffered from the same sort of difficulty in Switzerland, in their long-ago trip with Aunt Kate, and he was sorry not to be at her side to comfort her, as he had been then.[46]

William's wedding followed the announcement with great promptitude. He had escaped the sickroom air of home; Alice for her part seemed pleased and relieved to have William settled. She, like her parents, thought the new Alice, "William's Alice," was a paragon who would take him in hand. The newly married couple went off to a camp in the Adirondacks for a honeymoon that was also meant to be therapeutic for William's various ailments. There was not enough time for Henry even to consider returning for the wedding; when his mother's letter with the announcement arrived, Henry sent his most affectionate greeting to William:

> I have just heard from mother that you had decided to be married on the 10th [June], & as I was divorced from you by an untimely fate on this unique occasion, let me at least repair the injury by giving you, in the most earnest words that my clumsy pen can shape, a tender bridal benediction.[47]

Alice's health improved for a while after William's engagement and marriage;[48] but sometime later that summer, she suffered a new collapse into depression and helpless rage. The deepening of her illness may have coincided with the departure of her dear friend Fanny Morse for Europe and North Africa. The nursing of the invalid thereupon fell almost entirely upon Katharine Loring, who from this time forward became almost a member of the household. Katharine now administered the therapeutic massages that had been prescribed for Alice's hysteria, and these alone calmed her.

The aggravation of Alice's illness was mixed with a deep depression of spirits; it was somehow in the nature of the outbreak that it was directed at her father. Something in the mainspring of her affections had been injured. The memory of the two sensations—the deep injury to her selfhood and the patient grasp of Katharine Loring, like the strong nurse's hands that once bathed the children in the sea—fused into a single image.

Henry seems to have known something of what Alice felt that summer and fall. Her letters have been lost, but she recalled that summer in two passages in her journal, written fifteen years later, when she was deep in her final illness.

> This long slow dying is no doubt instructive, but . . . the fact is, I have been dead so long and it has been simply such a grim shoving of the hours behind me as I faced a ceaseless possible horror, since the hideous summer of '78, when I went down to the deep sea, its dark waters closed over me and I knew neither hope nor peace; that now it's only the shrivelling of an empty pea pod that has to be completed.[49]

The second entry was written after Katharine Loring had administered a massage, which even after fifteen years was the only treatment that relieved Alice's attacks of anxiety:

> These last [anxiety attacks], Katharine has completely under the control of her rhythmic hand, so I go no longer in dread. Oh the wonderful moment when I felt myself floated for the first time into the deep sea of divine *cessation*, and saw all the dear old mysteries and miracles vanish into vapour! That first experience doesn't repeat itself, fortunately, for it might become a seduction.[50]

By the fall, under Loring's care, Alice was beginning to report herself improved, although still in need of constant attention; Alice did not really begin to recover until Katharine took her away from Cambridge the following spring.[51] She wrote to her friends, longingly, of a desire to spend her convalescence with her companion in Europe.[52] And soon, freed from duty to her father by her illness, she and Katharine would indeed join Henry in England, eventually to remain there— after her father's death, and in the face of Aunt Kate's continuing dis-approval—in a household of their own.

In what had become his second family, the Boott household, there also was marrying and deep unhappiness. Anne Bartlett had decided to return to the United States to marry a Texan. The athletic Bartlett, excellent horsewoman as she was, "will break in mustangs, and wear a lassoo over her shoulder, and be the Diana of the Far West," James mildly observed.[53]

Elizabeth Boott had been obliged to revise the plan of her life. There was very little reason for her now to keep her studio in Rome, and if she were to pursue a career as a painter, she felt she must make a mark and sell her pictures in a world capital. James encouraged her to aim for London, to come there herself, or to send him one or two examples of her best work—something striking, something brilliant, that would establish her. And Elizabeth, who had been experiment-ing with decorative art, sent him two paintings of flowers on large wooden panels. They were striking, indeed; James loaded them, in their massive wooden box, into a hansom cab and carried them to an art dealer, Agnew, who praised them very highly. But he only dealt in paintings, in Gainsboroughs, principally, and recommended Trol-lope's, the decoration and furniture room in Belgravia. James dutifully loaded the great box back into the cab, and went on to Trollope's, but the proprietor was away, and he left the pictures with his card.[54]

Thus began a long, weary round of galleries and exhibition rooms. The flower panels were loaded into cabs, carried to galleries where they remained unsold, were moved, and moved again. Lizzie fretted over the price she was asking—twenty pounds plus the gallery's com-mission—but Henry assured her that this was not the obstacle. Eliza-beth thought perhaps other subjects would be better, and sent a series of portraits of children. But these, too, were in the French Impres-sionist manner, and London taste—which had already rejected James Whistler's experiments in impressionism—found them fatally lacking in "finish." Lady Gordon entered the fray in behalf of Elizabeth, and she too tried unsuccessfully to place the flower panels. Henry persevered with the portraits of children, slowly descending the scale from the best galleries to the Decorative Needlework Society, the Woman's Works showroom, and then to a little shop near the British Museum. He argued with gallery owners over the way in which the pictures were hung, and fought to get them advantageously placed. For a long time the pictures stood on his sofa, in the place where Zhukovsky's portrait of Lady Selina Bidwell had been displayed, but no earls or countesses came to see them. At last, most humiliatingly, they went to an auction room, in the hope of recouping some of the expense of the materials that had gone into them, but James was ashamed to report that the portraits of children brought only one pound, from which was deducted six shillings for the auctioneer. Through the whole agony he lay awake at night worrying over the unsold pictures, and, reporting in his monthly letters upon their progress, always advising courage and optimism.[55]

Lizzie held in abeyance her plan to come to London to pursue her career, and in the end gave it up. Her paintings had been shown in Boston to unfavorable reviews, and with the unfriendly reception her pictures had received in London, it seemed necessary to change direction. She decided to go to Munich. The young American painter, Frank Duveneck, whose work she had so much admired in Boston five years earlier, had established a studio near Munich, and was taking pupils.[56]

The duties of friendship and society constantly threatened to drain the resources of energy that James needed for his unremitting struggle to earn enough money and time for his proper work. Macmillan brought out in London a volume of Henry's essays on French writers that had been so long under discussion, *French Poets and Novelists*. This was well received, but sales were modest, and there were no royalty payments. He buckled down to the task of filling magazine pages, and his pockets, in preparation for the serious novel. The anonymous travel pieces he did for *The Nation* were not sufficiently well paid; he asked to become *The Nation*'s London correspondent and to send them regular, signed, political commentaries, for which they paid him more. *The Atlantic* was running his serial, *The Europeans*, and would take no more from him for a time. He wrote a connected series of short stories, like those he had produced in Paris two years before, and sent them to *Harper's* and *Scribner's*, in New York; with *The Galaxy* gone, he began sending stories to a Philadelphia magazine, *Lippincott's*. He continued to decline invitations from the British journals *Cornhill Magazine* and *Twentieth Century*, which simply did not pay as well.

The series of a half-dozen stories he wrote that spring and summer made a pattern. The characters gathered in a boardinghouse in Switzerland or Paris. They were American, British, French, German, Italian; the boardinghouse served as a stage or a laboratory, where the characters were displayed, turned in the light to exhibit their facets, and returned to the surrounding darkness.[57]

These stories were coolly written, and often very funny. Details of dress and manners were carefully described—the muslin, silk, linen, and lace of the ladies' dresses; the way an American businessman pushed his hat forward on his forehead. Over this hard, factual scene played the light of imagination. The brave, innocent American girl was called Daisy, and a cosmopolitan young woman, the moral hope of the future, was Aurora Church. The stories were written rapidly, and often the characters were only types, hardly more than stereotypes. The Americans said, "I guess," and "got to"; the Britons said, "Oh, I say." They often seemed artificial, as if posed for a group portrait: a harassed American businessman, whose pretty, empty-headed wife and daughter were shopping themselves into bankruptcy; an equally pretty and empty-headed young English lord; several little Frenchmen, with nothing in their field of vision except sexual conquest; a fat, blond German scientist who complacently looked forward to the racial conquest of Europe.

Only a few of these characters were surprising or unexpected. Plump, blond Mrs. Church, the mother of Aurora, approaching forty, with her wide experience of European pensions and her definite views, seemed to have an inner life, a reality denied to the other characters. She was a thoroughly Europeanized American, well but plainly dressed, rather careful with money. She was often to be found sitting alone, with a book in her hand, very much as James himself was likely to be. Her peculiarity was a settled determination to seek only the best, the very best.

And there was Diana Belfield, his American heroine: a tall, light figure, her nobly poised head weighted with a coronal of auburn braids, her frank, quick glance, and her rapid gliding step like that of Mary Temple. She now traveled through Europe with a female cousin, with whom she had formed an intimate, antique friendship.[58]

And there was Daisy Miller, of Schenectady, New York—traveling in Europe for the first time, with her helpless, ignorant mother and her uncivilized little brother. Daisy was an American type: young and wealthy, rather ignorant and common, but she was not merely a type, she was remarkably passionate and courageous, in her own characteristic way. She lacked, however, a mentor for her initiation into life.

> She was dressed in white muslin, with a hundred frills and flounces, and knots of pale-colored ribbon. She was bare-headed; but she balanced in her hand a large parasol, with a deep border of embroidery; and she was strikingly, admirably, pretty. "How pretty they are!" thought Winterbourne, straightening himself in his seat, as if he were prepared to rise.[59]

The cosmopolitan Winterbourne, who might have helped Daisy, saw her only as a type, as an "American girl," as a potential object of his attentions, and so he failed to befriend her. This failure proved to be fatal to her. For she was quite unprotected, and although she was driven by eager passions, she was absolutely innocent.

> "I'm very fond of society, and I have always had a great deal of it. I don't mean only in Schenectady, but in New York. I used to go to New York every winter. In New York I had lots of society, last winter I had seventeen dinners given me; and three of them were by gentlemen," added Daisy Miller. "I have more friends in Schenectady than in New York—more gentleman friends; and more young lady friends, too," she resumed in a moment. She paused again for an instant; she was looking at Winterbourne with all her prettiness in her lively eyes and in her light, slightly monotonous smile. "I have always had," she said, "a great deal of gentlemen's society."[60]

Cold-blooded Winterbourne had lived for many years in Geneva; he had lost his spontaneous instinct. He had known, in Europe, two or three women, provided for respectability's sake with husbands, who were great coquettes—dangerous, terrible women, with whom one's relations were liable to take a serious turn. But this young girl was not a coquette in that sense; she was only, he thought, a pretty American flirt. This was the only category in which he could place her. He condescended, and hesitated, and kept his distance.

She ventured on alone, bravely, into the European world. She was seen going about alone at night with a young Italian, her mother's servant, which caused a scandal among the Americans. She went with him to see the Colosseum in the moonlight, defiant of all dangers, and

Winterbourne gave up on her. In the end, shockingly, she died of the disease contracted that night, from the bad air that rose from the marshes of Rome. Standing rather coolly at her grave, Winterbourne came to see his own responsibility in the matter, but the understanding did not affect him greatly.

Lippincott's refused the story of "Daisy Miller," returning it without comment, which was alarming. James showed it to a friend, who said perhaps the Philadelphia editor had found it an "outrage on American girlhood"; but on later reflection, James thought perhaps the story was simply too long.[61] He did not risk submitting it to another American magazine, however, and instead gave it to Leslie Stephen, who had been asking for something for *The Cornhill*. It appeared in the June and July numbers, and was an immediate hit in London, where people were perfectly content to treat Daisy as typical. The *Spectator* praised it; the story and its author were talked of and mentioned in the newspapers, and James was particularly encouraged because it seemed that the story was understood.

He had found an audience, in London, in a matter of months.[62] Young Frederick Macmillan and he began to dine frequently, and the publisher seemed to accept him as a critic, a man of letters. Macmillan's, early the following year, brought out two volumes of the boardinghouse stories in which "Daisy Miller" was given pride of place; asked him to do a book on Hawthorne, and another on Dickens; and then published yet another collection of his short stories.[63]

Magazines in Boston and New York reprinted the story of Daisy Miller without permission,[64] and to forestall further piracies he quickly authorized *Harper's* to publish it as a pamphlet, price twenty cents; and this too did very well indeed, selling ten thousand copies. His royalty was only the usual 10 percent, however—if only he had known beforehand what a success it would be, he could have driven a harder bargain—and so he received only two hundred dollars for his huge American sales. But, as he wrote home, one rarely earned much from a first success.[65] The important thing was that he had been launched. American newspapers gave the story warm notices; they always found it easier to see the merits of work that had already succeeded in London.[66] They approved of James's highly principled, didactic intentions; the story should be a valuable lesson to American girls and their families.[67]

The American women themselves were more divided in opinion. "Harry James has waked up all the women with his 'Daisy Miller,' "

Howells bemusedly reported to Lowell. "The thing went so far that society almost divided itself into Daisy Millerites and anti-Daisy Millerites. . . ."[68] Women were indeed in conflict on the question of Daisy Miller, and many were angry with James. Elizabeth Lynn Lynton, a writer on political questions, a friend of the Bootts, sent him a long letter asking—as if Daisy Miller were an actual person— whether in truth she was "obstinate and defying," or whether on the contrary she was only "superficial and careless."[69] James answered, a trifle disingenuously:

> The whole idea of the story is the little tragedy of a light, thin, natu-
> ral, unsuspecting creature being sacrificed as it were to a social rum-
> pus that went on quite over her head. . . .[70]

This was true, in its way, but there was more to it than that. Daisy's courage, her liberty, had been sacrificed not to gossip but to disease; she was not only an innocent but a victim, and it was her beautiful helplessness, the vulnerability revealed by her death, that was the secret of her attractiveness.

James remained in London through the summer and fall, with only a brief excursion to Scotland to interrupt the monotony and the heat. He could not afford another visit to the Continent just then; all of his new prosperity was needed to pay the debts of the past year. Writing steadily, he finished his international boardinghouse stories, and corrected proofs for Macmillan's book edition of *The Europeans*. He hastened to give inscribed copies of the book to Fanny Kemble, Lord Houghton, and others of Fanny's circle when it appeared in the fall.[71]

The autumn was notable in memory for visits to Tennyson and George Eliot. It was late October, and both were in the country. Fanny Kemble's friend Mrs. Greville, who seemed to James the very personification of early Victorian good nature and innocent fatuity, had invited him for a weekend. Her little cottage in Surrey, with its red-shaded candles, remained with him, inexplicably, as the representative of that whole era, of the innocent complacency of those who stood on the right side of the social line, and were respectable.[72]

James and Mrs. Greville drove in her brougham through the cold rain to have lunch with Tennyson at Aldworth, on the noble height of Blackdown. The poet laureate was not in the least the person that he had imagined; James experienced something like the shock he had

had on meeting Renan. Tennyson was not ugly, but he was not in the least graceful or refined; he was not, in fact, Tennysonian. His talk ran to questions of food and wine. When they were seated in the drawing room, Mrs. Greville, to James's horror, began to recite, badly, the poet's own work "Locksley Hall" while Tennyson growled along and submitted. When they began to talk, however, it appeared that Tennyson, incredibly, inconceivably, had read one of James's stories—not only read but admired, and not only admired but understandingly referred to it; James could hardly believe his ears. The old man said it was more to his taste than anything else of the kind; the author of "In Memoriam" had liked his story, and James felt that a kind of grace had been conferred upon him.[73]

After lunch, Tennyson brought James up to his study, and offered to recite something, whatever James cared to hear; and the younger man named "Locksley Hall," which Mrs. Greville had attempted. "I sat in one of the windows that hung over space," he recalled for Miss Bosanquet, a lifetime later, "noting how the windy, watery autumn day, sometimes sheeting it all with rain, called up the dreary, dreary moorland or the long dun wolds; I pinched myself for the determination of my identity, and hung on the reader's deep-voiced chant. . . ."[74] It was an extraordinary moment—and yet James was unmoved, almost disappointed. Tennyson read in a solemn, sonorous chant,[75] and the wonderful poem, into which James, reading it as a young man, had once put so much of his own thought and feeling, seemed to empty itself.

> "When I dipt into the future, far as human eye could see,
>   Saw the Vision of the world, and all the wonders that would be . . .
>
> "Saw the heavens fill with commerce, argosies of magic sails,
>   Pilots of the purple twilight, dropping down with costly bales:
>
> "Heard the heavens fill with shouting, and there rain'd a ghastly dew
>   From the nations' airy navies grappling in the central blue; . . .
>
> "Not in vain the distance beacons. Forward, forward let us range;
>   Let the great world spin for ever down the ringing grooves of change."

The deep, growling song continued, and as it went on James strangely felt more and more that these favorite verses were being drained of meaning. Tennyson did not give the poem a gloss of intelligence; his was a song by the fireside, a celebration, a performance complete in itself, opaque. Tennyson was not a poet, like Browning, but a bard—a singer.[76] In later years, when James read poetry aloud—especially the poetry of Whitman, the American bard—he would chant the lines as Tennyson had done.[77] But on that October afternoon in 1878 he was still a young man, not a singer but a writer of texts, and he was disappointed.

On the next day Mrs. Greville brought him to see George Eliot and Henry Lewes in their own little house, Witley Villa. On the dreadful, cold, and rainy Sunday when they called, the novelist and her husband were alone, huddled beside their fire. George Eliot was cordial, benign, commiserating; she seemed glad to have the dreary afternoon interrupted. She asked about the Nortons, and James gave her their news.[78] Henry Lewes sat on the other side of the fireplace and said almost nothing at all, but the brief visit passed painlessly, to James's relief, who had been worried about their welcome. When he and Mrs. Greville were on the point of departure, Lewes saw them to the door and briefly became talkative as he saw them out—from relief, James suspected. And as James handed Mrs. Greville into the carriage in the rain under a raised umbrella, Lewes suddenly called him back. Mrs. Greville had lent them a book, and he must return it! James returned to the door, and waited.

> I still see him reissue from the room we had just left and hurry toward me across the hall shaking high the pair of blue-bound volumes. . . . "Ah those books—take them away, please, away, away!"—I hear him unreservedly plead while he thrusts them again at me, and I scurry back into our conveyance. . . .[79]

Seated at last in the carriage, James gradually realized that the books in his hand were the two slim volumes of his own *The Europeans*, an inscribed copy of which he had given to the misguided Mrs. Greville, and which she had lent to George Eliot. James, after the first sharp hurt, smiled to himself, but he kept quiet for fear of hurting poor benevolent Mrs. Greville. They rode home in silence, James holding the rejected books and trying not to laugh.[80]

On his return to London he began a notebook of topics and characters and words, of *names*, that had occurred to him but he could not stop to use. He was writing at top speed, and yet his mind was filled with still more visions than he had time for.

November 7, 1878.—A young Englishman, travelling in Italy twenty years ago, meets, in some old town—Perugia, Siena, Ravenna—two ladies, a mother & daughter, with whom he has some momentary relation: the mother a quiet, delicate, interesting, touching, high-bred woman—the portrait of a perfect lady, of the old English school, with a tone of sadness in the picture; the daughter a beautiful, picturesque high-tempered girl; generous, ardent, even tender, but with a good deal of coquetry & a certain amount of hardness. . . .[81]

Names. Mrs. Parlour—Mrs. Sturdy—Mrs. Silverlock . . . Dainty—Slight—Cloake—Beauchemin—Lord Demesne . . . Gilbert Osmond—Raymond Gyves—Mrs. Gift—Name in *Times:* Lucky Da Costa—Name in Knightsbridge—Tagus Shout—Other names: Couch—Bonnycastle—Theory—Cridge—Arrant—Mrs. Tippet—Noad.

He was immensely busy—dining out, weekending, omnivorously consuming London, and writing, writing. In the mornings, after an early breakfast, he wrote stories, essays, travel articles, and a new novel, all his voices speaking at once. In addition to the shorter magazine articles, he was at work more or less simultaneously on his book-length study of Hawthorne for Macmillan, and on two long critical pieces on French authors for the *North American Review.* Macmillan, pleased with his success, was planning to bring out all his previous novels in new editions, and he was now correcting proofs for a reissue of *The American* and a three-volume edition of *Roderick Hudson.* He would have his noon *déjeuner* at the chophouse on Piccadilly or at his club; he had been elected to the liberal Reform Club shortly after his guest membership in the Athenaeum expired. He usually walked to and fro for the sake of the exercise. Then he would go back to writing or correcting proofs, until it was time to dress for dinner. After dinner he would walk home, when the weather permitted, saving the expense of a cab and allowing the fumes of wine and conversation to clear. When he was at home, he would light his candle and work, or write letters, for an hour or two before sleep. In memory, one could hardly distinguish between the vividly imagined and the intensely lived. The letters were as varied in tone as his stories, essays, and reviews—he was alternately son and brother, man of the world, man of letters, courtier, gallant, and friend.

The circles in which he moved were correspondingly diverse. He was collecting materials for a Balzacian portrait of Europe. He spent

Saturday to Monday at the extraordinary, pseudo-Gothic castle where
Horace Walpole, the great leader of society and man of letters of the
eighteenth century, had held court:[82]

> Strawberry Hill is an enchanting place—[it] was filled with a multi-
> tude of "smart" people—the Crown Prince of Sweden, Duchess of
> Manchester, Lord Hartington (whose curiously public intimacy with
> the Duchess carries them everywhere together)—and twenty more
> members of the British peerage. The most entertaining to me was a
> famous old woman—a certain Maria Marchioness of Ailesbury—. . .
> who has been a figure in the London world since time immemorial
> and who looked exactly the same forty years 'ago as she does today.
> On the Sunday morning, coming into breakfast I found her there
> alone, doing sums on the tablecloth. . . .[83]

It was only on long walks in the streets that he had glimpses of
working-class London; but he felt that he had at least a glimpse, aided
by imagination, of every sort of life.

The winter was remarkably severe; there had been deep snowfalls
and hard frosts of a kind that he had not seen since his childhood. He
spent Christmas with Lord Houghton and his young cousin Charles
Gaskell—James now called him Carlo—in Yorkshire. At midnight on
Christmas, in an elevated mood that was delicately balanced on the
edge of dark depression he wrote to Lizzie Boott a long letter. He was
tired, and lonely amid all the company, and weary of the demands of
constant society. A letter from her had been forwarded from his
London lodgings, with the only season's greetings he had received.[84]
He had heard nothing from home for a long time; among the remaining family in Quincy Street only his mother was able to write, and she
was preoccupied with the care of her shrunken family of invalids. His
ties to Cambridge were all but dissolved.

After the first of the year the pace quickened, and designedly he
had no time for depression. For the first time, he went to an engraver
and ordered notepaper—"3, Bolton Street. Piccadilly. W."—in dignified, conventional lettering. Invitations required replies, and in the
winter of 1878–79, he dined out more than one hundred times,[85]
passed on from hostess to guest, who became hostess in turn. He
dined often that season with Hamilton Aïdé, "an amiable—very amiable—literary bachelor, who has charming rooms. . . ."[86] And his

growing prosperity allowed him for the first time to return invitations by entertaining at the Reform.[87]

With the beginning of the London season in the spring, James dined out every weeknight, although he steadily refused to attend the after-dinner parties, and his weekends again were filled with visits to country houses. As an American, he would always be somewhat an outsider, but he was now on close personal terms both with the older generation of the leaders of society and with the younger men and women of his own generation. He had already met and would soon come to know well three future prime ministers—Herbert Asquith, Arthur Balfour, and Lord Rosebery; the future commander in chief of the British armed forces, Sir Garnet Wolsely (as he was then); the leading scientist and future head of the Imperial University, Sir Thomas Huxley; and all the principal men and women of letters and arts. He dined occasionally with the Rabelais Club, of which Matthew Arnold, Thomas Hardy, and Anthony Trollope were all members; he was pleased to learn that Matthew Arnold had called him a "de-ah."

He was a true cosmopolite, a European, and as he reported in a letter home, at a "literary gathering" the famous Edmond About, whose *Tolla* was so influential a part of his own early reading, insisted on being introduced to him.

> About seized me by both hands & told me that what he wished of me
> (beyond the pleasure of making my acquaintance) was that I should
> promise to give him a translation of my next novel. . . .[88]

About insisted on a commitment, for, as he said, James was capable of everything, and would make a great figure in London; and James agreed to provide the advance sheets of his next novel, but in the end nothing came of it. And when two women separately asked Lizzie Boott to intercede for them and obtain permission for German translations, he simply declined. The pirated translations in Germany had failed, and the remainders had been sold for trivial prices, to his deep irritation. The value of his work depended on complexities of meaning, and people who read it in translation for the story were bound to be disappointed. He would rather it not be translated at all.[89]

The new novel, at which indeed he was already at work, was *Confidence*, another hasty composition whose serial publication would give him enough cash to get away from England for an extended time to work at the big, serious book that he had been planning for more than two years. *Scribner's* had asked for a short novel, and this was to be it. The first installments would appear that summer, and would pay his way to Europe. He began in March, and sent the first half of the novel to the publisher just six weeks later. By the fall the novel would have run its course.[90]

The added press of the season, with its breakfasts, lunches, and dinners, the relentless invitations that he found difficult to refuse— these were the lines of connection that he had so diligently constructed. And there was always the burden of love and friendship. William and his Alice were expecting a child, and yet had no money for a house of their own. They were living in rented rooms, and William was desperately writing articles on popular psychology, hoping for a commercial success. Henry carried the articles about to editors, as he had carried Zhukovsky's and Elizabeth Boott's pictures—once again without success.

In May the child was born; it was a son, whom Alice and William named Henry, and in London, Henry James, namesake and godfather, for all the sweet pleasure of this, felt a new burden of duty. London, society, friendship, and the demands of work were overwhelming him. Twice in one letter he returned to the theme:

> I am quite satiated just now with London, its crowds, its dinners, its interruptions, its chatter, its jargon, its topics, its mill-round of "so-called" pleasures. I long for a change—for a good long absence— a bath in a different sort of life, & shall try to get it in the autumn.[91]

And then, again, and with a more desperate note:

> I am much pressed. I know too many people, & shall never again undertake a season in London with work on my hands to do.[92]

As soon as he finished *Confidence*, he promised himself, in another six weeks, he would go to Paris, where he expected to find Zhukovsky. The Russian would have returned to Paris by early September, as usual. The Bootts were in Munich for the summer again, where Lizzie was visiting Frank Duveneck's studio and taking instruction from the young master. They planned to return to Florence in the fall.

James decided to spend some weeks in Paris with Zhukovsky and other friends, and then go on to Italy to visit the Bootts; then he would have his six months' restorative bath of solitude and at last have time and leisure to begin his big novel.[93] He would be prosperous, at last, and could come and go as he liked.

It was presumably with these thoughts in mind that he wrote the second half of *Confidence;* the first half already having appeared, there was no opportunity to harmonize the two. For as it began, it was meant as a tragic, somewhat sensational murder story, but it ended very happily in a pair of marriages.[94]

The initial, murderous setting was a familiar one: a young woman intruded upon the intimate friendship of two men. They each fell in love with her, but one of the men, with characteristic masculine violence, conceived a jealous suspicion. The young woman, Angela, was in truth virtuous, but the violent tragedy would be played out between the two men.

As he sat down to his writing desk on Bolton Street, in the waxing English summer, the two men took on a more distinct resemblance to William and himself. The William character was an angry young amateur scientist; he and the Henry character met in Europe and had their confrontation. They fought over Angela. But now in the second half of the tale, instead of remaining murderous, the William character returned to America, married another woman, and was happy. The Henry character remained with Angela in Europe.

The Henry character and Angela discussed their friends, virtuously scheming to help them, as Henry and Zhukovsky would do, as Henry and Louis De Coppet had done so many years before. The Henry character was curiously free of jealousy; he answered violence with love, and with Angela's masterly help he managed to persuade the William character that he loved his wife, after all.

Henry was very pleased with this novel, and told his friends that it was his best to date, and then he cheerfully prepared for a long visit to the Continent.

Just before leaving London, he met a young man named Robert Louis Stevenson at a lunch for a circle of literary men hosted by Andrew Lang. Present were Edmund Gosse, a pleasant young man of letters, oddly like Bill Howells, whom he also was meeting for the first time, and John Morley, an editor at Macmillan. Stevenson was the youngest of the group, and was the star attraction—he had had a striking success with a pair of travel books. Very tall and very thin, Stevenson had a long, straggling mustache, and lounged, rather than stood, with his hands in his pockets. He was an attractive man, but very young, and to James he seemed (in an inoffensive way) something of

a *poseur*.[95] It would be more than five years before the two men became intimate friends.

James arrived in Paris by the first of September and quickly found
an apartment in the still-empty city, in his old familiar Rue de Luxembourg. He made his presence known to the Turgenevs, Huntington,
Theodore Child, and Henrietta Reubell. Although he sought quiet
and composure, he was unable to be alone, and he paid his usual
calls and had his usual dinners. Andrew Lang and his circle descended
on Paris, and while Lang knew French literature very well, James
was pleased to find that he himself knew Paris better and was able
to show the Britons around. Among their quiet amusements, he conducted Lang and Hamilton Aïdé to Bougival, and introduced them
to Turgenev.

James had expected to find Zhukovsky in Paris, but he quickly
learned that the Russian had quarreled with Princess Urusova and
Pauline Viardot, had given up his studio and gone to Italy. James obtained an address in Venice from the Nicholas Turgenevs, and sent a
letter and a photograph of himself, as one did to establish a more personal note, after their long separation—it had been two years since
they had last met in Paris. James was planning to go on to Italy from
Paris; perhaps he would find Zhukovsky there. In due course a letter
returned from the young Russian.

> My dear friend, this is just to press your hand after a long absence and
> at a moment when I lack the tranquility to tell you everything that I
> have to tell you. I will soon write to you from home, that is from
> Punta di Posilipo, from the Villa Postiglione, half an hour from the
> noisy city of Naples, at the extremity of a point from which one sees,
> to the right, a view of the open sea toward Vesuvius and the Sorrento
> shore, to the left Naples with its profile that laughs and at the same
> time is severely Medieval. But I am surrounded by the adorable gulf,
> like the arms of a true friend, for every time that I have turned to this
> friend, he has soothed me. And your happy and dear face resembles
> my beloved gulf, it was good to see it again, and I thank you.
>
> How charming it would be if you two were united. Come if you
> can. The Villa Postiglione is an admirably well kept pension, clean,
> good food, excellent wine, heavenly view, excellent air. But I won't
> build up hopes that probably will not be realized. The longer I live,
> the less hold that time and distance have on me; you are as present,

as everyday,[96] and as dear as formerly. A long talk with you certainly would be a great joy, but if that cannot be, let us write to each other. I will be back in Naples, I hope, by October 7.[97]

There would be other guests. Zhukovsky explained that he had invited his sister, Alexandra, and her husband, Count Belyevski, and several others, to join him in the pension at Posilipo. The villa would be a house "filled with friends," and Henry was invited to immerse himself in the golden light and passivity of Zhukovsky's life. The Russian made almost a virtue of his indolence:

> For a Slav belonging to a nation that has yet to wake up or to reveal itself, it would be enough to live thus in a gentle somnolence, dreaming of everything and thus arriving without feeling it at death with an unanswered question in one's heart.[98]

James carefully kept this charming, characteristic letter with its dangerous invitation. He would now remake his plans. Rather than a short stay in Paris, followed by an extended visit to Italy, he would remain in Paris until November, and then go on to Naples. The charming little flat on the Rue de Luxembourg, between courtyard and garden, had been let for the remainder of the fall to someone else, however; and so James removed himself to the best quarters he could find on short notice in the midst of the busy season: furnished rooms in a shabby little hotel just off the Rue de la Paix, the curiously named Choiseul and Egypt hotel.[99]

There were masses of proofs to read—the Hawthorne study was to appear in December, as was a collection of his short stories; the installments of *Confidence* had to be revised into book form—the magazine pages had been hardly more than a hasty draft. The serial novel was already appearing in *Scribner's*, and the book edition was to be published in London by Chatto & Windus in December. It was essential that the book appear in London before the American edition was published, to secure British copyright, but not so long before as to allow a pirated American edition.

As the fall advanced into winter, he struggled to finish with the proofs of *Confidence* and the other volumes, and get free. Elizabeth Boott invited him to come to Florence upon their return from Munich; she added the surprising information that Duveneck was returning with them. She—or, rather, her father, at her request—was bringing Duveneck and his studio to Florence for the winter. The memories that would become the great completed work of James's maturity *The Golden Bowl* were forming.

> My good—my best—Lizzie . . . Yes, I know I owe you two or three letters; but I owe you so much besides, & shall owe you so much forever, that these mere items have seemed to lose themselves in the great sea of my indebtedness. It is charming to hear from you, & you must not measure my appreciation of your letters, which are among the consolations of my existence, by my occasional & involuntary dumbness. . . . I expect to leave Paris for Florence p.m. Dec. 1st. . . . I have promised to go & see my old friend P. Zhukovsky (the Russian whom you saw in Paris) at Naples where he has fixed himself. But I shall get a clear fortnight with you, & the quality will prevail against the quantity.[100]

But this last delay was to prove to be a choice between two paths; almost as soon as he had written to Elizabeth, the way to Italy was blocked.

He had his train ticket and was ready to depart for Italy when all travel came to a halt. As he described it to Miss Bosanquet thirty years later, it was a snowstorm of rare violence, and it raged without intermission for the better part of two days. He remained trapped in his plain little hotel off the Rue de la Paix, where he had expected to spend only a few hours more, the snow muffling him noiselessly into the small, shiny, shabby salon of the hotel. He was not concerned about the forced delay; his deadlines had been met, and he luxuriated in his temporary solitude. The silence and isolation prompted a deep concentration, in which he wrote at one long sitting a short story, another of his boardinghouse studies.[101]

When the snowstorm abated and he could venture out, he discovered that the Mont Cenis railroad tunnel was blocked, and that it would be days before the trains returned to their normal schedule. There was snow in Rome—even in Naples! And then, new deadlines were looming: he was hounded by awareness of all the new books he would have to see through the presses of two publishing houses.

> My admirable Lizzy—. . . I have thought it best therefore to go straight back to London now (I shall leave on Tuesday or Wednesday,) transact my business, &, as soon as I have done so, start afresh

for Italy, with a longer stretch of time before me & no obligation to be back at a fixed period. As far as I can tell at present this will be about the 20th January. . . . I am greatly obliged for your invitation to dine with Duveneck on "his favorite macaroni." Pray on this occasion have one of *my* favorite dishes for *him*![102]

Without a shade of apprehension, he returned to London, firing off a hasty good-bye to Child as he departed, leaving the manuscript of his story and very tender sentiments to be given to Huntington, "whom I count on finding in Florence *plus tard*."[103]

Delays accumulated again, however, and it was early in March before he left London. He would not linger in Florence, and he would quickly go on to Zhukovsky in Naples, but all the same he would be too late.

22

THE PORTRAIT OF A LADY

He again spent Christmas with Gaskell in Yorkshire. A letter from Lizzie brought him Christmas greetings and reminded him of how bitterly cold the winter was on the Continent, but in England the weather was humid and mild. He was impatient, constrained, but vigorously alive; he seemed to be living in all his senses. He liked, intensely, the muted colors of England, even the constant rain, even the odors. He could bury his nose in the sleeve of a new woolen coat and enjoy the scent. He rose on the morning of New Year's Eve, bathed and dressed, with the windows open and the mild air playing on his bare skin; it was a measure of the intimacy he and Elizabeth had achieved that he wrote to her about the experience.[1]

Back in the reassuring and depressing darkness of London, James hastily began writing another short novel to pay for long delays and repeated visits to the Continent, and to allow him, before his next departure, to send substantial checks to the Jameses of Cambridge. For he was now the only member of the family earning his living; and Father's disastrous investments had reduced the family's already shrunken capital by half.[2]

James worked surrounded by uproar—not only the ceaseless uproar of London but also the uproar over his recent books. *Hawthorne* had been very well received in London. It was the first biography, and the first serious appreciation, of an American author in England, and it was all the better received for its modesty. James wrote upon the background of his own now fully developed critical theory; the theory was insistent, a trifle pugnacious. In later life, James would do homage in less doctrinaire fashion to the works of his predecessor,[3] but just then he was a young man establishing his position. As he had cut himself free from Balzac, now he distinguished himself from Hawthorne.

He said again that there was a sharp distinction between the realistic novel and the romance; Hawthorne was evidently a practitioner of romance. James observed how difficult it would have been to write realistic fiction in the America of forty years before, in the wilderness, and how remarkable, accordingly, Hawthorne's accomplishment had been. If Hawthorne had not written novels, strictly speaking, it was only because he had lacked the materials.

> For myself, as I turn the pages of his journals, I seem to see the image of the crude and simple society in which he lived. I use these epithets, of course, not invidiously, but descriptively; if one desires to enter as closely as possible into Hawthorne's situation, one must endeavor to reproduce his circumstances. We are struck with the large number of elements that were absent from them, and the coldness, the thinness, the blankness. . . . It takes so many things, as Hawthorne must have felt later in life, when he made the acquaintance of the denser, richer, warmer, European spectacle—it takes such an accumulation of history and custom, such a complexity of manners and types, to form a fund of suggestion for a novelist. . . . No State, in the European sense of the word, and indeed barely a specific national name. No sovereign, no court, no personal loyalty, no aristocracy, no church, no clergy, no army, no diplomatic service, no country gentlemen, no palaces, no castles, nor manors, nor old country-houses, nor parsonages, nor thatched cottages nor ivied ruins; no cathedrals, no abbeys, nor little Norman churches. . . .[4]

And so he went on, enumerating the settings of English and French novels, omitting only the slums of London and Paris, that were lacking in Hawthorne's native land. For an American to say these things was terrible, a contravention of the national creed, as James knew perfectly well. He had brushed aside the American boast, the boast of every revolution, the fantastic claim that the new republic had broken with history. No, there had been no revolution in human affairs; America only lacked cultivation.

A howl arose, as James expected, from American reviewers, who quoted this passage repeatedly, and denounced the man who had written it. But he was surprised by the virulence of the reaction. As he wrote to Lizzie,

> The American press, with 2 or 3 exceptions, seems furious with my poor little Hawthorne. It is a melancholy revelation of angry vanity, vulgarity & ignorance. I thought they would protest a good deal at my calling New England life unfurnished, but I didn't expect they would lose their heads and their manners at such a rate. We are clearly the most thin-skinned idiots in the world & I blush for my compatriots. A presto, dear friend. Kind love to your father. . . .[5]

Confidence, however, which appeared at the same time in book form and was a celebration of the new moral character that James thought was distinctive of the American race, pleased the American critics no better. This book, too, provoked a certain agitation. The ending of the book was utterly unbelievable. How could two male rivals be reconciled so easily, so softly? Where was the jealousy, the violence, the passion? There was something almost effeminate here; one hesitated to say what, exactly, was missing from the character of the author. It was that old complaint of William's, voiced by the men who were the object of his lesson, and knew it: they said he lacked passion, lacked blood.

But his books were both very popular, all the same, in America and in England, and James—conscious of having written truthfully, and of making a hit—watched the uproar like a general who observes his troops occupying the field of battle.

He was already engaged on yet another novel, another brief masterwork like *The Europeans*. It was set—evidently with deliberate and slightly malicious humor—in the barren America of the 1840s.[6] James set to work at portraying the wilderness in which Hawthorne had withered and almost died. The title of the new tale was "Washington Square."

It was a beautiful novel constructed, once again, as if it were a French stage play,[7] and as a result it was another triumph of form. Nearly the whole of the action took place in the parlor of his own grandmother Robertson's house on Washington Square, and he, as a little boy, made an appearance of his own, kicking up the rank-smelling ailanthus leaves in the parade ground. It was difficult to portray the barren world of his childhood at length, and for long chapters the reader might have tired a little of the simplicity of the characters and their tale, but it was perfectly done, all the same, a tour de force.

Fanny Kemble had given him the story the winter before, and he had only moved it to America. Her younger brother, Henry, had been a beautiful boy, but selfish and indolent. A plain, rather stupid girl, Mary Anne Thackeray, had fallen in love with him. She was the only child of George Thackeray, the master of King's College. The old doctor had a very nice private fortune, four thousand pounds a year, and Henry Kemble, for the sake of the money, had made love to poor Miss T. The doctor disapproved, however, and said that if she married Henry Kemble, he would leave her nothing.

Fanny knew all about it, because the girl had come to see her in great tribulation. She had warned the girl that Henry was selfish, but she was still ready to marry the handsome lad. Fanny's brother, however, fearing that the doctor would never relent, extricated himself from the engagement.

Twenty years later, when the old man was dead, Fanny said, Henry Kemble returned and proposed once again, but Miss Thackeray refused him—it was too late. "And yet," Fanny concluded, "she cared for him—and she would have married no other man." Henry Kemble's selfishness had overreached itself and this was the retribution of time.[8]

There was James's story, with characters, plot, and even the moral, ready-made, and writing rapidly, he departed very little from it. He evidently took great pleasure in inserting a portrait of Fanny as a young woman, plump and pretty, in the story, playing her proper role as the sister of the handsome young adventurer.

Yet, as he wrote, the tale grew and changed. The doctor, a shadowy presence in Fanny's version, gradually revealed himself as a deeply egotistical man. It was he, and not the handsome young Europeanized adventurer, who became the villain. The doctor was no longer a Cambridge don but an American physician. He was perfectly correct and conventional, a very clever fellow, and was always in the right. But he did not love his daughter. And yet she had her moral triumph in the end, the only one that her circumstances permitted.

The transposition of the story to the New York of Henry's childhood, and the way in which he conferred his own memories upon the heroine, proved to be a useful exercise for the big novel that he was preparing. It also awakened more recent memories and feelings. His own sister, Alice, had recently passed through a crisis of her own. The simple, plain young heroine of James's new novel was the opposite, in every way, of clever, imperious Alice James. The fictional father, the clever, worldly doctor, was also the reverse of Henry James, Sr. Yet, and perhaps even for this reason, as the story unfolded it became a parable of a daughter's unhappy disappointment and her father's selfishness that might have been Alice's tale as well as Catherine Sloper's.

James continued to dine out every night, writing in the mornings, writing letters before bed, saving his money for a long visit to Italy. William wrote to say that he was planning to come to Europe for an extended visit; he thought he and his new family could live more cheaply there, and he himself might make the acquaintance of European men of science. But William characteristically and abruptly abandoned the plan, and Henry gave it no more thought for the time being.[9]

By the first week of March 1879 he had delivered the new novel, *Washington Square*, to Leslie Stephen for *The Cornhill Magazine*, in time for George Du Maurier to begin work on the illustrations. Macmillan in London, and Harper & Brothers in New York, had agreed to simultaneous magazine and book publication, and both were to include the Du Maurier drawings.

With all of this accomplished, and with the prospect of serial payments and royalties sufficient to support him for several months, he set off for an extended visit to Italy, to see Zhukovsky and the Bootts, to escape the London season, and to begin work, at last, on his big novel.

The visit to Zhukovsky in Naples, which James undertook promptly upon his arrival in Italy, was nevertheless, for a number of reasons, very cautious. He allowed himself only a fortnight in Naples and Rome, and he undertook to stay at Zhukovsky's pension near Naples for only five days, to begin with.[10] This caution derived in part from anxiety about Naples itself. He had received a strange warning not to stay overnight in Naples:

Two old friends of mine, a delightful old gentleman and his wife, have just been killed simultaneously, by spending a week there. They stopped on their way to Cairo, & on arrival at Cairo were instantly "taken ill" & in a few days died—side by side in the same room.[11]

Anxiety about contagion was perhaps an aspect of a general uneasiness about Zhukovsky's invitation and the dangerous sunlit passivity it promised. There had been a number of changes in Zhukovsky's circumstances, which also prompted caution. There was a crowd of Russians at the villa whom as yet James had not met, and a stocky young Neapolitan folksinger, Pepino, was living with Zhukovsky at the villa. Zhukovsky apparently considered the young singer an adopted son, and had undertaken his musical education. Zhukovsky was quite charming as the adoptive father of this very simple young man.[12] Of more troubling importance was that Richard Wagner had established himself nearby, and both Zhukovsky and Pepino had all but become members of his household.

Zhukovsky's encounter with Wagner was fortuitous. Wagner had been ill, and had come to southern Italy on his doctor's recommendation early in the new year. He had taken a large country house, the Villa d'Angri, on the seaward slope of the Posilipo, not far from Zhukovsky's pension. Zhukovsky quite naturally called. He had known Frau Cosima Wagner since his visit to Bayreuth, and now he was introduced to the composer himself, a vigorous and powerful man of sixty-six years.

The composer presided over a large and complex enterprise, more like an imperial court than an ordinary household. There was Cosima, herself a regal figure, the daughter of Franz Liszt and his mistress, the countess d'Agoult. Cosima was the ruler and manager of the household. There were her five children—three of whom Wagner had fathered while Cosima was still married to her first husband, Hans von Bülow. There was a nurse, an English governess, and a tutor for the children. The tutor, Heinrich von Stein, was one of a circle of handsome young aristocrats who had attached themselves to Wagner and whom he kept close beside him. In addition to Stein, living at the villa when James arrived were the pianist Josef Rubenstein; Karl von Gersdorff, a young friend of both Nietzsche and Wagner; and a young musician, Engelbert Humperdinck. They planned to found a sort of aesthetic colony at Bayreuth.

Zhukovsky had joined the circle of aristocratic bachelors around Wagner; he had become, in effect, the court painter. He who had grown up in the court of the czar easily adapted himself to this house-hold; indeed he seemed for the first time since he left Moscow to feel at home. When James arrived, he was painting Cosima's portrait. The Russian went to the Wagner villa for brief sittings every morning; on most days he would politely stay for lunch with the family. He gener-ally would return to the Villa d'Angri in the evening, when there was a regular salon. Pepino and the Wagner children played together and sang the master's music, and also performed *tableaux* designed by Zhukovsky, for the company.[13] It had already been decided that Zhukovsky would return to Bayreuth with the Wagners and design the sets and costumes for the performances of a new opera, *Parsifal*.[14] Wagner was at work on the orchestration, and together he and Zhukovsky visited houses and churches that might serve as models for the sets.

The old man kept people close by him, and never liked anyone whom he regarded as belonging to himself to go away. When he saw roses blooming in the garden, he liked to show them to Zhukovsky, who was so susceptible to beauty, and half his pleasure would be destroyed if Zhukovsky was not there to share it.[15]

There were bitter hostilities among the young men, as there were bound to be in a court circle. Rubenstein was intensely jealous, but Cosima, Zhukovsky's mentor, smoothed over all disagreements. It was she who created and maintained the structure of the court, upon which the whole great work depended.[16]

All of this James learned quickly enough upon his arrival at Posilipo, where the deep-colored oranges hung, like Japanese lanterns, in the gardens and orchards, amid the tangle of their own foliage and the silvery dusk of the olives. The blue water of the Bay of Naples was spread like a vast, pale blue floor, streaked in all sorts of fantastic ways with currents both of lighter and darker color. The coast of Sorrento was wonderfully distinct in the clear light.[17]

After his first welcome, Zhukovsky offered to bring James to the Villa d'Angri, but James declined. The conversation there was con-ducted in German, which James did not speak;[18] he was not at all mu-sical; and then he had come to see Zhukovsky, expecting in some degree to renew their old relation—he had not come to join a new master's court.

It was quickly plain that Zhukovsky regarded his new mentors with a veneration that was close to worship. Cosima was a woman of beauty and intelligence; Wagner himself, aside from being (as James noted a little irritably), a fount of wisdom, was a man of immense personal charm. Zhukovsky later said of this time: "No one who has not known Wagner in the intimacy of his home can have any idea of the goodness of his nature, his childlike lovableness . . . he was a child in spirit, with a whole world within him."[19]

James and Zhukovsky spent three days and nights together, in which they had time for long conversations, despite the young painter's frequent attendance at Villa d'Angri. The new life he was leading and Zhukovsky's new attraction to nihilism cast an odd light over their talks, however, that had once been so congenial. James could not reconcile the young painter's confident plan to live at Bayreuth, to design the sets of *Parsifal*—what Zhukovsky called "taking part in the great work"—with his apparent expectation that all European institutions would soon be destroyed. Zhukovsky much admired a Russian nihilist who was a great artist, he said; it was deeply moving to find so creative a person building solely on destruction.[20] Such sentimental talk about violence and death struck James as absurdly out of keeping with the collection of bric-a-brac with which Zhukovsky was surrounded.[21] But Zhukovsky had a new mentor.

James did not meet Wagner, and paid court only to the broken Psyche in the museum at Naples. The new musical drama that was being invented at the Villa d'Angri, the new art of pure action, the unmediated expression of the strong forces, would remain a closed book to him for many years. After three days he left Posilipo, and turned northward to Florence. Nothing would be allowed to deflect his determination to work.

Once more he had chosen Florence as the place in which to begin a serious novel. More prosperous than he had been in earlier years, however, now he took a suite of rooms on an upper floor of the Hôtel de l'Arno, overlooking the Lung' Arno, the sunny quay beside the yellow river where the bright-faced inns familiar to tourists stood in a row.[22] His deeply recessed parlor window, where he set his writing table, looked down upon the Ponte Vecchio. A stroll across this ancient bridge and through the palace and gardens of Eleanora, out through the ancient Roman Gate of the city and up the walled, winding road among the olive groves of Bellosguardo brought him to a little stone-flagged village square at the top of the hill. The Villa Castellani, where the Bootts had taken a large apartment, presented a blank façade to the square, but once inside the villa, one entered into a private domain, a cool, shady interior court. There the high windows let in a cool diffused light, ideal for work. The true front of the villa looked away from the square, over a little garden and a magnificent view of the valley of the Arno, bounded by distant hills.

Frank Duveneck had taken an apartment in Florence, and had all but joined the household. He was a wiry, inarticulate westerner and radiated physical assurance. James liked him, and liked his work. The portraits Duveneck had been doing were masterworks of psychological perception; he had managed to marry the technology of impressionism to the precise observation of the academic tradition, as La Farge had done, as Sargent would do. Lizzie was modeling her own painting upon Duveneck's work, which James thought a great improvement, and she had received a fine commission to paint the portrait of a bishop. It was the beginning that she had been struggling to achieve. The move to Florence was as much to Duveneck's benefit as to Elizabeth's, however; his school was prospering, and he seemed as fond of Lizzie as she of him. All that was lacking, it seemed to James, was for Lizzie and Duveneck to marry.[23] And he was of the genial view that their joint school needed to be better *publicized*.

It all seemed a remarkable contrast with Naples. Since his visit to Posilipo, James in his letters had repeatedly contrasted the "admirable, honest, wholesome" nature of his Anglo-Saxon friends with the "fantastic immoralities & aesthetics" of the circle he had left at Naples;[24] now again, as May was dawning, he remarked on the "pure-minded" Bootts.[25]

And so it was evidently in a curious temper, very much like that in which he had abandoned Paris, that he began work, at long last, on his big novel, on *The Portrait of a Lady*. The opening scenes were set in an English country house, and they were like a return to Eden, a long immersion in youthful innocence.[26]

He worked, as always, among distractions. There were the fond Bootts to see, almost daily, on their hilltop. He was a celebrity now, and this entailed a new difficulty he had not encountered before: people from America and Great Britain came to his door with letters of introduction and sought his attention. For the most part they could be dealt with briefly, but some required more attention than others. One, for instance, Constance Fenimore Woolson, had sought him through the cities of Europe, bearing a letter of introduction from, of all people, the late Mary Temple's youngest sister, Henrietta.[27] Woolson was a writer of real talent, she seemed to admire his work, and she had gone to a great deal of trouble to find him. She left her letter at his hotel; he called on her, and on several occasions showed her Florence.

Woolson was forty years old, three years his senior, but this was her first visit to Europe. She was stout and plain, and rather deaf, which were all serious defects in James's eyes, and their initial encounters were rather cool. Yet she had lovely, intelligent eyes; she was sympathetic, and if she was a spinster, she had a high moral sense of the place a spinster could occupy. When her father died, she had begun writing to support herself and her mother. Annie Fields had taken her up for *The Atlantic*, and she had just published a collection of short stories, most of which had appeared there, that showed real ability.[28] Miss Woolson admired, almost to the point of resentment, James's work, and in the end they became good friends. He did not venture to introduce her into Florentine society, but he called on her two or three mornings a week, and they went to museums and galleries or walked in the Boboli Gardens. Fifteen years later, after her death, he assisted in the weary task of sorting through the papers she had left, among which were her accounts of these puzzled, exciting first exposures to European life and art:

> Mr. James is . . . rather taller than John Hay, and with a larger frame, a beautiful regular profile, brown beard and hair, large light grey eyes from which he banishes all expression, and a very quiet, almost cold, manner. . . . He has many acquaintances in Florence and he was constantly invited out to lunch and dinner parties; yet with all this, he found time to come in the mornings and take me out. . . .[29]

> At present, I confess, Giotto remains beyond me. And H.J. says calmly, "Some day, you will see it." May be.[30]

> The statute of "Lorenzo" in the new Sacristy of San Lorenzo is the finest statue, a thousand times over, I have ever seen; and at once completely satisfies my expectations of Michelangelo, which were extremely great. What I have said is very strong when you consider that in the Uffizi stand the antiques—the Venus de Medici, Dancing Faun, the young Apollo and the Niobe group. But I confess frankly that it is going to take some time for me to appreciate the "nude." I have no objections to it, I look at it calmly, but I am not sufficiently acquainted with torsos, flanks, and the lines of anatomy, to know when

they are "supremely beautiful." Now "Lorenzo" is clothed and therefore comes within my comprehension and oh! he is superb. . . . The strange half-reclining figures at the base of the two statues, called somewhat arbitrarily, "Day," "Night," "Evening" and "Dawn" are rather beyond me—as yet. . . . In speaking of these statues, Henry James said—"Of course you admired those grand reclining figures?" "No," I replied honestly, "I did not. They looked so distracted." "Ah yes," he said, "*distracted*. But then!" Here words failed him. . . .[31]

He showed her the lovely Giotto frescoes in the second cloister of the church of Santa Maria Novella, and expatiated on the third, which seemed to Constance a picture of a little Virgin going up impossible steps; it was far superior, he said, to Titian's *Assumption* in Venice, which he described. But Titian's portraits, in the Pitti, he greatly admired, and they lingered together for a long time before the *Ritratto Virile*, the dark young man in black clothes with the inscrutable, violent expression in his eyes.[32]

And so they went about together in the mornings, and became friends. James did not take emotional advantage of her innocence and loneliness, but he did the honors of his beloved Italy, where Woolson was to remain until her unhappy death.

William reappeared. He wrote to say that he must come to Europe; the provincialism of American science was stifling him; he must spend a few weeks among European philosophers and psychologists. He would arrive in Europe in the middle of June.

This letter, forwarded from Bolton Street, reached Henry in Florence, and it must have brought with it echoes of that earlier visit. But Henry had no intention of repeating that episode, and he was ready, in any case, to return to his own nest. He yearned for the comforts of his club. He would not meet William in Italy, therefore, but would intercept him in London. And so on the first of June, he returned to London, and arranged to take the ground-floor flat at 3 Bolton Street (as he himself had long before been given Mr. Rutson's ground floor) for his brother.

The two men were now most cautious and respectful of each other's privacy. William spent four weeks in London, at the height of the season, and Henry offered to bring him along to many of the daily breakfasts and nightly dinners to which he was invited, but William did not care to make the effort to meet strangers whom he was not likely to see again. Henry did arrange a pleasant dinner at the Reform, to which he invited a number of the young philosophers and psychologists with whom William was anxious to open relations. For the most part, however, William knocked about the city on foot, alone, as Henry had done a decade earlier. They had the opportunity for a few good talks, which gave Henry a much more vivid sense of the family's life in Cambridge than he had had before. And if William tended to dwell a good deal on his own sensations and ailments, that could not be helped. At forty, he seemed tired and frail, and his sleep was a good deal disturbed. But as in the past, his visit gradually invigorated him, and he seemed to be restored to his old energy and cheerfulness before he departed for the Continent in July. He had not lost any of his clerical manner, nor his air of moral judgment. He criticized Henry's expatriation[33] and was eager, again, to bring Henry home with him, but he accepted that now even if he succeeded it would only be for a visit. Henry was visibly, irretrievably, committed to London, which William could not understand or approve. He reported home, like a missionary among the heathen on the eve of the Apocalypse:

> I think he is so thoroughly at home in England that he will always prefer to make it his headquarters. That Club is a tremendous material bribe to a man: such solid comfort, with no effort of any sort. Then I think as he grows older that he is better suited by a superficial contact with things at a great many points than by a deeper one at a few points. The way he worked at paying visits and going to dinners and parties was surprising to me, especially as he was all the time cursing them for so frustrating his work. It shows the perfect fascination of the whirlpool of a capital when once you are in it. You detest it and yet you can't bear to let go your hold. However it will all suddenly stop on a certain day.[34]

Henry's doorbell rang persistently, as American visitors, coming to London for the season, presented their letters of introduction. And this new burden, added to the pressures of the London season, and of William's visit, drove him close to distraction. But he continued to work at his novel, just the same.

In July, on the eve of William's departure, they paid a call together at Hardwicke, in the country west of London. Henry had declined all invitations to visit the house until then, but it seemed an admirable excursion for William, an opportunity to gain a glimpse of English country-house life while remaining in a circle of relatives and friends. And so it proved to be.

It was a handsome, early Tudor house on the Thames. Their cousin Charlotte Temple, aunt to the orphaned Temple girls, had married a Canadian banker, Sir John Rose, and had become Lady Rose, the proprietress of Hardwicke. In *The Portrait of a Lady*, Hardwicke became "Gardencourt":

> The large, low rooms, with brown ceilings and dusky corners, the deep embrasures and curious casements, the quiet light on dark, polished panels, the deep greenness outside, that seemed always peeping in, the sense of well-ordered privacy in the center of a "property"—a place where sounds were felicitously accidental, where the tread was muffled by the earth itself and in the thick mild air all friction dropped out of contact and all shrillness out of talk. . . .[35]

The carved marble mantel, plaster moldings, and oak wainscoting in the drawing room had been installed in anticipation of a visit from Queen Elizabeth three hundred years earlier; the portrait of the Virgin Queen as a helmeted, bare-breasted warrior smiled down from the ceiling. A side garden, the deep lawn bounded by hedges and overhung with an ancient oak, was like a drawing room, where the family served tea. It was a highly evolved Lawton's Valley, with the comforts of Mayfair and the pleasures of the cultivated outdoors combined.[36]

The brothers arrived at teatime, when tables had been set on the lawn; the genial banker who owned the house and their stout cousin who was its hostess welcomed them into an enclave of American luxury and innocence, nestled in the privacy and cultivation of a European garden. The striking characteristic of the house was that it had turned its back to the carriage road; the true front faced long lawns running down to the river. The house was the literal embodiment of the privacy that one could find only in the Old World,[37] and tea on a summer afternoon, on a private lawn, evoked his earliest memories of luxury and freedom.

The visit was a success: William had been bright, had shone socially for the first time during his visit.[38] When Henry returned to London, he revised the opening scene of his novel to include a description of this lovely place.[39]

In the procession of Americans whom Henry had by then introduced to Europe there was a vacant place. Mary Temple had yearned to join him in Europe, and now, in his novel, with the greatest tenderness he welcomed her.[40]

She stepped through the broad double doors of the Tudor house, Gardencourt, through doors that opened onto a lawn. Under the trees, tea had been set in the golden light of a summer afternoon. It was the house, the doorway, the very moment into which Henry had led William.[41] Waiting for her on the lawn were her cousins. One of them, a young man named Ralph Touchett, had lived his whole life in England. He was an Oxford man, tall, thin, and rather frail, but charming, attenuated into delicacy by the disease of which he was dying. She had been in the doorway for a moment before he saw that she was there, but his little black dog ran up to her, barking hard:

> whereupon, without hesitation, she stopped and caught him in her hands, holding him face to face while he continued his quick chatter. His master now had had time to follow and to see that Bunchie's new friend was a tall girl in a black dress, who at first sight looked pretty. She was bare-headed, as if she were staying in the house. . . . The girl spoke to Ralph, smiling, while she held up the terrier. "Is this your little dog, sir?"
>
> "He was mine a moment ago; but you've suddenly acquired a remarkable air of property in him."
>
> "Couldn't we share him?" asked the girl. "He's such a perfect little darling."
>
> Ralph looked at her a moment, she was unexpectedly pretty. "You may have him altogether," he then replied.

She remained standing in the doorway, tall and slim and charming, waiting for the men to come up to her. She looked about her with perfect confidence—at Ralph, at the two other gentlemen under the trees, at the beautiful scene that surrounded her. "I've never seen anything so lovely as this place. . . ."

Mary Temple had been transmuted into Isabel Archer. To poor Mary, racked with doubt as she had been, he gave his own strong sense of a central, controlling self. This core of certainty was the trait that Mary had lacked, in his eyes, and he had regretted the lack; it had left her tortured by uncertainties and fears. Now he conferred upon her, like a bequest, a consciousness of genius, of a calling.[42]

Ralph Touchett was the epitome of the charming Oxford man, rendered still more charming, in James's eyes, by his illness: like the consumptive young man he had helped on the train from the Riviera; like the blind young man he had befriended at Malvern; like Mary Temple herself. To this young man, too, he gave some of his own traits: above all, the passion to be a teacher, a mentor, to his beloved. Prevented by illness from thinking of marriage, Ralph became the ideally charming mentor. Exercising the arts of the indirectly powerful, he persuaded his father to confer a fortune in money, which meant freedom, upon his young cousin. He brought Isabel to Italy, and led her through the museums and galleries through which Henry had conducted his sister, Alice, his brother William, his new protégée Miss Woolson, and so many others.

Even in Gardencourt, however, there was evil, in the person of a remarkable villain: Serena Merle. She was a woman of forty years, just a trifle older than James; but she was of the Old World, of the old order. Isabel, coming into the drawing room at Gardencourt that rainy afternoon, found Madame Merle in possession of the place, Madame Merle seated, all absorbed but serene, at the piano, and she deeply recognized—in the striking of such an hour, in the presence there, among the gathering shades, of this personage, of whom a moment before she had never so much as heard—a turning point in her life.[43]

Madame Merle was Vautrin, a villain in perfect possession of her appearance; even her body was an expression of the part she wished to play. She was deeply attractive: tall, broad, rounded, replete; her thick blond hair was wound into smooth braids and arranged classically; she was Juno, a goddess—old, old, indeed. Her face was expressive, responsive, communicative; it spoke of a large nature, of quick and free motions. She inhabited every muscle of her body, and there was never a moment in which she was surprised or out of control. "Her manner expressed the repose and confidence which come from a large experience. . . . She was, in a word, a woman of strong impulses kept in admirable order."[44]

She played the piano for Isabel, and her music and her conversation quickly made a conquest of the girl. She was by far the most intelligent person that Isabel had yet encountered: she knew how to think, and she knew how to feel. She was a cosmopolitan American, long a resident of Italy; and it seemed to Isabel that she was an aristocrat. "To be so cultivated and civilized," she thought, "so wise and so easy, and still to make light of it—that was really to be a great lady."[45]

She had not a fault; she was one of the most brilliant women of Europe. While the men who sought Isabel's affections failed to interest the younger woman, Madame Merle captivated her. Isabel had never met a more agreeable or interesting figure. "The gates of the girl's confidence were opened wider than they had ever been; she said things to this amiable auditress that she had not yet said to anyone."[46]

James worked slowly at the story. One morning, he seemed to remember, he had all the principal characters: Isabel Archer, Ralph Touchett, and Madame Merle, of course, the most important; and further circles of satellite characters ringing the principal planets. Only the central characters were to have their consciousness displayed, and Isabel was to remain at the center of the center, the others shown only in relation to her. The figures that were only satellites were shown from the outside, as objects of her gaze.[47] By maintaining her point of view, as James had long ago learned, he rendered the setting truthfully, as if in single-point perspective, and he obliged the reader to exercise the faculty of imagination, to imagine what was out of sight, to do his or her part of the work of creation.

Madame Merle had a friend, an old lover, Gilbert Osmond, who had lived for many years in Naples. They had known each other in Naples, and there was a villa at Posilipo that Madame Merle still often visited.

Osmond was rather thin and weak, passive; distinguished by good taste and a certain aristocratic manner, he had lived in Italy for thirty years. Except that he was blond, and had been born in America, he might have been Paul Zhukovsky. And, like Zhukovsky, he was educating a child—not Pepino, but Pansy. The author lifted and carried him, and his little daughter, Pansy, from Naples and put them into the Bootts's villa on Bellosguardo. Osmond was a man who could be immensely charming; he had Zhukovsky's strangely attractive passivity.

> Oh yes, he paints if you please. . . . Fortunately, he is very indolent, so indolent that it amounts to a sort of position. He can say, "Oh, I do nothing; I'm too deadly lazy. You can't do anything today unless you get up at five o'clock in the morning." In that way he becomes a sort of exception; you feel he might do something if he would only rise early. He never speaks of his painting—to people at large. He's too clever for that.[48]

It was not a portrait, it was a wicked caricature; James emptied the Zhukovsky character of interior life. Osmond lived passively, and therefore selfishly—holding himself aloof to create the illusion of superiority.

Madame Merle determined to make a marriage between Isabel and her former lover, this hollow man, Gilbert Osmond. With infinite art, she enlisted Osmond in the scheme; she brought the two together; she remained with Isabel and guided her toward the consummation of the plan. Isabel did not precisely fall in love with Osmond—that was more than anyone could arrange—but she gradually came to believe that she should marry him, that she should confer comfort and wealth upon him and his little daughter. Serena Merle played upon what was best in her, her generosity.

Merle's matchmaking was a work of art, of a kind; it was skillfully accomplished, a performance. Osmond himself thought of it as a kind of opera, in which Isabel would put music to his text. It was immoral, in a profound sense. Madame Merle treated people as tools, as if they were soley means and not ends in themselves. "Isn't she meant for something better than that?" even Osmond protested.

"I don't pretend to know what people are meant for," said Madame Merle. "I only know what I can do with them."[49]

This was chilling. And yet the portrait of the two villains was as tenderly, as lovingly drawn as the portrait of the heroine herself. Madame Merle's love for the arid Osmond and the little girl, Pansy, was the strong force driving the tale. She had loved him with a helpless passion; now at forty, in absolute control of herself, she still loved him. All her ambition was for him, and for the little girl. She was not materialistic, she was flesh itself. Thick features, a powerful body, thick blond hair—thickness, power, solidity, and a crooked smile were her essential feature. Costumed as Madame Merle, James performed his greatest impersonation.

Married by this priestess to Gilbert Osmond, poor Isabel was obliged to live with him, not in the golden light of summer afternoons in the sheltered privacy of Gardencourt, but in a lamplit, cavernous palace in Rome, where it seemed always to be night. There she was on display, an infinitely valuable addition to Osmond's collections.

As the tale slowly unfolded, the possibilities of which life had been so full closed like so many shutting doors; Isabel was trapped in a windowless fortress. Osmond, who also was trapped, treated her coldly; his empty self-regard began to seem horrible. As in George Eliot's tale, the universe of fact forced itself with a slow, inexorable pressure into a narrow, complacent, and yet extremely sensitive mind, making it ache with the pain of knowledge.

One night, sitting beside the dying fire, Isabel struggled to understand what had happened to her; gradually, in the climax of the tale, she began to understand that she had been used, that Madame Merle, whom she loved, had used her.

The long passage in which Isabel achieved her knowledge of the existence of evil was the best, James knew, that he had yet written.[50] It was the perfect expression of his theory and his practice of realism. Here he portrayed one of the true pivots of history, an event in the consciousness of a person deeply engaged in living.[51]

Isabel was his reader, intelligently applying her imagination to the text around her, trying to understand the reality that lay behind the scattered clues of the fiction. The reader of the tale and the reader within the tale together came to a dawning understanding. Like James before the damaged *Last Supper*, imagination completed the work of art, and the reader became an author. Transformed by understanding from victim to actor, Isabel became an active shaper of her own future. The knowledge of good and evil bestowed not guilt but freedom.

The deepest horror that Isabel found was this: Pansy was Madame Merle's daughter. Merle and Osmond had conceived this illegitimate child in Naples; Madame Merle was now prepared to sacrifice everyone, even the child herself, to the ambitions she cherished for Pansy.

Armed with knowledge and understanding, Isabel became Madame Merle's conscious antagonist. Simply by hinting that she knew her secret, Isabel was able to banish Merle to the purgatory of America (here James surely allowed himself a smile). Now free to choose truly, in the light of her understanding, Isabel herself chose to remain in Rome, as Pansy's protector.[52]

Her own benevolent mentor, Ralph, was now free to die, and his death was an affectionate consummation, not undesirable in itself, of their friendship. Isabel envied his death, but her own fate was to live. Life still held the promise of love.

To house these central characters, James constructed the architecture of the novel, a beautifully symmetrical edifice.[53] The images he used were of landscape and architecture, but the form was that of a play, a French play. The novel was given shape by the structure of entrances and exits in carefully described settings. Minor characters were arranged in pairs around the heroine, so as to display her complex character in all its facets.

On Isabel's left hand, as it were, James placed a great Liberal lord, Warburton, who was very much like George Howard. This attractive and desirable figure was made to fall in love with Isabel, and the reader was allowed to see her innocent pleasure in the exercise of power over him.

On her right, James placed an American capitalist, an example of the new man, Caspar Goodwood, the owner of a cotton mill. He was all masculine violence and aggression, a warrior; and at the end of the novel, against her protests, he seized Isabel and held her:

> His kiss was like a flash of lightning; when it was dark again she was free.

Free to choose, she freed herself from his embrace, returning to her onerous marriage and the care of Pansy. She would live for others, rather than for herself.[54]

Late in life, when James reread this concluding passage, he thought it too spare, and audaciously added a fuller description:

> His kiss was like white lightning, a flash that spread, and stayed; and it was extraordinarily as if, while she took it, she felt each thing in his hard manhood that had least pleased her, each aggressive fact of his face, his figure, his presence, justified of its intense identity and made one with this act of possession. So had she heard of those wrecked and under water following a train of images before they sink. But when darkness returned she was free.[55]

She was free, and set off on straight steel rails for Rome, a new moral force unleashed in Europe; the new man, Caspar Goodwood, remained behind to learn his own lesson of patience.

Across Europe, steel rails were being laid that would someday carry a tide of violence. But James's part in that war was still distant, unimaginable. He had set Isabel in motion, and that was as much as he could do.

23

VENICE

He spent the winter in London, as quietly as he could, working. The opening chapter of *The Portrait of a Lady* appeared in October, in *Macmillan's* magazine, and in November, in *The Atlantic*, but only about half the novel had been written. He sketched the story of the remaining episodes for himself,[1] and then wrote them out in careful detail. For the first time he was extensively revising and recopying his manuscript, instead of sending a lightly revised first draft to the press. The work went steadily, but slowly,[2] as he nosed himself into the story, moment by moment, exploring and describing. Remarkably harsh weather, the most severe winter London had experienced in fifty years, was a great aid to steady work. For ten days the snow was piled high in the streets, putting a stop to milk, butter, coals, cabs, water, gas, dinners.[3]

The first chapters of *The Portrait* were being very well received, and letters bearing praise came from Lowell, from Grace Norton, from Henrietta Reubell. Someone told him that the editor of the Liberal journal, the *Spectator*, had "devoured" the first installment, and then had gone back and reread it. He paid James the great compliment of writing about the opening chapter at length in his journal, which made the novel an important event. He did not speak entirely favorably; like many English readers, he would fail to admire the portrayal of James's American heroine, Isabel Archer. Even Fanny Kemble, for all her admiration of his work, had reservations about the portrait.

Shortly after the beginning of the new year of 1881, as a foggy thaw set in and the heaped snow rapidly melted, he became restless and apprehensive; he decided to flee from London's darkness and the rapidly intensifying pressures of society. He wanted light and quiet in which to finish the big novel, and he thought of going south, not to Florence or Naples, where there were so many ties and distractions, but simply south—to the Riviera, which he had only glimpsed on his brief visits ten years before; perhaps he would continue on to Rome or Venice. Early in February he set off, fleeing depression and duty. He paused at Folkestone, within sight—if the weather had been clear—of Boulogne-sur-Mer, vividly remembered from his childhood.

> It has been very wild on the Channel [he wrote to Henrietta Reubell]. The sea is a good deal the worse for it, & yesterday there was no boat. Today there is only a bad one, so that I shall wait for tomorrow. Meanwhile, pour charmer mes ennuis, I write to you. What could be more effectual? it almost reconciles me to the dark depression of an English inn, or, at least almost lifts me out of it.[4]

The waters gradually subsided, and James continued southward—stopping, as he said, to pay toll in Paris, calling on Child, Huntington, Reubell, and the others whom he had not seen for months—and making obligatory calls on the American expatriates. The Childes gave a dinner in his honor for a few elite guests, where Guillaume Guizot, professor of English literature at the Sorbonne, said that he had desired to meet James; he greatly admired his book on Hawthorne. Guizot was most effusive and friendly, and repeated whole passages of the book in a most extraordinary accent. James was tickled to hear him admire the genius with which Hawthorne overcame the provinciality of his training and circumstances: Hawthorne had done it all in those little holes, Boston and—how does one say?—Salem.[5]

There were several very pleasant, if brief, visits with Turgenev, who was laid up with gout. But as always, Pauline Viardot seemed to thwart his efforts to get Turgenev away from the Rue de Douai.

James spent two weeks in a pleasant apartment with a little balcony overlooking the gardens of the Tuileries. Then he set off again southward, tracing in reverse the path he had followed twelve years before, when he returned from his first long visit to Italy: Avignon, Marseilles, Nice, Menton, San Remo.

He stopped for three weeks in San Remo, awakening memories of the single afternoon spent there more than a decade earlier. It had doubled in size since his first visit and had lost much of its ancient quality, but the feel of the warm air was very pleasant, and he took a room that looked out on the cobalt-blue of the Mediterranean. In San Remo, James returned to his work, which went well, and that made him very happy.[6]

He wrote for about four hours every afternoon, after his midday *déjeuner*, or late breakfast.

> I used in the morning to take a walk among the olives, over the hills
> behind the queer little black, steep town. Those old paved roads that
> rise behind and above San Remo, and climb and wander through the
> dusky light of the olives, have an extraordinary sweetness. Below and
> beyond, were the deep ravines, on whose sides old villages were
> perched, and the blue sea, glittering through the grey foliage.[7]

Then he would go for another walk in the fading, golden light, and read late into the night. He had received from London the proof sheets for the June and July *Macmillan's*, which he read with care and forwarded to the press in Cambridge, to set in type for *The Atlantic*.

After three weeks of steady work, restlessness struck him again, and he passed into Italy; he went by rail to Genoa, and then to Milan, where he paused for a week. In Milan he had no calls to make, and as a consequence again worked steadily and well. He did pay one visit, as it were, to an old friend, the "moldering old fresco" of Leonardo's *Last Supper*, which was "so magnificent in its ruin," he reported to Fanny Kemble, to whom, in lieu of calls, he sent monthly letters.[8] Milan otherwise was cold and inhospitable, but he continued to hesitate over his ultimate destination. Rome would be very pleasant, but it was crowded at this time of year; Hamilton Aïdé and others of the bachelor circle were there, and he was tempted. At last, however, he went to Venice, where he knew no one.

He had purchased a new notebook in London for this trip; it was the first journey that he had taken in many years that was off his regular circuit. But all his writing was for *The Portrait of a Lady* now, and travel pieces were no longer needed to keep the pot boiling. His notebook remained unopened until the fall, when the novel was finished and he could bring it up to date.

> I remained [in Venice, he then wrote,] till the last of June—Between three and four months. It would take too long to go into that now; and yet I can't simply pass it by. It was a charming time; one of those things that don't repeat themselves; I seemed to myself to grow young again. The lovely Venetian spring came and went, and brought with it an infinitude of impressions.[9]

Settling down for a long stay, he did not look for a hotel or pension, but took furnished rooms on the Riva degli Schiavoni,[10] the broad curving embankment of the lagoon. His windows, four flights up, were directly across the lagoon from the remarkable pink Palladian church of San Giorgio Maggiore. He sat at his desk for four hours every day, writing and rewriting. He rose frequently and paced, fidgeting, looking for a word, a phrase. He found himself constantly at the windows.

> There are pages of the book which, in the reading over, have seemed to make me see again the bristling curve of the wide Riva, the large color-spots of the balconied houses and the repeated undulation of the little hump-backed bridges, marked by the rise and drop again, with the waves, of foreshortened clicking pedestrians. The Venetian footfall and the Venetian cry . . . come in once more at the window. . . .[11]

Venice had not greatly changed in the ten years since his last visit, when he had accompanied Alice and Aunt Kate. But the mysterious silence of the lagoon, then broken only by the splash of the oars of the gondolas, was now disrupted by the roaring of steamboats, the vaporetti. The new Italian regime was ruthlessly restoring the Cathedral of Saint Mark, cleaning and replacing and repainting in what seemed to James a hideous manner. But the city still lacked a central water supply or sewage system; it was not wise to remain during the hot months of summer, and when one once took a few paces away from the Riva and the Piazza San Marco, it was a quiet, half-deserted place. It was an old city, in which girls came arm in arm to an ancient well in the center of a little campo; dressed in limp linen that fell in graceful folds, the girls filled their pitchers.

He took his morning coffee at Florian's, on the Piazza San Marco, and afterward rode a gondola across the mouth of the Grand Canal near the church of Santa Maria della Salute, to a respectable bathhouse, Stabilimento Chitarin, where he had a heated saltwater bath. He would then go for a walk or a gondola ride, until he had his proper noon breakfast at the Café Quadri. Then it was time to work; he remained at his desk until six, or perhaps only until five, so that he could stroll or float about on a gondola for two hours, until dinner. After dinner he would return to the Piazza San Marco, crossing it again to Florian's, where he might linger late into the evening listening to the music and talking with chance acquaintances.

The charming young women with their bare arms and unruly curls, filling their pitchers at the well; the idle young men in the piazza; and the handsome old beggars at the water gate of the Doge's Palace were all part of the city's beauty, and reminders of its poverty. Away from the Riva, it was remarkable how many palaces were crumbling into ruin and had been abandoned.

He was not more solitary than he wished or needed to be. Again there was an American colony, which gathered at a salon where he could call two or three evenings in the week, as if at a café on the boulevard. It was the drawing room of Katherine De Kay Bronson, widowed mother of a marriageable daughter, an acquaintance of James's from New York and Newport days, whom he had glimpsed with her late husband on his long-ago first visit to Venice, and who in her widowhood now had settled in a small house—small by comparison, in a city of palaces—the Casa Alvisi, at the wide mouth of the Grand Canal, just opposite the Salute church. Here she presided with tact and generosity over the little circle of Americans in Venice. She had learned to speak the Venetian dialect, and was slowly becoming acquainted with Venice itself. Her drawing room was like a private box at the opera for James, where he found easy polyglot talk, artfully concocted drinks, and artful cigarettes, served by the hostess herself. Mrs. Bronson, a plump, dark-haired matron, made an art, a performance, of the nightly gatherings: she could

> place people in relation and keep them so, take up and put down
> the topic, cause delicate tobacco and little gilded glasses to circu-

late, without ever leaving her sofa-cushions or intermitting her good nature.[12]

In Mrs. Bronson's drawing room, James met Daniel and Ariane Curtis, who had taken an apartment in a palace a little way up the Grand Canal, and who would become lifelong friends.[13] He met again Mrs. Van Rensselaer, a charming and wealthy young American matron whom he had known well in his visits to Rome. She had been one of the circle who gathered in Anne Bartlett's apartment; a certain widowed Mrs. Huntington, who had wanted greatly to remarry in those days, and especially to marry him, had conceived of Mrs. Van Rensselaer as a rival. It was perfectly true that Mrs. Van Rensselaer had a great fondness for him, but there was no misunderstanding between them. James went on frequent excursions with her to the Lido, carrying a lapful of peaches and figs for their lunch, and he took a brief excursion down to Rome with her, all but cohabiting for two weeks very pleasantly.[14]

It was also at Mrs. Bronson's that an excursion of another sort began. He met Herbert Pratt,[15] who was spending a month in Venice on his way to the Orient.

> I saw him tolerably often; he used to talk to me about Spain, about the East, about Tripoli, Persia, Damascus; till it seemed to me that life would be *manquée* altogether if one shouldn't have some of that knowledge. He was a most singular, most interesting type, and I shall certainly put him into a novel. I shall even make the portrait close and he won't mind. Seeing picturesque lands, simply for their own sake, and without making any use of it—that, with him, is a passion—a passion of which if one lives with him a little (a little I say; not too much) one feels the contagion. He gave me the nostalgia of the sun, of the south, of colour, of freedom, of being one's own master, and doing absolutely what one pleases. He used to say, "I know such a sunny corner, under the south wall of old Toledo. There's a wild fig tree growing there; I have lain on the grass, with my guitar. There was a musical muleteer, etc." I remember one evening he took me to a queer little wine shop, haunted only by gondoliers and *facchini*,[16] in an out of the way corner of Venice. We had some excellent muscat wine; he had discovered the place himself and made himself quite at home there. Another evening I went with him to his rooms—far

down the Grand Canal, overlooking the Rialto. It was a hot night; the
cry of the gondoliers came up from the Canal. He took out a couple
of Persian books and read me extracts from Firdousi and Saadi.[17]

James became passionately fond of Venice, of the people, of the life,
of the habits. The vast, intricate, thousand-year-old dwelling floated
between ocean and sky, an immense, perfect country house. He
walked in the little grass-grown campos, looking for the white slips of
paper, flapping in windows, that signaled unfurnished apartments to
let; he fancied himself dividing the years between London and Venice,
coming back every year in the spring.[18] "The simplest thing to tell you
of Venice is that I adore it—have fallen deeply & desperately in love
with it," he wrote to Grace Norton in June.[19]

He was thirty-eight years old; his big novel was finished, or virtually so; his duties were all discharged. Alice, William, Elizabeth Boott,
even Zhukovsky, were all settled in their distant families; he had
done his duty to them, and to the memories of the dead. Despite all
obstacles, he would keep up his powerful friendships with the living;
he was free. Alice wrote to say that she was on her way to London,
with Katharine Loring, for a brief visit, but his presence was not required, and much as he would have liked to see her, he did not hasten
his return.

It had been a remarkably productive time. In the little more than
three years since relocating himself from Paris to London he had
written four novels, three of which would become classics; a biography of Nathaniel Hawthorne; a volume of short stories, of which
"Daisy Miller" would become one of the most widely read in the English language; and almost one hundred essays and reviews. His long
apprenticeship as a man of letters had culminated in this outpouring of masterpieces; at the end was a great novel, *The Portrait of a
Lady*, a cathedral of the imagination for which all the rest had been
preparation.

James himself, the most private of men, had become a public figure; not yet popular with critics or scholars, he was immensely popular with his public, and the sales of these latest works would allow him
the years of travel and leisure he would need for the next great burst
of creativity. In truth it would require fifteen years to prepare for another outpouring of greatness, one that would all but overshadow the

first. But for the moment he was at rest and at peace, feeling his force in its fullness.

The Portrait of a Lady ran for fourteen numbers in both *Macmillan's* and *The Atlantic*, dominating both magazines for more than a year. It was a cultural event of significant magnitude, heatedly discussed and repeatedly reviewed even before it appeared as a book. It was profitable financially, and a popular success. More than seven thousand copies were sold of the American edition alone. The reviews, although not all were glowing, uniformly treated the publication as a major occasion. A few months after it appeared, an American novelist, Edgar Fawcett, wrote a long essay on James's work for the *Princeton Review*, in which he said what many young writers felt. James had become a hero, a mentor: he had not compromised, and in his own indirect way, he had become a shaper of history.

> Mr. James, as we understand, is still in middle life. His career has thus far been enviably brilliant. He has secured heed, place and note in England; he is honorably known throughout Germany and France. In his own country he has stimulated eager debate, caused sides to be formed for and against him, won his lovers and his haters in the manner of all literary men who have ever risen high above mediocrity. . . . He has put his stamp upon the literature of his age; he has employed a bewitching, resonant, cultivated style in which to express, not merely himself, but the best of himself—not merely his ideas, but his most careful, solid and durable ideas. . . . Fame has rarely crowned so young a writer with bays of so fine a verdure. But he has won them, when all is said, very honestly. He bears the palm because he merits it. Let him merit new honors and these are sure to reward him. As it is, there is little doubt that he deserves today to be called the first of English-writing novelists.[20]

APPENDIX

In his memoir *Notes of a Son and Brother,* James described the writing of the review that follows, in the winter of 1862–63, as the beginning of his career: "I first sat down beside my view of the Brighton Hills to enroll myself in the bright band of the fondly hoping and fearfully doubting who count the days after the despatch of manuscripts." The waiting, however, probably was no more than a single day. He wrote a review of the opening-night performance of Miss Maggie Mitchell in *Fanchon the Cricket,* and the review appeared the next evening—his first published work.

James wrote a letter to Miss Mitchell, perhaps sending a copy of the published review, and she answered, enclosing a copy of the acting edition of the play, apparently inscribed in a manner sufficiently romantic to make James think of the love affair between the nineteen-year-old hero and a thirty-year-old actress that opens Thackeray's *Pendennis.*

Although James devoted several pages to this incident in his memoir, and emphasized its importance—the beginning of his effort to define himself as an American man of letters—he did not name the journal to which he submitted his review and it has not been identified before. The review reprinted below is evidently James's; it appeared in the evening edition of a Boston newspaper, *The Daily Traveller,* on January 6, 1863. It appeared anonymously, but it is plainly the review described by James in his memoir. The youthful style—"characteristic" is already a favorite word—the adaptation of French critical theory, and the gratuitous assertion of familiarity with German forests would mark it as James's even without the description in his memoir.

"Miss Maggie Mitchell" was Julia Margaret Mitchell; *Fanchon* had been her stock performance from 1860 onward. James described the play as a translation of a German theatrical setting of George Sand's *La Petite Fadette*. He saw it in Boston at the old Howard Athenaeum, which has long since been torn down.

DRAMATIC

Miss Maggie Mitchell—This charming comedienne opened at the Howard, last night, in her highly successful character of Fanchon, the Cricket, and enchanted the splendid audience which witnessed the performance, by one of the most bewitching and natural of impersonations. Miss Mitchell does not study for courtly attitude, indeed her slight form is too fragile for that, but she makes the heart and body labor in concordant action; she does not express the throbbings and tremors of emotion, by the recognized rules of declamatory eloquence, but by the guiding impulses of the heart. She leaps upon the stage like the child of nature skipping over the green fields of waning spring, and her face looks flushed with the health of fresh breezes which course over the green mantled fields. She seems to lose sight of the stifled auditory, and plays the most fantastic romps upon the mimic field, relieving herself of the joyous pleasures brimming over the cup which holds the burthen of her artless happiness.

Her whole acting emanates apparently from impulse, and an intuitive perception of the actual sentiment of her character. The wild and reckless scenes of childhood she delivers with the most delicious vivacity and effect, while the tenderest chords of pathos are exhibited in that untutored sorrow which we might anticipate in a roving child whose life has been encompassed by enjoyments without the pale of society. And the exquisite abandon which she throws into every scene and incident of the play is among the most characteristic and entertaining features of her acting. Mr. Marshall has placed this play upon the stage supported by a company of no ordinary ability, and the scenery is, to say the least, exceedingly beautiful and picturesque, conveying a correct and appropriate idea of the chasms, mountains and weird-like prospects of the German forests, and besides greatly enhancing its dramatic effect.

Fanchon has been almost interminably before the most appreciative of New York audiences, with unqualified success; and every Western city has testified to its merits in the most unequivocal manner, and pronounced their favor by the most flattering receptions. The play will therefore be presented upon every night of this week.

BIBLIOGRAPHY

The following is a list of the principal works cited or referred to in this book. It is by no means a complete bibliography of the James literature, which would fill several volumes. I have had to be selective even in listing the works that have been helpful to me; a more complete review of the literature will be appended to the final volume of this biography.

Nor, with some exceptions, have I listed James's own works here. A separate word as to these is required. The excellent bibliography by Edel and Laurence, listed below, gives complete citations for all of Henry James's publications, except the first, which is identified for the first time in this volume and reprinted here as an appendix. Unfortunately, there is no standard edition of James's works, although the Library of America has begun to assemble one. Henry James is the only author whose complete work they plan to publish, and when this ambitious project is complete it will be possible to refer to a single, easily accessible edition. Until then, a number of sources must be assembled. When I have referred to a particular edition in the text, a complete citation is given in the Notes. Where no particular edition of a novel is referred to, the citation is from the Penguin editions. *Watch and Ward* and *Confidence*, which are not available as Penguins, are cited from the admirable Library of America edition. Ruhm's edition of the *Confidence* manuscript is cited as "Rhum." James's stories are cited from the *Complete Tales*, edited by Edel. Essays and reviews are cited from the original publication, and from the Library of America volumes, except his letters from Paris to the *New York Tribune*, which are cited from Edel and Lind's collection, *Parisian Sketches*. Plays are cited from Edel's edition, *The Complete Plays of Henry James*. James's three volumes of memoirs and his biography of William Wetmore Story are cited from the original book publications, which are listed here. I have also listed all the editions of James's letters to which I refer, in abbreviated form, in the Notes. Citations from the prefaces written by James for the New York edition are from the Blackmur edition, *The Art of the Novel;* since I began this work the prefaces have also been reprinted in the Library of America series.

About, Edmond, *Tolla: A Tale of Modern Rome.* Boston: Whittemore, Niles, and Hall, 1856 (translated anon: taken from *Constable's Foreign Miscellany*).

Adams, Henry, et al., *John La Farge: Essays.* New York: Abbeville Press, 1987 (published jointly with the Carnegie Museum of Art, the National Museum of Art, and the Smithsonian Institution; "On the occasion of the exhibition *John La Farge*").

Agassiz, Louis, *A Journey in Brazil* ("by Professor and Mrs. Conti Agassiz"). Boston: Houghton, Mifflin, 1884 (revised edition). (Copyright 1867 by Ticknor & Fields.)

Alcott, Bronson, *The Journal of Bronson Alcott* (Odell Shepard, ed.). Boston: Little, Brown & Co., 1938.

Aldrich, Mrs. Thomas Bailey (Lilian Woodman), *Crowding Memories.* Boston: Houghton Mifflin Co., 1920.

Allen, Gay Wilson, *William James: A Biography.* New York: Viking Press, 1967.

Anderson, Charles R., *Person, Place, and Thing in Henry James's Novels.* Durham, N.C.: Duke University Press, 1977.

Anderson, James William, "In Search of Mary James," *Psychohistory Review*, Vol. 8 (1979), p. 63.

Anderson, Quentin, *The American Henry James.* New Brunswick, N.J.: Rutgers University Press, 1957.

Andreas, Osborn, *Henry James and the Expanding Horizon: A Study of the Meaning and Basic Themes of James's Fiction.* Seattle: University of Washington Press, 1948.

Anesko, Michael, *"Friction with the Market," Henry James and the Profession of Authorship.* New York: Oxford University Press, 1986.

Annan, Noel, *Leslie Stephen: The Godless Victorian.* New York: Random House, 1984.

Armstrong, William M., *E. L. Godkin: A Biography.* Albany: State University of New York Press, 1978.

Atherton, Gertrude, *Adventures of a Novelist.* New York: Liveright, Inc., 1932.

Auchincloss, Louis, *Reading Henry James.* Minneapolis: University of Minnesota Press, 1975.

Auden, W. H., "Introduction," in *The American Scene, Together with Three Essays from 'Portraits of Places,'* by Henry James (W. H. Auden, ed.). New York: Charles Scribner's Sons, 1946.

Auerbach, Erich, *Mimesis: The Representation of Reality in Western Literature* (Willard R. Trask, trans.). Princeton: Princeton University Press, 1953.

Barry, Michael, *The Mystery of Robert Emmet's Grave: A Fascinating Story of Deception, Intrigue and Misunderstanding.* Fermoy, Co. Cork: Saturn Books, 1991.

Barzun, Jacques, "Henry James, Melodramatist," *Kenyon Review*, August 1943. Updated in Dupee, *The Question of Henry James*, p. 254.

Bayley, John, "Henry James, Women, and the Ghost Story," unpublished talk given at Rye Festival, September 2, 1991.

———, "The Master at Home," reviewing three books on HJ, in *The New York Review of Books*, Vol. 36, No. 19 (December 7, 1989), p. 21.

———, *The Short Story: Henry James to Elizabeth Bowen.* New York: St. Martin's Press, 1988.

Baym, Nina, "Early Histories of American Literature: A Chapter in an Institution of New England," *American Literary History*, Vol. 1, No. 3 (Fall 1989), p. 459.

Beach, Joseph Warren, *The Method of Henry James*. Philadelphia: Albert Saifer, 1954 (1st ed. 1918).

Beer, Thomas, *Stephen Crane: A Study in American Letters* (with an introduction by Joseph Conrad). New York: Alfred A. Knopf, 1923.

Bell, Ian F. A., *Henry James: Fiction as History*. London: Vision Press, 1984 (in U.S. by Barnes & Noble, 1985.)

Bell, Millicent, *Edith Wharton and Henry James: The Story of a Friendship*. New York: George Braziller, 1965.

———, "Henry James: The Man Who Lived," 14 *Massachusetts Review*, Vol. 14, No. 2 (Spring 1973), p. 391. (Review of Edel, *The Life of Henry James*).

———, *Meaning in Henry James*. Cambridge, Mass.: Harvard University Press, 1991.

Benedict, Clare, *Constance Fenimore Woolson*. London: Ellis [1945].

Benson, Arthur Christopher, *The Diary of Arthur Christopher Benson*, edited by Percy Lubbock. London: Hutchinson & Co. [1926].

———, *Edwardian Excursions: From the Diaries of A. C. Benson*, edited by David Newsome. London: John Murray, 1981.

———, *The House of Quiet: An Autobiography*. London: John Murray, 1906 (first published anonymously, 1904).

———, *Memories and Friends*. London: John Murray, 1924.

Benson, E. F., *Final Edition: Informal Autobiography*. London: Longman's Green & Co., 1940.

Benstock, Shari, *No Gifts from Chance: A Biography of Edith Wharton*. New York: Charles Scribner's Sons, 1994.

[Beresford, Louisa,] *A Catalogue of the Loan Exhibition of Water Colour Paintings by Louisa Marchioness of Waterford (with a short memoir, written in 1892)* ("Held at 8 Carlton House Terrace, April, 1910"). Privately printed, no date, "price six pence." Print sold at exhibition in 1910.

Beresford, Louisa Anne, *Life Songs: Being Original Poems Illustrated and Illuminated by Louisa Marchioness of Waterford and the Countess of Tankerville*. London: James Nisbet & Co., 21 Berners St. W., 1884.

Bersani, Leo, "The Jamesian Lie," *Partisan Review*, Vol. 36, No. 1 (1969), p. 53.

———, "The Subject of Power" (review of three works by Michel Foucault), *diacritics*, September 1977, p. 2.

Besant, Sir Walter, *Autobiography of Sir Walter Besant* (with a prefatory note by S. Squire Sprigge). New York: Dodd, Mead & Company, 1902.

Blackmur, R. P., "In the Country of the Blue." Autumn 1943 issue of *Kenyon Review*.

Boott, Francis, *Recollections of Francis Boott: for His Grandson F.B.D.* Boston: Southgate Press–T.W. Ripley Co., 1912.

———(ed.), *The Art of the Novel: Critical Prefaces by Henry James* (foreword by R.W.B. Lewis). Boston: Northeastern University Press, 1984 (first ed. New York: Charles Scribner's Sons, 1934).

Boren, Lynda S., *Eurydice Reclaimed: Language, Gender, and Voice in Henry James*. Ann Arbor, Mich.: UMI Research Press, 1989.

Bosanquet, Theodora, *Henry James at Work*. London: Hogarth Press, 1927.

Bowden, Edwin T., *The Themes of Henry James: A System of Observation Through the Visual Arts*. New Haven: Yale University Press, 1956.

Bradbury, Nicola, *An Annotated Critical Bibliography of Henry James*. New York: St. Martin's Press, 1987.

Bradford, Gaurgliel, *American Portraits: 1875–1900*. Boston: Houghton Mifflin Co., 1922.

Brent, Joseph, *Charles Sander Peirce: A Life*. Bloomington: Indiana University Press, 1993.

Briggs, Asa (ed.), *Gladstone's Boswell: Late Victorian Conversations*, by Lionel A. Tollemache. New York: St. Martin's Press, 1984 (first published 1898: this edition based on third edition, 1903).

Brooke, Rupert, *Letters from America* (with a preface by Henry James). London: Sidgwick & Jackson, 1916.

Brooke, Sylvia, Lady, The Ranee of Sarawak, *Queen of the Head Hunters: An Autobiography of H.H. the Hon. Sylvia, Lady Brooke, The Dame of Sarawak*. Oxford: Oxford University Press, 1990 (first published London: Sidgwick & Jackson, 1970).

Brookfield, Frances M., *The Cambridge "Apostles."* New York: Charles Scribner's Sons, 1906.

Brooks, Van Wyck, *The Pilgrimage of Henry James*. New York: E. P. Dutton & Co., 1925.

Brownstein, Rachel M., *Tragic Muse: Rachel of the Comédie-Française*. New York: Alfred A. Knopf, 1993.

Bryce, James, *Studies of Contemporary Biography*. New York: The Macmillan Co., 1903.

Buitenhuis, Peter, *Twentieth Century Interpretations of the Portrait of a Lady*. Englewood Cliffs, N.J.: Prentice-Hall, Inc., 1968.

Burd, Van Akin, *John Ruskin and Rose La Touche: Her Unpublished Diaries of 1861 and 1867* (reproduced and edited by Van Akin Burd). Oxford: Clarendon Press, 1979.

Cameron, Sharon, *Thinking in Henry James*. Chicago: University of Chicago Press, 1989.

Cary, Elisabeth Luther, *The Novels of Henry James: A Study* (with a bibliography by Fredrick A. King). New York: G. P. Putnam's Sons, 1905.

Chalfant, Edward, *Both Sides of the Ocean: A Biography of Henry Adams; His First Life, 1838–1862*. Hamden, Conn.: Archon Books, 1982.

———, *Better in Darkness: A Biography of Henry Adams; His Second Life, 1862–1891*. Hamden, Conn.: Archon Books, 1994.

Christy, Marian, "William Morris Hunt: An Artist Remembered: An Interview with William Morris Hunt II" [grandson of the artist]. In Vose, *The Return*, pp. 34–35: reprinted from *Boston Globe*, July 2, 1986 (courtesy of the *Los Angeles Times*, syndicated).

Cole, T. W. (Tamie Watters), "Rhoda Broughton: A Thesis submitted for the Degree of Doctor of Philosophy, at Oxford University." Oxford, St. Anne's College, October 1963 (typescript).

Colvin, Sidney, "Speech of Sidney Colvin at the dinner given him at the Imperial Restaurant, 1st November 1912." "Privately printed by request."

Conrad, Joseph, *Henry James: An Appreciation*. London: privately printed, 1919.

Corner, George W., *A History of the Rockefeller Institute, 1901–1953: Origins and Growth*. New York: The Rockefeller Institute Press, 1964.

Cortissoz, Royal, *John La Farge: A Memoir and a Study*. Boston: Houghton Mifflin Co., 1911.

Croly, Herbert, "Henry James and His Contemporaries," *Lamp*, February 1904.

Crothers, Samuel McChord, "Henry James," in *Later Years of the Saturday Club* (1927), 385. (M. A. DeWolfe Howe, ed.). Boston: Houghton Mifflin Co., 1927.

Dana, Richard Henry, *Hospitable England in the Seventies: The Diary of a Young American 1875–1876*. Boston: Houghton Mifflin Co., 1921.

Daugherty, Sarah B., "Henry James and George Eliot: The Price of Mastery," *Henry James Review*, Vol. 10, No. 3 (Fall 1989), p. 153.

Davenport-Hines, Richard, "Making Up the Universe," a review of Ford Madox Ford, *A History of our Own Times. Times Literary Supplement*, March 24–30, 1989, p. 297.

Davis, Philip, *The Experience of Reading*. London: Routledge, 1992.

Duberman, Martin, *James Russell Lowell*. Boston: Beacon Press, 1966.

Dupee, Frederick W., *Henry James*. New York: William Sloane Associates, 1951 ("The American Men of Letters Series").

—— (ed.), *Henry James: Autobiography*. Princeton: Princeton University Press, 1956.

—— (ed.), *The Question of Henry James: A Collection of Critical Essays*. New York: Henry Holt & Company, 1945.

Dwight, Eleanor, *Edith Wharton: An Extraordinary Life*. New York: Harry N. Abrams, Inc., 1994.

Edel, Leon (ed.), *The Complete Plays of Henry James*. Philadelphia: J. B. Lippincott Co., 1949; revised edition, New York: Oxford University Press, 1990.

—— (ed.), *Guy Domville, by Henry James*. Philadelphia: J. B. Lippincott Co., 1960 (paperback).

—— (ed.), *Henry James: A Collection of Critical Essays*. Englewood Cliffs, N.J.: Prentice-Hall, Inc., 1963.

——, *Henry James: A Life*. New York: Harper & Row, 1985.

——, *Henry James: Les Années Dramatiques*. Paris: Joyce & Cie., 1931.

——, *Henry James: The Untried Years, 1843–1870; The Conquest of London, 1870–1881; The Middle Years, 1882–1895; The Treacherous Years, 1895–1901*; and *The Master, 1901–1916*. Philadelphia: J. B. Lippincott & Co., 1953–1972.

——, and Dan H. Laurence, *A Bibliography of Henry James*. Oxford: Clarendon Press, 1982 (3d ed.; 1st ed. 1957).

——, and Ilse Dusoir Lind (eds.), *Parisian Sketches: Letters to the* New York Tribune *1875–1876*. London: Rupert Hart-Davis, 1958.

Egan, Michael, *Henry James: The Ibsen Years*. London: Vision Press, 1972.

Elliott, Maud Howe, *This Was My Newport*. Cambridge, Mass.: The Mythology Company, A. Marshall Jones, 1944.

Ellmann, Richard, *Oscar Wilde*. New York: Alfred A. Knopf, 1988.

Feinstein, Howard M., *Becoming William James*. Ithaca, N.Y.: Cornell University Press, 1984.

[Fields, Annie (Adams), ed.], *James T. Fields: Biographical Notes and Personal Sketches; with unpublished fragments of tributes from men and women of letters*. Boston: Houghton, Mifflin & Co., 1881.

Fields, Mrs. James T. [Annie Adams], *A Shelf of Old Books*. New York: Charles Scribner's Sons, 1894.

Fisher, Philip, "Appearing and Disappearing in Public: Social Space in Late-Nineteenth Century Literature and Culture," in Sacvan Bercovitch, *Reconstructing American Literary History*. Cambridge, Mass.: Harvard University Press, 1986.

Fogel, Daniel Mark, *Daisy Miller: A Dark Comedy of Manners*. Boston: Twayne Publishers, 1990.

Foley, Richard Nicholas, *Criticism in American Periodicals of the Works of Henry James from 1866 to 1916*. ("A dissertation submitted to the faculty of the Graduate School . . .") Washington, D.C.: Catholic University of America Press, 1944.

[Ford, Worthington Chauncey, ed.], *War Letters 1862–1865 of John Chipman*

Gray, Major Judge Advocate, and John Codman Ropes, Historian of the War. Boston: Houghton, Mifflin, 1927.

Fourier, Charles, *Design for Utopia: Selected Writings of Charles Fourier* (with an introduction by Charles Gide, new foreword by Frank E. Manuel, translated by Julia Franklin). New York: Schocken Books, 1971.

Fussell, Edwin Sill, *The Catholic Side of Henry James.* Cambridge: Cambridge University Press, 1993.

———, *The French Side of Henry James.* New York: Columbia University Press, 1990.

———, "Time and Topography in *The American,*" in *Henry James Review,* Vol. 10, No. 3 (Fall 1989), p. 167.

Gard, Roger (ed.), *Henry James: The Critical Muse—Selected Literary Criticism.* London: Penguin Books, 1987.

Gibbons, Sarah L., *Kant's Theory of Imagination: Bridging Gaps in Judgement and Experience.* Oxford: Oxford University Press, 1994.

Gilbert, Sandra M., and Susan Gubar, *The Madwoman in the Attic: The Woman Writer and the Nineteenth Century Literary Imagination.* New Haven: Yale University Press, 1984 (2d ed.).

Godden, Rumer, *A House with Four Rooms.* New York: William Morrow & Co., 1989.

Godkin, E[dwin] L[awrence], *The Gilded Age Letters of E. L. Godkin* (William Armstrong, ed.). Albany: State University of New York Press, 1974.

———, *Life and Letters of Edwin Lawrence Godkin* (edited by Rollo Ogden). New York: Macmillan Co., 1907 (2 vols.).

Goode, John, *The Air of Reality: New Essays on Henry James.* London: Methuen & Co., 1972.

Gosse, Edmund C. B., *Aspects and Impressions.* London: Cassell & Co., 1922.

Grant Duff, Sir Mountstuart E., *Ernest Renan: In Memoriam.* London: Macmillan & Co., 1893.

Grattan, C. Hartley, *The Three Jameses: A Family of Minds.* London: Longmans, Green & Co., 1932.

Greene, Graham, "Henry James: The Private Universe," in *The English Novelists* (Derek Verschoyle, ed.). London: Chatto & Windus, 1936.

Griffiths, Mary Darden Rodgers, "Reminiscences," compiled by Mary Darden Rodgers Griffith, of her great-grandfather Alexander Robertson [and others]. Typescript, n.d., approx. 1890; Houghton Library, James Papers.

Habegger, Alfred, "Dupine Tracks, J.J.", in *The Southern Review,* Vol. 27, No. 4 (October 1991, "Fall 1991"), p. 803.

———, *The Father: A Life of Henry James, Sr.* New York: Farrar, Straus & Giroux, 1994.

———, *Gender, Fantasy and Realism in American Literature.* New York: Columbia University Press, 1982.

———, *Henry James and the "Woman Business."* New York: Cambridge University Press, 1989.

———, "The Lessons of the Father: Henry James Sr. on Sexual Difference," *Henry James Review,* Vol. 7, No. 1 (Fall 1986).

Hagberg, Garry, "Wittgenstein, Henry James, and Epistemological Fiction," *Philosophy and Literature,* Vol. 13, No. 1 (April 1989), p. 75.

Hale, Edward Everett, *James Russell Lowell and His Friends.* Boston: Houghton, Mifflin & Co., 1899.

Hardwick, Elizabeth, "On Washington Square," *The New York Review of Books,* November 22, 1990, p. 25.

Hare, Augustus J. C., *The Story of Two Noble Lives,* being memorials of Charlotte,

Countess Canning, and Louisa, Marchioness of Waterford. London: George Allen, 1893.

Harlow, Virginia, *Thomas Sergeant Perry: A Biography (and letters to Perry from William, Henry, and Garth Wilkinson James)*. Durham, N.C.: Duke University Press, 1950.

Hassall, Christopher, *Rupert Brooke: A Biography*. London: Faber & Faber Ltd., 1964.

Hastings, Katharine (Bogg) (Mrs. Russel Hastings), *William James of Albany, N.Y. (1771–1832) and Some of His Descendants; with notes on some collateral lines* ("compiled and contributed by Katharine (Bogg) Hastings"). Albany, 1924 ("reprinted from the *New York Genealogical and Biographical Record*, 1924).

Hawley v. *James*, 16 Wend. 60 (1836) (NY, Court for the Correction of Errors), reversing 5 Paige Ch. 64 (3 N.Y. Chancery Rep. 734) (1835). (Construing William James of Albany's will.)

Heilbrun, Carolyn G. (ed.), *Lady Ottoline's Album: Snapshots and Portraits of her famous contemporaries (and of herself), photographed for the most part by Lady Ottoline Morrell*. London: Michael Joseph Ltd., 1976.

———, *Writing a Woman's Life*. New York: W. W. Norton & Co., 1988.

Higginson, Thomas Wentworth, *Harvard Memorial Biographies*. Cambridge, Mass.: Sever & Francis, 1866.

Himmelfarb, Gertrude, *The Idea of Poverty: England in the Early Industrial Age*. New York: Alfred A. Knopf, 1984.

———, *Poverty and Compassion: The Moral Imagination of the Late Victorians*. New York: Alfred A. Knopf, 1991.

Hocks, Richard A., *Henry James and Pragmatistic Thought: A study in the relationship between the philosophy of William James and the literary art of Henry James*. Chapel Hill: University of North Carolina Press, 1974.

Hogg, Robert, *George Howard and his Circle: 1843–1911*. Carlisle: City Art Gallery, 1968.

Holroyd, Michael, *Lytton Strachey: A Biography*. London: William Heinemann, Ltd., 1973 (1 vol.). (The two-volume "critical biography" published 1967–68.)

Honan, Park, *Matthew Arnold: A Life*. Cambridge, Mass.: Harvard University Press, 1983.

Horne, Philip, *Henry James and Revision*. The New York Edition. Oxford: Clarendon Press, 1990.

Howard, Michael, *The Franco-Prussian War: The German Invasion of France, 1870–1871*. New York: Dorset Press, 1990 (reprint of 1961 edition, first published by Routledge).

Howe, Julia Ward, *Reminiscences: 1819–1899*. Boston: Houghton, Mifflin & Company, 1900.

Howe, M. DeWolfe, "The Letters of Henry James to Mr. Justice Holmes," *Yale Review*, Spring 1949, p. 410.

Howe, M. A. DeWolfe, *Boston Common: Scenes from Four Centuries*. Boston: Atlantic Monthly Press, 1921.

———, *Later Years of the Saturday Club: 1870–1920*. Boston: Houghton, Mifflin & Co., 1927.

———, *Memories of a Hostess: A Chronicle of Eminent Friendships; drawn chiefly from the diaries of Mrs. James T. Fields*. Boston: Atlantic Monthly Press, 1922.

Howells, Elinor Mead, *If Not Literature: Letters of Elinor Mead Howells* (Ginette de B. Merrill and George Arms, eds.). Columbus: Miami University and Ohio State University Press, 1988.

Howells, William Dean, "Mr. Henry James's Later Work," *North American Review*, January 1903.

Howells, W[illiam] D[ean], *Years of My Youth*. New York: Harper Brothers, 1916.

Hoy, Helen, "Homotextual Duplicity in Henry James's, 'The Pupil,' " *Henry James Review*, Vol. 14, No. 3.

James, Alice, *Alice James: Her Brothers—Her Journal* (Anna Robeson Burr, ed.). New York: Dodd, Mead & Co., 1934.

James, Henry (Sr.), *The Literary Remains of the late Henry James* (William James, ed.). Boston: James R. Osgood & Company, 1885.

James, Henry

    Novels: (As noted above, where a specific edition is not cited, reference is made to the Penguin editions, not separately listed here, which for the most part are excellently edited by Geoffrey Moore, with admirable notes by Patricia Crick. Tony Tanner's introduction to the Penguin edition of *The Europeans* was also helpful, as was Gore Vidal's introduction to *The Golden Bowl*. Citations from *Watch and Ward* and *Confidence* are from the Library of America volume in which they are included. Six later novels, which at present are available in neither Penguin nor Library of America editions, fall into the second volume of this biography and are not mentioned here.)

        Confidence (1880), by Henry James ("now first edited from the manuscript, with notes, introduction, and bibliography") (Herbert Rhum, ed.). New York: Grosset & Dunlap, 1962.

        Henry James: Novels 1871–1880 (Watch and Ward, Roderick Hudson, The American, The Europeans, Confidence) (William T. Stafford, ed.). New York: Library of America, 1983.

    Stories and Novellas:
    The Complete Tales of Henry James. (12 vols.; Leon Edel, ed.) Philadelphia: J. B. Lippincott Company, 1961–62.

    Essays and Reviews:
    The American Essays of Henry James. (Leon Edel, ed.) Princeton: Princeton University Press, 1956.

    The Art of the Novel: Critical Prefaces by Henry James. (R. P. Blackmur, ed., foreword by R.W.B. Lewis.) Boston: Northeastern University Press, 1984 (1st ed. 1934).

    Henry James: Literary Criticism—Essays on Literature; American Writers; English Writers. (Leon Edel, ed.) New York: Library of America, 1984.

    Henry James: Literary Criticism—French Writers; Other European Writers; The Prefaces to the New York Edition. (Leon Edel, ed.) New York: Library of America, 1984.

    The Painter's Eye: Notes and Essays on the Pictorial Arts. (John L. Sweeney, ed.) Madison: University of Wisconsin Press, 1989.

    Parisian Sketches: Letters to the New York Tribune *1875–1876*. (Leon Edel and Ilse Dusoir Lind, eds.) London: Rupert Hart-Davis, 1958.

    The Scenic Art: Notes on Acting and The Drama, 1872–1901. (Allan Wade, ed.) New Brunswick, N.J.: Rutgers University Press, 1948.

Travel Writings:

Henry James: Collected Travel Writings—The Continent (A Little Tour in France, Italian Hours, Other Travels). (Richard Howard, ed.) New York: Library of America, 1993.

Henry James: Collected Travel Writings—Great Britain and America (English Hours, The American Scene, Other Travels). (Richard Howard, ed.) New York: Library of America, 1993.

Biographies:

The Middle Years. New York: Charles Scribner's Sons, 1917.

Notes of a Son and Brother. New York: Charles Scribner's Sons, 1914.

A Small Boy and Others. New York: Charles Scribner's Sons, 1913.

William Wetmore Story and His Friends. New York: Da Capo Press, 1969 (first published by Houghton, Mifflin & Co., 1903).

Letters:

Harlow, Virginia, *Thomas Sergeant Perry: A Biography and Letters to Perry from William, Henry and Garth Wilkinson James.* Durham, N.C.: Duke University Press, 1950.

Henry James Letters. (4 vols.; Leon Edel, ed.) Cambridge, Mass.: Harvard University Press, 1974.

Lubbock, Percy, *The Letters of Henry James* (2 vols.) New York: Charles Scribner's Sons, 1920.

Monteiro, George, *Henry James and John Hay: The Record of a Friendship.* Providence, R.I.: Brown University Press, 1965. (In addition to all surviving HJ–Hay letters, an invaluable introduction and notes include previously unpublished letters of the principals to other correspondents.)

The Correspondence of Henry James and Henry Adams, 1877–1914. (George Monteiro, ed.) Baton Rouge: Louisiana State University Press, 1992.

The Correspondence of Henry James and the House of Macmillan, 1877–1914. (Rayburn S. Moore, ed.) Baton Rouge: Louisiana State University Press, 1993.

Selected Letters of Henry James to Edmund Gosse, 1882–1915: A Literary Friendship. (Rayburn S. Moore, ed.) Baton Rouge: Louisiana State University Press, 1988.

"WJ-HJ Letters"—The Correspondence of William James. (Ignas K. Skrupskelis and Elizabeth M. Berkeley, eds.) Vol. I, *William and Henry 1861–1884;* Vol. II, *William and Henry 1885–1896;* Vol. III, *William and Henry 1897–1910.* Charlottesville: University Press of Virginia, 1992–94.

Journals and Notebooks:

The Notebooks of Henry James. (F. O. Matthiessen and Kenneth B. Murdock, eds.) New York: Oxford University Press, 1947.

The Complete Notebooks of Henry James. (Leon Edel and Lyall H. Powers, eds.) New York: Oxford University Press, 1987.

James, William, *The Letters of William James* (edited by his son Henry James). Boston: Little, Brown & Co., 1926 (1 vol.; first published 1920).

Jobe, Steven H., "A Calendar of the Published Letters of Henry James," *Henry James Review:* Part I, Winter 1990 (Vol. 11, No. 1), p. 2; Part II, Spring 1990 (Vol. 11, No. 2), p. 77.

———, *A Partial Calendar of the Correspondence of Henry James.* Hanover, Ind.: Hanover College, 1994.

Kaplan, Fred, *Henry James: The Imagination of Genius; A Biography.* New York: William Morrow & Company, Inc., 1992.

Kaston, Carren O., *Imagination and Desire in the Novels of Henry James.* New Brunswick, N.J.: Rutgers University Press, 1984.

Kaufman, Marjorie, "Beside Maisie on the Bench in Boulogne," *Henry James Review,* Vol. 15, No. 3 (Fall 1994), p. 257.

Kazin, Alfred, *On Native Grounds: An Interpretation of Modern American Prose Literature.* New York: Reynal & Hitchcock, 1942.

Kee, Robert, *The Laurel and the Ivy: The Story of Charles Stewart Parnell and Irish Nationalism.* London: Hamish Hamilton, 1993.

Kelley, Cornelia Pulsifer, "The Early Development of Henry James," *University of Illinois Studies in Language and Literature,* Vol. 15, Nos. 1 and 2. Urbana, Ill.: University of Illinois Press, 1930.

Kelley, Mary, *Private Woman, Public Stage: Literary Domesticity in Nineteenth-Century America.* New York: Oxford University Press, 1984.

Kemble, Fanny [Frances Anne], *The American Journals* (Elizabeth Mavor, ed.). London: Weidenfeld & Nicolson, 1990.

Kemble, Frances Anne, *Further Records 1848–1883: A series of letters by Frances Anne Kemble.* New York: Henry Holt & Company, 1891.

———, *Records of a Girlhood.* New York: Henry Holt & Co., 1879 (2d ed.).

———, *Records of Later Life.* New York: Henry Holt & Co., 1882.

Kenton, Edna, "Henry James in The World," *Hound & Horn,* April–May 1934.

Kern, John Dwight, *Constance Fenimore Woolson: Literary Pioneer.* Philadelphia: University of Pennsylvania Press, 1934.

Krook, Dorothea, *The Ordeal of Consciousness in Henry James.* Cambridge: Cambridge University Press, 1962.

Leavis, F. R., *The Great Tradition: George Eliot, Henry James, Joseph Conrad.* London: Chatto & Windus, 1948.

Lebovitz, Naomi, *The Imagination of Loving: Henry James's Legacy to the Novel.* Detroit: Wayne State University Press, 1965.

Le Clair, Robert C., "Henry James and Minny Temple," *American Literature,* Vol. 21, March 1949, p. 35.

———, *Young Henry James: 1843–1870.* New York: Bookman Associates, 1955.

Lesser, Wendy, *His Other Half: Men Looking at Women Through Art.* Cambridge, Mass.: Harvard University Press, 1991.

Lewis, R.W.B., *The Jameses: A Family Narrative.* New York: Farrar, Straus & Giroux, 1991.

Lind, Ilse Dusoir, "The Inadequate Vulgarity of Henry James," *PMLA,* Vol. 66 (December 1951), p. 886.

Loyer, François, *Paris Nineteenth Century: Architecture and Urbanism* (translated by Charles Lynn Clark). New York: Abbeville Press, 1988.

Lubbock, Percy (ed.), *The Letters of Henry James* (2 vols.). New York: Charles Scribner's Sons, 1920.

Luedtke, Luther S., *Nathaniel Hawthorne and the Romance of the Orient.* Bloomington: Indiana University Press, 1989.

Lynn, Kenneth S., *William Dean Howells: An American Life*. New York: Harcourt Brace Jovanovich, Inc., 1971.

Mackay, Margaret, *The Violent Friend: The Story of Mrs. Robert Louis Stevenson*. New York: Doubleday & Co., 1968.

Magarshack, David, "Introduction," to *Ivan Turgenev: Literary Reminiscences and Autobiographical Fragments*. (David Magarshack, trans.) London: Faber & Faber, 1959.

Maher, Jane, *Biography of Broken Fortunes: Wilkie and Bob, brothers of William, Henry and Alice James*. Hamden, Conn.: Archon Books, 1986.

Maitland, Frederic William, *The Life and Letters of Leslie Stephen*. London: Duckworth & Co., 1908.

Martineau, Harriet, *Biographical Sketches*. New York: Leopold & Holt, 1869.

Matthiessen, F. O. (ed.), *Henry James: The Major Phase*. New York: Oxford University Press, 1944.

——, *The James Family: A Group Biography*. New York: Alfred A. Knopf, 1961.

——, *Sarah Orne Jewett*. Boston: Houghton Mifflin Co., 1929.

——, *Stories of Writers and Artists by Henry James*. New York: New Directions Books [1945].

McCall, Dan, "What Maisie Saw," *Henry James Review*, Vol. 16, No. 1 (Winter 1995), p. 48.

McElderry, Bruce R., Jr., *Henry James*. New York: Twayne Publishing, 1965.

Miller, J. Hillis, *The Ethics of Reading: Kant, de Man, Eliot, Trollope, James and Benjamin*. New York: Columbia University Press, 1987.

Milnes, Richard Monckton [Lord Houghton], *Poems of Many Years*. Boston: William D. Tinknar & Co., 1841.

[Milnes, Richard Monckton] Lord Houghton, *Monographs: Personal and Social*. New York: Holt & Williams, 1873.

Milosz, Czeslaw, *The Land of Ulro* (translated by Louis Iribarne). New York: Farrar, Straus & Giroux, 1984 (first published by Institut Littéraire in Polish as *Ziemia Ulro*, 1977).

Mitchell, Juliet, "*What Maisie Knew*: Portrait of the Artist as a Young Girl," in John Goode, ed., *The Air of Reality: New Essays on Henry James*. London: Methuen & Co., 1972.

Moncreiffe, Iain, of Easter Moncreiffe, *The Robertsons: Clan Donnachaidh of Atholl*. Edinburgh: W. & A. K. Johnston & G. W. Bacon, Ltd., 1954.

Montgomery Hyde, H., *Henry James at Home*. London: Methuen & Co., 1969.

——, *Oscar Wilde: A Biography*. London: Eyre Methuen, 1976.

Moore, Harry T., *Henry James and His World*. London: Thames & Hudson, 1974.

Moore, Rayburn S., *Selected Letters of Henry James to Edmund Gosse, 1882–1915—A Literary Friendship*. Baton Rouge: Louisiana State University Press, 1988.

Morse, John T., Jr., *Thomas Sergeant Perry: A Memoir*. Boston: Houghton Mifflin Co., 1929.

Mott, Lewis Freeman, *Ernest Renan*. New York: D. Appleton & Co., 1921.

Myers, Gerald E., *William James: His Life and Thought*. New Haven: Yale University Press, 1986.

Nadal, E. S., *Impressions of London Social Life; with other papers: suggested by an English Residence*. New York: Scribner, Armstrong & Co., 1875.

Neville, Hastings M., *Under a Border Tower: Sketches and Memories of Ford Castle, Northumberland, and its Surroundings, with a memoir of its late noble Châtelaine, Louisa, Marchioness of Waterford*. Newcastle-on-Tyne: Mawson, Swan & Morgan, 1896.

Newman, Ernest, *The Life of Richard Wagner: Volume Four: 1866–1883*. New York: Alfred A. Knopf, 1946.

Nochlin, Linda, *Realism*. Harmondsworth: Penguin Books, 1971.

Noyes, John Humphrey, *History of American Socialisms*. Philadelphia: J. B. Lippincott & Co., 1870.

O'Meara, Kathleen, *Madame Mohl: Her Salon and Her Friends, A Study of Social Life in Paris*. London: Richard Bentley & Sons, 1885.

Pater, Walter, *Walter Pater: Three Major Texts (The Renaissance, Appreciations, and Imaginary Portraits)* (William E. Buckler, ed.). New York: New York University Press, 1986.

Payne, Robert, *The White Rajahs of Sarawak*. London: Robert Hale Ltd., 1960.

Peirce, Charles, "The Secret of Swedenborg: being an Elucidation of his doctrine of the Divine Natural Humanity," by Henry James; book review, *North American Review*, April 1870, p. 463.

Perosa, Sergio, *Henry James and the Experimental Novel*. Charlottesville: University Press of Virginia, 1978.

Perrot, Jean, *Henry James: Une écriture énigmatique*. Paris: Aubier-Montaigne, 1982.

———, "L'inconnue sur le tapis: Un amour de James," *Magazine Littéraire*, September 1985, p. 27.

Perry, Ralph Barton, *The Thought and Character of William James*. Boston: Little, Brown & Co., 1935.

Perry, Thomas Sergeant, *Selections from the Letters of Thomas Sergeant Perry*, edited with an introduction by Edwin Arlington Robinson. New York: Macmillan Co., 1929.

Peterson, Dale E., *The Clement Vision: Poetic Realism in Turgenev and James*. Port Washington, N.Y.: Kennikat Press, 1975.

Plante, David, "The Secret of Henry James," *The New Yorker*, November 28, 1994, p. 91.

Poirier, Richard, *The Comic Sense of Henry James: A Study of the Early Novels*. New York: Oxford University Press, 1960.

———, *The Performing Self: Compositions and Decompositions in the Languages of Contemporary Life* (foreword by Edward W. Said). New Brunswick, N.J.: Rutgers University Press, 1992 (1st ed. 1971).

Pope-Hennessy, James, *Monckton Milnes: The Years of Promise, 1809–1851* (2 vols.). London: Constable, 1949.

Posgate, Helen B., *Madame de Staël*. New York: Twayne Publishers, 1968.

Pritchett, V. S., *The Gentle Barbarian: The Life and Work of Turgenev*. New York: Random House, 1977.

Purdy, Strother B., *The Hole in the Fabric: Science, Contemporary Literature, and Henry James*. Pittsburgh, Pa.: University of Pittsburgh Press, 1977.

Putt, Gorley, *A Preface to Henry James*. London: Longman's, 1986.

Raverat, Gwen, *Period Piece*. New York: W. W. Norton & Company, 1976 (first published 1952).

"Red and Gold" Guides, No. 4, *An Illustrated Guide-Book to the Principal Summer Resorts of the United States*. New York: The American and Foreign Publication Co., 1875.

Reid, T. Wemyss, *The Life, Letters, and Friendships of Richard Monckton Milnes, First Lord Houghton*. London: Cassell & Co., Ltd., 1890 (2 vols.).

Renan, Ernest, *Brother and Sister: A Memoir and the Letters of Ernest and Henriette Renan*. New York: Macmillan & Co., 1896.

———, *The Poetry of the Celtic Race, and other studies by Ernest Renan*. London: Walter Scott, Ltd., [1896] (no publication date — introduction dated 1896).

———, *Recollections and letters of Ernest Renan* (Isabel F. Hapgood, trans.). New York: Cassell Pub. Co., 1892.

———, *Recollections of My Youth* (C. B. Pitman, trans.). New York: G. P. Putnam's Sons, 1883.

———, *La Vie de Jésus* (deuxième édition). Paris: Michel Lévy Frères, 1863.

Rourke, Constance, "The American," in Rourke, *American Humor*, Harcourt, Brace & Co., 1931.

Rovit, Earl, "James and Emerson: The Lesson of the Master," *American Scholar*, Vol. 33 (1964), p. 434.

Rowe, John Carlos, *The Theoretical Dimensions of Henry James*. Madison: University of Wisconsin Press, 1984.

Ruhm, Herbert (ed.), *Confidence*, by Henry James, "Now first edited from the manuscript, with notes, reproduction, and bibliography by Hubert Ruhm." New York: Grosset & Dunlap, 1962.

Ruskin, John, *The Elements of Drawing* (with an introduction by Lawrence Campbell). New York: Dover, 1971 (first published 1857).

———, *Ruskin's Venice* ("The Venetian Index" by John Ruskin, with modern notes, and a preface), Arnold Whittick, ed. New York: Watson-Guptill Pub., 1976.

Sainte-Beuve, Charles Augustin, *Saint-Beuve: Selected Essays* (translated and edited by Francis Steegmuller and Norbert Guterman). New York: Doubleday & Co., 1963.

Sargent, John T., Mrs. (ed.), *Sketches and Reminiscences of the Radical Club of Chestnut Street, Boston*. Boston: James R. Osgood & Co., 1880.

Sarotte, Georges-Michel, *Like a Brother, Like a Lover: Male Homosexuality in the American Novel and Theater from Herman Melville to James Baldwin* (Richard Miller, trans.). New York: Anchor Press/Doubleday, 1978. (Originally published as *Comme un frère, Comme un amant*. Paris: Flammarion, 1976.)

Saum, Lewis O., "Henry James's Christopher Newman: 'The American' as Westerner," in *Henry James Review*, Vol. 15, No. 1 (1994).

Schapiro, Leonard, *Turgenev: His Life and Times*. New York: Random House, 1978.

Schouler, William, *A History of Massachusetts in The Civil War*. Boston: E. P. Dutton & Co., 1868.

Scudder, Horace Elisha, *James Russell Lowell: A Biography*. Boston: Houghton, Mifflin & Co., 1901 (2 vols.).

Sedgwick, Eve Kosovsky, *Between Men: English Literature and Male Homosocial Desire*. New York: Columbia University Press, 1985.

———, *Epistemology of the Closet*. Berkeley: University of California Press, 1990.

Semenko, Irina M., *Vasily Zhukovsky*. Boston: Twayne Publishers, 1976.

Sennett, Richard, *The Fall of Public Man*. New York: Alfred A. Knopf, 1977.

Seymour, Miranda, *A Ring of Conspirators: Henry James and His Literary Circle— 1895–1915*. London: Hodder & Stoughton, 1988.

Shannon, Martha A. S., *Boston Days of William Morris Hunt*. Boston: Marshall Jones Co., 1923.

Sherman, Stuart P., "The Aesthetic Idealism of Henry James," in Sherman, *Contemporary Literature*. New York: Henry Holt & Co., 1917; reprinted in Dupee, *The Question of Henry James*, p. 70.

Showalter, Elaine, "Syphilis, Sexuality, and the Fiction of the *Fin de Siècle*," in Yeazell, ed., *Sex, Politics, and Science in The Nineteenth-Century Novel*. Baltimore: Johns Hopkins Press, 1986, p. 88.

Skelton, Geoffrey, *Richard and Cosima Wagner: Biography of a Marriage*. Boston: Houghton Mifflin, 1982.

Smalley, George W., M.A., *Anglo-American Memories*. New York: G. P. Putnam's Sons, 1911.

Spender, Stephen, "The Golden Bowl," in Spender's *The Destructive Element*. London: Jonathan Cape, 1936.

Springer, Mary Doyle, *A Rhetoric of Literary Character: Some Women of Henry James*. Chicago: University of Chicago Press, 1978.

Stallman, R. W., "Some Rooms from 'The Houses That James Built,' " *Texas Quarterly*, Winter 1958, pp. 181–84, 189–92.

Stebbins, Theodore E., Jr., *The Lure of Italy: American Artists and The Italian Experience 1760–1914* (catalog of an exhibition). Boston: Museum of Fine Arts, 1992 ("in association with Harry N. Abrams, Inc., Publishers, New York").

———, Carol Troyen and Trevor J. Fairbrother, *A New World: Masterpieces of American Painting 1760–1910* (catalog of an exhibition). Boston: Museum of Fine Arts, 1983.

Stein, Gertrude, *The Autobiography of Alice B. Toklas*. New York: Vintage Books, 1990 (first published by Harcourt Brace, 1933).

Stevens, Hugh, "Sexuality and the Aesthetic in *The Golden Bowl*," *Henry James Review*, Vol. 14 (Winter 1993), p. 55.

Stevenson, Robert Louis, *Vailima letters: Being correspondence addressed by Robert Louis Stevenson to Sidney Colvin, November 1890–October 1894* (Sidney Colvin, ed.). London: Methuen & Co., 1895.

Stokes, John, *In The Nineties*. Hemel Hempstead, U.K.: Harvester Wheatsheat, 1989.

Strouse, Jean, *Alice James: A Biography*. Boston: Houghton Mifflin Co., 1980.

Stuart, Gen. Charles, *Short Sketch of The Life of Louisa, Marchioness of Waterford*. London: Spottiswoode & Co., 1892.

Sturgis, Howard Overing, *Belchamber*. London: Oxford University Press, 1935 (first published 1909).

Sturgis, Julian, *From Books and Papers of Russell Sturgis by his son Julian Sturgis*. Oxford: printed at the University Press "For private circulation only." n.d. (acquired by Baker Library, at Dartmouth College, in 1936).

Swan, Michael, *Henry James*. London: Longmans, Green & Co. Ltd., 1950.

Symonds, John Addington, *The Memoirs of John Addington Symonds* (Phyllis Grosskurth, ed.). New York: Random House, 1984.

Taintro, Charles, *The Hudson River Route, New York to Albany, Saratoga Springs, etc*. New York: Tainter Brothers, copyright 1869; updated in 1870s.

Tanner, Tony, *Henry James and the Art of Nonfiction*. Athens, Ga.: University of Georgia Press, 1995.

———, *The Reign of Wonder; Naivety and Reality in American Literature*. Cambridge: Cambridge University Press, 1965.

Tharp, Louise Hall, *Mrs. Jack: A Biography of Isabella Stewart Gardner*. New York: Congdon & Weed, Inc., 1965.

———, *The Peabody Sisters of Salem*. Boston: Little, Brown & Co., 1950.

The Thousand and One Nights; or An Arabian Nights Entertainment, Translated by Rev. Edward Forster . . . with some additions, amendments, and notes, from the work of E. W. Lane. New York: C. S. Francis and Co.; Boston: J. H. Fracis, 1847.

Thwaite, Ann, *Waiting for the Party: The Life of Frances Hodgson Burnett, 1849–1924*. London: Secker & Warburg, 1974.

Todorov, Tzvetan, *The Poetics of Prose* (Richard Howard, trans.; Foreword by Jonathan Culler). Ithaca, N.Y.: Cornell University Press, 1977 (originally published as *La Poetique de la prose*, Éditions du Seuil, 1971).

Tollemache, Honorable Lionel A., *Talks with Mr. Gladstone*. London: Edward Arnold, 1898. (3d ed., 1903, reprinted with introduction by Asa Briggs).

Troubridge, Una, Lady (Una Vicenzo Troubridge), *The Life and Death of Radclyffe Hall*. London: Hammond, 1961. (Foreword is dated 1945).

Troy, William, "The Altar of Henry James," *The New Republic*, February 15, 1943.

Tryon, W. S., *Parnassus Corner: A Life of James T. Fields, Publisher to the Victorians*. Boston: Houghton Mifflin Co., 1963.

Turgenev, Ivan, *Literary Reminiscences and Autobiographical Fragments*. ("With an essay on Turgenev by Edward Wilson.") David Magarshark, trans. London: Faber & Faber, 1984 (paperback; first issued as hardback, 1959).

———, Polnoe subranie sochinenii i pisem v dvadtsati vos'ini tomakh. Pis'ma v trinadtsati tomakh. Moscow—Leningrad. [Pushkin House] 1961–68.

———, *Tourgueneff and his French Circle*. (Letters edited by E. Halperine-Kaminsky, translated by Ethel M. Arnold). London: T. Fisher Unwin, 1898.

Vidal, Gore, "Introduction," *The Golden Bowl* by Henry James. (reprinted edition, 1985).

Vose, Robert C., Jr., *The Return of William Morris Hunt*. (Catalog of a show at the Vose Galleries). Boston: Vose Galleries, 1986.

Wagenknecht, Edward, *William Dean Howells: The Friendly Eye*. New York: Oxford University Press, 1969.

Wagner, Cosima [Liszt], *Cosima Wagner's Diaries: Volume I: 1869–1877; Volume II: 1878–1883*. (Martin Gregor-Dellin and Dietrich Mack, eds.); (Geoffrey Skelton, trans.) New York: Harcourt Brace Jovanovich, 1980 (German ed. 1977).

Ward, Mrs. Humphry (Mary Augusta), *Robert Elsmere* (Rosemary Ashton, ed.). Oxford: Oxford University Press, 1987 (first published 1898).

Wardley, Lynn, "Woman's Voice, Democracy's Body, and *The Bostonians*," *ELH*, Vol. 56, No. 3 (Fall 1989), p. 639.

Warren, Austin, "Henry James: Symbolic Imagery in the Later Novels," in *Rage for Order*. Ann Arbor: University of Michigan Press, 1959.

———, *The Elder Henry James*. New York: Macmillan Co., 1934.

Waugh, Evelyn, *A Little Learning: The First Volume of an Autobiography*. Boston: Little, Brown & Co., 1964.

Webster, Sally, *William Morris Hunt, 1824–1879*. Cambridge: Cambridge University Press, 1991.

Weimer, Joan Myers, *Women Artists, Women Exiles: "Miss Grief" and Other Stories*. New Brunswick, N.J.: Rutgers University Press, 1988.

Wells, H. G., *Experiment in Autobiography: Discoveries and Conclusions of a Very Ordinary Brain (since 1866)*. New York: Macmillan, 1934.

West, Rebecca, *Henry James*. New York: Henry Holt & Co., 1916.

Wharton, Edith, *A Backward Glance*. New York: Charles Scribner's Sons, 1934.

Whitman, Walt, *Complete Poetry and Collected Prose* (Justin Kaplan, ed.). New York: Library of America, 1982.

Whittick, Arnold (ed.), *Ruskin's Venice*. New York: Waston-Guptill Publications, 1976.

Williams, Susan S., "The Tell-Tale Representation: James and *The Sense of The Past*," *Henry James Review*, Vol. 14, No. 3 (Winter 1993), p. 72.

Wilson, Edmund, "The Ambiguity of Henry James," in Wilson, *The Triple Thinkers*. New York: Harcourt, Brace & Co., 1930.

Wilson, Raymond J., III, "The Possibility of Realism: 'The Figure in the Carpet' and Hawthorne's Intertext," *Henry James Review*, Vol. 16, No. 2 (Spring 1995), p. 142.

————, "Turgenev and The Life-Giving Drop," in Ivan Turgenev, *Literary Reminiscences and Autobiographical Fragments*. London: Faber & Faber, 1959 (reprinted in paperback, 1984). First published in *The New Yorker* in 1957.

Winner, Viola Hopkins, *Henry James and the Visual Arts*. Charlottesville: University of Virginia Press, 1970.

Wolff, Geoffrey, *Black Sun: The Brief Transit and Violent Eclipse of Harry Crosby*. New York: Random House, 1976.

Woolf, Judith, *Henry James: The Major Novels*. Cambridge: Cambridge University Press, 1991.

Wright, Chauncey, "The Evolution of Self-Consciousness," *North American Review*, Vol. 116 (1873), p. 245.

Yeazell, Ruth Bernard (ed.), *Sex, Politics, and Science in the Nineteenth-Century Novel* ("Selected Papers from the English Institute 1983–84," New Series, no. 10"). Baltimore: Johns Hopkins Press, 1986.

Zacharias, Greg W., *Henry James and the Morality of Fiction*. New York: Peter Lang, 1993.

Zhitova, Anne V., *The Turgenev Family*. London: Harvill Press, 1947.

Zorzi, Rosella Mamoli, "Titian and XIX Century American Writers," in *Annali Di Ca Foscari*, Vol. 30, Nos. 1–2, 1991, pp. 173–201.

NOTES

I have used an abbreviated citation form throughout; the full citations are given in the Bibliography. When referring to Henry James's novels, where no other edition is indicated the reference is to the Penguin edition. (Until the Library of America completes its standard edition, the excellently edited Penguins are the best and most widely available.) The citations of the early novels not available in Penguin are from the Library of America volumes that have appeared. James's book reviews and travel writings in most cases are cited from both the original publication and the Library of America edition or from the specialized collections listed under his name in this bibliography.

Henry James's biographical works are abbreviated as follows:

NSB: *Notes of a Son and Brother.*
SBO: *A Small Boy and Others.*
STORY: *William Wetmore Story and His Friends.*
TMY: *The Middle Years.*

Abbreviated citations for published letters refer to the works listed with full references in the Bibliography. For unpublished works, I have drawn upon these manuscript collections:

Albany Institute of History and Art, Albany.
Austin: Humanities Research Center, University of Texas at Austin.
Barrett: C. Waller Barrett Collection, University of Virginia.
Benson Diary: A.C. Benson Diaries, Pepys Library, Magdalene
     College, Cambridge.
Berg: Berg Collection, New York Public Library.
BL: British Library.
Bodleian Library, Oxford University.
BPL: Boston Public Library.

Church: William Conant Church Correspondence [Galaxy
    Magazine], New York Public Library.
Colby: Special Collections, Colby College, Waterville, Maine.
Fales: Fales Collection, Bobst Memorial Library, New York
    University.
Fields, Annie, Journal: Annie Adams Fields Papers, 1852–1912,
    Massachusetts Historical Society.
Gardner: Isabella Stewart Gardner Papers, Gardner Museum,
    Boston.
Houghton: The James Family Papers, Houghton Library, Harvard
    University.
Hove: Viscount and Lady Wolseley Papers, Hove Central Library,
    Hove, East Sussex.
Hunt: Leigh Hunt Papers, Keats House, London.
Huxley: Thomas Huxley Papers, Imperial College, London.
Jordan: Elizabeth Jordan [Harper's Bazaar Magazine] Papers, New
    York Public Library.
Leeds: Brotherton Collection, Leeds University Library.
LoC: Manuscript Division, Library of Congress.
MHS: Massachusetts Historical Society, Boston.
NYHS: New-York Historical Society, New York City.
NYPL: Research Division, New York Public Library.
OWH Jr. Holmes Papers: The Oliver Wendell Holmes, Jr., Papers,
    Harvard Law School Library.
O. W. Holmes Papers: The Oliver Wendell Holmes (Sr.) Papers,
    Houghton Library, Harvard University.
Pushkin House: Institute of Russian Literature, St. Petersburg.
TsGALI: Central State Archive of Literature and Art, Moscow.
Vaux: Robertson James archive, Henry J. Vaux, Berkeley, California.
Waterlow Diary: Sir Sidney Waterlow's Diary, Berg Collection,
    New York Public Library.

In citations from letters, the following abbreviations are used for
members of the James family:

AJ: Alice James (sister).
AHJ: Alice Howe James (sister-in-law).
CBJ: Catherine Barber James (grandmother).

CW: Catherine Walsh (Aunt Kate).

GWJ: Garth Wilkinson James (Wilky, brother).

HJ: Henry James.

HJ Sr.:   Henry James (father).

MRJ: Mary Robertson James (mother).

RJ: Robertson James (Bob, brother).

WJ: William James (brother).

1   EARLIEST MEMORIES: ALONG THE HUDSON

1. Bosanquet, 4.
2. SBO, 28 ("I seem to have more or less begun life . . . with impressions of New Brighton"). New Brighton was a village on the north side of Staten Island.
3. The memories are given at SBO, 28–29. New Brighton is described in *Francis' Picture of New York* (1851), 21–22.
4. *The Portrait of a Lady.* See Chapter 22.
5. See SBO, 5. Her father's father had come to the United States from County Longford, Ireland. Her mother was Jennet Rea, of Montgomery County, New York. Hastings, 5. HJ says that both his grandmother's parents were of "English blood"; Dupee and other American commentators have taken this as an error, but it is reasonable to suppose that the Barbers and the Reas were Anglo-Irish.
6. SBO, 178.
7. *The Portrait of a Lady,* 76–77.
8. SBO, 8–9, where HJ says he has put both this incident and the interior of his grandmother's house into a "work of imagination"; this is evidently *The Portrait of a Lady,* 77–78. The house, which stood at the northeast corner of North Pearl and Steuben Streets, has long since been torn down. The entrance seems to have been on Steuben Street, which ran uphill to the Albany Academy (not, as HJ remembered, the state capitol), whose gilded dome was visible above the trees.
9. SBO, 5.
10. SBO, 5–6. Compare the otherwise autobiographical "The Pupil," where the protagonist is described as a throwback accounted for only by "the mysteries of transmission, the far jumps of heredity. Where his detachment from most of the things they [his parents] represented had come from was more than an observer could say—it certainly had burrowed under two or three generations." "Lesson of the Master," 133.
11. As well as three children who died in infancy. Hastings, 16–17.
12. In the winter of 1845–46 the Jameses probably were visiting at 19 Washington Square. Henry's reminiscence is inserted in *Washington Square,* 40.
13. No. 19 Washington Square, now Washington Square North. The house still stands, and is the property of New York University. It has been cut up into eight apartments.
14. Apparently in the summer of 1845–46. The memories are recorded in *Washington Square,* 40.
15. Compare *Washington Square,* 77–78. The house in the novel is evidently

the Walsh house at No. 19, except that a balcony has been added under the drawing-room windows, and the trim is marble instead of brownstone.

16. SBO, 122–23.

17. That is, they leased the house, and completed the purchase in 1851. The lease-purchase agreement was probably an early form of purchase-money mortgage, and suggests that the Jameses had to husband their resources even after the first distribution of the Albany estate. As Edel, Lewis, and others have described HJ's family as wealthy, a word may be in order concerning this inheritance.

At his death in 1832, grandfather William James (usually called William of Albany) left an estate officially valued at $1.2 million, consisting principally of real estate in Albany and Syracuse. The actual market price at the time it was distributed would be difficult to estimate now. A newspaper story that HJ quotes in NSB, p. 267, said that the estate was worth $3 million and that William of Albany was the wealthiest man in the state of New York except for John Jacob Astor. This newspaper story has often been repeated in biographies of the Jameses (see, e.g., Edel, Lewis, Habegger, Kaplan on HJ; Allen on WJ, p. 4). The story seems greatly exaggerated. The James house in Albany was large but not unusually so, judging by street maps and insurance maps of the time, and the Jameses were far overshadowed even in Albany by the Van Rensselaers, Clintons, and other families.

William of Albany was certainly wealthy, however, and he left a peculiarly inept and ambiguous will, which has been the subject of a great deal of psychological commentary. The facts are these. After a number of specific bequests, the residue of the estate was placed in a trust, which was not to be distributed to the named heirs until the youngest of them had reached twenty-one years of age. The principal assets were real estate and mills in Syracuse. The two surviving children of William's first wife were given favored treatment over the ten children of his widow, who had been his third wife. The trustees were given discretion to award a portion of the trust, however; it was unclear whether they had discretion to include William and HJ Sr., sons of the third wife, in the final distribution. The trustees asked the probate court to clarify the provisions of the will; the widow and her sons William and Henry all filed bills asking that the will be interpreted or reformed. The Supreme Court of Errors and Appeals eventually dissolved the will because the terms of the trust were uncertain in a manner that violated the rule against perpetual trusts, as codified in New York statutes. See *Hawley* v. *James*, 16 Wend. 60 (1836), reversing 5 Paige Ch. 64 (3 N.Y. Chancery Rep. 734) (1835).

The final result was that the widow, Catherine Barber James, chose to receive one third of the income from the estate during her lifetime. After some negotiations she agreed to accept a fixed income of $18,800, which suggests her share of the residuary estate was on the order of $400,000, which is in accord with the official valuation. Two thirds of the estate, apparently about $1 million, was then distributed to surviving children and grandchildren. HJ Sr. received about one twelfth of the residuary estate. Contemporary press put his share at $100,000, which is roughly consistent with these figures. His income from this property was probably from $3,000 to $5,000. This was an upper-middle-class income for a large family. A contemporary account says families on Washington Square had about $10,000 a year. Comparisons are difficult to make because of the very different mode of life in the 1850s, but HJ Sr.'s income was roughly equivalent to $60,000–$75,000 in 1995 dollars. This income was evidently supplemented by gifts from his mother, transmitted by Gideon Hawley, one of the trustees appointed by the will to administer the remainder of the estate. Hawley had dispensed allowances to the heirs until the estate was distributed. Because the estate consisted largely of real estate and the trustees were reluctant to sell, the distribution was not completed until 1847 or 1848.

The financial arrangements reveal the family structure. Catherine Barber James, her trustees and attorneys played the active role in the litigation throughout. She ended with a life estate in the Albany house and an income about five times larger than that of her son Henry. Gideon Hawley was her friend and trustee, as well as administrator of William of Albany's estate, and it is likely that it was only at her direction the children received from Hawley disbursements in excess of their own incomes. In short, until the death of grandmother Catherine Barber James when HJ was sixteen years old, the extended James family was a matriarchy headed by her, and while the family was wealthy, and had wealthy connections, HJ Sr.'s own independent means never rose beyond the upper middle class.

18. MRJ to Mrs. Garth Wilkinson, November 29, 1946, Houghton; unpub.
19. NSB, 176–78.
20. MRJ to Catherine Barber James, January 14, 1849, Houghton; unpub.
21. Carlyle, in a letter to Emerson, says that James confirmed the impression that a stammering man was always valuable, but the more detailed description in Edward Emerson's capsule biography, in *Early Years of the Saturday Club*, says that the elder Henry James hesitated on initial consonants, which we would call a stutter rather than a stammer. Wharton describes the stutter of both father and son in *A Backward Glance*, an account that Edel for some reason refers to as "apochryphal."
22. NSB, 178.
23. At 11 Fifth Avenue. In Henry's lifetime the house was demolished to make way for the Brevoort Hotel, which has long since vanished in its turn.
24. A famous story of HJ Sr.'s conversion to Swedenborgianism is told in a fictionalized, autobiographical fragment published in Henry James (Sr.), *The Literary Remains of Henry James* (William James, ed.). In this tale, the father while visiting Windsor "in the spring of 1844" was overcome by a terrible foreboding, a daydream of a squatting figure of evil, which precipitated a severe depression. In this tale, the father did not recover his health for months, despite consulting all the famous physicians of London, until a Mrs. Chichester explained that he had undergone a "vastation." He thereupon read the works of Swedenborg, which brought the cure. HJ repeats the story in NSB, 173–74, giving the published version as his source, and disclaiming any firsthand knowledge ("It was all a play I hadn't 'been to' ").

There is no independent evidence that the story of the conversion experience is anything other than fiction. The elder James was familiar with the works of Swedenborg before going to England; one of his purposes in going was to meet J. J. Garth Wilkinson, who was leading a revival of Swedenborgian thought in England. On their return, Mary James wrote regularly to the Wilkinsons, the Jameses' close friends and mentors in Swedenborgianism, and these letters have survived. Although the letters are intimate and filled with reports of the state of health of the family, and fond reminiscences of their visit with the Wilkinsons in England, there is no hint in them of either an illness or a dramatic conversion experience on her husband's part. It is very unlikely that in these friendly, confiding letters—she and Mrs. Wilkinson had both been pregnant at the time, and each child was given a name from the other family—she should not have mentioned the dramatic events of the previous spring, or commented on Henry's recovery.

25. See Warren, 132.

26. For the relation to Joseph Henry, see R.W.B. Lewis, 33–34, citing the Papers of Joseph Henry, Vol. 3 (1979), 344–499.

27. Swedenborg was a scientist, and in the text I summarize the views of his American followers—notably the founders of Brook Farm, and HJ Sr. himself—in the 1840s. In HJ Sr.'s writings, Swedenborg is portrayed as a cosmologist, mapping the universe. HJ notes that he was always disgusted at descriptions of Swedenborg as a "mystic." Compare Emerson's essay, "Swedenborg," in *Representative Men*. Hawthorne's novels contain a self-conscious account of the Swedenborgian sensibility among HJ Sr.'s contemporaries, especially in *The House of Seven Gables* and *The Blythedale Romance*, which again is primarily empirical or scientific. See for instance the description of Clifford Pyncheon's breakfast, in which the subtle influence of a cup of coffee renders his material body translucent, and reveals his moral nature; and the incident in which Alice Pyncheon is mesmerized and becomes an instrument of investigation, a sort of telescope into the spiritual world. In our materialist era it may seem odd to describe Swedenborg as a scientist (although his followers still consider him one), but Fourier's scientific socialism (see below) seemed to follow from Swedenborg's idealist philosophy. HJ Sr., in this tradition, believed the material world was a shadow or reflection of the spiritual: the impress of the divine substance upon nothingness. The sense of a separate self was a consciousness of sin; redemption was the loss of separate individuality, a merging into the substance of humanity as a whole, which was just another name for the divine spirit.

28. See Noyes, *History of American Socialisms* (1870).

29. *What Constitutes the State*, HJ Sr.'s first publication; a pamphlet edition of the speech is quoted in Warren, 90–91.

30. There are similarities of personality between HJ Sr. and Hollingsworth, the "philanthropist" in Hawthorne's *Blythedale Romance*, a parable of the Brook Farm experience. Although this character is usually taken to be modeled on George Ripley, the editor of *The Harbinger*, the physical resemblance is too neat. Hawthorne seems to have put homely Margaret Fuller's character into the flourishing beauty, Zenobia; and the halt, stammering James into the vigorous blacksmith, Hollingsworth.

31. On December 18, 1847, J. J. Garth Wilkinson—the leader of Fourierism and the Swedenborg revival in England—wrote, "glad your spare cash goes into *The Harbinger*." Warren, 248*n*. Brook Farm had begun as a transcendentalist settlement, in 1841, in which Elizabeth Peabody's mild, tolerant Christian socialism was dominant. About 1845 it was converted to Fourier, and became a phalanx; the famous journal *The Dial* became *The Phalanx* and then *The Harbinger*. Noyes in his history and Hawthorne in his novel both blame the men in the colony for importing the French socialist creed and ultimately wrecking the experiment; Hawthorne described it as a conscious subversion by the single-minded "philanthropist."

32. See Le Clair, 159.

33. See for example, James's review of the Swedenborgian journal *The New Christian Repository*, in *The Harbinger*, Saturday, February 19, 1848, from which the quoted phrase is taken. His view was that Christian belief was simply rational. Human nature in all its details was an expression of the divine nature; this was the great meaning of the incarnation of Christ. Human

passions were expressions of the divine spirit, and society, if these passional forces were allowed to operate freely, would break through the empty shells of material forms and laws, the illusions of self-importance, the errors of government and laws, and establish itself on the basis of true spontaneous morality. "Every faculty of man, and every exercise of such faculty, derive their constant animation from the spiritual sphere. . . ." Ibid., 126. Science was now discovering the laws by which the sexual passions, the religious sentiments, the ties of family, could be harnessed like magnetism.

34. Warren, 114.

35. HJ a little later, in the summer of 1853 or 1854, was intensely disappointed at being told he was too young for a novel, *Hot Corn*, by Solon Robinson, about a little girl who "hawked that familiar American luxury in the streets." SBO, 75.

36. Insurance maps at the New-York Historical Society show that the house was only twenty feet wide, was built in 1848, and was in a row of attached houses that still contained some gaps and a carpenter's establishment. The other details are from SBO. Edel, HJ, Vol. 1, 88, incorrectly describes this as the renovation of an old "mansion."

37. "[*The New Times*] will aim to maintain in the social sphere, the essential and permanent interests of man; in philosophy, to discover and set forth the laws of order, which govern the spiritual as well as the natural universe; and in religion, to assert and illustrate the distinctive hope of Christianity, which is the universal establishment of fraternal relations among men. . . ." From an advertisement in *The Harbinger*, January 1848. The list of expected contributors included J. J. Garth Wilkinson and most of the leaders of Brook Farm.

38. By 1855, with some fluctuations, the staff had increased to three female servants and a governess for Alice. See Habegger, 303. The census data that Habegger quotes are difficult to interpret, but confirm the modesty of the domestic establishment by the standards of the day.

39. In England and America, a manservant and a carriage were among the indicia of the upper class; the Jameses had neither, and Mary James did her own marketing.

40. MRJ to RJ, January 14, 1874; Vaux Papers, quoted Strouse, 24. Robertson had asked advice about his first child's constipation, and his mother replied, "this is not a weak, but a strong point in the little man."

41. Bronson Alcott Journal, March 2, 1851, 241, 242. The guest was Emerson, who repeated the saying to Alcott.

42. HJ to Elizabeth Jordan, May 3, 1907; Elizabeth Jordan Papers, NYPL. Jordan was then editor of *Bazar*, and had asked for James's favorite fairy tale. See Jordan, *Favorite Fairy Tales, The Childhood Voices of Representative Men and Women* (1907); James, "Henry James and the *Bazar* Letters," Bulletin of the New York Public Library (1958), 75. Compare *What Maisie Knew*, 51.

43. NSB, 166.

44. SBO, 70–71. Robertson also took this walk with her when he was old enough, and recalled it in a letter to Alice Howe James, February 24, 1898, Houghton; unpub.

45. Sixth Avenue is now the Avenue of the Americas, and has been extended southward, obliterating the little streets. There is now a park on the site of the old Washington Market, which was much like the better-remembered Fulton Street market across town.

46. In SBO, HJ associated the shabby red paint with Irish immigrants, his father's democracy, but in truth the great wave of immigration from Ireland, the flight from the famine and oppressive landlords, had only just begun.

The shabby red houses sheltered the Dutch and Scots-Irish immigrants of an earlier time.

47. In SBO, James said that he began school on the south side of Waverly Place; this would have been in the fall of 1848. He remembered the schoolteacher as Irish, a Mrs. Daly, but this seems to be wrong. It is highly unlikely that an Irishwoman, given the prejudices of the day, would have kept a school for the children of the well-to-do in Washington Square, and city directories show no entry for a Mrs. Daly (in any possible spelling) on Waverly Place or any nearby address. In 1848 there were two schools on the south side of Waverly Place, west of Washington Square: the Misses Taylors' school, and Miss Meeker's. By 1851 there was an Ann Day school at 108 Waverly Place, which is tantalizing, but there is no entry under this name in the 1848–1849 Doggett's directory. The Taylors' school took in both boys and girls, as Harry's school and few others did, and we have an almost exactly contemporary description by Euphemia P. Olcott, who attended the Taylors' school a year or two after Harry, that matches his description: "The house consisted of two stories and an attic, and had a low stoop. . . ." ("A Fashionable Dame's School of a Bygone Type," in Brown, 208). Details of the school are taken from Olcott's account. It is possible that "Mrs. Daly" worked for the Misses Taylor, but it is more likely that Harry either mixed up his teacher with an Irish nurse or mistook the name. Possibly he confused "the Misses Taylor" with "Mrs. Daly." In *The American Scene*, the chronicle of his visit to the United States in 1904–5, he stopped in Washington Square and found "Mrs. Daly's" house on Waverly Place somewhat decayed and absorbed into a general dilapidated Irish tone, and perhaps this general impression colored his later memories and his description in SBO. There were no identifiably Irish names in the neighborhood in 1848. The school is also mentioned in *Washington Square*, where he gives his teacher a broad bottom, and has her drink tea from an unmatched cup and saucer.

48. Many contemporary accounts mention Henry James's stutter or stammer, which persisted into adulthood. Edith Wharton in her autobiography described the stutter and said it had been discovered in the "kindergarten days" in Albany.

49. "George du Maurier," in *Partial Portraits*, 327.

50. There is, rather oddly, a substantial literature praising Henry James, Sr.'s method of educating his children. Le Clair has devoted an entire volume, *Young Henry James: 1843–1870*, to the theory that his superlative method accounted for the production of two geniuses among the children. Harry himself, in his memoirs of the father, was strongly critical, and denied that there was any system in the frequent changes of venue. (He calls them "vain and unintended," although he is able to "convert" them to a successful education, quite "as if" his parents had intended them so. SBO, 214.) Nor is there anything in the father's surviving letters that suggests a system. By and large the reasons he gave for the changes, when he mentioned them, were related to his own needs—i.e., to save money, to move to another city—or were perfectly random; for instance, the family went to Switzerland because of the wonderful schools; and HJ Sr. immediately decided that the Swiss schools were overrated. They then traveled to England for the famous schools, and HJ Sr. instead engaged a tutor. Then the family moved to Paris, and the tutor was fired; the boys were put into a phalangist school; and so on. It is a sad commentary, and most unnerving, that this abusive behavior is generally praised or viewed with amused tolerance by the family's biographers.

51. The only open criticism in Harry's memoir of his father—but he dwells on

it—is of the constant turmoil in domestic arrangements, the rapid disappearances of nurses and tutors of whom Harry often was fond, the succession of inappropriate schools, and the movements of the family itself every few weeks or months. In SBO, Harry makes it plain that he believed his father was responsible for the turmoil, and although Harry made the best of it, that turmoil marked him for all his later life. A villain who constantly reappeared in Harry's fiction was the egotistical father. Often there was a tutor or other outsider who tried to rescue a child from the parent's embrace. Strouse discusses HJ Sr.'s abusiveness and the damage done to Alice. The biography of the two youngest boys, Jane Maher's *Biography of Broken Fortunes,* I think also shows the parents' neglect and the father's manipulations.

52. After bearing five children in seven years, Mary James perhaps had closed her bedroom door to her husband; as noted above, after at last having a daughter she apparently decided not to have more children. For whatever reason, in any case the pregnancies, after following each other in quick succession, ceased; and the family's tortured travelings began shortly thereafter. Habegger, 290, speculates that Mary James underwent a miscarriage in the summer of 1849; but this speculation rests on the single word "hemorrhage" in a letter from Wilkinson to HJ Sr., referring to Mary James's illness. There is no mention in the surviving letters of a pregnancy, and it seems quite arbitrary to infer, as Habegger does, a "uteral" hemorrhage following a miscarriage.

53. Bosanquet, 33.

54. *What Maisie Knew,* 20, from which the preceding paragraph is paraphrased. Maisie was just six years old. She learned, in substance, that her parents were using her to carry on their own quarrel, were *willing* to use her as a means to further their love affairs and quarrels; which is substantially the discovery Isabel Archer makes about her husband and a beloved friend in *The Portrait of a Lady.* In *Washington Square* the daughter made the similar discovery that her father did not love her, and had treated her as a means, an object. The identity of HJ and Maisie has often been noted, as for example by Tony Tanner (1965), more recently by Kaufman, and Mitchell ("A Portrait of the Artist as a Young Girl"). McCall's "What Maisie Saw" (1995) is an unequaled evocation of the HJ/Maisie experience of evil as the absence of love. The positive side of HJ/Maisie's revelation, her awareness of a central core of certainty within herself, is well described by Kaston.

2   TEMPORARY QUARTERS IN UNION SQUARE

1. *American Scene,* 74. This is a ferry ride taken in 1905, but I venture to suppose that it was the memory of rides taken in childhood that made him describe the view of New York harbor as the defining vision of America. In SBO James says that he was twelve years old when the daguerreotype was taken, but in the summer of 1855 the family went abroad, and 1854 is more likely.

2. Bronson Alcott's Journal, entry for March 2, 1851, 242.

3. Compare *Bostonians,* 57. The now archaic phrase "enthusiasm of humanity" was roughly equivalent to 1970s "Movement."

4. Alcott Journal, November 4, 1851, 257.

5. Quoted in Grattan, 43–44. Emerson knew how to play this game. In his own diary, referring to his visits to New York and Philadelphia, he said, "The

people who fill them oppress me with their excess virility, and would soon become intolerable, if it were not for a few friends, who, like women, tempered the acrid mass. Henry James was true comfort. . . ." April 1859, quoted in Porte, 412 (1982).

6. Letter to Julia Kellogg, no date, probably from 1860s, quoted in Warren, 184–85.

7. "The Horse-Car Our True Shechinah at the Day," in *Society the Redeemed Form of Man*.

8. See O. W. Holmes to Lady Castletown, April 4, 1916 (on reading *Notes of a Son and Brother*), Holmes Papers, Harvard Law School Library, B26 F13; unpub.

9. RJ to his daughter Mary, "Saturday," probably in January 1882, Vaux; quoted *Alice James's Diary*, Burr ed., 55.

10. This is Mr. Moreen, in "The Pupil," in *The Lesson of the Master*, 128.

11. HJ Sr. to Samuel G. Ward, Houghton; unpub.

12. SBO, 234.

13. *Society the Redeemed Form of Man*, 81.

14. Ibid., 218.

15. Warren, 224. This is not critical; Warren, like Matthiessen, was sympathetic to the elder James's views. Warren perhaps means "characteristic" rather than "unique," as Fourier and his followers identified the social and the spiritual, as indeed did most early-nineteenth-century socialists. Noyes's *History of American Socialisms* is a long meditation on this topic.

16. HJ Sr. to Edmund Tweedy, May 30, 1851, Houghton; unpub.

17. SBO, 44.

18. SBO, 74. Uncle John drank and gambled, had love affairs, and apparently died a suicide in 1855, when HJ and his family were abroad. See Habegger (1991), an amusing fictionalized account of Uncle John's difficulties. Habegger correctly noted the theme of suicide in HJ's work, but attributed it—I think without adequate basis—to Uncle John James's unhappy suicide, of which there is no evidence that HJ ever knew.

19. "Frances Anne Kemble," in *Essays in England*, 90 (1893). This incident probably occurred in the winter of 1848–49, when Mrs. Kemble was giving readings of Shakespeare in New York. Her horseback-riding costume became famous when she published her *Journal* of life on a Southern plantation.

20. Houghton, bMS Am 1094 (1326). This undated note, probably from the fall of 1854, is the earliest surviving of James's letters. Edel, 1 HJ Letters, 5, dates it 1855–56, the winter the family was in Paris, apparently because the notepaper is embossed "Paris." Master Van Winkle was in New York, and this seems an unlikely message to have sent him from Paris. In Houghton the letter is associated with an envelope addressed to "Master E. Van Winkle," but without postage or postmark, and sealed with red wax. The frugal, constantly moving Jameses often used notepaper acquired abroad years before; many of their letters from this period are on notepaper purchased in Windsor, presumably in 1844. They probably had given Harry notepaper from that earlier visit to Europe, and this note was probably delivered by hand in the fall of 1854 while they were still in New York.

21. Catherine ("Kitty") James, daughter of Augustus James (Uncle Gus), had married Robert Emmet; three of Augustus's daughters married Emmet brothers. HJ places her "assembly" on Washington Place, but I cannot find any Emmet on the maps of that street in the 1850s. The house at No. 2 Washington Place in which HJ was born had been purchased originally from Uncle Gus for a modest sum, and then rapidly resold, probably, as Le Clair

speculates, as a device to give HJ Sr. some money in the years before their father's estate was distributed. Robert and Kitty Emmet may have *rented* the house in 1854.
22. SBO, 174.
23. SBO, 175.
24. SBO, 30.
25. SBO, 35.
26. SBO, 227.
27. Edel, in *Les Années Dramatiques* (1932), argued that James's recollection could not be correct. The performance of *The Comedy of Errors* described in the text, which Harry remembered as his first play, was not performed until 1855, according to Edel, by which time HJ would have seen many other plays. See *Complete Plays*, 22; "The Dramatic Years," in *Guy Domville*, 18–19. Edel thinks James saw the play at another theater in 1851. Le Clair accepts Edel's conclusion. Burton's theater opened in 1848, however, and records of the theater in those years are by no means complete, so James's memory may have been correct; it was an extraordinarily good one.
28. SBO, 116–17.
29. SBO, 106.
30. SBO, 109.
31. Henry James used this now famous picture to illustrate the frontispiece of SBO.
32. SBO, 186.

3   FATHER'S ASSAULT ON PARIS

1. James remembered this short-lived magazine as a quarto, but like other things remembered from childhood, it was smaller; the catalog of the British Museum lists it as octavo.
2. SBO, 170. HJ has "Christ and Disciples."
3. SBO, 266–67.
4. SBO, 260–62.
5. Le Clair puts James's total investment in the paper at ten thousand dollars at this time.
6. HJ Sr. to S. G. Ward June 19, 1855, Houghton; unpub.
7. Ibid.
8. HJ Sr. to CBJ, July 11, 1855, Houghton; unpub.
9. SBO, 278–79. See, for instance, MJ's letters concerning the chronic back trouble that afflicted HJ Sr. and his two eldest sons, below.
10. SBO, 279. HJ has "June afternoon" but this is poetic, as they did not sail from New York until June 27, and therefore did not arrive in London until July.
11. SBO, 280. Compare the similar passage in *What Maisie Knew*, on Maisie's first visit to France.
12. SBO, 283–85.
13. HJ in SBO has only William and Wilky there, and is silent as to Bob, but HJ Sr. to his mother August 13, 1855, has all three in the school. Edel has the boys also attending the Institution Haccius, but this is apparently a misreading of SBO, 292–93. LeClair correctly says that there is no evidence for this.
14. Phonetically "Gerebsoff" in SBO; see Le Clair, 164–65.
15. HJ Sr.'s letter to the New York *Daily Tribune*, September 3, 1855 (the let-

ter is dated August 13, 1855, and is quoted Le Clair, 159, 162). It was HJ's inability to intrude on his friends' privacy that doomed the success of his own letters to the *Tribune*, exactly twenty years later. The theme of newspaper invasions of privacy runs all through his fiction.

16. HJ Sr. letter to *Tribune*, September 3, 1855, reprinted Le Clair, 159, 163.
17. HJ Sr. to J. J. Garth Wilkinson, October 13, 1855, Houghton; unpub.
18. HJ Sr. to CBJ, September 25, 1855, Houghton; unpub.
19. See J.J.G. Wilkinson's letter to HJ Sr., October 13, 1855, Houghton, unpub., advising home tuition to save money.
20. SBO, 308–10.
21. "Frances Anne Kemble," *Temple Bar Review* (1893), reprinted in *Essays in London and Elsewhere*, 81, 91 (1893). I have added details to the description from Armstrong, 320, and Lucas, 330–31.
22. James remembered a white dress, but Armstrong says violet or lavender, see above.
23. See especially "The Pupil," 136. A similar exchange between a child and a tutor is in "Gabrielle de Bergerac," *Complete Tales*, II, 137. There is a similar exchange in *What Maisie Knew*, between the female child and her governess. By an odd coincidence, Robert Louis Stevenson was taught by the same Mr. Thomson. In SBO, HJ spells the name "Thompson."
24. Now the Avenue of the Bois-de-Boulogne.
25. The last passage is quoted from SBO, 332.
26. HJ Sr. to CBJ, August 13, 1865, Houghton; unpub.
27. MJ to CBJ, August 25, 1856, Houghton; unpub.
28. SBO, 337–38; compare "The Pupil," 139, in almost identical terms.
29. SBO, 340.
30. Remembered by HJ as "Page with a Falcon," SBO, 342.
31. Ibid.
32. SBO, 351–53; "The Pupil," 137–39.
33. "Around a Spring, by Gustave Droz," book review, *Nation*, August 1871, reprinted in Lit. Crit.: French and European, 368–69.
34. SBO, 347–48. At least he later remembered having such a premonition, after a dream late in life recalled it to him. Ibid.
35. SBO, 367.
36. "Or Clémentine or Augustine," SBO, 382.
37. SBO, 383.
38. *Christianity the Logic of Creation*. London: privately printed, 1857.
39. For HJ Sr.'s fascination with rail travel, see HJ Sr. to S. G. Ward, September 27, 1858, Houghton; unpub.
40. RJ to AJ, February 24, 1898, Houghton; quoted Perry, *The Life and Letters of William James*, Vol. I, 184, 185.
41. HJ Sr. to CBJ, December 24, 1857, Houghton; unpub.
42. SBO, 400–5.
43. HJ Sr. to MRJ, December 14, 1857, Houghton; unpub.
44. Edmond About, *Tolla* (1856). An English translation was published in Boston in 1856, and it is from that edition that I have drawn the paraphrase in the text. HJ in 1 *Story*, 360–61, says that he read this volume with his parents' encouragement in the summer of 1857. The reader familiar with HJ's works will recognize the germs of several later characters and stories here. I do not want to make too strong a case for influence, however: About's novel, like James's later productions, relies on literary conventions, which HJ may have absorbed from any number of sources, or from the cultural air itself.
45. HJ Sr. to CBJ, July 23, 1857, Houghton; reprinted Le Clair, 257.

46. HJ Sr. to William James, October 28, 1857, referring to letters to mother and other brothers; Houghton; unpub.
47. HJ Sr. to William James (brother), October 28, 1857, Houghton; unpub.
48. In the closing paragraphs of SBO, HJ departed from strict chronology in order to combine, in one paragraph, his fainting collapse and his recollection of the sinister M. Ansiot. In *Maisie*, HJ set the little heroine's awakening awareness of sexual love in Boulogne. Woolf has noted the similarity of the description to that in SBO. In the 1850s, the onset of puberty in boys was at about fifteen years, or Harry's age in the winter of 1857–58. In *The Turn of the Screw* and "The Pupil," young boys die at the moment of sexual awareness, precipitated by tutors.
49. HJ Sr. to Anna Ward (Mrs. Samuel G. Ward), November 2, 1857, Houghton; unpub. Compare *What Maisie Knew*, 184.

4   THE FAMILY RETREATS TO NEW ENGLAND

1. The same characteristic expression is observable in the Brady photograph of 1854, John La Farge's portrait of about 1862, and Sargent's birthday-portrait of 1913. HJ's coloring at this time is described from La Farge's portrait. The estimate of the education Harry had received is from SBO; a similar description is given of the James-ish protagonist of "The Pupil."
2. NSB, 67–68 ("the reminiscentially desperate").
3. NSB, 71. HJ conflated the family's two trips to Newport from Europe; this particular reminiscence seems to belong to the first.
4. William Morris Hunt, known as Bill, was not related to his contemporary the British Pre-Raphaelite William Holman Hunt.
5. This was the Berkeley Institute, named for Bishop Berkeley who in Newport's heyday had planned to found an institution of learning there.
6. The concupiscent New Englander in "A Bundle of Letters" was named Leverett. See Chapter 21.
7. HJ Sr. to Fanny MacDaniel, May 13, 1858, and August 15, 1858, Houghton; unpub.
8. Allen, 47–48.
9. Edward Emerson, "William James," in *Later Years of the Saturday Club*, 156–57.
10. AJ to HJ Sr., March 11 [1860], Houghton.
11. Thomas Sergeant Perry was also a grandson of the Admiral Perry who gained fame in the War of 1812 against the British, and the great-great-grandson of Benjamin Franklin, "by direct descent," as he said in later years, when he had become a clubman.
12. See HJ's letters to Perry, appended to Harlow; especially HJ to Thomas Sergeant Perry, March 27, 1860, and June 13, 1860.
13. T. S. Perry's memorandum to Percy Lubbock, quoted in Lubbock, 7–8.
14. Shannon, 47. HJ mentions the back-door entrance a little ruefully in NSB, 81.
15. The eyeglasses are not mentioned in the works on La Farge that I have seen, but HJ with his sensitivity to personal attractions mentioned them twice in NSB. Cortissoz, without mentioning the eyeglasses, said that La Farge's poor eyesight kept him from joining the Union army as he had wished; surely an interesting datum about a painter. Cortissoz, 26.
16. Houghton, 1092.9 (4600).

17. Then styled an "Academy."
18. Act I, Scene 3; Margaret Rawlings's translation.
19. NSB, 9.
20. "Wilhelm Meister's Apprenticeship and Travels," English translation reviewed *North American Review*, July 1865, in Lit. Crit.: French and European, 944. The suggestion is that the reviewer has read the novel before, presumably while in Germany.
21. See HJ Sr. to Edmund Tweedy, July 24, 1860, Houghton; unpub.
22. NSB, 61–62.
23. Shannon, 47, quoting Miss Watson's memoir of the studio. HJ's own recollection in NSB is partial and self-effacing; in NSB he described only his solitary sketching of plaster casts, and his surrender in the face of the life class, see below.
24. This ambition was achieved with his two masterpieces of the 1860s, *The Last Valley—Paradise Rocks*, and *Paradise Valley*. The latter he kept for years in a shed at the site, which he visited at the appropriate time of day and season, doing a little more on each visit, in the manner of the late Monet.
25. Cortissoz, 39.
26. Cortissoz, 25.
27. John La Farge, S.J., *The Manner is Ordinary*, 6. Quoted H. Adams, "The Mind of John La Farge," in Adams, *John La Farge*, 14.
28. See Perry memorandum in Lubbock.
29. Ruskin, *Modern Painters*, Vol. III (1856), Part IV, Chapter 16, § 28; quoted Campbell, Introduction to *Elements of Drawing* (1971).
30. HJ always used this word in this sense, which I believe Ruskin gave it. In his later works he applies it to moral character, see the closing paragraph of *The Sacred Fount* for a good example. See "tone," OED definition.
31. NSB, 95–96.
32. NSB, 96–97, where William's picture of Kitty is reproduced. The portraits of Katherine Temple by Hunt, La Farge, and William James have all survived. Hunt's is *The Lost Profile*. See Webster, 57, 59. There is, however, a tradition that the subject of *The Lost Profile* is Hunt's wife, and that he set the same pose for Kitty, who sat for the students. William's portrait has been dated 1859, but this cannot be correct because William did not become Hunt's student until 1860, the date of Hunt's *Lost Profile*. See Webster, 57, 59. HJ's account in NSB is not clear as to whether all three portraits were painted at the same time. Webster on the evidence of the paintings and Hunt's practice believes they were, and that *The Lost Profile* was a demonstration picture the teacher had painted for his students. Webster, 59. This seems the better reading of NSB.
33. Cortissoz, 23–24.
34. Freely paraphrased from HJ's review, "'Azarion: An Epistle,'" in *North American Review*, January 1865, reprinted in Lit. Crit.: American and English, 603, 608.

5 HENRY BECOMES AN AMERICAN

1. HJ Sr. to R. W. Emerson, no date, dated by HJ in 1862, NSB, 207; quoted NSB, 209.
2. NSB, 119.

3. HJ Sr.'s address at Trinity Church, "The Social Significance of Our Institutions," quoted Matthiessen, *Family*, 59. Lewis also gives extensive extracts from the address taken from newspaper reports.
4. HJ Sr., fragment of letter; no date or addressee; Vaux. This much quoted page is reproduced in Habegger, 430; he persuasively dates it approximately April 17, 1861, and identifies the addressee as Christopher or Elizabeth Cranch.
5. T. S. Perry memorandum, Lubbock, Vol. I, 9.
6. NSB, 102–3.
7. This at least is the account he gave in NSB. HJ attributed the beginning of his lifelong back troubles to this incident, but there has been much debate over the accuracy of his account. See note 16, below.
8. See HJ to Katy Rodgers January 23 [1864?], Houghton; unpub.
9. MRJ to HJ, July 24, 1869, Houghton; unpub. ("You know Father used to say to you, that if you would only fall in love it would be the making of you.")
10. *A Harlot High and Low* (Penguin ed.), 529.
11. *Lost Illusions* (Penguin ed.), 641–44.
12. Throughout his career HJ used the device of a ghost or mythic figure to represent sexual passions that could not be directly described; the best-known example is "The Turn of the Screw," in which the ghosts of servants seduce and corrupt two children.
13. See NSB, 93–94; *Prosper Mérimée*, 3 Literature 66 (July 23, 1898). In 1874, HJ wrote "The Last of the Valerii," which is a variation on Mérimée's story, see below. HJ's narrator in that story was a painter who wore John La Farge's eyeglasses.
14. T. S. Perry to Percy Lubbock, quoted Lubbock I, 8. HJ's first published story, "A Tragedy of Error," is from this period.
15. HJ to Howard James, April 12 [1862], Houghton; unpub.
16. A great deal has been written from a psychoanalytic point of view about the "obscure hurt," as HJ called his back trouble in NSB, 298. Although he did not like to be specific in print about details of his health, in letters HJ was very plain that the difficulty was back trouble. In a letter to Howard Sturgis he traced his lifelong troubles with his back to strain and subsequent neglect in 1862. HJ to Howard Sturgis, May 19, 1899, Houghton; unpub. In NSB, 299, he says that the trouble became painful in the spring, and after a little talk it is plain he means the spring of 1862 (NSB, 301). Unfortunately, HJ muddied the chronology by linking his injury with the beginning of the war. He seemed to say that the injury was caused by a strain, pumping at a fire, in April 1861. Edel claimed that the strain occurred at a fire in a stable in October 1861, which was reported in the local press. Edel has psychoanalytic reasons for linking HJ's sense of injury to a fire very much like the one in which HJ Sr. lost his leg; but the evidence makes the coincidence extremely unlikely. There is no evidence HJ was at the fire in October, to begin with. HJ visited his brother William in Cambridge three days later, without any apparent difficulty. William's letter home describing the visit says nothing about Harry's supposed back injury. In a family that monitored their own and each other's health as closely as the Jameses, it is not credible that Harry could have visited William, shortly after injuring his back, without provoking comment. His father, elder brother, and younger sister all suffered from back trouble, and it seems plainly to have been a hereditary weakness. Careful reading of HJ's own account shows his back seriously troubled him for the first time in the spring of 1862, and that the link with the outbreak of war in the spring of 1861 is purely suppositional, see note 7, above.

17. NSB, 299.
18. Or so one is led to suppose by HJ Sr.'s behavior, NSB, 299–301.
19. M. A. DeW. Howe, *Boston Common* (1921), 62–63.
20. HJ does not record his name, but the evil father in *Washington Square*, who is another such clever doctor, is Harry's judgment on this anonymous person, and perhaps to some degree on HJ Sr. as well.
21. NSB, 300–301.
22. NSB, 301.
23. *Nathaniel Hawthorne*, reprinted Lit. Crit.: English and American, 358–59.
24. The camp itself was at Portsmouth Grove.
25. NSB, 309–16. HJ did not read *Specimen Days* until long afterward, but as he drew the comparison in NSB I have made use of it here. Whitman emphasizes the multiplicity and variety of the soldiers, however, while Harry remarks on their essential unity and similarity. Writing in light of his visit in 1905, when he was struck with the changes in America, Harry goes out of his way to say that there were as yet no Irish or other recent immigrants among the soldiers, but this was probably not correct. There was a substantial Irish presence in Rhode Island and there were many soldiers with Irish surnames, as well as German immigrants, in the army. But HJ dates his own racialist Americanism from this experience.
26. *Specimen Days*, in Whitman, Poetry and Prose, 727.
27. Ibid., 730–31.
28. NSB, 310.
29. GWJ's recollection of the event, quoted Maher, 25.
30. NSB, 243.
31. *American Scene*, 62.
32. NSB, 295–96.
33. NSB, 303.
34. NSB, 331.
35. "The Ghostly Rental," *Scribner's Monthly*, September 1876; 4 *Complete Tales*, 49.
36. NSB, 120–21.
37. NSB, 372.
38. NSB, 243.
39. Quoted in Lewis, 128.
40. His first story of the war, "Story of a Year," is written from the point of view of such a young woman.
41. NSB, 344–45.
42. Quoted in Guterman-Steegmuller, xi–xii.
43. HJ evidently was familiar with the 1847 edition by Rev. Edward Forster, published in four volumes, in New York and Boston, by C. S. Francis, which drew very heavily on the Lane translation, as he put this book into the hands of one of the characters in *The Europeans*, which is set in Cambridge just prior to the revolutions of 1848. I cannot establish when he read it, but it was evidently before he wrote *The Europeans* in 1877. As he puts it in the hand of a young woman, very much like himself, who is living in Cambridge and is on the threshold of her awakening to life, I conjecture that this reference was a private joke—it was extremely unlikely that an unmarried woman would be reading this book in her family's parlor, as she was made to do in HJ's story—and that he himself had read it in Cambridge before his own "epochal spring" in 1865. This would have been in the term he spent at Harvard.
44. I have followed the 1847 edition, which HJ evidently knew (see above). This

story is referred to explicitly, and made to carry a portion of the narrative weight, in *The Europeans*. The prince and princess are combined into a single character, the Princess Casamassima, in *Roderick Hudson* and, of course, *The Princess Casamassima* itself. The name seems meant to convey the polymorphous power of beauty, the "sacred terror" HJ referred to more explicitly in his later novels. A footnote in the 1847 edition, taken from Lane, gives the derivation as "Kamar ez-Zaman, signifying 'The Moon of the Age,' " which adds a kind of mythic superlative degree. The tale was well known; George Eliot used it to characterize her Jewish hero in *Daniel Deronda*; as did HJ in "The Impressions of a Cousin," evidently expecting the reference to be understood without explanation.

    The text of *The Thousand and One Nights* that James's generation knew was in part a recent French invention; but for James it was simply some of the mythology that he inherited from the Old World, and that seemed to embody moral truths.

45. NSB, 340.
46. "James Russell Lowell," *Atlantic Monthly*, January 1892, reprinted *Essays in London*, and *American Essays*, 77, 81.
47. "Miss Maggie Mitchell" of James's reminiscences was Julia Margaret Mitchell, who was thirty years old when Harry admired her acting. *Fanchon* was her stock performance from 1860 onward.
48. See the Appendix for the text of the published review, and a brief note as to the circumstances. Although clearly described in NSB, 355–57, HJ's first published work has not before been identified.
49. NSB, 357. It is a tradition of HJ biography to treat this as an early romantic infatuation, but HJ makes fun of the idea.
50. NSB, 374.
51. Harvard Law School records show that James was enrolled for only two terms, from September 2, 1862, until July 10, 1863. See Le Clair 409, n.6. The requirement for graduation at this time was to have attended three semesters of lectures.
52. Allen, 92.
53. NSB, 311.
54. Quoted HJ Sr. to Elizabeth Peabody, July 30, 1863, Houghton; quoted Maher, 39–40.
55. GWJ to HJ Sr., July 18, 1863, Houghton; quoted Maher, 41–42.
56. NSB, 244–47; "Story of a Year," 91. The incident of a blanket's odors calling up the sense of the battlefield is given in HJ's notebooks, the recollection having been summoned by a visit to Cambridge; in NSB, where it is associated with his "premier initiation"; and in "Story of a Year," where he gives a very circumstantial account of a wounded soldier's return home that is otherwise identical with Wilky's return, and adds what is apparently the same blanket.
57. Ibid., 96.

6 ARRIVING AT MANHOOD IN THE WAR YEARS

1. 1 *Complete Tales*, 23.
2. Although published anonymously, the story was identified as HJ's in a contemporary letter, see Edel and Laurence, 291.

3. HJ to TSP, March 25, 1864, Colby; Harlow, 272; Mrs. George De Kay of Newport to Charles De Kay, February 29, 1864, cited Edel and Laurence, 291.

4. Mrs. George De Kay to Charles De Kay, February 29, 1864, quoted 1 Edel, 215.

5. NSB, 359.

6. "The Story of a Year," 1 *Complete Tales*, 62.

7. HJ to TSP, March 25, 1864, Houghton, reprinted Harlow, 272.

8. This was published as a book notice: "Essays on Fiction, by Nassau W. Senior," in the *North American Review*, October 1864; reprinted Lit. Crit.: American and English, 1196, 1202.

9. Ibid., 1204.

10. Annie Fields diary, book 8, entry for "January 19" 1864 (but evidently February 19 by place in sequence). On September 15, when the family was in a rented house in Boston, HJ Sr. wrote to Park Godwin that he had settled down "here for the remainder of our lives," but this seems only a characteristic manner of expressing his satisfaction at the change. NYPL. But Le Clair, 410 n.13, credits HJ Sr. with carefully laid, long-term plans to remain in the United States at this point, on the basis of this letter.

11. The move may have been prompted by concern for William. The eldest son, alone in Cambridge, had not been entirely in good health, and had suffered from a variety of vague ailments. In the fall of 1863 he wrote home about the uncertainty of his plans. The "too-fond mother," he said, wanted him to go into business and be prosperous; but Father, he knew, held him steadfastly to the life of the mind. Whichever direction he swung, however, he thought that Cambridge would be a good place for the family to settle. Letters of WJ 1, 45–46 (letter dated September 1863); 1 Perry, 215–26 (where date is corrected to November 2, 1863). He was evidently anxious, and when his mother came up to see him, William neglected to meet her at the depot in Boston, so that after a long wait she was obliged to return to Newport by the next train. The next day he wrote to apologize, and ended his letter with a gruesome joke, imagining that she had been run down by a horsecar and that he would find her corpse in the morgue. WJ to MJ, undated, probably fall 1863, Houghton. Anderson comments on the pathology exhibited by this letter, and dates it from early 1864, which is probably not correct. WJ began his medical courses late in 1863, see 1 Perry, 216, "I embraced the medical profession a couple of months ago," fragment to unidentified recipient, February 21, 1864. Medicine appears to have been a compromise between Father and Mother, science and business; it is interesting in that light to compare the opening of HJ's *Washington Square:* "Dr. Sloper's . . . learning and skill were very evenly balanced; he was what you might call a scholarly doctor. . . ."

12. See HJ to Kitty Rodgers, from Ashburton Place, January 24 [1865?], Houghton; unpub.

13. HJ to TSP, October 28 [1864], Duke; Harlow, 275.

14. NSB, 414. HJ declines to give a street number for this door—it is "defiant of vulgar notation"—but says it was "at the opposite end from Beacon." Both the Fieldses and Holmeses lived on Charles Street, but the door at the opposite end of Charles Street from Beacon was the Holmeses'.

15. *The Bostonians*, 45; HJ put Olive Chancellor into Annie Fields's house.

16. "A Most Extraordinary Case," 1 *Complete Tales*, 330–31; first published *Atlantic Monthly*, April 1868. Except that Holmes was twenty-three when they met, and Harry made Mason an orphan for purposes of the story, this stands

without change as an acute description of Holmes at the time of their friendship. The plot also bears interesting parallels to what we know of the course of this friendship, see Chapter 7.

17. As noted by Louis Auchincloss, the character Basil Ransome in HJ's *The Bostonians* strongly resembles Holmes, turned into a Southerner by one of James's characteristic inversions. HJ attributed to this character an interesting summary of Holmes's philosophy as it had evolved in the early 1870s.

18. From the autobiographical (see below) "Poor Richard," 1 *Complete Tales*, 207.

19. NSB, 407.

20. Addressing himself both to the business office in Boston and to the journal's editor in Cambridge. Both letters, dated July 30, 1864, are in Houghton.

21. NSB, 404.

22. The preceding paragraphs are paraphrased from NSB, 405.

23. "Emily Chester," in Lit. Crit.: English and American, 588, 592.

24. Ibid., 594.

25. We are reminded that HJ did not care for Poe, and did not yet know Whitman, whom he would later admire. HJ never was aware of Melville, who had by this time sunk into obscurity.

26. The firm's name at this time was Ticknor, Reed, and Fields. Reed's name shortly dropped away, and I have used throughout the more familiar Ticknor & Fields, which has been revived in recent years as an imprint of Houghton Mifflin.

27. "Puffing"—paying for favorable reviews—was common, and other book publishers also used captive magazines to promote book sales. See M. Kelley, 9–10. *Harper's* (1850) and *Putnam's Monthly* (1853) had preceded Fields, but with Annie's assistance he did a better job in capturing the allegiance of authors.

28. A. Fields diary, July 31, 1864. This is the first appearance in her diary, at any rate, in which she seems to have assiduously recorded every visit of Ticknor & Fields authors, including HJ Sr.

29. A. Fields diary, July 31, 1864.

30. [A. Fields] Biog Notes of JTF, 120, quoting Agassiz in 1866, after his return from the Brazilian expedition. I do not know if HJ was present at that dinner, but I have put the passage here because it gives a sense of the term "imagination" as HJ used it. This sense of the word "imagination" as the mental faculty whose active operation produces knowledge or understanding, as opposed to mere sense data, derives from Kant. Kant's imagination is the active principle uniting concepts, which otherwise would be empty, and intuitions—sense impressions—which otherwise would be blind. See generally Gibbons, *Kant's Theory of Imagination* (1994). This is the sense in which Coleridge and Ruskin used the term, and it is perhaps from Ruskin that HJ acquired it. But the usage was widespread in the Victorian era. Darwin defined the word in this way in *The Descent of Man*, Vol. 1, p. ii (1871) (imagination is creative, unites "images" and "ideas"). See OED "imagination," sense 4. Without a proper definition of this word much of HJ's theoretical writings are difficult to understand. He describes his long memoir, *Notes of a Son and Brother*, for instance, as the history of "an imagination," but this is wildly misleading if we understand the term in the sense of "imaginary," an escapist fancy. Imagination was the faculty that made possible realism in art, in HJ's Victorian sense: moral realism as opposed to mere naturalism or imitation of sense data. (As I make final corrections in these notes I find this point made by Philip Davis, "Keeping Faith with Real Reality," TLS, May 12, 1995, 13.)

31. HJ to Haviland, May 17 [1865?], in Edel, *Letters*, 11, "Ms Lynn Jachney." The dates of James's stay at Northampton, from August to November 1864, are set by the return addresses of his letters to Charles Eliot Norton, in Houghton, the only regular correspondence from this period that has survived.

32. This paragraph is paraphrased from *Roderick Hudson*, p. 69. HJ explained in his preface to the New York edition of this novel that these opening pages were set in Northampton. The companion of his frequent walks was Haviland, see above.

33. We in the United States have forgotten what an upheaval the new historical and linguistic studies of the Bible produced at this time. Both HJ and OWH recalled these as critical influences, and in general they were far greater challenges to orthodox religion than was Darwinism. See, for instance, Samuel Butler's *Way of All Flesh*, and Mrs. Ward's novels, for graphic portrayals of the way in which scientific history was shaking people's faiths.

34. *La Vie de Jésus*, "Introduction," liv–lix. "Fusion" became a very important word for HJ, signifying the active union of form and content, concept and intuition, mind and body, through the exercise of the imagination. See, for example, NSB, 406–7, concerning the *"fusions"*—the important experiences—of the epochal spring of 1865. For other examples of this usage see Tanner (1995), 13.

35. Concerning the use of the term "imagination" for the active process of understanding, derived ultimately from Kant, see n. 30, above.

36. Reading this book was one of the signal events of a year that James was later to call his "prime." In his early reviews he repeatedly expressed the view, never altered, that Ernest Renan was the first man of letters in France— which was to say, in Europe. In 1908 he wrote to Edmund Gosse that Renan was "one [of] the blessings of my youth & idols of my prime & influences, generally, of my life." (February 22, 1908, Leeds; Moore, 235). The "prime" was the period of which he was then writing, from the summer of 1864 to the summer of 1866. The only works of Renan he was likely to have known then were *L'Avenir de Science* which appeared in 1849 in French, and *La Vie de Jésus* which appeared in French and English in 1863, and was a best-seller in the United States. (Renan had an immense impact in England as well, in part through T. H. Green and the novels of Mrs. Humphrey Ward, who was to be James's closest professional friend.)

37. GWJ to parents, December 31, 1864, quoted from AJ Diary, Burr ed., 35–36. Freed slaves were referred to as "contraband" because they were property seized in order to suppress the rebellion. Until the Thirteenth Amendment was passed in 1865, slaves were constitutionally protected property, as the Supreme Court had held in the notorious Dred Scott case.

38. GWJ to parents, January [1865?], Houghton; quoted from NSB, 394.

39. NSB, 394–95.

40. WJ's most famous address, *The Moral Equivalent of War*, called for universal conscription into a war to tame "Nature." It was a reply to Holmes's *The Soldier's Faith*; to Holmes's disgust it was extensively republished as an antiwar tract on the eve of the First World War. WJ was implicitly defending his own choice, which Holmes continued to treat with polite contempt.

41. See "Frances Anne Kemble," in *Essays in London*, 97–98, reprinted in Lit. Crit.: English and American, where one would hardly expect to find it.

42. The notebook is with the James Family Papers at Houghton Library, and is accurately reproduced in Notebooks, Matthiessen, ed., 319; Edel, ed., 238. This passage seems impossible to misunderstand. HJ had his sexual initiation in Cambridge and Ashburton Place, but it would be impossible, fatal, to ex-

pand on that in the book for which these are notes. After a few more lines, *l'initiation première* becomes, in James's characteristic late Franglais style, his "prime," and he refers to this incident as his "prime" in *Notes of a Son and Brother*, thereby preserving a breath of that divine initiation without sacrificing propriety.

43. This is the opening scene of Book Ninth, *The Wings of the Dove*, quoted from the Penguin edition, 399–400 (which is the revised, New York edition). This key passage was only slightly altered from the first English edition of 1902, which is reproduced in the Norton Critical Edition, 441–42. (The recollection of "what had come to pass" was in the first edition, "all melted memories and harmonies." In the New York edition this was revised to "a cluster of pleasant memories," which clarifies the meaning and points up the activity of the imagination working on a manifold of sense memories.) The character Morton Densher, whose memory this is, greatly resembles the HJ of the spring of 1865. I don't know why we should suppose the sexual images are unintended or unconscious. In his memoir, HJ referred to the several "fusions" he achieved in the spring of 1865 as "various climaxes . . . that lifted the moment in the largest embrace." All the fusions—including his first receipt of some greasy dollars in payment for an article and the receipt of the news of Hawthorne's and Lincoln's deaths—are described as occurring in his bedroom at Ashburton Place (NSB, 404–7, 430).

44. NSB, 436. It is worth quoting at some length the passage in which HJ speaks of the fusion of the sexual and literary experiences, and of writing as a kind of secret lovemaking (or a kind of reminiscent masturbation):

> I of course truly cared for them [his short stories], as we say, more than for aught else whatever—cared for them with that kind of care, infatuated though it may seem, that makes it bliss for the fond votary never to so much as speak of the loved object, makes it a refinement of piety to perform his rites under cover of a perfect freedom of mind as to everything *but* them. These secrets of the imaginative life were in fact more various than I may dream of trying to tell; they referred to actual concretions of existence as well as to the suppositious; the joy of life, indeed, drawbacks and all, was just in the constant quick flit of association, to and fro, and through a hundred open doors, between the two great chambers (if it be not absurd, or even base, to separate them) of direct and indirect experience . . . it is of the great comprehensive *fusion* that I speak as the richest note of all these hours. . . .

NSB, 436. As his example of the fusion, he then goes on to speak of his mingled feelings, the "perfect muddle of pleasure," at having his stories accepted by his intimate friend William Dean Howells. I don't see how any of this can be misunderstood, and most people who write creatively will probably recognize the feeling. HJ's heightened feelings for his characters are especially notable in the late novels, which seem to drip with sexuality, and can induce a certain discomfort in the reader who does not share them.

45. As noted above, HJ consistently used the term "imagination" in the sense of a creative faculty that fused ideas and the memories of sense impressions into understanding; and it was in this sense that he referred to himself as a man of imagination. Gibbons's account of Kant's theory of imagination is a wonder-

ful work of reconstruction and seems to me to render very well, among other things, the Jamesian understanding. It is important to remember that imagination is the organ that one uses to bridge gaps and fill in blanks and silences; and as we shall see, HJ believed that the secret of successful art was, by creating "interest," to induce the reader or viewer to exercise this faculty to complete the work of art. HJ's contribution to theory seems to have been his idea that the force behind the imagination was physical passion. See Chapter 22, below. Compare Wilson (1995), who makes the central point correctly (the pattern in the carpet, of meaning in HJ's work, is derived from "the warm red light of caring engagement") but does not make the link to Kant.

46. The "fusions" of NSB, 404–7. These were the experience of being paid in cash, for the first time, in greasy dollars; the vicarious experience of death; and his first sexual experience; in short, the knowledge of good and evil, which he acquired in his Ashburton Street bedroom in the spring of 1865. The experience of the knowledge of good and evil is the central event in many of HJ's novels, notably *The Portrait of a Lady*, *What Maisie Knew*, and *The Golden Bowl*. The image he used for this understanding is the warm light of late summer afternoons; it was an image from Italian Renaissance paintings, the fusion of the harsh flattening light of materialist noon and the dim shadowy lamplight of fable. In "The Figure in the Carpet" he suggests that sexual experience is necessary for understanding, at least for the understanding of his stories; compare Wilson (1995). The figure in the carpet in his own stories, as we shall see, and as Wilson points out, was the story of the acquisition of this knowledge, the power and freedom it confers, and of the exercise of power over others. To HJ, moral principles were not simply abstractions, they were objective facts, a dimension of all experience, which is why he preferred his method of realism to the merely naturalistic tales of his French contemporaries.

47. HJ to OWH, July 6, 1911; OWH Jr. Papers, HLS, quoting OWH's letter. See also OWH letters of this time to mutual friends Alice Stopford Green and Lucy Clifford.

48. The hints in HJ's notebook and memoir direct one's attention to a recently returned veteran; Holmes, of whom HJ plainly was very fond, was someone with whom he might have been intimate in Cambridge and Ashburton Place—the locations of their respective bedrooms. I thought I might be reading too much into HJ's hints until I came upon an essay HJ published shortly after Annie Fields's death ("Mr. and Mrs. Fields," published in *Cornhill Magazine* and *The Atlantic Monthly*, July 1915; reprinted *American Essays* 261 (1989)), in which he gradually shifts his focus from the Fieldses' household to the Holmeses', reminisces about the doctor, turns from the doctor to the son, and uses an essay of the doctor's to introduce a welter of suggestive language, an image of the doctor's son being put tenderly to bed, and ends with a command to "see . . . the Bunker Hill obelisk point as sharply as ever its beveled capstone against the sky." This is startling and funny, and from an author who not long before had named a weakly female character, "Fanny Assingham," seems unmistakable.

49. NSB, 430.

7   HENRY DIRECTS A SCENE

1. NSB, 434–35.
2. NSB, 436–37; see the preceding chapter.
3. In his preface to *The American* in the New York edition, James described the plot of the novel coming to him on a Boston horsecar. *Art of the Novel*, 22.
4. The preceding two paragraphs are paraphrased from NSB, Chapter XII, in which he describes his "prime," especially 434–37. In the preceding chapter and notes there I discuss the probability that the "concrete experience" he mentions as fusing with his indirect experience was his sexual initiation with Wendell Holmes.
5. Paraphrased from NSB, 436. This passage, as it relates to HJ's sexual initiation, is discussed in the notes to the preceding chapter. I have interpolated the expression "the rites of love and art," which seems to be what is meant. One of the themes of HJ's work is the importance of privacy, and of secrets. Awareness of an inner self that is not accessible to others, without leave, is an important stage in moral development, and is central to the female protagonists in *The Bostonians*, *What Maisie Knew*, and other works. The fact that HJ's first sexual experiences involved another man, and could not be spoken of, evidently deepened this sense for him.
6. NSB, 428–29.
7. See, e.g., "Mr. and Mrs. Fields," *Cornhill Magazine*, July 1915, reprinted *American Essays*, 261, 262. Compare the character and history of Christopher Newman in *The American*.
8. OWH Sr. to unidentified New Yorker (presumably E. L. Godkin), May 5, 1865, saying he thinks very well of the plan for a new publication. O. W. Holmes Papers (copy in Mrs. Holmes's hand).
9. "The Founding of the Nation: Recollection of the 'Fairies' That Attended Its Birth," *Nation*, July 8, 1915; reprinted American Essays, 283.
10. Neither American nor British copyright statutes at this time protected works published abroad. American publishers, who relied on reprints of British books, had arranged among themselves to avoid destructive competition in the pirating of British books. They would bid for the rights to receive advance sheets of an English edition, in exchange for payment of a flat fee; and the American publisher who bought such a right generally could expect that no other publisher would bring out a rival edition. When Fields began to offer successful British authors like Dickens royalties rather than a flat fee, breaching this tacit agreement, he brought British writers to Ticknor & Fields, but he also set off a war of pirated editions that eventually destroyed the old gentlemanly system.
11. "Essays in Criticism," reprinted in Lit. Crit.: American and English, 711, 715, quoting Arnold's "Duty of Criticism."
12. Ibid.
13. HJ to TSP, "Friday morn," from Ashburton Place; apparently 1865; Harlow, 276.
14. NSB, 469. James here is remembering her in the parlor of her sister's house in Pelham, New York, in 1869.
15. NSB, 461.
16. Howe, 213.
17. The secondary characters in *The Bostonians*, for instance, are drawn from these salons, see below; and Mrs. Newsome in *The Ambassadors* appears to be modeled on Julia Ward Howe.

18. HJ to Julia Ward Howe, from 102 Mt. Vernon Street, "April 18th," no year date; Eliot, 86. The correct year perhaps is not 1865, where I have placed the letter here, as HJ was in Boston on April 15; but the letter is characteristic.

19. Quoted in M. A. DeW. Howe (1922), 125. M. A. DeW. Howe was not related to Julia Ward Howe.

20. *The Bostonians* is peopled from this circle, and the name of its leading character, Verena Tarrant, seems to suggest the doctor's novel *Elsie Venner*. "Tarrant" is evidently a play on "Tarantella," the mythic involuntary dance of those bitten by a spider. Verena Tarrant is portrayed as being under the influence of her mesmerist tyrant of a father; like many of James's bad heroines, she is the involuntary victim of an evil inheritance, which is the theme of *Elsie Venner*, but unlike the doctor's heroine she is still free to choose.

21. NSB, 415.

22. "The Light Woman."

23. See "A Light Man," in Chapter 10, below.

24. Oliver Wendell Holmes, Jr., Papers, Harvard Law School Library. I have expanded abbreviations used in the text.

25. At least he was not on the list of those in attendance compiled by one of the Shattuck sisters; Shattuck Papers, 1860–70, Vol. 23, MHS.

26. I must stop to say at this point, for the benefit of James scholars, that the single most famous incident in the received version of Henry James's life seems never to have occurred: The scene that was sketched somewhat cautiously in the first of Edel's five volumes, and after being seized upon and worked very hard by a generation of commentators, was then amplified and exaggerated in Edel's own one-volume summary.

   The canonical scene is this: Henry James, Oliver Wendell Holmes, and John Chipman Gray travel together by carriage along the "old carriage road" from Boston to North Conway. They visit Minny Temple, who is in North Conway alone with her aunt. Holmes and Gray are "bronzed, muscled" veterans of the war, "apparently" still in uniform, and they flirt and compete for Minny's favor. Henry James, who "adores" Minny Temple in Edel's first version, and flatly "loves" her in the second, is put in the shade by these handsome and virile warriors. HJ fumes with silent rage and frustration, and finally retires to a passive role, as first Holmes and then Gray succeed with the girl. For the rest of his life, he relives this scene of frustration and jealousy in book after book.

   The actual basis of Edel's account was a story, "Poor Richard," written in 1866–67. 1 Edel, 237. The story concerns three men competing for a woman, and one of the three, the eponymous "poor Richard," retires from the rivalry in silent rage and frustration. Edel told his own version of the story as if it were James's biography, and then in support of this somewhat circularly quoted "Poor Richard." HJ's nonfiction account (NSB, 457–63), contradicts this version, however. The facts we have are these: In August 1865, Mary Temple and her three sisters were all staying with a great-aunt, Ellen Gourlay, in North Conway (NSB, 459). James invited Wendell Holmes, alone, to come up to North Conway with him, apparently using the young ladies' presence as bait. (James's letters to Holmes are quoted in the text.) The two men traveled by railroad, probably from the Boston & Maine depot, changing in Dover. It was only the last stage of the journey, from Conway to North Conway, about five miles along the Saco River, which was by carriage. This trip is described in *The American Scene*. There was no "old carriage road" from Boston to North Conway. Holmes had left the army more than a year before, and most certainly was not in uniform. He was never at any time "bronzed and muscled," and in 1865, although more than six feet tall he weighed less than 150 pounds. The inclusion of so many imaginary details in Edel's account is disquieting.

Gray was not present on this visit. HJ says that Gray came "a little later," at Holmes's invitation (NSB, 459–60), and this is confirmed by what I have been able to learn of Gray's movements. Gray probably first visited North Conway the next year, in the summer of 1866. When Gray eventually did make the acquaintance of the Temple girls, he seems to have taken an interest in Kitty, rather than Minny. In short, rather than three young men competing for Minny Temple on one traumatic summer afternoon, we have HJ bringing Holmes to meet her, her two sisters, and a maiden aunt. See below. There is no evidence that the scene of the three men competing for Minny Temple's attention ever happened; and there is very good reason to think that it was Holmes, rather than Minny, with whom HJ was in "love."

27. Compare this description of a similar scene:

> The head, the features, the color, the whole facial oval and radiance had a wonderful purity; the deep grey eyes—the most agreeable, I thought, that I had ever seen—brushed with a kind of wing-like grace every object they encountered.

This is red-haired Flora Saunt, in "Glasses," recognizably Mary Temple. Flora Saunt is not dying, as Minny was, she is going blind.

28. *The Bostonians*, 8–9. This is Olive Chancellor meeting Basil Ransome, whom Auchincloss and others have noted is recognizably modeled on Holmes. In the novel, Olive envies him the opportunity for martyrdom. Compare Minny Temple's letter to John C. Gray:

> Isn't Christ the only man who ever lived and died *entirely* for his faith, without a shadow of selfishness? And isn't that reason enough why we should all turn to Him. . . . And if I believe this, which I think I do, how utterly inconsistent and detestable the life I lead, which so far from being a loving and cheerful surrender of itself once for all to God's service, is at best a base compromise. . . .

August 29, 1869, Houghton. This passage with some alterations was reprinted in NSB. It is characteristic of Mary Temple's letters.

29. "Glasses".
30. *Watch and Ward*, Library of America edition, 159.

8 FORMING AN IMAGE OF GREATNESS

1. "I can only feel, however, that what particularly drew the desired circle sharpest for me was the contribution to it that I had been able to effect by introducing the companion of my own pilgrimage," i.e., Holmes; NSB, 459.
2. John Chipman Gray, attorney and law professor. See NSB, 459–60.
3. MT to John C. Gray, June 27, 1869, Houghton. This passage is quoted, somewhat altered by HJ, in NSB, 489.

4. NSB, 457–59.
5. This is a paraphrase of NSB, 458–59.
6. See *Ambassadors*, Book Eleven, III (Penguin ed., 452–53). HJ apparently saw Lambinet's *Le Passeur sur La Seine, près Bougival*, and in the novel presumably recorded his *sensation* when he first visited the scene of the painting, on a visit to Turgenev at Bougival. The picture described in his novel is not this one, however, but Monet's *La Seine à Vétheuil*, painted at a similar spot on the Seine but a few miles closer to Paris (Anderson, 272–73). This use of details from his own memory to give the air of reality to stories that are borrowed or invented is characteristic.
7. Maria Ellery Mackaye to Jim Mackaye, December 1865, quoted, Mackaye I, 121.
8. WJ to HJ?, fall 1865?, quoted in Burr, 49.
9. "À Julie./On me demande, par les rues,/Pourquoi je vais bayant aux grues,/ Fumant mon cigare au soleil. . . . Ta bouche est brûlant, Julie;/Inventons donc quelque folie/Qui nous perde l'âme et le corps." As we have seen, James admired Musset, of whom he had learned from La Farge, as the greatest of French poets of his time. I have chosen this well-known excerpt because, aside from its being characteristic of Musset as he presents himself in his autobiography, James throughout his fiction equates love and death in this metaphorical way, and furthermore treats it as a literary convention with which the reader is expected to be familiar (as in the endings of several stories, notably "The Pupil," "The Middle Years," and "The Turn of the Screw," in all of which a boy or young man expires ecstatically in the arms of a mentor or tutor). There is no sign that James knew the English metaphysical poets and the most likely reason for treating this as a convention was the French romantic literature he admired in his youth. I have somewhat freely translated ("grue" is literally a crane, slang for "tart" or "streetwalker"), to emphasize the distinction that James always made between the poetry of Musset, and the materialist aestheticism that he disliked and that began with Gautier. See below.
10. "The Art of Fiction," in *Art of Criticism* (Veeder & Griffin), 177.
11. Despite all the attention paid to James's writings, little has been said about the remarkable first spate of essays he wrote from the summer of 1865 to the fall of 1866, the period he always referred to as his "prime." They ran from September 14, 1865, to the October 11, 1866, numbers of *The Nation*, with breaks for his contributions to *North American Review* for October 1865 and April 1866, and the two short stories described in the text. Steven Jobe has written very interestingly (and helpfully to me) on the review of Higginson's *Epictetus*. Habegger has written about James's reviews of Miss Braddon, but his psychologizing, although such speculations have their own interest, obscures the workman's tasks that James faced at this stage of his career.
12. "Aurora Floyd," Lit. Crit.: American and English, 744.
13. Ibid., 741.
14. "Noble Life," in Lit. Crit.: American and English, 845.
15. "Aurora Floyd," supra at 745.
16. "Miss Mackenzie," Lit. Crit.: American and English, 1313–14.
17. HJ seems not to have been aware of Herman Melville, who had sunk into obscurity by this time. He, too, was a realist author who wrote in the idealist tradition, believing in the objective reality of moral principles. Modern examples include Cynthia Ozick, Zora Neale Thurston, Saul Bellow. (I don't speak of influence, only the common attitude toward the moral dimension.)
    The other philosophical and critical path, of materialism and existential-

ism, was taken by western and southern writers whose popularity has always been more secure—Mark Twain, Stephen Crane, and many others. James in later life became much less doctrinaire, and even in his youth he greatly admired *Madame Bovary*, the great masterpiece of this tradition. He himself brought Stephen Crane to critical notice, as we shall see in the next volume, and in his late work tried to achieve a position outside or beyond textual dualisms. But at this time, he was marking out his own course, and setting himself in opposition to all potential rivals.

18. "The Journal of Eugénie de Guérin," Lit. Crit.: French and European, 429, 430.
19. Ibid., 430–33.
20. "Epictetus" in Lit. Crit.: American and English, 8, 13.
21. NSB, 364–66.
22. NSB, 367–68.
23. To HJ, his father's doctrine was a form of weakness, a yearning for passivity, for sleep and for death. His father wished to submerge himself into the spirit of humanity, to let God play on him as on a pipe. James was full of tender affection for the old man and his yearning for death, but he now put his own foot on a different path. Yet he remained in the world of his father's discourse, the world of idealist philosophy and advanced Unitarian belief.
24. "Day of Days," 1 *Complete Tales*, 140–41.
25. Ibid., 145–47.
26. Ibid., 139, 164.
27. "A Landscape-Painter," in 1 *Complete Tales*, 99, 118. Compare the lesson in patience taught to Caspar Goodwood at the end of *The Portrait of a Lady*. John Bayley has selected this tale for special and acute attention, and has described the delicate way in which the eponymous painter's victimization, the loss of freedom, is portrayed (Bayley, 1988). Like many commentators, he dwells on the victim in the story, but in an unpublished talk he noted that this story showed that in James's fiction, Todorov's "absent, unattainable absolute," was often a woman (Bayley, 1991).
28. "Walt Whitman's *Drum Taps*," Lit. Crit.: American and English, 629–30.
29. Ibid., 634. The "you" addressed here is Walt Whitman.
30. "Edmond Scherer," Lit. Crit.: French and European, 803.

9   FLEEING TOWARD THE LIGHT

1. WJ to MRJ, undated, probably fall 1863, Houghton; quoted J. W. Anderson. Compare the opening description of Dr. Sloper in *Washington Square*.
2. William thought he had hurt his back, romantically, by working long hours at the dissecting table. Aunt Kate's more prosaic theory was that he had hurt it carrying things when the family moved to Cambridge in October. MRJ to WJ, November 21, 1867, Houghton; unpub.
3. HJ Notebook for 1905, Matthiessen, ed., 319. The entry goes on to suggest that this was the germ of HJ's own "vision-haunted migration" to England ten years later.
4. Mrs. Holmes to OWH, May 21, 1866, OWH Jr. Papers.
5. Mrs. Holmes to OWH, July 22, 1866, OWH Jr. Papers. The account in NSB is incorrect in small details. The visit was in July, not August, and he was received by Amelia, not Mrs. Holmes.

6. Ibid., 318–19. In the same journal passage in which he recalls his sexual initiation, in the "epochal spring of 1865," HJ includes the summer of 1866 in the same "pathetic, heroic little *personal* prime of my own, which stretched over into the following summer at Swampscott," ibid., 319. The Swampscott months are intriguingly described as weeks of "unforgettable gropings and findings and sufferings and strivings and play of sensibility and inward passion there . ... little thrills and throbs and daydreams," ibid. Recalling the same period in NSB, he refers to "unspeakable memories," and makes them part of the same "imaginative life" with its "great comprehensive *fusion*" that began in the spring, NSB, 436–37. My guess is that all this is a record of a summer spent writing, amid intense and perhaps autoerotic imaginings apparently involving Holmes on his trip abroad, but there is no direct evidence, and the "gropings and findings" may involve someone or something else entirely.

7. NSB, 442–43.

8. By December he was actively seeking one. See WJ to AJ December 12, 1866, Houghton; 1 R. B. Perry, 231.

9. AJ to F. R. Morse, February 8, 1866, Houghton; unpub.

10. AJ Diary, February 21, 1890. In this passage AJ describes her growing awareness of herself, at age fourteen, "my young soul struggling out of its swaddling-clothes as the knowledge crystallized within me of what Life meant for me, one simple, single [illegible] before which all mystery vanished. A spark then kindled which every experience great and small has fed into a steady flame which has illuminated my little journey. . . . How profoundly grateful I am for the temperament which saves [me] from the wretched fate of those poor creatures who never find their bearings, but are tossed like dry leaves hither, thither and yon. . . ." I think it is in the context of this experience of her selfhood, so like the experiences of HJ's heroines, that one must read the preceding sentence in which AJ says that she spent the years of her adolescence learning self-control, "absorbing into the bone that the better part is to clothe oneself in neutral tints, walk by still waters, and possess one's soul in silence." This sounds like a young woman coming out to herself, as one says now.

11. AJ Diary, October 1, 1890. AJ dates this first "acute" episode of hysteria to "1867 or 1868," but the correspondence of the time shows she was already in New York City for treatment in the winter of 1866–67. HJ's letters to WJ early in 1867 describe her returning to Cambridge, seemingly fully recovered.

12. *Middle Years*, 62–64. See "Felix Holt, the Radical," review by HJ, *Nation*, August 16, 1866; Lit. Crit.: American and English, 907.

13. "The Novels of George Eliot," *Atlantic Monthly*, October 1866; Lit. Crit.: American and English, 912.

14. MY, 62.

15. "Novels of George Eliot," 922.

16. *Atlantic Monthly*, June–August 1877; 1 *Complete Tales*, 191.

17. The names of the characters are nearly all literary. "Richard Maul" is a reference to Hawthorne's *House of Seven Gables*, and "the Captain" at this time and place was a reference to Dr. Holmes's article in *The Atlantic*, "My Hunt for the Captain," which recounted his search for the wounded Wendell Holmes after the battle of Antietam. James tenderly associated this story with his own love for Holmes, see Chapter 6, above.

18. WDH to Edmund C. Stedman, December 5, 1866, 1 WDH Selected Letters, 271 and 272 n. 3. Howells's biographer propounded the theory that Howells was responsible for James's early success at *The Atlantic*, Fields al-

legedly having soured on him. Kenneth Lynn, 157; see also 1 Edel, 269. The story is mildly supported by HJ's effusive and friendly letter on Howells's seventy-fifth birthday, see American Essays, and his friendly reminiscence in NSB, 436–37, where HJ is speaking of the fusion of his affection for Howells and the pleasure he had on the acceptance of "Poor Richard." HJ was already a regular contributor to *The Atlantic* when Howells joined it, however, and there is no evidence at all that Fields then or later soured on HJ. The correspondence of the time shows that Howells was only a reader for his first five years, and that Fields made all editorial decisions of any consequence until his retirement. Fields did show "Poor Richard" to Howells when he assumed his duties in the fall of 1866, and Howells wrote the letter of acceptance. The fee is deduced from WJ's frequent gibes about the "$200 story" in his letters to HJ during the spring and summer of 1868 (see 1 WJ–HJ Letters).

19. HJ to T. S. Perry, September 20 [1867]; Harlow, 282, 285. See also WJ to AJ, November 1866, quoted in Lewis, 181.

20. Morrison, Harvard College, 313.

21. HJ to Grace Norton, May 20, 1870, Houghton; 1 HJL, 238.

22. WJ's biographers have treated his abandoning the medical profession that winter as something of a mystery, but it seems plain from an undated letter to Tom Ward, apparently written in September 1867, that WJ had in fact secured an appointment at the Massachusetts General Hospital. This is not mentioned by Perry or Allen. WJ's persistent back problem evidently obliged him to give up the appointment and to travel abroad, in search of treatment. Selected Letters of WJ, 27. WJ apparently did not tell his family what was the matter until the eve of his departure for Germany the following April. The secret of their shared disabilities was the premise for the friendship between William and Henry from this time forward.

23. Alice described the crisis in her diary, March 4, 1892, p. 232 (see note 50 for Chapter 21), but its precise nature was not clear. In later correspondence there is a suggestion that her parents did not approve of her close friendship with Fanny Morse and Katharine Loring, who became her companion.

24. Yeazell, 10 n.20. Modern commentary on AJ's illness has tended to focus on the treatment of bed rest that was then prescribed for "neurasthenia," and which was so damaging to HJ. But AJ's diagnosis was hysteria, and the vigorous exercise prescribed for her was benign and often helpful.

25. HJ to T. S. Perry, September 15 [1866], Colby; Harlow 277; OWH diary, October 28, 1866, OWH Jr. Papers, HLS. See following note.

26. Holmes's diary shows visits to HJ about once a month that winter, visits that presumably were returned at about the same frequency.

27. HJ to W. C. Church, October 9, 1866, Church Collection, NYPL.

28. HJ Jr. (HJ's nephew) to Percy Lubbock, May 20, 1919, Gosse Papers, Leeds.

29. For a characteristic incident, see, e.g., HJ to Lilla Cabot, undated letter, Colby. The letter appears to have been written in May of 1867 or 1868. An explanation of the letter was written in a microscopic hand by Lilla Cabot on the envelope in which HJ's letter arrived; HJ had struck up an acquaintance with the schoolgirl, a cousin of OWH's, and kept up the friendship through visits and correspondence to the end of his life.

30. In the catalog of HJ's letters being assembled by Stephen Jobe and Susan Gunter more than 800 correspondents have been identified, and except for business letters each seems to be part of a continuing relationship.

31. In *The Europeans*, HJ drew affectionate portraits of the Cambridge circle; Robert Acton is recognizably Lowell. (Longfellow's house, known as the

Craigie House, was moved by HJ to the site of Elmwood, however, and Emerson installed there. Lowell was obliged to live across the road.)

32. *The Ambassadors*, for instance, which is premised on an anecdote about Howells; see also "The Jolly Corner."

33. Howells later hinted that he alone was responsible for the acceptance of this story, 2 Life in Letters, 397, quoting 3 *Century* mag., November 1882, 25 ff. Howells's biographer Lynn amplified these hints, and the story has become canonical. But Fields made all editorial decisions of importance until 1871, when he retired.

34. *The Europeans*, 78.

35. E. Howells diary, May 1866, Howells papers, Houghton; unpub.

36. WDH to T. W. Higginson, November 20, 1866; 1 WDH Selected Letters, 270.

37. E. Howells to A. Howells, June 16, 1867, in E. M. Howells Letters.

38. HJ to W. D. Howells, February 19, 1912; 2 Lubbock, 221, 222.

39. HJ to T. S. Perry, September 20, [1867], Colby; Harlow, 282–85.

40. MJ to AJ [January 1867?], Houghton; unpub.

41. "My Friend Bingham," *The Atlantic*, March 1867; 1 *Collected Tales*, 189.

42. Ibid., 189.

43. HJ to WJ, May 10 [1867], Houghton; reprinted WJ–HJ Letters, 13–14.

44. MJ to WJ, May 27, 1857, Houghton; unpub.

45. AJ to WJ, October 13, 1867, Houghton; Yeazell, 50, 52.

46. HJ to TSP, September 20, 1867; Harlow, 282, 285.

47. WJ to HJ, May 3, 1867, Houghton; 1 WJ–HJ Letters, 11, 12 (in French).

48. Ibid.

49. *Voyages en Italie* (1866). See HJ to WJ, May 21, 1867, 1 WJ–HJ Letters, 15, 16. See also HJ's 1868 review of *Italy: Rome and Naples* (Lit. Crit.: European Writers, 828–29), the first volume of the English translation of *Voyages en Italie* that he had read the previous summer.

50. See, e.g., MRJ to WJ, May 27, 1867 (Houghton). Harry is only "so-so"; worried about demands that La Farge's visit may make; June 10, 1867 (same: includes Harry in her list of family "invalids"); November 21, 1867: "Harry brightened up very much for a while, but seems I grieve to say to have gone back to the old state."

51. HJ to T. S. Perry, September 20, 1867, Colby; Harlow, 282.

52. After the outpouring of the previous year, he published only one review (in August) between June and November 1867.

53. *Nation*, May 30, 1867, 432.

54. Ibid.

55. WDH to C. E. Norton, August 10, 1867, WDH Selected Letters.

56. Ibid., 282, 283. The story appeared in *The Atlantic Monthly*, February 1868.

57. HJ to T. S. Perry, August 15, 1867, Colby; HJ to WJ, November 22, 1867, 1 WJ–HJ Letters, 25.

58. Dickens had given Fields the exclusive right to publish all his books in America, in exchange for the right to royalties on the American edition. The lecture tour, which was wildly popular, capped this new triumph, and hotly fueled the demand for Dickens's books. American publishers, outraged by this breach of the long-standing, tacit agreement to share foreign authors, howled in outrage and then in retaliation began to pirate Dickens's books. War had been declared in the publishing business, and the Fieldses were fully occupied with the task of defending and enlarging their newly conquered territory.

59. MJ to WJ, November 21, 1867, Houghton; unpub.

60. HJ to Francis P. Church, October 2 [1867]; Church Collection, NYPL. This

apparently refers to "The Story of a Masterpiece," which appeared with illustrations in *The Galaxy* in January and February 1868.

61. HJ to F. P. Church, October 23, 1867, Church Collection, NYPL; reprinted 1 HJ Letters, 73.

62. "A Most Extraordinary Case," 1 *Complete Tales*, 332.

63. HJ Sr. to AJ, December 21, 1867, Houghton; Strouse, 111.

64. "Historical Novels," *Nation*, August 15, 1867; reprinted as "Anne E. Manning," Lit. Crit.: American and English, 1152.

65. "Short Studies on Great Subjects," reviewed *Nation*, October 31, 1867; Lit. Crit.: American and English, 1014.

66. "Waiting for the Verdict," *Nation*, November 21, 1867; Lit. Crit.: American and English, 218.

67. (Mrs. A.M.C. Seemüller,) "Opportunity: A Novel," *Nation*, December 5, 1867; Lit. Crit.: American and English, 595.

68. "The Friendships of Women," *Nation*, December 26, 1867; Lit. Crit.: American and English, 198.

69. "The Huguenots in England," *Nation*, January 9, 1868; Lit. Crit.: American and English, 1221.

70. "Short Studies on Great Subjects," *Nation*, October 31, 1867; Lit. Crit.: American and English, 1014, 1015.

71. "Italian Journeys," *North American Review*, January 1868.

72. "The Jesuits in North America in the Seventeenth Century," *Nation*, June 6, 1867; Lit. Crit.: American and English, 568.

73. "Historical Novels," supra, 1157; "Taine's Italy," *Nation*, May 7, 1868 (holding up Taine as a model of the scientific historian).

74. "Contemporary French Painters," *North American Review*, April 1868.

75. "Sainte-Beuve's Portraits," June 4, 1868. In this essay HJ for the first time gives the judgment, often later repeated, that Isabelle de Charrière was the founder of the realist novel in French. See "The Lesson of Balzac," etc. Her influence on James has never been explored.

76. "Historical Novels," supra; "Taine's Italy," supra; "Sainte-Beuve's Portraits," *Nation*, June 4, 1868.

77. "Father Lacordaire," *Nation*, January 16, 1868; Lit. Crit.: French and European Writers, 197.

78. Ibid., 201–2.

79. The preceding paragraphs are closely paraphrased from "Father Lacordaire," *Nation*, January 16, 1868, 53–55; reprinted Lit. Crit.: French and European Writers, 197–204. I have tried to give a shortened version without altering the tone. There is just the faintest hint of a snicker in James's account, and we needn't suppose he was unaware of the sadomasochistic frisson that he conveyed. The theme of the monastery as a form of living death reappeared throughout his writings, and despite his great sympathy he certainly meant to be critical of the Church in this passage. We also see in his later work and even in his conversation the continued message that one's duty is to live— which means to live within heterosexual society. See, e.g., "The Author of Beltraffio."

80. HJ to T. S. Perry, March 27, 1868; Harlow, 286, 288.

81. WJ to HJ, March 4, 1868; 1 WJ–HJ Letters, 19.

82. "The Story of a Masterpiece," 1 *Complete Tales*, 259; HJ to T. S. Perry, March 27, 1867; Harlow, 286, 288.

83. WJ to HJ, December 26, 1867; 1 WJ–HJ Letters, 27, 28.

84. WJ to HJ, September 26, 1867, Houghton; 1 WJ–HJ Letters, 18.

85. WJ to HJ, December 16, 1867, Houghton; 1 WJ–HJ Letters, 27.

86. WJ to HJ, February 12, 1868, Houghton; 1 WJ–HJ Letters, 30.
87. WJ to HJ, March 4, 1868, Houghton; 1 WJ–HJ Letters, 36–37.
88. HJ to T. S. Perry, March 27, 1868, Harlowe, 286–87:

> I rec'd yesterday a letter from Willy from Teplitz, March 4th, which
> cost me a great deal of deep regret & pain. His "cure" had turned out
> a failure & he was worse than before. He spoke of coming home. But
> I wrote him a long letter & I can't bear to talk about it.

The reply to WJ has not been preserved, but from William's subsequent
letters asking HJ about the criticisms expressed in the March 4 letter, it is
plain he never responded to them.
89. WJ to HJ, April 23, 1868, Houghton; 1 WJ–HJ Letters, 46.
90. See HJ to O.W. Holmes, July 29 [1868], OWH Jr. Papers, HLD, recapitulating previous exchanges.
91. Review of William Morris, "The Earthly Paradise," *North American Review*, July 1868; Lit. Crit.: American and English, 1186.
92. HJ reviewed Eliot's "The Spanish Gypsy" in *The Nation*, June 13, 1868, Lit. Crit.: English and American, 933, and in *North American Review*, October 1868. In *The Nation* review he speaks of her "maturity and manhood," and in both of her primarily intellectual quality. He reviewed Sand's *Mademoiselle Merquem* in *The Nation*, July 16, 1868, Lit. Crit.: French and European Writers, 696, and used the review as an occasion for assessing Sand's lifework.
93. "Camors: Or, Life under the Second Empire," *Nation*, July 30, 1868; Lit. Crit.: French and European Writers, 281.
94. This seems to have been the germ of *Watch and Ward*, see below; and the theme of a daughter being raised like a prize peach for her future husband, in an Old World atmosphere, reappears in *Roderick Hudson*, *The American*, *The Portrait of a Lady*, and *The Ambassadors*. In "Madame de Mauves," the French husband falls in love with his American wife, who holds him in contempt, and kills himself.
95. "Life and Letters of Madame Swetchine," *North American Review*, July 1868; Lit. Crit.: French and European Writers, 819, 824.
96. Ibid., 825. I have enlarged a little on HJ's essay, making explicit the theory that seems implied there, and is elaborated elsewhere in his writings.
97. "De Grey: A Romance." Also that summer, "A Problem," a lighter piece, concerns the working through of a pair of curses.
98. "Osborne's Revenge." James was very modern, as it seems now, in supposing that the same-sex tie was primary, and the heterosexual one derivative. See, for instance, "The Jolly Corner." This is now taken for granted in the psychology of women, but James saw the same mechanism operating between boys and their fathers, brothers, and friends.
99. HJ to OWH, July 29 [1868], OWH Jr. Papers; reprinted M. DeW. Howe [1949], 414. Howe misdated the letter "1865."
100. HJ to OWH, undated; evidently late July or early August 1868; Howe (1949), where it is misdated "1865."
101. HJ to WJ, May 30, 1869, Houghton; 1 WJ–HJ Letters, 74.
102. HJ to WJ, February 15, 1870, 1 WJ–HJ Letters, 142, 143. The timing of the two months of lifting is not certain, and there may have been only one course of exercise, but it appears from this letter that HJ did work out with weights immediately before his trip abroad.

1. Mary Temple to John C. Gray, January 7, 1869, Houghton. This letter with many alterations was reprinted in NSB, 455–57. Gray had given Mary Temple's letters to William, and they came to Henry on William's death. He transcribed some of them, editing them as he went, for NSB, and then destroyed the originals. Holograph copies had been made, however, apparently by William's widow, before sending them to Henry; and it is these copies that are preserved in the Houghton Library and that I have relied on here and elsewhere. While there may be errors of transcription in these copies, they are certainly closer to the originals than Henry's consciously revised version.
2. NSB, 507–8.
3. NSB, 469.
4. HJ to WJ, March 8, 1870; 1 WJ–HJ Letters, 155.
5. NSB, 470.
6. In TMY, James says very positively that he arrived on March 1, a Monday, but the chronology of his arrival and a letter to his mother dated March 2, from 7 Half Moon Street, make Saturday, February 27, a more likely date.
7. In James's autobiographical *The Middle Years*, he said he had already described his arrival in Liverpool in another work; in fact he had described it at least twice—in "London," which became the opening essay of *English Hours;* and in Lambeth Strether's arrival in Liverpool, in the opening pages of *The Ambassadors*. I have put elements of the *Ambassadors* account in chronological order with the others, and removed references to the fictional errand that gave the excuse for bringing Strether to Europe. Rearranged in that fashion it meshes perfectly with the accounts in TMY and "London," from which I have added some details.
8. TMY, 549.
9. TMY, 550. At the time, James attributed this odd sense of familiarity to the memory of his childhood visits; HJ to AJ, March 10–12, 1869, Houghton; 1 HJ Letters, 92. When he described the coffee-room scene some years later, in the opening passages of "Partial Portraits," HJ imputed the sense of familiarity to his reading, and also hinted at a kind of racial memory (see 240, 248). Compare the double consciousness of Strether in the opening scenes of *The Ambassadors;* and also *The Sense of the Past*, in which an American historian magically visits the Regency London that he has studied, and feels this odd double sense of being a stranger and yet miraculously knowing the context. In TMY, where James is continuing the story of the growth of his writer's imagination, he gives yet another gloss: the muffins are so thoroughly connected, so imbedded in their context, that remembered and imagined details lead him to understand everything else. Characteristically, his memory of the sensation is vivid, eidetically accurate over the years, but he continues to search and examine it for meaning.
10. The old sinister Thames-side was later obliterated by the Embankment; in 1874, Northumberland House and the little streets behind it were cleared away to make a broad avenue, Northumberland, connecting Charing Cross Road to the Embankment.
11. HJ to AJ, March 10–12, 1869, Houghton; 1 HJ Letters, 92.
12. It is now well known that the famous London fogs were a form of air pollution, from ubiquitous coal fires, and vanished almost overnight when the city forbade the burning of high-sulfur coal. James came to like the fog and haze, which he often compared to the patina on old pictures, but on this first visit he complained bitterly of the darkness.

13. "London," in *English Hours*, 7–8.
14. HJ to MRJ, March 2, 1869, Houghton; Le Clair, 429.
15. TMY, 565.
16. "Partial Portraits," 228.
17. TMY, 567.
18. TMY, 558–561; HJ letters to WJ and other family members in March 1869.
19. Dr. John Bridges, the translator of Auguste Comte's works into English, and Sir John Simon, a noted sanitary reformer.
20. HJ to AJ, March 10–12, 1869, 1 HJ Letters, 92.
21. HJ to WJ, March 19, 1869, 1 WJ–HJ Letters, 50, 59.
22. HJ to MRJ, March 20 [1869], Houghton; 1 HJ Letters, 102.
23. HJ to AJ, March 10–12, 1869; 1 HJ Letters, 92, 94.
24. Ibid., 95.
25. Ibid.
26. HJ to WJ, March 19, 1869; 1 WJ–HJ Letters, 58. Lord Middleton's son is presumably St. John Brodrick, later ninth Viscount and first Earl Middleton, the war minister during the Boer War who would relieve James's friend Viscount Wolseley of command.
27. "Passionate Pilgrim," 2 *Complete Tales*, 240.
28. TMY, 21.
29. HJ to MRJ, March 26, 1869, Houghton; 1 Lubbock, 19.
30. TMY, 552.
31. TMY, 571.
32. The story appeared in *The Galaxy* in July. Kaplan assumes that it was written in New York, before James's departure. Judging by the usual interval it would have been written in March or April—that is, while James was in England. There is a gap in the Church papers at the New York Public Library at this point, so we cannot tell exactly when it was submitted. Both the timing and the markedly new tone seem to me to mark it as the first of James's works to show the influence of his visit to Europe.
33. Edel, in the preface to his edition of this story, points out that it was a favorite of James's. Edel avoids any mention of the subject matter, and dwells on the diary form. Feinstein noticed the erotic passage quoted in the text, but assumed that James was unconscious of describing a homosexual act. Feinstein offered the unsubstantiated notion that this was an unconscious fantasy about incestuous relations with brother William.
34. This is the view from the neighborhood of "Lockley Park" in "A Passionate Pilgrim," which James set in the "Malvern Hills." It is evidently the view he saw on his arrival in Malvern.
35. HJ to Grace Norton, April 6, 1869, Houghton; 1 HJ Letters, 106.
36. HJ to WJ, April 8, 1869, 1 WJ–HJ Letters, 62, 64.
37. NSB, 472.
38. NSB, 480.
39. WJ to HJ, March 22, 1869, 1 WJ–HJ Letters, 61.
40. HJ to WJ, April 8, 1869, Houghton; 1 WJ–HJ Letters, 62.
41. HJ to WJ, April 26, 1869, 1 WJ–HJ Letters, 67; HJ was skeptical about the authorship of the plays. See his preface to *The Tempest*, and compare "The Birthplace," his satire of the English national religion.
42. HJ to WJ, March 26 [1869], Houghton; 1 WJ–HJ Letters, 67.
43. Ibid.
44. It seems likely that he wrote "A Light Man" for *The Galaxy* and had payment sent to him in London, to avoid drawing on his line of credit.
45. WJ to HJ, April 23, 1869, Houghton; 1 WJ–HJ Letters, 66.

46. HJ to WJ, May 13, 1869, 1 WJ–HJ Letters, 72–73.
47. HJ to WJ, May 30, 1869, 1 WJ–HJ Letters, 74, 77.
48. HJ to AJ, May 7, 1869, Houghton; unpub. Emphasis in the original.
49. See, e.g., "London."
50. HJ to HJ Sr., May 10, 1869, Houghton; 1 HJ Letters, 114.
51. TMY, 574–77.
52. "Swiss Notes," in CTW, 624, 626.
53. Ibid., 628.
54. "Swiss Notes," 624.
55. HJ to MJ, June 28 [1869], Houghton; 1 HJ Letters, 122, 125.
56. Ibid.
57. HJ to WJ, July 12, 1869, 1 WJ–HJ Letters, 84, 86.
58. Ibid., 86.
59. Ibid., 87.
60. HJ to WJ, July 12, 1869, 1 WJ–HJ Letters, 84, 87–88.
61. HJ to WJ, 1 WJ–HJ Letters, 90, 91.
62. "Swiss Notes," 625–26.
63. Mary Temple to HJ, June 3, 1869, Houghton; Le Clair, "Henry James and Minny Temple," 41–42.
64. WJ to HJ, June 12, 1869, Houghton; 1 WJ–HJ Letters, 81.
65. WDH to HJ, June 26, 1869, 1 WDH Selected Letters, 328. There is no mention of the story in the copious letters to and from Henry's family at this time, which suggests that he did not make a point of it, and perhaps arranged for payment to be sent to him in Europe (otherwise his father generally was his banker); see above.
66. MT to HJ, July 24, 1869, Houghton; Le Clair, supra.

11   THE LESSONS OF ITALY

1. "Travelling Companions," *Atlantic Monthly*, November 1870; 2 *Complete Tales*, 171–72. The protagonist of the story followed the itinerary and had the impressions that HJ had had on his recently completed journey, and struck up a friendship with a father and daughter who resembled the Bootts. See Chapter 13.
2. "Venice: An Early Impression," in CTW: *The Continent*, 337.
3. Ibid., 339. This incident may have occurred on his visit in 1872, with Alice, but as he makes it emblematic of his "early impressions" of Venice I put it here.
4. "Aspern Papers," 379.
5. J. La Farge to HJ, August 26 [1869], Houghton; unpub.
6. MJ to HJ, August 7, 1869, Houghton; unpub.
7. HJ to WJ, September 25 [1869], Houghton; 1 WJ–HJ Letters, 92.
8. "Venice: An Early Impression," in CTW: *The Continent*, 337.
9. The third volume of *The Stones of Venice*, published in 1867, and in 1877 separately published as a guide to Venice.
10. HJ to WJ, September 25 [1869], Houghton; 1 WJ–HJ Letters, 92, 94.
11. At the San Giorgio.
12. "Venice: An Early Impression," in CTW: *The Continent*, 341.
13. The Church of "San Cassano." (This was the spelling that Ruskin used, and James followed him; the more common spelling is "Cassiano.")

14. This is adapted from Ruskin's description in the "Venetian Index," reprinted in Whittick, pp. 34–37. In his letter to William September 25 HJ refers to this description as better than any he could provide. I have added the reference to the brow of a hill or a stage; Ruskin has the viewer lying down among the brambles.
15. "Venice: An Early Impression," in CTW: *The Continent*, 342.
16. HJ to WJ, September 25 [1869], Houghton; 1 WJ–HJ Letters, 96.
17. HJ to AJ, October 6, 1869, Houghton; reprinted 1 HJ Letters, 144.
18. WJ to HJ, October 25 [1869], Houghton; 1 WJ–HJ Letters, 112, 113.
19. HJ to MRJ, October 13 [1869], Houghton; 1 HJ Letters, 149.
20. MT to HJ, August 15–22, 1869, Houghton; Le Clair, "Henry James and Mary Temple," 46–47.
21. This imaginary Bronzino, a combination of two actual pictures, may be the eponymous "Portrait of a Lady," see below. It is explicitly made one of the central images of *The Wings of the Dove*, 195–97. The physical resemblance to Bronzino's portrait of Lucrezia Panciatichi has been noted—see Miriam Allott, "The Bronzino Portrait in *The Wings of the Dove*," Modern Language Notes LXVIII (January 1953), 23–25. The portrait of Lucrezia has Mary Temple's features and coloring, but nothing could be less dove-like than her expression. In the novel, the portrait is introduced principally for the purpose of inducing Mark to say silently, "Do let a poor fellow who isn't a fool take care of you a little." The portrait of Eleanor has precisely the expression to prompt such a remark, as well as the magnificently brocaded dress, that James describes in his imaginary composite, both of which the portrait of Panciatichi lacks.
22. HJ to WJ, October 30, 1869, Houghton; 1 WJ–HJ Letters, 115, 117.
23. HJ to WJ, October 30 [1869], Houghton; 1 WJ–HJ Letters, 115, 116; 1 Story, 360.
24. Ibid. Descriptions of Rome in the Story biography are a compound of HJ's 1869–70 and 1873 visits; I have followed HJ's account, although surviving letters allow us to disentangle the two visits, for convenience in conveying what was in memory a single impression.
25. 1 Story, 342.
26. Paraphrased from 2 Story, 207–8. As noted above, HJ combined into one account his visits of 1869–70 and 1873, for the sake of giving a single impression of the city. The meeting with Arnold probably occurred in March 1873, but I have given it here for the same reason.
27. 1 Story, 335–36.
28. *Italian Hours*, pp. 153–54, describing the "first ride" he took. Possibly this was the first horseback ride, however, which would have been in February 1873; his first carriage ride was in 1869–70, and when he returned to Rome it was with the plan of horseback riding on the Campagna again. See below.
29. HJ to MRJ, February 1 [1873], Houghton, recalling his plan; 1 HJ Letters, 333.
30. 1 Story, 331.
31. 1 Story, 347–48.
32. 1 Story, 348–49.
33. 2 Story, 210–11.
34. HJ to WJ, December 27 [1869], Houghton; I WJ–HJ Letters, 133, 134–35.

12   ENGLAND, AGAIN: THE ANCHOR CHAIN IS BROKEN

1. HJ to HJ Sr., January 14, 1870, Houghton; 1 HJ Letters, 187, 189.
2. 2 Story, 95–96.
3. See Francis Boott to HJ, June 14 [1874], Houghton; unpub. It was apparently published in a collection of her poems, which I have not been able to find.
4. Mary Temple to HJ, November 7, 1869, Houghton; Le Clair (1949).
5. HJ to MRJ, February 5 [1870], Houghton; 1 HJ Letters, 193.
6. HJ to HJ Sr., January 14, 1870, Houghton; 1 HJ Letters, 187.
7. HJ to HJ Sr., January 4, 1870, Houghton; 1 HJ Letters, 187, 191.
8. HJ to AJ, January 25, 1870, Houghton; unpub.
9. HJ to HJ Sr., January 14, 1870, Houghton; 1 HJ Letters, 187, 190.
10. HJ to AJ, January 25, 1870, Houghton; unpub.
11. HJ to HJ Sr., January 14, 1870, Houghton; 1 HJ Letters, 187.
12. HJ to AJ, January 25, 1870, Houghton; unpub.
13. *A Little Tour in France*, CTW, 232–33.
14. HJ to AJ, January 25, 1870, Houghton; unpub.
15. Rue Neuve St.-Augustin, now Rue Daunou.
16. The description that follows is taken from HJ's "The Théâtre Français," *Galaxy*, April 1877; reprinted *The Scenic Art* (Wade, ed., 1948). He gives this as a stranger's experience of visiting the theater for the first time. He shifts into the first person when describing the play by Augier, which he saw "the first time I ever went to the Théâtre Français," in 1872. See also his letters to AJ, WJ, and his mother at this time. The drinking scene many years later was to be the model for a similar scene in his play *Guy Domville*.
17. By Émile Augier.
18. HJ to WJ, February 5, 1870, 1 WJ–HJ Letters, 193, 195. This performance was evidently the model for the ironically named Eugenia in James's *The Europeans*, whose plot is taken from Augier's play. See below.
19. HJ to AJ, February 27, 1870, Houghton; unpub.
20. Ibid.
21. HJ to WJ, March 8, 1870, Houghton; 1 WJ–HJ Letters, 147, 149.
22. HJ to AJ, February 27, 1870, Houghton; unpub.
23. Ibid.
24. Ibid.
25. Ibid., postscript.
26. For details of the visit, see Mary Temple to Ellen Temple Emmet, November 19, 1869, Houghton; unpub.
27. HJ to WJ, March 8, 1870, Houghton; 1 WJ–HJ Letters, 147, 148.
28. HJ to MRJ, March 29, 1870, Houghton; Le Clair, "Henry James and Minny Temple," 38. A slightly edited version is given in 1 HJ Letters, 218, where it is misdated March 26.
29. HJ to WJ, March 29, 1870, 1 WJ–HJ Letters, 153; HJ to MRJ, February 29, 1870, Houghton; reprinted Le Clair (1949).
30. Isabel Archer in *The Portrait of a Lady* and Minny Theale in *Wings of the Dove* are among the heroines modeled on Mary Temple.
31. HJ to WJ, March 29 [1870], Houghton; 1 WJ–HJ Letters, 153, 154. The hint of pleasure or release in James's letters about Mary Temple's death has been noted by the psychoanalytic biographers Edel, Kaplan, and Habegger, but I think misunderstood. There is no evidence James ever felt burdened by or frightened of a heterosexual relationship with Mary Temple. On the other hand, there is a distinct ambiguity in his lifelong fondness for victims.

13 RETURNING TO THE HUDSON, AS A VISITOR FROM ABROAD

1. NSB, 515.
2. NSB, 480ff.
3. Boott published under the name "Telford"; sheet music for some of his earliest songs is in Baker Library, Special Collections, Dartmouth College.
4. Arthur Sedgwick to HJ, January 30, 1870, Houghton; unpub.
5. Ibid.
6. HJ to Grace Norton, May 20, 1870, Houghton; reprinted, lightly edited, in 1 HJ Letters, 238. The text is taken from the original.
7. "Travelling Companions," *Atlantic Monthly*, November–December 1870; 2 *Complete Tales*, 171.
8. Annie Fields Diary, July 16, 1870; excerpted M. A. DeW. Howe (1922), 119–20. She gives the title of the story as "Compagnons de Voyages," and this was likely the name HJ had given it, but Fields published it as "Travelling Companions."
9. *The Atlantic*, November–December 1870, reprinted in the collection of that name, and in 2 *Complete Tales*.
10. "Passionate Pilgrim," which Fields held for the March and April 1871 numbers of *The Atlantic*; and a review of Disraeli's "Lothair," which appeared in August 1870.
11. He probably also wrote his review of "Selections from De Musset," *The Atlantic Monthly*, September 1870, 379, at this time, containing some reflections on the French theater, which pretty much completed the principal impressions of his trip.
12. Ibid.
13. "Saratoga," CTW: Great Britain and America, 750.
14. "Red and Gold Guide," 64–65.
15. See Tainter.
16. "Saratoga," ibid., 751.
17. Saum has pointed out that Christopher Newman, the typical American HJ was soon to describe, is pointedly made to be a westerner. HJ's personal acquaintance was limited to New York and New England; George Abbott James, who had a vaguely western and southern background, was an exception. Newman is probably compounded of GAJ and glimpses of presumed businessmen at Saratoga, which constituted his whole nonliterary acquaintance with the type.
18. "Saratoga Springs," 753.
19. Ibid., 754–55.
20. This is the outline of HJ's first novel, *Watch and Ward*, about a man who adopts a young girl and raises her to be his wife. In Saratoga he began his ruminations on the American woman, and in each of the two travel pieces he wrote for *The Nation* on leaving Saratoga HJ said he was holding back certain scenes for use in his "great American novel." See "From Lake George to Burlington," and "Newport," CTW: Great Britain and America, 749, 762–63. The opening of the novel itself is set in one of the Saratoga hotels.
21. "Lake George," in CTW: Great Britain and America, 741.
22. Ibid., 745–46.
23. "Newport," in CTW: Great Britain and America, 766.
24. Ibid., 760.
25. Ibid., 759, 761 et passim.
26. See, e.g., HJ to Grace Norton, September 26, 1870, Houghton; 1 HJ Letters, 242.

27. HJ to Grace Norton, April 13, 1871, Houghton; unpub.
28. "Master Eustace," *Galaxy*, November 1871; 2 *Complete Tales*, 343.
29. HJ to F. P. Church, July 21, 1871, Church Collection, NYPL. The balance of this letter is missing. It shows that the title, "Master Eustace," was chosen by HJ, and as this is a clinical study, perhaps the name is a reference to Eustachio, the well-known Renaissance anatomist. Compare "The Author of Beltraffio," below.
30. *Watch and Ward*, 17.
31. Ibid., 22.
32. Ibid., 159.
33. HJ to C. E. Norton, August 9, 1871, Houghton; 1 HJ Letters, 259, 262.
34. The story of the duty of the mentor or parent has been traced through HJ's novels recently by Zacharias (1993).
35. HJ to WJ, September 22, 1872, 1 WJ–HJ Letters, 169; I take it that "purpurine" refers to Peirce's complexion.
36. Wright himself was a Germanophile and a materialist of the most advanced kind, and had written a long article addressing the central question of the dispute: How could inert matter, even if animated by some still-unknown principle, have given rise to consciousness and self-awareness, to the precious *self*? Wright (1873).
37. NSB, 283. Holmes later acknowledged Wright's influence. At this time the young men organized themselves into an informal Metaphysical Club, which met irregularly in the Jameses' parlor or William's bedroom, as often as anywhere else, since Wright had no space in which to entertain them. Among early members of the circle, in addition to Holmes and William James, were Charles S. Peirce, Josiah Royce, and Nicholas St. John Green. Peirce in later life tried to claim that he had launched "pragmatism" at these early discussions of the Metaphysical Club, a claim that has prompted a substantial literature. The claim seems greatly inflated, and that the club had even existed in any formal sense was doubted for some time; indeed I was one of those who doubted. It was certainly not more than an informal association. But HJ refers to it unmistakably in a letter: "My brother has just helped to found a metaphysical club in Cambridge, (consisting of Chauncey Wright, Charles Peirce, & c.) to which you may expect to be appointed corresponding member." HJ to E. Boott, January 24, 1872, Houghton; unpub. Since HJ in this letter is catching up events from the previous summer and fall, the "just" might refer to any time in the previous six months. It seems very unlikely, however, that Peirce delivered a paper on pragmatism to the club, and it is sad to see him deprive Wright's memory of the credit for having served as mentor to a remarkable group of young men. He was in his way a key figure in American intellectual history, a part of its secret history, if you will.
38. HJ to E. Boott, January 24, 1872, Houghton. In a published version of this letter, 1 HJ Letters, 267, "Hooper" is mistranscribed as "Harper," and Clover Hooper therefore becomes an unidentified "C.H."
39. Marion Hooper to Eleanor Shattuck, January 10, 1871, Shattuck Papers, MHS; unpub.
40. WDH to his father, March 12, 1871, Selected Howells Letters.
41. HJ to Grace Norton, April 13, 1871, Houghton; unpub.
42. "Still Waters," reprinted in *Collected Plays*. The setting is a piazza in Newport, at sunset. A cosmopolitan young man is fond of an innocent young woman. She in turn is in love with a handsome, empty fellow. The cosmopolitan hero sees what is between the other two, and deftly brings them together. He then departs for the greener pastures of "Europe." At the close,

the ingenue gazes out over the Atlantic, dimly beginning to realize that she has chosen foolishly. The fatuous young man she has chosen complains at her momentary inattention, and then contents himself with a cigar.

43. HJ to E. Boott, January 24, 1872, Houghton; 1 HJ Letters, 267.

44. HJ to Grace Norton, April 13, 1871, Houghton; unpub.

45. "Around a Spring," by Gustave Droz, book review in *The Nation*, August 1871; Lit. Crit.: French and European Writers, 268, 269.

46. Ibid., 273.

47. "Quebec," in CTW: Great Britain and America, 772.

48. Ibid., 774.

49. "Niagara," in CTW: Great Britain and America, 771, 781.

50. HJ to E. Boott, January 24, 1872, Houghton; 1 HJ Letters, 267, 268.

51. HJ to Grace Norton, March 17, 1872, Houghton; unpub. The references are to Theodora Sedgwick and Jane Norton, Grace's sister-in-law and sister, respectively.

52. "Guest's Confession," *Atlantic Monthly*, October, November 1872; 2 *Complete Tales*, 375, 397.

53. "Guest's Confession," supra. To complete the parable, the heroine is a Unitarian. She and David meet in a church, and her love and forgiveness supersede the hard Calvinist doctrine of predestined damnation. The point is made that he is Episcopalian—an adherent of the Anglican communion in America—and his Church presumably has the richness of tradition that allows it to embrace both the Old Testament and the New. HJ himself when in Europe appears to have attended Anglican and Catholic services; a few weeks after finishing this story he visited the cathedral at Chester and wrote: "you become conscious of that sweet, cool mustiness in the air which seems to haunt these places as the very climate of Episcopacy, you may grow to feel that they are less the empty shells of a departed faith than the abodes of a faith which may still affirm a presence and awaken echoes. Catholicism has gone, but Anglicism has the next best music." "Chester," *Nation*, July 4, 1872, reprinted in CTW: Great Britain and America, 63–64.

This account of the story may seem rather schematic, but the intensity of the story itself carries the reader along and the evocation of the Old and New Testaments is gracefully done. The same theme, which shows the marks of Renan's influence, is carried forward in James's American novels, most explicitly in *The American* itself. The central situation of HJ's unfinished novel *The Ivory Tower* is precisely the one in "Guest's Confession": a hard little man, a wealthy stock trader, comes to a resort and dies, passing a secret paper to the young man who is his heir. The earlier story perhaps gives an indication of how the unfinished novel would have concluded.

54. This departure from Cambridge was meant to be final—when the three arrived in England, HJ booked return berths for the ladies, but not for himself. The decision to leave Cambridge has been obscured by the loss of the notebook he began keeping on this journey; HJ's later notebooks pick up the thread in 1875, when after a brief, dutiful trial of living in New York, he decided to settle in Paris; see below; and his unfinished memoir *The Middle Years*, which begins with an account of his trips to London in 1869 and 1876. The gap in the record has contributed to the slighting of the years spent in Italy and France; and his later adoption of English nationality led HJ himself to minimize the importance of this period.

14   HENRY OPENS THE DOORS OF EUROPE FOR ALICE

1. For example in *The Portrait of a Lady*, see below. In *The Ambassadors*, Maria Gostrey conducts Lambert Strether on the same walks through Chester on which James took Alice. The companionable walks are described in the travel letter he wrote for the *Nation* at the time: "Chester," reprinted in CTW: Great Britain and America, 52.
2. "Chester," CTW: Great Britain and America, 52, 62. Most of the preceding description is taken from this article.
3. CW to MJ, June 1, 1872, Houghton; unpub.
4. "Chester," supra, 64.
5. "North Devon," *Nation*, August 8, 1872, reprinted in CTW: Great Britain and America, 82.
6. HJ Sr. to HJ, August 9, 1872, Houghton; quoted Perry 24 (1954).
7. HJ Sr. to HJ, March 18, 1873, published in slightly revised form, NSB, 262 (but misdated "1869," apparently to conceal William's years of illness and inactivity); Allen, *William James*, 179–80. I have taken this letter out of strict chronology for the convenience of having all the family news in one place; and HJ Sr.'s pleasure in WJ's new career does seem to date from this time. See HJ Sr. to HJ, August 9, 1872, Houghton; unpub.
8. NSB, 264–65. William's journals show that he had carried out a systematic study of idealist philosophy, beginning with a reading of his father's works, over the past two years. The first major work he would publish would be his study of his father's books, *The Literary Remains of Henry James* (1884).
9. AJ to E. Boott, July 2 [1872], Houghton; unpub. This interesting letter is apparently the only one of Alice's letters written on her Grand Tour to have survived. It seems not to have been referred to in print before.
10. HJ to E. Boott, July 2 [1872], Houghton; unpub.
11. See CW to MJ, July 20, 1872, Houghton; unpub.
12. HJ to WJ, July 24 [1872], Houghton; 1 WJ–HJ Letters, 161.
13. HJ to E. Boott, August 2 [1872], Houghton; unpub.
14. HJ to parents, September 9 [1872], Houghton; 1 HJ Letters, 295.
15. HJ to WJ, September 22 [1872], Houghton; 1 WJ–HJ Letters, 170.
16. Ibid., 169.
17. W. D. Howells to HJ, October 28, 1872, 1 Howells Selected Letters, 404–5.
18. *Au point où nous en sommes.*
19. HJ to WJ, September 22 [1872], Houghton; 1 WJ–HJ Letters, 168, 170.
20. HJ to E. Boott, November 16 [1872], Houghton; unpub.
21. "James Russell Lowell" *Atlantic*, January 1892, reprinted *American Essays*, 77, 82.
22. Ibid., 80–82. It was presumably under the continued influence of these talks that Henry later made extensive references to the Song of Roland in his first serious novel, *Roderick Hudson*, where the chivalrous New Englander is named Rowland Mallet.
23. Ibid., 82. See also HJ to AJ, February 16 [1872], Houghton, unpub.; Hale, 206–8; Scudder, 158 ff.
24. "The Parisian Stage," *Nation*, January 9, 1873; reprinted *The Scenic Art*, 3, 4.
25. Ibid., 3.
26. "Théophile Gautier," *North American Review*, April 1873; Lit. Crit.: French and European Writers, 355.
27. Ibid., 374–75.
28. "Henri Regnault" (unsigned review of *Correspondance de Henri Regnault*),

Nation, January 2, 1873; reprinted Lit. Crit.: French and European Writers, 619. HJ's review of Regnault's correspondence was written in Paris, and it was in this book that HJ found Gautier's reviews and learned of his role in Regnault's career. The essay on Gautier was written shortly thereafter, in January 1873 in Rome. For convenience I have summarized both works together here. Henry also put Regnault in a tale he wrote while in Paris, "The Sweetheart of M. Briseux," *Galaxy*, June 1873, reprinted 3 *Complete Tales*, 53. The fictional Briseux's great portrait of a woman is a portrait of an intellect; the red velvet of Regnault's picture is replaced by a yellow shawl in Briseux's. HJ first sent this story to a Gail Hamilton, who was planning a new magazine for women, *Wood's Household*, but the plan foundered and James was obliged to recover the story and send it to *The Galaxy*, where it appeared long after the other two works on Gautier-Regnault.

29. HJ to E. Boott, December 14, 1872, Houghton; unpub.
30. Ibid.; HJ to AJ, December 16 [1872], Houghton; unpub.

15 SETTLING IN ITALY

1. *Italian Hours*, 136–37.
2. E. Boott to HJ, June 13, 1874, Houghton; unpub.
3. HJ to HJ Sr., December 25 [1872], Houghton; 1 HJ Letters, 315.
4. HJ to MJ, December 29 [1872], Houghton; 1 HJ Letters, 316, 318.
5. HJ Journal, January 21, 1873; *Italian Hours*, 203–4. The journal itself has not survived; HJ refers to it in his later notebooks, and passages were published in *Italian Hours*.
6. HJ to HJ Sr., January 19 [1873], Houghton; 1 HJ Letters, 327, 328.
7. HJ to MJ, December 29 1872, Houghton; 1 HJ Letters, 316.
8. HJ to AJ, February 10 [1873], Houghton; 1 HJ Letters, 337.
9. Ibid.
10. HJ Journal, April 10, 1873, *Italian Hours*, 211.
11. Mrs. Terry, as she then was, had a son and daughter by her former marriage to the sculptor Thomas Crawford. HJ frequently mentioned the daughter Annie, later the countess von Rabe, in his letters but not the son, the future novelist F. Marion Crawford, then twenty years old and perhaps beneath HJ's notice.
12. "Roman Rides," in *Italian Hours*, 157. HJ has split himself into two characters and has them converse for the sake of rendering this description in dialogue.
13. "Roman Rides," 158. HJ here has his dopplegänger riding with a lady whom he "extremely admires"; there were a number of such rides, some of which were with Anne Bartlett, with whom he often galloped; see letters to his mother in February.
14. HJ to E. Boott, May 23, 1874, Houghton; unpub.
15. "Roman Rides," 169, Elizabeth Boott is identified as his companion in these rides in his letter to her of May 23, 1874, Houghton; unpub.
16. HJ to E. Boott, May 23, 1874, Houghton; unpub. It is difficult to capture the flavor of this long letter in a brief quotation. In another passage he says, "Everything that happened last winter now takes on the most iridescent hues. . . ."
17. "From a Roman Notebook," in *Italian Hours*, 212–13, where his companion was identified as "L.B." Edel translates this as "Lizzie Boott," but this is not

possible because the Bootts had left Rome before the villa was opened to the public. See also "The After-Season in Rome," in *Italian Hours*, 193–94. The initials by which HJ identified persons in the published version of his essay (the Tauschnitz edition that Edel cites as a discovery is the same as *Italian Hours*) are used artfully, to create quasi-fictional personages. Thus "G.G." probably is given the appearance of Count Primoli ("Gégé"), but the incidents attributed to him can be identified from HJ's contemporary letters as involving not the count but first, Aunt Mary's coachman, and second, an American named Wurt.

I have not been able to identify "Mr. Ireland," who accompanied HJ to the Villa Ludovisi. The Greek "Juno" behind a shutter is evidently the Juno of "The Last of the Valerii," and the same incident appears again more literally in *Roderick Hudson*, see below, when the narrator is showing the place to a young man, as HJ actually did.

18. *Roderick Hudson*, 103.
19. *Roderick Hudson*, 103. The visit of "our two young men" is recognizably that described in his journal.
20. HJ to AJ, June 8 [1873], Houghton; unpub.
21. Ibid.
22. Ibid.
23. HJ to E. Boott, June 12 [1873], Houghton; unpub.
24. The premise for the review was the appearance of a German translation of two novels, *The Torrents of Spring* and *A Lear of the Steppes*, in one volume. But this was no more than a pretext for the essay, and HJ does not refer specifically to the German translations. The review contains his own translations, apparently from the French, from other novels.
25. "Frühlingsfluten. Ein König Lear des Dorfes. Zwei Novellen. Von Iwan Turgéniew" (review), *North American Review*, April 1874, reprinted as "Ivan Turgénieff," in *French Poets and Novelists* (1878); and as "Ivan Turgenev" in Lit. Crit.: French Writers, 968 (1984). I have substituted the current American transliteration "Turgenev" here as elsewhere.
26. Ibid., 969.
27. Ibid., 972.
28. Ibid., 978.
29. Ibid., 982.
30. Ibid., 998. No summary can do justice to this detailed statement of a critical method and personal philosophy, which was evidently intended as a prospectus for the first great American novel. I do not want to exaggerate Turgenev's influence—HJ found in him similarity and reassurance, rather than ideas or methods. Nor should one minimize the importance of the reassurance Turgenev provided, however, as well as the crystallization of ideas that might otherwise have remained chaotic and HJ's determination to outdo the master.
31. On this last point, see e.g. "The Sweetheart of M. Brisieux," in which a young Englishwoman whose name would never be known, decides a part of the history of France. HJ was a student of scientific philosophy, not a philosopher in his own right; his ideas about national character amounted to little more than an application of the "advanced" or progressive thought of his time, a romantic idealism derived in part from Herder and Goethe, and popularized by Hippolyte Taine. The summary given in the text is abstracted from the stories and essays he wrote in the spring and summer of 1873. We no longer accept the ideas of national type and progressive evolution as "scientific," although they are still common enough, and HJ himself later pretty much

abandoned them. At the time of which we are speaking, however, he still clung to a sort of naïve racialism that mars much of his early work.

32. See R. West, 28–30. The importance of this summer in HJ's development has been noted by critics but ignored by recent biographers.

33. He did write one story about American commerce that summer, a sad little Hawthornish tale, told by a traveling salesman, about a fantastic professor who put his daughter on the public stage to sell his ideas of progress. "Professor Fargo," *Galaxy*, August 1874; reprinted 3 *Complete Tales*, 259. The father and daughter are the predecessors of the Tarrants in *The Bostonians*.

34. See HJ's preface to volume XIII of the New York edition, containing "Madame de Mauves" and other stories on the international theme, reprinted in *The Art of the Novel*, 180, 192–94. He did make an American businessman the hero of the international theme in *The American*, but the climax of the tale, in which the hero triumphs through his superior moral character, has seemed to most critics not to follow from the character's personality or history. The American businessman at last appears as a rounded character, an older man, in HJ's last novels *The Golden Bowl* and *The Ivory Tower*, in which the racialist international theme has been abandoned.

35. Ibid., 193. Compare "The Story in It," in which he dwells on the difficulty of writing an interesting story about a virtuous married woman, for whom by definition there were no great choices to make, and hence no story to tell. HJ's tendency to treat women purely as sexual beings, especially in his early work, has been noted and criticized. See, for instance, Rebecca West. As he was a little defensive on this point in the prefaces to the New York edition, it may be appropriate to point out that older women do appear as forceful, individual personalities from the start: the grandmother in "Madame de Mauves," itself, for instance, and Madame Merle in *The Portrait of a Lady*. They generally appear as villains, for whom there is a wider range of choice and so of drama. HJ's virtuous, autobiographical characters did grow older as he himself aged, however, and his female doppelgängers eventually reached middle age; in *The Spoils of Poynton* he made a mother of grown children the heroine of a novel for the first time. But his characteristic stories continued to center on sexual secrets, and virtuous mothers were not useful heroines in such tales. Middle-aged men, by the way, figure as heroes just as rarely, and for the same reasons: Lambert Strether in *The Ambassadors* is the only clear example of such a hero.

36. "The Last of the Valerii," "Madame de Mauves," and HJ's long essay on Turgenev were all written during the summer of 1873, but it is not possible now to establish in what order. On August 3 he told William that he had been reading Turgenev for some time, and he sent the Turgenev piece to the *North American Review* sometime in August. See HJ to AJ, September 3 [1873], Houghton; unpub. Most likely HJ wrote "The Last of the Valerii," which was set in Rome, while in Switzerland or Homburg, in June. He probably then turned to the Turgenev piece, which occupied most of the summer, and then last of all wrote "Madame de Mauves," which seems to show the influence of Turgenev most, and which is set in a suburb of Paris (Saint-Germain-en-Laye, where HJ had visited the Nortons the previous fall). The three pieces all deal in different ways with the heroine of the international theme, and should be taken as a single complex work defining HJ's views.

37. "The Last of the Valerii," *Atlantic Monthly*, January 1874, 69; 3 *Complete Tales*, 89.

38. The narrator of this tale resembled John La Farge (a painter who wore spectacles when he was working), HJ's own mentor, who might be said to em-

body the hopeful fusion of Europe and America; but HJ can hardly have expected a reader to see this. It was just one of the private jokes with which his work is filled. The "Last of the Valerii" is the first of HJ's highly complex, mature tales, which are often self-reflexive: the form of the story is also its subject, and the author is writing about the act of writing as much as about the characters and events portrayed. It was a romance, a fantastic tale in the tradition of Hawthorne. It was also a retelling of Mérimée's story, and so the story itself became an example of its theme: Henry James had conquered Mérimée. In the French setting, in the Europe of the old regime, Venus had been all-powerful, and had brushed aside the Church along with the other vanities of men. In Henry's tale, the ancient goddess herself is conquered by the new spirit of Christianity; Juno is overcome by the spirit of Lawton's Valley and Renan's *Life of Jesus*.

39. Preface, supra, 197.
40. "Madame de Mauves," *Galaxy*, February–March 1874; 3 *Complete Tales*, 123.
41. "Madame de Mauves," 3 *Complete Tales*, 125.
42. Preface, 197.
43. Ibid.
44. "Camors," in Lit. Crit.: French Writers, 285.
45. Ibid.
46. HJ to AJ, September 3 [1873], Houghton; unpub.
47. HJ to WJ, September 15 [1873], Houghton; 1 WJ–HJ Letters, 220.
48. See, e.g., WJ to RJ, September 27 [1873], Vaux; unpub.: "Considering then the example of Alice's improvement in Europe & how easy life will be there this winter with Harry. . . ."
49. MJ to HJ, April 27, 1873, Houghton; unpub.
50. WJ to HJ, May 1, 1873, Houghton; 1 WJ–HJ Letters, 203.
51. WJ to HJ, April 6, 1873, Houghton; 1 WJ–HJ Letters, 193.
52. Ibid.
53. WJ to HJ, May 25, 1873, Houghton; 1 WJ–HJ Letters, 207, 208–9.
54. WJ to HJ, July 14, 1873, Houghton; 1 WJ–HJ Letters, 214.
55. MRJ to RJ, May 17, 1873, Vaux; unpub.
56. Perry's letter, if there was one, has not been preserved, but the published essay is far more systematic and academic in its method of presentation (and more clear), than any of HJ's previous criticism.
57. HJ to HJ Sr., October 26 [1873], Houghton; 1 HJ Letters, 405. Edel's note states that HJ Sr. returned the essay on his own, with his own suggestions for revision. This is improbable, and is evidently Edel's own conjecture; it seems plain from the letters that Perry requested the revisions.
58. WJ to HJ, September 2, 1873, Houghton; 1 WJ–HJ Letters, 219–20.
59. HJ to WJ, September 26 [1873], Houghton; 1 WJ–HJ Letters, 222.

16 THE AMBASSADOR FROM LAWTON'S VALLEY

1. WJ to RJ, October 10, 1873, Vaux; unpub. "I shall make pretty straight tracks for Harry in Florence and try to bring him home with me in June."
2. WJ to GWJ, November 16, 1873, Vaux; published in part, 1 R. B. Perry, 351–52.
3. See HJ's portrayal of him on this visit, as Babcock in *The American*; see Chapter 18, and this chapter, below.

4. See WJ letters to HJ, March 22, 1874, and April 18, 1874, first apologizing for and then renewing this harangue; also WJ to GWJ, November 16, 1873, supra.

5. WJ to GWJ, November 16, 1873, Vaux.

6. WJ to HJ Sr., November 30, 1873, Houghton; 1 R. B. Perry, 162–63.

7. See WJ to HJ, April 18, 1874, Houghton; 1 WJ–HJ Letters, 229, 230–1, where he rehearsed some of these arguments, and WJ's letters to father and Bob during his visit with HJ.

8. This letter seems to have been lost, but its arrival and contents are described, WJ to AJ, December 7, 1873, Houghton, unpub.; see also WJ to RJ, December 8, 1873, Vaux; unpub.

9. WJ to RJ, December 8, 1873, Vaux; unpub.

10. Ibid.

11. HJ to HJ Sr., December 22, 1873, Houghton; 1 HJ Letters, 419–20.

12. WJ to GWJ, November 16, 1873, Houghton; 1 R. B. Perry, 351.

13. HJ to HJ Sr., December 22, 1873, Houghton; 1 HJ Letters, 420.

14. HJ to AJ, January 13, 1874, Houghton; unpub.

15. Henry did not immediately write home, but after following William to Florence he wrote to Howells in Cambridge a letter in which he surprisingly said, for the first time, that he planned to return home in the fall. HJ to WDH, January 9, 1874, Selected Letters.

16. HJ to AJ, January 13, 1874, Houghton; unpub.

17. Ibid.

18. Ibid.

19. Just before setting sail for America William wrote to say that he would wait in Dresden if Henry wished. But Henry answered that he would linger in Florence just a little while longer, and that William should suit his own convenience. HJ to WJ, "Saturday" [February 28, 1874], 2 WJ–HJ Letters, 224. WJ's letter from Dresden to which this is the answer has been lost or destroyed. From HJ's reply it seems it may have contained some discussion of the reasons for WJ's abrupt departure. "Babcock's" letter in *The American* was written under very similar circumstances and may be a paraphrase of William's, see below.

20. In addition to *The American* and *Confidence*, described in the text, William's visit also appeared in *The Ambassadors*; he is Waymarsh, although elements of later visits have been added to the account.

21. See HJ to Grace Norton, August 5, 1876, Houghton; unpub.; see Chapter 18, below.

22. *The American*, 110–11.

23. HJ to Grace Norton, August 5, 1876, Houghton; unpub. Norton's letter has not survived, but HJ paraphrases it in reply.

24. *The American*, 112. The hero quickly recovers his good spirits, however, and sends the William character, Babcock, an ironical little ivory carving of an aesthetic monk; "through one of the rents in his gown, you espied a fat capon hung round the monk's waist." The narrator comments that it was not supposable that this was a satire on Babcock.

25. The outline HJ prepared in his notebook is substantially different from the manuscript as finally submitted to the publisher. The notebook version has a somewhat melodramatic plot; it calls for the William-ish character to murder his wife. But at the crux of the story, the confrontation between the two men, the completed tale begins to veer sharply away from the prepared outline. The circumstances at the point of departure are suggestively like those during William's visit to Rome.

26. *Confidence*, 1174.
27. Ibid., 1186.
28. The encounter is in *Confidence*, 1210. The Henry-ish character is Bernard Longueville, perhaps a reference to London (compare the punning "Long-don" in *The Awkward Age*), where he was then living. The lover in the tale is a woman called Angela, which sounds like a name for Henry's own better nature, and what Longueville reveals is their engagement. The dialogue is nevertheless strikingly like what we would now call "coming out." As noted above, HJ portrayed William's visit also in *The Ambassadors*, where he is Waymarsh, although by 1900 there had been a series of visits of a similar pattern. In the later, less sarcastic, accounts the William character is understood to be frightened by his own feelings, although he blames Henry's.
29. "The Autumn in Florence," *Nation*, January 1, 1874, 6; reprinted *Italian Hours*, 269; CTW: Continent, 533.
30. F. Boott to HJ, June 14 [1874], Houghton; unpub.
31. See "James Russell Lowell," American Essays, 77, 83.
32. He from the first had intended it for *The Atlantic*, but a letter from Scribner's asking him to submit a novel for serialization gave him a chance to force an advantageous bargain. He wrote to his father, telling him to invite Howells to bid against Scribner's for the novel. He directed his father to ask twelve hundred dollars for a novel in twelve installments—about what he would receive for twelve short stories—and to accept one thousand dollars. Howells was pressed to pay at least a part of the money in advance, to feed the letter of credit. HJ to HJ Sr., March 9, 1874, Houghton; 1 HJ Letters, 434.
33. HJ to WDH, May 3, 1874, Selected Letters of WDH.
34. The "bad heroine" became a stock description for him in his journals in later years for the Princess Casamassima character. In his essay on Turgenev, HJ had criticized the older novelist's *femmes fatales*. They were too relentlessly wicked to be real, HJ thought; and he evidently set out to better the master in this novel.
35. Lit. Crit., Preface to *Roderick Hudson*, 1040. See also Preface to "What Maisie Knew," 1157 ("Sketchily clustered, even, these elements gave out the vague pictorial glow . . ."). An important point to note here is that this is an idealist method; relations, and not material objects, are the subject of the portrait. HJ never doubts that the relations have objective existence. Particular relations are the colored threads that he uses to fill his imagined tapestry. Compare, e.g., Morris R. Cohen, *An Introduction to Logic*.
36. This I take it is the meaning of the often quoted passage, "Really, universally, relations stop nowhere. . . ." Ibid., 1041.
37. See, for example, the Preface to "The Spoils of Poynton," in Lit. Crit., 1138–39 (a dog nosing out a bone), and elsewhere the comparison to a pig searching for truffles.
38. Preface to *Roderick Hudson*: "Until then he had hugged the shore, bumping about in the shallow waters and sandy coves of the short story. Now he put out to sea, and immediately as he dared to set out the blue southern sea spread out before him."
39. Ibid., 113–14.
40. Ibid., 168.
41. Ibid., 162.
42. I have omitted from this summary a plot device that seems to me simply a contrivance. Roderick Hudson has been engaged to be married to Mary Garland from the beginning of the tale. Rowland is made to fall in love with Mary, but he does not learn she is engaged to Roderick Hudson until after he

has undertaken to sponsor the young sculptor's career. Rowland honorably keeps his love for Mary a secret, and it is this secret that is the MacGuffin of the story. The angry outburst in which Rowland reveals the secret to Roderick is what destroys the sculptor's last remaining shreds of volition and sends him wandering into the mountains. I have omitted this element of the story from the summary given in the text because it seems to be a contrivance overlaid upon the central situation—the relation of the mentor to his pupil, in the context of the temptations of Rome. Rowland is a virtuous Vautrin, and Roderick is very much like Balzac's effeminate poet, Lucien Chardon, who is similarly deficient in will, and who under Vautrin's sway falls victim to the seductions of Paris, where he dies. Writing for an English-speaking audience, unlike Balzac, HJ was obliged to find a harmless female object for his Vautrin's passion, a passion that nevertheless had to be kept secret. The device is unpersuasive and adds nothing to the tale, which is stronger if Mary Garland is simply ignored (as the characters do through most of the novel). There is a moving scene toward the end of the tale, for instance, in which Roderick, sunk in his selfishness, arrogantly says that Rowland does not understand passion because he does not feel it. (There is a startling realism to this scene.) Rowland answers with a moving recital of his own carefully suppressed feelings, and of the excellent reasons that compel him to conceal and control his passion. Rowland is here speaking for HJ, and announcing his (their) moral superiority to the weak and selfish Roderick. This scene would have been a good deal stronger, and Roderick's dismayed reaction more probable, if Rowland had been able to say, "I have loved you from the beginning, you ass." Mary Garland plainly is introduced only as a convenient object upon which to fasten Rowland's affections. A similar device is used in the novel *Confidence*, where the James-ish protagonist is given reasons for hiding his love, which he again reveals in an angry outburst. But HJ was never able to tell this story successfully with a male protagonist.

43. E. Boott to HJ, June 13 [1874], Houghton; unpub.
44. Ibid.

17   A DUTIFUL EXPERIMENT: A YEAR IN MANHATTAN

1. There was an odd incident on Henry's brief visit: Alice's puppy escaped from his arms while Alice drove Henry in a pony cart, and the dog was run over and killed. It was replaced by a terrier, "Bunch," who later would make an appearance in the opening scene of *The Portrait of a Lady*. HJ was very fond of dogs, but he was not sentimental about them, and the dog's death at his hands, as it were, seemingly did not distress him.

2. Compare "The Impressions of a Cousin," in which the setting reproduces the circumstances of HJ's return to New York in 1874. His own thoughts and impressions are conferred on the narrator, a woman who has dutifully moved from Rome to New York, where she is confronted with an entirely suitable suitor. She answers, "I am an old maid. What should I want with a husband?" Given the conventions of the day, he and Elizabeth could not have spent so much time together without their—and their friends' and family's—being conscious of this question. Henry may have made an explicit or tacit offer to Elizabeth; I imagine he would have been refused, if he had done so, but I don't think he did. HJ was always deeply opposed to a marriage of conve-

nience, a marriage of less than passionate intensity, and there is no sign of his having such feelings toward Elizabeth.

3. Turgenev to HJ, August 7, 1874, in 10 Collected Papers of I. S. Turgenev, 269.

4. *Transatlantic Sketches*. Boston: J. R. Osgood and Company, 1875. Osgood was cautious, perhaps because he would also be bringing out Henry's first novel that year, and asked Henry to share the risk if the book failed to meet expenses. The publisher agreed to pay the usual 15 percent royalty on all books sold, but these royalties would be paid only after the cost of making the "stereotype" plates from which the book would be printed had been met. There has been some confusion about these business arrangements. Lewis and Kaplan, following Edel, say that HJ Sr. lent money to have the book printed, as if it were a vanity-press arrangement. HJ now being on the scene, however, HJ Sr. was no longer serving as his agent and was not involved in the transaction at all. Nor was there any need for money to be lent. Osgood treated the cost of the stereotypes as an advance against royalties. HJ was billed for them on the first statement from the publisher, but as royalties quickly exceeded the costs, he had nothing to pay. See HJ to J. R. Osgood & Co., August 18, 1875, 1 HJ Letters, 480. ("I have just received your account . . . for stereotyped plates.")

5. *A Passionate Pilgrim*. Boston: H. O. Houghton & Co., 1875. Houghton too was cautious; these were difficult times, and the market for Henry's work was as yet unknown. Houghton agreed to assume all the risk, but offered only a 10 percent royalty. This was agreed upon, and the book appeared promptly the following January.

6. See "Impressions of a Cousin," among many other diatribes against the number addresses; similarly *The Bostonians*, 195, HJ's letters of this time, and again in *The American Scene*.

7. This was his constant refrain in descriptions of New York. See "The Impressions of a Cousin," 5 *Complete Tales*, 111–13; and similar passages in *The Bostonians* and *The American Scene*.

8. As a child, I rode not only on the elevated tracks on Third Avenue but in the last of the wooden cars, which I remember as having little platforms at the ends for boarding, like streetcars. By then the line had been electrified, but in HJ's day the trains were drawn by coal-fired steam locomotives.

9. HJ to Sarah Wister, January 23 [1875], 1 HJ Letters, 469.

10. "Frances Anne Kemble," in *Essays in London*, 103–5. See also HJ to WDH, January 13 [1875], 1 HJ Letters, 468, 469.

11. HJ to WDH, January 13 [1875], 1 HJ Letters, 468–69.

12. In all, he wrote more than seventy articles that winter, half of them for *The Nation*.

13. "Madame Ristori," *Nation*, March 18, 1875; reprinted *The Scenic Art*.

14. "Notes on the Theatres," *Nation*, March 11, 1875; reprinted *The Scenic Art*.

15. "Impressions of London Social Life," by E. S. Nadal, reviewed by HJ in *The Nation*, October 7, 1865; Lit. Crit.: American and English, 554, 558–59.

16. Ibid., 559.

17. Nordhoff's account of the Oneida community provided part of the impetus for the novel *The Bostonians*. See note 25, below.

18. "The Communistic Societies of the United States," in Lit. Crit.: American and English, 560, 563.

19. Ibid., 567.

20. See John Humphrey Noyes, *History of American Socialisms*. Philadelphia: J. B. Lippincott, 1870.

21. Nordhoff, 294.

22. Ibid.
23. Ibid., 292–93.
24. "The Communistic Societies of the United States," supra; Lit. Crit.: American and English, 567. HJ refers to the man who is the object of the criticism as "Henry"; this is evidently a mistake for "Charles," and perhaps shows how vividly he imagined himself in his place.
25. Ibid., 567. HJ enlarged on this theme in *The Bostonians*. The heroine of that novel, Verena Tarrant, seems to have been raised in the Oneida community, and her socialist father's domination of her personality ends when the lovers Verena and Basil begin their intimacy with the sharing of a secret. HJ's reading of Nordhoff seems to have merged in memory with Fanny Kemble's anecdote to produce the plot of the novel, see below.
26. Elizabeth visited New York in February, and they lunched at Delmonico's: HJ to E. Boott, January 27 [1875]; March 8 [1875], Houghton. The first letter is unpublished; the second is in Italian, but an English translation appears at 1 HJ Letters, 473. Boott saw and admired the Duveneck pictures in Boston (Neuhaus, 32) but had not yet met Duveneck. When HJ next visited Boston, he puffed the Duveneck pictures, see below.
27. See 2 *Life and Letters*, 104–8.
28. See Armstrong, 138 ff.
29. Notebooks, 24.
30. "Mr. Roosevelt's Creed," *New York Times*, October 19, 1884, 2, quoted HJ–John Hay Letters, 5–6. Roosevelt was a Republican loyalist, supporting James G. Blaine for president; Godkin was one of the leaders of the Mugwumps, the ludicrous-sounding Sachem word for "wise men," who had abandoned the party and were supporting Cleveland, in protest against corrupt patronage politics. Roosevelt's attack on Godkin's circle probably was a purposeful piece of what we would now call homophobia—perhaps the first use of this weapon in national politics. James was in England by then, but was aware of the attack. See HJ to Grace Norton, November 14 [1884], Houghton; unpub.
31. "I could remember without effort with what an irresistible longing I turned to Europe . . . Europe for me then meant simply Italy." Notebooks, 24–25; compare "Impressions of a Cousin," in which the narrator, Catherine Condit, returns to New York in 1873, and where "Italy" has become simply "Rome."
32. "Benvolio," 3 *Complete Tales*, 351, 401.
33. HJ to WDH, "Friday evening," [March 1875] Houghton; see Selected Letters of WDH.
34. *New York Tribune*, April 29, 1875, 8; reprinted Monteiro, the HJ–John Hay Letters, 149 n.
35. "I recall perfectly the maturing of my little plan to get abroad and remain for years, during the summer of 1875"; Notebooks, 24.
36. *Nation*, June 3, 1875, 3–4. HJ also wrote a favorable review for *The Galaxy*, "On Some Pictures lately Exhibited," July 1875, and then a full-length review for *The Nation*, which appeared September 9, 1875; both the latter are reprinted in *The Painter's Eye*. As the reviews were all anonymous, this must have seemed to be a whole chorus of praise, and undoubtedly helped to boost Duveneck's reputation in the United States. Duveneck, however, departed for Munich in July.
37. Notebooks, Matthiessen, ed., 25 ("it loomed before me one summer's day, in Quincy St.").
38. HJ to John Hay, July 23, 1875, Brown; HJ–John Hay Letters, 81–2.

39. Reid's letter of dismissal to HJ a year later seems deliberately insulting; W. Reid to HJ, August 10, 1876, in *Parisian Sketches*, 217. The antipathy seemed to be personal, and long-lasting. See the malicious, possibly homophobic, description of HJ in W. Reid to John Hay, October 25, 1881; Monteiro, 17–17.
40. HJ to John Hay, August 3, 1875, Brown; HJ–John Hay Letters, 83.
41. "Three French Books," *Galaxy*, August 1875; Lit. Crit.: French Writers, 205.
42. "Honoré de Balzac," *Galaxy*, December 1875; Lit. Crit.: French Writers, 31. HJ compares Balzac to an ambitious hairdresser, p. 65.
43. "The Two Ampères," *Galaxy*, November 1875, reprinted as "André-Marie and Jean-Jacques Ampère," in Lit. Crit.: French Writers, 9, 30.
44. "Three French Books," reviewing Wallon, *Jeanne d'Arc*.
45. Ibid.
46. Ibid., 213.
47. Ibid.
48. HJ to family, November 1, 1875, Houghton; reprinted 1 HJ Letters, 484.

18   HENRY'S ASSAULT ON PARIS

1. "Paris Revisited," November 22, 1875, *New York Tribune*, December 11, 1875; *Parisian Sketches*, 3, 7.
2. See HJ to WJ, December 3, 1875, Houghton; 1 WJ–HJ Letters, 244–45. This interesting incident is recounted by Perrot (1985), whose acute reading of HJ suggests that HJ had an unhappy love affair—with Mme. Bentzon. The letter cited above suggests that he knew her. Apparently he was wrong about the translation, however; the editors of the WJ–HJ Letters assert that it was by a Lucien Biart. I believe Perrot was right about the unhappy love affair, and wrong only about the other party. See Chapter 19, below, and "La rencontre de Henry James et d'Ivan Tourguéniev à Paris," *Cahiers d'Ivan Tourguéniev*, No. 17–18 (1993–94), 189 (translated by Roger Asselineau).
3. Now Rue Cambon. Nos. 29 and 30 are now Chanel headquarters.
4. W. H. Huntington to John Hay, December 17, 1877; HJ–John Hay Letters, 20 (noting that on moving to London HJ had grown whiskers, which were becoming to him).
5. C. S. Peirce to WJ, December 16, 1875, Houghton; quoted Brent, 103–4.
6. HJ to WJ, July 4 [1876], Houghton; 1 WJ–HJ Letters, 266.
7. HJ to F. P. Church, December 1 [1875], Church Collection, NYPL.
8. Turgenev to HJ, November 20, 1875, in *Polnoe sobranie*, Vol. 11, 151.
9. HJ to CW, December 3 [1875], Houghton; unpub.
10. Ibid. See also James's letters to other family members in December 1875, and *Turgenev and His French Circle*, 36.
11. HJ to HJ Sr., December 20, 1875, Houghton; 2 HJ Letters, 14.
12. This is Alphonse Daudet's description of the Sunday afternoons at about the time James visited, quoted in *Turgenev and His French Circle*, 40.
13. HJ to TSP, February 3, 1876, Colby; Harlow, 291 ("Tu devrais le ton que prennent ces messieurs [chez Flaubert] à l'égard de Cherbuliez & de Gustave Droz"); in HJ's January 18 letter to the *Tribune*, *Parisian Sketches*, 54, 55, the English dialogue quoted in the text is given, but the description makes it plain he is speaking of the same incident.
14. HJ to CW, December 3, 1875, Houghton; unpub.

15. "Paris Revisited," dated November 22, 1875, in *New York Tribune*, December 11, 1875; *Parisian Sketches*, 3, 10–11.
16. This was Taine's point in *The Origins of Contemporary France*, from which HJ borrowed freely.
17. Ibid., 32–33. See also, for the eighteenth-century origins of polite society, Taine's *Ancien Régime*, which HJ was then reading.
18. *The American*, 34–35.
19. "Your second installment of the American is prime. The morbid little clergyman is worthy of Ivan Sergeitch [Turgenev]. I was not a little amused to find some of my own attributes in him—I think you found my 'moral reaction' excessive when I was abroad." WJ to HJ, July 5 [1876], Houghton; 1 WJ–HJ Letters, 267, 268. Even in the act of recognizing the portrait, William displayed Babcock's obtuseness. Grace Norton also recognized the portrait, HJ to Grace Norton, August 5 [1876], Houghton; unpub.
20. See Preface to *The American*, Vol. II of the New York edition, in *The Art of the Novel*, 39. HJ's judgment thirty years later is that he had written no more than a romance, detached from fact or verisimilitude; the tether had been cut that should have anchored his imagination in fact, but that he had not been aware of this at the time.
21. "Versailles as It Is," dated Paris, December 16, 1875; *New York Tribune*, January 8, 1876; *Parisian Sketches*, 24–26.
22. Ibid., 27–28.
23. HJ to TSP, February 3, 1876, Colby; Harlow, 291.
24. HJ to E. Gosse, October 15, 1912, and October 17, 1912, HJ–Gosse Letters, 278–281. HJ characteristically was most interested by the monkey, the voiceless victim, his jealousy and death. Edel gives another version of this anecdote, taken from Gosse—see 2 Edel, 217–8—and omits HJ's reaction. Edel cites the October 15 letter, which was in the Warren Collection at the University of Virginia; he may not have been aware of the October 17 letter, which contains HJ's criticism of French homophobia, and which is now in the Library of Congress.
25. "Parisian Sketches," December 28, 1875, *New York Tribune*, January 22, 1876; *Parisian Sketches*, 33, 40–41.
26. Ibid., 41.
27. Ibid., 42.
28. HJ to E. Boott, December 31, 1875, Houghton; unpub.
29. "Divertir moi."
30. TMY, 89–90.
31. Renan, *Recollections*, vii, xxi–xxii.
32. *Recollections*, 106–8. The note of this bell is a dominant image in Christopher Newman's moment of self-realization in *The American*.
33. "Paris in Election Time," February 11, 1876, *New York Tribune*, March 4, 1876, reprinted *Parisian Sketches*, 78. Renan is identified not by name but only as a "literary critic [this is perhaps the newspaper's rendering of "man of letters"] of much eminence, [who] had for many years delighted me by his writings." This can only be Renan, and the views are those he expressed in similar terms in *Recollections*. See also HJ to WJ, February 8, 1876, 1 WJ–HJ Letters, 252, 253, describing the dinner but omitting this exchange.
34. HJ to Mary James, January 24 [1876], Houghton; 2 HJ Letters, 18, 20.
35. Compare the Bellegardes' ball in *The American*, when Newman is introduced to their aristocratic circle, 280.
36. HJ to WJ, February 8, 1876, Houghton; 2 WJ–HJ Letters, 252, 253.
37. "Paris in Election Time," February 11, 1876; reprinted *Parisian Sketches*, 74, 77.

38. HJ to Mrs. Reubell, undated, Houghton; unpub.; HJ to Henrietta Reubell, February 26, 1889, Houghton; unpub.
39. HJ to WJ, April 25 [1876], Houghton; 2 WJ–HJ Letters, 258, 259.
40. "Parisian Life," January 18, 1876, *New York Tribune*, February 5, 1876; reprinted *Parisian Sketches*, 54, 55.
41. These two paragraphs, my summary of what I take to have been HJ's settled views on France, are based on HJ's January 18 *Tribune* letter, supra.
42. See HJ to WJ, March 14, 1876, Houghton; 2 WJ–HJ Letters, 255, 256–57.
43. "Nous avons commencé, Mme. Viardot et moi, à lire votre livre. . . ." I. S. Turgenev to HJ, January 31, 1876, *Polnoe sobranie*, Vol. 11, 203–4. Dr. Alexandre Zviguilsky, president of the Society of Friends of Turgenev, explained this passage rightly, I think, at a colloquium at Bougival in December 1993. According to Zviguilsky, Turgenev and Pauline Viardot read aloud to each other, a companionable custom that some European couples still observe; which explains the slowness with which they progressed through *Roderick Hudson*. This passage otherwise might seem a polite evasion from a man who had not continued reading.
44. Turgenev to HJ, January 31, 1876, Complete Works of I. S. Turgenev, Vol. 11, 203–4.
45. HJ to WJ, February 8, 1876, 1 WJ–HJ Letters, 252, 253.
46. HJ to WJ, February 8 [1876], Houghton; 1 WJ–HJ Letters, 252, 253.
47. "Si vous ne voulez faire la dépense d'un domino, il y aura dans le vestibule des toques et des tabliers de marmiton pour les messieurs en habit." Turgenev to HJ, undated, 12 *Polnoe sobranie*, 53. The date is given by HJ to WJ, February 8 [1876], 2 WJ–HJ Letters, 252, 253, and HJ to AJ, February 22, 1876. As HJ explained to Alice, *marmiton* was a scullion who wore a characteristic white cap and apron, like a cook's.
48. In *The American*, Madame Urbain de Bellegarde makes Newman promise to bring her to this scandalous entertainment.
49. HJ to WJ, April 25 [1876], Houghton; 1 WJ–HJ Letters, 258, 259.
50. HJ to E. Boott, April 1, 1876, Houghton; unpub.
51. An example is among the Turgenev Papers, TsGALI, Moscow, Fond 509, Opisi No.1, dello No. 14 (no date):

Matinée Littéraire et Musicale
50, Rue de Douai, 50

——

1.ᵉ Scène du ballet		DE MM. BÉRIOT
PAR M. PAUL VIARDOT		

2.ᵉ *Les Reliques vivantes*		TOURGUÉNIEFF
LU PAR L' AUTEUR		

3.ᵉ Air de Rousslane		GLINKA
PAR MME. PAULINE VIARDOT		

[etc.]

52. "Crawford's Consistency," *Scribner's Monthly*, August 1876; "The Ghostly Rental," *Scribner's Monthly*, September 1876.

53. HJ to AJ, February 22 [1876], Houghton; 2 HJ Letters, 28, 30.

54. HJ to WJ, March 14 [1876], Houghton; 1 WJ–HJ Letters, 255.

55. HJ was bitter at his insulting dismissal by Reid, see below, and the account of this episode has been greatly muddied by him and others. Edel and Lind convey the impression that his columns had been too refined and literary; they make him a highbrow who was too delicate and artistic to meet the demands of the marketplace. But in fact the letters are written in a vigorous and clear style for a general audience; nor was the *Tribune* especially less highbrow than *The Nation*. The single convoluted sentence that Edel and Lind quote is not typical. The early letters are little gems, conveying the visitor's fresh impressions of Paris. But as James grew settled and preoccupied, he increasingly relied on reviews of plays and paintings, and abstract observations on the political scene, that were less and less vigorous or personal. He was aware of the falling off in quality, but he somewhat defensively attributed the failure of the column in the end to his refusal to provide gossip. It was only in this sense that he failed to be sufficiently "vulgar."

56. "Carrière" in original.

57. HJ to E. Boott, April 3 [1876], Houghton; unpub.

58. I. S. Turgenev to HJ, February 28, 1877, *Polnoe sobranie*, Vol. 12, 98.

59. HJ to WJ, April 25 [1876], 1 WJ–HJ Letters, 258, 259.

60. "Chartres Portrayed," dated April 9, 1876; published *New York Tribune*, April 29, 1876, reprinted *Parisian Sketches*, 115.

61. HJ to WJ, April 25 [1876], Houghton; 1 WJ–HJ Letters, 258, 259.

62. HJ to AJ, May 24 [1876], Houghton; 2 HJ Letters, 348, 49.

63. WJ to HJ, July 5, 1876, Houghton; 1 WJ–HJ Letters, 267.

64. HJ to WDH, May 28, 1876, Houghton; 2 HJ Letters, 51–52.

65. "Parisian Festivity," April 22, 1876, *New York Tribune*, May 27, 1876; *Parisian Sketches*, 126, 131–32.

66. "Parisian Topics," June 9, 1876, *New York Tribune*, July 1, 1876; *Parisian Sketches*, 168, 174–75.

67. "Parisian Festivity," supra, 129–31.

68. HJ to E. Boott, April 3 [1876], Houghton; unpub.

69. We know from Cosima Wagner's diaries that Zhukovsky spent the summer of 1876 at Bayreuth, witnessing the first performance of the *Ring of the Nibelung* there. See below.

70. HJ to E. Boott, June 1 [1876], Houghton; unpub.

71. HJ to WJ, June 22 [1876], Houghton; 1 WJ–HJ Letters, 263. By an interesting coincidence, some years later, Frank Duveneck painted Boott as a Titian nobleman. In *The Golden Bowl*, Boott became Adam Verver, an American reincarnation of a Venetian merchant-prince.

72. *Nation*, October 5, 1876, 213.

73. See "The Four Meetings," whose central scene is the arrival of an American spinster at Le Havre, where she is cheated by her cosmopolitanized cousin and obliged to return to America.

74. HJ's *Tribune* letters of July 22 and August 4, reprinted in *Parisian Sketches*, describe his journey down the Seine to Le Havre, and his visit to Étretat. They dovetail exactly with the opening pages of Chapter 19 of *Confidence*, in which "Bernard Longueville," who greatly resembles James himself, goes from Le Havre to a seaside resort called "Blanquais-les-Galets," whose description tallies exactly with Étretat, a village on a shingle beach, enclosed by an encircling cliff with "two white arms," a casino or market hall at the end of the beach, and grassy downs above the cliffs. Bernard Longueville takes the same walks that Henry James describes himself taking in his *Tribune* letters.

75. This paragraph is taken from almost identical passages in the *Tribune* letter of August 4, *Parisian Sketches*, 202–5, and *Confidence* (Library of America ed.) E.g., in the *Tribune*: "The great occupation and amusement is the bathing. . . . The whole beach seems to be a large family party, in a family which should have radical views as regards some prudish prejudices. There is more or less costume," etc. James bathes, then dresses and lies on the beach, watching the other bathers. In *Confidence*: "Bathing in the sea was the chief occupation of these good people. . . . The little world of Blanquais appeared to form a large family party, of highly developed amphibious habits, which sat gossiping all day on the warm pebbles . . . without any relaxation of personal intimacy," etc. The hero goes for a swim, then dresses and lies on the beach and watches the other bathers, and so forth.

76. Judging by the tone of his letters and his published reports and reminiscences, this was one of the happiest moments of his life. But a July 29 letter to William is in marked contrast. In it, HJ deprecated Étretat and the French, said, "I have done with 'em, forever, & am turning English all over," and concluded that he would move to England "tomorrow" if he had only one friend there. 1 WJ–HJ Letters, 270, 271. This is so much out of key with HJ's surviving letters to Alice, Lizzie Boott, Tom Perry, and others from this time, that I think it must be discounted. HJ's letters to William often have this sour tone, which is not entirely dissimulated, but which was plainly part of the compromise on which their friendship was founded. In William's last letter to HJ, after remarking on how HJ seemed to be settled on the "gilded & snobbish heights" of Paris, he admired the manly English, and deprecated the effeminate French influence on HJ's letters. It is understandable that HJ, in reply, deprecated the French and affirmed his affection, which was genuine enough, for things English.

77. *Confidence* (Library of America ed.), 1170–71. This is a fictional account of the plainly autobiographical character, Bernard Longueville. The setting, as already noted, is a detailed description of HJ's own visit to Étretat. As there is independent evidence for HJ's having fallen in love while in Paris, it is reasonable to suppose that James re-created his visit to Étretat in such detail for the purpose of giving verisimilitude to the experience he wished his character to undergo.

78. Ibid., 1174. This is the first appearance of this theme in James's fiction, the moral correctness of a love that may be contrary to convention; and the mirror image, the immorality of loves that are perfectly conventional. This moment of realization, also on a Normandy beach, is beautifully given in the closing pages of *What Maisie Knew*, another autobiographical novel. See Kaston's moving explication of the passage in her *Imagination and Desire in the Novels of Henry James*.

79. HJ to HJ Sr., September 16 [1876], Houghton; 2 HJ Letters, 64–65.

80. HJ to Whitelaw Reid, July 25, 1876, from Étretat; reprinted *Parisian Sketches*, 216–17.

81. WJ to HJ, July 5 [1876], Houghton; 1 WJ–HJ Letters, 267.

19   THE ASSAULT IS REPULSED

1. HJ to MJ, January 31 [1877], Houghton; 2 HJ Letters, 92, 93.

2. HJ to E. Boott, August 19, 1876, Houghton; unpub.

3. Whitelaw Reid to HJ, August 10, 1876, *Parisian Sketches*, 217.
4. Ibid., 218.
5. Ibid.
6. HJ to Whitelaw Reid, August 30, 1876, *Parisian Sketches*, 219–20.
7. HJ to AJ, September 6, 1876, Houghton; unpub.
8. HJ to E. Boott, October 10 [1876], Houghton; unpub.
9. Gosse, "Henry James," in *Aspects and Impressions*, 43. Gosse is not an entirely reliable source. He was often careless about facts and dates, and concealed a good deal, but I am not aware of any evidence that he made up stories out of whole cloth, and this anecdote seems genuine. The detail of specifying a third-story window is very Jamesian, and very unlike Gosse. The same story was reported by Hugh Walpole, as having been told to him by HJ, but he may have heard it from Gosse.
10. HJ to MJ, November 11, 1876, Houghton; 2 HJ Letters, 73, 74.
11. HJ to E. Boott, October 10 [1876], Houghton; unpub.
12. HJ to WJ, October 13 [1876], Houghton; 1 WJ–HJ Letters, 272, 273.
13. HJ to MJ, May 4 [1877], Houghton; unpub. See Chapter 20, below.
14. See, e.g., HJ to MJ, September 26 [1876], Houghton; unpub.; HJ to E. Boott, October 10, 1876, supra; HJ to HJ Sr., October 11, 1876, Houghton; unpub. ("Paris, where I feel again like an old inhabitant . . . Paris seems agreeable . . . I expect to spend a brief & tranquil winter.")
15. HJ to WJ, October 13 [1876], Houghton; 1 WJ–HJ Letters, 272, 273.
16. HJ to WJ, October 23 [1876], Houghton; 1 WJ–HJ Letters, 274, 275. In his brief notebook entry, years later, describing this incident, HJ said: "I settled myself again in Paris—or attempted to do so (I linger over these details and like to recall them one by one); I had no intention of giving it up." HJ Notebooks, November 25, 1881, Houghton; Matthiessen, ed., 26. Explaining why he had, nevertheless, given it up, he mentioned the failure of his *Tribune* letters, and the difficulties over his apartment. He said that he had realized he would always be an outsider. Of his acquaintances in Paris, he recalled only Zhukovsky, Turgenev, and Flaubert; and of Zhukovsky he told his notebook there was to be no discussion—he would simply make note and pass on: "Non ragioniam—ma guarda e passa."
17. HJ to MJ, September 26 [1876], Houghton; unpub.
18. HJ to E. Boott, November 11 [1876], Houghton; unpub.
19. HJ to Henrietta Reubell, March 26 [1877], Houghton (where it is dated [1878?], but plainly was written shortly after his removal to London, over Reubell's protests). See Notebook supra, 24.
20. *New York Tribune*, January 16, 1877, 4; HJ–Hay letters, 17.

20 LONDON

1. TMY, 49. On the site of the house in which HJ lived for so long there now stands a block of flats built in 1894.
2. Notebook, November 25, 1881, Matthiessen, ed., 28. HJ is recalling his first weeks in London in December 1877.
3. *English Hours*, 130.
4. HJ to E. Boott, December 26 [1877], Houghton; unpub.
5. Ibid.
6. W. H. Huntington to J. Hay, December 17, 1877 (commenting on HJ's new

beard), HJ–John Hay Letters, 20. I am not quite sure when the beard was grown, as Huntington did not see it until the following fall; but it seems likely that James grew it in the quiet winter before he began dining out.

7. HJ to Howells, October 24 [1876], Houghton; 2 HJ Letters, 70.

8. HJ to F. P. Church, May 26, 1877, Church Collection, NYPL; unpub. Referring to a proposal for a serial made "some weeks ago" to which Church had not yet responded.

9. See preface to the New York Edition, *The Portrait of a Lady*, reprinted *Art of the Novel*, 41, 42–43.

10. HJ's correspondence with editors in the spring of 1877 showed that he was already well advanced on the plan of *The Portrait of a Lady*, which did not appear until 1881; but he was unable to find a magazine in which to serialize a long novel immediately. Church failed to respond to repeated inquiries, and Lippincott refused. *The Atlantic* was the best vehicle for a serious novel, but Howells was not willing to undertake something so serious, so soon after the yearlong *American*. James accordingly agreed to write a brief comic novel (*The Europeans*) with a happy ending, which was serialized in four numbers of *The Atlantic*, before undertaking the longer work, and in fact he wrote two more hastily composed novels, *Confidence* and *Washington Square*, in the interval, simply to keep his pot boiling. But it is clear he had begun planning the longer work late in 1876 or early in 1877, shortly after reading *Daniel Deronda*. Most of the contemporary reviews noted the similarity of the two novels. Nevertheless, in his preface for the New York edition he credits Turgenev, and not Eliot, with encouraging him to write of a young girl. Turgenev and not Eliot was the fashioner of heroines who were both morally strong and physically beautiful, and the combination is central to James's theme, which is the exercise of power. In Eliot heroines tend to be either one or the other—hence powerless.

11. "Daniel Deronda: A Conversation," *Nation*, February 24, 1877, 130; Lit. Crit.: American and English, 974, 990.

12. Ibid.

13. See, e.g., HJ to WJ, January 28 [1878], Houghton; 1 WJ–HJ Letters, 294, 295. Compare *Portrait*, *Wings of the Dove*, and *Sense of the Past*, in each of which the central situation is a young person from America entering a small circle of socially powerful elders in London. In *The Awkward Age*, the older generation (and London itself) are personified in "Longdon." In *Sense of the Past*, James imagined himself literally entering the world of Fanny Kemble's generation, as he evidently yearned to do.

14. *Further Records*, 225.

15. HJ to MJ, January 18 [1879], Houghton; 2 HJ Letters, 210, 212.

16. F. Kemble to HJ, November 8 [1879], Houghton; unpub.

17. Kemble (1879), 129.

18. Ibid., 129–30.

19. This anecdote is most certainly the germ from which HJ's *The Bostonians* grew; the principal female characters and their relation in the novel are here encapsulated. The source of the novel has long been a subject of speculation, as James did not include it in the New York edition of his collected works, and so did not write a preface describing its origin, as he did for most of his major novels. HJ's usual starting point—the central characters and their relation—was evidently taken from Kemble's anecdote.

20. F. Kemble to Harriet St. Leger, April 18, 1877, in *Further Records*, 224, 225–26.

21. TMY, 115–17.

22. I take it these are the "conditions of beauty" in which there had been an advance since Lady Waterford's time, TMY, 110.

23. Hon. Louisa Stuart [as she was then] to Lady Jane Bouverie, September 7, 1839; Hare, 204.

24. TMY, 115; compare *Sense of the Past*, in which HJ imagines himself actually entering her world (compare also "The Great Good Place"), becoming one of the early Victorians in his own person.

25. HJ to WJ, January 28 [1878], Houghton; 1 WJ–HJ Letters, 294, 297.

26. Ibid. Compare HJ's obituary for Fanny Kemble, in which he speaks of her in essentially the same terms that he later uses in his memoir for Lady Waterford.

27. See, e.g., Brookfield.

28. This is Frederick Carlyle's description in a letter to Emerson, quoted Reid, xiv.

29. There is a persistent error that James went to Lord Houghton with a letter of introduction from Henry Adams. Not important in itself, this mistake obscures the nature of the welcome James received from Kemble's generation. He did indeed have a letter of introduction, one of a half dozen from Adams, but he did not use it. As he wrote to Elizabeth Boott, he hesitated because he had heard (correctly) that Houghton's house in York had burned, destroying the larger part of his magnificent library. It is all the more remarkable that under these circumstances Houghton called on James, and suggests to my mind the intervention of Kemble. In writing to Adams, HJ nevertheless thanked him courteously for the letters, which in fact he did not use (except for an introduction to the sculptor Woolner).

30. Brookfield, 234.

31. HJ to HJ Sr., February 13 [1877], Houghton; 2 HJ Letters, 98.

32. HJ to WJ, February 9 [1877], Houghton; 1 WJ–HJ Letters, 279.

33. HJ to WJ, February 28 [1877], Houghton; 1 WJ–HJ Letters, 279, 281.

34. HJ to E. Boott, February 11 [1877], Houghton; unpub.

35. Ibid.

36. HJ saw the exhibition soon after it opened, HJ to Church, May 26, 1877, NYPL, unpub. The celebrated Ruskin review appeared somewhat later, in *Fors Claviger*, July 2, 1877. HJ referred in his article, however, to violent criticisms of the Whistler painting that Ruskin made, and I have quoted in the text the phrase that prompted Whistler's celebrated libel suit, in which he won nominal damages of a shilling.

37. See "The Picture Season in London," *Galaxy*, August 1877, reprinted *The Painter's Eye*, 130, 143; "The Grosvenor Gallery," ibid., 161, 165.

38. "London," reprinted in English Hours; see especially 48–49.

39. HJ to AJ, April 8 [1877], Houghton; unpub. This letter is marked [1878?] in the Houghton catalog, and in pencil annotations on the letter itself, but references to events such as the appearance of Turgenev's *Virgin Soil* in French translation date it positively as 1877.

40. Ibid.

41. HJ to E. Boott, January 30 [1878], Houghton; unpub.

42. *Portrait*, 61.

43. HJ to AJ, April 8 [1877], Houghton; unpub. See above concerning date of this letter. The notion of the "two Brownings" HJ later expanded into a wickedly funny story, "The Private Life," in which the poet whose private personality never appears in society is called Clare Vawdry.

44. HJ to MJ, May 4 [1877], Houghton; unpub.

45. HJ to Henry Adams, May 5 [1877], Houghton; HJ–HA Letters, 34, 36.

46. HJ to Grace Norton, June 7 [1877], Houghton; unpub.

47. HJ to E. Boott, August 22 [1877], Houghton; unpub.

48. HJ to E. Boott, September 7 [1877], Houghton; unpub.

49. HJ to AJ, May 21 [1877], Houghton; unpub. Marked [1878?] in Houghton but references to events—Bob's first piece for a newspaper, Anne Bartlett's visit—place it in 1877.

50. "Two Excursions," English Hours, 189.

51. Ibid., 194–95. The college is not named in the article, but in a letter HJ mentions lunching that day at All Souls, HJ to WJ, June 28 [1877]; 2 WJ–HJ Letters, 286.

52. Ibid., 195–96.

53. In James's later story, he portrayed Symonds as "The Author of 'Beltraffio.' " Beltraffio, by the way, was a Renaissance artist, a student of da Vinci, whose sensual portraits of young men had made him something of a cult figure. Symonds had just made a splash with the first volume of his The Renaissance in Italy.

54. "The Author of 'Beltraffio,' " 5 Complete Tales, 323. This is an accurate portrayal of what we now know of Symonds's feelings; and it has long been well known that Symonds was the model for this character. See HJ to E. Gosse, June 9 [1884], Leeds; HJ–Gosse Letters, 31–32.

55. "The Author of 'Beltraffio.' " Some years later, when Symonds's son died, it was rumored that his wife had allowed the child to die rather than to fall under the father's influence; and this, too, James with revulsion put into "The Author of 'Beltraffio.' " In "The Beast in the Jungle," a woman is sacrificed to a man's meaningless self-regard, the fantasy that something of importance will happen to him. In the end, all that happens to mark him as singular is his failure to love.

56. This was not used in the modern sense. HJ was displaying his command of local dialect, which he did whenever he traveled. "Cad" was contemptuous Oxford slang for townspeople, and at this time seems to have been applied to anyone whose appearance or manners were common. See OED, "cad," definition 2.

57. HJ to MJ, May 4 [1877], Houghton; unpub. Evidently W.E.H. Lecky, whose works of literary history were much admired in New England, and J. R. Green, whose Short History of the English People had just appeared, and which Alice presumably had given to HJ on his removal to England (not T. H. Green the philosopher). The quoted passage in this manuscript letter is marked in pencil, "omit," apparently by Edel.

58. HJ to HJ Sr., June 9 [1877], Houghton; unpub.

59. See, for instance, "The Author of 'Beltraffio,' " published in 1884, and The Tragic Muse, 1889.

60. In "The Great Good Place," heaven appears to be a sort of compound of All Souls and the Athenaeum Club.

61. "An English Easter," in English Hours, 139–40.

62. Ibid., 141.

63. HJ to MJ, January 13 [1878], Houghton; unpub. ("Did I tell you it had been reprinted here by Ward & Cook, in the railway library, with a wonderful picture on the cover?")

64. HJ to MJ, August 26 [1877], Houghton; unpub. For details of Lowell's appointment and request for HJ, see Duberman 282–83, and 456 n.

65. "London at Midsummer," in English Hours, 170–73.

66. See "London at Midsummer," 173.

67. HJ to MJ, May 4 [1877], Houghton; unpub.

68. HJ to MJ, June 9 [1877], Houghton; unpub.
69. "London," in English Hours, 45.
70. HJ to MJ, June 9 [1877], Houghton; unpub.
71. HJ to MJ, September 4 [1877], Houghton; unpub.
72. HJ to E. Boott, September 7 [1877], Houghton; unpub. The words in square brackets are interpolated by me, as there is a page missing from the letter at this point. It is the only missing page, I believe, in the Boott letters, and its absence is certainly curious. The letter picks up again only after the discussion of Zhukovsky has concluded.

21   HENRY JAMES BECOMES A COSMOPOLITE

1. HJ to Grace Norton, August 7, 1877, Houghton; unpub. ("I think the Emperor of R. might have been treated like a gentleman"); and to WJ, May 1 [1878], Houghton; 1 WJ–HJ Letters, 299, 302 ("to think that a clever Jew should have juggled old England into it"). This is how people spoke, HJ with the others. Mr. Caliph, "the clever Jew" who is the villain of "Impressions of a Cousin"—the name and references to Prince Camaralzaman remind us once more that HJ has absorbed Renan's Orientalism—is probably derived from Disraeli, whom HJ disliked on political grounds. Mr. Caliph was an aristocrat of the utmost polish and charm, but HJ withheld from his character the moral sense that would have kept him from using others for his own profit—a sense that in his early work HJ considered peculiarly Christian and American. This dreary, repetitious racialism mars much of the thought of his generation. By the time of his late works HJ had recognized these stereotypes as elements of "romance," or fable, lacking in historical basis; like the French aristocrats in *The American* they would gradually disappear, to be replaced by fully realized individuals (who often are also, it is true, "types," but in the late novels are rarely stereotypes).
2. Compare HJ's "The Altar of the Dead," in which a private religion is formed upon the art of remembering the dead.
3. HJ to Grace Norton, June 7 [1877], Houghton; unpub.(!) Compare HJ's essay "Is There a Life After Death," in *Bazar*, reprinted *In After Days* (1910), by which time he had come to believe that only the strongest selves were candidates for eternal life; his views had become a little Calvinistic with age. HJ's somewhat hesitant belief in an afterlife has been sadly deleted from all published biographies. His private religion, as this letter shows, was essentially Unitarian—he believed in the reality of the world of spirit, and the fundamental beneficence of the moral order, without believing in a personal God. The moral order that he perceived would not seem unfamiliar to a modern Catholic.
4. HJ to AJ, September 15, 1878, 1 Lubbock, 62, 64; 2 HJ Letters, 184, 186. The holograph is not among HJ's letters to AJ at Houghton and seems to have been lost.
5. HJ to Grace Norton, August 7 [1877], Houghton; 1 Lubbock, 54, 55.
6. "Paris Revisited," *Galaxy*, January 1878; reprinted *Portraits of Places*; CTW: Europe, 721.
7. HJ to Grace Norton, August 7, 1877, 1 Lubbock, 54, 55; 2 HJ Letters, 132, 135 (where the letter is incorrectly dated August 9).

8. HJ to Grace Norton, November 7 [1880], Houghton; 2 HJ Letters, 313, 314.
9. HJ to Grace Norton, December 28 [1880], Houghton; 2 HJ Letters, 322, 323.
10. HJ to TSP, March 22, 1878, Colby; Harlow, 298.
11. AJ to Sara [Sedgwick] Darwin, in England, August 9, 1879; Yeazell, 80, 82. There is a similar encomium, AJ to F. R. Morse, October 7, 1879; Yeazell, 83, 84. By this time, HJ had heard a similar description from his mother, and presumably from AJ as well; see HJ to WJ, May 1 [1878], Houghton; 1 WJ–HJ Letters, 299, 302. ("She [mother] told me all about Miss Catherine [sic] Loring, whose strength of wind and limb, to say nothing of her nobler qualities, must make her a valuable addition to the Quincy Street circle. . . .")
12. Fanny Morse introduced them at a lunch on December 17, 1872; we know the date because the two women thereafter kept the anniversary of their meeting. K. P. Loring to F. R. Morse, December 17, 1892, F. R. Morse Papers, Schlesinger Library, Box 1, folder 9; unpub. (Alice had died the previous March.) Both Edel and AJ's biographer Jeanne Strouse say AJ and Loring met in 1873, but this is evidently not correct.
13. As to the cottage, see Habegger, 491.
14. "I delight in the thought of her [Miss Loring] & she [Alice] must send me her photo." HJ to WJ, May 1 [1878], Houghton; 1 WJ–HJ Letters, 299, 302.
15. HJ to AJ, November 2 [1877], Houghton; unpub.
16. Ibid.
17. HJ to MJ, October 2 [1877], Houghton; unpub. The Turgenev villa at Bougival has been restored and is maintained by L'Association des Amis d'Ivan Tourgueniev, Pauline Viardot, et Maria Malibran (the last named also lived in the villa).
18. See, e.g., HJ to E. Boott, September 28 [1877], Houghton; unpub.
19. HJ to E. Boott, September 28 [1877], Houghton; unpub.
20. HJ to AJ, November 2 [1877], Houghton; unpub.
21. HJ to AJ, April 20 [1880], Houghton; 2 HJ Letters, 286, 287.
22. HJ to Grace Norton, December 15 [1877], 1 Lubbock, 56, 57.
23. HJ to HJ Sr., November 10 [1877], Houghton; unpub.
24. HJ to AJ, November 2 [1877], Houghton; unpub.
25. HJ to HJ Sr., December 9 [1877], Houghton; unpub.
26. HJ to AJ, November 2 [1877], Houghton; unpub.
27. HJ to E. Boott, May 26 [1877], Houghton; unpub.
28. Ibid.
29. HJ to HJ Sr., December 9 [1877], Houghton; unpub.
30. HJ to MRJ, December 21 [1877], Houghton; unpub.
31. Ibid.
32. HJ to AJ, December 27 [1877], Houghton; 2 HJ Letters, 147.
33. HJ to AJ, supra; Kemble, Further Records, 233.
34. "The Birthplace." It is a light treatment of what we should now call "drag," a possible predecessor of Genet's The Maids.
35. HJ to Howells, October 24, 1876; 2 HJ Letters, 70. This was The Europeans.
36. HJ to WJ, January 28 [1878], Houghton; unpub.
37. Preface to Volume 14, "Lady Barberina" and other stories, NYE, reprinted Art of the Novel, 212.
38. HJ to E. Boott, December 21 [1877], Houghton; unpub. Maria was the Boott's Italian cook, for whom HJ always professed a mock-heroic, gallant passion, to her evident delight.
39. HJ to E. Boott, April 3 [1878], Houghton; unpub.

40. See Chapter 12, above.
41. HJ evidently had purchased and read these plays, which he was studying. See "M. Émile Augier," *Nation*, June 27, 1878, reprinted *The Scenic Art*, 116.
42. See HJ to WJ, May 1 [1878], Houghton; 2 WJ–HJ Letters, 301. HJ had been studying the French dramatists, and had put the forms of French comedy to good use in his novel. Here he responds jocularly to WJ's suggestion that he write actual plays, as Howells was doing, for the sake of the money to be made. The passage has been somewhat misunderstood, since taken alone it suggests HJ was studying the French plays with a sort of helpless longing. HJ was not a frustrated playwright, as Edel implies, but a novelist who made good use of French forms throughout his career.
43. She is an American who has married Adolph, prince of Silberstadt-Shreckenstein, morganatically, and become Baroness Münster. The situation and the ludicrous princedom may have been inspired by Bessie Ward's marriage to Baron Schönberg Roth-Schönberg, whom HJ had met the previous spring. See HJ to AJ, May 21 [1877], Houghton; unpub. This letter was incorrectly marked [1878?] by the Houghton cataloger; see notes to Chapter 20.
44. *The Europeans*, 52. HJ was probably familiar with the Boston edition of 1847, the approximate year in which the novel is set, and as noted above, Prince Camaralzaman and Princess Badoura, sometimes separately and sometimes conflated into one character, notably the "Princess Casamassima," appear in several of HJ's novels and stories. See Chapter 5, above.
45. HJ to WJ, May 1 [1878], Houghton; 1 WJ–HJ Letters, 299, 302. One must piece the bits of information together, and it is not possible to be sure; I have given my understanding of what HJ tells WJ about what MRJ told him.
46. HJ to AJ, June 5 [1878], Houghton; unpub.
47. HJ to WJ, July 15 [1878], Houghton; 2 WJ–HJ Letters, 304.
48. HJ to E. Boott, June 15 [1878], Houghton; unpub. (Alice is "a good deal better; & I hope she has seen the worst.") As her illness preceded William's engagement, and she grew better when it was announced, there is little evidence for the theory advanced by Edel and Strouse that the illness was a symptom of her jealousy of William's marriage. She welcomed her sister-in-law into the family and into Cambridge society, and the two always got on well.
49. February 2, 1892, Diary, 230.
50. March 4, 1892; Diary, 232.
51. As this episode has been central to accounts of AJ's life, perhaps a word is in order. AJ apparently was suffering from the combined back trouble and constipation that afflicted both her older brothers. At some point, Alice also developed a hysterical paralysis of the legs, which perhaps had appeared at earlier episodes. Finally, there is some evidence in HJ Sr.'s letters to his younger sons, which are now in the Vaux collection, that AJ discussed suicide at this time, and that he rather coldly gave his permission.

There is danger in viewing the events of that summer, from a great distance, as all one. AJ's biographer, Strouse, following Edel, treats AJ's illness and depression as a single event, and characterizes it as a hysterical reaction to William's engagement to Alice Gibbens. This seems suspiciously novelistic and tidy; even if we view the whole progression of events over six months or a year as a single emotional event, and with all due respect to the Freudian science, there is no particular evidence for this reading of it. Previous episodes of hysterical paralysis, if that is what it was, seem connected to her relations with female friends. The attack in 1864 occurred while she was visiting Fanny Morse, and the episode in Switzerland that HJ referred to was connected with Elizabeth Boott's departure. The illness in the spring of 1878, similarly, many have been related to Fanny Morse's departure on a grand tour. In the late summer or fall of 1878, Katharine Loring took over the nursing of Alice. It seems possible that Alice was thwarted in her wish to leave home, and to live with Morse or Loring. The hysterical symptoms successfully if painfully allowed her to achieve this aim.

Alice and Henry often confided in each other, but Henry destroyed her letters, so we do not know what she told him of her feelings at this time. It is striking, however, that very shortly afterward, in 1879, HJ wrote a novel about a father and daughter, and set the tale in their grandmother Robertson's house on Washington Square. The characters are direct opposites, even mirror images, of Alice and Henry Sr.—a dull young girl and a clever, worldly doctor. In the novel, the father thwarts the daughter's improper love affair (with a male fortune hunter—again, perhaps, Katharine Loring's direct opposite); and the crisis of the story occurs when the daughter realizes that her father has acted with selfish motives, and does not love her. See below. We have no direct evidence that *Washington Square* is Alice's story, seen in a mirror that reversed genders, but if one must have a psychological account, I prefer Henry's tale to the Oedipal one.

HJ did draw a recognizable portrait of Katharine Loring—not in *Washington Square*, however, but in *The Bostonians*, where she is the unkindly named but sympathetically portrayed Dr. Mary J. Prance. James often equated doctors and lovers in his tales; see, for instance, *The Middle Years*.

52. AJ to Fanny Morse, November 25, 1878, Houghton; Yeazell, 77.
53. HJ to E. Boott, May 22 and June 15, 1878, Houghton; unpub.
54. Ibid.
55. HJ wrote monthly letters to E. Boott in 1878 and 1879, in which the whole weary tale is told in great detail.
56. See HJ letters to E. Boott spring and summer, 1879, Houghton; unpub.
57. In homage to Balzac's Maison Vaquer, which HJ reminds us was "*pension bourgeoise des deux sexes et autres*," see "Pension Beaurepas," *Atlantic Monthly*, April 1879, reprinted 4 *Complete Tales*, 329.
58. "Longstaff's Marriage," *Scribner's Monthly*, August 1878, reprinted 4 *Complete Tales*, 209.
59. "Daisy Miller," *Cornhill Magazine*, June-July 1878, in 43 *Complete Tales*, 141, 144–45.
60. Ibid., 150.
61. NYE Preface to Vol. 18, reprinted *Art of the Novel*, 267, 268.
62. HJ to WJ, July 23 [1878], Houghton; 1 WJ–HJ Letters, 305–6.
63. All were published in 1879 except the Dickens, which he declined to write.
64. *Litell's Living Age*, in Boston, and the *Home Journal* in New York.
65. HJ to WJ, June 15 [1879], Houghton; 1 WJ–HJ Letters, 312, 315.
66. This was a phenomenon he would later use to launch American writers via London reviews; Stephen Crane would be the greatest success of the method.
67. November 10, 1878, 10; quoted Fogel, *Daisy Miller*, 15.
68. WDH to JRL, June 22, 1879; 1 WDH Life in Letters, 270, 271.
69. The incident is described in a biography by George S. Layard, *Mrs. Lynn Linton: Her Life, Letters, and Opinions*. See 2 HJ Letters, 304 n.1.
70. HJ to Elizabeth Linton [August 1880], reprinted 2 HJ Letters, 303, 304.
71. TMY, 84; HJ to Lord Houghton, October 6 [1878?], Houghton papers, Trinity College, Cambridge; unpub. *The Europeans* was published by Macmillan in September 1878.
72. TMY, 74–78.

73. TMY, 97–98. There is some confusion about the date of this event in HJ's account. He has Tennyson making these remarks at a gathering in London, with Lowell present, but he also says that it happened *before* he went to Aldworth. HJ visited Aldworth on October 30, 1878; see HJ to Elizabeth Boott, of that date, but Lowell did not move to London until he took up his post as ambassador in May 1880. For convenience, I have combined both this incident, which evidently was early in their acquaintance, and the visit to Aldworth into one, which may have been the case.

74. TMY, 104–5.

75. HJ to E. Boott, October 30 [1878], Houghton; 2 HJ Letters, 189, 190.

76. TMY, 106.

77. Edith Wharton, *A Backward Glance*, 185–86.

78. HJ to C. E. Norton, November 17, 1878, Houghton; 2 HJ Letters, 194, 196.

79. TMY, 83.

80. TMY, 85–86. HJ does not say which book was being returned, but his "latest" at this point was *The Europeans*, which Macmillan had published in two volumes.

81. This was to be the opening scene of the novel *Confidence*. See below.

82. HJ to MJ, July 6 [1879], Houghton; the visit to Strawberry Hill was to be the premise and the setting of the novel left unfinished at his death, *The Sense of the Past*, in which an American historian is magically able to visit the London of an earlier day and meets a "Horace-Walpole-ish" character.

83. HJ to MJ, July 6 [1879], Houghton; 1 HJ Letters, 247, 249.

84. HJ to E. Boott, Christmas [1878], Houghton; unpub.

85. HJ to Grace Norton, June 8, 1879, Houghton; 2 HJ Letters, 237, 240.

86. HJ to Grace Norton, January 4, 1879, Houghton; unpub.

87. HJ to AJ, May 19 [1879], Houghton; 1 HJ Letters, 232, 234.

88. HJ to WJ, June 15 [1879], Houghton; 1 WJ–HJ Letters, 312, 315.

89. HJ to E. Boott, July 21 [1879], Houghton; unpub.

90. See HJ to WJ, March 4 [1879], Houghton; 1 WJ–HJ, Letters, 309–10; HJ to MJ, May 14 [1879], Houghton; 2 HJ Letters, 230, 233.

91. HJ to E. Boott, July 21 [1879], Houghton; unpub.

92. Ibid.

93. He was negotiating with Macmillan and with Howells, arranging to have the novel appear serially in both Great Britain and the United States simultaneously (to protect his copyright and to double the revenue from serialization). He asked Howells for $250, and Macmillan for £250, for each installment, and expected six or seven installments; see HJ to Howells, August 23, 1879. In the event, the novel was more than twice as long, ran for more than a year, and he received more than $6,000 from the two magazines. HJ to MJ, July 20, 1870, Houghton.

94. We have an unusually complete record of the process of composition, because HJ's outline for the novel in his notebook, the manuscript for the serial magazine version showing his corrections, and the successive print versions have all survived. This is the only one of HJ's novels for which we have such a record. The manuscript version, with the variants noted, was published in an excellent and valuable edition by Herbert Rhum (1962).

95. HJ to TSP, September 14, 1879, Colby; Harlow, 302–3.

96. "Commune."

97. Zhukovsky to HJ, September 25, 1879, Houghton; unpub. The original is in French; I am indebted to Scott R. Russell, Ph.D., for transcribing and translating Zhukovsky's letter. I have slightly altered Dr. Russell's English rendering.

98. Ibid.

99. On the Rue Neuve Saint-Augustin, now the Rue Daunou. Notebooks, 29.
100. HJ to E. Boott, November 20 [1879], Houghton; unpub.
101. See the Preface to Vol. 14 of the New York edition, reprinted *Art of the Novel*, 198, 212–13. The story was "A Bundle of Letters," *Parisian*, December 1879; 4 *Complete Tales*, 427, 440.
102. HJ to E. Boott, December 7 [1879], Houghton; unpub.
103. HJ to T. Child, December 15 [1879], Barrett Collection; unpub.

22   *THE PORTRAIT OF A LADY*

1. HJ to E. Boott, December 31 [1879], Houghton; unpub.
2. HJ to E. Boott, May 4 [1879], Houghton; unpub. The previous year he had paid the last of his debt, the expense of moving to London that he had charged to his letter of credit, and presumably had begun sending gifts to his family when he heard this news. He refers directly to the checks he has been sending November 28, 1880, in an unpublished letter to his mother, because she has failed to acknowledge receipt of the last. As he refers to several checks sent at one time, I assume he was sending money to William, and perhaps Bob, as well as to his parents.
3. Especially in his ghost stories, culminating with the novel *The Sense of the Past*, which as T. S. Eliot long ago pointed out is an homage to Hawthorne.
4. Hawthorne, in Lit. Crit.: American and English, 351–52.
5. HJ to E. Boott, February 22 [1880], Houghton. This letter has not been published, but part of the quoted portion appears, with changes in punctuation, in the Matthiessen edition of HJ's Notebooks, 29, n.1.
6. See, for instance, HJ to TSP, February 22 [1880], Colby; Harlow, 305: "I hold it a great piece of good luck to have stirred up such a clatter. The whole episode projects lurid light upon the state of American 'culture' & furnishes me with a hundred wonderful examples."
7. A successful dramatization, *The Heiress*, is running in revival at Lincoln Center in New York as this is written; the novel had earlier been made into a successful film and a television play as well.
8. February 21, 1879, HJ Notebook, reprinted in Matthiessen, ed., 12–13. James put Fanny Kemble in the story: she is the little plump sister of the adventurer, Morris Townsend. The advice that he records Kemble as having given to Miss Thackeray is reproduced almost verbatim, but is spoken by another character, Dr. Sloper's clever sister.
9. William's letters have not been preserved. They were answered in HJ to WJ, December 16, 1879, and following letters, 2 WJ–HJ Letters, 321.
10. HJ to HJ Sr., March 30 [1880], Houghton; 2 HJ Letters, 276, 278.
11. HJ to E. Boott, February 22 [1880], Houghton; unpub.
12. Newman, in his biography of Wagner, refers to Pepino as an adopted son. Cosima, in her diaries, refers to him as a "servant," and speaks of the love he must feel for Zhukovsky, who has rescued him from the streets; the sense of both perhaps is the same.
13. Zhukovsky's movements are described in Cosima's diary.
14. Zhukovsky's introduction into the household and the daily routine are described in Cosima's diaries for the months of January through June 1880.
15. Newman, Vol. 4, 639 n.6, quoting Glasenapp.
16. Newman, Vol. 4, 640–41.

17. HJ to Grace Norton, April 9, 1880, Houghton; 2 HJ Letters, 281, 282. HJ at this point is describing the view in the other direction, from Sorrento toward Posilipo.
18. HJ to Grace Norton, April 9, 1880, Houghton; 2 HJ Letters, 281, 283.
19. Newman, Vol. 4, 623 n.11, quoting Zhukovsky's unpublished reminiscences, from Glasenapp.
20. Cosima's Diary, February 23, 1880, 444; HJ to AJ, April 29, 1880, Houghton; 2 HJ Letters, 287. In this letter HJ referred to a nihilist who for a time had been Zhukovsky's mentor, as "Onéguin, the original of Nezhdanov" in Turgenev's recent novel, *Virgin Soil*. I have not been able to identify such a person. The character Nezhdanov is a romantic revolutionary, who ends by committing suicide. Suggested models for Nezhdanov have included B. M. Markevich and M. N. Longinov, of Turgenev's generation, and the youthful Turgenev himself; the Onéguin HJ refers to has not been identified.
21. HJ to AJ, April 25, 1880, 2 HJ Letters, 286, 287.
22. HJ to C. E. Norton, March 31 [1880], Houghton; 2 HJ Letters, 279; *The Portrait of a Lady*, 504. In the novel, HJ put Caspar Goodwood into his own rooms, and Henrietta Stackpole into the pension where Lowell had stayed. The effect was to endow the characters in the novel with actual memories; when Henrietta Stackpole walked along the Lung' Arno from her pension to Caspar's, she was taking a walk familiar to HJ in similar circumstances.
23. See his letters to his family from this time. They would marry in 1884. The situation was evidently the pattern for *The Golden Bowl*, with James characteristically using certain figures as models for their mirror opposites: Duveneck was transformed into an Italian prince, and Anne Bartlett into a villain. The Bootts became the immensely wealthy Ververs.
24. HJ to AJ, April 25 [1880], Houghton; 2 HJ Letters, 286, 288. Edel's footnote here is: "HJ seems to have been greatly shocked to find his old Parisian friend in a veritable nest of homosexuals." Taking "aesthetics" as code for "homosexuals," a term and a concept that did not exist in 1880, this is partly correct; but of course HJ was neither shocked nor surprised, as is plain from this letter itself—Edel is just taking an opportunity to giggle and point.
25. Ibid.
26. The opening chapters, which now seem to be the weakest in the novel, were drafted in May 1880 in Florence. HJ evidently began work on them only about a week after his return from Naples. Many commentators have noted the lightness, the conventionality, and the lack of wit in the conversation of the leading characters. But the evident intention was to portray a group of very young and rather innocent people, rather like the circle that had gathered at North Conway, and their healthy, robust Anglo-Saxon elders, in all the freshness of their Eden. The book does not become interesting, perhaps, until the appearance of the villain, Madame Merle, the only character who speaks with real intelligence.
27. Who had married Leslie Pell-Clarke of Newport.
28. *Rodman the Keeper* (1880). This was her second collection of stories, but HJ had not read the first, *Castle Nowhere* (1875). For his opinion of the second book, see his "Miss Constance Fenimore Woolson," *Harper's Weekly*, February 12, 1887; reprinted as "Miss Woolson," in *Partial Portraits*, 177, 179–80.
29. "Letter," quoted in Benedict, 185.
30. Benedict, 186.
31. Ibid., 187–88.
32. This paragraph is taken from "Florentine Experiment," a lightly fictionalized

account of Woolson's excursions with James, reprinted in Benedict, 192, 194.

33. See HJ's letters to WJ, especially November 13, 1880, 1 WJ–HJ Letters, 326, for echoes of this criticism. WJ's letters to HJ from this period have not survived.

34. WJ to parents, July 13 [1880], Houghton; quoted in Burr, 41–42.

35. *Portrait*, 108. Hardwicke was identified by Simon Blackburn as the original of Gardencourt; the house is the subject of the photograph that illustrates this volume of the New York edition. The present Lady Rose has preserved the diary of the Lady Rose of HJ's time, née Charlotte Temple, in which HJ's visits are recorded. In the novel, a side garden in which the family sit in good weather, and which is very much like a room, has been shifted to the front of the house and made to run down to the river. This would have either spoiled the roomlike quality or blocked the view; but presumably HJ made the rearrangement so that he could use the single setting as a stage set.

36. As noted above, in *Portrait* James for his own convenience combined the side garden and the front lawn into one outdoor room.

37. The façade facing the river is used to illustrate the New York edition of *Portrait*, and this curious characteristic of the house identifies it as the Gardencourt of the novel.

38. HJ to MRJ, July 20 [1880], Houghton; 2 HJ Letters, 294, 297. See also WJ to AJ, July 13, 1880, quoted in Burr, 41, 42.

39. The early installments of the novel were already in type at the time of their visit to Hardwicke, which HJ's letters home suggest was his first.

40. The resemblance of the heroine of *Portrait* to Mary Temple has many times been noted, and was promptly conceded by HJ. See below. He said later that he began the novel with this figure in mind; and when he began to think about the plot, he asked himself, "What will she 'do'? Why, the first thing she'll do will be to come to Europe. . . ." Preface, in *Art of the Novel*, 56.

41. "Gardencourt" was the Roses' house, Hardwicke, see above; the Elizabethan parlor was turned into an Elizabethan bedstead.

42. Preface, in *Art of the Novel*, 49, quoting George Eliot in *Daniel Deronda*. It is well known that the character is based upon Mary Temple. HJ had written to Grace Norton, who recognized the portrait: "I had her in mind & there is in the heroine a considerable infusion of my impression of her remarkable nature. But the thing is not a portrait. Poor Minny was essentially *incomplete* & I have attempted to make my young woman more rounded, more finished." HJ to Grace Norton, December 28, 1880, Houghton; 2 HJ Letters, 322, 324.

43. Preface, in *Art of the Novel*, 56.

44. *Portrait*, 229.

45. Ibid., 243.

46. Ibid., 239.

47. Preface, in *Art of the Novel*, 53, 51. HJ claims not to recall the origin of any of these characters in his own experience.

48. *Portrait*, 249.

49. Ibid., 291.

50. That is, it was the best passage in the best book he had yet written; Preface, in *Art of the Novel*, 56–57.

51. Ibid., 57.

52. This was fundamentally the same story that HJ later told in *The Ambassadors*, to which in his prefaces he constantly compared *The Portrait of a*

Lady. In the later novel, however, the protagonist was HJ himself—lightly disguised as his friend Howells. The repeated image of the female villain in *The Golden Bowl*, like Madame Merle, is of a cracked vessel; see, e.g., Anderson, 82; and she too is banished to America.

53. Preface, 52–53.
54. Some modern criticism has tended to attribute her decision to a neurotic fear of sex. This, of course, empties the novel of its central meaning, and reduces it to a formalist exercise.
55. This is the text of the New York edition of 1907–8; see Horne for the history of the revision. It seems to me that in this scene as well as the scene by the fireside in the palace, in each of which Isabel assembles her understanding from the manifold of memories by the aid of imagination, HJ is presenting a Kantian understanding of consciousness and the role of imagination. This particular understanding of imagination seems to have been present from his early description of *The Last Supper* in his short story "Travelling Companions," and is the central core of his critical theory and practice. See Chapter 6; Kant's theory of the imagination has been brilliantly revivified by Gibbons.

23   VENICE

1. Undated Notebook entry, between March 18, 1880, and January 17, 1881; probably late fall 1880, Houghton; Matthiessen, ed., 15–18.
2. American Notebook, November 25, 1881, Houghton; Matthiessen, ed., 30.
3. HJ to AJ, January 30, 1881, Houghton; 2 HJ Letters, 335, 336.
4. HJ to Henrietta Reubell, February 9, 1881, Houghton; unpub.
5. HJ to HJ Sr., February 24, 1881, Houghton; 1 HJ Letters, 344, 345.
6. Notebook, November 25, 1881, Houghton; Matthiessen, ed., 30.
7. Ibid.
8. HJ to Fanny Kemble, March 24, 1881, Houghton; 1 Lubbock, 78.
9. Notebook, November 25, 1881, Matthiessen, ed., 31.
10. No. 4161, now the Albergo Paganelli.
11. Preface to *Portrait of a Lady*, Vol. 3 of New York edition, in *Art of the Novel*, 41.
12. "Casa Alvisi," in *Italian Hours*, 79.
13. This was the first season in which they rented the upper floors of the Palazzo Barbaro, an apartment they would eventually purchase. James would be their guest on visits to Venice in the 1890s, and he would use their apartment as the setting for *Wings of the Dove*.
14. HJ to Grace Norton, June 18, 1881, 1 HJ Letters, 355; HJ to Henrietta Reubell, September 28, 1881, Houghton; unpub.
15. A Herbert James Pratt, a Bostonian who studied medicine and was apparently practicing in Paris in 1869, is mentioned in two letters from William James; editors of both William's and Henry's letters have assumed he is the Pratt of the journal, and this may be, but there is no evidence other than the coincidence of their names. Edel and Powers in their recent edition of the Notebooks embroider somewhat further: "Herbert Pratt, WJ's Cambridge friend and fellow medical student . . . The character of Gabriel Nash in *The Tragic Muse* derives to some extent from Pratt." Three citations are given, but neither Pratt nor the character Nash is mentioned in any of them, and none supports the assertion.

16. Porters.
17. Notebook, Matthiessen, ed., 31.
18. Ibid.
19. HJ to Grace Norton, June 12, 1881, Houghton; 1 HJ Letters, 354, 355.
20. "Henry James's Novels," *Princeton Review*, July 1884, 68, 86; excerpted in Gard, 144, 146–47.

Acknowledgments

I worked on this biography for six years and accumulated a great many debts. The late Alexander R. James kindly answered questions and granted permissions whenever I asked; I am sorry not to have been able to thank him more fully. I am grateful to him for permissions that were needed to gain access to collections of James's letters, and to Henry J. Vaux for permission to make use of transcripts made from his collection. My thanks to Bay James for granting permission to reproduce portions of Henry James's published and unpublished works. Peter Duveneck kindly shared family memorabilia; he and Elizabeth B. Dana allowed me to reproduce pictures by Frank Duveneck and Elizabeth Boott, some of which have not been published before. The Houghton Library, Harvard, and the Harvard Law School Library granted permission for the use of James Family letters cited here.

Lady Rose very kindly allowed me to visit Hardwicke, the setting of *The Portrait of a Lady*, and I thank her for her hospitality. Although the results will not be evident until the next volume appears, I would also like to thank Ione and William Martin, tenants of Lamb House when I visited, for making me feel at home, and Patricia Curtis-Viganò and Ralph Curtis for their hospitality at the Palazzo Barbaro.

Scott R. Russell, Ph.D., gracefully transcribed and translated Paul Zhukovsky's surviving letters to Henry James, for which I am endlessly grateful.

I have elsewhere mentioned my debt to Steven Jobe and Susan Gunter, who shared their carefully assembled calendar of Henry James's letters as a work in progress; I could not easily have done without it.

My work has depended on the help of librarians all over Europe and North America. Many of the libraries I visited were suffering reductions in staff and funds, and I am especially grateful for the courtesy and diligence with which my requests nevertheless were almost always met. The librarian of the Pepys Library and the Fellows of Magdalene College granted access to A. C. Benson's handwritten diaries. My thanks to Nina Tumarkin and Dmitri Urnov for their help and advice in gaining access to libraries in what was then the Soviet Union. I wish I knew the name of the librarian at TsGALI, who served tea to a foreigner and helped him spell his way through Cyrillic indexes. The wonderful nineteenth-century holdings of the Baker Library at Dartmouth allowed me to step back into Henry James's world at will; I am especially grateful to the staff of the special collections department. Above all, the patient staff of the Houghton Library reading room have helped in numberless ways over the years. When I was not able to travel, Susan Jorgensen of the Vermont Law School library patiently brought the world's libraries to me, a book at a time.

Leon Edel, early in the project, courteously answered my questions about sources, and his editions of James's plays and short stories as well as his selections of James's letters are frequently cited throughout this volume. If I have often disagreed with his conclusions I have nevertheless been greatly aided by his lifetime's work. Fred Kaplan generously shared his notes and transcriptions of letters from the Vaux collection; his biography of Henry James has been a valuable reference. Tamie Waters generously shared her unpublished work on James and Rhoda Broughton. Susan Gunter patiently read and commented on successive drafts; her comments and her research have been of immense value to me. The following persons also read and commented on the typescript in whole or in part: Roger Asselineau, Carolyn Clinton, Adele de Cruz, Carren O. Kaston, Rachel Kurland, Mary Marshall, and Mark Treanor. They helped me to avoid a great many errors and infelicities; for those that remain I alone am responsible.

I am also indebted to Carren Kaston for explaining the iconography of Henry James's portraits, and for her encouragement. There are portions of this book in which I am not sure whether the understandings are mine, independently arrived at, or are those expressed in her fine book *Imagination and Desire in the Novels of Henry James*. I am grateful to Jean Gaulmier for helping me to clarify the relation of James to Renan.

This is the third time over a period of ten years that I have thanked Claire Reinhardt for helping with research; I am glad to thank her once more. I thank Patricia Bradford as well. My dear cousin Joanne Legg lent me invaluable aid in her travels about Europe; Laura Gillen, Judy Hilts, Virginia Fifield, and Mary Aschenberg of Vermont Law

School helped with other aspects of the work that required more practical intelligence and skill than I could muster unaided.

Daniel Mark Fogel, then editor of the *Henry James Review*, who did so much during his tenure to open the doors of literary scholarship, kindly gave me an opportunity to present my work in progress at the Henry James sesquicentennial celebration, conducted jointly by New York University and the Henry James Society in June 1993. Alexandre Zviguilsky, in addition to his generous help with research in Russian and French sources, kindly gave me an opportunity to describe my work at another sesquicentennial conference—at Bougival, December 1993, under the auspices of Les Amis d'Ivan Tourguéniev, Pauline Viardot, and Maria Malibran. The participants in these two conferences were tremendously generous and helpful to a newcomer, and I am grateful for their encouragement and their criticisms.

Conversations of the *Vermont Review* group at Vermont Law School were of great value to me, and I would like to thank once again all my generous friends at Vermont Law School who continue to encourage my excursions into history and literature, and who have supported my work in so many ways, spiritual as well as material, over the years. Finally, I am glad to acknowledge the patience and tolerance of my neighbors in Strafford, Vermont, especially the staff of the South Strafford Cafe, where the last pages of this book were written.

It has been a privilege to work with the patient Bob Loomis, jewel among editors, to whom this work owes more than I can easily say; and with Elizabeth Kaplan, who over the years has spoken for my books so magnificently well.

Carolyn M. Clinton, to whom this book is dedicated, gave me her wise counsel at every stage of this project, for which I cannot begin to acknowledge my debt.

With so much help this should be a better book than it is; all of its faults are on my own head.

INDEX

PHOTO: BELTRAMI STUDIO, WEST LEBANON, NEW HAMPSHIRE

SHELDON M. NOVICK is the author of *Henry James: The Mature Master, Honorable Justice: The Life of Oliver Wendell Holmes*, and editor of *The Collected Works of Justice Holmes*. He is Adjunct Professor of Law and History at Vermont Law School and lives in Norwich, Vermont.

ABOUT THE TYPE

This book was set in Berling. Designed in 1951 by Karl Erik Forsberg for the Typefoundry Berkingska Stilgjuteri AB in Lund, Sweden, it was released the same year in foundry type by H. Berthold AG. It is a classic old-face design, and its generous proportions and inclined serifs make it highly legible.

THE PIONEERS OF ANGLO-IRISH FICTION 1800-1850

IRISH LITERARY STUDIES

THE PIONEERS OF ANGLO-IRISH FICTION 1800-1850

Barry Sloan

Irish Literary Studies 21

COLIN SMYTHE
Gerrards Cross, Bucks

BARNES AND NOBLE BOOKS
Totowa, New Jersey

First published in 1986 by Colin Smythe Limited
Gerrards Cross, Buckinghamshire

British Library Cataloguing in Publication Data
Sloan, Barry
The Pioneers of Anglo-Irish fiction 1800-1850.—
(Irish literary studies, ISSN 0140-895X; 21)
1. English fiction—Irish authors—History and
criticism   2. English fiction—19th century—
History and criticism
I. Title   II. Series
823′ .009′ 9415   PR8801

ISBN 0-86140-205-7

First published in the United States of America in 1987
By Barnes & Noble Books, Totowa, N.J. 07512

Library of Congress Cataloging in Publication Data
Sloan, Barry.
The pioneers of Anglo-Irish fiction, 1800-1850.
(Irish literary studies)
Bibliography: p.
Includes index.
1. English fiction—Irish authors—History and
criticism.   2. English fiction—19th century—History
and criticism.   3. Ireland in literature.   I. Title.
II. Series.
PR8801.S56   1987   823′ .7′ 099415   86-17438
ISBN 0-389-20662-8

Printed in Great Britain
Set by Grove Graphics, Tring, Herts
and printed and bound by Billing & Sons Ltd.
Worcester

For Diane and my Mother,
and to the memory of my Father

Our pioneers keep striking
Inwards and downwards,

Every layer they strip
Seems camped on before.
The bogholes might be Atlantic seepage.
The wet centre is bottomless.

Seamus Heaney: 'Bogland'.

CONTENTS

FOREWORD

The years between 1800 and 1850 saw the emergence in Ireland of a number of novelists and story writers who took as their subject-matter their native country, its people and its social, economic and political problems. Their pioneering work is not only a unique record of life in rural Ireland in the late eighteenth and early nineteenth centuries before the disasters of the great famine in the 1840s changed many things irreversibly; it also initiated a tradition of Anglo-Irish fiction which, in the twentieth century, has achieved international stature and recognition.

This book examines the origins of that tradition and the particular circumstances, both literary and social, from which the earliest Anglo-Irish fiction sprang. It is comprehensive in scope, considering not only the major writers – Maria Edgeworth, Lady Morgan, the Banim brothers, Gerald Griffin, and William Carleton – but also lesser figures such as Charles Maturin, Mrs S. C. Hall, Samuel Lover, the early work of Charles Lever and Joseph Sheridan Le Fanu, and other minor contributors. This inclusiveness helps to generate a picture of the diversity of theme and character found in the novels, and illustrates how effectively the texture of certain aspects of Irish life is evoked in them.

The early years of the century were politically dominated by the aftermath of the 1798 rebellion and the Act of Union, through which the Irish lost their Parliament. Thereafter Daniel O'Connell established himself as the champion of Catholic opinion with his campaigns for emancipation and repeal, until, in the 1840s, his political leadership was challenged by the members of the Young Ireland movement. In social and economic terms the period brought a mounting crisis on the land as absenteeism among the great property owners increased, while the financial burdens placed upon the tenants became ever more impossible. Famine caused by failure of the potato crop occurred at intervals, but most devastatingly, of course, in the late 1840s. All these factors influenced the novelists, and I have organized the material chronologically to highlight the shifting response to the historical situation in the fiction. Furthermore, the book explores the Irish preoccupation with history itself and examines how it is used as subject-matter by many of the writers.

One of the major problems facing the early Anglo-Irish novelists was that of audience: who were they writing for, and how could they simultaneously appeal to English readers and also justify Irish attitudes and opinions? I have sought to open up this complex issue and to consider the effect it had upon the writers and their work. Likewise I have investigated the equally difficult challenges facing those novelists who were writing in a 'foreign' language (English), using an alien literary tradition which was replacing an older oral culture, and who were at the same time trying to give voice to their own perception of experience.

In considering the subject-matter and characters in the novels, I have aimed to show how certain themes and particular types of character recur, and the powerful sense of environment which pervades work after work. I also suggest how the origins of Irish literary stereotypes are apparent in some of the fiction, and relate all these points to the novelists' interest in articulating a credible and truthful view of the nature of Irish character, temperament and nationality. This argument informed Thomas Flanagan's valuable book *The Irish Novelists*, published twenty-five years ago, but my chronological approach and discussion of both authors and works not treated by him are intended to extend the scope of such study.

A serious practical diffculty facing would-be readers of nineteenth-century Anglo-Irish fiction is its general inaccessibility. Very few of the works analysed here are available in popular modern editions, and some are almost totally unobtainable even from libraries. To compensate the reader for this problem, I have used generous quotations and have indicated the broad development of plots where this is relevant. By these means I hope to enhance popular understanding and appreciation of the work of the first Anglo-Irish novelists, and of the circumstances in which they were writing. Between them they produced two masterpieces – Maria Edgeworth's *Castle Rackrent* and William Carleton's *Traits and Stories of the Irish Peasantry* – and if the rest of their output is more uneven in merit, it is never without significance or interest.

ACKNOWLEDGEMENTS

An earlier version of this book was submitted as a doctoral thesis to the National University of Ireland after study undertaken through University College Cork.

I am indebted to a number of people for their suggestions and help, most notably Professor Séan Lucy of University College Cork, who supervised my original research, and Stephen Roud, formerly assistant librarian in Cricklade College, Andover, without whose invaluable support my work could not have been completed. My thanks also go to Diana Stephens and Elizabeth Fearn who typed my handwritten and revised manuscripts with expertise and patience. The final word of gratitude must be reserved for my wife, Diane, whose encouragement and loyalty throughout this enterprise have been unfailing.

Barry Sloan

CHRONOLOGY
Introductory Note

The chronology starts at 1767, the year in which Maria Edgeworth was born, and continues through to 1850, the date at which this study concludes. It sets the lives and works of the novelists discussed in the book against the literary, social and political contexts of their times, both in Ireland and abroad. Thus the reader may see at a glance a range of events which influenced the early Anglo-Irish novelists or which were of contemporary significance elsewhere.

YEAR	IRISH NOVELISTS MENTIONED IN THIS STUDY	IRISH NOVELS DISCUSSED IN THIS STUDY	OTHER IRISH WRITERS AND THEIR WORK
1767	Maria Edgeworth born		
1768			Laurence Sterne – *A Sentimental Journey through France and Italy* L. Sterne died
1770			O. Goldsmith – *The Deserted Village*
1771			
1773			O. Goldsmith – *She Stoops to Conquer*
1774			O. Goldsmith died
1775			R. B. Sheridan – *The Rivals*
1776	Sydney Owenson (Lady Morgan) born		
1777			R. B. Sheridan – *The School for Scandal*
1778			

SOME CON-TEMPORARY ENGLISH NOVELISTS AND THEIR WORK	SOME CON-TEMPORARY EUROPEAN/ AMERICAN NOVELS	POLITICAL, CULTURAL AND SOCIAL EVENTS IN IRELAND	MAJOR POLITICAL EVENTS ELSEWHERE
Tobias Smollett – *Humphrey Clinker* Sir Walter Scott born.			
	J. W. von Goethe – *Die Leiden des Jungen Werthers*		
Jane Austen born			
Fanny Burney – *Evelina*			

YEAR	IRISH NOVELISTS MENTIONED IN THIS STUDY	IRISH NOVELS DISCUSSED IN THIS STUDY	OTHER IRISH WRITERS AND THEIR WORK
1779			R. B. Sheridan – *The Critic* Thomas Moore born
1781			
1782	Charles Maturin born		
1783			Eoghan Ruadh Ó Súilleabháin died
1784			
1785			
1789			Charlotte Brooke – *Reliques of Irish Poetry*
1790			Edmund Burke – *Reflections on the French Revolution*
1791			
1792			

SOME CONTEMPORARY ENGLISH NOVELISTS AND THEIR WORK	SOME CONTEMPORARY EUROPEAN/ AMERICAN NOVELS	POLITICAL, CULTURAL AND SOCIAL EVENTS IN IRELAND	MAJOR POLITICAL EVENTS ELSEWHERE
W. Beckford – *Vathek* (1781-82)			
		Grattan's Parliament	American War of Independence in progress
T. L. Peacock born			
		Royal Irish Academy established	
			French Revolution in progress
		Founding of the United Irishmen	
		Harp Festival in Belfast	

YEAR	IRISH NOVELISTS MENTIONED IN THIS STUDY	IRISH NOVELS DISCUSSED IN THIS STUDY	OTHER IRISH WRITERS AND THEIR WORK
1793			
1794	William Carleton born		
1795			J. Callanan born
1796	Michael Banim born		Edward Bunting – *Ancient Irish Music*
1797	Samuel Lover born		Edmund Burke died
1798	John Banim born		
1800	Anna-Marie Hall (née Fielding) born	Maria Edgeworth – *Castle Rackrent*	T. Moore – *Odes of Anacreon*
1802			M. and R. L. Edgeworth – *Essay on Irish Bulls*
	Gerald Griffin born		J. C. Mangan born

SOME CON-TEMPORARY ENGLISH NOVELISTS AND THEIR WORK	SOME CON-TEMPORARY EUROPEAN/ AMERICAN NOVELS	POLITICAL, CULTURAL AND SOCIAL EVENTS IN IRELAND	MAJOR POLITICAL EVENTS ELSEWHERE
		Penal Laws relaxed	Execution of Louis XVI and Marie Antoinette; reign of terror in France; Britain and France at war.
Mrs Radcliffe – *Mysteries of Udolpho*			
W. Godwin – *Caleb Williams*; M. C. Lewis – *The Monk*	J. W. von Goethe – *Wilhelm Meisters Lehrjahre* (1795-6)	Maynooth founded. Orange Order established	
		United Irishmen's uprising; Wolfe Tone executed	
		Act of Union between Great Britain and Ireland	
		First Christian Brothers School	Peace of Amiens between Great Britain and France
		Robert Emmet's uprising and death	

YEAR	IRISH NOVELISTS MENTIONED IN THIS STUDY	IRISH NOVELS DISCUSSED IN THIS STUDY	OTHER IRISH WRITERS AND THEIR WORK
1804			
1805			B. Merriman died Lady Morgan – *Novice of St Dominick* and *Twelve Original Hibernian Melodies*
1806	Charles Lever born	Lady Morgan – *The Wild Irish Girl*	
1807			T. Moore – *Irish Melodies*
1808		Charles Maturin – *The Wild Irish Boy*	J. P. Curran – *Speeches*
1809		Maria Edgeworth – *Tales of Fashionable Life* (1809-12) (includes *Ennui*)	
1810			Sir S. Ferguson born
1811			
1812		Maria Edgeworth – *The Absentee* Charles Maturin – *The Milesian Chief*	

SOME CON-TEMPORARY ENGLISH NOVELISTS AND THEIR WORK	SOME CON-TEMPORARY EUROPEAN/ AMERICAN NOVELS	POLITICAL, CULTURAL AND SOCIAL EVENTS IN IRELAND	MAJOR POLITICAL EVENTS ELSEWHERE

B. Disraeli born

Elizabeth
Gaskell born

W. M.
Thackeray born
J. Austen –
*Sense and
Sensibility*

C. Dickens born

YEAR	IRISH NOVELISTS MENTIONED IN THIS STUDY	IRISH NOVELS DISCUSSED IN THIS STUDY	OTHER IRISH WRITERS AND THEIR WORK
1813			
1814	J. S. Le Fanu born	Lady Morgan – *O'Donnel*	T. Davis born
1815			T. Moore – *National Airs*
1816			R. B. Sheridan died
1817		Maria Edgeworth – *Ormond*	T. Moore – *Lalla Rookh*
1818		Charles Maturin *Women;* Lady Morgan – *Florence Macarthy*	
1819			
1820			C. Maturin – *Melmoth The Wanderer* D. Boucicault born

SOME CONTEMPORARY ENGLISH NOVELISTS AND THEIR WORK	SOME CONTEMPORARY EUROPEAN/ AMERICAN NOVELS	POLITICAL, CULTURAL AND SOCIAL EVENTS IN IRELAND	MAJOR POLITICAL EVENTS ELSEWHERE
J. Austen – *Pride and Prejudice*			
Sir W. Scott – *Waverley* J. Austen – *Mansfield Park*			
A. Trollope born			British victory against French at Waterloo
T. L. Peacock – *Headlong Hall* J. Austen – *Emma* C. Bronte born			
Jane Austen died		Potato Famine	
T. L. Peacock – *Nightmare Abbey* Jane Austen – *Northanger Abbey* and *Persuasion* Mary Shelley – *Frankenstein* E. Bronte born			
George Eliot and Charles Kingsley born			Massacre of 'Peterloo'
Sir W. Scott – *Ivanhoe* A. Bronte born			Accession of George IV

YEAR	IRISH NOVELISTS MENTIONED IN THIS STUDY	IRISH NOVELS DISCUSSED IN THIS STUDY	OTHER IRISH WRITERS AND THEIR WORK
1821			
1822			H. Grattan – *Speeches*
1823			
1824	C. R. Maturin died		T. C. Croker – *Researches in the South of Ireland* William Allingham born
1825		(John and Michael Banim) – *Tales by the O'Hara Family* – first series	T. C. Croker – *Fairy Legends and Traditions of the South of Ireland*
1826		*Tales by the O'Hara Family* – second series John Banim *The Boyne Water*	Rev. C. Otway founded the *Christian Examiner* *Life of Theobald Wolfe Tone* – ed. by his son
1827		Gerald Griffin – *Holland-Tide* and *Tales of the Munster Festivals*; Lady Morgan – *The O'Briens and the O'Flahertys*	Sir J. Barrington – *Personal Sketches of his Own Time* (2 vols; 3rd Vol in 1833)

SOME CON-TEMPORARY ENGLISH NOVELISTS AND THEIR WORK	SOME CON-TEMPORARY EUROPEAN/ AMERICAN NOVELS	POLITICAL, CULTURAL AND SOCIAL EVENTS IN IRELAND	MAJOR POLITICAL EVENTS ELSEWHERE
Sir W. Scott – *Kenilworth*	J. W. von Goethe – *Wilhelm Meisters Wanderjahre* (1821-29)		
		Potato Famine	
		Catholic Association established by O'Connell	
B. Disraeli – *Vivian Grey*	James Fenimore Cooper – *The Last of the Mohicans*		

YEAR	IRISH NOVELISTS MENTIONED IN THIS STUDY	IRISH NOVELS DISCUSSED IN THIS STUDY	OTHER IRISH WRITERS AND THEIR WORK
1828		Michael Banim – *The Croppy* John Banim – *The Anglo-Irish of the Nineteenth Century*	
1829		Gerald Griffin – *The Collegians* William Carleton – *Father Butler* and *The Lough Derg Pilgrim*	J. Callanan died T. C. Croker – *Legends of the Lakes*
1830		John Banim – *The Denounced* Gerald Griffin – *The Rivals* and *Tracy's Ambition*	J. Callanan – *The Recluse of Inchidony*
1831		William Carleton – *Traits and Stories of the Irish Peasantry* Mrs S. C. Hall – *Sketches of Irish Character*	S. Lover – *Legends and Stories of Ireland*
1832			*Dublin Penny Journal* started W. H. Maxwell – *Wild Sports of the West of Ireland*
1833		William Carleton – *Traits and Stories* (second series)	*Dublin University Magazine* started

SOME CON- TEMPORARY ENGLISH NOVELISTS AND THEIR WORK	SOME CON- TEMPORARY EUROPEAN/ AMERICAN NOVELS	POLITICAL, CULTURAL AND SOCIAL EVENTS IN IRELAND	MAJOR POLITICAL EVENTS ELSEWHERE
George Meredith born		O'Connell wins the Clare election	
		Catholic Emancipation Act	
	Stendhal – *La Rouge et la Noir*	Society for the Repeal of the Union established by O'Connell	
T. L. Peacock – *Crotchet Castle*	V. Hugo – *Notre-Dame de Paris*	National School system established Start of anti-tithe campaign	
Sir W. Scott died		Great Reform Bill	
	H. de Balzac – *Eugénie Grandet*		

YEAR	IRISH NOVELISTS MENTIONED IN THIS STUDY	IRISH NOVELS DISCUSSED IN THIS STUDY	OTHER IRISH WRITERS AND THEIR WORK
1834			
1835		Gerald Griffin *Tales of my Neighbourhood* John Banim – *The Mayor of Windgap* Harriet Martin – *Canvassing*	Anthony Raftery died
1836			
1837		Samuel Lover – *Rory O'More Legends and Stories of Ireland Popular Tales and Legends of the Irish Peasantry*	
1838		John Banim – *The Bit O'Writin'* Mrs S. C. Hall – *Lights and Shadows of Irish Life*	
1839		William Carleton – *Fardorougha the Miser* Charles Lever – *Harry Lorrequer*	

SOME CONTEMPORARY ENGLISH NOVELISTS AND THEIR WORK	SOME CONTEMPORARY EUROPEAN/AMERICAN NOVELS	POLITICAL, CULTURAL AND SOCIAL EVENTS IN IRELAND	MAJOR POLITICAL EVENTS ELSEWHERE
	H. de Balzac – *Le Père Goriot*	Tolpuddle Martyrs Abolition of slavery in the British Empire	
Samuel Butler born	N. Gogol – *Dead Souls*		
Charles Dickens – *Sketches by Boz* and *Pickwick Papers*			
	Nathaniel Hawthorne – *Twice-Told Tales*	Poor Law Relief Act	Accession of Queen Victoria
C. Dickens – *Oliver Twist*; *Nicholas Nickleby*			Anti-Corn League; beginnings of Chartism
	E. A. Poe – *The Fall Of the House of Ussher* Stendhal – *La Chartreuse de Parme*		Chartist riots

YEAR	IRISH NOVELISTS MENTIONED IN THIS STUDY	IRISH NOVELS DISCUSSED IN THIS STUDY	OTHER IRISH WRITERS AND THEIR WORK
1840	Gerald Griffin died		
1841		Charles Lever – *Charles O'Malley*	D. Boucicault – *London Assurance Cork Examiner* started
1842	John Banim died	Samuel Lover – *Handy Andy*	The *Nation* founded
1843		Charles Lever – *Jack Hinton*	
1844			
1845		Charles Lever – *The O'Donoghue* Mrs S. C. Hall *The Whiteboy* J. S. Le Fanu – *The Cock and Anchor*	Thomas Davis died J. C. Mangan – *Anthologia Germanica*

SOME CON-TEMPORARY ENGLISH NOVELISTS AND THEIR WORK	SOME CON-TEMPORARY EUROPEAN/ AMERICAN NOVELS	POLITICAL, CULTURAL AND SOCIAL EVENTS IN IRELAND	MAJOR POLITICAL EVENTS ELSEWHERE
Thomas Hardy born	E. A. Poe – *Tales of the Grotesque* M. Lermontov – *A Hero of our Time*	Loyal National Repeal Association formed by O'Connell	Union of Canada Act
C. Dickens – *The Old Curiosity Shop*			New Zealand declared British; Sovereignty over Hong Kong
			Chartist riots
Henry James born C. Dickens – *Christmas Carol*		O'Connell's Monster Meetings and his retreat from Clontarf	Natal British
C. Dickens – *Martin Chuzzlewit* B. Disraeli – *Coningsby* W. M. Thackeray – *Barry Lyndon*	A. Dumas – *Le Comte de Monte Christo*		
B. Disraeli – *Sybil*			

YEAR	IRISH NOVELISTS MENTIONED IN THIS STUDY	IRISH NOVELS DISCUSSED IN THIS STUDY	OTHER IRISH WRITERS AND THEIR WORK
1845 (cont.)		William Carleton – *Art Maguire; Parra Sastha; Valentine McClutchy; Rody the Rover*	
1846			Thomas Davis – *Poems and Essays* Standish James O'Grady born
1847		Charles Lever – *The Knight of Gwynne* William Carleton – *The Black Prophet*	J. Callanan – *Poems*
1848		William Carleton – *The Emigrants of Ahadarra*	John O'Donovan – *The Annals of the Four Masters* (1848-51); *United Irishman* founded by John Mitchel

SOME CONTEMPORARY ENGLISH NOVELISTS AND THEIR WORK	SOME CONTEMPORARY EUROPEAN/ AMERICAN NOVELS	POLITICAL, CULTURAL AND SOCIAL EVENTS IN IRELAND	MAJOR POLITICAL EVENTS ELSEWHERE
	F. Dostoevski – *Poor Folk* H. Melville – *Typee* H. de Balzac – *Cousine Bette*	1846-48 Great Famine 1846 Split between O'Connell and Young Irelanders	Repeal of the Corn Laws
W. M. Thackeray – *Vanity Fair* A. Trollope – *The Macdermots of Ballycloran* C. Bronte – *Jane Eyre* E. Bronte – *Wuthering Heights* A. Bronte – *Agnes Grey* B. Disraeli – *Tancred*		Daniel O'Connell died	
E. Gaskell – *Mary Barton* A. Trollope – *The Kellys and the O'Kellys* E. Bronte died C. Dickens – *Dombey and Son*		Young Ireland uprising	Revolutions throughout Europe Chartist Petition Marx and Engels publish *Communist Manifesto*

YEAR	IRISH NOVELISTS MENTIONED IN THIS STUDY	IRISH NOVELS DISCUSSED IN THIS STUDY	OTHER IRISH WRITERS AND THEIR WORK
1849	Maria Edgeworth died	William Carleton – *The Tithe Proctor*	J. C. Mangan died
1850			William Allingham – *Poems*

SOME CON-TEMPORARY ENGLISH NOVELISTS AND THEIR WORK	SOME CON-TEMPORARY EUROPEAN/ AMERICAN NOVELS	POLITICAL, CULTURAL AND SOCIAL EVENTS IN IRELAND	MAJOR POLITICAL EVENTS ELSEWHERE
C. Dickens – *David Copperfield* C. Bronte – *Shirley* A. Bronte – *Tenant of Wildfell Hall* A. Bronte died			
C. Kingsley – *Alton Locke* W. M. Thackeray – *Pendennis* R. L. Stevenson born	Nathaniel Hawthorne – *The Scarlet Letter* I. Turgenev – *The Diary of a Superfluous Man*	Tenant League founded Appointment of Archbishop Cullen	

ONE

CASTLE RACKRENT TO THE DEATH OF MATURIN (1800–1824)

Earnestness of purpose and desire to serve
> Lady Morgan:
> Preface to the 1846 edition of
> *The Wild Irish Girl*

Defeat and the attendant consequences have been such a prominent part of Irish history that it comes as no surprise to find that many of the dates and events which live on in popular memory are commemorations of disaster rather than celebrations of victory. One of the most emotionally potent of these dates, 1798, marks the abortive military uprisings which were the culmination of a decade of intense political activity, revolutionary intrigue and liberal thinking. The crushing reprisals exacted in physical terms that year had their political counterpart in 1800 when, by the Act of Union, the Irish lost their Parliament in Dublin. Thus an observer at the beginning of the nineteenth century might have concluded that this double defeat, both on the battlefield and in the Parliament house, had imposed a greater measure of subservience to the English colonial master than ever before. The idea of a separate Irish identity was, perhaps, never more obviously in jeopardy, for the English aim was to limit Irish independence and to reduce a troublesome colony to a state of respectful duty and obligation.

Initially the policy might well have appeared to succeed in its purposes. Even the issue of Catholic emancipation, which Pitt was unable to resolve after the passage of the Act of Union, lost its urgency in the opening years of the century. There was no longer a national cause – a fact clearly demonstrated in the tragi-comic events of Robert Emmet's uprising in 1803 which drew little or no support, but which provided Irish popular history with its next emotive date. According to Robert Kee: 'The success of the Emmet myth lay in the need to ennoble failure.'[1] But Emmet's gesture was not the only significant attempt to generate self-respect and to assert a distinctive

1

identity for the Irish at a time of national humiliation and oppression.

The Act of Union may have ended five hundred years of Irish parliamentary life, but in 1800 a short novel was published which is justly accepted as the first work of prose fiction to make a serious endeavour to explore certain critical aspects of Irish life without caricature or contempt. *Castle Rackrent* initiates a process of exploration which is still continuing, but which in the nineteenth century played a considerable part in shaping both the Irishman's view of his own people and country, and also the Englishman's view of a race and land about which so often he knew little and cared less, as long as the natives were quiet. Curiously enough *Castle Rackrent*, sometimes held to be its author's masterpiece because least influenced by her father, was written while Richard Lovell Edgeworth was away from home in Dublin voting on the Act of Union. Indeed one new tradition of self-expression was being born at the very moment when another was being extinguished. The novel lacked the impact of the political decision, but it signals the beginning of a certain kind of Anglo-Irish literature, a literature with a distinctively national character and preoccupied with national affairs.

Under the eighteenth-century penal laws Catholics were forbidden to practise their religion or to receive education. Socially ambitious Catholics usually found it necessary to conform to the Established Church and to serve the Dublin Castle administration. This was the cynical way to material prosperity. One of the most decisive cultural effects of these restrictions and pressures was the decline of the Irish language. As English increasingly became the first language of a majority of the population, so the need arose for people to express themselves imaginatively through literature written in English. Significantly the novel, which is not an indigenous Irish literary form, only assumes prominence as a mode of expression after the English language had superseded the native Irish. Furthermore, the first three Anglo-Irish novelists, Maria Edgeworth, Lady Morgan and Charles Maturin, were native English speakers who had enjoyed untypical educational advantages. The writings of the two women who dominate the first twenty years of the nineteenth century – Maturin is a rather special case who merits separate consideration – were crucially influenced by their social backgrounds and the personalities of their fathers.

Maria Edgeworth, the daughter of a prosperous landlord, was born in England but spent most of her eighty-two years in Ireland where, in addition to her activities as a writer, she assisted in the administration of her father's estates. Indeed her role as administrator, which brought her into close contact with ordinary Irish people, stimulated her insight into their strengths, weaknesses and aspirations and gave authority to her depiction of them.

Castle Rackrent is a seminal novel, not only because it initiates a tradition of fiction, nor because of its impact on other writers (most notably Sir Walter Scott), but because of the astonishing sense of historical process which emerges from this deceptively easy tale. The story as such may be summarized in a few words: Thady Quirk, an old servant of the Rackrent family, recalls his memories of life under four generations of Rackrents, and reveals, often with unconscious irony, the progressive collapse of their fortunes and estates and the decline in the lives of the tenants. In the end the land is no longer in the power of its traditional owners, but has been mortgaged to a legal agent who, by a final twist of irony, is Thady's own son Jason.

Simple as this may seem, the story announces some essential and recurring themes of nineteenth-century Anglo-Irish fiction: landownership, the relationship between landlords and their tenants, and how the fates of both parties depended upon the way the land was managed. Nor are these merely literary preoccupations, but abiding political and social problems in Ireland. The very fact that Maria Edgeworth's account of crisis on the land was published in 1800 – and therefore describes what she observed in the late eighteenth century – indicates how longstanding and deeprooted it was.

The use of Thady Quirk as her narrator was a stroke of genius, and the success of the novel stems largely from this. His lifetime of service to the Rackrent family and his apparent blind loyalty to them enable Maria Edgeworth to exploit the ironic tension between Thady's interpretation of events and characters and the reader's own perspective. But Thady's 'faithfulness' to the family he has worked for is, as James Newcomer has argued, 'actually a perceptive revelation of the Rackrents' errors', and he continues: 'The Rackrents play always into Thady's and Jason's hands, though, if a reader were inattentive, he might think exactly the opposite.'[2]

Sir Patrick, the first of the Rackrents in the tale, is seen indirectly, and his reputation has already achieved legendary status before the opening of Thady's account. He is celebrated for his extravagant lifestyle, hunting, drinking and eating, for his generosity to all-comers to his home, and for his kindness. Thady says 'The whole country rang with his praises!', but the very behaviour that earned his popularity also ruined his finances and set up the debts which eventually engulf his descendants.

The meanness of spirit and harsh treatment shown to the peasantry by Sir Murtagh Rackrent (Sir Patrick's heir) may perhaps be justified in part as a necessary reaction against his predecessor's excesses. But this is an insufficient explanation because Sir Murtagh is not simply careful; he is devious, eager to exploit every possible right over his tenants by exercising the threat of legal action, and at odds with his neighbours. His use of litigation to assert his power rather than to secure justice and establish equity marks a stage in the conversion of mutual feudal obligations between masters and their servants or tenants into a network of legal trickery and blackmail. As fear replaces love under Sir Murtagh, so servility replaces respect; and servility reflects a negative attitude of mind, leading at one extreme to an odious, fawning flattery, and at the other acting as a mask to conceal bitter or vengeful hatred. In either case it destroys self-respect.

The third of the Rackrents, Sir Kit, has the spendthrift temperament of Sir Patrick, but in addition he is an absentee, and this factor is crucial in understanding the further growth of alienation between landlord and tenants. Thady is left to formulate one of the vital questions in both nineteenth-century Irish history and Anglo-Irish literature when he says:

Sir Kit Rackrent, my young master, left all to the agent, and though he had the spirit of a Prince, and lived away to the honour of his country abroad, which I was proud to hear of, what were we the better for that at home?[3]

In this situation the tenants had the worst of all worlds: denied even a share in the improvidence of their landlord, unlike Sir Patrick's people, they were left responsible to an agent whose sole concerns were to finance his employer's follies and to line his own pocket. Land agents in Anglo-Irish fiction tend to be of two kinds – the very good and the very bad. The good ones, like Mr McLeod in *Ennui*, Mr Burke in *The Absentee*, or Mr Hickman in Carleton's *Valentine McClutchy*, are men of honour, concerned to improve the lives and education of their charges as well as returning a fair sum to their absentee masters. The villains – such as Mr Hardcastle in *Ennui*, Mr Garraghty in *The Absentee* and Valentine McClutchy himself – are, in varying degrees, treacherous, deceitful and utterly unscrupulous in exploiting the poor. By the end of *Castle Rackrent*, Jason Quirk is set fair to become just such a villain.

Thady responds to the increasing hardship faced by the Rackrent tenants under the administration of the agent by excusing Sir Kit's behaviour on the grounds that injustice flourishes merely because his master is oblivious of what is going on. But the reader is left to conclude that the landlord simply does not care so long as he has a ready supply of money. Moreover he does not mention the further irony – that his own son is gaining power precisely because of Sir Kit's behaviour. Thus Thady Quirk's apparently simple faith in the capacity of a resident landlord to set matters right on the estate requires careful scrutiny. This belief is offered repeatedly in nineteenth-century Anglo-Irish fiction as the panacea for all of Ireland's problems, and it rings ever more hollow. Here, in the first novel of its kind, Maria Edgeworth introduces the idea in a way that already makes it suspect. Such insight and shrewdness of presentation are a rare combination, even in her own writing.

While Thady seems to rely on a progressively forlorn cause, his son Jason is openly taking steps to ensure his emergence as the man of the future. He becomes assistant to the agent and his growing legal expertise is decisive in his dealings with Sir Condy, the last of the Rackrents, and the closest in spirit to the legendary Sir Patrick. In Sir Condy, writes H. R. Krans,

are seen in operation the curious code of honor and the conflicting characteristics that made the Irishman so startlingly strange and incomprehensible to other peoples; so wayward and wrong-headed, and yet so truly good-natured; combining in a remarkable way generosity and selfishness, unscrupulousness and honorable feeling, kind-heartedness and ferocity.[4]

Despite his hopeless financial position, he strives to emulate the popular extravagance of his ancestor.

The final collapse of the Rackrent estate marks another critical stage in the relationship between landowners and peasants. With Jason Quirk the agent in control, the tenants lose even the nominal protection and support of the feudal system without gaining greater independence or an increased capacity to be self-sufficient. On the contrary, here as elsewhere, the victims of irresponsibility became the subjects of heartless greed and often of sectarian hostility. The crisis is grasped vividly and succinctly, and no sleight-of-hand relieves the gloomy future.

The book, however, has its limitations. Maria Edgeworth's background inevitably dictated that her understanding of the landlord class was greater than her sense of identification with the peasants. Although her concern for the victims of exploitation was genuine, there is a difference between sympathy, however deep or imaginative, and a sure knowledge based on lived experience. She was always at a remove from her father's tenants, not only socially but intellectually and temperamentally, and there are aspects of peasant life unrepresented in her work. It is also true that she was primarily intrigued by the peculiarities of behaviour she observed among the Irish peasantry rather than with understanding their ways of thought and feeling.[5] This indeed is the key to her purpose: she wished to share her fascination with her readers. In doing so she was singularly successful and she must be judged accordingly. Furthermore Maria Edgeworth's own detachment from the peasantry was an essential precondition of her achievement.

Above all she took the Irish seriously, and the novel is not a cheap parody of stereotyped Irishness. She also took seriously the scale of duties and rights upon which the traditional landlord and peasant relationship depended. *Castle Rackrent* is not a subversive novel advocating peasant landownership. Maria Edgeworth may make a plea for the rights of the Irish poor, but those rights are conditional upon them serving good and responsible landlords who will fulfil their obligations to the tenantry. Her position is conservative insofar as it assumes the existence of the landlord class, but radical in that it reveals the inadequacy of many members of that class, and implies their betrayal of the peasants. It also shows how the people are further outsmarted by the more cynical of their fellow tenants, who are prepared to act as agents for their absentee masters. In other words, Maria Edgeworth did not want a fundamental change in the structure of Irish society – and indeed she lapsed into a long silence as the social structures gradually began to alter during the course of the century – but she hoped the old system might regenerate itself and function efficiently, embracing the duties of privilege as well as its rights.

Not surprisingly, therefore, absenteeism and its effects are central preoccupations in *Ennui* (1809) and *The Absentee* (1812), although in both these novels, and in *Ormond* (1817), the author complicates the action by introducing romantic subplots and scenes of fashionable life in the well-to-do salons of the time. But this is to anticipate, for before Maria Edgeworth published *Ennui*, another novelist appeared who introduced a new dimension to Anglo-Irish fiction.

Lady Morgan, born Sydney Owenson, could hardly be more different to Maria Edgeworth both as a person and as a writer. If irony, satire and restraint are characteristics of the latter novelist's style, extravagance, romance and atmosphere are Lady Morgan's distinguishing marks. Her mode of writing is remote from late-twentieth-century preferences, and the over-simplification and naivety of the author, whose reputation at one time stood equally high in literary circles in both London and Dublin, may cause added difficulties.

The fact of the matter is that Lady Morgan created a considerable impact among her contemporaries. Speaking of her book *The Wild Irish Girl*, which appeared in 1806, Thomas Flanagan says it is

a bad novel. But it is one of those oddities of literature which, regardless of merit, are deeply influential. . . . Together with Moore's *Irish Melodies* it established a sentimental image of Ireland of a specific kind. It was this image which aroused among English readers a sympathetic interest in Ireland's plight and gave first form to the rhetoric of Irish nationalists.[6]

The emphasis on the sentimental nature of the image of Ireland and on the link between this and its effects both upon the English view of the Irish and on the rhetoric of Irish nationalists is critical. Perhaps it is true to say that whereas *Castle Rackrent* influenced other writers, *The Wild Irish Girl*, and to a lesser extent the works that followed it, moulded the feelings and emotions of readers, both at home and in England, about Ireland and the Irish.

Lady Morgan is believed to have been born on Christmas Day 1776 while her mother was crossing on the mail boat from her native England to rejoin her husband Robert Owenson in Dublin. Owenson himself began life as Robert MacOwen, the son of a dashing ne'er-do-well farmer who made a runaway

marriage with Sydney Crofton, a daughter of the master of
Longford House, Sligo, after impressing her by his hurling
prowess. She was disowned by her family, but established a
reputation as a harpist and singer of Irish songs. Thus the lives
of Sydney Owenson's paternal grandparents contain some of
the romance and music which were to characterize her own
career. The element of showmanship came directly from her
father. Robert MacOwen, who claimed to be a distant relation
of Oliver Goldsmith, made a career as a comic actor in the
London theatre – where he changed his name to Owenson –
but in 1776 he returned to Ireland, and having been
enthusiastically received in Dublin, decided to stay. In this
way it came about that his wife was travelling to Ireland when
Sydney was born. Robert Owenson, who was an Irish speaker,
exercised a decisive influence over his daughter, especially as
her mother died early and Sydney and her sisters travelled the
provinces of Ireland with him in his capacity as an actor-
manager committed to fostering what he called 'the national
mind' by presenting dramatic and musical entertainment
based on native materials. He declared it his aim to promote
civilization in rural areas by erecting theatres, 'like Martello
towers', all across the country. The experiences of these days
were of incalculable importance for the young woman, and
they established once and for all the nationalist fervour and
sense of racial pride that dominated the writings of her adult
years. In her *Memoirs: Autobiography, Diaries and
Correspondence*, she told how her father would

narrate in broken episodes traits and incidents of his own story and
of the times in which he lived, mingled with relations of habits,
customs and manners still existing in Ireland down to the close of the
last century.[7]

Furthermore she admits that these recollections formed the
basis of *The Wild Irish Girl*, and she also records how her
meeting in her teens with officers of the Irish Brigade who had
returned in poverty to Kilkenny after the French Revolution
gave her the basis for her heroes in *O'Donnel*, *Florence
Macarthy* and *The O'Briens and the O'Flahertys*, and helped to
form her belief in the need for Catholic emancipation.

The Wild Irish Girl was not her first venture into print – she
had published earlier a volume of sentimental verses, which
were followed by a collection of Irish tunes with English
words. Although these attracted little or no attention, they

show her involvement with Irish material from the outset. In his biography of Lady Morgan, Lionel Stevenson quotes from a letter written after her first visit to England in which she explains the impulses behind her conception of the novel that established her literary reputation. Lady Morgan declares:

It was requisite I should leave my native country to learn the turpitude, degradation, ferocity, and inconsequence of her offspring; the miseries of her present, and the falsity of the recorded splendours of her ancient state. . . . in the course of one of the many conversations which occurred on the subject of my (always termed) 'unhappy country', . . . a hint casually suggested, formed the origin of a little work, which has since appeared under the title of *The Wild Irish Girl*. . . . as a *woman*, a *young woman*, and an *Irishwoman*, I felt all the delicacy of undertaking a work which had for the professed theme of its discussion circumstances of national import and national interest.[8]

The book is written as a series of letters concerning a young man, the son of an absentee landlord, who has been banished by his father for profligate living to a remote part of Connaught. Here he encounters the Prince of Inismore, his daughter, Glorvina, and Father John, the Prince's priest. He wins their confidence by pretending he is an artist on tour in the country — a device of the disguised outsider which was used again by other novelists later in the century. He conceals his real identity because he fears rejection, especially by the Prince, one of whose noble forebears was murdered by an ancestor of Mr Mortimer, the young man.

There are two main strands to the novel: it follows the course of Mortimer's love for Glorvina and, as Lady Morgan's letter indicated, indulges in special pleading, aimed at improving the image of Ireland and her people among English readers. The ancient roots, traditions, learning and courtesy of the Irish are all emphasized and, as the narrative is presented through the eyes of Mortimer, his disillusionment and his discovery of the true nature of the natives is intended to be the reader's experience also. The result is that there are long, highly contrived and improbable discourses on a variety of subjects which fit uneasily into the general progress of the novel. Yet the author herself regarded these interpolations as an essential part of the book's popularity. She wrote:

The great secret of the success of *The Wild Irish Girl* was, that it conveyed in a vivid and romantic story, curious information about the social condition, the manners, customs, literature and antiquities of

Ireland. There was in it a passionate pleading against the wrongs and injustice to which the people and country were subjected. . . . As these pleas were put forth in an interesting form, they were eagerly read.[9]

Her book was indeed an immediate success and became something of a cult novel among fashionable ladies in Dublin and London, many of whom adopted the hairstyle of the Princess of Inismore, pinned back with golden bodkins which were known as Glorvinas. There was a Glorvina mantle, and Sydney Owenson herself promoted this little industry by wearing a red Celtic cloak, based on the design allegedly affected by Granuille and fastened with a gold Tara brooch, when she went to London parties. These facts suggest the nature of the popular response generated by the book: it made 'going Irish' socially acceptable and fashionable; whether and how it impinged upon the moral and political consciences of the wealthy and the English is more problematic.

Early in the novel the stereotyped English notion of the 'natural character' of the Irish is given. They are said to be 'turbulent, faithless, intemperate, and cruel; formerly destitute of arts, letters, or civilization, and still but slowly submitting to their salutary and ennobling influence,' although Lady Morgan gives little *specific* evidence either to justify or overthrow this point of view.[10] The main Irish characters – the Prince of Inismore, his daughter and his priest – are in no sense typical or representative – as, for example, the Rackrents were representative of different kinds of landlord – and the peasants are merely cap-touching, amiable, welcoming, inoffensive ciphers who form a small part of the background scenery. There is no equivalent to Thady Quirk or to his grasping son Jason. The greedy agent in *The Wild Irish Girl*, Glendinning, is a shadowy and insubstantial figure. True, the impressionable Mortimer is driven to reassess his own prejudices against the Irish when he hears of the luckless Murtoch O'Shaughnassy, who is the victim of a bad agent and is unable to pay his rent; yet he shows true humanity for his family and their cow by his stoical and unprotesting labours on their behalf. This image of the suffering peasant is offered to win sympathy for the Irish and to increase the understanding of the English. But its limitations raise real questions.

First of all, while acknowledging that the man is a victim, his misfortune and injustice are not explained. This contrasts with *Castle Rackrent* where Maria Edgeworth revealed by implication the inequity of the treatment suffered by the peasantry. Here the reader is invited to feel sorry for people like Murtoch O'Shaughnassy, but not to make the intellectual effort to understand them or their predicament, a shortcoming which is a basic weakness of the novel's structure.

Second, the passivity and humble submissiveness of Murtoch are extolled as virtues – Glorvina may be the wild Irish girl, but Murtoch is no wild Irish man. He is in fact a good citizen in a colonial situation, a motif which recurs in Lady Morgan's work. The inference is that the Irish deserve to be treated reasonably because they are good colonial subjects whose reputation abroad has been sullied by the excesses of a small number of trouble-makers. The problem of the relationship between England and Ireland, and the exact degree of authority England should have, was of course one of the great divisive issues in nineteenth-century politics, and it appears in various ways in the literature. Lady Morgan did not envisage an Ireland free of English rule and governing itself: all her work implies that Ireland will continue to be ruled from across the water, although in a less repressive way.

The next series of problems arises with the central Irish characters, the Prince of Inismore and his daughter Glorvina. According to Lionel Stevenson,

Every trait of the Prince of Inismore contributes to a full length portrait of Robert Owenson in his later years, growing querulous with age, failure and ill-health, but still unreasonable, passionate, charming, pathetically dignified, and unconsciously dependent on the better sense of his daughter.[11]

He is a figure very much in the mould of King Corny in Maria Edgeworth's *Ormond*, and like him he is an anachronism. There was no future for Ireland in men like the Prince of Inismore and King Corny; they were already remnants of a past age, existing significantly on the very fringes of society – or, in the case of King Corny, on an island.

The Prince has been deprived of his lands because 'he would neither cut his glibbs, shave his upper lip, nor shorten his shirt', these being the ritual humiliations imposed upon the Irish chiefs by their English conquerors.[12] He is cultured, steeped in the stories and customs of the ancient Irish, and practises his Catholic religion in spite of its illegality. But he lives in a world of surviving fragments, romantic and heroic memories and legends, actual poverty and ruins. The hall of his half-derelict castle, once the centre of conviviality and hospitality, now serves as 'an armoury, a museum, a cabinet of national antiquities, and national curiosities', while his hatred of the Saxons is symbolized by the bricked-up windows which formerly overlooked his ancestral demesnes.[13] Ironically the Prince himself is another curiosity. There is no effective possibility of leadership from an intolerant recluse, however noble his spirit, and only under the influence of whiskey does he forget 'that he is the ruined possessor of a visionary title' and feel 'that he is a man – and an Irishman!'[14]

Whatever the need to define the present by reference to the past, this novel views Ireland exclusively as a shattered culture, and so produces a lop-sided picture. Lady Morgan exploits the ruins of former grandeur for sheer effect, and the description of Inismore in the setting sun is typical of the verbal ecstasy generated on many occasions:

Towards the extreme western point of this peninsula, which was wildly romantic beyond all description, arose a vast and grotesque pile of rocks, which at once formed the scite (*sic*) and fortifications of the noblest mass of ruins on which my eye ever rested. Grand even in desolation, and magnificent in decay – it was the Castle of Inismore![15]

The impact of the physical beauty of the Irish landscape has coloured the writings and speeches of numerous Irish artists and politicians alike – as Robert Kee noted in his study of Irish nationalism; but for Lady Morgan the focal point of most such breathless rhapsodies is a ruined building of erstwhile magnificence, as if the very fact that the old way of life existed only in fragments gave it an added exotic and nostalgic potency which she, with the Gothic novelist's delight in sensation, was quick to utilize. Everything about the life of the Prince and the environment in which he is presented reveals the author's romantic attachment to a bygone age and her delight in its vestigial remains. Lady Morgan shares, as it were, the excitement of the archaeologist, and her nationalism is retrospective.

The case is rather different with Glorvina, the Prince's daughter, who is obviously a self-projection of the novelist. As the destined bride of Mortimer and heiress of the future, her fate demands more forward-looking solutions. Glorvina is an idealized child of nature whose beauty, intelligence, sympathetic temperament and musical talent come as no surprise; but her views on the reconciliation of religious differences are relevant to a perennial Irish problem.

She argues that the human mind is 'propelled towards truth' by a 'divine and invariable law' so that the time will come when people's

affections, like their privileges, will be in common; the limited throb with which their hearts now beat towards each other, under the influence of a kindred fate, will then be animated to the nobler pulsation of universal philanthropy.[16]

Regrettably there is no further exploration or development of this idea or of how it might come to fulfilment, but at least it acknowledges a real social tension and the need to resolve it. The fact is particularly notable in a novel which contains so many unrealities.

In addition to Glorvina's tolerance we have the arguments of the priest – whose character is modelled on that of the Rev. Dr Flynn, Catholic Dean of Sligo – in favour of the industry, geniality, generosity and intelligence of the Irish people. All of these qualities, the novel insists, would be encouraged by respect and fair treatment from the English. This view leads to the concluding theory – that good landlords would be the answer to every ill. Although this solution implies the author's awareness that land possession and management were *the* critical issues, she proposes it with virtually no first-hand exploration of the conditions of those people whom it was meant to help.

In the highly improbable climax Mortimer's father – who has appeared periodically and in disguise at Inismore in order to help restore the Prince to an influential position of leadership – is revealed as the secret wooer of Glorvina. The disguise was necessitated by the Prince's Milesian pride, which caused him to refuse a previous offer of aid from Mortimer's father, and because of his hatred for the family which had killed his ancestor. The novelist appears ready to condone the devious altruism of the English landlord, although nothing suggests that it resulted in any practical benefits to the Prince or his people. Furthermore, while the Earl of M. emerges as a man whose conscience is troubled by his Irish affairs, there is no evidence that he tried to instil his belief in justice for the Irish into his sons. From any point of view this part of the novel lacks reason or credibility.

When the Earl gives up his attachment to Glorvina in favour

of his son Mortimer, the letter which he sends him resounds with pious hopes and advice, but again the point is inconsistent with what has gone before. His honourable wish to see an end to distinctions of race and religion is compromised by the inbuilt assumption which informs the whole epistle: namely, that English rule is justified and that the English are the best masters for the Irish. This is difficult to reconcile with the novelist's earlier concern to present the intellectual, cultural and political worth and ancestry of the Irish.

In one respect at least the Earl's advice is both sound and prophetic. He warns his son to be

more anxious to remove *causes* than to punish *effects*; for, trust me, that is only to 'Scotch the snake – not kill it', to confine error, and to waken vengeance.[17]

But the encouragement to 'cherish by kindness into renovating life' the 'national virtues' of the Irish ignores the part played by the English in Ireland in producing the 'fatality of circumstances' which 'blighted' its development.[18] Thus the question of how the destroyers are also to be the restorative force in Irish life is unanswered. Condescension, however unintentional, informs the passage and suggests exactly where this panacea fails. Mortimer is urged to

place the standard of support within their sphere; and like the tender vine, which has been suffered by neglect to waste its treasures on the sterile earth, you will behold them naturally turning and gratefully twining round the fostering stem, which rescues them from a cheerless and groveling destiny. . . . when the light of instruction shall have dispelled the gloom of ignorance and prejudice from their neglected minds, and their lightened hearts shall again throb with the cheery pulse of national exility:– then, and *not till then*, will you behold the day-star of national virtue rising brightly over the horizon of their happy existence.[19]

Ironically the final impression of the Irish, in a book committed to arguing their virtues, is of a race of rather wild, bitter and undisciplined people who really have hearts of gold, and who may yet with due care and management be reduced to sound colonial citizens. Clearly 'the day-star of national virtue' will be obedience and respect for the colonial master. The author, for all her earlier enthusiasm, does not finally allow any weight to the notion of the self-sufficiency of Irish culture, and she accepts that English influence will be civilizing and beneficial. No equal stress is given to the idea that Irish culture on its own merits will enrich the English, and thus it is not a true vision of brotherhood. The English, according to this thesis, will only benefit from the Irish *after* the Irish have been duly moulded to English expectations.

Such a judgment may be harsh and ungenerous, and it is only fair to mention a statement of Lady Morgan's in her Prefatory Address to the 1846 edition of the novel. There she wrote:

> at the moment *The Wild Irish Girl* appeared, it was dangerous to write on Ireland, hazardous to praise her, and difficult to find a publisher for an Irish tale which had a political tendency.[20]

Given these practical problems, the author's caution and restraint are understandable, and however limited, rhetorical and illogical her nationalism, there remains her undeniable success in articulating feelings and stirring emotions which were far more important in themselves than *The Wild Irish Girl* could ever be as a work of art.

The tendency to preach in the undisguised and somewhat heavy-handed way apparent in *The Wild Irish Girl* is also found in Maria Edgeworth's novels *Ennui* (1809) and *The Absentee* (1812). Both begin in an English setting but transfer to Ireland where they become examinations of the obligations of a landlord, and both present the discovery of Ireland and the Irish through the eyes of a central character who revisits his native soil. In *Ennui* the hero, the Earl of Glenthorn, returns to Ireland from which he had been removed by his father at the age of two. He holds inherited prejudices against the country which he expects to be backward and dull – an expectation which is reversed both here and in *The Absentee*, where Maria Edgeworth shows not only Colambre's discovery of Ireland but the folly of his mother's anti-Irish pronouncements in London.

Glenthorn's first adult encounter with his past is when his old nurse Ellinor O'Donoghoe – who by a subsequent twist in the plot turns out to be his mother – travels to England to see him. The amused superiority of his attitude towards Ellinor typifies his general view of the Irish:

> The very want of a sense of propriety, and the freedom with which she talked to me, regardless of what was suited to her station, or due to my rank, instead of offending or disgusting me, became agreeable; besides, the novelty of her dialect, and of her turn of thought, entertained me as much as a sick man could be entertained.[21]

Glenthorn's fascination with her dialect (her pronunciation is hinted at by the use of italics in words where the spelling is deliberately unorthodox, such as 'plased', 'asy', and 'contint'), with her picturesque account of his glorious ancestors, and with her religious and superstitious eccentricity (she hopes to die on Christmas Day 'because the gates of Heaven, they say, will be opened all that day; and who knows but a body might slip in unknownst?'), all indicate his remoteness from his own roots.[22]

If Glenthorn's position is one of ignorance and indifference, Lady Clonbrony in *The Absentee* consciously rejects her background, and in her vain attempts to pass as an Englishwoman in polite society she becomes the butt of cruel snubs, mockery and contempt. Glenthorn learns to appreciate aspects of Irish life about which he knew nothing; Lady Clonbrony is forced, not altogether convincingly, to acknowledge the cant and hypocrisy of high society in London and to review her opinions of Ireland.

Maria Edgeworth used the hero's journey to his home estates to introduce a variety of ideas in both novels. Lord Colambre's journey is a much more comprehensive affair than Glenthorn's, constituting a tour of four different estates run in varying ways. Glenthorn heads directly to his own castle, but soon discovers that the Irish gift for talk which had so intrigued him can also be used for less disinterested purposes. He finds that the image of 'feudal power . . . in (his) vast territory over tenants, who were almost vassals, and amongst a numerous train of dependants', which Ellinor had drawn for him, is less glamorous than it sounded.[23]

The further he travels from Dublin – which pleasantly surprised him by its mixture of buildings, magnificent and paltry, grand and incomplete – the rougher the journey becomes and the more improvised the transport arrangements. This, a favourite point in numerous novels, allows the author to write a marvellous description of man, carriage and beasts which must have seemed as eccentric to most readers as to the hero of the story itself:

From the inn yard came a hackney chaise, in a most deplorably crazy state; the body mounted up to a prodigious height, on unbending springs, nodding forwards, one door swinging open, three blinds up, because they could not be let down, the perch tied in two places, the iron of the wheels half off, half loose, wooden pegs for linch-pins, and ropes for harness. The horses were worthy of the harness; wretched little dog-tired creatures . . . held at arms' length by a man dressed like a mad beggar, in half a hat and half a wig, both awry in opposite directions; a long tattered greatcoat, tied round his waist by a hay-rope; the jagged rents in the skirts of this coat showing his bare legs, marbled of many colours; while something like stockings hung loose about his ankles.[24]

Although these details may seem stereotyped now, that is largely because they conform in their essentials to many such portraits, but they would not have done so in Maria Edgeworth's time. The original readers, especially in England, may have felt that such an account confirmed their worst suspicions about the Irish – Glenthorn reacts this way himself – but the absurdity of the situation and of the man's appearance is balanced by the wit and special cleverness of the conversation which follows. This is the second significant point: Maria Edgeworth's Paddy – for that is his name – is not as mad as he might appear at first sight. When Glenthorn exclaims at the crippled state of one of the horses, the reply comes back:

'Oh, plase your honour, tho' he can't stand, he'll *go* fast enough. He has a great deal of the rogue in him, plase your honour. He's always that way at first setting out.'
'And that wretched animal with the galled breast!'
  'He's all the better for it, when once he warms; it's he that will go with the speed of light, plase your honour.'[25]

Such conversation is not simply perverse or ridiculous, an example of the Irish bull which so intrigued the author and her father. It encapsulates one of the most characteristic styles – or, perhaps more accurately, mechanisms – of conversation attributed to the peasantry in their dealings with their social superiors or the forces of law. The distinguishing hallmark is an apparent readiness to agree with the questioner, while the answers themselves are full of equivocation and generally amount to an oblique denial of the original proposition. So, while seemingly agreeing with Glenthorn's observation that one of the horses can scarcely stand, Paddy maintains that far from being a handicap, this is a veritable advantage when it comes to galloping.

  The Irish peasant's genius for equivocation should not be dismissed as a kind of national weak-mindedness, nor regarded as part of the whimsical charm of an unsophisticated race of bog dwellers – these types of judgment are satirized in *Ennui* in the figure of Lord Craiglethorpe. A close examination of such ambiguities reveals that they constitute a series of calculated insults and defiantly individual stands against the people in power, be they landlords, agents or officers of the law. Conversation thus becomes a species of subversive warfare, often disguised as flattery or fawning, and always conducted from a defensive position. This tactic of the oppressed, of people who dare not be too forthright, who can only score indirect hits against their masters, at worst lends weight to one stereotyped view of the Irish as untrustworthy, cowardly and deceitful.

In *Ennui* Glenthorn encounters flattery and servility from his tenants who greet him with an inseparable mixture of best wishes and personal requests. His own handling of the situation is incompetent, for his indiscriminate acts of benevolence only serve to increase the number of people seeking favour. Furthermore Glenthorn is very insensitive in his would-be kindness. His attempt to re-house his nurse in a cottage built to an English design leaves the old woman feeling hopelessly strange and fails abysmally. Glenthorn is disillusioned to find that she has soon reduced her new home to the same level of dirt and damage as marked her former abode. Maria Edgeworth's point is not to mock Ellinor O'Donoghoe. Instead, like William Carleton thirty-five years later, she realized that social change among the Irish poor was possible, but could only be achieved gradually. In the twentieth century the idea of the cultural shock received by underdeveloped peoples when confronted with modern western technology and values is familiar. A hundred years ago writers such as Maria Edgeworth and William Carleton recorded an equivalent process in rural Ireland.

Despite an early antagonism towards M\u1d9cLeod, the agent, Glenthorn grows to value his advice. M\u1d9cLeod and his wife are models of diplomacy and intelligence in their dealings with the peasantry, encouraging small changes first, then using these as the basis for bigger improvements, fostering education and working to bridge sectarian differences. Clearly Maria Edgeworth favoured this approach, and there is one notable and tell-tale remark. On M\u1d9cLeod's estate Glenthorn observes, 'I almost thought myself in England', and here, as with Lady Morgan, English values and methods are implicitly upheld as providing the measure of orderliness and propriety.[26] Improvement in Ireland will involve a shift towards English standards. The perspective is again that of a colonial settler looking with longing at a more efficiently run country.

In *Ennui* Maria Edgeworth made her one attempt to write about secret societies, another popular topic in later fiction, for Glenthorn's support of the poor and of his foster brother Christy O'Donoghoe (who is the true Earl of Glenthorn) leads to a belief that he sympathizes with the 'united-men'. The author is perhaps at her weakest in attempting to describe how a group of peasants plan to kidnap Glenthorn with the intention of making him their captain in a popular insurrection. Needless to say the plan is foiled, but the reader is offered no reasons to explain why or with what justifications rebellious organizations might exist. These rebels are even tamer than Mrs Hall's Whiteboys, and placed beside Michael Banim's Croppies or some of Carleton's Ribbonmen, they have no substance whatever. Maria Edgeworth was obviously less involved with any conspiratorial groups than, say, Carleton was in his youth, but she certainly knew the violence of which the secret societies were capable and was outraged by it. Thus her difference of class, religion and background cannot fully explain her reticence on the subject, and, paradoxically, it may be that by withholding a full presentation of their viciousness she was actually showing pro-Irish sympathies.

The tale concludes when Christy O'Donoghoe, who has taken his title, recalls the narrator, who has qualified in law since handing over the estate he had formerly believed to be his own. In his new role as Lord Glenthorn Christy had reduced the estate to chaos, and therefore, when the title is voluntarily surrendered to the narrator, he is enthusiastically welcomed back by the tenants, now finally freed from his ennui and newly married to Cecilia Delamere who is, conveniently enough, heiress-at-law to the estates. Thus improbable events are contrived to justify the anglicized hero of the story as the worthiest man to manage land and property. Clearly an estate managed by the true Lord Glenthorn is a less desirable prospect than one run by the narrator, especially after he has overcome his follies and has decided to settle in Ireland. But this is unacceptable as a moral example with a general significance and illustrative of peasant incompetence in land management. Christy O'Donoghoe's fortunes are in no way representative or typical: his sudden change of role, responsibility and wealth are so total and unexpected that to blame him in any way for failure makes as little sense as to criticize the winner of enormous wealth in the pools who cannot manage his new finances prudently. Furthermore the chances of such a discovery as that made by Christy O'Donoghoe must be at least as remote as those of winning a fortune in the pools. The ending of Maria Edgeworth's next novel *The Absentee* is optimistic, but at least it is based on a more acceptable argument.

The book explores absenteeism from two points of view. First, there is the dilemma of the absentee family in England – a situation which receives little treatment in Anglo-Irish fiction. Lady Clonbrony refuses to concede that 'having the misfortune to be born in a country should tie one to it in any sort of way', whereas her husband maintains that 'if people would but, as they ought, stay in their own country, live on their own estates, and kill their own mutton, money need never be wanting'.[27] The working out of the practical consequences of these two basically conflicting attitudes provides the substance of the novel.

The familiar details of peasant hardship are complemented by a revelation of the extent to which life in London could be an expensive and disillusioning experience for the Irish gentry. Lady Clonbrony's fierce anti-Irish sentiments exacerbate her social position rather than render her more acceptable to the fashionable society she is so anxious to court and penetrate. She discovers painfully that the most sought after ladies attend her parties only to insult and snub her, and that she herself is deliberately overlooked when they are issuing the invitations. Her own vulgar desire for recognition and acceptance as an English, as opposed to an Irish, lady is seen and rejected.

Second, her social aspirations are very costly, and this shows how easily an absentee might come to depend on money provided by his agent and how, from his point of view, a good agent was one who furnished regular and substantial returns. Money is a perpetual source of anxiety to the Clonbronys. Neither Lord nor Lady Clonbrony is wicked, but they are selfish, unimaginative people and lack any appreciation of what their extravagant living implies for the peasants at home who are obliged to finance their follies. The point is all the more striking because seldom made. It is easy enough to derive a picture of villainous absentees from Anglo-Irish fiction. In truth, most of them were probably more like the Clonbronys – weak, struggling to make ends meet, genuinely unaware that others were much worse off than themselves, and petulantly exasperated by any interruption to their income.

The picture of the Clonbrony family in London is balanced

by the account of their son, Lord Colambre, travelling through Ireland, where Maria Edgeworth presents both the reader and her central character with a variety of landscapes, and establishes moral points about the links between particular types of landlord and their estates. Colambre visits three households before reaching his father's lands, and each introduces a different kind of regime, much in the way that each generation of the Rackrents sheds new light on the relationships between masters and tenants in that family.

His encounter with the Killpatricks confronts him with the folly of unnecessary extravagance. Rather like Sir Patrick Rackrent, they keep open house and anyone asserting the most tenuous relationship with the family is shown indiscriminate hospitality, but they fail to comprehend the real needs of their tenants. Colambre is invited to note – as Glenthorn did on first entering Dublin – that on every hand there is evidence of 'sumptuous and unfinished' projects. Furthermore the superficiality of the improvements made to their estate and the hypocritical humanitarianism which only seeks to reform what offends the eye are defined precisely:

Lord and Lady Killpatrick, who had lived always for the fashionable year, had taken little pains to improve the condition of their tenants: the few attempts they had made were injudicious. They had built ornamented, picturesque cottages within view of their demesne; and favourite followers of the family, people with half a century's habit of indolence and dirt, were *promoted* to these fine dwellings.[28]

The Killpatricks are less concerned with a general change in the lot of their peasants than with preserving the aesthetic harmony of the vista commanded from their own dwelling. The importation of favoured tenants to the new cottages is as misjudged and insensitive a manoeuvre as Glenthorn's imposition of a new home on Ellinor O'Donoghoe.

Colambre next meets Count O'Halloran, a new type of character in Miss Edgeworth's fiction, and a forerunner of King Corny in *Ormond*. He is, perhaps, to be taken as her equivalent to Lady Morgan's Prince of Inismore (and indeed to such later heroes as O'Donnel, Florence Macarthy or Murrogh O'Brien). Count O'Halloran represents the old, native Irish rulers, steeped in traditional lore, an antiquarian, and a landlord who has not capitulated to the pressures to leave his country. His castle is partly in ruins – again recalling Lady Morgan – 'and part repaired with great judgement and taste', and the good sense and care shown here typify the man.[29] He is overtly critical of absentees, regarding them as the true enemies of Ireland. Whereas the Prince of Inismore or King Corny may be dismissed with some justification as eccentric survivors, Count O'Halloran's links with the richness of the Irish past make him an attractive example and a potent influence on young Lord Colambre as he endeavours to discover his own country and identity. He voices hopes for mutual benefit from improved Anglo-Irish political and cultural relations, but this idea is introduced in a perfunctory way – with King Corny it is dropped altogether even as a gesture – and the author offers little explanation of how this mutual benefit is to manifest itself.

Count O'Halloran is ultimately, perhaps, more charming than believable. He lacks substance, unlike King Corny, who may be foolish, extravagant and committed to an impossible way of life but who is a character, nonetheless, who lives in the imagination. The truth of this may be measured by the change in the writing of *Ormond* which follows King Corny's early demise. Thereafter a vital element is missing. O'Halloran is a device rather than a character; King Corny is a character who also has a symbolic role. Both show the author's concern to elaborate a positive relationship between the past and the present in Ireland. This concern unites Maria Edgeworth with writers as different from her as Lady Morgan, John and Michael Banim, Gerald Griffin and William Carleton, and makes her one of the pioneer explorers of the question of nationality in Anglo-Irish fiction.

Lord and Lady Oranmore, Colambre's third host and hostess, exemplify fairmindedness and responsibility in their treatment of their tenants. They live on their estate where the improvements they have supervised are in obvious contrast to those of the Killpatricks:

Lord and Lady Oranmore showed him the neat cottages, and well-attended schools in their neighbourhood. They showed him not only what could be done, but what had been done, by the influence of great proprietors residing on their own estates, and encouraging the people by judicious kindness.[30]

The choice of the word 'judicious' is significant because the alterations made by the Killpatricks were specifically described as 'injudicious'. Here reason and conscience are actively at work and the Oranmores fulfil Maria Edgeworth's belief in the duties of landowners as well as their privileges.

As Colambre travels towards his own family's estates, he is confronted with the stark consequences of absenteeism and the harsh realization that even an agent with a conscience about his treatment of the poor cannot survive the system. Such is the case of Mr Burke, Lord Clonbrony's agent, a man of honesty and a defender of the peasants against unreasonable demands. But Mr Burke is himself answerable to Mr. Garraghty, the chief agent, who is a grasping and unscrupulous dealer. Conveniently enough, Colambre arrives at the very moment when Burke is under greatest pressure from Clonbrony to extort more money from his tenants, but Maria Edgeworth uses the situation effectively to evoke both a general picture of desolation and specific examples of personal suffering. The description of Nugent's Town, which Colambre is told was a 'snug' place before the landlord went to England, contains details of squalor and poverty that are to be found again and again in later fiction:

This *town* consisted of one row of miserable huts, sunk beneath the side of the road, the mud walls crooked in every direction; some of them opening in wide cracks, or zigzag fissures, from top to bottom, as if there had just been an earthquake – all the roofs sunk in various places – thatch off, or overgrown with grass – no chimnies, the smoke making its way through a hole in the roof, or rising in clouds from the top of the open door – dunghills before the doors, and green standing puddles – squalid children, with scarcely rags to cover them, gazing at the carriages.[31]

The degradation of the peasants themselves is most obvious in their dealings with the agents. It might be argued that if the Irish peasantry are frequently depicted as lawless, they learnt the trait in part from those appointed to manage the estates of absentee landlords. The chief agent's corruption includes a money-lending racket whereby he only accepts rents in gold coin, but simultaneously employs another man to sell the gold to the peasants for interest. In another case the agent uses his power to try and gratify his lust for an attractive girl, whose family is threatened with eviction if she does not co-operate. Such instances expose the endemic lawlessness of a system whereby the best servant was the man with least conscience about exploiting his charges for the material benefit of his master. Abuse, cynicism and rapacity were its inevitable symptoms; violence, hatred and division (often on sectarian lines) its equally inevitable products.

Curiously enough Maria Edgeworth's attempt to depict the agents at work collecting rent from the tenants is a rather pallid affair, terminated prematurely by Colambre's revelation of his true identity and his assurance of justice for all, including the offenders – a thoroughly unconvincing solution. Indeed the tone of the writing almost suggests that the author was more distressed at the thought of the agents 'throwing off their greasy hats on a damask sofa' and flicking ink onto the Wilton carpet in the presence-chamber of Clonbrony Castle than by the fraud perpetrated against the worthy Widow O'Neill.[32] At the moment of crisis and confrontation, Maria Edgeworth's art or imagination fails her. When Brian, the son of the mistreated widow, springs to her defence, his manner and language are not those of a peasant; rather they are closer to the voice of Lord Colambre; and the scene becomes progressively more operatic as his mother and fiancée appeal to the disguised stranger for help, not realizing who he is.

The episode, like the conclusion, again exposes Maria Edgeworth's uneasiness in writing about the peasantry, and Colambre's equally remote understanding is seen in the words he addresses to his mother to persuade her to return to Ireland:

Return to an unsophisticated people – to poor, but grateful hearts, still warm with the remembrance of your kindness – still blessing you for favours long since conferred – ever praying to see you once more.[33]

The irony of this, which is surely unintended, becomes obvious when the earlier descriptions of Nugent's Town and Clonbrony, reduced to desolation as a direct consequence of absenteeism, are recalled. It is no more ironic, however, than the wild enthusiasm with which the peasants welcome the Clonbronys home, as if their return in itself were a guarantee of future justice and prosperity for all. The peasants unharness the horses and draw the carriage to the house themselves in a scene described with very different implications in Gerald Griffin's story 'The Aylmers of Ballyaylmer'. Here there is no hint of resentment harboured against the absentees for the misery they have helped to create, and, of course, it must be taken on trust that Lord Clobvrony's financial incompetence and his wife's social ambitions have been left behind in

London. This requires remarkably durable optimism on the part of the reader. The truth of the matter is that whether or not the Clonbrony family return, absenteeism such as theirs had done irreparable damage to the social fabric of Irish society, a fact that is more obvious with historical hindsight than it may have been to Maria Edgeworth. This also explains why her accounts of exploitation and its effects are more persuasive than the final euphoria of Larry Brady's letter to his brother in London where he maintains that 'it's growing the fashion not to be an Absentee'.[34]

Unreal optimism also informs Lady Morgan's novel *O'Donnel* (1814), in which the author saw herself as moving openly into the arena of current political controversy. More specifically, the book was intended as a contribution to the arguments in support of Catholic emancipation. In a Preface to the 1835 edition she wrote:

O'Donnel was the first of a series of National Tales, undertaken with an humble but zealous view to the promotion of a great national cause, the emancipation of the Catholics of Ireland.[35]

The Preface to the first edition is even more revealing because Lady Morgan explains how her plan for the book changed as she became aware of the provocative nature of its originally intended content. Her initial idea was to draw 'the ground work of a story, and the character of a hero' from 'the romantic adventures and unsubdued valour of O'Donnel the Red, Chief of Tirconnel in the reign of Elizabeth'.[36] The aim was to reconcile opposing forces and opinions in Irish society, but, Lady Morgan continues,

when I fondly thought to send forth a dove bearing the olive of peace, I found I was on the point of flinging an arrow winged with discord. I *had* hoped . . . to extenuate the errors attributed to Ireland, by an exposition of their causes, drawn from historic facts; but I found that . . . in proceeding, I must raise a veil which ought never to be drawn, and should renew the memory of events, which the interests of humanity require to be for ever buried in oblivion.[37]

This statement does much to account for the peculiar awkwardness between the writer and his or her subject-matter which is a feature of so many nineteenth-century Anglo-Irish novels. When Lady Morgan elected to explore Irish history, she soon realized its potential to stir anti-English feelings. To tackle such material seriously in a novel was more than she dared, partly no doubt because of a genuine wish to heal rather than re-open old wounds, but partly also because she was business woman enough to know how far she could strain the sympathies of her English publisher and readers. This latter fact repeatedly influenced Anglo-Irish novelists and caused them to make the most unlikely concessions and adjustments in favour of the English.

O'Donnel is a case in point. The author's insight into Irish history led to the abandonment of her plan to write about the Red O'Donnel, and, in her own words, she

took up a happier view of things, advanced my story to more modern and more liberal times, and exchanged the rude chief of the days of old, for his polished descendant in a more refined age.[38]

The change of direction reveals Lady Morgan's political conservatism, more especially as her argument for Catholic emancipation is of the gentlest and most restrained kind. Indeed it amounts to little more than an appeal to English good sense, which in itself involves an unintentional irony because, almost without exception, the English are shown to be vain, inept, frivolous and irresponsible. This apparent self-contradiction is symptomatic of the division between sense and feeling in the writer, and of her wish to support the Catholics without alienating the Protestants and English.

The novel suffers from its divided purpose. It portrays the dignity, restraint, intelligence and gentlemanly breeding of Colonel O'Donnel who suffers all things without compromising his character – even to the extent of helping to disinherit his own family by providing the necessary documents to validate a rival claim to the O'Donnel lands. The hero is initially seen in his native environment where he encounters a party of travellers which includes a Mr Glentworth, who is representative of the ideal Augustan English gentleman, and a Mr Dexter, an Irishman who '*lived* by the country he *reviled*, like the wild and noxious weed that preys on the stately ruin, out of which it draws its existence'.[39] The simile is relevant: Dexter, whose anti-Irishness is reminiscent of Lady Clonbrony's, is a sycophantic adherent to Lady Singleton, an English woman based on the real Lady Cahir. He prospers by abusing his own fellow countrymen, painting them to conform to the stereotyped Anglo-Saxon image of the Irish as ignorant, rebellious, untrustworthy and contemptible, whereas O'Donnel represents the state of ruin to which the natural leaders of the Irish had been reduced by English oppression and anti-Catholic legislation.

The penal laws, which enabled one member of a Catholic family to disinherit the rest simply by conforming to the Established Church, split O'Donnel's family, like many others, and his father and uncle fought. O'Donnel's father was killed and his ancestral lands were confiscated as a result. The hero was then reared in a mountain wilderness by his great-uncle, an Abbé, and a man of fierce and violent sectarian feelings. Significantly the possible impact of such feelings on O'Donnel is ignored, for he wishes only for appeasement and the restoration of the forfeited lands.

Although he may exemplify the old adage that everything comes to him who waits, O'Donnel shows little initiative and less leadership. His humiliation when he finds he has been invited into English high society merely to be paraded by Lady Llanberis as 'a genuine Irish chief', and therefore a 'most amazingly interesting' sideshow for the idle rich, arouses sympathy for his predicament, while his honour and nobility are stressed when he defends the legal rights of the Duchess of Belmont to his own ancestral property – indeed the injustice of the legal process against Catholics seems all the greater just because he does behave with restraint.[40] The problem throughout is that O'Donnel's good sense, his culture, his understanding of how the peasants have been degraded, his awareness of how his own family and many others have been driven to seek service in foreign armies, his lack of sectarian or historical bitterness, all these virtues seem capable of expressing themselves *only* in sighs of regret. As a result his passivity and restraint appear in the long run very similar to acquiescence. He is a hero who grows in the reader's estimation because of what he does *not* do, and because in contrast with other people he is so much more admirable and scrupulous. The total effect is a circuitous demonstration that a man could be not only Irish and Catholic, but also a gentleman, and this, of course, accords with Lady Morgan's purpose of winning sympathy for her hero and people like him.

The second aim of the novel is to satirize the rich, idle gentlefolk in late-eighteenth-century high society. It is unnecessary to say much about this here other than to note that the greater part of the book is set in England, and as the author became increasingly absorbed in recounting the intrigues and inanities of Lady Llanberis's social set, with whom O'Donnel himself has nothing in common, so the first aim – to promote the cause of Catholic emancipation – tends to fade from sight.

The ending has a fairy tale quality, for the hero is retrieved from the nadir in his fortunes by an unsuspected act of conscience on the part of the Duchess of Belmont who had won his lands from him at law. Not only that, O'Donnel marries the Duchess, and thus by a brace of convenient over-simplifications he is reinstated in his ancestral properties, albeit that

he would have wished to have obtained the repossession of his rights by means more consonant to the spirit of a gentleman, the dignity of the man, and the general interests of his country.[41]

This conclusion may achieve poetic justice, but it strains credulity as much as the ending of *Ennui*.

The closing lines, in which McRory, O'Donnel's faithful servant, suggests that there is no reason why his master should not become 'a great parli'mint man', point to the way in which the author anticipated that the talented and intelligent native Irish might in time become involved again in shaping the destiny of the nation. The sentiment takes up an idea expressed earlier by O'Donnel himself when Dexter had maintained that education of the peasants would be tantamount to inciting rebellion. O'Donnel observed that it is

an odd paradox, a most irrational expectation, that a participation in the blessings of good government, and a share in the conduct of the state, should dispose any set of men the more readily to conspiracy and rebellion.[42]

The common sense of this view may seem undeniable, but the question of educating the poor, especially poor Catholics, would remain a vexed issue for some time, and the arguments against it were broadly similar to those implied here. Clearly, from the context of the passage, the author intends her readers to endorse O'Donnel's opinions rather than Dexter's, and in this at least the novel shows a liberal and progressive commitment.

Although O'Donnel is not as anachronistic a figure as the Prince of Inismore, the book still fails to articulate a coherent view of Irish nationalism. Perhaps Lady Morgan was trying to please too many people for this to be possible; perhaps while she enjoyed the feelings and emotions of nationalist fervour, she was less enthusiastic about the prospect of a self-governing Ireland; perhaps she was swayed by a mixture of these reasons, but in the end, while *O'Donnel* is not written in as breathlessly excited and headstrong a style as *The Wild Irish Girl*, there is little apparent progress in the author's intellectual dedication to Irish nationalism. Her self-confessed turning away from some of the more controversial episodes of Irish history, her continuing faith in the effectiveness of mere appeals to English good sense and fairness, and the contrived ending which gives restitution to the hero without the English having to make any concessions, indicate the limits on her willingness to argue the cause of the Irish in 1814.[43] Finally there is the failure to present a range of representatives of the Irish people in fiction. McRory, O'Donnel's servant, is a quaint combination of caricature and good sense, but apart from him, as in *The Wild Irish Girl*, the Irish peasantry are talked about in general rather than specific terms.[44] Likewise the figure of the grasping land agent – Glendinning in *The Wild Irish Girl*, Costello in *O'Donnel* – is not developed. In her next novel *Florence Macarthy* Lady Morgan moved into new areas of characterization and opened up the treatment of her themes in hitherto unexplored directions. First, however, there is Maria Edgeworth's last fictional contribution to Anglo-Irish literature.

If *Castle Rackrent* is Maria Edgeworth's greatest artistic achievement, *Ormond* (1817) is surely one of her most fascinating books. Set in the 1770s and 1780s it studies the possibilities which the author saw for Ireland, although some of these were already redundant by the time she was writing. The novel is organized around two pairs of characters from two generations and explores the similarities and differences between the four individuals and the implications of their values and ways of life. In addition, a number of other characters provide further variations on the theme and highlight strengths and defects in the behaviour of the main protagonists.

The older generation is represented on the one hand by Sir Ulick O'Shane, a pro-Union high-society political jobber and egotist, and on the other by his cousin Cornelius O'Shane (also known as King Corny), who dwells on the Black Islands and stands for the survival of the unspoilt traditions of Irish life. Sir Ulick is worldly, cynical in his attitude towards his tenants, a convert to Protestantism because of its social and financial advantages, and uninterested in the culture and history of his country; King Corny's mode of life is self-contained, self-reliant and self-complete, based on consciously maintained ways of the past and a denial of present political realities. The author defines the moral contrast between these two men in a passage which goes far to indicate why they are unable to agree with each other:

The one [Sir Ulick] living in the world, and mixing continually with men of all ranks and characters, had, by bending easily, and being all things to all men, won his courtier-way onwards and upwards to the possession of a seat in Parliament, and the prospect of a peerage. . . . The other [King Corny], inhabiting a remote island, secluded from all men but those over whom he reigned, caring for no earthly consideration, and for no human opinion but his own – had *for* himself, and *by* himself, hewed out his way to his own objects – and then rested, satisfied: 'Lord of himself, and all his (little) world his own!'[45]

The essential point here is the inadequacy of both ways of life. Sir Ulick's opportunism and indifference towards his tenants are as damaging as that of the Rackrents. This is highlighted by contrasting his behaviour as a landlord with that of his neighbour Sir Herbert Annaly. Whereas the latter banishes certain tenants of his coastal lands who earn an income and pay their rent by smuggling and deliberate ship-wrecking, Sir Ulick wilfully ignores the source of his wealth so long as it is forthcoming. Ultimately, however, he is ruined and disgraced by his own wheeling and dealing, and his estates are left in a disastrous condition.

King Corny lives among his 'subjects' and there is a reciprocal warmth and affection between ruler and people. Some of his behaviour is morally reprehensible, such as his prolonged drinking sessions and the foolish but binding marriage pledge he makes for his daughter while in a state of intoxication. More importantly, Corny's existence on the Black Islands symbolizes his limited sphere of authority and his detachment from reality. His insularity is so complete that he uses the threat of banishment to the mainland – 'the continent of Ireland' – as his key disciplinary measure against refractory tenants. This is a purely parochial way of living, in Patrick Kavanagh's sense of that term when he wrote: 'The parochial mentality . . . is never in any doubt about the social and artistic validity of his parish.'[46] The advantages of such a mentality are very real and not to be disregarded. There is a warmth of personality and humanity about Corny that no other character in Maria Edgeworth's fiction shares. These are reflected in his impulsiveness, loyalty to his friends and implacable antagonism towards his enemies, and his active delight in native tradition. But he is also a vulnerable person, and ultimately his charm does not compensate for his inadequacies. To be as uncompromising as he is should not be mistaken for a sign of strength. King Corny's absolute refusal to deal with Sir Ulick does not stem from his superior position and power, but from his innate dislike of political opportunism and from the facts of life in late-eighteenth-century Ireland. But the reader cannot fail to see that pure dislike, no matter how strong, does not alter reality, and thus Corny is a weaker person than Count O'Halloran in *The Absentee*, who was prepared to negotiate with his opponents rather than offering them simple denials.

Harry Ormond, Corny's self-appointed heir, raises a question concerning another aspect of the King's mode of life:

he began to doubt, whether it were worthy of a king, or a gentleman, to be his own shoemaker, hatter, and taylor; whether it were not better managed in society, where these things are performed by different tradesmen.[47]

Not only is it socially compromising for a nobleman to do all these tasks, but, more importantly, it breeds incompetence and inefficiency; the possibilities of a society are severely limited if there is no room for division of labour. Corny's death is the author's final comment on this point, for he perishes in a shooting accident when a gun of his own making explodes in his face.

Maria Edgeworth may have sympathized with King Corny in her heart, but she knew in her head that his way of life held no future for his people. Sir Ulick's political and financial immorality were clearly abhorrent to her, but King Corny is defending an outpost which has no base to supply or reinforce it. This is where Ormond himself fits into the story, for he is a kind of child of nature who is influenced by both these men at different stages in his youth, and who grows to see the limitations of each. Furthermore, he is contrasted with Marcus O'Shane, Sir Ulick's son, who inherits his father's meanness and egotism, but lacks his style and flamboyance. Sir Ulick and King Corny reject each other, and their inability to agree is the inability of the modernist and the traditionalist to join forces and produce a set of values which transcend the significance of those held by either of the individuals. In this sense Ormond is held up as the hope for the future, since he embodies the moral strength of King Corny with at least some of the worldly wisdom of Sir Ulick, and, in the end, he is a less selfish person than either of his guardians. But even this solution has its flaws, as will be seen.

In addition to Sir Ulick and King Corny, Ormond has significant encounters with a number of other characters with different kinds of experience. His first insight into the wider world comes when he meets Black Connal, the destined husband of Corny's daughter, who has served in the Irish Brigade and lived in Paris – thus illustrating another of the courses of action open to disinherited Irish gentlemen. Ormond finds his sophistication, worldly manner and morality hard to accept, but at the same time curiously fascinating. Black Connal's amusement at Ormond's priggishness is perhaps also intended to indicate the latter's limited experience and his accordingly intolerant idealism. On the other hand, when Ormond himself goes to France and mixes freely in Parisian society, his puritanical streak enables him to exercise self-discipline in potentially tempting and compromising situations. His experiences there mature him, convince him of the rectitude of his principles, and assure him of the depth of his affection for his own country and people, particularly its women. The structure of the novel – allowing Ormond to travel abroad, define his values and make his choices against a background of wider knowledge and experience – is a successful and unusual pattern for an Anglo-Irish novelist to follow, reversing the more familiar formula whereby an absentee or exile returns to Ireland and decides to stay.

Another beneficial influence on Ormond's development is his friendship with the Annaly family. Sir Herbert Annaly is a model landlord, whose attitudes contrast with those of Sir Ulick, King Corny and Marcus O'Shane. His strictness in evicting tenants guilty of smuggling and shipwrecking has been mentioned, but this must be balanced by adding that he gives incentives to his worthy tenants, and provides opportunities of employment for them in building a lighthouse and in manufacturing sailcloth. Above all his way of dealing with his people is emphasized:

Sir Herbert governed neither by threats, punishments, abuse, nor tyranny; nor yet did he govern by promises nor bribery, *favour* and *protection*, like Sir Ulick. – He neither cajoled nor bullied – neither held it as a principle, as Marcus did, that the people must be kept down, nor that the people must be deceived. . . . He treated them as reasonable beings, and as his fellow-creatures, whom he wished to improve, that he might make them and himself happy.[48]

This is perhaps Maria Edgeworth's fullest attempt to suggest the mixture of authority and tolerance, sympathy and firmness, mutual respect and fairness which she believed necessary to ensure a fruitful and contented estate.

A key feature of Sir Herbert's policy is his readiness to communicate with and his availability to his tenants, whereas Sir Ulick O'Shane simply ignores what he does not choose to see, makes promises which are never kept, and helps his people only in the dubious way of showing them loopholes in acts of Parliament. The result is that his tenants have a low respect for the law, and his own popularity is worthless because his susceptibility to flattery and bribery is generally known.

Having grown to manhood amidst these varied personalities and standards, and having experienced life in a wider sense during his visit to the continent, Ormond is offered the chance to purchase both Sir Ulick's estate and the Black Islands. His decision in favour of the Black Islands is crucial, as are his reasons for making it:

He should hurt no-one's feelings by this purchase – and he might do a great deal of good, by carrying on his old friend's improvements, and by further civilizing the people of the Islands, all of whom were warmly attached to him. They considered prince Harry as the lawful representative of their dear King Corny, and actually offered up prayers for his coming to reign over them.[49]

This ending ignores the example which Ormond learnt from Sir Herbert: it is the easier course of action because the people are already orderly and loyal, and it is a retreat from the present and future into a backwater of time and history. If Corny's régime was eccentric, Ormond's is certain to be still more so, and he is unlikely to inherit the moral authority which enabled his predecessor to hold his small community together because he is so alien from it in his feelings and responses.

The reader is left with the gnawing anxiety that the moral education of the hero which the novel documents is thrown away and wasted by his decision to opt for the Black Islands. Ormond's choice may well reflect the author's own growing pessimism. On the other hand, there is a renewed attempt to suggest that the way forward is through a unity of English practicality and morality and the warmth and humanity of the Gaelic past. Once again the isolation of Ormond's position weakens this idea. Ironically, in the novel which explores the Irish situation most comprehensively and in the most varied way, Maria Edgeworth's conclusion is particularly inadequate, lacking both the sombre realism of *Castle Rackrent* and the heady optimism of *Ennui* and *The Absentee*. The tensions at the end of *Ormond* are greater than in any of the previous books, for the author's two dominant driving forces – her practical awareness of reality and her desire to offer a morally improving example – are uneasily locked together. Although she lived until 1849 and would see sights and changes both social and political, which would alter Irish life more profoundly than anything that had taken place between her birth in 1767 and 1817 when *Ormond* was published, this was to be her last significant contribution to Anglo-Irish literature. As the nineteenth century advanced, Maria Edgeworth, who was so essentially a product of the late eighteenth century, felt herself increasingly remote from events she could not understand and was unable to act as their spokeswoman. Thus her long silence was maintained. Meanwhile Lady Morgan was developing a new depth of awareness of Irish society and its problems in her next book.

Complex plots are a regular feature of nineteenth-century Anglo-Irish fiction, and *Florence Macarthy* is a typical example. Here disguise, deception, mistaken identity and numerous red herrings all serve to reflect the intricate and often confusing fates of many of the old Irish families and their great estates. This theme was obviously present in *The Wild Irish Girl* and *O'Donnel*, but in *Florence Macarthy* and then again in *The O'Briens and the O'Flahertys* it is taken to new limits.

Throughout *Florence Macarthy* there is a remarkable change of emphasis in the information with which the author confronts the reader. Not only is Irish life more closely observed, but there is also an impressive concern to relate effects to their causes. Early on one of the characters establishes the case the writer intends to convey when he says: 'The mind starts beyond the mere impulse of sympathy here; it rushes at once from the *effect* to the cause.'[50] This comment arises from a view of the appalling living conditions of the poor in Ringsend, many of whom are forced to solicit charity from travellers arriving on the Holyhead packet boat. A complementary account of one of the men waiting by the docks in hope of chance employment as porters to the passengers illustrates the new seriousness of Lady Morgan's endeavour to face the behaviour and social conditions of the common people, and to show them as the victims of bad government:

Miserably clad, disgustingly filthy, squalid, meagre, and famished, the practitioner for employment had yet humour in his eye, and observation in his countenance. Occasionally ready to assist, and always prompt to flatter, he did neither gratuitously. Taunt and invective seemed the natural expression of his habit; for though debasingly acquiescent to a destiny, which left him without motive for industry, in a country where industry is no refuge from distress, he yet preserved the vindictiveness of conscious degradation; and there was frequently a deep-seated sincerity in his curse, which was sometimes wanting to his purchased benediction.[51]

The deliberate method by which the man's manner and speech are interpreted as the effects of oppression, degradation and failed opportunity is new and radical. There is a concerted effort to pass beyond either simple revulsion at his external appearance and hardened behaviour, or a mere dismissal of him as a creature undeserving of attention. His condition is recognized to be as much the result of a spiritual malaise as of hunger and unemployment. The ambiguity of his apparent cynicism conceals a profound desire for improvement, while his enforced passivity obscures a violent potential.

No longer is Lady Morgan's social commentary presented in footnotes or as authorial intrusion: the citizens of post-Union Dublin express their own disillusionment. As they enter College Green the porter tells his employers: 'That's the ould parliament-house, Sir. Why, then there was *grate* work going on there *oncet*, quiet and aisy as it stands now, the cratur!', and the effects of the Union he calls the 'murther' of Ireland.[52]

The tradesman's point of view is given in the reported words of a Dublin optician, who says:

The effect of the Union is to ruin Ireland: since that epoch her debt has increased, her resources diminished, her taxes augmented, her manufactures languishing, her gentry self-exiled, her peasantry turbulent from distress, and her tradesmen, like myself, drained to the last farthing, and sighing to remove to that country, where they will not be obliged to pay a large rent to the government, for leave to live; to America.[53]

Thus the reader begins to appreciate the economic, social and political realities of the Act of Union for all classes of people in Ireland, rather than simply for Princes and disinherited Colonels. Nor is this all. Lady Morgan directs attention to significant details which document the government-encouraged bigotry and official terrorism. For example there is the statue in Dublin of William III, decked in orange and blue ribbons as a calculated insult to Catholics, and, as the porter knows, the kind of socially divisive gesture upon which the ruling powers depend. On a more sinister note, the postillion on the coach taken by the gentlemen observes that a traveller in the Dublin mountains might come across barrack after barrack, and 'never get sight of inn, or house, man or baste, only sogers, Sir'.[54] Then at Naas the travellers see a croppy's head spiked outside the gaol and left to announce 'triumph to one party and subjection to another'.[55] These points combine to provide a comprehensive geography of political oppression and social humiliation.

The former romantic view of forelock-touching peasants, whose misery – if noted at all – was rapidly minimized, is almost gone. Lady Morgan shows a keen understanding of the psychological effects of brutality, systematic deprivation and defeat. One character, observing a peasant labourer, notes how 'the quick intelligence of his careless glances mingled with the lurking shyness of distrust, – the instinctive self-defence of conscious degradation'.[56] The details of the children's malnutrition and the social consequences of separation to the family mentioned also by Maria Edgeworth in *The Absentee*, when the father goes to England for the harvest season, are harsh facts faced squarely for the first time.

The joy and merriment traditionally presented as characteristic of the Irish peasants' way of life are missing. Indeed the elderly Mr Daly is able to cast his mind back over thirty years and to describe the destruction of native culture. He relates how

Wakes and fairs, patterns, and Sunday evening cake, are almost wholly laid aside: these, and the hurling matches, that noble, athletic, and national sport, are quite gone by: and of the troops of pipers and harpers that used to perform daily in their villages, or resort to the houses of the gentry, where welcome entertainment and ample remuneration awaited them, there scarce remain any of the order. . . . It warms one's old blood . . . to think of the native energy, force, and spirit of the genuine Irish character; and it chills it . . . when one thinks upon the means which must have been employed within the last thirty years to weaken and turn it from its natural bias.[57]

This is not a simple or sentimental longing for the good old days: the tone of loss and deprivation is unmistakable, and the author's awareness of the many facets of that loss, from the small social custom to the fullest expression of national identity through music and sport, is impressive. She shows here an eye for a kind of detail which is not to be discovered in Maria Edgeworth's writing.

Nowadays it is acknowledged that victims of a natural disaster or of a prolonged period of extreme harassment and stress are prone to fall into a state of deep apathy and depression which is difficult to relieve. Fitzwalter, the hero of the novel, perceives just such a look in the Irish peasants:

There is a mixture of indolence and laboriousness in these miserable people that is singular, they have neither the activity of savages nor the industry of civilization. They want energy for the one, and motive for the other.[58]

The sober realism of this comment and its practical implications help to expose the hopelessness of the optimism which saw the solution to Ireland's problems in terms of the return of absentee landlords and marriages between English and Irish gentlefolk.

Even Lady Morgan's abiding delight in dramatic landscapes is redirected and assumes new significance. The inevitable ruins she describes are now said to be 'desolated and deserted', and this is consistent with the fate of many of the great estates following the departure of their former owners. The new men of power, the agents, whose petty tyranny is endorsed by the cynicism and indifference of their masters and of government, are typified and convincingly portrayed in the aptly named Crawley family.

Their characters and behaviour are explored with a thoroughness that is new in Anglo-Irish fiction, and which makes them worthy forerunners of Carleton's monster of greed and power, Valentine McClutchy. Their sectarianism is reflected in the 'New-Town Mount Crawley supplementary auxiliary yeomanry legion', which they organize and run to inflate their leader's pretensions and to provoke deliberately the feelings of their Catholic neighbours. These troops, described as a 'little image of local power, and petty ascendancy', are raised and clothed at the expense of the country, while the very existence of the Crawleys in positions of power is connected directly to the aftermath of the 1798 uprising.[59]

There are three leading members of this family of opportunists: Darby Crawley, the agent, who deceives the landlord by his misrepresentations of the state of the country and who administers local justice according to the rules of sectarianism, favouritism and financial corruption; Major Thaddeus Crawley, a 'handsome, good-humoured, vulgar and self-sufficient' dasher; and Conway Townsend Crawley, a bitter caricature of Lady Morgan's longstanding critic and implacable enemy, John Wilson Croker. This triumvirate operates a network of total power over the people in the area, the effects of which are highlighted in a number of ways.

For example, they engineer an alleged conspiracy led by one Padreen Gar against two of the visiting ladies, partly out of spite because he rescued the women when their coach ran out of control while they were travelling with the Crawleys on an electioneering visit to a forty-shilling freeholder. The incident reveals the petty spitefulness of the Crawley family: their lawlessness hides behind a facade of supposed loyalty to crown and parliament. Furthermore, the farce of an electoral procedure based on the votes of forty-shilling freeholders is exposed in the portrait of the family visited by Lady Dunore and Lady Georgina: the man wore clothes which

were a patchwork of every colour. His worn-out brogues were stuffed with straw. His beard half an inch in length; his long black hair clotted and over-shadowing his eyes, indicated the neglect of hopelessness and irremediable poverty. . . . Such in general is . . . the Irish forty-shilling freeholder; a class which is daily multiplied, to the ruin of agriculture and the misery of the population, according to the exigencies and interests of intriguing landlords.[60]

The corruption of the system derived from the way in which it could be manipulated at will, so that a 'loyal' electorate could be created as required to comply with the parliamentary aspirations of a designing absentee candidate. This was also the system which O'Connell learnt how to harness to his own advantage in the 1820s.

Finally, the alleged conspiracy by Padreen Gar leads to his appearance before two judges whose personal philosophies and attitudes towards the administration of justice provide a striking contrast. One, Baron Boulter, is the champion of the Protestant Ascendancy and defender of the landed gentry, concerned only to maintain the status quo and not to understand or question its inequity; the other, Judge Aubrey, is committed to the disenfranchised and expropriated poor and is ready to relate their rebellious behaviour, regrettable as he regards it to be, to the sources of their dissatisfaction. The fact that Judge Aubrey regards Ireland as 'his object' introduces a key nationalist concept of one's country as one's vocation, a concept which recurs in the case of Murrogh O'Brien in *The O'Briens and the O'Flahertys*.

Padreen Gar's clash with the Crawleys illustrates Lady Morgan's maturing insight into the complex relationships between landlords, agents, peasants and legal officials, and shows her positive response to the daunting intricacies of the current political and cultural situation. The problem is that while she carefully relates the rise of the Crawleys and the decline of the country and of government to the after-effects of the 1798 Rebellion and the Act of Union, and while she links this moral point with a renewed appeal for good and responsible resident landlords, her account of existing hardship is much more convincing than her prescriptions for improvement. She introduces the idea that a necessary stage in changing the standards of living of the Irish poor must be to increase their expectations and aspirations, and this potentially revolutionary proposal is directly related to the degree of humiliation and hopelessness felt by the peasants. Although she shies from suggesting any kind of agitation or education to raise the level of political consciousness – her views on O'Connell are recorded below – practical plans of aid are formulated in the novel by Lady Cloncare for her tenants. These plans, the very modesty and caution of which further testify to Lady Morgan's expanding sense of the complexity of Irish social problems, are based upon limited initial objectives – for instance, persuading people to eat bacon as well as potatoes, or to wear shoes rather than always going barefoot. As Lady Cloncare says:

A few insulated examples of well-meaning individuals are not sufficient to effect a very general reformation, which will not take place till artificial wants become as pressing as the natural ones.[61]

Thus, while admitting both the value and the inadequacy of such genteel liberalism, Lady Morgan is unwilling or unable – or both – to carry her argument a stage further and anticipate how widescale reform might be achieved. It would be unfair, however, to ignore the realistic and perceptive admission that individual gestures of liberalism alone are unlikely to be enough to solve Irish grievances.

The most successfully created native Irish character in *Florence Macarthy* is a truly new addition to Lady Morgan's fiction. In Terence Oge O'Leary, fosterer, seanachee, and hedge-schoolmaster, the author drew a convincing figure who exudes a vitality through his language and personal eccentricity which far exceeds that of the priest in *The Wild Irish Girl* or MᶜRory in *O'Donnel*. While his cultural role gives him kinship with King Corny, his wonderfully captured conversational style brings him closest of all to Thady Quirk. O'Leary is the living link between an older way of life and a heritage that was already disappearing and the harshness of the nineteenth century. As a schoolmaster he is a genuine forerunner of Carleton's Pat Frayne, rich in absurdly pedantic knowledge and half-knowledge, violent towards his pupils, blindly obsessed with his commitments to the Macarthy More family, dangerously prejudiced in his affections, unable to discriminate between past history and present reality, overfond of his drink, but supremely irresistible in his conversation:

Them's my first class, plaze your honor: sorrow one of them gassoons, but would throw you off a page of Homer into Irish while he'd be clamping a turf stack. – Come forward here, Padreen Mahoney, you little mitcher, ye. Have ye no better courtesy than that, Padreen? Fie upon your manners. Then for all that, Sir, he's my head philosopher, and am getting him up for Maynooth. Och! then I wouldn't axe better than to pit him against the provost of Trinity College this day, for all his ould small cloathes, Sir, the cratur! troth, he'd puzzle him, great as he is, aye, and bate him too; that's at the humanities, Sir.[62]

It is a pity that O'Leary has only a small part in the novel, for not only is he an entertaining figure, but he also typifies a peculiar breed of man whose influence among the aspiring poor in the Irish countryside should not be forgotten. Carleton's accounts of hedge-schools are fuller and more complete, but O'Leary's inclusion in *Florence Macarthy* is another sign of Lady Morgan's widening vision.

In examining this novel the emphasis has been on the ways in which it differs from its predecessors, in order to show Lady Morgan's deepening relationship with her primary subject-matter, Ireland and the Irish. But *Florence Macarthy* deals mainly with the nobility — be they Irish or English — and with the restitution of old wrongs against an Irish heir, and in these respects it is consistent with the earlier books, as it is also in its assumption that the nobility are the natural leaders of the people and have only to be recognized as such by the general population for support to follow automatically. Thomas Flanagan has written that this was 'the first literary work of the nineteenth century to set forward the passions and the ultimate commitments of those members of the Ascendancy who espoused the nationalist movement'; but, as he points out, Lady Morgan — and later Yeats — was to be proved wrong in her conviction that the peasants would be roused to recognize and follow their noble masters.[63]

Although *Florence Macarthy* was the last Anglo-Irish novel of importance to be published before 1825, when the tales of the Banim brothers came before the public eye, this quarter of the nineteenth century also belongs to Charles Maturin. He was born in Dublin in 1782, the son of a well-to-do government official with French Protestant origins, went to Trinity College when he was fifteen — an experience to which he referred critically several times in his fiction —, married at the age of twenty, and entered the Established Church where he acquired a high reputation for his preaching and pastoral care. Maturin's religious vocation was at odds with his literary aspirations, and his eccentric behaviour, extravagant style of dress and the unconventional morality of some of the characters in his books emphasize the paradoxes in his life.

In 1808, prompted by the success of *The Wild Irish Girl*, Maturin published *The Wild Irish Boy*. The close similarity of the titles was intended to appeal to the audience Lady Morgan had captured, and in some measure the plot resembles that of the earlier work. In particular Maturin set out to exploit Lady Morgan's discovery that a regional novel based on Ireland could be developed in the style of Gothic romances; that the formula of bringing a sophisticated, reluctant and bored stranger into a romantic Irish setting and then permitting a love affair with a native to develop provided the basis for a good plot; and that an Irish chieftain and his chaplain could be used to convey semi-anthropological lore about the country.[64] Although he used these aspects of *The Wild Irish Girl*, Maturin's novel is not simply an act of plagiarism and, especially as the action develops and abandons the epistolary form, the author's individual views of events and values assert themselves.

The hero Ormsby Bethel, the illegitimate son of 'an enervated libertine', does not meet his parents or encounter his native background until he is an adult. Reared in England by various guardians, he passes a particularly formative period of his life in the Lake District where, inspired by the landscape, he dreams of

some fortunate spot, some abode peopled by fair forms, human in their affections, their habits, in everything but vice and weakness. . . . I resolved that they should be such as held a latent affinity with virtue, or could be easily reconciled to it by legislative discipline and cultivation. I therefore imagined them possessed of the most shining qualities that can enter into the human character, glowing with untaught affections, and luxuriant with uncultivated virtue; but proud, irritable, impetuous, indolent, and superstitious; conscious of claims they knew not how to support, burning with excellencies, which, because they wanted regulation, wanted both dignity and utility; and disgraced by crimes which the moment after their commission they lamented. . . .[65]

His guardian obligingly tells him that this is a vision of Ireland and the Irish people, and Bethel imagines himself becoming their legislator and benefactor. H. W. Piper and A. Norman Jeffares have shown that the influence of Wordsworth's romanticism on Maturin distinguishes his nationalism from that of Maria Edgeworth and Lady Morgan, so it is fitting that Bethel's vision of Ireland should occur in Cumberland. Notably, too, he not only contemplates the innate, if untutored, virtues of the Irish, but also implies that they may be brought to realize their potential under the guiding hand of Anglo-Irish gentlemen, such as himself, rather than by subjection to English authority. Maturin never argues in favour of Irish independence – indeed in *The Milesian Chief*, Connal O'Morven, the rebel leader, actually acknowledges the futility of his cause – but in Piper's and Jeffares' words he wanted to impress the rulers of England with the reliability of the Anglo-Irish and their ability to run Ireland, however much he disapproved of their apparent desertion of it after the Union.[66]

Ironically Ormsby Bethel's claim to be a ruler is severely compromised by his temperamental instability and absurd behaviour, both of which are accentuated by the confusions of the plot.

Summoned to Ireland by his father, Bethel attends the University of Dublin for a limited period before travelling west to his father's estates where he is exposed to contrasting influences: his father is unhealthy, cynical, arrogant, and as extravagant as his diminishing resources permit; whereas his rich and childless Milesian uncle is a man of 'wild and original dignity', 'lofty with unborrowed grandeur and habitual command', pious and moderate in his way of life, cultured and widely travelled, disappointed in love.[67] Bethel is confronted with the squalor, disorder, moral laxity and waste which characterize the lives of most of the landlords in the area, one household even being described as 'a castle-rackrent'.

Into this scene arrive Lord and Lady Montrevor, obliged to seek refuge on their Irish estates after a scandal in England, bringing with them a reputation for glamour, extravagance and riotous living. Ormsby Bethel's entanglement in their affairs, his consuming and frustrated passion for Lady Montrevor – 'a veteran woman of fashion' – and his eventual marriage to her daughter, undertaken mainly in the hope of enjoying a less compromising intimacy with his mother-in-law, form the basis of the plot. Overawed by the Montrevors and flattered by their attention to him, he not only discovers the cold cynicism of their heady social life and the deadness of their marriage, but is humiliated in their presence when the governess employed by his father to educate Sybilla, his sister, is revealed to be his own mother. Thus Bethel, the child of hedonism and immorality, becomes drawn into its snares in his own turn. Part of Maturin's aim in *The Wild Irish Boy* was to expose the vices and callousness of English fashionable society as opposed to Irish purity represented by the Milesian chief and Mr Corbett, an earnest clergyman who conveniently stimulates the consciences of the hero and Lady Montrevor on a number of critical occasions. This contrast is unsatisfactorily developed with the result that, as E. F. Bleiler has observed, Maturin has been accused of immorality in his work.[68]

The intricate plot and the long emotional outpourings of the principal characters obscure the exploration of the differences between the Irish and English people, and only intermittently does the issue resume a central place. One such incident follows Bethel's return to Dublin, where he mixes with the financially straitened but lavishly pleasure-loving professional classes. He contrasts the sobriety, reserve and selfishness of the English with the passion, spontaneity and social charms of the Irish, laments the limited mental horizons of his fellow countrymen, their desultory attempts to educate themselves or improve their lot, and their haphazard way of life; but he concludes that 'with all their errors, the Irish are an amiable people, and will yet be a great one.'[69] This belief in Irish amiability does not prevent Bethel, and Maturin, from revealing less desirable traits of character. In particular the peasantry appear to be irresponsible and blundering; De Lacy, Bethel's uncle, is cheated of money by his own foster brother and steward; and Lady Montrevor complains that Ireland offers no scope to men of talent because 'a kind of mental absenteeism pervades this country'.[70] Above all, after Bethel has gone to England where he is almost destroyed by the life of feckless dissipation and sexual intrigue, he vents his anger on the 'renegade nobility' and 'unnational gentry' who have deserted and exploited their country. He also criticizes the indifference of English government ministers towards Irish interests and speaks of the Act of Union as a 'fatal measure' which destroyed the economy, encouraged absenteeism and removed all status from Dublin without even providing the promised benefits of equal trading rights or internal security; but his real venom is reserved for Catholicism, which he accuses of seeking to subvert law and order, of destroying national culture and of resisting any system of secular education.

The passion and sincerity of Bethel's attack are in contrast to the aloof hostility with which it is received and are a further measure of how his basic virtue has remained uncorrupted, unlike that of his cynical table companions. As E. F. Bleiler remarks, although the hero is sexually compromised, he retains his innocence in the vicious power struggles that beset English high society.[71] Bethel, unlike almost everyone else, is honest, unsuspecting and essentially decent. He is also fortunate enough to have a wife who can see the folly and self-destructiveness of his London life, and the need for him to extricate himself from it and return to Ireland.

The Wild Irish Boy is neither a good nor a successful novel, and it did not even earn the financial rewards its author had expected. The plot is inadequately organized and Maturin's purpose is confused because the endless romantic intrigues of the hero and his sporadic nationalist fervour and wish to see an improvement in the lot of his countrymen are not reconciled.

In *The Milesian Chief* (1812) Maturin justified his choice of an Irish setting in a most unusual way. Dedicating his book to the reviewers who had received his earlier work with antagonism, he declares that his talent is for 'painting life in extremes, and representing those struggles of passion when the soul trembles on the verge of the unlawful and the unhallowed'. He then continues:

I have chosen my own country for the scene, because I believe it the only country on earth, where, from the strange existing opposition of religion, politics, and manners, the extremes of refinement and barbarism are united, and the most wild and incredible situations of romantic story are hourly passing before modern eyes.[72]

The plot does indeed abound in incredible situations, romance, passion, refinement and barbarism. More significantly, the opposition and contrast between Irish virtue and nobility, as embodied in the hero Connal O'Morven, and English cynicism and cold selfishness in the person of the army officer Wandesford, are clearly developed as the two men contend with each other for the love of Armida Montclare, the rich, proud and well-educated heroine of half-Italian origins. Here Maturin achieved the unity of themes which eluded him in *The Wild Irish Boy*.

Armida is a reluctant visitor to her father's Irish estate which had been purchased from a 'ruined Milesian family', but soon after her arrival she is moved by the landscape on the rugged Atlantic seaboard, and Maturin's belief in the impact of nature on human feelings and thought reappears:

the effect of such a scene was like that of a new world. She shuddered at the idea of becoming the inhabitant of such a country; and she thought she felt already the wild transforming effect of its scenery.[73]

The solitude of the place enables Armida to discover certain truths about herself and her real feelings: she realizes that she is indifferent to Wandesford, whereas her imagination is fired by her encounters with the 'proud savage' who rescues her from a variety of hazardous situations and refuses her offer of a financial reward. Connal O'Morven is an idealized figure, romantically attired and loftily refusing to have any truck with the Montclares, whom he regards as usurpers. He is alienated from his father, who is prepared to work as their agent, and has an uneasy relationship with his brother, a soldier of the crown. Connal's purity is thrown into relief by his dealings with Wandesford, because as the plot unfolds he is found to have accepted responsibility for the care of the Englishman's discarded mistress and child, rescued him from death several times and mistakenly trusted in his honour. He is a defender of the Irish language and music and is steeped in native culture. When Wandesford sneers at Irish boasts of a glorious past, Connal subdues him forcefully, and Armida is surprised by her feelings for this 'savage . . . native' of the 'abhorred country' where she believes she has been 'buried'.[74]

Maturin faced a dilemma when Connal O'Morven becomes the leader of an uprising against the government, because he wished to preserve his hero's unsullied reputation, and yet he could not condone armed revolt. The problem is resolved in an ingenious, though improbable, way when Connal explains to Armida that he is a victim of circumstances rather than a creator of trouble. He was formatively influenced by his grandfather, with whom he lived after his father's acceptance of service with the Montclares, a man of implacable pride

fierce from want, and intoxicated by solitary grandeur, and the loyal homage of his remaining followers, [who] shut himself up in the old tower on his ancient demesne, and listened to the tales of his bards and the songs of his harpers, who told him he was the sovereign of the western isles.[75]

This character, obviously a successor to the Prince of Inismore, instilled his delusions of grandeur into the young Connal – 'the child of mist and storm, of wandering and loneliness, of pride and melancholy' – until he believed in their reality and dedicated himself to their realization by leading a rebellion.[76] Connal then claims that with maturity he saw the practical impossibility of Irish independence, but since he could find no way to leave the rebel movement without apparently betraying his comrades, he resolved to lead them to destruction – until his meeting with Armida finally prompted him to break free. Even as he was addressing his men, Wandesford arrived and, having pretended to accept that

the rebels were disbanding, he treacherously returns to attack
them, thus forcing Connal to retaliate. In this way the hero
becomes involved in armed insurrection while yet retaining
his moral credibility and purity. Maturin makes no attempt to
idealize the rebel peasants who are ill-disciplined and untrustworthy. They fail to obey Connal's orders and his self-
chosen bodyguard for Armida attempts to rape her in his
leader's absence, and then plots to assume command himself. These peasants are shown to be wholly unsuitable as
revolutionary troops; nor are they credited with all manner of
virtues simply because of their humble origins. In the words of
H. W. Piper and A. Norman Jeffares: 'Maturin was not only a
post-revolutionary romantic, he was a post-'98-rebellion, post-
Robert-Emmet-rebellion romantic'; and *The Milesian Chief*
clearly establishes the lessons that he had learnt from recent
history.[77] The failure of Connal O'Morven and his fellow
rebels is a foregone conclusion, and their futile retreat to an
island from which they hope to emigrate *en masse* to America
is symbolic of their lost cause. It is paralleled by the private
misfortunes of the hero and heroine in their blighted love
relationship, so that both the personal and social themes of the
novel draw to an unhappy end.

Maturin's third work with a specifically Irish background,
Women (1818), explores the turmoil in the lives of Charles de
Courcy, a young orphan heir, and the two women with whom
he becomes involved. Eva Wentworth is young, inexperienced,
simple and innocent; above all, she is the victim of a rigid
Calvinist upbringing in her uncle's household, and one of the
most striking aspects of the novel is its successful critical
exposure of this kind of religious fanaticism. Her rival – who
ultimately turns out to be her long-lost mother – is a singer
known as Madame Zaira Dalmatiani; she is glamorous,
sexually enticing, worldly wise and highly educated. De
Courcy is torn by his feelings for the two sharply contrasting
women, and they, in turn, are equally tormented by his
fluctuating commitments to them. The book charts these
relationships, and although Maturin takes opportunities to
satirize the inanities of society life in Dublin and to lament the
sorry changes there since the Act of Union, it remains
essentially 'a study of inner life'.[78]

In his other fiction, including *Melmoth the Wanderer*,
Ireland and the Irish figure less prominently, and Maturin's
contribution to Anglo-Irish literature rests mainly on these

three books. He is a difficult figure to place, influenced by Lady Morgan, Wordsworth's romanticism and Gothic horror stories. His plots range from the ramshackle structure of *The Wild Irish Boy* to the astonishing ingenuity of *Melmoth*, while his leading characters are extravagant, passionate and melodramatic in their behaviour. The relationships he depicts are repeatedly promiscuous, amoral and emotionally self-indulgent, and the feelings of his females in particular are explored in ways that are unique in early Anglo-Irish fiction. At times he is clumsy and now seems unfashionably given to maudlin sentimentality, but he ventures to write about areas of experience which were not usually mentioned in a less permissive age.

Maturin's nationalism emerges through his portrayal of the relationships of his characters rather than being a subject in its own right, as for example it was for Lady Morgan, and in this respect *The Milesian Chief* is his most revealing book. Thus, although prompted to begin writing fiction by the particular success of one of his contemporaries, Maturin's work was shaped by a variety of sources and coloured by his highly individual imagination. He has no clear descendant, with the possible exception of Sheridan Le Fanu, who shares something of his eccentric originality and his preoccupation with abnormal and grotesque relationships. In the main his brief career must be regarded as one of the curious offshoots of the Anglo-Irish novel rather than as central to the growth of the genre.

The fiction of these twenty-five years discloses a number of related points. Written in the aftermath of the disastrous uprising of 1798 and concurrently with the dissolution of the Irish parliament, almost at once it became committed fiction – a moral and imaginative weapon for protesting against the sufferings caused by absentee landlords and the unenviable position of Irish Catholics. *Castle Rackrent*, the masterpiece of this period, is also the least overtly propagandist work. The conjunction of these two facts is more than coincidence, because in other novels the commitment of Maria Edgeworth, Lady Morgan and, in some measure, Charles Maturin (and of their successors) to various aspects of the Irish cause repeatedly compromises their artistic achievements.

Maria Edgeworth was thirty-three, Lady Morgan was about twenty-four (the exact date of her birth is uncertain), and Charles Maturin was eighteen in 1800. Although both women

lived to see the consequences of the great famine – Maturin died
in 1824 – the events of these early years shaped all three writers'
understanding of Irish history and the Irish people. In a sense their
work is a reaction to the abortive rebellion and to the loss of the
Irish parliament which led to so much absenteeism. Lady Morgan
wrote fulsomely of the period of Grattan's parliament when 'the
light of national genius concentrated its long-scattered rays to a
point', and 'Public Spirit fell like a dew in the desert upon the
renovating nation'.[79] But she is equally decided in her views of
1798 and the Act of Union which 'at once converted a local disease
into a national pestilence' by causing absenteeism to increase
dramatically, with the result that 'a new race of vulgar upstarts,
of uneducated and capricious despots' usurped the place of
the gentry, a view shared by Maturin.[80] These 'upstarts', the
Crawleys of *Florence Macarthy*, could only rule by dividing the
people, and thus by activating 'the religious question and the
question between landlords and tenants, which are the hinges on
which all the misfortunes of Ireland turn'.[81] Perhaps the greatest
hope of Maria Edgeworth and Lady Morgan was that their novels
might have some effect in reversing the drift of the old landlords
away from Ireland. As it became increasingly obvious that most
of them would not return, and that reform would inevitably come
about in a different way, they lapsed into silence.

Daniel O'Connell was anathema to them both, and again,
characteristically, Lady Morgan voiced her reactions more
forcefully. In 1826 she wrote in her diary:

O'Connell wants back the days of Brian Boru, himself to be the King, with
a crown of emerald shamrocks, a train of yellow velvet, and a mantle of
Irish tabinet, a sceptre in one hand and a cross in the other, and the people
crying 'Long live King O'Connell'.[82]

The contemptuous tone of this entry is followed by a note of real
fear as it seemed to her that O'Connell's fortunes were rising ever
higher, and in 1831 she wrote to Thomas Moore that 'peace or war
(*civil war and extending woes*) now lies in the influence of
O'Connell over the passions of the people'.[83] The future for
Ireland, as far as Lady Morgan could see it, was 'between Bedlam
and a jail'.[84] For her part Maria Edgeworth wrote in a family
letter:

It is impossible to draw Ireland as she now is in a book of fiction – realities
are too strong, party passions too violent to bear to see, or care to look at
their faces in the looking-glass.[85]

As the course of moral reform which these two ladies had championed in the early years of the century became progressively less likely, and as new leaders and writers emerged, so their alienation from the situation became more complete. Maria Edgeworth remained on her family's estate, active and humane as ever until her life's end, whereas Lady Morgan, whose last Anglo-Irish novel, and many would say her best, did not appear until 1827, retired to England and severed most of her ties with the country about which she had written so passionately.

Although silenced by events, Maria Edgeworth and Lady Morgan, in their repeated exploration of the relationship between the Irish people and the possession and management of land, defined the theme which (more than any other) dominates the writing of their successors in the nineteenth century. Their other telling achievement was the creation of an art form in English in which the Irish people and Irish problems could be treated seriously and engagingly. The characters and situations in their novels may be limited and primarily centred on the upper class – the peasantry had to await other pens – but the sincere and real attempts to observe, to comment fairly and to apportion blame to both the English and Irish demand attention. With the exception of *Castle Rackrent*, the conclusions of their books are always over-optimistic, at least to readers with the benefit of hindsight, and the plots usually depend to an embarrassing degree upon coincidences or melodramatic revelations and arrivals; yet sentimentality has little place in their writings. While always sympathetic to the plight of the Irish, they are never blind to their shortcomings. Both women, but especially Maria Edgeworth, demonstrate something of a good schoolmistress's concern for a pupil who shows real promise but who lacks the self-discipline and supportive background to make the most of his talents. They wrote without precedent, and their work marks the local beginning of a movement in Anglo-Irish literature which would ultimately include masterpieces of universal significance.

TWO

EARLY TALES BY THE BANIMS AND
GERALD GRIFFIN (1825–1830)

a striking portraiture of national manners as exhibited in the middle
and inferior classes of Irishmen.

The Times – reviewing
Tales by the O'Hara Family.

Although only a relatively small number of Anglo-Irish novels
were published between 1800 and 1824, the next six years
changed this situation radically. By 1830 not only would the
names of John and Michael Banim and Gerald Griffin be
established as novelists of eminence, but indeed their best
books would already have been written. The fiction of these
men inaugurates a new phase in the evolution of the Anglo-
Irish novel and introduces characters, situations and perspectives which are not found in the earlier books. Attention is no
longer concentrated to the same extent on the Big Houses and
the gentry; instead the focal points become farms, cottages or
the homes of the aspiring middle class. The most successfully
drawn characters are common folk rather than titled lords and
ladies, and the circumstances in which they are portrayed,
melodramatic as they often are, have a sound basis in everyday
experience. Through the writings of the Banim brothers and
Griffin, the reader draws closer to the realities of life as it was
for the majority of Catholic country people in Ireland in the
late eighteenth and early nineteenth centuries.

The apparent upsurge of creativity in these years is an
intriguing phenomenon and must surely be explained in part
by the course of political events in Ireland during the same
period. The 1820s was the decade in which Daniel O'Connell
became a figure of national importance with his mounting
popular campaign for Catholic emancipation. O'Connell has
been described as 'the first man to mobilize Irish opinion
effectively on a national scale', and the consequence of this for
the morale of Catholics was of inestimable importance.[1]

51

The work of the Banim brothers and of Griffin is at least in part symptomatic of that importance. Gearóid Ó Tuathaigh has written that O'Connell

stood in a relationship to the Catholic masses that was quite unique. In this respect, at least, there was no Irish leader before or since quite like O'Connell. He shared their historic sense, their hopes and aspirations. He had no need to imagine what the experience of being a Catholic in Ireland might be. He was one of them, and he articulated in ringing phrases their deep resentment at past wrongs and their firm resolve to make their presence felt.[2]

So, too, with the novelists of these years, and again with William Carleton slightly later. O'Connell led his followers to emancipation in 1829, and although this modest concession only yielded practical benefits to middle-class Catholics, its symbolic and psychological impact as a victory *per se* was profound and much more generally felt. In political terms it capped a decade of growing self-confidence among the Catholic population and was an unambiguous affirmation of the newly felt self-respect which was slowly beginning to overcome the older sense of degradation, humiliation and defeat. Against this background the Banims and Griffin were writing. Their work is at once an expression of and a contribution to the newly found confidence of the period.

John and Michael Banim, writing under the pseudonyms of Abel and Barnes O'Hara, published *The Tales by the O'Hara Family* in 1825 and 1826. These stories, the best parts of which have a memorable power and intensity, introduce at least two characters, Crohoore and John Nowlan, whose vividness is immediately engaging. Thomas Flanagan has rightly noted that *Crohoore of the Bill-hook*, a story of eighteenth-century life as it was experienced by the Catholic peasants and strong farmers, introduces 'a world for which neither the novels of Maria Edgeworth nor those of Lady Morgan have prepared us – the secret, strangely self-sufficient Gaelic world'.[3] The intimacy and domestic warmth of some parts of that world are counterbalanced by feelings of alienation from other parts of the society – particularly the tithe proctor, and the forces of the law. Violence runs close to the surface of even the most orderly lives and frequently erupts in bloodthirsty actions. Indeed an horrendous crime provides the basis for the whole story in *Crohoore* – the murder with a bill-hook of Anthony Dooling and his wife, and the abduction of their daughter by force.

These events towards the beginning of the novel follow immediately after what is probably the first comprehensive fictional description of the interior of a well-to-do Irish farmer's house, and the close proximity of the two passages suggests how rapidly violence can break in upon domesticity. A clue is found in the character of Anthony Dooling, whose self-sufficiency in the provision of food and clothes for his family, and whose readiness to give generous hospitality to strangers are contrasted with

his dark side. He was of a violent temper, and would fall into paroxysms of passion with his workmen, and sometimes ill-treat them, for the purpose it almost seemed, of making it up with them when he became cool, and all was over.[4]

This 'dark side' of his personality incites him to argue with and assault Crohoore, an event taken by witnesses as leading directly to Dooling's murder.

At first, the atmosphere in the house on Christmas Eve is warm and inviting, and individual details – the hum of Mrs Dooling's spinning wheel, the five or six workmen at ease before the fire, the pewter and copper shining on the dresser, the preserved bacon hanging by the chimney, the simple elegance of young Alley Dooling's dress – combine to give it reality. The intimacy and apparent harmony of the scene in Dooling's house are compromised by the presence of Crohoore, who seems wholly alienated from the rest of the group not only by his physical ugliness, but by his anti-social behaviour. He sits away from everyone else and is preoccupied with whetting a rusty bill-hook. The sound of this unexplained but menacing operation provokes Anthony Dooling's temper, and in the consequent argument Crohoore is violently struck and injured, and he leaves the room with a fearsome look towards his master.

The subsequent murder of the Doolings, the abduction of Alley, and the simultaneous disappearance of Crohoore complete his isolation from and rejection by the community to which he had belonged only tenuously at the outset; while the effect of these sensational events upon Dooling's neighbours is traced in detail and provides insights into their mentality and beliefs. Crohoore is in fact innocent of the murders, and he rescues Alley Dooling (who turns out to be his sister) from her real abductors, but the author shows the power of rumour and superstition in generating a popular feeling of antagonism towards him. No sooner is the crime discovered than gossip begins to convert him into a fiery spirit possessed of the evil eye. One old woman, in a typical response, says:

That Crohoore was always a bad sight to me. . . . I never cared to see him crossing my road; there was something not right about him; an' the look of his two eyes wasn't like any other Christhen's I ever seen.[5]

The self-generating nature of such rumour leads the speakers to the conviction that Crohoore must be hunted and killed by a Christian as the 'good people' themselves have not the power to take away life. Similarly Crohoore's supposed love for Alley is translated into a bewitching spell which gave him power over her, and which he chose to use to abduct her because of her imminent marriage to Pierce Shea.

All this talk strikingly discloses how peasant beliefs are an inseparable mixture of Christian and pagan ideas, a fact which is particularly evident at the wake for the murder victims, where the ceremony, itself pagan in origin, passes from words in praise of the dead to a series of curses against the murderer uttered by the chief keener, who is actually described as a 'witchlike poetess'. The atmosphere is further heightened and the notoriety of Crohoore increased by his sudden and brief appearance among the mourners, followed by his easy escape when recognized. Here Banim reveals the power of super-stition and auto-suggestion in the reactions of the women at the wake:

No one could tell or conjecture how he had entered or approached the house; and when the women were angrily questioned as to why they had not given timely alarm, they solemnly and earnestly averred, one and all, that their senses had become paralyzed, fairy-stricken, in fact, by his presence.[6]

This is not intended as cheap mockery of the simplicity or gullibility of the peasants. On the contrary Banim is fully aware both of the reality of such beliefs and of their effects on the behaviour of the community about which he is writing. He passes beyond a merely external description of Irish peasant eccentricity and superstition, and enables the reader to perceive the forces which shaped the lives of these people and made them act as they did. In so doing he extends the range of Anglo-Irish fiction.

The personal story of Crohoore's alleged crime and the reactions it produces are also given a social context of more widespread social unrest and violence. Pierce Shea, Alley Dooling's intended husband, commits himself to taking revenge on Crohoore and is offered the assistance of Jack Doran, the lawless son of a gentleman farmer and the leader of a band of Whiteboys. Doran himself was a former wooer of Alley, and after rejection by her father attempted to carry her off by force with his gang, only to be foiled by Pierce Shea and a party of reapers who attacked them with sickles. In describing the activities of Doran's Whiteboys, Banim, unlike Maria Edgeworth in *Ennui*, comments on the grievances which nurtured agrarian secret societies. These originated in the harshness of the penal laws which so humiliated Catholics that

the Irish peasantry, neglected, galled, and hard driven, in poverty, bitterness, and ignorance, without competent advisers, without leaders a step above themselves, and scarcely with an object, wildly endeavoured to wreak vengeance upon, rather than obtain redress from, the local agents of some of the most immediate hardships that maddened them.[7]

The bitterness against the Protestant minority was further aggravated by the tithe payable by all Catholics towards the maintenance of the Established Church; not surprisingly the tithe proctor was one of the most hated and despised figures in the community.

Some twenty years later Carleton wrote a novel entirely centred on a tithe proctor and his family, but Michael Banim's creation in this novel, Peery Clancy, is a worthy forerunner of Matthew Purcel and his sons. Clancy is depicted as a social outcast, a middle-aged failure who has served time in prison for debt and for sheep-stealing and whose newly found power, and the wealth which it enables him to accrue for himself, render him not only contemptible but dangerous. Like others in his position Clancy exploits the law to humiliate and utterly crush his victims, by first allowing their debts to him to mount up until they become unpayable and then demanding a total settlement without further delay. The proctor's own profits are automatically increased by law once he instigates proceedings against a person, and so the racket continues and the position of the debtor deteriorates as his only horse or cow is carried off, his wife or daughter crudely propositioned, and any final vestiges of his own dignity destroyed. In this situation, as Banim sees it, a man is driven straight into the arms of the Whiteboys.

The Whiteboy gathering dramatizes the mentality and behaviour of the conspirators. Initially their drunken aggression expresses itself in a 'mad shouting' song:

> They must lave off their tithin' and rackin of acres,
> Or we'll roast 'em as brown as a loaf at the baker's;
> An' we'll nip off their ears, and we'll lave their heads bare,
> As they do wid the calves in the county Kildare.[8]

This is followed by an inflammatory declamation, delivered by the schoolmaster who, as so often in comparable scenes, acts as the official spokesman of the Whiteboys. He berates Pierce Shea for his previous failure to join 'the boys' against the enemies of the people:

what's the raison, I say once agin, that you're not like a son o' green Ireland, the crature, doin' as much as you can, an' sorry in your heart that you can't do more, against the rievin', plundherin', murtherin' rapperies o' tithe-proctors, the bitter foes in ould Ireland's land; – slingin' at home, becase the blow doesn't sthrike hard on youself, an' never heeding the moans o' the poor neighbours, that are left to starve, or rot like ould horses in the ditches, becase the sassenach clergy, that doesn't care a crooked sthraw for them or theirs, must have grand houses to live in, brave horses to hunt, coaches to take their pleasure in, an' costly tastes, where there's the mate iv all kinds, everyday of the year, Fridays an' all, an' wine galore to dhrink.[9]

The first notable feature here is the clear implication that any true 'son o' green Ireland' will be ready to dedicate himself to the violent overthrow of tithe proctors and the Protestant clergy. This aspiration and the vigorous, uncompromising, concrete terms in which it is articulated are in marked contrast to the equally determined, but much more genteel and accommodating nationalist ideals voiced by Judge Aubrey in *Florence Macarthy*. Where Aubrey felt compassion, pity and the need for a real standard of justice for all citizens, the schoolmaster wishes to respond to one type of sectarian misrule by destroying it with another version of the same thing.

Another aspect of the speech is the energy of its language, and this is reminiscent again of *Florence Macarthy*, and in particular of Terence Oge O'Leary's speech. The personification of Ireland, 'the crature', the accumulation of participles and verbs which generate a feeling of activity and urgency, and the stark contrast between the reduced state of the Irish peasantry and the affluence of the 'sassenach clergy', combine to give the harangue its driving force.

Any vestiges of rationality in the situation are lost when a wretched victim of the tithe proctor's cruelty begins to speak, using Irish, which he adopts instinctively

as the most ready and powerful medium of expressing his feelings; for one who boggles, and stammers, and is ridiculous in English, becomes eloquent in Irish.[10]

Here the Irish language, although already largely replaced by English, survives as the means of expressing the most deep-seated and intense emotions. The 'grafted tongue', as John Montague has called it, is not yet well enough established to be articulate in moments of crisis when instinctive responses take command. The man's account of his own misfortunes is the emotional climax of the Whiteboys' meeting; it converts the excitement and bravado into a determination to take desperate action. Even Pierce Shea, the opponent of reck-lessness, yields to the atmosphere of the situation. Banim clearly understands the logic whereby men are driven to commit atrocities, and also the depth of resentment felt by the poor towards their oppressors.

The punishment meted out to Peery Clancy is barbaric – he is made to swear on a prayer book never to resume his profession, and after having been buried up to the neck in a mock grave, his ears are sliced off. These events are complemented by the chanting of death-prayers to the accompaniment of the fiddle – a scene similar to that described by Samuel Lover in his story 'The Burial of the Tithe'. In the same vein Eyre Crowe, writing in his book *Today in Ireland* (1825), tells of offending agents and proctors being 'carded' – their backs were scraped open with the metal combs used for untangling wool – and underlines the fanaticism of rebel raiding parties by describing how men injured in an attack were buried alive to prevent them betraying their fleeing comrades. Banim, Lover and Crowe observe how these grim occasions are conducted with a bizarre mixture of cynicism and lightheartedness, and this characteristic of temperament is shown repeatedly in stories of the Irish peasantry, as if their own experience of suffering was such that it produced a defensive, mocking attitude when the tables were turned and the oppressor was temporarily reduced to the status of victim. Perhaps the Irishman's capacity to commit acts of appalling cruelty, or of tribal justice in the case of Peery Clancy, and to do so in an atmosphere of grotesque gaiety, is symptomatic of the indigenous violence of the society. Obviously religious beliefs and morality have little or no influence on the thinking of Banim's Whiteboys or Crowe's Carders. They are men for whom forgiveness is a luxury they cannot afford, a sign of mere weakness, whereas the nerve to carry out acts of vengeance provides a test of manhood and enables a compensatory gesture of defiance in the face of humiliation and poverty. *Crohoore* is the first Anglo-Irish novel to tap the feelings, intimacy, loyalties and hostilities of such desperate people.

Melodrama and complexity of plot are also features of *The Nowlans*, John Banim's first major contribution to *The Tales by the O'Hara Family*. Even more than in *Crohoore* coincidence and improbability challenge the reader's credulity and weaken the structure of the story as a whole, but the central character, John Nowlan, is a memorable and powerfully presented figure whose particular personal dilemma and crisis of conscience are recorded more vividly than anywhere else in Anglo-Irish fiction until Joyce's *Portrait of the Artist as a Young Man*. John Nowlan's conflict is between his vocation to train for the Catholic priesthood, and the strong, and sometimes masochistic, sexual passions which entangle him with two women. The complications are compounded by the fact that Letty Adams, the girl he eventually marries, is a Protestant. Thus even a brief description of the situation of the hero indicates how it is dominated by a preoccupation with two areas of experience – religion and sex – which become almost obsessive interests in much twentieth-century Anglo-Irish fiction. In its own time, and for long afterwards, *The Nowlans* was bold and pioneering in its subject matter and in the intensity of treatment given to it. In this last respect it differs greatly from William Carleton's magnificent tale of a spoilt priest, 'Denis O'Shaughnessy Going to Maynooth', where the richness of the comedy generates a much more joyful atmosphere.

Joy has little place in the *The Nowlans*, for John Nowlan is a tormented character, torn and destroyed by the contrary impulses in his nature, who brings grief and suffering to those associated with him. He is the son of a 'mixed' marriage, his father being Catholic and his mother Protestant, and the author suggests the social tension such a relationship involves. Yet, in spite of their differences, Daniel Nowlan and his wife have sufficient tolerance for one another to make their relationship work.

They have two sons and two daughters, John being the

younger of the boys, and trouble arises partly because of Daniel
Nowlan's ambitions for his sons. The older boy, Phelim, is to
inherit his father's land, but John's fortunes come to depend
upon his debauched and increasingly impoverished uncle, Aby
Nowlan, who disrupts his nephew's initial training for entry
into the priesthood by inviting him to his home. Here John
finds himself in a situation where anarchy, mismanagement,
drunkenness and sexual licence are the norms of behaviour.

Aby Nowlan's house and grounds reflect his irresponsible,
wasteful and disorganized way of life, but the personal chaos
of his existence is seen most dramatically in his relationships
with other people and in the attitudes of those who have
dealings with him. He fails to take charge of his affairs while
the chance exists, preferring to indulge his fair-weather friends
with food and hunting, only to be deserted by them when the
inevitable collapse finally comes.

The effects of a landlord like Aby Nowlan on his tenants are
aptly suggested in the following conversation between the
master and some of his men:

'And what are ye for doing with yourselfs today, gentlemen?'
   'Why, Master Aby, we war upon thinkin' iv' goin' down to the
bottom [valley], to see what way is the hay goin' on.'
   'An' take your time, a-vouchal; it's a bad thing to be over-hasty –
an' things are apt to spile wid hurry.' – These words were
volunteered in a jeering tone, with a voice that sounded like the
interrupted growl of a bear, by a big fellow, with a bull neck, rolling,
unmanageable eyes, broad caricature features, and tattered apparel,
visibly the fragments of Aby's cast-off wardrobe, as, his uncouth
person shambling along, almost sideways, he made his appearance
over a stile, from the post-office.
   'What's that you're sayin', you bosthoon, you?' queried Aby, with
a smile on the newcomer such as Kings of yore were wont to bestow
on their admired jesters.
   'I say, so I do, there's loock in lesure: as the boys well knows, an'
yourself can bear witness to the same along wid 'em.'
   'No talk wid you, Matthew,' said one of the idle men, adroitly
turning off 'the masther's' observation, and taking up the cue often
given before – 'no talk wid you, Matthew, an' beg o' th' ould bouchal
to let you along.'[11]

The tone and content of this dialogue reveal the mutual
contempt between Nowlan and his tenants. At the same time
the insolence of the men is qualified by a deliberately fawning
attempt to please the master. Such flattery indicates a total

lack of respect, and as often as not conceals real feelings of hatred which only lack of courage and principle prevent emerging. Master and men alike know each other to be incompetent, feckless and lazy, but social convention is just strong enough to ensure that they continue to play a debased version of their prescribed roles in the community. Neither side feels loyalty or obligation to the other: Aby indulges in delusions of himself as some kind of King or ruler, while his men, whom he regards as fools, know exactly how little they need to do to appease him. In this way the meeting enables Banim to dramatize vividly both the causes and the effects of a cynical relationship between a landlord and his tenants.

Above all, the impact of Aby Nowlan's self-destructive household is illustrated most forcefully in the case of his young nephew. John Nowlan is fourteen when he first goes to his uncle's, and he is initiated into the way of life there by being locked in a room with Aby and his cronies until they have drunk themselves stupid after dinner. Although he demonstrates considerable willpower in coping with this aspect of his uncle's riotous living – rather like Harry Ormond with King Corny in a similar situation – the sexual promiscuity in Aby's home proves less easy to resist. John Nowlan's conflict of conscience begins when he is given charge of the education of Maggy, one of his uncle's illegitimate children, towards whom he soon acknowledges a strong physical attraction, which he tries unsuccessfully to discipline. He is further afflicted by a deepening crisis of conscience between his worldly desires and the demands of the priesthood, for which he is still training:

Religion still had full influence over him; but it was rather the influence of terror than of persuasion; he heard its awakened voice in the thunders of reproof, not in the whispers of peace; and therefore he groaned and trembled.[12]

The similarity between this and the account of one stage in Stephen Dedalus' development is obvious, and in both cases guilt precipitates the dilemmas of the characters. John Nowlan is portrayed as a tempestuous and passionate man for whom sexual relationships are a natural expression of his personality; but because of a commitment to the Church forced upon him at an early age, he has learned to regard sexual experience with shame and guilt even before he discovers its importance to him. In tackling this theme – the interrelationship of sex, guilt and religion – John Banim shows remarkable courage and insight into a kind of crisis which, if not uniquely Irish, is certainly typically so.

The second half of the novel introduces a new group of characters around whom the rest of the increasingly melo-dramatic plot is centred. The main figures are Mr Long, a wealthy, childless landowner, and his nephew and niece, Frank and Letty Adams. A chance meeting with the Nowlans leads quickly to two crucial relationships: Frank, who is little more than a stereotype of the smiling, plausible villain, is attracted to Peggy Nowlan, while John himself is charmed by the grace and elegance of Letty. His contact with her and subsequent visit to Long Hall introduce him to a whole new world of poetry, music and cultural activities, and the fascination he feels for Letty is complicated by his sense of social inferiority to her. The religious difference between the two adds a further dimension to an already difficult situation. It was a problem which the author himself knew at first hand through his own unsuccessful and miserably unhappy love affair with a Protestant girl.

John Nowlan's behaviour becomes increasingly erratic and hurtful both to himself and to Letty Adams as he is torn between his actual feelings for her and the celibacy he thinks he ought to honour. He is unable to sever the relationship cleanly, and there follows a series of inconclusive attempts to part with increasingly histrionic and bizarre behaviour by the principal characters. Indeed perhaps only the improbability of some of the events modifies their distastefulness.

The Nowlans presents the critic with very real problems because it is of such uneven merit. The first part, which deals with John Nowlan's relationships with his uncle and with Maggy and which explores the crisis of conscience between his natural impulses and religious training, is undeniably powerful. His dealings with Letty Adams are rather harder to credit, and as the endless machinations of Frank Adams come to the fore, so the novel as a whole declines into melodrama. Complexity of plot dominates the characters, and they become little more than instruments of it. But the novel offers several fresh perspectives on Irish society. John Nowlan himself is a new type of character in Anglo-Irish fiction, the victim of conflict between his own nature and the values, constraints and expectations of a closely knit rural community and of the Catholic Church. Within that community there are extremes of behaviour – the debauchery of Aby Nowlan at one limit, the conservative and orthodox morality of the Church at the other – and John's misfortune is to be exposed to the full force of the tension between these extremes. The study of John Nowlan may be described fairly as the first exploration of the particular difficulties of an individual in Irish society caught between the intolerable weight of institutionalized values and his own personal desires which are irreconcilable with them, but which will not be denied. Thus he is driven to act in a morally unconventional way, only to be tormented by a sense of guilt for what he has done. The peculiar intolerance of Irish society, particularly in matters of sexual morality, is identified, and the burden of guilt that it generates in the conscience of the non-conformist is understood. Curiously, if John Nowlan's unorthodoxy had expressed itself in an act of violence against a representative of the law, he would probably have become a celebrated and protected hero. As it is, the deepest irony is the fact that the relationships with Maggy and Letty which he cannot resist are both ruined because of the trials of conscience which they cause him.

Aby Nowlan lacks all trace of his nephew's shame and the portrayal of his ruined grandeur, decadent lifestyle and ultimate bankruptcy is impressive. The character of the reckless man of property is not new, but the material details of Aby's increasingly hopeless state are noted in all their diversity. Banim's authority and knowledge in writing of this character are lacking in his account of Mr Long. The latter is much more of a stereotype than an individual, and the author is imaginatively remote from his creation. Mr Long is a function of the plot whereas Aby Nowlan is a vital part of it.

Religion has a decisive place in John Nowlan's life, but the novel also projects its importance in society on a wider scale. Banim emphasizes the special association between priest and people, a feature of Irish society which receives no real attention in the work of his predecessors. By implication, too, he shows how in a community where the power and privilege of the priest among his people are so great, the burden of guilt falling upon the man who fails in his commitment to the ministry must be all the heavier; but it is not until the stories and novels of Carleton that the full extent and complexity of the bond between priest and people are explored through incident and example.

Banim's realization that this relationship has been forged

not only on the basis of common faith, but also through shared suffering heralds a theme to which he and his brother would return in their subsequent historical novels – *The Boyne Water*, *The Last Baron of Crana*, *The Conformists* (by John), and *The Croppy* (mainly Michael's work). In these books the brothers demonstrate that religion is not simply the obsessive preoccupation of fanatical individuals like John Nowlan, but a fundamental part of the national consciousness, of the very experience of being Irish, whether Protestant or Catholic.

The Nowlans may focus essentially on the fate of the hero, but later novels show an increasing concern to interpret the lives of the characters against a full background of social and political events. Thus it would be erroneous to see a retreat from contemporary realities in the Banims' choice of earlier periods as the settings for their major works. On the contrary those times are chosen with unfailing deliberateness to reflect intervals in Irish history when religious tensions between Protestants and Catholics were greatest – the period immediately before and after the Battle of the Boyne, the period following Sarsfield's defeat, the days of the penal laws, and the time of the 1798 Rebellion. By writing fiction which identifies itself so inextricably with historical events, the authors were of necessity offering an interpretation of that history through their novels. The limitations of their interpretation are perhaps less important than the fact that they attempted it at all. It reflects the new-found and essentially Catholic concern for self-definition and self-expression typical of the 1820s.

Before turning to these books, the early publications of Gerald Griffin, the other important writer who emerged in the 1820s, must be mentioned. His first two collections of stories, *Holland-Tide* and *Tales of the Munster Festivals*, appeared in 1827, and they extend the attempt to portray the Irish peasantry initiated by the Banims. Griffin is in the main a more polished and sophisticated writer than either of the brothers or Carleton, as W. B. Yeats noted in his biographical sketch of the author which precedes a selection from his work in *Representative Irish Tales*. Elsewhere Yeats adds that Griffin lacks the power and knowledge of life found in the fiction of the Banims and Carleton, and continues:

In Gerald Griffin . . . I think I notice a new accent – not quite clear enough to be wholly distinct; the accent of people who have not the recklessness of the landowning class, nor the violent passions of the peasantry, nor the good frankness of either. The accent of those middle-class people who find Carleton rough and John Banim coarse, who when they write stories cloak all unpleasant matters, and moralise with ease, and have yet a sense of order and comeliness that may sometime give Ireland a new literature. . . . They are closer to the peasant than to the gentry, for they take all things Irish with conscience, with seriousness. Their main hindrances are a limited and diluted piety, a dread of nature and her abundance, a distrust of unsophisticated life. But for these, Griffin would never have turned aside from his art and left it for the monastery; nor would he have busied himself with anything so filmy and bloodless as the greater portion of his short stories.[13]

This analysis may reveal more about Yeats than about his subject, and it certainly seems too harsh a judgment of Griffin, but it also contains a fair measure of truth.

His accounts of peasant life and customs, of the relationship between men's lives and the geography of the landscape in which they dwell, of the power of superstition upon them, and of the latent or open violence of the society are accurately drawn. In some instances these forces are more coherently perceived than in the Banims' writing; but the perception is gained at the expense of much of the raw energy and intensity of feeling and involvement found in the other novelists. Griffin's tales are observed where the Banims' and later Carleton's are lived. His gifts were perhaps those of the novelist rather than the short-story writer, for in the longer work his discipline and management of plot pay off, particularly when compared with the ramshackle structures of most full-length nineteenth-century Anglo-Irish novels, and this is not the least factor in the success of *The Collegians*.

The tales endorse many of the impressions of the peasantry created by the Banims. Those in *Holland-Tide* are supposed to be told around the firesides in humble cottages on All Saints' Eve and, given the occasion, not surprisingly superstition plays a key role in many of the stories. For instance the events in 'St. Martin's Day' all result from the attempts of two sailors to bring their ship in to land on a day which is superstitiously believed to be unlucky for mariners, while in *Tales of the Munster Festivals* 'Card Drawing' deals with a character, Duke Dorgan, whose trials and tribulations are foreseen by a fortune-teller. Even more important is the way in which superstitious beliefs, acts of violence and acts of revenge or justice are shown to be related. In a community where the official process of law is ineffective or held in defiance, or both, a system of popular justice, akin to that in *Crohoore of the Bill-hook*, prevails. Thus in 'The Hand and the Word', following a murder and the arrest of suspects, Griffin informs his reader that

It was the custom in those days, and is still the custom in most parts of Ireland, where any person is supposed to have 'come by his end' unfairly, that all the inhabitants of his parish, or district, particularly those who, from any previous circumstances, may be rendered at all liable to suspicion, shall meet together and undergo a kind of ordeal, by touching the corpse, each in his turn. . . . it was a current belief among the peasantry, that in many instances where the perpetrator of the horrid deed possessed strength of mind, or callousness of heart sufficient to subdue all appearance of emotion in the moment of trial, some miraculous change in the corpse itself had been known to indicate the evil doer.[14]

In this way justice and superstition are inextricably bound up together, the atmosphere of the occasion producing a decision rather than any logical process of law.

Griffin shares with the Banims and with Carleton an awareness of the closeness of violence to the surface not only of peasant life, but of all levels of society; and violence, or the threat of violence, is indigenous to his stories. Sometimes it is the bizarre violence of fairy tales and evil spirits: 'The Brown Man' tells of a mysterious and evil figure who appears at the home of a poor woman and her daughter, takes the girl off to be his wife, and eventually kills and devours her after she discovers his satanic habit of raiding graveyards; in the 'Persecution of Jack Edy' a midget is haunted by spirits seeking to destroy him, and he is obliged to protect himself in his own home by spilling his washing water, hiding his reaping hook in the thatch, and tying his hand reel with a rush; and in 'The Unburied Legs' a pair of legs seen walking the countryside is followed by people to a churchyard where they learn the story of a brutal murder in which the victim's legs were hacked off and never buried in consecrated ground like the rest of his body.[15]

Elsewhere the violence is of a less exotic kind, stemming directly from greed or a simple lust for vengeance. This is particularly true in the *Tales of the Munster Festivals*, in 'Card Drawing', 'The Half Sir' and 'Suil Dhuv, the Coiner'. The first of these concerns the way in which Duke Dorgan is made to appear the murderer of Mr McLoughlan, the father of the girl he loves. In fact McLoughlan is hacked to death with a scythe for failing to heed a warning 'not to bid for a certain farm in the neighbourhood, the tenant farmer of which had been ejected for non-payment of rent'.[16]

In 'The Half Sir' the hero Eugene Hamond encounters an impoverished peasant whose wife is suffering from fever and who has been evicted by the combined efforts of a spiteful landlord and his agent; the latter also happens to be a Protestant clergyman. Griffin gives only a reported account of these events, whereas later Carleton dramatizes such scenes, giving them an immediacy that is lacking here. The same is true of the description of the effects of famine and fever in the countryside, where the undoubted sincerity of the author does not compensate for the remarkably detached tone of the writing:

Numbers of poor wretches, who seemed to have been worn down by the endurance of disease and famine to the very skeleton, were dispersed through the fields, some of them occupied in gathering nettles, the common food of the people for a long period, and prishoc weed from the hedges, for the purpose of boiling, in lieu of a more nutritious vegetable. . . . The red crosses which were daubed on almost every cabin-door as he passed, and the sounds of pain and sorrow which came on his hearing from the interior, afforded him a fearful evidence of the extent to which the ravages of the disease had been carried. . . .[17]

Typically, Griffin's fairness and balance make him equally ready to include a word of praise for the 'proverbially benevolent and generous inhabitants of the sister island' (England) in trying to alleviate Irish hardship.[18] Such impartiality of sentiment is unusual in Anglo-Irish fiction, and, ironically, its effect here is enfeebling in terms of the total account of the situation.

He comes nearer the mark in his observations on the Irish peasant's attitude to life and his limited, hand-to-mouth philosophy of subsistence. In *Holland-Tide*, he wrote that the peasant

is satisfied with the appearance of things about him. . . . he sees the potatoes, they are his and his pig's by right, and he and his pig are merry fellows while they last, and while they can procure a turfen fire, or the smoke of a fire, to warm the little cabin about them.[19]

Similarly the destitute peasant in 'The Half Sir' tells Hamond if I had only praties enough to keep above ground for a few years more just to make my soul (a thing I was ever too negligent of), I think a prince couldn't be better off.[20]

The author stresses that this very attitude and the lowliness of the man's expectations and aspirations contribute to the general inertia of the poor.

A particular feature of Griffin's work is his own sensitivity to the various beauties of the Irish rural landscape and his deep-seated sense of the active relationship between natural surroundings and the workings of an individual's conscience. This is illustrated especially well in 'Suil Dhuv, the Coiner', where the eponymous villain rides out to steal the chalice from an isolated church and is stirred by the sights around him. Griffin's account of the tranquillity of the prosperous-looking farmland in the evening light makes a comprehensive appeal to the senses through details of the various flowers in the hedgerow, the smoke from the cottage chimneys, the flax gardens and ridges of sprouting potatoes, the peasants at work on the turf bog, the milk maid calling in the cattle, the sounds of a song or of a disturbed bird or of the conversation between a group of women washing clothes by the river.[21] This scene is evoked with the knowledge and affection of a deeply felt personal response. In terms of the story even the hardened Suil Dhuv is touched by its 'tender beauty' and his conscience stirs within him: 'all these objects acted like fire upon the remorse that was already beginning to fester within the bosom of the guilty wanderer.'[22] This activity of conscience is further prompted, and becomes tinged with melancholy, when he passes by the house where he spent some of his happiest boyhood days only to see it in a state of delapidation and collapse.

The idea of the specific moral impact of a landscape upon an individual's conscience is interpreted elsewhere in terms of the relationship between the geography of a place and the values of the people living in it. In 'Card Drawing' the story is located on the extreme southwestern tip of the country, and Griffin deliberately relates the remoteness of the area to the way of life of its natives, observing that it 'presents a very remarkable contrast, in the condition and moral character of its inhabitants, to all the rest of Munster – perhaps, we might say, Ireland.'[23] The author's knowledge of the region penetrates its initial impression of bleakness and wildness to discern its fertility, unexpected density of population and, even more surprising, its prosperity. Whereas Lady Morgan was enraptured by unspoilt beauties of nature, Griffin focuses on people:

They are contradistinguished from Irish landholders in general, by their apparent poverty and real wealth (many a tenant of clay walls being able without much inconvenience to give a dowry of some hundreds to his daughter) – as well as by their regular persevering industry – their extreme ignorance – their want of curiosity in all speculative matters – and their perfect unacquaintance with those popular themes of debate, which set all the rest of the land by the ears. They till their gardens quietly, as their fathers did before them – learn little and care for less – obey their priests in all reasonable matters, and pay him like princes – go to market with their oats and potatoes – eat – drink – dance – laugh – sleep and die.[24]

This conveys the idea of a continuing and unbroken way of life within a small, self-complete world, a parish, which seems to have been for Griffin what the Aran Islands were for Synge in more recent times. The countryside is free from agrarian agitation, as it is from debate on the issue of Catholic emancipation, because the issues are irrelevant to the circumstances of a community where hard work is required by all its members. Significantly disorder and violence, when they occur, are associated with the return of a member of the community who has long been absent, although in fact he is not the responsible party. Again the similarity to Synge suggests itself, for in *The Playboy of the Western World* the arrival of Christy Mahon, the outsider, generates tensions within the community.

H. R. Krans has written that in the *Tales of the Munster Festivals*

the scenes from this wild coast are introduced not merely for their picturesqueness, but are used to bring together in a single impression the fearful in landscape and the dangerous and desperate in human passion, so that moral and physical gulfs and precipices combine to produce situations of poignant terror.[25]

The truth of this has been illustrated in the case of Suil Dhuv who is stirred by the landscape to face up to his criminal behaviour which has ruined other people and apparently eroded his capacity for moral judgment; and much the same applies to Pryce Kinchela in 'Card Drawing'. In a different way the hero of 'The Half Sir' Eugene Hamond is shown in two situations, first leaving and then later returning to Ireland, where his views of the landscape prompt him to consider his feelings about his native country. With heartfelt sincerity, which must reflect Griffin's own disillusioning experiences as an emigrant in London, Hamond perceives the hopelessness of the aspirations held by the adventurers who crowd the pier, and 'devoutly believed that gold and fame grew like blackberries upon hedges every where except in poor Ireland.'[26] He anticipates their subsequent discovery of the squalor, demeaning work, failure and loneliness that are the typical realities for the vast majority of these discontented fortune-seekers, contrasting it with the relatively happy poverty and 'careless simplicity' of a cottager on the Irish hills.

On the occasion of his hero's return to Ireland, Griffin describes the great natural beauty of the lower reaches of the Shannon where the boat has anchored. But he also intimates that the pleasing prospect of the cottages is compromised by the fact that 'they were the abode of sickness and misery'; and an incident witnessed by Hamond just after he disembarks – an assassination attempt made upon a well-to-do landowner – is representative of the internal restlessness of the country.

This consciousness of the dual nature of the beauty of the landscape extends to Griffin's portrayal of the contradictory and unpredictable temperament so readily attributed to the Irish by outside observers. Thus, for instance, in 'The Aylmers of Bally-Aylmer' Mr Hasset, an absentee landlord returning to his people, is given a loyal welcome by his tenants:

As his carriage turned the angle of a rock, some miles distant from his seat, the sound of all manner of villainous instruments rattling away to an awe-inspiring national planxty, announced the approach of the villagers, and in a few minutes he was encountered by their advanced guard, a mounted deputation, headed by a lame carpenter, who filled his seat on the bony ridge of a wall-eyed, unfed gelding's back, with the dignity of an orderly on a field-day; and with the resignation of a martyr. The music being hushed for the moment into a delicious silence, and the open carriage drawn up, the schoolmaster of the village inflicted a harangue on the occupant, which was borne with gracious patience, and suitably acknowledged; after which, with tremendous yells, the crowd bounded on the carriage, emancipated the four-footed cattle, cashiered the postillions, and fastening two ropes on either side, hurried the lumbering vehicle along the rough and stony road, with a velocity which caused an expression of real alarm to take place of the smiling condescension which had before diffused itself over the gracious countenance of the proprietor.[27]

Although affection and perhaps even a kind of respect for the powerful are elements in this scene, there is a deeper current of aggression and anarchy expressed here in basically friendly terms, but which would be equally capable of exploding into something much less pleasant. This is apparent in the language of the passage – the military references, the fact that the schoolmaster 'inflicted' his 'harangue' on Mr Hasset, the limited violence practised against the postillions, and the account of the reckless speed with which the carriage is towed, and which shatters the occupant's complacency and exposes his real vulnerability. These peasants are not mere ciphers who know their place and conduct themselves with whimsical eccentricity, like, for example, Samuel Lover's Rory O'More. On the contrary, despite this display of apparently illogical warmth towards an absentee landlord who has failed them miserably, the occasion indicates a capacity for cruelty and the excitement of undisciplined mob strength.

The volatile nature of the Irish temperament, often characterized by extreme loyalty or implacable hatred, is at once recognized and in some measure lamented by Griffin. Irish spirit, as he calls it, is positive and admirable, but only so long as it is not 'warped and tainted by the vapours of Irish pride'.[28] Its identifying signs are usually a combination of snobbery and stubbornness, and its practical effect is to produce inflexible attitudes towards people, ideas and social changes. Griffin is by no means alone in commenting on this seemingly typical Irish trait: it appears in the folly of Lady Clonbrony, the stubbornness of the Prince of Inismore, the self-respect of O'Donnel, and the snobbery of Mrs Nowlan. Subsequently there is the vanity of Carleton's Denis O'Shaughnessy, the nationalist fervour of Mrs Hall's Lawrence Macarthy, and the arrogant idiosyncracy of Lever's Bagenal Daly.

In 'The Half Sir', Griffin states categorically that 'pride – mere family pride is one of the grand national foibles which yet remain unshaken by the inroads of modern intelligence'; and many of Eugene Hamond's sufferings derive immediately from his own susceptibility to this weakness.[29] The social aspirations which he cannot finance and his acute sensitivity towards real or imagined snubs from the Dublin society folk with whom he tries to meet on equal terms are not manifestations of pride which exist in a vacuum. At the outset of the story Hamond's house is visited by a party of Wren Boys celebrating St Stephen's Day and their conversations about him reveal both their own prejudices and also explain the title of the tale. A half sir is defined as:

A man that has not got any blood in him. . . . A sort of small gentleman, that way; the singlings of a gentleman, as it were. A made man – not a born gentleman. Not great, all out, nor poor, that way, intirely. Betwixt and betune, as you may say.[30]

A footnote explains that 'the singlings' are 'the first running of spirits in the process of distillation', so Hamond's lack of worth as far as the peasants are concerned is specifically related to the fact that he has no inherited gentility or breeding. Their measure of a man's nobility and moral virtue is his willingness to participate in hunting, racing, dancing, and other such rural entertainments, his extravagance in giving money away, and his liking for drink. Since Hamond fails on these counts, his assistance to the sick and poor, his selfless house visits to fever victims, and his true charity are either disregarded or dismissed; so too is the fact that the 'real gentlemen', those given to 'drunkenness, prodigality and gambling' according to the peasants' definition of that term, were not half as generous as Hamond when the poor were in a distressed state.

A fascination with the extravagant character, in whatever sense of the word, appears to be a perpetual facet of the Irish personality. This is reflected not only in literature but in real life, where the boundaries between fact and fiction rapidly tend to become blurred. It is only necessary to think of the magical powers sometimes attributed to O'Connell, or of the absorbing enigma of Parnell, or of Eamon De Valera whose life combined the capacity for both military and political survival and success in a unique way. Even the nicknames given to these political figures – 'The Liberator', 'The Chief', 'The Long Fellow' – are indicative of the heroic stature granted to them by the people. In the sphere of literature Yeats turned for inspiration to Cuchulain and Oisin as well as to Swift, Berkeley and O'Leary, conjoining the mythological and the historical without awkwardness or embarrassment. Carleton's life and writings are another example, for the *Traits and Stories of the Irish Peasantry* includes a regular catalogue of parish heroes, the big fellows of the townlands, just as Carleton himself was once the big fellow of Prillisk, jumping further and throwing the stone greater distances than anyone before him.

Carleton is as inseparable from his own stories as that more recent half-legendary figure, Brendan Behan, is from *The Borstal Boy*. All nations have their heroes but perhaps the small size of the country enables Irish heroes to be both familiar and remote at one and the same time: if you do not know the man yourself, you almost certainly will be acquainted with someone who does.

The danger in all this is that heroes are expected to behave in a certain way, and if the Irish are generous in their praise, they can be vicious in their opposition and condemnation. This point is revealed by Maria Edgeworth and Gerald Griffin. Sir Murtagh Rackrent's greatest sin in the popular view is his failure to be as extravagant and reckless as his predecessor; Eugene Hamond's personal abstemiousness in 'The Half Sir' is regarded similarly, even when one of the Wren Boys argues his established heritage by recalling that his family is descended from Cromwellian settlers. The impulsiveness of judgment observed in the peasants' reaction towards Hamond is further commented upon by Griffin in 'Suil Dhuv, the Coiner', where it has more sinister implications. He remarks that

Irish crime, like Irish virtue, is not the creature of the mind but of the heart. They are a people more frequently betrayed into guilt by the impulses of strong feeling, than the cold suggestions of convenience; and in proportion to the violence of the stimulus applied, will be found the depth and atrocity of the outrage that is committed.[31]

This seeks to explain the paradoxical nature of the Irish temperament which is recognized as being at once good-humoured, hospitable and generous, and also vengeful, vicious and apparently void of all moral considerations. As is consistent with this view, Griffin argues that instances of truly hardened and cynical villainy are rare, because the headstrong force that may cause a man to commit an outrageous crime at one time will produce an equally strong sense of revulsion and guilt in its aftermath. There is a similarity here to the alternating flow of passion and remorse experienced by John Nowlan. Whether this interpretation is adequate may be open to question, but it is a genuine attempt to come to terms with the contradictions and extremes of certain features of Irish life. Not only that, it also faces up to the ugliness and danger of such temperamental instability, as well as celebrating the charm and quaintness which are the main point for later writers such as Lover, Lever and Somerville and Ross.

The Tales by the O'Hara Family and the early stories of Gerald Griffin advance the reader's understanding of Ireland and the Irish not least because of the spirit and sensibilities of the writers themselves, which make them so very different from Maria Edgeworth, Lady Morgan or Charles Maturin. Between them the Banims and Griffin record the darker side of the Irish temperament, the moodiness and the predilection for occasional acts of grim violence. They explore the central place both of religion and of superstition in shaping and influencing behaviour, in creating social tensions, and very often in fuelling the moodiness and violence. At the same time they indicate the legacy of bitterness deriving from the penal laws and the various phases of English oppression and anti-Catholicism – though this subject does not receive its full treatment until the Banims' historical novels – and they interpret Irish lawlessness and violence partly as a reaction to prolonged injustice.

In common with Maria Edgeworth and Lady Morgan, they share a deep-seated consciousness of the strength of feeling provoked by issues of land ownership and management. The difference is that whereas the earlier writers regarded the matter almost exclusively from the point of view of large estate owners, and dealt with the peasantry chiefly by implication, the Banims and Griffin tell their stories from a lower level in the social scale. Their characters are generally men of modest or small possessions, and they are all the more vulnerable to the waywardness of the harvests and the financial demands made upon them. For such people there is no easy escape into absenteeism, and many of the most desperate actions in the stories arise from issues connected with the land.

THREE

THE BANIMS' HISTORICAL NOVELS
(1825–1830)

We, here in Ireland, ought to be anxious to ascertain our position accurately, if for no other reason than that we may give ourselves a common country. At present, the Irish, as a people, have no country, while the children of every other soil boast a proud identity with their native land.

Introductory Letter by
Abel O'Hara (John Banim) to
The Boyne Water (1826)

The earliest of the historical novels by the Banim brothers, *The Boyne Water*, is the work of John and is a lengthy, complex and detailed book dealing with the period from 1685, when James II became King, up to the Flight of the Wildgeese following the signing of the Treaty of Limerick by Sir Patrick Sarsfield. The title draws attention to the particular battle fought during that period (in 1690) which saw the decisive turn in the fortunes of William III's forces in their campaign against the deposed King James. Following this military engagement, which brought William and James face to face, the ultimate outcome of the war is shown to have been inevitable, even if it took a lot more bloodshed before any treaty was signed.

The novel is constructed in such a way that the fortunes of certain members of two families, the Protestant Evelyns and the Catholic McDonnells, are presented in the context of the major historical events of the time – the siege of Derry, the Battle of the Boyne and the siege and surrender of Limerick – and also against Banim's attempt to evoke the general background atmosphere of fear, danger, distrust and random violence throughout the country. The families themselves meet initially by accident when Robert and Esther Evelyn, travelling with their aunt and uncle and an old family servant, are given help and shelter by the McDonnells after a freak storm has struck the Antrim coast. Despite their religious differences, deep friendship, and later love, develop between Robert Evelyn and Eva McDonnell, and between Edmund

74

McDonnell and Esther Evelyn. Ironically the wedding of Robert and Eva has just taken place, and that of Edmund and Esther is stopped midway by disclosure of the news that William of Orange's troops have landed in England, and that therefore all men are required to show their military loyalties. This necessity separates the newly weds and the bride and her husband-to-be at the altar, as the McDonnells naturally rally to James's cause while Robert has pledged service to the Protestant forces. In terms of the personal story, the rest of the novel deals with Robert Evelyn's efforts to preserve his relationship with Eva and his friendship with Edmund, to restore the damage done by their early and heated separation, and to overcome the numerous misunderstandings and mysteries that bedevil almost every move they make.

The involved plot serves to suggest the division and disorder generated by the unsettled state of the country and the profound social ruptures caused by sectarianism and civil war. Indeed in many ways *The Boyne Water* is best viewed as an exploration of the effects of sectarian agitation and divided loyalties upon a community in general and certain individuals in particular. Furthermore, for all its twists and turns, the novel is carefully constructed both in characterization and incident: the Evelyns and the McDonnells are posed against each other, as are King William and King James; George Walker, the fanatical Protestant cleric and leader, is balanced by Friar O'Haggerty, a Catholic extremist; the noble Sarsfield and the brutal Galmoy are the Irish generals, while Schomberg and Kirke are their opposites in personality and loyalties. In addition to this, just as the Evelyn and McDonnell families are driven asunder by the events of the period, so too the main historical protagonists, William and James, are divided on family as well as religious and political grounds, for James was William's father-in-law. As far as action is concerned the siege of Derry presents the Protestants under pressure, with Edmund McDonnell trapped in the city as Evelyn's prisoner, while the siege of Limerick reverses the situation and shows Evelyn held by Sarsfield. The Battle of the Boyne falls between these two events. The great mobility and freedom of movement between the opposing sides allowed to Robert Evelyn, so that he meets and talks to rival generals and kings, rapparees and citizens of Derry, make him the central character and the ubiquitous historical observer. He is a hero of little distinction, except perhaps for his moderation and religious tolerance, but, as

Bernard Escarbelt points out in his introduction to *The Boyne Water*, only such a muted character could be employed to move between the warring parties.[1] Indeed the need to use a figure such as Robert Evelyn highlights a fundamental problem for a novelist who is concerned, as John Banim was, both to tell an original story and also to present a serious historical account of real events and people. The considerable and detailed research of the period which both brothers undertook when the novel was being written fits uneasily into certain parts of the story, and as Escarbelt has observed:

Our feeling, when reading the novel, is . . . one of overscrupulousness which makes the author pile up facts, until at times the text savours more of a chronicle than of a novel.[2]

This modern response needs to be balanced against remarks in a review of the first edition where a writer in *The Times* attacked it as 'a compendium of mad Popery' and for being 'childishly weak in historical judgement as to the political facts'.[3]

Present-day readers are more likely to sympathize with Escarbelt's comment than with that of *The Times'* writer, but both judgments are inclined to ignore the declared purpose of the author in his introductory letter. Here he begins by stressing that he has taken 'all due pains . . . to get at the bottom of the (in Ireland) muddy well, where truth is to be found'; and continues by demanding that people be presented with 'realities . . . instead of delusions; and then, sound footing will be preferred to Will-o'-the Wisp erroneousness'.[4] Finally John Banim offers a specific definition of the moral and educational task to which he saw himself contributing by writing *The Boyne Water* and confronting people with this interpretation of a decisive period of history:

I would go far to assist in dispersing the mist that hangs over Irish ground. I would like to see those dwelling on the Irish soil looking about them in the clear sunshine – the murkiness dispelled – recognizing each other as belonging to a common country, and exchanging the password, 'this is my native land'.[5]

To achieve his declared aim Banim effectively acknowledges the need to explore the most sensitive and emotional events without re-opening the sectarian divisions and antagonisms that are an essential feature of them. The same dilemma faced Lady Morgan when she wrote *O'Donnel*, but whereas she elected to reject the controversial period in which she had originally intended to set her tale, Banim made no such compromise. Indeed one of the remarkable features of *The Boyne Water* is that, as far as is possible, it studiously avoids siding with the extremists of either party. The note of general disenchantment that emerges is as much the responsibility of James's behaviour as of William's. Both kings are presented in a somewhat unfavourable light: James is vain and a poor leader whereas William is aloof and opportunistic, and above all neither man shows care, respect or trust for his Irish supporters. By and large the Irish who suffer so much and who are so polarized by their religious convictions appear as expendable ciphers in a struggle between rivals who are much more concerned with political power than the defence of theological truth.

In considering Banim's view of history one other factor must be remembered. Writing as an Irish Catholic in 1826, when O'Connell's movement to win emancipation for his co-religionists was in full swing, he naturally wished to avoid causing offence to any section of influential public opinion. That he failed in this objective is suggested by the review in *The Times* already cited, but equally clearly he did not intend to provoke such an allegation of sectarian bias. His intro-ductory letter and, above all, his choice of a humane and tolerant supporter of William as his central character are ample evidence of his honest intentions. Ironically, in fact, the modern reader may feel that far from being 'a compendium of mad Popery', the novel ends up by being rather mealy-mouthed and insipid precisely because the author has declined a more positive commitment in it and in spite of his intrusions into the action at intervals throughout the book, when he comments and interprets, seeking to understand the present in terms of the past. The problem is that such a judgment ignores the self-imposed difficulties of Banim's undertaking and the inflammatory nature of much of his subject-matter. Bernard Escarbelt may tend to encourage this misunderstanding when he notes that

the regularity of the term-to-term oppositions leaves us somewhat at a loss as to where we all stand – a little like Evelyn who, between James's and William's 'Jesuits', no longer knows where to turn to find Christian tolerance and fair dealing.[6]

Certainly events as represented in *The Boyne Water* do have a symmetry which seems too perfect to be true, and which foils the instinctive human desire to take sides or to vindicate personal prejudices about this most controversial period of Irish history. What is striking, however, is the image of the Protestant and Catholic factions – particularly of the latter – which Banim chose to create. As a supporter himself of the emancipation movement, he must have been anxious to present a generally favourable view of his co-religionists, and to dispel the worst notions of Catholic treachery, deviousness and missionary intent which were, and to some extent still are, a central part of popular Protestant folklore. A number of specific incidents in the novel demonstrate how he achieved this.

At the outset Banim concerns himself almost exclusively with establishing the characters of the Evelyns and the McDonnells. Public events receive only passing reference or are introduced simply as background detail, while the personal stories are set in motion. This strategy permits the reader to meet the key fictional personalities before he becomes involved with historical figures. Moreover, given that Robert and Esther Evelyn are first encountered in the company of their aunt and uncle and the old Covenanter, Oliver Whittle, their mildness of religious faith emerges in contrast to the crude sectarianism of the others. The warmth and kindness shown to the travellers by the McDonnells following the storm affords a view of this Catholic family's genuine charity and generosity irrespective of the creed of those they are assisting. Their own principles are shown in their daily celebration of the Mass, and their tact when their Protestant visitors are in their home is evident in the way that they move the service to an earlier hour with the intention of having completed it before the Evelyns and Whittle awaken. This discretion is very different from the rudeness and intolerance of Robert's aunt and Oliver Whittle when they happen to discover that Mass is being celebrated. They insist on an immediate departure, and Robert Evelyn's strength of character asserts itself in his refusal to go with them and in his determination to treat the McDonnells with civility and respect. Thus this early fictional incident goes some way towards revealing the tensions, both real and potential, running through northern Irish society.

Additionally, in contrast to the Evelyns who are not given any particular family history, the McDonnells are steeped in knowledge of their own ancestry and of the loss and deprivation that have been their familiar experiences down the years. Nor is the McDonnells' historical awareness limited to family matters: the Cuchullin myths recited in their household to a harp accompaniment by Carolan, perhaps the most famous of seventeenth-century Irish musicians, indicate their interest and involvement in both past and present native traditions. Furthermore the particular part of the Cuchullin story recorded by Banim tells how the great Ulster hero killed his own son in combat without realizing his identity. The relevance of this tale of a divided family to the main body of the novel is obvious.

Pertinent as these details are, one speech – and it is a speech rather than part of a natural conversation – made by Edmund McDonnell to the Evelyns sums up the image of good Catholic citizens that the author wished to establish. He maintains that he and his family are

Irish . . . in feeling, and, I will say, in generosity; – Irish enough to forgive and forget all the wanton cruelties that have been practised upon us; to forget the rank we have lost, and be content with that which we toil and sweat to earn, if, indeed, that poor privilege of humanity be left to us. I would not draw a sword, this moment, for the recovery of my old right, when blood and convulsion must be the consequence. Sensible of my father's loss I must be, and prompt to speak of it, warmly. But I find myself born under a new order of things: the voice of law, and of a king, have sounded in my infantine ears, to command obedience to that new order; and I say to myself: As my ancestors gained their lands, so I forfeit them. It is the chance of the world, and I am content.[7]

Apart from its stilted language, a factor which affects much of the dialogue in the book, the content here is very carefully balanced. McDonnell appears noble and magnanimous, aggrieved, yet bearing the disgrace imposed upon his family with a measure of hurt dignity which immediately wins sympathy – as it is intended to do. He descends almost to the maudlin with his references to the reduced circumstances in which his people now live, but then shows responsibility, stoicism and a concern for the greater good in his rejection of rebellion as a means of revenge and restitution. His admission of loyalty to the king becomes even more important when the civil war starts and sides have to be chosen, while the resonance of his concluding comments and acceptance of the current state of affairs is positively theatrical in tone. Unlikely as this speech may be, it includes all the elements calculated to win favour both for the speaker and his family and also for the plight of Catholics in general.

One of the most crucial of these elements is the passivity of McDonnell; he specifically rejects military action as a means of retribution or of furthering his own ends. Elsewhere Evelyn and McDonnell mutually acknowledge the damage and division caused by civil war and reject it as a result. Ironically their moderation and clear-sightedness count for little when the extremist agitators, Walker and O'Haggerty, begin to exert their influence.

The basis of the sectarianism is shown to be fear. The Protestants, alarmed by James II's willingness to enable Catholics to occupy positions of military and civil responsibility, anticipate that they are witnessing the onset of a real 'Popish Plot' to overthrow them. Again Edmund is the spokesman for Catholic tolerance and justice, defending the right of Protestants to resist any attempt by Catholics to displace them wholly from power, while at the same time arguing the case for equality of treatment and opportunity for his co-religionists. The common sense of such liberal sentiments may seem self-evident, but it wins few friends when fear is abroad, and Banim indicates that the Protestant opinion was that James II would overrule Parliament and impose measures inclined to favour Roman Catholics.

The exploration of the tactics and effects of the extreme sectarian leaders, George Walker and Friar O'Haggerty, is particularly successful. The subject remains topical – only the names seem to have changed – which suggests that Banim was writing about a certain mentality and obsessiveness that are distinctly Irish, whether Protestant or Catholic. Neither Walker nor O'Haggerty has any concept of Christianity, their vision being purely sectarian and informed by utter detestation and hatred of the other's Church. Walker repeatedly uses the rumour of a massacre of Protestants to whip up feelings, and O'Haggerty resorts to inflammatory rhetoric based upon a selective use of the Old Testament. As biblical authority merges into clerical authority and rumour is asserted as fact, the long-standing grievances of Catholics and the paranoiac fears of Protestants are equally exploited to generate tensions which inevitably spill over into acts of violence. This is less a conflict of religion or politics than a racial conflict in which two religious creeds serve to distinguish the opposing parties. Paradoxically, whereas religion can be one of the great unifying forces in a society, here it lies at the very centre of division.

O'Haggerty's and Walker's wish to embark upon independent military action without permission or declared support from the kings they allegedly serve introduces that most convoluted and apparently contradictory article of faith, the Ulsterman's interpretation of loyalty to the throne. Banim's understanding of this phenomenon is extremely accurate and illuminating. On the one hand, for men like O'Haggerty, loyalty to James II and loyalty to his Church were the same thing. But as he himself says:

Where king and religion are both in imminent peril, it seems no more than the duty of loyal subjects, and children of the faith, to act, even of their own accord, for the protection of both.[8]

In other words, loyalty may at times necessitate acting in defiance of the leader to whom one is ostensibly committed. Where the subjects see more clearly than the king what is good for him, they must take the initiative. Thus apparent treachery is justified as an extreme manifestation of good faith.

George Walker's arguments may seem even more perverse. He maintains that loyalty demands all right-thinking men should combine to overthrow James II because of his attacks upon the constitution as specifically evidenced in his promotion of Catholics to positions of power. That is to say, loyalty to the king is conditional upon him maintaining Protestant privilege in a society where Catholics constitute by far the greater part of the population. English justice and influence are assumed by Walker – and by his latter-day successors – to be synonymous with a double standard which operates helpfully or oppressively according to a person's creed. Both Edmund McDonnell and Robert Evelyn experience moments of personal doubt and uncertainty, particularly as events lead them remorselessly into conflict, but O'Haggerty and Walker deal only in beliefs which they hold to be absolute and above question. As a result their fanaticism is all the more terrifying and irresistible.

The religious difference between the Evelyns and McDonnells only becomes a source of tension in the face of increasing political crisis and after the interference of O'Haggerty and Walker. Even then, although Robert and Edmund have grown somewhat wary of each other, they are still determined to marry Eva and Esther respectively. The two women are exposed to less overt sectarian pressures than the men, but a conversation concerning the faith in which any children they may have would be reared threatens to create coolness between them and suddenly lays bare a potential problem area in their intended marriages. Eva raises the issue only to find that Esther assumes as a matter of course that McDonnell would be willing to allow his family to be brought up in the Protestant faith. Abruptly the language or, more precisely, the *tone* of sectarianism enters Esther's conversation, and the ease with which this happens reveals the deep roots of prejudice even in the mind of a liberal Protestant. The argument grows as the women discover that they would endeavour to convert their respective husbands and rear their children in their own faith, but the most frustrating thing for the reader is that at this juncture their brothers and husbands-to-be arrive, and the dispute is broken off and never resumed. Even at the close of the novel when Robert and Eva are united and have children, Banim does not show how the question resolved itself in practice, but he at least touches on an extremely sensitive and divisive issue – indeed the conversation may have been abandoned just because of its crucial and emotive substance.

The potentially tragic dilemma of Robert and Eva is that they love one another but have rival allegiances and loyalties to which they are committed, and neither feeling will be denied. Such a relationship which might grow and prosper in a tolerant and peaceful society is well nigh impossible where the community as a whole is divided and where the grounds of division are, literally, a matter of life and death. A bond that would create new links and loyalties between traditionally opposed parties is interpreted simply as an act of treachery and a weakening of the will to defend the status quo. Fortunately for Robert Evelyn and his wife the convoluted plot of the nineteenth-century novel ensures the ultimate success of their marriage.

Even so, that success involves certain compromises, the most obvious of which is the separation of Eva from her brothers, who are obliged to accompany Sarsfield and many others to the continent. Furthermore the note of hope on which *The Boyne Water* concludes can scarcely be taken seriously. Evelyn admits the failure of the Treaty of Limerick to safeguard the interests of Catholics, but he argues against all the evidence that it 'will yet be kept':

let us not despair. Other times will naturally create another spirit; when, if only to redeem the memory of their fathers, the children of my erring friends will repair this fault. . . . A little time will teach us this lesson.[9]

The confidence of this judgment perhaps makes greater sense if it is seen in the context of events in the 1820s, when the novel was written, rather than against the background of the story itself. Significantly, although Evelyn speaks of 'other times' generating 'another spirit', there is no clear indication of when this change of heart might come about, but considering his portrayal of William and James, Banim does not encourage belief that Evelyn is anticipating any early improvement. William's dour, self-contained manner, his preference for Dutch rather than English or Irish supporters, and especially his evident readiness to employ Catholics as well as Protestants in positions of trust and authority soon cause doubts in the minds of even his most ardent champions.

For his part, following defeat at the Boyne, James reveals himself to be both tactless and insulting in his publicly expressed opinion of his Irish supporters. Having argued that he himself is 'the martyr of bigotry', he accuses the Irish of cowardice in battle, an allegation which stirs both Sarsfield and Eva McDonnell to protest bitterly. Similarly, when a deputation of Irish officers appeals to James to replace the elderly and undistinguished Tyrconnel as their leader, James displays appalling misjudgment by appointing the Frenchman St. Ruth as supreme commander. The abiding impression left with the reader is that Ireland became the key battleground in a conflict which divided the loyalties of the population between two men, neither of whom displayed sympathy, understanding or even interest in the country or its citizens for their own sakes.

The publication of *The Boyne Water* marked a new phase in the evolution of Anglo-Irish fiction. The novel remains topical in a way that is unfortunate because it records prejudices which have survived and events which are still celebrated for the most negative reasons. But this is not its chief significance. John Banim's recognition of the need to explore a crucial period in the shaping of modern Irish history, his boldness in tackling a subject that was bound to impinge upon some of the most sensitive areas of Irish consciousness, and his wish to integrate it into the new genre of Anglo-Irish literature, give *The Boyne Water* its status.

In his undertaking the author was inspired by the achievement of Sir Walter Scott – who in turn claimed to be stimulated by Maria Edgeworth, thus completing an intriguing circle of influences. Scott stood out as the great example of a national writer and historian of his people, and both Banim and, later, Carleton dreamed of becoming his Irish counterpart. Their attempts to do so were not always helped by their readiness to imitate features of the master's style and approach to his subject-matter, but in *The Boyne Water* the case is somewhat different. Commenting on Scott's characterization Georg Lukács has said that the typical hero in his novels

is always a more or less mediocre, average English gentleman. He generally possesses a certain, though never outstanding, practical intelligence, a certain moral fortitude and decency which even rises to a capacity for self-sacrifice, but which never grows into a sweeping human passion, is never the enraptured devotion to a great cause.[10]

In almost every respect this might also describe Robert Evelyn's impartiality, fairmindedness and central position both in terms of the novel's plot and of its ideas. Lukács maintains that precisely because Scott's heroes are such people he was able to overcome the Romantic obsession with the career of individuals and to allow historical events their full importance. The reader is primarily made aware of how events overshadow human personalities and only secondarily of the fate of the hero – although obviously there is a continual interaction between historical process and the people involved in it at any particular time. Lukács continues:

The principal figures in Scott's novels are also typical characters nationally, but in the sense of the decent and average, rather than the eminent and all-embracing. The latter are the national heroes of a poetic view of life, the former of a prosaic one. . . . It is their task to bring the extremes whose struggle fills the novel, whose clash expresses artistically a greater crisis in society, into contact with one another. Through the plot at whose centre stands the hero, a neutral ground is sought and found upon which the extreme, opposing social forces can be brought into a human relationship with one another.[11]

An examination of the relationships between Robert Evelyn and his sister and Edmund and Eva McDonnell, of the different cultural, religious and social backgrounds and traditions which they represent in moderate form, of the ways they are drawn into conflicts urged by fanatics from both sides, and of the carefully arranged series of encounters between agents of the opposing forces through the medium of Robert Evelyn in particular, makes plain the relevance of Lukács' observations to *The Boyne Water*. Scott's influence was benign in this case, for the combination of the representative power of the novel and the sense of historical process which it generates is effective.

Nor do the novel's limitations obscure the seriousness of intent. Banim shows more understanding of the northern Irish temperament and mentality than his predecessors, and he also is aware of the evil effects of bigotry. *The Boyne Water* may not 'disperse the mists of history' quite as the author hoped but it does not shun or deny them. This is a sign of progress and of the growing maturity of the literature, for now history is accepted as a suitable and urgent subject for fictional treatment, capable of providing imaginative insights into current beliefs and events rather than being simply a catalogue of abuses perpetrated by the English against the Irish.

In 1830 John Banim returned to the period following the Treaty of Limerick, and although he published *The Anglo-Irish of the Nineteenth Century* before *The Denounced*, it helps to consider the latter book next. The title refers to the position of Catholics in Ireland during the time when the penal laws were enforced most rigorously against them, and the two stories which make up the volume were a conscious contribution to O'Connell's campaign for Catholic emancipation, a point underlined by the dedication of the first edition to the then Prime Minister, the Duke of Wellington, under whose government these laws were repealed before *The Denounced* was actually published. Banim found himself in an awkward situation: since his wish to write a novel that would have a positive influence on the emancipation debate and that would not alienate public sympathy had been overtaken by events in Parliament, he had to ensure that his stories would not re-open old wounds or appear to lack gratitude. This kind of self-consciousness has a decidedly weakening effect, so the tales are much less impressive than *The Boyne Water* and are closer in spirit to Lady Morgan's emancipation novel *O'Donnel*.

The first story *The Last Baron of Crana* is set after the Battle of Aughrim and has certain similarities of structure to *The Boyne Water*, especially in that the main plot is built around a Protestant and a Catholic family who are united by a promise made by Miles Pendergast to the dying Sir Redmond O'Burke that he will protect his son. Pendergast finds the young Patrick O'Burke living a hand-to-mouth existence in the grounds of his family home, which has been wrecked by King William's men. Accompanied only by a loyal servant, Rory Laherty, and a proscribed priest, Father James, his fear of further persecution following the sack of the house has reduced him to a state of neurotic terror.

John Banim's preference for symmetry of character and incident is evident again. Pendergast and O'Burke are matched against each other, as are their respective servants John Sharpe and Rory Laherty, whose mutual suspicion and distrust of one another are carefully analysed. Ironically they become loyal defenders of each other's interests when their masters are threatened by increasing anti-Catholic pressures in Ulster. Pendergast's liberalism alienates him from the community in much the same way as Evelyn's and McDonnell's mutually sympathetic views made them the recipients of antagonism and abuse. The focal point of sectarian rancour in *The Last Baron of Crana* is a remarkable creation. Indeed the early scenes with John Gernon and his vicious bulldog, Maud, are arguably the most vivid and engaging in the whole novel.

Gernon enjoys the honorary title of Mayor of the Bull Ring, which refers to his function as master of ceremonies during bull-baiting sessions in a local town near Pendergast's estate. In addition he is the leader of The Bachelors' Company, a paramilitary organization dedicated to the suppression of popery, and the authority he enjoys from these two positions gives him immunity from the normal processes of law. Thus he openly poaches on Pendergast's lands, and when he comes on the fugitive Father James reading his breviary in the woods and subsequently encounters Patrick O'Burke himself, Gernon is quick to charge him with his failure to attend the Established Church and his breach of the prohibition against Catholics carrying weapons. The hostility and rivalry between O'Burke and Gernon are symbolized by a ferocious fight between Brann, a magnificent Irish wolfhound and the only survivor of its kind from the assault by King William's men on the O'Burke home, and Maud, the savage bull dog. The latter wins an early success by getting its teeth into the wolfhound's neck, but Brann saves himself and when the conflict is subsequently renewed, Maud is killed. The victory is expensive, however, because it prompts Gernon to lead his Bachelors' Company against Pendergast and his Catholic guests, forcing them to flee the area.

Thereafter the novel becomes an increasingly involved account of pursuit and escape, disguise and discovery, mistaken identity and deliberate deception. There is a virtual re-enactment of the Antrim coast adventures of Evelyn and McDonnell as the Catholics flee from Pendergast Hall to seek refuge with Philip Walshe, another protector of Patrick O'Burke, in the south. The plot is further complicated by the activities of a rapparee leader, Randall Oge O'Hagan, who is really the brother of Philip Walshe and the true last Baron of Crana. He is portrayed sympathetically, another example of a good citizen driven into subversive behaviour and nomadic wandering because of 'unfriendliness, ill-neighbourhood, cold faces, finings, and at last imprisonment'.[12] Needless to say, despite his disillusionment and humiliation, he and his followers are honourable rogues, not unscrupulous high-waymen, but the broken spirit of Roger Walshe (O'Hagan's real name) is made plain when he pays a fleeting visit to the castle and lands which he should rightfully occupy:

It was pitiable to note the self-undervaluing air and the expression of countenance, with which he entered − after having stealthily gained it − one of the rooms in the house of his fathers − in his own castle.[13]

Moments like this, and the reactions of the individual involved, are much more convincing than the intricacies of plot whereby lives are saved in the nick of time and escapes are negotiated from the most improbable situations.

Another instance of insight into character occurs when John Sharpe, the arch-northerner, travels south and reacts with predictable prejudice to the sights he encounters on the way. As Banim puts it, he 'grew proportionately sour and critical after having passed the borders of Ulster'.[14] He criticizes the Irish language as sub-human and responds negatively to the farming methods, breed of livestock, landscape, and to the castle of Crana itself:

He could not understand, he said, the use or purpose of so much old stone and mortar in a residence for a few quiet Christian people, or, at least, a few who ought to be quiet and Christian, though he left all that to themselves . . . and asked − (he was thinking of Pendergast Hall) − why could they not build solid well-shaped, square, sensible houses, of comfortable-looking brick, three storeys high?[15]

This portrayal of narrow-mindedness, chauvinism and deliberate refusal to be impressed by, or even interested in, the unfamiliar highlights the racial and cultural differences between natives of the northern and southern parts of Ireland and the enormous gaps in their knowledge and understanding of each other. In general, however, such perception is infrequent, and *The Last Baron of Crana* lacks distinction.

Much the same is true of *The Conformists* which makes up the second part of *The Denounced*. Set in the mid-eighteenth century it explores the difficulties that beset the sons of a family where the father is Catholic and the mother Protestant. Because they have been raised as Catholics, the two boys are disqualified from educational opportunities by the penal laws; but they are also victims of their mother's overriding concern for them to receive schooling. The novel examines the unjust treatment meted out to the family of a mixed marriage – an issue that was evaded in *The Boyne Water*.

The difficulty is that the penal laws and the awkward social position of the D'Arcy family count less in determining their fate than the temperamental instability and, in the end, the unbelievable stupidity of the various members, particularly the mother and the younger son Daniel. The brothers Marks and Daniel are totally different in character: the former responds well to his mother's scholastic ambitions for him, going to Spain to complete his education, while the latter displays neither the will nor the ability to study. Ideally Daniel would live a simple peasant existence and would mix easily and happily with other humble farming folk, but his mother wishes to marry him to the daughter of a well-to-do family. This places him under great stress since she insists that it will only be possible when he has acquired a certain amount of learning, and because she violently resists his drunken flirtation with Jinny Haggerty (the daughter of a family evicted from the D'Arcy lands after a quarrel between Daniel and Jinny's brother Dinny). Daniel alternates between an instinctive contempt for education, and hence resentment of his mother for trying to impose it upon him, and a pathetic wish to please her. His problems are compounded by his abrupt rejection of Jinny Haggerty and by his readiness to accept the friendship of her brother, despite their earlier argument. Dinny Haggerty, in fact, turns out to be utterly treacherous and the proffered friendship merely enables him to ruin the D'Arcy family.

Temperamentally Daniel D'Arcy is the brother of John Nowlan – passionate, lacking self-discipline, extreme in his reactions, and brought to the brink of destruction by his own behaviour. But D'Arcy's torment is not as purely internal as John Nowlan's; he is the victim of an astonishingly complicated series of plots and pressures generated by a variety of people. At times indeed the story reads like a debased version of *Othello*, with Dinny Haggerty playing Iago to Daniel D'Arcy's Moor, maliciously driving him into a state of grotesque sexual jealousy and suspicion. The plot is as far-fetched as that of *Othello* but, unlike the play, it fails to transcend its improbability.

Very occasionally the reader glimpses how the penal laws could be used spitefully or to destroy a person's life. For example, on Dinny Haggerty's advice, Daniel arranges a secret meeting with a hedge-school master to improve his learning. They are betrayed to the bailiff, and though the teacher escapes, Daniel is arrested for refusing to inform against him. The episode hints at how whole sections of the Catholic community were forced to live double existences, forever afraid of being identified in their true roles. Another aspect of this theme concerns Catholic landownership. Daniel's father Hugh D'Arcy bought his estate in 1703, just before the law was changed to ban Catholics from land purchase, and although his property was not confiscated his position is highly vulnerable, for if denounced as a Catholic or if one of his family turned Protestant – 'conformed' – he would be liable to lose everything. In addition the law was framed actually to deprive tenants who struggled to improve their lands. They risked losing everything if their farms produced a profit in excess of one-third of its rent value. This system resulted in a decline in the effort and enterprise of Catholic farmers, deliberate neglect of land and buildings, and an increased rate of emigration.

The Conformists has even fewer moments of insight than *The Last Baron of Crana*. These are John Banim's last major novels with an Irish setting, and they reveal the author, already a very sick man, writing well below his abilities. Indeed these tales reproduce some of the worst features of his fiction – melodrama, extremely complex plots, unconvincing characterization – without much evidence of his compensating merits. Even his perception of the details of a landscape or building and his ear for the nuances of conversation fail him for the most part. The tales make a sorry end to a career which promised so much more at the outset.

There remain two other major novels by the Banim brothers, both published in 1828 – two years before *The Denounced*.

The Croppy, which is primarily Michael's work, deals with the 1798 uprising, while John's book, *The Anglo-Irish of the Nineteenth Century*, appeared anonymously and took a critical and embittered look at contemporary Irish politics. Surprisingly Thomas Flanagan's influential study, *The Irish Novelists, 1800–1850*, pays little attention to *The Croppy* and none at all to *The Anglo-Irish*, because both novels have an urgency and power of expression in their treatment of events which were either current realities or drawn from an immediate past that was remembered with great vividness.

The Croppy manifests all that is best and worst in the Banims' fiction. The plot is impossibly complicated and improbable, and the behaviour of some of the main characters is undiluted melodrama. Furthermore, when the author is dealing with upper-class gentlefolk, he produces characters that are stereotyped and 'flat', in E. M. Forster's sense of that word. Where he rises to distinction is in his portrayal of the passions, humour, cruelty, recklessness and anarchy of the peasantry prior to the outbreak of the 1798 rising, and in his accounts of the attacks on Enniscorthy, Wexford and New Ross. There is also a genuine attempt to represent the reasons for the uprising and the certainty of its failure without either justifying it or siding with the attitudes of the Protestants and the Government authorities. Perhaps understandably, Michael Banim is rather evasive in disclosing where his own sympathies lay, although he openly displays his horror at the sectarian excesses that accompanied the rebellion. The novel merits close attention because of its sustained effort to come to terms with one of the critical periods in modern Irish history; but it also has other literary and imaginative qualities which deserve recognition.

Banim begins with an exposition of the historical origins of sectarian rivalry and tension in the time leading up to 1798, an explanation which may appear to rest uneasily in a work of fiction but which is clearly intended to provide readers – particularly English readers – with a grasp of the explosive situation that had evolved. He perceives the source of anti-Catholicism to be the insecurity of the poorer Protestants who were not recruited into the genuinely nonsectarian Volunteer movement of the early 1790s, and in whom 'the old spirit of the admirers of Oliver Cromwell or of George Walker continued'.[16] The problem is summed up succinctly and indicates the basic failure of liberal thinkers to influence the minds of humble folk: 'Between reasoning men of the rival persuasions a philosophical feeling of brotherhood rapidly went on; – their inferiors were, meantime, cutting each other's throats.'[17] A sense of escalating violence is created by the account of how the Protestant Peep-o'-day-boys terrorized Catholics in County Armagh during the 1780s. Their activities, which were sanctioned by the penal laws, justified legal surveillance and the confiscation of Catholic weapons. Eventually the victims of this oppression formed a self-protective organization, The Defenders, which soon spread its membership away from areas of sectarian tension into districts where only Catholics lived. In so doing it became a focal point for drawing attention to local grievances against the Government or its agents, and thus diverged from its original character. An attempted insurrection in 1795 was crushingly defeated and many of The Defenders were sent to the fleets without even a trial, while the peasantry was exposed to undisciplined assaults by the military. Banim regards these events as decisive in provoking a readiness among the Catholic peasants to use force against the Government, and in making them susceptible to the influence of the United Irishmen, although they did not share the liberal and non-sectarian ideals of that organization.[18]

He develops his analysis by indicating how the Peep-o'-day-boys, encouraged by the crushing of The Defenders to renew their own hostilities against Catholics and having renamed themselves Orangemen, set about trying to expel all adherents to the Roman 'heresy' from Ulster. This, linked with the Orangemen's claim that they acted with Government authority, added to the mounting hostility of the Catholic peasants and to their sense of alienation from all the processes of law. In much the same way as *The Boyne Water* showed how Protestants lived in dread of a supposed massacre planned by the Catholics, so this novel, set a hundred years further on, reveals Catholic fears of a genocidal campaign to be waged against them by the Orangemen with the active connivance of the Government. The polarization of the community was completed by the Catholic suspicion that all Protestants were Orangemen, and therefore arch enemies, and the pressure upon Protestants by those of their own persuasion to join the Orange Order or else risk the stigma of disloyalty. Banim's impressive grasp of the irony of this situation provides a historical framework which enables the reader to make sense of, if not to justify, the atrocities recounted later in the book. Furthermore, writing some thirty years after the events he describes, he shows his awareness not only of the physical suffering and brutality of '98, but also of the profound psychological effects of the uprising and its suppression, and of the social and religious divisions it served to reinforce.

The most striking and memorable passages of the novel deal with the peasantry and with the acts of violence in which they become involved. Prior to the actual commencement of the Wexford rebellion, the growing expectation and likelihood of open aggression are evoked convincingly, as in the account of a military review where the Protestant forces flaunt their readiness for action. Despite their shabby appearance and rusty or makeshift weapons, the mindless fanaticism of the country corps makes them a force to be reckoned with. But the infantry are even more menacing. Socially they were the lowest and most under-equipped men on parade, but Banim understands precisely their uncompromising determination and ruthlessness:

they were persons who would ram the cartridge home, pull the trigger with unshaken nerve, and blanch not at the sight of blood, whether shed in the battle-field, or at the lonely road-side.[19]

Void of idealism, they are volunteers solely to intimidate or, if necessary, kill Catholics, and the fact that their existence is both legal and actively approved of by the Government is irrefutable evidence that the fears of the Catholic population were not entirely the result of hysterical rumours.

Rumour fuels the tension among Catholics, especially when mixed with accounts of individual persecution at the hands of Orangemen, or when deliberately stirred by an *agent provocateur*. For example, at a meeting held to discuss current events, a fugitive from the north tells how he is

but one of thousands of souls, hunted out of hoose an' home, and sent roaming over the country, without shed to shelter us or bit or sup for our lips: and hundreds of our religion, who didn't flee, were killed.[20]

His wife, who had just given birth, tried to accompany him, but she and her baby both died in the attempt. This personal grief has translated itself into a desire for revenge and a conviction that all Protestants are Orangemen, and that all Orangemen are as callous as those who brought disaster to his family.

The power of the man's story upon his listeners is considerable, leading them to consider their own position more closely, and to remember that the Protestants of Wexford are being recruited and armed. Suddenly the threat becomes more specific as someone recalls – or imagines – a fragment of overheard conversation: 'I hard a dozen o' Capt'n Whaley's Yeomen in Enniscorthy callin' us all gallows Papishes, an' swearin' oath upon oath that they'd cut us down like thistles.'[21] The magic word 'oath' is taken up by Rattlin' Bill Nale, a mysterious fortune-teller whose own history is a source of much local gossip and rumour, and he reads a document purporting to be the oath taken by all members of the Yeomanry, pledging themselves to exterminate the Catholics of Ireland and to 'wade ankle deep in Papist blood'. The author deliberately casts doubt on the authenticity of this oath, but shows how, in the emotionally charged atmosphere of the forge where the meeting is taking place, its discovery is decisive, so that, led by Shawn-a-Gow the blacksmith, the men urge Nale to administer to them the oath of allegiance to the United Irishmen.

Similar types of rumour played a tragically real part in provoking some of the worst excesses in the actual '98 uprising. Thomas Pakenham records how both Protestants and Catholics were affected. For example there is a story of a Catholic baker at Rathcoole who tried to dispose of the Dublin garrison by poisoning their bread; another report tells of a maid who confessed while drunk that twenty thousand Catholic serving girls had sworn to join the rebels. Elsewhere a harmless Protestant schoolmaster and a gardener were killed and mutilated, and a third man, again a Protestant, was put in a cauldron of boiling pitch. During the month of May 1798 a rumour was current in Wexford that the Protestants had taken an Orangeman's oath, almost identical with the one referred to by Rattlin' Bill Nale, and tension mounted to near hysteria among the Catholic population. The absurdity of the oath, given the overwhelming Catholic majority in the area, did nothing to improve the situation, and acts of brutality by the Protestant military authorities appeared to give it credibility.[22]

Banim draws a picture in which the ironies multiply. Rattlin' Bill Nale, the recruiting officer for the United Irishmen, is a double-agent working on behalf of the Government, and suddenly the connection between the red glow from the forge, which provides light to see the false documents and heat to shape iron into pikes, and the fires of Hell becomes explicit. Nale is recruiting men on the basis of their sectarian fears and hatred, yet the words of the oath state: 'In the awful presence of God, I do voluntarily declare, that I will persevere in endeavouring to form a *brotherhood of affection among Irishmen of every religious persuasion'* (Banim's italics).[23] The contradiction between the ideals laid down here and the intentions of those pledging themselves to them does not trouble the men. The only part of the oath that really means something to them comes in a later section where they swear never to inform against fellow members of the society, whatever the temptation or inducement. In the light of this vow the cynicism of the treacherous recruiting officer is again underlined.

If Rattlin' Bill Nale personifies the type of informer whose activities betrayed numerous conspiratorial groups in eighteenth- and nineteenth-century Ireland, the figure of Shawn-a-Gow, the blacksmith, represents the local leader and organizer of military preparations. His forge, like many others in the 1790s, becomes the focal point for political discussion among the disaffected peasants, the airing of grievances, and ultimately the fabrication of weapons.

By indicating these elements at work in society – the extremist Protestant group, the double-agent, the local Catholic peasant organizations – the author lays bare the deep divisions, distrust and mutual ignorance that existed. The problems were compounded by the lack of harmony among the peasants themselves, even as they prepared to resist the anticipated Protestant pogrom. Banim explores this, first, by giving an account of a chaotic meeting of the rebels on the eve of the uprising and, second, in his descriptions of events during the rebellion itself.

The description of the meeting satirizes the petty jealousies, clashes of personality, and total inability to distinguish between the trivial and important issues, that typify local peasant politics. The gathering, called to hear the words of an enigmatic representative of the higher echelons of the United Irishmen, immediately becomes entangled in an argument about parochial politics which, linked with the peasants' refusal to look at a map of the country as a whole, symbolizes their lack of national awareness. Their analysis of the situation is neither abstract nor intellectual, but a matter of planning particular punishments for specific enemies. The fact that the stranger, MacNevitt, fails to appreciate the implications of this indicates his remoteness from the realities of deep-seated townland grievances.

The local tailor's account of the preference of many peasants for random acts of terrorism carried out when an opportunity offers itself, as opposed to a centrally controlled national plan of action, is a prologue to the anarchy of the rebellion and reveals one of the difficulties facing the organizers. Similarly MacNevitt's attempt to convince his audience that not all Protestants detest Catholics and that many of the most eminent United Irishmen are Protestants is silenced by the knowing cynicism of the local peasantry:

There's no use in thrying to persuade ourselves, or the poor people round us, that the Protestants of Wexford are our friends. Aren't all the Orangemen Protestants? And haven't all the Protestants here, firelocks in their hands, swearing our downfall?[24]

This summarizes concisely the gap between the United Irishmen and the Wexford peasants. MacNevitt's distinctions are meaningless to them because they are fully aware of the prevailing attitude of local Protestants.

Even after the flat rejection of MacNevitt's argument, a telling exception is shown when, at the start of the uprising, the peasants gather at the house of the influential Protestant landowner, Sir Thomas Hartley, and ask him to be their leader. He refuses the request, but the fact that it was made is convincing evidence that a fair and just landlord could inspire the loyalty and affection of his Catholic tenants despite his religion. Argued in another way, Protestantism only became a focal point for aggression and bitterness when it was associated with sectarianism. Where a landlord was seen to be unprejudiced on religious grounds, and equitable in his dealings, then his creed ceased to be a provocative issue.

Although a former sympathizer with the United Irishmen, Sir Thomas Hartley refuses to lead the rebels because of the movement's loss of idealism and subsequent slide into sectarianism and internal feuding, which he sees as having replaced the struggle against England. Furthermore he abhors the prospect of a civil war, referring to the French situation to justify his feelings, and considers sectarian strife as the inevitable and uncontrollable result of any Irish uprising. Hartley's interpretation of the situation, like his suspicion that the Government was happy to encourage any means of reinforcing national disunity and sectarian emotions, is historically endorsed. The failure to win the support and leadership of Sir Thomas and his kind is of incalculable importance in considering the course of the '98 uprising. His refusal to join the rebels ensures that their progress will be anarchic and, in the end, self-destructive.

Rebellion finally breaks out in the novel after an outrageous attack on Shawn-a-Gow's smithy led by the bigoted Protestant magistrate and local yeomanry officer, Captain Whaley, in search of pikes and other evidence of violent intent. In the course of the assault Shawn-a-Gow's son is half-hanged, then revived for interrogation; and the torture is repeated until the boy eventually dies of exhaustion. This incident serves to typify the barbarous sectarian terrorism to which isolated Catholic communities were exposed. Here there is a total breakdown of any legal or judicial procedure, and the anarchy is created by the authorities themselves. Brute force is the order of the day and the least scrupulous are the most powerful.

This crude lesson is not lost on the victims of Whaley's attack, as descriptions of random acts of butchery and burning carried out by Protestants and Catholics alike on the elderly or stragglers and on deserted cabins clearly illustrate. Such early successes as the rebels enjoy, for instance at Owlard Hill, result from bungled military operations by the opposition rather than from any strategic or tactical skill on their own part. A series of victories in skirmishes leads the peasants to brave themselves for an assault on the town of Enniscorthy. Michael Banim portrays the reckless enthusiasm, the lack of an effective command structure, and the petty power struggles that characterize this improvised army.

Most memorable of all the closely observed scenes is the description of the Croppies' encampment on Vinegar Hill, first taking in the view afforded from its height across a countryside disfigured by burning houses and with Enniscorthy nearby, ransacked and strewn with the bodies of the dead and of drunken rebels sleeping off their debauch. Finally the focus moves to the people on the hill-side and to the bizarre confusion of their feelings: on the one hand, they are inspired by a 'ferocious exultation' but, on the other, they are terrified of vengeance being wreaked upon themselves. Eventually, after the majority of the rebels have left Vinegar Hill to advance on Wexford, the fears, bloodlust and sheer brutality of those remaining emerge in a grotesque series of mock trials of Protestant prisoners, almost all of whom are subsequently piked to death. The last shreds of idealism are shown to have deserted these people who, interested only in food, drink and killing supposed enemies, illustrate in their behaviour the full horror of civil war. At this decisive point Michael Banim offers a symbol to express the hard reality of the situation. A green flag inscribed with the words 'Liberty or Death' had been raised above the windmill in which Protestant captives were held before their fates were decided:

but the summer-breeze, as if disgusted from its agency, had fled the summit of Vinegar Hill, leaving that baleful flag to droop over the scene beneath it, until within its heavy folds the word 'Liberty' became hidden, and 'Death' alone was visible.[25]

Although *The Croppy* is less carefully constructed than *The Boyne Water* and ranges less widely in character and incident, it tackles an emotive era of Irish history with imagination and insight. The author's engagement with his subject-matter, his undisguised sincerity and earnestness of purpose, and his strength of feeling are evident. He generally succeeds in providing both a factual historical framework and an intensely realized series of accounts of individual suffering and privation. This combination gives the novel value as an interpretation – albeit a fictional interpretation – of the origins and course of part of the 1798 uprising. The book is weakest in its main plot where romance, narrow escapes and melodramatic encounters abound; the best parts concern the Catholic peasantry and the general background to the period, but Banim's perception of the fear and weakness of the Protestants shown in their very acts of aggression is particularly notable. In a curious way he anticipates Jean-Paul Sartre's theory that in a situation between a torturer and his victim, as long as the victim refuses to capitulate totally, thus confirming his worthlessness and justifying the cruelty inflicted on him, the torturer is left in the more agonizing position because his own humanity is in doubt.

The novel contemplates the horrors of civil warfare more fully than any of its predecessors, and this lends weight to the author's regrets for the lost idealism and unification of Protestant and Catholic interests originally aimed for by the United Irishmen. In as far as Michael Banim reveals a personal sympathy for the followers of Wolfe Tone, the book may be taken to support republican ideals, but he also seems to share the doubts and disappointments of Sir Thomas Hartley with the way in which events were developing. Certainly *The Croppy* is less concerned to argue the merits of a particular political philosophy than to interpret what to the English was yet another troublesome Irish uprising and further indication of the disloyalty of the natives; to explain, though not always to justify, Catholic feelings and behaviour; to expose the corruption and cynicism of the Government and its Protestant agents; and to portray the devastation caused by civil strife. When focusing on these issues the novel has a powerful insistence.

If *The Croppy* enunciated certain doubts and disappointments about the course of recent Irish history, *The Anglo-Irish of the Nineteenth Century* looked at contemporary attitudes towards Ireland with a degree of cynicism and disillusionment which takes the reader by surprise. John Banim published the novel anonymously in 1828, the same year as *The Croppy* first appeared, and the immediacy and relevance it was felt to have are reflected in the words of a reviewer in the *Scotsman*:

This novel will be much read. Its great topic – the policy of England towards Ireland – the question, What ought now to be done with the Irish Catholics? is uppermost at present in the public mind, and is momentous if not engrossing; its great staple – the feelings of the English and the Irish towards each other, or rather of the provincializing Anglo-Irish, or Orange, faction, towards their half countrymen – would have been interesting at any time, from its requiring at once a portraiture of manners and an analysis of motives; but it is doubly so now, from the feelings of which it consists, and the manner in which they are dealt with, involving the quiet and prosperity of an empire.[26]

This reviewer rightly stressed the urgent questions of political and national identity raised in the novel, for they give it its bite and are treated with an unaccustomed frankness.

At one level *The Anglo-Irish* follows a formula already seen in *The Absentee* and *Ennui* – the leading character Gerald Blount, the son of an absentee landlord, begins by maintaining his dislike and even his embarrassment with all things Irish, but following a variety of exotic adventures he grows to recognize the error of his ways and ends by settling in Ireland and marrying an Irishwoman. Apart from this general similarity of structure, however: John Banim's book has little in common with those of Maria Edgeworth. Indeed the dismissive manner and tone at the conclusion of *The Anglo-Irish* may even suggest that the author is wilfully parodying the conventional optimistic ending of the earlier books. Certainly its sincerity is scarcely credible following the bitter analysis of the state of Irish affairs which forms the core of the novel.

All the events are viewed through the eyes of Gerald Blount, who is the ubiquitous mediator in the same way as Robert Evelyn was in *The Boyne Water*. At the outset he is orphaned and as a minor is placed under the guardianship of three men – a character referred to as 'The Minister' (in fact, an unflattering portrait of Castlereagh), Sir Robert Flood, a General of Irish origin, and Mr Knightly, an Anglo-Irish landlord who lives at home on his estate. These details matter because the various characters have attitudes towards Ireland and the Irish which are significant both in themselves and in the influence they have on Gerald. Through them John Banim approaches the problem of Anglo-Irish relations primarily in racial – rather than religious or political – terms. This interpretation also informed *The Boyne Water*, but *The Anglo-Irish* pursues it much more fully. Religious antagonism and political difficulties clearly exist, but these are symptomatic of the racial difference rather than the fundamental causes of tension and distrust. Gerald Blount and his older brother begin by feeling contempt for the Irish – they liken Mr Knightly to Peter Bell, the simple-minded hero of Wordsworth's poem, and to Caliban, the monster on the island in *The Tempest* – but their attitudes are not merely adolescent humour and bad taste; they represent the views held by much older and more experienced men of the world. The Minister and General Flood are critical of Mr Knightly's failure to conform to their idea of social etiquette, and assume that, because he is Irish and lives at home, he must automatically be a boorish, uneducated provincial. This is despite the fact that Mr Knightly is a Protestant man of property – not 'mere Irish', to use the parlance of the Minister and General – and thus merits their support.

The *hauteur* they display towards Mr Knightly as an individual turns to open dislike of the Irish as a whole when the gentlemen consider the unrest in the country. Knightly appears to acquiesce in the Government's view of Ireland as a perpetual source of trouble, and he also agrees with General

Flood's model colonial theory that the only way for the country to become quiet, prosperous and worth living in is for 'the great majority of the population . . . [to] cease to be merely Irish, and become, like the only portion of it who are now respectable, intelligent – ay, or civilized, – English-Irish.'[27] This crucial idea forms the key to Gerald Blount's Irish philosophy and it is tested out in various situations within the novel. Ironically, of course, Flood is himself of Irish background, and the argument coming from him is reminiscent of Lady Clonbrony's belief in the superiority of English polite society.

The Minister and General are irritated, almost petulant, because the Irish appear to be unwilling or unable to benefit from the examples of civilization and character shown to them by the English. Typically the General argues that the most effective way of producing the desired change of character would be for the native population to suffer a 'salutary humiliation' at the hands of English soldiers, in the aftermath of which they might be expected to embrace the values of their conquerors. His logic is curious but not unique.

Gerald Blount himself is repeatedly embarrassed and discomfited by his encounters with Irish folk living in England. His brother warns him to guard against 'the manners, temper, and even the brogue' which they regard as the tell-tale signs of an undesirable background.[28] This demonstrates the total alienation from Ireland felt by the brothers and also suggests their own insecurity and sense of inferiority in English society, since such matters assume a major importance to them. In a way there is something more endearing in Lady Clonbrony's idiomatic blunders among English gentlewomen than in the studied purity of language sought after by the Blounts.

At Cambridge University Gerald utters renewed expressions of regret for his own ancestry which precludes him from feeling 'perfect identity' with England, and experiences fresh shame at the loud-mouthed behaviour and drunken pranks of the Irish students. The fact that they are Protestant Irishmen who conduct themselves in such an unruly way makes him speculate what a 'genuine Hibernian' (that is native Irish Catholic) must be like. He also hears these undergraduates denounce the peasantry as ignorant and idle, the priests as bigoted and superstitious, and the middle-class Catholics as rude and vain. Gerald does not give much consideration to the anomaly that these accusations come from people who are themselves the epitome of irresponsibility and folly and who are also members of the most privileged section of Irish society; he is ashamed of the Irishmen primarily because they are not English. The reader, however, is not prevented from appreciating the irony.

A London society gathering attended by Gerald after the end of his Cambridge days makes plain the depth of John Banim's disillusionment and his loss of hope in conciliatory politics towards Ireland. Here the Irish are dismissed as a race who, unlike the Scots, have never been taught to think. The former Parliament is mocked as 'absurd' and 'exquisitely Irish', while the worthless and bankrupt Dublin Ascendancy gentleman, Mr Gore, argues that whatever good conduct, industry, intellect, morality or rank exist in Ireland derive from the English. Mr Gore also endorses a plan for the conversion of Irish Catholics, maintaining that the people have no concept of truth or religion, but only superstitious fears of the half-educated priests. A Bishop of the Established Church denounces Catholicism in general and Jesuits in particular as the root of all evil and as a constant source of hostility towards England. In short these prejudices and opinions are an extension of the narrow-minded bigotry and intolerance of George Walker and Father O'Haggerty in *The Boyne Water*; but where their extremism appeared a limited, if influential, phenomenon, these conversations are now part of the general small-talk of polite society.

The same kind of cynicism is evident in the account of an emancipation debate in the House of Commons. Gerald, with all the naivety of youth, informs the Minister that he would support an Emancipation Bill, because he understands such a ruling to have been implied in the spirit of the Act of Union. This is, of course, historically accurate, but the Minister feels under no obligation to history: ' "Words may *seem* to *imply* many meanings," remarked the Minister, smiling.'[29] In practice the debate is a low-key affair ending in a negative vote on the basis of political expediency. Mr Gunning, a cynical old Scot who befriends Gerald, is left to explain to him the significance of what he has seen. Gunning is an important commentator, providing a disenchanted interpretation of events which must correspond closely with the views of the author himself. He regards Gerald's 'charitable politics' with contempt, pointing out how much money the Established Church in Ireland would stand to lose if Catholic emancipation were granted and an agitation against tithes were to follow, and cynically dismisses the apparent interest in the emancipation issue shown by the House of Commons as merely a safety valve to create the impression of action where no will to change the law exists. It is a deliberate blind to mislead the Irish and to ensure that disorder in the country does not become unmanageable, particularly while English military resources are deployed in fighting the Peninsula War. Such allegations are arresting and dramatic; they cut through the convention of politely restrained chiding and moral pleading characteristic of earlier novels on the emancipation subject and prepare the ground for the radical alternative put forward in the closing stages of the novel by Mr Knightly.

First, the hero has to be brought into contact with Irish people in Ireland, and this is achieved by allowing him to be shipwrecked on the Irish coast and rescued by the mysterious Miss Knightly – although Gerald does not know who she is – and a group of peasants with Rockite sympathies. Sadly Banim's portrayal of these characters is disappointing and unconvincing and there is no sustained attempt to evoke their way of life or hardships. As a whole the peasants serve primarily as aids to advance the plot or as decorative local colour.

Later Gerald's exploration of Dublin forces him to revise his views on its architectural and aesthetic merits, while the earnestness, realism and energy of the debate he attends between O'Connell and Shiel impress him. The climax to his stay in the city comes when he attends a party at Mr Gore's house and hears the inanities, prejudices and anti-Catholic venom of the Ascendancy freely expressed. The gathering takes place on the evening of a rumoured uprising by Captain Rock and his followers and an attempt to slaughter the Protestants in the capital. As the anti-Catholicism of the gathering becomes less and less restrained, one particular outburst from Mr Gore drives Gerald into voicing sympathies which earlier would have been inconceivable. Gore denounces Irish Catholics as

'a half-savage race who hate us, our religion, our superior station, and our English descent, just as the Caffers and Hottentots hate the members and subjects of our paternal Colonial Government at the Cape, and –'
'If you give them the same cause for hatred, as that Colonial Government, which you call paternal, gives to the Caffers and

Hottentots, I love *them* for hating *you* with all their hearts and souls,'
interrupted Gunning.
'And so do I,' said Gerald.[30]

Both Gerald's intelligence and his sense of decency are
outraged by Gore's mindless bigotry and arrogance, but he
finds that there are many others who agree with his host. Their
sentiments expose the fundamental lack of confidence and
insecurity of many Ascendancy gentlemen in the post-Union
period, and they speak from a position of weakness, whether
consciously recognized or not, rather than from strength.

That weakness is reflected in another way by an old landlord
who recalls the days when an awkward tenant was kept in
place by a horse-whipping or by setting the dogs on him, but
who knows that now the same man will threaten his master
with an action for assault if he is similarly abused. As passions mount the suggestions for keeping the Catholics in their
place become increasingly wild – forced labour, deliberate
starvation, transportation, forbidding them to marry, letting
them rebel and then massacring them – and the whole grim
ritual of hate culminates in a toast which Gunning and Gerald
refuse to drink: 'The Pope in the pillory, the pillory in h-ll,
pelted with priests by the d-l!'[31] Banim then mocks the scene
by allowing the party to believe that the Rockite rebellion has
started, when in fact nothing is happening; and Charles Flood
mischievously encourages them in their mistake, ordering the
men to discharge their guns into the fireplace to make an
impressive noise and directing the ladies to hide in the cellars.
Although the men admit their error when they see the trick
that has been played on them, the reader can have little doubt
that their antagonism towards Catholics, their fear of them,
and their readiness to use their weapons against them are all
real enough. As elsewhere Gunning's experience enables him
to perceive a basic truth about the psychology and behaviour
of the Anglo-Irish:

I never knew till now why it was that, whenever such of your half-
Irish as I have seen, come to visit us in England, they appeared to be
over-polite, over-conciliating, self-doubting, inferior kind of men. But
now I know it. They are tyrants at home under us, and they must be
inferiors *from* home, in our presence: they can't help it.[32]

This captures the dilemma of people bred with the expectation
of exercising authority, convinced of their racial and religious
superiority, yet lacking confidence in their position, aware

of their difference from the true English and of the dislike or contempt felt for them in England, and frequently crippled by debts and obligations that undermined their credibility. The only course open to them was to trumpet their own virtues at home, which effectively meant heaping abuse upon the rest of the community, and hope that England, which had deprived them of their Parliament and, as it seemed to them, eroded their position by allowing the penal laws to lapse, would not desert them still further. Banim's grasp of the problem is perceptive, imaginative and bolder than any treatment of it since Maria Edgeworth. In a sense he carries the Rackrent story forward into another generation.

Now that the scales have begun to fall from Gerald Blount's eyes and his doubts about the worthiness of the Anglo-Irish Ascendancy to occupy any position of responsibility have become very real, the story moves towards its climax – his voluntary journey into the country to visit his sister and the Knightlys. On this journey his conversation with an unrecognized fellow-traveller – in fact Mr Knightly himself – introduces the novel's most radical ideas, which challenge and upset Gerald's prejudices and long-established opinions. Thus a casual comparison between the slums of Dublin and the St Giles district of London where Irish emigrants live produces agreement from the stranger, followed by criticism of the Act of Union which allows the English to abuse, mistreat and corrupt the Irish, and causes them to clan together for mutual protection and support. Far from assuming that because they live differently, the English must be superior, Knightly draws attention to the debilitating effect of city life upon Irish emigrants and the actively insulting and damaging attitudes of the English towards them. He points out that the insult is even enshrined in English law, which proclaims that a marriage between two Catholics in England, celebrated by a Catholic priest, is null and void (whereas this would not be so in Ireland); and thus many Irish couples are forced to live in sin, according to the institutions of state, and the less scrupulous of them can abandon their partners at will without committing any crime or incurring any liability. Gerald cannot reply to these facts, nor can he deny Mr Knightly's claim that, against all the odds, many Irish Catholics have achieved positions of distinction in English society, especially in the sphere of journalism and editorial work, and have preserved impeccable characters in all their dealings. Mr Knightly even defends the fighting in London-Irish slums, contrasting its warm-blooded spontaneity and short-lived fury with the cold-blooded, professional prize-fighting so popular among the English. His view may be oversimplified but it passes beyond the convenient stereotyped image of the Irish as wild, drunken and aggressive, commenting instead on a temperament which is volatile, prone to strong expressions of feeling and ready to argue and defend a person or idea with utmost intensity.

Mr Knightly rejects any scheme for anglicizing the Irish and appeals to seven hundred years of failure as his justification. He recommends instead a new plan:

In fact, Sir, since we plainly see that Ireland *cannot* be made English, suppose we just allow her to make herself what she is everyday becoming in spite of us – Irish?[33]

This forthright demand for the recognition of Ireland as an independent, self-governing nation is the most radical political statement in early Anglo-Irish fiction. Knightly continues by insisting that only a minority of the descendants of the planters and invaders regard themselves as opposed to the native Irish. The majority of the people of Ireland

now amount to numbers fitted to form a great nation; and they are at last united, firm; talky, if you like; but still firm; reflective and full of purpose; united by a riveting of every link of the social chain; united in religion, – or at least their fellow-countrymen who join them in *purpose*, care nothing for the difference, – and above all, Sir, they are – United Irish.[34]

These claims continue the radical philosophies that originate with Wolfe Tone and the United Irishmen, and anticipate the nationalism of Thomas Davis and the Young Irelanders. Knightly does not insist on armed struggle as the necessary route to freedom, but neither does he exclude it as a possibility. What he does uphold as absolutely inevitable is the eventual establishment of Ireland as

a nation, free, and able to work out its own resources . . . when once a country has come to a certain step, she must go further; there is a moral necessity – a necessity sown in the elements of human nature, then manifesting itself, that she should. Every country that ever gained that certain step, has done so; Ireland has gained it, and she must do so.[35]

The insistence that Ireland's future must lie within herself and her own people, rather than in subjection or lip-service to

England, is crucial. So too is Knightly's realization that religious differences between the descendants of former invaders are much less important than the cause of the nation as a whole. Implied here is the acknowledgement that the true cause of the Anglo-Irish, and their potential for practical and constructive influence, lies not in aping and kow-towing to the English, who will never accept them on equal terms anyway, but in siding with the best interests of the native Irish. This is, of course, the insight that gave strength and inspiration to Davis, Butt and Parnell in later days. Indeed Mr Knightly's words anticipate almost uncannily the famous declaration made nearly sixty years later by Charles Stewart Parnell, when he asserted that 'No man has the right to set a boundary to the onward march of a nation. No man has a right to say: "Thus far shalt thou go and no further." ' In response to Gerald's scepticism about how the unity of minds among Irishmen of all kinds is to be achieved, Knightly sees no need to root out or annihilate those who resist the progress of the nation towards autonomy, because they will simply be rendered redundant by the passage of history:

Ireland must, at last, become a nation in the teeth of that disunion, as far as it goes, and those who made it, and who obstinately and foolishly keep it up, must abide the consequences. They have made their bed; let them lie down on it. They have spurned every opportunity of getting on along with the Irish people, when both might have gone on well together, to the end of the world; and now the Irish people will get on without them.[36]

The English policy of permitting trifling reforms or of displaying hypocritical or half-hearted concern for the Irish will not serve to delude or impress for much longer. Ironically, in Knightly's view, the biggest error of judgment made by the English was in repealing the penal laws which were truly effective in demoralizing, humiliating and crushing the spirit of the nation. Having granted certain freedoms, though no power, the English themselves have created the irrepressible demand for total liberation and an uncompromised national identity: 'The whole slave may be kept stationary, the half freedman never.'[37] Conversely, there is no way that the English will be able to re-introduce penal legislation, and any attempt at a genocidal solution would cause international disgrace and censure.

Gerald Blount's last attempt to discredit Knightly's ideas

collapses when he discovers that the speaker is a Protestant, not, as he assumed, a Catholic, and a landlord. Thereafter the novel is something of an anti-climax, as if Banim, having exposed the cynicism and inadequacy of the English authorities and certain representatives of the Anglo-Irish Ascendancy in their relationship to Ireland, and having voiced a radical alternative policy through Mr Knightly, felt that his task was completed. The unsatisfactory nature of the account of Gerald Blount's renewed adventures among the Rockites, and the closing paragraphs, in which the reader is told that, having become Lord Clangore on his brother's premature death, he shortly afterwards 'married a mere Irishwoman, and since then continues to live in Ireland, as a mere Irishman', can only be taken as a dismissal. The author promises the possibility of future volumes in which the course and details of Gerald Blount's change of heart may be traced, but this book was never written and the writer's loss of interest in the subject is obvious. In addition the events of history caught up with the novel, for in 1828, when it was published, O'Connell won his famous Clare election victory and within two years Catholic emancipation was on the statute books.

The Anglo-Irish of the Nineteenth Century is an unusual and, in places, a forceful work. But as fiction it is even more compromised by the author's bias than most novels of its kind. The actual story of Gerald Blount is much less memorable than some of the opinions and ideas contained in the book. Indeed the fortunes of Gerald serve largely as a framework to support the impassioned satire and the heartfelt disillusionment of the author with the objects of his attack. In its own time the assault on English political deviousness and on the petty tyranny and bigotry of the Dublin Ascendancy must have seemed even more abrasive than it does now, whereas a modern reader may find matter of more enduring interest in Mr Knightly's anticipation of the future role and identity of those members of the Anglo-Irish community wishing to take an active part in the progress of the Irish nation and in his view of the development of Ireland as an independent entity. Here he finally states an idea which earlier writers seemed anxious to avoid, namely the desirability of separating Irish and English politics and institutions and of permitting the unimpeded growth and expression of Irish nationality. The apparent optimism of Mr Knightly is not justified by history, for even O'Connell's success and the Emancipation Bill were limited victories, but his radical opinions are early examples of a mode of thought which grew in prominence and practical influence as the century advanced. Gradually ideas voiced in a rather undistinguished, anonymous novel of the 1820s would become issues of principle for radical politicians in the 1840s. John Banim may not have been the originator of Mr Knightly's political philosophy, but its inclusion in *The Anglo-Irish of the Nineteenth Century* shows his radical sympathies. Where *The Boyne Water* (and, to some extent, the later tales *The Last Baron of Crana* and *The Conformists*) endeavoured to come to terms with crucial periods in Ireland's past, *The Anglo-Irish* is John Banim's novel of the present and future, and it again distinguishes him as a writer with a passionate concern to establish as accurately as possible the position of the Irish people and their national identity.

FOUR

LADY MORGAN'S DEPARTURE AND GRIFFIN'S MAJOR WORKS (1825–30)

> . . . a softening corollary to the more exciting moral chronicles of other writers, to bring forward the sorrows and the affections more frequently than the violent and fearful passions of the people
>
> Gerald Griffin
> from the Conclusion of the
> *Tales of the Munster Festivals*

Four more novels published between 1825 and 1830 remain to be considered. Three by Gerald Griffin effectively conclude his contribution to Anglo-Irish literature, and the other, by Lady Morgan, is also her last novel to deal with Irish subject matter. This book, *The O'Briens and the O'Flahertys*, is the most complex of her Irish novels and probably the best remembered of all her works. Set in the period 1780-1800 it describes the political intricacies and social convulsions of the time from the point of view of two families. The O'Briens, an ancient Catholic family, have suffered and lost in the face of numerous struggles with the English and as a result of penal legislation. Despite this they have remained in Ireland whereas the equally ancient O'Flaherty family has sought refuge on the continent and, particularly, in the Catholic Church. These alternatives – to remain in poverty in Ireland or to seek better fortunes in Europe – represent the choices open to the Catholic gentry of the eighteenth century, whom as elsewhere Lady Morgan champions in their position of hardship.

The hero Murrogh O'Brien is the focal point of a number of key social tensions. Thus he comes from a lapsed Catholic family, but was secretly educated in Catholicism in his youth. His experiences during a period spent on the continent have given him a sceptical attitude towards his faith, and have also made him aware of the revolutionary philosophies and ideals of freedom current in France in the second half of the eighteenth century. Murrogh is an independent thinker attracted by the objectives of the United Irishmen, yet he is also, at least for a time, a member of the ultra-conservative University of Dublin. Furthermore he is introduced to vice-regal society in Dublin, with which he has a kind of love-hate relationship. Although the very diversity of Murrogh's experiences makes him intriguing, it is so great that is stretches credulity, while the plot of the novel becomes progressively more fantastic.

Lady Morgan's absorption with family histories and with the effects upon Catholics of penal legislation and military defeat typifies the permanent fascination which history has for most Irish people. The nationalist movement has always been ready to cite the roll of Irish defeats and oppression, and in this respect *The O'Briens and the O'Flahertys* is representative. Indeed the Abbé O'Flaherty interprets the 'common affliction of the country' in purely sectarian terms, seeing its commercial misfortunes as stemming directly from 'the monopoly enjoyed by the merchants of the established church'.[1] But Lady Morgan endeavours to show the situation from the Protestant perspective as well. She notes how the complicated and prolonged acts of confiscation and redistribution of land deprived the country of capital, 'awoke the spirit of litigation, that has long been a ridicule and a reproach to the national character', and also reduced the new Protestant landholders to a general state of insecurity regarding their own rights of possession, even though they themselves had instigated the legal process against their Catholic counterparts.[2] This analysis reveals an unexpected dimension to the social tensions in the country – allusions to the victimization of the Catholics are predictable, but the insight into the uneasiness of the Protestants enlarges the reader's view of affairs.

A similar breadth of understanding is found in the author's comments on the Volunteer movement where, for the first time, she refers to 'the eloquence of men with arms in their hands', and links this 'eloquence' to the granting of free trade and legislative independence.[3] In addition her observations on the suppression of the Irish Volunteers after their open demonstration of sympathy for the French Revolution are accurate:

It was then that the government, taking new alarm, resolved upon the destruction of a force, which if it had no other demerit, must have at once been odious and suspicious, because it was – national.[4]

The harshness of tone and the open sneer at the government are, perhaps, surprising given the general conservatism of Lady Morgan's politics, but are consistent with the satirical picture of the Dublin Castle rulers around whom a considerable part of the novel revolves. They are referred to as oligarchs, the autocrats of fashion and politics alike, unscrupulously damaging the lives and tranquillity of the Irish people by their selfish, uncaring exercise of power.

The attack on government is more full-blooded throughout than in the earlier novels, while the picture of poverty and squalor in Dublin, first observed in the description of Ringsend in *Florence Macarthy*, is now seen as the specific responsibility of the country's rulers rather than simply as a distressing circumstance without a cause. There is no concession to high society, no appeal to good sense and conscience – the author, by implication, reveals that good sense and conscience cannot be expected from such people; the time for them to show willing has passed.

The criticism of government continues in the study of the University of Dublin, with its account of legislation depriving Catholics of educational opportunities. To their lasting credit there was a movement amongst the students of Trinity College to debate and discuss the history and political future of the country, but again Lady Morgan is quick to show how the University authorities responded to such gestures of nationalism by rusticating those who offended. Murrogh O'Brien himself is expelled, and ironically this precipitates his involvement with the United Irishmen and his recognition that: 'Ireland is my vocation . . . . here, in this unhappy land, stands the altar of my first and warmest vows.'[5] With these words, simultaneously suggestive of a religious and a sexual bond, Murrogh expresses a central idea in Irish nationalism, both literary and political. The concept of dedication to the country – so often and so tragically transmuted into a readiness to die for Ireland rather than to live for her – is fundamental. Furthermore Murrogh's radicalism is more clearly defined by his acceptance of the argument that in Ireland the only merit rewarded by the law is 'political subserviency', that the Church is 'a broad road to intellectual and moral nothingness', and that the education offered by the establishment is the enemy of 'those students who presume to scan men or combine realities'.[6]

The contrast between the midnight gathering of United

Irishmen which Murrogh attends and that portrayed at Shawn-na-Gow's forge in *The Croppy* (or in Carleton's tale 'The Midnight Mass') is at once irresistible and striking. The Back Lane conspirators are cultured, disciplined, idealistic, and convinced of their ability to achieve

national redemption by its sole means – *a national union!* – that brotherhood of affection, that community of interest, which operating from its centre, to the remotest verge of society, will effect a regeneration by a means as constitutional as they are effectual.[7]

The remoteness of both the language and the ideals expressed here from those of the Wexford croppies is obvious, and likewise the civilized debate of the Dublin United Irishmen is worlds apart from the hellish glow of Shawn-na-Gow's forge and the feverish business of making and concealing pikes. These expressions of heady idealism and the account of the secret meeting are as much as Lady Morgan presumes to show of the United Irishmen, but she succeeds in conveying, however locally, the fervour, sincerity and purity of intention characteristic of those early days.

Murrogh O'Brien's adventures in Connemara allow Lady Morgan to interpret the landscape for the first time as a pictorial history book as well as a beautiful sight. There are references to 'vast tracts' of the countryside made over to new proprietors and to the feebleness of their efforts to reclaim or improve the land. She singles out ruined castles, representative of past grandeur, or else occupied by the agents of absentee landlords. Finally, and most notable of all, the hero's nationalist feelings are directly inspired and heightened by the impact of the landscape on his emotions and mind:

he wondered that in regions so sublime the Irish heart ever quailed, the Irish spirit ever drooped; and that men, who were masters of such natural ramparts, had not rather died in their defiles than have submitted to the oppressor.[8]

Here is the appeal of O'Connell, Davis and Pearse, the characteristic attitude of emotionally expressed defiance and racial pride in the face of a hostile reality, expressed with greater eloquence than, perhaps, anywhere else in Lady Morgan's work.

Nonetheless the failure of the United Irishmen to arouse widespread support is evident as is the readiness of many of the more prosperous Catholics to accept their situation and be grateful that things are not worse. As Lord Walter Fitzwalter, Murrogh O'Brien's United Irishman friend, tells him:

Ireland is not America, still less is it France. The knowledge, the philosophy of the one, the energy, the freshness of the other, are wanting to this land of helots. The lever by which this inert mass is to be moved, is one of infinite delicacy.[9]

The hero's own experience demonstrates the correctness of this analysis – as does the entirety of *The Croppy* in another way.

Although Murrogh O'Brien's story culminates in his successful escape from Ireland, where he is wanted for his political activities, it is ultimately one of failure. The Superior of the Abbey of Moycullen, Beavoin O'Flaherty, sums up the dilemma of the would-be patriot in words which are relevant not only to this novel but to the fate of many men and women who have made Ireland their vocation:

To be born an Irishman is a dark destiny at the best. . . . Here virtue is made to turn traitor to itself; and the same passions that rouse the patriot to any sacrifice, urge him into the snares of the profligate. Here the fortitude of long endurance corrupts into obsequiousness; and the spirit of the gallant maddens into lawless intemperance. Here genius is the object of suspicion to dull rulers, and of insult to petty underlings; and all that bends not – falls.[10]

These words prove not only to be perceptive but also deeply ironic, for while the Abbess urges Murrogh to flee and save his life, she avows it to be her intention to run a religious house which will liberalize the members of her sect and free them from the influence of bigotry. This aim is in marked contrast to the Abbot O'Brien's mission to Connemara to promote a revival of fundamental Catholicism on narrow sectarian principles. The fate of both undertakings is doomed, however, for the Abbot O'Brien dies at the altar, a martyr in the eyes of the congregation, during a raid by soldiers searching for Murrogh. Meanwhile the reader's last view of the Abbess, who has sworn to 'live in Ireland' as 'the purest proof of patriotism, that those, unprotected by power and faction, can give', comes when she reappears in the closing pages of the book, at the opera in Paris in 1802, as the wife of Murrogh O'Brien, now a French general.[11]

With each novel from the time of *The Wild Irish Girl*, Lady Morgan's confidence and optimism noticeably waned. *The O'Briens and the O'Flahertys*, the least conclusive and the most pessimistic of her Irish tales, is also the most complex in approach to its subject and in its presentation of the various attitudes active within late eighteenth-century Irish society. It comes as no surprise that this was Lady Morgan's last significant work about Ireland – her *Dramatic Sketches from Real Life* (1833) was her only other specifically Irish publication – and that she eventually made her permanent home in England. Although she had championed the cause of Catholic emancipation for twenty odd years, and would see that ambition fulfilled soon after the publication of *The O'Briens and the O'Flahertys*, Lady Morgan's disillusionment had set in, and in 1837 she retreated to Belgravia and the security of a pension awarded for services rendered to the world of letters.

To be cynical and dismissive of this retirement is to ignore its point and to be grossly unfair to an extraordinary woman whose long life – she was probably fifty-two when *The O'Briens and the O'Flahertys* appeared in 1828 and was to live on until 1859 – spanned many of the achievements, disappointments, false starts and disasters out of which modern Ireland arose. Like Maria Edgeworth, with whom she shared the doubtful privilege of longevity, she found the reality of nineteenth-century Ireland increasingly incomprehensible as it grew remote from the situation of her formative years. And yet Lady Morgan's novels are part of the history of that period and should not be forgotten. As one critic has written in a recent article: 'Between the seanachies of old Ireland and Douglas Hyde of the late nineteenth century came Sydney Owenson, Lady Morgan.'[12] Admittedly she misconstrued the future: she was wrong to pin her hopes on the return of the absentees and the restoration of the old Irish families; and she underestimated the extent to which the peasants would be capable of violence, conspiracy and agrarian terrorism. In such misjudgments she was not alone. On the positive side there is much more to be allowed. Lady Morgan was an early expositor of nationalist feelings and emotions in prose fiction, of that patriotism of the heart which has stirred men to action again and again down the years. She also expressed the anguish and frustration which she identified as another very real aspect of the experience of being Irish, and her deepening awareness of the psychological damage resulting from repression is one of her most incisive revelations. In short Murrogh O'Brien's claim that service to Ireland was his vocation was also Lady Morgan's claim.

Her nationalism was emotionally radical but politically naive and conservative, while her romantic commitment to the nobility and her faith in their ultimate willingness to return to Ireland to serve and to save the country are crucial limitations of her vision. Even in *The O'Briens and the O'Flahertys* the noble characters excite the writer's imagination – Murrogh O'Brien himself, his foster-brother, the romantic and improbable Shane-na-Brien, the beautiful Beavoin O'Flaherty, and the doyenne of high society, Countess Knocklofty. Lady Morgan also reveals genteel poverty in the masterly comic scenes involving the Misses MacTaaf. Here she shows how arrogance and consciousness of social niceties exist alongside bankruptcy and ruin. But there is no such perception of the details of life among the poor, and this helps to explain her lack of understanding and sympathy for the peasants when they became politically active.

The life and writings of Lady Morgan reveal a growing uncertainty of relationship between the novelist, her native country and her potential readers; the tension that was always implicit between her commitment to Ireland and the Irish and the knowledge that her audience would be largely English is a considerable shaping influence in her fiction. Other Anglo-Irish novelists of the period were conscious of similar difficulties, and one of the most telling illustrations of the peculiarity of the author's relationship to subject-matter and audience is *The Collegians* by Gerald Griffin.

First published in 1829, this is the book for which Griffin's name is remembered, although more people may be familiar with Dion Boucicault's melodrama *The Colleen Bawn* or Benedict's opera *The Lily of Killarney*, both based upon it, than with the novel itself. *The Collegians* presents a broader cross-section of Irish society than any earlier fiction, and much of the richness of the book derives from the variety of life, language and characters portrayed in it. Likewise its very scope generates a new awareness in the reader of the social divisions and confusions within the community it describes. As Thomas Flanagan has written:

The Collegians is a 'social' novel, embracing all classes and conditions. But what strikes one immediately about the culture which Griffin has created is its lack of cohesiveness.[13]

This is a view shared by John Cronin, who also points out how the novel differs importantly from fiction of the exclusively 'Big House' kind, in which the authors are generally concerned with Irish society only at its two extremes. Griffin, clearly, works very hard to enrichen and amplify the public's sense of the complexity and density of the social fabric of Ireland.[14]

Specifically, Griffin goes to great lengths to depict a hitherto unacknowledged sector of Irish society, the Catholic middle class, and to show their solid respectability and worth.

One of the curiosities of Anglo-Irish fiction in the nineteenth century, and one of its most striking differences from English fiction of the same period, is that whereas novelists in the latter tradition frequently wrote from a middle-class point of view for a largely middle-class audience, no such situation obtained in Ireland. In England there already existed bonds of understanding, shared values and recognition between writers and their readers which facilitated communication and enabled the novel to achieve the sophistication and complexity of great art. No such coherent community of interest and understanding is to be found in nineteenth-century Ireland, and probably no novel illustrates the point better than *The Collegians* where the author was obliged, as it were, to explain and describe the kind of middle-class family which an English novelist could have assumed to be immediately recognizable to his readers. The lack of a stable Irish middle class must be attributed largely to the history of the country as an English colony and to the socially crippling effects of the penal laws on the Catholic population. Thus Gerald Griffin's portrayal of the decency and respectability of the Daly family, who are both Catholic and middle class, is a significant attempt to persuade foreign readers to accept the existence of a section of the community which many of them had never suspected to be there at all. The case has, perhaps, a kind of added urgency for Griffin himself since his own background was somewhat similar to that of the Dalys. Ironically the degree to which the Dalys have become respectable and middle class corresponds closely to the degree to which they have assumed typically English middle-class values and attitudes. In fact Gerald Griffin, writing to make the case for middle-class Irish Catholics with their English counterparts, ends up by showing the extent to which the Dalys have succumbed to colonial influences and drifted away from their native culture. This drift is by no means final, and some of the most engaging and moving moments in the novel occur when the tension between the old ways and the new becomes acute.

The Daly family is first introduced at home, where certain domestic details emphasize their social ambitions. The picture prints that hang on the walls are noticeably un-Irish in their associations: Hogarth's 'Roast Beef', 'Prince Eugene', 'Mr Betterton playing Cato'. Even the picture of 'Schomberg at the Boyne' seems rather odd in a Catholic household since Schomberg was one of King William's generals. Yet despite this apparent English bias Mr Daly is said to be an enthusiast for Irish history and is forever quizzing his children on events from the past. Another important clue is in the title of the book itself. The collegians are Kyrle Daly and Hardress Cregan, and the college in question is the University of Dublin where both have studied. Although the university does not feature directly in the story, the fact of their having attended it indicates how, especially in the case of Kyrle Daly, they have aspired to an education in the establishment which was virtually synonymous with the Protestant Ascendancy.

Mr Daly's own self-confidence and social status are neatly illustrated by his employment of Lowry Looby, a small farmer brought to bankruptcy by the impact in Ireland of an English economic recession, as a messenger between his farms. This also reveals the middleman farmer's susceptibility to flattery, for Lowry Looby is a particularly attractive recipient of aid because of the ingenuous way in which he gently panders to his benefactor's weakness. That weakness, which is fairly harmless in the case of Mr Daly, together with the new access of power and possessions by men like him following the departure of many of the gentry from the country, would in the end prove self-destructive to the middlemen.

The sober-mindedness, sense of honour and responsibility, and even the unintended dullness of Mr Daly's son Kyrle, provide both the model of middle-class respectability and the obvious contrast to Hardress Cregan's volatile, passionate and reckless behaviour. Regarded as lovers the difference between the two men is clearly visible. Kyrle Daly begins the novel as the suitor to Anne Chute, the refined and genteel daughter of a well-to-do landowner, and the author declares that

the love which Kyrle entertained for this lady was so sincere, so rational, and regulated by so fine a principle of judgment, that the warmest, the wisest, and the best of men might condescend to take an interest in its success.[15]

Hardress Cregan, on the other hand, having eloped with Eily O'Connor, the luckless daughter of a rope-maker, chances to meet Kyrle Daly just after his rejection by Anne Chute, and a conversation which follows reveals the attitudes of the two young men. For Kyrle one of Anne Chute's greatest attractions is her educated mind, whereas Hardress maintains the opposite view:

I hold that this system of polishing girls ad unguem, is likely to be the destruction of all that is sincere and natural and unaffected in the sex. It is giving the mind an unwholesome preponderance over the heart . . . by the intervention of reason.'[16]

His friend is left to suggest that elegance and education are not necessarily synonymous with artificiality and hypocrisy, and to defend Anne Chute against the charge that her upbringing has destroyed her natural spirit and feeling, leaving her cold and distant.

The family pride and impetuosity of the Cregans are repeatedly emphasized and, blended with Hardress's inexperience, they motivate him in most of his decisive actions and attitudes. So his pride is offended by Anne Chute's apparent indifference towards her old childhood playmate, but his vanity is flattered by the almost unquestioning affection and respect which Eily O'Connor shows him. Eily's spontaneity and simplicity touch the heart of a man who admits awkwardness and 'social cowardice' in polite company, and so he is inclined to reject rashly all the customs of formal society. In so doing, however, he turns his back on certain standards which his pride insists upon. He falls into the very trap foreseen by Kyrle Daly when he warns his friend of the need to accept responsibility in one's relationships as well as merely indulging momentary whims, and of the danger of rushing into a commitment to simplicity if he should later discover the value of elegance.

The humorless pedantry and sobriety of Kyrle Daly's opinions, which make him sound years older than he is, do not invalidate their truth, and the reader is also aware of their irony in view of Hardress's situation. Cregan's love for Eily does not outweigh his social vanity: he will only elope with her and keep her in secret where his relationship is not open to public scrutiny because he fears disinheritance. Furthermore the rural innocence and uncultivated female mind which he warmly defended against Kyrle Daly's arguments soon begin to lose their attraction, and he knows he would be ashamed to bring a girl with Eily's accent and lack of sophistication into the kind of society in which he wishes to shine. As might be expected the problem becomes acute as his relationship with Anne Chute is renewed and matures.

Gerald Griffin's dilemma throughout the presentation of these two characters was that whereas Kyrle Daly is obviously the figure whose values, attitudes and behaviour are correct at every turn, Hardress Cregan, for all his many shortcomings, steals the story. The author does the best he can for Kyrle, stressing that his goodness and generosity are not simply acquired virtues but innate and natural to him. Regrettably this does not succeed in making him more likeable, a fact which Griffin himself knew all too well. He confesses that the reckless and unreasoning generosity of Hardress, the obvious place of emotion in ruling his behaviour, made him the darling of the peasantry while Kyrle Daly was known simply as a good master. Ironically the one man's weaknesses earn him an easy popularity while the other's dependability and earnestness are not fully valued or understood, and his capacity for strong and sincere feeling is almost wholly unsuspected.

The emotional side of Kyrle's nature is best seen following his mother's death. The wake and keening for the dead are specifically Irish, as opposed to English, rituals and, as is also shown in the account of King Corny's death in *Ormond*, they were looked upon by the English with a mixture of incomprehension and contempt. Both involve open and unabashed expressions of emotion which are largely alien to the English temperament, and it is a measure of Kyrle Daly's distance from his own native traditions and culture that initially he is unable to release his grief in the customary manner. The first people to gather at the house to pay their respects after Mrs Daly's death are distant relatives and dependants, and Griffin states that though their sympathy was cordial and sincere, 'he could not receive from them the delicate condolence which his equals might have afforded'.[17] The mourners themselves are sensitive to the restrained atmosphere, and during the night there is only whispered conversation and a general refusal of drink, usually a central part of any wake. The account of the callers' behaviour in controlling their own feelings further reveals the difference between the Dalys and the common people. This restraint is maintained until, finally, on the evening of the second day, Kyrle's own feelings break through and he bursts into 'a loud and hysterical passion of grief', an action which is followed almost immediately by a similar show of emotion from Mr Daly senior. Only then does courtesy permit the other mourners in the house to vent their own cries of sorrow.

Thomas Flanagan writes that this incident demonstrates that the Dalys are 'cut off from the instinctual life of their people, yet remain, at the core, unassimilated to the culture whose manners and whose stoicism they emulate'.[18] The aptness of his judgment is illustrated by Griffin's attention to the precise stimulus which breaks down Kyrle Daly's resistance to a free expression of grief. He describes how the young man, sitting by the window in the room where his mother's corpse is laid out, sees an old man leaning heavily on a blackthorn stick making his way towards the house:

He figured, involuntarily, to his own mind, the picture of this poor old fellow in his cottage, taking his hat and stick, and telling his family that he would 'step over to Mrs. Daly's wake'. To Mrs. Daly's wake! His mother, with whom he had dined on the Christmas day just past, in perfect health and security! The incident was slight, but it struck the spring of nature in his heart.[19]

Kyrle responds from the inner recesses of his being to this sudden moment of identification with the community from whose roots he seemed to have been cut off. It is not so much the figure of the anonymous old man that prompts his outburst, but an unconscious awareness of the culture and traditions symbolized by him 'stepping over' to the wake. Despite his moment of recognition, however, Kyrle Daly remains at a remove from the old ways.

Images and incidents of anarchy and lawlessness, which were recurrent in Griffin's earlier tales, again form a clear part of the author's vision of a confused society. Kyrle Daly's attitude to law differs markedly from that of almost every other character, and this further illustrates his middle-class respectability. Thus in a conversation between Kyrle and Mihil O'Connor, the father of Eily, shortly after his daughter's disappearance, O'Connor responds to what has happened by declaring: 'if I knew the one that robbed me, I'd find him out, if he was as cunning as a rabbit, an' I'd tear him between my two hands if he was as strong as a horse'.[20] The violence of the language reflects not only the man's distress and strength of feeling; it also indicates his desire for personal vengeance, the wish to settle his own scores. When Kyrle Daly soberly suggests laying information with a magistrate, O'Connor rejects the idea with the proud assertion that his 'back' (faction) is not so feeble that he needs to do such a 'mean' thing.

Numerous further instances demonstrate this contempt for formal law and order, and confirm the impression that justice is distributed in an improvised, arbitrary and often violent way. The system of delivering individual judgment and punishment, of standing up for oneself, appears to be connected with admiration accorded to a person who shows independence of spirit. This introduces the difference between the respect felt for Kyrle Daly by the people and the warm affection they have for Hardress Cregan. The former is a fairminded and just man, but the latter is a man of spirit. His spirit is inseparable from his pride and quickness of temper which are displayed, for example, in his sudden and violent retaliation against a group of men whom he hears teasing his boatman, the hunchbacked Danny Mann, at the Garryowen fair. Ironically Cregan's readiness to fight for Danny Mann reflects an uneasy conscience perhaps more than a generous spirit, for the boatman's deformity is the consequence of a throw he received from Cregan when the latter was in a temper as a child. Violence is integral to their relationship throughout, for Mann murders Eily and finally informs against Hardress before being executed himself.

Griffin goes to considerable lengths to explain the paradoxical nature of Hardress Cregan and its self-destructive tendency:

he was not without the peculiar selfishness of genius, that selfishness which consists . . . in a luxurious indulgence of all one's natural inclinations, even to an effeminate degree. His very generosity was a species of self-seeking. . . . He liked for liking's sake, and as long only as his humour lasted. It required but a spark to set him all on fire, but the flame was often as prone to smoulder, and become extinct, as it was hasty to kindle.[21]

So it is in his relationship with Eily O'Connor. Not only is he drawn to her by her good looks, important as they are, but he is also reacting against the distance he feels has developed between Anne Chute and himself during his absence as a student. Accordingly part of Eily's appeal is her difference from Anne, but equally that difference soon makes him uncomfortable with her.

The turbulence of Hardress Cregan's emotions and behaviour,

which the novel traces in particular detail, is consistent with the general mood of anarchy that typifies his family and their friends. Hunting, duelling, drinking and defying the bailiffs, these are the primary concerns of men like Cregan senior and his cronies, Connolly and Creagh. Their way of life, which is degenerate, selfish and pleasure-seeking, revolves around a private code of honour with pride as its basis and the duel as its accepted mode of settling disputes.

But above all the hunt symbolizes the anarchy and disorder which lie so close to the surface of the society Griffin describes. Here are found both the dash and excitement of life among the squireens and its brutality and chaos. The incident in which Danny Mann is set upon and severely beaten by Connolly, Creagh and Cregan senior illustrates the point vividly. Danny hears the hunting cries of the drunk riders as he journeys by night past a ruined church and graveyard, and suddenly, at the same time as the character, the reader realizes that Danny will become the object of the 'hunt'. The squireens mistake him for a bailiff and begin to horse-whip him and to threaten him with their swords. Only the fortuitous arrival of Hardress, also in a state of intoxication, and his recognition of Danny Mann save the victim's life, but the barbarism and ferocity of the episode are wholly typical of the lives of the participants in it.

Similarly, the discovery of Eily O'Connor's murdered body occurs during an actual fox hunt. Griffin builds up the scene faultlessly, telling how

The fox was said to have kennelled in the side of a hill, near the riverside, which, on one side was grey with lime-stone crag, and on the other covered with a quantity of close furze.[22]

At first the hounds search to no avail, while the author describes the dank, misty weather and the fine drizzle which settles on everything. Hardress himself, his marriage to Anne Chute approaching rapidly, is tormented by morbid reflections on death, his lost youth and freedom. Suddenly the dogs appear to pick up the scent of the fox, but instead they lead the hunters to the very spot where Eily's corpse is lying in the marsh water. Grim as this is, an even more powerful moment follows, for Hardress, who finds himself able to view the body without emotion, is shocked into reaction by a fresh outburst of barking from the hounds:

'The hounds! The hounds!' he exclaimed, 'Mr.Warner, do you hear them? Keep off the dogs! They will tear her if ye let them pass! Good sir, will ye suffer the dogs to tear her? I had rather be torn myself, than look upon such a sight. . . . If this ground should open before me, and I should hear the hounds of Satan yelling upward from the deep, it would not freeze me with a greater fear!'[23]

The chopping of the hounds is to Hardress what the knocking on the castle door was to Macbeth, and indeed the scene is conceived with the insight of a dramatist. Hardress's tormented display of fear and guilt is finely balanced against the accumulated details of the hunt and the discovery of the body, and against his own father's grotesque joke about the magistrate having caught 'a fine fat fox', because of the fee he will earn for conducting the inquest. Griffin is writing at the peak of his powers, integrating references to landscape and weather with the actions and reactions of the characters to create a richly suggestive moment in which events assume a significance far beyond their literal meaning. The hunt is no longer a mere recreational activity; it is the occasion which brings Hardress Cregan face to face with the truth about himself and his own behaviour; it is a matter of human life and death, justice and injustice, rather than the simple pursuit of a luckless animal; and it provides the moment of reckoning for the self-indulgent, irresponsible lifestyle followed not only by Hardress, but by all the squireens who ride with him.

Following the recovery of Eily O'Connor's body, the mental anguish and fear of detection experienced by Hardress become obsessive. Appropriately enough, his trials of conscience are described in terms of a hunt in which the guilty man imagines himself to be the quarry. While his nightmares indicate the corruption of his powers of imagination, his loss of judgment and self-control is typified by an incident when, while shooting snipe, Hardress accidentally kills his own dog rather than a bird. He is greatly agitated by references to death and murder made by one of the peasants following this unfortunate error. Through such episodes, and by means of showing how Hardress Cregan suffers increasingly from mental flashes back to his relationship with Eily O'Connor and her cruel fate, Griffin convinces the reader of the destruction of his character. The wild and proud spirit so much admired at the outset is humiliated and brought low by the consequences of his behaviour.

What also impresses is the richness of the background against which Hardress Cregan's story is set. His predicament may be extreme but it is not without antecedents of a less extravagant kind. Hepton Connolly, for example, boasts freely about his defiance of the law and his refusal to pay his debts. Indeed the ingenuity with which the workings of the law are confounded usually wins the greatest popular respect, as is magnificently demonstrated when Phil and Poll Naughten are questioned by the magistrate after the discovery of Eily's body. Here the ensuing comedy derives from the couple's brilliantly frustrating equivocation, assumed stupidity, and sudden inability to understand or use the English language, which combine to deflect awkward enquiries and render their examination a hopeless task.

The reader may well be amused by such trickery and have an instinctive sympathy for the cunning of the underdogs which empowers them to cock a snook at officialdom. On the other hand there are serious implications to their behaviour. If the legal process is deliberately foiled as a point of principle, then the law is indeed made an ass, and in order to function at all it comes to depend upon tyranny and the word of informers. In the case of *The Collegians* Hardress Cregan is only brought to justice because Danny Mann betrays him out of spite following an argument between them. Even as he denounces him, Danny shows his contempt for the legal system in Ireland:

I knew your laws of old. It isn't for nothing that we see the fathers of families, the pride and the sthrength of our villages, the young an' the old, the guilty, and the innocent, snatched away from their own cabins, and shared off for transportation an' the gallows. It isn't for nothing, our brothers, our cousins, an' our friends are hanged before our doores from year to year. They teach us something of the law, we thank 'em.[24]

Because the law is identified with oppression, and regarded as the agent of the people's natural enemies, it can only operate unjustly; and this in turn confirms the popular suspicion that it is not to be trusted. But the vindictiveness of Danny Mann's betrayal of Cregan is nothing compared to his own self-disgust and anguish when he realizes the disgrace he has brought upon himself and his family by being an informer, because he knows the Irish peasant's scorn and detestation of a traitor.

Mutual contempt for the due process of the law is not the only point of similarity between the squireens and the peasantry. They also share an overweening pride, even in dire poverty, although in the case of the poor it manifests itself in ingratiation and flattery. This is illustrated by the comic antics of Myles-na-Coppulleen, the horse trader, who is forced to plead with Mrs Chute following the trespass of his animals upon her land. The eccentric Myles incurs no loss of face because his natural ease of presence in the company of his social superiors and, above all, his ready capacity to humour and flatter every person present in the room at Chute Castle prove quite irresistible, so that he wins a discharge for his ponies without receiving punishment.

Set in the closing quarter of the eighteenth century, the novel moves from scenes of remembered tranquillity, good-humour and innocent happiness, through the initial rowdy incident and fateful meeting when Hardress Cregan rescues Mihil and Eily O'Connor from the boisterousness of the St Patrick's Day revellers, into a society which is increasingly seen to be violent, selfish and treacherous. John Cronin speaks of the opening as

a carefully orchestrated evocation of a bygone age, an age of lost innocence, a paradisal era set quite literally in a garden, since Garryowen, the scene of the action, has an Irish name which means 'Owen's garden'.[25]

The ruin of the picturesque Garryowen setting in the period between the 1770s and 1829, when the novel was written, is like the ruin which overtakes Hardress Cregan and Eily O'Connor. The initial freedom from cares and innocence, both personal and communal, is lost in the series of conflicts, tensions and weaknesses which are gradually shown to embrace all levels of provincial Irish life. These facts led H. R. Krans to comment that 'no other novel has made so complete a synthesis of Irish society. No other novel has presented faithfully and effectively so many phases of Irish life.'[26] Griffin may have known less of the landlord class than Maria Edgeworth and been further removed from the intimate details of peasant life than William Carleton, but in *The Collegians* he shows a more comprehensive understanding of Irish life as a whole and of the tensions that beset it than either of his contemporaries. W. B. Yeats wrote to Father Matthew Russell that Griffin gives the impression of being 'Irish on purpose', and goes on to add that 'he could have written like an Englishman had he chosen'.[27] His middle-class values and self-consciousness in writing for an English audience are no doubt responsible for Yeats's remarks. True, *The Collegians* may lack some of the raw energy found in the Banims' or Carleton's fiction, and it possesses a certain refinement of style and sentiment which may be more reminiscent of nineteenth-century English than Irish novels. Yet in spite of this, Griffin remains wholly within the field of Anglo-Irish fiction; even Yeats concedes that he shares with Carleton and John Banim 'a square-built power' which 'no later Irishman has approached', and by this phrase he refers specifically to the capacity of these writers to see 'the whole of everything they looked at'. In *The English Novel* Walter Allen is dismissive of *The Collegians*, as indeed he is of the work of the other Anglo-Irish novelists of the period. He describes it as

almost unreadable now; garrulous, the working out of the plot buried beneath a mass of unselected detail, and with altogether too much scope given to the longeurs of the humour of comic Irish peasants.[28]

Admittedly Allen's comments must be understood in the context of his study of the development of English fiction, but even so they are less than just to Griffin and show little understanding of the book's place in the evolution of the Anglo-Irish novel. *The Collegians* may not be a great book, but neither is it 'unreadable now', and as a social document of its time it retains a very real interest.

In his recent critical biography of Griffin, John Cronin proposes a further reason to explain the unique success of this novel over all the rest of the author's work. He sees Hardress Cregan, melodramatic and simple-minded as he is, as the key to the book's impact, which is a judgment that readily invites agreement. But he goes on to argue that the bond between writer and character is particularly intense and important:

Hardress's social morality is as simple and unsophisticated as Griffin's artistic morality. They are both sensitive, warm-hearted, full of 'nature', passionate and intense. They both have an oversimplified view of life and they both murder what they love: Hardress murders Eily; Griffin tries to destroy his work. Surely Griffin's penetration of the ambiguities of Hardress is made possible because of some war within himself between two sharply opposed views of life and art, views which might be described in Kyrle Daly's words as 'simplicity' and 'elegance'. . . . *The Collegians* is Griffin's greatest work because it combines a hero whose psychology paralleled the author's own with a vivid depiction of a society in decay. It is the combination of personal with social which makes this novel memorable.[29]

Cronin's thesis that *The Collegians* dramatizes and reveals Griffin's personal crisis of conscience as well as that of his hero is a new departure, and extends modern appreciation of its richness and complexity. Earlier critics had recognized it as an important social novel, but now it may be seen as the climax of Griffin's achievement as an artist, embodying the very elements which were to destroy him as a writer in the course of the next few years. Naturally it remains intriguing to speculate about how he might have developed had he not given up his career as a novelist and journalist soon after in favour of joining the Christian Brothers. This decision was prompted in part by the moral dilemma provoked by his recognition that, in the popular eye, the unprincipled Hardress Cregan would always be more memorable than the moral and upright Kyrle Daly. But the question of what might have followed is rendered even more tantalising because in his next books, *The Rivals* and *Tracy's Ambition*, Griffin seemed to be on the verge of breaking fresh ground in Anglo-Irish fiction.

Sectarianism, violence and the struggle for land possession, these are the common themes of the two stories. They present a society in which bitterness and cruelty are everywhere apparent and where the balance of power is maintained by terrorism. In *The Rivals* the harsh and unscrupulous behaviour of Richard Lacy, landowner and magistrate, is pitted against Francis Riordan's patriotism and readiness to defend the poor and oppressed. At one level the tale is very simple and extremely melodramatic: returning from a self-imposed exile necessitated by an earlier clash with Lacy, Riordan finds that the girl he loves, Esther Wilderming, has made a promise of marriage to his rival. Soon after he learns of Esther's death and determines to see her body in the family vault at Glendalough, but at the same time Lacy hears of Riordan's return and plans to capture him. Following the mysterious and unexplained resurrection of Esther, and her reunion with Riordan, the rivals meet and Lacy is badly wounded in a fight that ensues. He is taken for shelter to the house where Riordan and Esther are staying, and here Esther appears before him like a ghost warning him to flee. Subsequently Riordan becomes involved in the defence of two brothers who have been undeservedly persecuted by Lacy, and he is successful in discrediting the magistrate in court through a further series of enigmatic revelations. Lacy's character undergoes a total reform after this, and Esther urges him to lead a benevolent and constructive life, advice which he implements during the brief remaining time before his death.

This summary of the main plot shows that *The Rivals* strains the credulity and patience of the reader to the very limits. Yet in spite of its crude structure some of the background detail depicting the characters' entrenched attitudes and conflicts – religious, social and political – is convincingly introduced. In these parts Griffin grapples with issues which remained controversial throughout much of the nineteenth century, and which again relate the origin of the tension and unrest to the differing cultural backgrounds of the parties concerned.

This point is established in various ways. Early in the novel a conversation between Esther Wilderming's guardian, the wealthy landowner Mr Damer and his brother-in-law Mr Leonard, has the former deploring the mockery he has been subjected to by the Catholic poor because of his endeavours to convert them to Protestantism. But Damer's own patronising complacency is attacked by his brother-in-law who points out that

it is an easy matter to be a saint, when one has an income of four thousand a year, with a mansion like this on one's estate. . . . It is not difficult to be punctual at church, in defiance of distance and of weather, when one can go there in a close carriage and four; nor to meet round the fire at evening and read the Bible, and shudder at the poor deluded peasant, who is shivering, meanwhile, all alone, by his cold cottage hearth, and offering up the idolatrous devotion that moves our horror.[30]

The liberalism and humanity of Mr Leonard and his identification of the weakness in Mr Damer's position and actions are striking but have little impact upon events in the novel.

Religious intolerance is matched by political hostilities which are equally absolute. Thus Mr Damer regards Francis Riordan as a 'dissolute young villain' and 'a baffled murderer', while Leonard maintains that he is 'a patriot. . . [an] adventurer in the cause of Columbia, the cause of freedom'.[31] Riordan's popular reputation is further enhanced by Damer's old housekeeper Mrs Keleher, whose attitude typifies the almost sentimental affection felt by the Irish poor for a rebel who has defied the legal authorities. Her roots in an older cultural tradition that has little in common with Mr Damer's Methodism are evident when she accounts for Riordan's ill luck and troubled life as the result of his being looked at by someone with an evil eye when he was a child.

Perhaps the biggest problem in the story of Lacy and Riordan's rivalry is the extreme nature of their positions. Riordan's patriotism which, like Murrogh O'Brien's in *The O'Briens and the O'Flahertys*, is stirred and stimulated by his sensitivity towards the beauties of the mountain landscape to which he returns from exile, makes him a type of Robin Hood figure, a defender of the poor and downtrodden rather than a participant in any organized political opposition. Accordingly his adventures are the romantic exploits of an attractive and bold individual rather than part of any wider resistance movement, while his patriotism is inseparable from his sense of justice for himself and others, his self-respect and his fearless defiance of petty tyranny.

Lacy, on the other hand, is self-seeking, unscrupulous and cruel. He is described as one of those magistrates who

sought preferment by an emulative display of zeal and activity in the discharge of their duties. . . and earned the applause of his patrons, by rendering himself an object of detestation in his neighbourhood.[32]

One obvious expression of his villainy is his employment of the much-hated process server, Tobin, as a spy and informer against his fellow peasants. Their relationship is one of mutual contempt and greed, with the histrionic posturing and declaiming of Lacy matched against the cool cynicism of his stooge.

The ease with which Griffin appoints his characters to be heroes or villains precludes any complexity of the kind found in the portrayal of Hardress Cregan. He is at his best when minor figures dominate the action. There is a marvellous public house discussion among the peasantry concerning two pieces of legislation, the Sub-letting Act and the Vestry Act, in which Davy Lenigan, the hedge-school master, reminds his rowdy audience of the earlier days when priests and schoolmasters were the object of persecution and when Catholics were restricted in their possession of property; but his cynicism emerges when he comments on the reform of penal legislation:

Now, spakin' in truth, they repealed these dismal, unpolitical laws, not for any feelin' of friendship or humanity towards us, but merely to secure the pace o' the Empire, an' to remove the disgrace they resaved in all the polished Coorts o' the known world they visited, as they looked upon them as base, savage, and unpolished people.[33]

This remarkably candid interpretation of reform as little more than English political opportunism leads the speaker to consider recent acts of law which he sees as designed to impoverish the people and curb the population growth by forbidding the sub-division of land amongst the members of a family. Then Lenigan's argument takes an unexpected direction. Far from inciting rebellion, he urges acquiescence on the grounds that the effects of this law will be to weaken the armies of the Empire – because of a lack of Irish recruits – and thus lead to the English becoming 'a prey to some Napoleon, or some other haro of his kind'. But Davy Lenigan's appeal for non-violence is ambiguous, for shortly afterwards he entertains the company with a song which mocks the tyranny and authority of the police, telling how a 'Banshee Peeler' met a goat on the road and threatened him with transportation.

The plot and characterization of *The Rivals* are not particularly successful, though glimpses emerge of the author's concern at mounting social disorder and sectarianism. He makes the reader aware in a general way of active and growing tensions but fails to provide an adequate framework within which to write about them. In *Tracy's Ambition*, the companion piece to *The Rivals*, Griffin overcomes many of these problems, and the result is powerful and imaginative. Where *The Rivals* implies that all might still be well if the law were to be justly implemented, *Tracy's Ambition* admits no such easy resolution. As John Cronin has written:

Griffin's Ireland, as depicted in *Tracy's Ambition*, is a small world of dubiously respectable citizens straddling a pullulating pit of restless helots. Maria Edgeworth had seen the peasantry through the cracked window-panes of Castle Rackrent. Griffin enfleshes the people Thady saw and, in this short but intensely powerful novel, we stumble with them along the muddy roads of a barbarous and bitter land, we feel them huddling their wretched rags about them, we inhabit with them their miserable cabins and feel their winter cold.[34]

The themes of *Tracy's Ambition* are similar to those of *The Rivals* but are entered into with much greater complexity and detail.

One major improvement is in the characterization of the chief protagonists, and of the title hero in particular. Abel Tracy, who is also the narrator of the story, was once a happy and prosperous landowner, but his ambition to be appointed a magistrate and his friendship with Dalton, a cruel 'weeder-out of disaffection', lead to increasing suffering and misfortune for his own family. The miseries that befall them are precipitated by the conjunction of Tracy's desire for material gain and social recognition by the gentry with his decision to respond to a request of Dalton's to lend him money to pay off his spend-thrift son's debts. The money which Tracy loans is the marriage portion set aside for his beloved daughter's wedding to Rowan Clancy. Needless to say it is not repaid when Tracy needs it, while in the meantime he himself has become increasingly involved in and compromised by the activities of Dalton and his men.

Tracy becomes openly identified with Dalton and his Peelers following an abortive night attack by a group of agrarian conspirators, during which he is injured while also managing to shoot dead one of the insurgents. Like the reader, he is left in no doubt about Dalton's cynicism and tyranny, for he is told how, having assisted Tracy to a tenant's house, Dalton first accuses the woman of having a son who is a croppy because of the evidence of a pair of muddy brogues, and then furtively implants two parcels in the thatch of her cottage. These parcels are, of course, subsequently 'discovered' and used as incriminating evidence against the family. Moreover Dalton denounces Shanahan, the woman's husband, for allegedly threatening and assaulting his son. The incident underlines how the magistrate exercises power to victimize individuals, to settle personal feuds whether real or imagined, and to give vent to his own sectarian passions. The situation is rendered even worse by the discovery that Tracy has killed Shanahan's brother, for this provokes the man to swear a grotesque blood oath of vengeance against Tracy for shooting someone who never harmed him. The oath is directed against Dalton as well because of the disappearance of Shanahan's sister, who it is believed has been ruined by the magistrate's son. Thus the circle of violence is completed and future acts of disorder and bloodshed are guaranteed. The mood and events of *Tracy's Ambition* have their basis in this bleak vision of life in Ireland in the 1820s.

Abel Tracy's alienation from his neighbourhood is progressive. Following the shooting of Shanahan and the threat against his life, Dalton instals policemen in Tracy's house, supposedly to protect him in the event of an attack, but also

to facilitate further punitive raids upon the Catholic population. Apart from the inevitable unpopularity of such a
move among Tracy's tenants, he himself is uneasy about this
decision because his wife and daughter are both Catholics, and
thus domestic tensions are generated by the presence of the
agents of sectarianism in the household. The problem is
exacerbated by the great affection felt by the poor for Abel's
wife, Mary Tracy, because her kind ministrations to them are
compromised by the association of the family with the police.
Tracy's reluctance to assume his new role in the community
is contrasted with the undisguised contempt and hatred of
Dalton for all poor folk. He dismisses the Irish peasantry as

a base, fawning, servile, treacherous, smooth-tongued, and black-
hearted race of men; bloody in their inclinations, debauched and
sensual in their pleasures, beasts in their cunning, and beasts in their
appetites.[35]

Ironically, of course, much of this abuse has some justification: the peasantry *are* seen to be capable of flattery,
servility, treachery, and many of them do plan or become
involved in plots for revenge and acts of extreme brutality. But
Dalton's view of the poor takes no account of the pressures and
injustices to which they are continually subjected, and one
of the most distinctive features of *Tracy's Ambition* is its
concern throughout to interpret and understand the conduct of
all parties in a social context. The behaviour of the characters
is not merely the result of individual temperament or passions,
strong and relevant as these factors are, but derives from the
conflicts and stresses that beset the society as a whole. Abel
Tracy is almost as memorable a creation as Crohoore or John
Nowlan, but his way of life, the events in which he becomes
involved, show him more fully as the member of a wider
community than is the case with the Banims' protagonists. So,
too, his personal ruin is also a metaphor for the kind of
destruction that awaits anyone who seeks to exploit the forces
of division and disorder for selfish ends.

The author's pessimism emerges clearly on the occasion of
a renewed meeting between Tracy and the mother of the man
he shot. She reiterates her threat of vengeance and then
declares: 'Ah, Abel Tracy, there is no law for the poor in
Ireland, but what they make themselves, and by that law my
child will have blood for blood before the year is out.'[36] The
horrifying implications of this statement indicate the ordinary

person's total loss of confidence in the process of law other than as a vehicle of oppression operated against him. Tracy's moralistic response ill becomes him, but it enables Griffin to put forward some of his own opinions. He permits his hero to round on the woman, accusing her of being the true murderer of her own son because

When he was an infant on your lap, you filled his mind with thoughts of revenge and discord. You sung him to sleep with songs of guilt and passion, you taught him to fight out his own will among his own brothers and play-fellows. . . . From you he learned that riot and revenge were glory and honour, and that blind rebellion was patriotism. You made him a bad child, a worse man, a factious neighbour, a rebel, a blood-spiller, and thus, having bound his soul to perdition, you became his murderer.[37]

The reader senses the author's concern to make a general appeal to the consciences of all Irish people involved in sectarian or agrarian strife; and perhaps this explains why the sentiments, although they come awkwardly from Abel Tracy, have an undeniable urgency of tone. Griffin wishes the events of the novel to be viewed as a small-scale example of a pattern that is repeated throughout the society of which he is writing. He knows that, whereas the details may vary from case to case, the origins and consequences of discontent, hostile feelings and conflict are invariably the same.

Furthermore these words are aimed directly at Irish readers, because in *Tracy's Ambition* Griffin resolved for himself the vexed question of the audience for whom he was writing. The book is addressed specifically to Irish readers, and by liberating himself from the need to be an apologist as well as a novelist, Griffin makes an important advance in the development of Anglo-Irish fiction. He did not consolidate this achievement because his career as a writer was approaching its close, and nor is it followed up, except in occasional instances, in the fiction of his immediate successors. Carleton's best writing shows similar independence of mind, but much of his work was undertaken for other reasons and to appeal to particular audiences, while writers such as Mrs Hall, Samuel Lover and Charles Lever had their eyes firmly set on the English market. In *Tracy's Ambition*, however, Griffin moved some way towards making Anglo-Irish fiction a self-sufficient entity, rather than a humble and self-conscious imitation of an English art form.

The novel deals effectively with the general causes of conspiratorial activity and discontent abroad in the country. Hunger, distress, hardship and the desire for whiskey, these are the pressures which drive the poor into the secret societies according to the informers treacherously employed by the supposed law enforcement officer Dalton. This theme is taken up more fully in a conversation between Tracy and Morty Shanahan, when the latter argues that prosperity is not the result of abstinence from violence and alcohol alone. As they view a snug farmhouse Shanahan observes:

The man that owns that house is a Palentin an' a Protestant, he has his ground for five shillings an acre, on a long lase; he has a kind landlord over him that will never *distress* him for a small arrear, he isn't like a poor Catholic that has a mud cabin, an acre o' pratie ground, an' seven landlords above him, an' that has no feelings nor kindness to look for, when times run hard an' poverty strikes him between the cowld walls.[38]

These remarks penetrate the superficial image of the Irish peasant as drunken and aggressive and define the cause of his apparently irresponsible behaviour. Above all else that cause is the insecurity of the tenant, his knowledge that he and his family may be evicted at any time, his feeling of remoteness from his landlord, and the total lack of incentive to improve his land or property. The effect of this is to drive men to drink, and that in turn leads to fighting.

Shanahan's words explain but do not seek to excuse or justify. So too with his reaction to Tracy's criticism of the seeming indolence of the peasantry, their failure to undertake even simple maintenance of their homes and out-buildings. He points out that the peasant's first obligation is to his landlord and to farming his landlord's estates. Time spent in tilling his own smallholding or in re-thatching his cabin is unprofitable and therefore a luxury he cannot afford. The impression derived from this account of the plight of the Irish peasantry is of a people living precariously at subsistence level, and so over-exploited by their masters that no opportunity for self-improvement is possible. The conversation serves Griffin's moral purpose of exposing the inequities and debilitating features of the Irish social structure. Such intrusions may upset the artistic balance of the novel, for Griffin, to borrow D. H. Lawrence's image, is unashamedly putting his finger in the pan and tilting the scales in a particular direction; but his analysis is engaging and his bias is stated with a refreshing lack of equivocation and apology. Again, as in the story of Abel Tracy's personal fortunes, the reader is forced to realize that the implications of Shanahan's remarks extend far beyond the immediate occasion which provoked them. The author's vision of events was parochial and anecdotal in *Holland-Tide* and the *Tales of the Munster Festivals*, but widened and deepened in *The Collegians*; now it strives to embrace the general condition of the poor and of their relations with landlords and magistrates throughout the country. The attempt may not be wholly successful, but the aspiration is both bold and worthy.

Looking back over the fiction published in the closing years of the 1820s, certain clear changes of direction and tone may be delineated. These changes are not wholly unexpected because the work of the Banims earlier in the decade had an enormous impact upon Gerald Griffin, while Lady Morgan's career led her logically to the position and attitudes expressed in *The O'Briens and the O'Flahertys*. Perhaps the most striking difference between these books and earlier fiction is the increasingly frank and unapologetic tone with which they treat their subject matter. Thus Lady Morgan's portrayal of Dublin Castle society and its political machinations, and the candid way in which Griffin lays bare various forms of legal corruption, are bolder and less circumspect than similar incidents in earlier novels. This new directness exists alongside a rapidly diminishing store of optimism. *The O'Briens and the O'Flahertys* denies itself the luxury of an easy solution such as that which ended *The Wild Irish Girl* or *O'Donnel*, or Maria Edgeworth's *Ennui*, *The Absentee* and *Ormond*. Griffin's novels convey a growing impression of a country gripped and divided by petty, but vicious, local arguments and disputes. Moreover in *The Rivals* and *Tracy's Ambition* Griffin was moving away from fiction that deals with a past period of history and turning his attention to bleak contemporary realities.

The new mood of sobriety is reflected in a number of ways. Lady Morgan's last Anglo-Irish novel is the least exotic of her works. No longer is she satisfied with or convinced of the efficacy of appealing to the English for reform, or of trusting in their sense of justice and fair play to put things right. The same is true of Gerald Griffin. The ideal world of old Garryowen has been obliterated and is no more than a memory even before the grim action of *The Collegians* begins, while *The Rivals* and more especially *Tracy's Ambition*, show a society almost wholly devoid of idealism. Maria Edgeworth's Harry Ormond, young, attractive, intelligent and principled, is succeeded by Hardress Cregan, young, attractive, intelligent, but also self-destructive, selfish and lacking in moral values. The note of optimism on which *Ormond* concluded may have rung somewhat hollow, but the ending of *The Collegians* is quite unambiguously restrained.

The widening range of social analysis and perspective, particularly in Griffin's work, creates an irresistible image of the unchanging oppression of the poor. Even with the phasing out of the harshest penal laws, and on the threshold of Catholic emancipation, there is an abiding sense that nothing has really altered from the eighteenth century. Equally clearly the new landlords and squireens are just as irresponsible and indifferent towards the poor as the older type of estate owner typified by the Rackrents. The new men may not be absentees, but the extreme selfishness and self-indulgence of the lives of many of them are equally damaging to the welfare of the country and its poorer inhabitants. One obvious symptom of the harm done by their profligate living to the social fabric as a whole is their general contempt for all the processes of law. The law and its agents are not simply forces to be resisted by the poor; they are also forces to be defied openly and arrogantly by the squirearchy in general. Thus the section of the community whose interests are normally served by the law, and who would therefore endorse it, are unashamedly abusive of it. The dangers of widespread social disorder, and the certainty of continuing local violence are shown most decisively by this failure of the law to establish itself as a credible and effective standard of justice in nineteenth-century Ireland. Time soon showed that the dark future for Ireland implied in these novels of the 1820s would prove to be tragically accurate in reality, for bit by bit social breakdown and alienation between different classes and creeds were reducing the entire country to a state of crisis—a crisis which could not be solved by the belated and ungenerous passing of the Emancipation Act in 1829.

FIVE

SKETCHES OF IRISH CHARACTER AND TRAITS AND STORIES OF THE IRISH PEASANTRY (1830-1833)

I found . . . a class unknown in literature, unknown by their own landlords, and unknown by those in whose hands much of their destiny was placed. If I became the historian of their habits and manners, their feelings, their prejudices, their superstitions and their crimes; if I have attempted to delineate their moral, religious and physical state, it was because I saw no person willing to undertake a task which surely must be looked upon as an important one.

> William Carleton
> from his Introduction to *Tales of Ireland* (1834)

In 1829, under the auspices of an evangelical Protestant cleric, Caesar Otway, two stories were published by a Tyrone peasant who, having failed to become a Catholic priest, had travelled to Dublin to seek his fortune. A year later the writer of these tales, William Carleton, produced the first volume of his *Traits and Stories of the Irish Peasantry*, and a second volume followed in 1833. 'Father Butler' and 'The Lough Derg Pilgrim', the 1829 stories, were written with the specific purpose of high-lighting the superstition, intolerance and undesirability of the Catholic church. Their intention is unashamedly propagandist, and yet in spite of that the reader finds, particularly in 'The Lough Derg Pilgrim', an energy, humour and close observation of life that are unusual in moralistic tracts, and feels that he is in the presence of a writer with greater talents than those of the hack pamphleteer. In the *Traits and Stories of the Irish Peasantry* the artist emerges triumphant, and even where there are lapses into dogmatism, these do not compromise the work as a whole. The tales are an undoubted milestone in the course of Anglo-Irish fiction, and are all the more remarkable because, in a sense, they appear without precedent and have no real successors. If Maria

Edgeworth's *Castle Rackrent* was the first great surprise in modern Anglo-Irish literature, Carleton's *Traits and Stories* must surely be the second. From the outset Carleton's stories were recognized both as different from the work of his predecessors and also as a unique record of a culture that was passing away even as the author was writing about it. Thomas Davis expressed the point in the following way:

Well may Carleton say that we are in a transition state. The knowledge, the customs, the superstitions, the hopes of the People are entirely changing. . . . It is chiefly in this way we value the work before us. In it Carleton is the historian of the peasantry rather than a dramatist.[1]

Carleton's work has abiding importance as an indispensable aid to any real understanding of Irish peasant life in the late eighteenth and early nineteenth centuries – a fact well illustrated by comparing his work with a collection of tales published under the title *Sketches of Irish Character* which also came out in 1829.

The author, Mrs S. C. Hall, set out to describe her experience of life in the parish of Bannow, Co. Wexford, not merely to provide her readers with amusement, but to portray the Irish character in such a way as to make it 'more justly appreciated, more rightly estimated, and more respected in England'; and to point out 'in a kindly and affectionate spirit . . . the errors and faults that prevail most among my countrymen and countrywomen, [so] as to be of some use in inducing a removal of them'.[2] Thus her dogmatic purpose here, as in her later collections of stories *Lights and Shadows of Irish Life* (1838) and *Stories of the Irish Peasantry* (1840), is readily admitted.

This in itself is not a new approach in Anglo-Irish fiction, but what is different, and what makes these tales striking to look at in conjunction with Carleton's *Traits and Stories*, is the specific attention they give to the Irish peasantry. Mrs Hall herself did not come from a peasant background. Her family was well-to-do, her husband was a clergyman, and she was strongly influenced by English values and ways of living. Not surprisingly these facts have considerable bearing upon the way in which she regarded her subject-matter, the weaknesses of character which she identified and the tone in which she wrote about them.

In 'We'll See About it' ' and 'Take It Easy' the procrastination and laziness of the Irish peasant are criticized, and shown to result in financial ruin. The custom of offering hospitality far in excess of what could be afforded ('Hospitality'), of failing to provide for the future ('Larry Moore'), of intemperance ('Good Spirits and Bad'), and of giving legendary status to outlaws and law-breakers ('The Rapparee'), all these are gently castigated. In time Carleton too would write critically about many of these shortcomings. For example, he attacks improvidence, idleness and fecklessness in *Parra Sastha: or the history of Paddy Go-easy and his wife Nancy*; intemperance in *Art Maguire: or the broken pledge*; and the credibility of law-breakers in numerous places, including *Rody the Rover: or the Ribbonman*.

Carleton, however, could never look at his subject with the detachment and lack of personal feeling that characterize Mrs Hall's writing. This is not to question the sincerity of Mrs Hall's aims nor to doubt the genuineness of her concern, but rather to define a crucial difference of perspective between the two writers: Mrs Hall saw the Irish peasantry and felt sorrow and sympathy for them; Carleton *was* an Irish peasant, and there was no distance between his own feelings and way of thought and those of his characters. Mrs Hall wrote from a position of privilege, albeit a position which she wanted to use for the good of others; Carleton wrote as an equal, and often with the simple mercenary ambition of earning enough to provide for himself and his family. Mrs Hall wrote as an observer of most of the behaviour recounted in her tales; Carleton had participated in many of the incidents and experiences he describes in his.

The effect of these differing perspectives perhaps is measured most obviously by comparing the tone of the two writers. In the following extract from 'Lilly O'Brien', Mrs Hall tells of the appearance of a well-kept cottage:

The farm-yard is stocked with ricks of corn, hay, and furze; with a puddle-like pond for ducks and geese, and a sty for a little grunting animal, who thinks it a very unjust sentence that consigns a free-born Irish pig to such confinement. How beautiful is the hawthorn hedge! – one sheet of snowy blossom – and such a row of bee-hives! while the white walls of the cottage are gemmed over with the delicate green, half-budded leaves of the noble rose-tree, that mounts even to the chimney top; the bees will banquet rarely there, by-and-by. A parlour in an Irish cabin! yes, in good truth, and a very pretty one – the floor strewed with the ocean's sparkling sand; pictures of, at all events, half the head saints of the calendar, in black frames, and bright green, scarlet, and orange draperies; a corner cupboard, displaying china and glass for use and show, the broken parts carefully turned to the wall – the inside of the chimney lined with square tiles of blue earthenware; and over it an ivory crucifix, and a small white chalice, full of holy water; six high-backed chairs, like those called 'education', of modern days; a well-polished round oak table, and a looking-glass of antique form, complete the furniture.[3]

The details in this description are observed closely. The reader is, as it were, walked around the exterior of the cottage and his attention directed to salient points there before he is led indoors. Evidently the writer wishes to impress him by the orderliness and cleanliness of the establishment, probably in order to counteract the outsider's commonplace view of the Irish peasant as dirty, squalid and impoverished. The well-stocked farm-yard is indicative of modest prosperity, while the accounts of the ducks, geese and, especially, of the pig make them sound almost picture-book creatures. The hawthorn hedge, bee-hives and rose-covered walls of the cottage add further to the idyllic setting.

The portrayal of the interior of the house is equally purposeful. The author's expectation that her readers will be surprised to learn that the cottage has a parlour is seen in the way she introduces the topic. As with the description of the exterior, details are carefully selected for comment, and an impression of neatness, piety, and respectability is built up. The mention of the china cupboard with its display of items which have their cracks and chips turned towards the wall is a gently humorous aside upon the vanity and social aspirations of the mistress of the house. The one real shortcoming of this whole account is its detachment from the business of living. This is not surprising since the parlour of such cottages was only used on highdays and holidays, but because Mrs Hall concentrates on it she conveys an impression which, though easy to visualise in the mind's eye, sounds as if she was telling of a cottage in a folk museum: the artefacts are all there, but no-one lives in this dwelling. This curious effect is a measure of the writer's own distance, however genuine and warm her feelings, from her subject. She is only an observer, not a participant in the life of a cottage like the one she describes.

By way of contrast, the extract below shows William Carleton introducing the household of Mary Sullivan in his short story 'The Lianhan Shee'.

Mrs. Sullivan was the wife of a wealthy farmer, and niece to the Rev. Felix O'Rourke; her kitchen was consequently large, comfortable, and warm. Over where she sat jutted out the 'brace' well lined with bacon; to the right hung a well-scoured salt-box, and to the left was the jamb, with its little gothic paneless window to admit the light. Within it hung several ash rungs, seasoning for flail-sooples, a dozen of eel-skins, and several stripes of horse-skin, as hangings for them. The dresser was a 'parfit white', and well furnished with the usual appurtenances. Over the door and on the 'threshel' were nailed, 'for luck', two horse-shoes that had been found by accident. In a little 'hole' in the wall, beneath the salt-box, lay a great bottle of water to keep the place purified; and against the copestone of the gable, on the outside, grew a large lump of house-leek, as a specific for sore eyes.

In the corner of the garden were a few stalks of tansy, 'to kill the thievin' worms in the childhre, the crathurs', together with a little Rosenoble, Solomon's Seal and Bugloss, each for some medicinal purpose. The 'lime wather' Mrs. Sullivan could make herself, and the 'bogbane' for the linh roe, or heartburn, grew in their own meadow-drain. . . . Lying on the top of the salt-box was a bunch of fairy-flax, and sewed in the folds of her own scapular, was the dust of what had once been a four-leafed Shamrock, an invaluable specific 'for seein' the good people', if they happened to come within the bounds of vision. Over the door in the inside, over the beds, and over the cattle in the outhouses, were placed branches of withered palm, that had been consecrated by the priest on Palm Sunday; and when the cows happened to calve, this good woman tied, with her own hands, a woollen thread about their tails, to prevent them from being overlooked by evil eyes, or elf-shot by the fairies, who seem to possess a peculiar power over females of every species during the season of parturition.[4]

One immediate difference between this passage and the extract from Mrs Hall's story is that Carleton begins with the mistress of the house. Besides, this link between the occupant and the place is inseparable throughout. Carleton starts by establishing and explaining the prosperity of the family, a fact which he achieves easily by reference to Mary Sullivan's husband and uncle, a wealthy farmer and a priest respectively. He also focuses attention on the kitchen, rather than the parlour, thus choosing the natural centre of activity and life in any farmhouse. This, in turn, enables him to draw attention to details associated with cooking (the bacon, salt and dresser with all its bits and pieces), work (the drying ash rungs, eel-skins and stripes of horse-skin), religion (the holy water), and superstition (the horse shoes for luck). Religion and superstition are at once central to the life of the family and inextricably bound up together. Thus the consecrated palm branch is preserved with equal care to the bunch of fairy flax and the dust of the four-leafed shamrock. Carleton's presentation makes it clear that Mary Sullivan sees no contradiction or problem of belief in practising this combination of Christian and pagan observances. So, too, with her herb-growing and homemade remedies. Some of these cures are acknowledged to work from experience, but the idea of shielding a cow that is in calf from the evil eye by tying a woollen thread round its tail is obviously mere superstition.

The inclusion in a descriptive passage of odd words and phrases recorded as they would have been spoken – 'threshel', 'to kill the thievin' worms in the childher, the crathurs', 'for seein' the good people', and so on – may at first appear a rather artificial ploy. On the other hand, it reflects the directness with which Carleton's imagination worked: he is hearing Mary Sullivan's voice as he tells of her kitchen and garden, and he knows precisely the idioms she would use. Mrs Hall was closer to her reader's sensibility than that of the cottager whose house she was describing, hence the calculated tone of surprise when she mentions the parlour; but Carleton's instinctive identity is with his character rather than with his audience. Mary Sullivan's house is not a museum piece, but a place permeated with the evidence of daily living.

Mrs Hall's moral concern and her wish to enlighten the Irish peasants and show them the folly of some of their practices often communicate themselves in a patronizing way. So, for example, in 'Mark Connor's Wooing and Wedding', having shown the stubbornness of Mrs Connor, an elderly woman who is enraged by her prospective daughter-in-law's wish to introduce various 'English', and therefore unpatriotic, reforms into the organization of the household and farm, the story concludes with the following exchanges:

'Helen, do you know it is very hard to convince an Irishman; he has so many quips, and cranks, and puzzling sayings, and would prefer being reduced to expedient, to attaining anything by straightforward means – provided it was not too troublesome.'

'There is truth in all that,' replied Helen, thoughtfully, 'and no good will ever be effected by flying in the face of their prejudices; they are a people that must be led, not driven. Preconceived ideas cannot be hammered out of their heads – but they may be directed to other objects; though you cannot stop the source of a river, you may turn its course.'[5]

Here, at one stroke, is a return to the language and tone first noticed in the closing pages of Lady Morgan's *The Wild Irish*

Girl where M's father wrote to advise him how to handle his Irish tenants. The basic goodness of the Irish peasant is not in question, but it is necessary to be long-suffering and patient in dealing with his recalcitrance and reluctance to accept advice. A similar notion is conveyed in the short story 'Independence', where Mrs Hall laments the general lack of understanding of this word in Ireland. She sees the people as too ready to submit to existing circumstances, however bad, with a demeaning calmness and indifference. The author's attitude here is ambiguous, because, as with other writers before her, her call to the Irish peasants to reform their way of life and hold their heads higher amounts to an oblique summons to them to become more anglicized. To make such an appeal in Ireland without attending in some measure to the history of Anglo-Irish relations and the impositions placed upon the peasants by the colonialists is to tell only half the story. Mrs Connor's contempt for new ideas simply because they come from England is clearly foolish and self-punishing; but the prejudice derives from a certain kind of rationale, and Mrs Hall's story makes no attempt to demonstrate this. Equally, to chide the Irish peasantry for their acceptance of the status quo sounds like the prerogative of a person in a privileged position. After all in 1829 there were no channels for orthodox political representation for the poor, and, until the Act of Emancipation, none of any kind for Catholics. The memory of 1798 was still fresh enough in people's minds to make them reluctant to envisage a wide-spread uprising – not that Mrs Hall would have advocated rebellion as a means of winning independence. (Her exploration of this theme comes in *The Whiteboy*, a full-length novel published in 1845). No doubt her observation of the peasantry as acquiescent and apathetic is true enough, but if the peasants did not share the enthusiasm of their would-be reformer, it was because their experience of many years had taught them to be cynical of promises of improvement. The extent to which Mrs Hall grasped this brute fact is a matter for speculation.

The same question poses itself when, in 'Kelly the Piper', the author criticizes the improvidence and anarchy of the Kelly household. As she primly remarks: 'The family of this village musician was managed like many Irish families – that is, not managed at all.'[6] Entertainment is the sole concern of the Kellys, and the local enjoyment of music and dancing is described as 'an excuse for idleness, uniform and premeditated'. The reader may well balk at such a puritanical and censorious attitude, even though drunkenness, quarrelling and often violence were regular features of a pattern or a fair. To dismiss these occasions as merely an 'excuse for idleness' is to misunderstand their social and recreational function within a community where the possibilities of enjoyment were often limited and infrequent. Carleton would never have adopted this view, even in his own most moralizing moods, but then Carleton himself had been a dancer and by all accounts a very graceful one in his day. He knew what dancing and music meant to the participants whereas Mrs Hall saw only social disorder and recklessness as their direct outcome.

The one curious exception to Mrs Hall's generally disapproving attitude towards morally reprehensible behaviour is her romantic view of certain kinds of law-breaker. In 'The Rapparee' she explores the legendary status among the peasants of Freney, an outlaw who successfully makes a fool of the forces of authority. Significantly his gallantry is not limited to the military sphere, for his reputation is high among women; above all, he has no record of killing, but is loved for his acts of personal charity and generosity to the poor. In fact Freney, who does not operate within any political context, is really another Irish brother of Robin Hood. The author is merely concerned to portray him as a popular champion rather than a blood-thirsty criminal. Whether this is naivety or a deliberately tactful refusal to show Irish rebels as they really were, it strikes quite a different note from that found in Carleton's work, and Mrs Hall's censure is at its mildest in this story.

The deeply moralistic tone of these *Sketches of Irish Character* recalls Mrs Hall's female predecessors Maria Edgeworth and Lady Morgan, although she lacks the artistry of the former and the flamboyance of the latter. Her particular achievement, and her main relevance here, is her concentration upon the lives of the peasantry. Unlike the Banim brothers and Griffin, whose tales are usually set against studies of landlords and gentry, Mrs Hall saw the lives of the poor as subject enough in itself. This emphasis is perhaps her strongest common bond with Carleton. Both writers are moralists. For Mrs Hall didacticism was inseparable from her view of the nature and purpose of fiction, whereas Carleton, for all he sold his talent to a variety of causes, wrote the best of his *Traits and Stories* first and foremost as an artist and only secondly as a conscious moralist.

Two of the most striking and memorable features of Carleton's stories are the completeness and immediacy with which they conjure up a whole way of life. Although many of the superficial details and customs he describes may have long since vanished, they survive here with an irresistible vitality, a fact which led Thomas Davis to assert that: 'No man, who does not know the things he tells, knows Ireland – no man who knows it ever doubted the perfection of those *Traits and Stories*.'[7] This is not simply a rhetorical flourish, for the accuracy, truth and realism of Carleton's best works have always been something of a cliché among his readers and admirers.

Undoubtedly the strengths of his writing derive from his background and upbringing, as Carleton himself was duly aware. Not only were his social origins unique amongst his fellow writers of the period, but, according to his own testimony, he was particularly fortunate in his parents, from both of whom he learnt much of the folklore and many of the beliefs, superstitions and country customs that are the basis of his best writing. In his unfinished *Autobiography* Carleton pays handsome and moving tributes to his parents. He maintains there that his father's stock of tales, charms, poems, ranns and prophecies was so complete that even when he came to move in wider social and intellectual circles, he never heard any legend or tradition that was wholly new to him. Carleton also comments on how his father told his stories as often in Irish as in English:

a circumstance which enabled me in my writings to transfer the genius, the idiomatic peculiarity and conversational spirit of the one language into the other, precisely as the people themselves do in their dialogues, whenever the heart or imagination happens to be moved by the darker or better passions.[8]

The richness of Carleton's language at its best, particularly of his dialogue, is one of his great virtues – and much of its idiomatic colour and energy derives from the bilingual elements in it. Likewise, in his account of his mother, renowned in her day for the sweetness of her singing and the 'sorrowful but solitary beauty' of her keening, Carleton shows the source of his inherited sensitivity to the differences between Irish and English:

she had a prejudice against singing the Irish airs to English words. .
. . I remember on one occasion when she was asked to sing the English
version of that touching melody, 'The Red-Haired Man's Wife', she
replied, 'I will sing it for you, but the English words and the air are
like a man and his wife quarrelling – the Irish melts into the tune but
the English doesn't.'[9]

More than any other novelist of his generation Carleton made
use of his first-hand knowledge of the two languages, which,
in common with his intimate grasp of the details of peasant
life, was acquired unconsciously during his boyhood and
youth. Only later, when he chanced to become a writer, did he
himself become aware of the rich store of language he
possessed, and by that time he declares, 'I could no more forget
it than I could forget my own name'.[10]

One additional point about Carleton's background not only
distinguishes him from his predecessors in Anglo-Irish fiction,
but also contributes to the feeling that he remains contemporary in a unique way. He was an Ulsterman and, as Sam Hanna
Bell noted in an article published in *Ulster Folklife*, 'even in
Carleton's day, the North was the North'.[11] Other writers
whose origins were in different parts of Ireland may have seen
and encountered sectarianism and anti-Catholicism, but the
Ulster experience has always been that much more abrasive,
urgent and unavoidable, as any Northerner knows. The effects
of this manifest themselves in several ways. Carleton's peasant
characters show an independence of mind which, in Mr Bell's
words, endows them with 'dignity, pathos, and the indignation
in the presence of injustice, lacking in the pages of Lever and
Lover'.[12] Furthermore his understanding of the sectarian
mentality is unique: he can distinguish between the moods that
precede a faction fight and a party fight ('The Battle of the
Factions'), or expose the apparatus of sectarianism in action in
Valentine McClutchy. Unlike John Banim's treatment of this
subject, Carleton's is no mere historical reconstruction; it is
written with the grim intensity of a man who had seen his sister
prodded in the side by a local Orangeman's bayonet as she lay in
bed during an insolent house-search.

Carleton's Ulster origins were at least as influential in
shaping his attitudes as Dublin would be for Joyce in a later
generation. His biography reveals a career that embraced many
of the contradictions that are particularly important in the
North. Born and raised a Catholic in an area where Irish was still
widely spoken, and intended for the priesthood, he moved

to Dublin, became a Protestant convert, and wrote in English. Tricked into becoming a Ribbonman in his youth, he flirted with the Young Ireland movement in his middle years, but also wrote unashamedly propagandist fiction against subversive organizations. Contrary, opinionated and often lonely in his later life, he used every devious means at his disposal to gain a pension for services to literature. This, then, is the background to the remarkable series of tales which Carleton presented to the public in 1830 and 1833. They launched him on his literary career; indeed some would say they took him at once to the pinnacle of his achievement, and that most of what followed over the next thirty years was inferior. Be that as it may, *Traits and Stories of the Irish Peasantry* was immediately acknowledged for its truth and vitality, a reputation it has never since lost.

One story which introduces a number of characteristic themes in Carleton's work, and which also partly reflects events in his own life, is 'The Poor Scholar'. Education is a recurrent topic, for in addition to 'The Poor Scholar', it is central to 'Denis O'Shaughnessy Going to Maynooth' and 'The Hedge School'. This is not surprising, because Carleton's *Autobiography* reveals how he himself was a student at a series of hedge-schools that existed intermittently in and around his home area during his youth and early manhood. Furthermore, when he set off on the travels which eventually led him to Dublin, he encountered other hedge-schools and even tried his hand at teaching. Although Carleton's accounts of hedge-schools are not unprecedented, they are unique in their detail. These schools, which were already in decline by the time Carleton was writing, existed on a most haphazard basis, but were of enormous social importance in providing the children of ambitious peasants and small farmers with basic learning, especially at times when anti-Catholic legislation was stringently enforced. The name 'hedge-schools' derives from the irregular meeting places of such gatherings, since under the penal laws the teacher and his pupils could only afford to assemble in improvised circumstances. Often when the schools were compelled to disband, the master would have to move on and a new school would emerge elsewhere.

The determination and perseverance which alone kept the schools functioning against all the odds are a clear indication of the value that the Irish poor attached to education. From the point of view of the Catholic peasant the training derived from a hedge-school was often the first step on the long road to the priesthood, and to see a son become a priest was the highest ambition of many parents. If a boy showed interest in gaining entry to Maynooth, not only would his immediate family support him in his endeavour, but local neighbours and friends would also subscribe money or gifts to help him on his way. To assist a young man who was committed to attaining sufficient education to embark upon his formal religious training was regarded as an act of faith as well as an act of charity; and for a family to have a son return to them as an ordained priest was an occasion of profound pride and honour. These facts form the basis of 'The Poor Scholar'.

The story begins with a striking image of Catholic dispossession, a description of Dominick McEvoy and his son, Jemmy, digging potatoes in mid-November 'on the side of a hard barren hill, called Esker Dhu'. The account continues:

The day was bitter and wintry, the men were thinly clad, and as the keen blast swept across the hill with considerable violence, the sleet-like rain which it bore along, pelted into their garments with pitiless severity. The father had advanced into more than middle-age; and having held, at a rack-rent, the miserable waste of farm which he occupied, he was compelled to exert himself in its cultivation, despite either obduracy of soil, or inclemency of weather. This day, however, was so unusually severe, that the old man began to feel incapable of continuing his toil. The son bore it better; but whenever a cold rush of stormy rain came over them, both were compelled to stand with their sides against it, and their heads turned, so as that the ear almost rested back upon the shoulder, in order to throw the rain off their faces. Of each, however, that cheek which was exposed to the rain and storm was beaten into a red hue; whilst the other part of their faces was both pale and hunger-pinched.

The father paused to take breath, and supported by his spade, looked down upon the sheltered inland which, inhabited chiefly by Protestants and Presbyterians, lay rich and warm-looking under him.

'Why thin', he exclaimed to his son – a lad about fifteen, – 'sure I know well I oughtn't to curse yees, anyway, you black set! an'yit, the Lord forgive me my sins, I'm almost timpted to give yez a volley, an' that from my heart out! Look at thim, Jimmy agra – only look at the black thieves! how warm and wealthy they sit there in our own ould possessions, an' here we must toil till our fingers are worn to the stumps, upon this thievin' bent.'[13]

The combined information about the weather, the men's physical privations and the motive for their labours constitutes a detailed portrait of the alienated position of Ulster Catholics like Dominick McEvoy. The single sentence which stands as the second paragraph is perhaps the most telling of all, for it introduces both the sharp contrast between Dominick's and Jemmy's situation and the snugness, warmth and prosperity of their Protestant neighbours, and also the facts of history to which Dominick McEvoy alludes in his words to his son: these lands occupied by 'Protestants and Presbyterians' are not held by traditional right, but because McEvoy and his kind were driven off them and forced to search out a living on barren hillsides like Esker Dhu.

One detail which Dominick McEvoy focuses upon from his vantage point on the hillside is decisive in determining his son's future. He observes the smoke rising from a neighbour's house in which the priest is holding a Station, and he knows that part of the responsibility of the host on such occasions is to provide an ample spread of food in honour of the priest and his visitors. This leads him to an envious contemplation of the treatment given to the priest, and also to Jemmy's dramatic gesture of hurling away his spade, cursing the slavery of his present life, and vowing to set off to Munster in order either to study and be trained as a priest himself or else never to return. Jemmy's decision has no religious or vocational basis, but is taken because to become a priest was also to become a gentleman with a recognized status and authority in the community. For a person like Jemmy McEvoy it was almost the only way to gain a measure of respectability and influence, and the boy specifically relates his intention to his determination to improve the lot of his family. Clearly his success in becoming a priest would not alter the material circumstances of his parents in itself, but it would give them a kind of distinction, as people whose son had entered the church, in their own community. Furthermore, as a priest, Jemmy presumably hopes that he may be able to influence the way in which his family are treated by agents and landlords, and in this the story shows him to be exceptionally effective.

Having decided to journey to Munster in quest of education, Jemmy McEvoy finds himself the recipient of many good-will gifts. (In the story of Denis O'Shaughnessy, he, too, is treated in a similar fashion when he seeks to become a priest, but Denis's character and the uses to which he puts his donations are very different.) The local priest, Father Kavanagh, shows his support for Jemmy by making him a promise of two guineas towards his collection, which he also organizes. Dominick

McEvoy's reaction to the priest's offer is at once surprising and, as Carleton himself points out, illustrative of the mixture of superstition and shrewdness of the peasant's way of thought. On the one hand, he is wary of receiving money from the priest lest it bring his son bad luck because it may have been paid out as the price of absolution for someone's sins. On the other hand, so his reasoning continues,

it's best to take it, anyway. We can asily put it off on some o' these black-mouthed Presbyterians or Orangemen, by way of changin' it, an' if there's any hard fortune in it, let them have full benefit of it.[14]

Carleton is not poking fun at Dominick McEvoy for this highly individual species of logic. On the contrary, he shows the complexity of the man's thought – Dominick is no mere stereotype – and the hard-headed practicality of a poor man who cannot afford to indulge his own finer scruples, but who sees a method both of accepting the gift and of using it in such a way as to enjoy its benefits and simultaneously inflict an underhand blow against a local enemy.

The power of the priest is a recurrent theme in Carleton's writing, and he presents the numerous ways in which priestly authority impinged upon the peasants' lives – spiritually, morally, politically, and socially. His clerics are the best monument in fiction to the very special relationship between priests and people in the period after the lapse of the strictest penal laws and before the reforming era of Cardinal Cullen in the mid-nineteenth century. Although he became a convert to Protestantism, Carleton's knowledge of Catholicism and of the place of the priest in a peasant community was so deeply ingrained that he recognized and was sensitive to their every nuance and detail. Thus, as a peasant himself, he identifies the finely tuned mixture of pathos and humour present in the sermon and appeal for money made by Father Kavanagh, the hedge-school priest. Carleton feels obliged to express regret for the way in which the priest uses his rude eloquence to arouse sectarian and political prejudices, but he is too honest an artist to deny that that *is* part of the technique.[15] He also shows how Protestants attended a service at which their own faith was attacked and gave financial assistance to a boy whose declared aim was to train for the ministry of the Catholic church. Neither party regarded this behaviour as either inconsistent or stupid; instead, it was interpreted as a sign of good neighbourly intentions and accepted as such.

On his journey to Munster Jemmy McEvoy soon discovers
that his special position as a poor scholar earns him the respect
and assistance of families who feed and shelter him in
exchange for a promise that he will say a Mass for them when
he has been ordained as a priest. But not all Jemmy's
adventures are fortunate, and his experiences in the hedge-
school run by Mr Corcoran – based upon Carleton's own
treatment at the hands of a hedge-schoolmaster called Pat
Frayne – are brutal and shocking. The poor scholar becomes
the object of the master's greed, mockery, bad temper and
physical violence. In another autobiographical incident we see
that the master is wily enough to be concerned about his own
job when the scholars rebel against a general assault upon
them. Carleton gives an irresistibly amusing account of how
the master, relieved to have his students return the following
morning, delivers an address of appeasement with as much
dignity as a man with a black eye, broken nose, and numerous
bruises can muster:

You treated my ribs as if they were the ribs of a common man; my
shins you took liberties wid even to excoriation; my head you made
a target of for your hardest turf; and my nose you dishonoured to my
face. Was this ginerous? was it discreet? was it subordinate? and,
above all, was it *classical*? However, I will show you what greatness
of mind is. I will convince you that it is more noble and god-like to
forgive an injury, or rather five dozen injuries, than to avenge one;
when – hem – yes, I say, when I – I – *might* so easily avenge it.[16]

This speech typifies Carleton's ability to capture the energy,
flow and vitality of the spoken word. With characters like
Corcoran, and indeed with most of his peasants, his ear seldom
lets him down. Here he pinpoints the pomposity, preten-
tiousness, absurdity and cunning of the coward and bully,
embedded in a debased version of formal rhetoric.

In another of the *Traits and Stories*, 'The Hedge School', the
author comments further on both the masters and their
schools. Discussing the privileged position of hedge-
schoolmasters he writes that they

were a class of men, from whom morality was not expected by the
peasantry; for, strange to say, one of their strongest recommendations
to the good opinion of the people, as far as their literary talents and
qualifications were concerned, was an inordinate love of whiskey, and
if to this could be added a slight touch of derangement, the character
was complete.[17]

Lady Morgan's portrait of Terence Oge O'Leary in *Florence Macarthy* conforms closely to this description, as does Matt Kavanagh in Carleton's own story. Equally intriguing is the claim that, for all their idiosyncrasies and unpredictability, the hedge-schoolmasters 'were as superior in literary knowledge and acquirements to the class of men who are now engaged in the general education of the people, as they were beneath them in moral and religious character'.[18] In other words, whatever the spiritual and ethical advantages of the formal system of national schools which began to emerge during Carleton's lifetime, and which struck the final blow against the existence of the hedge-schools, he had a higher regard for the confused but encyclopaedic knowledge of the old-fashioned polymaths of the barn or ditch.

Both 'The Poor Scholar' and 'The Hedge School' show that these seats of learning operated entirely on the principle of the survival of the fittest, either physically or intellectually, and the privileged. For a scholar to emerge and begin on the road to establishing himself as a hedge-schoolmaster was a difficult business, for a boy must challenge and defeat his own teacher in a public literary contest. If successful he would then travel as a poor scholar to another school, and study there until he could challenge and defeat his new teacher. After three or four years of travel, study and public debate, the scholar usually returned home to confront the incumbent in the hope of driving him out and installing himself in his place.

So strong was the desire for education that however cruel a master might be to a pupil, legal action would never follow, and whereas a local boy who had suffered unduly might be avenged by members of his own family assaulting the teacher, or even driving him out of the neighbourhood, the poor scholar had no such protection. Carleton recalls, both in his stories and in his *Autobiography*, examples of ferocious beatings given by the masters to their entire class using a furze or thorn branch against the bare legs of the children, or kicking on the shins with the nailed edge of a brogue, of cudgelling and of punching, all carried out in the name of punishment.

In addition to the brutalizing effects of so much of the behaviour in the schools, Carleton records the frequent involvement of the schoolmasters in spreading ideas of disaffection, rebellion and religious indifference – for example, Matt Kavanagh in 'The Hedge School' narrowly escapes hanging as an agent of the Ribbonmen. He also points out how much of the knowledge they imparted was dangerously limited or inaccurate. Despite these reservations, the story of Jemmy McEvoy exemplifies the triumph of the individual against enormous odds, and the hedge-school plays an indispensable part in that success.

Yet 'The Poor Scholar' concludes on a note of muted joy. Jemmy's father receives restitution for the unjust practices of Yellow Sam, the corrupt agent, because Colonel B – the landowner, undertakes a visit to his property and an investigation into the running of it after Jemmy has brought the plight of his family to the Colonel's attention. When he arrives at his estate the Colonel sees on all sides the standard evidence of neglect – overgrown grounds, broken hedges and gates, uncultivated fields, a decaying mansion – but his presence and sense of justice soon earn him the love of his tenants and lead to new activity and industry in the neighbourhood. Carleton's faith in the power and effectiveness of a good resident landlord is almost as great as that of Maria Edgeworth and Lady Morgan, as is his belief in the readiness of the peasants to forgive and forget. There is difficulty in accepting his premises without question, not least because the appearance of the good landlord, both here and in, for example, *Valentine McClutchy*, is such a contrived event.

The real climax to the story is obviously the return of Jemmy as an ordained priest, and the scenes of rejoicing and thanksgiving that accompany it. But despite this happiness, the tale ends with a brief note that Jemmy McEvoy did not live long to serve in the ministry. Weakened by hardship and disease he died soon after the completion of his training. Even this sombre detail is true to the spirit of the story: the gesture of defiance with which it opened, and the determination with which it was followed up, are impressive, but are paid for at an appallingly expensive rate. Oppression and humiliation may not be overcome without great sacrifices. Jemmy McEvoy succeeds in creating an identity for himself amongst a dispossessed people, and, incidentally, he enables his father to regain his self-respect, but the reader cannot avoid wondering at the injustice of a system which imposed such suffering upon certain members of the community.

The natural counterpart to 'The Poor Scholar' among the *Traits and Stories* is 'Denis O'Shaughnessy Going to Maynooth', but where the former is distinguished by its pathos and dark mood, the latter is an outstanding example of

Carleton's skill as a writer of comedy. In some respects it repeats the subject-matter of 'The Poor Scholar', with the major differences that whereas Jemmy McEvoy's persistence in striving to achieve his goal was unflagging, Denis O'Shaughnessy's determination is forever wavering and ultimately he abandons his quest to become a priest. Herein there is a much stronger link between the story of Denis and that of his creator than there is with 'The Poor Scholar'. Denis has the vivacity, waywardness, liking for the girls, and the strange mixture of pomposity and lack of confidence which Carleton attributes to himself in his *Autobiography*. Above all Denis's situation, unlike Jemmy's which was self-chosen, derives from the pressures and expectations placed upon him by his father. 'The Poor Scholar' showed the peasants' respect for education and for the benefits it could bring, but 'Denis O'Shaughnessy' explores how that same respect for learning and for the church becomes a snare which traps the hero of the tale. As Maurice Harmon has written,

The peasant reverence for the church and its figures, including the potential or aspiring priest, are some of the nets against which Denis has to struggle. Largely because of their historical force, he accepts the part of the philomath-priest in this vain drama. The tragedy lies in his unthinking or immature indulgence of a part determined for him by social and historical contexts.[19]

The comedy, however, results from the ironic way in which the story is related.

From the outset the narrative tone is at once affectionate and mocking, and this odd combination infuses the tale with genuine feeling and sympathy for Denis's position, and yet saves it from becoming self-indulgent or merely quixotic. Denis makes countless laughable blunders, but he is no stereotyped stage Irishman, nor is he the kind of lovable fool for whom events always work out right in the end, like Rory O'More in Samuel Lover's novel of the same name. The secret of Carleton's success is that he bases Denis's whole life firmly within the community to which he belongs: his family and his parish make him into the kind of person he is as much as anything that he himself does. Writing of *The Playboy of the Western World*, Raymond Williams observes how Christy Mahon's fantasy of killing his father is not simply personal, but is stimulated and encouraged by the community in which he seeks refuge, and as the story grows, so too does his belief in it. Christy's character is changed, or liberated, by the status he achieves, and although the illusion is shattered at the end, Christy retains his newfound confidence.[20] This situation is at once both similar to and different from that of Denis O'Shaughnessy, for although Denis is largely shaped by the community in which he lives, he is trapped rather than liberated by it. This is not surprising, for Christy Mahon's freedom was only attained when he fled from home and sought concealment amongst strangers. Denis never makes such a break, and Carleton's story is concerned with showing how his hero is encircled by the pressures of his community, and how those pressures place impossible demands upon him.

The reputation of young Denis derives from his alleged ability to engage in successful public controversy on any conceivable subject, and from the sheer nerve he shows in doing so. His talent is promoted by his father, although, ironically, he is usually the victim of his son's arguments, and unlike Jemmy McEvoy, who made his own decision to train for the priesthood, Denis's career is effectively chosen for him by his doting parent. Once his alleged vocation is declared, the boy's position and importance within the family change, as does his role within the local community, where his youthful learning is regarded with a degree of awe and respect that is directly proportional to its obscurity and pomposity. Herein lies the tragi-comedy of Denis O'Shaughnessy's predicament, for, like his creator, he lacks any real wish to enter the Church, but he greatly enjoys his prestige and authority as an aspiring priest.

Denis's language is characterized by idioms associated with physical action or drawn from rural life, which fill it with an energy and vividness that have an immediate appeal. He speaks of rubbing down an opponent with a Greek towel, of giving him a plaster of Latin to heal the injuries he has received in debate, and of bruising a few Greek roots to lay on his victim's 'caput'. Elsewhere, having denounced his father's ignorance for using the word 'prove' instead of 'probate' or 'probe', he proceeds to explain that the 'ancisthor' of the word is '*probo*, a deep Greek word – *probo, probas, probass* – that is to say, I'm to *probe* Phadrick here to be an *ass*'.[21] The comedy of such nonsense is heightened by the gravity of the listeners, but the social implications of granting pride of place to such a half-taught scholar have yet to be considered.

Young Denis is not a complete fool, however, for even his

most ludicrous arguments demonstrate a native cunning and wittiness that are memorable. An example of this is the 'proof' he offers a neighbour, Patrick Murray, that there is no difference between black and white. Here the dialogue belongs to an Anglo-Irish tradition which extends from Swift's remorseless logic in *A Modest Proposal* down to the ingenuities of Joyce, or Flann O'Brien's atomic theory in *The Third Policeman*. It deploys some of the trappings of rational argument and proof, but rests upon premises that render the entire case absurd:

'So, Phadrick, your preamble is that white is white and black is black? . . . Now, stretch out your ears, till I probate or probe to you the differ atween black an' white. . . . here's the griddle, an' here's a clane plate– do you see them here beside one another?'
    'I'm lookin' at them.'
    'Now shut your eyes.'
    'Is that *your* way, Denis, of judgin' colours?'
    'Shut your eyes, I say, till I give you *ocular* demonstration of the differ atween these two respectable colours.'
    'Well, they're shut.'
    'An' keep them so. Now, what differ do you *see* atween them?'
    'The sorra taste, man alive; I never *seen* anything in my whole life so clearly of a colour as they are both this minute.'
    'Don't you see now, Phadrick, that there's not the smallest taste o' differ in them, an' that's accordin' to Euclid.'
    'Sure enough, I see the divil a taste o' differ atween the two.'
    'Well, Phadrick, that's the point settled. There's no discrimination at all atween black an' white. They're both of the same colour– so long as you keep your eyes shut.'[22]

In this 'proof', which is representative of several that Denis propounds, Carleton allows his character to reveal himself through talk rather than description. Its comic effects derive from the awe of Patrick Murray on the one hand and the self-confident pomposity of Denis who knows exactly how to exploit his reputation for being 'long-headed' on the other. In this respect the story is different to 'The Poor Scholar' where straight narrative played a much bigger part.

    Having established Denis with his readers by means of his conversation, Carleton then looks more closely at other aspects of his hero's privileged position. He understands that as Denis becomes a showpiece for the rest of his family, performing to their credit, he is therefore justified in being exempted from the ordinary working lives of the rest of the community. But not only is Denis excused from labour that might demean him; he is also ready to exploit his reputation for his own material ends. His concern with his personal appearance assumes an increasing importance to him as he approaches manhood and endeavours to adopt the manners, dress and dignity of a priest. Ironically the more successful he is in playing the role, the more isolated he becomes from his family and neighbours. Their very admiration and pride in him have the effect of distancing them from him, and the pedantry with which he overawed them earlier diminishes because he no longer permits himself to engage in discussion with them.

The tragi-comedy of Denis's progress is heightened by the fact that, for all his posturing and detachment, he is also an eighteen-year-old with an eye for the girls. Carleton's accounts of Denis's attempts to steal a kiss and a caress, and of his explanation to the young lady that he is 'only feeling [her] cheek as a philosophical experiment', provide moments of high comedy. They also reveal the tension of Denis's situation, because his high-falutin' language, ponderously worded expressions of emotion and justifications of his flirtatious behaviour reveal that the role into which he is trying to force himself is unnatural and increasingly difficult for him to sustain. Miss Norah's words when he lectures her on decorum – 'You're a fool, Misther O'Shaughnessy! Why didn't you take the kiss an' spare the king's English!' – penetrate to the centre of Denis's dilemma.[23]

Another aspect of Denis's mounting arrogance is less humorous and indicates how hurtful his behaviour can be to the very people who most admire him. He comes to demand better food than the rest of his family can have, arguing that it 'increases the weight of the brain', and that a man in a black clerical coat should not be expected 'to be placed among the other riff-raff of the family'.[24] Perhaps even more offensive is his insistence that everyone, his parents included, must address him as Master Dionysius rather than Dinny. The confused submission of his mother and father to these outrageous pretensions is pathetic; it is as if they have created a monster over whom they can no longer exercise control. Denis's behaviour places great strain upon the bonds of family affection. As his sister says,

I'd beg . . . for him, sooner nor he should want; but I can't bear to be callin' my brother Dinny – *Sir* – like a stranger; it looks as if *I* didn't love him, or as if *he* was forgettin' us, or carin' less about us nor he used to do.[25]

The girl sees what her brother misses: that he confuses part of his preparation for the priesthood with an insensitive rejection of the people who love and support him. Denis's pomposity is a sign of his weakness rather than his strength and even in this Carleton encourages sympathy for him.

The rapid approach of the crisis point in Denis's career – his interview with the Bishop who alone has the power to recommend him for acceptance at Maynooth – is heralded in three ways, each of which furthers awareness of his insecurity. First, Denis becomes involved in a rather unsavoury arrangement with Father Finnerty, his local priest, whereby the latter will receive the gift of a horse provided that the Bishop is persuaded to allow Denis to proceed to Maynooth. In fact the Bishop discovers this attempted bribery, which adds to the humiliation of Denis's failure at the first interview. The introduction of Father Finnerty at this juncture is notable, because Carleton has so far been careful not to compare Denis's conduct with that of an ordained priest. Far from being a detached and vain man, Father Finnerty is deeply involved in the life of his parishioners and is regular, if informal, in carrying out his duties. His all-too-human weaknesses are seen in his readiness to exploit the generous hospitality of the O'Shaughnessys in exchange for flattering their favourite son, and in accepting the proposed bribe in exchange for persuading the Bishop to back a candidate whom he knows to be unready and unsuitable for the priesthood.

The second sign of Denis's insecurity is his rejection of Susan O'Connor with whom he had exchanged a hand-promise of marriage. He again seeks refuge in long words and specious reasoning to justify his breach of faith – and a hand-promise was a very serious form of oath – urging the girl to believe that it would be a sin of great enormity to prevent 'such a-a-a-galaxy', 'a rara avis in terris', as himself from entering the priesthood. Like the members of his own family, Susan is impressed by such statements and is ready to accept them, however painful, but again Denis blunders on and turns his remarks into an unkind insult:

There is one argument which I am anxious to press upon you. It is a very simple but a very respectable one after all. I am not all Ireland. You will find excellent good husbands even in this parish. There is, as the old proverb says, as good fish in the say as ever were caught. Do you catch one of them. For me, Susan, the vineyard claims me; I must, as I said, cultivate the grape. We must consequently – hem! – we must – hem! hem! – consequently strive to forget – hem! – I say to forget each other. . . . destiny will be triumphant. What is decreed, is decreed – I must go to Maynooth.[26]

Carleton carefully guides the reader's responses at this critical point, underlining the sincerity of Denis's feelings for Susan, but also emphasizing that one passion has been defeated by another, namely ambition.

The third indication of insecurity comes on the eve of his interview with the Bishop, when Denis is suddenly struck by the full implications of his situation. His family's hour of greatest pride and confidence in his ability to walk into Maynooth without let or hindrance is Denis's time of extreme loneliness and fear. True, he indulges them by imagining his way of life and conduct when he is an ordained priest, but these self-erected barriers of arrogance and superiority give way to expose him as a vulnerable and home-leaving peasant boy. The course he is embarked upon cannot be altered, and the humiliation Denis receives from the Bishop is made worse because his parents have prepared a massive feast to welcome him home in triumph. Even in disgrace and disappointment Denis's family remain incapable of admitting any inadequacy in their paragon, yet they are superstitiously cautious of being overcritical of the clergy. His mother reacts to the approval of Father Malony's nephew in preference to her son by remarking:

As for Father Malony, we wish him well, but undher the roof of this house, at a Station, or anything else of the kind, he will never sit, barrin' I thought he was either dhry or hungry, that I wouldn't bring evil upon my substance by refusin' him.[27]

Their confused mixture of awe before the priest, superstition and fear of attracting bad luck, and blind family loyalty, is centred on Denis, thus making him the focal point for an entire community and giving the tale the particular richness which makes it greater than, say, 'Phelim O'Toole's Courtship'.

Phelim is another magnificent creation – grotesque, eccentric, roguish and highly amusing – who is acknowledged by his neighbours to be an unusual character, so that when he ends up engaged to three women, all of whom he is to marry on the same day, and is called to account by the priest in front of the congregation, they are neither shocked nor surprised but simply amused: it is just what they expect of him. The impact of this splendid tale is different to that of 'Denis O'Shaughnessy Going to Maynooth', for Phelim exists in a kind of isolation from his family and friends which is never true of Denis. He is an object of curiosity, local indulgence and comedy, whereas the myth of Denis is largely a creation of the community in general and of his family in particular. Phelim would have provoked a similar response in any community: his freakish appearance, with the drooping left eyelid – the legacy of an attack of smallpox in childhood that makes him look as if he is permanently winking –, his outsize clothes, and his flattering way with women of all ages ensure that this is so. Denis, on the other hand, begins with a certain native talent, but this is taken over and built up by the people around him, who are as much concerned with living out their own aspirations and frustrated ambitions through him as with the well-being of Denis himself.

Thomas Flanagan is probably right to argue that Carleton should have finished the tale of Denis with the account of the feast and the hero's sorry return from the Bishop's palace. Instead it goes on to show how, by a further act of bribery and manipulation involving the Bishop himself, Denis does finally get to Maynooth. Even then Denis's feelings for Susan Connor are stronger than his vocation, and a year after entering college and following the death of his father, he abandons Maynooth and returns to marry his true love. But the verbal magic fades in these closing episodes, demonstrating just how much the success of the earlier part derived from its sparkling dialogue.

The comparison between 'Denis O'Shaughnessy Going to Maynooth' and *The Playboy of the Western World* may be extended here, for, in the same way that Christy Mahon has to 'kill' his father, at least in his own imagination, so too Denis's father has to die before he can rid himself of the burden laid upon him and act as a free agent. Only then can he abandon the enforced role of scholar-priest and live out the kind of life that he himself chooses, no longer alienated from his society but an integrated member of it.

Carleton's intermittent anti-Catholicism influences some of his work, particularly in the early stages of his career when the impact of the Protestant evangelical Caesar Otway was strongest upon him. Thus *Father Butler*, an early story not included in the *Traits and Stories*, contains a deliberate attack on Catholicism in general and the Jesuits in particular. It tells of the author's encounter with a priest who is dying of consumption and at the same time undergoing a crisis of faith. Father Butler had been blackmailed into entering the priesthood because of a vow taken on his behalf by his parents. To make matters worse, he also was forced to break an earlier promise of marriage to a Protestant girl, Ellen Upton. She dies of grief as a consequence, and Butler himself becomes increasingly antagonistic towards Roman Catholicism, the power of the priests, the deliberate ignorance in which the peasantry are kept and the denial of the individual's right of conscience.

Carleton scores a number of easy points against the Catholic Church, contrasting Father Butler's rational critique of its harsh authoritarianism with the stereotyped responses of Paddy Diminick, a sectarian bigot and hypocritical rogue. The crisis of faith described here, however, is dull compared with that of John Nowlan, for Carleton's hero is obviously little more than an excuse for a series of anti-Catholic attacks, whereas John Banim's character is agonisingly real.

The astonishing thing is that Carleton's natural gift for story-telling, his intuitive understanding of what makes a good yarn, emerged rapidly and in spite of the pressures upon him to slant his tales in support of a particular cause. So the confusion of religious faith and superstition which he attempts to satirize in *Father Butler* reappears in a tale like 'Ned McKeown', where, stimulated by whiskey and the bleak weather outside, the characters in Ned's isolated inn begin by telling each other frightening stories and end up by believing that the Devil has joined them by the fireside. By this device Carleton *enacts* the beliefs and values of the peasantry rather than simply telling of their existence. In 'Ned McKeown' he is an artist; in *Father Butler* a tract writer. Similarly in 'Shane Fadh's Wedding', after the wedding ceremony, there is a crazy race between the guests to be the first back to the house in order to win a bottle of whiskey. The race culminates in a fight which is ended by the priest, Father Corrigan, and his curate, Father James, who move amongst the contestants with whips and denounce their behaviour vehemently:

'What, you murderers,' says his Reverence, 'are you bint to have each other's blood upon your heads; ye vile infidels, ye cursed unchristian Hottentots? are ye going to get yourselves hanged like sheep-stalers?

down with your sticks, I command you: do you know – will ye give yourselves time to see who's spaking to you – you bloodthirsty set of Africans? I command you, in the name of the Catholic Church and the Blessed Virgin Mary to stop this instant, if you don't wish me,' says he, 'to turn you into stocks and stones where you stand, and make world's wonders of you so long as you live.'[28]

Not only the forcefulness of this speech, but also the way in which it is introduced, using a narrator but quoting the supposed words of the priest, reveal Carleton's maturing skill as a writer. Father Corrigan's abuse of the troublemakers, whom he accuses of being like uncivilized or pagan people, and his own threat to use his authority as a Catholic cleric to employ magical powers to punish anyone who continues to fight, make for more effective satire and at the same time more entertaining reading than the tedious *Father Butler*. The incongruity of the priest's words trouble neither priest nor people, and his intervention is wholly successful: even if they do not entirely believe in Father Corrigan's capacity to petrify limbs, no-one is prepared to put him to the test.

'The Lough Derg Pilgrim' (1829) is different again, indeed something of a hybrid. Based loosely on an experience of the author himself, it describes a serio-comic pilgrimage made by a gullible and self-important youth who aspires to the priesthood and who undertakes the journey to Lough Derg as an act of faith. The story is told by a narrator whose tone veers between anti-Catholic moralizing and affectionate good-humour. It tells how the youthful pilgrim is tricked of his money and good clothes by an elderly female vagabond who haunts the roads leading to Lough Derg for this very purpose, and is overlaid with a satirical attack on the superstition of Catholics and the unscrupulousness of their priests.

It is hard to believe that the speaker, if he is a prospective priest making a serious pilgrimage, would be so openly critical of the clergy and their conduct. He mocks the way in which one priest hearing confessions rushes to absolve the pilgrims before they have finished; he indicates the undisguised amusement of others when an unfortunate hare-lipped man is leading the party in prayers; and he exposes the fawning greed of Sol Donnel, a professional pilgrim who survives by the charity of others. These points are made too self-consciously and intrusively, and the best parts come when Carleton lets the mask fall and writes naturally. The narrator's account of his vain attempt to walk on water, his observation and enjoyment of the countryside he passes through on his way to Lough Derg, his flattered vanity when two women whom he joins *en route* appear to take him for a priest, and the description of how he was cheated by Nell McCollum, the tinker's wife, these are the memorable events. 'The Lough Derg Pilgrim' shows how right from the outset Carleton was prone to compromise his fiction by making it the servant of one cause or another. Without exception this had a damaging – in some instances a disastrous – effect, and it partly explains why he is such an uneven writer; why, in his novels especially, the good passages are often embedded uneasily in the midst of long sections of inferior hack work.

Carleton did not always write mockingly of the Catholic Church. 'The Midnight Mass', a powerful and melodramatic tale of revenge and bloodshed, opens with a magnificent scene of the kind which perhaps only he could evoke. The occasion is Christmas Eve and this particular Mass, intended to commemorate not only the day but also the supposed hour of Christ's birth, was regarded with the greatest respect by most Catholics at the period of the story (around the turn of the nineteenth century). Because of the large numbers who attended, the Mass was usually held in the open air, and there is a vivid account of the sight of many dozens of people making their way through the night carrying burning bog-fir torches to guide them. The event is at once mysterious and enjoyable, spiritual and worldly, sober and intoxicated. Carleton is not sentimental , however affectionately he remembers the scene, for he also records that arguments, fights, and assaults on the young women were frequent occurrences, usually prompted by excessive drinking. Less sinister behaviour – secret meetings of lovers, and families gathering for a few drinks before the Mass in a public-house or shebeen near to the chapel green – was also commonplace. These accumulated details convey the sense of a great social gathering which is also a religious festival: indeed the two are inseparable.

The setting and the celebration of the Mass combine to add to the inherent drama of the situation. There is something wild, almost pagan, in the description of the huge, silent crowd, the faces illuminated by the torches, awaiting the climax of the open-air ceremony. As so often at moments of particular tension and power in his work, Carleton responds not only to events themselves but also quite effortlessly, even instinctively, to the landscape in which they are taking place:

the stars scattered thinly over the heavens, twinkled with a faint religious light that blended well with the solemnity of this extraordinary worship, and rendered the rugged nature of the abrupt cliffs and precipices, together with the still outline of the stern mountains, sufficiently visible to add to the wildness and singularity of the ceremony.[29]

The scene, linked with the 'spectre-like appearance of the white-robed priest', not only makes the experience almost supernatural but also exemplifies and helps to explain the easy fusion of superstition and religion in the minds of the peasants. As soon as the Mass is completed, there is renewed noise, movement and laughter, and the shebeens are quickly filled again, emphasizing once more the close co-existence of sacred and secular in such a community.

The scene in 'The Midnight Mass' contains no imposed comments on the desirability or otherwise of the Catholic religion, and it is the better for it. In his introduction to *Representative Irish Tales*, W. B. Yeats commented that

Carleton . . . when he began writing, knew nothing about the public and its tastes. He had little more education than may be picked up at fair greens and chapel greens, and wrote, as a man naturally wants to write, of the things he understood.[30]

The account of the midnight Mass is a good example of this kind of writing. Whether or not Carleton was a believing Catholic, a Protestant convert or a free thinker is irrelevant. What counts is the surefootedness of his description, the atmosphere he conveys, and the ease with which he himself responds to his own memories. Here, as always, he is most reliable and effective when his imagination acts upon his own experiences, rather than when he endeavours to treat his subject in an intellectual or abstract way. Then he tends towards the simplistic and he cuts himself off from the humour, colour, conversations and descriptions of people and places which are the flesh and blood of his best stories.

These positive features are all found in a group of tales which deal with the intricacies of another aspect of peasant life: sectarian, political and inter-family disputes and fights. The Irish have a long-established reputation for belligerence and squabbling, and while Carleton's stories may appear to confirm the truth of such an impression, they also penetrate the stereotyped image of the drunken, shillelagh-swinging Paddy and explore the society which generated this cartoon figure. Carleton himself deplored the outrages and fights which split communities and spread distrust, secrecy and desire for revenge, but he was too much a product of that society to underestimate the indigenous nature of many of the arguments and their power over the minds and actions of the peasantry. Thus his dislike of faction and party fighting, and his denunciations of it, are not a matter of simple moralizing, but derive from an informed awareness of how these battles are also complex social rituals.

One of his earliest and most graphic accounts of violence occurs in 'Wildgoose Lodge', which tells of an attack by Ribbonmen on an isolated farmhouse and the consequent destruction of the occupants and their property. The incident, including the eventual arrest and execution of ring-leaders, is based upon an historical incident which took place in Co. Louth. The author had seen the horrific remains of the gibbeted schoolmaster, Devaun, and twenty-three of his confederates hanging as a warning near the site of their crime. The purpose of this tale is not merely to shock, although the lurid details of the ferocious attack are certainly gruesome: the inmates of the house are burnt alive, and one particularly grotesque incident appears to symbolize the barbarity of the entire action. Following a cry for mercy from a burning woman,

the only reply to this was the whoop from the Captain and his gang of 'No mercy – no mercy!' and that instant the former, and one of the latter, rushed to the spot, and ere the action could be perceived, the head was transfixed with a bayonet and a pike, both having entered it together. The word mercy was divided in her mouth; a short silence ensued; the head hung down on the window but was instantly tossed back into the flames.[31]

This bizarre episode not only suggests the melodramatic nature of the story, but also Carleton's emphasis upon the absolute ruthlessness of the attackers. In this it recalls Michael Banim's portrayal of the brutality and heartlessness of the slaughter of Protestants on Vinegar Hill.

The so-called captain of the Ribbonmen, Paddy Devaun, proves particularly fascinating because of the apparent contradictions in his way of life. In addition to being a terrorist, he is also the local schoolmaster and the clerk to the priest. Such confusion of religious and political beliefs and values and the capacity to accept philosophies which seem to be utterly incompatible intrigue both the author and his readers. Moreover the problem remains a contemporary issue. The fact that the conspirators meet to plan their raid in a church may seem unnecessarily melodramatic, perhaps a detail that belongs merely to the genre of Gothic horror tales, but the grim reminder which the captain gives his men after they have completed the attack sounds a note of cold truth:

Remember, every man of you, what you've sworn this night on the book an' altar of God – not on a heretic Bible. If you perjure yourselves, you may hang us; but let me tell you, for your comfort, that if you do, there is them livin' that will take care the lase of your own lives will be but short.[32]

Here again is the sinister and pitiless world of fanaticism and terror. Fear of discovery and execution is conjoined with fear of breaking a sacred oath – and Paddy Devaun was too experienced to allow any of his fellows to get away with false oaths or thumb-kissing – and thus men are intimidated into silence just as some of them had been unwillingly pressured into attending the meeting in the first place.

This confusion of values extends beyond the crime itself, for Carleton concludes his story by telling how, after Devaun's execution for the raid on Wildgoose Lodge, the peasants still speak of him as 'Poor Paddy'. The Irish love martyrs and are quick to bestow the title on those who die at the hands of the authorities, especially if that authority is associated with English rule; they are sometimes less ready to examine the actions for which the offender has been punished. Here is another aspect of that traditional contempt for law imposed from without which is illustrated repeatedly in Anglo-Irish fiction. Carleton was perplexed by this problem, and in his 'Essay on Irish Swearing' he even suggests that there is almost an innate temperamental element in the Irish attitude towards criminal behaviour. He writes:

It is not in Ireland with criminals as in other countries, where the character of a murderer or incendiary is notoriously bad, as resulting from a life of gradual profligacy and villainy. Far from it. In Ireland you will find those crimes perpetrated by men who are good fathers, good husbands, good sons, and good neighbours – by men who would share their last morsel or their last shilling with a fellow-creature in distress – who would generously lose their lives for a man who had obliged them, provided he had not incurred their enmity – and who would protect a defenceless stranger as far as lay in their power.[33]

This observation touches upon a truth about Irish attitudes which is as valid today as it was a hundred and fifty years ago: the Irish have developed an inbuilt ambivalence in their views on violence in general, and on political violence in particular. Whereas an Irishman will condemn armed robbery, rape or murder for personal gain as roundly as his fellow Englishman, he will often be less willing to denounce killings and attacks on people or property which are linked with a political motive. In the minds of many Irishmen such activities are a contribution to a longstanding national feud, are selfless rather than selfish, and arouse neither the repugnance nor the pity that the same deed carried out without a political justification would immediately generate. To this extent the Provisional IRA of today are the true heirs of the Ribbonmen and Whiteboys, and insofar as there exists a genuine hesitation in condemning their excesses for reasons other than simple fear of reprisals, it is based upon this ambiguity of attitude which Carleton described. This same equivocation made the English contemptuous of Irish acts of political violence in the nineteenth century, and bewilders their attempts to understand certain Irish responses to more recent events.

The predilection for violence is shown not only in attacks of the kind described in 'Wildgoose Lodge', but also in accounts of party and faction fights. The former clashes are motivated by political or sectarian disputes, whereas the latter stem from rivalry between different families within the community. Party fights tend to be premeditated and are altogether more fierce and vengeful than faction fights, which are, according to the account in 'The Battle of the Factions', 'all song, dance, good-humour, and affection'.[34] Faction fighting stimulates trade, because people flood into a local town before a confrontation, but if there is word of a potential party fight, many folk stay away and the shopkeepers lose business. The narrator of 'The Battle of the Factions' gives an account of cudgel-making with a grotesque enthusiasm that might remind the reader of Gulliver's gleeful conversation with the King of Brobdingnag on the human genius for designing weapons of destruction: in both cases the irony is heightened by the passionate delight of the speaker in his theme. According to Pat Frayne,

a real Irish cudgel must be root-growing, either oak, black-thorn, or crab-tree — although crab-tree, by the way, is apt to fly. They should not be too long — three feet and a few inches is an accommodating length. They must be naturally top-heavy, and have around the end that is to make acquaintance with the cranium, three or four natural lumps, calculated to divide the flesh in the natest manner, and leave, if possible, the smallest taste in life of pit in the skull. But if a good root-growing kippeen be light at the fighting end, or possess not the proper number of knobs, a hole, a few inches deep, is to be bored in the end, which must be filled with melted lead. This gives it a widow-and-orphan-making quality, a child-bereaving touch, altogether very desirable.[35]

The tone and style of these comments make it hard to remember the grim nature of the subject; the deadpan delivery and semi-scientific instructions are aspects of a literary sophistication not usually associated with Carleton.

Pat Frayne's account of the fight shows how it draws in all members of the community. Even the women are active combatants, and the wives and sweethearts of members of the opposite faction may take part against their own blood relations or, alternatively, may attack their husbands or lovers. He sums up the whole business of faction fighting in a characteristically witty and perceptive remark: 'Ireland ought to be a land of mathemathitians; for I'm sure her population is well-trained, at all events, in the two sciences of *multiplication* and *division*.'[36]

Whereas in 'The Battle of the Factions' Pat Frayne told his story from within the community he described, the narrator of 'The Funeral and Party Fight' is a man returning after an absence of fourteen years to his neighbourhood, where he finds himself involved in the funeral ceremonies for one Denis Kelly, a former fighter of local renown. Carleton's account of his narrator's reactions as he journeys through increasingly familiar country is relevant not only to the character, but also offers an oblique comment on the inhabitants of the area:

as I advanced nearer home, the names of hills, and lakes, and mountains that I had utterly forgotten, as I thought, were distinctly revived in my memory. . . . The name of a townland would instantly return with its appearance; and I could now remember the history of families and individuals, long sunk into the dark recesses of my memory.

But what is even more singular is, that the superstitious terrors of my childhood began to come over me, as formerly, whenever a spot noted for supernatural appearances met my eye. It was in vain that I exerted myself to repel them, by throwing the barrier of philosophic reasoning in their way; they still clung to me, in spite of every effort to the contrary.[37]

This testifies to the intimate relationship between the Irish peasant and his environment, and to the indestructibility of that bond. Even a long absence and an acquired sophistication of thought have little effect on the narrator's responses to the landscape and its associations which are as immediate and primitive as ever. Since these recollections return with such vivid reality to a man who has been away from the neighbourhood for many years, their grip would be even stronger on the minds of those who had never lived anywhere else. In a similar fashion family or sectarian divisions and feuds became enshrined in local memory, thus ensuring their perpetuation from generation to generation, even after the original cause for dispute between the parties may have been forgotten.

One part of Carleton's description of the difference between the Protestant and Catholic combatant in the party fight highlights the superior physical hardiness of the Ribbonmen, although the Orangemen were taller and more sturdily built. The Protestants have the advantage of possessing firearms, whereas the Catholics depend upon their murderous cudgels – no doubt a legacy from the prohibition banning them from bearing weapons imposed under the penal laws. These contrasts between the rival parties reflect the history of the area, for the Catholics are mountain dwellers, having been driven out of the more fertile parts by the Protestants in earlier civil feuding. Carleton concludes that

The characteristic features produced by these causes are such as might be expected – the Catholic being, like his soil, hardy, thin and capable of bearing all weathers; and the Protestants, larger, softer, and more inactive.[38]

Significantly the Orangemen's victory in the ferocious party fight is only secured after they use their weapons on the Ribbonmen.

Carleton's account of Denis Kelly's wake conforms in the main to the kind of picture drawn by Griffin in *The Collegians*, but since Kelly dies as the result of a party fight rather than of natural causes, there are a number of decisive differences. Here the keening and lamentations are accompanied by equally passionate vows that revenge will be taken for Denis Kelly's death. His fourteen-year-old son publicly swears to have blood for blood, again a response which is not seen by his family and friends to contradict their Christian hope of salvation, which is symbolized by their care to leave the corpse's feet and toes loose in his grave-clothes so that he will be unimpeded on the day of the general resurrection. This curious combination of faith in God's goodness and justice and determination to make sure that scores are also settled on earth is further exemplified by events during the funeral procession. In cases of murder the body of the victim was taken past the house of the killer, if he was known, and the mourning family would stop outside and call down Heaven's justice on the offender. If there was doubt about the murderer's identity, then the suspect could only clear himself by touching the corpse or the coffin and swearing his innocence. Denis Kelly's death is not a clearcut matter, for although the deliverer of the fatal blow is known, because it was struck in the course of a party fight, the case is not a simple murder. Carleton uses this fact to bring about a recognition of the need for forgiveness and reconciliation between the two families rather than revenge, but while such a conclusion may be admirable and morally desirable, the son's oath of revenge carries a greater ring of truth.

'No other peasantry', wrote Thomas Davis, 'have had their tale told so well as the Irish by this Ulsterman.'[39] Whether this is literally true or not may be open to question, but the feeling which prompted Davis's remark is understandable, and it remains a sorry fact that Carleton's *Traits and Stories* should be as little known and as inaccessible as it is today. It is an astonishing achievement. Davis and Yeats were both right in their evaluation of Carleton's contribution. They recognized how his stories, more than those of any other writer, form a bridgehead between the dying Gaelic world of the eighteenth century and the increasingly Anglicized, turbulent and hungry people of the nineteenth century. His role as social historian has sometimes received fuller acknowledgement than his artistic merits, and Carleton himself certainly regarded his writing as, among other things, a memorial to the old ways, but he was also, in Sam Hanna Bell's words, 'the mentor of his people'.[40]

As such he was at once the defender, interpreter and critic of the Irish peasantry in all the fullness and variety of their lives. His general introduction to the 1843 edition of the *Traits and Stories* attacks the popular English notion of the Irish which saw them all as 'the Captain O'Cutters, O'Blunders, and Dennis Bulgrudderies of the English stage', and argues that these characters were the creations of writers 'who were as ignorant of the Irish people as they were of their language and feelings'.[41] In assuming this stance Carleton is, of course, following his predecessors, Maria Edgeworth, Lady Morgan, the Banims, and Gerald Griffin, but by referring to his own background in Co. Tyrone he is able to develop the argument instructively. Alluding to the fact that the Irishman's reputation for stupidity is often based upon his confused use of language, Carleton continues:

The language of our people has been for centuries, and is up to the present day, in a transition state. The English tongue is gradually superseding the Irish. In my own native place, for instance, there is not by any means so much Irish spoken now, as there was about twenty or five-and-twenty years ago. This fact, then, will easily account for the ridicule which is, and I fear ever will be, unjustly heaped upon those who are found to use a language which they do not properly understand.[42]

Carleton was a product of this transition, and perhaps one of his most original and significant literary achievements is that some of his best writing, and his dialogue in particular, captures the idiom of the changing language. In this at least he is unmatched by any of his contemporaries, and he succeeds in giving Anglo-Irish fiction its first unique *voice*, as opposed to theme or characters. D. J. O'Donoghue seized on this point in the introduction to his four-volume edition of the *Traits and Stories* when he stated that 'The accent of old Ireland is more truly and faithfully preserved in [them] than if it were treasured up in the most perfect phonographs'.[43] More recently Patrick Kavanagh emphasized the same idea: 'Carleton's *Traits and Stories* contain the most authentic dialect and . . . most racy dialogue, which reads like a translation direct from the necessities of early nineteenth-century Irish life.[44]'

Modern Anglo-Irish literature is generally taken to have a distinctive language, or, more accurately, to employ English in a distinctive and identifiable way. In the recognition and early use of this special 'Irish English', Carleton's place has never been thoroughly examined or his importance assessed.

Certainly there is evidence to suggest that he saw himself as striving to give the Irish an articulate voice in English which would be capable of conveying the full range of human emotions and experiences, as opposed to mere comic blunders. He praises the endeavours of all his major predecessors in pursuing this common aim, and he defines the vacuum that exists when a country lacks, or is deprived of, a coherent cultural identity:

For nearly a century we were completely at the mercy of our British neighbours, who probably amused themselves at our expense with the greater licence, and a more assured sense of impunity, inasmuch as they knew that we were utterly destitute of a national literature.[45]

The extension of this argument, which Carleton also makes, is that whereas a nation may produce eminent men, until they succeed in fostering *within* the country a love and concern for literature and science, their talents remain unfulfilled. That is to say the people of a country must learn to recognize and take pride in the achievements of their creative men and women, or else they remain unsophisticated and impoverished, and force their talented citizens into exile. In Irish terms this means that the creative geniuses, like so many landlords, become absentees. The cynic might read this appeal as evidence of Carleton's own undoubted self-interest, but he has also to take account of the acccuracy of this analysis of the fate of Irish writers. After all the pattern can be observed almost as clearly today as in the mid-nineteenth century.

Carleton never became a highly sophisticated writer, and indeed his worst novels are inferior in every way to his early *Traits and Stories*. He is a good example of untutored genius, a kind of rural Dickens without that great writer's discipline and vision. Yet the comparison is not wholly inappropriate, for Carleton does have an eye for details of appearance and character and an ear for individual uses of language, idiom or gesture which are usually taken as facets of Dickens' enormous creativity. Furthermore, in the same way as Dickens generates a sense of the complexity and multiplicity of Victorian society, so Carleton gives an impression of the fullness and variety of peasant life in rural Ireland before the Famine, and of the nature of the Irish temperament. Commenting, as all his critics must do, on the inequalities of merit in his fiction, Roger McHugh has written:

In Carleton's works man and nature are closely identified in their swift changes of mood, their interlacing shades, their triumphant vitality. He worked with two moulds: one narrow and sectarian, one as wide as Ireland. If the first is cracked and broken, the second remains, and one readily forgives its defects for the life it contains.[46]

To blame Carleton for his carelessness, his frequently ill-constructed plots, his unabashed self-contradictions of attitude and sympathy, his painful moralizing, or his prejudices is understandable. They are all defects and set limits to his greatness; but they are also the inevitable self-damage incurred in writing in the very way that gives him his status. Above all Carleton's skill as a communicator of oral traditions is the key to understanding his genius. He is the seanachie who has turned to written records, the story-teller who has become a novelist; but his real talents remained rooted in the old oral culture rather than absorbing the newer and less familiar literary modes. He himself spoke of giving a 'linked embodiment' to people and incidents he had known at first hand, and the phrase cannot be bettered as a description of the process behind his writing. As part of the seanachie's function was to preserve the memories of a family or community, so Carleton's *Traits and Stories of the Irish Peasantry* gathers together in a uniquely complete and varied way his knowledge of a people whose lives were changing irreversibly. This is what W. B. Yeats perceived when he wrote the finest of all tributes to the Ulster story-teller:

The history of a nation is not in parliaments and battle-fields, but in what the people say to each other on fair days and high days, and in how they farm, and quarrel, and go on pilgrimage. These things has Carleton recorded.[47]

SIX

MISCELLANEOUS MINOR FICTION, AND NOVELS BY LOVER, CARLETON AND LEVER (1834-44)

It is better to leave the debased and profligate in oblivion than drag their doings before the day; and it is with happy consciousness an Irishman may assert that there is plenty of subject afforded by Irish character and Irish life honourable to the land, pleasing to the narrator, and sufficiently attractive to the reader, without the unwholesome exaggerations of crime which too often disfigure the fictions which pass under the title of 'Irish', alike offensive to truth as to taste – alike injurious both of private and public considerations.

> Samuel Lover,
> *Handy Andy* (1842)

In the first thirty-three years of the nineteenth century Anglo-Irish fiction was born and grew precociously. Carleton's *Traits and Stories* is an obvious highpoint in its early development, but there follows an apparent hiatus in which little of distinction was published. The last works of the Banims, such as *The Ghost-Hunter and his Family* (1833), *The Mayor of Windgap* (1835) and *The Bit o' Writin'* (1838), do not break any new ground. Gerald Griffin's long historical novels, *The Invasion* (1832) and *The Duke of Monmouth* (1836), and his collections of stories, *Tales of My Neighbourhood* (1835) and the posthumously published *Talis Qualis, or Tales from the Jury-Room* (1842), are more notable as symptoms of his artistic decline – a point explored fully in John Cronin's critical biography of the author – than for their place in the expansion of Anglo-Irish fiction.[1] Towards the end of the 1830s two new writers, Samuel Lover and Charles Lever, began to publish, and in 1839 Carleton produced his first novel *Fardorougha the Miser.* Much of the other writing of the period shows a slipping away from the greatest achievements of the previous decade, although one notable exception must be recorded.

Harriet Martin's story 'Canvassing' effectively combines two themes, an account of a political campaign in Ireland by Lord Warringdon, an English gentleman, and a revelation of the scheming of Lady Anne Wilmot to marry off her two daughters, the beautiful Isabel and the shrewish Maria. Warringdon, a former rake, weds Isabel while Maria accepts Mr Barham, his vapid English friend. Both marriages end in estrangement and unhappiness and, as a tale of fashionable romance, 'Canvassing' penetratingly satirizes the cruelties of the mercenary marriage market.

It also provides some of the best insight since *Castle Rackrent* into landlord-servant relationships and on the effects of absenteeism and overspending. Even the dry, ironic tone of the narrative is reminiscent of Maria Edgeworth's style. Thus, for instance, Mr Wilmot is described as

The owner of an estate, like most old Irish ones, a little the worse for wear, and living away, like most such proprietors, as if the said estate was spick and span new.[2]

The extravagance of the house-keeping in the Big House is also pointed out:

An ox a week, and three sheep a day, was the minimum of provision disposed of in the kitchen, and servants'-hall; and all other things were on the same 'grandee' scale of expenditure.[3]

If these passages conjure up recollections of the Rackrents' mismanagement, the strange loyalty of Mr Wilmot's servants bears some likeness to the blind devotion of Thady Quirk. Having shown one of the servants, Pat Murphy, avow his readiness 'to go to the hottest place in the other world' for his master's family, and, more specifically, to fight off 'them blood-thirsty-Orangemen of process-servers', Miss Martin goes on to define the difference between a good servant in England and in Ireland. She concludes that the latter may be

an individual who may be troublesome, drunken, and negligent, even disrespectful, but who would stand up for his master's dignity, and defend his person at the peril of his own neck; very useful qualifications, it may be added, in a country, where, now and then, its gentry owe their personal liberty to their inaccessible roads and a devoted tenantry.[4]

The last part of this sentence is a significant comment not only on the servants, but also on the landlords and on their irresponsible and anarchic way of life. Unlike *Castle Rackrent* the story does not follow the deterioration of the Wilmot estate through to eventual collapse and ruin, but they are clearly implicit in many episodes.

The English visitors, Lord Warringdon and Mr Barham, are easily duped by Irish flattery. The latter is overwhelmed by what he regards as the eccentric, funny, foolish but harmless and lovable speech and behaviour of the Irish. He sees all Irishmen as caricatures, stage figures, and never imagines the amusement his own conduct causes among the servants. Ironically, too, Barham's attitudes and his behaviour, such as dancing a jig, are viewed with horror and disdain by his social equals who, like Lady Clonbrony in *The Absentee*, are anxious to dissociate themselves from anything specifically Irish. Thus Miss O'Higgerty exclaims: 'I hope you don't form so unfavourable an idaa (*sic*) of us to imagine you would see anything in good society in Ireland different from what you would see in England?'[5] The speaker's words express her sense of inferiority and inadequacy, and she attempts to compensate by trying to be like the English – note how her speech is free of any trace of Irish pronunciation. The story is largely successful in identifying and recording those moments of social comedy and self-revelation which expose the values of the characters.

There is even a curious diversion when Lord Warringdon, already in love with Isabel Wilmot, believes he has a rival in the form of a handsome and sophisticated young man with a fine singing voice. This person, Mr O'Reilly, turns out unexpectedly to be a priest, and although he has only a small part in the tale, he is a new type of figure in Anglo-Irish fiction. O'Reilly, who is totally different from the hedge-school priests of Carleton, is well-educated, at ease in genteel surroundings, and never seen in the context of the humble and poor. It is impossible to imagine him breaking up the fight at Shane Fadh's wedding, or presiding over the feast in honour of Denis O'Shaughnessy.

The other topic in 'Canvassing', alluded to in the title, is the process of electioneering in Ireland. This noisy, violent and controversial business is a topic which later writers – for example Charlotte Riddell in *Maxwell Drewitt* (1865) and Mary Laffan Hartley in *Hogan MP* (1876) – would return to in similar vein. Here the election campaign and voting have little connection with ideas or policies, but are closely bound up with physical force and compelled loyalty to landlords. Miss Martin sums up the occasion tersely:

The freed freeholders of the McAlpine estate, found their newly accorded liberty of thinking, and acting for themselves a perilous as well as puzzling privilege, beset on the one side by Father John's eloquence, and the Warringdon shillelagh; and on the other, by Mr. Archer's money, and fear of their master.[6]

The authority of the priest, the authority of violence, the authority of bribes, and the authority of the Big House make up a powerful complex of pressures acting upon the electorate. They are bewildered by threats of hell-fire and damnation on the one hand if they ignore the priest, and with the risk of dispossession if they defy their landlord. The inevitable fight between rival elements has to be broken up by the military at the cost of several lives and numerous injuries, and even the women join in a fierce attack on the supporters of Mr Archer. Such was the exercise of democracy in a nineteenth-century rural Irish election where personated votes were often the critical factor in determining the final result.

'Canvassing' has real qualities of observation, an ironic tone, and a concern with social and political matters which give it a certain distinction. Although published only as an accompanying tale with Michael Banim's *The Mayor of Windgap*, it is the more engaging piece of the two.

Two other volumes of this period – *Legends and Stories of Ireland* (1837) and *Popular Tales and Legends of the Irish Peasantry* (1837) – show how the pioneers of Anglo-Irish fiction were beginning to attract emulators. Some of these stories assume new attitudes and directions which were to be important in more substantial writing of the next years. In particular characterization tends to become little more than the representation of eccentricity and rural peculiarity. This is, at least by implication, a reductive and belittling mode of writing, a turning away from serious attempts to understand and reveal Irish character in favour of producing a series of harmless, comical oddities. Self-parody is also found in a story like 'Barny O'Reirdon, the Navigator', which appears in *Legends and Stories of Ireland*, and is by Samuel Lover himself.

Briefly, it deals with O'Reirdon's endeavour to establish his claim to be the most experienced and widely travelled navigator in Kinsale. He sets about his record-breaking attempt by following a trading vessel out to sea, and soon runs into all sorts of difficulties. Addressed by the captain of the trading ship, who realizes his follower is lost, Barny's replies reveal a mixture of ignorance and cunning, vanity and fear. Asked if he has a compass and whether he can read its points, he retorts:

A compass! by my sowl an' it's not let alone a compass, but a *pair* of compasses I have, that my brother the carpinthir, left me for a keepsake whin he wint aboard; but, indeed, as for the points o'thim I can't say much, for the childher spylt thim intirely, rootin' holes in the flure.[7]

The confusion and misunderstanding reflected in this answer are obvious and amusing; Barny's naivety provokes laughter as does his assumption that the cardinal points have something to do with the Pope, or his fear of sliding off the world if it really is round.

Yet he also displays a certain kind of reasoning: it is not altogether stupid to wonder why the sea remains level if the earth is a globe, or to think that tea might grow like hay because it is called Bohea. In the context of the story, however, Barny is the butt of the humour; his blunders, despite some degree of credibility, are meant to amuse, and the entire account of his supposed voyage is preposterous. This character looks forward to figures like Rory O'More in Lover's novel of the same name, also published in 1837, and to a creation like Sean the Post in Boucicault's play *Arrah-na-Pogue* (1860). The reader is in fact being entertained by a likeable, if foolish, character who has a certain ready wit and speed of reply that make him more than an utter buffoon, but which are not sufficient to enable him to be taken entirely seriously.

A greater degree of realism is apparent in another story in the collection, 'The Burial of the Tithe', which tells of a grotesque celebration following the repeal of the hated tithe laws in 1832. The writer aims to show the peculiar combination of viciousness and pathos typical in the events he describes, but the story comes to life with the account of the mock funeral held after a feast to mark the passing of the Tithe. The chief mourners are a pair of local tithe proctors, specially kidnapped for the occasion, who are obliged to don mock religious vestments, are doused with ashes, and are given pitchforks in lieu of croziers. The procession itself, which culminates in the symbolic interment of the Tithe, is accompanied by the local fiddler and piper playing 'Go to the devil and shake yourself' as a further indication of the general mood of the ceremony.

The stance of the writer throughout is very detached: he is little more than an observer and recorder of quaint ways and eccentric people; the reader is never made to feel part of the action, and there is always a certain restraint in the behaviour of the characters. The tithe proctors may be forced to participate, but there is no danger of them having their ears sliced off or their houses fired. The element of violence, or of threatened violence, is muted and there is little to suggest the emotionally volatile temperaments of the peasants in Carleton's stories.

Much the same is true of *Popular Tales and Legends of the Irish Peasantry*, even though this volume contains contributions from William Carleton ('Alley Sheridan') and Mrs Hall ('Kate Connor'). Indeed Mrs Hall's tale typifies the moralistic approach of several of the writers whose work is featured in the book. She sets out to illustrate the precept that 'the Irish act only from impulse, not from principle', and the eponymous heroine, who exemplifies 'the aristocracy of virtue' which 'may be found, in all its lustre, in an Irish cabin', is as selfless, virtuous and exasperatingly upright as might be expected.[8]

Simplicity of a different kind is evident in a story involving the members of a secret society. In 'The Whiteboy's Revenge' by Denis O'Donoho there is a melodramatic account of a disastrous raid on the house of a proctor who had seized the farm belonging to the rebel leader. Little effort is made to relate the violence and passions of the attackers to social or political causes, and the terrorist attack is presented as scarcely more than an act of revenge. Similarly the moral of the tale is less concerned with the social injustice that precipitated the action than with the consequences that follow it. Edward MacCarthy, alias Captain Steel, is a romantic image of a Whiteboy rather than a real person, and his magnanimous speech when one of his confederates, black Dermod, fails to keep a rendezvous is very different from the drunken intimidation and bullying that preceded the raid on Wildgoose Lodge, although that story, too, is a lurid melodrama.

When MacCarthy – betrayed by black Dermod – dies in an ambush, his death is followed soon after by that of his beloved, and then by the mysterious murder of the offending tithe proctor: the cycle of violence continues, with one atrocity leading to the next and innocent people becoming involved as casualties. Clearly the reader is encouraged to feel sympathy for MacCarthy and his lover because of the waste of their lives, but this sympathy depends almost entirely upon the fact that he is glamorous and she is innocent. Likewise MacCarthy's enemy, Mike Reilly the proctor, is never seen in action nor are his motives disclosed. Ultimately 'The Whiteboy's Revenge' is a trivialization of a difficult and many-sided social and political problem, and a denial or, more likely, an act of turning away from its real implications.

This simplifying trend may also be observed in *Lights and Shadows of Irish Life*, a collection of stories by Mrs Hall published in 1838, although in one lengthy tale, 'The Groves of Blarney', the author creates a character who is more convincingly real than many of her figures. The events revolve around Connor O'Gorman, an attractive, popular, hot-headed but morally upright young Irishman, and Margaret Lee, a young widow and the daughter of an English Catholic living in Ireland. She agrees to marry O'Gorman if he abstains from drink and fighting for a year, but he is tricked by the villain of the piece, the Griffin – a mischievous, destructive and spiteful old woman of dubious origins, but not, the reader is assured, pure Irish – who makes him drunk and creates a situation in which he becomes involved in a fight in defence of the home of an elderly, helpless woman.

The Griffin is authentically malicious and grotesque, and O'Gorman's misfortune is to cross her, so that she strives to work his undoing. In the end, of course, he regains his credibility with Margaret Lee, but the melodrama of his words and actions –

Boys, Irishmen! give me six hours to seek that woman's child – her child whom you knew and liked – give me six hours, and I'll give you leave to cut my throat, if I don't come back![9]

– is much less believable than the hideous menace of the Griffin. Connor O'Gorman is tamed to make him into a wholly respectable Anglicized gentleman, and, as usual, this dogmatic purpose precludes the author from allowing her character to evolve in a more spontaneous way.

Another kind of limitation is apparent in the two novels for which Samuel Lover is best remembered. The first of these, *Rory O'More*, was published in 1837; it was followed in 1842 by the equally popular *Handy Andy*, one of the few Anglo-Irish novels of the period still in print.[10] These are important books not only because of their contemporary commercial success, but also because in each case the hero is the kind of endearing, bumbling, good-hearted and sometimes witty peasant who falls into adversity and out of it again with unfailing ease and inevitability. Both Rory and Andy face major setbacks – Rory is actually sentenced to death – but both emerge unscathed and better off than they were originally. The reader's composure is never disturbed, unless by the recurrent improbabilities of the plots, for he is confident throughout that nothing really serious will happen. This indeed seems to be the clue to understanding Lover's position, for whereas Maria Edgeworth, Lady Morgan, the Banims, Gerald Griffin and Carleton almost always conclude their stories in a way favourable to their leading characters, these 'happy endings' did not prevent them from embracing serious topics in the course of their writing. Lover, on the other hand, touches on little that is serious and, when he does so, he soon hurries his reader on to lighter matters. One particularly sharp instance of this occurs towards the end of *Rory O'More*. The novel is set at the time of the 1798 uprising, but, conveniently, the hero is in France when the uprising takes place, and the author writes of it as 'the awful year of 1798, whose acts seemed the work of fiends, and whose records are but of blood'; it is a subject

too fearful to be touched on here, – too tempting to the passion of party, or too forcibly appealing to the gentler feelings of human nature, for mortal pen to be trusted with.[11]

Thus the evasion is complete and, although the novel deals in the main with Rory's adventures among the United Irishmen, the natural climax of the story is omitted.

It tells of Rory O'More's exploits with Horace de Lacy, a Frenchman of Irish stock who has been sent to England and Ireland by the Directory to reconnoitre the possibilities for a French invasion of either or both countries. Rory makes his acquaintance with de Lacy by accident, and as the latter is taken ill and obliged to dwell for some time with the O'Mores, he is pressed into service as a messenger for the United Irishmen. The rebels are portrayed as an unsavoury and unreliable bunch, more interested in drinking and wenching than revolution, and influenced by the treacherous de Welskein, a smuggler, and the equally dangerous and miserly Solomon Sly, a vagabond tinker.

The second strand to the story concerns Rory's love for

Kathleen Regan, whose brother, Shan, is a bitter enemy of Rory because of the imagined insult of having been deceived by Rory's sister, Mary. Regan is also a United Irishman, and Lover uses him as an example of the kind of corrupt villain who, in his opinion, was influential in the movement. Indeed, apart from de Lacy, there is little discernible idealism among any of the United Irishmen presented in the book. As might be expected all the bad characters are punished (or executed), and the scope and success of their activity are never allowed to grow out of hand.

Lover subtitled his novel 'A National Romance', which furnishes a clue to his purpose. It is national in the sense that it uses an Irish setting and, for the most part, Irish characters, but it is not a nationalist novel concerned to justify, explain or promote Irish interests. On the contrary, the author gives certain deliberate indications of his wish to dissociate himself from his characters and their lives. The effect of this is significant, often making it appear that Lover regards the peasants as little more than a source of laughter, albeit affectionate rather than contemptuous mirth. But the result is belittling and condescending, and although readers may feel occasional embarrassment at the seriousness with which the earlier novelists regarded themselves and their fellow Irishmen, Lover's position is not an adequate alternative.

His detached tone and mode of presentation are soon apparent in a description of the peasants' cabins in the locality where the O'Mores live. He mentions how the houses have mud walls, that most have simply a hole in the roof for a chimney, and unglazed windows which may be partly blocked by a piece of board – 'or, as Pat says, a wooden pane of glass'.[12] The reference to 'Pat' as a generic name for Irishmen is essentially an English term; and the way in which the author introduces his parenthesis giving the Irishman's supposed description of the window board is clearly intended to amuse a non-Irish audience.

In a similar vein Rory O'More himself is introduced with a mention of the ham-fisted way in which he has embedded a broken looking-glass in the wall of the best bed-room, so that the image it produces is highly deceptive and often causes him to gash himself unexpectedly while shaving. This is followed by an account of the grotesque result produced by Rory on his late father's headstone because of his failure to measure out and space the words correctly. By selecting these incidents to bring Rory into the novel, within half a dozen paragraphs Lover has his audience smiling comfortably and confidently awaiting other foolish blunders. The reader is led away from characterization into the realms of caricature, which even Carleton, for all he created many bizarre eccentrics, had eschewed.

Lover is primarily interested in recording absurdity – the pride of Rory, despite his poverty, in the glory and ancestry of his family name, his mother's fear and distrust of Dublin and of city folk, the customs of Phelim O'Flanagan, hedge-schoolmaster and parish clerk, who wears a clean shirt on Sundays to serve Mass and then continues to use it for the rest of the week. He shows little concern to explore the society which produced these people, resting content, for example, with an easy laugh at the superstition of the peasants who deliberately try to become as wet as possible when Phelim splashes holy water on them using a bucket and brush. Dismissing the incident with lofty superiority, he observes 'Poor people! if it made them happy where was the harm of it?'[13] Here, indeed, is the tone of a colonialist, even though Lover was born and bred in Dublin.

When Carleton makes the reader laugh at Denis O'Shaughnessy's pretentious and inappropriate use of language, he also makes him aware of the reasons *why* the young man talks as he does. Rory O'More and, more especially, Handy Andy misuse language in a way that is merely amusing. This is, perhaps, harmless enough except insofar as it endorses the idea of the Irish peasant as an amiable simpleton, witty at times and obtuse in his logic, but by and large a creature to be laughed at and forgotten by the educated reader. Lover makes no attempt to place the speech of his characters in a social context, as Carleton did, and to that extent the humour is of a much lower kind.

This is apparent in *Handy Andy* when the hero, described by his creator as 'a blundering servant' whom 'no English or any other gentleman would like . . . in his service', goes to the post office to collect a letter for his employer Squire Egan.[14] Failing to obtain his object on the first enquiry Andy tries again:

'The directions I got was to get a letther here, – that's the directions.'
　'Who gave you those directions?'
　'The masther.'
　'And who's your master?'
　'What consarn is that o'yours?'

'Why, you stupid rascal! If you don't tell me his name, how can I give you a letter?'

'You could give it, if you liked; but you're fond of axin' impident questions, bekaze you think I'm simple.'

'Go along out o' this! Your master must be as great a goose as yourself, to send such a messenger.'

'Bad luck to your impidince,' said Andy; 'is it Squire Egan you dar to say goose to?'. . . .

Just at this moment a person to whom Andy was known entered the house, who vouched to the postmaster that he might give Andy the squire's letter.

'Have you one for me?'

'Yes, sir,' said the postmaster, producing one, – 'fourpence'.

The gentleman paid the fourpence postage, and left the shop with his letter.

'Here's a letter for the squire,' said the postmaster; 'you've to pay me elevenpence postage.'

'What 'ud I pay elevenpence for?'

'For postage.'

'To the divil wid you! Didn't I see you give Mr. Durfy a letther for fourpence this minit, and a bigger letther than this? and now you want me to pay elevenpence for this scrap of a thing. Do you think I'm a fool?'[15]

This incident is typical of numerous episodes which display Handy Andy's mixture of stupidity and ignorance. In his introduction to *Representative Irish Tales* W. B. Yeats noted that this character 'has been the cause of much misconception', but adds that the fault lies more with the reader who assumes that all Irishmen are like Andy than with the author who created him.[16] No doubt this is a fair enough comment, but the fact remains that Handy Andy confirms and panders to one of the most popular and regrettable Irish stereotypes.

Lover's humour is not always belittling, as may be seen in the delightful scene in *Rory O'More* when the hero, on a visit to Dublin, endeavours to buy a pair of boots to take home to his parish priest. Rory has never before been asked to give a shoe size, and he is amazed at the apparent incompetence of the salesman who lacks intuitive knowledge of Father Kinshela's fitting. Initially he assumes that the Dubliner is trying to make a fool of him because he is a countryman, and he immediately becomes defensive, but when he learns that it is normal city practice to purchase shoes according to size rather than depending on the local cobbler to produce a suitable match, he concludes that town folk are by no means as clever as their rural neighbours believe. This confrontation between country and city men is believable, and also particularly notable because it is not the kind of incident that finds much place in nineteenth-century Anglo-Irish fiction. Indeed one of the distinguishing features of Anglo-Irish fiction of this period is its almost total dependence on rural settings, whereas the English novel was becoming increasingly city orientated.

Similarly, despite Lover's generally light-hearted approach to the serious tensions and political issues of the 1790s, he occasionally interpolates a number of more substantial observations. Thus, for instance, he attacks the penal laws on the basis of their counterproductive effect: Catholicism not only survived but actually grew in strength precisely 'because penalty attended its profession', whereas the Irish language was dying out although it was never banned.[17] What is unclear is whether Lover himself was in agreement with the idea of eliminating Catholicism and that therefore he is critical of the penal laws because of their inefficiency rather than their inhumanity.

In two places he seems ready to grasp even the most sensitive political and social matters. The first occurs when de Lacy writes a letter to France to report on the state of the nation and to urge immediate intervention. He singles out the irresponsibility of the Irish landowners and their indifference towards their tenants' lives and well-being, emphasizing how these attitudes are quite opposite to those of the English gentry. The wretched state of the poor is further elaborated, but in terms so generalized and stereotyped that they do not suggest an intimate knowledge of poverty, even though de Lacy has been staying with the O'Mores. This, of course, may help to explain his misjudgment both of the political situation and of the readiness of the Irish people to commit themselves to revolution.

In one particular, however, de Lacy's analysis is perceptive, and perhaps he was wrong only in his estimation of its importance. He points out that whereas in English society, there is a complex class hierarchy, in Ireland there is only

a sort of mongrel middle rank, but consisting of too few to constitute anything like a class, in comparison with the others. In England there are many degrees between the peer and the peasant; – but not so here: the *cementing* portions of society are wanting; the wholesome links that bind it together exist not here; – in short, Ireland may be comprised under two great heads, – those who inflict, and those who suffer.[18]

De Lacy views the almost total polarity between rich and poor as another factor likely to generate revolutionary fervour, readily discounting the middle-class squireens as a relevant force. In practice these conclusions were incorrect, because the lack of an influential middle class in rural areas very often meant that the disaffected peasantry was only concerned with immediate parochial grievances (a point grasped by Michael Banim), while the power of local government to enforce law and order invested in the squireens made them a much more formidable body than de Lacy recognizes. He is right to say that the people hold officials of justice in contempt, but seems to underrate the tyranny of the petty despots.

This is not a mistake that Lover himself makes, as is clear from the graphic account of the summary execution of the United Irishman Solomon Sly by Captain Slink, magistrate and commander of the local yeomanry. In this episode alone, the narrative approaches the intensity and force that distinguish many parts of *The Croppy*, and although Solomon is a highly unpleasant character, the brutishness of his treatment still appals. Captain Slink's philosophy is that of Captain Crawley in *Florence Macarthy* and of Valentine McClutchy in Carleton's novel: he believes that the way to pacify the country is to hang men and not to worry about the abstract principles of justice and law. When Sly appeals for a priest, Slink regrets that there is not one available, because he could be executed as well, and when the hapless tinker fails to die at once by hanging, the Captain hastens the process with a bullet so as to avoid waiting in the rain for him to expire. Had Lover written more in this vein, his work would have had quite a different character, but this is not consistent with his aim to please and entertain, and so it remains an untypical incident.

The return to sentimentality and improbability is marked by Rory's wholly unlikely delivery from the murder charge he faces, and by the closing pages of the story which deal with the decision of de Lacy to emigrate to America, taking the O'More family with him. De Lacy's emigration is an act of convenience in terms of the plot, and also shows him reneging on his commitment to Ireland with the greatest of ease. More surprising, perhaps, is the willingness of Rory himself to abandon his native land. Carleton was to look at this problem in *The Emigrants of Ahadarra*, and although the issue of emigration is finally avoided there, thanks to a fortuitous twist in the plot, he manages to evoke the poignant emotions such an occasion produced in the parties concerned. Lover's story does not shirk the act of departure, but it produces only token expressions of feeling from Rory:

It goes agin me hard, I don't deny it, to lave the owld counthry, and the places my heart warms to at the sight of. Sure, I used to dhrame of thim when I was with you in France; and could see the river, and the hills, and the cottage, and the owld rath, as plain as if I was on the spot: and won't it be the same when I'm in another strange land? – my heart will always be longing afther my darlin' Ireland, and the owld tunes of her be ringin' in my ears all day. Oh, but the shamrocks is close at my heart![19]

But however strong his sense of place and his affection for home, Rory is quickly persuaded to accept the hopelessness of the situation in Ireland and the desirability of seeking his fortunes abroad. In this respect, perhaps Rory's reactions are rather similar to his creator's for although Lover did not go to America, except on a lecturing tour in 1846, he made his own career in London rather than at home in Dublin.

In *Rory O'More* and *Handy Andy* Lover used Ireland and the Irish as source material for a kind of light-hearted, commercial literature which has little in common with the earnest and sometimes anguished fiction of the earlier Anglo-Irish novelists. He did not share their anxiety to define and explore Irish nationality and the experience of being Irish, perhaps partly because he himself was Protestant, middle-class and born in a city, so that these problems did not press upon him as they did upon his predecessors. Furthermore Lover never had the personal commitment to literature of, say, Griffin or John Banim. He was a painter, illustrator and song-writer, and he came to write fiction almost by chance, although the song, novel, and dramatic adaptation of *Rory O'More* were his most substantial successes. Clearly Lover did have feelings of conscience about the state and treatment of Ireland: the Captain Slink episode in *Rory O'More* is evidence of this; so is the romantic poet and patriot, Edward O'Connor, in *Handy Andy*, with his comprehensive collection of books on Irish history, his sense of Ireland's wrongs, and his readiness to celebrate the country's ancient culture and riches. But Lover was not the man to allow a political conscience to disturb the enjoyment of life and his novels mark the arrival of the straightfoward entertainer in Anglo-Irish fiction.

A quite different development took place in 1839, when William Carleton published his first full-length novel, and thus entered upon a new stage in his literary career. Some would argue that as his *Traits and Stories* is his most distinguished contribution to short fiction, so *Fardorougha the Miser* is his best novel. Certainly it is a powerful and highly imaginative story, briefer than most of his later novels, and probably all the better as a result because the plot is less ramshackle and coincidental than is often the case subsequently. The key to the book's vivid power is its characterization, and Carleton readily admitted that most of the central figures were based upon people known to him. The miser himself was suggested by a man who lived in the author's home area, while his wife Honor O'Donovan derives from Carleton's fond recollections of his own mother. Bartle Flanagan, the villain of the piece, was prompted by an old school-fellow, and Mary Moan, the midwife, portrays an actual midwife in Clogher. Bodagh Buie O'Brien and his family were intended to represent typical members of the Catholic middle class, while Connor O'Donovan, the miser's son, is a purely fictional creation.

The lives of all these figures come to be affected to greater or lesser extent by the miserliness of Fardorougha. This is no case of ordinary meanness; Fardorougha is haunted by and utterly obsessed with the desire to accumulate money and the fear of losing it, or even spending the smallest portion of it. So warped is his way of thought that he exercises the most stringent economies within his own family, regretting even the expense of a christening feast for his only child born after thirteen years of marriage, and then, later, the money to pay for his son's education. Ironically, he justifies his parsimony as a token of love for Connor and of his concern to provide for his future.

Carleton shows the unscrupulous nature of Fardorougha's greed, for, having rejected the idea of Connor marrying Una O'Brien because he considers her father is not wealthy enough to provide a handsome dowry, he proposes that his son should make a runaway match with the girl and then refuse to wed her until O'Brien agrees to a good settlement. Even when he is

eventually persuaded to negotiate a marriage arrangement
with the girl's father, Bodagh Buie O'Brien, Fardorougha
wrecks the occasion by refusing to offer Connor and Una any
money within his own lifetime.

The depraved appetite of the miser is contrasted with the
simple piety, warmth and honesty of his wife. Frightened by
the avarice of her husband, she nevertheless remains loyal
to him, while always striving to do the best for her beloved
son. The artistry with which Carleton depicts Honor
O'Donovan's efforts to mediate in her difficult family
circumstances occasions some of his most accomplished
writing. He understands how the woman's mind works, her
faith, and the love she bears her husband and son. Because his
imaginative insight into her predicament is complete, he
resists any temptation to be sentimental about her.

When the treacherous Bartle Flanagan succeeds in making it
appear that Connor has fired Bodagh Buie O'Brien's barn,
Honor and the other heroine of the tale, Una O'Brien, stand by
him. Fardorougha himself, grief-stricken as he is by his son's
arrest, nevertheless pleads total poverty and refuses to hire an
attorney to defend the young man. Fate then deals him a
second, and in a sense more serious, blow, because his banker
absconds from the country taking the miser's money with
him. Connor's defence is eventually paid for from a legacy of
Una O'Brien's, but he is found guilty and sentenced to death,
though the penalty is later commuted to transportation for life.
Only when faced with the enormity of his losses, personal and
financial, is Fardorougha brought to some realization of the
hideousness of his avarice.

Connor O'Donovan's hardships bring out the best in his
character, for when his old friend Nogher McCormick hints
that vengeance will soon fall on Bartle Flanagan for informing
Connor insists that any such plans should be dropped. Even
when Nogher argues that Bartle's death would not be murder,
'only sarvin' honest people right', and tells him of the villain's
desire to abduct Una, Connor remains inflexible.[20] In the end,
however, Nogher's promise not to 'give pain to a single hair of
his [Bartle's] head' is deliberately ambiguous: not all methods
of killing entail pain to the hairs of a man's head.

This scene also shows the curiosities of the Irish tempera—
ment, as Carleton is quick to point out. On the one hand,
Nogher McCormick, a man known throughout his life for his
affectionate and innocuous nature, is prepared to plot the

murder of a person against whom he has no immediate personal grudge, simply because he believes him to have grossly wronged his friend. Thus the generosity of Nogher's feeling for Connor stirs him to undertake the most serious of crimes. On the other, Connor himself, having roundly condemned the suggestion of killing Bartle Flanagan, does not hold it against Nogher that he should have contemplated such an act. He is ready at once to embrace him as a dear friend and respond to his love without allowing his murderous intention to interfere. It may be that Connor's virtues are overdone, but not in a way that undermines the authority of the author's observations of the anomalies of Irish character.

Carleton's first venture into novel-writing is undoubtedly an impressive debut. In the 1840s his output was more prolific, but the quality of his work became increasingly uneven. This may have been the result perhaps of his commitment to the exposure of various social evils in these later books, which may make them more intriguing to the historian and sociologist than *Fardorougha the Miser*, but which regularly compromises their artistic integrity. In his portrayal of the miser Carleton explored one man's moral depravity in a particularly graphic way – Fardorougha is literally consumed and withered by his own avarice, and as with all vices, it does not exist in a social vacuum. The rural, peasant community within which Fardorougha lives is faithfully captured in all its variety and richness. Here the threat of violence is permanently present, justice is rough and ready, and the Ribbonmen exercise enough influence to frighten off those who could give evidence against Bartle Flanagan. The community embraces prosperous, strong farmers like O'Brien, whose home is comfortable and well-stocked, and families like the Flanagans who cannot pay their debts and can be evicted at the whim of Fardorougha. Deep, if unsophisticated, religious faith exists alongside unprincipled, ruthless greed and villainy. In reading this novel, as with the best of the *Traits and Stories*, the reader feels drawn into the very texture of the lives of the characters, and over all of them hangs the shadow of Fardorougha. Most nineteenth-century Anglo-Irish novels exhibit a primary interest in particular social, political or religious problems, and often only a secondary concern for the characters who are devised to serve these issues. The result is often an awkward relationship between themes and characters, the latter seeming at times little more than convenient instruments rather than full-blooded creations. All too frequently this is the case in Carleton's own fiction, but *Fardorougha the Miser* is a distinctive and distinguished exception. Here theme is revealed through character and action, rather than the reverse, so that the book has an individual force. For the most part Carleton resists the temptation to moralize, to intervene with cumbersome directives to the reader, and he lets his story speak for itself. The benefits he derived from this confidence in his own material were enormous, and it is ironic that he did not recognise them fully himself. Had he done so, and had *Fardorougha the Miser* been a real beginning to the development of his fiction rather than an isolated event in his career, Carleton's reputation might have been of a very different order of importance, and his name more widely known today. As it is B. G. MacCarthy has defined the novel's strengths:

With Fardorougha, Carleton cannot go wrong, and he shows us the mind expressing itself even in those apparently meaningless gestures which he significantly calls 'the hieroglyphics of human action'. Nor is Fardorougha the only superb portrait in this novel. There is also Fardorougha's wife, Carleton's most successful study of a woman.[21]

In later days Carleton achieved further successes, but they were of another kind. *Fardorougha the Miser* is truly a unique achievement.

In the same year that Carleton's novel appeared, 1839, a new and rising talent emerged and won almost instant success and popularity. This was Charles Lever, and his book was *The Confessions of Harry Lorrequer*, the chance end-product of a series of contributions made since 1837 to the *Dublin University Magazine*. It marked the start of a literary career that was to span almost forty years of prolific output, which established Lever's name more firmly in the minds of the English reading public than that of any Anglo-Irish novelist before him. Yeats wrote of him that 'more than any other Irish writer has he caught the ear of the world and come to stand for the entire nation'; more recently David H. Greene has added weight to this claim by pointing out that in America, whereas Carleton's works appeared in three unattractive volumes in 1882, Lever's were graced by a forty-volume collection.[22] Who was this enormously successful writer? Why was he so popular? And what happened to his reputation?

Charles Lever was the son of a prosperous builder from Lancashire who had settled in Dublin in 1787 and married the daughter of a Kilkenny planter family. Lever's education was capped by a period of riotous living at Trinity College, during which he managed to complete enough work to graduate and go on to study medicine. His medical training began in Ireland but continued on the continent, and this initiated the nomadic and spirited adventures in many countries which continued for much of the rest of his life. Lever was undoubtedly the most cosmopolitan of the early Anglo-Irish novelists, travelling far beyond literary London which was, in the main, the furthest destination of his predecessors. Not surprisingly his books reflect the diversity and scope of his experience, involving scenes set in America, Spain, Portugal, France or Austria just as readily as those placed in Ireland. Yet Ireland always remained important to him as a source of ideas and imagination, even though he left it in 1845 and never lived there again. In this one respect at least, as Roger McHugh has observed, Lever shows an unexpected affinity with James Joyce.

Harry Lorrequer and its immediate successors, *Charles O'Malley* and *Jack Hinton*, form the basis of their author's popularity, yet they are little more than collections of episodic adventures, anecdotes, songs and romantic encounters set partly in Ireland and partly in Europe. The eponymous heroes are in each case young soldiers who romp their way through large quantities of alcohol, several duels fought for honour, a number of hairbreadth escapes and improbable encounters; they ride recklessly in the chase, woo maidens who seem set to reject them but ultimately relent, and are surrounded by friends who are equally light-hearted, hot-headed and glamorous. In the end they marry, which brings an effective conclusion to their anarchic existences. It may seem an injustice to speak of the heroes of three separate novels as though they are the same, but it is this common identity of the hero that offers a clue to Lever's early work. Harry, Charles and Jack are indeed the same person, and even the situations in which they are placed vary little from novel to novel. Lever, surprised, perhaps, by the immediate success of his first novel, was sharp enough to realize he had struck upon a profitable formula, and he showed a sufficient fund of inventiveness to ring the changes on it in his next two tales. Compared with the moral sobriety of Mrs Hall or Gerald Griffin, or the grim moments in Carleton and the Banims' fiction, here the reader had a series of adventures that provoked laughter, confirmed foreign prejudices about the quaintness of the Irish peasantry, and challenged little or nothing of the complacency of mid-Victorian England in its policies towards Ireland. Quite consciously, he appealed to the literary tastes of his foreign readers in a way and to an extent greater than that of his contemporaries, with the possible exception of Samuel Lover. Significantly, when in his later work Lever assumed a more serious and critical attitude to various aspects of Irish life, many of his readers regretted the change and maintained that his first books were his best.

Undoubtedly these tales have an engaging freshness and energy, and Lever's considerable gift for dialogue lightens almost every page. Lorrequer's Cork, O'Malley's Trinity College and Hinton's Dublin are places where party-going, drinking, flirting, amateur theatricals, and more drinking are the social norm. There is little indication of the post-Union depression in Dublin recorded, for example, by Lady Morgan in *Florence Macarthy*. In *Jack Hinton*, where for the first time there are a few slight indications that Lever's thoughts are deepening, the squalor, unemployment and poverty of the majority of Dubliners are mentioned in passing, but the reader is promptly assured that they delight in observing the extravagance of their wealthy neighbours. Meanwhile Harry Lorrequer says:

Such was our life in Cork – dining, drinking, dancing, riding steeple-chases, pigeon-shooting, and tandem-driving – filling up any little interval that was found to exist between a late breakfast, and the time to dress for dinner.[23]

It is a way of life divorced from all social or political responsibility; even military matters, and Lorrequer is a soldier, are insignificant.

Jack Hinton is also in the army. While stationed in Dublin his life is passed in an equally giddy whirl of excess. Yet within the accounts of Dublin fashionable society the seeds of its own decadence and self-destruction are evident:

austere churchmen, erudite chief-justices, profound politicians, privy councillors, military officers of high rank and standing, were here mixed up together into one strange medley, apparently bent on throwing an air of ridicule over the graver business of life, and laughing alike at themselves and the world.[24]

This dizzy race to financial ruin and political discredit and impotence is explored again in the activities of a kind of Hell Fire Club called The Monks of the Screw, a real society that included many of the most eminent Dublin citizens, in which heavy drinking took place (hence the name of the organization) and riotous conduct was enshrined in a series of mock religious rituals.

Here is the image of the Irish middle and upper classes which, as Yeats pointed out, became the popular stereotype among Lever's foreign, and especially his English, readers. He shows a gentry already in decline, and his subsequent books concentrate on the less glamorous aspects of that downhill progress to bankruptcy and crisis on the land. But he never entirely lost sight of the gaiety and folly of early nineteenth-century Dublin or the exuberance and absurdly generous hospitality of the Galway landowners of the same period.

The problems of Ireland and the Irish people which so preocccupied the earlier Anglo-Irish novelists cause Lever's conscience little trouble in his first books. So, for example, in *Harry Lorrequer* the hero is sent to Clonmel on duty during the assizes. The country around has been restless, and there is a fleeting reference to the trial of a man who had resisted violently the efforts of an agent and three tithe proctors to make him pay his dues, and who, it is feared, may be rescued from the court by force. This, however, is the sum total of the information revealed about the situation or the role of the military in it. Nevertheless, by the end of the novel, the hero is set to assume responsibility as Under Secretary for Ireland!

Likewise, in *Charles O'Malley*, there are passing allusions to the increasing financial crisis in the hero's family leading finally to ruin in an unsuccessful lawsuit, and when O'Malley himself returns to Ireland from the Peninsula War he seeks to improve the state of his impoverished tenants. His activities are rattled off easily enough, but there are no specific details of the problems of the poor or how these were resolved.

Only in *Jack Hinton* is there any significant variation on this glib approach to the less pleasant side of life, and brief though the departure is, it deserves a mention. Travelling in the company of a priest through a mountainous region in Munster, the hero comes upon a scene of violence and grief: a young man killed and mutilated in a vain attempt to avenge himself against a land agent who had evicted him with his wife and child some time before. He had struggled to save enough money to emigrate, but then his son died of hunger and disease, and the man could not bear to leave the district where the body was interred, despite the fact that there was no future for him or for his wife there. The priest, Father Tom, denounces the use of violence as a means of resolving any issue, but later the reader learns that a further attack upon the land agent has achieved the revenge which eluded his previous would-be killer. Here, at last, Lever seems ready to write about the less jolly side of Irish life, but he promptly turns away from it. The priest tells Jack Hinton:

Never speak to me nor question me about what we saw last night, and try only to remember it as a dream. And now let me tell you how I mean to amuse you in the far West.[25]

Gravity is not allowed to disfigure the pages of *Jack Hinton*. The most overtly political comment comes when Father Tom appeals to the English to protect the Irish poor from the unscrupulous, and not to equate their restlessness with innate viciousness or stupidity, but to recognize the frustrations, injustices, famine, and poverty of their lives. On this occasion Hinton's attitude is significant:

In this strain did the good priest continue to develop his views concerning his country; the pivot of his argument being, that to a people so essentially different in every respect, English institutions and English laws were inadequate and unsuitable. Sometimes I could not only follow, but agree with him. At others, I could but dimly perceive his meaning, and dissent from the very little I could catch. Enough of this, however. In a biography so flimsy as mine, politics would play but an unseemly part; and even were it otherwise, my opportunities were too few, and my own incapacity too great, to make my opinions of any value on a subject so complicated and so vast. Still the topic served to shorten the road. . . .[26]

With such unblushing ingenuousness, Hinton, the man who claims to be interested in learning about Ireland and the Irish, hastily moves on to the interior of a public house where he feels much more at ease.

In his autobiography Anthony Trollope, who calls Lever his 'dear old friend', praises the author for his inimitable skills of conversation, and goes on to speak of his first novels as exemplifying their creator's genius in this respect. Notably Trollope also admits that he has never read Lever's subsequent fiction, and he predicts that because his books lack convincing characters, they will not live long, – even if they may be said to be alive now, – because it is so. What was his manner of working I do not know, but I should think that it must have been very quick, and that he never troubled himself on the subject except when he was seated with a pen in his hand.[27]

It is a provocative judgment, because Lever merits defence in some measure against the charge of failing to create convincing characters. One reply might be that Trollope read the wrong books. On the other hand, it remains true that Lever's reputation, unfortunately, came to rest on these early novels, and that it is their very superficiality which has since caused them generally to be forgotten. These are also the books which aroused the antagonism of later Anglo-Irish writers and critics precisely because they afford such a distorted and limited interpretation of nineteenth-century Ireland and her people. Lever had a strange career in that he was stereotyped by his early successes, and then he was unable to persuade his audience to take him seriously when he turned to more complex subjects. Yet his later fiction earns him his real place in the history of the Anglo-Irish novel, for it shows him to belong squarely in the tradition of the Big House writers who descend from Maria Edgeworth and Lady Morgan through Charles Lever to Somerville and Ross and George Moore at the close of the century.

SEVEN

NOVELS BY MRS HALL, LE FANU, LEVER AND CARLETON (1845-1850)

I have been so completely sickened by the bigoted on each side, that I have come to the determination, as every honest Irishman ought, of knowing no party but my country, and of devoting such talents as God has given me, to the promotion of her general interests, and the happiness of her whole people.

> William Carleton
> Preface to *Valentine McClutchy*
> (1845)

The revival of Anglo-Irish fiction in the closing years of the 1830s and the early 1840s coincides with a period of renewed political agitation, as O'Connell urged the English Government to repeal the Act of Union and stirred the hearts and minds of his supporters at a series of so-called 'monster meetings'. The Liberator may have been eclipsed by his retreat from Clontarf in October 1843, and his credibility was never fully restored before his death in 1847, but other men were claiming the authority to lead and speak for the Irish people. The 1840s was the decade of Thomas Davis, Charles Gavan Duffy, John Blake Dillon, John Mitchel and the *Nation* newspaper, a publication of inestimable importance in disseminating ideas of nationality and nationalism with a breadth of vision hitherto unprecedented in Irish history. Politically the Young Ireland Movement achieved little or nothing, ending in an attempted uprising in 1848 which was more ludicrous than threatening, although it soon acquired something of the mystique of Robert Emmet's equally abortive gesture in 1803. Intellectually and emotionally, however, it was enormously fruitful, and although Davis himself died at the age of thirty-one in 1845, he left a legacy of thought and writings of the most eclectic kind which continued to stimulate his successors more fully than any political essays since the time of Wolfe Tone.

Not only were the 1840s a watershed in the political history of Ireland; this was also the decade of the great famine.

Between 1845 and 1850 there were starvation, disease, abject suffering and desperation, appalling human degradation, and emigration on an unequalled scale. When the worst years were over, not only had the population of Ireland been radically and permanently altered by death and departure for new lands, but the minds of the survivors had been changed by an unforgettable experience which would be handed down to future generations both at home and abroad, for these events impinged upon popular consciousness more deeply than the most successful political propaganda or agitation.

Where, then, did the Anglo-Irish novelists fit into these traumatic years, and what were the subjects about which they chose to write? In 1845 Mrs Hall published her only full-length novel with an Irish subject, *The Whiteboy*, which, as the title indicates, attempts to come to terms with the Irish rebel tradition. The same year saw the appearance of the first novel by Joseph Sheridan Le Fanu, and although the bulk of his work falls outside the scope of this study, *The Cock and Anchor* established him as a writer of great individuality and considerable power. Throughout the period Charles Lever kept up a steady flow of published work, the best of which shows an unexpected maturity and complexity as well as a deepening concern for and awareness of the social problems in the country. But, above all, these years belong to Carleton whose three major novels – *Valentine McClutchy*, *The Black Prophet* and *The Emigrants of Ahadarra* – complete his right to be considered the major writer of Anglo-Irish fiction in the first half of the nineteenth century. He published other work as well, but in these three books he confronted the key problems of his time – sectarianism and the corrupt land system, famine and emigration – with memorable boldness and perseverance. First, though, there were the more modest achievements of the day.

The Whiteboy, 'a story of Ireland in 1822', explores the situation of the native Irish under the rule of an unscrupulous land agent whose activities are uncovered by the arrival in the country of a young absentee landlord Edward Spencer. Certain ingredients in this scenario are familiar. But whereas Mortimer in *The Wild Irish Girl*, Glenthorn in *Ennui*, and Gerald Blount in *The Anglo-Irish of the Nineteenth Century* are reluctant to visit Ireland and are convinced in advance of the wretchedness of the people and the land, Spencer is different in his open-minded approach. Indeed his determination to steer a middle course in Irish politics amuses the people to whom he first expounds his plans.

Mrs Hall defines the problem of moderation in Irish politics through the character of Lady Mary O'Brien, Spencer's first adviser. She tells her young idealist:

We are two nations on one soil; Celt and Saxon, Roman and Protestant, Irish Irish and English Irish; in England you do not understand this . . . . to dream of being allowed to steer a middle course . . . it is really too ridiculous.[1]

Lady O'Brien does not deny Edward Spencer's conviction that a course of moderation would be beneficial to the country, but she emphasizes the naivety of his philosophy in an Irish context by showing why such apparent common sense has made so little headway in the past. The outcome of the novel suggests that Mrs Hall herself does not believe in her character's 'two nation' theory and its negative consequences; indeed it might have been more realistic of her to have given the theory more weight, since it is clearly one possible way of accounting for the Irish problem.

Another character, Dean Graves, who meets Spencer on the boat to Ireland, regards the situation more optimistically. He maintains that the introduction of steam-powered ships will open up new opportunities for travel and trade between England and Ireland, thus forging mutual commercial bonds and understanding, and discouraging absenteeism which has so demoralized the Irish people. Graves does not dismiss Edward Spencer's faith in a middle course with the abruptness of Lady O'Brien, but gives him a sober warning that 'all knowledge of Ireland acquired only by hearsay, leads to dreams'.[2] Furthermore he maintains that the Irish peasantry themselves have dangerous dreams and need no encouragement to believe in their own glorious history and that, although dispossessed, they have never been conquered. Edward Spencer's response – that the distribution of 'even-handed justice' would overcome nationalist aspirations and the general rejection of the English as oppressors – implies the well-worn belief that English influence in Ireland is and must be beneficial and better for the country and its people than any native system of government or law. This does not impress Graves, who perceives how, in circumstances of poverty, hardship and suffering, an imaginative race like the Irish can only brood over memories of a remote and distinguished past which alone offer them dignity and self-respect. Thus history becomes distorted, the past dominates the present and generates bitterness towards the race which is identified with the wilful destruction of that culture and its traditions. The resultant atmosphere is ripe for social unrest and rebellion. By such carefully presented and stage-managed arguments, Mrs Hall provides a sense of the complexity of the situation in Ireland and prepares for the variety of action and attitudes which her hero encounters.[3]

In rather the same way the author is also painstaking in her introduction of the rebel leader Lawrence Macarthy. He is the last survivor of an old, noble family which has been dispossessed, and because of the circumstances of his birth – the child of a disapproved 'mixed' marriage whose father died prematurely and whose mother remarried – he regards himself as honour-bound to try to restore his family's position. This motive, linked with his somewhat impetuous and defiant nature, makes him a willing leader of the Whiteboys.

Mrs Hall's own sympathies do not lie with the methods espoused by the Whiteboys, nor indeed with the idea of rebellion itself, but she is concerned, nonetheless, to encourage her readers to accept Lawrence by understanding him. This she does by showing the pressures active upon him. He is left with his paternal grandmother's dying command to remember his name and his country, and is portrayed as the inheritor of a legacy of deprivation and persecution, so that his sense of history and the burden of responsibility for his family corrupt his judgment, in Mrs Hall's view, but do so in a way that is intelligible and by no means unique.

He believes that he is alienated from his half-sister Ellen MacDonnel, because her upbringing was well-to-do and her education and religion different to his own. At worst this blinds him to her virtues – an affectionate and loving nature, sympathy for the poor, and a sense of honour which is as strong as Lawrence's own but lacking his bitterness; at best he is doubtful of her, conscious of a certain inferiority to her, unwilling to accept the sincerity of her attitudes and her professed love for him. He charges her with forgetting the lessons of history and experience which they both learnt and which form a catalogue of Irish wrongs, and argues that to be true-hearted is to be a Whiteboy. Ellen rejects such a simple equation: without denying the past and the present evils inflicted on the Macarthy family by the grasping and unscrupulous land agent, Abel Richards, she cannot ignore certain acts of kindness and generosity performed by people whom Lawrence dismisses as oppressors. She retains tolerance and humanity, whereas he takes these to be signs of a weak will, discounting the charity of others as the actions of frightened men, and preferring instead to indulge in an idealistic vision of Ireland freed by the Whiteboys with the help of foreign aid, and proud beneath a national flag.

Ironically Lawrence Macarthy's dream of the future is seriously flawed by his proposed methods for securing the destiny of his native land. This is shown clearly by the clash of personalities and opinions that occurs when he is in the company of Louis, a refined and gentlemanly Whiteboy sympathizer who has come to the area to try and arrange foreign help for the rebels. In the same way that Michael Banim indicated the different perspectives of the United Irishman agent from Dublin and the local Wexford peasants, so Mrs Hall presents Louis arguing the case for total revolution, while Lawrence Macarthy insists on the need for short-term action and parochial terrorism, a view shared by the peasants who have little interest in the concept of a wider struggle.

Louis is an unlikely character as a rebel, for he is closer in his sympathies to Ellen MacDonnel than to Lawrence, and indeed his commitment to the Irish cause is based largely on his romantic interest in Ellen, who has filled his ears with 'the poetry of Irish revolt'.[4] Romanticism also colours his opinion of how the campaign should be conducted, for although he declares himself ready to face any personal evil in 'the hope of a patriot's death', he will not countenance assassination as a method worthy of the cause.[5] Even Louis' death-wish appears fanciful in comparison with the impassioned fanaticism of Macarthy who is blinded by his unquestioning belief in the flawless virtue of all Irish rebels.

Mrs Hall reveals something of the web-like structure of the Whiteboy organization throughout the community. She shows how Catholic servants employed in the Big Houses owned by Protestants were generally sympathetic towards the rebel cause, even if only by turning a blind eye to illegal activities. At a rebel meeting members furnish their leaders with comprehensive reports on the security and lay-out of potential targets, on the political affiliations of the owners, on whether they are known as enemies of the poor, and on the degree of support to be expected from the servants. Similarly the movement of troops and accumulation of arms or the plans of any landlord to make an unexpected journey are duly observed and reported through this comprehensive system of espionage.

Ultimately, however, *The Whiteboy* is seriously flawed by absurdities in the plot and the author's compulsive moralizing. The romantic evasion with which the story concludes ten years further on suggests that Edward Spencer has succeeded in imposing his version of English reason, justice and organization on his estates. The reader is told that

the people are now politically as well as morally exalted – their onward strides are becoming rapid as firm, firm as rapid; and though for a time they may be disturbed and distressed, though blood may even be spilt – yet, in the end, Ireland will become prosperous.[6]

Presumably these comments are meant to apply to the state of the country in 1832; but they were obviously untrue, except maybe in a few singular cases, even in 1845 when the novel was written, and, of course, history was about to unleash an even more cruel trick in the years immediately following. Edward Spencer's closing comments lack any real basis or justification in a tale which shows no peasant demands satisfied, no laws reformed, and nothing to indicate a general change in the attitudes of the landlords.

1845 was also the year in which Sheridan Le Fanu published his first novel, *The Cock and Anchor: A Chronicle of Old Dublin City*. Le Fanu is a difficult novelist to place, for while his subject-matter is usually Irish – although his best known book, *Uncle Silas*, takes place in England – it does not fall readily within the mainstream of Anglo-Irish fiction. Indeed his style is highly individual, even idiosyncratic in certain of its preoccupations. The novelist Elizabeth Bowen wrote an introduction to a new edition of *Uncle Silas* published in 1947, in which she makes some engaging suggestions about the link between Le Fanu's own family background and the particular way in which he viewed life through his fiction. Having observed that *Uncle Silas* strikes her 'as being an Irish story transposed to an English setting', she continues:

The hermetic solitude and the autocracy of the great country house, the demonic power of the family myth, fatalism, feudalism and the 'ascendancy' outlook are accepted facts of life for the race of hybrids from which Le Fanu sprang.[7]

The truth of these remarks is equally applicable to *The Cock and Anchor*, where the action revolves around the collapsing fortunes of the once wealthy Ashwoode family. Although the story is set in the early part of the eighteenth century, when there was still a covert Catholic movement dedicated to the restoration of the 'rightful' king, James, and the overthrow of William, the decadence and irresponsibility of the Anglo-Irish gentry are already far advanced.

At a moment of crisis, when young Sir Henry Ashwoode realizes that his gambling losses have made him the helpless victim of Nicholas Blarden, a money-lender, and his legal agent Mr Chancey, he looks around at the portraits of his ancestors in Morley Court and contemplates his own origins. The incident serves as a representative outline of the backgrounds of many such families, springing from the haughty men of old 'from whom was derived. . . pride and daring'. He sees the courtier of 'bluff king Hal' who had won the order of knighthood for the family; the soldier who had fought in Elizabeth's armies to crush the Irish rebels; the baronet who had held his position in the uprising of 1641, and had later taken part in Cromwell's campaign, 'and terribly avenged the sufferings of his Protestant countrymen'.[8] His own grandfather was a lord justice under Charles II, and his father had served with William of Orange. Distinguished as this pedigree might appear to be, it has another side, as the luckless Sir Henry realizes, because he is also the inheritor of bankruptcy and debts. Clearly his own reckless behaviour contributes to his ruin, but the roots of the problem extend further back in time.

The story consists of episodes in gambling clubs, in back-street dens and inns in Dublin, late at night on roads and in the fields near the city, occasionally at the social gatherings of the rich and bankrupt nobility, and above all at the Ashwoode family home Morley Court, which becomes more and more of a prison for Sir Henry and his sister Mary, as Blarden and Chancey tighten their grip. The deceit and furtiveness of much of the action is rendered more sinister because it takes place under cover of darkness, and the threat of violence always runs close to the surface and erupts into full view at regular intervals. Under cover of night Henry Ashwoode travels the road between his home and Dublin in an increasingly desperate search for pleasure and, ultimately, for survival itself. Similarly Edmond O'Connor, impoverished Catholic gentleman and son of a luckless follower of the fortunes of King James, encounters an old friend of his father disguised as a highwayman, who is engaged in organizing resistance to the Williamite regime; and later he meets a rebel priest who tries to recruit him for the same cause as he rides the roads at a late hour. Le Fanu portrays a society which comes to life after dark and where much of the intense business of those hours is dubious, if not openly corrupt.

Mary Ashwoode, the sister of Henry, is the focal point of the worst selfishness and cruelty in the story. Her innocence, helplessness and passivity are ruthlessly exploited, first by her father and then by her brother in their attempts to acquire money. Sir Richard tries unsuccessfully to marry her to Lord Aspenly, an aged and revolting roué with considerable wealth. He forbids her to meet the man she loves, Edmond O'Connor, and partly wheedles, partly compels his daughter to sign over her own inheritance to him in order that he may use it to pay off his own most urgent debts. He dies before he can do this, but his son and heir takes advantage of the property for a similar purpose. Worst of all Mary herself becomes the ultimate pawn in Nicholas Blarden's plot to ruin and humiliate Sir Henry, and Le Fanu evokes the kind of terror for which *Uncle Silas* is celebrated in his account of the money-lender's increasingly violent and abusive treatment of the girl as he moves towards the point of forcing her to marry him. The isolation, persecution and destruction of Mary Ashwoode – for she dies even though she foils Blarden's scheme – are more than the ingredients in a suspense story. They form a complex image of a society in which innocence and virtue have little place, and which, beneath a glib exterior of wealth and nobility, is cruel, unscrupulous and inordinately selfish. Even the good and principled characters – O'Connor, his friend Mr Audley and Mary's eccentric uncles, Major O'Leary and Mr French – are unable to help. Their efforts are rejected and swept aside by the arrogance and egocentricty of the Ashwoodes.

Le Fanu's book depicts a ruling class already in decline, its right to rule hopelessly compromised by its failure to exercise responsibility and control, and inwardly in an advanced state of self-destruction which it lacks the will and ability to arrest. The legal and political situation may ensure that those with power and privilege will continue to enjoy it for some time to come, but the end is inevitable. Le Fanu is, then, a novelist of the Big House tradition, imagining times earlier than those described by Maria Edgeworth, although she wrote her Anglo-

Irish novels almost half a century before him, and providing an odd contrast with his own contemporary Charles Lever, whose attention in the 1840s was directed towards the final stages in the collapse of various old land-owning families.

Lever's reputation, when he is still remembered, rests so firmly on *Harry Lorrequer*, *Charles O'Malley* and *Jack Hinton* that a stranger to his work might be surprised to discover that he wrote over thirty more novels, and that after his initial light-hearted, swashbuckling tales, his fiction altered significantly. H. R. Krans notes that:

The Irish novels that followed *Hinton* spread out into a broad transitional survey of Irish society, and may be considered in the main as an illustration of the process by which the old families of the land decayed, were uprooted from the soil in which they had grown for centuries, and finally supplanted by a new race of landlords.[9]

Thus Lever addressed himself to one of the great social issues in nineteenth-century Ireland, a topic which had figured largely in Anglo-Irish fiction from the time of Maria Edgeworth.

Furthermore his approach to this task recalls the historical novels of John Banim. In the same way that Banim chose periods in Irish history which he regarded as decisive in shaping the development of the country, so Lever explored his subject in certain carefully selected times. In the two novels considered here, *The O'Donoghue* takes place around the events of 1798 while *The Knight of Gwynne* deals with the Act of Union period. If the Banims and Carleton were the historians of these years for the Catholic peasantry, Lever records their impact and significance for the once wealthy and powerful Protestant landlord class whose fortunes were already eclipsed, but whose contribution to Irish society had been of the first importance. The novels deal primarily with decline, but they reveal a degree of sympathy and understanding which deserves more attention than is generally accorded to their author.

The O'Donoghue (1845) centres mainly on the relationships between an absentee landlord, Sir Marmaduke Travers, who visits Ireland briefly and the members of the O'Donoghue family who live in the ruins of their former ancestral castle. Although set in the time of 1798, the novel treats the uprising in the most superficial way, reducing its events to a tale of misguided romantic adventure. The plot is intricate and the love affairs of the main characters are fraught with misunderstandings, betrayal and excitement. In short it bears recognizable marks of Lever's earlier style with his predilection for turning everything into a rather boyish adventure with no clear scale of priorities.

What, then, makes this book different from its predecessors? In the first place, it focuses on Irish characters outside military circles; and it also admits that life is more than a prolonged series of celebrations with wine, women and song. There may be exaggeration and improbability – for example the rôle of Captain Hemsworth, the treacherous agent, in his endless manoeuvres against Mark O'Donoghue in the later part of the novel is highly melodramatic – but Lever admits reality in places, and makes some attempt to show its bleakness.

The O'Donoghue family are of a type that appears repeatedly in Lever's tales. Like Sir Patrick Rackrent, they are remembered by the older members of the community for their excessive and self-ruinous style of living, and the efforts of later generations to do things differently are regarded with a mixture of suspicion and contempt, indeed almost as signs of their inferiority. Thus they are trapped in history, unable to afford their former extravagance, their status and authority eroded to an empty gesture, yet proud of their name and conscious of distant glories in which it is too late for them to share. Young Mark O'Donoghue's sense of the past and his uncompromising antagonism towards the English, in whose offers of friendship he can see only betrayal, drive him into league with the United Irishmen. Ironically this association is revealed to the authorities by an Irishman, Lanty Lawler, who is a double agent, whereas the Englishman, Frederick Travers, deliberately enables him to elude capture and punishment after the abortive French attempt to land in Bantry Bay.

The novel provides no clear impression of the United Irishmen or their philosophy. There are fleeting references to French officers who are reconnoitring the state of the country and the readiness of the people, and allusions to the existence of a secret arms cache at Mary O'Kelly's shebeen; but these ideas, which are mentioned only to be dropped until needed again, are more like props than integral parts of the story. Mark O'Donoghue's own opinions are extremely unsophisticated and have as much to do with amorous jealousy as with politics. Since he is the most prestigious local recruit, this further undermines the credibility of the rebel movement.

Kate O'Donoghue, Mark's cousin and the woman loved both by him and by Frederick Travers, voices more coherent nationalist attitudes. Significantly, too, her experience of living and being educated in a convent abroad has not weakened her loyalty or affection for her family and home, but has made her aware of their defects and weaknesses as well as their virtues. She sees how Mark has been crushed and humiliated by misfortune, while his brother, Herbert, allows all events to pass him by without disturbing his innate apathy. Neither of them strikes her as a likely agent in the cause of restoring Ireland's honour and self-respect.

Her uncle, Sir Archy McNab, warns her against any popular movements designed to overthrow the existing order of government. His words shed light on the deliberately accommodating attitude towards the status quo of certain Catholic gentry, who prefer to live as depressed gentlefolk rather than to risk the loss of their standing in the chaos of a general rebellion. As Sir Archy explains to his niece,

The gentry . . . are better satisfied to live under a government they dislike than to be at the mercy of a rabble they despise . . . trust me, the poetry of patriotism has little relation to the revengeful fury of rebellion. You wish freedom for those who cannot enjoy the portion of it they possess. It is time to outlive the evil memories of the past; we want here – time, to blunt the acuteness of former and long-past sufferings – time, to make traditions so far forgotten as to be inapplicable to the present – time, to read the homely lesson, that one half the energy a people can expend in revolt will raise them in the rank of civilized and cultivated beings.[10]

This speech is a virtual code of reactionary conservatism with its unabashed admission of the self-interestedness of the gentry, despite the erosion of their power that has already taken place, and with its rejection of any challenge to authority. A rabble, after all, is not simply disorganized, but also mindless in its behaviour. Sir Archy's distinction between the eloquence of rebellion and the act itself is one thing, but his contempt for his social inferiors is ironic if the exercise of responsibility is taken as an inherent part of any real freedom. He himself and those of like mind, it may be argued, betray their own right to freedom by their failure to offer leadership to their people.

His call for time to heal the wounds of the past is equally dubious for two reasons. First, although it may be damaging to nurse the grievances of history, given the rest of Sir Archy's views, he appears to be arrogating any claim to a more equitable form of government for Ireland. This is particularly unsatisfactory in the context of the many disadvantages under which such a large section of the population, including Sir Archy himself, still labours. Second, his call to forget old traditions poses further questions, not least because it is unclear to what he is referring. If he means that the Irish should turn their backs finally on Gaelic culture, language and background, then he is proposing a total capitulation to English values and a severing of people from their native roots. His concluding comments are consistent with this opinion, implying that the untamed Irish lack civilization and sophistication, whereas a race of dutiful colonial citizens aping the customs of their rulers would earn some kind of respect from the people they copy. The reader may wonder what possible value respect gained on such terms could have.

Lever tries to show the active corruption and mismanagement stemming from the combination of an absentee landlord and the activities of an unscrupulous agent, Hemsworth, who has been scheming to ruin his employer and become the owner of the estate. His policy to achieve this end was twofold: to alienate the landlord and his tenants so totally that each party considered the other with contempt and despair, and to impose such exacting demands for 'duty-labour' and gifts for the agent upon the peasants that their own land remained untilled and unprofitable while that belonging to the Big House flourished and his own fortunes accumulated. Carleton's agent, Valentine McClutchy, may be the definitive model of heartless expropriation, but Lever's Captain Hemsworth is also penetratingly understood.

An example of how the ignorance of Sir Marmaduke Travers enables his agents to deceive him occurs when the landlord interviews Sam Wylie, a self-interested under-agent, concerning attempts to reform methods of agriculture and land distribution on part of his estate. Wylie reports a wholly negative response, thus actively encouraging his master's impression of the Irish as ungrateful, unreliable, aggressive and obtuse. As Lever points out, his ignorance of the true state of the peasantry and of their dissimilarity to English farm labourers blinds him to his own folly. Nor does he appreciate that the peasantry doubt the sincerity of his sudden benevolence and anxiety for them. Unlike Maria Edgeworth's peasants in, for example, *The Absentee*, where the very prospect of the landlord's return produces unqualified rejoicing, these people are cynical, and justifiably dismissive of many of Sir Marmaduke's ideas. He in turn interprets their refusal to co-operate in a most unfavourable way, more especially so with the help of a commentator like Sam Wylie.

Sir Marmaduke falls victim on the one hand to the flattery and smooth talk of some of his least worthy people, and on the other, to disillusionment and despair at the trickery and deceitfulness which seem to bedevil his every effort to help. To his cost he discovers that the ostensible docility and simple-mindedness of the poor, whom, he thinks, only need to be humoured, conceal depths and complexities of feeling far beyond his imagination or knowledge. Charles Lever was unable to reveal those depths and complexities in specific detail, but his very acknowledgement of their existence is part of the heightened social awareness and new seriousness which distinguish *The O'Donoghue* from his first novels. Furthermore, in addressing the question of land ownership and management, Lever contributes to a major, perhaps *the* major, theme in nineteenth-century Anglo-Irish fiction. His next books add to this contribution even more tellingly, because they concentrate closely on the aspect of that subject which Lever knew best of all: the decline and final collapse of old land-owning families.

In his preface added in 1872 to *The Knight of Gwynne*, the author explains how his novel is set around the period of the Act of Union and is concerned with showing

how the country gentleman of the time bore himself in the midst of solicitations and temptings the most urgent and insidious; what, in fact, was the character of that man whom no national fortunes could subdue, no Ministerial blandishments corrupt.[11]

The Knight is the owner of extensive, but heavily encumbered, estates in the west of Ireland. A man of great popularity among both his social equals and his tenants, his vote for the Union is urgently sought by Lord Castlereagh as one likely to influence the decision of others. He belongs to the tradition of landlords who, however weak their financial situation, commanded respect by their innate nobility, and who in this were quite unlike the newly *created* gentry of the time. In particular the Knight is contrasted with the Hickman family who gain control of his estates, but who are little more than unscrupulous social-climbing villains.

His grounds for refusing to endorse the Act of Union are notable. He tells Castlereagh that he will not be flattered into acceptance of the argument that the Irish party's influence will be undiminished by absorption into the Imperial Parliament; indeed he anticipates precisely how such a minority will be viewed in London: 'branded with provincialism as our badge, and accused of prejudice and narrow-sightedness, from the very fact of our nationality'.[12]

Furthermore he foresees that a leadership crisis will occur in Ireland after a union of parliaments, and that the way will be opened for

the demagogue, the public disturber, the licensed hawker of small grievances, every briefless lawyer of bad fortune and worse language, every mendicant patriot that can minister to the passions of a people deserted by their natural protectors. . . .[13]

Here the voice of inherited privilege prepares the reader for the hostile portrait of Daniel O'Connell which appears later. The question of the extent to which Darcy and his kind deserve to be considered the 'natural protectors' of the Irish reappears and remains unanswered, but his expectation of a changing social order after the Act of Union is significant. The Knight is even more perceptive when he argues that, once these new men become a force to be reckoned with, the government will find itself in an unenviable position, for coercion will make them martyrs, while conciliation will give them privileges; and he predicts a time when the English authorities will be criticized for the way in which they bought the votes to abolish the Irish Parliament, and when the blame for all that is wrong in the country will be linked with this one act. Yet despite Darcy's comprehensive grasp of the implications of the Act of Union, ironically when it comes to the vote, he misses the opportunity to make his stand because at that very time he hears of the flight of his agent with his money, and so is unable to attend the debate.

Following the abolition of the Irish Parliament, the novel traces the increasing financial straits of the Darcy family, but of greater significance are Lever's attempts to show in practice the general effects of the Union. The Knight himself argues that the sole purpose of the act was to make Ireland more easily governable; and here, at least, historians will agree with him. He also maintains that the new approach of governing by party, and of seeking to curry favour with individuals for political ends, can only have a divisive effect and tends to advance the most self-interested rather than the most able or suitable men. Darcy asserts that, however well the system works for a time, in the end

> your allies, grown exacting by triumph, will ask more than you dare, or even have to give; and the question will then arise, that the party who aspires to power must bid for it by further concession, and who is to vouch for the moderation of such demands, or what limit will there be to them?[14]

Thus, with one astonishing bound of vision, Darcy – and his creator – seems to anticipate the very situation that developed over the Home Rule issue half a century after the novel was written.

Another facet of Darcy's opposition to the Act of Union and of his fears for the future is his regret at the emergence of professional, career politicians who are eroding the authority of the noble statesmen. He alleges that

> suddenly acquired wealth can scarcely be intrusted with political power; it lacks the element of prudent caution, by which property is maintained as well as accumulated; it wants also the 'prestige' of antiquity as a claim to respect; and, legislate as you will, men will look back as well as forward.[15]

The irony of such a claim can scarcely escape the reader who knows that the Knight of Gwynne's own financial irresponsibility and incompetence have contributed the final blows to his family's estates. At the same time the representatives of the new class of men with power are portrayed in a generally unfavourable light. The Hickmans are contemptible and they receive poetic justice, for all their machinations fail or rebound upon them. A more successful opportunist is Con Heffernan, Castlereagh's helper in preparing for the Act of Union, and a political go-between without any illusions. He understands the English policy towards Ireland – to make the people 'become English in feeling as they are in law and in language' – and the means by which it is to be achieved: namely, through breaking down the old bonds of clanship.[16] His sole miscalculation concerns his own career, for he finds his services which were willingly accepted are soon forgotten by his English masters when it comes to giving rewards. Heffernan is shrewd, but not shrewd enough in the last analysis.

Most significant of all is the presentation of Daniel O'Connell. Lever makes no effort to disguise his hostility towards him, seeing him as an amalgam of all that is worst in the Irish temperament. His antipathy to O'Connell is evident in the second half of the novel, where a character named Counsellor O'Halloran is introduced as Hickman O'Reilly's lawyer and the implacable foe of Maurice Darcy. O'Halloran, a thinly disguised portrait of O'Connell, is described as 'the great orator at the bar, and the great speaker at public meetings, the rising patriot who, not being deemed of importance enough to be bought, was looked on as incorruptible'.[17] The account stresses his self-centredness, his confidence in his own legal knowledge and oratorical genius, and the boldness with which he asserts his democratic opinions, however unpopular both these and the common tone in which he voices them might be. He seems to be a man, Lever claims, who even in these early days has a kind of assurance that his views would command respect and attention in time.

The conclusion of *The Knight of Gwynne* is wholly weak and unconvincing, for it shows Darcy restored to his ancestral estates thanks to the efforts of his eccentric friend Bagenal Daly, the overthrow of the Hickmans, and the legal defeat of O'Halloran – yet nothing in the earlier development of the novel suggests the likelihood or reality of this resolution. Indeed most of the evidence points in the opposite direction, and the Knight's ruin is to be expected rather than his miraculous return to Gwynne Abbey. Perhaps the problem derives from Lever's apparent change of strategy in the second volume where the action ranges so widely that the Union issues often fade into the background. Certainly the final outcome is a flat denial of the very insights expressed by the Knight himself concerning the effects of the Act of Union.

Lever depicted more completely than other novelists of the period the hedonism, arrogance and attitudes of the estate owners whose debts destroyed them within a generation. Although he could see the error of their ways, he shared something of their spirit. W. B. Yeats, commenting on Lever's popularity amongst English readers, states that he

has never won a place beside Carleton and Banim, or even Griffin, in the hearts of the Irish people. His books, so full of gaiety and animal laughter, are true merely to the life of the party of ascendancy, and to that of their dependants. It will be a long time before the world tires altogether of his gay, witty, reckless personages, though it is gradually learning that they are not typical Irish men and women.[18]

Yeats is right insofar as Lever's stories centre on the landed gentry and not on the native Irish about whom the Banims and Carleton wrote; but to dismiss the Anglo-Irish ascendancy as if they were a minor and insignificant faction in the history of the country is to deny the facts. Similarly the reader may acknowledge that the native Irish and the Anglo-Irish were, in general terms, people of different racial and cultural origins; but it is also true that the nineteenth-century Anglo-Irish were not synonymous with the English, despite their common ancestral roots. Like it or not, the destiny of the Anglo-Irish ascendancy forms part of Irish history and development, and their contribution, both positive and negative, can only be seen in its Irish context. Lever, as one of the novelists who captured something of the lives of these people in his fiction, should not be discounted in quite such a cavalier manner.

Lever was not the only novelist whose output was prolific during these years. For Carleton, too, this was a highly productive period, which saw the appearance of three of his most important novels and four other works of lesser significance. These books illustrate all the author's strengths and weaknesses as a writer of fiction: his humanity and his prejudices, his insensitivity and his lack of judgment, his morality and his unscrupulousness.

Two of the lesser books, *Parra Sastha, or the History of Paddy Go-Easy and His Wife Nancy* and *Art Maguire, or the Broken Pledge,* show Carleton at his most doctrinaire and sententious. The former was written very rapidly to replace a volume in the Library of Ireland series which was to have been contributed by Thomas Davis had he not been taken fatally ill. Its moralistic intention is quite clearly defined:

[to] inculcate habits of industry, punctuality, cleanliness, comfort, intelligence, and that principle of social progress which the landlords of Ireland have seldom or never made any earnest attempt to develop among their tenantry. . . .[19]

Presumably in order to convey the message as unambiguously as possible, the main characters, Paddy and Nancy, are reduced to diagrammatic figures. The man is a model of indolence, carelessness and prejudice against progress, while his wife exemplifies the virtues of hard work, self-discipline and prudence as she struggles to improve her standard of living. The problem is that they are so simplistic and one-dimensional that they lack individuality and even reality. The total reformation of Paddy through the good offices of his wife surpasses belief: everything depends on his basically good and decent nature, and all it takes is a walk round the farm with Nancy pointing out its deficiences for her husband to see the error of his ways. While the spirit of such writing may be admirable, Carleton might have done better if he had dropped the pretence of writing fiction and offered a straightforward practical guide to domestic and farm improvement. It seems doubtful if many of the Paddy Go Easys would be able or likely to read his book, and, if they were, it is even less probable that they would have been favourably impressed by it.

Much the same applies to the temperance tract *Art Maguire*. Dedicated to the great pioneer of abstinence, Father Theobald Matthew, this is another doctrinaire and moralistic tale thinly disguised as fiction. Addiction to drink, the author argues, erodes self-reliance and confidence and produces servility, domestic unhappiness, poverty, violence and even death. Clearly there is truth in such allegations, all of which are exemplified in the life of Art Maguire, but they are introduced in a way that makes the account little more than a paradigm of a drunkard's progress. The sources of the problem are Art Maguire's absurd vanity, his claim to be descended from an ancient Fermanagh family, and his indiscriminate love of company. He is contrasted with his brother, Frank, who is sober-minded, industrious, loyal and selective in the society he keeps. Both men learn to be carpenters and do well until Art discovers his weakness for whiskey and is humiliated by his supposed friends. Furthermore he makes an implacable enemy in one Toal Finigan by marrying Margaret Murray, because although Art was betrothed to her, it was a secret arrangement and Finigan feels betrayed.

Art forswears drink for seven years, and keeps his word, during which time he establishes himself as a master crafts-man and a model family man. At the end of this period he resumes drinking, and the decline and collapse of his business and domestic life are rapid and total. Once again he is rescued from the depths, for, having attended a temperance rally held by Father Matthew himself, Art takes the pledge and proceeds to become as determined a devotee of abstinence as he was of drunkenness. All is well until Toal Finigan plays on his vanity and boastfulness after Art has gone to a public house to drink temperance cordial, and this temptation accompanied by Toal and his friends discreetly lacing Art's drink with whiskey soon reduce him to drunkenness again. This time the consequences are tragic, for he goes to hit his wife, strikes his favourite son by mistake, and leaves the child a simpleton as a result. Art deteriorates into a regular drunkard and subsequently dies of consumption in the workhouse, after which his son miraculously recovers his reason.

Carleton is undoubtedly attempting to tackle a very serious social problem in Ireland. The misery and damage which Art Maguire causes himself and other people are not in themselves unbelievable, and the schematic way in which the story develops is consistent with its specific moral purpose. But Art Maguire is unacceptable as a complete or 'round' character because the stages in his career are too abruptly marked, and his personality and relationships are too narrowly defined. The issue is less simple in two of the novels he published during this period, for although *Rody the Rover* and *The Tithe Proctor* carry vigorous attacks on the Ribbonmen and Whiteboys, these are set in more fully developed fictional contexts. *Rody the Rover* is the weaker book, reflecting the author's innate conservatism and abhorrence of the Ribbon movement and all that it stood for. The intention is propagandist and the method for the most part is diagrammatic. He shows how the village of Ballybracken, which was once impoverished and disorderly, achieves peace and prosperity because of a well managed mining project in the area, but it is reduced to a condition worse than that from which it started by the machinations of the Ribbonmen.

In addition the credibility of the Ribbon movement is totally destroyed because the leaders are in league with the government, deliberately fomenting local unrest and thus justifying the refusal of greater liberties to the Catholic population on whose behalf they are supposedly campaigning. The cynical manipulators make their own fortune out of these activities and destroy the happiness and stability of the communities in which they operate. Rody the Rover himself is a treacherous, machiavellian, hypocritical polygamist, while his boss, Mr Sharpe, is an unscrupulous and embittered Orange sympathizer.

The villainy of Rody is heightened by the careful way in which the harmony and industry of Ballybracken in general and of the MacMahon family in particular are established before he arrives. There is a cameo view of the destitution, dirt and ignorance prevalent in the village before the mine opened, and this is contrasted with the improved material and educational standards achieved under the direction of the good agent who runs the new industrial concern. Drunkenness and party and faction feuds have withered away, so that on the evening that Rody first appears in Ballybracken the life of the villagers has almost a prelapsarian innocence.

Rody claims to be on the run after a fight with Orangemen in which he allegedly killed a man. The readiness of his welcome by the MacMahon family not only shows their hospitable generosity, but also their ambiguous attitude towards the law. In this instance their instinctive sympathy for his predicament – which Carleton neither questions nor criticizes – has far-reaching consequences. The MacMahons typify all that the author loved to celebrate in Irish peasant life: honesty, sobriety, female beauty and virtue, dignity and friendliness. Rody is the plausible enemy and exploiter of these qualities. He proceeds by recruiting one new Ribbonman, binding him under an oath of secrecy and furnishing him with papers, and then employing him to involve others. All the arguments used to seduce the villagers are based upon suggestions of conspiracy against their welfare and happiness. Thus distrust and suspicion spread throughout the community, and the initial harmony is exposed as a very fragile state of equilibrium.

The situation in Ballybracken deteriorates when the Ribbonmen provoke a strike for higher pay among the miners, and here Carleton goes to some lengths to remove any justification for the action by emphasizing that their wages are already above average. Tom MacMahon, who disapproves of the strike, is framed as being one of the main agitators, and this prepares for his ultimate undoing when the agent is shot and fatally wounded and Tom is accused of the murder. Ironically he is not only innocent of the assassination, but had already decided to break off his association with the Ribbon movement. He was present at the scene of the shooting solely to try and prevent trouble. All these factors add to the terrifying moral lesson which the novel expounds, for Tom, having been relieved by Rody of the membership fees he had collected from Ribbon recruits, sees his destroyer elope with his sister, Alice, and is himself sentenced and executed for a murder he did not commit. In more general terms the village is ruined because the mine closes, the Insurrection Act is enforced in the area, while Mr Sharpe, Rody's government-inspired employer, gains wealth and power.

Towards the conclusion, which takes a jaundiced view of events even by Carleton's regularly partisan standards, the author indulges in deliberate scare-mongering. He warns the Irish people that

> they are, at this moment, surrounded by an invisible body of spies and detectives, trained and disciplined into the deepest reaches of treachery and iniquity, under the very sanction of government, which is not ashamed to degrade itself by the double guilt of employing a class of men whose services are calculated to destroy the confidential intercourse of society at large, and are clearly at variance, besides, with the spirit of a free constitution.[20]

Undoubtedly governments did use informers, spies and double agents throughout Ireland's troubled history, but Carleton's paranoia seems more likely to contribute to the breakdown of 'the confidential intercourse of society at large' than to heal wounds or create loyalty. He wrote *Rody the Rover* out of distrust and fear, probably with a vivid remembrance of his own brush with the Ribbonmen as an impressionable youth; in the end his book does little more than add to the negative feelings in which it originated. The novel, maybe, says more about the author and his own concern to achieve respectability and favour, even from the government he was castigating, than about the Ribbonmen and their mode and purpose of action.

Carleton never claimed to be writing with fairness and impartiality in *Rody the Rover*, but he does so in *The Tithe Proctor*, published in 1849. In the preface he defines the changes which he believed had taken place in the behaviour and attitudes of the Irish peasantry since the days of his boyhood. He laments the erosion of the moral and social principles of the nation, and their replacement by slavish insolence, deceitfulness and cowardice, which he sees as the pernicious effects of the repeal movement. Such a beginning seems to herald another strident and reactionary treatise, and indeed this is what we find in many places. But the novel also contains scenes and characters which represent Carleton at his best, showing the humour and imagination that often deserted him after his early stories.

The Tithe Proctor is a study of the tyranny and arrogance of

Matthew Purcel and his sons, whose despised employment is to collect from the Catholic peasantry the tax which is used to pay the clergy of the Established Church. In the course of his duties the proctor himself makes a rich living, thus adding further to his own notoriety. Although the violent, overbearing and greedy behaviour of the Purcels is contemptible, there is something almost admirable in their fearlessness as they continue to live in and travel about a neighbourhood where almost everyone is their sworn enemy. For once Carleton views his subject from more than one angle, because he is also critical of the Whiteboys who use their influence to pressure the peasants into withholding their tithe payments and thus exposing themselves to the bullying of the proctor and his sons. He shows a real understanding of how young men are forced to commit acts of violence and terrorism simply to remain in favour with their friends. Furthermore he offers a sympathetic account of the hardship and undeserved suffering of certain worthy members of the Protestant ministry and their families, while also showing how others are justifiable victims. Even here the situation is complicated because some Catholics are still prepared to help popular Protestant clergymen in secret, despite the injunctions of the Whiteboys. Thus, although the details of the plot are often far-fetched and unconvincing, the atmosphere of mounting social unrest and violence is effectively evoked and certain incidents and characters are particularly well drawn.

Carleton did not support the tithe agitation, but he shows a critical attitude towards the Established Church of his day, and is careful to give the popular opposition to it a real context. He states that

The Established Church in Ireland . . . in its unpurged and unreformed state, was very little else than a mere political engine for supporting and fostering British interests, and British principles in this country; and no one here had any great chance of preferment in it who did not signalize himself some way in favour of English policy. The Establishment was indeed the only bond that bound the political interests of the two nations together.[21]

As might be expected in such a situation, corruption, self-indulgence and arrogance were rife, and most senior positions were given as political rewards rather than on the basis of a genuine interest in or sympathy for Ireland or its people. This, of course, added to the rancour felt by the Catholic peasantry who had to subsidize the Church either by direct payment or through increased rents to their landlords. Against this background popular agitators soon generated a widespread unity of action when the idea of refusing tithe payments was inaugurated.

Carleton charges the Catholic priesthood with inciting crime and debasing religious practice by their support for a repeal of the Act of Union and resistance to tithe payments. At the same time he reveals the eccentric behaviour and humanity of individual priests. The account of how Father Anthony Casey, ostensibly an ardent supporter of the tithe agitation, attempts to provide secret relief to the Rev. Goodison and his family is one of the best written and most humorous episodes in the novel. Having heard from his curate of the pitiful state of the Goodisons, Father Casey denounces the Established Church as an English garrison, and appears to justify all the hardship its clergy are now suffering as their fit deserts after so many years of unscrupulous privilege. Yet, as soon as he has dispatched the young man to bed, the priest sets out with a sack of oatmeal and a flitch of bacon, 'for a distressed person in the neighbourhood that wants it badly', urging on his servants the need for the utmost secrecy.[22] The rich comedy of the situation develops when, to his embarrassment, he meets one of his parishioners engaged upon a like errand of mercy to the same family. Father Casey is too sharp-witted to be discountenanced for long, and the mutual justification by which he and Con McMahon excuse their charity is worked out in magnificent style. Having stressed the need to distinguish between the tithes and the parsons themselves, the priest continues:

And by the way, now, I don't know but it would be our duty . . . to render the same parsons, now that they're suffering, as much good for evil as possible. It would be punishing the thieves by heaping, as the Scripture says, coals of fire upon their heads. . . . That's the way to punish them like a Christian.[23]

Con McMahon is quick to see the priest's purpose in this obtuse logic, and he immediately seizes it to explain his own charitable conduct as an act of 'revenge' against a heretic clergyman. This incident is not merely amusing, it also smacks of reality. The two men, both of whom are compromised by their own generosity in the extraordinary situation that prevails, part from their chance encounter with their integrity intact. Father Casey's authority provides a pseudo-religious reason for their conduct, and Con McMahon is tactful enough to accept this without question and to use it to show that he was only following the advice of his parish priest. They understand each other completely and respect their relative positions, so that no further explanation is necessary between them.

When Carleton turns his attention to the darker passions of some of the members of illegal organizations, the mood at once becomes sombre. He comments in general terms upon how such societies dedicated to violence appeal to the psychologically unstable, the psychotic and the congenitally vicious, as well as to those with genuine political convictions; and so arise the anarchic and dangerous operations of rebel groups. He also specifically attacks O'Connell for inciting people to oppose the laws without breaking them – a course which Carleton dismisses as impossible in the first place, and which tends to lead to disorder and bloodshed in the long run.

The action in *The Tithe Proctor* as a whole creates a conspiratorial atmosphere which involves virtually everyone in the community, an impression that is reinforced by the presence of the Cannie Soogah, a rebel leader who, in his guise of a pedlar, moves through the community without drawing suspicion upon himself. He gains legitimate access to most houses, including that of Matt Purcel, and is able to observe details of buildings and engage in conversations with servants which furnish him with a wealth of information. At the same time the Cannie Soogah is no pitiless villain like Rody the Rover. He actually helps the Rev. and Mrs Temple, a humble and faithful Protestant couple who are brought to dire poverty by the tithe campaign. He also warns Julia Purcel, daughter of the hated proctor, not to venture out alone because he knows of a plan to abduct her. When the long-expected attack on the proctor's house takes place, again the Cannie Soogah is a friend to the females of the house, ensuring their escape to safety although he will do nothing to save Matt Purcel and his sons, who die in the vain defence of their property, having been condemned to this fate at a mock trial held beforehand by the representatives of Captain Right. Carleton's anger and passionate condemnation of violence are evident in *The Tithe Proctor*, and the balance of art threatens to tilt in the direction of narrow propaganda and bigotry. Later books, such as *The Squanders of Castle Squander* (1852), show no saving graces but are the outpourings of a confused mind and a spent imagination.

But this is to anticipate, for in the 1840s Carleton wrote his last great, if flawed, novels and these works alone would entitle him to serious attention. The first of these books, *Valentine McClutchy*, has been described by H. R. Krans as 'the most daring picture of Irish country life ever executed'; while Benedict Kiely claims that: 'From several points of view it is the most important book of the Irish nineteenth century.'[24] At least part of its significance derives from the fact that here Carleton tries once and for all to define his view of the perennial question that hangs over the Irish people, their writers and their politicians throughout the century: the control, administration and tenancy arrangements of the land. Anglo-Irish fiction first expresses itself in a novel concerned with the land, and *Valentine McClutchy* has been described as Carleton's *Castle Rackrent*, thus acknowledging its place in the tradition of works dealing with the subject.[25] Maria Edgeworth's indictment of land mismanagement is subtle, ironic and understated; Carleton's is swingeing, passionate, at times crude and elsewhere profoundly moving, but always demanding to be noticed and difficult to deny as a powerful statement of the core of so much Irish suffering and grief. Moreover, written from the point of view of the exploited Catholic peasantry in the early years of the nineteenth century, it reflects the writer's own background and experience.

Carleton was sufficiently aware of the personal advantages of keeping in favour with the establishment to restrain in part his bitterness against absentee landlords, despite the fact that in his preface to *Valentine McClutchy* he speaks of bad landlords and bad agents as 'the two great curses of Ireland'.[26] The focal points for his attack are the eponymous agent, his son Phil, and the religious attorney Solomon McSlime, who embody every possible evil and vice that an agent or lawyer might have. Valentine McClutchy is greedy, deceitful, spiteful, power-mad, unscrupulous and hypocritical; he is also illegitimate, and this appears to add to his viciousness of character. His son is less cunning and more cowardly, while his sectarianism is more pronounced than his father's, amounting merely to a mindless hatred without even Val's political motivation to justify it. His cowardice makes him dangerous because his bullying is increased by it, and as the novel progresses drunkenness and lechery are added to his catalogue of depravity. McSlime is an arch religious hypocrite whose outward manner, suggested by his name, is meant to conceal his fundamental greed, lechery, sectarianism, self-interest, and lust for power and wealth. In brief these villains are creatures of melodrama as even their physical appearances suggest: Val, for example, is stout and broad-shouldered with knock-knees, heavy brows, a squinting eye and a hooked nose. None of the three is fully credible as a real man, though they are recognizable as almost Jonsonian distillations of corruption. Similarly their knavery is comprehensive, concentrating many of the kinds of tyranny practised against the Catholic peasantry in one place. The result is that a deliberate compressing of experience gives an impression of heightened and intensified reality which survives the unlikeliness of the three main characters, the inadequacies of the plot, and the utterly contrived happy ending.

It is not only the wicked characters who are exaggerated. Brian McLoughlin, who becomes the prime target of McClutchy's viciousness, is an idealized figure, while his daughter Mary, on whose behalf McLoughlin contemptuously rejects Val's proposal of a marriage with his son, is a familiar model of Irish female beauty and virtue. Her physical perfection reflects her innocence and purity of character, but she becomes the object of Phil McClutchy's lust, and, because of her family's refusal to subject her to him, the McLoughlins are made to suffer bitterly. Yet she is a source of strength and dignity in even the most exacting circumstances.

The struggle between these good and evil characters derives from the power wielded by McClutchy, and that in turn stems from the authority vested in him by the absentee landowner, Lord Cumber. Unlike the good agent Mr Hickman, McClutchy is willing to resort to the most unscrupulous means to meet his master's financial demands, while at the same time he lines his own pocket.

Early in the book Mr Hickman outlines five essential guidelines for promoting happy landlord/tenant relationships. These involve respect for the tenantry and recognition of their influence in supporting the landlord's authority and position; acceptance and fulfilment of the obligations of a landowner to his people; tolerance towards those of a different creed and careful protection of civil and religious liberties; humane concern for the needs and feelings of tenants; and finally great caution not to provoke rebellion by unreasonable, rapacious or cruel behaviour. All these principles are violated by Valentine McClutchy who is scornful of Hickman's reluctance to allow tenants to fall into arrears, precisely because he knows that those who have paid their dues can afford to be more independently minded and cannot be intimidated so easily. McClutchy also opposes education for the poor, preferring to keep them in their ignorance rather than encouraging the capacity for free thought. Elsewhere, in a discussion on the increasingly desperate state of things on the Castle Cumber property, Francis Harman, Mary McLoughlin's lover, insists that educating the people to know their own value in society and their moral and civic duties is the only way to eradicate

that humiliating and slavish error, that the landlord is everything and themselves nothing. . . . At present they [i.e. the landlords] disregard public opinion, because it is too feeble to influence them; and, consequently, they feel neither fear nor shame. So long as the landlords and the people come together as opposing or antithetical principles, it is not to be supposed that the country can prosper.[27]

Here is the theory of what should be, and a vision of how it might be achieved. But, positive and constructive as these suggestions are meant to be, they make dull and uninspiring reading. The true vigour and emotion of the book only emerge in the scenes of staggering cruelty, sectarian excess and cynicism that are the products of the unjust system which Hickman and Harman wish to see swept away.

One of the most harrowing incidents tells of the eviction on Christmas Eve of a number of Catholic families who had refused to promise their votes to Lord Cumber. The agent is supported in his task by a body of heavily armed Orange yeomanry, known as Deaker's Dashers, who are little more than a gang of bully boys disguised as a legal force, and committed to the violent suppression of Catholicism. McClutchy jeers at and threatens the wretched people in the village, while McSlime assures them that the eviction is part of God's purpose to help chastise and purify His misguided children. Their frantic appeals for mercy are ignored, and the action proceeds relentlessly, even when McClutchy finds his own mother begging for a stay of execution. The most inhumane action of all occurs when a young boy, Torley O'Regan, lying gravely ill from a ruptured blood-vessel, dies after being dragged roughly into the winter air. Even after the boy's death McClutchy insists on completing the ejections, but then, as a supposed act of mercy, he allows the people to re-occupy their houses until the weather is milder. The episode dramatizes the full tyranny and cruelty of the agent's power in practice: on the one hand, he inflicts suffering and death on the villagers, and then, as if to underline his absolute authority, he allows his victims to re-enter the very places they had originally begged to be left in undisturbed.

As if anticipating that he would be accused of extravagance or misrepresentation of the behaviour of the yeomanry and of McClutchy's Blood Hounds, Carleton insists in his preface that

there is not an *honest man*, on either side, who has lived in the north of Ireland, and reached the term of fifty years who will not recognize the conduct and language of the northern Orangemen as just, truthful, and not one whit exaggerated.[28]

For once his claim seems entirely justified, particularly in view of the author's Ulster background. There was in those days, as Carleton recorded years later in his *Autobiography*, 'no law *against* an Orangeman, and no law *for* a Papist', and punitive raids were often conducted by men who were well known to the victims.[29]

Carleton's formative years coincided with the aftermath of the 1798 rebellion, and *Valentine McClutchy* is set in the early years of the nineteenth century when old grievances were still close to the surface, a situation that helps to explain – though not to justify – the roughness of the treatment meted out to the Catholic population. Similarly the particular activity of the Orange Lodges in this period may be related to the same cause. There is a memorable account of an Orange Lodge meeting, which consists, for the most part, of a heavy-drinking session accompanied by the singing of sectarian songs, and toasts to the King, Protestant Ascendancy, Church and State, and other less well-known institutions, such as the Castle Cumber press, an organ of militant Orange scurrility.

The description captures perfectly the voices and idioms of Ulster Protestant bigotry and sectarianism. A particularly telling moment comes in a speech made by Mr Yellowboy, editor of the local paper, in response to an allegation made in a rival publication that he had been found lying drunk in the gutter. Denying this rumour, Yellowboy's definition of his own political and religious position forms a classic statement of the paradoxical Ulster Protestant view of freedom and liberty. He claims to be:

a bold, honest, uncompermising Pruddestant – who will support the church and constitution for ever – who will uphold the Pruddestant Ascendancy to the day of judgment – keep down Popery and treason – and support civil and religious liberty over the world to all eternity.[30]

The contradictions of this may amuse outsiders, but Carleton did not mean them as joke any more than Mr Yellowboy did. Out of just such illogicalities repeated suffering and discrimination have come. Mr. Yellowboy's words reflect a society in which the lines of loyalty are drawn decisively and with stark simplicity, and where judgments are so absolute that the worst kind of traitor is not the Papist, whose treachery to the state is assumed as a matter of course, but the Prostestant who refuses to side openly with the sectarian Orange movement and who thus remains an unreliable enigma in the eyes of his co-religionists.

The effects of the McClutchy régime on the lives of the Castle Cumber tenants are variously shown. The landscape bears all the characteristic signs of mismanagement and the tyrannical exercise of power. Leases are granted not with regard to the merits of the tenants, but as political rewards; those peasants who know the insecurity of their position refrain from making any improvements to their land or property; evicted and poverty-stricken families haunt the roads and ditches in a desperate, improvised struggle to survive from one day to the next; often the menfolk are forced to leave their wives and children to seek employment elsewhere. The total impression is of large numbers of the population who are vulnerable to every mischance, and who lack even the most rudimentary securities in life, so that this novel written in 1845 and recording events set in 1804 anticipates exactly why the great famine would be so devastating and inevitable.

Whereas in *Rody the Rover* Carleton presented the evils of Ribbonism in a purely arbitrary way, never setting the behaviour of the people of Ballybracken in a convincing context, in *Valentine McClutchy* the growth of the movement is entirely understandable. The conduct of McClutchy and his kind, backed locally by the entire partisan apparatus of law and justice, inflames the feelings of the peasantry, and the author is decidedly more generous towards these rebels than he usually is towards violent agitators. He stresses that the apparent wildness and ferocity of the conspirators belie their true natures, and that their secret gathering to 'try' and 'sentence' the McClutchys is solemn and dreadful, but not melodramatic and histrionic:

in what light did they view this terrible determination? Simply as a redress of grievances; as the only means left them of doing that for themselves, which the laws refused to do for them.[31]

Carleton hastily adds his moral censure of a system of government which drives people to these exigencies, but as he proceeds to introduce the heart-broken, embittered and deranged victims of McClutchy's reign of terror, the reader's sympathies are soon actively engaged on the part of the peasantry. The agent and his son are condemned to be shot by the unanimous decision of the 'jury', but this judgment is compromised, for with impeccable timing the good Father Roche appears and commands that his parishioners forswear their intentions. He insists on them accepting the Christian alternative of loving their enemies and teaching them by example, and thus, ironically, Valentine and Phil McClutchy's lives are saved by the intervention and prayers of a Catholic priest. Father Roche's success is incomplete, however, for one man slips away unnoticed and avoids the obligation to refrain from violence, thus ensuring that the threat remains real. In the end Owen O'Regan's silent departure is as decisive as Father Roche's authority, for Valentine McClutchy dies at his hands, conveniently allowing Carleton both to express his disapproval of bloodshed and to provide a worthy fate for his villain.

Finally the rôle of the Established Church in the midst of so much corruption and sectarianism attracts strong adverse comment. In particular there is the phenomenon known as the New Reformation, a movement to convert Catholics to Anglicanism by simple bribery at times of the year when fuel and food are scarce, the weather appalling, and cold, hunger and lack of adequate clothing commonplace. This practice posits a strange concept of Christian charity which takes advantage of destitution and which offers help only after imposing the harshest conditions, namely, that the recipient should abandon his religious beliefs and adopt an alien form of faith. The opportunism of many, or most, of the supposed converts is less easy to condemn, for the instinct to survive is basic and in extreme circumstances may justify actions that would otherwise be unthinkable.

In fairness Carleton does not suggest that the New Reformation was universally endorsed and Mr Clement, a humble but hard-working and caring Anglican cleric, denounces fake conversions, seeing exactly how they undermine the authority and credibility of his own church and insult the faith of those Catholics who are driven into a change of religion out of mere desperation and dire material hardship. Needless to say Mr Clement himself benefits little from his own position as a Protestant minister, and his meagre stipend and widespread duties and services to the poor are contrasted to the bigotry, luxurious standard of living and lack of work done by his superior, Rev. Phineas Lucre.

The conclusion to *Valentine M⁄cClutchy* is disappointing, for Carleton resorts to the old cliché of ensuring the accession of a landlord who has undergone the necessary change of heart to make him take up his responsibilities to his tenants. The villains are neatly disposed of and the good agent recognized for his integrity, so that the future looks rosy for the occupants of the Castle Cumber lands. No reader can imagine that Carleton believed in his own story at this point: if all that he revealed earlier was true – and that seems likely – then a miraculous cure is incredible. It is merely a diplomatic juggling of the facts and a rejection of experience in order to produce a less abrasive tone at the end. The strength of other parts of the novel, for all its unevenness, may be gauged by the fact that it survives this final capitulation to artistic dishonesty and remains in the memory as such a powerful satire upon the social and religious injustices in early nineteenth-century Ulster.

Much the same applies to *The Black Prophet*. Written during the course of the great famine, it recalls scenes remembered by the author from 1817 and 1822 when there had also been crop failures and severe hardship, though not on the scale of 1846–49. The book includes some of the most powerful and harrowing scenes in Carleton's fiction and, indeed, in the fiction of the whole period between 1800 and 1850. Yet, as so often, the plot is weak and flawed. B. G. MacCarthy has stated the problem thus:

Carleton continually shows a lack of judgment in his over-writing of a situation, in his exaggeration, his melodrama, his evident inability to 'cut'. . . . instead of basing his plot on the famine period, he used the famine merely as a background for a flashy and hollow story which has really no connection with the famine. . . . For such trumpery Carleton lost the opportunity of writing what, with his material, might have been a great novel.[32]

The justice of these comments leaves the reader pondering over the extraordinary paradox of this writer whose work was so crude and unpolished on the one hand, and yet so convincing and uniquely accomplished on the other.

Dedicated to Lord John Russell in his capacity as head of a government which had failed to show humanitarian concern for the Irish people and to legislate to prevent such scenes as are described, Carleton assumes an attacking and embittered stance from the outset. Early in the novel Donnel Dhu, the Black Prophet whose sinister presence hangs over the tale but is somehow inadequate as a symbol for the evil of the famine, remarks ominously on the wet weather and overcast sky:

The airth is softened for the grave, an' in the black clouds of heaven you may see the death-hearses movin' slowly along – funeral afther funeral – funeral afther funeral – an' nothin' to folly them but lamentation an' woe, by the widow an' orphan – the fatherless, the motherless, an' the childless – woe an' lamentation – lamentation an' woe.[33]

There is an eerie quality to this litany of anticipated disaster, an effect heightened by the trick of repeated key phrases. It creates a feeling of evil and danger which are all around, from the earth to the sky. The sense of impending doom is complete and chilling, and the grotesquely sensuous image of the soil 'softened for the grave' is especially resonant.

The cheerlessness of the scene is further intensified by the lack of sound across the landscape; even the animals and birds seem subdued by the prevailing mood, and all that is heard are the noises of water flowing, dripping and squelching. Paradoxically there is a kind of sunset, but this is distorted by the other weather conditions and is interpreted as a sinister warning from God of the bad things to come.

Initially the atmosphere of impending evil appears to relate to the curious and intricate events in the plot, many of which are launched in the first few chapters. But Carleton is also busy establishing contrasts between the living conditions of various members of the community he describes. The declining fortunes of the Sullivan family, for example, are illustrated by the squalor and collapse of their house and land, and above all by their scant supply of food: life here is carried on at subsistence level, or below it.

This contrasts with the establishment maintained by Darby Skinadre, a miser, and one of the most successfully created characters in the novel. Skinadre is a cruel symptom of a land where food is scarce and need is great. He has built up a fortune by a steady exploitation of shortage, hoarding his meal and grain supplies until people are desperate, then driving merciless bargains which cannot be refused. His own style of life has all the appearance of frugality and piety, but he is dedicated to grasping avarice, for unlike Carleton's other great study of a miser, Fardorougha, Skinadre is presented as a man already fully committed to his vice rather than one who is increasingly consumed by it.

The symbolic centre of his house is a set of dishonestly balanced scales and weights with which this hypocritically religious fraud weighs out his false measures. His personal harvest season corresponds with the poverty of everyone else, and the greater their hardship the greater his glut of prosperity. Carleton catches the horror of his business perfectly when he calls him

the very Genius of Famine, surrounded by distress, raggedness, feeble hunger, and tottering disease, in all the various aspects of pitiable suffering, hopeless desolation, and that agony of the heart which impresses wildness upon the pale cheek, makes the eye at once dull and eager, parches the mouth, and gives to the voice of misery tones that are hoarse and hollow.[34]

If the degradation and humiliation felt by the tenants on the Castle Cumber estates were distressing, the state of Darby Skinadre's suppliants is outrageous, an affront to all that is decent or humane. Shortage of money is one kind of poverty, but shortage of food is quite another thing, as Carleton knew, and it produces different reactions. No-one is immune to the ravages of hunger, and the people who gather at Skinadre's door represent all sections of the community. They are reduced to begging with a desperate urgency because of the immediate hardship that afflicts them; meanwhile the miser responds to their appeals by urging charity on others and denying his own ability to help.

The potential violence of the situation first manifests itself when young Tom Dalton – having heard of Skinadre's refusal to serve a starving girl, who is, in fact, the mother of his illegitimate child – assaults and half-strangles the extortionist. He forces him to weigh out a measure of meal, but on going to lift it for the girl, Tom himself collapses from sheer exhaustion and weakness, and although he recovers later, the girl dies of similar causes. Meanwhile Skinadre hastily returns the meal to his store chest. This individual gesture of revolt anticipates the wider breakdown of order recorded later as the situation deteriorates further, and more and more people are driven to acts of desperation.

The heightened self-interest and loss of scruple resulting from hunger are movingly portrayed in the account of the wake held for Tom Dalton's dead mistress and infant, in which Carleton describes not only the emaciated physical appearances of the starving people who gather to pay their last respects, but also their zombie-like behaviour and haunted thoughts:

They were all mostly marked also by what appeared to be a feeling of painful abstraction, which, in fact, was nothing else than that abiding desire for necessary food, which in seasons of famine keeps perpetually gnawing, as they term it, at the heart, and pervades the system by that sleepless solicitation of appetite, which, like the presence of guilt, mingles itself up, whilst it lasts, with every thought and action of one's life.[35]

Most pitiful of all are the parents of the dead girl, on whose behalf she had been seeking food at the time of her collapse, because they are incapable of responding with any kind of normality to their loss. Two passions grip them, hunger and grief, and the former is more powerful and obvious. Even as he mourns his child, the old man is found searching the cottage in a hopeless quest for food. Here again Carleton creates an effective image of general suffering out of a specific case.

When famine conditions developed in nineteenth-century Ireland, they were regularly accompanied by outbreaks of cholera and typhus fever. Indeed writers such as Cecil Woodham-Smith in *The Great Hunger* suggest that these diseases caused more actual deaths than malnutrition. In *The Black Prophet* both typhus and cholera are rampant, the former producing a lingering death, the latter striking much more suddenly and devastatingly. These human miseries are reflected in the prevailing gloom of the weather meanwhile on the earth 'the roads were literally black with funerals', and more and more families adopted a desperate nomadic existence that often ended in disease or starvation in the fields or under some temporary shack:

all the lingering traces of self-respect – all recollection of former independence – all sense of modesty was cast to the winds. Under the terrible pressure of the complex destitution which prevailed everything like shame was forgotten, and it was well known that whole families, who had hitherto been respectable and independent, were precipitated, almost at once, into all the common cant of importunity and clamour during this frightful struggle between life and death.[36]

There are well-substantiated accounts of the effects of famine in Ireland from numerous other sources, and the following observations by William Steuart Trench are typical and serve to endorse Carleton's words. Trench was a land agent during the great famine, and here he is writing about the devastation caused by hunger and disease in the region around Kenmare. There the people

died on the roads, and they died in the fields; they died on the mountains, and they died in the glens; they died at the relief works, and they died in their houses; so that little 'streets' or villages were left almost without an inhabitant: and at last some few, despairing of help in the country, crawled into the town, and died at the doors of the residents and outside the Union walls. Some were buried underground, and some were left unburied in the mountains where they died, there being no-one able to bury them.[37]

Trench was not, perhaps, so disposed to sympathize with the predicament of the Irish peasantry as Carleton, but this demonstrates that he too was moved and shocked by what he saw in the 1840s just as the novelist had been by his view of famine earlier in the century.

Carleton and Trench concur on another point. Both state categorically that throughout these times of direst hardship, food supplies were held in reserve by greedy farmers and racketeers. Skinadre is thus a representative rather than a unique figure. Similarly, as is well authenticated, food stuffs were being exported from Ireland, even at the height of these crises. Little wonder, then, that outbreaks of violence and mob rioting should have become increasingly commonplace, and these also form part of the action of *The Black Prophet*, where appropriately enough the property and person of Darby Skinadre provide the targets for one such assault.

The problems of famine, disease, and the iniquitous failure to provide against them are the major issues in *The Black Prophet*, and they are not resolved. Carleton cannot be blamed for this; his aim, in part, was to draw the attention of the political authorities to a specific aspect of the Irish situation, which they alone had the power to take effective action to redress. The irony that the writer himself became, as it were, the Black Prophet of the worst of all the Irish famines adds to the historical force of this strange novel where the fates of the principal characters, the successful unravelling of the various pieces of villainy, and the ultimate preservation and restoration of the innocent and wrongly accused, are much less engaging than the general descriptions of a society stretched beyond its limits and breaking down under pressures of hunger and disease. Even the characters of Mave Sullivan and the unhappy Sarah McGowan, striking as they are in their courage, humanity and personalities, fade from the memory sooner than the evocations of the funereal clouds, the oppressive weather, and the panoramic views of sheer human misery.

In *The Boyne Water* John Banim set out to recapture one of the decisive periods in Irish history, and in *The Black Prophet* Carleton found himself writing a fictional account of another of the great watersheds in the life of the nation. Neither man really succeeded in his task. Banim was partly constrained by events which were already complete, and his plot is too carefully schematized to be wholly satisfactory. The particular famine seasons about which Carleton was writing were also over, although obviously this issue of history was still very much alive, yet he too fails to write the epic novel that the subject might have inspired. He sacrifices the greater cause for the lesser, the 'national calamity', as he calls it in one place, for the parochial skullduggery, and the reader is left with a glimpse of what might have been, and a certain disappointment in what actually was achieved. In his defence Benedict Kiely has observed that while novelists are drawn powerfully to abstract consideration of matters of birth, death, life and the afterlife, few have written of death in the middle of an apparently universal holocaust. Carleton's shortcomings are manifest, but perhaps his rather foolish and halting plot was the necessary device he had to use to place enough distance between himself and his true subject – famine – in order to write at all. Perhaps only an imperfect story could be written amidst such immediate and personal anguish, even by a greater novelist than Carleton. Certainly there is cause to be grateful that he made the attempt, and that he left a book that manages as much as *The Black Prophet*, despite all its limitations.

In *The Emigrants of Ahadarra* (1848) Carleton reconsidered the need for land reform, insisting that, unless and until changes were instituted, the people would never rest content, acts of violence would continue, and emigration would go on increasing. Once again the novelist spoke better than he knew, for although emigration had become quite commonplace in the earlier part of the century, the exodus during the famine years could never have been anticipated. He also took the opportunity of attacking priests of any denomination who turn from their ministry to preaching politics or denouncing political offenders, and, indeed, one of the best scenes records the public shaming of a man by a priest in the presence of his congregation over a political matter.

The heavy-handed and crudely coincidental plot employs all the elements of a typical Carleton melodrama in which the injured innocents are eventually given fair treatment and the rogues are punished according to their misdemeanours. In fact, the title turns out to be a misnomer, for the McMahons, who have been the victims of various schemes to destroy them, are saved from having to emigrate by the timely intervention of their new landlord, Squire Chevydale, and his former political opponent, Major Vanston. The story of the McMahons is used to show how even improving tenants have no immunity from the arbitrary decisions of agents and bad or absentee landlords. Carleton declares that the loss of hardworking tenants 'enfeebles and impoverishes the country, by depriving her of all that approaches to anything like a comfortable and independent yeomanry'.[38] The essential point is that the very poorest people did not constitute the majority of emigrants – they simply could not afford to go; however, those farmers who had succeeded in achieving a modest degree of prosperity, which they then saw threatened by the conditions in the country, chose to leave while they still had enough money to do so. Thus, in many cases, the care of the land was left to the least able, the laziest, or the most destitute peasants.

Carleton is also keen to explain emigration in its social and political context. Earlier novelists had shown absenteeism, mismanagement of estates, exorbitant rents, sub-letting and the dependence of the poor upon the potato as the precursors of disorder, penury and injustice, but now they contribute directly to the flow of people from the land, as if the old consequences are taken a stage further. The involvement of priests in political disputes, and the divisions between the political aspirations of the landlords and those of the common people create additional animosity and tensions, often heightened by the corruption encouraged by the forty-shilling franchise system. On all counts, too, there is repeated evidence of the unwillingness of the English Parliament to legislate against abuses and in the interests of the majority of Irish citizens.

In reply to the charge that the Irish have a predilection for leaving home, Carleton insists that no people are more fondly attached to their native soil, and that the flow of emigrants is evidence only of 'the love of honest industry, enterprise, and independence, by which our countrymen, when not degraded by neglect and poverty, are actuated'.[39] The departure of many, perhaps most, emigrants is enforced by dire necessity and the instinct to survive, rather than being symptomatic of a temperamental wanderlust common to the Irish people as a whole.

In an account of a contested Parliamentary election, Carleton focuses on the forty-shilling franchise for specific criticism, arguing that this 'civil right' did more harm than good in the hands of unscrupulous landlords who manipulated their tenants in order to sustain electoral majorities. The subdivision of already small properties in order to multiply votes certainly did increase the pauper population by eroding the status of the strong farmers, and it created in the long run insupportable numbers of families without means of maintaining themselves. Such people were the most immediate victims of famine and disease, and at best were a wretched burden on the flimsy economic resources of the nation. Carleton concludes that

unless some wholesome and humane principle either of domestic employment or colonial emigration, or perhaps both, shall be adopted, they will continue to embarrass the country, and to drive out of it, always in connexion with other causes, the very class of persons that constitute its remaining strength.[40]

In fact just such a system of subsidized emigration became commonplace during and after the years of the great famine, as, for example, W. S. Trench records in his own dealings with tenants.

The criticism of Irish politics becomes more individual in the account of the treatment meted out to the hero, Bryan McMahon, following his controversial decision to vote for the Protestant candidate Major Vanston. The general abuse to which he is subjected by his neighbours is given impetus and respectability by his public denunciation from the altar, while the words of the priest show the ominous link between politics and religion, and his assumption that a man's creed imposes a moral obligation upon his voting conduct. Echoes of this pulpit rhetoric reverberate down the years:

Little did I think that anyone, bearing the once respectable name of McMahon upon him, should turn from the interests of his holy church, spurn all truth, violate all principle, and enter into a lague of hell with the devil and his enemies of the church. . . . You sould yousself to his agent and representative, Vanston . . . an' if that's not sellin' yourself to the devil, I don't know what is. Judas did the same thing when he betrayed our Saviour – the only difference is – that he got a thirty shilling note – an' God knows it was a beggarly bargain – when his hand was in he ought to have done the thing dacent – and you got the fine taken off you; that's the difference – that's the difference.[41]

The wit and humour of this harangue do not ameliorate its vindictiveness or disguise its abuse of authority, but they typify a style of clerical oratory that was to become – and, at least in some places, still remains – a significant force in influencing the behaviour of voters. This priest is the direct descendant of the fanatical O'Haggerty in *The Boyne Water*. Carleton's character may not carry a sword, but the effect of his words is to have McMahon violently ejected from the church and beaten up.

The episode is much more believable than the book's contrived ending, which enables Carleton to reiterate some of his favourite cautionary verdicts. In a sense he ends in 1848 where he had started almost twenty years before: he appeals for a change of heart and an acceptance of duty by the landlords; he castigates the confusion of politics with religion; he regrets passionately the misery and poverty of the lives of so many of the Irish peasantry; yet he eschews both local and national attempts to reform or radicalize the institutions of government in the country, either by organized agitation or acts of terrorism. Liberal in spirit but conservative in action, he reminds one again of his greater English contemporary, Charles Dickens. Six years after *The Emigrants of Ahadarra*, Dickens published *Hard Times*, and there too the author champions the downtrodden and unrepresented – in this case, the industrial workers; yet the same novel contains a most biased and inadequate account of the Trades' Union movement, the very organization designed to help the people for whom Dickens was concerned. Like Carleton, Dickens also was frightened by a movement which, in his view, threatened the stability of government and the rule of law, unhappy as he was with features of that government and law. Carleton and Dickens were both desirous of greater humanity in the dealings between rulers and people, but both baulked at the political implications, and with every repetition their continued appeals for a change of heart, admirable as they are, become less and less convincing as a practical resolution to major social problems. It may not be an artist's job to find solutions to political problems, but if he chooses political themes and seeks to pronounce upon them, he must be judged according to political criteria.

Carleton never lost his peasant cunning, his basic will to survive, and his capacity to be almost ruthlessly self-interested. Even in the novels where he is most scathing about the abuses within Irish society, he is always ready in the end to hold out an olive branch to the authorities. Often this seems a betrayal of what has gone before, but it is rather a function of his essential opportunism, the same quality that launched him on his literary career almost by accident. This is the quality, too, which Sean O'Faolain has detected throughout the career of that political giant of the period Daniel O'Connell, and which, as he points out, in another man might have made him one of the villains of history. Yet for all his self-interest, his endless attempts to curry favour and earn for himself a government pension, his increasingly embittered complaints against the ingratitude of the Irish people towards him, and the loneliness he experienced in his later years, Carleton never lost touch with his origins among the peasantry of Co. Tyrone. His stories and the best of his novels are always redeemed, even if only intermittently, by the sure knowledge with which he writes of the lives of the Irish, and specifically the small farmers and tenants of Ulster. The wit, humour, extravagance, mirth, poverty and desperate hardship he recorded in his tales are so vivid and convincing because they are not contrived or imagined; rather they are written out of the heartfelt experience of the novelist. On these aspects of Irish life Carleton could not go wrong, for he wrote as himself, and no writer of the period is his equal. Asked by Francis Davis, a journalist for the *Nation*, whether his characters were imaginary or real, Carleton replied:

I found them . . . some at school or at college, or amid the lanes and hill-sides of my native Tyrone. I found them at Mass, in 'stations', and pilgrimages, in dances and diversions, and in the company of the priests.[42]

When he endeavoured to reach for greater and more complex achievements, he usually fell foul of other pressures and influences which were bad for him as an artist, but which it is impossible to see how he could have escaped. Perhaps the real tragedy was his failure to understand how rich and how good was his early *Traits and Stories*, especially after he had shed the influence of Caesar Otway, and his continuing need to try to prove himself within conventions of fiction to which he was never suited. In his old age Carleton seems to have recognized the uniqueness of his own position, and the fact that the literary future of Ireland would inevitably be different, for he wrote in 1863 to Dr T. C. S. Corry that

The only three names which Ireland can point to with pride are Griffin's, Banim's, and – do not accuse me of vanity when I say it – my own. Banim and Griffin are gone, and I will soon follow them – ultimus Romanorum, and after that will come a lull, an obscurity of perhaps half a century, when a new condition of civil society and a new phase of manners and habits among the people – for this is a transition state – may introduce new fields and new tastes for other writers, for in this manner the cycles of literature and taste appear, hold their day, displace each other, and make room for others.[43]

In this self-assessment and prophecy at least, Carleton's judgment proved to be just and accurate. It is surely fitting that he should have had the last word.

EIGHT

CONCLUSION: THE PROBLEMS AND SUCCESSES OF THE FIRST FIFTY YEARS

> At last we are beginning to see what we are, and what is our destiny.
>
> Thomas Davis
> (1845)

The achievements of the first fifty years of Anglo-Irish fiction may appear modestly undistinguished in comparison with the best English or European novels of the period, and marred by inadequacies and frequent awkwardness of both subject and style. The case proves the truth of Dr Johnson's maxim that time is the ultimate test of what is finest and most enduring in literature. Most of the novels considered here have long been out of print in popular editions, and the situation is not likely to alter significantly. Indeed there are those who would question the whole point of bothering about these writers. The question contains its own answer, for as T. S. Eliot wrote:

> no artist of any art, has his complete meaning alone. His significance, his appreciation is the appreciation of his relation to the dead poets and artists. You cannot value him alone; you must set him, for contrast and comparison, among the dead.[1]

The great Anglo-Irish writers of this century have their literary forbears, and if Anglo-Irish literature has its own characteristics which set it apart from the mainstream of English literature, then they have specifically Irish literary predecessors. And among these must be numbered the early Anglo-Irish novelists.

This fact is all the more easily forgotten or neglected just because of the prestigious reputation of later writers, and the meteoric rise of Anglo-Irish literature to universal attention. It seems astonishing now to find Thomas MacDonagh declaring in 1916 that

> this is an age of beginnings rather than of achievements; for a hundred years now writers in this land have been translating, adapting,

experimenting – working as the writers of the sixteenth century worked in many countries.[2]

Yet his statement emphasizes how very suddenly the status of Anglo-Irish literature changed, and also acknowledges the long period of artistic journeyman work which preceded the flowering of the early twentieth century.

There is a need to define the contribution made by the early Anglo-Irish novelists to their successors, to trace the links from the past to the present, to try and understand the present in terms of the past. It is useful to start by acknowledging what is perhaps the central fact about the work of the early writers: their stumbling attempts to write in a foreign language, and at the same time to shape that language and impose their own Irish identity upon it. Here above all was their legacy to later generations. By the late eighteenth century the Irish language was in an advanced state of crisis. English was establishing itself irresistibly as the first language in the land, but it had still to become the vehicle of native literary expression. Yeats once wrote that 'there is no fine nationality without literature and . . . there is no fine literature without nationality': and, as if unconsciously they realized this, the early Anglo-Irish novelists and poets began to write in the once foreign language.[3] They may not have produced much 'fine literature', but they were taking the necessary steps that would enable others to do so in the fullness of time.

Several of these writers – particularly Maria Edgeworth, Lady Morgan, Charles Maturin and Mrs Hall – used a language that is closely similar to that of their English contemporaries; but their actual subject-matter introduced a new regional emphasis and, more specifically, made Ireland and Irish characters acceptable in fiction. The problem of writing in English for novelists such as the Banims, Griffin and Carleton may be interpreted at one level as a matter of basic skill and confidence: the English were writing within a tradition that was already well established and accepted, whereas the Irish were endeavouring to graft themselves onto that tradition. When they did succeed in adding an original dimension to literature written in English, it was only after they had mastered what MacDonagh calls 'the plenary use of the English language'.[4] That is to say, Anglo-Irish literature could only become a full and individual expression of Irish life and manners when the population in general and the writers in particular had mastered both spoken and literary English. (On these grounds, MacDonagh rejects the so-called Anglo-Irish literature of the eighteenth century because it is not an expression of the dominant culture of the period by its typical representatives.) From the outset English spoken and written by the Irish has varied from that employed in England. Thus, for instance, the voices of Thady Quirk and Terence Oge O'Leary show how, despite other literary influences, Maria Edgeworth and Lady Morgan *listened* to the Irish speaking English and responded sensitively to the peculiarities of their speech. The reasons for these variations are complex, perhaps even indeterminable in certain respects.

Not only are there differences of idiom, but the rhythms and even the syntax of an Irishman's English are quite distinctive. Clearly this owes much to the Gaelic influence which lingered on long after Irish had ceased to be the common language. Furthermore, whereas in England by the start of the nineteenth century, there was a well established tradition of literary culture, in Ireland this was not the case. The Irish for the most part had recorded their experience not in written, but in oral, forms – the seanachies and bards who recited or sang their stories, poems and histories were the key figures in Irish culture rather than the literary poet, the dramatist or the novelist. Naturally, when the early novelists came to write, they were influenced by this background. This may be especially obvious with Carleton whose *Traits and Stories* begins as a series of tales told beside the fire in Ned McKeown's bar, but there are also Gerald Griffin's stories which revolve to greater or lesser extent around well-known annual feasts – Candlemas, St Stephen's Day, St John's Eve, St Patrick's Day, May Day, Christmas Day, St Bridget's Day, Palm Sunday. Similarly the early works of the Banims were conceived of as a set of stories that might easily have been narrated rather than written. It is reasonable to speculate that the oral tradition with which these writers must all have been familiar may have added to their problems in creating effective plots, but it also may have contributed to their frequent success in writing vivid dialogue. The episodic or loosely constructed plot which may be perfectly adequate to the needs of a seanachie will not necessarily withstand the closer scrutiny given by readers of novels. On the other hand, dialogue, and the spoken word in all its forms, has particular value and richness in a culture where oral traditions are of primary importance; and Anglo-Irish literature has always been characterized by its colloquial energy.

Nor is the linguistic background to Anglo-Irish literature the only feature which distinguishes it from its English counterpart. The entire social, political, economic and religious *milieux* of the two nations were decisively different, and this prompted the oft-repeated desire to define and explain these differences to the English, as well as to articulate them for the Irish themselves. Gerald Griffin suggests the success of this enterprise when, in his conclusion to the *Tales of the Munster Festivals*, he remarked that

The Irish peasant has, by a combination of circumstances become better known within the last few years to his English ruler, than he had been since the conquest. . . . One fact is now generally known and admitted by candid men, – that the Irish peasant possesses in a high degree, all those qualities which are considered essential to the formation of a good and useful member of society. The very extravagance of his excesses, while they increase the passion of the true philanthropist, must also confirm the hope of an easy amelioration of his condition.[5]

But much of the fiction was gravely compromised by the tension of trying at the same time to arouse the interest, understanding and sympathy of the English, and to give new literary form to emotions and aspirations of the Irish people. When the appeal to the English dominated a writer, then he or she was most likely to ape English forms, values and styles, as for example with Maria Edgeworth, Lady Morgan, Maturin, Mrs Hall, and sometimes with Griffin and Carleton; but when the writers were able, if not to forget, then at least to discipline their need to attract English attention, their writing has the originality and power of a language reshaped to convey their own experience. This is found in the best passages and stories of Carleton, Griffin and the Banims.

The most productive years for the early novelists correspond closely to the periods of greatest political activity and social upheaval. Three main phases may be determined, the first coming in the aftermath of the 1798 uprising and the Act of Union; the second during the years of O'Connell's mounting campaign for Catholic emancipation; and the third overlapping with the Repeal movement, the launching of the *Nation* newspaper and the Young Ireland movement, and the great famine. Behind these significant Irish developments lie two eruptions of much more general import on European life and thought: the American War of Independence and the French Revolution. Despite its remoteness from the centre of the action, Ireland did not remain untouched by the philosophies of freedom, national independence and self-respect generated abroad. The story of Wolfe Tone, who was obliged to live in America for a time, and who supported the ideals of the French Revolution and courted its leaders to persuade them of the appropriateness of landing in Ireland, is well known. Tone's thought, his awareness of what might be achieved in Ireland, was far in advance of the readiness or understanding of the majority of his countrymen; but the desire for change, for liberty, for an end to the old order, which he voiced coherently, was stimulated and born among many people in a much less specific and clearcut way.

Georg Lukács has claimed that the French Revolution first made history a mass experience, and he goes on to comment on the upsurge of national feeling and the desire for national independence which were active, especially, in the period between 1789 and 1814. He asserts that

the appeal to national independence and national character is necessarily connected with a reawakening of national history, with memories of the past, of past greatness, of moments of national dishonour, whether this results in a progressive or a reactionary ideology.[6]

The truth of this in Ireland is clearly seen in the fictional accounts of events leading up to the 1798 uprising: in, for example, *The O'Briens and the O'Flahertys* and, above all, in the opening pages of Michael Banim's *The Croppy*. These same accounts also make plain that, although English rule in Ireland may have been – however briefly – 'ripe for shaking', the Irish were not of one mind to carry out the task.

A triumph of early Anglo-Irish fiction is its exposure of the sources of social division and religious antagonism in the country. Additionally *The Boyne Water* endeavours to place nineteenth-century tensions in their long-term historical perspective, and in so doing sheds light on past and present alike. The quest to understand and interpret the relationships between the events of history and current reality may have been John Banim's particular concern, but his brother Michael, Gerald Griffin, William Carleton, Lady Morgan and Maria Edgeworth also based much of their work on conditions in the mid and late eighteenth century. Even Charles Lever resorted to this period in certain of his more serious novels, and Le Fanu, too, placed his fiction in earlier times. In a word, history, whether recent or of a more distant period, is a notable influence *and subject* in many of the novels written between 1800 and 1850. Furthermore this act of turning to the past is inseparable from the endeavours of the nineteenth-century novelists and poets to recreate an idea of Irish national identity through literature, in rather the same way as the popular political leaders attempted a like task through reform or rebellion at intervals throughout the period.

To assert and rediscover national identity when the independence of the Irish was almost wholly eroded and their humiliation greatest was indeed a challenge. Not surprisingly the early novelists found it a formidable and obsessive task, and their level of success was very mixed. If their fiction often seems to strike a defensive note – justifying the behaviour and temperament of the Irish people – this is a reflection of lost confidence. Perhaps it may even indicate a national inferiority complex born of years of systematic oppression and defeat. At its most demoralized it has all the marks of the literature of enslavement, projecting images of a people who are engagingly irresponsible, quaint and quarrelsome in their conduct, contradictory in their moods and opinions, ingratiating and fawning in their attitudes to outsiders or their social superiors, and woefully ignorant of anything more than the immediate conditions of their lives. Peasants who display most or all of these characteristics appear in the novels of Maria Edgeworth, Lady Morgan, Mrs Hall and Samuel Lover. At best they are viewed with a condescending charity; at worst as treacherous, dishonest and idle. Significantly the one true peasant among the early novelists, William Carleton, provides a more complete view of the negative, destructive and dangerous aspect of the Irish peasant's mentality than these other writers who were distanced from him by background and experience. Carleton knew not only the love and affection of Jemmy McEvoy's family, but also the desperate barbarism of Paddy Devaun and his cronies; not only the eccentricity of Phelim O'Toole, but also the cruelty of Valentine McClutchy.

The best English novels of the period introduce a much wider range of interests, and generally contain more complex and profound explorations of character and morality than their Irish counterparts. This locates a key thematic difference between nineteenth-century fiction in the two countries, for the Irish were only beginning to answer questions of national identity which were well established certainties for the English, and which they felt no need to debate endlessly. The abolition of the Irish Parliament, the erosion of the power of the Protestant nation, and the growing strength and self-consciousness of the Catholics throughout these fifty years gave to national identity an added interest and new directions. But the subject also limited the scope of early Anglo-Irish novels. This is apparent in the work of all the novelists of the time.

The writers demonstrate that the question of Irish nationality was essentially one of who owned and controlled the land, for if there is any truth in the old adage that an Englishman's home is his castle, then its complement must be that an Irishman's plot of land is the measure of his identity. Thus references to the land and the landscape are a recurrent source of image and allusion to describe the state of the nation. Land hunger was a prime motivating force for most of the subversive organizations which flourished among the peasantry throughout the period, and the greed and unfairness of the landlords and their agents in managing the land are the direct cause for many of the horrific acts of vengeance recorded in the novels. Without a plot capable of supporting his family, a peasant was condemned to the most insecure and vulnerable existence, while the position of the small-holder was little better because, as the novelists again record, there was often no incentive to improve property, and in any case the gales and tithes payable to agents, landlords and the Established Church placed crippling restrictions upon him.

Ironically the problems of the land did not rest simply with the poor and the exploited, but also with the large estate owners. If nineteenth-century Anglo-Irish fiction tells on the one hand of the miseries and injustices of the peasantry, its accompanying preoccupation is the decline and collapse of the gentry. The same inability or lack of interest in managing their land efficiently or fairly which produced peasant unrest was an immediate cause of the ruin which overtook so many of the once great landlords. Maria Edgeworth grasped this with prophetic clarity when she wrote *Castle Rackrent*, and in novel after novel which followed, other writers re-affirmed her vision. Because the truth of these pictures of decline is so self-evident, the figure of a reforming landlord introduced to provide a happy ending to many tales is utterly unconvincing. There *were* good landlords who were genuine in their concern for their tenants; the Edgeworths were a shining example of this. But then the Edgeworths were not absentees, nor did they suddenly arrive on their property to the general acclaim of the peasantry to begin a series of immediate reforms. Whatever they achieved by way of improvement was the result of a painstaking process.

The problem of the unsatisfactory ending through the introduction of a benevolent landlord points to another difficulty faced by the early Anglo-Irish novelists – the audience for whom they were writing. Given the general ignorance and unfamiliarity with a literary culture in Ireland, aspiring writers naturally turned to London for a publisher. Maria Edgeworth, Lady Morgan and Charles Maturin found English publishers, and John Banim and Gerald Griffin eked out straitened existences as journalists and would-be creative writers in London. The consequences of this English connection are complex. According to John Banim it created the 'necessity of endeavouring, cautiously and laboriously, to make fiction the vehicle of fact', in order to persuade the foreign reader to adopt a more understanding attitude to the Irish.[7] It also imposed problems of intelligibility, of ensuring that the appeal of these regional novels was not diminished by the obscurity of the colloquial dialogue or of details of life described in them. The novelists attempted to resolve these difficulties by providing notes and parentheses designed to enlighten a foreign audience.[8] The issue was not only one of intelligibility, but also of humouring English readers, and this is where the contrived endings are relevant. The Anglo-Irish novelists were in a paradoxical situation: they were laying bare the truth of injustice, exploitation and government-backed sectarianism, and at the same time they were seeking sympathy from the very people against whom the accusations were made, if only by implication; small wonder, then, that they never really found a fictional means to cope with this situation. Ironically, for all they achieved by way of changing opinion significantly, they might as well have abandoned their cautiousness and spoken their minds freely.

The deep social, religious, political and cultural divisions within Irish society itself added further complications to the writers' task. Their attempts to find or create unity amidst such deep-seated contradictions may often seem forced and false, but the task was crucial, and it paved the way for what one critic has called 'a new, synthetic culture . . . created by the nationalism of the late nineteenth century and the artistic leadership of Yeats and his friends in the Celtic Revival'.[9] The efforts of the Banims, Griffin and Carleton in this particular direction give them pre-eminence among the first generation of Anglo-Irish novelists, and make them at least the spiritual brothers of the Young Irelanders with their ideal of a unified nation-state, where the aspirations of each group within it would be informed by a wish to serve the common good of all.

The same cannot be said of Maria Edgeworth, important as she clearly is, particularly in the development of regional fiction. *Castle Rackrent* is a masterpiece of its kind, and her subsequent Irish novels each introduce characters and themes that have obvious successors in later work by other writers. Yet Maria Edgeworth's social position and her English background and relation to English culture and literature set her apart from the novelists who come after her. Furthermore her Anglo-Irish novels form only a small part of her total output, and she wrote with at least as much ease in the traditions of the English eighteenth-century novel. The same cannot be said of the native Irish writers who, when they tried to follow suit, are at their most tortuous.

Daniel Corkery spoke of Maria Edgeworth as a colonial novelist seeking to explain 'the quaintness of the humankind of this land, especially the native humankind, to another humankind that was not quaint, that was standard, normal'.[10] There is undoubtedly a sense in which this is true, although when Corkery speaks of colonial writers – and presumably he is not making a special allowance for Maria Edgeworth – being 'condemned' to a strange land, he appears to overstate his case. Her affection and concern for her tenants and her enduring love of Ireland are summed up in lines she wrote a few days before her death to her sister Honora Beaufort:

> Ireland, with all thy faults, thy follies too,
> I love thee still: still with a candid eye must view
> Thy wit, too quick, still blundering into sense,
> Thy reckless humour: sad improvidence,
> And even what sober judges follies call,
> I, looking at the Heart, forget them all![11]

These are hardly the words of an estranged and resentful colonial.

Perhaps Maria Edgeworth's greatest contribution to Anglo-Irish literature was that she showed it was possible to write about a people and a country traditionally regarded by the English with contempt or patronage when they bothered to regard them at all, and to do so in an engaging way. Her achievement is of inestimable significance, and in her continual references to the need for good land management, she singles out the abiding theme of nineteenth-century Anglo-Irish fiction. As a daughter of the Big House her perspective on this subject is predictably different from that of, say, William Carleton, but this does not invalidate it. Finally, with *Castle Rackrent*, Maria Edgeworth produced not only a pioneering novel, but the most artistically perfect specimen of Anglo-Irish fiction for many decades to come.

The process of establishing an English market and audience for this new breed of fiction was carried on by Lady Morgan, who today is among the least remembered of the first generation of Anglo-Irish novelists. She never wrote with the accomplishment of Maria Edgeworth at her best, nor with the passion and intensity of the Banims, Griffin and Carleton, yet she deserves her place in the story. Her romantic disposition, which eventually led her to self-imposed exile, infuses her books with a distinctive spirit of nationalism, and makes her a contributor to the growth of a mode of thought and feeling about Ireland that grew in importance throughout the century. If Lady Morgan's fiction seems more remote than that of some of her fellow writers, this may be partly explained by the subsequent fate of that romantic point of view. Her chosen symbols of ancient Ireland – ruined halls and castles, harps, and fragments of Irish culture, dress and conduct – were used so extensively by later writers that to the modern sensibility they are little more than clichés from which it is now necessary to escape. Difficult as it may be to accept the fact, in Lady Morgan's novels these symbols were not regarded as debased but were active stimuli to the imaginations of numerous artists.

Maturin was less missionary in his nationalism than Lady Morgan, his chief interest being the complexities of human emotions and sensibilities. His repeated formula of bringing together lovers of Irish and English backgrounds inevitably throws into relief certain cultural and temperamental differences between the two races, and leads on occasion to a broader view of the situation in Ireland as a result of English rule.

But it is the novels of the Banim brothers which launched Anglo-Irish fiction on a wholly new phase. Their work first gives full expression to the native Irish influence and offers the earliest attempts to produce an original species of fiction with its own unique characteristics resulting from a combination of the traditions of the realistic novel and the highly imaginative, almost visionary otherworldliness of Gaelic folklore and traditions.[12] The practical consequences of drawing on two such different sources of inspiration are seen in the ease and unselfconsciousness with which the tales move between the levels of hard political or economic reality and the impact of superstition and the supernatural. Both kinds of experience are commonly represented in the same story; thus there are the fairy powers attributed to Crohoore, or the mysterious behaviour of Oona in *The Boyne Water*, and yet these novels also deal with events which are wholly realistic. Similarly a tale like *The Fetches* is entirely dependent on belief in a particular superstition, while *The Ghost-Hunter* is an involved saga of murder and conspiracy that rests upon the hero's belief in ghosts and the general superstitions and fears of the community as a whole when confronted with an apparently inexplicable event. Even lighter works such as *The Mayor of Windgap* and *The Bit o' Writin'* incorporate elements from the world of folklore and superstition and blend them with scenes of conventional realism. From the reader's point of view the vital necessity is that he should accept both types of experience with an equal degree of seriousness. That is to say, he must not allow himself to be convinced that the slaughter of Anthony Dooling and his wife was an horrific deed, and then reject the terror felt by the peasants when Crohoore appears briefly in their midst, and their belief that he could fairy blast them, as incredible or farfetched. Both reactions were real for John and Michael Banim and for the kind of people about whom they were writing. Indeed what a modern reader may be inclined to dismiss as the unreal world was often, precisely because of its unpredictable and uncontrollable nature, a far more frightening type of reality than the realm of material objects and observable experience.

In this process of drawing together the diverse worlds of material fact and supernatural belief, the Banims forged one of the chief distinguishing features of much Anglo-Irish fiction, and they revealed something fundamental about the Irish temperament which had not been grasped by their predecessors. Mark D. Hawthorne argues that for Irish readers this fiction reflected the contradictions of the society in which they lived:

its lack of respect for English law, its fierce temper, its intense sense of justice, its tenderness and deep affection, its drunkenness and its sober faith, its wide diversity of behaviour.[13]

On the other hand, for an English audience the Banims presented a series of insights into the Irish character and the experience of being Irish which had no real precedent. They also extended the range of fiction by their mixture of actuality and wonder, a mixture which had existed previously only in popular Gothic romances, and seldom, if ever, as part of the portrayal of ordinary men and women, especially those of humble origins.

The writing of the Banim brothers is, above all, the first real expression of Irish nationality in English fiction. This state-ment is not equally true of every novel and story. In many places there emerges the defensively aggressive tone of nationalist, as opposed to national, literature. At their best, however, they create successfully the speech and manner of a particular place, people and experience, and they do so to a greater extent and in a less self-conscious way than Maria Edgeworth, Lady Morgan or Charles Maturin, because they were closer to the lives of the ordinary Irish people. Their attempts to develop and exploit a vocabulary, syntax, rhythms and subject-matter reflecting the real attitudes of the Irish to each other and to the world were necessarily defective or inadequate on many occasions. The same is true of Gerald Griffin and William Carleton, while the other novelists – Lover, Lever, Mrs Hall – never really addressed themselves to these artistic problems. Even so the incompleteness of their success should not obscure the fact that they recognized and sought to resolve the difficulties of forging a genuine national literature, a distinctive type of fiction. There is after all much truth in T. S. Eliot's declaration that 'no man can invent a form, create a taste for it, and perfect it too.'[14] The Banims, Griffin and Carleton demonstrate this as much by their shortcomings as by their achievements.

W. B. Yeats perceived the essential place of the early novelists for later generations of Irish readers. In a letter written in 1895 to the editor of the *Daily Express*, he comments specifically on two novels – John Banim's *The*

Nowlans and Carleton's *Fardorougha the Miser*. These works, he says,

> can only have been prevented from taking their place as great literature because the literary tradition of Ireland was, when Carleton and Banim wrote, so underdeveloped that a novelist, no matter how great the genius, found no fit convention ready to his hands, and no exacting public to forbid him to commingle noisy melodrama with his revelations. England can afford to forget these books, but we cannot, for with all their imperfections they contain the most memorable records yet made of Irish habits and passions.[15]

Despite all that has happened since 1895, Yeats's statement stands; relatively inferior as such novels may be, they are a genuine part of what has subsequently become a great tradition.

The case of Gerald Griffin has its own individual characteristics. The problem of audience is particularly acute in his fiction, but it is part of the larger problem of the contradictory pressures under which he laboured. This conflict is itself recurrent in the lives and work of many Anglo-Irish artists, most famously, perhaps, in the case of James Joyce, but also in writers such as Shaw and O'Casey. It amounts to an inability to reconcile artistic vision and honesty with the values, politics, religious beliefs and conservatism of Irish society. John Cronin, Griffin's recent biographer, has argued persuasively that his subject is an early example of the talented writer-in-exile with whom all students of Anglo-Irish literature are familiar. Where Joyce left Ireland to break from Catholicism at least far enough to survive as an artist, Griffin went in the opposite direction, forsaking fiction in favour of the Church. The personal conflict is also a representative one, and is most successfully captured by Griffin in the dichotomy between Kyrle Daly and Hardress Cregan. Thus *The Collegians* has at its very core a crisis recognizable to many Irish readers, and this may help to explain its contemporary popularity and the affection with which it was long regarded.

Nor was his success limited to the particular story of Daly and Cregan. *The Collegians* encapsulates a fuller, more complete view of Irish society than any other novel of its time; and above all it conveys a sense of cultural confusion which is unique in early Anglo-Irish fiction. This vision also informs *Tracy's Ambition* where so many of the tensions and contradictions of nineteenth-century rural Ireland are laid bare through the dilemma – part personal, part environmental – of the central character. Tracy, writes John Cronin, inhabits 'a moral no-man's land which Griffin charts with instinctive skill'.[16] The phrase is well chosen, because for Griffin, perhaps more than for any of his contemporaries, the problem of national identity was essentially a moral question. With the possible exception of John Nowlan, it is Griffin's heroes, especially Hardress Cregan and Abel Tracy, who are faced with moral choices of the kind common enough in English fiction of the period, but rare in the early Anglo-Irish novel. This may be what prompted Yeats's opinion that Griffin could have written like an Englishman if he had wanted, and that he sought to be Irish on purpose. On this occasion, however, Yeats did not notice all that is there, for the unflagging affection for the countryside and the sure knowledge of the divided society from which he came suggest that in his own way Griffin, like the Banims and Carleton, did indeed write out of 'the necessity of his blood'.[17]

The truth of this appears all the stronger when the fiction of any of these writers is compared with the novels and tales of Mrs Hall, Samuel Lover and Charles Lever. The earnestness and good intentions of Mrs Hall are beyond question, but her moral purposes governed her creativity in a negative way. She presents carefully selected, edited and arranged episodes of life set against an Irish background, as opposed to a revelation of indigenous Irish life. Carleton once boasted that the superiority of his peasant characters to those of Mrs Hall resulted from the fact that he had been drunk in the company of such people whereas she had not. The brag is not as inane as it might appear to be at first sight. Mrs Hall wanted to cultivate greater gentility, refinement, organization and providence amongst the Irish poor. Her Victorian sensibility was offended by their dirt, wildness, lack of thrift and pre-dilection for violence. Unable to surrender herself and to feel unselfconsciously as a native Irish person would feel or think, she approached fiction in the spirit of a preacher – sincere in her charitable concern, but convinced that she was there to help change the people about whom she wrote, rather than to represent them or learn from them.

With Samuel Lover and Charles Lever, Anglo-Irish fiction tends to become popular entertainment for a specifically foreign audience. Even allowing for Lever's greater seriousness in his less well-known novels, there is still a discernible difference between the work of these writers and that of their predecessors or of Carleton. Here comedy becomes self-parody, the deliberate cult of the charming and quixotic which often panders to the stereotyped English view of Irish buffoonery and wildness. But the characters in these novels are emasculated, passionless, often thoughtless and reduced to figures of fun. This is not fiction concerned with 'the reality of experience' or with forging 'the uncreated conscience' of the Irish people.[18] Likening Lover and Lever to the poet William Allingham, Yeats observed that the weakness common to all three was apparent in the flippant attitude they adopted towards the people, and that in this respect they are not national writers, but exploiters of Ireland and 'Irishness' as mere ploys to amuse outsiders, whereas Carleton wrote out of the immediate painfulness and joys of lived experience.

This immediacy, accompanied by an astonishing wealth of detail, gives the Ulsterman's best work its unique distinction. Furthermore his peasant background was the enabling factor which freed his tales from the misunderstanding and incomprehension of the ordinary people that marred the writing of his contemporaries and predecessors. This is why John Montague has asserted that 'almost singlehanded' Carleton 'effected a literary discovery of the Irish people'.[19] He goes on to suggest that this achievement has no real complement until the appearance of Liam O'Flaherty and Patrick Kavanagh in this century, but since so much had changed irreparably in the interim, in a sense Carleton has no direct heirs. Ironically the tales and stories, which revealed a way of life with unprecedented fullness and instinctive assurance, are not only a celebration but also an obituary. The processes of change which had already started to erode the old traditions, language and values of the Irish peasant were accelerated by the pressure of events in the first half of the century, so that after the famine in the 1840s, there was much that was unrecognizable to the older members of the community. Even within his own lifetime Carleton the story teller was transformed into Carleton the social historian, and his fiction is itself reflective of the changes.

1850 is not an entirely arbitrary date with which to conclude this study. Historically it marks the conclusion of some of the worst years in the troubled story of Ireland. The period that followed was, inevitably, a gradual re-emergence from the suffering, loss and changes brought about by the famine. In the short term it was not distinguished by a political leader of O'Connell's stature, by an idealist of Thomas Davis's vision, or by a novelist of Carleton's eminence. Although he lived on until 1869 Carleton's significant contribution to Anglo-Irish fiction, with the exception of his unfinished *Autobiography*, was already complete by the mid-century. Even in this fact his life and career seem representative of the enormous alteration that took place in Ireland, and which left him stranded, cut off from his roots until he returned to them one last time by delving back into his own early days. Then he was true to what he knew with incomparable and incontestable authority.

Thus 1850 is also the point at which it may be said with some accuracy that Anglo-Irish fiction ended the first phase of its existence as an art form. From Maria Edgeworth through to William Carleton there was an overlapping of the careers and publications of the novelists. After this there is a distinct hiatus, and when the next Anglo-Irish prose fiction writers began to make their names, they belonged to a different generation: Charles Kickham, Somerville and Ross, George Moore, Canon Sheehan, and, supremely, James Joyce. These were new talents responding to new times, but behind them lay the solid achievements and the modest tradition pioneered by a disparate group of writers who had by their own efforts created a mode of expression where none had existed before. Eudoxus, one of the spokesmen in Edmund Spenser's *A View of the State of Ireland*, pronounced that 'it hath ever been the use of the conqueror, to despise the language of the conquered, and to force him by all means to learn his'.[20] The novelists in the first half of the nineteenth century had demonstrated that even when 'the conqueror' had been successful in imposing his language, 'the conquered' still retained enough initiative and independence to adapt it into an individual idiom.

In his Preface to *John Bull's Other Island*, Bernard Shaw wrote:

A conquered nation is like a man with cancer: he can think of nothing else, and is forced to place himself in the hands of quacks who profess to treat or cure cancer. . . . Nationalism stands between Ireland and the light of the world. . . . A healthy nation is as unconscious of its nationality as a healthy man of his bones. But if you break a nation's nationality it will think of nothing else but getting it set again.[21]

There are certainly moments in the fiction of this period when the conscious need to assert Irish national identity as a subject in its own right seems to be obsessive. The tendency is especially obvious when the tone of the writing is half apologetic, almost pleading for acceptance. In these cases the wisdom of Shaw's remarks is apparent; the attitude indicates ill-health. Perhaps only Carleton – and there again, only in certain places – achieves the freedom from self-conscious nationalism that Shaw holds up as indicative of full health. This happens when the writer is taken over wholly by his story, when it runs away with him and he tells it with the spontaneity of a man talking to his friends over a drink, at the market, or after Mass. Then Carleton is a national writer, an Irishman relating his tale in his own way, but without the felt necessity of having to draw attention to the fact.

Daniel Corkery accused most Anglo-Irish literature of failing 'to speak the secret things in the nation's soul', and of selling itself out to the type of yarns that appeal to foreigners.[22] This dilemma did confront all the early novelists to greater or lesser extent, yet even Corkery goes on to suggest that the student who wishes to encounter the interplay of the three forces which he distinguishes as primary influences upon 'the Irish national being' – the religious consciousness of the people, Irish nationalism, and the land – must turn back to men like Carleton and the Banims.[23] These writers, he maintains, for all their clumsiness, were less compromised and confused than some of their successors who were not as intimately involved in their subject-matter. The argument is provocative, as it was intended to be, but it is also a reminder of a debt to the past which is so often ignored or unrecognized. Although some of their material may be history that is complete, in many of their themes, attitudes, moods and contradictions these novels and stories are living links with contemporary Anglo-Irish literature. W. B. Yeats said that:

The old men tried to make one see life plainly but all written down in a kind of fiery shorthand that it might never be forgotten.[24]

To ignore that 'fiery shorthand' is to deny a small but significant stage in Irish cultural evolution; and to be the poorer for it.

NOTES

Chapter 1: *Castle Rackrent* to the death of Maturin (1800–1824)

1 Robert Kee, *The Green Flag* (London: Weidenfeld & Nicolson, 1973), p. 169.
2 James Newcomer, *Maria Edgeworth* (Lewisburg: Bucknell University Press, 1973), p. 66.
3 Maria Edgeworth, *Castle Rackrent* (London: J. Johnson, 1800), p. 28.
4 H. R. Krans, *Irish Life in Irish Fiction* (New York: Columbia University Press, 1903), p. 29.
5 These points are argued by Roger McHugh, 'Maria Edgeworth's Irish Novels', in *Studies* (December 1938), pp. 556–70.
6 Thomas Flanagan, *The Irish Novelists 1800–1850* (New York: Columbia University Press, 1959), pp. 119–20.
7 Lady Morgan, *Memoirs: Autobiography, Diaries and Correspondence*, 2 vols. arr. by W. Hepworth Dixon (London: W. H. Allen, 1863), I, p. 40.
8 Lionel Stevenson, *The Wild Irish Girl* (London: Chapman and Hall, 1936), p. 68.
9 Lady Morgan, *Memoirs*, I, pp. 277–78.
10 Lady Morgan, *The Wild Irish Girl* (London: Phillips, 1806), I, p. 37.
11 Lionel Stevenson, *The Wild Irish Girl*, p. 73.
12 Lady Morgan, *The Wild Irish Girl*, I, p. 114.
13 *Ibid.*, II, pp. 52–53. The matter of the blocked windows is based on the actual conduct of a well-known Connaught man, the MacDermott of Coolavin.
14 *Ibid*, II, p. 54.
15 *Ibid.*, I, p. 136.
16 *Ibid.*, III, pp. 58–59.
17 *Ibid.*, III, p. 261.
18 *Ibid.*, III, p. 262.
19 *Ibid.*, III, pp. 262–64.
20 Lady Morgan, *The Wild Irish Girl*, revised edition (London: H. Colburn, 1846), p. xxv.
21 Maria Edgeworth, *Tales of Fashionable Life* (London: J. Johnson, I–III, 1809, IV–VI, 1812), I, pp. 36–37.
22 *Ibid.*, I, p. 37.
23 *Ibid.*, I, p. 39.
24 *Ibid.*, I, pp. 61–62.
25 *Ibid.*, I, pp. 62–63.
26 *Ibid.*, I, p. 158.

27 *Ibid.*, V, pp. 376, 247–48.
28 *Ibid.*, VI, p. 71.
29 *Ibid.*, VI, p. 84.
30 *Ibid.*, VI, p. 122.
31 *Ibid.*, VI, pp. 162–63.
32 *Ibid.*, VI, p. 218.
33 *Ibid.*, VI, pp. 298–99.
34 *Ibid.*, VI, p. 466.
35 Lady Morgan, *O'Donnel* (London: H. Colburn, 1814, revised 1835), p. viii.
36 Lady Morgan, *O'Donnel* (London: H. Colburn, 1814), I, p. ix.
37 *Ibid.*, I, pp. x–xi.
38 *Ibid.*, I, pp. xi–xii.
39 *Ibid.*, I, p. 52.
40 Lady Llanberis is modelled on the Marchioness of Abercorn.
41 Lady Morgan, *O'Donnel*, 1814, III, p. 307.
42 *Ibid.*, I, p. 211.
43 Even the conclusion of the novel is a compromise in favour of polite feelings. According to her diaries, in the original draft of the story O'Donnel was to have been hanged. (Lady Morgan, *Memoirs*, II, p. 37.)
44 This remains true in spite of Richard Lovell Edgeworth's praise of *The Wild Irish Girl*, in which he congratulated the author on 'the just character you have given to the lower Irish, and for the sound and judicious observations you have attributed to the priest'. (Lady Morgan, *Memoirs*, I, p. 293.)
45 Maria Edgeworth, *Ormond*, in *Harrington, a tale: and Ormond, a tale* (London: R. Hunter, etc, 1817), II, pp. 111–12.
46 Patrick Kavanagh, *Collected Pruse* (London: MacGibbon & Kee, 1967), p. 282.
47 Maria Edgeworth, *Ormond*, II, p. 109.
48 *Ibid.*, III, pp. 108–09.
49 *Ibid.*, III, p. 351.
50 Lady Morgan, *Florence Macarthy* (London: H. Colburn, 1818), I, p. 44.
51 *Ibid.*, I, p. 21.
52 *Ibid.*, I, p. 47.
53 *Ibid.*, I, pp. 81–82.
54 *Ibid.*, I, p. 86.
55 *Ibid.*, I, p. 89.
56 *Ibid.*, I, p. 92.
57 *Ibid.*, III, pp. 117–18.
58 *Ibid.*, I, p. 194.
59 *Ibid.*, I, p. 315.
60 *Ibid.*, II, pp. 239–41.
61 *Ibid.*, III, pp. 270–71.
62 *Ibid.*, II, pp. 288–89.
63 Thomas Flanagan, *The Irish Novelists 1800–1850*, p. 155.
64 These points are made by H. W. Piper and A. Norman Jeffares, 'Charles Robert Maturin the Innovator', in *Huntingdon Library Quarterly*, XXI, 3 May 1958, pp. 261–84.
65 C. R. Maturin, *The Wild Irish Boy*, (London: Longman etc, 1808), I, pp. 102–03
66 Piper & Jeffares, *op.cit.*, p. 272
67 C. R. Maturin, *The Wild Irish Boy*, I, p. 182.

68 *Ibid.*, I, p. vii.
69 *Ibid.*, II, p. 254.
70 *Ibid.*, II, p. 311.
71 *Ibid.*, I, p. vii.
72 C. R. Maturin, *The Milesian Chief.* (London: H. Colburn, 1818), I, pp. iv-v.
73 *Ibid.*, I, p. 55.
74 *Ibid.*, I, p. 136.
75 *Ibid.*, III, p. 49.
76 *Ibid.*, III, p. 50.
77 Piper & Jeffares, *op.cit.*, p. 275.
78 *Ibid.*, p. 278.
79 Lady Morgan, *Absenteeism* (London: H. Colburn, 1825), pp. 92, 113.
80 *Ibid.*, pp. 153–54.
81 *Ibid.*, p. 158.
82 Lady Morgan, *Memoirs*, II, p. 225. Ironically O'Connell himself appears to have admired Lady Morgan, for Lionel Stevenson quotes him as saying of her in 1828:
    'To Irish female talents and patriotism we owe much. There is one name consecrated by a generous devotion to the best interests of Ireland – a name sacred to the cause of Liberty, and of everything great, virtuous, and patriotic – the name of an illustrious female who has suffered unmanly persecution for her talented and chivalrous adherence to her native land. Need I say that I allude to Lady Morgan? Her name is received with enthusiasm by the people of the country where her writings create and perpetuate among the youth of both sexes a patriotic ardour in the cause of everything that is noble and dignified.' (Lionel Stevenson, *The Wild Irish Girl*, p. 267.)
83 Lady Morgan, *Memoirs*, II, p. 319.
84 *Ibid.*, II, p. 379.
85 Augustus J. C. Hare (ed.), *The Life and Letters of Maria Edgeworth* (London: Arnold, 1892), II, p. 202.

Chapter 2: Early Tales by the Banims and Gerald Griffin (1825–1830)

1 Robert Kee, *The Green Flag*, p. 195.
2 Gearoid Ó Tuathaigh, *Ireland Before the Famine 1798–1848* (Dublin: Gill & Macmillan, 1972), p. 65.
3 Thomas Flanagan, *The Irish Novelists 1800–1850*, pp. 176, 374–75. The same might also be said of *John Doe* which has an account of a faction fight, records the violent activities of a band of peasant rebels against a corrupt land agent and – a wholly original feature – describes the interior of an illicit poteen still. The basic narrative device is familiar from earlier works: all the action is observed by two young English military officers who are swept into it by a mixture of accident, romantic adventure and official duties.
4 John and Michael Banim, *Tales by the O'Hara Family* (London: Simpkin & Marshall, 1825), I, p. 6.
5 *Ibid.*, I, p. 40.
6 *Ibid.*, I, p. 48.
7 *Ibid.*, I, pp. 102–03.

8   *Ibid.*, I, p. 191.
9   *Ibid.*, I, pp. 191–92.
10   *Ibid.*, I, p. 197.
11   John and Michael Banim, *Tales by the O'Hara Family: The Nowlans* (London: H. Colburn, 1826), I, pp. 83–84.
12   *Ibid.*, I, p. 34.
13   W. B. Yeats (ed.) *Representative Irish Tales* (1891; reissued with a foreword and list of sources by M. H. Thuente, Gerrards Cross: Colin Smythe, 1979), p. 31.
14   Gerald Griffin, *Holland-Tide* (London: W. Simpkin & R. Marshall, 1827), pp. 259–60.
15   All these stories appear in *Holland-Tide*.
16   Gerald Griffin, *Tales of the Munster Festivals*, 3 vols. (London: Saunders & Otley, 1827), I, p. 84.
17   *Ibid.*, II, pp. 66–67.
18   *Ibid.*, II, pp. 66, 375. In fairness to Griffin, it should be added that elsewhere he is critical of the policy of exporting grain from Ireland as long as the natives experience a regular food shortage in the winter season (*ibid.*, III, pp. 185–86).
19   Gerald Griffin, *Holland-Tide*, pp. 4–5.
20   Gerald Griffin, *Tales of the Munster Festivals*, II, p. 53.
21   *Ibid.*, III, pp. 126–31.
22   *Ibid.*, III, p. 136.
23   *Ibid.*, I, p. 11.
24   *Ibid.*, I, p. 12.
25   H. R. Krans, *Irish Life in Irish Fiction*, pp. 154–55.
26   Gerald Griffin, *Tales of the Munster Festivals*, I, pp. 347–48.
27   Gerald Griffin, *Holland-Tide*, pp. 95–96.
28   Gerald Griffin, *Tales of the Munster Festivals*, II, p. 151.
29   *Ibid.*, I, p. 269.
30   *Ibid.*, I, p. 202.
31   *Ibid.*, III, p. 122.

Chapter 3: The Banims' Historical Novels (1825–1830)

1   John Banim, *The Boyne Water* (2nd edition, 1865; reissued with an introduction by Bernard Escarbelt, Lille: Universite de Lille III, 1976), Introduction, pp. 20–21.
2   *Ibid.*, Introduction, p. 19.
3   *Ibid.*, cited in Introduction by Escarbelt, p. 13.
4   *Ibid.*, Introductory Letter, p. xiii.
5   *Ibid.*, p. xiii.
6   *Ibid.*, Introduction, p. 21.
7   *Ibid.*, pp. 60–61.
8   *Ibid.*, p. 133.
9   *Ibid.*, pp. 564, 563.
10   Georg Lukács, *The Historical Novel*, trans. H. and S. Mitchell (London: Merlin Press, Atlantic Highlands, N.J.: Humanities Press, 1962), p. 33.
11   *Ibid.*, p. 36.
12   John Banim, *The Denounced* (London: Colburn and Bentley, 1830), II, p. 167.

13 *Ibid.*, II, pp. 161–62.
14 *Ibid.*, II, p. 97.
15 *Ibid.*, II. p. 98.
16 Michael Banim, *The Croppy: A Tale of 1798* (London: Colburn, 1828), I, pp. 17–18.
17 *Ibid.*, I, p. 18.
18 *The Croppy* is not unique in indicating the gap between the city-based activists in the United Irishmen and the people in the country. In *The O'Briens and the O'Flahertys* Murrogh O'Brien writes in despair to Lord Walter Fitzwalter, warning him of the lack of readiness for an uprising in the far-flung parts of Connaught. He described the 'total absence of all immediate discontent in the Catholic gentry, who (remote from official persecution, and living in habits of kindly intercourse with the old protestant families, their rents well-paid, their cellars well-stocked), slept over the degradation of their caste, and were ignorant or unmoved by the events which were passing in the distant capital' (Lady Morgan, *The O'Briens and the O'Flahertys*, London: H. Colburn, 1827, IV, p. 283). Although Michael Banim and Lady Morgan emphasize different aspects of the problem, they are alike in their perception of national disunity.
19 Banim, *The Croppy*, I, p. 165.
20 *Ibid.*, II, p. 26.
21 *Ibid.*, II, p. 27.
22 Thomas Pakenham, *The Year of Liberty* (London: Panther, 1969, reprint. 1978), pp. 145, 164, 167.
23 Banim, *The Croppy*, II, pp. 29–30.
24 *Ibid.*, II, p. 13.
25 *Ibid.*, III, pp. 26–27.
26 Quoted from advertisement at the end of Volume I of Anonymous [Eyre Crow], *Yesterday in Ireland* (London: H. Colburn, 1829), and cited by Robert Lee Wolff in his essay 'The Fiction of the O'Hara Family', which appears in Anonymous [John Banim], *The Anglo-Irish of the XIXth Century* (1828, reprinted New York: Garland, 1978), I, p. xxviii.
27 *Ibid.*, I, p. 23.
28 *Ibid.*, I, pp. 30–31.
29 *Ibid.*, I, p. 177.
30 *Ibid.*, II, pp. 262–63.
31 *Ibid.*, II, p. 272.
32 *Ibid.*, III, p. 2–3.
33 *Ibid.*, III, p. 120.
34 *Ibid.*, III, p. 121.
35 *Ibid.*, III, pp. 121–22.
36 *Ibid.*, III, p. 124.
37 *Ibid.*, III, p. 127.

Chapter 4: Lady Morgan's departure and Griffin's major works (1825–1830)

1 Lady Morgan, *The O'Briens and the O'Flahertys*, I, p. 24.
2 *Ibid.*, I, p. 106.
3 *Ibid.*, I, p. 142.
4 *Ibid.*, I, pp. 145–46.

5   *Ibid.*, III, p. 66.
6   *Ibid.*, III, pp. 68–70.
7   *Ibid.*, III, pp. 71–72.
8   *Ibid.*, III, p. 286.
9   *Ibid.*, III, p. 74.
10 *Ibid.*, IV, pp. 244–45.
11 *Ibid.*, IV, p. 270.
12 James Newcomer, 'Lady Morgan: Generalization and Error', in *Études Irlandaises*, No. 3, new series (December 1978), p. 32.
13 Flanagan, *The Irish Novelists 1800–1850*, p. 222.
14 John Cronin, *The Anglo-Irish Novel*, Vol. 1 (Belfast: Appletree Press, 1980), p. 67.
15 Gerald Griffin, *The Collegians* (London: Saunders and Otley, 1829), I, p. 126.
16 *Ibid.*, I, p. 272.
17 *Ibid.*, III, p. 35.
18 Flanagan, *The Irish Novelists 1800–1850*, p. 229.
19 Griffin, *The Collegians*, III, pp. 38–39.
20 *Ibid.*, I, p. 148.
21 *Ibid.*, I, pp. 325–27.
22 *Ibid.*, III, p. 80–81.
23 *Ibid.*, III, pp. 94–95.
24 *Ibid.*, III, p. 247.
25 Cronin, *The Anglo-Irish Novel*, I, p. 69.
26 Krans, *Irish Life in Irish Fiction*, p. 304.
27 W. B. Yeats, *The Letters of W. B. Yeats*, ed. Allan Wade (London: Rupert Hart Davies, 1954), p. 143; *The Collected Letters of W. B. Yeats*, edited by John Kelly (Oxford: Clarendon Press, 1986), I, p. 199.
28 Walter Allen, *The English Novel* (1954. Harmondsworth: Pelican, 1970), p. 131.
29 John Cronin, *Gerald Griffin (1803–1840): A Critical Biography* (Cambridge: Cambridge University Press, 1978), pp. 68–69.
30 Gerald Griffin, *The Rivals and Tracy's Ambition* (London: Saunders and Otley, 1830), I, p. 61.
31 *Ibid.*, I, pp. 63–64.
32 *Ibid.*, I, p. 165.
33 *Ibid.*, II, pp. 37–8.
34 Gerald Griffin, *The Rivals and Tracy's Ambition* (1851. Reprint with Introduction by John Cronin, Lille: Universite de Lille, III, 1978), p. xv.
35 Griffin, *The Rivals and Tracy's Ambition* (1830), II, pp. 188–189.
36 *Ibid.*, II, p. 207.
37 *Ibid.*, II, pp. 207–08.
38 *Ibid.*, III, p. 168.

Chapter 5: *Sketches of Irish Character* and *Traits and Stories of the Irish Peasantry* (1830–1833)

1   Thomas Davis, *Thomas Davis: Memoir, Essays and Poems* (Dublin: Gill, 1945), p. 112.
2   Mrs S. C. Hall, *Sketches of Irish Character* (London: F. Westley and A.H. Davis, 1829. Second edition 1842), p. vi.

Mrs Hall does not state her purpose in such explicit terms in the introduction to the first edition of her book. There, in her dedication to Miss Mitford, she states simply that she was 'desirous of introducing [her] "to an Irish village" ', and goes on to admit that Bannow is a particularly 'favourable specimen'.

3 Mrs Hall, *Sketches of Irish Character* (1829), I, pp. 5–6.
4 William Carleton, *Traits and Stories of the Irish Peasantry* second series, (Dublin: W. F. Wakeman, 1833), II, pp. 4–5.
5 Mrs S. C. Hall, *Sketches of Irish Character*, second series (London: F. Westley and A. H. Davies, 1831), pp. 310–11.
6 Mrs Hall, Sketches of Irish Character, I, p. 93.
7 Davis, *Thomas Davis: Memoir, Essays and Poems*, p. 112.
8 William Carleton, *Autobiography* (1896. Revised edition, with Preface by Patrick Kavanagh, London: McGibbon & Kee, 1968), p. 19.
9 *Ibid.*, p. 20.
10 *Ibid.*, p. 128.
11 Sam Hanna Bell, 'William Carleton and his Neighbours', in *Ulster Folklife*, Vol. 7 (Holywood, Co. Down: Ulster Folk and Transport Museum, 1961), p. 40.
12 *Ibid.*, p. 40.
13 Carleton, *Traits and Stories of the Irish Peasantry*, second series, II, pp. 59–60.
14 *Ibid.*, II, p. 76.
15 The influence of the priest in persuading his congregation to give generously is also seen in 'The Funeral and Party Fight', where, at the funeral of Denis Kelly who died of injuries received in a fight, he calls for offerings to help the deceased's family. The priest then announces the names of the donors and the size of their gifts, thus precipitating competitive charity.
16 *Ibid.*, II, pp. 161–62.
17 William Carleton, *Traits and Stories of the Irish Peasantry* (Dublin: W. Curry, 1830), II, pp. 110–11.
18 *Ibid.*, II, p. 112.
19 William Carleton, *Traits and Stories of the Irish Peasantry*, ed. Maurice Harmon (Cork: Mercier Press, 1973), II, p. viii.
20 Raymond Williams, *Drama from Ibsen to Eliot* (1952. Harmondsworth: Peregrine, 1967), pp. 180–82.
21 Carleton, *Traits and Stories of the Irish Peasantry*, second series, III, p. 12.
22 *Ibid.*, III, pp. 13–15.
23 *Ibid.*, III, pp. 53–54.
24 *Ibid.*, III, pp. 63, 64.
25 *Ibid.*, III, p. 74.
26 *Ibid.*, III, pp. 101–02.
27 *Ibid.*, III, pp. 166–67.
28 Carleton, *Traits and Stories of the Irish Peasantry*, I, p. 126.
29 Carleton, *Traits and Stories of the Irish Peasantry*, second series, I, pp. 67–68.
30 W. B. Yeats (editor), *Representative Irish Tales* (1891. Gerrards Cross: Colin Smythe, 1979), p. 30.
31 Carleton, *Traits and Stories of the Irish Peasantry*, second series, II, p. 328.
32 *Ibid.*, II, p. 335.

33 *Ibid.*, I, pp. 280–81.
34 Carleton, *Traits and Stories of the Irish Peasantry*, I, p. 255.
35 *Ibid.*, I, p. 252.
36 *Ibid.*, I, p. 228.
37 *Ibid.*, II, pp. 12–13.
38 *Ibid.*, II, p. 72.
39 Davis, *Thomas Davis: Memoir, Essays and Poems*, p. 111.
40 Bell, *Ulster Folklife*, p. 39.
41 William Carleton, *Traits and Stories of the Irish Peasantry* (Dublin: . W. Curry; London: W. Orr, 1843), I, p. ii.
42 *Ibid.*, I, p. ii.
43 William Carleton, *Traits and Stories of the Irish Peasantry*, ed. D. J. O'Donoghue (London: Dent, 1896), I, p. x.
44 Carleton, *Autobiography*, p. 9.
45 Carleton, *Traits and Stories of the Irish Peasantry* (1843), I, p. v.
46 Roger McHugh, 'William Carleton: A Portrait of the Artist as Propagandist', in *Studies* (Dublin), XXVII (1938), p. 62.
47 W. B. Yeats, 'Introduction' to *Stories from Carleton* (1889), reprinted in Yeats, *Representative Irish Tales*, p. 363.

Chapter 6: Miscellaneous minor fiction, and novels by Lover, Carleton and Lever (1834–1844)

1   Cronin, *Gerald Griffin (1803–1840): A Critical Biography*.
2   Harriet Martin, 'Canvassing', in *The Mayor of Windgap* by the O'Hara Family (1835. Reprinted New York: Garland, 1979), II, p. 237.
3   *Ibid.*, II, p. 238.
4   *Ibid.*, II, p. 265.
5   *Ibid.*, III, pp. 106–07.
6   *Ibid.*, III, p. 203.
7   Samuel Lover, *Legends and Stories of Ireland*, second series (London: Baldwin, 1834), p. 32.
8   *Popular Tales and Legends of the Irish Peasantry* (Dublin: W. F. Wakeman, 1834), pp. 60, 61.
9   Mrs S. C. Hall, *Lights and Shadows of Irish Life* (London: H. Colburn, 1838), I, p. 240.
10 Between 1978 and 1980 Garland Publishing Inc. of New York reissued seventy-seven nineteenth-century Anglo-Irish titles (the list does not include any of Lover's work); however these are so expensive that they are not generally available. *Handy Andy* is published by Dent (London) and Dutton (New York) in the Everyman Series.
11 Samuel Lover, *Rory O'More* (London: Bentley, 1837), III, p. 126.
12 *Ibid.*, I, p. 2.
13 *Ibid.*, I, p. 14.
14 Samuel Lover, *Handy Andy* (London: F. Lover, 1842), p. x.
15 *Ibid.*, pp. 11–12.
16 Yeats (editor), *Representative Irish Tales*, p. 26.
17 Lover, *Rory O'More*, II, p. 122.
18 *Ibid.*, II, p. 181.
19 *Ibid.*, III, p. 284.
20 William Carleton, *Fardorougha the Miser* (Dublin: W. Curry, 1839), p. 323.

21   B. G. MacCarthy, 'Irish Regional Novelists of the Early Nineteenth
      Century', in *The Dublin Magazine* (July–September 1946), p. 37.

22   Yeats (editor), *Representative Irish Tales*, p. 27. Greene's article is quoted
      by John Cronin in *The Anglo-Irish Novel*, I, p. 8.

23   Charles Lever, *The Confessions of Harry Lorrequer* (Dublin: W. Curry,
      June & Co., and Edinburgh: Fraser & Crawford, 1839), p. 10.

24   Charles Lever, *Our Mess: Jack Hinton, the Guardsman* (Dublin: W.
      Curry, etc., 1843), p. 21.

25   Lever, *Ibid.*, p. 236.

26   *Ibid.*, p. 237.

27   Anthony Trollope, *An Autobiography* (1883. Oxford: Oxford University
      Press, 1974), p. 217.

Chapter 7: Novels by Mrs Hall, Le Fanu, Lever, and Carleton (1845–1850)

1   Mrs S. C. Hall, *The Whiteboy* (London: Longman, etc., 1845), I, pp. 8–9.

2   *Ibid.*, I, p. 26.

3   Her technique here is akin to Michael Banim's synopsis of the social
      tensions and attitudes in Ireland prior to 1798 with which he opens *The
      Croppy*.

4   Mrs Hall, *The Whiteboy*, II, p. 6.

5   *Ibid.*, II, p. 31.

6   *Ibid.*, II, p. 301.

7   J. S. Le Fanu, *Uncle Silas* (1864. With Introduction by Elizabeth Bowen,
      London: Cresset Press, 1947), p. 8. This point is also elaborated upon in
      W. J. McCormack's critical biography *Sheridan Le Fanu and Victorian
      Ireland* (Oxford: Clarendon Press, 1980).

8   J. S. Le Fanu, *The Cock and Anchor* (Dublin: W. Curry, 1845), II, pp.
      265–66.

9   Krans, *Irish Life in Irish Fiction*, pp. 90–91.

10   Charles Lever, *The O'Donoghue* (Dublin: W. Curry, 1845), p. 199.

11   Charles Lever, *The Knight of Gwynne* (London: Chapman & Hall, 1847),
      I, p. vi.

12   *Ibid.*, p. 136.

13   *Ibid.*

14   *Ibid.*, pp. 236–37.

15   *Ibid.*, p. 254.

16   *Ibid.*, p. 354.

17   *Ibid.*, p. 348.

18   Yeats (editor), *Representative Irish Tales*, p. 287. More recently the
      balance has been redressed in Lever's favour by A. Norman Jeffares, who
      praises his intelligence, education and his range of experience as a rural
      Irish dispensary doctor, a traveller, an editor and a diplomat. These helped
      to mature his understanding of the Irish character and shaped his
      perception of the tragic consequences of English rule in Ireland. Jeffares
      concludes that:

         Lever loved his country; he surveyed its politics sardonically, at times
         detachedly; he was Anglo-Irish in his enjoyment of scenery and

complexity of character; and he had a sharp awareness of the differences in Irish and English sensibilities.

He then poses the witty but pertinent question: 'How could Yeats (and a horde of lesser writers after him) have got hold of the wrong Lever?' 'Yeats and the Wrong Lever' in A. Norman Jeffares (editor), *Yeats, Sligo and Ireland* (Gerrards Cross: Colin Smythe, and New York: Barnes & Noble, 1980), pp. 98–111.

19 William Carleton, *Parra Sastha, or the History of Paddy Go-Easy and His Wife Nancy* (Dublin: Duffy, 1845), p. xv.

20 William Carleton, *Rody the Rover, or the Ribbonman* (Dublin: Duffy, 1845), p. 232.

21 William Carleton, *The Tithe Proctor* (London and Belfast: Simms & M'Intyre, 1849, and New York: Garland, 1979), p. 98.

22 *Ibid.*, p. 211.

23 *Ibid.*, p. 213.

24 Krans, *Irish Life in Irish Fiction*, p. 312; Benedict Kiely, *Poor Scholar: A Study of William Carleton* (Dublin: Talbot Press, 1947, reprint 1972), p. 92.

25 Flanagan, *The Irish Novelists*, p. 315.

26 William Carleton, *Valentine McClutchy, the Irish Agent* (Dublin: Duffy; London: Chapman & Hall; Edinburgh: Oliver & Boyd, 1845), I, p. viii.

27 *Ibid.*, III, p. 123.

28 *Ibid.*, I, p. vi.

29 Carleton, *Autobiography*, p. 37, and see also p. 40 where he states that the portrayal of the Orangemen in *Valentine McClutchy* derived from his boyhood memories.

30 Carleton, *Valentine McClutchy*, II, p. 311.

31 *Ibid.*, III, p. 141.

32 B. G. MacCarthy, in *The Dublin Magazine* (July–September 1946), p. 35.

33 William Carleton, *The Black Prophet* (Belfast: Simms & M'Intyre, 1847), pp. 20–21.

34 *Ibid.*, p. 70.

35 *Ibid.*, p. 154.

36 *Ibid.*, pp. 212–13.

37 W. Steuart Trench, *Realities of Irish Life* (1868. London: McGibbon & Kee, 1966), p. 73.

38 William Carleton, *The Emigrants of Ahadarra* (London and Belfast: Simms & M'Intyre, 1848), p. 86.

39 *Ibid.*, p. 88

40 *Ibid.*, p. 168.

41 Ibid., p. 224.

42 William Carleton and D. J. O'Donoghue, *Life of Carleton* (London: Downey, 1896), II, p. 305.

43 *Ibid.*, II, p. 293.

Chapter 8: Conclusion. The Problems and successes of the first fifty years.

1 T. S. Eliot, *The Sacred Wood* (1920. London: Methuen, 1966), p. 49.

2 Thomas MacDonagh, *Literature in Ireland* (London: T. Fisher Unwin, 1916), p. 13.

3   W. B. Yeats, *Letters to the New Island*, edited by H. Reynolds (Cambridge, Mass.: Harvard University Press, 1934, reprint Oxford: Oxford University Press, 1970), p. 76.
4   MacDonagh, *Literature in Ireland*, p. 24.
5   Griffin, *The Rivals and Tracy's Ambition*, pp. 381–82.
6   Lukács, *The Historical Novel*, p. 25.
7   P. J. Murray, *The Life of John Banim* (London: Lacy, 1857), p. 254.
8   This point is elaborated by John Cronin in *The Anglo-Irish Novel*, p. 11.
9   Mark D. Hawthorne, *John and Michael Banim (The 'O'Hara Brothers'): A Study in the Early Development of the Anglo-Irish Novel* (Salzburg: Universität Salzburg, 1975), p. 13.
10 Daniel Corkery, *Synge and Anglo-Irish Literature* (Dublin & Cork: Cork University Press; London: Longmans, Green, 1931), pp. 7–8.
11 Maria Edgeworth, *The Life and Letters of Maria Edgeworth*, edited by A. Hare (London: Arnold, 1894), II, p. 332.
12 Mark D. Hawthorne, in *John and Michael Banim (The 'O'Hara Brothers')*, p. 28, elaborates on this idea.
13 *Ibid.*, p. 31.
14 Eliot, *The Sacred Wood*, p. 62.
15 Yeats, *The Letters of W. B. Yeats*, p. 248; *The Collected Letters of W. B. Yeats*, I, p. 442.
16 Cronin, *Gerald Griffin (1803–1840): A Critical Biography*, p. 77.
17 Yeats, *The Letters of W. B. Yeats*, p. 199; *The Collected Letters of W. B. Yeats*, I, p. 199.
18 James Joyce, *A Portrait of the Artist as a Young Man* (1916. Harmondsworth: Penguin, 1965), p. 253.
19 John Montague, 'Tribute to William Carleton', in *The Bell* (Dublin), XVIII (April 1952), p. 13.
20 Edmund Spenser, *Works* (Dublin: Washbourne, 1850), p. 499.
21 G. B. Shaw, *John Bull's Other Island and Major Barbara* (London: Constable, 1907), p. xxxiv.
22 Corkery, *Synge and Anglo-Irish Literature*, p. 17.
23 *Ibid.*, p. 25.
24 Yeats, *The Letters of W. B. Yeats*, p. 143; *The Collected Letters of W. B. Yeats*, I, p. 199.

BIBLIOGRAPHY

PRIMARY SOURCES:

Books, Essays and other works by the authors under study.

Banim, John and Michael. *The Bit o' Writin'* (and other stories). 3 vols., London: Saunders and Otley, 1838, rpt. with intro. by Robert Lee Wolff, New York: Garland, 1979.

Banim, John and Michael. *Tales by the O'Hara Family* (first series). 3 vols, London: Simpkin and Marshall, 1825.

Banim, John and Michael. *Tales by the O'Hara Family* (second series). 3 vols., London: H. Colburn, 1826.

Banim, John. *The Anglo-Irish of the Nineteenth Century*. 3 vols., London: H. Colburn, 1828, rpt. with intro. by Robert Lee Wolff, New York: Garland, 1978.

The Boyne Water. 3 vols., London: Simpkin and Marshall, 1826: 2nd. edn. 1 vol., Dublin: Duffy, 1865, rpt. with intro. by Bernard Escarbelt, Lille: Universite de Lille, 1976.

The Celt's Paradise. London: John Warren, 1821.

The Denounced. 3 vols., London: Colburn and Bentley, 1830.

The Ghost-Hunter and his Family. London: Smith and Elder, 1833.

The Smuggler, A Tale. 3 vols., 1831, reset 1 vol., London: Ward and Lock, 1856.

Banim, Michael. *The Croppy: A Tale of 1798*. 3 vols., London: H. Colburn, 1828.

The Mayor of Windgap. 3 vols., London: Saunders and Otley, 1835, rpt. with intro. by Robert Lee Wolff, New York: Garland, 1979.

Carleton, William. *Art Maguire, or The Broken Pledge*. Dublin: Duffy, 1845.

Autobiography. 1896, reset with intro. by Patrick Kavanagh, London: MacGibbon and Kee, 1968.

The Black Prophet. London: Simms and McIntyre, 1847; also reset 1899 and rpt. with intro. by Timothy Webb, Shannon: Irish University Press, 1972.

The Clarionet and other Stories. 3 vols., Dublin: Curry, 1841.

The Emigrants of Ahadarra. London and Belfast: Simms and McIntyre (The Parlour Library Series, No. x), 1848.

Fardorougha the Miser, or the Convicts of Lisnamona. Dublin: Curry, 1839.

Father Butler and The Lough Derg Pilgrim. Dublin: Curry, 1829.

Parra Sastha, or the History of Paddy Go-Easy and His Wife, Nancy. Dublin: Duffy, 1845.

Rody the Rover, or the Ribbonman. Dublin: Duffy, 1845.

The Squanders of Castle Squander. 2 vols., London: Illustrated London Library, 1852.

The Tithe Proctor. London: Simms and McIntyre, 1849, rpt. with intro. by Robert Lee Wolff, New York: Garland, 1979.

Traits and Stories of the Irish Peasantry. 2 vols., Dublin: Curry, 1830.

Traits and Stories of the Irish Peasantry (second series). 3 vols., Dublin: W. F. Wakeman, 1833.

Traits and Stories of the Irish Peasantry (first and second series). 4 vols., reset with intro. by D. J. O'Donoghue, London: Dent, 1896.

Traits and Stories of the Irish Peasantry (first and second series). 4 vols., reset with intro. by Maurice Harmon, Cork: Mercier, 1973. (N.B. This series is incomplete.)

Valentine McClutchy, the Irish Agent. 3 vols., Dublin: Duffy; London: Chapman and Hall; Edinburgh: Oliver and Boyd, 1845.

Carleton, W. and O'Donoghue, D. J.,*Life of William Carleton*. 2 vols., London: Downey, 1896.

Edgeworth, Maria. and R. L. *Essay on Irish Bulls*. London: R. Hunter 1825.

Edgeworth, Maria. *Castle Rackrent*. London: J. Johnson, 1800.

Harrington, a tale: and Ormond, a tale. 3 vols., London: R. Hunter, 1817.

Tales of Fashionable Life. 6 vols. Vols. 1–3, London: J. Johnson, 1809; vols. 4–6, London: J. Johnson, 1812. (*Ennui* is in vol. 1; *The Absentee* is in vols. 5 and 6.)

ed. Hare, Augustus. *The Life and Letters of Maria Edgeworth*. 2 vols., London: Arnold, 1894.

Griffin, Gerald. *The Collegians*. 3 vols., London: Saunders and Otley, 1829.

Holland-Tide. London: Simpkin and Marshall, 1827.

The Invasion. 4 vols. London: Saunders and Otley, 1832.

Poetical Works. London: Simpkin and Marshall, 1843.

The Rivals and Tracy's Ambition. 3 vols., London: Saunders and Otley, 1830; reset as 1 vol., London: Maxwell and Co., 1842 and Belfast: Parlour Library, 1851. (This last edn. rptd. with intro. by John Cronin, Lille: Universite de Lille, 1978.)

Tales of the Munster Festivals. 3 vols., London: Saunders and Otley, 1827.

Tales of My Neighbourhood. 3 vols., London: Saunders and Otley, 1835.

Talis Qualis, or Tales of the Jury Room. London: Maxwell and Co., 1842.

Hall, Mrs S. C. *Lights and Shadows of Irish Life*. 3 vols. London: H. Colburn, 1838.

Sketches of Irish Character (second series). London: F. Westley and
A. H. Davis, 1831.

The Whiteboy, a story of Ireland. 2 vols., London: Chapman and
Hall, 1845.

Le Fanu, J. S. *The Cock and Anchor, a chronicle of old Dublin City.*
3 vols., Dublin: Curry, 1845.

Uncle Silas, a tale of Bartram-Haugh. 3 vols., 1864; reset 1 vol. with
intro. by Elizabeth Bowen, London: Cresset Press, 1947.

Lever, Charles. *Charles O'Malley, the Irish Dragoon.* 2 vols., Dublin:
Curry, 1841.

The Confessions of Harry Lorrequer. Dublin: W. Curry, June and
Co., and Edinburgh: Fraser and Crawford, 1839.

The Knight of Gwynne, a tale of the time of the Union. London:
Chapman and Hall, 1847.

The O'Donoghue, a tale of Ireland fifty years ago. Dublin: Curry,
1845.

Our Mess. 3 vols., Dublin: Curry, 1843–44. (Vol. 1 contains *Jack
Hinton, the Guardsman*; vols. 2 and 3, published 1844, contain
Tom Burke of 'Ours'.)

Roland Cashel. 2 vols., London: Chapman and Hall, 1850.

Lover, Samuel. *Handy Andy, a tale of Irish Life.* London: Lover, Reid
and Groombridge, 1842.

Legends and Stories of Ireland. London: Baldwin, 1834.

Popular Tales and Legends of the Irish Peasantry. Dublin:
Wakeman, 1834.

Rory O'More, a national romance. 3 vols., London: Bentley, 1837.

Martin, Harriet. *Canvassing.* (published with *The Mayor of Windgap*)
3 vols., London: Saunders and Otley, 1835, rpt. with intro. by
Robert Lee Wolff, New York: Garland, 1979.

Maturin, Charles Robert. *Melmoth the Wanderer.* 3 vols., London:
Bentley, 1820, reset with memoir of the author's life, 1892.

The Milesian Chief. 4 vols., London: H. Colburn, 1812.

The Wild Irish Boy. 3 vols., London: Longman, Hurst, Rees and
Orme, 1808, rpt. with intro. by E. F. Bleiler, New York: Arno Press,
1977.

Women: or Pour et Contre. 3 vols., London: Longman, Hurst, Rees
and Orme, 1818.

Morgan, Lady S. *Absenteeism.* London: H. Colburn, 1825.

Florence Macarthy, an Irish Tale. 4 vols., London: H. Colburn,
1818.

Memoirs: Autobiography, Diaries and Correspondence. 2 vols., arr.
W. Hepworth Dixon, London: W. H. Allen, 1863.

The O'Briens and the O'Flahertys, a national tale. 4 vols., London:
H. Colburn, 1827.

O'Donnel, a national tale. 3 vols., London: H. Colburn, 1814.

The Wild Irish Girl. 3 vols., London: Phillips, 1806, rpt. with intro.
by Robert Lee Wolff, New York: Garland, 1979.

The Wild Irish Girl. 3 vols., London: Phillips, 1806, rev'd London: H.Colburn 1846.

Yeats, W. B. (editor) *Representative Irish Tales*. 1891, reissued with foreword and list of sources by M. H. Thuente, Gerrards Cross: Colin Smythe, 1979.

SECONDARY SOURCES

Allen, Walter. *The English Novel*. London: Phoenix House, 1954; Harmondsworth: Penguin, 1970.

Allingham, William. *Laurence Bloomfield in Ireland*. London: Macmillan, 1864, rpt. New York: A.M.S. Press Inc., 1972.

Baker, Ernest A. *The History of the English Novel*. (vol. 6) London: H. F. and G. Witherby, 1924.

Beckett, J. C. *The Making of Modern Ireland*. London: Faber and Faber, 1966.

Bell, Sam Hanna. 'William Carleton and his Neighbours'. *Ulster Folklife*, VII (1961), 37–40.

Boucicault, D. *The Dolmen Boucicault*. Ed. and with an intro. by D. Krause, Dublin: Dolmen, 1964.

Brown, Malcolm. *The Politics of Irish Literature*. London: Allen and Unwin, 1972.

Brown, Stephen J. *Ireland in Fiction*. 1915. Reprinted Shannon: Irish University Press, 1969.

Brown, Terence. 'The Death of William Carleton 1869'. *Hermathena* CX (1970), 81–5.

Callanan, J. J. *The Poems of J. J. Callanan*. Cork: Daniel Mulcahy, 1861.

Campbell, Mary. 'The Wild Irish Girl – an Anniversary'. *The Irish Times* (6 Jan. 1977), 8.

Chesnutt, Margaret. *Studies in the Short Stories of William Carleton*. Göteborg: Acta Universitatis Götoburgenis, 1976. (Gothenburg Studies in English No. 34.)

Colum, Patrick. 'Maria Edgeworth and Ivan Turgenev'. *British Book Review* 11 (1915), 109–113.

Corkery, Daniel. *Synge and Anglo-Irish Literature*. Cork: University Press, 1931.

Cronin, John. *The Anglo-Irish Novel*. (vol. 1) Belfast: Appletree Press, 1980.
Gerald Griffin (1803–1840): A Critical Biography. Cambridge: University Press, 1978.

Crowe, Eyre. *Today in Ireland*. 3 vols., London: Charles Knight, 1825.
Yesterday in Ireland. 3 vols., London: H. Colburn, 1829.

Davie, Donald. *The Heyday of Sir Walter Scott*. London: Routledge and Kegan Paul, 1961.

Davis, Thomas. *Essays and Poems, with a Centenary Memoir*. Dublin: Gill, 1945.

270   *The Pioneers of Anglo-Irish Fiction 1800–1850*

Duffy, C. G. *My Life in Two Hemispheres*. 2 vols., 1898, rpt. with intro. by John H. Whyte, Shannon: Irish University Press, 1969.

Edgeworth, R. L. *Memoirs of Richard Lovell Edgeworth, Esq.* 2 vols., London: R. Hunter, 1820.

Eliot, T. S. *The Sacred Wood*. 1920. London: Methuen, 1966.

Flanagan, Thomas. *The Irish Novelists, 1800–1850*. New York: Columbia University Press, 1959.

Foster, John Wilson. *Forces and Themes in Ulster Fiction*. Dublin: Gill and Macmillan, 1974.

Griffin, Daniel. *Life of Gerald Griffin*. London: Simpkin and Marshall, 1843.

Harmon, Maurice. *Modern Irish Literature 1800–1967: A Reader's Guide*. Dublin: Dolmen, 1967.

Select Bibliography for the Study of Anglo-Irish Literature and its Backgrounds. Portmarnock: Wolfhound, 1977.

Hartley, Mary Laffan. *Hogan M. P.* 3 vols., London: Henry King, 1876; rpt. with intro. by Robert Lee Woolf, New York: Garland, 1979.

Hawthorne, Mark D. *John and Michael Banim (The 'O'Hara Brothers'): A Study in the Early Development of the Anglo-Irish Novel*. Salzburg: Institut für Englische Sprache und Literatur, Universität Salzburg, 1975.

Hayley, Barbara. (ed.) *Carleton's Alterations to Traits and Stories of the Irish Peasantry: An Appendix*. Gerrards Cross: Colin Smythe, 1986.

Carleton's Traits and Stories and the Nineteenth Century Anglo-Irish Tradition. (Irish Literary Studies 12) Gerrards Cross: Colin Smythe, 1983.

A Bibliography of the Writings of William Carleton. Gerrards Cross: Colin Smythe, 1985.

Ibarra, Eileen. 'William Carleton: an Introduction'. *Eire-Ireland*, V, 1 (1970), 81–6.

Jeffares, A. Norman. *Anglo-Irish Literature*. Dublin: Gill and Macmillan, 1982.

(ed.) *Yeats, Sligo and Ireland*. Gerrards Cross: Colin Smythe, 1980.

Joyce, James. *A Portrait of the Artist as a Young Man*. 1916. Harmondsworth: Penguin, 1965.

Kavanagh, Patrick. *Collected Pruse*. London: MacGibbon and Kee, 1967.

Kee, Robert. *The Green Flag*. London: Weidenfield and Nicolson, 1973.

Kiely, Benedict. *Poor Scholar: A Study of William Carleton*. Dublin: Talbot Press, 1947, reset 1972.

'The Two Masks of Gerald Griffin'. *Studies* 61, (1971), 241–51.

Krans, H. R. *Irish Life in Irish Fiction*. New York: Columbia University Press, 1903.

Leclaire, Lucien. *A General Analytical Bibliography of the Regional Novelists of the British Isles, 1800–1950*. Paris: Les Belles Lettres, 1954.

Lukács, Georg. *The Historical Novel*. Trans. H. and S. Mitchell, London: Merlin Press and New Jersey: Humanities Press, 1962.

MacCarthy, B. G. 'Irish Regional Novelists of the Early Nineteenth Century'. *The Dublin Magazine* (July–Sept. 1946), 28–37.

McCormack, W. J. *Sheridan Le Fanu and Victorian Ireland*. Oxford: Clarendon Press, 1980.

MacDonagh, Thomas. *Literature in Ireland*. London: Fisher Unwin, 1916.

McDowell, R. B. (ed.) *Social Life in Ireland 1800–1845*. Cork: Mercier Press, 1957, new edition, 1973.

McHugh, Roger. 'Charles Lever', *Studies* XXVII (June 1938), 247–60. 'Maria Edgeworth's Irish Novels'. *Studies* XXVII (Dec. 1938), 556–570.
'A Portrait of the Artist as Propagandist'. *Studies* XXVII (1938), 47–62.

McKenna, Brian. *Irish Literature 1800–1975*. Detroit: Gale Research Co., 1978. (Vol. 13 in the American Literature, English Literature, and World Literatures in English Information Guide Series.)

McWhorter, Harden O. Elizabeth. *Maria Edgeworth's Art of Prose Fiction*. The Hague: Mouton, 1971. (Studies in English Literature Vol. LXII.)

Martin, A. (ed.) *The Genius of Irish Prose*. Cork: Mercier, 1984.

Mercier, Vivian. *The Irish Comic Tradition*. Oxford: University Press, 1962.

Montague, John. *The Rough Field*. Dublin: Dolmen Press, 1972.
'A Tribute to William Carleton'. *The Bell* XVII (April 1952), 13–20.

Moore, Thomas. *The History of Ireland*. 4 vols., London: Longman, Rees, Orme, Brown, Green and Longman, I, 1835; II, 1837; III, 1840; IV, 1846.
Memoirs of Captain Rock, the Celebrated Irish Chieftain. London: Longman, Hurst, Rees, Orme, Brown and Green, 1824.
Poetical Works. London: Gill and Inglis, n.d.

Moody, T. W. and Martin, F. X. (eds) *The Course of Irish History*. Cork: Mercier Press, 1967, 2nd ed. 1973.

Murray, P. J. *The Life of John Banim*. London: Lacy, 1857.

Newby, P. H. *Maria Edgeworth*. London: Arthur Baker, 1950.

Newcomer, James. 'Lady Morgan: Generalization and Error'. *Études Irlandaises*, No. 3 Nouvelle Serie (Dec. 1978), 27–34.

Newcomer, James. *Maria Edgeworth*. Lewisburg: Bucknell University Press, 1973.

O'Faolain, Sean. *The Irish*. Harmondsworth: Pelican, 1969.
King of the Beggars, a Life of Daniel O'Connell. 1938. Swords: Poolbeg Press, 1980.

Ó'Tuathaigh, Gearóid. *Ireland before the Famine 1798–1848*. Dublin: Gill and Macmillan, 1972.

Pakenham, Thomas. *The Year of Liberty*. London: Panther, 1972, new ed. 1978.

272 The Pioneers of Anglo-Irish Fiction 1800–1850

Piper, H. W. and Jeffares, A. Norman. 'Maturin the Innovator'. *The Huntington Library Quarterly* 21, No. 3 (1957–58, rpt. New York: Krauss Reprint Co., 1969), 261–284.

Rafroidi, Patrick. *Irish Literature in English: The Romantic Period.* 2 vols., Gerrards Cross: Colin Smythe, 1980.

Riddell, C. H. *Maxwell Drewitt.* 3 vols., London: Tinsley Brothers, 1865; rpt. with intro. by Robert Lee Woolf, New York: Garland, 1979.

Sadleir, M. *XIX Century Fiction: a Bibliographical Record.* 2 vols., London: Cooper Square Publications, 1951.

Sartre, J.-P. *What is Literature?* Trans Bernard Frechtman, 1950. London: Methuen, 1967.

Shaw, G. B. *John Bull's Other Island.* (pub'd with *Major Barbara*) 1907, new edition London: Constable, 1927.

Sloan, Barry. 'Mrs Hall's Ireland'. *Eire-Ireland* (Fall 1984), 18–30.
'Samuel Lover's Irish Novels'. *Études Irelandaises*, No. 7 Nouvelle Serie (Dec. 1982), 31–42.

Spenser, Edmund. *Works.* Dublin: Washbourne, 1850.

Stevenson, Lionel. *Dr. Quicksilver: The Life of Charles Lever.* London: Chapman and Hall, 1939.
The Wild Irish Girl. London: Chapman and Hall, 1936.

Trench, William Steuart. *Realities of Irish Life.* 1868. Issued with Preface by Patrick Kavanagh, London: MacGibbon and Kee, 1966.

Trollope, Anthony. *An Autobiography.* 1883. World's Classics no. 239, Oxford: University Press, 1974.
Castle Richmond. 3 vols., London: Chapman and Hall, 1860.
An Eye for an Eye. 1879. London: Anthony Blond, 1966.
The Kellys and the O'Kellys. 1848. World's Classics no. 341, Oxford: University Press, 1978.
The Land Leaguers. London: Chatto and Windus, 1884.
The MacDermots of Ballycloran. 1847. London: Chapman and Hall, 1866.

Watson, George (ed.) *New Cambridge Bibliography of English Literature.* Vol. 3, Cambridge: University Press, 1967.

Williams, Raymond. *Drama from Ibsen to Eliot.* London: Chatto and Windus, 1952; Harmondsworth: Peregrine, 1967.

Woodham-Smith, C. *The Great Hunger.* London: Hamish Hamilton, 1962.

Yeats, W. B. *The Collected Letters of W. B. Yeats.* (Ed. John Kelly) 12 + vols., Oxford: University Press, 1986–.
The Letters of W. B. Yeats. (Ed. Allan Wade) London: Rupert Hart Davis, 1954.
W. B. Yeats: Letters to the New Island. (Ed. H. Reynolds) Cambridge Mass.: Harvard University Press, 1934, reprinted Oxford: University Press, 1970.

INDEX

Note: For references to a particular work, please consult under the title, rather than under the author's name.